At a Glance Chapter Summary

The At a Glance chapter summary ties everything together and helps you stay on course! First, the Key Points recap the chapter content for each Learning Objective. Second, the related Key Learning Outcomes list all of the expected student performance capabilities that come from completing each objective. In case you need further practice on a specific outcome, the last column references the related Example Exercises. In addition, the At a Glance grid guides you from the Key Learning Outcomes to the page reference in the textbook where the material is covered.

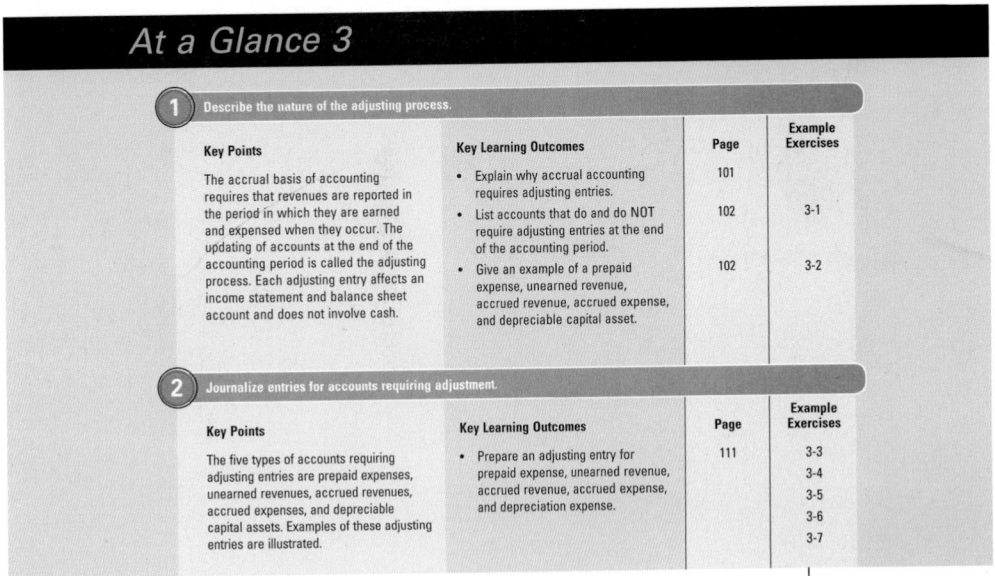

End-of-chapter Practice Exercises parallel the Example Exercises for further reinforcement and self-study. If you struggle with a Practice Exercise, you can return to the Example Exercise to see a model solution.

PE 3-4
Adjustment for unearned revenues

On August 1, 2014, Treadwell Co. received $10,500 for the rent of land for 12 months. Journalize the adjusting entry required for unearned rent on December 31, 2014.

EE 3-4 p. 115

ACCOUNTING

Second Canadian Edition

Carl S. Warren
Professor Emeritus of Accounting
University of Georgia, Athens

James M. Reeve
Professor Emeritus of Accounting
University of Tennessee, Knoxville

Jonathan E. Duchac
Professor of Accounting
Wake Forest University

Sheila F. Elworthy
Vice President of Learning
CA School of Business

Tana M. Kristjanson
Instructor, School of Business
Camosun College

Barrie E. Tober
Professor and Coordinator of Accounting
Niagara College

NELSON / EDUCATION

NELSON / E D U C A T I O N

Accounting, Volume 1, Second Canadian Edition

by Carl S. Warren, James M. Reeve, Jonathan E. Duchac,
Sheila F. Elworthy, Tana M. Kristjanson, and Barrie E. Tober

Vice President, Editorial Higher Education:
Anne Williams

Senior Acquisitions Editor:
Amie Plourde

Acquisitions Editor:
Rod Banister

Executive Marketing Manager:
Sean Chamberland

Technical Reviewer:
Ross Meacher

Developmental Editor:
Lisa Berland

Photo Researcher/Permissions Coordinator:
Natalie Barrington

Senior Content Production Manager:
Imoinda Romain

Production Service:
Integra Software Services Pvt. Ltd.

Copy Editor:
Mariko Obokata

Proofreader:
Margaret DeWind

Indexer:
Jeanne Busemeyer, Hyde Park
Publishing Services

Manufacturing Manager:
Joanne McNeil

Design Director:
Ken Phipps

Managing Designer:
Franca Amore

Interior Design Modifications:
Greg Devitt Design

Cover Design:
Liz Harasymczuk

Cover Image:
Scott Gilchrist/Masterfile

Compositor:
Integra Software Services Pvt. Ltd.

Printer:
R.R. Donnelley

**Library and Archives Canada
Cataloguing in Publication**

Accounting / Carl S. Warren ...
[et al.]. — 2nd Canadian ed.

Includes indexes.
Contents: v. 1. Chapters 1–10 —
v. 2. Chapters 11–17.

ISBN 978-0-17-650973-6 (v. 1).—
ISBN 978-0-17-650974-3 (v. 2)

1. Accounting—Textbooks.
I. Warren, Carl S

HF5636.A315 2013
657'.044   C2012-905659-6

ISBN-13: 978-0-17-650973-6
ISBN-10: 10: 0-17-650973-9

BRIEF CONTENTS

VOLUME 1

VOLUME 2

CONTENTS

1 Introduction to Accounting and Business 1

2 Analyzing Transactions 45

3 The Adjusting Process 99

4 Completing the Accounting Cycle 165

5 Accounting for Merchandising Businesses 235

6   *Inventories* 303

7   *Internal Control and Cash* 349

8   *Receivables* 413

9   *Property, Plant, and Equipment and Other Long-Term Assets* 459

10   *Current Liabilities and Payroll* 503

THE AUTHOR TEAM

In His Image Studios

Carl S. Warren

Dr. Carl S. Warren is Professor Emeritus of Accounting at the University of Georgia, Athens. Dr. Warren has taught classes at the University of Georgia, University of Iowa, Michigan State University, and University of Chicago. Professor Warren focused his teaching efforts on principles of accounting and auditing. He received his Ph.D. from Michigan State University and his B.B.A. and M.A. from the University of Iowa. During his career, Dr. Warren published numerous articles in professional journals, including *The Accounting Review, Journal of Accounting Research, Journal of Accountancy, The CPA Journal*, and *Auditing: A Journal of Practice & Theory*. Dr. Warren has served on numerous committees of the American Accounting Association, the American Institute of Certified Public Accountants, and the Institute of Internal Auditors. He has also consulted with numerous companies and public accounting firms. Warren's outside interests include playing handball, golfing, skiing, backpacking, and fly-fishing.

Charles Garvey, Garvey Photography

James M. Reeve

Dr. James M. Reeve is Professor Emeritus of Accounting and Information Management at the University of Tennessee. Professor Reeve taught on the accounting faculty for 25 years, after graduating with his Ph.D. from Oklahoma State University. His teaching effort focused on undergraduate accounting principles and graduate education in the Master of Accountancy and Senior Executive MBA programs. Beyond this, Professor Reeve is also very active in the Supply Chain Certification program, which is a major executive education and research effort of the College. His research interests are varied and include work in managerial accounting, supply chain management, lean manufacturing, and information management. He has published over 40 articles in academic and professional journals, including the *Journal of Cost Management, Journal of Management Accounting Research, Accounting Review, Management Accounting Quarterly, Supply Chain Management Review*, and *Accounting Horizons*. He has consulted or provided training around the world for a wide variety of organizations, including Boeing, Procter & Gamble, Norfolk Southern, Hershey Foods, Coca-Cola, and Sony. When not writing books, Professor Reeve plays golf and is involved in faith-based activities.

Ken Bennett

Jonathan E. Duchac

Dr. Jonathan Duchac is the Merrill Lynch and Co. Professor of Accounting and Director of the Program in Enterprise Risk Management at Wake Forest University. He earned his Ph.D. in accounting from the University of Georgia and currently teaches introductory and advanced courses in financial accounting. Dr. Duchac has received a number of awards during his career, including the Wake Forest University Outstanding Graduate Professor Award, the T.B. Rose award for Instructional Innovation, and the University of Georgia Outstanding Teaching Assistant Award. In addition to his teaching responsibilities, Dr. Duchac has served as Accounting Advisor to Merrill Lynch Equity Research, where he worked with research analysts in reviewing and evaluating the financial reporting practices of public companies. He has testified before the U.S. House of Representatives, the Financial Accounting Standards Board, and the Securities and Exchange Commission; and has worked with a number of major public companies on financial reporting and accounting policy issues. In addition to his professional interests, Dr. Duchac is the Treasurer of The

Special Children's School of Winston-Salem, a private, nonprofit developmental day school serving children with special needs. Dr. Duchac is an avid long-distance runner, mountain biker, and snow skier. His recent events include the Grandfather Mountain Marathon, the Black Mountain Marathon, the Shut-In Ridge Trail run, and NO MAAM (Nocturnal Overnight Mountain Bike Assault on Mount Mitchell).

Sheila F. Elworthy

Dr. Sheila Elworthy, C.A., is the Vice President of Learning at the CA School of Business (CASB), the professional school for aspiring chartered accountants in western Canada. Dr. Elworthy has taught introductory, intermediate, and advanced accounting, and general business courses for 20 years at Camosun College in Victoria, B.C.; University of Victoria in Victoria, B.C.; Eastern Institute of Technology in Napier, New Zealand; and in the Executive Certified Management Accounting (ECMA) program. Her professional interest in successful learning processes for accounting students extends from the introductory stages in college and university settings through to the successful completion of the students' chosen designation. Dr. Elworthy received her M.B.A. from the Richard Ivey School of Business in London, Ontario, and her Doctor of Education from Simon Fraser University in Burnaby, B.C. In 1984, Dr. Elworthy qualified as a Chartered Accountant in Ontario. In addition to her professional pursuits, Dr. Elworthy is active in Big Brothers Big Sisters, currently serving as a member of the board and of the Fund Development Committee and previously as the Treasurer and the Chair of the Finance Committee. Sheila is also a founding member of the CPA Professional Education Program Working Group, tasked with the design of the national program for Canadian accounting education and accreditation. Her personal interests include spending time with her husband and her three children, playing bridge, cycling, kayaking, and skiing.

Tana M. Kristjanson

Tana M. Kristjanson, C.A., C.F.E., is an instructor in the School of Business at Camosun College, in Victoria, B.C. She has also taught accounting at North Island College in Courtenay, B.C.; Vancouver Island University (formerly Malaspina College) in Nanaimo, B.C.; in the Certified Management Accounting (CMA) program; and the Chartered Accountant School of Business (CASB). Ms. Kristjanson currently teaches introductory and intermediate courses in financial accounting and auditing and has developed a college-level fraud awareness course. She is an investigator for the Professional Conduct and Ethics Committee of the Institute of Chartered Accountants of B.C. Her professional interests focus on the use of reflection and student feedback as mechanisms to improve teaching. She is currently working on her Masters of Education at Simon Fraser University. Ms. Kristjanson spent five years in public practice working on reviews, audits, and taxes for clients such as not-for-profits, businesses, and Native Councils. She became a Chartered Accountant in 2004. Her personal interests include hiking, travelling, and spending time with her husband, friends, and family.

Barrie E. Tober

Barrie E. Tober, C.M.A, is a professor in the School of Business and Management at Niagara College, Niagara-on-the-Lake, Ontario, where she teaches introductory financial accounting, managerial accounting, and operations management. She is also the program coordinator for the two- and three-year accounting diplomas at Niagara College. She has taught managerial accounting, advanced financial accounting, and accounting information systems at Brock University in St. Catharines, Ontario. Professor Tober completed her B.Comm at the University of Windsor, received her C.M.A. designation in 1992, and earned a Master of Accountancy degree from Brock in 2005. Prior to becoming a full-time professor, she spent eight years working in public accounting and two years as a consultant for new entrepreneurs in the Business Development Centre at Niagara College. Her personal interests include camping and travelling with her husband and four children.

PREFACE

In the second Canadian edition of *Accounting*, we have continued with the tradition of focusing on the changing needs of accounting students and their instructors by utilizing feedback from student reviews, an Editorial Advisory Board, and other reviewers. Accounting faculty from all over the country contributed to our book development process in a direct and creative way. Many of the features and themes in this text reflect the suggestions and feedback received from both instructors and students.

Textbooks play an invaluable role in the teaching and learning environment at postsecondary institutions. Designed for today's students, this text uses a high-impact writing style that emphasizes topics in a concise and clearly written manner. Direct sentences, concise paragraphs, numbered lists, and step-by-step calculations provide students with an easy-to-follow structure for learning accounting. This is achieved without sacrificing content or rigour.

Walkthrough of Pedagogical Features

Accounting, Second Canadian Edition, is unparalleled in pedagogical innovation. Our goal is to provide a logical framework and pedagogical system that cater to how today's students study and learn. Our student surveys and review board of accounting faculty from across Canada significantly influenced the textbook presentation. Here is a preview of the important features that are used throughout the textbook:

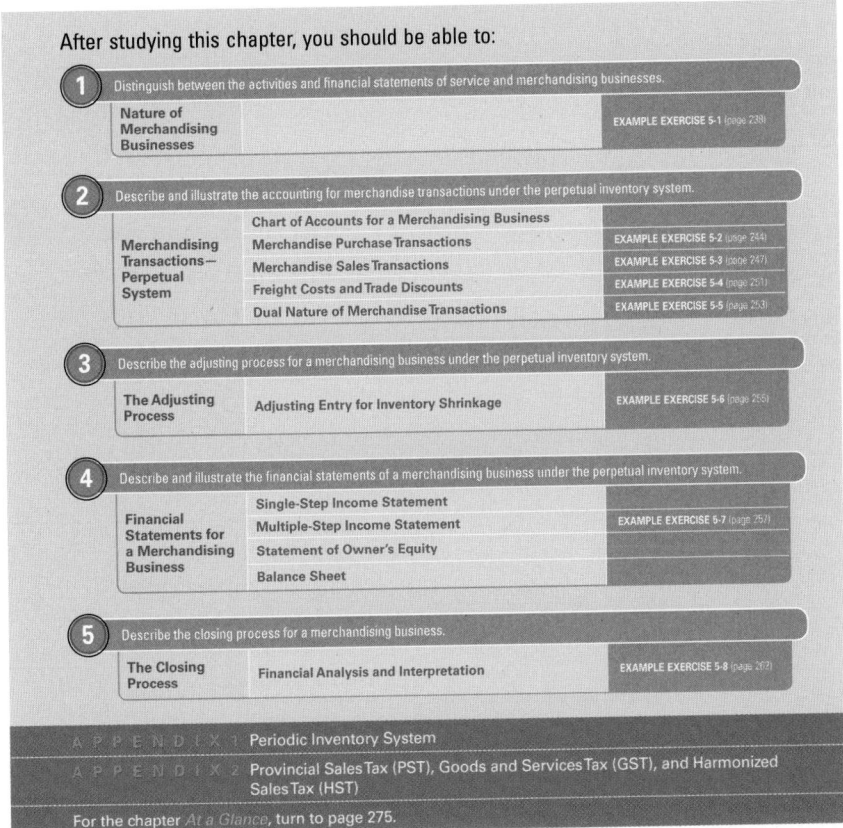

Guiding Principles System

Students can easily locate the information they need to master course concepts with the Guiding Principles System (GPS). At the beginning of every chapter, this innovative system plots a course through the chapter content by displaying the chapter objectives, major topics, and related Example Exercises. The GPS reference to the chapter At a Glance summary completes this proven system.

Clear Objectives and Key Learning Outcomes

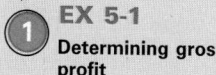

To help guide students, the authors provide clear chapter objectives and important learning outcomes. All aspects of the chapter materials relate back to these key points and outcomes, which keeps students focused on the most important topics and concepts to help them succeed in the course.

1 Distinguish between the activities and financial statements of service and merchandising businesses.

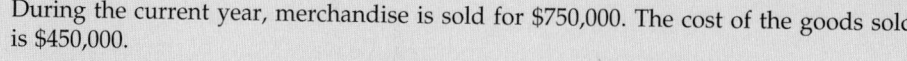

EXERCISES

1 **EX 5-1**
Determining gross profit

During the current year, merchandise is sold for $750,000. The cost of the goods sold is $450,000.
a. What is the amount of the gross profit?
b. Compute the gross profit percentage (gross profit divided by sales).
c. Will the income statement necessarily report a net income? Explain.

Example Exercises

Example Exercises were developed to reinforce concepts and procedures in a bold, new way. Similar to following the instructor's example in the classroom, students follow the authors' example to see how to complete accounting applications as they are presented in the text. This feature also provides a list of Practice Exercises that parallel the Example Exercises to provide students with the practice they need. In addition, the Practice Exercises also include references back to the Example Exercises so that students can easily cross-reference when completing homework.

See the example of the application being presented.

Follow along as the authors work through the Example Exercise.

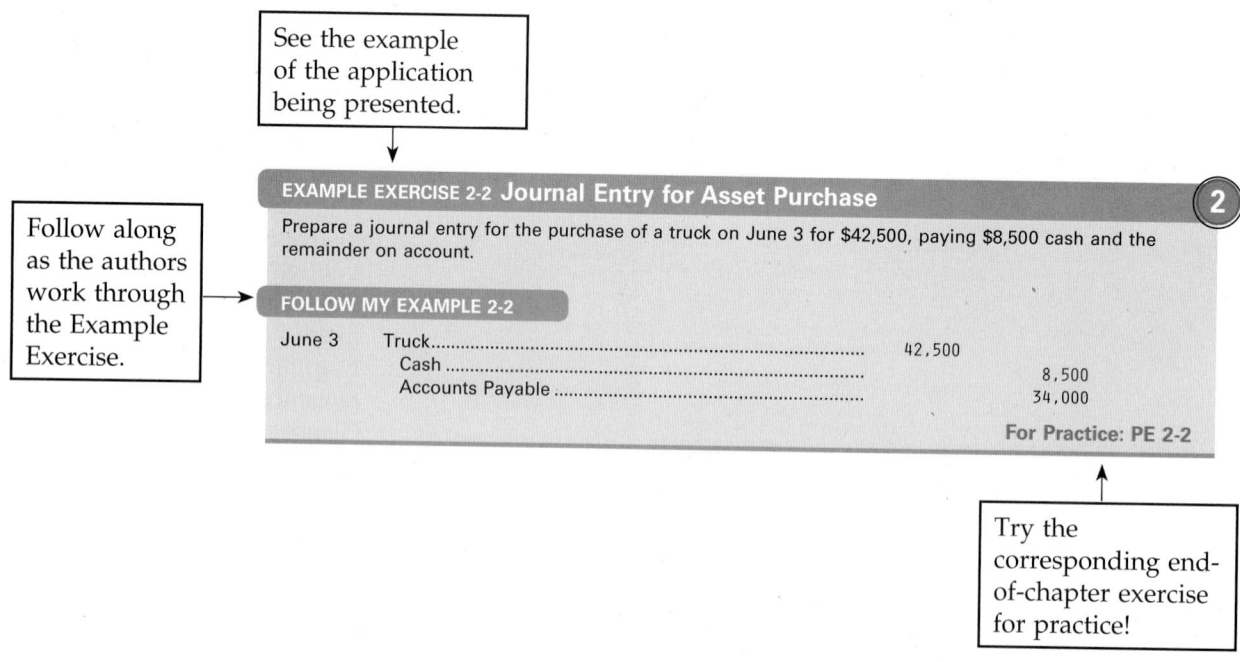

EXAMPLE EXERCISE 2-2 Journal Entry for Asset Purchase

2

Prepare a journal entry for the purchase of a truck on June 3 for $42,500, paying $8,500 cash and the remainder on account.

FOLLOW MY EXAMPLE 2-2

June 3	Truck	42,500	
	Cash		8,500
	Accounts Payable		34,000

For Practice: PE 2-2

Try the corresponding end-of-chapter exercise for practice!

At a Glance Chapter Summary

The At a Glance summary grid ties everything together and helps students stay on course. First, the Key Points recap the chapter content for each Learning Objective. Second, the related Key Learning Outcomes list all the expected student performance capabilities that result from completing each objective. The Key Learning Outcomes are referenced by page number in the next column, to guide students to the related content in the chapter. For students needing further practice on a specific outcome, the last column references the related Example Exercise. Through this intuitive grid, all of the chapter pedagogy links together in one cleanly integrated summary.

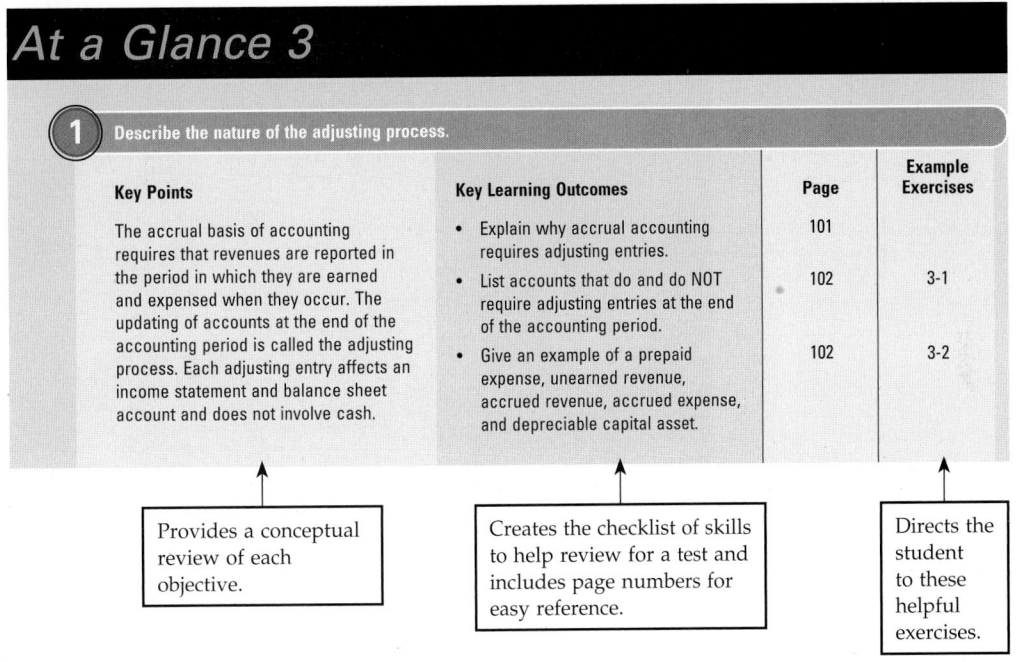

At a Glance 3

1 Describe the nature of the adjusting process.

Key Points	Key Learning Outcomes	Page	Example Exercises
The accrual basis of accounting requires that revenues are reported in the period in which they are earned and expensed when they occur. The updating of accounts at the end of the accounting period is called the adjusting process. Each adjusting entry affects an income statement and balance sheet account and does not involve cash.	• Explain why accrual accounting requires adjusting entries.	101	
	• List accounts that do and do NOT require adjusting entries at the end of the accounting period.	102	3-1
	• Give an example of a prepaid expense, unearned revenue, accrued revenue, accrued expense, and depreciable capital asset.	102	3-2

Provides a conceptual review of each objective.

Creates the checklist of skills to help review for a test and includes page numbers for easy reference.

Directs the student to these helpful exercises.

Practice Exercises

The Example Exercises direct students to the Practice Exercises. These Practice Exercises parallel the Example Exercises and provide the opportunity for further reinforcement and course mastery. Students who have difficulty with the Practice Exercises can return to the Example Exercises to see a model solution.

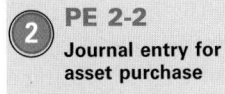

PE 2-2
Journal entry for asset purchase

Prepare T accounts and a journal entry for the purchase of office supplies on October 14 for $9,000, paying $1,800 cash and the remainder on account. Office supplies has a zero opening balance, cash has an $800 opening balance, and accounts payable has a $700 balance.

EE 2-2 p. 54

Real-World Chapter Openers

Chapter openers relate the accounting and business concepts in the chapter to familiar companies and activities in students' lives. These openers employ examples of real companies and provide invaluable insight into real business practices. Several of the openers focus on familiar companies, such as Facebook, Jones Soda Co., Tim Hortons, and Cirque du Soleil.

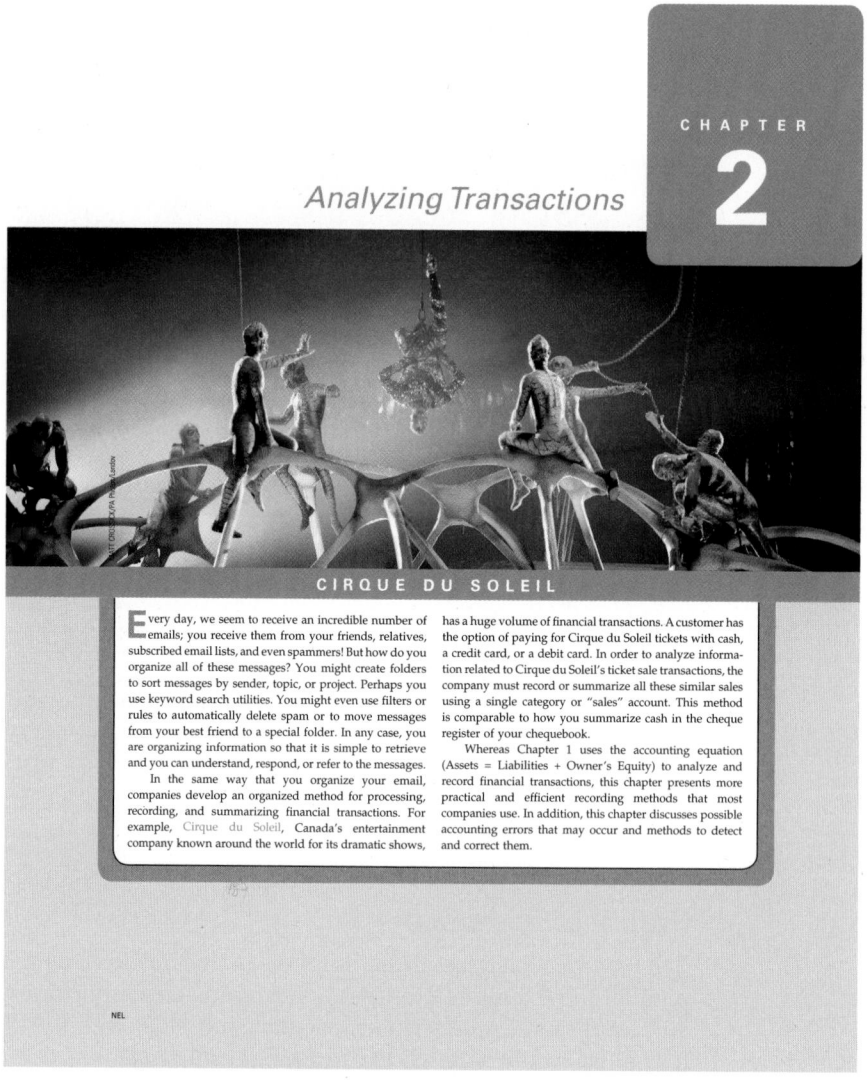

Analyzing Transactions

CHAPTER 2

CIRQUE DU SOLEIL

Every day, we seem to receive an incredible number of emails; you receive them from your friends, relatives, subscribed email lists, and even spammers! But how do you organize all of these messages? You might create folders to sort messages by sender, topic, or project. Perhaps you use keyword search utilities. You might even use filters or rules to automatically delete spam or to move messages from your best friend to a special folder. In any case, you are organizing information so that it is simple to retrieve and you can understand, respond, or refer to the messages.

In the same way that you organize your email, companies develop an organized method for processing, recording, and summarizing financial transactions. For example, Cirque du Soleil, Canada's entertainment company known around the world for its dramatic shows,

has a huge volume of financial transactions. A customer has the option of paying for Cirque du Soleil tickets with cash, a credit card, or a debit card. In order to analyze information related to Cirque du Soleil's ticket sale transactions, the company must record or summarize all these similar sales using a single category or "sales" account. This method is comparable to how you summarize cash in the cheque register of your chequebook.

Whereas Chapter 1 uses the accounting equation (Assets = Liabilities + Owner's Equity) to analyze and record financial transactions, this chapter presents more practical and efficient recording methods that most companies use. In addition, this chapter discusses possible accounting errors that may occur and methods to detect and correct them.

NEL

Morning Java Financial Statements

Beginning in Chapter 6, "Inventories," and continuing through Chapter 15, "Investments," chapters contain excerpts from the full financial statements for Morning Java, a coffee company. These statements show students the big picture of accounting by providing a consistent reference point for users who want to see a set of financial statements and how each chapter topic relates to the different financial statements. The financial statements were crafted by the authors to be consistent with the presentation in each chapter and are prepared using Accounting Standards for Private Enterprises (ASPE) in Volume 1 and International Financial Reporting Standards (IFRS) in Volume 2. Any significant differences in financial statement presentation when using ASPE or IFRS are mentioned. The Morning Java statements in Appendix A of each volume follow this same pattern. In Appendix A of Volume 1, the ASPE version of the statements is presented with IFRS differences pointed out. In Appendix A of Volume 2, the IFRS version of the statements is presented with ASPE differences pointed out.

User-Friendly Design

Based on students' testimonials of what they find most useful, this streamlined presentation includes a wealth of helpful resources without the clutter. Some exhibits use computerized spreadsheets to better reflect the changing environment of business. Visual learners will appreciate the generous number of exhibits and illustrations used to convey concepts and procedures.

Exhibit 4

The Closing Process

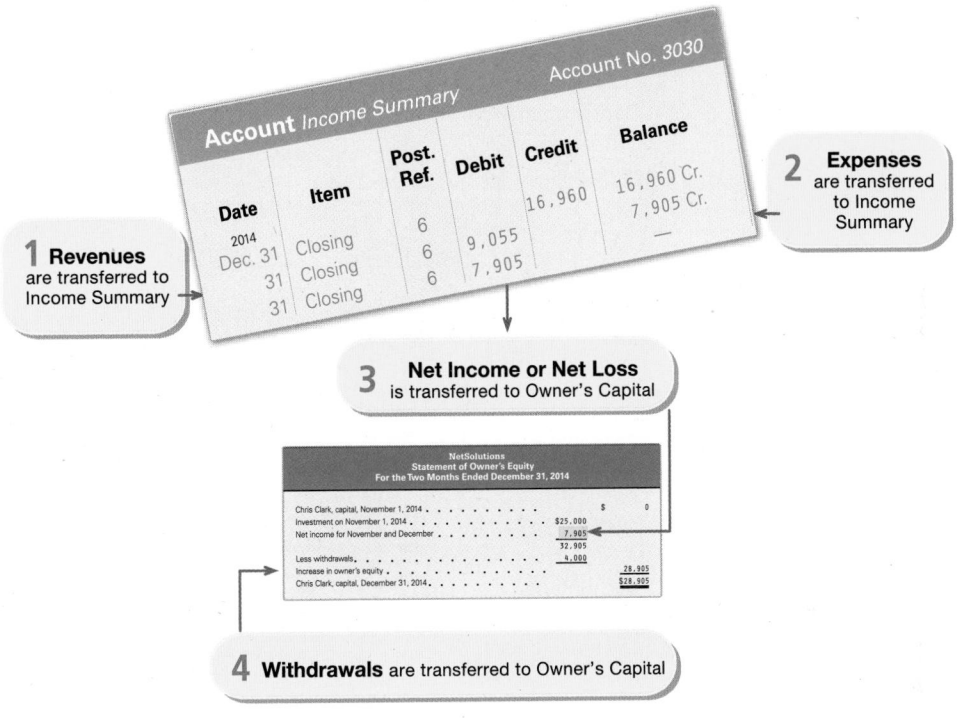

Financial Records Colour Coding

Accounting, Second Canadian Edition, introduces a new colour scheme to help students learn to identify the different types of accounting records.

Financial statements →

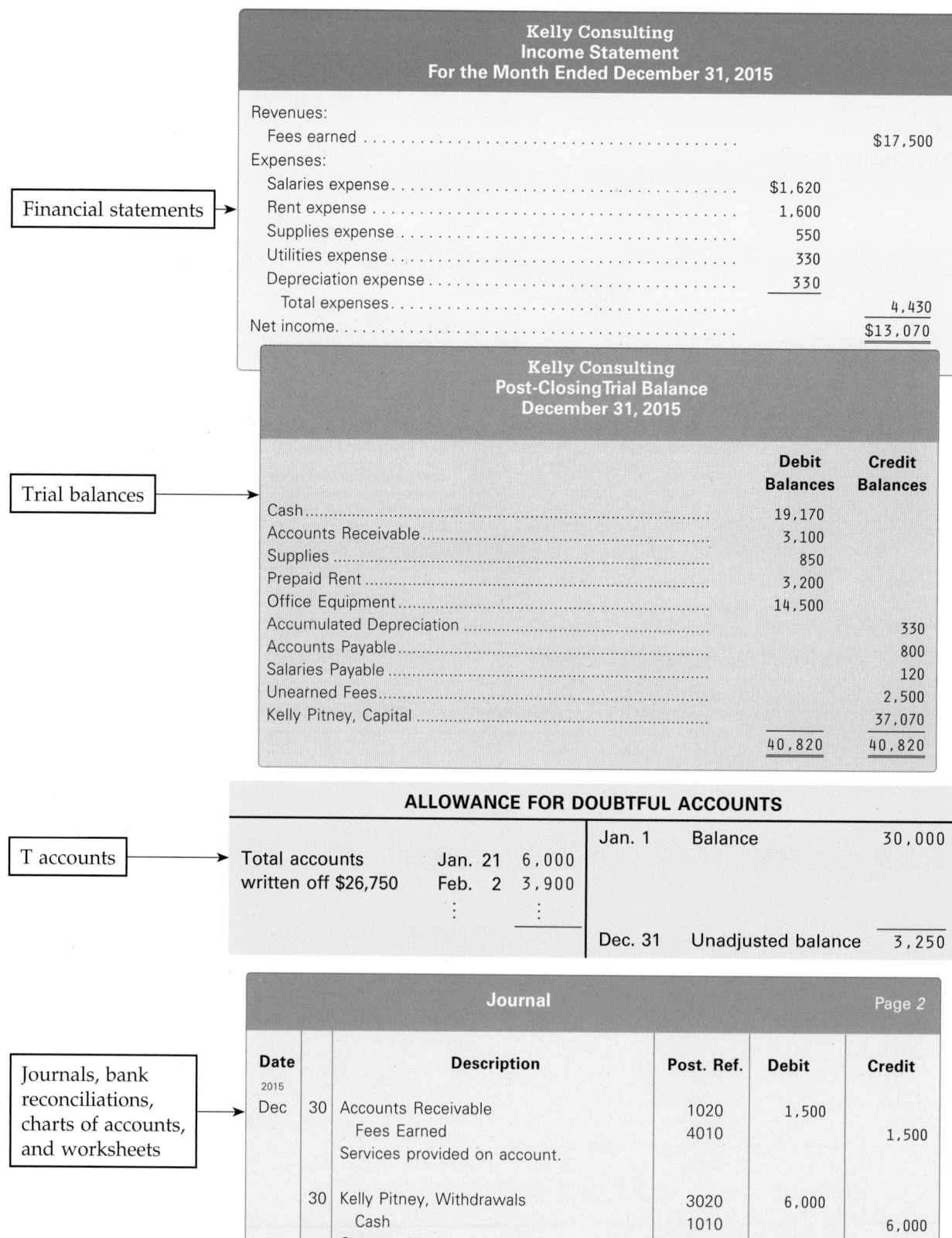

Kelly Consulting
Income Statement
For the Month Ended December 31, 2015

Revenues:		
Fees earned		$17,500
Expenses:		
Salaries expense	$1,620	
Rent expense	1,600	
Supplies expense	550	
Utilities expense	330	
Depreciation expense	330	
Total expenses		4,430
Net income		$13,070

Trial balances →

Kelly Consulting
Post-Closing Trial Balance
December 31, 2015

	Debit Balances	Credit Balances
Cash	19,170	
Accounts Receivable	3,100	
Supplies	850	
Prepaid Rent	3,200	
Office Equipment	14,500	
Accumulated Depreciation		330
Accounts Payable		800
Salaries Payable		120
Unearned Fees		2,500
Kelly Pitney, Capital		37,070
	40,820	40,820

T accounts →

ALLOWANCE FOR DOUBTFUL ACCOUNTS

Total accounts written off $26,750	Jan. 21	6,000	Jan. 1	Balance		30,000
	Feb. 2	3,900				
	⋮	⋮	Dec. 31	Unadjusted balance		3,250

Journals, bank reconciliations, charts of accounts, and worksheets →

Journal — Page *2*

Date		Description	Post. Ref.	Debit	Credit
2015					
Dec	30	Accounts Receivable	1020	1,500	
		Fees Earned	4010		1,500
		Services provided on account.			
	30	Kelly Pitney, Withdrawals	3020	6,000	
		Cash	1010		6,000
		Owner withdrawal.			

Financial Analysis and Interpretation

The Financial Analysis and Interpretation, or FAI, section at the ends of Chapters 4 to 16 introduces relevant key ratios used throughout the textbook. Students connect with the business environment as they learn how stakeholders interpret financial reports. This section covers basic analysis tools that students will use again in Chapter 17, "Financial Statement Analysis." Furthermore, a related Example Exercise has been added after each FAI in this edition, and students can test their proficiency with these tools through special activities and exercises at the end of each chapter. To ensure a consistent presentation, a unique icon is used for both the section and in the margin beside related end-of-chapter materials.

FINANCIAL ANALYSIS AND INTERPRETATION

Long-term assets can be evaluated by their ability to generate income. The **return on assets** ratio measures the profitability of total assets used within the company and is computed as follows:

$$\text{Return on Assets} = \frac{\text{Net Income}}{\text{Average Total Assets}}$$

To illustrate, the following information is used for WestJet:

	December 31, 2011 (in millions)	December 31, 2010 (in millions)
Total assets	$3,474	$3,384
Net income	149	

Thus, the return on assets ratio is calculated as follows:

$$\text{Return to Assets} = \frac{\$149}{(\$3,384 + \$3,474)/2} = 4.3\%$$

The larger this ratio, the more efficiently a business is using its assets. This ratio can be compared across time within a single company or to other companies in the industry to evaluate overall asset performance.

The return on assets for a number of different companies is shown below. The smaller ratios are associated with companies that require large investments in long-term assets. The larger ratios are associated with firms that are more labour intensive and require smaller investments in long-term assets.

Company (Industry)	Return on Assets
Canadian Pacific Railway Ltd. (railroad)	4.7%
Google Inc. (Internet)	17.3%
Tim Hortons Inc. (restaurant)	28.3%

Integrity, Objectivity, and Ethics in Business

In each chapter, these cases help students develop their ethical compass. Often coupled with related end-of-chapter activities, these cases can be discussed in class, or students can consider the cases as they read the chapter. Both the section and related end-of-chapter materials are indicated with a unique icon for a consistent presentation.

INTEGRITY, OBJECTIVITY, AND ETHICS IN BUSINESS

ETHICAL BEHAVIOUR AS A MARKETING TOOL

Consumers are concerned with the environmental impact of their purchases on the planet, and so ethical behaviour of corporations is becoming an increasingly important selling feature. More and more companies are focusing their efforts on ensuring the products sold in their stores are produced in an environmentally friendly and socially responsible manner. A movement is growing to ensure that producers in developing countries are paid a fair price for their products. Ethical Soles Trading Company, for example, is a Canadian distributor of ethical footwear and apparel. Coffee distributors are another example, with more fair-trade brands being offered all the time. Fair trade can apply to the local market as well. Wolfville, Nova Scotia, was proclaimed the first fair-trade town in Canada when it committed to buying local produce in support of its farmers.

Critical Thinking

Boxed critical thinking features in each chapter present samples of the ambiguities, risks, and uncertainties that students may encounter in their accounting practice. Using a question and answer format, this feature helps students develop their ability to consider multiple factors and use their judgment in applying accounting concepts to realistic and ambiguous situations. The critical thinking icon is also used in end-of-chapter materials to indicate the need for analysis or deeper thinking.

CRITICAL THINKING

Employers often say their employees are their most valuable asset. **Does an employee meet the definition of an asset?**

An employee meets two of the three essential characteristics of an asset: (1) an employee contributes to future cash flows, and (2) the event giving rise to the benefit has already occurred—the employee has been hired. The third essential characteristic, however, is not met: the business cannot control access to the benefit because an employee has the right to resign at any time. Thus, an employee does not appear on the financial statements as an asset, despite what many employers say!

Mid-Chapter Illustrative Problem and Solution

A problem and its solution illustrate one or more concepts from the first half of the chapter. Students are thus able to apply their knowledge early in the chapter.

MID-CHAPTER ILLUSTRATIVE PROBLEM

On December 31, 2014, the following data were accumulated to assist the accountant in preparing the adjusting entries for Chocolate Bakery:

a. The supplies account balance on December 31 is $2,105. The supplies on hand are $1,603.
b. The unearned sales account balance on December 31 is $4,200, representing work that will be completed over three months, December, January, and February.

Journalize the adjusting entries required at December 31, 2014.

MID-CHAPTER ILLUSTRATIVE SOLUTION

2014				
Dec.	31	Supplies Expense	502	
		Supplies		502
		Supplies used ($2,105 − $1,603).		
	31	Unearned Sales	1,400	
		Sales Revenue		1,400
		Sales earned ($4,200/3 months).		

Continuing Case Study and Problem

Throughout Chapters 1–5, students follow a fictitious company, NetSolutions, which demonstrates a variety of transactions. The continuity of using the same company facilitates student learning, especially for Chapters 1–4, which cover the accounting cycle. Also, using the same company allows students to follow the transition of the company from a service business in Chapters 1–4 to a merchandising business in Chapter 5.

The practice material for Chapters 1–4 also includes a continuing problem, featuring a fictitious enterprise called Music Depot, which allows students to practise completing the accounting cycle for one company.

End-of-Chapter Illustrative Problem and Solution

A solved problem models one or more of the chapter's assignment problems so that students can apply the modelled procedures to end-of-chapter materials.

Market-Leading End-of-Chapter Material

Students need to practise accounting so that they can understand and use it. To give students the greatest possible advantage in the real world, *Accounting*, Second Canadian Edition, goes beyond presenting theory and procedure by including comprehensive end-of-chapter material.

New to the Second Canadian Edition

Textbooks continue to play an invaluable role in the teaching and learning environments. Continuing our focus from the previous edition, we reached out to accounting instructors in an effort to improve the textbook presentation. Our research indicated a need to remain current in the areas of emerging topics and trends, while continuing to look for ways to make the book more accessible to students. The results of the collaboration with instructors from across Canada are reflected in the following major improvements to the second Canadian edition.

Accounting Standards for Private Enterprise (ASPE) and International Financial Reporting Standards (IFRS)

Today's accounting educators face the challenge of teaching introductory accounting in an environment that uses more than one set of corporate accounting standards. Based upon feedback from instructors, we have organized the volumes so that Volume 1 emphasizes ASPE and discusses the IFRS differences, while Volume 2 includes both ASPE and IFRS treatments. We feel this approach will allow students to learn both accounting treatments without being overly confused or overwhelmed. In Volume 1, Appendix A presents the ASPE version of the financial statements for our fictitious company, Morning Java, with IFRS differences pointed out. In Volume 2, both IFRS versions of the financial statements for Morning Java are presented, with ASPE differences pointed out.

The Accounting Equation and the Accounting Cycle

To help students understand that a transaction ultimately affects the accounting equation, T accounts are now shown for each journal entry in Chapters 2 and 3.

Also, an image of the accounting cycle has been referenced throughout Chapters 2 to 4, to ensure that students know where they are working in the accounting cycle and how each step relates to prior and subsequent steps.

Additional Example and Practice Exercises

Example Exercises and Practice Exercises were developed to reinforce concepts and provide students with opportunities to practise the chapter content. This edition adds more Example Exercises and Practice Exercises for chapter material and for the Financial Analysis and Interpretations (FAIs).

Critical Thinking

A new feature of *Accounting*, Second Canadian Edition, is the introduction of Critical Thinking boxes, designed with the assistance of Dr. Susan Wolcott, CMA, CPA, Ph.D. These boxes allow students to explore ambiguous accounting issues or accounting treatments. This feature gives students the opportunity to use the conceptual framework to resolve situations that have more than one correct answer.

End-of-Chapter Exercises and Problems

This edition increases the number of end-of-chapter exercises and problems by 30% over the previous edition. Many of the end-of-chapter materials have been updated for both fictitious and real-world companies. The longer questions are now shorter in response to feedback that they were too time-consuming, and the number of questions has increased substantially.

Chapter-by-Chapter Enhancements

The following specific content changes can be found in *Accounting,* Second Canadian Edition.

Volume 1

Chapter 1: Introduction to Accounting and Business

- The chapter opener features Facebook.
- Subtotals have been removed from the accounting equation analysis throughout the chapter.
- The continuing case study and longer problems are shorter.
- Discussions have been added on the Chartered Professional Accountant (CPA) designation and the merger of the accounting professions.
- Definitions have been added for assets and liabilities.
- More of the conceptual framework elements are discussed.
- New end-of-chapter exercises and problems have been added.

Chapter 2: Analyzing Transactions

- T accounts have been added to help students better understand the accounting equation.
- A new table summarizes common transaction terminology and the related accounts to be debited or credited.
- The steps of the accounting cycle are emphasized and each step is tied to the accounting cycle.
- Prepaid insurance and unearned revenue are introduced to lead to better flow when introducing adjusting entries in the next chapter.
- New end-of-chapter exercises and problems have been added.

Chapter 3: The Adjusting Process

- T accounts are used to describe and illustrate adjusting entries.
- The chapter features five new exhibits summarizing the five types of adjusting entries, as a reference for identifying the differences between adjusting entries and the journal entries required.
- The continuing problem is shorter.
- The coverage of depreciation is more comprehensive and introduces the calculations for straight-line depreciation.
- New end-of-chapter exercises and problems have been added.

Chapter 4: Completing the Accounting Cycle

- The steps of the accounting cycle are emphasized, and each step is tied to the accounting cycle.
- A new Example Exercise and Practice Exercise correspond with the new FAI, Working Capital and Current Ratio.
- New end-of-chapter exercises and problems have been added.

Chapter 5: Accounting for Merchandising Businesses

- Chapter 5 from the first Canadian edition, "Accounting Systems," has moved to Appendix E, in response to reviewer feedback on the best way to treat this material. Accounting Systems for Merchandisers, which was an appendix to "Accounting for Merchandising Businesses" in the previous edition, now forms part of Appendix E.
- Treatment under ASPE is presented, and the IFRS differences are identified and discussed.
- Coverage, exercises, and problems for Appendix 2 now allow instructors to teach PST only, PST and GST, or HST only. The accounting treatment of refund entries has also been added.
- Problems are shorter.
- A new Financial Analysis and Interpretation box features gross profit and gross margin using the real-world retailer Le Château.
- A new Example Exercise and Practice Exercise correspond with the new FAI.
- New end-of-chapter exercises and problems have been added.

Chapter 6: Inventories

- The steps have been added for calculating the moving weighted average cost using the perpetual inventory method.
- The discussion of the periodic inventory system has moved to Appendix 2 to be consistent with Chapter 5.
- A new Example Exercise and Practice Exercise correspond with the FAI.
- Treatment of inventories under ASPE is presented, and the IFRS differences are identified and discussed.
- New end-of-chapter exercises and problems have been added.

Chapter 7: Internal Control and Cash

- A new discussion addresses the responsibilities of internal and external auditors.
- An example of an online bank statement is presented to be consistent with statements that students are familiar with.
- The steps for completing a bank reconciliation have been condensed.
- New end of chapter exercises and problems have been added.

Chapter 8: Receivables

- Content and exercises address the percent of receivables allowance method.
- Problems now show more than one allowance method used throughout the year.
- Merchandise transactions have been added to reinforce inventory chapter coverage.
- Treatment under ASPE is presented, and the IFRS differences are identified and discussed.
- A new Example Exercise and Practice Exercise correspond with the FAI.
- New end-of-chapter exercises and problems have been added.

Chapter 9: Property, Plant, and Equipment and Other Long-Term Assets

- Discussion of impairment losses for long-term assets has been expanded, and more related exercises have been added.
- The discussion on goodwill has been updated to reflect recent changes in accounting standards.
- A new discussion addresses the revaluation model.
- New problems have been added that require balance sheet preparation for consecutive years.
- Content and exercises on lump-sum purchases have been added.
- The discussion of depreciation for partial years is simplified.
- T accounts have been added to illustrate the impact of property, plant, and equipment disposals on account balances.
- Treatment under ASPE is presented, and the IFRS differences are identified and discussed.
- A new Financial Analysis and Interpretation features return on assets, using the real-world company WestJet Airlines Ltd.
- A new Example Exercise and Practice Exercise correspond with the FAI.
- New end-of-chapter exercises and problems have been added.

Chapter 10: Current Liabilities and Payroll

- Discussion has been expanded on different types of liabilities such as accrued liabilities and unearned revenues.
- An explanation of Harmonized Sales Tax (HST) and examples of HST have been added.
- The discussion of discounted notes payable has been omitted.
- Provisions have been added to the chapter content.
- Updated payroll calculations now include excerpts of payroll charts supplied by Canada Revenue Agency (CRA).
- Federal and provincial income taxes are now shown separately throughout the chapter.
- New Example Exercises and Practice Exercises have been added to calculate gross pay and deductions and record remittance of payroll deductions.
- The material has been rearranged to show single employee information all together.
- New end-of-chapter exercises and problems have been added.

Volume 2
Chapter 11: Partnerships

- New Example Exercises and Practice Exercises have been added for recording closing entries, division of income when allowances exceed net income, and partner withdrawals.
- The Mid-Chapter Illustrative Problem is shorter.
- The asset revaluation Example Exercise now includes an allowance for doubtful accounts to be consistent with examples used in exercises and problems.
- The same partnership scenario is used throughout the chapter.
- More of the examples and exercises now show an unequal division of profits to better reflect real-world scenarios.
- The balance sheet presentation for partnerships has been added.

- The liquidation section has been rearranged to embed the journal entries within the explanation of the steps.
- The coverage on characteristics of corporations has been moved to Chapter 12.
- New end-of-chapter exercises and problems have been added.

Chapter 12: Corporations: Organization, Share Transactions, and Shareholders' Equity

- The chapter opener features Leon's Furniture Limited.
- The characteristics of corporations have been moved to this chapter from Chapter 11.
- New Example Exercises and Practice Exercises compare the three business forms, closing entries for corporations, and the statement of changes in equity.
- A more detailed discussion has been added on retained earnings, including closing entries.
- A discussion has been added on other comprehensive income and accumulated other comprehensive income.
- The discussion on common and preferred shares rights and privileges has been expanded.
- The option of recording cash dividends to a cash dividends account and closing it to retained earnings at year-end has been added.
- The presentation of shareholders' equity has been reorganized to cover IFRS first in this chapter, and Morning Java's equity is shown under both IFRS and ASPE for comparison purposes.
- The FAI has been expanded to discuss the industry comparison between the returns on common shareholders' equity for Bank of Montreal and for Royal Bank of Canada.
- The statement of shareholders' equity has been omitted.
- New end-of-chapter exercises and problems have been added.

Chapter 13: Corporations: Additional Share Transactions, Income Statement, and Accounting Changes

- The chapter opener features Shoppers Drug Mart.
- New Example Exercises and Practice Exercises address share splits.
- The explanation of weighted average common shares has been expanded to include share splits and share dividends.
- The Mid-Chapter Illustrative Problem has been expanded.
- An example has been added to demonstrate the "tax effect" on discontinued operations.
- Extraordinary items have been omitted.
- An example has been added to show the accounting treatment for correction of an error.
- Objective 5 has been revised to address the statement of comprehensive income.
- New end-of-chapter exercises and problems have been added.

Chapter 14: Long-Term Liabilities: Bonds and Notes

- The chapter opener features WestJet Airlines Ltd.
- The Mid-Chapter Illustrative Problem is shorter.
- IFRS is used, and the differences under ASPE are discussed.
- A new Example Exercise shows the issuing of bonds at face value.
- The coverage of financing corporations is simplified and now opens the chapter.

- New problems address adjusting entries, the effective interest method of bond amortization, bond retirement, and financial statement presentation.
- New problems integrate current liabilities from Chapter 11 with long-term liabilities transactions.
- New T accounts illustrate the impact of bond redemptions on the general ledger accounts.
- A new Example Exercise and Practice Exercise correspond with the FAI.
- New end-of-chapter exercises and problems have been added.

Chapter 15: Investments

- The chapter opener features Shaw Communications Inc.
- The chapter has been reorganized to enable students to understand and apply the current standard. A new appendix describes the upcoming changes affecting investments for corporations reporting under IFRS.
- Chapter material has been updated to reflect current IFRS.
- A new discussion addresses the effective method and the straight line method of amortizing bond discounts and premiums.
- The direct valuation method of tracking investments has been added.
- For comparison purposes, Morning Java investments are illustrated for IFRS and ASPE.
- New end-of-chapter exercises and problems have been added.

Chapter 16: Statement of Cash Flows

- A new Example Exercise and Practice Exercise correspond with the FAI.
- Cash flows are presented using IFRS, with a discussion of the differences under ASPE.
- New end-of-chapter exercises and problems have been added.

Chapter 17: Financial Statement Analysis

- The chapter opener features Potash Corporation of Saskatchewan, Inc.
- The problems are shorter and critical thinking questions have been added.
- New end-of-chapter exercises and problems have been added.

Appendices

The complete annual report of Leon's Furniture Limited and the partial report of Shoppers Drug Mart illustrate financial statements prepared according to IFRS.

Custom Publishing

Nelson Education Ltd. is pleased to offer instructors greater flexibility in the choice of material covered in their textbooks by offering the opportunity to customize the textbook resources. If you are an instructor who is interested in selecting an alternative organization, adding or omitting chapters from what is currently presented in the two volumes, or other variations on this textbook, please contact your Nelson Sales and Editorial Representative to discuss the options available to you.

Online Support: Homework Management for Students and Instructors

Aplia

Founded in 2000 by economist and Stanford professor Paul Romer, Aplia is an educational technology company dedicated to improving learning by increasing student effort and engagement. Currently, Aplia products have been used by more than a million students at more than 1,300 institutions.

For students, Aplia offers a way to stay on top of coursework by working through regularly scheduled homework assignments that increase their practice time and provide prompt feedback. Interactive tools and additional content further increase students' engagement and understanding.

For instructors, Aplia offers high-quality, auto-graded assignments that ensure students apply effort on a regular basis throughout the term. These assignments can easily be customized to suit individual teaching schedules. To ensure consistency between the Aplia course and the textbook, the Aplia course for *Accounting*, Second Canadian Edition, was prepared by two of the textbook authors, Sheila Elworthy and Tana Kristjanson.

To help improve the homework system, a Technology Advisory Board provided competitive reviews and direction for the development of the Aplia course. The following people were members of the Technology Advisory Board:

Jerry Aubin
Algonquin College

Anu Goel
Seneca College

Cheryl Wilson
Durham College

Tamara Ebl
Okanagan College

Kerry Hendricks
Fanshawe College

Julie Wong
Dawson College

Deirdre Fitzpatrick
George Brown College

For more information, please contact your Nelson Education sales and editorial representative or go to **www.aplia.com/accounting**.

Instructor Support

When it comes to supporting instructors, Nelson Education Ltd. is unsurpassed. *Accounting*, Second Canadian Edition, continues this tradition with powerful print and digital ancillaries aimed at facilitating greater course successes.

Nelson Education Teaching Advantage

The Nelson Education Teaching Advantage (NETA) program delivers research-based instructor resources that promote student engagement and higher-order thinking to enable the success of Canadian students and educators.

Instructors today face many challenges. Resources are limited, time is scarce, and a new kind of student has emerged: one who balances school with work, has gaps in his or her basic knowledge, and is immersed in technology in a way that has led to a completely new style of learning. In response, Nelson Education has gathered a group of dedicated instructors to advise us on the creation of richer and more flexible ancillary materials that respond to the needs of today's teaching environments.

Instructor's Resource CD

Key instructor ancillaries are provided on the Instructor's Resource CD (ISBN 0-17-666107-7), providing instructors with the ultimate tool for customizing lectures and presentations.

(Downloadable web versions are also available at **www.warren2ce.nelson.com**.) The following NETA items are available on the IRCD:

Enriched Instructor's Manual The Enriched Instructor's Manual was written by one of the textbook authors, Barrie Tober. It is organized according to the textbook chapters and addresses eight key educational concerns, including typical stumbling blocks students face and how to address them. Other features include at least two alternative lesson plans per chapter, activities for large and small classes, exploration of learning objectives, and opportunities for students to interact with the material in different ways.

Test Bank The Test Bank was written by Maria Belanger of Algonquin College. It includes more than 2,800 multiple-choice questions written according to NETA guidelines for effective construction and development of Bloom's higher-order questions. Also included are true/false questions and problems. The test bank provides a grid for each chapter that correlates each question to the chapter's objectives and a ranking of difficulty. Test bank files are provided both online and in Word for easy editing.

The Computerized Test Bank by ExamView® includes all the questions from the test bank. The easy-to-use ExamView software is compatible with Microsoft Windows and Mac OS. Create tests by selecting questions from the test bank, modifying these questions as desired, and add new questions you write yourself. You can administer quizzes online and export tests to WebCT, Blackboard, and other formats.

Solutions Manual Prepared by the authors of this textbook, the Solutions Manual contains answers to all exercises, problems, and activities in the textbook. As always, the solutions are author-written and have been verified multiple times for numerical accuracy and consistency with the core text.

NETA Presentation Microsoft PowerPoint lecture slides for every chapter have been created by Sheila Elworthy and Tana Kristjanson, authors of the textbook. Each chapter contains objectives followed by a thorough outline of the chapter that together provide an entire lecture model. Exhibits from each chapter, such as Example Exercises, have been recreated as PowerPoint slides to create a powerful, customizable tool. NETA principles of clear design and engaging content have been incorporated throughout.

Image Library This resource consists of digital copies of figures, short tables, and photographs used in the book. Instructors may use these files to create their own PowerPoint presentations.

 Instructor Excel® Templates Prepared by Paul Elworthy, these templates provide the solutions for the problems and exercises that have Enhanced Excel® templates for students. By using these files, instructors can see the solutions in the same format as the students. All problems with accompanying templates are marked in the book with an icon. These templates are available for download at **www.warren2ce.nelson.com** and are on the IRCD.

DayOne Day One—Prof InClass is a PowerPoint presentation that you can customize to orient your students to the class and their text at the beginning of the course.

TurningPoint® Another valuable resource for instructors is TurningPoint® classroom response software customized for *Accounting,* Second Canadian Edition. Now you can author, deliver, show, access, and grade, all in PowerPoint—with no toggling back and forth between screens! JoinIn on Turning Point is the only classroom response software tool that gives you true PowerPoint integration. With JoinIn, you are no longer tied to your computer. You can walk about your classroom as you lecture, showing slides and collecting and displaying responses with ease. There is simply no easier or more effective way to turn your lecture hall into a personal, fully interactive experience for your students. If you can use PowerPoint, you can use JoinIn on TurningPoint! (Contact your Nelson publishing representative for details.)

Student Support

Students come to accounting with a variety of learning needs. *Accounting*, Second Canadian Edition, offers a broad range of supplements in both printed form and easy-to-use technology. We refined our entire supplement package around the comments instructors have provided about their courses and teaching needs.

Working Papers for Exercises and Problems Prepared by the authors of this textbook, the traditional working papers include problem-specific forms for preparing solutions for Exercises, A & B Problems, the Continuing Problem, and the Comprehensive Problems from the textbook. These forms, with preprinted headings, provide a structure for the problems, which helps students get started and saves them time. Additional blank forms are included.

 Enhanced Excel® Templates Prepared by Paul Elworthy, these templates are provided for selected long or complicated end-of-chapter exercises and problems and provide assistance to students as they set up and work through the problem. Certain cells are coded to display a red asterisk when an incorrect answer is entered, which helps students stay on track. Selected problems that can be solved using these templates are designated by an icon.

Product Companion Website The companion site at **www.warren2ce.nelson .com** provides students with a wealth of introductory accounting resources, including Interactive Quizzes to test their understanding, Crossword Puzzles, Flashcards, Online Glossary, and downloadable Enhanced Excel® templates for selected exercises and problems in the text. The Interactive Quizzes were prepared by Maria Bergeron of Algonquin College.

Acknowledgments

Throughout our development of *Accounting*, Second Canadian Edition, we had the privilege to work alongside our Editorial Advisory Board and Technology Advisory Board. Nelson Education Ltd. brought these talented and creative individuals together to serve on the boards to help guide the direction of the textbook. Through countless reviews, phone calls, emails, and an intensive meeting in Toronto, their comments and feedback had a profound impact on the presentation and core themes of this text. We are forever indebted to our advisory board members for the contribution to this textbook:

Maria Belanger
Algonquin College

David Fleming
George Brown College

Darlene Lowe
Grant MacEwan University

Darla Lutness
NAIT

Pina Salvaggio
Dawson College

David Van Rijt
St. Clair College

Harvey Willows
Centennial College

We also thank our Technology Advisory Board, mentioned earlier, for their contributions:

Jerry Aubin
Algonquin College

Tamara Ebl
Okanagan College

Deirdre Fitzpatrick
George Brown College

Anu Goel
Seneca College

Kerry Hendricks
Fanshawe College

Cheryl Wilson
Durham College

Julie Wong
Dawson College

Our thanks also go to Susan K. Wolcott, of WolcottLynch Associates, for her analysis of the critical thinking components in *Accounting* and for her recommendations for how *Accounting* can support and develop critical thinking among students.

We want to take this opportunity to thank the following reviewers for their perspectives and feedback on textbook use:

Karina Brassard
Champlain College

Walt Burton
Okanagan College

Derek Cook
Okanagan College

Paul Griffin
Humber College

Ken Hartford
St. Clair College

Kerry Hendricks
Fanshawe College

Shelley Johnson
Okanagan College

Gerry La Rocca
Vanier College

Darlene Lowe
Grant MacEwan University

Karen Matthews
Okanagan College

Doug Ringrose
Grant MacEwan University

David Sale
Kwantlen Polytechnic University

Pina Salvaggio
Dawson College

Elaine Sonberg
Dawson College

Dan Wong
SAIT Polytechnic

We also want to thank the following people who made significant contributions to our previous Canadian edition.

Adrian Fontenla
Okanagan College

Amy Greene
triOS College

Barbara Likar
Sprott Shaw Community College

Barbara Moore
triOS College

Betty Cook
CompuCollege

Cynthia Lone
Red River College

Dan Wong
SAIT Polytechnic

Dave Fleming
George Brown College

David Mills
SAIT Polytechnic

Debbie Musil
Kwantlen Polytechnic University

Don Hutton
Durham College

Don Smith
Georgian College

Doug MacDonald
CompuCollege

Doug Mann
Georgian College

Doug Ringrose
MacEwan College

Douglas Leatherdale
Georgian College

Geoff Stephenson
Olds College

Glenn Ankrom
CDI College

Glen Stanger
Douglas College

Graeme Gomes
Everest College

Heather Martin
Nova Scotia Community College

Ian Hutchinson
Acadia University

Jerry Aubin
Algonquin College

Joan Wallwork
Kwantlen Polytechnic University

Joe Pidutti
Durham College

Joy Atkinson
NSCC/CompuCollege

Kim Dyck
Red River College

Maria Belanger
Algonquin College

Patrick Hamilton
Nova Scotia Community College

Penny Parker
Fanshawe College

Raymond Leung
University of the Fraser Valley

Rhonda Fenner
University College of the North

Susan Johnston Emberly
Maritime Business College

Traven Reed
Canadore College

Vanessa Oltmann
Vancouver Island University

Sheila and Tana would like to thank the following Camosun College instructors who approached them personally with very helpful suggestions:

Stu Berry

Leelah Dawson

Barbara Edwards

Amy Hoggard

Jolene Kendrew

Michelle Lysak

Keri Norrie

Alison Parker

Jennifer Reed

Stephen Scott

Lyle Widdifield

Thanks also to Diane McDonald and Shan Thomas, who provided guidance on technical accounting issues.

We also thank all those involved in helping us through this entire writing process. Specifically, we thank our Acquisitions Editor, Rod Banister, who provided answers and direction to countless questions; Amie Plourde, Senior Acquisitions Editor; Lisa Berland, Developmental Editor; our Copy Editor, Mariko Obokata; and Sean Chamberland, Executive Marketing Manager; Dave Stratton, Marketing Manager; and Imoinda Romain, Senior Content Production Manager.

Quality Control

Over the years, we have all used books where we have encountered problems with errors. One of our goals with *Accounting*, Second Canadian Edition, was to minimize the possibility that errors would slip through. Many people have been involved in checking this textbook for errors and ensuring its accuracy, and we believe it is as free of mistakes as we can make it. Any that remain are, of course, the responsibility of the authors. We would like to thank Ross Meacher, C.A., for the detailed accuracy check that he performed on our text, the assignment materials, and the accompanying Solutions Manual. If by chance you do identify what you believe to be an error, please report your findings to kristjansontextbook@camosun.bc.ca.

Conclusion

Mastering introductory accounting can be a daunting task for many students. Through careful planning and execution of our development plan, we feel that this textbook will help your students master the course and assist you with the challenging task of teaching introductory accounting. If you have any thoughts or suggestions, please email us at kristjansontextbook@camosun.bc.ca, barrietober@gmail.com, or sheilaelworthy@gmail.com. Our goal is to produce the best possible textbook by recognizing that change is the only constant, and by actively seeking innovative methods to provide the best possible accounting textbook for Canadian students and instructors.

Sheila Elworthy
Tana Kristjanson
Barrie Tober
January 2013

Introduction to Accounting and Business

FACEBOOK

When two teams play hockey, there is often a lot of noise. The organ plays, the fans cheer, horns blare, and the scoreboard lights up when there is a goal. Obviously, the fans are committed and care about the outcome of the game. Just like fans at a hockey game, the owners of a business want their business to "win" against their competitors in the marketplace. Although having our hockey team win can be a source of pride, winning in the marketplace goes beyond pride and has many tangible benefits. Companies that are winners are better able to serve customers, to provide good jobs for employees, and to make more money for the owners.

One such successful company is Facebook, one of the most visible companies on the Internet. This social networking company was started by Mark Zuckerberg when he was a 20-year-old Harvard undergraduate. People are increasingly using Facebook for their communication needs. Each day, 526 million users worldwide log on to Facebook, where they post 3.2 billion "likes" and comments to be read by 125 billion connections, or "friends." And yet, Facebook is a free service—you can use any of Facebook's applications and no one will ever ask for your credit card. So, do you think Facebook has been a successful company? Does it make money? How would you know? Accounting helps to answer these questions.

In this textbook, we will introduce you to accounting, the language of business. In this chapter, we begin by discussing what a business is, how it operates, and the role that accounting plays.

After studying this chapter, you should be able to:

1 Describe the nature of a business, the role of accounting, and the role of ethics in business.

Nature of Business and Accounting	Types of Businesses	
	Role of Accounting in Business	
	Role of Ethics in Accounting and Business	
	Role of Regulators in Accounting	
	Opportunities and Training for Accountants	

2 Summarize the development of accounting principles and relate them to practice.

Generally Accepted Accounting Principles	Framework for Accounting Decision Making	
	Underlying Assumptions, Principles, and Constraints	EXAMPLE EXERCISE 1-1 (page 9)
	Qualitative Characteristics of the Conceptual Framework	

3 State the accounting equation and define each element of the equation.

The Accounting Equation	EXAMPLE EXERCISE 1-2 (page 11)

4 Describe and illustrate how business transactions can be recorded in terms of the resulting change in the elements of the accounting equation.

Business Transactions and the Accounting Equation	

5 Describe the financial statements of a proprietorship and explain how they interrelate.

Financial Statements	Income Statement	EXAMPLE EXERCISE 1-3 (page 17)
	Statement of Owner's Equity	EXAMPLE EXERCISE 1-4 (page 18)
	Balance Sheet	
	Cash Flow Statement	EXAMPLE EXERCISE 1-5 (page 20)
	Interrelationships among Financial Statements	

For the chapter *At a Glance*, turn to page 21.

 # Nature of Business and Accounting

Describe the nature of a business, the role of accounting, and the role of ethics in business.

A **business**[1] is an organization in which basic resources (inputs), such as materials and labour, are assembled and processed to provide goods or services (outputs) to customers. Businesses come in all sizes, from a local coffeehouse to Tim Hortons, which sells almost $2 billion of coffee and related products each year.

The objective of most businesses is to earn a profit. **Profit** is the difference between the amounts received from customers for goods or services provided and the amounts paid for the inputs used to provide the goods or services. In this text, we focus on businesses operating to earn a profit. However, many of the same concepts and principles also apply to not-for-profit organizations, such as charities, churches, and government agencies.

1 A complete glossary of terms appears at the end of each chapter.

Types of Businesses

Three types of businesses operated for profit are service, merchandising, and manufacturing businesses.

Each type of business and some examples are described below.

Service businesses provide services rather than products to customers.

Air Canada (transportation services)

Astral Media (entertainment services)

Merchandising businesses purchase products from other businesses and sell these products to customers.

Walmart (general merchandise)

Amazon.ca (books, music, videos)

Manufacturing businesses change basic inputs into products that are sold to customers.

General Motors Corporation (cars, trucks, vans)

Dell Inc. (personal computers)

Role of Accounting in Business

What is the role of accounting in business? The simplest answer is that accounting provides information that managers use in operating their business. In addition, accounting provides information to other users for assessing the economic performance and condition of the business.

Thus, **accounting** can be defined as an information system that provides reports to users about the economic activities and condition of a business. You may think of accounting as the "language of business." Accounting is the means by which businesses' financial information is communicated to users.

The process by which accounting provides information to users is as follows:

1. Identify users.
2. Assess users' information needs.
3. Design the accounting information system to meet users' needs.
4. Record economic data about business activities and events.
5. Prepare accounting reports for users.

As illustrated in Exhibit 1, users of accounting information can be divided into two groups: internal users and external users.

Note: Accounting is an information system that provides reports to users about the economic activities and condition of a business.

Exhibit 1

Accounting as an Information System

Internal Users Internal users of accounting information include managers and employees. These users are directly involved in managing and operating the business. The area of accounting that provides internal users with information is called **managerial accounting** or **management accounting**.

The objective of managerial accounting is to provide relevant and timely information for managers' and employees' decision-making needs. Often, such information is sensitive and is not distributed outside the business. Examples of sensitive information include information about customers, costs, and plans to expand the business. Managerial accountants employed by a business are employed in **private accounting**.

External Users External users of accounting information include customers, creditors, investors, and the government. These users are not directly involved in managing and operating the business. The area of accounting that provides external users with information is called **financial accounting**.

The objective of financial accounting is to provide relevant and timely information for the decision-making needs of users outside of the business. For example, financial reports on the operations and condition of the business are useful for banks and other creditors when deciding whether to lend money to the business. **General-purpose financial statements** are one type of financial accounting report that is distributed to external users. The term *general-purpose* refers to the wide range of decision-making needs that these reports are designed to serve. Later in this chapter, we describe and illustrate general-purpose financial statements.

Role of Ethics in Accounting and Business

The objective of general-purpose financial reporting is to provide financial information about the reporting entity. This information is useful to those who decide whether to provide resources to the entity, such as creditors and investors.[2] Accountants must behave in an ethical manner so that the information they provide will be trustworthy and, thus, useful for decision making. Managers and employees must also behave in an ethical manner in managing and operating a business. Otherwise, no one will be willing to invest in the business or loan it money.

Ethics are moral principles that guide the conduct of individuals. Unfortunately, some business managers and accountants behave in an unethical manner. Some managers of the companies listed in Exhibit 2 engaged in accounting or business fraud. Their ethical violations led to fines, firings, and lawsuits. In some cases, managers were criminally prosecuted, convicted, and sent to prison.

What went wrong for the managers and companies listed in Exhibit 2? The answer normally involved one or both of the following two factors:

> **Failure of Individual Character.** Ethical managers and accountants are honest and fair. However, managers and accountants often face pressures from supervisors to meet company and investor expectations. In many of the cases in Exhibit 2, managers and accountants justified small ethical violations to avoid such pressures. However, these small violations became big violations as the company's financial problems became worse.
>
> **Culture of Greed and Ethical Indifference.** By their behaviour and attitude, senior managers set the company culture. In most of the companies listed in Exhibit 2, the senior managers created a culture of greed and indifference to the truth.

Role of Regulators in Accounting

The financial accounting and reporting failures of Enron, WorldCom, and Nortel shocked the investing public. The disclosure that some of the largest and best-known

---

2 *CICA Handbook–Accounting*, 2013 edition, Part I, The conceptual framework, Ch. 1, OB2, and Part II, 1000.09.

INTEGRITY, OBJECTIVITY, AND ETHICS IN BUSINESS

ETHICAL BEHAVIOUR AS A MARKETING TOOL

Consumers are concerned with the environmental impact of their purchases on the planet, and so ethical behaviour of corporations is becoming an increasingly important selling feature. More and more companies are focusing their efforts on ensuring the products sold in their stores are produced in an environmentally friendly and socially responsible manner. A movement is growing to ensure that producers in developing countries are paid a fair price for their products. Ethical Soles Trading Company, for example, is a Canadian distributor of ethical footwear and apparel. Coffee distributors are another example, with more fair-trade brands being offered all the time. Fair trade can apply to the local market as well. Wolfville, Nova Scotia, was proclaimed the first fair-trade town in Canada when it committed to buying local produce in support of its farmers.

corporations had overstated profits and misled investors raised the question: Where were the accountants?

As a response to this question, additional laws, including the Sarbanes-Oxley Act of 2002 (SOX), were passed in the United States; in Canada, the Canadian Public Accountability Board (CPAB) was created. The major focus of this board is to review work completed by accounting firms for publicly traded companies in order to promote public confidence in the integrity of financial reporting in Canada. You can learn more about CPAB from the "How We Work – Overview" section of its website at www.cpab-ccrc.ca.

Opportunities and Training for Accountants

Numerous career opportunities are available for students majoring in accounting. These opportunities are partly due to the increased regulation of business caused by the accounting and business frauds shown in Exhibit 2. Also, more businesses have come to recognize the importance and value of high-quality accounting information.

As we indicated earlier, accountants employed by a business are said to be employed in private accounting. Private accountants have a variety of possible career options

Exhibit 2

Accounting and Business Fraud in the 2000s

Company	Nature of Accounting or Business Fraud	Result
Bre-X	"Salting" of gold in core samples to inflate share price.	Collapse of company. $6 billion in stock market losses.
Enron	Fraudulently inflated its financial results, using methods such as not disclosing special-purpose entity liabilities.	Bankruptcy. Criminal charges against senior executives, more than $60 billion in stock market losses.
Hollinger International	Failure to disclose payments to Chairman/CEO Lord Conrad Black and senior executives.	CEO and senior executives convicted of $6 million fraud and obstruction of justice. CEO sentenced to prison.
Nortel	Fraudulently inflated its financial results by prematurely recording $1 billion of revenues and manipulating reserves.	Millions of dollars of financial restatements over four years. CEO and senior executives fined $36 million.
WorldCom	Misstated financial results by nearly $9 billion, using methods such as capitalizing billions of dollars of expenses.	Bankruptcy. Criminal conviction of CEO and CFO. More than $100 billion in stock market losses. Directors forced to pay $18 million.

within a company, such as accountant, payroll clerk, budget analyst, cost accountant, internal auditor, or information technology auditor.

Auditors are accountants who provide audit services. They verify the accuracy of financial records, accounts, and systems. Internal auditors are employed in private accounting as employees of the company they audit.

Accountants and their staff who provide services on a fee basis are said to be employed in **public accounting**. Public accounting includes a number of services, such as external audits, accounting, tax, and consulting. An accountant may practise public accounting as an individual or as a member of a public accounting firm. Canada has traditionally had three main accounting designations: **Chartered Accountant (CA), Certified General Accountant (CGA),** and **Certified Management Accountant (CMA).** In May 2012, these organizations merged in Quebec into one organization that will issue a new designation, **Chartered Professional Accountant (CPA).** At press time, the rest of the Canadian provinces and territories were in discussions and considering a similar decision. Current information about the proposed merger status is available at www.cpacanada.ca, and at www.cpaone.ca. In Quebec, accountants from the three original organizations will add "CPA" to their titles for the next 10 years. For example, Jane Smith, CGA will become Jane Smith, CPA, CGA. Aspiring accountants must complete an undergraduate degree and professional courses, pass professional examinations, and gain practical experience as an accountant in order to become a professional accountant in Canada. Professional accountants who want to perform external audits require additional training.

Because all functions within a business use accounting information, experience in private or public accounting provides a solid foundation for a career. Many varied positions in industry and in government agencies are held by individuals with accounting backgrounds.

Generally Accepted Accounting Principles

Summarize the development of accounting principles and relate them to practice.

If a company's management could record and report financial data as it saw fit, comparisons among companies would be difficult, if not impossible. Thus, financial accountants follow accounting principles in preparing financial statements.

Accounting principles and concepts develop from research, accepted accounting practices, and pronouncements of regulators.

Accounting standards in Canada are known as **Canadian generally accepted accounting principles (GAAP)**. GAAP consists of all the accounting standards that can be used by Canadian organizations. The **Accounting Standards Board (AcSB)** of the **Canadian Institute of Chartered Accountants (CICA)** has the primary responsibility for approving the accounting standards, or GAAP, contained in the *CICA Handbook*.

In 2006, AcSB decided to adopt **International Financial Reporting Standards (IFRS)** for Canadian publicly accountable enterprises. These global accounting standards were developed by the **International Accounting Standards Board (IASB). Publicly accountable enterprises** include companies that have shares or bonds listed on stock exchanges and other organizations, such as credit unions or investment dealers, whose business dealings affect large or diverse groups of stakeholders.[3] These international accounting standards have been adopted by many countries, including Russia, China, Africa, Australia, New Zealand, and member states of the European Union (EU). As a result of this widespread adoption, use of IFRS makes it easier for companies to attract foreign investors and simplifies the preparation of financial reports for companies that have operations in many countries.

Since 2011, all Canadian publicly accountable enterprises use IFRS to prepare their financial statements. IFRS comprises Part I of the five parts of the *CICA Handbook*.

Many Canadian companies are **private enterprises**—profit-oriented organizations that do not issue shares or bonds through stock exchanges.[4] The information needs of

---

3 *CICA Handbook–Accounting*, 2012 edition, Preface, para. 3(a).

4 *CICA Handbook–Accounting*, 2012 edition, Preface, para. 3(b).

Conceptual Framework for Accounting Decision Making

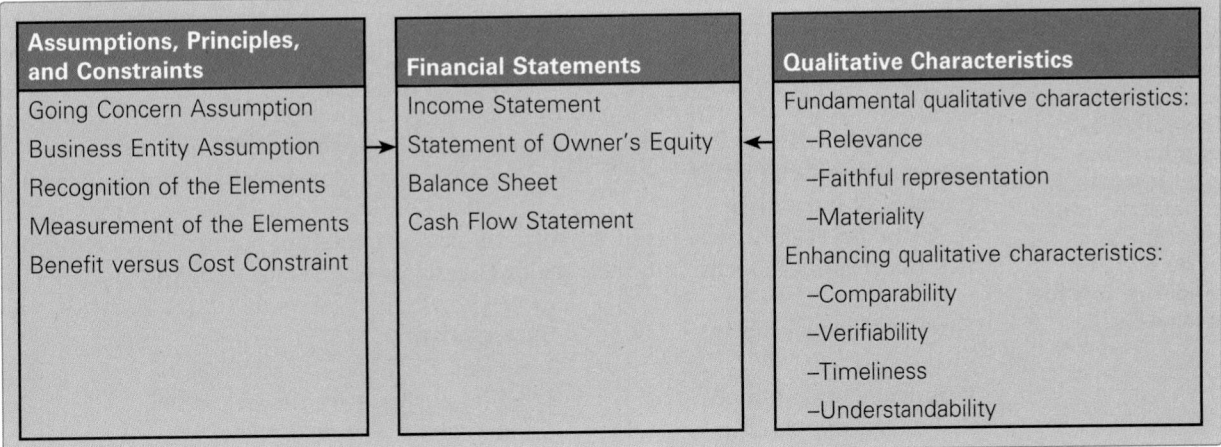

the users of private companies' financial information differ from the needs of those who use public companies' information. Because owners of private companies are closely related to the company, they can easily access sources of information other than financial statements and so private companies are not required to report the detailed financial information required of public companies. This distinction led to AcSB developing different standards for private companies, referred to as Part II of the *CICA Handbook*, or **Accounting Standards for Private Enterprises (ASPE)**. A private enterprise may choose to use IFRS in preparing its financial information. Using IFRS is especially suitable for a private company that is considering going public in the near future or for a subsidiary of a foreign company that reports in accordance with IFRS. Both sets of standards, IFRS and ASPE, are considered Canadian GAAP.

Framework for Accounting Decision Making

The basic objective of financial accounting is to produce financial information that presents fairly the results of the operation of the business and its financial position in order to help users make decisions. How do we ensure we meet this goal, particularly since Canadian accounting standards are based upon principles rather than detailed rules? When accountants consider how to record accounting transactions, they often have choices. Making those choices requires accountants to use professional judgment. Having a conceptual framework of underlying principles also helps accountants to choose the most appropriate accounting treatment. The conceptual frameworks that exist within Part I (IFRS) and Part II (ASPE) of the *CICA Handbook* are based on common, but not identical, conceptual frameworks. The main elements of the conceptual framework for IFRS are illustrated in Exhibit 3 and will be discussed in this chapter.

Underlying Assumptions, Principles, and Constraints

The framework for accounting includes some assumptions, principles, and constraints. The underlying elements being considered in this chapter are the going concern assumption, the business entity assumption, recognition of the elements, measurement of the elements, and the benefit versus cost constraint.

Going Concern Assumption When preparing financial statements, one fundamental assumption is the **going concern assumption**. If a business is a going concern, then it is appropriate to prepare financial statements using the accounting principles in the *CICA Handbook*. But if the business is in financial trouble and is not likely to be operating in the following year, then that method is no longer appropriate. Instead, all items should be valued at what they could be sold for, their net realizable value, and long-term items should all be classified as current items. This treatment will better reflect the economic reality for that business. Although some businesses do fail, the going concern assumption is appropriate for most companies.

Note: Under the business entity assumption, the activities of a business are recorded separately from the activities of its owners, creditors, or other businesses.

Business Entity Assumption

The **business entity assumption** limits the economic data in an accounting system to data related directly to the activities of the business. In other words, the business is viewed as an entity separate from its owners, creditors, or other businesses. For example, the accountant for a business with one owner records the activities of the business only and does not record the personal activities, property, or debts of the owner.

A business entity may take the form of a proprietorship, partnership, or corporation. Each of these forms and their major characteristics are listed below.

Form of Business Entity	Characteristics[5]
Proprietorship is owned by one individual.	• 35% of business entities in Canada, generating 7% of total revenues. • Easy and cheap to organize. • Resources are limited to those of the owner. • Used by small businesses.
Partnership is owned by two or more individuals.	• Less than 10% of business entities in Canada, generating less than 5% of total revenues. • Combines the skills and resources of more than one person.
Corporation is organized under a provincial, territorial, or federal charter as a separate legal entity.	• More than 50% of business entities in Canada, generating more than 70% of total revenues. • Ownership is divided into shares. • Can obtain large amounts of resources by issuing shares. • Used by large businesses.

The three types of businesses we discussed earlier—service, merchandising, and manufacturing—may be organized as proprietorships, partnerships, or corporations. Because of the large amount of resources required to operate a manufacturing business, most manufacturing businesses, such as Bombardier Inc., are corporations. Most large retailers, such as Sears Canada and Home Depot, are also corporations.

Recognition of the Elements

A transaction element is considered to be "recognized" when it is included in the financial statements of the business entity. In order to be recognized, a transaction must meet the following criteria:

a) It is likely to generate a future economic benefit to the business.

b) A cost for the item can be measured reliably.

The **revenue recognition principle**, for example, suggests revenue should be recognized when it is earned, which normally is when the work is performed or the goods are delivered. At that point, the recognition criteria have been met, and revenue can be recorded in the accounting records.

Measurement of the Elements

Although an item can be measured according to numerous bases, financial statements primarily use the **historical cost basis**, by recognizing transactions and events by the amount of cash paid or received.[6] To illustrate, assume that, on February 20, 2013, Bapco Publishers purchased land that had the following values:

---

5 The balance of business entities and revenues are attributable to joint ventures, government businesses, and other unknown businesses (Statistics Canada, 2009).

6 *CICA Handbook–Accounting*, 2012 edition, Part II, Section 1000.48.

List price	$500,000
Purchase price on February 20, 2013	450,000
Assessed value for property taxes	440,000
Estimated selling price on December 31, 2015	650,000

Using the historical cost basis, often referred to as the *cost principle*, Bapco Publishers records the purchase of the land at the purchase price of $450,000. The other amounts listed above have no effect on the accounting records.

The estimated selling price of $650,000 on December 31, 2015, indicates that the land has increased in value. If a company is preparing financial statements using ASPE, then the historical cost is the basis for measurement, and the increase in value is not recorded. Under IFRS, a company may choose either the cost model or the revaluation model, in which the land is valued at the estimated selling price of $650,000.[7] The revaluation model, however, is beyond the scope of an introductory accounting text.

EXAMPLE EXERCISE 1-1 Measurement of the Elements   ② 2

On August 25, Gallatin Repair Service extended an offer of $125,000 for land that had been priced for sale at $150,000. On September 3, Gallatin Repair Service accepted the seller's counteroffer of $137,000. On October 20, the land was assessed at a value of $98,000 for property tax purposes. On December 4, Gallatin Repair Service was offered $160,000 for the land by a national retail chain. At what value should the land be recorded in Gallatin Repair Service's records?

FOLLOW MY EXAMPLE 1-1

$137,000. The land should be recorded at the historical cost to Gallatin Repair Service.

For Practice: PE 1-1

Benefit versus Cost Constraint The **benefit versus cost constraint**, or **cost constraint**, suggests that a trade-off exists between the accuracy of the financial information being produced and the cost to produce that information.[8] For example, a wastepaper basket meets the definition of an asset, but would be classified as an expense because the cost to track the wastepaper basket as an asset is not justified. Accountants face many situations where they must choose between treating an item as an asset or as an expense. For both convenience and consistency, many companies choose a dollar amount and agree to treat items costing less than that amount as expenses.

Qualitative Characteristics of the Conceptual Framework

The IFRS conceptual framework identifies three characteristics as fundamental to producing financial information: relevance, faithful representation, and materiality.

Information is considered to have **relevance** when it helps investors and others make financial decisions. **Faithful representation**, or **representational faithfulness**, suggests that a transaction should be recorded in a manner that reflects the substance of the event. For example, a company might enter into a lease for a piece of equipment with the option to purchase the asset outright at the end of the lease. Even though the company does not legally own the asset until the end of the lease, the item is recorded as an asset on the balance sheet to reflect the essence of the situation. To be a faithful representation of a transaction, the information should be *complete, neutral,* and *free of error*.[9]

The final fundamental characteristic is **materiality**. Information is considered material if omitting it or misstating it could influence decisions that users make on the basis of the financial statements. Materiality will vary depending upon the nature

---

7 *CICA Handbook–Accounting*, 2013 edition, Part I, IAS 16, para. 29.

8 *CICA Handbook–Accounting*, 2013 edition, Part I, The conceptual framework, QC 35 and Part II, Section 1000.48.

9 *CICA Handbook–Accounting*, 2013 edition, Part I, The conceptual framework, QC 12.

and size of the item relative to the size of the business entity. For example, omitting a $10,000 expense may be material for a very small company but immaterial for a large company, such as WestJet Airlines Ltd.

According to the IFRS conceptual framework, financial information is enhanced if it meets the characteristics of comparability, verifiability, timeliness, and understandability.[10] **Comparability** suggests that information about a business is more useful if it allows a potential investor to compare the financial results of one company with those of other companies in the industry, and to compare a company's results from one year with results from prior years. The goal of comparability is met by applying accounting choices consistently over periods of time and by choosing an accounting treatment that is similar to that used by other companies in the industry. **Verifiability** refers to the ability of different knowledgeable individuals to agree on the financial information as reported, usually by comparing information against supporting documentation, such as an invoice. **Timeliness** refers to information being more useful when produced on a frequent or timely basis, which has led to publicly accountable enterprises producing financial statements, called *interim statements*, every three months. Financial information also requires a level of **understandability**, an attribute that is improved by including notes to explain the numbers in the financial statements.

 # The Accounting Equation

State the accounting equation and define each element of the equation.

The resources owned by a business are its assets. An **asset** is defined as an economic resource controlled by an entity as a result of past transactions or events and from which future economic benefits may be obtained.[11] Ownership is not an essential component. Assets have three essential characteristics:

1. They embody a future benefit that will contribute directly or indirectly to future cash flows.
2. The business can control access to the benefit.
3. The transaction or event giving rise to the benefit has already occurred.

In other words, an asset is a tangible or intangible item that will benefit the company. Examples of assets include cash, accounts receivable, land, buildings, and equipment. A **liability** is defined as an obligation to give up either services or assets.[12] Liabilities have three essential characteristics:

1. They embody a duty to others that involves giving up a service or asset.
2. The duty or responsibility is unavoidable.
3. The transaction or event giving rise to the obligation has already occurred.

Examples of liabilities include accounts payable, salaries payable, and unearned revenue. The rights of the owners are called **owner's equity**. Owner's equity is defined as the assets that remain after deducting the liabilities.[13]

The following equation shows the relationship among assets, liabilities, and owner's equity:

$$\text{Assets} = \text{Liabilities} + \text{Owner's Equity}$$

This equation is called the **accounting equation**. Liabilities usually are shown before owner's equity in the accounting equation because creditors have first rights to the assets.

Given any two amounts, the accounting equation may be solved for the third unknown amount. To illustrate, if the assets owned by a business amount to $100,000 and the liabilities amount to $30,000, the owner's equity is equal to $70,000, as shown on the following page.

---

10 *CICA Handbook–Accounting*, 2013 edition, Part I, The conceptual framework, QC 4.

11 *CICA Handbook–Accounting*, 2013 edition, Part I, The conceptual framework, para. 4.4 (a) and Part II, Section 1000.24 and 1000.25.

12 *CICA Handbook–Accounting*, 2013 edition, Part I, The conceptual framework, para. 4.4 (b) and Part II, Section 1000.28 and 1000.29.

13 *CICA Handbook–Accounting*, 2013 edition, Part I, The conceptual framework, para. 4.4 (c) and Part II, Section 1000.31.

Assets	**= Liabilities + Owner's Equity**
$100,000	= $30,000 + Owner's Equity
Owner's Equity	= $70,000

EXAMPLE EXERCISE 1-2 Accounting Equation   ③

John Joos is the owner and operator of You're A Star, a motivational consulting business. At the end of its accounting period, December 31, 2014, You're A Star has assets of $800,000 and liabilities of $350,000. Using the accounting equation, determine the following amounts:

a. Owner's equity, as at December 31, 2014.

b. Owner's equity, as at December 31, 2015, assuming that assets increased by $130,000 and liabilities decreased by $25,000 during 2015.

FOLLOW MY EXAMPLE 1-2

a.   Assets = Liabilities + Owner's Equity

   $800,000 = $350,000 + Owner's Equity

Owner's Equity = $450,000

b. First, determine the change in owner's equity during 2015 as follows:

      Assets = Liabilities + Owner's Equity

   $130,000 = –$25,000 + Owner's Equity

Owner's Equity = $155,000

Next, add the change in owner's equity during 2015 to the owner's equity on December 31, 2014, to arrive at owner's equity on December 31, 2015, as shown below.
Owner's Equity on December 31, 2015 = $450,000 + $155,000 = $605,000

For Practice: PE 1-2

CRITICAL THINKING

Employers often say their employees are their most valuable asset. **Does an employee meet the definition of an asset?**

An employee meets two of the three essential characteristics of an asset: (1) an employee contributes to future cash flows, and (2) the event giving rise to the benefit has already occurred—the employee has been hired. The third essential characteristic, however, is not met: the business cannot control access to the benefit because an employee has the right to resign at any time. Thus, an employee does not appear on the financial statements as an asset, despite what many employers say!

---

④

Describe and illustrate how business transactions can be recorded in terms of the resulting change in the elements of the accounting equation.

Business Transactions and the Accounting Equation

Paying a telephone bill of $168 affects a business's financial condition because it now has less cash on hand. Such an economic event that directly changes an entity's financial condition or its results of operations is a **business transaction**. For example, purchasing land for $50,000 is a business transaction. In contrast, a change in a business's credit rating does not directly affect cash or any other asset, liability, or the amount of owner's equity.

All business transactions can be stated in terms of changes in the elements of the accounting equation. We illustrate how business transactions affect the accounting equation by using some typical transactions. As a basis for illustration, we use a business organized by Chris Clark.

Assume that on November 1, 2014, Chris Clark begins a business that will be known as NetSolutions. The first phase of Chris's business plan is to operate NetSolutions as a service business assisting individuals and small businesses in developing Web pages and installing computer software. Chris expects this initial phase of the business to

Note: All business transactions can be stated in terms of changes in the elements of the accounting equation.

last one to two years. During this period, Chris plans on gathering information on the software and hardware needs of customers. During the second phase of the business plan, Chris plans to expand NetSolutions into a personalized retailer of software and hardware for individuals and small businesses.

Each transaction during NetSolutions' first month of operations is described in the following paragraphs. The effect of each transaction on the accounting equation is then shown.

Transaction A

Nov. 1, 2014   Chris Clark deposited $25,000 in a bank account in the name of NetSolutions.

This transaction increases the asset cash (on the left side of the equation) by $25,000. To balance the equation, the owner's equity (on the right side of the equation) increases by the same amount. The equity of the owner is identified using the owner's name and "Capital," such as "Chris Clark, Capital."

The effect of this transaction on NetSolutions' accounting equation is shown below.

Assets	=	Liabilities	+	Owner's Equity
Cash	=			Chris Clark, Capital
a. 25,000				25,000

Because Chris Clark is the sole owner, NetSolutions is a proprietorship. Also, the accounting equation shown above is for NetSolutions only. Under the business entity concept, Chris Clark's personal assets, such as a home or personal bank account, and his personal liabilities are excluded from the equation.

Transaction B

Nov. 5, 2014   NetSolutions paid $20,000 for the purchase of land as a future building site.

The land is located in a business park with access to transportation facilities. Chris Clark plans to rent office space and equipment during the first phase of the business plan. During the second phase, Chris plans to build an office and a warehouse on the land.

The purchase of the land changes the makeup of the assets, but it does not change the total assets. The effect of the transaction is shown below.

Assets	=	Liabilities	+	Owner's Equity
Cash + Land	=			Chris Clark, Capital
b. −20,000 + 20,000				

Transaction C

Nov. 10, 2014   NetSolutions purchased supplies for $1,350 and agreed to pay the supplier in the near future.

You have probably used a credit card to buy clothing or other merchandise. In this type of transaction, you received clothing in return for a promise to pay your credit card bill in the future. That is, you received an asset and incurred a liability to pay a future bill. NetSolutions entered into a similar transaction by purchasing supplies for $1,350 and agreeing to pay the supplier in the near future. This type of transaction is called a **purchase on account** and is often described as follows: *Purchased supplies on account, $1,350.*

The liability created by a purchase on account is called an **account payable**. Items such as supplies that will be used in the business in the future are called **prepaid expenses,** which are assets. Thus, the effect of this transaction is to increase assets (Supplies) and liabilities (Accounts Payable) by \$1,350, as follows:

	Assets	=	Liabilities + Owner's Equity
	Cash + Supplies + Land	=	Accounts Payable + Chris Clark, Capital
c.	+1,350		+1,350

Transaction D

Nov. 18, 2014   NetSolutions received cash of \$7,500 for providing services to customers.

You may have earned money by babysitting or mowing lawns. If so, you received money for rendering services to a customer. Likewise, a business earns money by selling goods or services to its customers. This amount is called revenue. **Revenues** are increases in economic resources, through either an increase in assets or a decrease in liabilities, caused by the normal activities of the business.

During its first month of operations, NetSolutions received cash of \$7,500 for providing services to customers. The receipt of cash increases NetSolutions' assets and also increases Chris Clark's equity in the business. The revenues of \$7,500 are recorded in a Fees Earned column to the right of Chris Clark, Capital. The effect of this transaction is to increase Cash and Fees Earned by \$7,500, as shown below.

	Assets	=	Liabilities +	Owner's Equity	
	Cash + Supplies + Land	=	Accounts Payable +	Chris Clark, Capital +	Fees Earned
d.	+7,500				+7,500

Different terms are used for the various types of revenues. As illustrated above, revenue from providing services is recorded as **fees earned**. Revenue from the sale of merchandise is recorded as **sales**. Other examples of revenue include rent, which is recorded as **rent revenue**, and interest, which is recorded as **interest revenue**.

Instead of receiving cash at the time services are provided or goods are sold, a business may accept payment at a later date. Such revenues are described as **fees earned on account** or **sales on account**. For example, if NetSolutions had provided services on account instead of for cash, transaction (d) would have been described as follows: *Fees earned on account, \$7,500.*

In such cases, the firm has an **account receivable**, which is a claim against the customer. An account receivable is an asset, and the revenue is earned and recorded as if cash had been received. When customers pay their accounts, Cash increases and Accounts Receivable decreases.

Transaction E

Nov. 30, 2014   NetSolutions paid the following expenses during the month: wages, \$2,125; rent, \$800; utilities, \$450; and miscellaneous, \$275.

During the month, NetSolutions spent cash in earning revenue. Assets used in this process of earning revenue are called expenses. **Expenses** are decreases in economic resources, through either a decrease in assets or an increase in liabilities, caused by the normal activities of the business. Expenses include supplies used and payments for employee wages, utilities, and other services.

NetSolutions paid the following expenses during the month: wages, \$2,125; rent, \$800; utilities, \$450; and miscellaneous, \$275. Miscellaneous expenses include small amounts paid for such items as postage, coffee, and newspapers. The effect of expenses is the opposite of revenues in that expenses reduce assets and owner's equity. Like fees earned, the expenses are recorded in columns to the right of Chris Clark, Capital. However, because expenses reduce owner's equity, the expenses are entered as negative amounts. The effect of this transaction is shown below.

Assets	=	Liabilities +	Owner's Equity					
Cash + Supplies + Land	=	Accounts Payable +	Chris Clark, Capital	Fees + Earned	Wages − Exp.	Rent − Exp.	Utilities − Exp.	Misc. − Exp.
e. −3,650					−2,125	−800	−450	−275

Businesses usually record each revenue and expense transaction as it occurs. However, to simplify, we have summarized NetSolutions' revenues and expenses for the month in transactions (d) and (e).

Transaction F

Nov. 30, 2014   NetSolutions paid creditors on account, $950.

When you pay your monthly credit card bill, you decrease the cash in your chequing account and decrease the amount you owe to the credit card company. Likewise, when NetSolutions pays $950 to creditors during the month, it reduces assets and liabilities, as shown below.

Assets	=	Liabilities +	Owner's Equity					
Cash + Supplies + Land	=	Accounts Payable +	Chris Clark, Capital	Fees + Earned	Wages − Exp.	Rent − Exp.	Utilities − Exp.	Misc. − Exp.
f. −950		−950						

Paying an amount on account is different from paying an expense. The paying of an expense reduces owner's equity, as illustrated in transaction (e). Paying an amount on account reduces the amount owed on a liability.

Transaction G

Nov. 30, 2014   Chris Clark withdrew $2,000 from NetSolutions for personal use.

At the end of the month, Chris Clark withdrew $2,000 in cash from the business for personal use. This transaction is the opposite of an investment in the business by the owner. Withdrawals by the owner should not be confused with expenses. Withdrawals *do not* represent assets or services used in the process of earning revenues. Instead, withdrawals are a distribution of capital to the owner. Owner withdrawals are identified by the owner's name and "Withdrawals." For example, Chris Clark's withdrawal is identified as "Chris Clark, Withdrawals." Like expenses, withdrawals are recorded in a column to the right of Chris Clark, Capital. The effect of the $2,000 withdrawal is shown as follows:

Assets	=	Liabilities +	Owner's Equity						
Cash + Supp. + Land	=	Accounts Payable +	Chris Clark, Capital	Chris Clark, − Withdrawals	Fees + Earned	Wages − Exp.	Rent − Exp.	Utilities − Exp.	Misc. − Exp.
g. −2,000				−2,000					

Summary The transactions of NetSolutions are summarized below. Each transaction is identified by letter.

	Assets			=	Liabilities +		Owner's Equity					
	Cash	+ Supp. +	Land	=	Accounts Payable +	Chris Clark, Capital −	Chris Clark, Withdrawals +	Fees Earned −	Wages Exp. −	Rent Exp. −	Utilities Exp. −	Misc. Exp.
a.	+25,000					+25,000						
b.	−20,000		20,000									
c.		+1,350			+1,350							
d.	+7,500							+7,500				
e.	−3,650								−2,125	−800	−450	−275
f.	− 950				−950							
g.	−2,000						−2,000					
Bal.	5,900	1,350	20,000		400	25,000	−2,000	7,500	−2,125	−800	−450	−275

You should note in the preceding summary:

1. The effect of every transaction is *an increase or a decrease in one or more of the accounting equation elements.*
2. The two sides of the accounting equation are *always equal.*
3. The owner's equity is *increased by amounts invested by the owner* and is *decreased by withdrawals by the owner.* In addition, the owner's equity is *increased by revenues* and is *decreased by expenses.*

The effects of these four types of transactions on owner's equity are illustrated in Exhibit 4.

Exhibit 4

Types of Transactions Affecting Owner's Equity

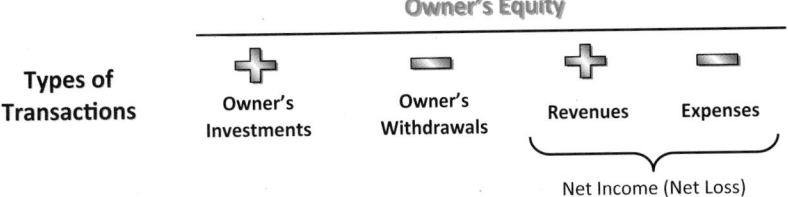

MID-CHAPTER ILLUSTRATIVE PROBLEM

Lawrie Delivery Service is owned and operated by Janis Lawrie. The following selected transactions were completed by Lawrie Delivery Service during February, the first month of operations:

1. Janis invested $35,000 in the proprietorship.
2. Purchased supplies on account, $800.
3. Received cash from customers for deliveries, $2,000.
4. Paid creditors on account, $500.
5. Paid staff wages, $550.
6. Janis withdrew $1,000 for personal use.

In tabular form below the equation, indicate the increases and decreases resulting from each transaction and the final balances after all transactions.

	Assets		=	Liabilities +		Owner's Equity			
Trans.	Cash +	Supplies	=	Accounts Payable +	Janis Lawrie, Capital −	Janis Lawrie, Withdrawals +	Fees Earned −	Wages Exp.
1.	+35,000				+35,000			
2.		+800		+800				
3.	+2,000						+2,000	
4.	− 500			−500				
5.	− 550							−550
6.	−1,000					−1,000		
Bal.	34,950	800		300	35,000	−1,000	2,000	−550

⑤ Financial Statements

Describe the financial statements of a proprietorship and explain how they interrelate.

After transactions have been recorded and summarized, reports are prepared for users. The accounting reports providing this information are called **financial statements**. The primary financial statements of a proprietorship are the income statement, the statement of owner's equity, the balance sheet, and the cash flow statement. The order in which the financial statements are prepared and the nature of each statement are described as follows:

Order Prepared	Financial Statement	Description of Statement
1.	Income statement	A summary of the revenues and expenses *for a specific period of time*, such as a month or a year. For companies reporting under IFRS, this statement is also known as **statement of comprehensive income**.
2.	Statement of owner's equity	A summary of the changes in the owner's equity that have occurred *during a specific period of time*, such as a month or a year. This statement is also known as **statement of retained earnings** for corporations reporting under ASPE, and as **statement of changes in equity** for corporations reporing under IFRS.
3.	Balance sheet	A list of the assets, liabilities, and owner's equity *as at a specific date*, usually at the close of the last day of a month or a year. For companies reporting under IFRS, this statement is also known as **statement of financial position**.
4.	Cash flow statement	A summary of the cash receipts and cash payments for a *specific period of time*, such as a month or a year. For companies reporting under IFRS, this statement is also known as **statement of cash flows**.

@netsolutions

The four financial statements and their interrelationships are illustrated in Exhibit 5 on page 19. The data for the statements are taken from the summary of transactions of NetSolutions on page 15.

All financial statements are identified by the name of the business, the title of the statement, and the *date* or *period of time*. The data presented in the income statement, the statement of owner's equity, and the cash flow statement are for a period of time. The data presented in the balance sheet are for a specific date.

Income Statement

The income statement reports the revenues and expenses for a period of time. The excess of the revenue over the expenses is called **net income**. If the expenses exceed the revenue, the excess is a **net loss**.

The revenue and expenses for NetSolutions were shown in the equation as separate increases and decreases in each item. Net income for a period increases the owner's equity (capital) for the period. A net loss decreases the owner's equity (capital) for the period.

The revenue, expenses, and the net income of $3,850 for NetSolutions are reported in the income statement in Exhibit 5 on page 19. The order in which the expenses are listed in the income statement varies among businesses. Most businesses list expenses in order of size, beginning with the larger items.

EXAMPLE EXERCISE 1-3 Income Statement   ⑤

The assets and liabilities of Chickadee Travel Service at December 31, 2015, the end of the current year, and its revenue and expenses for the year are listed below.

Accounts payable	$ 12,200	Miscellaneous expense	$ 12,950
Accounts receivable	31,350	Office expense	63,000
Cash	53,050	Supplies	3,350
Fees earned	263,200	Wages expense	131,700
Land	80,000		

Prepare an income statement for the current year ended December 31, 2015.

FOLLOW MY EXAMPLE 1-3

CHICKADEE TRAVEL SERVICE
INCOME STATEMENT
For the Year Ended December 31, 2015

Revenues:		
Fees earned............................		$263,200
Expenses:		
Wages expense....................	$131,700	
Office expense.....................	63,000	
Miscellaneous expense........	12,950	
Total expenses.................		207,650
Net income		$ 55,550

For Practice: PE 1-3

Statement of Owner's Equity

The statement of owner's equity reports the changes in the owner's equity for a period of time. It is prepared *after* the income statement because the net income or net loss for the period must be reported in this statement. Similarly, the statement of owner's equity is prepared *before* the balance sheet because the amount of owner's equity at the end of the period must be reported on the balance sheet. Thus, the statement of owner's equity is often viewed as the connecting link between the income statement and balance sheet.

The three transactions that affected the owner's equity for NetSolutions during November were

1. the original investment of $25,000,
2. the revenue and expenses that resulted in net income of $3,850 for the month, and
3. a withdrawal of $2,000 by the owner.

The preceding information is summarized in the statement of owner's equity in Exhibit 5.

EXAMPLE EXERCISE 1-4 Statement of Owner's Equity (5)

Using the data for Chickadee Travel Service shown in Example Exercise 1-3, prepare a statement of owner's equity for the current year ended December 31, 2015. The capital of the owner, Adam Cellini, was $80,000 at January 1, 2015. Adam invested an additional $50,000 in the business during the year and withdrew cash of $30,000 for personal use.

FOLLOW MY EXAMPLE 1-4

CHICKADEE TRAVEL SERVICE
STATEMENT OF OWNER'S EQUITY
For the Year Ended December 31, 2015

Adam Cellini, capital, January 1, 2015		$ 80,000
Additional investment by owner during year..........	$ 50,000	
Net income for the year	55,550	
	105,550	
Less withdrawals...	30,000	
Increase in owner's equity		75,550
Adam Cellini, capital, December 31, 2015		$155,550

For Practice: PE 1-4

Balance Sheet

The balance sheet in Exhibit 5 reports the amounts of NetSolutions' assets, liabilities, and owner's equity as at November 30, 2014. The asset and liability amounts are taken from the last line of the summary of transactions on page 15. Chris Clark, Capital as at November 30, 2014, is taken from the statement of owner's equity. The form of balance sheet shown in Exhibit 5 is called the **account form** because it resembles the basic format of the accounting equation, with assets on the left side and the liabilities and owner's equity sections on the right side.[14]

The assets section of the balance sheet presents assets in the order that they will be converted into cash or used in operations. Cash is presented first, followed by receivables, supplies, prepaid insurance, and other assets. The assets of a more permanent nature are shown next, such as land, buildings, and equipment.

In the liabilities section of the balance sheet in Exhibit 5, accounts payable is the only liability. When there are two or more liabilities, each should be listed and the total amount of liabilities presented as follows:

Liabilities

Accounts payable	$12,900	
Wages payable	2,570	
Total liabilities		$15,470

Cash Flow Statement

The cash flow statement, as shown in Exhibit 5, explains the changes to the cash account that occur from the beginning to the end of the accounting period. These changes are categorized into three sections: changes resulting from the business operations or operating activities, from investing activities, and from financing activities.

---

14 Normally, the balance sheet is in the **report form**. It presents the liabilities and owner's equity sections below the assets section and is illustrated in Chapter 4.

Exhibit 5

Financial Statements for NetSolutions

NetSolutions
Income Statement
For the Month Ended November 30, 2014

Revenues:		
Fees earned		$7,500
Expenses:		
Wages expense	$2,125	
Rent expense	800	
Utilities expense	450	
Miscellaneous expense	275	
Total expense		3,650
Net income		$3,850

NetSolutions
Statement of Owner's Equity
For the Month Ended November 30 2014

Chris Clark, capital, November 1, 2014		$ 0
Investment on November 1, 2014	$25,000	
Net income for November	3,850	
	28,850	
Less withdrawals	2,000	
Increase in owner's equity		26,850
Chris Clark, capital, November 30, 2014		$26,850

NetSolutions
Balance Sheet
November 30, 2014

Assets		Liabilities	
Cash	$ 5,900	Accounts payable	$ 400
Supplies	1,350	**Owner's Equity**	
Land	20,000	Chris Clark, capital	26,850
Total assets	$27,250	Total liabilities and owner's equity	$27,250

NetSolutions
Cash Flow Statement
For the Month Ended November 30, 2014

Cash flows from operating activities:		
Cash received from customers	$ 7,500	
Cash payments for expenses and payments to creditors	(4,600)	
Net cash flow from operating activities		$ 2,900
Cash flows from investing activities:		
Cash payments for purchase of land		(20,000)
Cash flows from financing activities:		
Cash received as owner's investment	25,000	
Cash withdrawal by owner	(2,000)	
Net cash flow from financing activities		23,000
Net cash flow and November 30, 2014, cash balance		$ 5,900

EXAMPLE EXERCISE 1-5 Balance Sheet (5)

Using the data for Chickadee Travel Service shown in Example Exercises 1-3 and 1-4, prepare the balance sheet as at December 31, 2015.

FOLLOW MY EXAMPLE 1-5

CHICKADEE TRAVEL SERVICE
BALANCE SHEET
December 31, 2015

Assets		Liabilities	
Cash	$ 53,050	Accounts payable	$ 12,200
Accounts receivable	31,350	**Owner's Equity**	
Supplies	3,350		
Land	80,000	Adam Cellini, capital	155,550
Total assets	$167,750	Total liabilities and owner's equity	$167,750

For Practice: PE 1-5

This statement is the most challenging of the four financial statements to prepare. Consequently, it will be discussed in theory here, and detailed preparation will be explained in Chapter 16.

Interrelationships among Financial Statements

Financial statements are prepared in the following order: the income statement, statement of owner's equity, balance sheet, and cash flow statement. This order is important because the financial statements are interrelated. These interrelationships for NetSolutions are shown in Exhibit 5 and are described below.

Interrelationships among Financial Statements	**NetSolutions Example (Exhibit 5)**
Net income or net loss is reported on the income statement *and* the statement of owner's equity.	NetSolutions' net income of $3,850 for November is added to Chris Clark's investment of $25,000 in the statement of owner's equity.
End-of-period owner's capital is reported on the statement of owner's equity *and* the balance sheet.	Chris Clark, Capital of $26,850 as at November 30, 2014, on the statement of owner's equity also appears on the November 30, 2014, balance sheet as Chris Clark, Capital.
Cash is reported on the balance sheet *and* the cash flow statement.	Cash of $5,900 reported on the balance sheet as at November 30, 2014, is also reported on the November cash flow statement as the end-of-period cash.

The preceding interrelationships are important when analyzing financial statements and the impact of transactions on a business. In addition, these interrelationships serve as a check on whether the financial statements have been prepared correctly. For example, if the ending cash on the cash flow statement doesn't agree with the balance sheet cash, then an error has occurred.

At a Glance 1

1 Describe the nature of a business, the role of accounting, and the role of ethics in business.

Key Points	Key Learning Outcomes	Page	Example Exercises
A business provides goods or services to customers with the objective of earning a profit. Three types of businesses include service, merchandising, and manufacturing businesses.	• Distinguish among service, merchandising, and manufacturing businesses.	3	
Accounting is an information system that provides users with reports about the economic activities and condition of a business.	• Describe the role of accounting in business and explain why accounting is called the "language of business."	3	
Ethics are moral principles that guide the conduct of individuals.	• Define ethics and list the two factors affecting ethical conduct.	4	
	• Describe private accounting and public accounting.	5	

2 Summarize the development of accounting principles and relate them to practice.

Key Points	Key Learning Outcomes	Page	Example Exercises
Generally accepted accounting principles (GAAP) are used in preparing financial statements so that users can rely on the information. Canadian GAAP includes IFRS for publicly account-able enterprises and ASPE for private enterprises, though private enterprises may choose to use IFRS for preparing financial information. The fundamental qualitative characteristics that should define financial information are relevance, faithful representation, and materiality. The enhancing character-istics are comparability, verifiability, timeliness, and understandability. Other elements to consider when preparing financial information are the going concern assumption, the business entity assumption, the recognition of the elements, the measurement of the elements, and the benefit versus cost constraint. Businesses may be organized as proprietorships, partnerships, or corporations.	• Explain generally accepted accounting principles and how they are developed.	6	
	• Identify two sets of standards that are part of Canadian GAAP and the enterprises to which they apply.	7	
	• Describe the going concern assumption.	8	
	• Describe and give an example of the business entity assumption.	8	
	• Describe the characteristics of a proprietorship, partnership, and corporation.	8	
	• Describe and give an example of the revenue recognition principle.	8	
	• Describe and give an example of the historical cost principle.	9	1-1
	• Describe and give an example of the cost constraint.	9	
	• Describe the fundamental and enhancing qualitative character-istics to be applied to financial statements.	9	

3 State the accounting equation and define each element of the equation.

Key Points	Key Learning Outcomes	Page	Example Exercises
The resources owned by a business and the rights or claims to these resources may be stated in the form of an equation, as follows: Assets = Liabilities + Owner's Equity	• State the accounting equation.	10	
	• Define assets, liabilities, and owner's equity.	10	
	• Given two elements of the accounting equation, solve for the third element.	10	1-2

4 Describe and illustrate how business transactions can be recorded in terms of the resulting change in the elements of the accounting equation.

Key Points	Key Learning Outcomes	Page	Example Exercises
All business transactions can be stated in terms of the change in one or more of the three elements of the accounting equation.	• Define a business transaction.	11	
	• Using the accounting equation as a framework, record transactions.	12	

5 Describe the financial statements of a proprietorship and explain how they interrelate.

Key Points	Key Learning Outcomes	Page	Example Exercises
The primary financial statements of a proprietorship are the income statement, the statement of owner's equity, the balance sheet, and the cash flow statement. The income statement reports a period's net income or net loss, which is also reported on the statement of owner's equity. The ending owner's capital reported on the statement of owner's equity is also reported on the balance sheet. The ending cash balance is reported on the balance sheet and the cash flow statement.	• List and describe the financial statements of a proprietorship.	16	
	• Prepare an income statement	17	1-3
	• Prepare a statement of owner's equity.	17	1-4
	• Prepare a balance sheet.	18	1-5
	• Explain how the financial statements of a proprietorship are interrelated.	20	

GLOSSARY

account form – The form of balance sheet that resembles the basic format of the accounting equation, with Assets on the left side and Liabilities and Owner's Equity sections on the right side. (p. 18)

account payable – The liability created by a purchase on account. (p. 12)

account receivable – A claim against the customer created by selling merchandise or services on account. (p. 13)

accounting – An information system that provides reports to users about the economic activities and condition of a business. (p. 3)

accounting equation – Assets = Liabilities + Owner's Equity. (p. 10)

Accounting Standards Board (AcSB) – The authoritative body of the CICA that has the primary responsibility for approving and developing accounting standards in Canada. (p. 6)

Accounting Standards for Private Enterprises (ASPE) – The guidelines that constitute Part II of the *CICA Handbook*, which private enterprises may choose to use for the preparation of financial information. (p. 7)

asset – An economic resource controlled by an entity as a result of a past transaction and from which future economic benefit may be obtained. (p. 10)

balance sheet – A list of the assets, liabilities, and owner's equity as at a specific date, usually at the close of the last day of a month or a year. (p. 16) Also known as *statement of financial position* under IFRS.

benefit versus cost constraint – The trade-off that exists between the accuracy of financial information and the cost to produce that information. (p. 9) Also known as *cost constraint.*

business – An organization in which basic resources (inputs), such as materials and labour, are assembled and processed to provide goods or services (outputs) to customers. (p. 2)

business entity assumption – An assumption of accounting that limits the economic data in the accounting system to data related directly to the activities of the business. (p. 8)

business transaction – An economic event or condition that directly changes an entity's financial condition or directly affects its results of operations. (p. 11)

Canadian generally accepted accounting principles (Canadian GAAP) – All of the Canadian accounting standards, including Accounting Standards for Private Enterprises (ASPE) and International Financial Reporting Standards (IFRS). (p. 6)

Canadian Institute of Chartered Accountants (CICA) – A private organization that has primary responsibility for approving and developing accounting standards in Canada. (p. 6)

cash flow statement – A summary of the cash receipts and cash payments for a specific period of time, such as a month or a year. (p. 16) Also known as *Statement of cash flows* under IFRS.

Certified General Accountant (CGA) – An individual who has passed the professional examinations and practical experience requirements of the Certified General Accountants Association of Canada (CGA-Canada). (p. 6)

Certified Management Accountant (CMA) – An individual who has passed the professional examinations and practical experience requirements of the Society of Management Accountants of Canada (CMA-Canada). (p. 6)

Chartered Accountant (CA) – An individual who has passed the professional examinations and practical experience requirements of the Canadian Institute of Chartered Accountants (CICA). (p. 6)

Chartered Professional Accountant (CPA) – An individual who has passed the Chartered Professional Accountants' professional examinations and practical experience requirements. (p. 6)

CICA Handbook – A document containing accounting standards and guidance for Canadian organizations, published by the Canadian Institute of Chartered Accountants. (p. 6)

comparability – A preferred characteristic of accounting information whereby information for one company is comparable to information prepared for another organization. (p. 10)

corporation – A business organized under provincial, territorial, or federal charter as a separate legal entity. (p. 8)

cost constraint – The trade-off that exists between the accuracy of financial information and the cost to produce that information. (p. 9) Also known as *benefit versus cost constraint.*

cost principle – In financial statements, the recognition of transactions at the amount of cash paid or received. (p. 9) Also known as the *historical cost basis.*

ethics – Moral principles that guide the conduct of individuals. (p. 4)

expenses – Assets used up or services consumed in the process of generating revenues. (p. 13)

faithful representation – Recording an event in a manner that reflects the substance of the transaction. (p. 9) Also known as *representational faithfulness.*

fees earned – Revenue from providing services. (p. 13)

fees earned on account – Revenue from providing services when payment is received at a later date. (p. 13)

financial accounting – The branch of accounting that is concerned with recording transactions using generally accepted accounting principles (GAAP) for a business or other economic unit and with a periodic preparation of various statements from such records. (p. 4)

financial statements – Financial reports that summarize the effects of events on a business. (p. 16)

general-purpose financial statements – A type of financial accounting report that is distributed to external users. The term "general purpose" refers to the wide range of decision-making needs that the reports are designed to serve. (p. 4)

going concern assumption – An assumption that the business will continue for the foreseeable future. (p. 7)

historical cost basis – In financial statements, the recognition of transactions at the amount of cash paid or received. (p. 8) Also known as the *cost principle.*

income statement – A summary of the revenues and expenses for a specific period of time, such as a month or a year. (p. 16) Also known as *statement of comprehensive income* under IFRS.

interest revenue – Money received for interest. (p. 13)

International Accounting Standards Board (IASB) – An organization that issues International Financial Reporting Standards for many countries. (p. 6)

International Financial Reporting Standards (IFRS) – Guidelines, contained in Part I of the *CICA Handbook* for the preparation of financial statements for publicly accountable enterprises. (p. 6)

liability – An obligation to give up either services or assets. (p. 10)

management (or managerial) accounting – The branch of accounting that provides accounting information for internal users' decision making. (p. 4)

manufacturing business – A business that changes basic inputs into products that are sold to customers. (p. 3)

materiality – Information is considered material if omitting it or misstating it could influence decisions that users make on the basis of financial information of an entity. (p. 9)

merchandising business – A business that purchases products from other businesses and sells them to customers. (p. 3)

net income – The amount by which revenues exceed expenses. (p. 17)

net loss – The amount by which expenses exceed revenues. (p. 17)

owner's equity – Assets less liabilities, being the amount that the owner is entitled to. (p. 10).

partnership – An unincorporated business form consisting of two or more persons conducting business as co-owners for profit. (p. 8)

prepaid expenses – Items such as supplies that will be used in the business in the future. (p. 12)

private accounting – The field of accounting whereby accountants are employed by a business or a not-for-profit organization. (p. 4)

private enterprises – Profit-oriented organizations that do not issue shares or bonds through stock exchanges. (p. 6)

profit – The difference between the amounts received from customers for goods or services provided and the amounts paid for the inputs used to provide the goods or services. (p. 2)

proprietorship – A business owned by one individual. (p. 8)

public accounting – The field of accounting where accountants and their staff provide services on a fee basis. (p. 6)

publicly accountable enterprises – Companies with shares or bonds listed on stock exchanges and other organizations, such as credit unions or investment dealers, that impact large or diverse groups of stakeholders. (p. 6)

purchase on account – Items purchased by agreeing to pay the supplier in the near future. (p. 12)

relevance – Ability of financial information to be helpful to investors and others making financial decisions. (p. 9)

rent revenue – Money received for rent. (p. 13)

report form – The form of balance sheet that presents the liabilities and owner's equity sections below the assets section. (p. 18)

representational faithfulness – Recording an event in a manner that reflects the substance of the transaction. (p. 9) Also known as *faithful representation*.

revenue recognition principle – Revenue transactions that meet the recognition criteria, normally when goods are provided or services are performed. (p. 8)

revenues – Increases in owner's equity as a result of selling services or products to customers. (p. 13)

sales – The total amount charged customers for merchandise sold, including cash sales and sales on account. (p. 13)

sales on account – The amount charged customers for merchandise sold when payment is received at a later date. (p. 13)

service business – A business providing services rather than products to customers. (p. 3)

statement of cash flows – For companies reporting under IFRS, a summary of the cash receipts and cash payments for a specific period of time, such as a month or a year. (p. 16) Also known as *cash flow statement*.

statement of changes in equity – For companies reporting under IFRS, a summary of the changes in the owner's equity that have occurred during a specific period of time, such as a month or a year. (p. 16) Also known as *statement of owner's equity* and as *statement of retained earnings* for corporations reporting under ASPE.

statement of comprehensive income – For companies reporting under IFRS, a summary of the revenues and expenses for a specific period of time, such as a month or a year. (p. 16) Also known as *income statement*.

statement of financial position – For companies reporting under IFRS, a list of the assets, liabilities, and owner's equity as at a specific date, usually at the close of the last day of a month or a year. (p. 16) Also known as *balance sheet*.

statement of owner's equity – A summary of the changes in the owner's equity that have occurred during a specific period of time, such as a month or a year. (p. 16) Also known as *statement of retained earnings* for corporations reporting under ASPE, and as *statement of changes in equity* for corporations reporting under IFRS.

statement of retained earnings – For corporations reporting under ASPE, a summary of the changes in the owner's equity that have occurred during a specific period of time, such as a month or a year. (p. 16) Also known as *statement of owner's equity* and as *statement of changes in equity* for corporations reporting under IFRS.

timeliness – Ability of financial information to be produced on a timely basis so that it is helpful to investors and others making financial decisions. (p. 10)

understandability – Ability of information to improve the reader's comprehension of financial information, such as notes to the financial statements. (p. 10)

verifiability – A characteristic of financial information such that the information can be confirmed by source documents. (p. 10)

END-OF-CHAPTER ILLUSTRATIVE PROBLEM

Cathy Black, Solicitor, is a proprietorship owned and operated by Cathy Black. On July 1, 2014, Cathy Black, Solicitor, has the following account balances: cash, $1,000; accounts receivable, $3,200; supplies, $850; accounts payable, $1,530; Cathy Black, Capital, $3,520. Business transactions during July are summarized as follows:

   a. Received cash from clients for services, $4,000.
   b. Paid creditors on account, $1,055.
   c. Received cash from Cathy Black as an additional investment, $3,700.
   d. Paid office rent for the month, $1,200.
   e. Charged clients for legal services on account, $2,025.
   f. Purchased supplies on account, $245.

   g. Received cash from clients on account, $3,000.

   h. Paid the following: wages expense, $850; utilities expense, $325; and miscellaneous expense, $75.

   i. Black withdrew $1,000 in cash from the business for personal use.

Instructions

1. State the assets, liabilities, and owner's equity as at July 1 in equation form, similar to that shown in this chapter. In tabular form below the equation, indicate the increases and decreases resulting from each transaction and the final balances after all the transactions.

2. Prepare an income statement for July, a statement of owner's equity for July, and a balance sheet as at July 31, 2014.

Solution

1.

	Assets				=	Liabilities +				Owner's Equity					
			Accts.				Accts.		Cathy Black,	Cathy Black,		Fees	Wages	Rent	Utilities	Misc.
	Cash	+	Rec.	+ Supp.	=		Pay.	+	Capital	− Withdrawals	+ Earned	− Exp.	− Exp.	− Exp.	− Exp.
Bal.	1,000		3,200	850			1,530		3,520						
a.	+4,000										+4,000				
b.	−1,055						−1,055								
c.	+3,700								+3,700						
d.	−1,200												−1,200		
e.			+2,025								+2,025				
f.				+245			+245								
g.	+3,000		−3,000												
h.	−1,250											−850		−325	−75
i.	−1,000									−1,000					
Bal.	7,195		2,225	1,095			720		7,220	−1,000	6,025	−850	−1,200	−325	−75

2.

CATHY BLACK, SOLICITOR
Income Statement
For the Month Ended July 31, 2014

Revenues:		
Fees earned		$6,025
Expenses:		
Rent expense	$1,200	
Wages expense	850	
Utilities expense	325	
Miscellaneous expense	75	
Total expenses		2,450
Net income		$3,575

CATHY BLACK, SOLICITOR
Statement of Owner's Equity
For the Month Ended July 31, 2014

Cathy Black, capital, July 1, 2014		$3,520
Additional investment by owner	$3,700	
Net income for the month	3,575	
	7,275	
Less withdrawals	1,000	
Increase in owner's equity		6,275
Cathy Black, capital, July 31, 2014		$9,795

(continued)

CATHY BLACK, SOLICITOR
Balance Sheet
July 31, 2014

Assets		Liabilities	
Cash	$ 7,195	Accounts payable	$ 720
Accounts receivable	2,225	**Owner's Equity**	
Supplies	1,095	Cathy Black, capital	9,795
		Total liabilities and	
Total assets	$10,515	owner's equity	$10,515

EYE OPENERS

1. What is the objective of most businesses?
2. What is the difference between a manufacturing business and a service business? Is a restaurant a manufacturing business, a service business, or both?
3. Name some users of accounting information.
4. What is the role of accounting in business?
5. Why are most large companies, such as Microsoft, Bombardier, and Finning Tractor, organized as corporations?
6. The new company bookkeeper decided to record the $50 lamp purchase as an asset. Discuss, referencing GAAP in your answer, whether this treatment is appropriate.
7. On April 2, Gremlin Repair Service extended an offer of $100,000 for land that had been priced for sale at $125,000. On May 10, Gremlin Repair Service accepted the seller's counteroffer of $115,000. Describe how Gremlin Repair Service should record the land purchase.
8. Is a publicly accountable enterprise allowed to use ASPE? Is a private enterprise allowed to use IFRS?
9. Describe the difference between an account receivable and an account payable.
10. A business had revenues of $600,000 and operating expenses of $715,000. Did the business (a) incur a net loss or (b) realize net income?
11. What particular item of financial or operating data appears on both the income statement and the statement of owner's equity? What item appears on both the balance sheet and the statement of owner's equity? What item appears on both the balance sheet and the cash flow statement?

PRACTICE EXERCISES

② PE 1-1
Measurement of the elements

EE 1-1 p. 9

On February 7, Snap Repair Service, a private company, extended an offer of $75,000 for land that had been priced for sale at $85,000. On February 21, Snap Repair Service accepted the seller's counteroffer of $81,000. On April 30, the land was assessed at a value of $125,000 for property tax purposes. On August 30, Snap Repair Service was offered $130,000 for the land by a national retail chain. At what value should the land be recorded in Snap Repair Service's records?

③ PE 1-2
Accounting equation

EE 1-2 p. 11

Shannon Cook is the owner and operator of Galaxy Ltd., a motivational consulting business. At the end of its accounting period, December 31, 2014, Galaxy Ltd. has assets of $800,000 and liabilities of $450,000. Using the accounting equation, determine the following amounts:

a. Owner's equity, as at December 31, 2014.

b. Owner's equity, as at December 31, 2015, assuming that assets increased by $175,000 and liabilities increased by $60,000 during 2015.

PE 1-3
⑤
Income statement

The assets and liabilities of Escape Travel Service at December 31, 2015, the end of the current year, and its revenue and expenses for the year are listed below.

EE 1-3 p. 17

Accounts payable	$ 52,500	Miscellaneous expense	$ 15,875
Accounts receivable	94,375	Office expense	391,625
Cash	56,750	Supplies	6,375
Fees earned	942,500	Wages expense	562,500
Land	362,500		

Prepare an income statement for the current year ended December 31, 2015.

PE 1-4
⑤
Statement of owner's equity

Using the data for Escape Travel Service shown in Practice Exercise 1-3, prepare a statement of owner's equity for the current year ended December 31, 2015. The capital of the owner, Nancy Coleman, was $475,000 as at January 1, 2015. Nancy invested an additional $45,000 in the business during the year and withdrew cash of $25,000 for personal use.

EE 1-4 p. 18

PE 1-5
⑤
Balance sheet

Using the data for Escape Travel Service shown in Practice Exercises 1-3 and 1-4, prepare the balance sheet as at December 31, 2015.

EE 1-5 p. 19

EXERCISES

EX 1-1
①
Types of businesses

a. Indicate whether each of the following companies is primarily a service, merchandise, or manufacturing business. If you are unfamiliar with the company, use the Internet to locate the company's home page or use the finance website of Yahoo.ca.

1. Century 21
2. eBay Inc.
3. Ford Motor Company
4. Bank of Montreal
5. WestJet Airlines Ltd.
6. Procter & Gamble
7. Purolator
8. The Bay
9. Days Inn
10. Bombardier Inc.
11. Finning Tractor & Equipment Co. Ltd.
12. The Dow Chemical Company

b. For which of the preceding companies is the accounting equation relevant?

EX 1-2
②
Business entity concept

Rocky Mountain Sports sells hunting and fishing equipment and provides guided hunting and fishing trips. Rocky Mountain Sports is owned and operated by Mike Webber, a well-known sports enthusiast and hunter. Mike's wife, Sarah, owns and operates Sable Boutique, a women's clothing store.

a. For each of the following transactions, identify which of the entities listed should record the transaction in its records.

Entities	
R	Rocky Mountain Sports
S	Sable Boutique
X	Neither of the above

1. Mike paid for an eye examination, which was required by the workers' compensation insurance policy carried by Rocky Mountain Sports.
2. Mike received a cash advance from customers for a guided hunting trip.
3. Sarah paid her dues to the YWCA.
4. Mike paid a breeder's fee for an English springer spaniel to be used as a hunting guide dog.
5. Sarah deposited a $5,000 personal cheque in a trust fund established to finance their children's postsecondary education.

(continued)

6. Mike paid for an advertisement in a hunters' magazine.
7. Sarah donated several dresses from inventory to a local charity auction that will benefit a women's shelter.
8. Mike paid for dinner and a movie to celebrate their 15th wedding anniversary.
9. Sarah purchased two dozen spring dresses from a Vancouver designer for a special spring sale.

b. What is a business transaction?

---

② EX 1-3
Accounting principles

Identify which of the conceptual framework elements have or have not been implemented in the following situations.

a. TRK Company invented a puncture-free bike tire, spending $80,000 on its development. The owner expects to generate $500,000 from this invention next year and so he has recorded $580,000 in an asset account entitled Puncture-Free Tire Asset.

b. The owner of TRK Company purchased an expensive bike trailer for transporting his children. When preparing the company financial statements, he did not include the bike trailer as a company asset.

---

② EX 1-4
Accounting principles

In 2012, Mary Frances established a boutique wine store in Victoria. After operating for three years, Mary hired her brother, Fred, to help with her accounting. Fred produced the first set of financial statements. Mary's office is in her house, and so Fred included Mary's house as an asset and valued it at $800,000, its market value in 2015. Mary's accounts receivable balance is $50,000, but Mary thinks that some of those accounts are not collectible. Fred feels it is reasonable to leave the accounts receivable balance at $50,000 until Mary knows for certain which accounts are not collectible. Fred decides not to include any notes to the financial statements because he feels they reveal too much information. Since Mary does not own the building in which the wine store is located, Fred feels it is appropriate to expense the $25,000 Mary spent in 2015 on leasehold improvements to the wine store.

Instructions

1. In groups, discuss which of the conceptual framework elements Fred has violated and the cause of the violation.
2. Where possible, identify the action that Fred should take to produce financial statements in accordance with generally accepted accounting principles.

---

② EX 1-5
Accounting principles

Identify which of the conceptual framework elements have been violated by the following events. Some questions have more than one acceptable answer.

1. The owner is in the process of purchasing a building, and the closing date for the transaction is next month. The building is shown as an asset on the balance sheet.
2. Office furniture was donated to the company by the owner's mother. The owner listed the furniture on the balance sheet with a value of $1,000.
3. The financial statements were produced eight months after the year-end.
4. The accountant prepared the financial statements without following Canadian GAAP.
5. The owner bought a piece of equipment on sale, paying $1,500 instead of $2,800. The accountant recorded the equipment with a value of $2,800.
6. An advance payment for future work was recorded as revenue.

---

② EX 1-6
Accounting principles

Identify which of the conceptual framework elements have been violated by the following events. Some questions have more than one acceptable answer.

1. The company's building has increased in value since it was purchased 10 years ago. Since the owner intends to sell the building next year, he recorded the building at market value on the balance sheet.
2. The notes to the financial statements were omitted.

3. The company's balance sheet listed the owner's personal vehicle as an asset.
4. The accountant recorded the office staplers as assets on the balance sheet.
5. The accountant is planning to alternate use of ASPE and IFRS in preparing the financial statements.
6. The owner listed his employees as an asset entitled "Intellectual Property" on the balance sheet.

---

③ EX 1-7
Accounting equation

✔ a. $1,030,000

Determine the missing amount for each of the following:

	Assets	=	Liabilities	+	Owner's Equity
a.	✕	=	$250,000	+	$780,000
b.	$125,000	=	✕	+	39,500
c.	60,000	=	7,500	+	✕

---

③④ EX 1-8
Accounting equation

✔ b. $530,000

Todd Olson is the owner and operator of Alpha, a motivational consulting business. At the end of its accounting period, December 31, 2014, Alpha has assets of $800,000 and liabilities of $350,000. Using the accounting equation and considering each case independently, determine the following amounts:

a. Todd Olson, capital, as at December 31, 2014.
b. Todd Olson, capital, as at December 31, 2015, assuming that assets increased by $150,000 and liabilities increased by $70,000 during 2015.
c. Todd Olson, capital, as at December 31, 2015, assuming that assets decreased by $60,000 and liabilities increased by $20,000 during 2015.
d. Todd Olson, capital, as at December 31, 2015, assuming that assets increased by $100,000 and liabilities decreased by $40,000 during 2015.
e. Net income (or net loss) during 2015, assuming that as at December 31, 2015, assets were $975,000, liabilities were $400,000, and there were no additional investments or withdrawals.

---

③ EX 1-9
Asset, liability, owner's equity items

Indicate whether each of the following is identified with (1) an asset, (2) a liability, or (3) owner's equity:

a. accounts payable
b. cash
c. fees earned
d. accounts receivable

e. land
f. supplies
g. wages expense
h. Mark Flinn, Withdrawals

---

③④ EX 1-10
Effect of transactions on accounting equation

Describe how the following business transactions affect the three elements of the accounting equation.

a. Invested cash in the business.
b. Received cash for services performed.
c. Paid for utilities used in the business.
d. Purchased supplies for cash.
e. Purchased supplies on account.

---

③④ EX 1-11
Effect of transactions on accounting equation

✔ a. (1) increase $140,000

a. A vacant lot acquired for $150,000 is sold for $290,000 in cash. What is the effect of the sale on the total amount of the seller's (1) assets, (2) liabilities, and (3) owner's equity?
b. Assume that the seller owes $80,000 on a loan for the land. After receiving the $290,000 cash in (a), the seller pays the $80,000 owed. What is the effect of the payment on the total amount of the seller's (1) assets, (2) liabilities, and (3) owner's equity?
c. Does a transaction always affect two or more elements of the accounting equation (i. e., assets, liabilities, or owner's equity)? Explain.

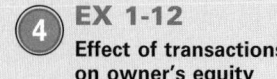

EX 1-12

Effect of transactions on owner's equity

Indicate whether each of the following types of transactions will (a) increase owner's equity or (b) decrease owner's equity:

1. expenses
2. revenues
3. owner's investments
4. owner's withdrawals

EX 1-13

Transactions

The following selected transactions were completed by Speedy Delivery Service during October:

1. Received cash from owner as additional investment, $30,000.
2. Purchased supplies for cash, $1,500.
3. Paid rent for October, $4,000.
4. Paid advertising expense, $2,500.
5. Received cash for providing delivery services, $18,750.
6. Billed customers for delivery services on account, $41,500.
7. Paid creditors on account, $6,000.
8. Received cash from customers on account, $26,200.
9. Paid cash to owner for personal use, $2,000.

Indicate the effect of each transaction on the accounting equation by listing the numbers identifying the transactions, (1) through (9), in a column and inserting at the right of each number the appropriate letter from the following list:

a. Increase in an asset, decrease in another asset.
b. Increase in an asset, increase in a liability.
c. Increase in an asset, increase in owner's equity.
d. Decrease in an asset, decrease in a liability.
e. Decrease in an asset, decrease in owner's equity.

EX 1-14

Nature of transactions

✔ d. $15,000

Jeremy Zabel operates his own catering service. Summary financial data for February are presented in equation form below. Each line designated by a number indicates the effect of a transaction on the equation. Each increase and decrease in owner's equity, except transaction (5), affects net income.

	Assets			=	Liabilities +		Owner's Equity			
						Jeremy	Jeremy			
					Accounts	Zabel,	Zabel,	Fees		
	Cash	+ Supplies	+ Land	=	Payable	+ Capital	− Withdrawals	+ Earned	− Expenses	
Bal.	25,000	2,000	75,000		12,000	90,000				
1.	+29,000							+29,000		
2.	−20,000		+20,000							
3.	−14,000								−14,000	
4.		+1,000			+1,000					
5.	− 2,000						−2,000			
6.	− 7,000				−7,000					
Bal.	11,000	3,000	95,000		6,000	90,000	−2,000	29,000	−14,000	

a. Describe each transaction.
b. What is the amount of net decrease in cash during the month?
c. What is the amount of net increase in owner's equity during the month?
d. What is the amount of the net income for the month?
e. How much of the net income for the month was retained in the business?

EX 1-15

Net income and owner's withdrawals

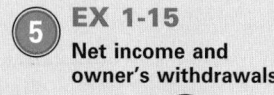

The income statement of a proprietorship for the month of December indicates a net income of $120,000. During the same period, the owner withdrew $130,000 in cash from the business for personal use.

Would it be correct to say that the business incurred a net loss of $10,000 during the month? Discuss.

⑤ EX 1-16

Net income and owner's equity for four businesses

✔ Leo: Net income $60,000

Four different proprietorships, Aries, Gemini, Leo, and Pisces, show the same balance sheet data at the beginning and end of a year. These data, exclusive of the amount of owner's equity, are summarized as follows:

	Total Assets	Total Liabilities
Beginning of the year	$400,000	$100,000
End of the year	750,000	300,000

On the basis of the above data and the following additional information for the year, determine the net income (or loss) of each company for the year. (*Hint:* First determine the amount of increase or decrease in owner's equity during the year.)

Aries: The owner had made no additional investments in the business and had made no withdrawals from the business.

Gemini: The owner had made no additional investments in the business but had withdrawn $40,000.

Leo: The owner had made an additional investment of $90,000 but had made no withdrawals.

Pisces: The owner had made an additional investment of $90,000 and had withdrawn $40,000.

---

⑤ EX 1-17

Balance sheet items

From the following list of selected items taken from the records of Hoosier Appliance Service as at a specific date, identify the items that would appear on the balance sheet:

1. Accounts Payable
2. Cash
3. Fees Earned
4. Land
5. Sarah Neil, Capital
6. Supplies
7. Supplies Expense
8. Utilities Expense
9. Wages Expense
10. Wages Payable

---

⑤ EX 1-18

Income statement items

From the data presented in Exercise 1-17, identify the items that would appear on the income statement.

---

⑤ EX 1-19

Statement of owner's equity

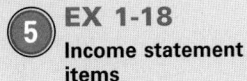

✔ Penny Beall, capital, June 30, 2015: $482,000

Financial information related to Lost Trail Company, a proprietorship, for the month ended June 30, 2015, is as follows:

Net income for June	$125,000
Penny Beall's withdrawals during June	18,000
Penny Beall's capital, June 1, 2015	375,000

a. Prepare a statement of owner's equity for the month ended June 30, 2015.
b. Why is the statement of owner's equity prepared before the June 30, 2015, balance sheet?

---

⑤ EX 1-20

Income statement

✔ Net income: $449,000

Universal Services was organized on October 1, 2015. A summary of the revenue and expense transactions for October follows:

Fees earned	$800,000
Wages expense	270,000
Rent expense	60,000
Supplies expense	9,000
Miscellaneous expense	12,000

Prepare an income statement for the month ended October 31, 2015.

5 **EX 1-21**

Missing amounts from balance sheet and income statement data

✔ a. $45,000

One item is omitted in each of the following summaries of balance sheet and income statement data for the following four different proprietorships:

	Aquarius	Libra	Scorpio	Taurus
Beginning of the year:				
Assets	$300,000	$500,000	$100,000	$ (d)
Liabilities	120,000	260,000	76,000	120,000
End of the year:				
Assets	420,000	700,000	90,000	248,000
Liabilities	110,000	220,000	80,000	136,000
During the year:				
Additional investment in the business	(a)	100,000	10,000	40,000
Withdrawals from the business	25,000	32,000	(c)	60,000
Revenue	190,000	(b)	115,000	112,000
Expenses	80,000	128,000	122,500	128,000

Determine the missing amounts, identifying them by letter. (*Hint:* First determine the amount of increase or decrease in owner's equity during the year.)

---

5 **EX 1-22**

Balance sheets, net income

✔ b. $136,275

Financial information related to the proprietorship of Plexiglass Interiors for the last day of October and November 2015 is as follows:

	October 31, 2015	November 30, 2015
Accounts payable	$ 46,200	$ 49,800
Accounts receivable	102,000	117,375
Claudia Symonds, capital	?	?
Cash	180,000	306,000
Supplies	9,000	7,500

a. Prepare balance sheets for Plexiglass Interiors as at October 31 and November 30, 2015.

b. Determine the amount of net income for November, assuming the owner made no additional investments or withdrawals during the month.

c. Determine the amount of net income for November, assuming the owner made no additional investments but withdrew $37,500 during the month.

---

5 **EX 1-23**

Financial statements

Each of the following items is shown in the financial statements of EnCana Corporation.

1. Accounts payable and accrued liabilities
2. Cash and cash equivalents
3. Operating expenses
4. Income taxes payable
5. Revenues, net of royalties
6. Long-term debt
7. Other liabilities and provisions
8. Property, plant and equipment, net
9. Investments and other assets
10. Transportation expenses

Instructions

a. Identify the financial statement (the balance sheet or the income statement) where each item would appear.

b. Which item(s) would appear on more than one financial statement?

PROBLEMS SERIES A

4 **PR 1-1A**

Transactions

✔ Cash bal. at end of September: $37,700

On September 1 of the current year, Linda Cross established a business to manage rental property. She completed the following transactions during September:

a. Opened a business bank account with a deposit of $40,000 from personal funds.

b. Purchased supplies on account, $2,200.

c. Received cash from fees earned for managing rental property, $6,000.

d. Paid rent on office and equipment for the month, $2,700.

e. Paid creditors on account, $1,000.

f. Billed customers for fees earned for managing rental property, $5,000.
g. Paid automobile expenses for the month, $600, and miscellaneous expenses, $300.
h. Paid office salaries, $1,900.
i. Withdrew cash for personal use, $1,800.

Instructions

1. Indicate the effect of each transaction using the following tabular headings:

Assets			= Liabilities +		Owner's Equity						
Cash +	Accounts Receivable +	Supplies =	Accounts Payable +	Linda Cross, Capital −	Linda Cross, Withdrawals +	Fees Earned −	Rent Expense −	Salaries Expense −	Auto Expense −	Misc. Expense	

2. Briefly explain why the owner's investment and revenues increased owner's equity, while withdrawals and expenses decreased owner's equity.
3. Determine the net income for September.
4. How much did September's transactions increase or decrease Linda Cross' capital?

PR 1-2A
Transactions

✔ Cash bal. at end of July: $50,450

Jean Howard established an insurance agency on July 1 of the current year and completed the following transactions during July:

a. Opened a business bank account with a deposit of $50,000 from personal funds.
b. Purchased supplies on account, $1,600.
c. Paid creditors on account, $500.
d. Received cash from fees earned on insurance commissions, $9,250.
e. Paid rent on office and equipment for the month, $2,500.
f. Paid automobile expenses for the month, $900, and miscellaneous expenses, $300.
g. Paid office salaries, $1,900.
h. Billed insurance companies for sales commissions earned, $11,150.
i. Withdrew cash for personal use, $2,700.

Instructions

1. Indicate the effect of each transaction using the following tabular headings:

Assets			= Liabilities +		Owner's Equity						
Cash +	Accounts Receivable +	Supplies =	Accounts Payable +	Jean Howard, Capital −	Jean Howard, Withdrawals +	Fees Earned −	Rent Expense −	Salaries Expense −	Auto Expense −	Misc. Expense	

2. Briefly explain why the owner's investment and revenues increased owner's equity, whereas withdrawals and expenses decreased owner's equity.

PR 1-3A
Financial statements

✔ 1. Net income: $40,000

The following are the amounts of the assets and liabilities of New World Travel Agency at December 31, 2015, the end of the current year, and its revenue and expenses for the year. The capital of Kris Taber, owner, was $120,000 on January 1, 2015, the beginning of the current year. During the current year, Kris withdrew $10,000.

Accounts payable	$ 25,000	Rent expense	$45,000
Accounts receivable	60,000	Supplies	5,000
Cash	110,000	Supplies expense	3,000
Fees earned	200,000	Utilities expense	18,000
Miscellaneous expense	4,000	Wages expense	90,000

Instructions

1. Prepare an income statement for the current year ended December 31, 2015.
2. Prepare a statement of owner's equity for the current year ended December 31, 2015.
3. Prepare a balance sheet as at December 31, 2015.
4. What item appears on both the income statement and statement of owner's equity?

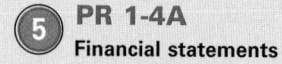

(5) PR 1-4A
Financial statements

Doug Van Buren established Ohm Computer Services on July 1, 2015. The effect of each transaction for July is shown below.

✔ 1. Net income: $24,500

Instructions

1. Prepare an income statement for the month ended July 31, 2015.
2. Prepare a statement of owner's equity for the month ended July 31, 2015.
3. Prepare a balance sheet as at July 31, 2015.

	Assets			=	Liabilities +		Owner's Equity						
	Cash	+ Accounts Receivable	+ Supplies	=	Accounts Payable	+ Doug Van Buren, Capital	– Doug Van Buren, Withdrawals	+ Fees Earned	– Salaries Expense	– Rent Expense	– Auto Expense	– Misc. Expense
a.	+30,000					+30,000						
b.			+2,600		+2,600							
c.	+29,500							+29,500				
d.	–8,000									–8,000		
e.	–1,250				–1,250							
f.		+20,750						+20,750				
g.	–5,750										–3,875	–1,875
h.	–12,000								–12,000			
i.	–7,500						–7,500					
Bal.	25,000	20,750	2,600		1,350	30,000	–7,500	50,250	–12,000	–8,000	–3,875	–1,875

---

(4)(5) PR 1-5A
Transactions; financial statements

On January 1, 2015, Carlton Myers established Vista Realty. Carlton completed the following transactions during the month of January:

✔ 2. Net income: $13,800

a. Opened a business bank account with a deposit of $25,000 from personal funds.
b. Purchased supplies on account, $2,500.
c. Paid creditor on account, $1,600.
d. Earned sales commissions, receiving cash, $25,500.
e. Paid rent on office and equipment for the month, $5,000.
f. Withdrew cash for personal use, $8,000.
g. Paid automobile expenses for the month, $2,500, and miscellaneous expenses, $1,200.
h. Paid office salaries, $3,000.

Instructions

1. Indicate the effect of each transaction using the following tabular headings:

Assets		=	Liabilities +		Owner's Equity						
Cash	+ Supplies	=	Accounts Payable	+ Carlton Myers, Capital	– Carlton Myers, Withdrawals	+ Sales Commissions	– Office Salaries Expense	– Rent Expense	– Auto Expense	– Misc. Expense

2. Prepare an income statement for January, a statement of owner's equity for January, and a balance sheet as at January 31, 2015.

---

(4)(5) PR 1-6A
Transactions; financial statements

Colfax Dry Cleaners is owned and operated by Marie Lapointe. A building and equipment are currently being rented, pending expansion to new facilities. The actual work of dry cleaning is done by another company at wholesale rates. The assets and the liabilities of the business on November 1, 2015, are as follows: Cash, $34,200; Accounts Receivable, $40,000; Supplies, $5,000; Land, $50,000; Accounts Payable, $16,400. Business transactions during November are summarized as follows:

✔ 3. Net income: $18,200

a. Marie Lapointe invested additional cash in the business with a deposit of $35,000 in the business bank account.
b. Purchased land for use as a parking lot, paying cash of $30,000.
c. Paid rent for the month, $4,500.

d. Charged customers for dry cleaning revenue on account, $18,250.

e. Paid creditors on account, $9,000.

f. Purchased supplies on account, $2,800.

g. Received cash from cash customers for dry cleaning revenue, $31,750.

h. Received cash from customers on account, $27,800.

i. Received monthly invoice for dry cleaning expense for November (to be paid in December), $14,800.

j. Paid the following: wages expense, $8,200; truck expense, $1,875; utilities expense, $1,575; miscellaneous expense, $850.

k. Withdrew $10,000 for personal use.

Instructions

1. Determine the amount of Marie Lapointe's capital as at November 1.
2. State the assets, liabilities, and owner's equity as at November 1 in equation form. In tabular form below the equation, indicate increases and decreases resulting from each transaction.
3. Prepare an income statement for November, a statement of owner's equity for November, and a balance sheet as at November 30, 2015.

---

⑤ PR 1-7A

Financial statements

✔ Correct amount of total assets is $176,400

Driftwood Realty, organized July 1, 2015, is owned and operated by Steffy Owen. The following statements were prepared after its second month of operations.

Driftwood Realty
Income Statement
August 31, 2015

Revenues:		
Sales commissions		$467,100
Expenses:		
Office salaries expense	$291,600	
Rent expense	99,000	
Automobile expense	22,500	
Miscellaneous expense	7,200	
Supplies expense	2,700	
Total expenses		423,000
Net income		$134,100

Steffy Owen
Statement of Owner's Equity
August 31, 2015

Steffy Owen, capital, August 1, 2015	$ 93,600
Less withdrawals during August	18,000
	75,600
Additional investment during August	22,500
	98,100
Net income for the month	134,100
Steffy Owen, capital, August 31, 2015	$232,200

Balance Sheet
For the Month Ended August 31, 2015

Assets		Liabilities	
Cash	$29,700	Accounts receivable	$128,700
Accounts payable	34,200	Supplies	18,000
		Owner's Equity	
		Steffy Owen, capital	232,200
Total assets	$63,900	Total liabilities and owner's equity	$378,900

Instructions

1. List the errors found in the Driftwood Realty financial statements.
2. Prepare an income statement for the month ended August 31, 2015.
3. Prepare a statement of owner's equity for the month ended August 31, 2015.
4. Prepare a balance sheet as at August 31, 2015.

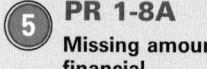

PR 1-8A

Missing amounts from financial statements

✔ i. $515,610

The financial statements at the end of Four Corners Realty's first month of operations are shown below.

Four Corners Realty
Income Statement
For the Month Ended July 31, 2015

Revenues:		
Fees earned		$239,700
Expenses:		
Wages expense	$ (a)	
Rent expense	24,480	
Supplies expense	20,400	
Utilities expense	13,770	
Miscellaneous expense	8,415	
Total expenses		121,890
Net income		$ (b)

Four Corners Realty
Statement of Owner's Equity
For the Month Ended July 31, 2015

Jeremy Parks, capital, July 1, 2015		$ (c)
Investment on July 1, 2015	$ (d)	
Net income for July	(e)	
	(f)	
Less withdrawals	(g)	
Increase in owner's equity		(h)
Jeremy Parks, capital, July 31, 2015		$ (i)

Four Corners Realty
Balance Sheet
July 31, 2015

Assets		Liabilities	
Cash	$150,450	Accounts payable	$12,240
Supplies	10,200	**Owner's Equity**	
Land	(j)	Jeremy Parks, capital	(l)
Total assets	$ (k)	Total liabilities and owner's equity	$ (m)

Four Corners Realty		
Cash Flow Statement		
For the Month Ended July 30, 2015		

Cash flows from operating activities:		
Cash received from customers.	$ 239,700	
Cash payments for expenses and payments to creditors	(119,850)	
Net cash flow from operating activities		$119,850
Cash flows from investing activities:		
Cash payments for acquisition of land		(367,200)
Cash flows from financing activities:		
Cash received as owner's investment	459,000	
Cash withdrawal by owner.	(61,200)	
Net cash flow from financing activities.		(397,800)
Net cash flow and July 31, 2015, cash balance		$150,450

Instructions

By analyzing the interrelationships among the four financial statements, determine the proper amounts for (a) through (m).

PROBLEMS SERIES B

PR 1-1B
Transactions

✔ Cash bal. at end
of January: $73,500

Alec Lee established an insurance agency on January 1 of the current year and completed the following transactions during January:

a. Opened a business bank account with a deposit of $75,000 from personal funds.
b. Purchased supplies on account, $3,000.
c. Paid creditors on account, $1,000.
d. Received cash from fees earned on insurance commissions, $11,800.
e. Paid rent on office and equipment for the month, $4,000.
f. Paid automobile expenses for the month, $600, and miscellaneous expenses, $200.
g. Paid office salaries, $2,500.
h. Billed insurance companies for sales commissions earned, $12,500.
i. Withdrew cash for personal use, $5,000.

Instructions

1. Indicate the effect of each transaction using the following tabular headings:

Assets			= Liabilities +		Owner's Equity						
	Accounts		Accounts	Alec Lee,	Alec Lee,	Fees	Rent	Salaries	Auto	Misc.
Cash +	Receivable +	Supplies =	Payable +	Capital	– Withdrawals +	Earned –	Expense –	Expense –	Expense –	Expense

2. Briefly explain why the owner's investment and revenues increased owner's equity, while withdrawals and expenses decreased owner's equity.
3. Determine the net income for January.
4. How much did January's transactions increase or decrease Alec Lee's capital?

PR 1-2B
Transactions

✔ Cash bal. at end of
November: $28,100

On November 1 of the current year, Rhea Quade established a business to manage rental property. She completed the following transactions during November:

a. Opened a business bank account with a deposit of $30,000 from personal funds.
b. Purchased supplies on account, $1,750.
c. Received cash from fees earned for managing rental property, $3,600.
d. Paid rent on office and equipment for the month, $1,300.

(continued)

e. Paid creditors on account, $500.

f. Billed customers for fees earned for managing rental property, $4,800.

g. Paid automobile expenses for the month, $500, and miscellaneous expenses, $200.

h. Paid office salaries, $1,000.

i. Withdrew cash for personal use, $2,000.

Instructions

1. Indicate the effect of each transaction using the following tabular headings:

Assets			= Liabilities +		Owner's Equity						
Cash +	Accounts Receivable +	Supplies =	Accounts Payable +	Rhea Quade, Capital	Rhea Quade, – Withdrawals +	Fees Earned	Rent – Expense	Salaries – Expense	Auto – Expense	Misc. – Expense	

2. Briefly explain why the owner's investment and revenues increased owner's equity, whereas withdrawals and expenses decreased owner's equity.

---

⑤ **PR 1-3B**

Financial statements

✔ 1. Net income: $80,000

The amounts of the assets and liabilities of St. Simon Travel Service at December 31, 2015, the end of the current year, and its revenue and expenses for the year are listed below. The capital of Gwen Perez, owner, was $150,000 at January 1, 2015, the beginning of the current year, and the owner withdrew $30,000 during the current year.

Accounts payable	$ 25,000		Rent expense	$ 75,000
Accounts receivable	90,000		Supplies	12,000
Cash	123,000		Supplies expense	18,000
Fees earned	500,000		Utilities expense	36,000
Miscellaneous expense	11,000		Wages expense	280,000

Instructions

1. Prepare an income statement for the current year ended December 31, 2015.

2. Prepare a statement of owner's equity for the current year ended December 31, 2015.

3. Prepare a balance sheet as at December 31, 2015.

4. What item appears on both the income statement and statement of owner's equity?

---

⑤ **PR 1-4B**

Financial statements

✔ 1. Net income: $10,300

Ashley Rhymer established Fair Play Financial Services on January 1, 2015. Fair Play Financial Services offers financial planning advice to its clients. The effect of each transaction for January is shown below.

Instructions

1. Prepare an income statement for the month ended January 31, 2015.

2. Prepare a statement of owner's equity for the month ended January 31, 2015.

3. Prepare a balance sheet as at January 31, 2015.

	Assets			= Liabilities +		Owner's Equity						
	Cash +	Accounts Receivable +	Supplies =	Accounts Payable +	Ashley Rhymer, Capital	Ashley Rhymer, – Withdrawals +	Fees Earned	Salaries – Expense	Rent – Expense	Auto – Expense	Misc. – Expense	
a.	+15,000				+15,000							
b.			+2,180	+2,180								
c.	−600			−600								
d.	+28,000						+28,000					
e.	−7,500								−7,500			
f.	−5,700									−4,500	−1,200	
g.	−16,000							−16,000				
h.		+11,500					+11,500					
i.	−5,000					−5,000						
Bal.	8,200	11,500	2,180	1,580	15,000	−5,000	39,500	−16,000	−7,500	−4,500	−1,200	

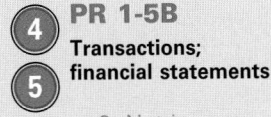

PR 1-5B

**Transactions;
financial statements**

✔ 2. Net income:
$10,000

On June 1, 2015, Lindsey Brown established Equity Realty. Lindsey completed the following transactions during the month of June:

a. Opened a business bank account with a deposit of $15,000 from personal funds.
b. Paid rent on office and equipment for the month, $4,000.
c. Paid automobile expenses for the month, $1,200, and miscellaneous expenses, $800.
d. Purchased supplies on account, $1,000.
e. Earned sales commissions, receiving cash, $18,500.
f. Paid creditor on account, $600.
g. Paid office salaries, $2,500.
h. Withdrew cash for personal use, $5,000.

Instructions

1. Indicate the effect of each transaction using the following tabular headings:

Assets	=	Liabilities	+	Owner's Equity					
Cash + Supplies	=	Accounts Payable	+	Lindsey Brown, Capital	− Lindsey Brown, Withdrawals	+ Sales Commissions	− Rent Expense	− Office Salaries Expense	− Auto Expense	− Misc. Expense

2. Prepare an income statement for June, a statement of owner's equity for June, and a balance sheet as at June 30, 2015.

PR 1-6B

**Transactions;
financial statements**

✔ 3. Net income:
$25,000

Swan Dry Cleaners is owned and operated by Peyton Keyes. A building and equipment are currently being rented, pending expansion to new facilities. The actual work of dry cleaning is done by another company at wholesale rates. The assets and the liabilities of the business on July 1, 2015, are as follows: Cash, $17,000; Accounts Receivable, $31,000; Supplies, $3,200; Land, $36,000; Accounts Payable, $10,400. Business transactions during July are summarized as follows:

a. Peyton Keyes invested additional cash in the business with a deposit of $25,000 in the business bank account.
b. Paid $24,000 for the purchase of land as a future building site.
c. Received cash from cash customers for dry cleaning revenue, $19,500.
d. Paid rent for the month, $3,000.
e. Purchased supplies on account, $1,550.
f. Paid creditors on account, $5,100.
g. Charged customers for dry cleaning revenue on account, $24,750.
h. Received monthly invoice for dry cleaning expense for July (to be paid in August), $8,200.
i. Paid the following: wages expense, $5,100; truck expense, $1,200; utilities expense, $800; miscellaneous expense, $950.
j. Received cash from customers on account, $26,750.
k. Withdrew $18,000 cash for personal use.

Instructions

1. Determine the amount of Peyton Keyes's capital as at July 1 of the current year.
2. State the assets, liabilities, and owner's equity as at July 1 in equation form. In tabular form below the equation, indicate increases and decreases resulting from each transaction.
3. Prepare an income statement for July, a statement of owner's equity for July, and a balance sheet as at July 31, 2015.

⑤ PR 1-7B

Financial statements

✔ Correct amount
of total assets is
$88,200.

Empire Realty, organized May 1, 2015, is owned and operated by Bertram Mitchell. How many errors can you find in the following statements for Empire Realty, prepared after its first month of operations?

Empire Realty
Income Statement
May 31, 2015

Revenues:		
Sales commissions		$233,550
Expenses:		
Office salaries expense	$145,800	
Rent expense	49,500	
Automobile expense	11,250	
Miscellaneous expense	3,600	
Supplies expense	1,350	
Total expenses		211,500
Net income		$ 67,050

Bertram Mitchell
Statement of Owner's Equity
May 31, 2014

Bertram Mitchell, capital, May 1, 2015	$ 46,800
Less withdrawals during May	9,000
	37,800
Additional investment during May	11,250
	49,050
Net income for May	67,050
Bertram Mitchell, capital, May 31, 2015	$116,100

Balance Sheet
For the Month Ended May 31, 2015

Assets		Liabilities	
Cash	$14,850	Accounts receivable	$ 64,350
Accounts payable	17,100	Supplies	9,000
		Owner's Equity	
		Bertram Mitchell, capital	116,100
Total assets	$31,950	Total liabilities and owner's equity	$189,450

PR 1-8B

Missing amounts from financial statements

✔ f. $278,400

The financial statements at the end of Eastern Realty's first month of operations are shown below.

Eastern Realty
Income Statement
For the Month Ended November 30, 2015

Revenues:		
Fees earned	$	(a)
Expenses:		
Wages expense	$51,000	
Rent expense	19,200	
Supplies expense	(b)	
Utilities expense	10,800	
Miscellaneous expense	6,600	
Total expenses		105,600
Net income		$ 74,400

Eastern Realty
Statement of Owner's Equity
For the Month Ended November 30, 2015

Laura Biddle, capital, November 1, 2015	$	(c)
Investment on November 1, 2015	$240,000	
Net income for November	(d)	
	(e)	
Less withdrawals	36,000	
Increase in owner's equity		(f)
Laura Biddle, capital, November 30, 2015	$	(g)

Eastern Realty
Balance Sheet
November 30, 2015

Assets		**Liabilities**	
Cash	$ 26,700	Accounts payable	$9,600
Supplies	21,300	**Owner's Equity**	
Land	240,000	Laura Biddle, capital	(i)
Total assets	$ (h)	Total liabilities and owner's equity	$ (j)

Eastern Realty
Cash Flow Statement
For the Month Ended November 30, 2015

Cash flows from operating activities:		
Cash received from customers	$ 180,000	
Cash payments for expenses and payments to creditors	(117,300)	
Net cash flow from operating activities		$ 62,700
Cash flows from investing activities:		
Cash payments for acquisition of land		(240,000)
Cash flows from financing activities:		
Cash received as owner's investment	240,000	
Cash withdrawal by owner	(36,000)	
Net cash flow from financing activities		204,000
Net cash flow and November 30, 2015, cash balance		$ 26,700

(continued)

Instructions

By analyzing the interrelationships among the four financial statements, determine the proper amounts for (a) through (j).

CONTINUING PROBLEM

✔ 2. Net income: $3,400

Pat Sharpe enjoys listening to all types of music and owns countless CDs. Over the years, Pat has gained a local reputation for knowledge of music from classical to rap and the ability to put together sets of recordings that appeal to all ages.

During the past several months, Pat served as a guest disc jockey on a local radio station. In addition, Pat has entertained at several friends' parties as the host deejay.

On November 1, 2015, Pat established a proprietorship known as Music Depot. Using an extensive collection of music MP3 files, Pat will serve as a disc jockey on a fee basis for weddings, parties, and other events. During November, Pat entered into the following transactions:

Nov. 1. Deposited $9,000 in a chequing account in the name of Music Depot.
  2. Received $3,600 from a local radio station for serving as the guest disc jockey for November.
  4. Purchased supplies from City Office Supply Co. for $700. Agreed to pay $100 within 10 days and the remainder by December 5, 2015.
  6. Paid $450 to a local radio station to advertise the services of Music Depot twice daily for two weeks.
  13. Paid City Office Supply Co. $100 on account.
  22. Served as disc jockey for a wedding party. The father of the bride agreed to pay $1,250 the 1st of December.
  30. Paid $1,000 royalties (music expense) to Society of Composers, Authors and Music Publishers of Canada (SOCAN) for use of various artists' music during the month.
  30. Withdrew $500 of cash from Music Depot for personal use.

Instructions

1. Indicate the effect of each transaction using the following tabular headings:

Assets			=	Liabilities	+	Owner's Equity				
Cash +	Accts. Rec. +	Supplies =		Accounts Payable	+	Pat Sharpe, Capital	−	Pat Sharpe, Withdrawals +	Fees Earned −	Music Exp. −	Advertising Exp.

2. Prepare an income statement for Music Depot for the month ended November 30, 2015.
3. Prepare a statement of owner's equity for Music Depot for the month ended November 30, 2015.
4. Prepare a balance sheet for Music Depot as at November 30, 2015.

SPECIAL ACTIVITIES

SA 1-1

Ethics and professional conduct in business

Group Project

Vince Hunt, president of Sarrant Enterprises, applied for a $175,000 loan from TD Bank. The bank requested financial statements from Sarrant Enterprises as a basis for granting the loan. Vince has told his accountant to provide the bank with a balance sheet. Vince has decided to omit the other financial statements because a net loss occurred during the past year.

In groups of three or four, discuss the following questions:

1. Is Vince behaving in a professional manner by omitting some of the financial statements? Which qualitative characteristics is Vince not following?

2. a. What types of information about their businesses would owners be willing to provide bankers? What types of information would owners not be willing to provide?
    b. What types of information about a business would bankers want to receive before extending a loan?
    c. What common interests are shared by bankers and business owners?

SA 1-2

Net income

On August 1, 2014, Dana Hendley established Advice, a business-consulting firm organized as a proprietorship. The following conversation occurred the following February between Dana and a former classmate, Ed Monroe, at a business convention in Winnipeg.

Ed: Dana, good to see you again. Why didn't you call when you were in Ottawa? We could have had dinner together.

Dana: Actually, I never made it to Ottawa this year. My husband and kids went up to our cabin in the Muskokas twice, but I got stuck in Toronto. I opened a new consulting practice in August and haven't had any time for myself since.

Ed: I heard about it . . . Advice . . . something . . . right?

Dana: Yes, Advice. My husband chose the name.

Ed: I've thought about doing something like that. Are you making any money? I mean, is it worth your time?

Dana: You wouldn't believe it. I started by opening a bank account with $30,000, and my January bank statement has an ending balance of $75,000. Not bad for six months—all pure profit.

Ed: Maybe I'll try it in Ottawa! Let's have breakfast together tomorrow and you can fill me in on the details.

Comment on Dana's statement that the difference between the opening bank balance ($30,000) and the January statement balance ($75,000) is pure profit.

SA 1-3

Transactions and financial statements

Jan Martinelli, a college student, has been seeking ways to earn extra spending money. As an active sports enthusiast, Jan plays tennis regularly at the North Fulton Tennis Club, where her family has a membership. The president of the club recently approached Jan with the proposal that she manage the club's tennis courts. Jan's primary duty would be to supervise the operation of the club's four indoor and six outdoor courts, including court reservations.

In return for her services, the club would pay Jan $300 per week, plus Jan could keep whatever she earned from lessons and the fees from the use of the ball machine. The club and Jan agreed to a one-month trial, after which both would consider an arrangement for the remaining year of Jan's college program. On this basis, Jan organized Topspin. During June 2014, Jan managed the tennis courts and entered into the following transactions:

a. Opened a business account by depositing $1,000.
b. Paid $300 for tennis supplies.
c. Paid $200 for the rental of video equipment to be used when offering lessons during June.
d. Arranged for the rental of two ball machines during June for $250. Paid $150 in advance, with the remaining $100 due July 1.
e. Received $1,600 for lessons given during June.
f. Received $500 in fees from the use of the ball machines during June.
g. Paid $800 for salaries of part-time employees who answered the telephone and took reservations while Jan was giving lessons.
h. Paid $225 for miscellaneous expenses.
i. Received $1,200 from the club for managing the tennis courts during June.
j. Withdrew $270 for personal use on June 30.

As a friend and accounting student, you have been asked by Jan to aid her in assessing the venture.

(continued)

1. Indicate the effect of each transaction using the following tabular headings:

Assets		= Liabilities +			Owner's Equity				
Cash +	Supplies	= Accounts Payable +	Jan Martinelli, Capital −	Jan Martinelli, Withdrawals +	Service Revenue −	Salaries Expense −	Rent Expense −	Misc. Expense	

2. Prepare an income statement for June.
3. Prepare a statement of owner's equity for June.
4. Prepare a balance sheet as at June 30, 2014.
5. a. Assume that Jan Martinelli could earn $9 per hour working 30 hours a week as a waitress. Evaluate which of the two alternatives, working as a waitress or operating Topspin, would provide Jan with more income per month.
   b. Discuss any other factors that you believe Jan should consider before negotiating a long-term arrangement with the North Fulton Tennis Club.

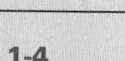

SA 1-4

IFRS versus ASPE

Internet Project

Go to the two CICA websites, **www.cica.ca** and **www.frascanada.ca**, and answer the following questions:

1. What sort of information is contained on each of these sites? Which user groups might find this information useful?
2. Are the accounting standards in Canada changing or constant? What evidence can you find for your answer?

SA 1-5

Financial analysis of Enron Corporation

The now-defunct Enron Corporation, once headquartered in Houston, Texas, provided products and services for natural gas, electricity, and communications to wholesale and retail customers. Enron's operations were conducted through a variety of subsidiaries and affiliates that involved transporting gas through pipelines, transmitting electricity, and managing energy commodities. The following data were taken from Enron's financial statements:

	In millions
Total revenues	$100,789
Total costs and expenses	98,836
Operating income	1,953
Net income	979
Total assets	65,503
Total liabilities	54,033
Total owners' equity	11,470
Net cash flows from operating activities	4,779
Net cash flows from investing activities	(4,264)
Net cash flows from financing activities	571
Net increase in cash	1,086

The market price of Enron's shares was approximately $83 per share when those financial statement data were taken. However, eventually Enron's shares were selling for $0.22 per share.

Review the preceding financial statement data and search the Internet for articles on Enron Corporation. Briefly explain why the price of Enron's shares dropped so dramatically.

Analyzing Transactions

MATT CROSSICK/PA Photos/Landov

CIRQUE DU SOLEIL

Every day, we seem to receive an incredible number of emails; you receive them from your friends, relatives, subscribed email lists, and even spammers! But how do you organize all of these messages? You might create folders to sort messages by sender, topic, or project. Perhaps you use keyword search utilities. You might even use filters or rules to automatically delete spam or to move messages from your best friend to a special folder. In any case, you are organizing information so that it is simple to retrieve and you can understand, respond, or refer to the messages.

In the same way that you organize your email, companies develop an organized method for processing, recording, and summarizing financial transactions. For example, Cirque du Soleil, Canada's entertainment company known around the world for its dramatic shows,

has a huge volume of financial transactions. A customer has the option of paying for Cirque du Soleil tickets with cash, a credit card, or a debit card. In order to analyze information related to Cirque du Soleil's ticket sale transactions, the company must record or summarize all these similar sales using a single category or "sales" account. This method is comparable to how you summarize cash in the cheque register of your chequebook.

Whereas Chapter 1 uses the accounting equation (Assets = Liabilities + Owner's Equity) to analyze and record financial transactions, this chapter presents more practical and efficient recording methods that most companies use. In addition, this chapter discusses possible accounting errors that may occur and methods to detect and correct them.

After studying this chapter, you should be able to:

1 Describe the characteristics of an account and a chart of accounts.

Using Accounts to Record Transactions	Accounts	
	T Accounts	
	Chart of Accounts	

2 Describe and illustrate journalizing transactions using the double-entry accounting system.

Double-Entry Accounting System	Balance Sheet Accounts	
	Income Statement Accounts	
	Owner Withdrawals	
	Normal Balances	EXAMPLE EXERCISE 2-1 (page 50)
	The Accounting Cycle	
	Journalizing	EXAMPLE EXERCISE 2-2 (page 54) EXAMPLE EXERCISE 2-3 (page 55) EXAMPLE EXERCISE 2-4 (page 56)

3 Describe and illustrate the posting of transactions to accounts.

Posting Journal Entries to Accounts	Posting Transactions	

4 Prepare an unadjusted trial balance and explain how it can be used to discover errors.

Unadjusted Trial Balance	Errors Affecting the Trial Balance	EXAMPLE EXERCISE 2-5 (page 67)
	Errors Not Affecting the Trial Balance	
	Correcting Journal Entries	EXAMPLE EXERCISE 2-6 (page 69)

For the chapter *At a Glance*, turn to page 70.

Using Accounts to Record Transactions

Describe the characteristics of an account and a chart of accounts.

In Chapter 1, we recorded the November transactions for NetSolutions using the accounting equation format shown in Exhibit 1. However, this format is not efficient or practical for companies that need to record thousands or millions of transactions daily. As a result, accounting systems are designed to show the increases and decreases in each accounting equation element as a separate record. This record is called an **account**.

To illustrate, the Cash column of Exhibit 1 records the increases and decreases in cash. Likewise, the other columns in Exhibit 1 record the increases and decreases in the other accounting equation elements. Each of these columns can be organized into a separate account.

Accounts

An account, in its simplest form, has three parts.

1. A title, which is the name of the accounting equation element recorded in the account. These titles are common English words for the type of items in the account.

Exhibit 1

NetSolutions November Transactions

	Assets			=	Liabilities +		Owner's Equity						
					Accounts	Chris Clark,	Chris Clark,	Fees	Wages	Rent	Utilities	Misc.	
	Cash	+ Supp. +	Land	=	Payable	+ Capital	– Withdrawals +	Earned –	Exp. –	Exp. –	Exp. –	Exp.	
a.	+25,000					+25,000							
b.	−20,000		+20,000										
c.		+1,350			+1,350								
d.	+7,500							+7,500					
e.	−3,650								−2,125	−800	−450	−275	
f.	−950				−950								
g.	−2,000						−2,000						
Bal.	5,900	1,350	20,000		400	25,000	−2,000	7,500	−2,125	−800	−450	−275	

2. A space for recording increases in the amount of the element.
3. A space for recording decreases in the amount of the element.

Note: Amounts entered on the left side of an account are debits, and amounts entered on the right side of an account are credits.

T Accounts

Many times when accountants analyze complex transactions, they use T accounts to simplify the thought process. T accounts are a tool to help accountants decide which accounts are affected and how transactions balance. You may find T accounts a useful device in this and later accounting courses. The account form presented below is called a **T account** because it resembles the letter T. The left side of the account is called the *debit* side, and the right side is called the *credit* side.[1]

Title	
Left side	Right side
debit	*credit*

The amounts shown in the Cash column of Exhibit 1 can be recorded in a cash account using one of the following alternative methods:

Alternative 1

Cash

Debit Side of Account	(a) 25,000 (d) 7,500	20,000 (b) 3,650 (e) 950 (f) 2,000 (g)	Credit Side of Account
	Balance 5,900		

Balance of account ⬆

Alternative 2

Cash

Debit Side of Account	(a) 25,000 (d) 7,500	20,000 (b) 3,650 (e) 950 (f) 2,000 (g)	Credit Side of Account
	Balance 32,500 5,900	26,600	

Balance of account ⬆

1 The terms *debit* and *credit* are derived from the Latin *debere* and *credere*.

Recording transactions in accounts must follow certain rules. For example, increases in assets are recorded on the **debit** (left side) of an account. Likewise, decreases in assets are recorded on the **credit** (right side) of an account. The excess of the debits of an asset account over its credits is the **balance of the account**.

To illustrate, the receipt (increase in cash) of $25,000 in transaction (a) is entered on the debit (left) side of the cash account shown above. The letter or date of the transaction is also entered into the account. This information is entered so that, if any questions later arise related to the entry, the entry can be traced back to the underlying transaction data. In contrast, the payment (decrease in cash) of $20,000 to purchase land in transaction (b) is entered on the credit (right) side of the account. The balance of the cash account of $5,900 is the excess of the debits over the credits, as shown below.

Debits ($25,000 + $7,500)... $32,500
Less credits ($20,000 + $3,650 + $950 + $2,000)................. 26,600
Balance at Cash as at November 30, 2014........................... $ 5,900

The balance of the cash account is inserted in the account in the Debit column. In this way, the balance is identified as a debit balance. This balance represents NetSolutions' cash on hand as at November 30, 2014. This balance of $5,900 is reported on the November 30, 2014, balance sheet for NetSolutions as shown in Exhibit 5 of Chapter 1.

In an actual accounting system, a more formal account form replaces the T account. Later in this chapter, we illustrate this three-column account form. The T account, however, is a simple way to illustrate the effects of transactions on accounts and financial statements. For this reason, T accounts are often used in business to explain transactions.

Each of the columns in Exhibit 1 can be converted into an account form in a similar manner as was done for the Cash column of Exhibit 1. However, as we mentioned earlier, recording increases and decreases in accounts must follow certain rules. We discuss these rules after we describe and illustrate the chart of accounts.

Chart of Accounts

A group of accounts for a business entity is called a **ledger**. A list of the accounts in the ledger is called a **chart of accounts**. The accounts are normally listed in the order in which they appear in the financial statements. The balance sheet accounts are listed first in the order of assets, liabilities, and owner's equity. The income statement accounts are then listed in the order of revenues and expenses.

Assets are resources owned by the business entity that can provide the company with future benefits. These resources can be physical items, such as cash and supplies, or intangibles that have value. Examples of intangible assets include patent rights, copyrights, and trademarks. Examples of other assets include accounts receivable, prepaid expenses (such as insurance), buildings, equipment, and land.

Liabilities are debts owed to outsiders (creditors). Liabilities are often identified on the balance sheet by titles that include the word *payable*. Examples of liabilities include accounts payable, notes payable, and wages payable. Cash received before services are delivered creates a liability to perform the services. These future service commitments are called *unearned revenues*. Examples of unearned revenues are magazine subscriptions received by a publisher and tuition received by a university at the beginning of a term.

Owner's equity is the owner's right to the assets of the business after all liabilities have been paid. For a proprietorship, the owner's equity is represented by the balance of the owner's **capital account**. A **withdrawals** account represents the amount of withdrawals, also known as **drawings**, made by the owner.

Revenues are increases in owner's equity as a result of selling services or products to customers. Examples of revenues include fees earned, fares earned, commissions revenue, and rent revenue.

Expenses result from using up assets or consuming services in the process of generating revenues. Examples of expenses include wages expense, rent expense, utilities expense, supplies expense, and miscellaneous expense.

Exhibit 2

Chart of Accounts for NetSolutions

Balance Sheet Accounts	Income Statement Accounts
Assets	**Revenues**
1010 Cash	4010 Fees Earned
1020 Accounts Receivable	**Expenses**
1040 Supplies	5010 Wages Expense
1050 Prepaid Insurance	5020 Rent Expense
1070 Office Equipment	5040 Utilities Expense
1090 Land	5090 Miscellaneous Expense
Liabilities	
2010 Accounts Payable	
2030 Unearned Rent	
Owner's Equity	
3010 Chris Clark, Capital	
3020 Chris Clark, Withdrawals	

A chart of accounts should meet the needs of a company's managers and other users of its financial statements. The accounts within the chart of accounts are numbered for use as references. A numbering system is normally used, so that new accounts can be added without affecting other account numbers.

Exhibit 2 is NetSolutions' chart of accounts that we will use in this chapter. Additional accounts will be introduced in later chapters. In Exhibit 2, each account number has four digits. The first digit indicates the major account group of the ledger in which the account is located. Accounts beginning with 1 represent assets; 2, liabilities; 3, owner's equity; 4, revenues; and 5, expenses. For example the 1000s will be set aside for assets, 2000s for liabilities, etc. The second, third, and fourth digits indicate the location of the account within the group.

You should note that each of the columns in Exhibit 1 has been assigned an account number in the chart of accounts shown in Exhibit 2. In addition, we have added accounts for accounts receivable, prepaid insurance, office equipment, and unearned rent. These accounts will be used in recording NetSolutions' December transactions.

Double-Entry Accounting System

Describe and illustrate journalizing transactions using the double-entry accounting system.

All businesses use what is called the **double-entry accounting system**. This system is based on the accounting equation and requires that every business transaction be recorded in at least two accounts. In addition, this system requires that the total debits recorded for each transaction equal the total credits recorded. The double-entry accounting system also has specific **rules of debit and credit** for recording transactions in the accounts. See Exhibit 3 for a summary chart of the rules. An understanding of these rules is essential in accounting.

Balance Sheet Accounts

The double-entry accounting system is based on the accounting equation and specific rules for recording debits and credits. The debit and credit rules for balance sheet accounts are as follows:

Balance Sheet Accounts					
ASSETS Asset Accounts		=	**LIABILITIES** Liability Accounts	+	**OWNER'S EQUITY** Owner's Equity Accounts
Debit for increases (+)	Credit for decreases (−)	Debit for decreases (−)	Credit for increases (+)	Debit for decreases (−)	Credit for increases (+)

Income Statement Accounts

The debit and credit rules for income statement accounts are based on their relationship with owner's equity. As shown above, owner's equity accounts are increased by credits. Because revenues increase owner's equity, revenue accounts are increased by credits and decreased by debits. Because owner's equity accounts are decreased by debits, expense accounts are increased by debits and decreased by credits. Thus, the rules of debit and credit for revenue and expense accounts are as follows:

Income Statement Accounts			
Revenue Accounts		**Expense Accounts**	
Debit for decreases (−)	Credit for increases (+)	Debit for increases (+)	Credit for decreases (−)

Owner Withdrawals

The debit and credit rules for recording owner withdrawals, also known as drawings, are based on the effect of owner withdrawals on owner's equity. Owner's equity accounts are decreased by debits, and owner's withdrawals decrease owner's equity. Because owner's equity accounts are decreased by debits, the owner's withdrawal account is increased by debits and decreased by credits. Thus, the rules of debit and credit for the owner's withdrawals account are as follows:

Withdrawals Account	
Debit for increases (+)	Credit for decreases (−)

Normal Balances

The sum of the increases in an account is usually equal to or greater than the sum of the decreases in the account. Thus, the **normal balance of an account** is either a debit or a credit depending on whether increases in the account are recorded as debits or credits. For example, because asset accounts are increased with debits, asset accounts normally have debit balances. Likewise, liability accounts normally have credit balances.

The rules of debit and credit and the normal balances of the various types of accounts are summarized in Exhibit 3. Debits and credits are often abbreviated as Dr. for debit and Cr. for credit.

EXAMPLE EXERCISE 2-1 Rules of Debit and Credit and Normal Balances   ②

State for each account whether it is likely to have (a) debit entries only, (b) credit entries only, or (c) both debit and credit entries. Also, indicate whether its normal balance is a debit or a credit.

1. Amber Saunders, Withdrawals
2. Accounts Payable
3. Cash
4. Fees Earned
5. Supplies
6. Utilities Expense

FOLLOW MY EXAMPLE 2-1

1. Debit entries only; normal debit balance
2. Debit and credit entries; normal credit balance
3. Debit and credit entries; normal debit balance
4. Credit entries only; normal credit balance
5. Debit and credit entries; normal debit balance
6. Debit entries only; normal debit balance

For Practice: PE 2-1

Exhibit 3

Rules of Debit and Credit, Normal Balances of Accounts

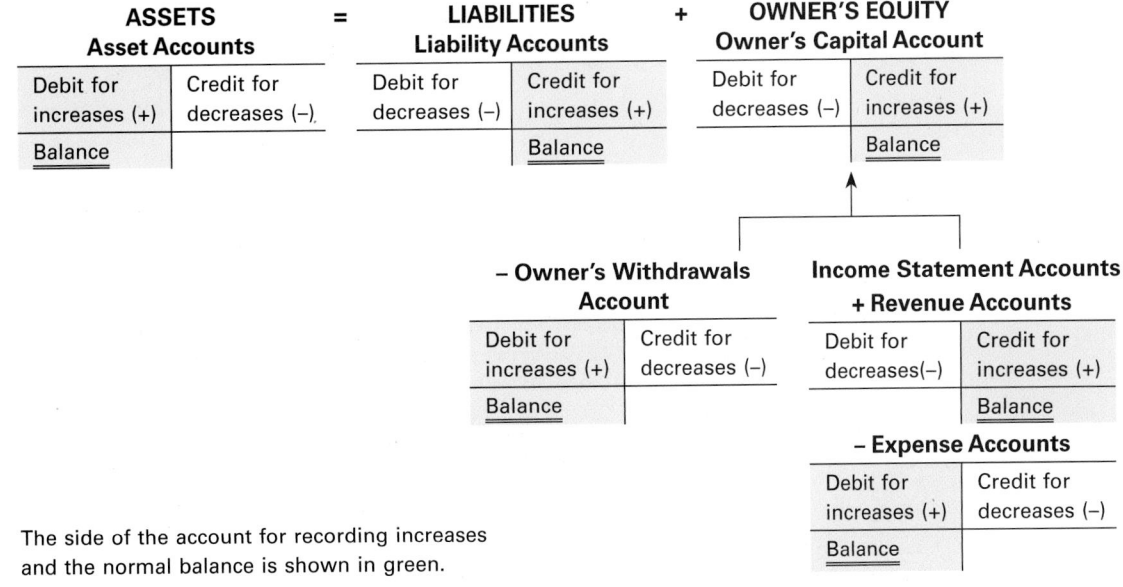

The side of the account for recording increases and the normal balance is shown in green.

Net income or net loss

When an account normally having a debit balance has a credit balance or vice versa, an error may have occurred or an unusual situation may exist. For example, a credit balance in the office equipment account could result only from an error. A business cannot have more decreases than increases of office equipment. On the other hand, a debit balance in an accounts payable account could result from an overpayment. Accountants use either a computerized accounting program or a manual system to record transactions and summarize them in financial statements. The steps involved in the accounting cycle are shown in Exhibit 4.

The Accounting Cycle

The accounting cycle consists of steps that the accountant follows to ensure that all necessary information has been collected and reported correctly in the financial statements. The cycle starts with source documents that arise outside of the accounting department and ends after the financial statements have been prepared. Accountants use either a computerized accounting program or a manual system to record transactions and summarize them in financial statements. The steps involved in the accounting cycle are shown in Exhibit 4.

Step 1: Source Documents A source document is received and reviewed. It is a piece of paper or an electronic document, such as a purchase invoice, sales receipt, cheque stub, or bank statement.

Journalizing

Step 2: Journal Entries Using the rules of debit and credit, transactions are initially entered in a record called a **journal.** This is step 2 in the accounting cycle. In this way, the journal serves as a record of when transactions occurred and were recorded. We will use NetSolutions' November transactions from Chapter 1 to illustrate the first four steps of the accounting cycle. Source documents from outside the company have arrived (step 1) and entries need to be made (step 2).

Chris Clark's first transaction (a) on November 1 was to deposit $25,000 in a bank account in the name of NetSolutions. The effect of this transaction on the balance sheet is to increase assets (Cash) and owner's equity (Chris Clark, Capital) by $25,000. This transaction is recorded in the journal in the following manner:

Exhibit 4

Steps of the Accounting Cycle

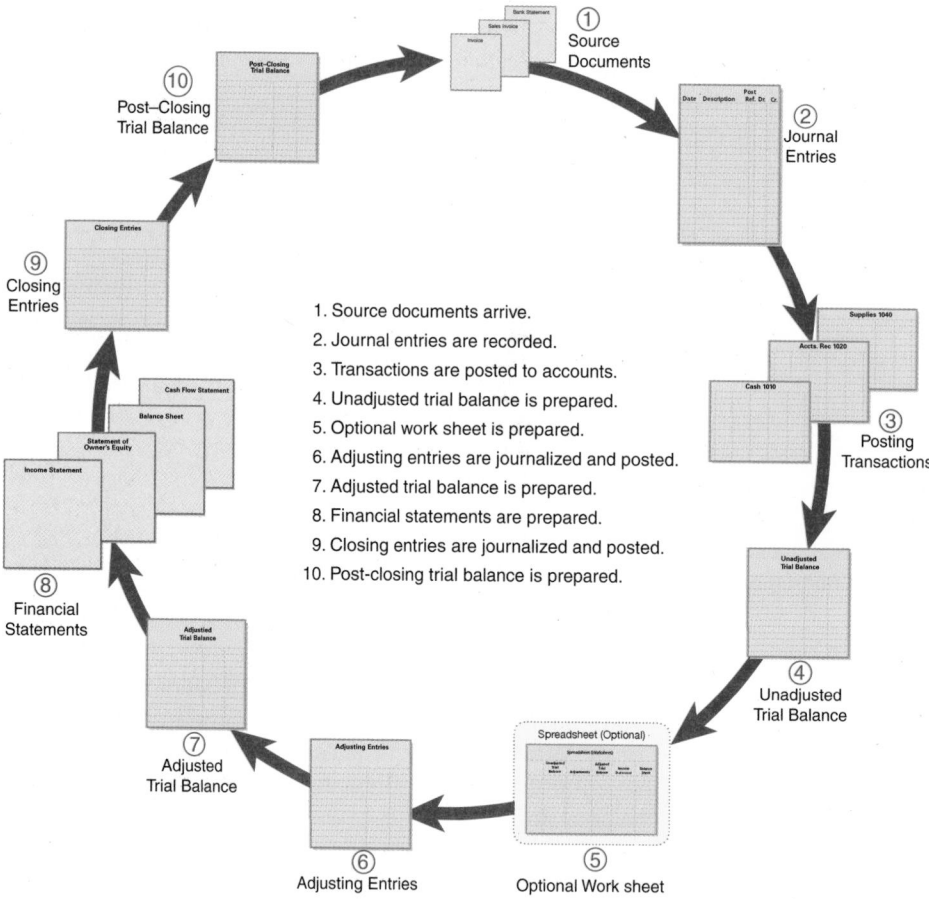

1. Source documents arrive.
2. Journal entries are recorded.
3. Transactions are posted to accounts.
4. Unadjusted trial balance is prepared.
5. Optional work sheet is prepared.
6. Adjusting entries are journalized and posted.
7. Adjusted trial balance is prepared.
8. Financial statements are prepared.
9. Closing entries are journalized and posted.
10. Post-closing trial balance is prepared.

Transaction A

⊟netsolutions

1. The date of the transaction is entered in the Date column.
2. The title of the account to be debited is recorded at the left-hand margin under the Description column, and the amount to be debited is entered in the Debit column.
3. The title of the account to be credited is listed below and to the right of the debited account title, and the amount to be credited is entered in the Credit column.
4. A brief description may be entered below the credited account.
5. The Post. Ref. (Posting Reference) column is left blank when the journal entry is initially recorded. We will use this column later in this chapter when we transfer the journal entry amounts to the accounts in the ledger.

Transaction (a) is recorded in the journal as follows:

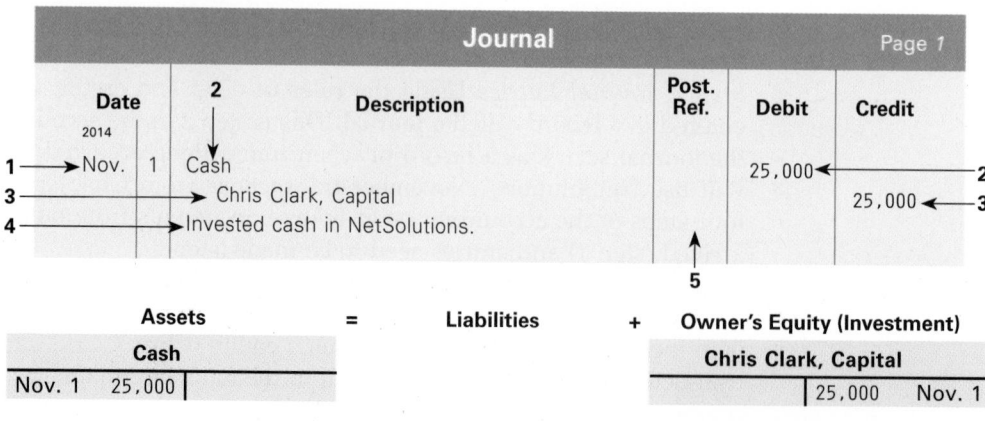

The process of recording a transaction in the journal is called **journalizing**. The entry in the journal is called a **journal entry**. The journal being used in this textbook is called a two-column journal because it shows two columns of numbers.

The following is a useful method for analyzing and journalizing transactions:

@netsolutions

A. Carefully read the description of the transaction to determine whether it affects an asset, a liability, an owner's equity, a revenue, an expense, or a withdrawals account.

B. For each account affected by the transaction, determine whether the account increases or decreases.

C. Determine whether each increase or decrease should be recorded as a debit or a credit, following the rules of debit and credit shown in Exhibit 3.

D. Record the transaction using a journal entry.

The following table summarizes terminology that is often used in describing a transaction along with the related accounts that would be debited and credited.

Common transaction terminology	Journal Entry Account	
	Debit	**Credit**
Received cash for services provided	Cash	Fees Earned
Services provided on account	Accounts Receivable	Fees Earned
Received cash on account	Cash	Accounts Receivable
Purchased on account	Asset Account	Accounts Payable
Paid on account	Accounts Payable	Cash
Paid cash	Asset or Expense Account	Cash
Owner investments	Cash and/or other assets	(Owner's Name), Capital
Owner withdrawals	(Owner's Name), Withdrawals	Cash

Next, the remaining transactions of NetSolutions for November are analyzed and journalized.

Transaction B

> Nov. 5   NetSolutions paid $20,000 for the purchase of land as a future building site.

Analysis This transaction increases one asset account and decreases another. It is recorded in the journal as a $20,000 increase (debit) to Land and a $20,000 decrease (credit) to Cash.

Journal Entry

Nov.	5	Land		20,000	
		Cash			20,000
		Purchased land for building site.			

Assets	=	Liabilities	+	Owner's Equity

Land

Nov. 5	20,000	

Cash

	20,000	Nov. 5

Transaction C

Nov. 10   NetSolutions purchased supplies on account for $1,350.

Analysis This transaction increases an asset account and increases a liability account. It is recorded in the journal as a $1,350 increase (debit) to Supplies and a $1,350 increase (credit) to Accounts Payable. As noted in Chapter 1, the term "on account" is used when a company agrees to pay the amount in the future. Because NetSolutions is agreeing to pay for the supplies in the future, its purchase "on account" represents a liability for NetSolutions.

Journal Entry

Nov.	10	Supplies	1,350	
		Accounts Payable		1,350
		Purchased supplies on account.		

Assets	=	Liabilities	+	Owner's Equity
Supplies		**Accounts Payable**		
Nov. 10 1,350		1,350 Nov. 10		

EXAMPLE EXERCISE 2-2 Journal Entry for Asset Purchase   2

Prepare a journal entry for the purchase of a truck on June 3 for $42,500, paying $8,500 cash and the remainder on account.

FOLLOW MY EXAMPLE 2-2

June 3	Truck...	42,500	
	Cash		8,500
	Accounts Payable		34,000

For Practice: PE 2-2

Transaction D

Nov. 18   NetSolutions received cash of $7,500 from customers for services provided.

Analysis This transaction increases an asset account and increases a revenue account. It is recorded in the journal as a $7,500 increase (debit) to Cash and a $7,500 increase (credit) to Fees Earned.

Journal Entry

Nov.	18	Cash	7,500	
		Fees Earned		7,500
		Received fees from customers.		

Assets	=	Liabilities	+	Owner's Equity (Revenue)
Cash				**Fees Earned**
Nov. 18 7,500				7,500 Nov. 18

EXAMPLE EXERCISE 2-3 Journal Entry for Fees Earned   ②

Prepare a journal entry on August 7 for fees earned on account, $115,000.

FOLLOW MY EXAMPLE 2-3

Aug. 7   Accounts Receivable.. 115,000
         Fees Earned..   115,000

For Practice: PE 2-3

Transaction E

Nov. 30   NetSolutions paid the following expenses: wages, $2,125; rent, $800; utilities,
          $450; and miscellaneous, $275.

Analysis This transaction increases various expense accounts and decreases an asset
(Cash) account. You should note that regardless of the number of accounts, *the sum
of the debits is always equal to the sum of the credits in a journal entry*. The transaction is
recorded in the journal as an increase (debit) to Wages Expense, $2,125; Rent Expense,
$800; Utilities Expense, $450; Miscellaneous Expense, $275; and a decrease (credit) to
Cash, $3,650.

This is an example of a **compound journal entry** because it has more than one debit
entry or more than one credit entry.

Journal Entry

Nov.	30	Wages Expense		2,125	
		Rent Expense		800	
		Utilities Expense		450	
		Miscellaneous Expense		275	
		Cash			3,650
		Paid expenses.			

Assets   =   Liabilities   +   Owner's Equity (Expenses)

Cash			Wages Expense	
	3,650 Nov. 30		Nov. 30 2,125	

Rent Expense	
Nov. 30 800	

Utilities Expense	
Nov. 30 450	

Miscellaneous Expense	
Nov. 30 275	

Transaction F

Nov. 30   NetSolutions paid creditors $950 of the accounts payable.

Analysis This transaction decreases a liability account and decreases an asset account.
It is recorded in the journal as a $950 decrease (debit) to Accounts Payable and a $950
decrease (credit) to Cash.

Journal Entry

Nov.	30	Accounts Payable		950	
		Cash			950
		Paid creditors on account.			

Assets	=	Liabilities	+	Owner's Equity
Cash		**Accounts Payable**		
	950	Nov. 30	Nov. 30	950		

INTEGRITY, OBJECTIVITY, AND ETHICS IN BUSINESS

WILL JOURNALIZING PREVENT FRAUD?

Although journalizing transactions reduces the possibility of fraud, it does not eliminate fraud. For example, embezzlement can be hidden within the double-entry bookkeeping system by creating fictitious suppliers to whom cheques are issued.

Transaction G

Nov. 30   Chris Clark withdrew $2,000 from NetSolutions for personal use.

Analysis This transaction decreases assets and owner's equity. This transaction is recorded in the journal as a $2,000 increase (debit) to Chris Clark, Withdrawals and a $2,000 decrease (credit) to Cash.

Journal Entry

Nov.	30	Chris Clark, Withdrawals		2,000	
		Cash			2,000
		Chris Clark withdrew cash for personal use.			

Assets	=	Liabilities	+	Owner's Equity (Withdrawals)
Cash				**Chris Clark, Withdrawals**
	2,000 Nov. 30			Nov. 30	2,000	

EXAMPLE EXERCISE 2-4 Journal Entry for Owner's Withdrawal   ②

Prepare a journal entry on December 29 for the payment of $3,000 to the owner of Smartstaff Consulting Services, Jessie Algeo, for personal use.

FOLLOW MY EXAMPLE 2-4

| Dec. 29 | Jessie Algeo, Withdrawals... | 3,000 | |
| | Cash... | | 3,000 |

For Practice: PE 2-4

MID-CHAPTER ILLUSTRATIVE PROBLEM

Volfir Industries had the following transactions in the month of April.

Apr. 17. Blaine Ferguson invested $5,000 in Volfir Industries.
Apr. 20. Paid $1,000 for a $600 desk and $400 of supplies to set up an office for the business.
Apr. 25. Volfir Industries received an invoice for consulting expenses from Small Business Consulting (SBC) for $1,350. The invoice is to be paid next month.
Apr. 28. Received $600 for services supplied by Volfir.

Instructions

Journalize the above transactions for the month of April.

MID-CHAPTER ILLUSTRATIVE SOLUTION

Journal					
Date		**Description**	**Post. Ref.**	**Debit**	**Credit**
Apr.	17	Cash		5,000	
		Blaine Ferguson, Capital			5,000
		Owner invested in business.			
	20	Furniture		600	
		Supplies		400	
		Cash			1,000
		Purchased furniture and supplies.			
	25	Consulting Expenses		1,350	
		Accounts Payable			1,350
		Purchased consulting services on account.			
	28	Cash		600	
		Fees Earned			600
		Received fees from customers.			

Posting Journal Entries to Accounts

Describe and illustrate the posting of transactions to accounts.

Step 3: Posting Transactions As illustrated, a transaction is first recorded in a journal. Periodically, the journal entries are transferred to the accounts in the ledger. The process of transferring the debits and credits from the journal entries to the accounts is called **posting**.

The first December transaction of NetSolutions is used to illustrate step 3 of the accounting cycle, posting from the journal to the ledger. The ledger is a three-column ledger because it shows three columns of numbers. Reviewing the December transactions provides an additional review of analyzing and journalizing.

Transaction

Dec. 1 NetSolutions paid a premium of $2,400 for an insurance policy for liability, theft, and fire. The policy covers a one-year period.

Analysis Advance payments of expenses, such as for insurance premiums, are called prepaid expenses. Prepaid expenses are assets. For NetSolutions, the asset purchased is insurance protection for 12 months. This transaction is recorded as a $2,400 increase (debit) to Prepaid Insurance and a $2,400 decrease (credit) to Cash.

Journal Entry

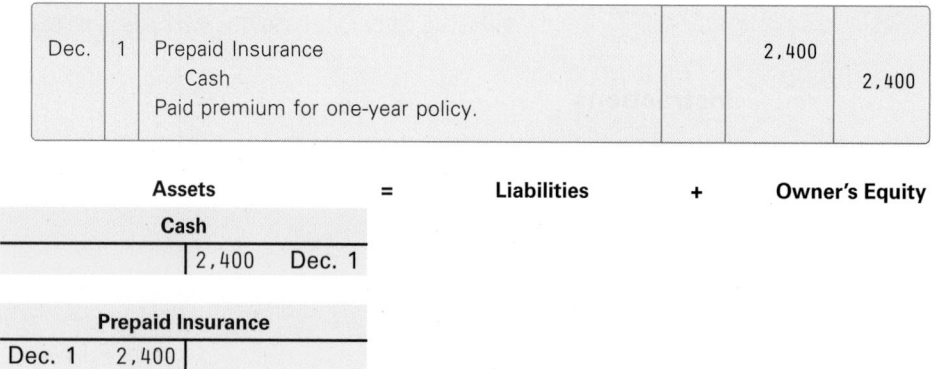

The posting of the preceding December 1 transaction is shown in Exhibit 5. You will notice that the T account form is not used. In practice, the T account is usually replaced with a standard account form similar to that shown in Exhibit 5.

The debits and credits for each journal entry are posted to the accounts in the order in which they occur in the journal. To illustrate, the debit portion of the December 1 journal entry is posted to the prepaid insurance account in Exhibit 5 using the following four parts:

Part 1. The date (Dec. 1) of the journal entry is entered in the Date column of Prepaid Insurance.

Part 2. The amount (2,400) is entered in the Debit column of Prepaid Insurance.

Part 3. The journal page number (2) is entered in the Posting Reference (Post. Ref.) column of Prepaid Insurance.

Part 4. The account number (1050) is entered in the Posting Reference (Post. Ref.) column in the journal.

As shown in Exhibit 5, the credit portion of the December 1 journal entry is posted to the cash account in a similar manner.

The remaining December transactions for NetSolutions are analyzed and journalized in the following paragraphs. These December transactions are posted to the ledger in Exhibit 6, on page 64. To simplify, some of the December transactions are stated in summary form. For example, cash received for services is normally recorded on a daily basis. However, only summary totals are recorded at the middle and end of the month for NetSolutions.

Transaction *Dec 1 NetSolutions paid rent for December, $800.*

NetSolutions' store is a rented property. The building's owner has informed NetSolutions that payment of rent is now required on the first of each month, not at the end of the month.

Analysis The advance payment of rent is an asset, much like the advance payment of the insurance premium in the preceding transaction. However, unlike the insurance premium, this prepaid rent will expire in one month. When an asset is purchased with the expectation that it will be used up in a short period of time, such as a month, an expense account is usually debited. Debiting the expense account at the time of the purchase avoids the need to transfer the balance from an asset account (Prepaid Rent) to an expense account (Rent Expense) at the end of the month. Thus, this transaction is recorded as an $800 increase (debit) to Rent Expense and an $800 decrease (credit) to Cash.

Exhibit 5

Diagram of the Recording and Posting of a Debit and a Credit

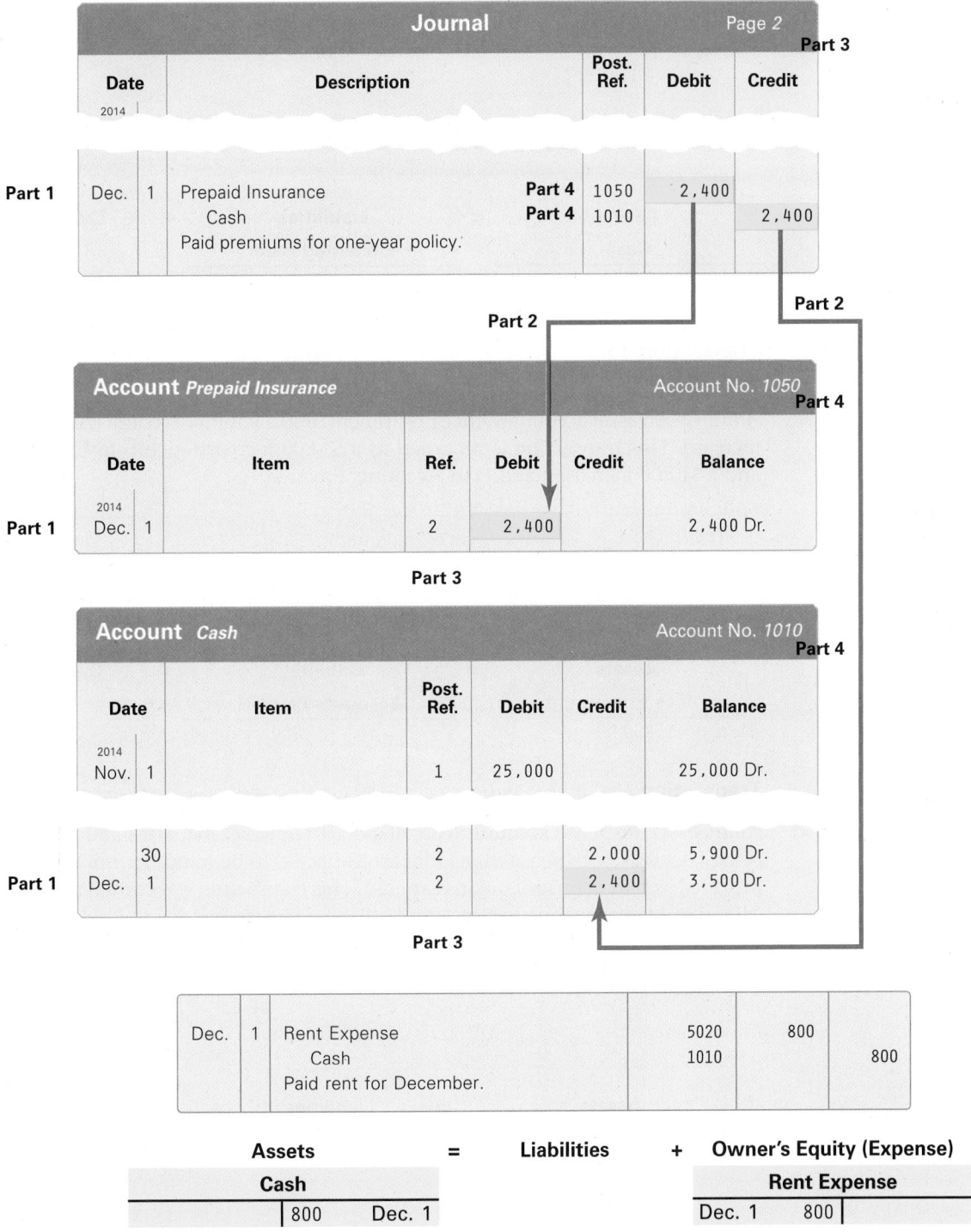

Transaction *Dec. 1 NetSolutions received an offer from a local retailer to rent the land purchased on November 5. The retailer plans to use the land as a parking lot for its employees and customers. NetSolutions agreed to rent the land to the retailer for three months, with the rent payable in advance. NetSolutions received $360 for three months' rent beginning December 1.*

Analysis By agreeing to rent the land and by accepting the $360, NetSolutions has incurred an obligation (a liability) to the retailer. This obligation is to make the land available for use for three months and to not to interfere with its use. The liability created by receiving the cash in advance of providing the service is called **unearned revenue**. As time passes, the unearned rent liability will decrease and will become revenue. Thus, this transaction is recorded as a $360 increase (debit) to Cash and a $360 increase (credit) to Unearned Rent.

Dec.	1	Cash	1010	360	
		Unearned Rent	2030		360
		Received advance payment for three months' rent on land.			

Assets	=	Liabilities	+	Owner's Equity
Cash		**Unearned Rent**		
Dec. 1 360		360 Dec. 1		

Transaction *Dec. 4 NetSolutions purchased office equipment on account from Executive Supply Co. for $1,800.*

Analysis An asset account (Office Equipment) and a liability account (Accounts Payable) increase. This transaction is recorded as a $1,800 increase (debit) to Office Equipment and a $1,800 increase (credit) to Accounts Payable.

Dec.	4	Office Equipment	1010	1,800	
		Accounts Payable	2010		1,800
		Purchased office equipment on account.			

Assets	=	Liabilities	+	Owner's Equity
Office Equipment		**Accounts Payable**		
Dec. 4 1,800		1,800 Dec. 4		

Transaction *Dec. 6 NetSolutions paid $180 for a newspaper advertisement.*

Analysis An expense account (Miscellaneous Expense) increases and an asset account (Cash) decreases. Expense items that are expected to be minor in amount are normally included as part of miscellaneous expense. This transaction is recorded as a $180 increase (debit) to Miscellaneous Expense and a $180 decrease (credit) to Cash.

Dec.	6	Miscellaneous Expense	5090	180	
		Cash	1010		180
		Paid for newspaper advertisement.			

Assets	=	Liabilities	+	Owner's Equity (Expense)
Cash				**Miscellaneous Expense**
180 Dec. 6				Dec. 6 180

CRITICAL THINKING

What prevents bookkeepers from posting all expenses as miscellaneous expense?

Bookkeepers and accountants need to use their professional judgment to decide on the expense categories that are appropriate. The goal is to provide categories that will inform the users of the financial statements where the expenses truly are. If miscellaneous expenses are too high, Canada Revenue Agency may request further details regarding the expenses and may audit the miscellaneous expense account to ensure that the expenses are appropriate for the business.

Transaction *Dec. 11 NetSolutions paid creditors $400.*

Analysis A liability account (Accounts Payable) and an asset account (Cash) decrease. This transaction is recorded as a $400 decrease (debit) to Accounts Payable and a $400 decrease (credit) to Cash.

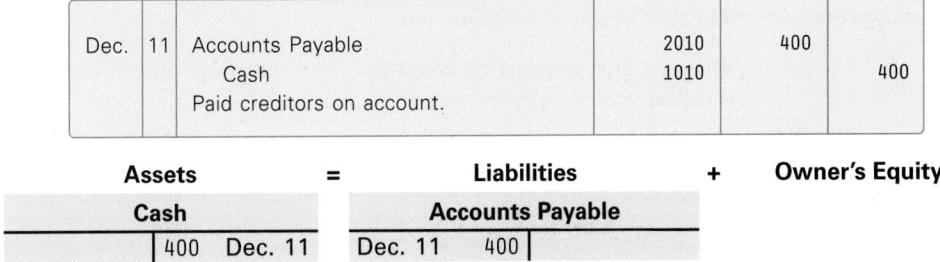

Transaction *Dec. 12 NetSolutions paid a receptionist and a part-time assistant $950 for two weeks' wages.*

Analysis This transaction is similar to the December 6 transaction: an expense account (Wages) increases and an asset account (Cash) decreases. This transaction is recorded as a $950 increase (debit) to Wages Expense and a $950 decrease (credit) to Cash.

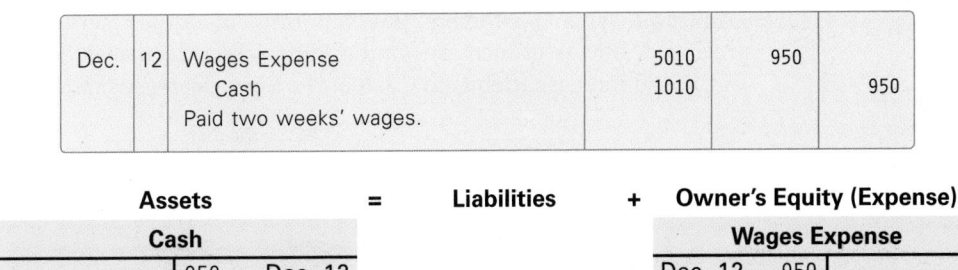

Transaction *Dec. 16 NetSolutions received $3,100 from fees earned for the first half of December.*

Analysis An asset account (Cash) and a revenue account (Fees Earned) increase. This transaction is recorded as a $3,100 increase (debit) to Cash and a $3,100 increase (credit) to Fees Earned.

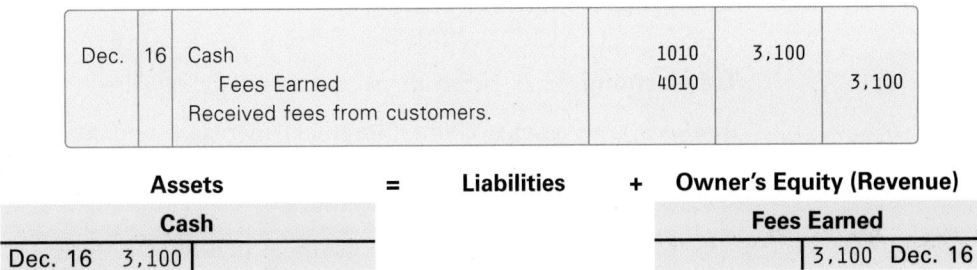

Transaction *Dec. 16 Fees earned on account totalled $1,750 for the first half of December.*

Analysis When a business agrees that a customer may receive services and pay for them at a later date, the business creates an account receivable. An account receivable is a claim against the customer. An account receivable is an asset, and the revenue is earned even though no cash has been received. Thus, this transaction is recorded as a $1,750 increase (debit) to Accounts Receivable and a $1,750 increase (credit) to Fees Earned.

Dec.	16	Accounts Receivable	1020	1,750	
		Fees Earned	4010		1,750
		Fees earned on account.			

Assets	=	Liabilities	+	Owner's Equity (Revenue)

Accounts Receivable		Fees Earned
Dec. 16 1,750		1,750 Dec. 16

Transaction *Dec. 20 NetSolutions paid $900 to Executive Supply Co. on the $1,800 debt owed from the December 4 transaction.*

Analysis This transaction is similar to the transaction of December 11. This transaction is recorded as a $900 decrease (debit) to Accounts Payable and a $900 decrease (credit) to Cash.

Dec.	20	Accounts Payable	2010	900	
		Cash	1010		900
		Paid creditor on account.			

Assets	=	Liabilities	+	Owner's Equity

Cash		Accounts Payable
900 Dec. 20	Dec. 20 900	

Transaction *Dec. 21 NetSolutions received $650 from customers in payment of their accounts.*

Analysis When customers pay amounts owed for services they have previously received, one asset increases and another asset decreases. This transaction is recorded as a $650 increase (debit) to Cash and a $650 decrease (credit) to Accounts Receivable.

Dec.	21	Cash	1010	650	
		Accounts Receivable	1020		650
		Received cash from customers on account.			

Assets	=	Liabilities	+	Owner's Equity

Cash	
Dec. 21 650	

Accounts Receivable	
650 Dec. 21	

Transaction *Dec. 23 NetSolutions paid $1,450 for supplies.*

Analysis One asset account (Supplies) increases and another asset account (Cash) decreases. This transaction is recorded as a $1,450 increase (debit) to Supplies and a $1,450 decrease (credit) to Cash.

Dec.	23	Supplies	1040	1,450	
		Cash	1010		1,450
		Purchased supplies.			

Assets	=	Liabilities	+	Owner's Equity

Supplies	
Dec. 23 1,450	

Cash	
1,450 Dec. 23	

Transaction *Dec. 26 NetSolutions paid a receptionist and a part-time assistant $1,200 for two weeks' wages.*

Analysis This transaction is similar to the December 12 transaction. This transaction is recorded as a $1,200 increase (debit) to Wages Expense and a $1,200 decrease (credit) to Cash.

Dec.	26	Wages Expense	5010	1,200	
		Cash	1010		1,200
		Paid two weeks' wages.			

Assets	**=**	**Liabilities**	**+**	**Owner's Equity (Expense)**
Cash				**Wages Expense**
1,200 Dec. 26				Dec. 26 1,200

Transaction *Dec. 31 NetSolutions paid a $310 telephone bill for the month.*

Analysis This transaction is similar to the transaction of December 6. This transaction is recorded as a $310 increase (debit) to Utilities Expense and a $310 decrease (credit) to Cash.

Dec.	31	Utilities Expense	5040	310	
		Cash	1010		310
		Paid telephone bill.			

Assets	**=**	**Liabilities**	**+**	**Owner's Equity (Expense)**
Cash				**Utilities Expense**
310 Dec. 31				Dec. 31 310

Transaction *Dec. 31 NetSolutions paid its $225 electric bill for the month.*

Analysis This transaction is similar to the preceding transaction. This transaction is recorded as a $225 increase (debit) to Utilities Expense and a $225 decrease (credit) to Cash.

Dec.	31	Utilities Expense	5040	225	
		Cash	1010		225
		Paid electric bill.			

Assets	**=**	**Liabilities**	**+**	**Owner's Equity (Expense)**
Cash				**Utilities Expense**
225 Dec. 31				Dec. 31 225

Transaction *Dec. 31 NetSolutions received $2,870 from fees earned for the second half of December.*

Analysis This transaction is similar to the transaction of December 16. The transaction is recorded as a $2,870 increase (debit) to Cash and a $2,870 increase (credit) to Fees Earned.

Dec.	31	Cash	1010	2,870	
		Fees Earned	4010		2,870
		Received fees from customers.			

Assets	**=**	**Liabilities**	**+**	**Owner's Equity (Revenue)**
Cash				**Fees Earned**
Dec. 31 2,870				2,870 Dec. 31

Transaction *Dec. 31 Fees earned on account totalled $1,120 for the second half of December.*

Analysis This transaction is similar to the transaction of December 16. This transaction is recorded as a $1,120 increase (debit) to Accounts Receivable and a $1,120 increase (credit) to Fees Earned.

Dec.	31	Accounts Receivable	1020	1,120	
		Fees Earned	4010		1,120
		Fees earned on account.			

Assets	=	Liabilities	+	Owner's Equity (Revenue)

Accounts Receivable			Fees Earned
Dec. 31 1,120			1,120 Dec. 31

Transaction *Dec. 31 Chris Clark withdrew $2,000 for personal use.*

Analysis This transaction decreases owner's equity and assets. The transaction is recorded as a $2,000 increase (debit) to Chris Clark, Withdrawals and a $2,000 decrease (credit) to Cash.

Dec.	31	Chris Clark, Withdrawals	3020	2,000	
		Cash	1010		2,000
		Chris Clark withdrew cash for personal use.			

Assets	=	Liabilities	+	Owner's Equity (Withdrawals)

Cash			Chris Clark, Withdrawals
2,000 Dec. 31			Dec. 31 2,000

Exhibit 6

Ledger NetSolutions

Ledger

Account *Cash*   Account No. *1010*

Date	Item	Post. Ref.	Debit	Credit	Balance
2014					
Nov. 1		1	25,000		25,000 DR.
5		1		20,000	5,000 DR.
18		1	7,500		12,500 DR.
30		1		3,650	8,850 DR.
30		1		950	7,900 DR.
30		1		2,000	5,900 DR.
Dec. 1		2		2,400	3,500 DR.
1		2		800	2,700 DR.
1		2	360		3,060 DR.
6		2		180	2,880 DR.
11		2		400	2,480 DR.
12		2		950	1,530 DR.
16		3	3,100		4,630 DR.
20		3		900	3,730 DR.
21		3	650		4,380 DR.
23		3		1,450	2,930 DR.
26		3		1,200	1,730 DR.
31		3		310	1,420 DR.
31		4		225	1,195 DR.
31		4	2,870		4,065 DR.
31		4		2,000	2,065 DR.

Account *Accounts Receivable*   Account No. *1020*

Date	Item	Post. Ref.	Debit	Credit	Balance
2014					
Dec. 16		3	1,750		1,750 DR.
21		3		650	1,100 DR.
31		4	1,120		2,220 DR.

Account *Supplies*   Account No. *1040*

Date	Item	Post. Ref.	Debit	Credit	Balance
2014					
Nov. 10		1	1,350		1,350 DR.
Dec. 23		3	1,450		2,800 DR.

Account *Prepaid Insurance*   Account No. *1050*

Date	Item	Post. Ref.	Debit	Credit	Balance
2014					
Dec. 1		2	2,400		2,400 DR.

(continued)

Exhibit 6

Ledger NetSolutions (*concluded*)

Account *Office Equipment*   Account No. *1070*

Date	Item	Post. Ref.	Debit	Credit	Balance
2014					
Dec. 4		2	1,800		1,800 Dr.

Account *Land*   Account No. *1090*

Date	Item	Post. Ref.	Debit	Credit	Balance
2014					
Nov. 5		1	20,000		20,000 Dr.

Account *Accounts Payable*   Account No. *2010*

Date	Item	Post. Ref.	Debit	Credit	Balance
2014					
Nov. 10		1		1,350	1,350 Cr.
30		1	950		400 Cr.
Dec. 4		2		1,800	2,200 Cr.
11		2	400		1,800 Cr.
20		3	900		900 Cr.

Account *Unearned Rent*   Account No. *2030*

Date	Item	Post. Ref.	Debit	Credit	Balance
2014					
Dec. 1		2		360	360 Cr.

Account *Chris Clark, Capital*   Account No. *3010*

Date	Item	Post. Ref.	Debit	Credit	Balance
2014					
Nov. 1		1		25,000	25,000 Cr.

Account *Chris Clark, Withdrawals*   Account No. *3020*

Date	Item	Post. Ref.	Debit	Credit	Balance
2014					
Nov. 30		1	2,000		2,000 Dr.
Dec. 31		4	2,000		4,000 Dr.

Account *Fees Earned*   Account No. *4010*

Date	Item	Post. Ref.	Debit	Credit	Balance
2014					
Nov. 18		1		7,500	7,500 Cr.
Dec. 16		3		3,100	10,600 Cr.
16		3		1,750	12,350 Cr.
31		4		2,870	15,220 Cr.
31		4		1,120	16,340 Cr.

Account *Wages Expense*   Account No. *5010*

Date	Item	Post. Ref.	Debit	Credit	Balance
2014					
Nov. 30		1	2,125		2,125 Dr.
Dec. 12		2	950		3,075 Dr.
26		3	1,200		4,275 Dr.

Account *Rent Expense*   Account No. *5020*

Date	Item	Post. Ref.	Debit	Credit	Balance
2014					
Nov. 30		1	800		800 Dr.
Dec. 1		2	800		1,600 Dr.

Account *Utilities Expense*   Account No. *5040*

Date	Item	Post. Ref.	Debit	Credit	Balance
2014					
Nov. 30		1	450		450 Dr.
Dec. 31		3	310		760 Dr.
31		4	225		985 Dr.

Account *Miscellaneous Expense*   Account No. *5090*

Date	Item	Post. Ref.	Debit	Credit	Balance
2014					
Nov. 30		1	275		275 Dr.
Dec. 6		2	180		455 Dr.

Unadjusted Trial Balance

Prepare an unadjusted trial balance and explain how it can be used to discover errors.

Errors may occur in posting debits and credits from the journal to the ledger. One way to detect such errors is by preparing a **trial balance**. This is step 4 in the accounting cycle. Double-entry accounting requires that debits must always equal credits. The trial balance verifies this equality. The stages in preparing a trial balance are as follows:

Stage 1: List the name of the company, the title of the trial balance, and the date the trial balance is prepared.

Stage 2: List the accounts from the ledger and enter their debit or credit balance in the Debit or Credit column of the trial balance.

Stage 3: Total the Debit and Credit columns of the trial balance.

Stage 4: Verify that the total of the Debit column equals the total of the Credit column.

The trial balance for NetSolutions as at December 31, 2014, is shown in Exhibit 7. The account balances in Exhibit 7 are taken from the ledger shown in Exhibit 6. Before a trial balance is prepared, each account balance in the ledger must be determined. The balance of each account appears in the balance column on the same line as the last posting to the account.

The trial balance shown in Exhibit 7 is titled an **unadjusted trial balance**. This title distinguishes it from other trial balances that we will prepare in later chapters. These other trial balances include an adjusted trial balance and a post-closing trial balance.[2]

Errors Affecting the Trial Balance

If the trial balance totals are not equal, an error has occurred. In this case, the error must be found and corrected. A method useful in discovering errors is as follows:

1. If the difference between the Debit and Credit column totals is 10, 100, or 1,000, an error in addition may have occurred. In this case, re-add the trial balance column totals. If the error still exists, recompute the account balances.

2. If the difference between the Debit and Credit column totals can be evenly divisible by 2, the error may be due to the entering of a debit balance as a credit balance or vice versa. In this case, review the trial balance for account balances of one-half the

Exhibit 7

Trial Balance

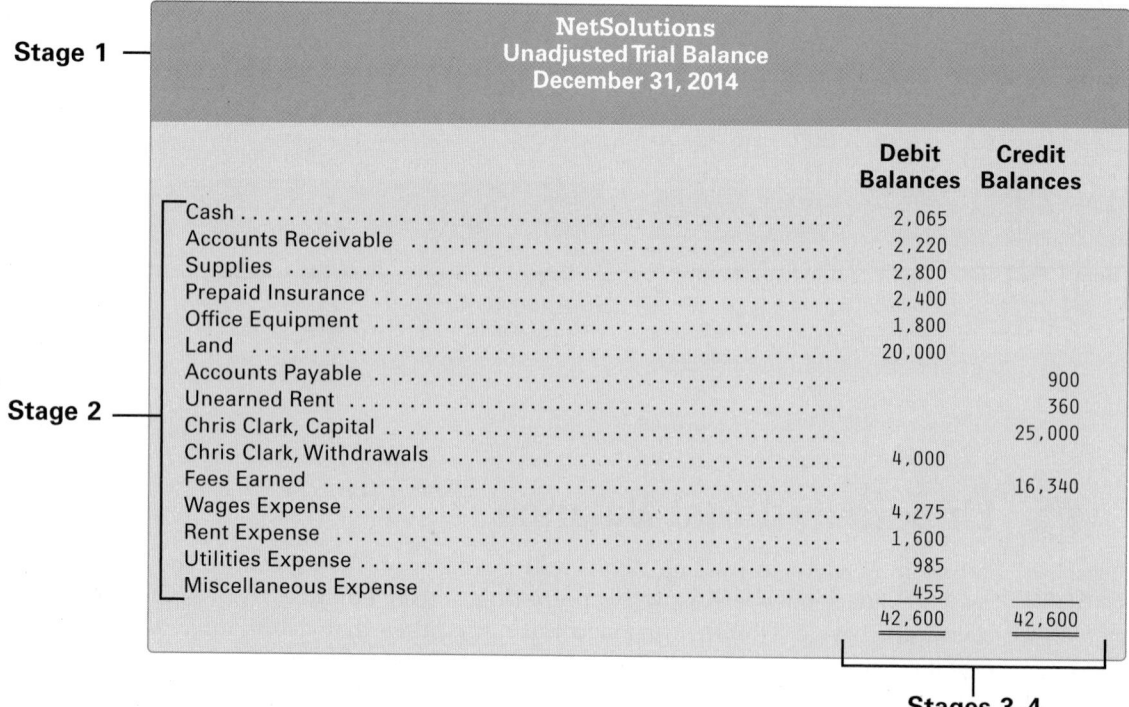

Stage 1 —

NetSolutions
Unadjusted Trial Balance
December 31, 2014

	Debit Balances	Credit Balances
Cash	2,065	
Accounts Receivable	2,220	
Supplies	2,800	
Prepaid Insurance	2,400	
Office Equipment	1,800	
Land	20,000	
Accounts Payable		900
Unearned Rent		360
Chris Clark, Capital		25,000
Chris Clark, Withdrawals	4,000	
Fees Earned		16,340
Wages Expense	4,275	
Rent Expense	1,600	
Utilities Expense	985	
Miscellaneous Expense	455	
	42,600	42,600

Stage 2 —

Stages 3–4

2 The adjusted trial balance is discussed in Chapter 3 and the post-closing trial balance is discussed in Chapter 4.

difference that may have been entered in the wrong column. For example, if the Debit column total is $20,640 and the Credit column total is $20,236, the difference of $404 ($20,640 - $20,236) may be due to a credit account balance of $202 that was entered as a debit account balance.

3. If the difference between the Debit and Credit column totals is evenly divisible by 9, trace the account balances back to the ledger to see if an account balance was incorrectly copied from the ledger. Two common types of copying errors are transpositions and slides. A **transposition** occurs when the order of the digits is copied incorrectly, such as writing $542 as $452 or $524. In a **slide**, the entire number is copied incorrectly one or more spaces to the right or the left, such as writing $542.00 as $54.20 or $5,420.00. In both cases, the resulting error will be evenly divisible by 9.

4. If the difference between the Debit and Credit column totals is not evenly divisible by 2 or 9, review the ledger to see whether an account balance in the amount of the error has been omitted from the trial balance. If the error is not discovered, review the journal postings to see whether a posting of a debit or credit may have been omitted.

5. If an error is not discovered by the preceding steps, the accounting process must be retraced, beginning with the last journal entry.

The trial balance does not provide complete proof of the accuracy of the ledger. It indicates only that the debits and the credits are equal. This proof is of value, however, because errors often affect the equality of debits and credits.

EXAMPLE EXERCISE 2-5 Trial Balance Errors   ④

For each of the following errors, considered individually, indicate whether the error would cause the trial balance totals to be unequal. If the error would cause the trial balance totals to be unequal, indicate whether the debit or credit total is higher and by how much.

a. Payment of a cash withdrawal of $6,700 was journalized and posted as a debit of $7,600 to Salary Expense and a credit of $7,600 to Cash.

b. A fee of $3,280 earned from a client was debited to Accounts Receivable for $3,820 and credited to Fees Earned for $3,280.

c. A payment of $6,200 to a creditor was posted as a debit of $6,200 to Accounts Payable and a debit of $6,200 to Cash.

FOLLOW MY EXAMPLE 2-5

a. The totals are equal since both the debit and credit entries were journalized and posted for $7,600.

b. The totals are unequal. The debit total is higher by $540 ($3,820 – $3,280).

c. The totals are unequal. The debit total is higher by $12,400 ($6,200 + $6,200).

For Practice: PE 2-5

Errors Not Affecting the Trial Balance

An error may occur that does not cause the trial balance totals to be unequal. Such an error may be discovered when preparing the trial balance or may be indicated by an unusual account balance. For example, a credit balance in the supplies account indicates an error has occurred because a business cannot have "negative" supplies. When such errors are discovered, they should be corrected. If the error has already been journalized and posted to the ledger, **correcting journal entries** are normally prepared.

Correcting Journal Entries

To illustrate, assume that on May 5, a $12,500 purchase of office equipment on account was incorrectly journalized and posted as a debit to Supplies and a credit to Accounts Payable for $12,500. This posting of the incorrect entry is shown in the following T accounts:

Incorrect:

Supplies		Accounts Payable	
May 5 12,500		12,500 May 5	

Before making a correcting journal entry, it is best to determine the debit(s) and credit(s) that should have been recorded. These are shown in the following T accounts:

Correct:

Office Equipment		Accounts Payable	
Dec. 31 12,500		12,500 Dec. 31	

Once you have identified the incorrect entry and the correct entry, apply a two-step process, using an entry to remove the original entry by debiting the credit and crediting the debit and then record the correct entry. First, remove the incorrect entry by completing the exact opposite entry—debiting Accounts Payable and crediting Supplies. Second, record the entry correctly.

May	31	Accounts Payable	12,500	
		Supplies		12,500
		To remove entry made in error on May 5.		
		See invoice from Bell Office Equipment Co.		
May	31	Office Equipment	12,500	
		Accounts Payable		12,500
		To correct entry made in error on May 5.		
		See invoice from Bell Office Equipment Co.		

These two entries make it easy for someone later to understand what had happened and why the entries were necessary. Although the journal entries can be recorded as a compound entry, the two-step process is better practice from an audit perspective.

EXAMPLE EXERCISE 2-6 Correcting Entries

The following errors took place in journalizing transactions:

a. A withdrawal of $6,000 by Cheri Ramey, owner of the business, was recorded as a debit to Office Salaries Expense and a credit to Cash.

b. Utilities Expense of $4,500 paid for the current month was recorded as a debit to Miscellaneous Expense and a credit to Accounts Payable.

Journalize the entries to correct the errors.

FOLLOW MY EXAMPLE 2-6

a. Cash	6,000	
Office Salaries Expense		6,000
To remove an incorrect entry.		
Cheri Ramey, Withdrawals	6,000	
Cash		6,000
To correct error.		
b. Accounts Payable	4,500	
Miscellaneous Expense		4,500
To remove an incorrect entry.		
Utilities Expense	4,500	
Cash		4,500
To correct error.		

For Practice: PE 2-6

CRITICAL THINKING

How does an accountant decide whether a transaction represents an asset or an expense?

An accountant evaluates whether the transaction meets the definition of an asset. If the transaction does not meet the definition of an asset, then it is considered to be an expense item. For example, suppose a business hires an interior designer to plan renovations to its building. The accountant can ask three questions to decide whether the cost of the plans should be considered an asset. Will the cost provide a future economic benefit? Yes, the building will be improved. Can the company control access to the benefit? Yes, the company owns the plans. And finally, is the item a result of a past transaction? Yes, the plans have been prepared and paid for. The transaction is recorded as an asset and the cost of the renovation plans is added to the building asset account. If any of these characteristics did not exist, then the costs would be recorded as an expense.

At a Glance 2

1 | Describe the characteristics of an account and a chart of accounts.

Key Points	Key Learning Outcomes	Page	Example Exercises
The form used for recording individual transactions is an account. A group of accounts is called a ledger. The simplest form of an account is a T account. Amounts entered on the left side of an account, regardless of the account title, are called debits to the account. Amounts entered on the right side of an account are called credits. Periodically, the balance of the account is determined. The system of accounts that make up a ledger is called a chart of accounts.	• Record transactions in T accounts. • Determine the balance of a T account. • Prepare a chart of accounts for a proprietorship.	47 47 48	

2 | Describe and illustrate journalizing transactions using the double-entry accounting system.

Key Points	Key Learning Outcomes	Page	Example Exercises
The double-entry accounting system is designed so that the sum of the debits always equals the sum of the credits for each journal entry. Transactions are initially entered in a record called a journal. The rules of debit and credit for recording increases or decreases in asset, liability, owner's equity, revenue, expense, and withdrawal accounts are shown in Exhibit 3. The normal balance of an account is indicated by the side of the account (debit or credit) that receives the increases.	• Indicate the normal balance of an account. • Journalize transactions using the rules of debit and credit.	50 51	2-1 2-2 2-3 2-4

3 | Describe and illustrate the posting of transactions to accounts.

Key Points	Key Learning Outcomes	Page	Example Exercises
Transactions are posted to the ledger using the rules of debit and credit. The debits and credits for each journal entry are posted to the accounts in the order in which they occur in the journal.	• Post journal entries to accounts.	57	

4 Prepare an unadjusted trial balance and explain how it can be used to discover errors.

Key Points

A trial balance is prepared by listing the accounts from the ledger and their balances. The totals of the Debit column and Credit column of the trial balance must be equal. If the two totals are not equal, an error has occurred. Errors may occur even though the trial balance totals are equal. Such errors may require correcting journal entries.

Key Learning Outcomes	Page	Example Exercises
• Prepare an unadjusted trial balance.	64	
• Discover errors that cause unequal totals in the trial balance.	67	2-5
• Prepare correcting journal entries for errors.	68	2-6

GLOSSARY

account – An accounting form that is used to record the increases and decreases in each financial statement item. (p. 46)

assets – The resources owned by a business that can provide the company with future benefits. (p. 48)

balance of the account – The amount of the difference between the debits and the credits that have been entered into an account. (p. 48)

capital account – In a proprietorship, the account that represents the owner's equity. (p. 48)

chart of accounts – A list of the accounts in the ledger. (p. 48)

compound journal entry – A journal entry that has more than one debit entry or more than one credit entry. (p. 55)

correcting journal entries – Entries that are prepared when an error has already been journalized and posted. (p. 68)

credit – Amount entered on the right side of an account. (p. 48)

debit – Amount entered on the left side of an account. (p. 48)

double-entry accounting system – A system of accounting for recording transactions, based on recording increases and decreases in accounts so that debits equal credits. (p. 49)

drawings – The account used to record amounts withdrawn by an owner of a proprietorship. (p. 48) Also known as *withdrawals*.

expenses – Assets used up or services consumed in the process of generating revenues. (p. 48)

journal – The initial record in which the effects of a transaction are recorded. (p. 51)

journal entry – The form of recording a transaction in a journal. (p. 53)

journalizing – The process of recording a transaction in the journal. (p. 53)

ledger – A group of accounts for a business. (p. 48)

liabilities – The rights of creditors that represent debts of the business. (p. 48)

normal balance of an account – The normal balance of an account can be either a debit or a credit depending on whether increases in the account are recorded as debits or credits. (p. 50)

owner's equity – The owner's right to the net assets of the business. (p. 48)

posting – The process of transferring the debits and credits from the journal entries to the accounts. (p. 57)

revenues – Increases in owner's equity as a result of selling services or products to customers. (p. 48)

rules of debit and credit – In the double-entry accounting system, specific rules for recording debits and credits based on the type of account. (p. 49)

slide – An error in which the entire number is moved one or more spaces to the right or the left, such as writing $542.00 as $54.20 or $5,420.00. (p. 67)

T account – The simplest form of an account. (p. 47)

transposition – An error in which the order of the digits is changed, such as writing $542 as $452 or $524. (p. 67)

trial balance – A summary listing of the titles and balances of accounts in the ledger. (p. 64)

unadjusted trial balance – A summary listing of the titles and balances of accounts in the ledger prior to the posting of adjusting entries. (p. 67)

unearned revenue – The liability created by receiving cash in advance of earning the revenue. (p. 60)

withdrawals – The account used to record amounts withdrawn by an owner of a proprietorship. (p. 48) Also known as *drawings*.

END-OF-CHAPTER ILLUSTRATIVE PROBLEM

J. F. Outz, D.D.S., has been practising as a dentist for three years. During April 2014, Outz completed the following transactions in her practice of dentistry:

Apr.   1.   Paid office rent for April, $800.
3.   Purchased equipment on account, $2,100.
5.   Received cash on account from patients, $3,150.
8.   Purchased X-ray film and other supplies on account, $245.
12.   Paid cash to creditors on account, $1,250.
17.   Paid cash for renewal of a six-month property insurance policy, $660.
27.   Paid cash from business bank account for personal and family expenses, $1,250.
30.   Recorded the cash received in payment of services (on a cash basis) to patients during April, $1,720.
30.   Paid salaries of receptionist and dental assistants, $1,725.
30.   Recorded fees charged to patients on account for services performed in April, $5,145.

Outz's account titles, numbers, and balances as at April 1 (all normal balances) are listed as follows: Cash, 1010, $4,588; Accounts Receivable, 1020, $6,725; Supplies, 1030, $290; Prepaid Insurance, 1040, $660; Equipment, 1080, $19,745; Accounts Payable, 2020, $765; J. F. Outz, Capital, 3010, $31,243; J. F. Outz, Withdrawals, 3020; Professional Fees, 4010; Salaries Expense, 5010; Rent Expense, 5030.

Instructions

1.   Open a ledger of standard three-column accounts for Dr. Outz as at April 1, 2014. Enter the balances in the appropriate balance columns and place a check mark (✔)

in the Posting Reference column. (*Hint:* Verify the equality of the debit and credit balances in the ledger before proceeding with the next instruction.)

2. Journalize each transaction in a two-column journal.
3. Post the journal to the ledger, extending the month-end balances after each posting.
4. Prepare an unadjusted trial balance as at April 30, 2014.

Solutions

1., 2., and 3.

Journal				Page 27
Date	**Description**	**Post. Ref.**	**Debit**	**Credit**
2014				
Apr. 1	Rent Expense	5030	800	
	Cash	1010		800
	Paid office rent for April.			
3	Equipment	1080	2,100	
	Accounts Payable	2020		2,100
	Purchased equipment on account.			
5	Cash	1010	3,150	
	Accounts Receivable	1020		3,150
	Received cash on account.			
8	Supplies	1030	245	
	Accounts Payable	2020		245
	Purchased supplies.			
12	Accounts Payable	2020	1,250	
	Cash	1010		1,250
	Paid creditors on account.			
17	Prepaid Insurance	1040	660	
	Cash	1010		660
	Prepaid insurance for six months.			

Journal				Page 28
Date	**Description**	**Post. Ref.**	**Debit**	**Credit**
2014				
Apr. 27	J. F. Outz, Withdrawals	3020	1,250	
	Cash	1010		1,250
	J. F. Outz withdrew cash for personal use.			
30	Cash	1010	1,720	
	Professional Fees	4010		1,720
	Received fees from patients.			
30	Salaries Expense	5010	1,725	
	Cash	1010		1,725
	Paid salaries.			
30	Accounts Receivable	1020	5,145	
	Professional Fees	4010		5,145
	Recorded fees earned on account.			

Account Accounts Receivable				Account No. 1020	
Date	**Item**	**Post. Ref.**	**Debit**	**Credit**	**Balance**
2014					
Apr. 1	Balance	✓			6,725 DR.
5		27		3,150	3,575 DR.
30		28	5,145		8,720 DR.

Account Cash				Account No. 1010	
Date	**Item**	**Post. Ref.**	**Debit**	**Credit**	**Balance**
2014					
Apr. 1	Balance	✓			4,588 DR.
1		27		800	3,788 DR.
5		27	3,150		6,938 DR.
12		27		1,250	5,688 DR.
17		27		660	5,028 DR.
27		28		1,250	3,778 DR.
30		28	1,720		5,498 DR.
30		28		1,725	3,773 DR.

Account Supplies				Account No. 1030	
Date	**Item**	**Post. Ref.**	**Debit**	**Credit**	**Balance**
2014					
Apr. 1	Balance	✓			290 DR.
8		27	245		535 DR.

(*continued*)

Account *Prepaid Insurance* Account No. *1040*

Date	Item	Post. Ref.	Debit	Credit	Balance
2014					
Apr. 1	Balance	✓			660 Dr.
17		27	660		1,320 Dr.

Account *Equipment* Account No. *1080*

Date	Item	Post. Ref.	Debit	Credit	Balance
2014					
Apr. 1	Balance	✓			19,745 Dr.
3		27	2,100		21,845 Dr.

Account *Accounts Payable* Account No. *2020*

Date	Item	Post. Ref.	Debit	Credit	Balance
2014					
Apr. 1	Balance	✓			765 Cr.
3		27		2,100	2,865 Cr.
8		27		245	3,110 Cr.
12		27	1,250		1,860 Cr.

Account *J. F. Outz, Capital* Account No. *3010*

Date	Item	Post. Ref.	Debit	Credit	Balance
2014					
Apr. 1	Balance	✓			31,243 Cr.

Account *J. F. Qutz, Withdrawals* Account No. *3020*

Date	Item	Post. Ref.	Debit	Credit	Balance
2014					
Apr. 27		28	1,250		1,250 Dr.

Account *Professional Fees* Account No. *4010*

Date	Item	Post. Ref.	Debit	Credit	Balance
2014					
Apr. 30		28		1,720	1,720 Dr.
30		28		5,145	6,865 Dr.

Account *Salaries Expense* Account No. *5010*

Date	Item	Post. Ref.	Debit	Credit	Balance
2014					
Apr. 30		28	1,725		1,725 Dr.

Account *Rent Expense* Account No. *5030*

Date	Item	Post. Ref.	Debit	Credit	Balance
2014					
Apr. 1		27	800		800 Dr.

4.

J. F. Outz, D.D.S.
Unadjusted Trial Balance
April 30, 2014

	Debit Balances	Credit Balances
Cash	3,773	
Accounts Receivable	8,720	
Supplies	535	
Prepaid Insurance	1,320	
Equipment	21,845	
Accounts Payable		1,860
J. F. Outz, Capital		31,243
J. F. Outz, Withdrawals	1,250	
Professional Fees		6,865
Salaries Expense	1,725	
Rent Expense	800	
	39,968	39,968

EYE OPENERS

1. What is the difference between an account and a ledger?
2. Do the terms *debit* and *credit* signify an increase or a decrease, or can they signify either? Explain.
3. Explain why the rules of debit and credit are the same for liability accounts and owner's equity accounts.
4. What is the effect (increase or decrease) of a debit to an expense account (a) in terms of owner's equity and (b) in terms of expense?
5. What is the effect (increase or decrease) of a credit to a revenue account (a) in terms of owner's equity and (b) in terms of revenue?
6. Weir Company adheres to a policy of depositing all cash receipts in a bank account and making all payments by cheque. The cash account as at March 31 has a credit balance of $3,190, and there is no undeposited cash on hand. (a) Assuming no errors occurred during journalizing or posting, what caused this unusual balance? (b) Is the $3,190 credit balance in the cash account an asset, a liability, owner's equity, a revenue, or an expense?
7. Resource Services Company performed services in February for a specific customer, for a fee of $11,250. Payment was received in March. (a) Was the revenue earned in February or March? (b) What accounts should be debited and credited in (1) February and (2) March?
8. What proof is provided by a trial balance?
9. If the two totals of a trial balance are equal, does it mean the accounting records have no errors? Explain.
10. Assume that a trial balance is prepared with an account balance of $21,740 listed as $2,174 and an account balance of $4,500 listed as $5,400. Identify the transposition and the slide.
11. Assume that when a purchase of supplies of $3,100 for cash was recorded, both the debit and the credit were journalized and posted as $1,300. (a) Would this error cause the trial balance to be out of balance? (b) Would the trial balance be out of balance if the $3,100 entry had been journalized correctly but the credit to Cash had been posted as $1,300?
12. Assume that Timberline Consulting erroneously recorded the payment of $9,000 of owner withdrawals as a debit to Salary Expense. (a) How would this error affect the equality of the trial balance? (b) How would this error affect the income statement, statement of owner's equity, and balance sheet?
13. Assume that Western Realty Co. borrowed $200,000 from the Canadian Imperial Bank of Commerce. In recording the transaction, Western erroneously recorded the receipt as a debit to Cash, $200,000, and a credit to Fees Earned, $200,000. (a) How would this error affect the equality of the trial balance? (b) How would this error affect the income statement, statement of owner's equity, and balance sheet?
14. In journalizing and posting the entry to record the purchase of supplies for cash, the accounts payable account was credited in error. What is the preferred procedure to correct this error?
15. Chequing accounts are the most common form of deposits for banks. Assume that Village Storage has a chequing account at ATB Financial. What type of account (asset, liability, owner's equity, revenue, expense, withdrawals) does the account balance of $8,750 represent from the viewpoint of (a) Village Storage and (b) ATB Financial?

PRACTICE EXERCISES

② PE 2-1

Rules of debit and credit and normal balances

EE 2-1 p. 50

State for each account whether it is likely to have (a) debit entries only, (b) credit entries only, or (c) both debit and credit entries. Also, indicate whether its normal balance is a debit or a credit.

1. Accounts Payable
2. Cash
3. Dorothy Holt, Withdrawals
4. Miscellaneous Expense
5. Rent Revenue

---

② PE 2-2

Journal entry for asset purchase

EE 2-2 p. 54

Prepare T accounts and a journal entry for the purchase of office supplies on October 14 for $9,000, paying $1,800 cash and the remainder on account. Office supplies has a zero opening balance, cash has an $800 opening balance, and accounts payable has a $700 balance.

---

② PE 2-3

Journal entry for fees earned

EE 2-3 p. 55

Prepare T accounts and a journal entry on April 2 for cash received for services rendered, $3,600. The opening balance for cash is $4,000, and the opening balance for services rendered is $12,000.

---

② PE 2-4

Journal entry for owner's withdrawal

EE 2-4 p. 57

Prepare T accounts and a journal entry on January 19 for the withdrawal of $6,000 by James Green for personal use. There have been no previous withdrawals during the year, and the cash account balance is $25,000.

---

④ PE 2-5

Trial balance errors

EE 2-5 p. 67

Consider each of the following errors and indicate whether the error would cause the trial balance totals to be unequal. If the error would cause the trial balance totals to be unequal, indicate whether the debit or credit total is higher and by how much.

a. The payment of cash for the purchase of office equipment of $6,000 was debited to Land for $6,000 and credited to Cash for $6,000.
b. The payment of $8,750 on account was debited to Accounts Payable for $875 and credited to Cash for $8,750.
c. The receipt of cash on account of $6,150 was recorded as a debit to Cash for $6,510 and a credit to Accounts Receivable for $6,150.

---

④ PE 2-6

Correcting entries

EE 2-6 p. 69

The following errors took place in journalizing transactions:

a. The receipt of $6,480 for services rendered was recorded as a debit to Accounts Receivable and a credit to Fees Earned.
b. The purchase of supplies of $1,960 on account was recorded as a debit to Office Equipment and a credit to Supplies.

Journalize the entries to correct the errors. Omit explanations.

EXERCISES

EX 2-1
Chart of accounts

The following accounts appeared in recent financial statements of Air Canada:

Accounts Payable and Accrued Liabilities
Aeroplan Miles Obligation
Aircraft Fuel Expense
Cargo Revenue
Commissions

Property and Equipment
Airport and Navigation Fees
Passenger Revenue
Deposits and Other Assets
Spare Parts, Materials, and Supplies

Identify each account as either a balance sheet account or an income statement account. For each balance sheet account, identify it as an asset, a liability, or owner's equity. For each income statement account, identify it as a revenue or an expense.

EX 2-2
Chart of accounts

Humvee Interiors is owned and operated by Tony Newbaurer, an interior decorator. In the ledger of Humvee Interiors, the first digit of the account number indicates its major account classification (1—assets, 2—liabilities, 3—owner's equity, 4—revenues, 5—expenses). The next three digits of the account number indicate the specific account within each of the preceding major account classifications.

Match each account number with its most likely account in the list below. The account numbers are 1010, 1020, 1030, 2010, 3010, 3020, 4010, 5010, and 5020:

Accounts Payable
Accounts Receivable
Cash
Fees Earned
Land

Miscellaneous Expense
Tony Newbaurer, Capital
Tony Newbaurer, Withdrawals
Wages Expense

EX 2-3
Chart of accounts

Monet School is a newly organized business that teaches people how to inspire and influence others. The list of accounts to be opened in the general ledger is as follows:

Accounts Payable
Accounts Receivable
Cash
Equipment
Fees Earned
Jamie Bjork, Capital

Jamie Bjork, Withdrawals
Miscellaneous Expense
Rent Expense
Supplies
Wages Expense

List the accounts in the order in which they should appear in the ledger of Monet School and assign account numbers. Each account number is to have four digits: the first digit is to indicate the major classification (1 for assets, etc.), and the rest identify the specific account within each major classification (010 for Cash, etc.).

EX 2-4
Identifying transactions

Southwest Tours Co. is a travel agency. The eight transactions recorded by Southwest Tours during February 2015, its first month of operations, are indicated in the following T accounts:

Cash		Equipment		Mickey O'Dell, Withdrawals	
(1) 25,000	(2) 1,750	(3) 18,000		(8) 2,500	
(7) 10,000	(3) 5,600				
	(4) 2,700				
	(6) 7,500				
	(8) 2,500				

Accounts Receivable		Accounts Payable		Service Revenue	
(5) 13,500	(7) 10,000	(6) 7,500	(3) 12,400		(5) 13,500

Supplies		Mickey O'Dell, Capital		Operating Expenses	
(2) 1,750			(1) 25,000	(4) 2,700	

(continued)

Indicate for each debit and each credit (a) whether an asset, liability, owner's equity, withdrawal, revenue, or expense account was affected and (b) whether the account was increased (+) or decreased (−). Present your answers in the following form, with transaction (1) given as an example:

Transaction	Account Debited		Account Credited	
	Type	Effect	Type	Effect
(1)	asset	+	owner's equity	+

EX 2-5
Journal entries

Based upon the T accounts in Exercise 2-4, prepare the eight journal entries from which the postings were made. Journal entry explanations may be omitted.

EX 2-6
Trial balance

Based upon the data presented in Exercise 2-4, prepare an unadjusted trial balance, listing the accounts in their proper order.

✔ Total Debit column: $43,400

EX 2-7
Normal entries for accounts

During the month, Iris Labs Co. has a substantial number of transactions affecting each of the following accounts. State for each account whether it is likely to have (a) debit entries only, (b) credit entries only, or (c) both debit and credit entries.

1. Accounts Payable
2. Accounts Receivable
3. Cash
4. Fees Earned
5. Insurance Expense
6. Nicki Swanson, Withdrawals

EX 2-8
Normal balances of accounts

Identify each of the following accounts of Advanced Services Co. as asset, liability, owner's equity, revenue, or expense, and state in each case whether the normal balance is a debit or a credit.

a. Accounts Payable
b. Accounts Receivable
c. Barbara Mallary, Capital
d. Barbara Mallary, Withdrawals
e. Cash
f. Fees Earned
g. Office Equipment
h. Rent Expense
i. Supplies
j. Wages Expense

EX 2-9
Rules of debit and credit

The following table summarizes the rules of debit and credit. For each of the items (a) through (l), indicate whether the proper answer is a debit or a credit.

	Increase	Decrease	Normal Balance
Balance sheet accounts:			
Asset	Debit	(a)	(b)
Liability	Credit	(c)	(d)
Owner's equity:			
Capital	(e)	Debit	(f)
Withdrawals	(g)	(h)	Debit
Income statement accounts:			
Revenue	(i)	(j)	(k)
Expense	(l)	Credit	Debit

EX 2-10
Capital account balance

As at January 1, Oh Kwon, Capital, had a credit balance of $37,100. During the year, withdrawals totalled $1,000, and the business incurred a net loss of $52,300.

Calculate the balance of Oh Kwon, Capital, as at the end of the year.

(1) (2) EX 2-11
Cash account balance

During the month, Raccoon Co. received $319,750 in cash and paid out $269,900 in cash.

a. Do the data indicate that Raccoon Co. earned $49,850 during the month? Explain.

b. If the balance of the cash account is $72,350 at the end of the month, what was the cash balance at the beginning of the month?

---

(1) (2) EX 2-12
Account balances

✔ c. $284,175

a. During July, $90,300 was paid to creditors on account, and purchases on account were $115,150. Assuming that the July 31 balance of Accounts Payable was $39,000, determine the account balance on July 1.

b. On May 1, the accounts receivable account balance was $36,200. During May, $315,000 was collected from customers on account. Assuming that the May 31 balance was $41,600, determine the fees billed to customers on account during May.

c. On April 1, the cash account balance was $18,275. During April, cash receipts totalled $279,100, and the April 30 balance was $13,200. Determine the cash payments made during April.

---

(2) EX 2-13
Transactions

Chalet Co. has the following accounts in its ledger: Cash; Accounts Receivable; Supplies; Office Equipment; Accounts Payable; Martin Kim, Capital; Martin Kim, Withdrawals; Rent Expense.

Journalize the following selected transactions for March 2014 in a two-column journal. Journal entry explanations may be omitted.

Mar.   1.   Paid rent for the month, $2,100.
       3.   Martin paid cash for a new sofa for his home, using a company cheque, $900.
       5.   Paid cash for supplies, $700.
       6.   Purchased office equipment on account, $12,300.
      10.   Received cash from customers in payment of receivables, $4,100.
      15.   Paid creditors $1,200 of the accounts payable.

---

(2) (3) EX 2-14
Journalizing and posting

On August 7, 2015, Mainsail Co. purchased $2,190 of supplies on account. In Mainsail Co.'s chart of accounts, the supplies account is No. 1050, and the accounts payable account is No. 2010.

a. Journalize the August 7, 2015, transaction on page 19 of Mainsail Co.'s two-column journal. Include an explanation of the entry.

b. Prepare a three-column account for Supplies. Enter a debit balance of $1,050 as at August 1, 2015. Place a check mark (✓) in the Posting Reference column.

c. Prepare a three-column account for Accounts Payable. Enter a credit balance of $15,600 as at August 1, 2015. Place a check mark (✓) in the Posting Reference column.

d. Post the August 7, 2015, transaction to the accounts.

---

(2) (3) EX 2-15
Transactions and T accounts

The following selected transactions were completed during February of the current year:

1. Billed customers for fees earned, $41,730.
2. Purchased supplies on account, $1,800.
3. Received cash from customers on account, $39,150.
4. Paid creditors on account, $1,100.
5. Owner purchased dinner on the way home from work, paying out of his own pocket, $35.

a. Journalize the above transactions in a two-column journal, using the appropriate number to identify the transactions. Journal entry explanations may be omitted.

b. Post the entries prepared in (a) to the following T accounts: Cash, Supplies, Accounts Receivable, Accounts Payable, Fees Earned. To the left of each amount posted in the accounts, place the appropriate number to identify the transactions.

④ EX 2-16
Trial balance

✔ Total of Credit
column: $482,400

The accounts in the ledger of Diva Co. as at December 31, 2015, are listed in alphabetical order as follows. All accounts have normal balances. The balance of the cash account has been intentionally omitted.

Accounts Payable	$28,000	Land	$125,000
Accounts Receivable	40,000	Miscellaneous Expense	12,000
Cash	?	Notes Payable	50,000
Cheryl Sievert, Capital	40,900	Prepaid Insurance	6,400
Cheryl Sievert, Withdrawals	25,000	Rent Expense	36,000
Fees Earned	350,000	Supplies	4,000
Insurance Expense	6,000	Unearned Rent	13,500
Wages Expense	195,000	Utilities Expense	18,000

Prepare an unadjusted trial balance, listing the accounts in their proper order and inserting the missing figure for cash.

---

④ EX 2-17
Effect of errors on trial balance

Consider each of the following errors individually and indicate which of the errors would cause the trial balance totals to be unequal:

a. A payment of $2,500 to a creditor was posted as a debit of $2,500 to Accounts Payable and a debit of $2,500 to Cash.

b. A fee of $5,000 earned and due from a client was not debited to Accounts Receivable or credited to a revenue account because the cash had not been received.

c. A receipt of $3,000 from an account receivable was journalized and posted as a debit of $3,000 to Cash and a credit of $3,000 to Fees Earned.

d. A payment of $9,000 for equipment purchased was posted as a debit of $9,000 to Equipment and a credit of $9,000 to Cash.

e. Payment of a cash withdrawal of $13,000 was journalized and posted as a debit of $3,000 to Salary Expense and a credit of $13,000 to Cash.

---

④ EX 2-18
Errors in trial balance

✔ Total of Credit
column: $174,600

The following preliminary unadjusted trial balance of Seats-For-You Co., a sports ticket agency, does not balance:

Seats-For-You Co.
Unadjusted Trial Balance
December 31, 2015

	Debit Balances	Credit Balances
Cash	47,350	
Accounts Receivable	22,100	
Equipment	6,500	
Accounts Payable		13,980
Gina Ness, Capital	82,420	
Gina Ness, Withdrawals	10,000	
Service Revenue		80,000
Wages Expense		42,000
Advertising Expense	7,200	
Miscellaneous Expense		1,425
	175,570	137,405

When the ledger and other records are reviewed, you discover the following: (1) the debits and credits in the cash account total $47,350 and $23,975, respectively; (2) a billing of $3,500 to a customer on account was not posted to the accounts receivable account; (3) a payment of $1,800 made to a creditor on account was not posted to the accounts payable account; (4) the correct balance of the equipment account is $65,000; and (5) each account has a normal balance.
Prepare a corrected unadjusted trial balance.

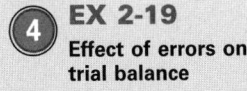

EX 2-19

Effect of errors on trial balance

The following errors occurred in posting from a two-column journal:

1. A credit of $7,210 to Accounts Payable was not posted.
2. A debit of $3,000 to Cash was posted to Miscellaneous Expense.
3. A credit of $120 to Cash was posted as $710.
4. A debit of $2,540 to Wages Expense was posted as $2,450.
5. An entry debiting Accounts Receivable and crediting Fees Earned for $10,000 was not posted.
6. A debit of $850 to Accounts Payable was posted as a credit.
7. A debit of $1,500 to Supplies was posted twice.

Considering each case individually (i.e., assuming that no other errors had occurred), indicate (a) by "yes" or "no" whether the trial balance would be out of balance; (b) if the answer to (a) is "yes," the amount by which the trial balance totals would differ; and (c) whether the Debit or Credit column of the trial balance would have the larger total. Answers should be presented in the following form, with error (1) given as an example:

	(a)	(b)	(c)
Error	Out of Balance	Difference	Larger Total
1.	yes	$7,210	debit

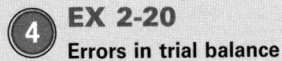

EX 2-20

Errors in trial balance

Identify the errors in the following trial balance and prepare a corrected trial balance. All accounts have normal balances.

✔ Total of Credit column: $1,456,800

Burgoo Co.
Unadjusted Trial Balance
For the Month Ended March 31, 2015

	Debit Balances	Credit Balances
Cash	90,000	
Accounts Receivable		196,800
Equipment.	600,000	
Accounts Payable	22,200	
Salaries Payable.		15,000
Estelle Chatman, Capital		518,400
Estelle Chatman, Withdrawals		72,000
Service Revenue		901,200
Salaries Expense	393,720	
Advertising Expense		86,400
Miscellaneous Expense.	17,880	
	1,789,800	1,789,800

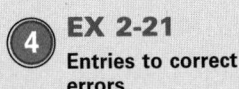

EX 2-21

Entries to correct errors

The following errors took place in journalizing and posting transactions:

1. Rent of $5,000 paid for the current month was recorded as a debit to Rent Expense and a credit to Prepaid Rent. The credit is in error.
2. A withdrawal of $19,000 by Rose Harding, owner of the business, was recorded as a debit to Wages Expense and a credit to Cash.

a. Journalize the entries to correct the errors. Include explanations.
b. Suppose the accountant used the definition of an asset to decide whether Prepaid Rent was the correct account. How would the definition of an asset have helped the accountant to realize that a credit entry was incorrect in part (a)?

EX 2-22

Entries to correct errors

The following errors took place in journalizing and posting transactions:

a. Cash of $3,750 received on account was recorded as a debit to Fees Earned and a credit to Cash.
b. A $150 purchase of items for a birthday party for cash was recorded as a debit to Miscellaneous Expense and a credit to Accounts Payable.

Journalize the entries to correct the errors. Include explanations.

PROBLEMS SERIES A

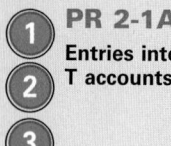

PR 2-1A

Entries into T accounts

Misha Zetkova opened a health food consulting business on October 1, 2015. During the month, the following transactions occurred:

a. Misha transferred $5,000 from a personal bank account to an account to be used for the business.
b. Paid advertising expense, $1,800.
c. A client called to book Misha's time in November; Misha gave a quote of $1,000.
d. Misha completed a review of a client's dietary intake for one week and charged the client $500. The client has not yet paid.
e. Paid cash for miscellaneous items, $50.
f. Paid telephone bill for the month, $180.
g. Withdrew cash for personal use, $2,000.

Instructions

Record the above transactions directly in the following T accounts, without journalizing: Cash; Accounts Receivable; Misha Zetkova, Capital; Misha Zetkova, Withdrawals; Advertising Expense; Miscellaneous Expense; Fees Earned; Telephone Expense. To the left of each amount entered in the accounts, place the appropriate letter to identify the transaction.

PR 2-2A

Entries into T accounts
Unadjusted trial balance

✔ 3. Total of Debit column: $49,700

Robin Godin, an architect, opened an office on April 1, 2015. During the month, he completed the following transactions connected with his professional practice:

a. Transferred cash from a personal bank account to an account to be used for the business, $30,000.
b. Paid April rent for office and workroom, $3,000.
c. Paid cash for supplies, $1,450.
d. Purchased office and computer equipment on account, $6,000.
e. Decided to purchase insurance but could not choose between a $1,000 plan and a $1,200 plan.
f. Received cash from a client for plans delivered, $7,500.
g. Paid cash for miscellaneous expenses, $500.
h. Received invoice for blueprint service, due in May, $1,000.
i. Recorded fee earned on plans delivered, payment to be received in May, $5,200.

Instructions

1. Record the above transactions directly in the following T accounts, without journalizing: Cash; Accounts Receivable; Supplies; Equipment; Accounts Payable; Robin Godin, Capital; Professional Fees; Rent Expense; Blueprint Expense; Miscellaneous Expense. To the left of each amount entered in the accounts, place the appropriate letter to identify the transaction.
2. Determine account balances of the T accounts. Accounts containing a single entry only (such as Supplies) do not need a balance.
3. Prepare an unadjusted trial balance as at April 30, 2015.

PR 2-3A

Entries into T accounts
Unadjusted trial balance

✔ 3. Total of Debit column: $29,710

James Weicker, a mechanic, opened a mobile repair business on June 1, 2015. The following are selected transactions from the first month:

a. Transferred cash from a personal bank account to an account to be used for the business, $15,000.
b. Purchased a used van for $19,500, paying $5,000 in cash and giving a note payable for the remainder.
c. Purchased equipment on account, $1,450.
d. Paid cash for insurance for the following year, $800.
e. Paid cash to creditors on account, $1,450.

f.   Received an invoice, due in July, for a new window on the van, $460.
g.   Paid salary of assistant, $1,200.
h.   Paid installment due on note payable, $250.
i.   Paid gas and oil for the van, $400.

Instructions

1.   Record the above transactions directly in the following T accounts, without journalizing: Cash; Prepaid Insurance; Automobiles; Equipment; Accounts Payable; Note Payable; James Weicker, Capital; Salary Expense; Automobile Expense. To the left of each amount entered in the accounts, place the appropriate letter to identify the transaction.
2.   Determine account balances of the T accounts. Accounts containing a single entry only (such as Prepaid Insurance) do not need a balance.
3.   Prepare an unadjusted trial balance as at June 30, 2015.

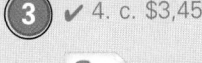

PR 2-4A

Journalizing and posting

✔ 4. c. $3,450

On October 1, 2015, Cody Doerr established Mudcat Realty, which completed the following transactions during the month:

a.   Cody Doerr transferred cash from a personal bank account to an account to be used for the business, $17,500.
b.   Purchased supplies on account, $1,000.
c.   Earned sales commissions, receiving cash, $12,250.
d.   Paid rent on office and equipment for the month, $3,800.
e.   Paid creditor on account, $600.
f.   Withdrew cash for personal use, $3,000.
g.   Bought a new flat screen television for his bedroom, using a company cheque, $1,000.
h.   Paid automobile expenses (including rental charge) for month, $1,500, and miscellaneous expenses, $400.
i.   Paid office salaries, $3,100.

Instructions

1.   Journalize entries for transactions (a) through (i), using the following account titles: Cash; Supplies; Accounts Payable; Cody Doerr, Capital; Cody Doerr, Withdrawals; Sales Commissions; Rent Expense; Office Salaries Expense; Automobile Expense; Miscellaneous Expense. Journal entry explanations may be omitted.
2.   Prepare T accounts, using the account titles in (1). Post the journal entries to these accounts, placing the appropriate letter to the left of each amount to identify the transactions. Determine the account balances after all posting is complete. Accounts containing only a single entry do not need a balance.
3.   Prepare an unadjusted trial balance as at October 31, 2015.
4.   Determine the following:
     a. Amount of total revenue recorded in the ledger.
     b. Amount of total expenses recorded in the ledger.
     c. Amount of net income for October.

PR 2-5A

Journalizing and posting
Unadjusted trial balance

✔ 3. Total of Credit column: $38,600

On July 1, 2015, Andrea Robson established an interior decorating business, Finishing Designs. During the month, Andrea completed the following transactions:

July 1.   Andrea transferred cash from a personal bank account to an account to be used for the business, $18,000.
      4.   Paid rent for period of July 4 to end of month, $1,750.
     13.   Purchased equipment on account, $7,000.
     14.   Purchased supplies for cash, $1,200.
     15.   Received cash for job completed, $7,500.
     21.   Paid creditor a portion of the amount owed for equipment purchased on July 13, $2,500.
     24.   Recorded jobs completed on account and sent invoices to customers, $8,600.
     27.   Paid utilities expense, $900.
     31.   Withdrew cash for personal use, $2,000.

(*continued*)

Instructions

1. Journalize each transaction in a two-column journal, referring to the following chart of accounts in selecting the accounts to be debited and credited. (Do not insert the account numbers in the journal at this time.) Journal entry explanations may be omitted.

1010	Cash		3010	Andrea Robson, Capital
1020	Accounts Receivable		3020	Andrea Robson, Withdrawals
1030	Supplies		4010	Fees Earned
1060	Equipment		5030	Rent Expense
2020	Accounts Payable		5040	Utilities Expense

2. Post the journal to a ledger of three-column accounts, inserting appropriate posting references as each item is posted. Extend the balances after each transaction is posted, and note whether the balance is a debit or credit.

3. Prepare an unadjusted trial balance as at July 31, 2015.

PR 2-6A

Journalizing and posting

Unadjusted trial balance

✔ 3. Total of Debit column: $24,900

On September 1, 2015, Colton Davies established an organizing business, Get Rid of It. During the month, Colton completed the following transactions:

Sep. 1. Colton deposited money into the business bank account, from his pocket, $300.
3. Colton borrowed $15,000 from his mother. She said that the company can owe her for the whole amount.
6. Colton purchased a one-year insurance policy, $1,200.
10. Recorded jobs completed but not yet paid and sent invoices to customers, $8,600.
12. Purchased a digital pocket camera on his own credit card as a gift for a relative in China, $750.
12. Received cash for a job to be started next month, $1,000.
20. Paid miscellaneous expenses, $315.
24. Received cash from customers on account, $3,600.
30. Paid wages of employees, $2,400.

Instructions

1. Journalize each transaction in a two-column journal, referring to the following chart of accounts in selecting the accounts to be debited and credited. (Do not insert the account numbers in the journal at this time.) Explanations may be omitted.

1010	Cash		3010	Colton Davies, Capital
1020	Accounts Receivable		4010	Fees Earned
1050	Prepaid Insurance		5010	Wages Expense
2020	Unearned Deposit		5090	Miscellaneous Expense
2030	Loan Payable			

2. Post the journal to a ledger of three-column accounts, inserting appropriate posting references as each item is posted. Extend the balances after each transaction is posted, and note whether the balance is a debit or credit.

3. Prepare an unadjusted trial balance as at September 30, 2015.

PR 2-7A

Journalizing and posting

Unadjusted trial balance

✔ 4. Total of Debit column: $536,250

Roundhouse Realty acts as an agent in buying, selling, renting, and managing real estate. The unadjusted trial balance on July 31, 2015, is shown below.

Roundhouse Realty
Unadjusted Trial Balance
July 31, 2015

	Debit Balances	Credit Balances
1010 Cash.	33,920	
1020 Accounts Receivable	57,200	
1040 Office Supplies.	1,600	
1060 Land.	—	
2010 Accounts Payable.		9,920
2030 Notes Payable		—
3010 Jeremiah Rilkoff, Capital.		38,480
3020 Jeremiah Rilkoff, Withdrawals	25,600	
4010 Fees Earned.		344,800
5010 Salaries and Commission Expense.	224,000	
5020 Rent Expense	28,000	
5030 Advertising Expense	22,880	
	393,200	393,200

The following business transactions were completed by Roundhouse Realty during August 2015:

Aug. 2.   Paid rent on office for month, $4,000.
   3.   Received cash from clients on account, $44,600.
   5.   Hired a new real estate agent, estimated income, $2,000/week. She starts next week.
   17.   Paid advertising expense, $5,500.
   23.   Paid creditors on account, $4,950.
   31.   Paid salaries and commissions for the month, $27,800.
   31.   Recorded revenue earned and billed to clients during the month, $83,000.
   31.   Purchased land for a future building site for $75,000, paying $10,000 in cash and giving a note payable for the remainder.
   31.   Withdrew cash for personal use, $5,000.

Instructions

1.   Record the August 1, 2015, balance of each account in a three-column ledger, noting if it is a debit or credit. Write *Balance* in the item section, and place a check mark (✓) in the Posting Reference column.
2.   Journalize the transactions for August in a two-column journal. Journal entry explanations may be omitted.
3.   Post the journal entries to the ledger, extending the account balance and noting debit or credit after each posting of the balance.
4.   Prepare an unadjusted trial balance as at August 31, 2015.

 **PR 2-8A**
Journalizing and posting
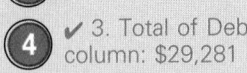 **Unadjusted trial balance**

 ✔ 3. Total of Debit column: $29,281

Ribbons & Lace Custom Sewing performs custom sewing for its clients. The unadjusted trial balance on September 30, 2015, is shown below:

(*continued*)

Ribbons & Lace Custom Sewing
Unadjusted Trial Balance
September 30, 2015

		Debit Balances	Credit Balances
1010	Cash	2,578	
1020	Accounts Receivable	2,891	
1030	Prepaid Insurance	1,100	
1040	Sewing Supplies	2,410	
2010	Accounts Payable		3,801
2020	Unearned Revenue		2,613
3010	Wendy Nicholson, Capital		1,036
3020	Wendy Nicholson, Withdrawals	7,200	
4010	Fees Earned		19,541
5010	Piecework Expense	1,741	
5030	Rent Expense	4,510	
5040	Automobile Expense	4,520	
5090	Miscellaneous Expense	41	
		26,991	26,991

The following business transactions were completed by Ribbons & Lace Custom Sewing during October:

Oct. 1. Purchased sewing supplies on account, $1,100.
  3. Signed and paid for a new insurance policy for the year, $850.
  9. Returned a portion of the sewing supplies purchased on October 1, receiving full credit for their cost, $300.
  15. Paid miscellaneous expense, $15.
  25. Received payment in advance from a client who has not received any sewing from Ribbons & Lace, $400.
  26. Paid automobile expense, $500.
  27. Received cash from customers on account, $600.
  30. Paid subcontractors for piecework sewing, $400.
  30. Recorded revenue earned and billed to clients during the month, $1,090.

Instructions

1. Record the October 1, 2015, balance of each account in a three-column ledger, noting if it is a debit or credit. Write Balance in the item section, and insert a check mark (✔) in the Posting Reference column.
2. Journalize the transactions for October in a two-column journal. Explanations may be omitted.
3. Post the journal entries to the ledger, extending the account balance and noting debit or credit after each posting of the balance.
4. Prepare an unadjusted trial balance as at October 31, 2015.

PR 2-9A

Errors in trial balance

✔ 7. Total of Credit column: $43,086.60

If the working papers correlating with this textbook are not used, omit Problem 2-9A.

The following records of Hallmark Electronic Repair are presented in the working papers:

- Journal containing entries for the period May 1–31.
- Ledger to which the May entries have been posted.
- Preliminary trial balance as at May 31, which does not balance.

Locate the errors, supply the information requested, and prepare a corrected trial balance according to the following instructions. The balances recorded in the accounts as at May 1 and the entries in the journal are correctly stated. If it is necessary to correct any posted amounts in the ledger, a line should be drawn through the erroneous figure and the correct amount inserted above. Corrections or notations may be inserted on the preliminary trial balance in any manner desired. It is not necessary to complete all of the instructions if equal trial balance totals can be obtained earlier. However, the requirements of instructions (6) and (7) should be completed in any event.

Instructions

1. Verify the totals of the preliminary trial balance, inserting the correct amounts in the schedule provided in the working papers.

2. Compute the difference between the trial balance totals.

3. Compare the listings in the trial balance with the balances appearing in the ledger. List the errors in the space provided in the working papers.

4. Verify the accuracy of the balance of each account in the ledger. List the errors in the space provided in the working papers.

5. Trace the postings in the ledger back to the journal, using small check marks to identify items traced. Correct any amounts in the ledger that may be necessitated by errors in posting. List the errors in the space provided in the working papers.

6. Journalize as at May 31 the payment of $120 for gas and electricity. The bill had been paid on May 31 but was inadvertently omitted from the journal. Post to the ledger. (Revise any amounts necessitated by posting this entry.)

7. Prepare a new unadjusted trial balance.

PR 2-10A

4

Corrected trial balance

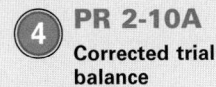

✔ 1. Total of Debit column: $468,600

Yin & Yang Video has the following unadjusted trial balance as at January 31, 2015:

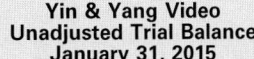

Yin & Yang Video Unadjusted Trial Balance January 31, 2015		
	Debit Balances	Credit Balances
Cash	19,000	
Accounts Receivable	34,100	
Supplies.	4,464	
Equipment.	108,000	
Notes Payable		45,000
Accounts Payable.		9,650
Chea Wynn, Capital		69,400
Chea Wynn, Withdrawals	23,500	
Fees Earned.		349,600
Wages Expense.	204,000	
Rent Expense.	41,700	
Advertising Expense.	19,800	
Gas, Electricity, and Water Expense	11,340	
	465,904	473,650

The debit and credit totals are not equal as a result of the following errors:

a. The balance of Cash was overstated by $10,000.

b. A cash receipt of $6,100 was posted as a debit to Cash of $1,600.

c. A debit of $3,500 to Accounts Receivable was not posted.

d. A return of $415 of defective supplies was erroneously posted as a $451 credit to Supplies.

e. The balance of Notes Payable was overstated by $9,000.

f. A credit of $1,450 in Accounts Payable was overlooked when the balance of the account was determined.

g. A debit of $2,500 for a withdrawal by the owner was posted as a debit to Chea Wynn, Capital.

h. The balance of $18,900 in Advertising Expense was entered as $19,800 in the trial balance.

i. Miscellaneous Expense, with a balance of $3,060, was omitted from the trial balance.

Instructions

1. Prepare a corrected unadjusted trial balance as at January 31, 2015.

2. Does the fact that the unadjusted trial balance in (1) is balanced mean that no errors occur in the accounts? Explain.

PR 2-11A
Correcting entries

4

The following errors took place in journalizing transactions:

a. A cash receipt of $6,100 was recorded as a debit to Cash of $1,600 and a credit to Accounts Receivable of $1,600.

b. A debit of $3,500 to Accounts Receivable was missed entirely, as was the credit entry to Fees Earned.

c. Supplies of $415 were returned and cash was received. This transaction was erroneously recorded as a $451 credit to Supplies and a $451 debit to Cash.

d. Supplies of $1,450 were purchased on account. The entry was not recorded.

Instructions

If necessary, use T accounts to record the original entry, the entry to remove it and, record the entry correctly.

PR 2-12A
Correcting entries

4

The following errors took place in journalizing transactions:

a. A purchase of a one-year insurance policy was recorded as a debit to Insurance Expense of $3,000 and a credit to Accounts Payable of $3,000. The company records its prepaid expenses to the balance sheet account.

b. The receipt of $3,500 for four months' rent was debited to Cash and credited to Fees Earned. The company records their unearned revenues to a balance sheet account.

c. A $15 cash purchase of supplies was erroneously recorded as a $51 debit to Supplies and a $51 credit to Accounts Payable.

d. A debit of $1,450 to Accounts Receivable and its balancing credit entry to Fees Earned were not recorded.

Instructions

1. Journalize the entries to correct the errors if necessary. Include explanations.
2. Explain why, in transaction a., the insurance policy is not considered an expense.

PROBLEMS SERIES B

PR 2-1B
Entries into T accounts

1
2
3

Daniel Hagell operates a gardening consulting business. His business had the following selected transactions:

a. Paid cash for miscellaneous items, $150.
b. Paid an insurance broker $900 in insurance premiums for two years' coverage.
c. Fees earned and billed to clients for the month, $4,000.
d. Paid the electricity bill, $50.
e. Paid creditors on account, $400.
f. Withdrew cash for personal use, $1,000.

Instructions

Record the above transactions directly in the following T accounts, without journalizing: Cash; Accounts Receivable; Prepaid Expense; Accounts Payable; Daniel Hagell, Capital; Daniel Hagell, Withdrawals; Miscellaneous Expense; Fees Earned; Utilities Expense. To the left of each amount entered in the accounts, place the appropriate letter to identify the transaction.

PR 2-2B
Entries into T accounts
Unadjusted trial balance

1
2
3
4

✔ 3. Total of Debit column: $35,125

Jay Lin, an architect, opened an office on July 1, 2015. During the month, he completed the following transactions connected with his professional practice:

a. Transferred cash from a personal bank account to an account to be used for the business, $20,000.
b. Paid July rent for office and workroom, $2,500.
c. Purchased office and computer equipment on account, $7,000.
d. Paid cash for supplies, $1,200.

e. Decided to purchase insurance, but could not choose between a $1,000 plan and a $1,200 plan.
f. Received cash from client for plans delivered, $4,175.
g. Received invoice for blueprint service, due in August, $800.
h. Recorded fee earned on plans delivered, payment to be received in August, $3,150.

Instructions

1. Record the above transactions directly in the following T accounts, without journalizing: Cash; Accounts Receivable; Supplies; Equipment; Accounts Payable; Jay Lin, Capital; Professional Fees; Rent Expense; Blueprint Expense. To the left of the amount entered in the accounts, place the appropriate letter to identify the transaction.
2. Determine account balances of the T accounts. Accounts containing a single entry only (such as Supplies) do not need a balance.
3. Prepare an unadjusted trial balance as at July 31, 2015.

PR 2-3B
Entries into T accounts
Unadjusted trial balance

✔ 3. Total of Debit column: $44,560

Karen Furber, a photographer, opened Gratitude in Photography on January 1, 2015. Selected transactions from the first month are below:

a. Transferred cash into the business, $20,000.
b. Purchased used automobile for $22,300, paying $5,000 in cash and giving a note payable for the remainder.
c. Paid cash for insurance for the following year, $900.
d. Purchased camera equipment on account, $7,000.
e. Received invoice, due in February, for van repairs, $560.
f. Paid installment due on note payable, $300.
g. Paid gas and oil on automobile for January, $400.

Instructions

1. Record the above transactions directly in the following T accounts, without journalizing: Cash; Prepaid Insurance; Automobiles; Camera Equipment; Accounts Payable; Note Payable; Karen Furber, Capital; Automobile Expense. To the left of each amount entered into the accounts, place the appropriate letter to identify the transaction.
2. Determine account balances of the T accounts. Accounts containing a single entry only (such as Prepaid Insurance) do not need a balance.
3. Prepare an unadjusted trial balance as at January 31, 2015.

PR 2-4B
Journalizing and posting
Unadjusted trial balance

✔ 4. c. $11,600

On August 1, 2015, Cheryl Newsome established Titus Realty, which completed the following transactions during the month:

a. Cheryl Newsome transferred cash from a personal bank account to an account to be used for the business, $25,000.
b. Paid rent on office and equipment for the month, $2,750.
c. Purchased supplies on account, $950.
d. Paid creditor on account, $400.
e. Earned sales commissions, receiving cash, $18,100.
f. Paid automobile expenses (including rental charge) for month, $1,000, and miscellaneous expenses, $600.
g. Paid office salaries, $2,150.
h. Withdrew cash for personal use, $2,000.
i. Paid for a new home stereo unit with personal cash, $785.

Instructions

1. Journalize entries for transactions (a) through (i), using the following account titles: Cash; Supplies; Accounts Payable; Cheryl Newsome, Capital; Cheryl Newsome, Withdrawals; Sales Commissions; Office Salaries Expense; Rent Expense; Automobile Expense; Miscellaneous Expense. Explanations may be omitted.

(continued)

2. Prepare T accounts, using the account titles in (1). Post the journal entries to these accounts, placing the appropriate letter to the left of each amount to identify the transactions. Determine the account balances after all posting is complete. Accounts containing only a single entry do not need a balance.

3. Prepare an unadjusted trial balance as at August 31, 2015.

4. Determine the following:

    a. Amount of total revenue recorded in the ledger.

    b. Amount of total expenses recorded in the ledger.

    c. Amount of net income for August.

PR 2-5B

①

Journalizing and posting

②

Unadjusted trial balance

③

④ ✔ 3. Total of Credit column: $37,000

On April 1, 2015, Alykhan Sunderji established an interior decorating business, Yaletown Interiors. During the month, Alykhan completed the following transactions:

Apr. 1. Alykhan transferred cash from a personal bank account to an account to be used for the business, $15,000.

       2. Paid rent for period of April 2 to end of month, $2,350.

       6. Purchased office equipment on account, $10,000.

      10. Purchased supplies for cash, $1,200.

      12. Received cash for job completed, $8,500.

      15. Sent his girlfriend flowers paid for on his own credit card, $90.

      23. Recorded jobs completed on account and sent invoices to customers, $6,000.

      29. Paid utilities expense, $1,100.

      30. Paid creditor a portion of the amount owed for equipment purchased on April 6, $2,500.

Instructions

1. Journalize each transaction in a two-column journal, referring to the following chart of accounts in selecting the accounts to be debited and credited. (Do not insert the account numbers in the journal at this time.) Explanations may be omitted.

1010	Cash	3010	Alykhan Sunderji, Capital
1020	Accounts Receivable	4010	Fees Earned
1030	Supplies	5030	Rent Expense
1060	Equipment	5040	Utilities Expense
2020	Accounts Payable		

2. Post the journal to a ledger of three-column accounts, inserting appropriate posting references as each item is posted. Extend the balances after each transaction is posted, and note whether the balance is a debit or credit.

3. Prepare an unadjusted trial balance as at April 30, 2015.

PR 2-6B

①

Journalizing and posting

②

Unadjusted trial balance

③

④ ✔ Total of Debit column: $18,260

On May 1, 2015, Alexis Nieuwkerk established an organizing business, GO! During the month, Alexis completed the following transactions:

May 1. Deposited money into the business bank account, $600.

      3. Borrowed $13,000 from her father, who said that the company can owe him for it.

      6. Purchased a one-year insurance policy, $900.

     10. Recorded jobs completed but not yet paid and sent invoices to customers, $3,200.

     12. Purchased T-shirts imprinted with GO! for advertising purposes, using her own credit card, $560.

     12. Received cash for a job to be started next month, $900.

     20. Paid miscellaneous expenses, $315.

     24. Received cash from customers on account, $2,200.

     30. Paid wages of employees, $2,400.

Instructions

1. Journalize each transaction in a two-column journal, referring to the following chart of accounts in selecting the accounts to be debited and credited. (Do not insert the account numbers in the journal at this time.) Explanations may be omitted.

1010	Cash	3010	Alexis Nieuwkerk, Capital
1020	Accounts Receivable	4010	Fees Earned
1050	Prepaid Insurance	5010	Wages Expense
2020	Unearned Revenue	5030	Advertising Expense
2030	Loan Payable	5090	Miscellaneous Expense

2. Post the journal to a ledger of three-column accounts, inserting appropriate posting references as each item is posted. Extend the balance after each transaction is posted, and note whether the balance is a debit or credit.
3. Prepare an unadjusted trial balance as at May 31, 2015.

PR 2-7B

Journal entries and trial balance

Unadjusted trial balance

✔ 4. Total of Debit column: $255,640

Kane Realty acts as an agent in buying, selling, renting, and managing real estate. The unadjusted trial balance on October 31, 2015, is shown below.

Kane Realty
Unadjusted Trial Balance
October 31, 2015

		Debit Balances	Credit Balances
1010	Cash	13,150	
1020	Accounts Receivable	33,750	
1040	Office Supplies	900	
1060	Land	—	
2010	Accounts Payable		6,510
2030	Notes Payable		—
3010	Nicole Russell, Capital		11,790
3020	Nicole Russell, Withdrawals	1,000	
4010	Fees Earned		128,500
5010	Salary and Commission Expense	74,100	
5020	Rent Expense	15,000	
5030	Advertising Expense	8,900	
		146,800	146,800

The following business transactions were completed by Kane Realty during November 2015:

Nov. 1. Paid rent on office for month, $3,000.
5. Hired a new secretary, $1,200 per week. She starts next week.
10. Received cash from clients on account, $25,000.
15. Purchased land for a future building site for $90,000, paying $10,000 in cash and giving a note payable for the remainder.
17. Paid creditors on account, $2,910.
23. Paid advertising expense, $1,250.
30. Recorded revenue earned and billed to clients during the month, $31,750.
30. Paid salaries and commissions for the month, $13,500.
30. Withdrew cash for personal use, $1,000.

Instructions

1. Record the November 1, 2015, balance of each account in a three-column ledger, noting if it is a debit or credit. Write *Balance* in the item section, and place a check mark (✔) in the Posting Reference column.
2. Journalize the transactions for November in a two-column journal. Journal entry explanations may be omitted.
3. Post the journal entries to the ledger, extending the account balance and noting debit or credit after each posting of the balance.
4. Prepare an unadjusted trial balance as at November 30, 2015.

PR 2-8B

1 **2** **3**

Journalizing and posting

Unadjusted trial balance

4 ✔ Total of Debit column: $223,342

Amplitude Productions Company produces documentaries. The unadjusted trial balance on April 30, 2015, is shown below:

Amplitude Productions Company
Unadjusted Trial Balance
April 30, 2015

		Debit Balances	Credit Balances
1010	Cash	125,845	
1020	Accounts Receivable	25,742	
1040	Office Supplies	1,410	
1050	Prepaid Insurance	—	
2010	Accounts Payable		5,723
2020	Unearned Revenue		15,753
3010	Thomas de Bastiani, Capital		47,482
3020	Thomas de Bastiani, Withdrawals	2,000	
4010	Fees Earned		145,784
5010	Salary Expense	55,432	
5040	Automobile Expense	3,863	
5090	Miscellaneous Expense	450	
		214,742	214,742

The following business transactions were completed by Amplitude Productions Company during May:

May 1. Purchased office supplies on account, $1,000
5. Returned a portion of the office supplies purchased on May 1, receiving full credit for their cost, $400.
8. Arranged and paid for insurance for the next documentary, $1,200 for the duration of the production.
10. Received cash from ticket sales on account, $15,000.
15. Discovered an error in computing salary; received cash from the producer for the overpayment, $2,000.
25. An interested party deposited $3,000 in the company's account, as a deposit to encourage the company to start work on a documentary in the following year.
26. Paid automobile expense, $750.
27. Paid miscellaneous expenses, $600.
30. Paid salaries for the month, $8,000.
30. Recorded revenue earned and billed to client for last documentary during the month, $5,000.

Instructions

1. Record the May 1, 2015, balance of each account in a three-column ledger, noting if it is a debit or credit. Write Balance in the item section, and place a check mark (✔) in the Posting Reference column.
2. Journalize the transactions for May in a two-column journal. Explanations may be omitted.
3. Post the journal entries to the ledger, extending the account balance and noting debit or credit after each posting of the balance.
4. Prepare an unadjusted trial balance as at May 31, 2015.

---

4 **PR 2-9B**

Errors in trial balance

✔ 7. Total of Debit column: $43,086.60

If the working papers correlating with this textbook are not used, omit Problem 2-9B.

The following records of Hallmark Electronic Repair are presented in the working papers:

- Journal containing entries for the period May 1–31.
- Ledger to which the May entries have been posted.
- Preliminary trial balance as at May 31, which does not balance.

Locate the errors, supply the information requested, and prepare a corrected trial balance according to the following instructions. The balances recorded in the accounts as at May 1 and the entries in the journal are correctly stated. If it is necessary to correct any posted amounts in the ledger, a line should be drawn through the erroneous figure and the correct amount inserted above. Corrections or notations may be inserted on the preliminary trial balance in any manner desired. It is not necessary to complete all of the instructions if equal trial balance totals can be obtained earlier. However, the requirements of instructions (6) and (7) should be completed in any event.

Instructions

1. Verify the totals of the preliminary trial balance, inserting the correct amounts in the schedule provided in the working papers.
2. Compute the difference between the trial balance totals.
3. Compare the listings in the trial balance with the balances appearing in the ledger. List the errors in the space provided in the working papers.
4. Verify the accuracy of the balance of each account in the ledger. List the errors in the space provided in the working papers.
5. Trace the postings in the ledger back to the journal, using small check marks to identify items traced. Correct any amounts in the ledger that may be necessitated by errors in posting. List the errors in the space provided in the working papers.
6. Journalize as at May 31 the payment of $175 for advertising expense. The bill had been paid on May 31 but was inadvertently omitted from the journal. Post to the ledger. (Revise any amounts necessitated by posting this entry.)
7. Prepare a new unadjusted trial balance.

PR 2-10B
Corrected trial balance

Damascus Carpet has the following unadjusted trial balance as at August 31, 2015.

✔ 1. Total of Debit
column: $347,670

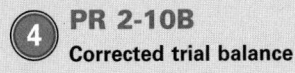

Damascus Carpet
Unadjusted Trial Balance
August 31, 2015

	Debit Balances	Credit Balances
Cash	8,650	
Accounts Receivable	21,760	
Supplies	4,195	
Equipment	98,000	
Notes Payable		45,675
Accounts Payable		13,825
Isaiah Betts, Capital		67,200
Isaiah Betts, Withdrawals	25,375	
Fees Earned		212,395
Wages Expense	122,500	
Rent Expense	29,050	
Advertising Expense	1,260	
Miscellaneous Expense	2,540	
	313,330	339,275

The debit and credit totals are not equal as a result of the following errors:

a. The balance of Cash was understated by $5,250.
b. A cash receipt of $3,600 was posted as a debit to Cash of $6,300.
c. A debit of $2,250 to Accounts Receivable was not posted.
d. The balance of Notes Payable was understated by $13,125.
e. A credit of $1,575 in Accounts Payable was overlooked when determining the balance of the account.
f. A debit of $6,125 for a withdrawal by the owner was posted as a credit to Isaiah Betts, Capital.
g. The balance of $12,600 in Advertising Expense was entered as $1,260 in the trial balance.
h. Gas, Electricity, and Water Expense, with a balance of $12,075, was omitted from the trial balance.

(continued)

Instructions

1. Prepare a corrected unadjusted trial balance as at August 31, 2015.
2. Does the fact that the unadjusted trial balance in (1) is balanced mean that there are no errors in the accounts? Explain.

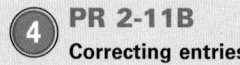

PR 2-11B
Correcting entries

The following errors took place in journalizing transactions:

a. A cash receipt of $3,600 was recorded as a debit to Cash of $6,300 and a credit to Accounts Receivable of $6,300.
b. A debit of $2,100 to Accounts Receivable and its corresponding credit entry to Fees Earned were missed entirely.
c. A return of $312 of defective supplies was erroneously posted as a $321 credit to Supplies and a debit to Cash.
d. A deposit of $2,000 for next month's rent was received. It was recorded as a debit to Cash and a credit to Fees Earned.

Instructions

If necessary, use T accounts to record the original entry, the entry to remove it and, record the entry correctly.

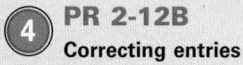

PR 2-12B
Correcting entries

The following errors took place in journalizing transactions:

a. A purchase of a one-year insurance policy was recorded as a debit to Insurance Expense of $2,730 and a credit to Accounts Payable of $2,730. The company records its prepaid expenses to the balance sheet account.
b. Cash was received for prepaid rent. A rent deposit for four months of $6,000 was debited to Cash and credited to Fees Earned. The company records prepaid rent to a balance sheet account.
c. A $65 cash purchase for refreshments for the staff was erroneously posted as a $56 debit to Miscellaneous Expense and a $56 credit to Accounts Payable.
d. A debit of $2,100 to Accounts Receivable and a credit of $2,100 to Fees Earned were missed.

Instructions

1. Journalize the entries to correct the errors. Include explanations.
2. Explain why, in transaction a., the insurance policy is not considered an expense.

CONTINUING PROBLEM

The transactions completed by Music Depot during November 2015 were described at the end of Chapter 1. The following transactions were completed during December, the second month of the business's operations:

✔ 4. Total of Debit
column: $30,800

December 1. Paid a premium of $2,700 for a comprehensive insurance policy covering liability, theft, and fire. The policy covers a one-year period.
2. Received $1,250 on account.
3. On behalf of Music Depot, Pat signed a contract with a local radio station, CHBD, to provide guest spots for the next three months. The contract requires Music Depot to provide a guest disc jockey for 80 hours per month for a monthly fee of $3,600. Any additional hours beyond 80 will be billed to CHBD at $40 per hour. In accordance with the contract, Pat received $7,200 from CHBD as an advance payment for the first two months.
3. Paid $250 on account.
5. Purchased office equipment on account from One-Stop Office Mart, $6,000.
8. Paid for a newspaper advertisement, $200.
11. Received $900 for serving as a disc jockey for a party.

23. Served as disc jockey for a party for $2,500. Received $760, with the remainder due January 4, 2016.

31. Paid $1,400 royalties (music expense) to Society of Composers, Authors and Music Publishers of Canada (SOCAN) for use of various artists' music during December.

31. Withdrew $1,500 cash from Music Depot for personal use.

Music Depot's chart of accounts and the balance of accounts as at December 1, 2015 (all normal balances), are as follows:

1010	Cash	$10,550	2020	Unearned Revenue	$ —
1020	Accounts Receivable	1,250	3010	Pat Sharpe, Capital	9,000
1040	Supplies	700	3020	Pat Sharpe, Withdrawals	500
1050	Prepaid Insurance	—	4010	Fees Earned	4,850
1070	Office Equipment	—	5040	Music Expense	1,000
2010	Accounts Payable	600	5050	Advertising Expense	450

Instructions

1. Enter the December 1, 2015, account balances, noting if it is a debit or credit. Write *Balance* in the Item column and place a check mark (✓) in the Posting Reference column. (*Hint:* Verify the equality of the debit and credit balances in the ledger before proceeding with the next instruction.)

2. Analyze and journalize each transaction in a two-column journal, omitting journal entry explanations.

3. Post the journal to the ledger, extending the account balance and noting whether it is a debit or credit after each posting of the balance.

4. Prepare an unadjusted trial balance as at December 31, 2015.

SPECIAL ACTIVITIES

SA 2-1

Ethics and professional conduct in business

At the end of the current month, Hannah Kinsey prepared a trial balance for Seaside Rescue Service. The credit side of the trial balance exceeds the debit side by a significant amount. Hannah has decided to add the difference to the balance of the miscellaneous expense account in order to complete the preparation of the current month's financial statements by a five o'clock deadline. Hannah will look for the difference next week when she has more time.

Discuss whether Hannah is behaving in a professional manner.

SA 2-2

Record transactions

The following discussion took place between Faye Lucas, the office manager of Blizzard Data Company, and a new accountant, Steve Haack.

Steve: I've been thinking about our method of recording entries. It seems that it's inefficient.

Faye: In what way?

Steve: Well—correct me if I'm wrong—it seems like we have unnecessary steps in the process. We could easily develop a trial balance by posting our transactions directly into the ledger and bypassing the journal altogether. In this way, we could combine the recording and posting process into one step and save ourselves a lot of time. What do you think?

Faye: We need to have a talk.

What should Faye say to Steve?

SA 2-3
Debits and credits

Group Project

The following excerpt is from a conversation between Barb Thiel, the president and chief operating officer of Diamond Construction Company, and her neighbour, Lloyd Crum.

Lloyd: Barb, I'm taking a course in night school, "Intro to Accounting." I was wondering—could you answer a couple of questions for me?

Barb: Well, I will if I can.

Lloyd: Okay, our instructor says that it's critical we understand the basic concepts of accounting, or we'll never get beyond the first test. My problem is with those rules of debit and credit...you know, assets increase with debits, decrease with credits, etc.

Barb: Yes, pretty basic stuff. You just have to memorize the rules. It shouldn't be too difficult.

Lloyd: Sure, I can memorize the rules, but my problem is I want to be sure I understand the basic concepts behind the rules. For example, why can't assets be increased with credits and decreased with debits like revenue? As long as everyone did it that way, why not? It would seem easier if we had the same rules for all increases and decreases in accounts. Also, why is the left side of an account called the debit side? Why couldn't it be called something simple...like the "LE" for Left Entry? The right side could be called just "RE" for Right Entry. Finally, why are there just two sides to an entry? Why can't there be three or four sides to an entry?

In a group of four or five, select one person to play the role of Barb and one person to play the role of Lloyd.

1. After listening to the conversation between Barb and Lloyd, help Barb answer Lloyd's questions.
2. What information (other than just debit and credit journal entries) could the accounting system gather that might be useful to Barb in managing Diamond Construction Company?

SA 2-4
Transactions and income statement

Cody Packwood is planning to manage and operate Ace Caddy Service at The Glen Golf and Country Club from June through August 2015. Cody will rent a small maintenance building from the country club for $600 per month and will offer caddy services, including cart rentals, to golfers. Cody has had no formal training in record keeping.

Cody keeps notes of all receipts and expenses in a shoe box. An examination of Cody's shoe box records for June revealed the following:

June 1. Withdrew $2,500 from personal bank account to be used to operate the caddy service.
      1. Paid rent to The Glen Golf and Country Club, $600.
      2. Paid for golf supplies, $750.
      3. Arranged for the rental of 25 regular (pulling) golf carts and 10 gasoline-driven carts for $2,000 per month. Paid $500 in advance, with the remaining $1,500 due June 20.
      7. Purchased supplies, including gasoline, for the golf carts on account, $500. The Glen Golf and Country Club has agreed to allow Cody to store the gasoline in one of its fuel tanks at no cost.
     15. Received cash for services from June 1–15, $2,350.
     17. Paid cash to creditors on account, $500.
     20. Paid remaining rental on golf carts, $1,500.
     22. Purchased supplies, including gasoline, on account, $400.
     25. Accepted IOUs from customers on account, $1,200.
     28. Paid miscellaneous expenses, $150.
     30. Received cash for services from June 16–30, $2,650.
     30. Paid telephone and electricity (utilities) expenses, $140.
     30. Paid wages of part-time employees, $450.
     30. Received cash in payment of IOUs on account, $800.

Cody has asked you several questions concerning his financial affairs to date, and he has asked you to assist with his record keeping and reporting of financial data.

a. To assist Cody with his record keeping, prepare a chart of accounts that would be appropriate for Ace Caddy Service.

b. Prepare an income statement for June to help Cody assess the profitability of Ace Caddy Service. For this purpose, the use of T accounts may be helpful in analyzing the effects of each June transaction.

c. Based on Cody's records of receipts and payments, calculate the amount of cash on hand on June 30. For this purpose, a T account for cash may be useful.

d. A count of the cash on hand on June 30 totalled $3,600. Briefly discuss the possible causes of the difference between the amount of cash computed in (c) and the actual amount of cash on hand.

SA 2-5
Opportunities for accountants

Internet Project

The increasing complexity of the current business and regulatory environment has created an increased demand for accountants who can analyze business transactions and interpret their effects on the financial statements. In addition, a basic ability to analyze the effects of transactions is necessary to be successful in all fields of business as well as in other disciplines, such as law. To better understand the importance of accounting in today's environment, search the Internet or your local newspaper for job opportunities. One possible Internet site is **www.monster.ca**. Then do one of the following:

1. Print a listing of at least two ads for accounting jobs. Alternatively, bring to class at least two newspaper ads for accounting jobs.

2. Print a listing of at least two ads for non-accounting jobs for which some knowledge of accounting is preferred or necessary. Alternatively, bring to class at least two newspaper ads for such jobs.

ROGERS MEDIA INC.

Do you subscribe to any magazines? Most of us sub-scribe to one or more magazines, such as *Flare*, *LouLou*, *Carguide*, *Cycle Canada*, *Reader's Digest*, or *The Hockey News*. Magazines usually require you to prepay the yearly sub-scription price before you receive any issues. When should the magazine company record revenue from subscriptions?

As we discussed in Chapter 2, sometimes revenues are earned and expenses are incurred when cash is received or paid. For transactions such as magazine subscriptions, the revenue is earned when the magazine is delivered, not when the cash is received. Most companies are required to account for revenues and expenses when the benefit is substantially provided or consumed, which may not be when cash is received or paid.

One company that records revenue from subscrip-tions is Rogers Media Inc. Rogers produces more than 70 different magazines and trade and professional publica-tions in Canada. Rogers not only publishes magazines but also handles radio and television broadcasting, including the Shopping Channel, and owns the Toronto Blue Jays Baseball Club and Rogers Centre.

Before preparing their financial statements, most companies, such as Rogers Media Inc., are required to update their accounting records for items such as revenues earned from magazine subscriptions. In this chapter, we describe and illustrate this updating process.

After studying this chapter, you should be able to:

1 Describe the nature of the adjusting process.

Nature of the Adjusting Process	The Adjusting Process	
	The Accounting Cycle	
	Types of Accounts Requiring Adjustment	EXAMPLE EXERCISE 3-1 (page 110) EXAMPLE EXERCISE 3-2 (page 110)

2 Journalize entries for accounts requiring adjustment.

Adjusting Entries	Prepaid Expenses	EXAMPLE EXERCISE 3-3 (page 114)
	Unearned Revenues	EXAMPLE EXERCISE 3-4 (page 115)
	Accrued Revenues	EXAMPLE EXERCISE 3-5 (page 117)
	Accrued Expenses	EXAMPLE EXERCISE 3-6 (page 119)
	Depreciation of Captial Assets	EXAMPLE EXERCISE 3-7 (page 120)

3 Summarize the adjustment process.

Summary of the Adjustment Process		EXAMPLE EXERCISE 3-8 (page 120)

4 Prepare an adjusted trial balance.

Adjusted Trial Balance	Financial Statements	EXAMPLE EXERCISE 3-9 (page 126)

A P P E N D I X 1 Alternative Methods of Recording Prepaid Expenses and Unearned Revenues

For the chapter *At a Glance*, turn to page 130.

Nature of the Adjusting Process

Describe the nature of the adjusting process.

When preparing financial statements, the economic life of the business is divided into time periods. These time periods are usually months, quarters, or years. Sole proprietorships, the types of businesses we have been discussing in Chapters 1 and 2, have December year-ends; their fiscal year-end is the same as the calendar year-end. Corporations, which will be covered in Chapters 12, 13, and 14, may have fiscal year-ends other than December. The **time period concept** requires that revenues and expenses be reported in the proper period. To determine the proper period, accountants use generally accepted accounting principles (GAAP). The use of the accrual basis of accounting is required by GAAP.

Under the **accrual basis of accounting**, transactions and events are reported in the income statement in the period in which they occur. For example, revenue is reported when the services are provided to customers because that is when the revenue is earned. Cash may or may not be received from customers during this period. The accounting principle supporting this reporting of revenues is called the **revenue recognition principle**.

Under the accrual basis, expenses are also reported in the same period that they occur. For example, utility expenses incurred in December are reported as an expense in December even though the utility bill may not be paid until January. This ensures that net income or loss for the period is properly reported on the income statement and reflects the economic reality of the business.

Although GAAP requires the accrual basis of accounting, some businesses use the **cash basis of accounting** if the difference between the two methods is small. Under the cash basis of accounting, revenues and expenses are reported in the income statement in the period in which cash is received or paid. For example, fees are recorded when cash is received from clients; likewise, wages are recorded when cash is paid to employees. The net income (or net loss) is the difference between the cash receipts (revenues) and the cash payments (expenses).

Some small businesses, such as fisheries, may use the cash basis because they have few receivables and payables. The cash basis provides financial statements similar to the statements provided by the accrual basis. For most large businesses, however, the cash basis will not provide accurate financial statements for user needs. For this reason, we use the accrual basis in this text.

The Adjusting Process

Steps 1 through 4 of the accounting cycle, discussed in Chapters 1 and 2, cover the journal entries made during an accounting period. At the end of the accounting period, many of the account balances in the ledger can be reported in the financial statements without change. For example, the balances of the cash and land accounts are normally the amounts reported on the balance sheet at the end of step 4.

Under the accrual basis, however, some accounts in the ledger require updating.[1] This updating is generated by the accounting department at the end of the month, quarter, or year. The number and type of adjusting entries depend on the underlying business. This chapter will cover some of the more common adjusting entries, which are required for the following reasons:

1. Some expenses are not recorded daily. For example, the daily use of supplies would require many entries with small amounts. Also, managers usually do not need to know the amount of supplies on hand on a day-to-day basis.

2. Some revenues and expenses are incurred as time passes rather than as separate transactions. For example, rent revenue received in advance (unearned rent revenue) expires and becomes revenue with the passage of time. Likewise, prepaid insurance expires and becomes an expense with the passage of time.

3. Some revenues and expenses may be unrecorded. For example, a company may have provided services to customers that it has not billed or recorded at the end of the accounting period. Likewise, a company may not pay its employees until the next accounting period even though the employees have earned their wages in the current period.

Note: All adjusting entries affect at least one income statement account and one balance sheet account and never involve cash.

The analysis and updating of accounts at the end of the period before the financial statements are prepared is called the **adjusting process**. The journal entries that bring the accounts up to date at the end of the accounting period are called **adjusting entries.** Step 5, the optional worksheet, is covered in Chapter 4, Appendix 2.

The Accounting Cycle

Step 6: Adjusting Entries Step 6 in the accounting cycle is the preparation of adjusting entries. See Exhibit 1 to locate the step in the overall cycle.

All adjusting entries affect at least one income statement account and one balance sheet account. Thus, an adjusting entry will *always* involve a revenue or an expense account *and* an asset or a liability account.

---

1 Under the cash basis of accounting, accounts do not require adjusting. This is because transactions are recorded only when cash is received or paid.

Exhibit 1

Steps of the Accounting Cycle

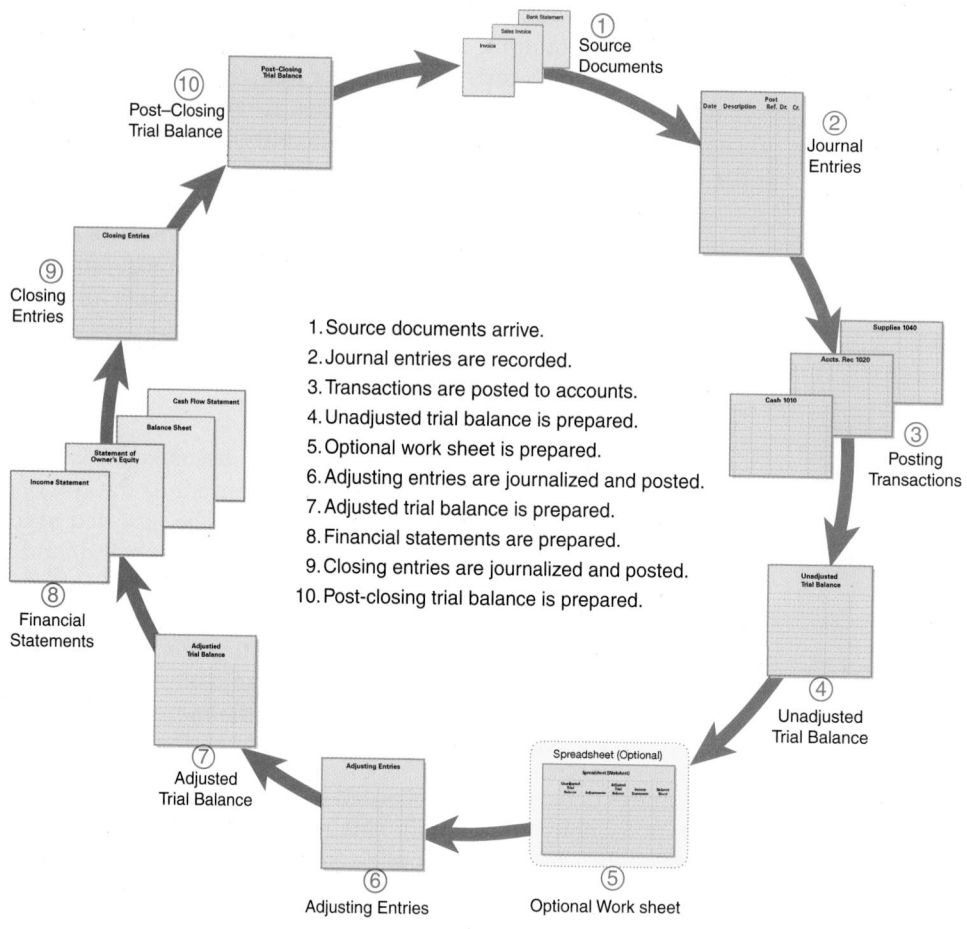

1. Source documents arrive.
2. Journal entries are recorded.
3. Transactions are posted to accounts.
4. Unadjusted trial balance is prepared.
5. Optional work sheet is prepared.
6. Adjusting entries are journalized and posted.
7. Adjusted trial balance is prepared.
8. Financial statements are prepared.
9. Closing entries are journalized and posted.
10. Post-closing trial balance is prepared.

Types of Accounts Requiring Adjustment

Five basic types of accounts require adjusting entries, as shown below.

1. Prepaid expenses
2. Unearned revenues
3. Accrued revenues
4. Accrued expenses
5. Depreciation of capital assets

Prepaid Expenses   Prepaid expenses are the advance payment of *future* expenses and are recorded as assets when cash is paid. They are not recorded as expenses because, although cash has traded hands, the expense has not occurred. Prepaid expenses fit the definition of an asset because they provide future benefits. Prepaid expenses become expenses over time or during normal operations. To illustrate, the following transaction of NetSolutions from Chapter 2 is used.

Note: The tuition you pay at the beginning of each term is an example of a prepaid expense to you, as a student.

Dec. 1   NetSolutions paid $2,400 as a premium on a one-year insurance policy.

On December 1, the cash payment of $2,400 is recorded as a debit to Prepaid Insurance and a credit to Cash for $2,400. At the end of December, only $200 ($2,400 divided by 12 months) of the insurance premium is expired and has become an expense. The remaining $2,200 of prepaid insurance will become an expense in future months.

Thus, the $200 is an insurance expense of December and should be recorded with an adjusting entry.

Other examples of prepaid expenses include supplies, prepaid advertising, and service contracts.

Exhibit 2 summarizes the nature of prepaid expenses

Prepaid Expenses

TRANSACTION *Cash is paid in advance for an expense.*

ANALYSIS Advance payments of future expenses are recorded as assets when the cash is paid. The transaction is recorded as a debit to a prepaid expense account and a credit to the cash account.

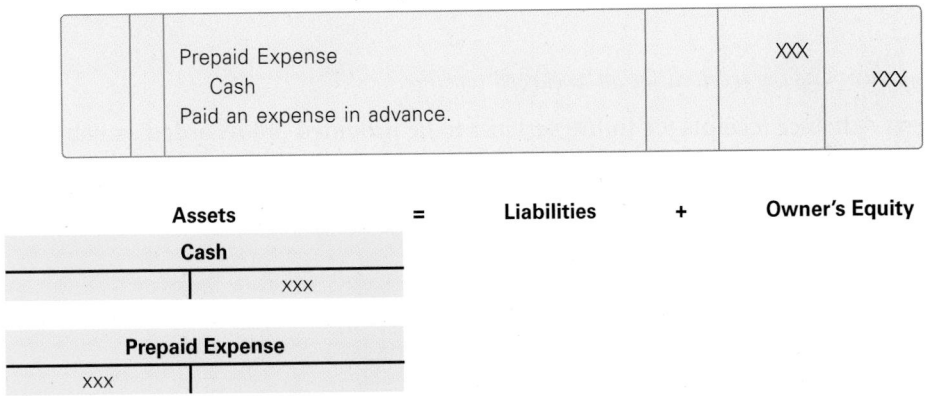

ADJUSTMENT *An end-of-period adjustment is needed to update the prepaid expense account.*

ANALYSIS The prepaid expense account is decreased (credited) by the amount of the prepaid expense that has expired or has been used, and the related expense account is increased (debited).

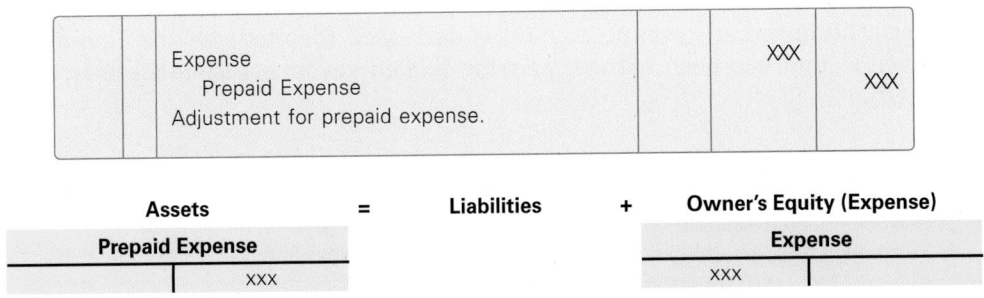

Unearned Revenues   Unearned revenues are the advance receipt of *future* revenues and are recorded as liabilities when cash is received. Unearned revenues become earned revenues over time or during normal operations. To illustrate, the following December 1 transaction of NetSolutions is used.

Dec. 1   NetSolutions received $360 from a local retailer to rent land for three months.

On December 1, the cash receipt of $360 is recorded as a debit to Cash and a credit to Unearned Rent for $360. The revenue recognition principle requires revenue to be earned before it is recognized. Because the payment received is for three months' rental of land, a portion of the revenue is recognized each month. Because the revenue has not been earned but the cash has been received, the unearned revenue represents a liability. At the end of December, $120 ($360 divided by 3 months) of the unearned rent has been earned. The remaining $240 will become rent revenue in future months. Thus, the $120 is rent revenue of December and should be recorded with an adjusting entry.

Other examples of unearned revenues include tuition received in advance by a school, a retainer fee received by a lawyer, premiums received in advance by an insurance company, and magazine subscriptions received in advance by a publisher as noted in the opening vignette on page 99.

Exhibit 3 summarizes the nature of unearned revenues.

Exhibit 3

Unearned Revenues

TRANSACTION *Cash is received for an unearned revenue.*

ANALYSIS Advance receipts for future services to be provided are recorded as liabilities when the cash is received. The transaction is recorded as a debit to the cash account and a credit to the unearned revenue account.

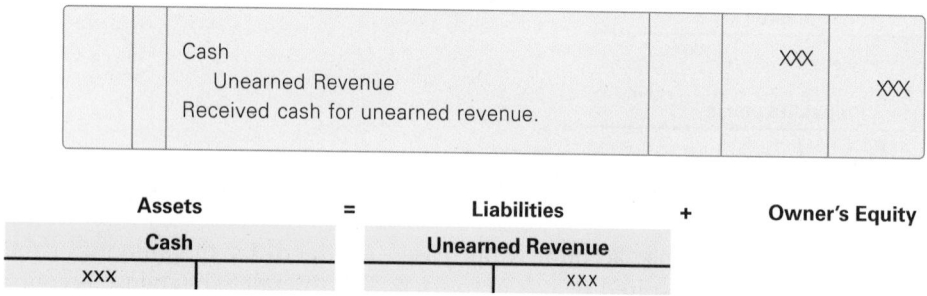

ADJUSTMENT *An end-of-period adjustment is needed to update the unearned revenue account.*

ANALYSIS The unearned revenue account is decreased (debited) for the amount of the revenue that has been earned, and the related revenue account is increased (credited).

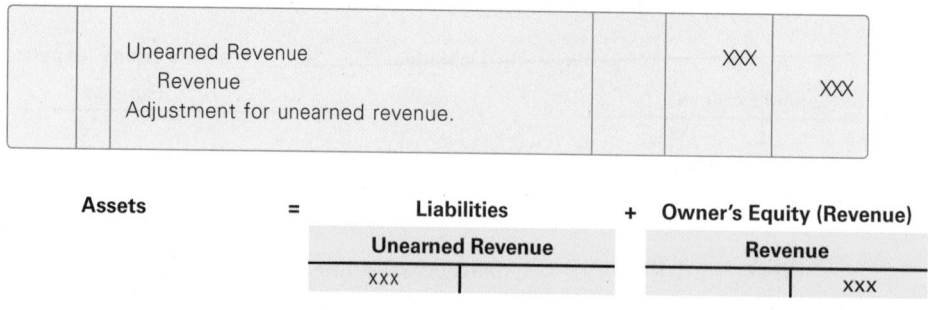

Accrued Revenues Accrued revenues are unrecorded revenues that have been earned and for which cash has yet to be received. An asset exists because a future inflow of economic benefit will be received—the cash. Fees for services that a lawyer or a consultant has provided but not yet billed are accrued revenues. The following example involving NetSolutions and one of its customers illustrates the adjustments needed to record accrued revenues.

> Dec. 15   NetSolutions signed an agreement with Dankner Co. to invoice Dankner Co. on the 15th of each month for services rendered during the previous month, at the rate of $20 per hour.

From December 16 to 31, NetSolutions provided 25 hours of service to Dankner Co. Although the revenue of $500 (25 hours × $20) has been earned, it will not be invoiced until January 15. Likewise, cash of $500 will not be received until Dankner pays its invoice. Thus, the $500 of accrued revenue and the $500 of fees earned should be recorded with an adjusting entry on December 31.

Other examples of accrued revenues include accrued interest on **notes receivable** and accrued rent on property rented to others.

Because Net Solutions does not have a note payable to illustrate, we use the following transaction:

A note receivable is a written promise from one party to another party to pay an amount and interest at an agreed-upon rate in the future. Assume that a company has a 90-day, 6% note receivable dated November 15, 2015. On November 15, the company records the note as follows:

2015				
Nov.	15	Note Receivable	6,000	
		Cash		6,000
		To record note receivable.		

In this example at the year-end of December 31, 2015, the other party owes interest on the note receivable. The business in our example will be receiving the interest in the future. Note that the interest is not due until the note receivable is paid. The company should record an adjusting entry for the accrued interest revenue at the end of the period. In this example, November has 30 days, and interest is owed on 15 days, from November 16 to 30. December has 31 days, making a total of 46 days of interest. The interest rate is stated as a yearly amount.

The interest on a note is computed as follows:

Interest = Principal × Interest Rate × (Term/365 days) or (Term/12 months)

In our example, the calculation is as follows:

Accrued Interest = $6,000 × 6% × 46/365

Accrued Interest = $45.37

The interest on the note is recorded by the following entry:

2015				
Dec.	31	Interest Receivable	45.37	
		Interest Income		45.37
		Accrued interest receivable ($6,000 × 6% × 46/365).		

Exhibit 4 summarizes the nature of accrued revenues.

Exhibit 4

Accrued Revenues

TRANSACTION *Revenue has been earned, but has not been recorded.*

ANALYSIS Revenues have been earned, but the revenue has not been recorded nor has cash been received. No journal entry has been recorded even though revenues have been earned.

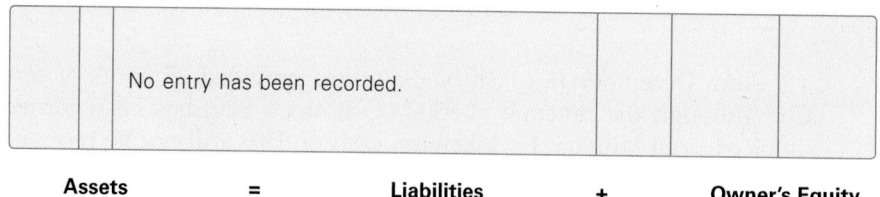

	No entry has been recorded.			

Assets	**=**	**Liabilities**	**+**	**Owner's Equity**

No impact since the revenue has not been recorded.

ADJUSTMENT *An end-of-period adjustment is needed to recognize accrued revenue.*

ANALYSIS An asset account is increased (debited) for the amount of the revenue that has been earned, and the related revenue account is increased (credited). The type of receivable account that is debited depends upon the type of revenue. For example, Accounts Receivable would be debited for fees earned. Interest Receivable would be debited for interest earned.

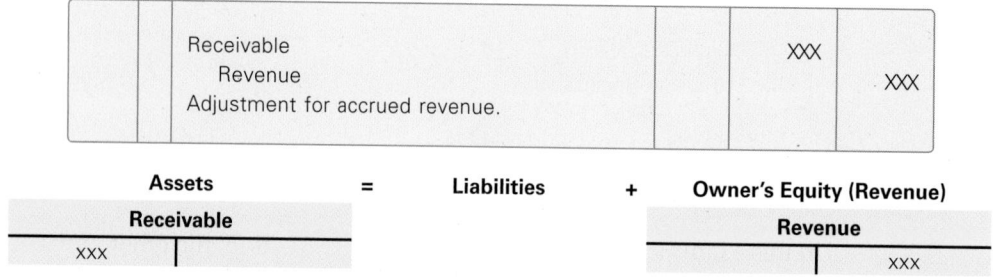

	Receivable		XXX	
	Revenue			XXX
	Adjustment for accrued revenue.			

Assets	**=**	**Liabilities**	**+**	**Owner's Equity (Revenue)**
Receivable				**Revenue**
XXX				XXX

Why would an accountant want to recognize revenue at a time other than when cash is received?

Accountants want to represent economic reality. Revenue is recognized when substantial performance has occurred, not when cash has traded hands. If the risks and rewards of ownership have transferred, the accountant records the revenue. For example, if a publisher has sold a magazine subscription but has not yet sent the magazine to the customer, then all the risks remain with the publisher. If the printer's computers break down, and the magazine cannot be sent to the customer, then the publisher would need to return a portion of the subscription money. The publisher holds all the risk.

Accrued Expenses Accrued expenses are unrecorded expenses that have been incurred and for which cash has yet to be paid. Wages owed to employees at the end of a period but not yet paid are an accrued expense. An obligation exists to pay out cash in the future. To illustrate, we use the following example involving NetSolutions and its employees:

Dec. 31   NetSolutions owed its employees wages of $250 for Monday, Tuesday, and Wednesday, December 29, 30, and 31.

NetSolutions paid wages of $950 on December 12 and $1,200 on December 26, 2014. These payments covered the biweekly pay periods that ended on those days. As at December 31, 2014, NetSolutions owed its employees wages of $250 for Monday, Tuesday, and Wednesday, December 29, 30, and 31. The wages of $250 will be paid on January 9, 2015; however, they are an expense of December. The employees were working to produce revenues in December and so the liability needs to be recorded. It is a liability because NetSolutions has a present obligation to pay wages that have been earned in the past and cannot be avoided in the future.[2] Thus, $250 of accrued wages should be recorded with an adjusting entry on December 31.

Other examples of accrued expenses include accrued interest on **notes payable** and accrued taxes. Because NetSolutions does not have a note payable, to illustrate, we use the following transaction:

A note payable is a written promise to pay an amount and interest at an agreed-upon rate in the future. Assume that a company has a 90-day, 6% note payable for $6,000 dated November 21, 2015. On November 21, the company records the note as follows:

2015				
Nov.	21	Cash	6,000	
		Note Payable		6,000
		To record note payable.		

At the year-end of December 31, 2015, the company owes interest on the note payable to the other party. It is not due until the note is paid. The company should record an adjusting entry for the accrued interest expense at the end of the period. In this example, interest is owed on nine days in November, from November 22 to 30. December has 31 days, making a total of 40 days of interest. The interest rate is stated as a yearly amount.

The interest on a note is computed as follows:

Interest = Principal × Interest Rate × (Term/365 days) or (Term/12 months)

In our example, the calculation is as follows:

Accrued Interest = $6,000 × 6% × 40/365

Accrued Interest = $39.45

The company would record the following entry:

2015				
Dec.	31	Interest Expense	39.45	
		Interest Payable		39.45
		Accrued interest payable ($6,000 × 6% × 40/365).		

Exhibit 5 summarizes the nature of accrued expenses.

Exhibit 5

Accrued Expenses

TRANSACTION *An expense has been incurred, but has not been recorded.*

ANALYSIS An expense has been incurred, but the expense has not been recorded nor has cash been paid. No journal entry has been recorded even though an expense has been incurred.

(*continued*)

2. *CICA Handbook–Accounting*, 2012 edition, Part I, 4.15; Part II, 1000.28 and 1000.29.

Exhibit 5

Accrued Expenses (*concluded*)

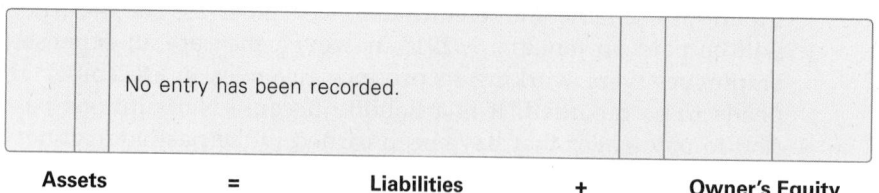

No entry has been recorded.

| Assets | = | Liabilities | + | Owner's Equity |

No impact since the expense has not been recorded.

ADJUSTMENT *An end-of-period adjustment is needed to recognize the accrued expense.*

ANALYSIS An expense account is increased (debited) for the amount of the expense that has been incurred and the related liability account is increased (credited). The liability account that is credited depends upon the type of expense. For example, Wages Payable would be credited for wages expense. Interest Payable would be credited for interest expense.

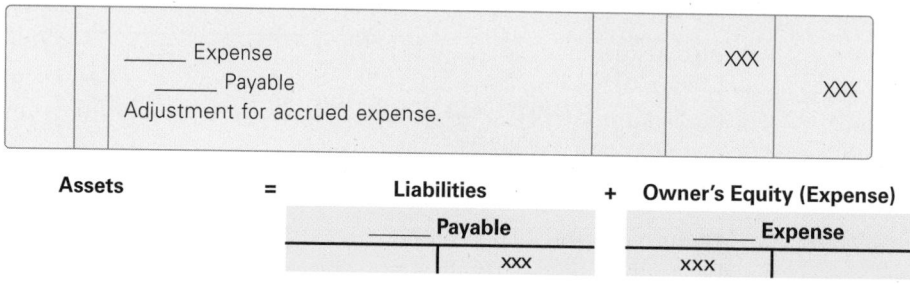

_____ Expense   XXX
_____ Payable   XXX
Adjustment for accrued expense.

Assets	=	Liabilities	+	Owner's Equity (Expense)
		_____ Payable		_____ Expense
		XXX		XXX

Prepaid expenses and unearned revenues are sometimes referred to as *deferrals*. This is because the recording of the related expense or revenue is deferred to a future period. Accrued revenues and accrued expenses are sometimes referred to as *accruals*. This is because the related revenue or expense should be recorded or accrued in the current period.

Depreciation Expense represents the "using up" of an asset[3]. Unlike short-term assets, such as supplies, long-term assets, such as equipment, do not incur a visible reduction in the quantity of the asset over time. Instead, the usefulness of the asset decreases as the asset is used from year to year. This reduction in value is called **depreciation**, also known as **amortization**. The following example is used:

> Dec. 31 Depreciation of equipment calculated at $50 for the year.

The company has calculated $50 of depreciation. This expense needs to be recognized during the period in which the equipment was used to earn income.

Examples of property, plant, and equipment are land, buildings, and equipment. They are physical resources that are owned and used by a business and are permanent or have a long life. In a sense, these **capital assets** are a type of *long-term* prepaid expense. Because of their unique nature and long life, they are discussed separately from other prepaid expenses, such as supplies and prepaid insurance.

Capital assets such as office equipment are used to generate revenue much like supplies are used to generate revenue. Unlike supplies, however, there is no visible

---

3. International Financial Reporting Standards (IFRS) use the term *depreciation* for tangible assets and reserve the term *amortization* for intangible assets. Accounting Standards for Private Enterprises (ASPE) state that "amortization may also be termed depreciation or depletion." We have chosen to use the IFRS term throughout this textbook. *CICA Handbook–Accounting*, 2012 edition, Part 1, IAS 16.6 and IAS 38; Part II, 3061.17.

reduction in the quantity of the equipment. Instead, as time passes, the equipment loses its ability to provide useful services. This decrease in usefulness is called **depreciation**.

All capital assets, except land, lose their usefulness and, thus, are said to **depreciate**. As the cost of the asset is allocated to the period of service provided by the asset, a portion of its cost should be recorded as an expense.[4] This periodic expense is called depreciation expense. Net income will then more closely approximate the earnings of the company less all the costs related to running the company. The discussion of depreciation will not include intangible assets and goodwill at this point; this issue will be revisited in Chapter 9.

The adjusting entry to record depreciation expense is similar to the adjusting entry for supplies used. The depreciation expense account is increased (debited) for the amount of depreciation. However, the capital assets account is not decreased (credited). This is because both the original cost of capital assets and the depreciation recorded since its purchase are normally reported on the balance sheet. Instead, an account entitled **Accumulated Depreciation** is increased (credited).

Accumulated depreciation accounts are called **contra accounts**, or contra asset accounts. This is because accumulated depreciation account balances are deducted from their related capital asset account balances on the balance sheet. The normal balance of a contra account is opposite to the account that it adjusts. Because the normal balance of a capital asset account is a debit, the normal balance of an accumulated depreciation account is a credit.

Note: Capital assets include both tangible and intangible assets.

The normal titles for capital asset accounts and their related contra asset accounts are as follows:

Capital Asset Account	Contra Asset Account
Land	None—Land is not amortized
Buildings	Accumulated Depreciation—Buildings
Store Equipment	Accumulated Depreciation—Store Equipment
Office Equipment	Accumulated Depreciation—Office Equipment

The straight-line method of calculating depreciation, covered in this chapter and revisited in Chapter 9, provides for the same amount of depreciation expense for each year of the asset's useful life. The useful life of the asset is the number of years that the asset is expected to be used.

To illustrate, assume that equipment was purchased on January 1 as follows:

Initial cost	$20,000
Expected useful life	5 years

The annual straight-line depreciation of $4,000 is computed below.

$$\text{Annual Depreciation} = \frac{\text{Cost}}{\text{Useful Life}} = \frac{\$20,000}{5 \text{ years}} = \$4,000$$

The journal entry for the first year is recorded as follows:

Dec.	31	Depreciation Expense	4,000	
		Accumulated Depreciation—Equipment		4,000
		To record depreciation for equipment.		

Exhibit 6 summarizes the nature of depreciation of capital assets.

4. *CICA Handbook—Accounting*, 2012 edition, Part II, 3061.17.

Depreciation of Capital Assets

TRANSACTION *Cash is paid for a capital asset.*

ANALYSIS Advance payments of future expenses are recorded as assets when the cash is paid. The transaction is recorded as a debit to a capital asset account and a credit to the cash account.

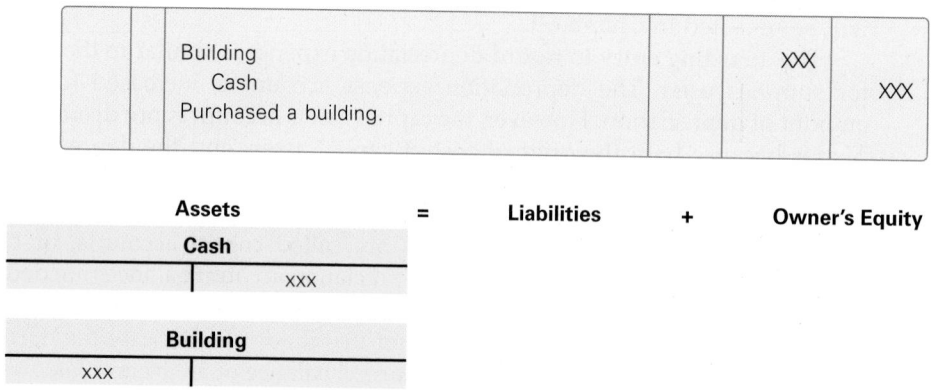

ADJUSTMENT *An end-of-period adjustment is needed to update the accumulated depreciation-building account.*

ANALYSIS The accumulated depreciation-building account is increased (credited) for the amount of the depreciation that has been "used up" and the depreciation expense account is increased (debited).

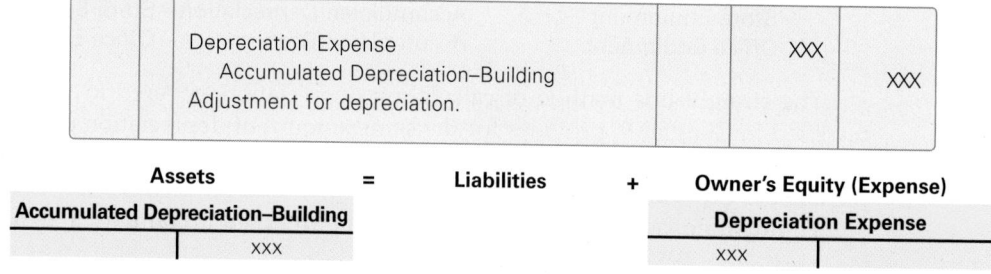

EXAMPLE EXERCISE 3-1 Accounts Requiring Adjustment

①

Indicate with a Yes or No whether each of the following accounts normally requires an adjusting entry.

a. Cash
b. Prepaid Rent

c. Wages Expense
d. Office Equipment

e. Accounts Receivable
f. Unearned Rent

FOLLOW MY EXAMPLE 3-1

a. No
b. Yes

c. Yes
d. Yes (to the contra account)

f. Yes
e. Yes

For Practice: PE 3-1

EXAMPLE EXERCISE 3-2 Type of Adjustment

Classify the following items as (1) prepaid expense, (2) unearned revenue, (3) accrued revenue, (4) accrued expense, or (5) depreciable capital asset.

a. Wages owed but not yet paid.

b. Supplies on hand.

c. Office equipment.

d. Fees received but not yet earned.

e. Fees earned but not yet received.

FOLLOW MY EXAMPLE 3-2

a. Accrued expense

b. Prepaid expense

c. Depreciable capital asset

d. Unearned revenue

e. Accrued revenue

For Practice: PE 3-2

② Adjusting Entries

Journalize entries for accounts requiring adjustment.

To illustrate adjusting entries, we will use the December 31, 2014, unadjusted trial balance of NetSolutions shown in Exhibit 7 on page 112. The expanded chart of accounts for NetSolutions is shown in Exhibit 8 on page 112. The additional accounts used in this chapter are shown in colour. The rules of debit and credit shown in Exhibit 3 of Chapter 2 are used to record the adjusting entries.

Prepaid Expenses

Supplies The balance in NetSolutions' supplies account on December 31 is $2,800. Some of these supplies (CDs, paper, envelopes, etc.) were used during December, and some are still on hand (not used). If either amount is known, the other can be determined. It is normally easier to determine the cost of the supplies on hand at the end of the month than to record daily supplies used. Assuming that on December 31 the amount of supplies on hand is $1,560, the amount to be transferred from the asset account to the expense account is $1,240, computed as follows:

Supplies available during December (balance of account)	$2,800
Supplies on hand, December 31	1,560
Supplies used (amount of adjustment)	$1,240

At the end of December, the supplies expense account should be increased (debited) for $1,240, and the supplies account should be decreased (credited) for $1,240 to record the supplies used during December. The adjusting journal entry and T accounts for Supplies and Supplies Expense are as follows:

Adjusting entry:

Journal				Page 5
Date	**Description**	**Post. Ref.**	**Debit**	**Credit**
2014				
Dec. 31	Supplies Expense	5050	1,240	
	Supplies	1040		1,240
	Supplies used ($2,800 – $1,560).			

Assets = Liabilities + Owner's Equity (Expense)

Supplies / Supplies Expense

Bal. 2,800 | Dec. 31 1,240 ; Adj. Bal. 1,560 ; Bal. 0 ; Dec. 31 1,240 ; Adj. Bal. 1,240

Exhibit 7

Unadjusted Trial Balance for NetSolutions

@netsolutions

NetSolutions
Unadjusted Trial Balance
December 31, 2014

	Debit Balances	Credit Balances
Cash	2,065	
Accounts Receivable	2,220	
Supplies	2,800	
Prepaid Insurance	2,400	
Office Equipment	1,800	
Land	20,000	
Accounts Payable		900
Unearned Rent		360
Chris Clark, Capital		25,000
Chris Clark, Withdrawals	4,000	
Fees Earned		16,340
Wages Expense	4,275	
Rent Expense	1,600	
Utilities Expense	985	
Miscellaneous Expense	455	
	42,600	42,600

Exhibit 8

Expanded Chart of Accounts for NetSolutions

Balance Sheet Accounts	Income Statement Accounts
Assets	**Revenues**
1010 Cash	4010 Fees Earned
1020 Accounts Receivable	4020 Rent Revenue
1040 Supplies	**Expenses**
1050 Prepaid Insurance	5010 Wages Expense
1070 Office Equipment	5020 Rent Expense
1080 Accumulated Depreciation—Office Equipment	5030 Depreciation Expense
1090 Land	5040 Utilities Expense
Liabilities	5050 Supplies Expense
2010 Accounts Payable	5060 Insurance Expense
2020 Wages Payable	5090 Miscellaneous Expense
2030 Unearned Rent	
Owner's Equity	
3010 Chris Clark, Capital	
3020 Chris Clark, Withdrawals	

The adjusting entry is shown in colour in the T accounts to separate it from other transactions. After the adjusting entry is recorded and posted, the supplies account has a debit balance of $1,560. This balance is an asset that will become an expense in a future period.

Prepaid Insurance   The debit balance of $2,400 in NetSolutions' prepaid insurance account represents a December 1 prepayment of insurance for 12 months. At the end of December, the insurance expense account is increased (debited), and the prepaid insurance account is decreased (credited) by $200, the insurance for one month. The adjusting journal entry and T accounts for Prepaid Insurance and Insurance Expense are as follows:

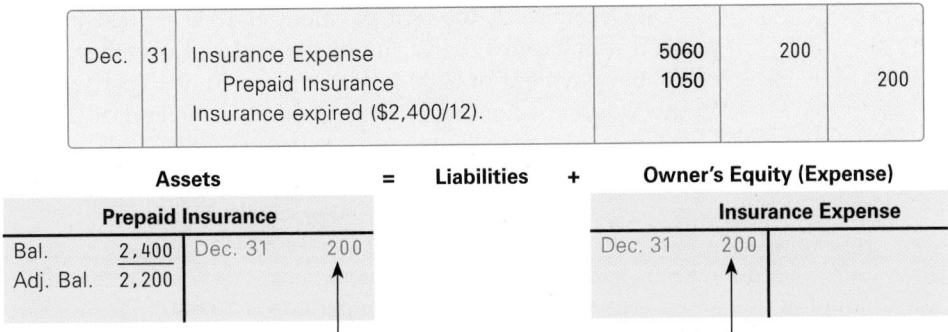

Dec.	31	Insurance Expense	5060	200	
		Prepaid Insurance	1050		200
		Insurance expired ($2,400/12).			

| Assets | = | Liabilities | + | Owner's Equity (Expense) |

Prepaid Insurance				**Insurance Expense**	
Bal.	2,400	Dec. 31	200	Dec. 31	200
Adj. Bal.	2,200				

After the adjusting entry is recorded and posted, the prepaid insurance account has a debit balance of $2,200. This balance is an asset that will become an expense in future periods. The insurance expense account has a debit balance of $200, which is an expense of the current period.

What Is the Effect of Omitting Adjusting Entries for Prepaid Expenses?

Note: The adjusted balance of a prepaid expense is an asset that will become an expense in a future period.

If the preceding adjustments for supplies ($1,240) and insurance ($200) are not recorded, the financial statements prepared as at December 31 will be misstated. On the income statement, total expenses will be understated by $1,440 ($1,240 + $200), and net income will be overstated by $1,440. On the balance sheet, Supplies and Prepaid Insurance will be overstated by a total of $1,440. Because net income increases owner's equity, the Capital account will also be overstated by $1,440 on the balance sheet. The effects of omitting these adjusting entries on the income statement and balance sheet are as follows.

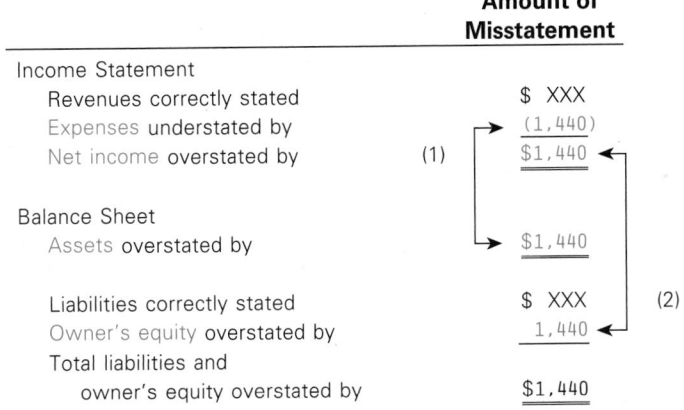

		Amount of Misstatement
Income Statement		
Revenues correctly stated		$ XXX
Expenses understated by		(1,440)
Net income overstated by	(1)	$1,440
Balance Sheet		
Assets overstated by		$1,440
Liabilities correctly stated		$ XXX (2)
Owner's equity overstated by		1,440
Total liabilities and		
owner's equity overstated by		$1,440

Arrow (1) indicates the effect of the understated expenses on assets. Arrow (2) indicates the effect of the overstated net income on owner's equity.

INTEGRITY, OBJECTIVITY, AND ETHICS IN BUSINESS

FREE ISSUE

Office supplies are often available to employees on a "free issue" basis. That is, employees do not need to "sign" for the release of office supplies but can simply obtain the necessary supplies from a local storage area as needed. Because supplies are easily available, however, does not mean they can be taken for personal use. In many instances, employees have been terminated for taking supplies home for personal use.

@netsolutions

Payments for prepaid expenses are sometimes made at the beginning of the period in which they will be *entirely used or consumed*. To illustrate, we use the following December 1 transaction of NetSolutions:

| Dec. 1 | NetSolutions paid rent of $800 for the month. |

On December 1, the rent payment of $800 represents prepaid rent. However, the prepaid rent expires daily, and at the end of December, no asset will be left. In such cases, the payment of $800 is recorded as Rent Expense rather than as Prepaid Rent. In this way, no adjusting entry is needed at the end of the period.[5]

EXAMPLE EXERCISE 3-3 Adjustment for Prepaid Expenses   ②

The prepaid insurance account had a beginning balance of $7,500 and was debited for $3,200 of premiums paid during the year. Journalize the adjusting entry required at the end of the year, assuming the amount of unexpired insurance related to future periods is $3,500.

FOLLOW MY EXAMPLE 3-3

Insurance Expense...	7,200	
Prepaid Insurance		7,200
Insurance expired ($7,500 + $3,200 − $3,500).		

For Practice: PE 3-3

Unearned Revenues

The December 31 unadjusted trial balance of NetSolutions indicates a balance in the unearned rent account of $360. This balance represents the receipt of three months' rent on December 1 for December, January, and February. At the end of December, one month's rent has been earned. Thus, the unearned rent account should be decreased (debited) by $120, and the rent revenue account should be increased (credited) by $120. The $120 represents the rental revenue for one month ($360/3). The adjusting journal entry and T accounts are shown below.

Dec.	31	Unearned Rent	2030	120	
		Rent Revenue	4020		120
		Rent earned ($360/3 months).			

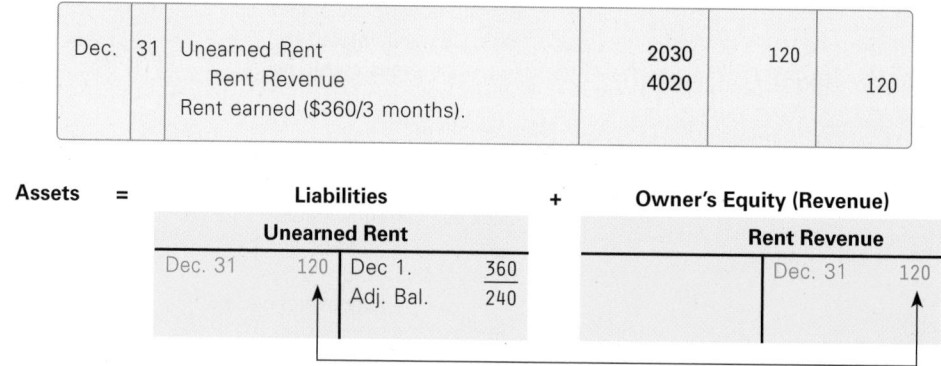

After the adjusting entry is recorded and posted, the unearned rent account has a credit balance of $240. This balance is a liability that will become revenue in a future period. Rent Revenue has a balance of $120, which is revenue of the current period.[6]

What Is the Effect of Omitting Adjusting Entries for Unearned Revenues?

If the preceding adjustment of unearned rent and rent revenue is not recorded, the financial statements prepared on December 31 will be misstated. On the income statement, Rent Revenue and the net income will be understated by $120. On the balance sheet, Unearned Rent will be overstated by $120, and the Capital account will be understated by $120. The effects of omitting this adjusting entry are shown as follows.

---

5. An alternative treatment of recording the cost of supplies, rent, and other prepayments of expenses is discussed in Appendix 1 of this chapter.

6. An alternative treatment of recording revenues received in advance of being earned is discussed in Appendix 1 of this chapter.

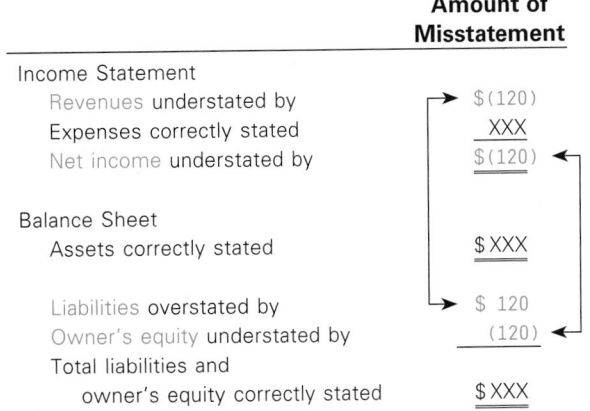

	Amount of Misstatement
Income Statement	
Revenues understated by	$(120)
Expenses correctly stated	XXX
Net income understated by	$(120)
Balance Sheet	
Assets correctly stated	$ XXX
Liabilities overstated by	$ 120
Owner's equity understated by	(120)
Total liabilities and	
owner's equity correctly stated	$ XXX

EXAMPLE EXERCISE 3-4   Adjustment for Unearned Revenues   ②

The balance in the unearned fees account, before adjustment at the end of the year, is $55,700. Journalize the adjusting entry required if the amount of unearned fees at the end of the year is $26,400.

FOLLOW MY EXAMPLE 3-4

Unearned Fees..	29,300	
Fees Earned		29,300
Fees earned ($55,700 − $26,400).		

For Practice: PE 3-4

MID-CHAPTER ILLUSTRATIVE PROBLEM

On December 31, 2014, the following data were accumulated to assist the accountant in preparing the adjusting entries for Chocolate Bakery:

a. The supplies account balance on December 31 is $2,105. The supplies on hand are $1,603.

b. The unearned sales account balance on December 31 is $4,200, representing work that will be completed over three months, December, January, and February.

Journalize the adjusting entries required at December 31, 2014.

MID-CHAPTER ILLUSTRATIVE SOLUTION

2014				
Dec.	31	Supplies Expense	502	
		Supplies		502
		Supplies used ($2,105 − $1,603).		
	31	Unearned Sales	1,400	
		Sales Revenue		1,400
		Sales earned ($4,200/3 months).		

Accrued Revenues

During an accounting period, some revenues are recorded only when cash is received. Thus, at the end of the accounting period, there may be revenue that has been earned *but has not been recorded*. In such cases, the revenue is recorded by increasing (debiting) an asset account and increasing (crediting) a revenue account.

To illustrate, assume NetSolutions signed an agreement with Dankner Co. on December 15. The agreement provides that NetSolutions will answer computer questions and render assistance to Dankner Co.'s employees. The services will be billed to Dankner Co. on the fifteenth of each month at a rate of $20 per hour. As at December 31, NetSolutions had provided 25 hours of assistance to Dankner Co. The revenue of $500 (25 hours × $20) will be billed on January 15. However, NetSolutions earned the revenue in December.

The claim against the customer for payment of the $500 is an account receivable (*an asset*). Thus, the accounts receivable account should be increased (debited) by $500 and the fees earned account should be increased (credited) by $500. The adjusting journal entry and T accounts are shown below.

2014					
Dec.	31	Accounts Receivable	1020	500	
		Fees Earned	4010		500
		Accrued fees (25 hrs. × $20).			

Assets		= Liabilities +	Owner's Equity (Revenue)	
Accounts Receivable			**Fees Earned**	
Bal.	2,220		Bal.	16,340
Dec. 31	500		Dec. 31	500
Adj. Bal.	2,720		Adj. Bal.	16,840

What Is the Effect of Omitting Adjusting Entries for Accrued Revenues?

If the adjustment for the accrued revenue ($500) is not recorded, Fees Earned and the net income will be understated by $500 on the income statement. On the balance sheet, Accounts Receivable and the Capital account will be understated by $500. The effects of omitting this adjusting entry are as follows.

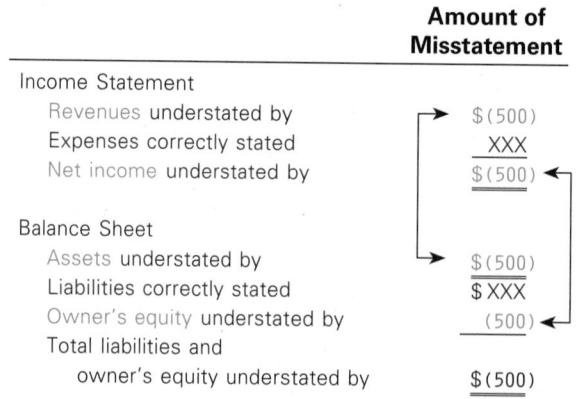

	Amount of Misstatement
Income Statement	
Revenues understated by	$(500)
Expenses correctly stated	XXX
Net income understated by	$(500)
Balance Sheet	
Assets understated by	$(500)
Liabilities correctly stated	$ XXX
Owner's equity understated by	(500)
Total liabilities and	
owner's equity understated by	$(500)

②

EXAMPLE EXERCISE 3-5 Adjustment for Accrued Revenues   ②

At the end of the current year, $13,680 of fees have been earned but have not been billed to clients. Journalize the adjusting entry to record the accrued fees.

FOLLOW MY EXAMPLE 3-5

Accounts Receivable	13,680	
Fees Earned		13,680
Accrued fees.		

For Practice: PE 3-5

Accrued Expenses

Some types of services used in earning revenues are paid for after the service has been performed. For example, wages expense is used hour by hour, but is paid only daily, weekly, biweekly, or monthly. At the end of the accounting period, the amount of such accrued but unpaid items is an expense and a liability.

For example, if the last day of the employees' pay period is not the last day of the accounting period, an accrued expense (wages expense) and the related liability (wages payable) must be recorded by an adjusting entry. This adjusting entry is necessary so that expenses are properly matched to the period in which they were incurred in earning revenue.

@net**solutions**

To illustrate, NetSolutions pays its employees biweekly. NetSolutions paid wages of $950 on December 12 and $1,200 on December 26. These payments covered pay periods ending on those days, as shown in Exhibit 9. As at December 31, NetSolutions owes $250 of wages to employees for Monday, Tuesday, and Wednesday, December 29, 30, and 31. Thus, the wages expense account should be increased (debited) by $250 and the wages payable account should be increased (credited) by $250. The adjusting journal entry and T accounts are shown below.

2014					
Dec.	31	Wages Expense	5010	250	
		Wages Payable	2020		250
		Accrued wages.			

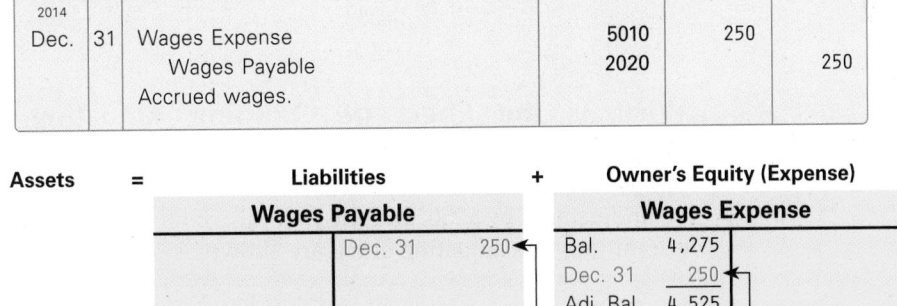

After the adjusting entry is recorded and posted, the debit balance of the wages expense account is $4,525. This balance of $4,525 is the wages expense for two months, November and December. The credit balance of $250 in Wages Payable is the liability for wages owed on December 31.

As shown in Exhibit 9 below, NetSolutions paid wages of $1,275 on January 9. This payment includes the $250 of accrued wages recorded on December 31. Thus, on January 9, the wages payable account should be decreased (debited) by $250. Also, the wages expense account should be increased (debited) by $1,025 ($1,275 – $250), which is the wages expense for January 1–9. Finally, the cash account is decreased (credited) by $1,275. The journal entry for the payment of wages on January 9 is shown below.[7]

---

7. To simplify the subsequent recording of the following period's transactions, some accountants use what is known as reversing entries for certain types of adjustments. Reversing entries are discussed in Appendix 1 of Chapter 4.

Exhibit 9	

Accrued Wages

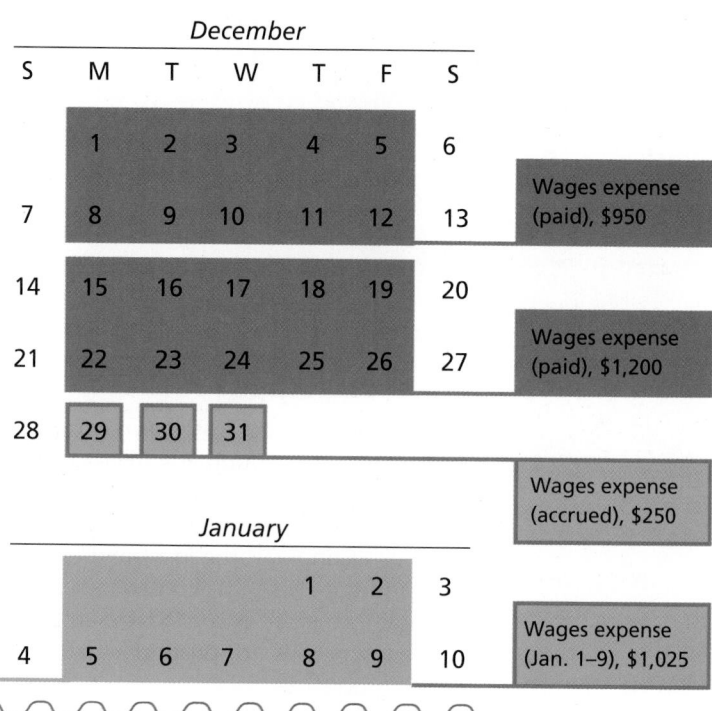

1. Wages are paid every two weeks on Friday for the two-week periods ended on those Fridays. The payments were $950 on December 12 and $1,200 on December 26.

2. The wages accrued for Monday, Tuesday, and Wednesday, December 29, 30, and 31, are $250.

3. Wages paid on Friday, January 9, total $1,275.

4. Wages expense, January 1–9, totals $1,025.

2015					
Jan.	9	Wages Expense		1,025	
		Wages Payable		250	
		Cash			1,275
		Payment of wages.			

What Is the Effect of Omitting Adjusting Entries for Accrued Wages?
On the income statement, Wages Expense will be understated by $250, and the net income will be overstated by $250. On the balance sheet, Wages Payable will be understated by $250, and the Capital account will be overstated by $250. The effects of omitting this adjusting entry are shown as follows:

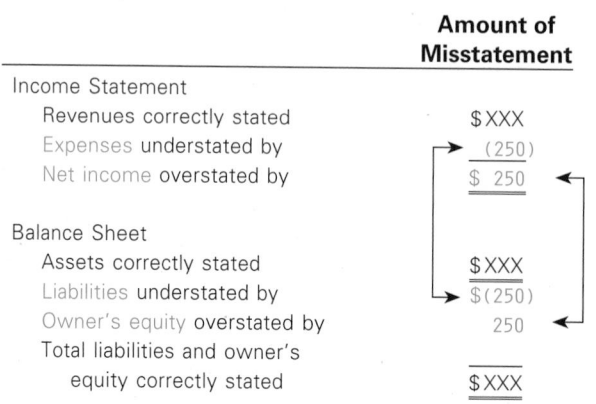

	Amount of Misstatement
Income Statement	
Revenues correctly stated	$ XXX
Expenses understated by	(250)
Net income overstated by	$ 250
Balance Sheet	
Assets correctly stated	$ XXX
Liabilities understated by	$(250)
Owner's equity overstated by	250
Total liabilities and owner's equity correctly stated	$ XXX

EXAMPLE EXERCISE 3-6 **Adjustment for Accrued Expense** (2)

First Realty Co. pays weekly salaries of $12,500 on Friday for a five-day week ending on that day. Journalize the necessary adjusting entry at the end of the accounting period, assuming that the period ends on Thursday.

FOLLOW MY EXAMPLE 3-6

Salaries Expense..	10,000	
Salaries Payable..		10,000
Accrued salaries [($12,500/5 days) x 4 days].		

For Practice: PE 3-6

Depreciation of Capital Assets

@netsolutions

The December 31, 2014, unadjusted trial balance of NetSolutions (Exhibit 8) indicates that NetSolutions owns two capital assets: land and office equipment. Land does not depreciate; however, an adjusting entry should be recorded for the depreciation of the office equipment for December. We assume that the office equipment has depreciated $50 during December. Thus, the depreciation expense account should be increased (debited) by $50 and the accumulated depreciation—office equipment account should be increased (credited) by $50. The adjusting journal entry and T accounts are shown below:

2014					
Dec.	31	Depreciation Expense	5030	50	
		Accumulated Depreciation—Office Equip.	1080		50
		Depreciation on office equipment.			

Assets	=	**Liabilities**	+	**Owner's Equity (Expense)**

Office Equipment			**Depreciation Expense**	
Bal.	1,800		Dec. 31	50

Accumulated Depr.—Office Equip.	
	Dec. 31	50

After the adjusting journal entry is recorded and posted, the office equipment account still has a debit balance of $1,800. This is the original cost of the office equipment. The accumulated depreciation—office equipment account has a credit balance of $50. The difference between these two balances of $1,750 ($1,800 – $50) is the cost of the office equipment that has not yet been depreciated. This amount of $1,750 is called the **carrying amount of the asset** (or **net book value**).

The office equipment and its related accumulated depreciation are reported on the December 31 balance sheet as follows:

Office equipment	$1,800	
Less accumulated depreciation	50	$1,750

The market value of a capital asset usually differs from its carrying value. This is because depreciation is an *allocation* method, not a *valuation* method. That is, depreciation allocates the cost of a capital asset to expense over its estimated life. Depreciation does not measure changes in market values, which vary from year to year. Thus, on December 31, the market value of the office equipment could be more or less than $1,750.

What Is the Effect of Omitting Adjusting Entries for Depreciation? If the adjustment for depreciation ($50) is not recorded, Depreciation Expense on the income statement will be understated by $50, and the net income will be overstated by $50. On the balance sheet, the book value of Office Equipment and Capital will be overstated by $50. The effects of omitting the adjustment for depreciation are as follows.

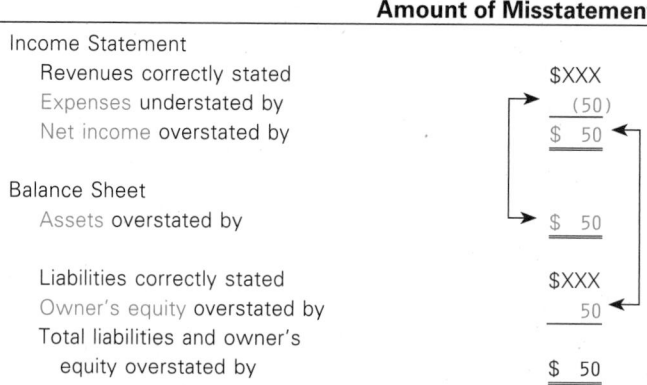

	Amount of Misstatement
Income Statement	
Revenues correctly stated	$XXX
Expenses understated by	(50)
Net income overstated by	$ 50
Balance Sheet	
Assets overstated by	$ 50
Liabilities correctly stated	$XXX
Owner's equity overstated by	50
Total liabilities and owner's equity overstated by	$ 50

EXAMPLE EXERCISE 3-7 Adjustment for Depreciation

The estimated amount of depreciation on equipment for the current year is $4,250. Journalize the adjusting entry to record the depreciation.

FOLLOW MY EXAMPLE 3-7

Depreciation Expense..	4,250	
Accumulated Depreciation—Equipment................................		4,250
Depreciation on equipment.		

For Practice: PE 3-7

---

3 Summary of the Adjustment Process

Summarize the adjustment process.

We have described and illustrated the basic types of adjusting entries in this chapter. A summary of these basic adjustments is shown in Exhibit 10 on page 121.

The adjusting entries for NetSolutions are shown in Exhibit 11 on page 122. The adjusting entries are dated as at the last day of the period. However, because collecting the adjustment data requires time, the entries are usually recorded at a later date. An explanation is included with each adjusting entry.

NetSolutions' adjusting entries have been posted to the ledger shown in Exhibit 12 on pages 123 and 124. The adjustments are shown in colour in Exhibit 12 to distinguish them from other transactions.

To see these adjustments in a visual presentation and to show how the entries are used to adjust the unadjusted trial balance and produce the adjusted trial balance, a worksheet follows at Exhibit 13, on page 125.

EXAMPLE EXERCISE 3-8 Effect of Omitting Adjustments

For the year ended December 31, 2015, Sulek Construction Co. mistakenly omitted adjusting entries for (1) $9,200 of unearned revenue that was earned, (2) earned revenue that was not billed of $13,300, and (3) accrued wages of $3,100. Indicate the combined effect of the errors on (a) revenues, (b) expenses, and (c) net income for the year ended December 31, 2015.

FOLLOW MY EXAMPLE 3-8

a. Revenues were understated by $22,500 ($9,200 + $13,300).

b. Expenses were understated by $3,100.

c. Net income was understated by $19,400 ($22,500 − $3,100).

For Practice: PE 3-8

Exhibit 10

Summary of Adjustments

Examples	Reason for Adjustment	Adjusting Entry		Examples from NetSolutions		Financial Statement Impact if Adjusting Entry Is Omitted	
PREPAID EXPENSES							
1. Supplies, Prepaid Insurance	Prepaid expenses (assets) have been used or consumed in the business operations.	Expense Dr. Asset Cr.		Supplies Expense 1,240 　Supplies 1,240 Insurance Expense 200 　Prepaid Insurance 200		Income Statement: 　Revenues 　Expenses 　Net income Balance Sheet: 　Assets 　Liabilities 　Owner's Equity 　(Capital)	No effect Understated Overstated Overstated No effect Overstated
UNEARNED REVENUES							
2. Unearned rent, magazine subscriptions received in advance, fees received in advance of services	Cash received before the services have been provided is recorded as a liability. Some services have been provided to customer before the end of the accounting period.	Liability Dr. Revenue Cr.		Unearned Rent 120 　Rent Revenue 120		Income Statement: 　Revenues 　Expenses 　Net income Balance Sheet: 　Assets 　Liabilities 　Owner's Equity 　(Capital)	Understated No effect Understated No effect Overstated Understated
ACCRUED REVENUES							
3. Services performed but not billed, interest to be received	Services have been provided to the customer, but have not been billed or recorded. Interest has been earned, but has not been received or recorded.	Asset Dr. Revenue Cr.		Accounts Receivable 500 　Fees Earned 500		Income Statement: 　Revenues 　Expenses 　Net income Balance Sheet: 　Assets 　Liabilities 　Owner's Equity 　(Capital)	Understated No effect Understated Understated No effect Understated
ACCRUED EXPENSES							
4. Wages or salaries incurred but not paid, interest incurred but not paid	Expenses have been incurred, but have not been paid or recorded.	Expense Dr. Liability Cr.		Wages Expense 250 　Wages Payable 250		Income Statement: 　Revenues 　Expenses 　Net income Balance Sheet: 　Assets 　Liabilities 　Owner's Equity 　(Capital)	No effect Understated Overstated No effect Understated Overstated
DEPRECIATION							
5. Depreciation of equipment and buildings	Fixed assets depreciate as they are used or consumed in the business operations.	Expense Dr. Contra Asset Cr.		Depreciation Expense 50 　Accum. Depreciation— 　　Office Equipment 50		Income Statement: 　Revenues 　Expenses 　Net income Balance Sheet: 　Assets 　Liabilities 　Owner's Equity 　(Capital)	No effect Understated Overstated Overstated No effect Overstated

Exhibit 11

Adjusting Entries—NetSolutions

Journal					Page 5
Date		**Description**	**Post. Ref.**	**Debit**	**Credit**
2014		Adjusting Entries			
Dec. 31		Supplies Expense	5050	1,240	
		Supplies	1040		1,240
		Supplies used ($2,800 – $1,560).			
	31	Insurance Expense	5060	200	
		Prepaid Insurance	1050		200
		Insurance expired ($2,400/12 months).			
	31	Unearned Rent	2030	120	
		Rent Revenue	4020		120
		Rent earned ($360/3 months).			
	31	Accounts Receivable	1020	500	
		Fees Earned	4010		500
		Accrued fees (25 hrs. × $20).			
	31	Wages Expense	5010	250	
		Wages Payable	2020		250
		Accrued wages.			
	31	Depreciation Expense	5030	50	
		Accum. Depreciation—Office Equipment	1080		50
		Depreciation on office equipment.			

CRITICAL THINKING

Why bother with adjusting entries? Wouldn't it be easier to record transactions when the cash trades hands?

Users rely on information in the financial statements when making decisions. The financial statements need to faithfully represent the results of the choices that the business has made. For example, assume a business paints a client's building in January and is paid for the work in February. If the revenue was recorded when the cash traded hands, the revenue would be recorded in February, even though the work was completed in January. By recording an adjusting entry, the business will correctly record revenue in January, and the monthly financial statements will truthfully represent that the business has earned the revenue, even though it has not yet been paid.

Exhibit 12

Ledger with Adjusting Entries—NetSolutions

Account *Cash*   Account No. *1010*

Date	Item	Post. Ref.	Debit	Credit	Balance
2014					
Nov. 1		1	25,000		25,000 DR.
5		1		20,000	5,000 DR.
18		1	7,500		12,500 DR.
30		1		3,650	8,850 DR.
30		1		950	7,900 DR.
30		1		2,000	5,900 DR.
Dec. 1		2		2,400	3,500 DR.
1		2		800	2,700 DR.
1		2	360		3,060 DR.
6		2		180	2,880 DR.
11		2		400	2,480 DR.
12		2		950	1,530 DR.
16		3	3,100		4,630 DR.
20		3		900	3,730 DR.
21		3	650		4,380 DR.
23		3		1,450	2,930 DR.
26		3		1,200	1,730 DR.
31		3		310	1,420 DR.
31		4		225	1,195 DR.
31		4	2,870		4,065 DR.
31		4		2,000	2,065 DR.

Account *Accounts Receivable*   Account No. *1020*

Date	Item	Post. Ref.	Debit	Credit	Balance
2014					
Dec. 16		3	1,750		1,750 DR.
21		3		650	1,100 DR.
31		4	1,120		2,220 DR.
31	Adjusting	5	500		2,720 DR.

Account *Supplies*   Account No. *1040*

Date	Item	Post. Ref.	Debit	Credit	Balance
2014					
Nov. 10		1	1,350		1,350 DR.
Dec. 23		3	1,450		2,800 DR.
31	Adjusting	5		1,240	1,560 DR.

Account *Prepaid Insurance*   Account No. *1050*

Date	Item	Post. Ref.	Debit	Credit	Balance
2014					
Dec. 1		2	2,400		2,400 DR.
31	Adjusting	5		200	2,200 DR.

Account *Office Equipment*   Account No. *1070*

Date	Item	Post. Ref.	Debit	Credit	Balance
2014					
Dec. 4		2	1,800		1,800 DR.

Account *Acc. Depr.—Office Equip* Account No. *1080*

Date	Item	Post. Ref.	Debit	Credit	Balance
2014					
Dec. 31	Adjusting	5		50	50 CR.

Account *Land*   Account No. *1090*

Date	Item	Post. Ref.	Debit	Credit	Balance
2014					
Nov. 5		1	20,000		20,000 DR.

Account *Accounts Payable*   Account No. *2010*

Date	Item	Post. Ref.	Debit	Credit	Balance
2014					
Nov. 10		1		1,350	1,350 CR.
30		1	950		400 CR.
Dec. 4		2		1,800	2,200 CR.
11		2	400		1,800 CR.
20		3	900		900 CR.

Account *Wages Payable*   Account No. *2020*

Date	Item	Post. Ref.	Debit	Credit	Balance
2014					
Dec 31	Adjusting	5		250	250 CR.

Account *Unearned Rent*   Account No. *2030*

Date	Item	Post. Ref.	Debit	Credit	Balance
2014					
Dec. 1		2		360	360 CR.
31		5	120		240 CR.

Account *Chris Clark, Capital*   Account No. *3010*

Date	Item	Post. Ref.	Debit	Credit	Balance
2014					
Nov. 1		1		25,000	25,000 CR.

(continued)

Exhibit 12

Ledger with Adjusting Entries—NetSolutions (*concluded*)

Account *Chris Clark, Withdrawals* Account No. *3020*

Date	Item	Post. Ref.	Debit	Credit	Balance
2014					
Nov. 30		1	2,000		2,000 DR.
Dec. 31		4	2,000		4,000 DR.

Account *Depreciation Expense* Account No. *5030*

Date	Item	Post. Ref.	Debit	Credit	Balance
2014					
Dec. 31	Adjusting	5	50		50 DR.

Account *Fees Earned* Account No. *4010*

Date	Item	Post. Ref.	Debit	Credit	Balance
2014					
Nov. 18		1		7,500	7,500 CR.
Dec. 16		3		3,100	10,600 CR.
16		3		1,750	12,350 CR.
31		4		2,870	15,220 CR.
31		4		1,120	16,340 CR.
Dec. 31	Adjusting	5		500	16,840 CR.

Account *Utilities Expense* Account No. *5040*

Date	Item	Post. Ref.	Debit	Credit	Balance
2014					
Nov. 30		1	450		450 DR.
Dec. 31		3	310		760 DR.
31		4	225		985 DR.

Account *Rent Revenue* Account No. *4020*

Date	Item	Post. Ref.	Debit	Credit	Balance
2014					
Dec 31	Adjusting	5		120	120 CR.

Account *Supplies Expense* Account No. *5050*

Date	Item	Post. Ref.	Debit	Credit	Balance
2014					
Dec. 31	Adjusting	5	1,240		1,240 DR.

Account *Wages Expense* Account No. *5010*

Date	Item	Post. Ref.	Debit	Credit	Balance
2014					
Nov. 30		1	2,125		2,125 DR.
Dec. 12		2	950		3,075 DR.
26		3	1,200		4,275 DR.
31	Adjusting	5	250		4,525 DR.

Account *Insurance Expense* Account No. *5060*

Date	Item	Post. Ref.	Debit	Credit	Balance
2014					
Dec. 31	Adjusting	5	200		200 DR.

Account *Miscellaneous Expense* Account No. *5090*

Date	Item	Post. Ref.	Debit	Credit	Balance
2014					
Nov. 30		1	275		275 DR.
Dec. 6		2	180		455 DR.

Account *Rent Expense* Account No. *5020*

Date	Item	Post. Ref.	Debit	Credit	Balance
2014					
Nov. 30		1	800		800 DR.
Dec. 1		2	800		1,600 DR.

Exhibit 13

Worksheet with Adjusting Entries—NetSolutions

Account Title	Unadjusted		Adjustments		Adjusted TB	
	Dr.	Cr.	Dr.	Cr.	Dr.	Cr.
Cash	2,065				2,065	
Accounts Receivable	2,220		500		2,720	
Supplies	2,800			1,240	1,560	
Prepaid Insurance	2,400			200	2,200	
Office Equipment	1,800				1,800	
Acc. Depreciation				50		50
Land	20,000				20,000	
Accounts Payable		900				900
Unearned Rent		360	120			240
Wages Payable				250		250
Chris Clark, Capital		25,000				25,000
Chris Clark, Withdrawals	4,000				4,000	
Fees Earned		16,340		500		16,840
Rent Revenue				120		120
Wages Expense	4,275		250		4,525	
Rent Expense	1,600				1,600	
Depreciation Expense			50		50	
Utilities Expense	985				985	
Supplies Expense			1,240		1,240	
Insurance Expense			200		200	
Miscellaneous	455				455	
	42,600	42,600	2,360	2,360	43,400	43,400

(4)

Adjusted Trial Balance

Prepare an adjusted trial balance.

@netsolutions

Step 7: Adjusted Trial Balance After the adjusting entries have been posted, an **adjusted trial balance** is prepared. The adjusted trial balance verifies the equality of the total debit and credit balances before the financial statements are prepared. If the adjusted trial balance does not balance, an error has occurred. However, as we discussed in Chapter 2, errors may occur even when the adjusted trial balance totals agree. For example, if an adjusting entry were omitted, the adjusted trial balance totals would still agree.

Exhibit 14 shows the adjusted trial balance for NetSolutions as at December 31, 2014. In Chapter 4, we discuss how financial statements can be prepared from an adjusted trial balance.

Financial Statements

In Chapter 3, we have introduced steps 6 and 7 of the accounting cycle. Step 6 involves journalizing and posting adjusting entries and step 7 prepares the adjusted trial balance. In Chapter 4, we complete the accounting cycle with step 8, preparation of the financial statements; step 9, closing entries; and, finally, step 10, the post-closing trial balance.

Financial statements were introduced in earlier chapters, we have included the option of completing financial statements in the end-of-chapter material.

Exhibit 14

Adjusted Trial Balance

NetSolutions Adjusted Trial Balance December 31, 2014	Debit Balances	Credit Balances
Cash	2,065	
Accounts Receivable	2,720	
Supplies	1,560	
Prepaid Insurance	2,200	
Office Equipment	1,800	
Accumulated Depreciation—Office Equipment		50
Land	20,000	
Accounts Payable		900
Unearned Rent		240
Wages Payable		250
Chris Clark, Capital		25,000
Chris Clark, Withdrawals	4,000	
Fees Earned		16,840
Rent Revenue		120
Wages Expense	4,525	
Rent Expense	1,600	
Depreciation Expense	50	
Utilities Expense	985	
Supplies Expense	1,240	
Insurance Expense	200	
Miscellaneous Expense	455	
	43,400	43,400

EXAMPLE EXERCISE 3-9 **Effect of Errors on Adjusted Trial Balance** 4

Consider each of the following errors individually, and indicate whether the error would cause the adjusted trial balance totals to be unequal. If the error would cause the adjusted trial balance totals to be unequal, indicate whether the debit or credit total is higher and by what amount.

a. The adjustment for accrued fees of $5,340 was journalized as a debit to Accounts Payable for $5,340 and a credit to Fees Earned of $5,340.

b. The adjustment for amortization of $3,260 was journalized as a debit to Amortization Expense for $3,620 and a credit to Accumulated Amortization for $3,260.

FOLLOW MY EXAMPLE 3-9

a. The totals are equal even though the debit should have been journalized to Accounts Receivable, not to Accounts Payable.

b. The totals are unequal. The debit total is higher by $360 ($3,620 − $3,260).

For Practice: PE 3-9

A P P E N D I X 1

Alternative Methods of Recording Prepaid Expenses and Unearned Revenues

In this chapter, prepaid expenses were debited to an asset account at the time of payment. As an alternative, the cost may be debited to an expense account at the time of payment. Also, in this chapter, unearned revenues were credited to a liability account at the time of receipt. As an alternative, the amount may be credited to a revenue account at the time of receipt. This appendix describes and illustrates these alternative methods of recording prepaid expenses and unearned revenues.

Prepaid Expenses

As a basis for illustrating the alternative methods of recording prepaid expenses, the insurance premium paid in the NetSolutions example on page 111 is used. The amounts related to this insurance are as follows:

Prepayment of insurance for 12 months, starting December 1	$2,400
Insurance premium expired during December	200
Unexpired insurance premium at the end of December	$2,200

Based on the above data, the entries to account for the prepaid insurance recorded initially as an *asset* are shown in the journal and T accounts in Exhibit 15. The adjusting entry in Exhibit 15 was shown in this chapter. The entries to account for the prepaid insurance recorded initially as an *expense* are shown in the journal and T accounts in Exhibit 16.

Either of the two methods of recording prepaid expenses may be used. As illustrated in Exhibits 15 and 16, both methods result in the same account balances after the adjusting entries have been recorded. Therefore, the amounts reported as expenses in the income statement and as assets on the balance sheet will not be affected by the method used. To avoid confusion, the method used by a business for each kind of prepaid expense should be followed consistently from year to year.

Exhibit 15

Prepaid Expense Recorded Initially as Asset

Initial entry (to record initial payment):

Dec.	1	Prepaid Insurance	2,400	
		Cash		2,400
		Paid insurance in advance.		

Adjusting entry (to transfer amount used to the proper *expense* account):

Dec.	31	Insurance Expense	200	
		Prepaid Insurance		200
		Adjustment for prepaid expense.		

Assets	= **Liabilities** +	**Owner's Equity (Expense)**
Prepaid Insurance		**Insurance Expense**
Dec. 1 2,400 | Dec. 31 Adjusting 200		Dec. 31 Adjusting 200 |

Exhibit 16

Prepaid Expense Recorded Initially as Expense

Initial entry (to record initial payment):

Dec.	1	Insurance Expense		2,400	
		Cash			2,400
		Paid insurance in advance.			

Adjusting entry (to transfer amount *unused* to the proper *asset* account):

Dec.	31	Prepaid Insurance		2,200	
		Insurance Expense			2,200
		Adjustment for prepaid expense.			

Assets	= Liabilities +	Owner's Equity (Expense)
Prepaid Insurance		**Insurance Expense**
Dec. 31 Adjusting 2,200		Dec. 1 2,400 | Dec. 31 Adjusting 2,200

Some businesses record all prepaid expenses using one method. Other businesses use one method to record the prepayment of some expenses and the other method for other expenses. Initial debits to the asset account are logical for prepayments of insurance, which are usually for periods of one to three years. On the other hand, rent on a building may be prepaid on the first of each month. The prepaid rent will expire by the end of the month. In this case, it is logical to record the payment of rent by initially debiting an expense account rather than an asset account.

Unearned Revenues

To illustrate the alternative methods of recording unearned revenues, we will use the rent received by NetSolutions on page 114. Land was rented on December 1 to a local retailer for use as a parking lot for three months, and $360 was received for the entire three months. On December 31, $120 (1/3 × $360) of the rent has been earned, and $240 (2/3 × $360) of the rent is still unearned.

Based on the above data, the entries to account for the unearned rent recorded initially as a liability are shown in the journal and the T accounts in Exhibit 17. The adjusting entry in Exhibit 17 was shown in this chapter. The entries to account for the unearned rent recorded initially as revenue are shown in the journal and the T accounts in Exhibit 18.

As illustrated in Exhibits 17 and 18, both methods result in the same account balances after the adjusting entries have been recorded. Therefore, the amounts reported as revenues in the income statement and as liabilities on the balance sheet will not be affected by the method used. Either of the methods may be used for all revenues received in advance. Alternatively, the first method may be used for advance receipts of some kinds of revenue and the second method for other kinds. To avoid confusion, the method used by a business for each kind of unearned revenue should be followed consistently from year to year.

Exhibit 17

Unearned Revenue Recorded Initially as Liability

Initial entry (to record initial receipt):

Dec.	1	Cash		360	
		Unearned Rent			360
		Received cash for three months' rent.			

Adjusting entry (to transfer amount *earned* to proper *revenue* account):

Dec.	31	Unearned Rent		120	
		Rent Revenue			120
		Rent earned for month of December.			

Assets	= Liabilities +	Owner's Equity (Expense)
Unearned Rent		**Rent Revenue**
Dec. 31 Adjusting 120	Dec. 1 360	Dec. 31 Adjusting 120

Exhibit 18

Unearned Revenue Recorded Initially as Revenue

Initial entry (to record initial receipt):

Dec.	1	Cash		360	
		Rent Revenue			360
		Received cash for three months' rent.			

Adjusting entry (to transfer amount *unearned* to proper *liability* account):

Dec.	31	Rent Revenue		240	
		Unearned Rent			240
		Adjustment for unearned rent.			

Assets	= Liabilities +	Owner's Equity (Expense)
Unearned Rent		**Rent Revenue**
	Dec. 31 Adjusting 240	Dec. 31 Adjusting 240	Dec. 1 360

At a Glance 3

1 Describe the nature of the adjusting process.

Key Points	Key Learning Outcomes	Page	Example Exercises
The accrual basis of accounting requires that revenues are reported in the period in which they are earned and expensed when they occur. The updating of accounts at the end of the accounting period is called the adjusting process. Each adjusting entry affects an income statement and balance sheet account and does not involve cash.	• Explain why accrual accounting requires adjusting entries.	101	
	• List accounts that do and do NOT require adjusting entries at the end of the accounting period.	102	3-1
	• Give an example of a prepaid expense, unearned revenue, accrued revenue, accrued expense, and depreciable capital asset.	102	3-2

2 Journalize entries for accounts requiring adjustment.

Key Points	Key Learning Outcomes	Page	Example Exercises
The five types of accounts requiring adjusting entries are prepaid expenses, unearned revenues, accrued revenues, accrued expenses, and depreciable capital assets. Examples of these adjusting entries are illustrated.	• Prepare an adjusting entry for prepaid expense, unearned revenue, accrued revenue, accrued expense, and depreciation expense.	111	3-3 3-4 3-5 3-6 3-7

3 Summarize the adjustment process.

Key Points	Key Learning Outcomes	Page	Example Exercises
A summary of adjustments, including the type of adjustment, reason for the adjustment, the adjusting entry, and the effect of omitting an adjustment on the financial statements, is shown in Exhibit 10.	• Determine the effect on the income statement and balance sheet of omitting an adjusting entry for prepaid expense, unearned revenue, accrued revenue, accrued expense, and depreciation expense.	121	3-8

4 Prepare an adjusted trial balance.

Key Points	Key Learning Outcomes	Page	Example Exercises
After all the adjusting entries have been posted, the equality of the total debit balances and total credit balances is verified by an adjusted trial balance. The financial statements are then prepared.	• Prepare an adjusted trial balance.	125	3-9
	• Determine the effect of errors on the equality of the adjusted trial balance.		
	• Prepare financial statements from the adjusted trial balance.		

GLOSSARY

accrual basis of accounting – Revenues and expenses are reported in the income statement in the period in which they are earned or incurred. (p. 100)

accrued expenses – Expenses that have been incurred but not recorded in the accounts. (p. 106)

accrued revenues – Revenues that have been earned but not recorded in the accounts. (p. 104)

accumulated depreciation – The contra asset account credited when recording the depreciation of a capital asset. (p. 109)

adjusted trial balance – The trial balance prepared after all the adjusting entries have been posted. (p. 125)

adjusting entries – The journal entries that bring the accounts up to date at the end of the accounting period. (p. 101)

adjusting process – An analysis and updating of the accounts before financial statements are prepared. (p. 101)

amortization – The systematic periodic transfer of the cost of a depreciable asset to an expense account during its expected useful life. (p. 108) Also known as *depreciation*.

capital assets – Long-term or relatively permanent tangible and intangible assets such as land, equipment, machinery, buildings, and patents that are used in normal business operations. (p. 108)

carrying amount of the asset – The difference between the cost of a capital asset and its accumulated depreciation. (p. 119) Also known as *net book value.*

cash basis of accounting – Revenues and expenses are reported in the income statement in the period in which cash is received or paid. (p. 101)

contra accounts – Accounts that are offset against another account. (p. 109)

depreciate – Decreasing in usefulness over time for all capital assets, except land. (p. 108)

depreciation – The systematic periodic transfer of the cost of a depreciable asset to an expense account during its expected useful life. (p. 108) Also known as *amortization.*

depreciation expense – The portion of the cost of a depreciable asset that is recorded as an expense each year of its useful life. (p. 108)

net book value – The difference between the cost of a capital asset and its accumulated depreciation. (p. 119) Also known as *carrying amount of the asset.*

notes payable – Written promises to pay an amount and interest at an agreed-upon rate. (p. 106)

notes receivable – Customers' written promises to pay company an amount and interest at an agreed-upon rate. (p. 106)

prepaid expenses – Items such as supplies that will be used in the business in the future. (p. 102)

revenue recognition principle – The accounting concept that supports reporting revenues when the services are provided to customers. (p. 100)

time period concept – The accounting concept that assumes that the economic life of the business can be divided into time periods. (p. 100)

unearned revenues – The liability created by receiving cash in advance of earning the revenue. (p. 103)

END-OF-CHAPTER ILLUSTRATIVE PROBLEM

Three years ago, T. Roderick organized Harbour Realty. At December 31, 2015, the end of the year, the unadjusted trial balance of Harbour Realty appears as shown below.

Harbour Realty
Unadjusted Trial Balance
December 31, 2015

	Debit Balances	Credit Balances
Cash	3,425	
Accounts Receivable	7,000	
Supplies	1,270	
Prepaid Insurance	620	
Office Equipment	51,650	
Accumulated Depreciation—Office Equipment		9,700
Accounts Payable		925
Wages Payable		0
Unearned Fees		1,250
T. Roderick, Capital		29,000
T. Roderick, Withdrawals	5,200	
Fees Earned		59,125
Wages Expense	22,415	
Depreciation Expense	0	
Rent Expense	4,200	
Utilities Expense	2,715	
Supplies Expense	0	
Insurance Expense	0	
Miscellaneous Expense	1,505	
	100,000	100,000

The data needed to determine year-end adjustments are as follows:
a. Supplies on hand at December 31, 2015, $380.
b. Insurance premiums expired during the year, $315.
c. Depreciation of equipment during the year, $4,950.
d. Wages accrued but not paid at December 31, 2015, $440.
e. Accrued fees earned but not recorded at December 31, 2015, $1,000.
f. Unearned fees on December 31, 2015, $750.

Instructions

1. Prepare the necessary adjusting journal entries. Include journal entry explanations.
2. Determine the balance of the accounts affected by the adjusting entries and prepare an adjusted trial balance.

Solution

1.

Journal					
Date		**Description**	**Post. Ref.**	**Debit**	**Credit**
2015 Dec. 31		Supplies Expense		890	
		Supplies			890
		Supplies used ($1,270 – $380).			
	31	Insurance Expense		315	
		Prepaid Insurance			315
		Insurance expired.			
	31	Depreciation Expense		4,950	
		Accumulated Depreciation—Office Equipment			4,950
		Depreciation expense.			
	31	Wages Expense		440	
		Wages Payable			440
		Accrued wages.			
	31	Accounts Receivable		1,000	
		Fees Earned			1,000
		Accrued fees.			
	31	Unearned Fees		500	
		Fees Earned			500
		Fees earned ($1,250–$750).			

2.

	Debit Balances	Credit Balances
Harbour Realty		
Adjusted Trial Balance		
December 31, 2015		
Cash	3,425	
Accounts Receivable	8,000	
Supplies	380	
Prepaid Insurance	305	
Office Equipment	51,650	
Accumulated Depreciation—Office Equipment		14,650
Accounts Payable		925
Wages Payable		440
Unearned Fees		750
T. Roderick, Capital		29,000
T. Roderick, Withdrawals	5,200	
Fees Earned		60,625
Wages Expense.	22,855	
Depreciation Expense	4,950	
Rent Expense	4,200	
Utilities Expense	2,715	
Supplies Expense	890	
Insurance Expense	315	
Miscellaneous Expense.	1,505	
	106,390	106,390

EYE OPENERS

1. How are revenues and expenses reported on the income statement under (a) the cash basis of accounting and (b) the accrual basis of accounting?
2. Fees for services provided are billed to a customer during 2014. The customer remits the amount owed in 2015. During which year would the revenues be reported on the income statement under (a) the cash basis? (b) the accrual basis?
3. Employees performed services in 2014, but the wages were not paid until 2015. During which year would the wages expense be reported on the income statement under (a) the cash basis? (b) the accrual basis?
4. Is the cash balance on the unadjusted trial balance the amount that should normally be reported on the balance sheet? Explain.
5. Is the supplies balance on the unadjusted trial balance the amount that should normally be reported on the balance sheet? Explain.
6. Why are adjusting entries needed at the end of an accounting period?
7. What is the difference between *adjusting entries* and *correcting entries*?
8. Identify the five different categories of adjusting entries frequently required at the end of an accounting period.
9. If the effect of the debit portion of an adjusting entry is to increase the balance of an asset account, which of the following statements most likely describes the effect of the credit portion of the entry?
   a. Increases the balance of a liability account.
   b. Increases the balance of a revenue account.
   c. Increases the balance of an expense account.

10. If the effect of the credit portion of an adjusting entry is to increase the balance of a liability account, which of the following statements most likely describes the effect of the debit portion of the entry?
    a. Increases the balance of an expense account.
    b. Increases the balance of a revenue account.
    c. Increases the balance of an asset account.
11. Does every adjusting entry have an effect on determining the amount of net income for a period? Explain.
12. What is the nature of the balance in the prepaid insurance account at the end of the accounting period (a) before adjustment? (b) after adjustment?
13. On July 1 of the current year, a business paid the July rent on the building that it occupies. (a) Do the rights acquired at July 1 represent an asset or an expense? (b) What is the justification for debiting Rent Expense at the time of payment?
14. (a) Explain the purpose of the two accounts: Depreciation Expense and Accumulated Depreciation. (b) What is the normal balance of each account? (c) Is it customary for the balances of the two accounts to be equal in amount? (d) In which financial statements, if any, will each account appear?

PRACTICE EXERCISES

① PE 3-1
Accounts requiring adjustment

EE 3-1 p. 110

Indicate with a Yes or No whether each of the following accounts normally requires an adjusting entry.
a. Building
b. Cash
c. Interest Payable
d. Miscellaneous Expense
e. Nath Luken, Capital
f. Prepaid Insurance

---

① PE 3-2
Type of adjustment

EE 3-2 p. 110

Classify the following items as (1) prepaid expense, (2) unearned revenue, (3) accrued revenue, (4) accrued expense, or (5) depreciable capital asset.
a. Cash received for use of land next month
b. Fees earned but not received
c. Office furniture
d. Rent expense owed but not yet paid
e. Supplies on hand

---

② PE 3-3
Adjustment for prepaid expenses

EE 3-3 p. 114

The prepaid insurance account had a beginning balance of $7,200 and was debited for $4,800 of premiums paid during the year. Journalize the adjusting entry required at the end of the year, assuming the amount of unexpired insurance related to future periods is $8,000.

---

② PE 3-4
Adjustment for unearned revenues

EE 3-4 p. 115

On August 1, 2014, Treadwell Co. received $10,500 for the rent of land for 12 months. Journalize the adjusting entry required for unearned rent on December 31, 2014.

PE 3-5
② **Adjustment for accrued revenues**

At the end of the current year, $12,400 of fees have been earned but have not been billed to clients. Journalize the adjusting entry to record the accrued fees.

EE 3-5 p. 117

PE 3-6
② **Adjustment for accrued expenses**

Colossal Realty Co. pays weekly salaries of $29,100 on Monday for a six-day workweek ending the preceding Saturday. Journalize the necessary adjusting entry at the end of the accounting period assuming that the period ends on Thursday.

EE 3-6 p. 119

PE 3-7
② **Adjustment for depreciation**

The estimated amount of depreciation on equipment for the current year is $5,500. Journalize the adjusting entry to record the depreciation.

EE 3-7 p. 120

PE 3-8
③ **Effect of omitting adjustments**

For the year ended December 31, 2015, Balboa Services Co. mistakenly omitted adjusting entries for (1) $1,520 of supplies that were used, (2) unearned revenue of $12,200 that was earned, and (3) insurance of $6,000 that expired. Indicate the combined effect of the errors on (a) revenues, (b) expenses, and (c) net income for the year ended December 31, 2015.

EE 3-8 p. 120

PE 3-9
④ **Effect of errors on adjusted trial balance**

Consider each of the following errors individually, and indicate whether the error would cause the adjusted trial balance totals to be unequal. If the error would cause the adjusted trial balance totals to be unequal, indicate whether the debit or credit total is higher and by what amount.

a. The adjustment for accrued wages of $4,150 was journalized as a debit to Wages Expense for $4,150 and a credit to Accounts Payable for $4,150.

EE 3-9 p. 126

b. The entry for $1,290 of supplies used during the period was journalized as a debit to Supplies Expense of $1,290 and a credit to Supplies of $1,920.

EXERCISES

EX 3-1
① **Classifying types of adjustments**

Classify the following items as (a) prepaid expense, (b) unearned revenue, (c) accrued revenue, or (d) accrued expense.
1. A two-year premium paid on a fire insurance policy.
2. Fees earned but not yet received.
3. Fees received but not yet earned.
4. Salary owed but not yet paid.
5. Subscriptions received in advance by a magazine publisher.
6. Supplies on hand.

7. Taxes owed but payable in the following period.
8. Utilities owed but not yet paid.
9. Interest earned but not yet received.

---

1 EX 3-2
Classifying adjusting entries

The following accounts were taken from the unadjusted trial balance of Orion Co., a lobbying firm. Indicate whether each account would normally require an adjusting entry. If the account normally requires an adjusting entry, use the following notation to indicate the type of adjustment:

> AE—Accrued Expense
> AR—Accrued Revenue
> PE—Prepaid Expense
> UR—Unearned Revenue

To illustrate, the answer for the first account is shown below.

Account	Answer
Accounts Receivable	Normally requires adjustment (AR).
Cash	
Interest Expense	
Interest Receivable	
Johann Atkins, Capital	
Land	
Office Equipment	
Prepaid Rent	
Supplies	
Unearned Fees	
Wages Expense	

---

2 EX 3-3
Adjusting entry for supplies

The balance in the supplies account, before adjustment at the end of the year, is $3,915. Journalize the adjusting entry required if the amount of supplies on hand at the end of the year is $1,750 and note the final balance. What principle requires an adjustment to supplies?

---

2 EX 3-4
Determining supplies purchased

The supplies and supplies expense accounts at December 31, after adjusting entries have been posted at the end of the first year of operations, are shown in the following T accounts:

Supplies		Supplies Expense	
Bal.	900	Bal.	2,750

Determine the amount of supplies purchased during the year.

---

2 EX 3-5
Adjusting entry for supplies

The supplies and supplies expense accounts for Tim's Trims and Cuts are shown at December 31 before adjustment at the end of the year. The final amount of supplies was counted and found to be $312.

Supplies				Supplies Expense		
Bal.	675			Jun. 30	421	
May 15	532	421	Jun. 30			
Oct. 28	732					

Journalize the required adjusting entry to bring the supplies account up to date for the year ended December 31.

EX 3-6
Effect of omitting adjusting entry

At December 31, the end of the first month of operations, the usual adjusting entry transferring prepaid insurance expired to an expense account is omitted. Because of the error, which items will be incorrectly stated on (a) the income statement for December and (b) the balance sheet as at December 31? Also indicate whether the items in error will be overstated or understated.

EX 3-7
Adjusting entries for prepaid insurance

The balance in the prepaid insurance account, before adjustment at the end of the year, is $14,800. Journalize the adjusting entry required under each of the following *alternatives* for determining the amount of the adjustment: (a) the amount of insurance expired during the year is $11,200; (b) the amount of unexpired insurance applicable to future periods is $3,600.

EX 3-8
Adjusting entries for prepaid insurance

The prepaid insurance account had a balance of $5,400 at the beginning of the year. The account was debited for $6,000 for premiums on policies purchased during the year. Journalize the adjusting entry required at the end of the year for each of the following situations: (a) the amount of unexpired insurance applicable to future periods is $1,000; (b) the amount of insurance expired during the year is $10,400.

EX 3-9
Adjusting entry for supplies and prepaid insurance

Scene Productions Inc. set up its operations on December 15 of the current year and chose a December 31 year-end for ease in future years. Prepare the required journal entries and adjusting entries for the following items:

a. A one-year insurance policy was purchased on December 15 for $2,280. Supplies totalling $1,652 were purchased on December 15.
b. A $1,500 three-month advertising contract was signed and paid for on December 15.
c. Supplies totalling $48 were used in December.

EX 3-10
Adjusting entry for unearned fees

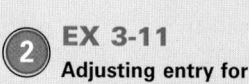

The balance in the unearned fees account, before adjustment at the end of the year, is $38,375.

a. Journalize the adjusting entry required if the amount of unearned fees at the end of the year is $17,200.
b. Why was this unearned fees account set up? What transaction occurred to require this account?

EX 3-11
Adjusting entry for unearned revenues

On June 1, 2013, Speed Secretarial Co. received two one-year contracts to perform services. Also on June 1, Speed Secretarial Co. received a deposit of half of the future revenue in cash for each contract. It will receive the balance upon completion of the contracts. The following information is available for the year ended December 31, 2013:

	Total Contract
Contract #1	$30,000
Contract #2	$16,500

a. Journalize the entry to record when the cash is received on June 1, 2013.
b. Journalize the adjusting entry to record the revenue earned at year-end.

EX 3-12
Adjusting entry for unearned revenues

On May 1, 2014, Joe's Computing negotiated a one-year contract to provide services for $8,400. The company received 25% of the payment upon receipt of the contract and will receive the remainder upon completion of the contract. Joe's Computing will do an equal amount of work on the contract each month. The company has no other outstanding contracts.

a. Journalize the required entry to record the May 1 transaction.
b. Journalize the adjusting entry for the year ended December 31, 2014.

EX 3-13

Effect of omitting adjusting entry

2
3

At the end of January, the first month of the business year, the accountant omitted the usual adjusting entry transferring rent earned to a revenue account from the unearned rent account. Because of the error, which items will be incorrectly stated on (a) the income statement for January and (b) the balance sheet as at January 31? Also indicate whether the items in error will be overstated or understated.

EX 3-14

Adjusting entry for accrued fees

2

At the end of the current year, $8,140 of fees has been earned but has not been billed to clients.

Journalize the adjusting entry to record the accrued fees.

EX 3-15

Adjusting entry for accrued fees

2

Zing Computing has a contract with a local business that began on July 1 of the current year. Zing Computing was contracted for a period of six months to assist the company in changing over to a new accounting system. The contract states that the client will be billed at the end of the term based on a $2,400 monthly rate.

Journalize the adjusting entry necessary for the year ended December 31.

EX 3-16

Adjusting entry for accrued fees

2

Decca Design Ltd. is a database design company. Its clients pay a $1,000 deposit and are billed for the remainder of the contract once the database is complete. All existing contracts were entered into in the current year.

	Total Value	Completion at Dec. 31 year-end
Contract #1	$12,800	25%
Contract #2	$ 6,250	60%
Contract #3	$14,900	90%

a. Journalize the adjusting entry to record the revenue earned at year-end.
b. Assume that Decca Design Ltd. has only these three contracts. What are the balances in the unearned revenue, accounts receivable, and revenue accounts at year-end?

EX 3-17

Adjusting entries for unearned and accrued fees

2

The balance in the unearned fees account, before adjustment at the end of the year, is $96,000. Of these fees, $78,500 has been earned. In addition, $23,600 of fees has been earned but has not been billed. Journalize the adjusting entries (a) to adjust the unearned fees account and (b) to record the accrued fees.

EX 3-18

Effect of omitting adjusting entry

2
3

The adjusting entry for accrued fees was omitted at December 31. Because of the omission, which items will be in error on (a) the income statement for the current year and (b) the balance sheet as at December 31? Also indicate whether the items in error will be overstated or understated.

EX 3-19

Adjusting entry for interest receivable

2

On May 10, 2015, Hallihan's Co-op provided cash of $4,000 to Chan Choi & Company for a year at 4%.

a. Journalize the required entry to record the May 10 transaction.
b. Journalize the adjusting entry for the year ended December 31, 2015.

EX 3-20

Adjusting entry for interest receivable

2

On September 5, 2015, McCrea Co. provided cash of $3,000 to Pilon & Company for a 150-day period at 4%.

a. Journalize the required entry to record the September 5 transaction.
b. Journalize the adjusting entry for the year ended December 31, 2015.

EX 3-21

Adjusting entries for accrued salaries

√ a. Amount of entry: $2,220

Ash Realty Co. pays weekly salaries of $3,700 on Friday for a five-day workweek ending on that day. Journalize the necessary adjusting entry at the end of the accounting period assuming that the period ends (a) on Wednesday, October 20 and (b) on Thursday, October 21.

Journalize the entries at payment assuming the period ended (c) on Wednesday and (d) on Thursday.

EX 3-22

Determining wages paid

The wages payable and wages expense accounts at December 31, after adjusting entries have been posted at the end of the first month of operations, are shown in the following T accounts:

Wages Payable		Wages Expense	
Bal.	3,175	Bal.	93,800

Determine the amount of wages paid during the month.

EX 3-23

Adjusting entry for accrued salaries

Steve's Stitchery Co. has 26 employees with a combined daily salary of $5,800. Year-end falls halfway through the two-week pay period. Assume that all employees worked every day during the pay period.
a. Calculate the accrued salaries and journalize the adjusting transaction for December 31.
b. Journalize the payment.

EX 3-24

Adjusting entry for accrued salaries

Salaries for each of the six employees at Live, Work, Play and Co. are $1,600 for each two-week period and are based on a five-day workweek. The December 31 year-end falls on the fourth day of the pay period.
a. Calculate the accrued salaries and journalize the adjusting transaction.
b. Journalize the payment.

EX 3-25

Effect of omitting adjusting entry

Accrued salaries of $4,950 owed to employees for December 30 and 31 are not considered in preparing the financial statements for the year ended December 31. Because of the error, which items will be erroneously stated on (a) the income statement for the year and (b) the balance sheet as at December 31? Also indicate whether the items in error will be overstated or understated.

EX 3-26

Effect of omitting adjusting entry

Assume that the error in Exercise 3-25 was not corrected and that the $4,950 of accrued salaries was included in the first salary payment in January. Because of the failure to correct the initial error, which items will be erroneously stated on (a) the income statement for the month of January and (b) the balance sheet as at January 31?

EX 3-27

Adjusting entries for prepaid insurance

√ b. $7,975

Andular Financial Services was organized on April 1 of the current year. On that day, Andular prepaid $9,000 for insurance for the year. The company later decided it needed more insurance coverage. On October 1, it purchased fire insurance for the next 12 months at a cost of $4,900 and recorded it as prepaid insurance.
a. Journalize the two adjusting entries required to bring the accounts affected by the two insurance policies up to date as at December 31.
b. What is the amount of the insurance expense for the current year?

EX 3-28

Adjustment for depreciation

The estimated amount of depreciation on equipment for the current year is $1,840. Journalize the adjusting entry to record the depreciation on December 31.

EX 3-29
② **Adjustment for depreciation**

On January 1, 2014, AJ Manufacturing paid $90,000 for a new machine that has an expected useful life of 15 years. AJ Manufacturing has a December 31 year-end.

a. Journalize the adjusting entry to record depreciation on the new machine for 2015.

b. What is the net book value of the machine at December 31, 2015?

EX 3-30
② **Adjustment for depreciation**

Net Programs Inc. purchased three new computer programs in 2014. The following information is available for the year ended December 31, 2014:

	Date of Purchase	Purchase Price	Useful Life
Program A	January 1, 2014	$ 8,800	1 year
Program B	January 1, 2014	$10,400	2 years
Program C	January 1, 2014	$19,700	2 years

a. Journalize the adjusting entry to record depreciation at December 31, 2014.

b. What is the net book value of each program at December 31, 2014?

EX 3-31
② **Determining capital asset's book value**

The balance in the equipment account is $925,700, and the balance in the accumulated depreciation—equipment account is $311,100.

a. What is the carrying amount of the equipment?

b. Does the balance in the accumulated depreciation account mean that the equipment's loss of value is $311,100? Explain.

EX 3-32
② **Book value of capital assets**

In a recent balance sheet, Microsoft Corporation reported *Property and Equipment* of $16,259 million and *Accumulated Depreciation* of $8,629 million.

a. What was the carrying amount of the property and equipment?

b. Would the carrying amount of these assests normally approximate their fair market values?

EX 3-33
② **Effects of errors on financial statements**

For a recent period, the balance sheet for Best Buy Co., Inc., reported accrued expenses of $1,685,000,000. For the same period, Best Buy reported income before income taxes of $1,043,000,000. Assume that the accrued expenses apply to the current period but were not recorded at the end of the current period. What would have been the income (loss) before income taxes?

EX 3-34
② **Effects of errors on financial statements**

For a recent year, the balance sheet for The Campbell Soup Company included accrued expenses of $623,000,000. The income before taxes for The Campbell Soup Company for the year was $1,149,000,000. Assume the accruals apply to the current year but were not recorded at the end of the year. By how much would income before taxes have been misstated?

EX 3-35
② ③ **Effects of errors on financial statements**

✔ 1. a. Revenue understated, $18,000

The accountant for Hallmark Co., a construction firm, mistakenly omitted adjusting entries for (a) unearned revenue earned during the year ($18,000) and (b) accrued wages ($3,000). Consider each error individually and indicate the effect on the income statement for December 31. Also indicate the effect of each error on the December 31 balance sheet. Set up a table as follows and record your answers by inserting the dollar amount in the appropriate spaces. Insert a zero if the error does not affect the item.

(*continued*)

		Error (a)		Error (b)	
		Over-stated	Under-stated	Over-stated	Under-stated
1.	Revenue for the year would be	$ _____	$ _____	$ _____	$ _____
2.	Expenses for the year would be	$ _____	$ _____	$ _____	$ _____
3.	Net income for the year would be	$ _____	$ _____	$ _____	$ _____
4.	Assets at December 31 would be	$ _____	$ _____	$ _____	$ _____
5.	Liabilities at December 31 would be	$ _____	$ _____	$ _____	$ _____
6.	Owner's equity at December 31 would be	$ _____	$ _____	$ _____	$ _____

EX 3-36

②③ Effects of errors on financial statements

If the net income for the current year had been $424,300 in Exercise 3-35, what would have been the correct net income if the proper adjusting entries had been made?

EX 3-37

②③ Adjusting entries for amortization; effect of error

On December 31, a business estimates depreciation on equipment used during the first year of operations to be $12,200.

a. Journalize the adjusting entry required as at December 31.

b. If the adjusting entry in (a) were omitted, which items would be erroneously stated on (1) the income statement for the year and (2) the balance sheet as at December 31?

Appendix EX 3-38

Alternative method for prepaid expenses and unearned revenue

The insurance expense account had a total of $13,200 of premiums debited for premiums paid during the year. Showing T accounts, journalize the adjusting entry required at the end of the year, assuming that the amount of unexpired insurance related to future periods is $4,200. Prepaid insurance had a $3,000 normal balance before the adjusting entry. What are the final balances in the prepaid insurance and insurance expense accounts?

Appendix EX 3-39

Alternative method for prepaid expenses and unearned revenue

On October 1, 2014, Workout Co. received $15,000 for the rent of land for 12 months and recorded the amount to rent revenue. Journalize the adjusting entry required for unearned rent as at December 31, 2014. The unearned rent account is at zero. Show T accounts.

Appendix EX 3-40

Alternative adjusting entries for office supplies

The office supplies purchased during the year total $4,570, and the amount of office supplies on hand at the end of the year is $460. Opening Office Supplies was $500.

a. Record the following transactions directly in T accounts for Office Supplies and Office Supplies Expense, using the system of initially recording supplies as an asset: (1) purchases for the period; (2) adjusting entry at the end of the period. Identify each entry by number.

b. Record the following transactions directly in T accounts for Office Supplies and Office Supplies Expense, using the system of initially recording supplies as an expense: (1) purchases for the period; (2) adjusting entry at the end of the period. Identify each entry by number.

Appendix EX 3-41

Alternative adjusting entries for prepaid insurance

During the first year of operations, insurance premiums of $11,400 were paid. At the end of the year, unexpired premiums totalled $4,175. Journalize the adjusting entry at the end of the year, assuming that (a) prepaid expenses were initially recorded as assets and (b) prepaid expenses were initially recorded as expenses.

**Appendix
EX 3-42**

Alternative adjusting entries for unearned revenue

The unearned advertising revenue collected in advance during the year totalled $482,800, and the unearned advertising revenue at the end of the year was $112,500. Unearned advertising revenue at the beginning of the year was zero.

a. Record the following transactions directly in T accounts for Unearned Advertising Revenue and Advertising Revenue, using the system of initially recording advertising fees as a liability: (1) revenues received during the period; (2) adjusting entry at the end of the period. Identify each entry by number.
b. Record the following transactions directly in T accounts for Unearned Advertising Revenue and Advertising Revenue, using the system of initially recording advertising fees as revenue: (1) revenues received during the period; (2) adjusting entry at the end of the period. Identify each entry by number.

**Appendix
EX 3-43**

Alternative adjusting entries for unearned revenue

In its first year of operation, Martin Publishing Co. received $3,275,000 in advance from advertising contracts and $9,195,000 in advance from magazine subscriptions, crediting the two amounts to Unearned Advertising Revenue and Circulation Revenue, respectively. At the end of the year, the unearned advertising revenue amounts to $396,000, and the circulation revenue amounts to $3,150,000. Journalize the adjusting entries that should be made at the end of the year.

PROBLEMS SERIES A

PR 3-1A
Adjusting entries

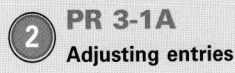

On December 31, 2015, the following data were accumulated to assist the accountant in preparing the adjusting entries for Dependable Realty:

a. Fees accrued but unbilled at December 31 are $4,900.
b. The supplies account balance on December 31 is $3,975. The supplies on hand at December 31 are $1,050.
c. Wages accrued but not paid at December 31 are $2,500.
d. The unearned rent account balance at December 31 is $11,000, representing the receipt of an advance payment on December 1 of three months' rent from tenants.
e. Amortization of office equipment is $1,100.

Instructions

1. Journalize the adjusting entries required at December 31, 2015.
2. Briefly explain the difference between adjusting entries and entries that would be made to correct errors, which was discussed in Chapter 2.

PR 3-2A
Adjusting entries

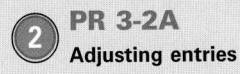

Selected account balances before adjustment for Oval Realty at December 31, 2015, the end of the current year, are shown below.

	Debits	Credits
Accounts Receivable	$ 65,000	
Accumulated Depreciation		$ 10,000
Depreciation Expense	—	
Equipment	100,000	
Fees Earned		379,500
Prepaid Rent	8,200	
Rent Expense	—	
Supplies	1,950	
Supplies Expense	—	
Unearned Fees		9,000
Wages Expense	128,000	
Wages Payable		—

(continued)

Data needed for year-end adjustments are as follows:
a. Supplies on hand at December 31, $600.
b. Depreciation of equipment during year, $1,000.
c. Rent expired during year, $6,000.
d. Wages accrued but not paid at December 31, $1,900.
e. Unearned fees at December 31, $3,750.
f. Unbilled fees at December 31, $4,500.

Instructions

Journalize the six adjusting entries required at December 31, using the data presented.

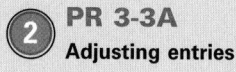 **PR 3-3A**
Adjusting entries

Calm Lake Outfitters Co., an outfitter store for fishing trips, prepared the following unadjusted trial balance at the end of its first year of operations:

Calm Lake Outfitters Co.
Unadjusted Trial Balance
December 31, 2015

	Debit Balances	Credit Balances
Cash	13,200	
Accounts Receivable	43,800	
Supplies	4,200	
Equipment	81,000	
Accounts Payable		6,100
Unearned Fees		9,600
Randy Huntsinger, Capital		112,000
Randy Huntsinger, Withdrawals	5,000	
Fees Earned		147,900
Wages Expense	76,400	
Rent Expense	27,500	
Utilities Expense	21,000	
Miscellaneous Expense	3,500	
	275,600	275,600

To prepare the adjusting entries, the following data were assembled:
a. Supplies on hand on December 31 were $900.
b. Fees earned but unbilled on December 31 were $3,500.
c. Depreciation of equipment was estimated to be $6,200 for the year.
d. Unpaid wages accrued on December 31 were $950.
e. The balance in unearned fees represented the December 1 receipt in advance for services to be provided. Only $2,100 of the services was provided between December 1 and December 31.

Instructions

Journalize the adjusting entries necessary on December 31.

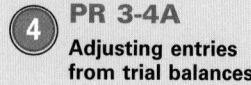 **PR 3-4A**
Adjusting entries from trial balances

The unadjusted and adjusted trial balances for McWay Services Co. on December 31, 2015, are shown below.

McWay Services Co.
Trial Balance
December 31, 2015 (in $ millions)

| | Unadjusted | | Adjusted | |
	Debit Balances	Credit Balances	Debit Balances	Credit Balances
Cash	16		16	
Accounts Receivable	38		44	
Supplies	12		9	
Prepaid Insurance	22		12	
Equipment	40		40	
Accumulated Depreciation—Equipment		8		11
Land	26		26	
Accounts Payable		26		26
Wages Payable		0		3
Chad McWay, Capital		94		94
Chad McWay, Withdrawals	8		8	
Fees Earned		74		80
Wages Expense	22		25	
Rent Expense	10		10	
Insurance Expense	0		10	
Utilities Expense	4		4	
Depreciation Expense	0		3	
Supplies Expense	0		3	
Miscellaneous Expense	4		4	
	202	202	214	214

a. Journalize the five entries that adjusted the accounts at December 31, 2015. None of the accounts was affected by more than one adjusting entry.

b. Prepare the income statement, statement of owner's equity, and balance sheet, assuming no new investment by Chad.

PR 3-5A

Adjusting entries from trial balances

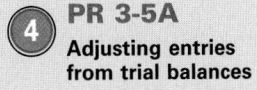

The accountant for Rooster Laundry prepared the following unadjusted and adjusted trial balances. Assume that all balances in the unadjusted trial balance and the amounts of the adjustments are correct. Identify the errors in the accountant's adjusting entries and show the corrected adjusted trial balance.

✔ Corrected trial balance totals, $621,900

Rooster Laundry
Trial Balance
December 31, 2015

| | Unadjusted | | Adjusted | |
	Debit Balances	Credit Balances	Debit Balances	Credit Balances
Cash	15,000		15,000	
Accounts Receivable	36,500		44,000	
Laundry Supplies	7,500		11,000	
Prepaid Insurance*	10,400		2,800	
Laundry Equipment	280,000		268,000	
Accumulated Depreciation		96,000		96,000
Accounts Payable		19,200		19,200
Wages Payable				2,400
Carlos Martinez, Capital		120,600		120,600
Carlos Martinez, Withdrawals	57,550		57,550	
Laundry Revenue		364,200		364,200
Wages Expense	98,400		98,400	
Rent Expense	51,150		51,150	
Utilities Expense	37,000		37,000	
Depreciation Expense			12,000	
Laundry Supplies Expense			3,500	
Insurance Expense			1,600	
Miscellaneous Expense	6,500		6,500	
	600,000	600,000	608,500	602,400

*$7,600 of insurance expired during the year.

PR 3-6A

2

Adjusting entries and adjusted trial balances

3

4

Kim's Nursery sells a wide variety of plants and offers courses on summer and winter garden maintenance. Kim Linge prepared the unadjusted trial balance at December 31, 2015, shown below.

Kim's Nursery
Unadjusted Trial Balance
December 31, 2015

	Debit Balances	Credit Balances
Cash	17,600	
Supplies	11,730	
Plant Inventory	36,980	
Prepaid Insurance.	1,960	
Tractor.	9,900	
Accumulated Depreciation—Tractor.		660
Building.	67,000	
Accumulated Depreciation—Building.		43,550
Land	148,000	
Accounts Payable		560
Unearned Revenue		2,700
Kim Linge, Capital.		281,890
Kim Linge, Withdrawals.	6,000	
Plant Revenue.		112,940
Course Revenue		7,200
Cost of Goods Sold	90,940	
Salaries Expense	42,000	
Utilities Expense.	16,250	
Maintenance Expense.	1,140	
	449,500	449,500

To prepare the adjusting entries, the following data were assembled:
a. An inventory count shows that $3,620 in supplies remain on hand.
b. The one-year insurance policy was purchased at the end of March of the current year. It was the only policy in the account.
c. The tractor was purchased in 2014 and has an estimated useful life of 15 years. The building depreciation is $1,675.
d. December 31 is the last working day of the calendar year for the seven employees, and they have been fully paid to year-end. They have each earned a $1,500 bonus to be paid to them on January 15, 2016.
e. Spaces fill up fast for the summer maintenance course. As a result, four people have paid in advance for next year's course at $350 per person, which has been recorded to Course Revenue. The $2,700 balance in the unearned revenue account relates to the winter maintenance course that took place in November.
f. Kim's Nursery has paid $300 in advance for the winter groundskeeper. The grounds-keeper does not start until January 15. This transaction has not yet been recorded in error.

Instructions

1. Journalize the adjusting and correcting entries. Add additional accounts as needed.
2. Determine the balances of the accounts affected by the adjusting and correcting entries and prepare an adjusted trial balance. There were no additional investments during the period.

PR 3-7A

2

Adjusting entries and adjusted trial balances

3

4

TRS Consulting, owned by Trevor Sultan, has a December 31 year-end. On January 20, 2015, all invoices and related information were provided for posting year-end adjusting entries. The prepaid expense accounts in the trial balance, shown below, have not been adjusted during the year. The information is as follows.

a. TRS has a three-and-a-half-year service contract that began October 1, 2014, for supplying consulting services at a monthly rate of $2,748. Invoicing is to be done quarterly. The first invoice was issued January 1, 2015.

b. TRS received a $13,000 deposit on December 31, 2014, for services to be rendered in May 2015. The total value of the services to be rendered for this contract is $52,000. No entry has been made for this transaction.

c. Depreciation for 2014 has not been recorded. The expected life of the assets listed on the trial balance are shown below. No assets have been purchased or sold in the current year. Complete a compound journal entry.

Asset	Estimated Life
Vehicle	10 years
Computers	1 year
Office Furniture	5 years
Building	25 years

d. Business insurance and auto insurance were purchased and paid for. Coverage for both policies begins on March 1, 2014. Both these policies are for 12-month periods.

TRS Consulting
Unadjusted Trial Balance
December 31, 2014

	Debit Balances	Credit Balances
Cash	7,460	
Accounts Receivable	17,350	
Prepaid Insurance	4,200	
Prepaid Auto Insurance	1,200	
Vehicle	30,000	
Accumulated Depreciation—Vehicle		6,000
Computers	9,000	
Accumulated Depreciation—Computers		9,000
Office Furniture	7,750	
Accumulated Depreciation—Office Furniture		4,650
Building	300,000	
Accumulated Depreciation—Building		18,000
Land	100,000	
Accounts Payable		950
Trevor Sultan, Capital		364,960
Trevor Sultan, Withdrawals	18,000	
Consulting Fees		264,300
Other Income		16,500
Salaries Expense	180,000	
Supplies Expense	3,260	
Utilities Expense	6,140	
	684,360	684,360

Instructions

1. Journalize the adjusting and correcting entries. Add additional accounts as needed.
2. Determine the balances of the accounts affected by the adjusting and correcting entries and prepare an adjusted trial balance. There were no additional investments during the period.

PR 3-8A
Adjusting entries

② ③ ④

Billy Board Company specializes in the maintenance and repair of signs, such as billboards. On December 31, 2015, the accountant for Billy Board Company prepared the following trial balances:

(continued)

Billy Board Company
Trial Balance
December 31, 2015

	Unadjusted		Adjusted	
	Debit Balances	Credit Balances	Debit Balances	Credit Balances
Cash	4,750		4,750	
Accounts Receivable	17,400		17,400	
Supplies	6,200		1,850	
Prepaid Insurance	9,000		3,600	
Buildings	120,000		120,000	
Accumulated Depreciation—Buildings		51,500		58,100
Trucks	75,000		75,000	
Accumulated Depreciation—Trucks		12,000		14,300
Land	50,000		50,000	
Accounts Payable		6,920		7,520
Salaries Payable		—		1,180
Unearned Service Fees		10,500		5,100
William Elkins, Capital		156,400		156,400
William Elkins, Withdrawals	7,500		7,500	
Service Fees Earned		162,680		168,080
Salaries Expense	80,000		81,180	
Depreciation Expense—Trucks	—		2,300	
Rent Expense	11,900		11,900	
Supplies Expense	—		4,350	
Utilities Expense	6,200		6,800	
Depreciation Expense—Buildings	—		6,600	
Taxes Expense	2,900		2,900	
Insurance Expense	—		5,400	
Miscellaneous Expense	9,150		9,150	
	400,000	400,000	410,680	410,680

Instructions

Journalize the seven entries that adjusted the accounts at December 31. None of the accounts was affected by more than one adjusting entry.

PR 3-9A

Adjusting entries and adjusted trial balances

② ③ ④

✔ 2. Total of Debit column: $333,050

Clarity Services Co., which specializes in appliance repair services, is owned and operated by Cindy Latty. Clarity Services Co.'s accounting clerk prepared the unadjusted trial balance at December 31, 2015, shown below.

Clarity Services Co.
Unadjusted Trial Balance
December 31, 2015

	Debit Balances	Credit Balances
Cash	10,200	
Accounts Receivable	34,750	
Prepaid Insurance	6,000	
Supplies.	1,725	
Building	80,750	
Accumulated Depreciation—Building.		37,850
Equipment.	45,000	
Accumulated Depreciation—Equipment		17,650
Land	50,000	
Accounts Payable		3,750
Unearned Rent		3,600
Cindy Latty, Capital		103,550
Cindy Latty, Withdrawals	8,000	
Fees Earned		158,600
Salaries and Wages Expense	56,850	
Utilities Expense	14,100	
Advertising Expense.	7,500	
Repairs Expense	6,100	
Miscellaneous Expense.	4,025	
	325,000	325,000

The data needed to determine year-end adjustments are as follows:
a. Depreciation of building for the year, $2,100.
b. Depreciation of equipment for the year, $3,000.
c. Accrued salaries and wages at December 31, $800.
d. Unexpired insurance at December 31, $1,500.
e. Fees earned but unbilled on December 31, $2,150.
f. Supplies on hand at December 31, $600.
g. Rent unearned at December 31, $1,500.

Instructions

1. Journalize the adjusting entries. Add additional accounts as needed.
2. Determine the balances of the accounts affected by the adjusting entries and prepare an adjusted trial balance.
3. Prepare an income statement, statement of owner's equity, and balance sheet, assuming no new investment by Cindy.

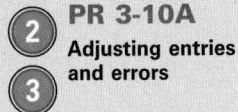

PR 3-10A

Adjusting entries and errors

✔ 2. Corrected Net Income: $135,375

At the end of December, the first year of operations, the following selected data were taken from the financial statements of Monita Forche, a lawyer:

Net income for year	$135,800
Total assets at December 31	750,000
Total liabilities at December 31	250,000
Total owner's equity at December 31	500,000

In preparing the financial statements, adjustments for the following data were overlooked:
a. Unbilled fees earned at December 31, $6,700.
b. Depreciation of equipment for December, $3,000.
c. Accrued wages at December 31, $2,150.
d. Supplies used during December, $1,975.

(*continued*)

Instructions

1. Journalize the entries to record the omitted adjustments.
2. Determine the correct amount of net income for the year and the total assets, liabilities, and owner's equity at December 31. In addition to indicating the corrected amounts, indicate the effect of each omitted adjustment by setting up and completing a columnar table similar to the following. Adjustment (a) is presented as an example.

	Net Income	Total Assets	=	Total Liabilities	+	Total Owner's Equity
Reported amounts	$135,800	$750,000		$250,000		$500,000
Corrections:						
Adjustment (a)	+6,700	+6,700		0		+6,700
Adjustment (b)						
Adjustment (c)						
Adjustment (d)						
Corrected amounts						

PR 3-11A

(2) (3) (4) Correcting entries, adjusting entries, and adjusted trial balances

On December 31, 2014, the following unadjusted trial balance was prepared, and the following data were accumulated to assist the accountant in preparing the adjusting entries and adjusted trial balance for Spur Publishing, owned by Kathleen Spur. When the trial balance did not balance, the records were reviewed and errors were identified.

Spur Publishing
Unadjusted Trial Balance
December 31, 2014

	Debit Balances	Credit Balances
Cash	46,850	
Accounts Receivable	64,480	
Prepaid Supplies	11,730	
Vehicle	17,900	
Accumulated Depreciation—Vehicle		3,780
Building	268,000	
Accumulated Depreciation—Building		28,800
Land	140,000	
Accounts Payable		2,685
Unearned Revenue		39,680
Kathleen Spur, Capital		209,665
Kathleen Spur, Withdrawals	120,000	
Publishing Revenue		2,111,820
Other Income		26,000
Salaries Expense	1,742,000	
Utilities Expense	10,980	
Supplies Expense	650	
Insurance Expense	1,140	
	2,423,730	2,422,430

a. The purchase of supplies on February 1, 2014, was incorrectly posted as a $650 debit to Supplies Expense and a $650 debit to Prepaid Supplies. Supplies used in 2014 were valued at $9,420.
b. The one-year insurance policy was purchased and incorrectly fully expensed on March 1, 2014. It is the only policy in Insurance Expense.
c. The $230 November hydro payment was incorrectly posted as a debit to Cash and a credit to Utilities Expense.
d. A $15,000 deposit for a contract beginning in January 2015 was incorrectly recorded as revenue on December 15, 2014.
e. As at December 31, 2014, $45,875 in fees was earned but unbilled. Of the unearned revenue recorded in the unearned revenue account, $30,000 was earned in December.

f. Spur Publishing has 15 employees who have a combined daily salary of $6,700. Year-end falls halfway through a two-week pay period. Assume that all employees worked every day during that period.

g. The vehicle was purchased in 2013 and has an estimated useful life of 10 years. The building has an estimated life of 20 years. Use the straight-line method for calculating depreciation.

Instructions

1. Correct any identified errors by creating both an entry to remove the error and a correcting journal entry.

2. Determine the balances of the accounts affected by the correcting entries and prepare another unadjusted trial balance.

3. Journalize the year-end adjusting entries. Add additional accounts as needed.

4. Determine the balances of the accounts affected by the adjusting entries and prepare an adjusted trial balance. Assume no additional investments during the period.

Appendix
PR 3-12A

Alternative adjusting entries

Selected account balances before adjustment for Close to Perfect Realty at December 31, 2015, the end of the current year, are as follows:

	Debits	Credits
Accounts Receivable	25,000	
Accumulated Depreciation		10,000
Depreciation Expense	—	
Equipment	55,000	
Fees Earned		62,000
Prepaid Rent	8,000	
Rent Expense	10,000	
Supplies	2,500	
Supplies Expense	4,000	
Unearned Fees		12,000
Wages Expense	5,000	
Wages Payable		200

Data needed for year-end adjustments are as follows:

a. Receipt of unearned fees during the year of $6,000 has been recorded in fees earned, and $7,000 of last year's unearned fees has been earned.

b. Supplies on hand, $3,000.

c. The total rent expense should be $8,000.

d. Depreciation of equipment during the year, $2,000.

e. Wages accrued but not paid at December 31, 2015, $600.

Instructions

Journalize the five adjusting entries required at December 31, 2015, using the data presented.

PROBLEMS SERIES B

② PR 3-1B

Adjusting entries

On December 31, 2015, the following data were accumulated to assist the accountant in preparing the adjusting entries for Oceanside Realty:

a. The supplies account balance on December 31 is $6,100. The supplies on hand on December 31 are $1,300.

b. The unearned rent account balance on December 31 is $4,500, representing the receipt of an advance payment on December 1 of three months' rent from tenants.

c. Wages accrued but not paid at December 31 are $3,000.

d. Fees accrued but unbilled at December 31 are $10,280.

e. Depreciation of office equipment is $1,400.

(continued)

Instructions

1. Journalize the adjusting entries required at December 31, 2015.
2. Briefly explain the difference between adjusting entries and entries that would be made to correct errors.

PR 3-2B
Adjusting entries

Selected account balances before adjustment for Perfect Realty at December 31, 2015, the end of the current year, are as follows:

	Debits	Credits
Accounts Receivable	$ 40,000	
Equipment	100,000	
Accumulated Depreciation		$ 12,000
Prepaid Rent	9,000	
Supplies	1,800	
Wages Payable		—
Unearned Fees		6,000
Fees Earned		215,000
Wages Expense	75,000	
Rent Expense	—	
Depreciation Expense	—	
Supplies Expense	—	

Data needed for year-end adjustments are as follows:

a. Unbilled fees at December 31, $2,900.
b. Supplies on hand at December 31, $400.
c. Rent expired, $6,000.
d. Depreciation of equipment during year, $3,000.
e. Unearned fees at December 31, $800.
f. Wages accrued but not paid at December 31, $1,400.

Instructions

Journalize the six adjusting entries required at December 31, using the data presented.

PR 3-3B
Adjusting entries

Browning Company, an electronics repair store, prepared the unadjusted trial balance shown below at the end of its first year of operations.

Browning Company
Unadjusted Trial Balance
December 31, 2015

	Debit Balances	Credit Balances
Cash	26,400	
Accounts Receivable	87,600	
Supplies	7,200	
Equipment	162,000	
Accounts Payable		12,200
Unearned Fees		19,200
Neal Salmon, Capital		222,800
Neal Salmon, Withdrawals	10,000	
Fees Earned		295,800
Wages Expense	152,800	
Rent Expense	55,000	
Utilities Expense	42,000	
Miscellaneous Expense	7,000	
	550,000	550,000

To prepare the adjusting entries, the following data were assembled:
a. Fees earned but unbilled on December 31 were $6,500.
b. Supplies on hand on December 31 were $1,850.
c. Depreciation of equipment was estimated to be $2,800 for the year.
d. The balance in unearned fees represented the December 1 receipt in advance for services to be provided. Only $3,000 of the services was provided between December 1 and December 31.
e. Unpaid wages accrued on December 31 were $1,275.

Instructions

Journalize the adjusting entries necessary on December 31, 2015.

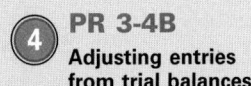

PR 3-4B

Adjusting entries from trial balances

The unadjusted and adjusted trial balances for BiWay Services Co. on December 31, 2015, are shown below.

BiWay Services Co.
Trial Balance
December 31, 2015 (in $millions)

	Unadjusted		Adjusted	
	Debit Balances	Credit Balances	Debit Balances	Credit Balances
Cash	20		20	
Accounts Receivable	58		66	
Supplies	14		12	
Prepaid Insurance	51		48	
Equipment	40		40	
Accumulated Depreciation—Equipment		20		24
Land	12		12	
Accounts Payable		15		15
Wages Payable		2		7
Ken Louis, Capital		101		101
Ken Louis, Withdrawals	5		5	
Fees Earned		89		97
Wages Expense	14		19	
Rent Expense	5		5	
Insurance Expense	0		3	
Utilities Expense	6		6	
Depreciation Expense	0		4	
Supplies Expense	0		2	
Miscellaneous Expense	2		2	
	227	227	244	244

a. Journalize the five entries that adjusted the accounts at December 31, 2015. None of the accounts was affected by more than one adjusting entry.
b. Prepare an income statement, statement of owner's equity, and balance sheet, assuming no new investment by Ken.

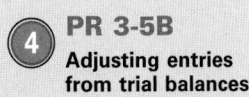

PR 3-5B

Adjusting entries from trial balances

✔ Corrected trial balance totals, $392,360

The accountant for Chicken Laundry prepared the following unadjusted and adjusted trial balances. Assume that all balances in the unadjusted trial balance and the amounts of the adjustments are correct. Identify the errors in the accountant's adjusting entries and show the corrected adjusted trial balance.

(continued)

Chicken Laundry
Trial Balance
December 31, 2015

	Unadjusted		Adjusted	
	Debit Balances	Credit Balances	Debit Balances	Credit Balances
Cash	18,000		18,000	
Accounts Receivable	25,500		25,500	
Laundry Supplies	6,470		8,880	
Prepaid Insurance	7,360		1,060	
Laundry Equipment	120,000		110,000	
Accumulated Depreciation—Laundry Equipment		40,000		40,000
Accounts Payable		53,500		53,500
Wages Payable		0		4,000
Sean Boone, Capital		53,260		53,260
Sean Boone, Withdrawals	25,750		25,750	
Laundry Revenue		225,600		231,600
Wages Expense	112,800		112,800	
Rent Expense	26,320		26,320	
Insurance Expense*	0		3,600	
Utilities Expense	25,600		25,600	
Depreciation Expense	0		10,000	
Laundry Supplies Expense	0		2,410	
Miscellaneous Expense	4,560		4,560	
	372,360	372,360	374,480	382,360

*3,600 of insurance expired during the year.

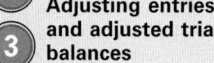

PR 3-6B

Adjusting entries and adjusted trial balances

Backfield Shoeing sells snowshoes and offers a wide variety of courses and guided tours through the backcountry. Dave Norton, the owner, prepared the unadjusted trial balance at December 31, 2015, shown below.

Backfield Shoeing
Unadjusted Trial Balance
December 31, 2015

	Debit Balances	Credit Balances
Cash	8,665	
Supplies	2,760	
Inventory	15,890	
Prepaid Insurance	3,840	
Equipment	12,800	
Accumulated Depreciation—Equipment		1,600
Building	42,000	
Accumulated Depreciation—Building		36,400
Land	178,000	
Accounts Payable		270
Unearned Revenue		1,350
Dave Norton, Capital		223,880
Dave Norton, Withdrawals	7,500	
Shoe Revenue		23,950
Course and Tour Revenue		46,750
Cost of Goods Sold	19,725	
Salaries Expense	32,000	
Utilities Expense	9,780	
Maintenance Expense	1,240	
	334,200	334,200

To prepare the adjusting entries, the following data were assembled:

a. An inventory count shows that $135 in supplies remain on hand.

b. The one-year insurance policy was purchased at the beginning of September of the current year.

c. The equipment was purchased in 2014 and has an estimated useful life of eight years. Depreciation for the building was calculated at $1,400.

d. December 31 is the last working day of the calendar year for the four employees and they have been fully paid to year-end. They have each earned a $600 bonus that will be paid to them on January 15, 2016.

e. Spaces fill up fast for the winter course in January. As a result, four people have paid in advance for next year's course at $150 per person. These payments have been recorded in Course and Tour Revenue. The balance in the unearned revenue account can be attributed to a course that completed in November.

f. Backfield has paid $800 in advance for the summer groundskeeper. The grounds-keeper does not start until March 1. This transaction has not yet been recorded in error.

Instructions

1. Journalize the adjusting and correcting entries. Add additional accounts as needed.
2. Determine the balances of the accounts affected by the adjusting and correcting entries and prepare an adjusted trial balance. Assume no additional investments during the period.

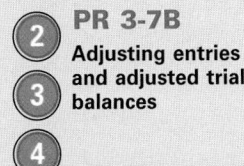

PR 3-7B

Adjusting entries and adjusted trial balances

LRB Consulting, owned by Lennox Bronson, has a December 31 year-end. On January 20, 2015, all invoices and related information were provided for posting year-end adjusting entries. The prepaid expense accounts in the trial balance, shown below, have not been adjusted during the year. The information is as follows.

a. On October 1, 2014, LRB began a three-and–a-half-year service contact to supply consulting services at an annual rate of $56,496. Invoicing is to be done quarterly.

b. On December 31, 2014, LRB received a $6,000 deposit for services to be rendered in February. The total value of the services to be rendered is $36,000. No entry has been made for this transaction.

c. Depreciation for 2014 has not been recorded. The expected lives for the assets listed on the trial balance are shown below. No assets have been purchased or sold in the current year. Complete a compound journal entry.

Asset	Expected Life
Computers	1 year
Office Furniture	5 years
Vehicle	10 years
Building	25 years

d. Business insurance and auto insurance were purchased and paid for. The insurance coverage begins on January 1, 2014, and March 1, 2014, respectively. Both policies are for 12-month periods.

(continued)

LRB Consulting
Unadjusted Trial Balance
December 31, 2014

	Debit Balances	Credit Balances
Cash	2,195	
Accounts Receivable	9,680	
Prepaid Insurance	3,960	
Prepaid Auto Insurance	1,656	
Computers	6,200	
Accumulated Depreciation—Computers		6,200
Office Furniture	6,775	
Accumulated Depreciation—Office Furniture		4,065
Vehicle	17,900	
Accumulated Depreciation—Vehicle		3,580
Building	216,000	
Accumulated Depreciation—Building		12,960
Land	119,000	
Accounts Payable		1,126
Lennox Bronson, Capital		247,639
Lennox Bronson, Withdrawals	16,000	
Consulting Fees		303,945
Other Income		18,000
Salaries Expense	187,350	
Supplies Expense	3,750	
Utilities Expense	7,049	
	597,515	597,515

Instructions

1. Journalize the adjusting and correcting entries. Add additional accounts as needed.
2. Determine the balances of the accounts affected by the adjusting and correcting entries and prepare an adjusted trial balance. Assume no additional investments during the period.

PR 3-8B
Adjusting entries

Luxor Company specializes in the repair of music equipment and is owned and operated by Amy Busby. On December 31, 2015, the accountant for Luxor Company prepared the trial balances shown below:

Luxor Company
Trial Balance
December 31, 2015

	Unadjusted		Adjusted	
	Debit Balances	Credit Balances	Debit Balances	Credit Balances
Cash	38,250		38,250	
Accounts Receivable	109,500		109,500	
Supplies	11,250		2,700	
Prepaid Insurance	14,250		4,500	
Equipment.	360,450		360,450	
Accumulated Depreciation—Equipment		94,500		102,000
Automobiles	109,500		109,500	
Accumulated Depreciation—Automobiles		54,750		61,200
Accounts Payable		24,930		26,400
Salaries Payable.		–		6,000
Unearned Service Fees		18,000		8,700
Amy Busby, Capital		394,020		394,020
Amy Busby, Withdrawals	75,000		75,000	
Service Fees Earned		733,800		743,100
Salaries Expense.	516,900		522,900	
Rent Expense	54,000		54,000	
Supplies Expense	–		8,550	
Depreciation Expense—Equipment	–		7,500	
Depreciation Expense—Automobiles.	–		6,450	
Utilities Expense	12,900		14,370	
Taxes Expense	8,175		8,175	
Insurance Expense.	–		9,750	
Miscellaneous Expense.	9,825		9,825	
	1,320,000	1,320,000	1,341,420	1,341,420

Instructions

Journalize the seven entries that adjusted the accounts at December 31. None of the accounts were affected by more than one adjusting entry.

PR 3-9B

Adjusting entries and adjusted trial balances

✔ 2. Total of Debit column: $822,180

Misfire Company is a small editorial services company owned and operated by Peter Borman. On December 31, 2015, Misfire Company's accounting clerk prepared the following unadjusted trial balance.

The data needed to determine year-end adjustments are as follows:
a. Unexpired insurance at December 31, $1,800.
b. Supplies on hand at December 31, $750.
c. Depreciation of building for the year, $2,000.
d. Depreciation of equipment for the year, $5,000.
e. Rent unearned at December 31, $2,850.
f. Accrued salaries and wages at December 31, $2,800.
g. Fees earned but unbilled on December 31, $12,380.

(continued)

Misfire Company
Unadjusted Trial Balance
December 31, 2015

	Debit Balances	Credit Balances
Cash	7,500	
Accounts Receivable	38,400	
Prepaid Insurance	7,200	
Supplies.	1,980	
Building	200,250	
Accumulated Depreciation—Building.		137,550
Equipment.	135,300	
Accumulated Depreciation—Equipment		97,950
Land	112,500	
Accounts Payable		12,150
Unearned Rent		6,750
Peter Borman, Capital		221,000
Peter Borman, Withdrawals	15,000	
Fees Earned		324,600
Salaries and Wages Expense.	193,370	
Utilities Expense	42,375	
Advertising Expense.	22,800	
Repairs Expense	17,250	
Miscellaneous Expense.	6,075	
	800,000	800,000

Instructions

1. Journalize the adjusting entries. Add additional accounts as needed.
2. Determine the balances of the accounts affected by the adjusting entries, and prepare an adjusted trial balance.
3. Prepare an income statement, statement of owner's equity, and balance sheet, assuming no new investment by Peter.

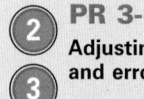

PR 3-10B

Adjusting entries and errors

✔ 2. Corrected Net Income: $136,850

At the end of December, the first month of operations, the following selected data were taken from the financial statements of Beth Cato, a lawyer:

Net income for December	$125,750
Total assets at December 31	500,000
Total liabilities at December 31	180,000
Total owner's equity at December 31	320,000

In preparing the financial statements, adjustments for the following data were overlooked:

a. Supplies used during December, $3,100.
b. Unbilled fees earned at December 31, $18,750.
c. Depreciation of equipment for December, $2,700.
d. Accrued wages at December 31, $1,850.

Instructions

1. Journalize the entries to record the omitted adjustments.
2. Determine the correct amount of net income for the year and the total assets, liabilities, and owner's equity at December 31. In addition to indicating the corrected amounts, indicate the effect of each omitted adjustment by setting up and completing a columnar table similar to the following. Adjustment (a) is presented as an example.

	Net Income	Total Assets	=	Total Liabilities	+	Total Owner's Equity
Reported amounts	$125,750	$500,000		$180,000		$320,000
Corrections:						
Adjustment (a)	−3,100	−3,100		0		−3,100
Adjustment (b)						
Adjustment (c)						
Adjustment (d)						
Corrected amounts						

PR 3-11B

2 3 4

Correcting entries, adjusting entries, and adjusted trial balances

On December 31, 2014, the following unadjusted trial balance was prepared, and the following data were accumulated to assist the accountant in preparing the adjusting entries and adjusted trial balance for Stark Advertising. When Henny Stark, the owner, realized the unadjusted trial balance did not balance, the records were reviewed and errors were identified.

Stark Advertising
Unadjusted Trial Balance
December 31, 2014

	Debit Balances	Credit Balances
Cash	53,870	
Accounts Receivable	74,150	
Prepaid Supplies	13,489	
Vehicle	21,700	
Accumulated Depreciation—Vehicle		4,340
Building	255,000	
Accumulated Depreciation—Building		27,360
Land	168,000	
Accounts Payable		3,088
Unearned Revenue		45,632
Henny Stark, Capital		358,231
Henny Stark, Withdrawals	138,000	
Advertising Revenue		1,646,968
Other Income		29,900
Salaries Expense	1,378,000	
Utilities Expense	12,630	
Supplies Expense	748	
Insurance Expense	1,428	
	2,117,015	2,115,519

a. The purchase of supplies on April 1, 2014, was incorrectly posted as a $748 debit to Supplies Expense and a $748 debit to Prepaid Supplies. Supplies used in 2014 were valued at $8,470.

b. The one-year insurance policy was purchased and incorrectly fully expensed on May 1, 2014. It is the only item in insurance expense.

c. The $418 September hydro payment was incorrectly posted as a debit to Cash and a credit to Utilities Expense.

d. A $17,250 deposit for a contract beginning in January 2015 was incorrectly recorded as revenue on December 15, 2014.

e. As at December 31, 2014, $52,750 fees are earned but unbilled. Of the unearned revenue posted, $34,500 was earned in December.

f. Stark Advertising has 10 employees with a combined daily salary of $5,300. Year-end falls halfway through a two-week pay period. Assume that all employees worked every day during the period.

g. The vehicle was purchased in 2012 and has an estimated useful life of 10 years. The estimated life of the building is 15 years. Straight-line depreciation is used.

(continued)

Instructions

1. Correct any identified errors by creating both a reversing journal entry and a correcting journal entry.
2. Determine the balances of the accounts affected by the correcting entries and prepare another unadjusted trial balance.
3. Journalize the year-end adjusting entries. Add additional accounts as needed.
4. Determine the balances of the accounts affected by the adjusting entries and prepare an adjusted trial balance. Assume no additional investments during the period.

Appendix PR 3-12B

Alternative adjusting entries

Selected account balances before adjustment for Kristjanson Realty at December 31, 2015, the end of the current year, are as follows:

	Debits	Credits
Accounts Receivable	20,000	
Accumulated Depreciation		8,000
Depreciation Expense	—	
Equipment	50,000	
Fees Earned		56,000
Prepaid Rent	4,000	
Rent Expense	8,000	
Supplies	2,000	
Supplies Expense	5,000	
Unearned Fees		9,000
Wages Expense	4,000	
Wages Payable		600

Data needed for year-end adjustments are as follows:

a. Receipt of unearned fees during the year of $8,000 has been recorded in fees earned. $5,000 of last year's unearned fees has been earned.
b. Supplies on hand, $3,200.
c. The total rent expense should be $6,000.
d. Depreciation of equipment during the year, $3,500.
e. Wages accrued but not paid at December 31, 2015, $400.

Instructions

Journalize the five adjusting entries required at December 31, 2015, using the data presented.

CONTINUING PROBLEM

The unadjusted trial balance that you prepared for Music Depot at the end of Chapter 2, on pages 94 and 95, should appear as follows:

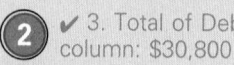

✔ 3. Total of Debit column: $30,800

Music Depot
Unadjusted Trial Balance
December 31, 2015

Acct. Numbers		Debit Balances	Credit Balances
1010	Cash	14,610	
1020	Accounts Receivable	1,740	
1030	Prepaid Insurance	2,700	
1040	Supplies	700	
1070	Office Equipment	6,000	
2010	Accounts Payable		6,350
2020	Unearned Revenue		7,200
3010	Pat Sharpe, Capital		9,000
3020	Pat Sharpe, Withdrawals	2,000	
4010	Fees Earned		8,250
5040	Music Expense	2,400	
5050	Advertising Expense	650	
		30,800	30,800

The data needed to determine adjustments for the two-month period ended December 31, 2015, are as follows:

a. During December, Music Depot provided guest disc jockeys for CHBD for a total of 120 hours. For information on the amount of the accrued revenue to be billed to CHBD, see the contract described in the December 3, 2015, on page 94.
b. Supplies on hand at December 31, 2015, $400.
c. The balance of the prepaid insurance account related to the December 1, 2015, transaction on page 94 in Chapter 2.
d. Depreciation of the office equipment, $75.
e. The balance of the unearned revenue account relates to the contract between Music Depot and CHBD, described in the December 3, 2015, transaction on page 94.
f. Accrued wages for a new assistant who started work three days before the year-end, $170.

Instructions

1. Prepare adjusting journal entries. You will need the following additional accounts:

        1080 Accumulated Depreciation—Office Equipment
        2030 Wages Payable
        5060 Supplies Expense
        5080 Depreciation Expense
        5090 Insurance Expense
        5100 Wages Expense

2. Post the adjusting entries, inserting balances in the accounts affected.
3. Prepare an adjusted trial balance.

SPECIAL ACTIVITIES

SA 3-1

Ethics and professional conduct in business

Cliff Hall opened Meridian Co. on January 1, 2014. At the end of the first year, the business needed additional capital. On behalf of Meridian, Cliff applied to Scotiabank for a loan of $300,000. Based on Meridian's financial statements, which had been prepared on a cash basis, the Scotiabank loan officer rejected the loan as too risky.

After receiving the rejection notice, Cliff instructed his accountant to prepare the financial statements on an accrual basis. These statements included $48,500 in accounts receivable and $15,650 in accounts payable. Cliff then instructed his accountant to record an additional $20,000 of accounts receivable for commissions on property for which a contract had been signed on December 28, 2014, but which would not be formally "closed" and the title transferred until January 5, 2015.

(*continued*)

Cliff then applied for a $300,000 loan from the Royal Bank, using the revised financial statements. On this application, Cliff indicated that he had not previously been rejected for credit.

Discuss the ethical and professional conduct of Cliff Hall in applying for the loan from the Royal Bank.

SA 3-2
Accrued expense

On December 30, 2015, you buy a Ford Expedition. It comes with a three-year, 60,000-km warranty. On March 5, 2016, you return the Expedition to the dealership for some basic repairs covered under the warranty. The cost of the repairs to the dealership is $1,645. In what year, 2015 or 2016, should Ford Motor Company recognize the cost of the warranty repairs as an expense?

SA 3-3
Accrued revenue

Roswell College requires students to pay tuition each term before classes begin. Students who have not paid their tuition are not allowed to enroll or to attend classes.

What journal entry should Roswell College use to record the receipt of the students' tuition payments? Describe the nature of each account in the entry.

SA 3-4
Accrued revenue

Group Project

The following is an excerpt from a conversation between Joel Loomis and Krista Truitt just before they board a flight to Paris on Air Canada. They are going to Paris to attend their company's annual sales conference.

Joel: Krista, aren't you taking an introductory accounting course at college?

Krista: Yes, I decided it's time I learned something about accounting. You know, our annual bonuses are based on the sales figures that come from the accounting department.

Joel: I guess I never really thought about it.

Krista: You should think about it! Last year, I placed a $750,000 order on December 28. But when I got my bonus, the $750,000 sale wasn't included. They said it hadn't been shipped until January 3, so it would have to count in the next year's bonus.

Joel: A real bummer!

Krista: Right! I was counting on that bonus including the $750,000 sale.

Joel: Did you complain?

Krista: Yes, but it didn't do any good. Ashley, the head accountant, said something about not recording revenues until the sale is final. I figure I'd take the accounting course and find out whether she's just jerking me around.

Joel: I never really thought about it. When do you think Air Canada will record its revenues from this flight?

Krista: Hmmm . . . I guess it could record the revenue when it sells the ticket . . . or . . . when the boarding passes are taken at the door . . . or . . . when we get off the plane . . . or when our company pays for the tickets . . . or . . . I don't know. I'll ask my accounting instructor.

Discuss when Air Canada should recognize the revenue from ticket sales to properly match revenues and expenses.

SA 3-5
Adjustments and financial statements

Several years ago, your brother opened Niagara Appliance Repairs. He made a small initial investment and added money from his personal bank account as needed. He withdrew money for living expenses at irregular intervals. As the business grew, he hired an assistant. He is now considering adding more employees, purchasing additional service trucks, and purchasing the building he now rents. To secure funds for the expansion, your brother submitted a loan application to the bank and included the most recent financial statements (shown below) prepared from accounts maintained by a part-time bookkeeper.

Niagara Appliance Repairs
Income Statement
For the Year Ended December 31, 2015

Service revenue		$112,500
Less: Rent paid	$31,200	
Wages paid	24,750	
Miscellaneous payments . .	9,100	
Supplies paid	7,000	
Utilities paid.	6,500	
Insurance paid	3,600	
Total expenses		82,150
Net income		$ 30,350

Niagara Appliance Repairs
Balance Sheet
December 31, 2015

Assets	
Cash	$ 15,900
Amounts due from customers. . .	18,750
Truck	55,350
Total assets	$ 90,000
Equities	
Owner's capital	$ 90,000

After reviewing the financial statements, the loan officer at the bank asked your brother whether he used the accrual basis of accounting for revenues and expenses. Your brother responded that he did, which is why he included an account for "Amounts Due from Customers." The loan officer then asked whether the accounts were adjusted prior to the preparation of the statements. Your brother answered that they had not been adjusted.

a. Why do you think the loan officer suspected that the accounts had not been adjusted prior to the preparation of the statements?

b. Indicate the accounts that might need to be adjusted before an accurate set of financial statements can be prepared.

c. Why did the loan officer ask your brother whether he used the accrual basis of accounting for revenues and expenses? Why would it have been important to use this method?

SA 3-6
Codes of ethics

Group Project

Obtain a copy of the student code of conduct for your college or university. In groups of three or four, answer the following questions:

1. Compare this code of conduct with the accountant's Codes of Professional Conduct, at the various websites.

2. One of your classmates asks you for permission to copy your homework, which your instructor will be collecting and grading for part of your overall term grade. Although your instructor has not stated whether one student may or may not copy another student's homework, is it ethical for you to allow your classmate to copy your homework? Is it ethical for your classmate to copy your homework?

Completing the Accounting Cycle

SLEEMAN BREWERIES LTD.

Most of us have had to file a personal tax return. During the year, you earn income and enter into tax-related transactions, such as making charitable donations. At the end of the year, your employer sends you the T4 tax information form, and you collect the tax records needed for completing your yearly tax return. As the next year begins, you start the cycle all over again.

Businesses also go through a cycle of activities. For example, Sleeman Breweries Ltd., a brewery based in Guelph, Ontario, brews beer for the Canadian market. This company begins its cycle by brewing the beer, with names such as Sleeman Cream Ale, Sleeman Honey Brown, and Sleeman Original Dark. This beer is then marketed and sold throughout the year. During the year, operating transactions of the business are recorded. For Sleeman's, such transactions include the salaries for staff, advertising expenditures, the cost of producing the beer, packaging costs, and revenues from sales. At the end of the year, financial statements are prepared to summarize the operating activities for the year. Finally, before the start of the next year, the accounts are readied for recording the operations of the next year.

As we saw in Chapter 1, the initial cycle for Net Solutions began with Chris Clark's investment in the business on November 1, 2014. The cycle continued with recording NetSolutions' transactions for November and December, as discussed and illustrated in Chapters 1 and 2. In Chapter 3, the cycle continued when the adjusting entries for the two months ended December 31, 2014, were recorded. In this chapter, we complete the cycle for NetSolutions by preparing financial statements and getting the accounts ready for recording transactions of the next period.

1 Describe the accounting cycle.

The Accounting Cycle		EXAMPLE EXERCISE 4-1 (page 167)

2 Prepare financial statements from adjusted account balances.

Financial Statements	Income Statement	EXAMPLE EXERCISE 4-2 (page 168)
	Statement of Owner's Equity	EXAMPLE EXERCISE 4-3 (page 170)
	Balance Sheet	EXAMPLE EXERCISE 4-4 (page 173)

3 Prepare closing entries

Closing Entries	Journalizing and Posting Closing Entries	EXAMPLE EXERCISE 4-5 (page 181)
	Post-Closing Trial Balance	

4 Illustrate the accounting cycle for one period.

Illustration of the Accounting Cycle	Steps of the Accounting Cycle	
	Calendar Year	
	Financial Analysis and Interpretation	EXAMPLE EXERCISE 4-6 (page 193)

APPENDIX 1 Reversing Entries

APPENDIX 2 End-of-Period Spreadsheet (Work Sheet)

For the chapter *At a Glance*, turn to page 199.

1 The Accounting Cycle

Describe the accounting cycle.

The **accounting cycle** is the process that begins by receiving documentation of a business transaction, involves journalizing transactions and producing financial statements, and ends with the post-closing trial balance. Exhibit 1, which you have seen in earlier chapters, illustrates the 10 steps of the accounting cycle in graphic form. The first seven steps of the accounting cycle, ending with the adjusted trial balance, were completed at the end of Chapter 3. The final three steps involved in completing the accounting cycle will be discussed and illustrated in this chapter.

You will notice that step 5, an optional end-of-period spreadsheet (work sheet), was not covered in Chapters 2 and 3. This step is covered in Appendix 2 of this chapter because it relates to producing the financial statements.

The steps in the accounting cycle are as follows:

1. Business transaction occurs, which results in a source document that is received by the accounting department.
2. Transactions are analyzed and recorded in the journal.
3. Transactions are posted to the ledger.
4. An unadjusted trial balance is prepared at the end of the accounting period.
5. An optional end-of-period spreadsheet (work sheet) is prepared. See Appendix 2 in this chapter.
6. Adjusting entries are journalized and posted to the ledger.
7. An adjusted trial balance is prepared.

Exhibit 1

The Accounting Cycle

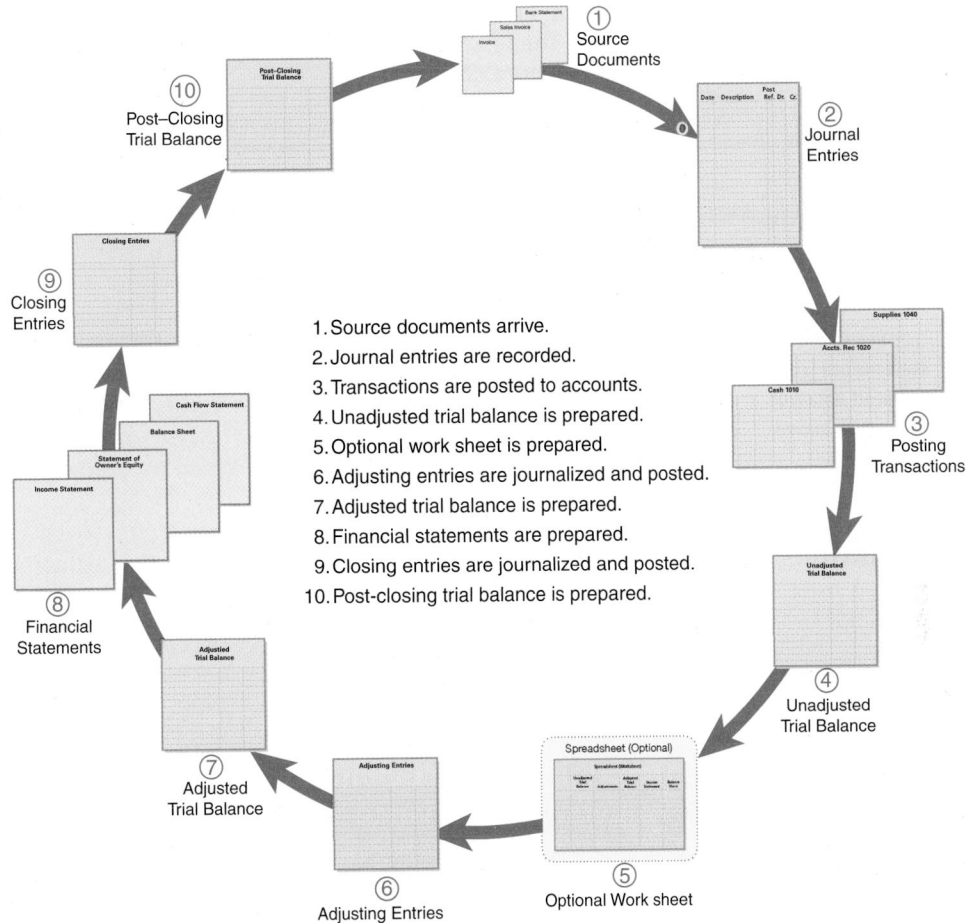

1. Source documents arrive.
2. Journal entries are recorded.
3. Transactions are posted to accounts.
4. Unadjusted trial balance is prepared.
5. Optional work sheet is prepared.
6. Adjusting entries are journalized and posted.
7. Adjusted trial balance is prepared.
8. Financial statements are prepared.
9. Closing entries are journalized and posted.
10. Post-closing trial balance is prepared.

8. Financial statements are prepared.
9. Closing entries are journalized and posted to the ledger.
10. A post-closing trial balance is prepared.[1] Not required in a computerized system.

EXAMPLE EXERCISE 4-1 Accounting Cycle   1

From the following list of steps in the accounting cycle, identify which two steps are missing.

a. Business transaction occurs, which results in a source document that is received by the accounting department.

b. Transactions are analyzed and recorded in the journal.

c. Transactions are posted to the ledger.

d. An optional end-of-period spreadsheet (work sheet) is prepared.

e. Adjusting entries are journalized and posted to the ledger.

f. Financial statements are prepared.

g. Closing entries are journalized and posted to the ledger.

h. A post-closing trial balance is prepared. Not required in a computerized system.

(continued)

---

1 Some accountants include the journalizing and posting of "reversing entries" as the last step in the accounting cycle. Because reversing entries are not required, we have not included them in the accounting cycle. Reversing entries are described and illustrated in Appendix 1 of this chapter.

The following two steps are missing: (1) the preparation of an unadjusted trial balance and (2) the preparation of the adjusted trial balance. The unadjusted trial balance should be prepared after step (c). The adjusted trial balance should be prepared after step (e).

For Practice: PE 4-1

 Financial Statements

Prepare financial statements from adjusted account balances.

Step 8: Financial Statements Using Exhibit 2, the adjusted trial balance that we assembled in Chapter 3, the financial statements for NetSolutions can be prepared. The income statement, the statement of owner's equity, and the balance sheet are shown in Exhibit 3.

Income Statement

@netsolutions

The income statement is prepared directly from the Adjusted Trial Balance beginning with fees earned of $16,840. The expenses in the income statement in Exhibit 3 are generally listed in order of size, beginning with the larger items, or in alphabetic order.

EXAMPLE EXERCISE 4-2 Determining Net Income from the Adjusted Trial Balance

2

The adjusted trial balance of Randall Consulting Co. has fees earned of $790,200 and total expenses of $462,360. In preparing the income statement from the adjusted trial balance, what is the amount of net income or net loss?

FOLLOW MY EXAMPLE 4-2

A net income of $327,840 ($790,200 – $462,360) would be reported. When the revenues exceed expenses, net income is reported. If the expenses exceed revenues, a net loss is reported.

For Practice: PE 4-2

Statement of Owner's Equity

The first item presented on the statement of owner's equity is the balance of the owner's capital account at the beginning of the period. The amount listed as owner's capital in the adjusted trial balance, however, is not always the account balance at the beginning of the period. The owner may have invested additional assets in the business during the period. Thus, for the beginning balance and any additional investments, it is necessary to refer to the owner's capital account in the ledger. These amounts, along with the net income (or net loss) and the withdrawals account balance, are used to determine the ending balance of the owner's capital account.

The basic form of the statement of owner's equity is shown in Exhibit 3. Other factors, such as additional investments or a net loss, require some change in the form, as shown below.

Allan Johnson, capital, January 1, 2014	$39,000	
Additional investment during the year	6,000	
Total		$45,000
Net loss for the year	5,600	
Withdrawals	9,500	
Decrease in owner's equity		15,100
Allan Johnson, capital, December 31, 2014		$29,900

Exhibit 2

Adjusted Trial Balance

NetSolutions
Adjusted Trial Balance
December 31, 2014

	Debit Balances	Credit Balances
Cash	2,065	
Accounts Receivable	2,720	
Supplies	1,560	
Prepaid Insurance	2,200	
Office Equipment	1,800	
Accumulated Depreciation—Office Equipment		50
Land	20,000	
Accounts Payable		900
Unearned Rent		240
Wages Payable		250
Chris Clark, Capital		25,000
Chris Clark, Withdrawals	4,000	
Fees Earned		16,840
Rent Revenue		120
Wages Expense	4,525	
Rent Expense	1,600	
Depreciation Expense	50	
Utilities Expense	985	
Supplies Expense	1,240	
Insurance Expense	200	
Miscellaneous Expense	455	
	43,400	43,400

INTEGRITY, OBJECTIVITY, AND ETHICS IN BUSINESS

THE ROUND TRIP

A common type of fraud involves artificially inflating revenue. One fraudulent method of inflating revenue is called "round tripping." Under this scheme, a selling company (S) "lends" money to a customer company (C). The money is then used by C to purchase a product from S. Thus, S sells product to C and is paid with the money just loaned to C! This transaction looks like a sale in the accounting records, but in reality, S is shipping free product. The fraud is exposed when it is determined that C had no intent to repay the original loan.

EXAMPLE EXERCISE 4-3 Statement of Owner's Equity   2

Zack Gaddis owns and operates Gaddis Employment Services. On January 1, 2014, Zack Gaddis, Capital had a balance of $186,000. During the year, Zack invested an additional $40,000 and withdrew $25,000. For the year ended December 31, 2014, Gaddis Employment Services reported a net income of $18,750. Prepare a statement of owner's equity for the year ended December 31, 2014.

FOLLOW MY EXAMPLE 4-3

GADDIS EMPLOYMENT SERVICES
STATEMENT OF OWNER'S EQUITY
For the Year Ended December 31, 2014

Zack Gaddis, capital, January 1, 2014		$186,000
Investment during year	$40,000	
Net income..	18,750	
	58,750	
Less withdrawals..	25,000	
Increase in owner's equity		33,750
Zack Gaddis, capital, December 31, 2014................		$219,750

For Practice: PE 4-3

Exhibit 3

Financial Statements Prepared from Adjusted Trial Balance

NetSolutions
Income Statement
For the Two Months Ended December 31, 2014

Revenues:		
Fees earned	$16,840	
Rent revenue	120	
Total revenues		$16,960
Expenses:		
Wages expense	$ 4,525	
Rent expense	1,600	
Supplies expense	1,240	
Utilities expense	985	
Miscellaneous expense	455	
Insurance expense	200	
Depreciation expense	50	
Total expenses		9,055
Net income		$ 7,905

NetSolutions
Statement of Owner's Equity
For the Two Months Ended December 31, 2014

Chris Clark, capital, November 1, 2014		$ 0
Investment on November 1, 2014	$25,000	
Net income for November and December	7,905	
	32,905	
Less withdrawals	4,000	
Increase in owner's equity		28,905
Chris Clark, capital, December 31, 2014		$28,905

NetSolutions
Balance Sheet
December 31, 2014

Assets			Liabilities		
Current assets:			Current liabilities:		
Cash	$ 2,065		Accounts payable	$ 900	
Accounts receivable	2,720		Wages payable	250	
Supplies	1,560		Unearned rent	240	
Prepaid insurance	2,200		Total liabilities		$ 1,390
Total current assets		$8,545			
Property, plant, and equipment:					
Office equipment	$1,800				
Less accum. depr.	50	1,750			
Land		20,000	**Owner's Equity**		
Total property, plant, and equipment		21,750	Chris Clark, capital		28,905
Total assets		$30,295	Total liabilities and owner's equity		$30,295

Balance Sheet

The balance sheet is prepared directly from the adjusted trial balance in Exhibit 2, beginning with Cash of $2,065.

Exhibit 3 shows the liabilities and owner's equity beside the assets, in the *account form* of the balance sheet. Balance sheets are often shown in the *report form*, with the liabilities and owner's equity below the assets. The Mid-Chapter Illustrative Problem shows the balance sheet in report form. The balance sheet in Exhibit 3 shows subsections for assets and liabilities. Such a balance sheet is a *classified balance sheet*. We describe these subsections below.

A classified balance sheet provides users of the financial statements with such information as the total value of the current assets compared with the total value of property, plant, and equipment. This extra information can lead to better conclusions about the company and its financial position. The data for calculating the current ratio and the working capital ratio are provided in the financial statements. The general aim of the balance sheet and the financial statements is to communicate economic information as clearly as possible to the users of the financial statements. See the Financial Analysis and Interpretation on page 192 to learn how the financial ratios are calculated.

Note: Three common classes of assets are current assets; property, plant, and equipment; and other assets.

Assets Assets are commonly divided into three sections on the balance sheet: (1) current assets; (2) property, plant, and equipment; and (3) other assets.

CURRENT ASSETS Cash and other assets that are expected to be converted to cash, sold, or used up within one year or less, through the normal operations of the business, are called **current assets**. In addition to cash, the current assets may include notes receivable, accounts receivable, supplies, and other prepaid expenses.

Notes receivable are amounts that customers owe. They are written promises to pay the amount of the note and interest. Accounts receivable are also amounts customers owe, but they are less formal than notes. Accounts receivable normally result from providing services or selling merchandise on account. Notes receivable and accounts receivable are current assets because they are usually converted to cash within one year or less.

PROPERTY, PLANT, AND EQUIPMENT The property, plant, and equipment includes assets such as equipment, machinery, buildings, and land. With the exception of land, as we discussed in Chapter 3, these assets depreciate over a period of time. The cost, accumulated depreciation, and book value of each major type of capital asset are normally reported on the balance sheet or in the notes to the financial statements.

OTHER ASSETS In addition, other classes may be shown within the asset subsection. Two **other assets** are Long-Term Investments, which are intended to be held for longer than one year, and Intangible Assets, which have no physical substance, such as licences, patents, and copyrights. Additional detail regarding these assets will be covered in future chapters.

Liabilities Liabilities are the amounts the business owes to creditors. Liabilities are commonly divided into two sections on the balance sheet: (1) current liabilities and (2) long-term liabilities.

CURRENT LIABILITIES Liabilities that will be due within a short time (usually one year or less) and that are to be paid out of current assets are called **current liabilities**. The most common liabilities in this group are notes payable and accounts payable. Other current liabilities may include wages payable, interest payable, taxes payable, current portion of long-term debt, and unearned fees.

Note: Two common classes of liabilities are current liabilities and long-term liabilities.

LONG-TERM LIABILITIES Liabilities that will not be due for a long time (usually more than one year) are called **long-term liabilities**. If NetSolutions had long-term liabilities, they would be reported below the current liabilities. When a portion of long-term liabilities comes due and is to be paid within one year, it is reported as a current liability. If liabilities are to be renewed rather than paid, they would continue to be reported as long term.

Owner's Equity The owner's right to the net assets of the business is presented on the balance sheet below the liabilities section. The owner's equity is added to the total liabilities, and this total must be equal to the total assets.

EXAMPLE EXERCISE 4-4 Classified Balance Sheet

②

The following accounts appear in an adjusted trial balance of Hindsight Consulting. Indicate whether each account would be reported in the (a) current asset; (b) property, plant, and equipment; (c) other assets; (d) current liability; (e) long-term liability; or (f) owner's equity section of the December 31, 2014, balance sheet of Hindsight Consulting.

1. Jason Corbin, Capital
2. Notes Receivable (due in 6 months)
3. Notes Payable (due in 2016)
4. Land

5. Cash
6. Unearned Rent (3 months)
7. Accumulated Depreciation—Equipment
8. Accounts Payable

FOLLOW MY EXAMPLE 4-4

1. Owner's equity
2. Current asset
3. Long-term liability
4. Property, plant, and equipment

5. Current asset
6. Current liability
7. Property, plant, and equipment
8. Current liability

For Practice: PE 4-4

MID-CHAPTER ILLUSTRATIVE PROBLEM

The adjusted trial balance for Curry's Consulting, for the first month of business, is as follows:

Curry's Consulting
Adjusted Trial Balance
December 31, 2015

	Debit Balances	Credit Balances
Cash	12,237	
Accounts Receivable	3,625	
Supplies	2,712	
Prepaid Rent	1,000	
Prepaid Insurance	500	
Office Equipment	6,544	
Accumulated Depreciation		100
Accounts Payable		4,645
Salaries Payable		457
Unearned Fees		1,247
Barb Curry, Capital		14,019
Barb Curry, Withdrawals	4,500	
Fees Earned		13,391
Depreciation Expense	100	
Insurance Expense	462	
Rent Expense	500	
Salaries Expense	1,355	
Supplies Expense	324	
	33,859	33,859

Instructions

Prepare an income statement, a statement of owner's equity (assuming no additional investments were made during the month), and a balance sheet.

MID-CHAPTER ILLUSTRATIVE SOLUTION

Curry's Consulting
Income Statement
For the Month Ended December 31, 2015

Revenues:		
Fees earned		$13,391
Expenses:		
Salaries expense	$1,355	
Rent expense	500	
Insurance expense	462	
Supplies expense	324	
Depreciation expense	100	
Total expenses		2,741
Net income		$10,650

Curry's Consulting
Statement of Owner's Equity
For the Month Ended December 31, 2015

Barb Curry, capital, December 1, 2015		$ 0
Investment during the month	$14,019	
Net income for the month	10,650	
	24,669	
Less withdrawals	4,500	
Increase in owner's equity		20,169
Barb Curry, capital, December 31, 2015		$20,169

Curry's Consulting
Balance Sheet
December 31, 2015

Assets

Current assets:		
Cash	$12,237	
Accounts receivable	3,625	
Supplies	2,712	
Prepaid rent	1,000	
Prepaid insurance	500	
Total current assets		$20,074
Property, plant, and equipment:		
Office equipment	6,544	
Less accumulated depreciation	100	
Total property, plant, and equipment		6,444
Total assets		$26,518

Liabilities

Current liabilities:		
Accounts payable	$4,645	
Salaries payable	457	
Unearned fees	1,247	
Total liabilities		$ 6,349

Owner's Equity

Barb Curry, capital		20,169
Total liabilities and owner's equity		$26,518

International Financial Reporting Standards (IFRS) Financial statements prepared under International Financial Reporting Standards (IFRS) for companies that are publicly accountable appear different than those prepared under Accounting Standards for Private Enterprises (ASPE) and may have different titles. The Balance Sheet, for instance, may be entitled the Statement of Financial Position. Generally, publicly accountable companies are more complicated than private enterprises and also have a higher number of varied users. These companies need to disclose additional information. The basic principles underlying the accounting equation and the double-entry system are the same. Even though differences in recording and reporting exist, the accounting equation holds true; the total assets still equal the total liabilities and owner's equity.

③ **Closing Entries**

Prepare closing entries.

@netsolutions

As discussed in Chapter 3, the adjusting entries are recorded in the journal at the end of the accounting period. For NetSolutions, the adjusting entries are shown in Exhibit 11 of Chapter 3.

After the adjusting entries are posted to NetSolutions' ledger, shown in Exhibit 12 (on pages 123–124), the ledger agrees with the data reported on the financial statements.

The balances of the accounts reported on the balance sheet are carried forward from year to year. Because they are relatively permanent, these accounts are called **permanent accounts**. For example, Cash, Accounts Receivable, Equipment, Accumulated Depreciation, Accounts Payable, and Owner's Capital are all permanent accounts.

The balances of the accounts reported on the income statement are not carried forward from year to year. Also, the balance of the owner's withdrawals account, which is reported on the statement of owner's equity, is not carried forward. Because these accounts report amounts for only one period, they are called **temporary accounts**. Temporary account balances are not carried forward because they relate only to one period. For example, the Fees Earned of $16,960 and Wages Expense of $4,525 for NetSolutions shown in Exhibit 3 are for the two months ended December 31, 2014, and should not be carried forward to 2015.

Note: Closing entries transfer the balances of temporary accounts to the owner's capital account.

At the beginning of the next period, temporary accounts should have zero balances. To achieve this, temporary account balances are transferred to permanent accounts at the end of the accounting period. The entries that transfer these balances are called **closing entries**. The transfer process is called the **closing process** and is sometimes referred to as **closing the books**.

Step 9: The Closing Process The closing process involves the following four steps:

1. Revenue account balances are transferred to an account called Income Summary.
2. Expense account balances are transferred to an account called Income Summary.
3. The balance of Income Summary (net income or net loss) is transferred to the owner's capital account.
4. The balance of the owner's withdrawals account is transferred to the owner's capital account.

Exhibit 4 diagrams the closing process.

Note: The income summary account does not appear on the financial statements.

Income Summary is a temporary account that is used only during the closing process. At the beginning of the closing process, Income Summary has no balance. During the closing process, Income Summary will be debited and credited for various amounts. At the end of the closing process, Income Summary will again have no balance. Because Income Summary has the effect of clearing the revenue and expense accounts of their

Exhibit 4

The Closing Process

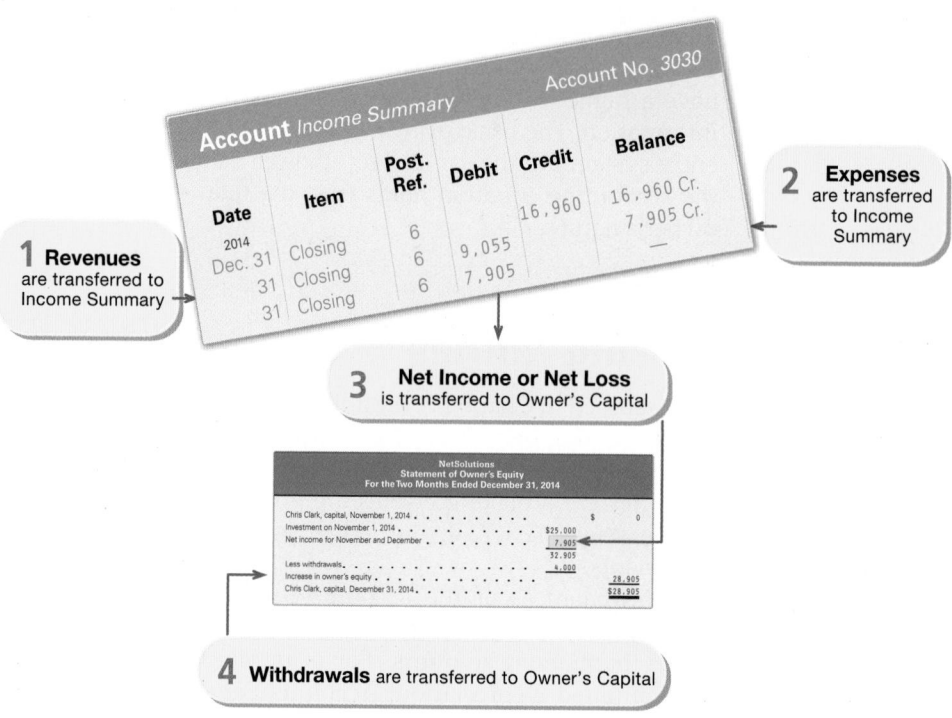

balances, it is sometimes called a **clearing account**. Other titles used for this account include Revenue and Expense Summary, Profit and Loss Summary, and Income and Expense Summary.

The four closing entries required in the closing process are as follows:

1. Debit each revenue account for its balance and credit Income Summary for the total revenue.

2. Credit each expense account for its balance and debit Income Summary for the total expenses.

3. Debit Income Summary for its balance and credit the owner's capital account. This amount represents the net income. In the case of a net loss, credit Income Summary for its balance and debit the owner's capital account.

4. Debit the owner's capital account for the balance of the withdrawals account and credit the withdrawals account.

Closing entries are recorded in the journal and are dated as at the last day of the accounting period. In the journal, closing entries are recorded immediately following the adjusting entries. Note that step 3 takes effect when a net income or net loss is shown on the income statement. When the income statement shows a net loss, the owner's capital account is debited for the amount of that loss. That amount will, in turn, decrease the owner's equity side of the accounting equation.

It is possible to close the temporary revenue and expense accounts without using a clearing account such as Income Summary. In this case, the balances of the revenue and expense accounts are closed directly to the owner's capital account. This process may be used in a computerized accounting system. In a manual system, the use of an income summary account aids in detecting and correcting errors. This is demonstrated in Exhibit 8 on page 180.

Journalizing and Posting Closing Entries

A flowchart of the four closing entries for NetSolutions is shown in Exhibit 5. The balances in the accounts are those shown in the Adjusted Trial Balance in Exhibit 2.

The closing entries for NetSolutions are shown in Exhibit 6. The account titles and balances for these entries may be obtained from the adjusted trial balance, the income statement, the statement of owner's equity, the ledger, or the end-of-period spreadsheet.

The closing entries are posted to NetSolutions ledger as shown in Exhibit 7 (pages 177–179). Income Summary has been added to NetSolutions' ledger in Exhibit 7 as account number 3030. After the closing entries are posted, NetSolutions' ledger has the following characteristics:

1. The balance of Chris Clark, Capital of $28,905 agrees with the amount reported on the statement of owner's equity and the balance sheet.
2. The revenue, expense, and withdrawals accounts have zero balances.

As shown in Exhibit 7, the closing entries are normally identified in the ledger as "Closing." In addition, a line is often inserted in both balance columns after a closing entry is posted. This line separates next period's revenue, expense, and withdrawal transactions from those of the current period. Next period's transactions will be posted directly below the closing entry.

Exhibit 5

Flowchart of Closing Entries for NetSolutions

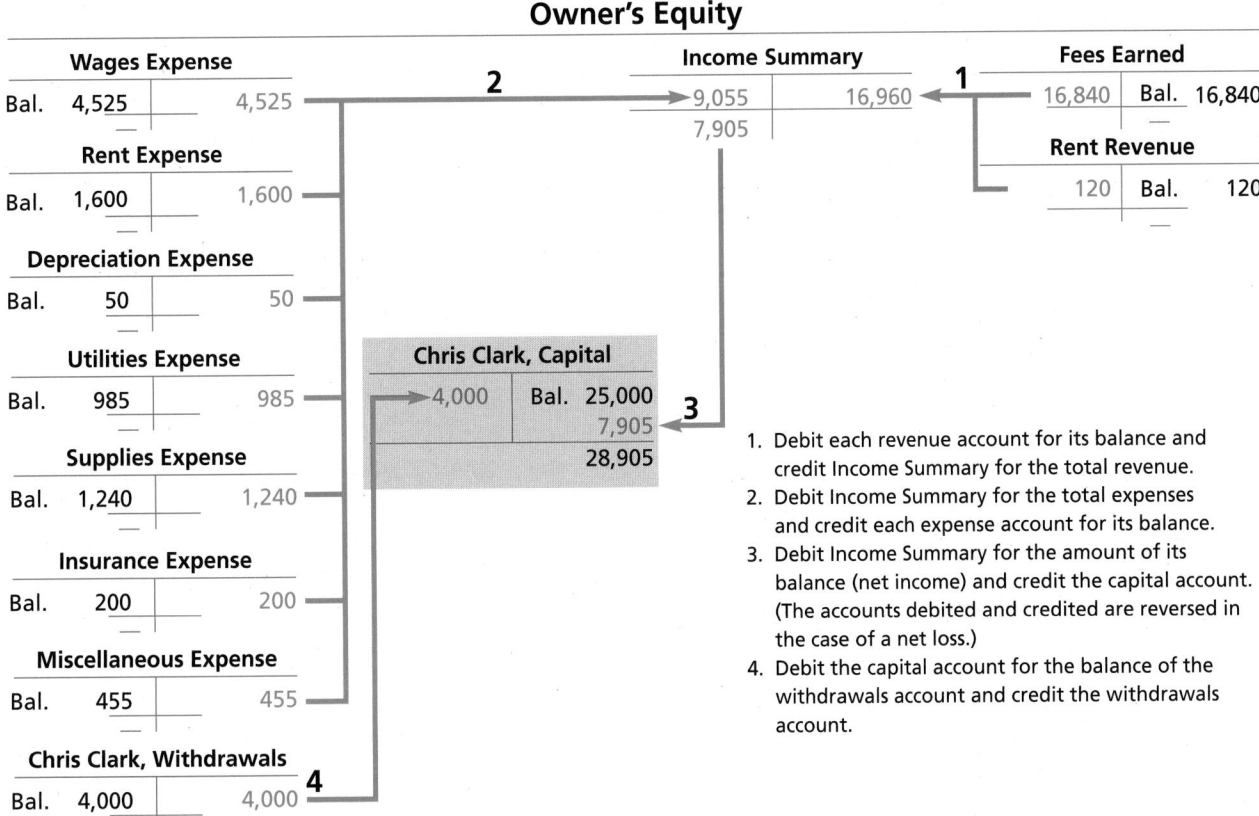

Owner's Equity

1. Debit each revenue account for its balance and credit Income Summary for the total revenue.
2. Debit Income Summary for the total expenses and credit each expense account for its balance.
3. Debit Income Summary for the amount of its balance (net income) and credit the capital account. (The accounts debited and credited are reversed in the case of a net loss.)
4. Debit the capital account for the balance of the withdrawals account and credit the withdrawals account.

Exhibit 6

Closing Entries for NetSolutions

Journal					Page 6
Date	**Description**		**Post. Ref.**	**Debit**	**Credit**
	Closing Entries				
2014 Dec. 31	Fees Earned		4010	16,840	
	Rent Revenue		4020	120	
	Income Summary		3030		16,960
	Closing entry for revenues.				
31	Income Summary		3030	9,055	
	Wages Expense		5010		4,525
	Rent Expense		5020		1,600
	Depreciation Expense		5030		50
	Utilities Expense		5040		985
	Supplies Expense		5050		1,240
	Insurance Expense		5060		200
	Miscellaneous Expense		5090		455
	Closing entry for expenses.				
31	Income Summary		3030	7,905	
	Chris Clark, Capital		3010		7,905
	Closing entry for Income Summary.				
31	Chris Clark, Capital		3010	4,000	
	Chris Clark, Withdrawals		3020		4,000
	Closing entry for withdrawals.				

Exhibit 7

Ledger for NetSolutions

Account Cash   Account No. 1010

Date	Item	Post. Ref.	Debit	Credit	Balance
2014					
Nov. 1		1	25,000		25,000 DR.
5		1		20,000	5,000 DR.
18		1	7,500		12,500 DR.
30		1		3,650	8,850 DR.
30		1		950	7,900 DR.
30		1		2,000	5,900 DR.
Dec. 1		2		2,400	3,500 DR.
1		2		800	2,700 DR.
1		2	360		3,060 DR.
6		2		180	2,880 DR.
11		2		400	2,480 DR.
12		2		950	1,530 DR.
16		3	3,100		4,630 DR.
20		3		900	3,730 DR.
21		3	650		4,380 DR.
23		3		1,450	2,930 DR.
26		3		1,200	1,730 DR.
31		3		310	1,420 DR.
31		4		225	1,195 DR.
31		4	2,870		4,065 DR.
31		4		2,000	2,065 DR.

Account Accounts Receivable   Account No. 1020

Date	Item	Post. Ref.	Debit	Credit	Balance
2014					
Dec. 16		3	1,750		1,750 DR.
21		3		650	1,100 DR.
31		4	1,120		2,220 DR.
31	Adjusting	5	500		2,720 DR.

Account Supplies   Account No. 1040

Date	Item	Post. Ref.	Debit	Credit	Balance
2014					
Nov. 10		1	1,350		1,350 DR.
Dec. 23		3	1,450		2,800 DR.
31	Adjusting	5		1,240	1,560 DR.

Account Prepaid Insurance   Account No. 1050

Date	Item	Post. Ref.	Debit	Credit	Balance
2014					
Dec. 1		2	2,400		2,400 DR.
31	Adjusting	5		200	2,200 DR.

Exhibit 7

Ledger for NetSolutions (*continued*)

Account *Office Equipment* — Account No. *1070*

Date	Item	Post. Ref.	Debit	Credit	Balance
2014 Dec. 4		2	1,800		1,800 DR.

Account *Acc. Depr.—Office Equip.* — Account No. *1080*

Date	Item	Post. Ref.	Debit	Credit	Balance
2014 Dec. 31	Adjusting	5		50	50 CR.

Account *Land* — Account No. *1090*

Date	Item	Post. Ref.	Debit	Credit	Balance
2014 Nov. 5		1	20,000		20,000 DR.

Account *Accounts Payable* — Account No. *2010*

Date	Item	Post. Ref.	Debit	Credit	Balance
2014 Nov. 10		1		1,350	1,350 CR.
30		1	950		400 CR.
Dec. 4		2		1,800	2,200 CR.
11		2	400		1,800 CR.
20		3	900		900 CR.

Account *Wages Payable* — Account No. *2020*

Date	Item	Post. Ref.	Debit	Credit	Balance
2014 Dec. 31	Adjusting	5		250	250 CR.

Account *Unearned Rent* — Account No. *2030*

Date	Item	Post. Ref.	Debit	Credit	Balance
2014 Dec. 1		2		360	360 CR.
31		5	120		240 CR.

Account *Chris Clark, Capital* — Account No. *3010*

Date	Item	Post. Ref.	Debit	Credit	Balance
2014 Nov. 1		1		25,000	25,000 CR.
Dec. 31	Closing	6		7,905	32,905 CR.
31	Closing	6	4,000		28,905 CR.

Account *Chris Clark, Withdrawals* — Account No. *3020*

Date	Item	Post. Ref.	Debit	Credit	Balance
2014 Nov. 30		1	2,000		2,000 DR.
Dec. 31		4	2,000		4,000 DR.
31	Closing	6		4,000	—

Account *Income Summary* — Account No. *3030*

Date	Item	Post. Ref.	Debit	Credit	Balance
2014 Dec. 31	Closing	6		16,960	16,960 CR.
31	Closing	6	9,055		7,905 CR.
31	Closing	6	7,905		—

Account *Fees Earned* — Account No. *4010*

Date	Item	Post. Ref.	Debit	Credit	Balance
2014 Nov. 18		1		7,500	7,500 CR.
Dec. 16		3		3,100	10,600 CR.
16		3		1,750	12,350 CR.
31		4		2,870	15,220 CR.
31		4		1,120	16,340 CR.
Dec. 31	Adjusting	5		500	16,840 CR.
31	Closing	6	16,840		—

Account *Rent Revenue* — Account No. *4020*

Date	Item	Post. Ref.	Debit	Credit	Balance
2014 Dec. 31	Adjusting	5		120	120 CR.
31	Closing	6	120		—

Account *Wages Expense* — Account No. *5010*

Date	Item	Post. Ref.	Debit	Credit	Balance
2014 Nov. 30		1	2,125		2,125 DR.
Dec. 12		2	950		3,075 DR.
26		3	1,200		4,275 DR.
31	Adjusting	5	250		4,525 DR.
31	Closing	6		4,525	—

Account *Rent Expense* — Account No. *5020*

Date	Item	Post. Ref.	Debit	Credit	Balance
2014 Nov. 30		1	800		800 DR.
Dec. 1		2	800		1,600 DR.
31	Closing	6		1,600	—

(continued)

Ledger for NetSolutions (concluded)

Account *Depreciation Expense*   Account No. *5030*

Date	Item	Post. Ref.	Debit	Credit	Balance
2014					
Dec. 31	Adjusting	5	50		50 DR.
31	Closing	6		50	—

Account *Insurance Expense*   Account No. *5060*

Date	Item	Post. Ref.	Debit	Credit	Balance
2014					
Dec. 31	Adjusting	5	200		200 DR.
31	Closing	6		200	—

Account *Utilities Expense*   Account No. *5040*

Date	Item	Post. Ref.	Debit	Credit	Balance
2014					
Nov. 30		1	450		450 DR.
Dec. 31		3	310		760 DR.
31		4	225		985 DR.
31	Closing	6		985	—

Account *Miscellaneous Expense*   Account No. *5090*

Date	Item	Post. Ref.	Debit	Credit	Balance
2014					
Nov. 30		1	275		275 DR.
Dec. 6		2	180		455 DR.
31	Closing	6		455	—

Account *Supplies Expense*   Account No. *5050*

Date	Item	Post. Ref.	Debit	Credit	Balance
2014					
Dec. 31	Adjusting	5	1,240		1,240 DR.
31	Closing	6		1,240	—

If the Income Summary account is not being used, then the third entry is removed and the other entries are completed straight to the owner's capital account. See the example in Exhibit 8.

Closing Entries for NetSolutions—Income Summary Not Used

Date		Description	Post. Ref	Debit	Credit
Dec.	31	Fees Earned	4010	16,840	
		Rent Revenue	4020	120	
		Chris Clark, Capital	3010		16,960
		Closing entry for revenues.			
	31	Chris Clark, Capital	3010	9,055	
		Wages Expense	5010		4,525
		Rent Expense	5020		1,600
		Depreciation Expense	5030		50
		Utilities Expense	5040		985
		Supplies Expense	5050		1,240
		Insurance Expense	5060		200
		Miscellaneous Expense	5090		455
		Closing entry for expenses.			
	31	Chris Clark, Capital	3010	4,000	
		Chris Clark, Withdrawals	3020		4,000
		Closing entry for withdrawals.			

EXAMPLE EXERCISE 4-5 Closing Entries

After the accounts have been adjusted at December 31, the following balances are taken from the ledger of Rio Services Co.:

Lisa Banks, Capital	$732,840
Lisa Banks, Withdrawals	30,000
Fees Earned	572,400
Wages Expense	300,000
Rent Expense	75,000
Supplies Expense	16,290
Miscellaneous Expense	7,200

Journalize the four entries required to close the accounts.

FOLLOW MY EXAMPLE 4-5

December	31	Fees Earned	572,400	
		Income Summary		572,400
		Closing entry for revenues.		
	31	Income Summary	398,490	
		Wages Expense		300,000
		Rent Expense		75,000
		Supplies Expense		16,290
		Miscellaneous Expense		7,200
		Closing entry for expenses.		
	31	Income Summary	173,910	
		Lisa Banks, Capital		173,910
		Closing entry for Income Summary.		
	31	Lisa Banks, Capital	30,000	
		Lisa Banks, Withdrawals		30,000
		Closing entry for withdrawals.		

For Practice: PE 4-5

CRITICAL THINKING

The owner's equity account balance is $15,000 on December 15. Suppose the company's year-end is December 31. **Will the owner's equity account have a balance of $15,000 at year-end?**

No. The $15,000 balance does not include any of the transactions related to revenues, expenses, or withdrawals that have occurred since the accounts were last closed. The $15,000 balance in the owner's equity account represents the total owner's equity at the end of the previous year (or month), provided no owner contributions have been made. All transactions related to revenues, expenses, and withdrawals during the time period being reported will move to the equity account after the closing entries have been recorded.

Exhibit 9

Post-Closing Trial Balance

	NetSolutions Post-Closing Trial Balance December 31, 2014		
		Debit Balances	**Credit Balances**
Cash		2,065	
Accounts Receivable		2,720	
Supplies		1,560	
Prepaid Insurance		2,200	
Office Equipment		1,800	
Accumulated Depreciation—Office Equipment			50
Land		20,000	
Accounts Payable			900
Wages Payable			250
Unearned Rent			240
Chris Clark, Capital			28,905
		30,345	30,345

Post-Closing Trial Balance

A post-closing trial balance is prepared after the closing entries have been posted. As noted in the steps of the accounting cycle on page 167, the post-closing (after closing) trial balance is not required in a computerized system. The computer program ensures that the debits are equal to the credits by testing the journal entries as they are entered into the records. The purpose of the post-closing trial balance is to verify that the ledger is in balance at the beginning of the next period. The accounts and amounts should agree exactly with the accounts and amounts listed on the balance sheet at the end of the period. The post-closing trial balance for NetSolutions is shown in Exhibit 9.

Illustration of the Accounting Cycle

Illustrate the accounting cycle for one period.

In this section, we will illustrate the complete accounting cycle for one period. As at December 1, 2015, Kelly Pitney decided to move to rented quarters and to operate a consulting business, Kelly Consulting, on a full-time basis. During December, Kelly Consulting entered into the following transactions:

Dec. 1. The following assets were received from Kelly Pitney: cash, $13,100; accounts receivable, $3,000; supplies, $1,400; and office equipment, $12,500. There were no liabilities assumed.

      1. Paid three months' rent on a lease rental contract, $4,800.

      4. Received cash from client as an advance payment for services to be provided and recorded it as unearned fees, $5,000.

      5. Purchased additional office equipment on account from Office Station Co., $2,000.

     12. Paid Office Station Co. for part of the debt incurred on December 5, $1,200.

     12. Recorded services provided on account for the period December 1–12, $4,200.

     14. Paid part-time receptionist for two weeks' salary, $750.

     17. Recorded cash from cash clients for fees earned during the period December 1–16, $6,250.

     26. Received cash from clients on account, $5,600.

     28. Paid part-time receptionist for two weeks' salary, $750.

29. Paid telephone bill for December, $330.
30. Recorded cash from clients for fees earned for the period December 25–30, $3,050.
30. Recorded services provided on account for the remainder of December, $1,500.
30. Kelly withdrew $6,000 for personal use.

Step 1: Source Documents Arrive

A business transaction occurs, resulting in a source document being generated by another business and received by the accounting department. Examples of source documents are invoices and bank statements. Instead of reading a description of the transaction, as done in step 2, the accountant reviews the source document and enters the transaction to reflect information in the document.

Step 2: Journal Entries Are Recorded

The second step in the accounting cycle is to analyze and record transactions in the journal using the double-entry accounting system. As illustrated in Chapter 2, transactions are analyzed and journalized using the following steps:

1. Carefully read the description of the transaction to determine whether an asset, liability, owner's equity, revenue, expense, or withdrawals account is affected.
2. For each account affected by the transaction, determine whether the account increases or decreases.
3. Determine whether each increase or decrease should be recorded as a debit or a credit, following the rules of debit and credit shown in Exhibit 3 of Chapter 2.
4. Record the transaction using a journal entry.

The company's chart of accounts is useful in determining which accounts are affected by the transaction. The chart of accounts for Kelly Consulting is as follows:

1010 Cash	3010 Kelly Pitney, Capital
1020 Accounts Receivable	3020 Kelly Pitney, Withdrawals
1040 Supplies	3030 Income Summary
1050 Prepaid Rent	4010 Fees Earned
1080 Office Equipment	5010 Salaries Expense
1090 Acc. Depr.—Office Equipment	5020 Rent Expense
2010 Accounts Payable	5030 Supplies Expense
2020 Salaries Payable	5040 Depreciation Expense
2030 Unearned Fees	5090 Utilities Expense

After analyzing each of Kelly Consulting's transactions for December, the journal entries are recorded as shown in Exhibit 10.

Step 3: Transactions Are Posted to Accounts

Periodically, the transactions recorded in the journal are posted to the accounts in the ledger. The debits and credits for each journal entry are posted to the accounts in the order in which they occur in the journal. As illustrated in Chapters 2 and 3, journal entries are posted to the accounts using the following four steps.

1. The date is entered in the Date column of the account.
2. The amount is entered into the Debit or Credit column of the account.
3. The journal page number is entered in the Posting Reference column.
4. The account number is entered in the Posting Reference (Post. Ref.) column in the journal.

The journal entries for Kelly Consulting have been posted to the ledger shown in Exhibit 17 on pages 191–192.

Exhibit 10

Journal Entries for December, Kelly Consulting

		Journal			Page *1*
Date		**Description**	**Post. Ref.**	**Debit**	**Credit**
2015					
Dec	1	Cash	1010	13,100	
		Accounts Receivable	1020	3,000	
		Supplies	1040	1,400	
		Office Equipment	1080	12,500	
		Kelly Pitney, Capital	3010		30,000
		Investing assets in business.			
	1	Prepaid Rent	1050	4,800	
		Cash	1010		4,800
		Payment of rent.			
	4	Cash	1010	5,000	
		Unearned Fees	2030		5,000
		Client deposit.			
	5	Office Equipment	1080	2,000	
		Accounts Payable	2010		2,000
		Purchased office equipment on account.			
	12	Accounts Payable	2010	1,200	
		Cash	1010		1,200
		Payment for accounts payable.			
	12	Accounts Receivable	1020	4,200	
		Fees Earned	4010		4,200
		Services on account.			
	14	Salaries Expense	5010	750	
		Cash	1010		750
		Paid salary.			
	17	Cash	1010	6,250	
		Fees Earned	4010		6,250
		Services provided for cash.			
	26	Cash	1010	5,600	
		Accounts Receivable	1020		5,600
		Received cash on account.			
	28	Salaries Expense	5010	750	
		Cash	1010		750
		Paid salary.			
	29	Utilities Expense	5090	330	
		Cash	1010		330
		Paid telephone bill.			
	30	Cash	1010	3,050	
		Fees Earned	4010		3,050
		Services provided for cash.			

Exhibit 10

Journal Entries for December, Kelly Consulting (_concluded_)

	Journal				Page _2_
Date	**Description**	**Post. Ref.**	**Debit**	**Credit**
2015				
Dec 30	Accounts Receivable	1020	1,500	
	Fees Earned	4010		1,500
	Services provided on account.			
30	Kelly Pitney, Withdrawals	3020	6,000	
	Cash	1010		6,000
	Owner withdrawal.			

Step 4: Unadjusted Trial Balance Is Prepared

An unadjusted trial balance is prepared to determine whether any errors have been made in posting the debits and credits to the ledger. The unadjusted trial balance does not provide complete proof of the accuracy of the ledger. It indicates only that the debits and the credits are equal. This proof is of value, however, because errors often affect the equality of debits and credits. If the two totals of a trial balance are not equal, an error has occurred that must be discovered and corrected.

The unadjusted trial balance for Kelly Consulting is shown in Exhibit 11. The unadjusted account balances shown in Exhibit 11 were taken from Kelly Consulting's ledger shown in Exhibit 17, on pages 191–192, before any adjusting entries were recorded.

Exhibit 11

Unadjusted Trial Balance, Kelly Consulting

Kelly Consulting
Unadjusted Trial Balance
December 31, 2015

	Debit Balances	Credit Balances
Cash	19,170	
Accounts Receivable	3,100	
Supplies	1,400	
Prepaid Rent	4,800	
Office Equipment	14,500	
Accumulated Depreciation—Office Equipment		0
Accounts Payable		800
Salaries Payable		0
Unearned Fees		5,000
Kelly Pitney, Capital		30,000
Kelly Pitney, Withdrawals	6,000	
Fees Earned		15,000
Salaries Expense	1,500	
Rent Expense	0	
Supplies Expense	0	
Depreciation Expense	0	
Utilities Expense	330	
	50,800	50,800

Step 5: Optional Work Sheet Is Prepared

Although an end-of-period spreadsheet (work sheet) is not required, it is useful to show the flow of accounting information from the unadjusted trial balance to the adjusted trial balance and financial statements. In addition, an end-of-period spreadsheet is useful for analyzing the impact of proposed adjustments on the financial statements. The end-of-period spreadsheet for Kelly Consulting is shown in Exhibit 20 in Appendix 2.

Step 6: Adjusting Entries Are Journalized and Posted

Before the financial statements can be prepared, the accounts must be updated. The four types of accounts that normally require adjustment are prepaid expenses, unearned revenues, accrued revenues, and accrued expenses. In addition, depreciation expense must be recorded for capital assets other than land. The following data have been assembled on December 31, 2015, for analysis of possible adjustments for Kelly Consulting:

a.   Supplies on hand on December 31 are $850.

b.   Depreciation of office equipment for December is $330.

c.   Accrued receptionist salary on December 31 is $120.

d.   Rent expired during December is $1,600.

e.   Unearned fees on December 31 are $2,500.

Adjusting entries for Kelly Consulting are prepared as shown in Exhibit 12. Each adjusting entry affects at least one income statement account and one balance sheet account. Explanations for each adjustment including any computations are normally included with each adjusting entry. Each of the adjusting entries shown in Exhibit 12 is

---

Exhibit 12

Adjusting Entries, Kelly Consulting

Journal				Page 3
Date		**Post. Ref.**	**Debit**	**Credit**
2015				
Dec 31	Supplies Expense	5030	550	
	Supplies	1040		550
	Supplies used ($1,400 − $850).			
31	Depreciation Expense	5040	330	
	Acc. Depr.—Office Equipment	1090		330
	Depreciation of office equipment.			
31	Salaries Expense	5010	120	
	Salaries Payable	2020		120
	Accrued salary.			
31	Rent Expense	5020	1,600	
	Prepaid Rent	1050		1,600
	Rent expired during December.			
31	Unearned Fees	2030	2,500	
	Fees Earned	4010		2,500
	Fees earned ($5,000 − $2,500).			

posted to Kelly Consulting's ledger shown in Exhibit 17 on pages 191–192. The adjusting entries are identified in the ledger as "Adjusting."

Step 7: Adjusted Trial Balance Is Prepared

After the adjustments have been journalized and posted, an adjusted trial balance is prepared to verify the equality of the total of the debit and credit balances. This is the last step before preparing the financial statements. The ledger balances, shown in Exhibit 17 on pages 191–192, are used to prepare the financial statements. If the adjusted trial balance does not balance, an error has occurred and must be found and corrected. The adjusted trial balance for Kelly Consulting as at December 31, 2015, is shown in Exhibit 13.

Step 8: Financial Statements Are Prepared

The most important outcome of the accounting cycle is the financial statements. The income statement is prepared first, followed by the statement of owner's equity and then the balance sheet. The statements can be prepared directly from the adjusted trial balance, or the ledger. The net income or net loss shown on the income statement is reported on the statement of owner's equity along with any additional investments by the owner and any withdrawals. The ending owner's capital is reported on the balance sheet and is added to total liabilities to equal total assets.

The financial statements for Kelly Consulting are shown in Exhibit 14. Kelly Consulting earned net income of $13,070 for December. As at December 31, 2015, Kelly Consulting has total assets of $40,490, total liabilities of $3,420, and total owner's equity of $37,070.

Exhibit 13

Adjusted Trial Balance, Kelly Consulting

Kelly Consulting
Adjusted Trial Balance
December 31, 2015

	Debit Balances	Credit Balances
Cash	19,170	
Accounts Receivable	3,100	
Supplies	850	
Prepaid Rent	3,200	
Office Equipment	14,500	
Accumulated Depreciation—Office Equipment		330
Accounts Payable		800
Salaries Payable		120
Unearned Fees		2,500
Kelly Pitney, Capital		30,000
Kelly Pitney, Withdrawals	6,000	
Fees Earned		17,500
Salaries Expense	1,620	
Rent Expense	1,600	
Supplies Expense	550	
Depreciation Expense	330	
Utilities Expense	330	
	51,250	51,250

Exhibit 14

Financial Statements, Kelly Consulting

Kelly Consulting Income Statement For the Month Ended December 31, 2015		
Revenues:		
Fees earned		$17,500
Expenses:		
Salaries expense....................................	$1,620	
Rent expense	1,600	
Supplies expense	550	
Utilities expense....................................	330	
Depreciation expense	330	
Total expenses....................................		4,430
Net income..		$13,070

Kelly Consulting Statement of Owner's Equity For the Month Ended December 31, 2015		
Kelly Pitney, capital, December 1, 2015		$ 0
Investment during the month	$30,000	
Net income for the month	13,070	
	43,070	
Less withdrawals...	6,000	
Increase in owner's equity		37,070
Kelly Pitney, capital, December 31, 2015............................		$37,070

Kelly Consulting Balance Sheet December 31, 2015					
Assets			**Liabilities**		
Current assets:			Current liabilities:		
Cash......................................	$19,170		Accounts payable	$ 800	
Accounts receivable...........................	3,100		Salaries payable	120	
Supplies	850		Unearned fees	2,500	
Prepaid rent	3,200		Total liabilities..........................		$ 3,420
Total current assets.........................		$26,320			
Property, plant, and equipment:					
Office equipment...............................	14,500				
Less accumulated depreciation	330				
Total property, plant,			**Owner's Equity**		
and equipment	14,170		Kelly Pitney, capital		37,070
Total assets................................		$40,490	Total liabilities and owner's equity		$40,490

Step 9: Closing Entries Are Journalized and Prepared

As described earlier in this chapter, four closing entries are required at the end of an accounting period. These four closing entries are as follows:

1. Debit each revenue account for its balance and credit Income Summary for the total revenues.
2. Credit each expense account for its balance and debit Income Summary for the total expenses.
3. Debit Income Summary for its balance and credit the owner's capital account. This amount represents the net income. In the case of a net loss, credit Income Summary for its balance and debit the owner's capital account.
4. Debit the owner's capital account for the balance of the withdrawals account and credit the withdrawals account.

The four closing entries for Kelly Consulting are shown in Exhibit 15. The closing entries are posted to Kelly Consulting's ledger as shown in Exhibit 17 (pages 191–192). After the closing entries are posted, Kelly Consulting's ledger has the following characteristics:

1. The balance of Kelly Pitney, Capital of $37,070 in Exhibit 17 on page 191, agrees with the amount reported on the statement of owner's equity and the balance sheet in Exhibit 14 on page 188.
2. The revenue, expense, and withdrawals accounts will have zero balances and only balance sheet accounts remain. The zero balances can be seen in the ledger in Exhibit 17 on pages 191–192.

The closing entries are normally identified in the ledger as "Closing." In addition, a line is inserted in the balance column after a closing entry is posted. This line separates the next period's revenue, expense, and withdrawal transactions from those of the current period.

Exhibit 15

Closing Entries, Kelly Consulting

Journal					Page 4
Date		**Description**	**Post. Ref.**	**Debit**	**Credit**
2015		Closing Entries			
Dec	31	Fees Earned	4010	17,500	
		Income Summary	3030		17,500
		Closing entry.			
	31	Income Summary	3030	4,430	
		Salaries Expense	5010		1,620
		Rent Expense	5020		1,600
		Supplies Expense	5030		550
		Depreciation Expense	5040		330
		Utilities Expense	5090		330
		Closing entry.			
	31	Income Summary	3030	13,070	
		Kelly Pitney, Capital	3010		13,070
		Closing entry.			
	31	Kelly Pitney, Capital	3010	6,000	
		Kelly Pitney, Withdrawals	3020		6,000
		Closing entry.			

Step 10: A Post-Closing Trial Balance Is Prepared

A post-closing trial balance is prepared after the closing entries have been posted. The purpose of the post-closing trial balance is to verify that the ledger is in balance at the beginning of the next period. The accounts and amounts in the post-closing trial balance should agree exactly with the accounts and amounts listed on the balance sheet at the end of the period.

The post-closing trial balance for Kelly Consulting is shown in Exhibit 16. The balances shown in the post-closing trial balance are taken from the ending balances in the ledger shown in Exhibit 17. These balances agree with the amounts shown on Kelly Consulting's balance sheet in Exhibit 14.

Calendar Year

Note: Financial statements are available for all publicly traded Canadian companies that are traded on SEDAR (The System for Electronic Document Analysis and Retrieval).

As discussed in Chapter 3, the fiscal year for businesses that are organized as sole proprietors and partnerships is the same as the **calendar year**. Thus, the year-end for all sole proprietors and partnerships is December 31. One reason for this is that sole proprietorships and partnerships do not pay taxes directly on their income. The owners pay taxes by including their business income in their personal tax returns, which are completed on a calendar year basis.

Businesses that are organized as corporations, file a corporate tax return. Therefore, they may select a year-end other than December 31. A **fiscal year** often begins on the first day of the month selected and ends on the last day of the following twelfth month. You will see year-ends other than December 31 in some of the business examples in this textbook.

Exhibit 16

Post-Closing Trial Balance, Kelly Consulting

Kelly Consulting
Post-Closing Trial Balance
December 31, 2015

	Debit Balances	Credit Balances
Cash	19,170	
Accounts Receivable	3,100	
Supplies	850	
Prepaid Rent	3,200	
Office Equipment	14,500	
Accumulated Depreciation—Office Equipment		330
Accounts Payable		800
Salaries Payable		120
Unearned Fees		2,500
Kelly Pitney, Capital		37,070
	40,820	40,820

Exhibit 17

Ledger, Kelly Consulting

Ledger

Account *Cash*   Account No. *1010*

Date	Item	Post. Ref.	Debit	Credit	Balance
2015					
Dec. 1		1	13,100		13,100 Dr.
1		1		4,800	8,300 Dr.
4		1	5,000		13,300 Dr.
12		1		1,200	12,100 Dr.
14		1		750	11,350 Dr.
17		1	6,250		17,600 Dr.
26		1	5,600		23,200 Dr.
28		1		750	22,450 Dr.
29		1		330	22,120 Dr.
30		1	3,050		25,170 Dr.
30		2		6,000	19,170 Dr.

Account *Accounts Receivable*   Account No. *1020*

Date	Item	Post. Ref.	Debit	Credit	Balance
2015					
Dec. 1		1	3,000		3,000 Dr.
12		1	4,200		7,200 Dr.
26		1		5,600	1,600 Dr.
30		2	1,500		3,100 Dr.

Account *Supplies*   Account No. *1040*

Date	Item	Post. Ref.	Debit	Credit	Balance
2015					
Dec. 1		1	1,400		1,400 Dr.
31	Adjusting	3		550	850 Dr.

Account *Prepaid Rent*   Account No. *1050*

Date	Item	Post. Ref.	Debit	Credit	Balance
2015					
Dec. 1		1	4,800		4,800 Dr.
31	Adjusting	3		1,600	3,200 Dr.

Account *Office Equipment*   Account No. *1080*

Date	Item	Post. Ref.	Debit	Credit	Balance
2015					
Dec. 1		1	12,500		12,500 Dr.
5		1	2,000		14,500 Dr.

Account *Acc. Depr.—Office Equip.*   Account No. *1090*

Date	Item	Post. Ref.	Debit	Credit	Balance
2015					
Dec. 31	Adjusting	3		330	330 Cr.

Account *Accounts Payable*   Account No. *2010*

Date	Item	Post. Ref.	Debit	Credit	Balance
2015					
Dec. 5		1		2,000	2,000 Cr.
12		1	1,200		800 Cr.

Account *Salaries Payable*   Account No. *2020*

Date	Item	Post. Ref.	Debit	Credit	Balance
2015					
Dec. 31	Adjusting	3		120	120 Cr.

Account *Unearned Fees*   Account No. *2030*

Date	Item	Post. Ref.	Debit	Credit	Balance
2015					
Dec. 4		1		5,000	5,000 Cr.
31	Adjusting	3	2,500		2,500 Cr.

Account *Kelly Pitney, Capital*   Account No. *3010*

Date	Item	Post. Ref.	Debit	Credit	Balance
2015					
Dec. 1		1		30,000	30,000 Cr.
31	Closing	4		13,070	43,070 Cr.
31	Closing	4	6,000		37,070 Cr.

Account *Kelly Pitney, Withdrawals*   Account No. *3020*

Date	Item	Post. Ref.	Debit	Credit	Balance
2015					
Dec. 30		2	6,000		6,000 Cr.
31	Closing	4		6,000	—

Account *Income Summary*   Account No. *3030*

Date	Item	Post. Ref.	Debit	Credit	Balance
2015					
Dec. 31	Closing	4		17,500	17,500 Cr.
31	Closing	4	4,430		13,070 Cr.
31	Closing	4	13,070		—

(continued)

Exhibit 17

Ledger, Kelly Consulting (*concluded*)

Account *Fees Earned* — Account No. *4010*

Date	Item	Post. Ref.	Debit	Credit	Balance
2015					
Dec. 12		1		4,200	4,200 CR.
17		1		6,250	10,450 CR.
30		2		3,050	13,500 CR.
30		2		1,500	15,000 CR.
31	Adjusting	3		2,500	17,500 CR.
31	Closing	4	17,500		—

Account *Salaries Expense* — Account No. *5010*

Date	Item	Post. Ref.	Debit	Credit	Balance
2015					
Dec. 14		1	750		750 DR.
28		1	750		1,500 DR.
31	Adjusting	3	120		1,620 DR.
31	Closing	4		1,620	—

Account *Rent Expense* — Account No. *5020*

Date	Item	Post. Ref.	Debit	Credit	Balance
2015					
Dec. 31	Adjusting	3	1,600		1,600 DR.
31	Closing	4		1,600	—

Account *Supplies Expense* — Account No. *5030*

Date	Item	Post. Ref.	Debit	Credit	Balance
2015					
Dec. 31	Adjusting	3	550		550 DR.
31	Closing	4		550	—

Account *Depreciation Expense* — Account No. *5040*

Date	Item	Post. Ref.	Debit	Credit	Balance
2015					
Dec. 31	Adjusting	3	330		330 DR.
31	Closing	4		330	—

Account *Utilities Expense* — Account No. *5090*

Date	Item	Post. Ref.	Debit	Credit	Balance
2015					
Dec. 29		1	330		330 DR.
31	Closing	4		330	—

FINANCIAL ANALYSIS AND INTERPRETATION

f·a·i

To provide important information to users, the balance sheet is divided into current and long-term items in both the assets and liabilities sections. Users can then review these category amounts to further analyze the company's performance. For example, these data can be used to calculate **working capital** and the **current ratio**.

Working capital is computed as follows:

Working Capital = Current Assets – Current Liabilities

Working capital informs the user of the company's ability to pay its current liabilities using its current assets. Working capital is thus an important indicator of the company's ability to stay in business.

The current ratio is computed as follows:

$$\text{Current Ratio} = \frac{\text{Current Assets}}{\text{Current Liabilities}}$$

As you can see, the formula for computing the current ratio has the same components as the formula for computing working capital. As a result, the current ratio is often called the **working capital ratio**. The current ratio is more useful than working capital because it can be compared with the current ratios of companies of varying sizes and with industry standards.

For example, Tryston Enterprises has current assets of $300,000 and current liabilities of $250,000. Its working capital is $300,000 – $250,000 = $50,000. This working capital illustrates that Tryston Enterprises can pay off all of its current liabilities using its current assets, and it will still have $50,000 to spare.

Tryston Enterprise's current ratio is $300,000 / $250,000 = 1.2. This current ratio indicates that the company can pay off its current liabilities 1.2 times using its current assets. If the industry standard is 2.0, then Tryston Enterprises has a much lower ratio than the industry generally and would be considered to have working capital problems, relative to other companies in the industry.

Appendix D includes working capital and current ratios in the liquidity measures.

EXAMPLE EXERCISE 4-6 Working Capital and Current Ratio

Bentley Excavating's current assets and current liabilities are detailed below:

	2015	2014
Current Assets	$650,000	$580,000
Current Liabilities	225,000	250,000

Calculate the working capital and the current ratio for Bentley Excavating. Note whether these amounts have increased or decreased from the previous year.

FOLLOW MY EXAMPLE 4-6

2014
Working capital = $580,000 – $250,000 = $330,000
Current ratio = $580,000 / $250,000 = 2.3

2015
Working capital = $650,000 – $225,000 = $425,000
Current ratio = $650,000 / $225,000 = 2.9

The amount of working capital has improved for Bentley Excavating. Its current asset amount improved by increasing, and its current liabilities amount improved by decreasing.

This improvement can also be seen in the increase in the current ratio, from 2.3 to 2.9. The company can now cover its current liabilities 2.9 times, compared with 2.3 times in 2014.

For Practice: PE 4-6

A P P E N D I X   1

Reversing Entries

Some of the adjusting entries recorded at the end of the accounting period affect transactions that occur in the next period. In such cases, a reversing entry may be used to simplify the recording of the next period's transactions.

To illustrate, an adjusting entry for accrued wages expense affects the first payment of wages in the next period. Without using a reversing entry, Wages Payable must be debited for the accrued wages at the end of the next period. In addition, Wages Expense must also be debited for only that portion of the payroll that is an expense of the current period.

Using a reversing entry, however, simplifies the analysis and recording of the first wages payment in the next period. As the term implies, a *reversing entry* is the exact opposite of the related adjusting entry. The amounts and accounts are the same as the adjusting entry, but the debits and credits are reversed.

@netsolutions

Reversing entries are illustrated by using the accrued wages for NetSolutions presented in Chapter 3. These data are summarized in Exhibit 18.

The adjusting entry for the accrued wages of December 29, 30, and 31 is as follows:

2014					
Dec.	31	Wages Expense	5010	250	
		Wages Payable	2020		250
		Accrued wages.			

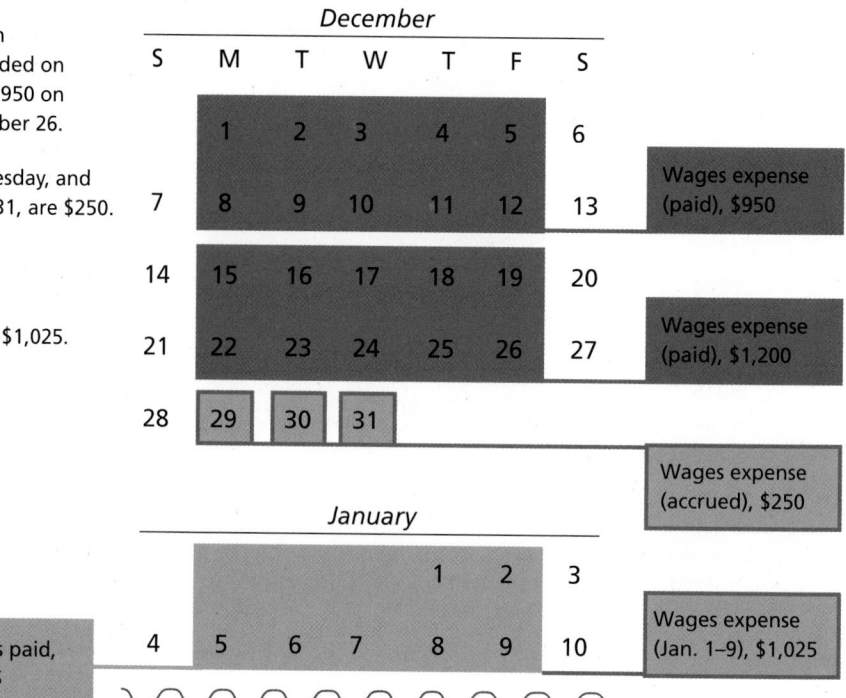

Exhibit 18

Accrued Wages

1. Wages are paid every two weeks on Friday for the two-week periods ended on those Fridays. The payments were $950 on December 12 and $1,200 on December 26.

2. The wages accrued for Monday, Tuesday, and Wednesday, December 29, 30, and 31, are $250.

3. Wages paid on Friday, January 9, total $1,275.

4. Wages expense, January 1–9, totals $1,025.

After the adjusting entry is recorded, Wages Expense will have a debit balance of $4,525 ($4,275 + $250), as shown on the next page. Wages Payable will have a credit balance of $250.

After the closing entries are recorded, Wages Expense will have a zero balance. However, because Wages Payable is a liability account, it is not closed. Thus, Wages Payable will have a credit balance of $250 as at January 1, 2015.

Without recording a reversing entry, the payment of the $1,275 payroll on January 9 would be recorded as follows:

2015						
Jan.	9	Wages Payable	2020	250	
		Wages Expense	5010	1,025	
		Cash	1010		1,275
		Payment of Jan. 9 payroll.			

As shown above, to record the January 9 payroll correctly, Wages Payable must be debited for $250. Thus, the employee who records the January 9 payroll must refer to the December 31, 2014, adjusting entry or to the ledger to determine the amount to debit Wages Payable.

Because the January 9 payroll is not recorded in the normal manner, there is a greater chance that an error may occur. This chance of error is reduced by recording a reversing entry as at the first day of the next period. For example, the reversing entry for the accrued wages expense would be recorded on January 1, 2015, as follows:

2015					
Jan.	1	Wages Payable	2020	250	
		Wages Expense	5010		250
		Reversing entry.			

The preceding reversing entry transfers the $250 liability from Wages Payable to the credit side of Wages Expense. The nature of the $250 is unchanged—it is still a liability. Because of its unusual nature, an explanation is written under the reversing entry.

When the payroll is paid on January 9, the following entry is recorded:

2015					
Jan.	9	Wages Expense	5010	1,275	
		Cash	1010		1,275
		Payment of Jan. 9 payroll.			

After the January 9 payroll is recorded, Wages Expense has a debit balance of $1,025. This amount is the wages expense for the period January 1–9, 2015.

Wages Payable and Wages Expense after posting the adjusting, closing, and reversing entries are shown below.

Account *Wages Payable*   Account No. *2020*

Date		Item	Post. Ref.	Debit	Credit	Balance
2014 Dec.	31	Adjusting	5		250	250 CR.
2015 Jan.	1	Reversing	7	250		—

Account *Wages Expense*   Account No. *5010*

Date		Item	Post. Ref.	Debit	Credit	Balance
2014 Nov.	30		1	2,125		2,125 DR.
Dec.	12		2	950		3,075 DR.
	26		3	1,200		4,275 DR.
	31	Adjusting	5	250		4,525 DR.
	31	Closing	6		4,525	—
2015 Jan.	1	Reversing	7		250	250 CR.
	9		7	1,275		1,025 DR.

In addition to accrued expenses (accrued liabilities), reversing entries are also used for accrued revenues (accrued assets). To illustrate, the reversing entry for NetSolutions' accrued fees earned as at December 31, 2014, is as follows:

2015					
Jan.	1	Fees Earned	4010	500	
		Accounts Receivable	1020		500
		Reversing entry.			

In the Appendix of Chapter 3, the alternative method of recording prepaid expenses and unearned revenues was described. Reversing entries may also be used for these adjusting entries.

The use of reversing entries is optional. However, in computerized accounting systems, data entry employees often input routine accounting entries. In such cases, reversing entries may be useful in avoiding errors.

A P P E N D I X 2

End-of-Period Spreadsheet (Work Sheet)

Accountants often use working papers for analyzing and summarizing data. Such working papers are not a formal part of the accounting records. This use of working papers is in contrast to the chart of accounts, the journal, and the ledger, which are essential parts of an accounting system. Working papers are usually prepared by using a computer spreadsheet program, such as Microsoft's Excel.™

@netsolutions
The end-of-period spreadsheet (work sheet) shown in Exhibit 19 is a working paper used to summarize adjusting entries and the account balances for the financial statements. In companies with few accounts and adjustments, an end-of-period spreadsheet may not be necessary. For example, the financial statements for NetSolutions can be prepared directly from the Adjusted Trial Balance. However, some companies use an end-of-period spreadsheet as an aid to analyzing adjustment data and preparing the financial statements.

Exhibit 19 on page 197 illustrates the step-by-step process of preparing an end-of-period spreadsheet. As a basis for this illustration, we use NetSolutions.

Exhibit 19 begins with the unadjusted trial balance as at the end of the period. The unadjusted trial balance verifies that the total of the debit balances equals the total of the credit balances. If the trial balance totals are unequal, an error has occurred. Any error must be found and corrected before the end-of-period process can continue.

The adjustments for NetSolutions from Chapter 3 are shown in the Adjustments columns of Exhibit 19. Cross-referencing (by letters) the debit and credit of each adjustment is useful in reviewing the impact of the adjustments on the unadjusted account balances. The adjustments are normally entered in the order in which the data are assembled. If the titles of the accounts to be adjusted do not appear in the unadjusted trial balance, the accounts are inserted in their proper order in the Account Title column. The total of the Adjustments columns verifies that the debits equal the credits for the adjustment data and adjusting entries. The total of the Debit column must equal the total of the Credit column.

The adjustment data are added to or subtracted from the amounts in the Unadjusted Trial Balance columns to arrive at the Adjusted Trial Balance columns. In this way, the Adjusted Trial Balance columns of Exhibit 19 illustrate the impact of the adjusting entries on the unadjusted accounts. The totals of the Adjusted Trial Balance columns verify the equality of the totals of the debit and credit balances after adjustment.

Exhibit 19 illustrates the flow of accounts from the adjusted trial balance into the financial statements as follows:

- The revenue and expense accounts are extended to (flow into) the Income Statement columns.
- At the bottom of the Income Statement columns, the net income or net loss for the period is the difference between the total Credit column (revenues) and the total Debit column (expenses). If the Income Statement Credit column total (revenues) is greater than the Income Statement Debit column total (expenses), the difference is the net income. If the Income Statement Debit column total is greater than the Income Statement Credit column total, the difference is a net loss. Exhibit 19 shows that NetSolutions had net income of $7,905 for the period.
- The assets, liabilities, owner's capital, and withdrawals accounts are extended to (flow into) the Balance Sheet columns.
- At the bottom of the Balance Sheet column, the net income or net loss for the period is the difference between the total Debit column and the total Credit column. Because net income increases owner's capital, NetSolutions' net income of $7,905 is shown in the Balance Sheet Credit column.

To summarize, Exhibit 19 illustrates the end-of-period process by which accounts are adjusted. In addition, it illustrates how the adjusted accounts flow into the financial

Exhibit 19

Spreadsheet (Work Sheet) with Unadjusted Trial Balance Entered

	A	B	C	D	E	F	G	H	I	J	K
1		NetSolutions									
2		End-of-Period Spreadsheet (Work Sheet)									
3		For the Two Months Ended December 31, 2014									
4		Unadjusted				Adjusted					
5		Trial Balance		Adjustments		Trial Balance		Income Statement		Balance Sheet	
6	Account Title	Dr.	Cr.	Dr.	Cr.	Dr.	Cr.	Dr.	Cr.	Dr.	Cr.
7											
8	Cash	2,065				2,065				2,065	
9	Accounts Receivable	2,220		500		2,720				2,720	
10	Supplies	2,800			1,240	1,560				1,560	
11	Prepaid insurance	2,400			200	2,200				2,200	
12	Office Equipment	1,800				1,800				1,800	
13	Acc. Depr.—Office Equip.				50		50				50
14	Land	20,000				20,000				20,000	
15	Accounts Payable		900				900				900
16	Unearned Rent		360	120			240				240
17	Wages Payable				250		250				250
18	Chris Clark, Capital		25,000				25,000				25,000
19	Chris Clark, Withdrawals	4,000				4,000				4,000	
20	Fees Earned		16,340		500		16,840		16,840		
21	Rent Revenue				120		120		120		
22	Wages Expense	4,275		250		4,525		4,525			
23	Rent Expense	1,600				1,600		1,600			
24	Depreciation Expense			50		50		50			
25	Utilities Expense	985				985		985			
26	Supplies Expense			1,240		1,240		1,240			
27	Insurance Expense			200		200		200			
28	Miscellaneous Expense	455				455		455			
29		42,600	42,600	2,360	2,360	43,400	43,400	9,055	16,960	34,345	26,440
30								►7,905			7,905
31								16,960			34,345
32											

The adjustments on the spreadsheet (work sheet) are used in preparing the adjusting journal entries.

The adjusted trial balance amounts are determined by adding the adjustments to or subtracting the adjustments from the unadjusted trial balance amounts. For example, the Wages Expense debit of $4,525 is the unadjusted trial balance amount of $4,275 plus the $250 adjustment debit.

The revenue and expense amounts are extended to (entered in) the Income Statement columns.

The asset, liability, owner's capital, and withdrawals amounts are extended to (entered in) the Balance Sheet columns.

The difference between the Income Statement column totals is the net income (or net loss) for the period. The difference between the Balance Sheet column totals is also the net income (or net loss) for the period.

The spreadsheet (work sheet) is used for summarizing the effects of adjusting entries. It also aids in preparing financial statements.

statements. The financial statements for NetSolutions can be prepared directly from Exhibit 19.

The spreadsheet in Exhibit 19 is not a required part of the accounting process. However, the spreadsheet is a useful demonstration of the flow of accounting information in the accounting cycle.

Illustration of the Accounting Cycle Using the Work Sheet

In this chapter, the accounting cycle was illustrated using Kelly Consulting. Exhibit 20 shows the worksheet for step 5, Preparing an Optional End-of-Period Spreadsheet (Work Sheet).

Exhibit 20

End-of-Period Spreadsheet (Work Sheet)

	A	B	C	D	E	F	G	H	I	J	K
1					Kelly Consulting						
2					End-of-Period Spreadsheet (Work Sheet)						
3					For the Month Ended December 31, 2014						
4		Unadjusted				Adjusted					
5		Trial Balance		Adjustments		Trial Balance		Income Statement		Balance Sheet	
6	Account Title	Dr.	Cr.	Dr.	Cr.	Dr.	Cr.	Dr.	Cr.	Dr.	Cr.
7											
8	Cash	19,170				19,170				19,170	
9	Accounts Receivable	3,100				3,100				3,100	
10	Supplies	1,400			(a) 550	850				850	
11	Prepaid Rent	4,800			(d) 1,600	3,200				3,200	
12	Office Equipment	14,500				14,500				14,500	
13	Accum. Depreciation				(b) 330		330				330
14	Accounts Payable		800				800				800
15	Salaries Payable				(c) 120		120				120
16	Unearned Fees		5,000	(e) 2,500			2,500				2,500
17	Kelly Pitney, Capital		30,000				30,000				30,000
18	Kelly Pitney, Withdrawals	6,000				6,000				6,000	
19	Fees Earned		15,000		(e) 2,500		17,500		17,500		
20	Salaries Expense	1,500		(c) 120		1,620		1,620			
21	Rent Expense			(d) 1,600		1,600		1,600			
22	Supplies Expense			(a) 550		550		550			
23	Depreciation Expense			(b) 330		330		330			
24	Utilities Expense	330				330		330			
25		50,800	50,800	5,100	5,100	51,250	51,250	4,430	17,500	46,820	33,750
26	Net income							13,070			13,070
27								17,500	17,500	46,820	46,820
28											

At a Glance 4

1 Describe the accounting cycle.

Key Points	Key Learning Outcomes	Page	Example Exercises
The 10 basic steps of the accounting cycle.	• List the 10 steps of the accounting cycle. • Determine whether any steps are missing, or out of order, in a listing of accounting cycle steps.	166 167	4-1

2 Prepare financial statements from adjusted account balances.

Key Points	Key Learning Outcomes	Page	Example Exercises
Using the Adjusted Trial Balance shown in Exhibit 2, the income statement, balance sheet, and the statement of owner's equity can be prepared.	• Describe how the net income or net loss for the period can be determined from an Adjusted Trial Balance. • Prepare an income statement, statement of owner's equity, and a classified balance sheet.	168 168	4-2 4-3 4-4

3 Prepare closing entries.

Key Points	Key Learning Outcomes	Page	Example Exercises
Four entries are required to close the temporary accounts. After the closing entries have been posted to the ledger, the balance in the capital account agrees with the amount reported on the statement of owner's equity and balance sheet. In addition, the revenue, expense, and withdrawal accounts will have zero balances.	• Prepare the four closing entries.	175	4-5

4 Illustrate the accounting cycle for one period.

Key Points	Key Learning Outcomes	Page	Example Exercises
The complete accounting cycle for Kelly Consulting for the month of December is described and illustrated on pages 182–192.	• Complete the accounting cycle for a period from beginning to end. • Working capital and current ratio	182 192	 4-6

GLOSSARY

accounting cycle – The process that begins with analyzing and journalizing transactions and ends with the post-closing trial balance. (p. 166)

calendar year – A year beginning on January 1 and ending December 31, used for sole proprietors and partnerships. (p. 190)

clearing account – An account to which are transferred the revenue and expense account balances. (p. 176) Also known as *income summary*.

closing entries – The entries that transfer the balances of the revenue, expense, and withdrawals accounts to the owner's capital account. (p. 175)

closing process – The process of transferring temporary account balances to permanent accounts at the end of the accounting period. (p. 175) Also known as *closing the books*.

closing the books – The process of transferring temporary account balances to permanent accounts at the

end of the accounting period. (p. 175) Also known as the *closing process*.

current assets – Cash and other assets that are expected to be converted to cash, sold, or used up, usually within one year or less, through the normal operations of the business. (p. 172)

current liabilities – Liabilities that will be due within a short time (usually one year or less) and that are to be paid out of current assets. (p. 172)

current ratio – current assets divided by current liabilities, a ratio of 1 indicates the company can cover their current liabilities with current assets. (p. 192) Also known as *working capital ratio*.

fiscal year – The annual accounting period adopted by a business. (p. 190)

income summary – An account to which the revenue and expense account balances are transferred at the end of a period. (p. 175) Also known as a *clearing account*.

long-term liabilities – Liabilities that usually will not be due for more than one year. (p. 172)

other assets – Other classes within the asset subsection, such as long-term investments and intangible assets. (p. 172)

permanent accounts – Balance sheet accounts that are relatively permanent and are carried forward from year to year. (p. 175)

temporary accounts – Accounts that report amounts for only one period. (p. 175)

working capital – Current assets less current liabilities, indicates company's abilities to pay off current liabilities with current assets. (p. 192)

working capital ratio – Current assets divided by current liabilities, a ratio of 1 indicates the company can cover their current liabilities with current assets. (p. 192) Also known as a *current ratio*.

END-OF-CHAPTER ILLUSTRATIVE PROBLEM

At December 31, 2015, the following adjusted trial balance was prepared:

Harbour Realty
Adjusted Trial Balance
December 31, 2015

	Debit Balances	Credit Balances
Cash	3,425	
Accounts Receivable	8,000	
Supplies	380	
Prepaid Insurance	305	
Office Equipment	51,650	
Accumulated Depreciation—Office Equipment		14,650
Long-Term Investments	5,000	
Intangible Assets	7,000	
Accounts Payable		925
Interest Payable		330
Unearned Fees		750
Wages Payable		440
Long-Term Liabilities		12,000
T. Roderick, Capital		20,580
T. Roderick, Withdrawals	5,200	
Fees Earned		60,625
Wages Expense	22,855	
Depreciation Expense	4,950	
Interest Expense	330	
Supplies Expense	890	
Insurance Expense	315	
	110,300	110,300

Instructions

1. Prepare an income statement, a statement of owner's equity (no additional investments were made during the year), and a balance sheet.
2. On the basis of the data in the adjusted trial balance, journalize the closing entries.

Solution

1.

Harbour Realty
Income Statement
For the Year Ended December 31, 2015

Fees earned		$60,625
Expenses:		
Wages expense	$22,855	
Depreciation expense	4,950	
Supplies expense	890	
Interest expense	330	
Insurance expense	315	
Total expenses		29,340
Net income		$31,285

Harbour Realty
Statement of Owner's Equity
For the Year Ended December 31, 2015

T. Roderick, capital, January 1, 2015		$20,580
Net income for the year	$31,285	
Less withdrawals	5,200	
Increase in owner's equity		26,085
T. Roderick, capital, December 31, 2015		$46,665

Harbour Realty
Balance Sheet
December 31, 2015

Assets			Liabilities		
Current assets:			Current liabilities:		
Cash	$ 3,425		Accounts payable	$ 925	
Accounts receivable	8,000		Unearned fees	750	
Supplies	380		Wages payable	440	
Prepaid insurance	305		Interest payable	330	
Total current assets		$12,110	Total current liabilities		$ 2,445
Property, plant, and equipment:					
Office equipment	51,650		Long-term liabilities		12,000
Less accumulated depreciation	14,650		Total liabilities		14,445
Total property, plant, and equipment		37,000	**Owner's Equity**		
Long-term investments		5,000			
Intangible assets		7,000	T. Roderick, capital		46,665
Total assets		$61,110	Total liabilities and owner's equity		$61,110

(continued)

2.

		Journal			Page *1*
Date		**Description**	**Post. Ref.**	**Debit**	**Credit**
		Closing Entries			
2015 Dec.	31	Fees Earned		60,625	
		Income Summary			60,625
	31	Income Summary		29,340	
		Wages Expense			22,855
		Depreciation Expense			4,950
		Interest Expense			330
		Supplies Expense			890
		Insurance Expense			315
	31	Income Summary		31,285	
		T. Roderick, Capital			31,285
	31	T. Roderick, Capital		5,200	
		T. Roderick, Withdrawals			5,200

EYE OPENERS

1. (a) What is the most important output of the accounting cycle? (b) Do all companies have an accounting cycle? Explain.
2. Describe the nature of the assets that compose the following sections of a balance sheet: (a) current assets; (b) property, plant, and equipment; and (c) other assets.
3. What is the difference between a current liability and a long-term liability?
4. What types of accounts are referred to as temporary accounts?
5. Why are closing entries required at the end of an accounting period?
6. What is the difference between adjusting entries and closing entries?
7. Describe the four entries that close the temporary accounts.
8. What is the purpose of the post-closing trial balance?
9. The reversing entry, completed at the start of the next period, is an alternative method of dealing with adjusting entries. Does it replace another entry, or is it an additional entry? Explain.
10. Why do some accountants prepare an end-of-period spreadsheet (work sheet)?
11. Is the end-of-period spreadsheet (work sheet) a substitute for the financial statements? Discuss.
12. In the Income Statement columns of the end-of-period spreadsheet (work sheet) for Hayward Consulting Co. for the current year, the Debit column total is $556,400 and the Credit column total is $792,600 before the amount for net income or net loss has been included. In preparing the income statement from the end-of-period spreadsheet (work sheet), what is the amount of net income or net loss?

PRACTICE EXERCISES

PE 4-1
Accounting cycle

EE 4-1 p. 167

From the following list of steps in the accounting cycle, identify which two steps are missing.

a. Business transaction occurs.
b. Transactions are analyzed and recorded in the journal.
c. Transactions are posted to the ledger.
d. An unadjusted trial balance is prepared.
e. An optional end-of-period spreadsheet (work sheet) is prepared.

f. An adjusted trial balance is prepared.

g. Financial statements are prepared.

h. A post-closing trial balance is prepared.

PE 4-2

Determining net income from the adjusted trial balance

In the adjusted trial balance of Stargate Consulting Co. for the current year, expenses are $192,700 and the revenues total $239,300. In preparing the income statement from the adjusted trial balance, what is the amount of net income or net loss?

EE 4-2 p. 168

PE 4-3

Statement of owner's equity

Meg Ostermiller owns and operates 4U Delivery Services. On January 1, 2014, Meg Ostermiller, Capital had a balance of $900,500. During the year, Meg made no additional investments and withdrew $60,000. For the year ended December 31, 2014, 4U Delivery Services reported a net loss of $24,900. Prepare a statement of owner's equity for the year ended December 31, 2014.

EE 4-3 p. 170

PE 4-4

Classified balance sheet

The following accounts appear in an adjusted trial balance of Gondola Consulting. Indicate whether each account would be reported in the (a) current asset; (b) property, plant, and equipment; (c) other assets; (d) current liability; (e) long-term liability; (f) owner's equity section; or (g) is not included in the December 31, 2014, balance sheet of Gondola Consulting.

EE 4-4 p. 173

1. Accounts Payable
2. Accounts Receivable
3. Accumulated Depreciation—Equipment
4. Cash
5. Interest expense
6. Unearned revenue
7. Holly Webb, Capital
8. Note Payable (due in 2018)
9. Supplies
10. Wages Payable
11. Patents
12. Fees earned

PE 4-5

Closing entries

After the accounts have been adjusted at December 31, the following balances were taken from the ledger of Lake Landscaping Co.:

EE 4-5 p. 181

Brian Orr, Capital	$956,400
Brian Orr, Withdrawals	45,000
Fees Earned	862,000
Wages Expense	342,000
Rent Expense	70,000
Miscellaneous Expense	12,400
Supplies Expense	8,500

Journalize the four entries required to close the accounts.

PE 4-6

Working capital and current ratio

f·a·i

Highland Enterprises' current assets and current liabilities are detailed below:

	2015	2014
Current Assets	$775,000	$900,000
Current Liabilities	350,000	375,000

EE 4-6 p. 193

Calculate the working capital and the current ratio for 2014 and 2015. Note whether the 2015 working capital and current ratio have increased or decreased from the previous year.

EXERCISES

EX 4-1
1
Steps in the accounting cycle

Rearrange the following steps in the accounting cycle in proper sequence:
a. An unadjusted trial balance is prepared.
b. Transactions are posted to the ledger.
c. An optional end-of-period spreadsheet (work sheet) is prepared.
d. An adjusted trial balance is prepared.
e. Financial statements are prepared.
f. A post-closing trial balance is prepared.
g. Transactions are analyzed and recorded.
h. Closing entries are journalized and posted to the ledger.
i. Adjusting entries are journalized and posted to the ledger.
j. Business transaction occurs.

EX 4-2
2
Preparing financial statements

The balances for the accounts listed below appear in the adjusted trial balance. Indicate whether each balance should appear on (a) the Income Statement or (b) the Balance Sheet.

1. Accounts Payable
2. Accounts Receivable
3. Cash
4. Dean Pinkerton, Withdrawals
5. Fees Earned
6. Supplies
7. Unearned Rent
8. Utilities Expense
9. Wages Expense
10. Wages Payable
11. Patents
12. Mortgage Payable

EX 4-3
2
Classifying accounts

Balances for each of the following accounts appear in an adjusted trial balance. Identify each as (a) asset, (b) liability, (c) revenue, or (d) expense.

1. Accounts Payable
2. Equipment
3. Fees Earned
4. Insurance Expense
5. Prepaid Advertising
6. Prepaid Insurance
7. Rent Revenue
8. Salaries Expense
9. Salaries Payable
10. Supplies
11. Supplies Expense
12. Unearned Rent

EX 4-4
2
Income statement

The following account balances were taken from the adjusted trial balance for On-Time Messenger Service, a delivery service firm, for the current fiscal year ended December 31, 2015:

Depreciation Expense	$ 7,000	Rent Expense	$ 70,100
Fees Earned	525,000	Salaries Expense	225,400
Insurance Expense	2,500	Supplies Expense	5,750
Miscellaneous Expense	3,750	Utilities Expense	23,500

Prepare an income statement.

EX 4-5
2
Income statement; net loss

The following revenue and expense account balances were taken from the ledger of Graphics Services Co. after the accounts had been adjusted on December 31, 2015, the end of the current fiscal year:

Depreciation Expense	$ 9,200	Service Revenue	$270,100
Insurance Expense	5,000	Supplies Expense	2,970
Miscellaneous Expense	3,950	Utilities Expense	19,200
Rent Expense	52,300	Wages Expense	185,300

Prepare an income statement.

EX 4-6
Income statement

Telus Corporation had the following revenue and expense account balances (in millions) at its fiscal year-end of December 31, 2010:

Depreciation	$1,333	Operations	6,062
Amortization of Intangible Assets	402	Other Expense (net)	32
Financing Costs	510	Restructuring Costs	74
Income Taxes	328	Revenues	9,779

a. Prepare an income statement.
b. Compare your income statement with the related income statement that is available at the TELUS Corporation website. What similarities and differences do you see?

SOURCES: Courtesy of TELUS

EX 4-7
Statement of owner's equity

Jackrabbit Systems Co. offers its services to residents in the Nepean area. Selected accounts from the ledger of Jackrabbit Systems Co. for the current fiscal year ended December 31, 2015, are as follows:

Terry Collins, Capital

Dec. 31	32,000	Jan. 1	611,900
		Dec. 31	320,000

Terry Collins, Withdrawals

Mar. 31	8,000	Dec. 31	32,000
Jun. 30	8,000		
Sep. 30	8,000		
Dec. 31	8,000		

Income Summary

Dec. 31	600,000	Dec. 31	920,000
31	320,000		

Prepare a statement of owner's equity for the year.

EX 4-8
Statement of owner's equity; net loss

Selected accounts from the ledger of Picasso Sports for the current fiscal year ended December 31, 2015, are as follows:

Margarita Castillo, Capital

Dec. 31	32,300	Jan. 1	237,600
31	4,000		

Margarita Castillo, Withdrawals

Mar. 31	1,000	Dec. 31	4,000
Jun. 30	1,000		
Sep. 30	1,000		
Dec. 30	1,000		

Income Summary

Dec. 31	511,900	Dec. 31	479,600
		31	32,300

Prepare a statement of owner's equity for the year.

EX 4-9
Classifying assets

Identify each of the following as (a) a current asset; (b) property, plant, and equipment; (c) other assets; or (d) not applicable.

1. Accounts receivable
2. Building
3. Cash
4. Unearned revenue
5. Wages expense
6. Equipment
7. Prepaid rent
8. Supplies
9. Trademarks
10. Investments

EX 4-10

2

Balance sheet classification

At the balance sheet date, a business owes a mortgage note payable of $360,000, the terms of which provide for monthly principal payments of $2,000.

Explain how the liability should be classified on the balance sheet.

EX 4-11

2

Balance sheet

My-Best Weight Co. offers personal weight-reduction consulting services to individuals. After all the accounts have been closed on December 31, 2015, the end of the current fiscal year, the balances of selected accounts from the ledger of My-Best Weight Co. are as follows:

Accounts Payable	$ 34,500	Land	$400,000
Accounts Receivable	83,120	Prepaid Insurance	19,200
Accumulated Depreciation—Equipment	103,900	Prepaid Rent	12,000
Bianca Tierney, Capital	692,000	Salaries Payable	13,500
Cash	?	Supplies	2,080
Equipment	300,000	Unearned Fees	10,000

Prepare a classified balance sheet that includes the correct balance for Cash.

EX 4-12

2

Balance sheet

List the errors in the following balance sheet. Prepare a corrected balance sheet.

Tent Services Co.
Balance Sheet
For the Year Ended December 31, 2015

Assets			Liabilities	
Current assets:			Current liabilities:	
Cash	$ 15,840		Accounts receivable	$ 41,250
Accounts payable	20,370		Accum. depr.—	
Supplies	4,950		building	260,100
Prepaid insurance	14,400		Accum. depr.—	
Land	180,000		equipment	55,440
Total current assets		$235,560	Net income	75,000
Property, plant, and			Total liabilities	$431,790
equipment:				
Building	470,100		**Owner's Equity**	
Equipment	129,000		Wages payable	4,020
Total property, plant,			Henry Dearborn, Capital	515,610
and equipment		715,860	Total owner's equity	519,630
			Total liabilities and	
Total assets		$951,420	owner's equity	$951,420

EX 4-13

3

Identifying accounts to be closed

From the following list, identify the accounts that should be closed to Income Summary at the end of the fiscal year:

a. Accounts Receivable
b. Accumulated Depreciation—Equipment
c. Depreciation Expense
d. Equipment
e. Erin Dowley, Capital
f. Erin Dowley, Withdrawals
g. Fees Earned
h. Land
i. Supplies
j. Supplies Expense
k. Wages Expense
l. Wages Payable

EX 4-14

3

Closing entries— income summary

Prior to its closing, Income Summary had total debits of $432,200 and total credits of $572,600.

Briefly explain the purpose served by the income summary account and the nature of the entries that resulted in the $432,200 and the $572,600.

EX 4-15

Closing entries with net income—income summary

After all revenue and expense accounts have been closed at the end of the fiscal year, Income Summary has a debit of $193,400 and a credit of $258,600. At the same date, Laurie Engan, Capital has a credit balance of $300,000, and Laurie Engan, Withdrawals has a balance of $25,000. (a) Journalize the entries required to complete the closing of the accounts. (b) Determine the amount of Laurie Engan, Capital at the end of the period.

EX 4-16

Closing entries with net income—capital account

Three accounts need to be closed at the end of the fiscal year: Fees Earned of $36,000 and the only two expense accounts, Salary Expense of $12,000 and Rent Expense of $10,000. At the end of the fiscal year, Nicholas Wong, Capital has a credit balance of $100,000, and Nicholas Wong, Withdrawals has a balance of $4,000.

a. Journalize the entries required to complete the closing of the accounts without using the Income Summary account.
b. Determine the amount of Nicholas Wong, Capital at the end of the year.

EX 4-17

Closing entries with net loss—income summary

Marina Services Co. offers its services to individuals desiring to improve their personal images. After the accounts have been adjusted at December 31, the following balances were taken from the ledger of Marina Services Co.

John O'Neil, Capital	$480,000	Rent Expense	$45,000
John O'Neil, Withdrawals	30,000	Supplies Expense	11,200
Fees Earned	215,000	Miscellaneous Expense	5,100
Wages Expense	190,000		

Journalize the four entries required to close the accounts.

EX 4-18

Closing entries with net loss—capital account

Regina Services Co. offers its services to individuals desiring to improve their mental state. After the accounts have been adjusted at December 31, the following balances were taken from the ledger of Regina Services Co.

Regina Schuhmann, Capital	$340,000	Rent Expense	$42,000
Regina Schuhmann, Withdrawals	25,000	Supplies Expense	10,000
Fees Earned	198,000	Miscellaneous Expense	4,800
Wages Expense	170,000		

Journalize the three entries required to close the accounts, closing directly to the capital account.

EX 4-19

Identifying permanent accounts

Which of the following accounts will usually appear in the post-closing trial balance?

a. Accounts Payable
b. Accumulated Depreciation—Office Equipment
c. Bo Erath, Capital
d. Bo Erath, Withdrawals
e. Cash
f. Depreciation Expense
g. Fees Earned
h. Office Equipment
i. Salaries Expense
j. Salaries Payable
k. Supplies

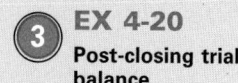

EX 4-20

Post-closing trial balance

An accountant prepared the following post-closing trial balance:

Gypsy Treasures Co.
Post-Closing Trial Balance
December 31, 2015

	Debit Balances	Credit Balances
Cash...	18,000	
Accounts Receivable..	31,000	
Supplies..		5,500
Equipment...		75,000
Accumulated Depreciation—Equipment...........................	19,000	
Accounts Payable..	11,000	
Salaries Payable..		1,000
Unearned Rent..	6,000	
Leticia Aloni, Capital...	92,500	
	177,500	81,500

Prepare a corrected post-closing trial balance. Assume that all accounts have normal balances and that the amounts shown are correct.

Appendix 1
EX 4-21

Journalize the optional reversing entries

The total balance in Accounts Receivable is $3,412. The balance in the Accounts Receivable related to amounts accrued at year-end is $782. Journalize the optional reversing entry required at the beginning of the next year.

Appendix 1
EX 4-22

Journalize the optional reversing entries

Colossal Realty Co. pays weekly salaries of $29,100 on Monday for a six-day workweek ending the preceding Saturday. Colossal used the option of recording reversing entries at the beginning of the year.

a. Journalize the necessary adjusting entry at the end of the accounting period, assuming that the period ends on Thursday.
b. Journalize the reversing entry.

Appendix 1
EX 4-23

Adjusting and reversing entries

On the basis of the following data, (a) journalize the adjusting entries at December 31, the end of the current fiscal year, and (b) journalize the reversing entries on January 1, the first day of the following year.

1. Sales salaries are uniformly $17,375 for a five-day workweek, ending on Friday. The last payday of the year was Friday, December 26.
2. Accrued fees earned but not recorded at December 31, $19,850.

Appendix 1
EX 4-24

Adjusting and reversing entries

On the basis of the following data, (a) journalize the adjusting entries at December 31, the end of the current fiscal year, and (b) journalize the reversing entries on January 1, the first day of the following year.

1. Wages are uniformly $25,900 for a five-day workweek, ending on Friday. The last payday of the month was Friday, December 27.
2. Accrued fees earned but not recorded at December 31, $36,100.

Appendix 1
EX 4-25

Entries posted to the wages expense account

Portions of the wages expense account of a business are shown below.

a. Indicate the nature of the entry (payment, adjusting, closing, reversing) from which each numbered posting was made.
b. Journalize the complete entry from which each numbered posting was made.

Account	Wages Expense				Account No. 5030	
Date	Item	Post. Ref.	Dr.	Cr.	Balance	
2014						
Dec. 26	(1)	49	32,000		1,500,000 Dr.	
31	(2)	50	19,200		1,519,200 Dr.	
31	(3)	51		1,519,200	—	
2015						
Jan. 1	(4)	52		19,200	19,200 Cr.	
2	(5)	53	32,000		12,800 Dr.	

Appendix 1
EX 4-26

Entries posted to the salaries expense account

Portions of the salaries expense account of a business are shown below.

Account	Salaries Expense				Account No. 5030	
Date	Item	Post. Ref.	Dr.	Cr.	Balance	
2014						
Dec. 27	(1)	29	17,500		910,000 Dr.	
31	(2)	30	7,000		917,000 Dr.	
31	(3)	31		917,000	—	
2015						
Jan. 1	(4)	32		7,000	7,000 Cr.	
2	(5)	33	17,500		10,500 Dr.	

a. Indicate the nature of the entry (payment, adjusting, closing, reversing) from which each numbered posting was made.
b. Journalize the complete entry from which each numbered posting was made.

Appendix 2
EX 4-27

Spreadsheet

The balances for the accounts listed below appear in the adjusted trial balance columns of the end-of-period spreadsheet (work sheet). Indicate whether each balance should be extended to (a) an Income Statement column or (b) a Balance Sheet column.

1. Amber Bablock, Withdrawals
2. Utilities Expense
3. Accumulated Depreciation—Equipment
4. Unearned Rent
5. Fees Earned
6. Accounts Payable
7. Rent Revenue
8. Supplies

Appendix 2
EX 4-28

Spreadsheet

The balances for the accounts listed below appear in the adjusted trial balance columns of the end-of-period spreadsheet (work sheet). Indicate whether each balance should be extended to (a) an Income Statement column or (b) a Balance Sheet column.

1. Accumulated Depreciation—Equipment
2. Cash
3. Commissions Earned
4. Insurance Expense
5. Intangible Assets
6. Prepaid Rent
7. Supplies
8. Svend Tisdale, Withdrawals
9. Wages Expense
10. Mortgage Payable

Appendix 2
EX 4-29
Spreadsheet

In the Balance Sheet columns of the end-of-period spreadsheet (work sheet) for Dimple Consulting Co. for the current year, the Debit column total is $678,450 and the Credit column total is $599,750 before including the amount of net income or net loss. In preparing the income statement from the end-of-period spreadsheet (work sheet), what is the amount of net income or net loss?

Appendix 2
EX 4-30
Spreadsheet

In the Balance Sheet columns of the end-of-period spreadsheet (work sheet) for Lancaster Consulting Co. for the current year, the Debit column total is $375,000 and the Credit column total is $505,200 before including the amount of net income or net loss. In preparing the income statement from the end-of-period spreadsheet (work sheet), what is the amount of net income or net loss?

Appendix 2
EX 4-31
Financial statements from the end-of-period spreadsheet (work sheet)

Mather Consulting is a consulting firm owned and operated by Ali Cask. The end-of-period spreadsheet (work sheet) shown below was prepared for the year ended December 31, 2015.

	A	B	C	D	E	F	G	H	I	J	K
1		Mather Consulting									
2		End-of-Period Spreadsheet (Work Sheet)									
3		For the Year Ended December 31, 2015									
4		Unadjusted				Adjusted					
5		Trial Balance		Adjustments		Trial Balance		Income Statement		Balance Sheet	
6	Account Title	Dr.	Cr.	Dr.	Cr.	Dr.	Cr.	Dr.	Cr.	Dr.	Cr.
7											
8	Cash	10,500				10,500				10,500	
9	Accounts Receivable	22,800				22,800				22,800	
10	Supplies	2,400			(a) 2,200	200				200	
11	Office Equipment	18,500				18,500				18,500	
12	Accumulated Depreciation		3,500		(b) 1,200		4,700				4,700
13	Intangible Assets	2,000				2,000				2,000	
14	Accounts Payable		6,100				6,100				6,100
15	Salaries Payable				(c) 400		400				400
16	Long-Term Liabilities		2,000				2,000				2,000
17	Ali Cask, Capital		22,900				22,900				22,900
18	Ali Cask, Withdrawals	3,000				3,000				3,000	
19	Fees Earned		53,800				53,800		53,800		
20	Salaries Expense	27,250		(c) 400		27,650		27,650			
21	Supplies Expense			(a) 2,200		2,200		2,200			
22	Depreciation Expense			(b) 1,200		1,200		1,200			
23	Miscellaneous Expense	1,850				1,850		1,850			
24		88,300	88,300	3,800	3,800	89,900	89,900	32,900	53,800	57,000	36,100
25	Net income							20,900			20,900
26								53,800	53,800	57,000	57,000
27											

Based on the preceding spreadsheet, prepare an income statement, statement of owner's equity, and balance sheet for Mather Consulting.

Appendix 2
EX 4-32
Financial statements from the end-of-period spreadsheet (work sheet)

Kermode Consulting is a consulting firm owned and operated by Jan Sullivan. The following end-of-period spreadsheet (work sheet) was prepared for the year ended December 31, 2015.

	A	B	C	D	E	F	G	H	I	J	K
1		Kermode Consulting									
2		End-of-Period Spreadsheet (Work Sheet)									
3		For the Year Ended December 31, 2015									
4		Unadjusted Trial Balance		Adjustments		Adjusted Trial Balance		Income Statement		Balance Sheet	
5											
6	Account Title	Dr.	Cr.	Dr.	Cr.	Dr.	Cr.	Dr.	Cr.	Dr.	Cr.
7											
8	Cash	7,500				7,500				7,500	
9	Accounts Receivable	18,500				18,500				18,500	
10	Supplies	3,000			(a) 2,250	750				750	
11	Office Equipment	30,500				30,500				30,500	
12	Accumulated Depreciation		4,500		(b) 900		5,400				5,400
13	Accounts Payable		3,300				3,300				3,300
14	Salaries Payable				(c) 400		400				400
15	Jan Sullivan, Capital		27,200				27,200				27,200
16	Jan Sullivan, Withdrawals	2,000				2,000				2,000	
17	Fees Earned		60,000				60,000		60,000		
18	Salaries Expense	32,000		(c) 400		32,400		32,400			
19	Supplies Expense			(a) 2,250		2,250		2,250			
20	Depreciation Expense			(b) 900		900		900			
21	Miscellaneous Expense	1,500				1,500		1,500			
22		95,000	95,000	3,550	3,550	96,300	96,300	37,050	60,000	59,250	36,300
23	Net income							22,950			22,950
24								60,000	60,000	59,250	59,250
25											

Based upon the preceding spreadsheet, prepare an income statement, statement of owner's equity, and balance sheet for Kermode Consulting.

Appendix 2
EX 4-33

Steps in completing an end-of-period spreadsheet (work sheet)

The steps performed in completing an end-of-period spreadsheet (work sheet) are listed below in random order. Indicate the correct order in which these steps are performed when preparing and completing a spreadsheet (work sheet).

a. Add the Debit and Credit columns of the Unadjusted Trial Balance columns of the spreadsheet (work sheet) to verify that the totals are equal.

b. Add the Debit and Credit columns of the Balance Sheet and Income Statement columns of the spreadsheet (work sheet) to verify that the totals are equal.

c. Add or deduct adjusting entry data to trial balance amounts and extend amounts to the Adjusted Trial Balance columns.

d. Add the Debit and Credit columns of the Adjustments columns of the spreadsheet (work sheet) to verify that the totals are equal.

e. Add the Debit and Credit columns of the Balance Sheet and Income Statement columns of the spreadsheet (work sheet) to determine the amount of net income or net loss for the period.

f. Add the Debit and Credit columns of the Adjusted Trial Balance columns of the spreadsheet (work sheet) to verify that the totals are equal.

g. Enter the adjusting entries into the spreadsheet (work sheet), based on the adjustment data.

h. Enter the amount of net income or net loss for the period in the proper Income Statement column and Balance Sheet column.

i. Enter the unadjusted account balances from the general ledger into the Unadjusted Trial Balance columns of the spreadsheet (work sheet).

j. Extend the adjusted trial balance amounts to the Income Statement columns and the Balance Sheet columns.

Appendix 2
EX 4-34

Adjustment data on an end-of-period spreadsheet (work sheet)

Zeidman Security Services Co. offers security services to business clients. The unadjusted trial balance for Zeidman Security Services Co. has been prepared on the end-of-period spreadsheet (work sheet) for the year ended December 31, 2015, shown below.

Zeidman Security Services Co.
End-of-Period Spreadsheet (Work Sheet) (in $000s)
For the Year Ended December 31, 2015

Account Title	Unadjusted Trial Balance Dr.	Unadjusted Trial Balance Cr.	Adjustments Dr.	Adjustments Cr.	Adjusted Trial Balance Dr.	Adjusted Trial Balance Cr.
Cash	12					
Accounts Receivable	80					
Supplies	8					
Prepaid Insurance	12					
Equipment	40					
Accum. Depr.—Equipment		4				
Land	100					
Accounts Payable		36				
Wages Payable		0				
Alex Zeidman, Capital		170				
Alex Zeidman, Withdrawals	8					
Fees Earned		90				
Wages Expense	20					
Rent Expense	12					
Insurance Expense	0					
Utilities Expense	6					
Depreciation Expense	0					
Supplies Expense	0					
Miscellaneous Expense	2					
	300	300				

The data for year-end adjustments are as follows:

a. Fees earned, but not yet billed, $9.
b. Supplies on hand, $3.
c. Insurance premiums expired, $8.
d. Depreciation expense, $4.
e. Wages accrued, but not paid, $1.

Enter the adjustment data, and place the balances in the adjusted trial balance columns.

Appendix 2
EX 4-35

Completing an end-of-period spreadsheet (work sheet)

Zeidman Security Services Co. offers security services to business clients. Complete the following end-of-period spreadsheet (work sheet) for Zeidman Security Services Co.

Zeidman Security Services Co.
End-of-Period Spreadsheet (Work Sheet)
For the Year Ended December 31, 2015 (in $000s)

Account Title	Adjusted Trial Balance Dr.	Adjusted Trial Balance Cr.	Income Statement Dr.	Income Statement Cr.	Balance Sheet Dr.	Balance Sheet Cr.
Cash	12					
Accounts Receivable	89					
Supplies	3					
Prepaid Insurance	4					
Equipment	40					
Accum. Depr.—Equipment		8				
Land	100					
Accounts Payable		36				
Wages Payable		1				
Alex Zeidman, Capital		170				
Alex Zeidman, Withdrawals	8					
Fees Earned		99				
Wages Expense	21					
Rent Expense	12					
Insurance Expense	8					
Utilities Expense	6					
Supplies Expense	5					
Depreciation Expense	4					
Miscellaneous Expense	2					
	314	314				
Net income (loss)						

Appendix 2
EX 4-36

Financial statements from an end-of-period spreadsheet (work sheet)

Based on the data in Exercise 4-35, prepare an income statement, statement of owner's equity, and balance sheet for Zeidman Security Services Co.

Appendix 2
EX 4-37

Adjusting entries from an end-of-period spreadsheet (work sheet)

Based on the data in Exercise 4-34, prepare the adjusting entries for Zeidman Security Services Co.

Appendix 2
EX 4-38

Closing entries from an end-of-period spreadsheet (work sheet)

Based on the data in Exercise 4-35, prepare the closing entries for Zeidman Security Services Co.

PROBLEMS SERIES A

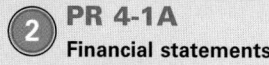

PR 4-1A
Financial statements

Hamlet Productions prepared the following adjusted trial balance at December 31, 2015.

Hamlet Productions
Adjusted Trial Balance
December 31, 2015

	Debit Balances	Credit Balances
Cash..	1,200	
Accounts Receivable......................................	623	
Equipment...	3,000	
Acc. Depreciation—Equipment........................		160
Accounts Payable..		894
Unearned Revenue..		645
Craig Logan, Capital..		1,786
Craig Logan, Withdrawals................................	4,000	
Fees Revenue..		7,563
Salaries and Wages Expense..........................	2,145	
Depreciation Expense.....................................	80	
	11,048	11,048

Instructions

1. Prepare an income statement for the year ended December 31.
2. Prepare a statement of owner's equity for the year ended December 31. No additional investments were made during the year.
3. Prepare a balance sheet as at December 31.
4. Journalize the closing entries.
5. Prepare a post-closing trial balance.

PR 4-2A
Financial statements and closing entries

Winter Consulting prepared the following adjusted trial balance at December 31, 2015, the end of the current fiscal year.

Winter Consulting
Adjusted Trial Balance
December 31, 2015

✔ 1. Net loss: $20,875

	Debit Balances	Credit Balances
Cash..	5,100	
Accounts Receivable......................................	13,950	
Prepaid Insurance...	2,700	
Building...	400,000	
Acc. Depreciation—Bldg.		92,500
Land..	80,000	
Accounts Payable..		9,750
Unearned Rent..		500
Greg Lewis, Capital...		439,875
Greg Lewis, Withdrawals.................................	20,000	
Fees Revenue..		81,200
Advertising Expense..	86,800	
Depreciation Expense.....................................	8,500	
Miscellaneous Expense...................................	5,875	
Insurance Expense..	900	
	623,825	623,825

Instructions

1. Prepare an income statement for the year ended December 31.
2. Prepare a statement of owner's equity for the year ended December 31. No additional investments were made during the year.
3. Prepare a balance sheet as at December 31.

4. Journalize the closing entries.
5. Prepare a post-closing trial balance.

PR 4-3A

2 3

Financial statements and closing entries

✔ 1. John Fairfield, Capital, December 31: $361,500

Fairfield Services Company is a financial planning services firm owned and operated by John Fairfield. As at December 31, 2015, the accountant for Fairfield Services Company prepared the following adjusted trial balance.

Fairfield Services Company
Adjusted Trial Balance
December 31, 2015

	Debit Balances	Credit Balances
Cash..	13,000	
Accounts Receivable...	29,100	
Prepaid Insurance...	8,500	
Buildings...	350,000	
Accumulated Depreciation—Bldg.		121,000
Land..	120,000	
Accounts Payable..		33,300
Salaries Payable..		3,300
Unearned Rent..		1,500
John Fairfield, Capital...		268,800
John Fairfield, Withdrawals..	20,000	
Service Fees..		500,000
Rent Revenue..		6,000
Salaries Expense	342,500	
Depreciation Expense	25,100	
Rent Expense..	17,500	
Miscellaneous Expense...	5,100	
Insurance Expense..	3,100	
	933,900	933,900

Instructions

1. Prepare an income statement, a statement of owner's equity (no additional investments were made during the year), and a balance sheet.
2. Journalize the entries that were required to close the accounts at December 31.
3. If the balance of John Fairfield, Capital increased $60,000 after the closing entries were posted and the withdrawals remained the same, what was the amount of net income or net loss?

PR 4-4A

2 3

T accounts, adjusting entries, financial statements, and closing entries

✔ 4. Net income: $36,700

The unadjusted trial balance of Surf Suds Laundry at December 31, 2015, is shown below.

Surf Suds Laundry
Unadjusted Trial Balance
December 31, 2015

	Debit Balances	Credit Balances
Cash..	4,350	
Laundry Supplies..	11,250	
Prepaid Insurance...	7,200	
Laundry Equipment...	163,500	
Accumulated Depreciation—Laundry Equipment............		61,500
Accounts Payable..		9,300
Hilda Dinero, Capital...		56,700
Hilda Dinero, Withdrawals	3,000	
Laundry Revenue..		247,500
Wages Expense	107,250	
Rent Expense..	54,000	
Utilities Expense...	20,400	
Miscellaneous Expense...	4,050	
	375,000	375,000

(continued)

The data needed to determine year-end adjustments are as follows:

a. Wages accrued but not paid at December 31 are $1,250.
b. Depreciation of equipment during the year is $9,500.
c. Laundry supplies on hand at December 31 are $2,900.
d. Insurance premiums expired during the year are $6,000.

Instructions

1. For each account listed in the unadjusted trial balance, enter the balance in a T account. Identify the balance as "Dec. 31 Bal." In addition, add T accounts for Wages Payable, Depreciation Expense, Laundry Supplies Expense, Insurance Expense, and Income Summary.
2. Journalize and post the adjusting entries. Identify the adjustments by "Adj." and the new balances as "Adj. Bal."
3. Prepare an adjusted trial balance.
4. Prepare an income statement, a statement of owner's equity (no additional investments were made during the year), and a balance sheet.
5. Journalize and post the closing entries. Identify the closing entries by "Clos."
6. Prepare a post-closing trial balance.

---

2 **PR 4-5A**

Ledger accounts, adjusting entries,

3 **financial statements, and closing entries**

✔ 4. Net income: $22,645

If the working papers correlating with this textbook are not used, omit Problem 4-5A.

The ledger and trial balance of Mechanical Services Co. as at December 31, 2015, the end of the first month of its current fiscal year, are presented in the working papers.

Data needed to determine the necessary adjusting entries are as follows:
a. Service revenue accrued at December 31 is $3,000.
b. Supplies on hand at December 31 are $1,475.
c. Insurance premiums expired during December are $1,200.
d. The building has a cost of $312,000 and its life is estimated at 20 years.
e. Equipment of $150,000 has a useful life of 10 years.
f. Unearned rent at December 31 is $1,700.
g. Wages accrued but not paid at December 31 are $500.

Instructions

1. Journalize and post the adjusting entries, inserting balances in the accounts affected.
2. Prepare an adjusted trial balance.
3. Prepare an income statement, a statement of owner's equity, and a balance sheet as at December 31, 2015.
4. Journalize and post the closing entries. Indicate closed accounts by inserting a line in the balance column opposite the closing entry. Insert the new balance of the capital account.
5. Prepare a post-closing trial balance.

---

2 **PR 4-6A**

Ledger accounts, adjusting entries,

3 **financial statements, and closing entries**

✔ 4. Net income: $43,425

The unadjusted trial balance of Loose Leaf Co. at December 31, 2015, is shown below. The data needed to determine year-end adjustments are as follows:
a. Supplies on hand at December 31 are $1,500.
b. Insurance premiums expired during the year are $2,500.
c. The equipment life is estimated at 23 years.
d. The trucks have a useful life of three years.
e. Wages accrued but not paid at December 31 are $750.

Loose Leaf Co.
Unadjusted Trial Balance
December 31, 2015

	Debit Balances	Credit Balances
1010 Cash	1,825	
1030 Supplies	4,820	
1040 Prepaid Insurance	7,500	
1060 Equipment	108,100	
1070 Accumulated Depreciation—Equipment		12,050
1080 Trucks	9,300	
1090 Accumulated Depreciation—Trucks		1,000
2010 Accounts Payable		12,015
3010 Reed Barmack, Capital		51,185
3020 Reed Barmack, Withdrawals	2,500	
4010 Service Revenue		120,950
5010 Wages Expense	48,010	
5030 Rent Expense	7,600	
5050 Truck Expense	5,350	
5090 Miscellaneous Expense	2,195	
	197,200	197,200

Instructions

1. For each account listed in the unadjusted trial balance, enter the balance in the appropriate Balance column of a three-column account and place a check mark (✔) in the Posting Reference column.
2. Journalize and post the adjusting entries, inserting balances in the accounts affected. The following additional accounts from Loose Leaf's chart of accounts should be used: Wages Payable, 2020; Supplies Expense, 5020; Depreciation Expense, 5040; Insurance Expense, 5070.
3. Prepare an adjusted trial balance.
4. Prepare an income statement, a statement of owner's equity (no additional investments were made during the year), and a balance sheet.
5. Journalize and post the closing entries. (Income Summary is account #3030 in the chart of accounts.) Indicate closed accounts by inserting a line in the balance column opposite the closing entry.
6. Prepare a post-closing trial balance.

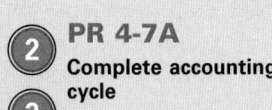

PR 4-7A

Complete accounting cycle

✔ 7. Net income: $38,500

For the past several years, Emily Page has operated a part-time consulting business from her home. As of December 1, 2015, Emily decided to move to rented quarters and to operate the business, to be known as Bottom Line Consulting, on a full-time basis. Bottom Line Consulting entered into the following transactions during December:

Dec. 1. The opening balances at December 1 are cash, $20,000; accounts receivable, $4,500; supplies, $2,000; office equipment, $12,000; and Emily Page, capital, $38,500. There were no liabilities.

1. Paid three months' rent on a lease rental contract, $6,000.

2. Paid the premiums on property and casualty insurance policies, $2,400.

4. Received cash from clients as an advance payment for services to be provided and recorded it as unearned fees, $2,700.

10. Paid cash for a newspaper advertisement, $200.

12. Recorded services provided on account for the period December 1–12, $5,100.

18. Paid cash for supplies, $750.

24. Recorded cash from cash clients for fees earned for the period December 17–24, $5,150.

26. Received cash from clients on account, $6,900.

(continued)

Dec. 29. Paid telephone bill for December, $150.

31. Recorded cash from cash clients for fees earned, $8,000.

31. Recorded services provided on account for the remainder of December, $4,100.

Instructions

1. Journalize each transaction in a two-column journal, referring to the following chart of accounts in selecting the accounts to be debited and credited.

1010	Cash		3010	Emily Page, Capital
1020	Accounts Receivable		3020	Emily Page, Withdrawals
1040	Supplies		4010	Fees Earned
1050	Prepaid Rent		5020	Rent Expense
1060	Prepaid Insurance		5030	Supplies Expense
1080	Office Equipment		5040	Depreciation Expense
1090	Accumulated Depreciation—Office Equipment		5050	Insurance Expense
2010	Accounts Payable		5090	Miscellaneous Expense
2030	Unearned Fees			

2. Post the journal to a ledger of three-column accounts.
3. Prepare an unadjusted trial balance.
4. At the end of December, the following adjustment data were assembled. Analyze and use these data to complete instructions 5 and 6.
   a. Insurance expired during December is $200.
   b. Supplies on hand on December 31 are $650.
   c. The office equipment has an estimated life of four years.
   d. Rent expired during December is $2,000.
   e. Unearned fees on December 31 are $1,875.
5. Journalize and post the adjusting entries.
6. Prepare an adjusted trial balance.
7. Prepare an income statement, a statement of owner's equity, and a balance sheet.
8. Prepare and post the closing entries. (Income Summary is account #3030 in the chart of accounts.) Indicate closed accounts by inserting a line in the balance column opposite the closing entry.
9. Prepare a post-closing trial balance.

 PR 4-8A
Complete accounting cycle

✔ 7. Net income:
$1,690

Maren Chawrun has been operating a part-time interior decorating business from her home. As of December 1, 2015, Maren expanded the business, Miss Fix It, and started operating it full-time.

Dec. 1. The opening balances at December 1 are cash, $13,600; accounts receivable, $4,200; supplies, $1,800; office equipment, $17,000; and Maren Chawrun, Capital, $36,600. There were no liabilities.

1. Purchased additional office equipment on account from Office Depot Co., $2,200.

6. Received cash from clients on account, $3,000.

12. Paid Office Depot Co. for part of the debt incurred on December 1, $800.

14. Paid part-time receptionist for two weeks' salary, $900.

17. Recorded cash from cash clients for fees earned during the period December 1–16, $5,000.

20. Recorded services provided on account for the period December 13–20, $1,300.

27. Paid part-time receptionist for two weeks' salary, $900.

31. Paid electricity bill for December, $300.

31. Maren withdrew $4,000 for personal use.

Instructions

1. Journalize each transaction in a two-column journal, referring to the following chart of accounts in selecting the accounts to be debited and credited.

1010	Cash		3010	Maren Chawrun, Capital
1020	Accounts Receivable		3020	Maren Chawrun, Withdrawals
1040	Supplies		4010	Fees Earned
1080	Office Equipment		5010	Salaries Expense
1090	Accumulated Depreciation		5030	Supplies Expense
2010	Accounts Payable		5040	Depreciation Expense
2020	Salaries Payable		5090	Miscellaneous Expense
2030	Unearned Fees			

2. Post the journal to a ledger of three-column accounts.
3. Prepare an unadjusted trial balance.
4. At the end of December, the following adjustment data were assembled. Analyze and use these data to complete instructions 5 and 6.
   a. Supplies in the amount of $700 were used during the month.
   b. Depreciation of office equipment needs to be estimated. The life of the equipment is four years.
   c. Accrued receptionist salary on December 31 is $210.
   d. Unearned fees on December 31 are $1,200. They have been recorded as fees earned.
5. Journalize and post the adjusting entries.
6. Prepare an adjusted trial balance.
7. Prepare an income statement, a statement of owner's equity, and a balance sheet.
8. Prepare and post the closing entries. (Income Summary is account #3030 in the chart of accounts.) Indicate closed accounts by inserting a line in the balance column opposite the closing entry.
9. Prepare a post-closing trial balance.

Appendix 1
PR 4-9A

Optional reversing entries

Sound Company made the following adjusting journal entries at December 31, 2015:

a.	Depreciation Expense		2,100	
	Accumulated Depreciation—Buildings			2,100
	Building depreciation.			
b.	Depreciation Expense		3,000	
	Accumulated Depreciation—Equipment			3,000
	Equipment depreciation.			
c.	Salaries and Wages Expense		800	
	Salaries and Wages Payable			800
	Accrued salaries and wages.			
d.	Insurance Expense		4,500	
	Prepaid Insurance			4,500
	Insurance expired.			
e.	Accounts Receivable		2,150	
	Fees Earned			2,150
	Accrued fees earned.			
f.	Supplies Expense		1,125	
	Supplies			1,125
	Supplies used.			
g.	Unearned Rent		2,100	
	Rent Revenue			2,100
	Rent earned.			

Instructions

Journalize the reversing entries required.

Appendix 1
PR 4-10A

Optional reversing entries

On December 31, 2015, the following data were accumulated to assist the accountant in preparing the adjusting entries for Blue Realty:
a. Fees accrued but unbilled at December 31 are $8,000.
b. The supplies account balance on December 31 is $3,000. The supplies on hand at December 31 are $850.
c. Wages accrued but not paid at December 31 are $1,350.

(*continued*)

d. The unearned rent account balance at December 31 is $9,249, representing the receipt of an advance payment on December 1 of three months' rent from tenants.
e. Depreciation of the equipment is $1,400.

Instructions

1. Journalize the adjusting entries required at December 31, 2015.
2. Journalize the optional reversing entries required at the beginning of the next year.

Appendix 2
PR 4-11A
End-of-period spread-sheet (work sheet)

Winter Consulting, from Problem 4-2A, prepared an end-of-period spreadsheet (work sheet) at December 31, 2015, the end of the current fiscal year (shown below).

Instructions

1. Prepare an income statement for the year ended December 31.
2. Prepare a statement of owner's equity for the year ended December 31. No additional investments were made during the year.
3. Prepare a balance sheet as at December 31.
4. On the basis of the end-of-period spreadsheet (work sheet), journalize the closing entries.
5. Prepare a post-closing trial balance.

	A	B	C	D	E	F	G	H	I	J	K
1						Winter Consulting					
2					End-of-Period Spreadsheet (Work Sheet)						
3					For the Year Ended December 31, 2015						
4		Unadjusted				Adjusted					
5		Trial Balance		Adjustments		Trial Balance		Income Statement		Balance Sheet	
6	Account Title	Dr.	Cr.	Dr.	Cr.	Dr.	Cr.	Dr.	Cr.	Dr.	Cr.
7											
8	Cash	5,100				5,100				5,100	
9	Accounts Receivable	12,750		(a) 1,200		13,950				13,950	
10	Prepaid Insurance	3,600			(b) 900	2,700				2,700	
11	Building	400,000				400,000				400,000	
12	Acc. Depr.—Building		84,000		(c) 8,500		92,500				92,500
13	Land	80,000				80,000				80,000	
14	Accounts Payable		9,750				9,750				9,750
15	Unearned Rent		500				500				500
16	Greg Lewis, Capital		439,875				439,875				439,875
17	Greg Lewis, Withdrawals	20,000				20,000				20,000	
18	Fees Revenue		80,000		(a) 1,200		81,200		81,200		
19	Advertising Expense	86,800				86,800		86,800			
20	Depreciation Expense			(c) 8,500		8,500		8,500			
21	Insurance Expense			(b) 900		900		900			
22	Miscellaneous Expense	5,875				5,875		5,875			
23		614,125	614,125	10,600	10,600	623,825	623,825	102,075	81,200	521,750	542,625
24	Net loss								20,875	20,875	
25								102,075	102,075	542,625	542,625
26											

Appendix 2
PR 4-12A
End-of-period spreadsheet (work sheet)

Fairfield Services Company, from Problem 4-3A, prepared an end-of-period spreadsheet (work sheet) a part of which is shown below, at December 31, 2015, the end of the current fiscal year (shown below).

Instructions

1. Prepare an income statement, a statement of owner's equity (no additional investments were made during the year), and a balance sheet as at December 31.
2. Journalize the entries that were required to close the accounts at December 31.
3. If the balance of John Fairfield, Capital increased $60,000 after the closing entries were posted, and the withdrawals remained the same, what would be the amount of net income or net loss?

	A	H	I	J	K
1	Fairfield Services Company				
2	End-of-Period Spreadsheet (Work Sheet)				
3	For the Year Ended December 31, 2015				
4		Income Statement		Balance Sheet	
5		Dr.	Cr.	Dr.	Cr.
6	Cash			13,000	
7	Accounts Receivable			29,100	
8	Prepaid Insurance			8,500	
9	Land			120,000	
10	Buildings			350,000	
11	Accumulated Depreciation—Building				121,000
12	Accounts Payable				33,300
13	Salaries Payable				3,300
14	Unearned Rent				1,500
15	John Fairfield, Capital				268,800
16	John Fairfield, Withdrawals			20,000	
17	Service Fees		500,000		
18	Rent Revenue		6,000		
19	Salary Expense	342,500			
20	Depreciation Expense	25,100			
21	Rent Expense	17,500			
22	Insurance Expense	3,100			
23	Miscellaneous Expense	5,100			
24		393,300	506,000	540,600	427,900
25	Net income	112,700			112,700
26		506,000	506,000	540,600	540,600
27					

**Appendix 2
PR 4-13A**

End-of-period spread-sheet (work sheet)

Refer to Surf Suds Laundry in Problem 4-4A. After completing instruction 1, enter the unadjusted trial balance for Surf Suds Laundry on an end-of-period spreadsheet (work sheet) and complete the spreadsheet. Add the accounts shown in instruction 1 as needed. Then complete instructions 2 through 6.

**Appendix 2
PR 4-14A**

End-of-period spread-sheet (work sheet)

Refer to Problem 4-5A. Before completing the steps, complete the end-of-period spreadsheet (work sheet) using the adjustment data. Complete the remaining steps.

**Appendix 2
PR 4-15A**

End-of-period spread-sheet (work sheet)

Refer to Problem 4-6A. Before completing the steps, enter the unadjusted trial balance on an end-of-period spreadsheet (work sheet) and complete the spreadsheet. Add the accounts listed in instruction 2 as needed. Complete the remaining steps.

**Appendix 2
PR 4-16A**

End-of-period spread-sheet (work sheet)

Refer to Problem 4-7A. After completing instructions 1 and 2, enter the unadjusted trial balance on an end-of-period spreadsheet (work sheet) and complete the spreadsheet. Complete the remaining steps. Step 6 will be completed on the spread sheet.

PROBLEMS SERIES B

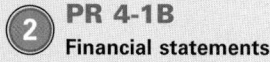

PR 4-1B
Financial statements

Comedy Productions prepared the following adjusted trial balance at December 31, 2015.

Comedy Productions
Adjusted Trial Balance
December 31, 2015

	Debit Balances	Credit Balances
Cash	3,100	
Accounts Receivable	924	
Equipment	2,000	
Accumulated Depreciation—Equipment		120
Accounts Payable		1,251
Unearned Revenue		734
Ken Louis, Capital		2,000
Ken Louis, Withdrawals	3,000	
Fees Revenue		8,253
Salaries and Wages Expense	3,274	
Depreciation Expense	60	
	12,358	12,358

Instructions

1. Prepare an income statement for the year ended December 31.
2. Prepare a statement of owner's equity for the year ended December 31. No additional investments were made during the year.
3. Prepare a balance sheet as at December 31.
4. Journalize the closing entries.
5. Prepare a post-closing trial balance.

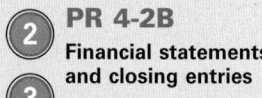

PR 4-2B
Financial statements and closing entries

✔ 1. Net loss: $6,620

Working Company maintains and repairs warning lights, such as those found on radio towers and lighthouses. Working Company prepared the following adjusted trial balance at December 31, 2015, the end of the current fiscal year:

Working Company
Adjusted Trial Balance
December 31, 2015

	Debit Balances	Credit Balances
Cash	5,800	
Accounts Receivable	22,200	
Prepaid Insurance	1,200	
Building	200,000	
Accumulated Depreciation—Bldg.		101,700
Land	98,000	
Accounts Payable		5,700
Unearned Rent		1,100
Mohammad Amin, Capital		235,320
Mohammad Amin, Withdrawals	10,000	
Fees Revenue		57,000
Advertising Expense	41,700	
Miscellaneous Expense	4,320	
Depreciation Expense	14,600	
Insurance Expense	3,000	
	400,820	400,820

Instructions

1. Prepare an income statement for the year ended December 31.
2. Prepare a statement of owner's equity for the year ended December 31. No additional investments were made during the year.

3. Prepare a balance sheet as at December 31.
4. Journalize the closing entries.
5. Prepare a post-closing trial balance.

PR 4-3B

② ③

Financial statements and closing entries

✔ 1. Walter Salva, capital, December 31: $171,400

Outsider Company is an investigative services firm that is owned and operated by Walter Salva. On December 31, 2015, the end of the current fiscal year, the accountant for Outsider Company prepared an adjusted trial balance, which is shown below.

Outsider Company
Adjusted Trial Balance
December 31, 2015

Cash..	12,000	
Accounts Receivable..	52,500	
Prepaid Insurance..	5,100	
Equipment..	150,000	
Accumulated Depreciation—Equipment............		39,000
Accounts Payable...		5,500
Salaries Payable...		1,200
Unearned Rent...		2,500
Walter Salva, Capital..		135,800
Walter Salva, Withdrawals................................	20,000	
Service Fees...		420,000
Rent Revenue...		20,000
Salaries Expense..	310,000	
Rent Expense...	61,000	
Depreciation Expense.......................................	6,100	
Miscellaneous Expense....................................	4,200	
Insurance Expense...	3,100	
	624,000	624,000

Instructions

1. Prepare a single-step income statement, statement of owner's equity (no additional investments were made during the year), and a balance sheet as at December 31, 2015.
2. Journalize the entries that were required to close the accounts at December 31.
3. If Walter Salva, Capital decreased $40,000 after the closing entries were posted, and the withdrawals remained the same, what was the amount of net income or net loss?

PR 4-4B

② ③

T accounts, adjusting entries, financial statements, and closing entries

✔ 4. Net income: $35,900

The unadjusted trial balance of Ocean Breeze Laundromat at December 31, 2015, is shown below.

Ocean Breeze Laundromat
Unadjusted Trial Balance
December 31, 2015

	Debit Balances	Credit Balances
Cash..	11,000	
Laundry Supplies..	18,900	
Prepaid Insurance..	8,600	
Laundry Equipment..	284,000	
Accumulated Depreciation—Laundry Equipment....		150,400
Accounts Payable...		9,800
Deanna Beaven, Capital....................................		107,600
Deanna Beaven, Withdrawals...........................	8,400	
Laundry Revenue..		232,200
Wages Expense..	104,000	
Rent Expense...	39,300	
Utilities Expense..	20,400	
Miscellaneous Expense....................................	5,400	
	500,000	500,000

(continued)

The data needed to determine year-end adjustments are as follows:

a. Laundry supplies on hand at December 31 are $4,000.
b. Insurance premiums expired during the year are $5,200.
c. Depreciation of equipment during the year is $6,000.
d. Wages accrued but not paid at December 31 are $1,100.

Instructions

1. For each account listed in the unadjusted trial balance, enter the balance in a T account. Identify the balance as "December 31 Bal." In addition, add T accounts for Wages Payable, Amortization Expense, Laundry Supplies Expense, Insurance Expense, and Income Summary.
2. Journalize and post the adjusting entries. Identify the adjustments by "Adj." and the new balances as "Adj. Bal."
3. Prepare an adjusted trial balance.
4. Prepare an income statement, a statement of owner's equity (no additional investments were made during the year), and a balance sheet.
5. Journalize and post the closing entries. Identify the closing entries by "Clos."
6. Prepare a post-closing trial balance.

---

② ③ PR 4-5B

Ledger accounts, adjusting entries, financial statements, and closing entries

✔ 3. Net income: $22,820

If the working papers correlating with this textbook are not used, omit Problem 4-5B.

The ledger and trial balance of Handy Man Services Co. as at December 31, 2015, the end of the first month of its current fiscal year, are presented in the working papers.

Data needed to determine the necessary adjusting entries are as follows:

a. Service revenue accrued at December 31 is $2,200.
b. Supplies on hand at December 31 are $1,450.
c. Insurance premiums expired during December are $800.
d. The building has a cost of $192,000 and its life is estimated at 16 years.
e. Equipment of $63,000 has a useful life of seven years.
f. Unearned rent at December 31 is $1,800.
g. Wages accrued at December 31 are $600.

Instructions

1. Journalize and post the adjusting entries, inserting balances in the accounts affected.
2. Prepare an adjusted trial balance.
3. Prepare an income statement, a statement of owner's equity, and a balance sheet as at December 31, 2015.
4. Journalize and post the closing entries. Indicate closed accounts by inserting a line in the balance column opposite the closing entry. Insert the new balance of the capital account.
5. Prepare a post-closing trial balance.

---

② ③ PR 4-6B

Ledger accounts, adjusting entries, financial statements, and closing entries

✔ 4. Net income: $35,635

The unadjusted trial balance of Fix-It Co. at December 31, 2015, the end of the current year, is shown below.

Fix-It Co.
Unadjusted Trial Balance
December 31, 2015

	Debit Balances	Credit Balances
1010 Cash	3,950	
1030 Supplies	15,295	
1040 Prepaid Insurance	2,735	
1060 Equipment	120,000	
1070 Accumulated Depreciation—Equipment		21,209
1080 Trucks	17,500	
1090 Accumulated Depreciation—Trucks		7,400
2010 Accounts Payable		4,015
3010 Benjamin Buck, Capital		72,976
3020 Benjamin Buck, Withdrawals	5,000	
4010 Service Revenue		119,950
5010 Wages Expense	39,925	
5030 Rent Expense	10,600	
5050 Truck Expense	7,350	
5090 Miscellaneous Expense	3,195	
	225,550	225,550

The data needed to determine year-end adjustments are as follows:

a. Supplies on hand at December 31 are $4,000.
b. Insurance premiums expired during year are $2,000.
c. The equipment has a life of 20 years.
d. The trucks have a useful life of 5 years.
e. Wages accrued but not paid at December 31 are $450.

Instructions

1. For each account listed in the trial balance, enter the balance in the appropriate Balance column of a three-column account and place a check mark (✔) in the Posting Reference column.
2. Journalize and post the adjusting entries, inserting balances in the accounts affected. The following additional accounts from Fix-It's chart of accounts should be used: Wages Payable, 2020; Supplies Expense, 5020; Depreciation Expense, 5040; Insurance Expense, 5070.
3. Prepare an adjusted trial balance.
4. Prepare an income statement, a statement of owner's equity (no additional investments were made during the year), and a balance sheet.
5. Journalize and post the closing entries. (Income Summary is account #3030 in the chart of accounts.) Indicate closed accounts by inserting a line in the balance column opposite the closing entry.
6. Prepare a post-closing trial balance.

PR 4-7B

Complete accounting cycle

✔ 7. Net income: $15,150

For the past several years, Kareem Ismail has operated a part-time consulting business from his home. As of December 1, 2015, Kareem decided to move to rented quarters and to operate the business, to be known as Iron Mountain Consulting, on a full-time basis. Iron Mountain Consulting entered into the following transactions during December:

Dec. 1. The opening balances at December 1 are as follows: Kareem Ismail, capital, $53,300; cash, $18,000; accounts receivable, $5,000; supplies, $1,500; and office equipment, $28,800. There were no opening balances for liabilities.

1. Paid three months' rent on a lease rental contract, $4,800.
2. Paid the premiums on property and casualty insurance policies, $2,700.
4. Received cash from clients as an advance payment for services to be provided and recorded it as unearned fees, $3,150.
10. Paid cash for a newspaper advertisement, $325.

(continued)

12. Recorded services provided on account for the period December 1–12, $5,750.

18. Paid cash for supplies, $600.

24. Recorded cash from cash clients for fees earned for the period December 17–24, $4,850.

26. Received cash from clients on account, $3,450.

29. Paid telephone bill for December, $250.

31. Recorded cash from cash clients for fees earned for the period December 25–31, $3,975.

31. Recorded services provided on account for the remainder of December, $2,500.

Instructions

1. Journalize each transaction in a two-column journal, referring to the following chart of accounts in selecting the accounts to be debited and credited.

1010	Cash	3010	Kareem Ismail, Capital
1020	Accounts Receivable	3020	Kareem Ismail, Withdrawals
1040	Supplies	4010	Fees Earned
1050	Prepaid Rent	5010	Salaries Expense
1060	Prepaid Insurance	5020	Rent Expense
1080	Office Equipment	5030	Supplies Expense
1090	Accumulated Depreciation—Office Equipment	5040	Depreciation Expense
2010	Accounts Payable	5050	Insurance Expense
2020	Salaries Payable	5090	Miscellaneous Expense
2030	Unearned Fees		

2. Post the journal to a ledger of three-column accounts.
3. Prepare an unadjusted trial balance.
4. At the end of December, the following adjustment data were assembled. Analyze and use these data to complete instructions 5 and 6.
   a. Insurance expired during December is $225.
   b. Supplies on hand on December 31 are $875.
   c. The office equipment has an estimated life of 10 years.
   d. Rent expired during December is $1,600.
   e. Unearned fees on December 31 are $1,150.
5. Journalize and post the adjusting entries.
6. Prepare an adjusted trial balance.
7. Prepare an income statement, a statement of owner's equity, and a balance sheet.
8. Prepare and post the closing entries. (Income Summary is account #3030 in the chart of accounts.) Indicate closed accounts by inserting a line in the balance column opposite the closing entry.
9. Prepare a post-closing trial balance.

PR 4-8B

2
3

Complete accounting cycle

✔ 7. Net loss: $755

Sheryl Jones has been operating a part-time interior decorating business from her home. As of December 1, 2015, Sheryl expanded the business, Star Bookkeeping, and started operating it on a full-time basis.

Dec. 1. The opening balances at December 1 are cash, $18,600; accounts receivable, $6,300; supplies, $1,200; office equipment, $11,800; and Sheryl Jones, capital, $37,900. There were no liabilities.

1. Purchased additional office equipment on account from Office Depot Co., $5,000.

6. Received cash from clients on account, $4,900.

12. Paid Office Depot Co. for part of the debt incurred on December 1, $2,400.

14. Paid part-time receptionist for two weeks' salary, $850.

17. Recorded cash from cash clients for fees earned during the period December 1–16, $4,800.

20. Recorded services provided on account for the period December 13–20, $2,100.

27. Paid part-time receptionist for two weeks' salary, $850.

31. Paid electricity bill for December, $275.

31. Sheryl withdrew $3,500 for personal use.

Instructions

1. Journalize each transaction in a two-column journal, referring to the following chart of accounts in selecting the accounts to be debited and credited.

1010	Cash	3010	Sheryl Jones, Capital
1020	Accounts Receivable	3020	Sheryl Jones, Withdrawals
1040	Supplies	4010	Fees Earned
1080	Office Equipment	5010	Salaries Expense
1090	Accumulated Depreciation	5030	Supplies Expense
2010	Accounts Payable	5040	Depreciation Expense
2020	Salaries Payable	5090	Miscellaneous Expense
2030	Unearned Fees		

2. Post the journal to a ledger of three-column accounts.
3. Prepare an unadjusted trial balance.
4. At the end of December, the following adjustment data were assembled. Analyze and use these data to complete instructions 5 and 6.
   a. Supplies in the amount of $500 were used during the month.
   b. Depreciation of office equipment needs to be estimated. The life of the equipment is seven years.
   c. Accrued receptionist salary on December 31 is $170.
   d. Unearned fees on December 31 are $1,500. They have been recorded in fees earned.
5. Journalize and post the adjusting entries.
6. Prepare an adjusted trial balance.
7. Prepare an income statement, a statement of owner's equity, and a balance sheet.
8. Prepare and post the closing entries. (Income Summary is account #3030 in the chart of accounts.) Indicate closed accounts by inserting a line in the balance column opposite the closing entry.
9. Prepare a post-closing trial balance.

Appendix 1
PR 4-9B
Optional reversing entries

Listening Company made the following adjusting journal entries at December 31, 2015:

a.	Depreciation Expense	4,100	
	Accumulated Depreciation—Buildings		4,100
	Building depreciation.		
b.	Depreciation Expense	7,000	
	Accumulated Depreciation—Equipment		7,000
	Equipment depreciation.		
c.	Salaries and Wages Expense	900	
	Salaries and Wages Payable		900
	Accrued salaries and wages.		
d.	Insurance Expense	2,500	
	Prepaid Insurance		2,500
	Insurance expired.		
e.	Accounts Receivable	2,750	
	Fees Earned		2,750
	Accrued fees earned.		
f.	Supplies Expense	1,125	
	Supplies		1,125
	Supplies used.		
g.	Unearned Rent	2,100	
	Rent Revenue		2,100
	Rent earned.		

Instructions

Journalize the reversing entries required.

Appendix 1
PR 4-10B
Optional reversing entries

On December 31, 2015, the following data were accumulated to assist the accountant in preparing the adjusting entries for Problem Solved Realty:

a. Fees accrued but unbilled at December 31 are $5,000.
b. The supplies account balance on December 31 is $4,100. The supplies on hand at December 31 are $850.

(continued)

c. Wages accrued but not paid at December 31 are $1,750.
d. The unearned rent account balance at December 31 is $9,249, representing the receipt of an advance payment on November 1 of three months' rent from tenants.
e. Depreciation of the equipment is $1,750.

Instructions

1. Journalize the adjusting entries required at December 31, 2015.
2. Journalize the optional reversing entries required at the beginning of the next year.

Appendix 2
PR 4-11B
End-of-period spread-sheet (work sheet)

Working Company, from Problem 4-2B, prepared an end-of-period spreadsheet (work sheet) at December 31, 2015, the end of the current fiscal year.

	A	B	C	D	E	F	G	H	I	J	K
1						Working Company					
2					End-of-Period Spreadsheet (Work Sheet)						
3					For the Year Ended December 31, 2015						
4		Unadjusted				Adjusted					
5		Trial Balance		Adjustments		Trial Balance		Income Statement		Balance Sheet	
6	Account Title	Dr.	Cr.	Dr.	Cr.	Dr.	Cr.	Dr.	Cr.	Dr.	Cr.
7											
8	Cash	5,800				5,800				5,800	
9	Accounts Receivable	18,900		(a) 3,300		22,200				22,200	
10	Prepaid Insurance	4,200			(b) 3,000	1,200				1,200	
11	Building	200,000				200,000				200,000	
12	Acc. Depr.—Building		87,100		(c) 14,600		101,700				101,700
13	Land	98,000				98,000				98,000	
14	Accounts Payable		5,700				5,700				5,700
15	Unearned Rent		2,100	(d) 1,000			1,100				1,100
16	Mohammad Amin, Capital		234,320				234,320				234,320
17	Mohammad Amin, Withdrawals	10,000				10,000				10,000	
18	Fees Revenue		53,700		(a) 3,300		57,000		57,000		
19	Rent Revenue				(d) 1,000		1,000		1,000		
20	Advertising Expense	41,700				41,700		41,700			
21	Depreciation Expense			(c) 14,600		14,600		14,600			
22	Insurance Expense			(b) 3,000		3,000		3,000			
23	Misc. Expense	4,320				4,320		4,320			
24		382,920	382,920	21,900	21,900	400,820	400,820	63,620	58,000	337,200	342,820
25	Net loss								5,620	5,620	
26								63,620	63,620	342,820	342,820
27											

Instructions

1. Prepare an income statement for the year ended December 31.
2. Prepare a statement of owner's equity for the year ended December 31. No additional investments were made during the year.
3. Prepare a balance sheet as at December 31.
4. On the basis of the end-of-period spreadsheet (work sheet), journalize the closing entries.
5. Prepare a post-closing trial balance.

Appendix 2
PR 4-12B

End-of-period
spreadsheet (work
sheet)

Outsider Company, from Problem 4-3B, prepared an end-of-period spreadsheet (work sheet), a part of which is shown below, at December 31, 2015, the end of the current fiscal year.

	A	H	I	J	K
1	Outsider Company				
	End-of-Period Spreadsheet (Work Sheet)				
2	For the Year Ended December 31, 2015				
3		Income Statement		Balance Sheet	
4		Dr.	Cr.	Dr.	Cr.
5	Cash			12,000	
6	Accounts Receivable			52,500	
7	Prepaid Insurance			5,100	
8	Equipment			150,000	
9	Accumulated Depreciation—Equipmemt				39,000
10	Accounts Payable				5,500
11	Salaries Payable				1,200
12	Unearned Rent				2,500
13	Walter Salva, Capital				135,800
14	Walter Salva, Withdrawals			20,000	
15	Service Fees		420,000		
16	Rent Revenue		20,000		
17	Salaries Expense	310,000			
18	Rent Expense	61,000			
19	Depreciation Expense	6,100			
20	Insurance Expense	3,100			
21	Miscellaneous Expense	4,200			
22		384,400	440,000	239,600	184,000
23	Net income	55,600			55,600
24		440,000	440,000	239,600	239,600
25					

Instructions

1. Prepare an income statement, a statement of owner's equity (no additional investments were made during the year), and a balance sheet as at December 31.
2. Journalize the entries that were required to close the accounts at December 31.
3. If the balance of Walter Salva, Capital increased $40,000 after the closing entries were posted and the withdrawals remained the same, what was the amount of net income or net loss?

Appendix 2
PR 4-13B

End-of-period
spreadsheet (work
sheet)

Refer to Ocean Breeze Laundromat in Problem 4-4B. After completing instruction 1, enter the unadjusted trial balance for Ocean Breeze Laundromat on an end-of-period spreadsheet (work sheet) and complete the spreadsheet. Add the accounts shown in instruction 1 as needed. Then complete instructions 2 through 6.

Appendix 2
PR 4-14B

End-of-period
spreadsheet (work
sheet)

Refer to Problem 4-5B. Before completing the steps, complete the end-of-period spreadsheet (work sheet) using the adjustment data. Complete the remaining steps.

Appendix 2
PR 4-15B

End-of-period
spreadsheet (work
sheet)

Refer to Problem 4-6B. Before completing the steps, enter the unadjusted trial balance on an end-of-period spreadsheet (work sheet) and complete the spreadsheet. Add the accounts listed in instruction (2) as needed. Complete the remaining instructions.

Appendix 2
PR 4-16B

End-of-period
spreadsheet (work
sheet)

Refer to Problem 4-7B. After completing instructions 1 and 2, enter the unadjusted trial balance on an end-of-period spreadsheet (work sheet) and complete the spreadsheet. Complete the remaining steps. Step 6 will be completed on the spreadsheet.

CONTINUING PROBLEM

✔ 2. Net income:
$6,920

The unadjusted trial balance of Music Depot as at December 31, 2015, along with the adjustment data for the two months ended December 31, 2015, are shown in Chapter 3, on pages 160–161.

Based upon the adjustment data, the adjusted trial balance shown below was prepared.

Music Depot
Adjusted Trial Balance
December 31, 2015

	Debit Balances	Credit Balances
Cash	14,600	
Accounts Receivable	3,350	
Prepaid Insurance	2,475	
Supplies	400	
Office Equipment	6,000	
Accumulated Depreciation—Office Equipment		75
Accounts Payable		6,350
Wages Payable		170
Unearned Revenue		3,600
Pat Sharpe, Capital		9,000
Pat Sharpe, Withdrawals	2,000	
Fees Earned		13,450
Music Expense	2,400	
Advertising Expense	650	
Supplies Expense	300	
Depreciation Expense	75	
Insurance Expense	225	
Wage Expense	170	
	32,645	32,645

Instructions

1. **Optional**. Using the data from Chapter 3, prepare an end-of-period spreadsheet (work sheet).
2. Prepare an income statement, a statement of owner's equity, and a balance sheet. (Note: Pat Sharpe made investments in Music Depot on November 1 and December 1, 2015.)
3. Journalize and post the closing entries. The Income Summary account is #3030 in the ledger of Music Depot. Indicate closed accounts by inserting a line in the balance column opposite the closing entry.
4. Prepare a post-closing trial balance.

COMPREHENSIVE PROBLEM 1

8. Net income, $8,955

Kelly Pitney began her consulting business, Kelly Consulting, on December 1, 2015. The accounting cycle for Kelly Consulting for December, including financial statements, was illustrated on pages 182–192. During January, Kelly Consulting entered into the following transactions:

Jan. 3. Received cash from clients as an advance payment for services to be provided and recorded it as unearned fees, $2,500.
   9. Paid cash for a newspaper advertisement, $300.
   13. Paid Office Station Co. for part of the debt incurred on December 5, $400.
   16. Paid part-time receptionist for two weeks' salary including the amount owed on December 31, $750.
   20. Purchased supplies on account, $400.
   21. Recorded services provided on account for the period January 1–20, $6,700.
   27. Received cash from clients on account, $9,500.
   28. Paid part-time receptionist for two weeks' salary, $750.
   30. Paid telephone bill for January, $120.
   31. Recorded cash from cash clients for fees earned for the period January 1–31, $3,875.

Instructions

1. The chart of accounts for Kelly Consulting is shown on page 183, and the post-closing trial balance as at December 31, 2015, is shown on page 190. For each account in the post-closing trial balance, enter the balance in the appropriate Balance column of a three-column account. Date the balances January 1, 2015, and place a check mark (✔) in the Posting Reference column. Journalize each of the January transactions in a two-column journal using Kelly Consulting's chart of accounts. (Do not insert the account numbers in the journal at this time.)
2. Post the journal to a ledger of three-column accounts.
3. Prepare an unadjusted trial balance.
4. At the end of January, the following adjustment data were assembled. Analyze and use these data to complete instructions 5 and 6.
    a. Supplies on hand on January 31 are $600.
    b. Depreciation of office equipment for January is $330.
    c. Accrued receptionist salary on January 31 is $240.
    d. Rent expired during January is $1,600.
    e. Unearned fees on January 31 are $2,000.
5. **Optional:** Enter the unadjusted trial balance on an end-of-period spreadsheet (work sheet) and complete the spreadsheet.
6. Journalize and post the adjusting entries.
7. Prepare an adjusted trial balance.
8. Prepare an income statement, a statement of owner's equity, and a balance sheet.
9. Prepare and post the closing entries. (Income Summary is account #3030 in the chart of accounts.) Indicate closed accounts by inserting a line in the balance column opposite the closing entry.
10. Prepare a post-closing trial balance.

SPECIAL ACTIVITIES

SA 4-1

Ethics and professional conduct in business

Pixel Graphics is a graphics arts design consulting firm. Marcie Biel, its treasurer and vice president of finance, has prepared a classified balance sheet as at December 31, 2015. This balance sheet will be submitted with Pixel Graphics' loan application to the company's credit union.

(continued)

In the Current Assets section of the balance sheet, Marcie reported a $75,000 receivable from Chas Gaddis, the president of Pixel Graphics, as a trade account receivable. Chas borrowed the money from Pixel Graphics in November 2013 for a down payment on a new home. He has orally assured Marcie that he will pay off the account receivable within the next year. Marcie reported the $75,000 in the same manner on the preceding year's balance sheet.

Evaluate whether it is acceptable for Marcie Biel to prepare the December 31, 2015, balance sheet in the manner indicated above.

SA 4-2
Financial statements

The following is an excerpt from a telephone conversation between Alice Lutz, president of DeSoto Supplies Co., and Victor Hood, owner of Hood Employment Co.

Alice: Victor, you're going to have to do a better job of finding me a new computer programmer. That last guy was great at programming, but he didn't have any common sense.

Victor: What do you mean? The guy had a master's degree with straight As.

Alice: Yes, well, last month he developed a new financial reporting system. He said we could do away with manually preparing our financial statements. The computer would automatically generate our financial statements with "a push of a button."

Victor: So what's the big deal? Sounds to me like it would save you time and effort.

Alice: Right! The balance sheet showed a minus for supplies!

Victor: Minus supplies? How can that be?

Alice: That's what I asked.

Victor: So, what did he say?

Alice: Well, after he checked the program, he said that it must be right. The minuses were greater than the pluses....

Victor: Didn't he know that Supplies can't have a credit balance—it must have a debit balance?

Alice: He asked me what a debit and credit were.

Victor: I see your point.

1. Comment on (a) the desirability of computerizing DeSoto Supplies Co.'s financial reporting system, (b) the elimination of manually preparing financial statements in a computerized accounting system, and (c) the computer programmer's lack of accounting knowledge.
2. Explain to the programmer why Supplies could not have a credit balance.

SA 4-3
Financial statements

Assume that you recently accepted a position with Canadian Imperial Bank of Commerce as an assistant loan officer. As one of your first duties, you have been assigned the responsibility of evaluating a loan request for $90,000 from Goldworks.ca, a small proprietorship. In support of the loan application, Yolanda Tovar, owner, submitted a "Statement of Accounts" (trial balance) for the first year of operations ended December 31, 2015.

Goldworks.ca
Statement of Accounts
December 31, 2015

Cash...	4,100	
Billings Due from Others	30,140	
Supplies (chemicals, etc.)	14,940	
Trucks...	52,740	
Equipment	16,180	
Amounts Owed to Others		5,700
Investment in Business		47,000
Service Revenue		147,300
Wages Expense	60,100	
Utilities Expense..	14,660	
Rent Expense..	4,800	
Insurance Expense..	1,400	
Other Expenses...	940	
	200,000	200,000

1. Explain to Yolanda Tovar why a set of financial statements (income statement, statement of owner's equity, and balance sheet) would be useful to you in evaluating the loan request.
2. In discussing the "Statement of Accounts" with Yolanda Tovar, you discovered that the accounts had not been adjusted at December 31. Analyze the "Statement of Accounts" and indicate possible adjusting entries that might be necessary before an accurate set of financial statements can be prepared.
3. Assuming that an accurate set of financial statements will be submitted by Yolanda Tovar in a few days, what other considerations or information do you require before making a decision on the loan request?

SA 4-4

Financial Statements

Group Project

In groups of three or four, review the balance sheet of Leon's Furniture Ltd., in Appendix B. Is it a classified balance sheet? Identify the parts of the balance sheet that are more complex than the classified balance sheet presented in the textbook on page 170.

SA 4-5

Financial Statements

Group Project

In groups of three or four, compare the balance sheets of two different companies. Prepare a summary of the two companies' similarities and differences and present your findings to the class. You can locate the balance sheets you need from one of the following sources:

1. SEDAR (System for Electronic Document Analysis and Retrieval) website, www.sedar.com. See below for more information on accessing information from this website.
2. The companies' websites.
3. The companies' investor relations departments.
4. Your school library or the public library.

The balance sheet is included as part of the annual report information that is a required disclosure to the Canadian Securities Administrators (CSA). CSA documents can be retrieved from SEDAR.

To obtain annual report information, click on Search Database, then click on Public Company. Enter the company name where it is indicated. Under Document Type, select Annual Report or Financial Statement (if you do not want the whole report). If your search has no results, try changing the dates. The American version of this site is EdgarScan™, available at www.sec.gov/edgar/searchedgar/webusers.htm.

Accounting for Merchandising Businesses

GREAT CANADIAN DOLLAR STORE

When you are low on cash but need to pick up party supplies, housewares, or other consumer items, where do you go? Many shoppers are turning to Great Canadian Dollar Stores, with franchise stores from Victoria, BC, to Twillingate, Newfoundland and Labrador, to Whitehorse, Yukon. For the price of $5 or less on most merchandise in its stores, this retailer has worked hard on its concept to provide new "treasures" every week for the entire family.

Despite most items costing no more than $5, the accounting for a merchandiser, like Great Canadian, is more complex than for a service company. This is because a service company sells only services and has no inventory. With Great Canadian's locations and merchandise,

the company must design its accounting system not only to record the receipt of goods for resale but also to keep track of what merchandise is available for sale and where the merchandise is located. In addition, Great Canadian must record the sales and costs of the goods sold for each of its stores. Finally, Great Canadian must record such data as delivery costs, merchandise discounts, and merchandise returns.

In this chapter, we focus on the accounting principles and concepts for a merchandising business. In doing so, we highlight the basic differences between merchandiser and service company activities. We then describe and illustrate the financial statements of a merchandising business and accounting for merchandise transactions.

After studying this chapter, you should be able to:

1   Distinguish between the activities and financial statements of service and merchandising businesses.

Nature of Merchandising Businesses	Provincial Sales Tax (PST), Goods and Services Tax (GST), and Harmonized Sales Tax (HST)	EXAMPLE EXERCISE 5-1 (page 238)

2   Describe and illustrate the accounting for merchandise transactions under the perpetual inventory system.

Merchandising Transactions— Perpetual System	Chart of Accounts for a Merchandising Business	
	Merchandise Purchase Transactions	EXAMPLE EXERCISE 5-2 (page 244)
	Merchandise Sales Transactions	EXAMPLE EXERCISE 5-3 (page 247)
	Freight Costs and Trade Discounts	EXAMPLE EXERCISE 5-4 (page 251)
	Dual Nature of Merchandise Transactions	EXAMPLE EXERCISE 5-5 (page 253)

3   Describe the adjusting process for a merchandising business under the perpetual inventory system.

The Adjusting Process	Adjusting Entry for Inventory Shrinkage	EXAMPLE EXERCISE 5-6 (page 255)

4   Describe and illustrate the financial statements of a merchandising business under the perpetual inventory system.

Financial Statements for a Merchandising Business	Single-Step Income Statement	
	Multiple-Step Income Statement	EXAMPLE EXERCISE 5-7 (page 257)
	Statement of Owner's Equity	
	Balance Sheet	

5   Describe the closing process for a merchandising business.

The Closing Process	Financial Analysis and Interpretation	EXAMPLE EXERCISE 5-8 (page 262)

For the chapter *At a Glance*, turn to page 275.

Nature of Merchandising Businesses

Distinguish between the activities and financial statements of service and merchandising businesses.

The activities of a service business differ from those of a merchandising business. These differences are illustrated in the following condensed income statements:

Service Business	
Fees earned	$XXX
Operating expenses	–XXX
Net income	$XXX

Merchandising Business	
Sales	$XXX
Cost of goods sold	–XXX
Gross profit	XXX
Operating expenses	–XXX
Net income	$XXX

The revenue activities of a service business involve providing services to customers. On the income statement for a service business, the revenues from services are reported as *fees earned*. The operating expenses incurred in providing the services are subtracted from the fees earned to arrive at *net income*.

Sales − Cost of Goods Sold = Gross Profit

Gross Profit − Operating Expenses = Net Income

In contrast, the revenue activities of a merchandising business involve the buying and selling of merchandise. A merchandising business first purchases goods to sell to its customers. When these goods are sold, the revenue is reported as sales, and the cost is recognized as an expense. This expense is called the **cost of goods sold**. The cost of goods sold is subtracted from sales to arrive at gross profit. This amount is called **gross profit** because it is the profit *before* deducting operating expenses.

Merchandise on hand (not sold) at the end of an accounting period is called **inventory**. Inventory is reported as a current asset on the balance sheet. The definition of inventory is the same for both Accounting Standards for Private Enterprises (ASPE) and International Financial Reporting Standards (IFRS).[1] Inventory is made up of all the costs to purchase the inventory, the costs related to making the product, and other costs related to bringing the inventory to the company's premises and making it ready for sale. These costs include the purchase price; import duties; and the costs of raw materials, services, and moving the product to the selling location.

If the inventory is being manufactured, then all manufacturing-related costs are included: direct costs, such as labour, and indirect costs, such as electricity and depreciation on the building where the inventory is manufactured. Note that any discounts received during the manufacturing stage are removed from the total cost of inventory. A summary of these costs is shown in Exhibit 1.

Any costs incurred after the inventory has been moved to the company's premises and is ready for sale are expensed. These expenses include the costs for storing the inventory and selling-related costs such as advertising. Freight costs should be recorded in the inventory or the operating expenses depending on where it is being shipped. When a retailer pays for freight to move the inventory from the manufacturer to the retail site, the freight costs are included in the inventory. But when the retailer pays to transport the goods to the customer, the freight costs are expensed as transportation costs in the operating section.

Provincial Sales Tax (PST), Goods and Services Tax (GST), and Harmonized Sales Tax (HST)

Merchandising business transactions also involve provincial sales tax and goods and services tax in some provinces and harmonized sales tax in other provinces. The complication of these different taxes for different provinces has been removed from

---

Exhibit 1

Costs of Acquiring Inventory

Inventory	Operating expense

• Purchase price
• Freight in
• Manufacturing costs such as
  – direct labour
  – indirect labour
  – depreciation
  – electricity
• Sales taxes
	• Freight to customers
	
	• Storage
	• Sales commissions
	• Sales salaries

---

1 For ASPE, *CICA Handbook–Accounting*, 2012 edition, Part II, 3031, para. 11; for IFRS, *CICA Handbook–Accounting*, 2013 edition, Part I, IAS 2, para. 10.

the transactions illustrated in this chapter. For more information on these taxes, see Appendix 2, Provincial Sales Tax (PST), Goods and Services Tax (GST), and Harmonized Sales Tax (HST) at the end of this chapter.

EXAMPLE EXERCISE 5-1 Gross Profit   **1**

During the current year, merchandise is sold for $250,000 cash and $975,000 on account. The cost of the goods sold is $735,000. What is the amount of the gross profit?

FOLLOW MY EXAMPLE 5-1

The gross profit is $490,000 ($250,000 + $975,000 − $735,000).

For Practice: PE 5-1

THE OPERATING CYCLE

The operations of a merchandising business involve the purchase of goods for sale (purchasing), the sale of the products to customers (sales), and the receipt of cash from customers (collection). This overall process is referred to as the *operating cycle*. Thus, the operating cycle begins with spending cash, and it ends with receiving cash from customers. The operating cycle for a merchandising business is shown to the right.

Operating cycles for retailers are usually shorter than for manufacturers because retailers purchase goods in a form ready for sale to the customer. Of course, some retailers will have shorter operating cycles than others because of the nature of their products. For example, a jewellery store or an automobile dealer normally has a longer operating cycle than a consumer electronics store, a grocery store, or a dollar store.

Businesses with longer operating cycles normally have higher profit margins on their products than businesses with shorter operating cycles. For example, it is not unusual for jewellery stores to price their jewellery at 30%–50% above cost. In contrast, grocery stores operate on very small profit margins, often less than 5%. Grocery stores make up the difference by selling their products more quickly.

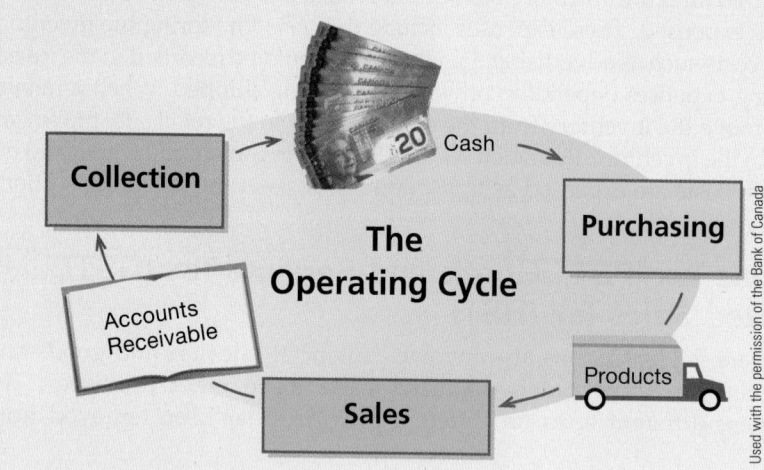

Used with the permission of the Bank of Canada

2

Describe and illustrate the accounting for merchandise transactions under the perpetual inventory system.

Merchandising Transactions—Perpetual System

In this section, we describe and illustrate the recording of merchandise transactions. Two systems are used to record merchandise transactions. These are called the **perpetual inventory system** and the **periodic inventory system**. Most retailers have computerized systems, and so can optimize the perpetual inventory system. For example, such systems may use bar codes, such as the one on the back of this textbook. An optical scanner reads the bar code to record merchandise purchased and sold. Because of this computerization, the perpetual inventory system is used more often, and so it is discussed in this chapter; the periodic inventory system is discussed in Appendix 1 at the end of this chapter. The perpetual inventory system tracks inventory and the cost of goods sold on a day-to-day basis. The periodic inventory system records day-to-day inventory costs in a purchases account, and the inventory account is adjusted only on an annual or quarterly basis. We begin by describing the chart of accounts for a merchandising business.

@netsolutions

Chart of Accounts for a Merchandising Business

In this section, we illustrate the chart of accounts for NetSolutions after it becomes a retailer of computer hardware and software. During 2015, Chris Clark implemented the second phase of NetSolutions' business plan. In doing so, Chris notified clients that beginning July 1, 2015, NetSolutions would no longer offer consulting services. Instead, it would become a retailer. NetSolutions' business strategy is to offer personalized service to individuals and small businesses that are upgrading or purchasing new computer systems. NetSolutions' personal service includes a no-obligation, on-site assessment of the customer's computer needs. By providing personalized service and follow-up, Chris feels that NetSolutions can compete effectively against such retailers as Grand & Toy and Office Depot. The chart of accounts for a merchandising business should reflect the elements of the financial statements. The chart of accounts for NetSolutions is shown in Exhibit 2. Note that Chris Clark has added many accounts and renumbered many accounts. The accounts related to merchandising transactions are shown in colour.

As shown in Exhibit 2, NetSolutions' chart of accounts consists of four-digit account numbers. The first digit indicates the major financial statement classification (1 for assets, 2 for liabilities, and so on). The second digit indicates the subclassification (e.g., 10 for current assets, 12 for noncurrent assets). The third and fourth digits identify the specific account (e.g., 1010 for Cash, 1230 for Store Equipment). Using a four-digit numbering system makes it easy to add new accounts as they are needed.

Inventory Control Account and Subsidiary Ledger   An accounting system is designed to provide information on the amounts in the accounts. The use of a control account and a subsidiary ledger provides this additional information.

The inventory account includes a large number of individual items, which can become difficult to manage effectively. To help control the inventory account, inventory details are grouped together in a separate ledger called a subsidiary ledger. The inventory subsidiary ledger is represented in the general ledger by the summarizing account, called a **controlling account**. In the NetSolutions' example, this inventory account is shown as 1050 Inventory. The sum of the balances of the accounts in the subsidiary ledger must equal the balance of the inventory account. Thus, the inventory **subsidiary ledger** is a secondary ledger that supports the controlling account in the general ledger. If the balance in the general ledger control account is $6,200, then the individual items in the inventory subsidiary ledger should also total $6,200, as shown below.

Inventory	Subsidiary Ledger
Item #5621	$2,100
Item #6211	4,000
Item #4128	100
Total inventory	$6,200

Merchandise Purchase Transactions

Under the perpetual inventory system, cash purchases of merchandise are recorded as follows:

		Journal			Page 24
Date		**Description**	**Post. Ref.**	**Debit**	**Credit**
2016					
Jan.	3	Inventory		2,510	
		Cash			2,510
		Purchased inventory from Bowen Co.			

Exhibit 2

Chart of Accounts for NetSolutions, a Merchandising Business

Balance Sheet Accounts	Income Statement Accounts
Assets	**Revenues**
1010 Cash	4010 Sales
1020 Accounts Receivable	4020 Sales Returns and Allowances
1050 Inventory	4030 Sales Discounts
1060 Office Supplies	**Costs and Expenses**
1070 Prepaid Insurance	5010 Cost of Goods Sold
1230 Store Equipment	5100 Sales Salaries Expense
1240 Accumulated Depreciation—Store Equipment	5110 Advertising Expense
1250 Office Equipment	5120 Depreciation Expense—Store Equipment
1260 Accumulated Depreciation—Office Equipment	5130 Delivery Expense
1270 Land	5140 Miscellaneous Selling Expense
Liabilities	5200 Office Salaries Expense
2010 Accounts Payable	5210 Rent Expense
2020 Salaries Payable	5220 Depreciation Expense—Office Equipment
2030 Unearned Rent	5230 Insurance Expense
2050 Notes Payable	5240 Office Supplies Expense
Owner's Equity	5250 Misc. Administrative Expense
3010 Chris Clark, Capital	**Other Income**
3020 Chris Clark, Withdrawals	6010 Rent Revenue
3030 Income Summary	**Other Expense**
	7010 Interest Expense

Purchases of merchandise on account are recorded as follows:

2016					
Jan.	4	Inventory		9,250	
		Accounts Payable—Thomas Corporation			9,250
		Purchased inventory on account.			

The terms of a sale are normally indicated on the **invoice** or bill that the seller sends to the buyer. An example of an invoice received by NetSolutions is shown in Exhibit 3.

The time requirements for the payment of merchandise are called the **credit terms**. If payment is required on delivery, the terms are *cash or net cash*. Otherwise, the buyer is allowed an amount of time to pay, known as the **credit period**.

The credit period usually begins with the date of the sale. If payment is due within a stated number of days after the invoice date, such as 30 days, the terms are *net 30 days*.[2] These terms may be written as *n/30*. If payment is due by the end of the month in which the sale was made, the terms are written as *n/eom*.

To encourage the buyer to pay before the end of the credit period, the seller may offer a discount. For example, the seller may offer a 2% discount if the buyer pays within 10 days of the invoice date. If the buyer does not take the discount, the total

2 The word *net* as used here does not refer to the number remaining after deductions have been subtracted, as in *net income*.

Exhibit 3

Invoice

Alpha Technologies   **INVOICE**

220 Yonge Street, Suite 110   Invoice No: 16424
Toronto, ON M5B 2H1   Date: March 12, 2016
416-578-8560

To: NetSolutions
     5101 Victoria Ave.
     Calgary, AB T2M 4E3

DESCRIPTION	AMOUNT
Computer equipment	$ 3,000.00
Total	$ 3,000.00

Payment terms
Payment within 30 days or 2/10, n/30

amount is due within 30 days. These terms are expressed as *2/10, n/30* and are read as 2% *discount if paid within 10 days, net amount due within 30 days.* The credit terms of 2/10, n/30 are summarized in Exhibit 4, using the invoice in Exhibit 3.

Purchases Discounts   Purchases discounts taken by a buyer reduce the cost of the merchandise purchased. Even if the buyer needs to borrow to pay within a discount period, it is normally to the buyer's advantage to do so. For this reason, accounting systems are normally designed so that all available discounts are taken.

To illustrate, assume that NetSolutions purchased merchandise from Alpha Technologies as follows:

Invoice Date	Invoice Amount	Terms
March 12	$3,000	2/10, n/30

The last day of the discount period is March 22 (March 12 + 10 days). Assume that in order to pay the invoice on March 22, NetSolutions borrows $2,940, which is $3,000 less the discount of $60 ($3,000 × 2%). Assuming a 365-day year and an annual interest rate of 6%, calculated using simple interest, the interest on the loan of $2,940 for the remaining 20 days of the credit period is $9.67 ($2,940 × 6% × 20/365).

The net savings to NetSolutions of taking the discount is $50.33, computed as follows:

Discount of 2% on $3,000	$60.00
Interest for 20 days at a rate of 6% on $2,940	9.67
Savings from taking the discount	$50.33

Exhibit 4

Credit Terms

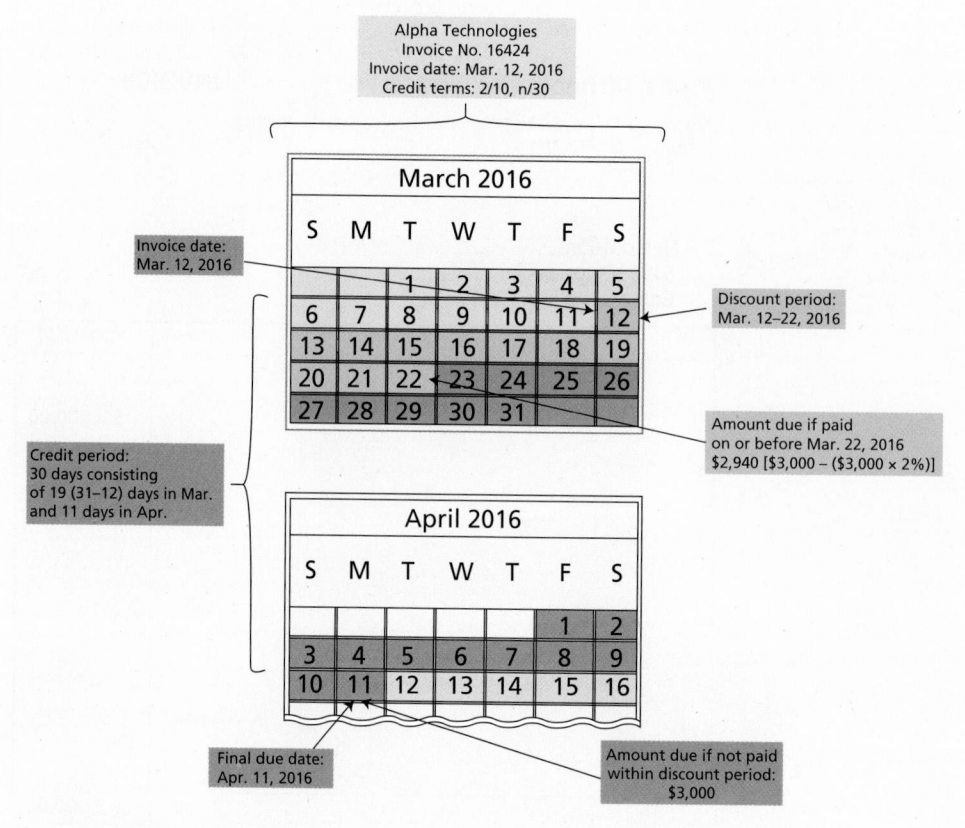

The savings can also be seen by comparing the interest rate on the money *saved* by taking the discount and the interest rate on the money *borrowed* to take the discount. The interest rate on the money saved in the prior example is estimated by converting 2% for 20 days to a yearly rate, as follows:

$$2\% \times \frac{365 \text{ days}}{20 \text{ days}} = 2\% \times 18.25 = 36.5\%$$

NetSolutions borrowed $2,940 at 6% to take the discount. If NetSolutions does not take the discount, it *pays* an estimated interest rate of 36.5% for using the $2,940 for the remaining 20 days of the credit period. Thus, buyers should normally take all available purchases discounts.

Under the perpetual inventory system, the buyer initially debits Inventory for the amount of the invoice. When paying the invoice within the discount period, the buyer credits Inventory for the amount of the discount. In this way, Inventory shows the *net* cost to the buyer.

To illustrate, NetSolutions records the Alpha Technologies invoice and its payment at the end of the discount period as follows:

2016				
Mar.	12	Inventory	3,000	
		Accounts Payable—Alpha Technologies		3,000
		Purchased inventory.		
	22	Accounts Payable—Alpha Technologies	3,000	
		Cash		2,940
		Inventory		60
		To record payment on account.		

Assume that NetSolutions does not take the discount, but instead pays the invoice on April 11. In this case, NetSolutions records the payment on April 11 as follows:

2016				
Apr.	11	Accounts Payable—Alpha Technologies	3,000	
		Cash		3,000
		To record payment on account.		

Purchases Returns and Allowances   A buyer may return merchandise (purchases return) or request a price allowance (purchases allowance) from the seller. In both cases, the buyer normally sends the seller a debit memorandum. A **debit memorandum**, often called a **debit memo**, is shown in Exhibit 5. A debit memo informs the seller of the amount the buyer proposes to *debit* to the account payable due the seller. It also states the reasons for the return or the request for the price allowance.

The buyer may use the debit memo as the basis for recording the return or allowance or wait for approval from the seller (creditor). In either case, the buyer debits Accounts Payable and credits Inventory.

To illustrate, NetSolutions records the return of the merchandise indicated in the debit memo in Exhibit 5 as follows:

2016				
Mar.	7	Accounts Payable—Maxim Systems	900	
		Inventory		900
		Debit Memo No. 18.		

A buyer may return merchandise or be granted a price allowance before paying an invoice. In this case, the amount of the debit memo is deducted from the invoice. The amount is deducted before the purchase discount is computed.

To illustrate, assume the following data concerning a purchase of merchandise by NetSolutions on May 2:

May   2.   Purchased $5,000 of merchandise on account from Delta Data Link, terms 2/10, n/30.

       4.   Returned $3,000 of the merchandise purchased on May 2.

       12. Paid for the purchase of May 2 less the return and discount.

Exhibit 5

Debit Memo

NetSolutions	**No. 18**
5101 Victoria Ave.	
Calgary, AB T2M 4E3	

DEBIT MEMO

TO	**DATE**
Maxim Systems	March 7, 2016
7519 East Willson Ave.	
Winnipeg, MB R2J 2C8	

WE DEBIT YOUR ACCOUNT AS FOLLOWS

10	Server Network Interface Cards, your Invoice		
	No. 7291, are being returned via parcel post.	@ 90.00	900.00
	Our order specified No. 825X.		

NetSolutions records these transactions as follows:

2016					
May	2	Inventory		5,000	
		Accounts Payable—Delta Data Link			5,000
		Purchased merchandise.			
	4	Accounts Payable—Delta Data Link		3,000	
		Inventory			3,000
		Returned portion of merchandise purchased.			
	12	Accounts Payable—Delta Data Link		2,000	
		Cash			1,960
		Inventory			40
		Paid invoice [($5,000 − $3,000) × 2% = $40;			
		$2,000 − $40 = $1,960].			

EXAMPLE EXERCISE 5-2 Purchase Transactions   ② 2

Rofles Company purchased merchandise on account from a supplier for $11,500, terms 2/10, n/30. Rofles Company returned $3,000 of the merchandise and received full credit.

a. If Rofles Company pays the invoice within the discount period, what is the amount of cash required for the payment?

b. Under a perpetual inventory system, what account is credited by Rofles Company to record the return?

FOLLOW MY EXAMPLE 5-2

a. $8,330. Purchase of $11,500 less the return of $3,000 less the discount of $170 [($11,500 − $3,000) × 2%].

b. Inventory

For Practice: PE 5-2

Merchandise Sales Transactions

Merchandise sales transactions are recorded using the rules of debit and credit that we described and illustrated in Chapter 2. Exhibit 3, shown on page 51 of Chapter 2, summarizes these rules.

Special journals may be used, or transactions may be entered, recorded, and posted using a computerized accounting system. To simplify, we will use a two-column general journal in this chapter.[3]

Cash Sales A business may sell merchandise for cash. **Sales** are the amount charged customers for merchandise sold. Cash sales are normally entered on a cash register and recorded in the accounts. To illustrate, assume that on January 3, NetSolutions sells merchandise for $1,800. These cash sales are recorded as follows:

Journal					Page 25
Date		**Description**	**Post. Ref.**	**Debit**	**Credit**
2016					
Jan.	3	Cash		1,800	
		Sales			1,800
		To record cash sales.			

3 Special journals for merchandising businesses are described in Appendix E at the end of this textbook.

Using the perpetual inventory system, the cost of goods sold and the decrease in inventory are also recorded. In this way, the inventory account indicates the amount of merchandise on hand (not sold).

To illustrate, assume the cost of goods sold on January 3 is $1,200. The entry to record the cost of goods sold and the decrease in the inventory is as follows:

2016				
Jan.	3	Cost of Goods Sold	1,200	
		Inventory		1,200
		To record the cost of goods sold.		

Credit Card Sales and Debit Card Sales Sales may be made to customers using credit cards such as MasterCard or VISA, or bank debit cards. Such sales are recorded as cash sales. This is because these sales are normally processed by a clearing house that contacts the bank that issued the card. The issuing bank then electronically transfers cash directly to the retailer's bank account. Thus, the retailer normally receives cash within a few days of making the credit card or debit card sale. The debit card will remove the money from the holder's account, whereas the credit card will add the amount to the total owed by the account holder.

If the customers in the preceding sales had used credit cards to pay for their purchases, the sales would be recorded exactly as shown in the preceding entries. Any processing fees charged by the clearing house or issuing bank are periodically recorded as an expense. This expense is normally reported on the income statement as an administrative expense. To illustrate, assume that NetSolutions paid credit card processing fees of $48 on January 31. These fees would be recorded as follows:

2016				
Jan.	31	Credit Card Expense	48	
		Cash		48
		To record service charges on credit card sales		
		for the month.		

Sales on Account A business may sell merchandise on account. The seller records such sales as a debit to Accounts Receivable and a credit to Sales. An example of an entry for a NetSolutions sale on account of $510 follows. The cost of goods sold was $280.

2016				
Jan.	12	Accounts Receivable—Sims Co.	510	
		Sales		510
		Invoice No. 7172.		
	12	Cost of Goods Sold	280	
		Inventory		280
		Cost of merchandise sold on Invoice No. 7172.		

Sales Discounts An example of a sales invoice for NetSolutions is shown in Exhibit 6. The credit period usually begins with the date of the sale, or the invoice date, in this case, January 12, 2016, as shown on the invoice. A discount would be given if paid by January 22, 2016. Note that the term *free on board*, or *FOB*, is discussed on page 249.

Discounts taken by the buyer for early payment are recorded as sales discounts by the seller. Managers usually want to know the amount of the sales discounts for a period. For this reason, sales discounts are recorded in a separate sales discounts account, which is a *contra* (or *offsetting*) account to Sales.

To illustrate, assume that NetSolutions receives $1,470 on January 22 for the invoice shown in Exhibit 6. Because the invoice was paid within the discount period (10 days),

Exhibit 6

Invoice

NetSolutions		106-8
5101 Victoria Ave.		
Calgary, AB T2M 4E3		

Invoice   Made in Canada.

SOLD TO	**CUSTOMER'S ORDER NO. & DATE**
Omega Technologies	412 Jan. 10, 2016
1000 Matrix Blvd.	
Sudbury, ON P3G 1G2	

DATE SHIPPED	**HOW SHIPPED AND ROUTE**	**TERMS**	**INVOICE DATE**
Jan. 12, 2016	Express Trucking Co.	2/10, n/30	Jan. 12, 2016

FROM	**F.O.B.**
Calgary	Calgary

QUANTITY	**DESCRIPTION**	**UNIT PRICE**	**AMOUNT**
10	3COM Wireless PC Card	150.00	1,500.00

the buyer deducted $30 ($1,500 × 2%) from the invoice amount. NetSolutions records the receipt of the cash as follows:

2016					
Jan.	22	Cash		1,470	
		Sales Discounts		30	
		Accounts Receivable—Omega Technologies			1,500
		Collection on Invoice No. 106-8, less 2% discount.			

Sales Returns and Allowances Merchandise sold may be returned to the seller (sales return). In other cases, the seller may reduce the initial selling price (sales allowance). This reduction might occur if the merchandise is defective, damaged during shipment, or does not meet the buyer's expectations.

If the return or allowance is for a sale on account, the seller usually issues the buyer a **credit memorandum**, often called a **credit memo**. A credit memo authorizes a credit to (decreases) the buyer's account receivable. A credit memo indicates the amount and reason for the credit. An example of a credit memo issued by NetSolutions is shown in Exhibit 7.

Exhibit 7

Credit Memo

NetSolutions	No. 32
5101 Victoria Ave.	
Calgary, AB T2M 4E3	

CREDIT MEMO

TO	**DATE**
Krier Company	January 13, 2016
7608 Melton Avenue	
Mississauga, ON L4Y 1L8	

WE CREDIT YOUR ACCOUNT AS FOLLOWS:

1	Graphic Video Card	225.00

Like sales discounts, sales returns and allowances reduce sales revenue. Also, returns often result in additional shipping and handling expenses. Thus, managers usually want to know the amount of returns and allowances for a period. For this reason, sales returns and allowances are recorded in a separate sales returns and allowances account, which is a *contra* (or *offsetting*) account to Sales.

The seller debits Sales Returns and Allowances for the amount of the return or allowance. If the sale was on account, the seller credits Accounts Receivable. Using a perpetual inventory system, the seller must also debit (increase) Inventory and decrease (credit) Cost of Goods Sold for the cost of the returned merchandise.

To illustrate, we use the credit memo shown in Exhibit 7. The selling price of the merchandise returned in Exhibit 7 is $225. Assuming that the cost of the merchandise returned is $140, the sales return and allowance would be recorded as follows:

2016				
Jan.	13	Sales Returns and Allowances	225	
		Accounts Receivable—Krier Company		225
		Credit Memo No. 32.		

2016				
Jan.	13	Inventory	140	
		Cost of Goods Sold		140
		Cost of merchandise returned, Credit Memo No. 32.		

A buyer may pay for merchandise and then later return it. In this case, the seller may do one of the following:

1. Issue a credit that is applied against the buyer's other receivables.
2. Issue a cash refund.

If the credit is applied against the buyer's other receivables, the seller records the credit with entries similar to those shown above. If cash is refunded, the seller debits Sales Returns and Allowances and credits Cash.

EXAMPLE EXERCISE 5-3   Sales Transactions   ②

Journalize the following merchandise transactions:

a. Sold merchandise on account, $7,500 with terms 2/10, n/30. The cost of the goods sold was $5,625.

b. Received payment less the discount.

FOLLOW MY EXAMPLE 5-3

a.	Accounts Receivable	7,500	
	Sales		7,500
	To record sales on account.		
	Cost of Goods Sold	5,625	
	Inventory		5,625
	To record the cost of goods sold.		
b.	Cash	7,350	
	Sales Discounts	150	
	Accounts Receivable		7,500
	Collection of invoice, less 2% discount.		

For Practice: PE 5-3

MID-CHAPTER ILLUSTRATIVE PROBLEM

Ruby Rose owns a flower shop. Selected transactions during the month related to inventory are as follows:

May 3	Purchase of vases from manufacturer for $4,000 on account using a 3% purchase discount.
10	Purchase of flowers from wholesaler for $2,000 cash.
13	Cash sale of vases with flowers for centrepieces for a wedding: 10 vases priced at $20 each (cost $4) and 10 bouquets priced at $50 each (cost $30).
20	Sold flowers and vases on account to Coastal Convention Centre as part of a monthly contract. Flowers total $4,000 (cost $2,500) and vases total $1,500 (cost $400).

Record journal entries for the above transactions, using the perpetual inventory system.

MID-CHAPTER ILLUSTRATIVE SOLUTION

Date		Account	Debit	Credit
May	3	Inventory	3,880	
		Accounts Payable		3,880
		Purchased vase inventory on account, 3% discount (4,000 × 0.97)		
	10	Inventory	2,000	
		Cash		2,000
		Purchased flower inventory.		
	13	Cash	700	
		Sales		700
		Sale of flowers and vases.		
		Cost of Goods Sold	340	
		Inventory		340
		To record the cost of goods sold.		
	20	Accounts Receivable—Coastal Convention Centre	5,500	
		Sales		5,500
		Sales on account.		
		Cost of Goods Sold	2,900	
		Inventory		2,900
		To record the cost of goods sold for flowers and vases on account.		

Note: The buyer bears the freight costs if the shipping terms are FOB shipping point.

Freight Costs and Trade Discounts

Purchases and sales of merchandise often involve freight costs and provincial and federal sales taxes. Also, the seller may offer buyers trade discounts. The provincial and federal sales taxes are discussed in Appendix 2 of this chapter.

Freight The terms of a sale indicate when ownership (title) of the merchandise passes from the seller to the buyer. This point determines whether the buyer or the seller pays the freight costs.[4] This point also dictates when inventory is recorded in the books as it tells us when the sale has occurred. In practice, the entry to record a purchase or sale is made when the invoie is received or paid. At year-end this is adjusted to reflect the ownership based on whether the item is FOB shipping point oer destination as discussed below.

The ownership of the merchandise may pass to the buyer when the seller delivers the merchandise to the freight carrier. In this case, the terms are said to be **FOB (free on board) shipping point**. This term means that the buyer pays the freight costs from the shipping point to the final destination. Such costs are part of the buyer's total cost of purchasing inventory and are added to the cost of the inventory by debiting Inventory.

Sometimes FOB shipping point and FOB destination are expressed in terms of the location at which the title to the merchandise passes to the buyer. For example, if Toyota Motor Corporation's assembly plant in Osaka, Japan, sells automobiles to a dealer in Toronto, FOB shipping point could be expressed as FOB Osaka. Likewise, FOB destination could be expressed as FOB Toronto. See Exhibit 8.

To illustrate, assume that on June 10, NetSolutions purchased merchandise as follows:

June 10.   Purchased merchandise from Magna Data, $900, terms FOB shipping point.

10.   Paid freight of $50 on June 10 purchase from Magna Data.

NetSolutions records these two transactions as follows:

2016					
June	10	Inventory	900	
		Accounts Payable—Magna Data		900
		Purchased merchandise, terms FOB shipping point.		
	10	Inventory	50	
		Cash		50
		Paid shipping cost on merchandise purchased.		

Note: The seller bears the freight costs if the shipping terms are FOB destination.

The ownership of the merchandise may pass to the buyer when the buyer receives the merchandise. In this case, the terms are said to be **FOB (free on board) destination**. This term means that the seller pays the freight costs from the shipping point to the buyer's final destination. When the seller pays the delivery charges, the seller debits Delivery Expense or Freight Out. Delivery Expense is reported on the seller's income statement as a selling expense.

To illustrate, assume that NetSolutions sells merchandise as follows:

June 15.   Sold merchandise to Kranz Company on account, $700, terms FOB destination. The cost of the merchandise sold is $480.

15.   NetSolutions pays freight of $40 on the sale of June 15.

NetSolutions records the sale, the cost of the sale, and the freight cost as follows:

2016					
June	15	Accounts Receivable—Kranz Company	700	
		Sales		700
		Sold merchandise, terms FOB destination.		
	15	Cost of Goods Sold	480	
		Inventory		480
		Recorded cost of merchandise sold to Kranz Company.		
	15	Delivery Expense	40	
		Cash		40
		Paid shipping cost on merchandise sold.		

4 The passage of title also determines whether the buyer or seller must pay other costs, such as the cost of insurance, while the merchandise is in transit.

The seller may prepay the freight, even though the terms are FOB shipping point. The seller then adds the freight to the invoice. The buyer debits Inventory for the total amount of the invoice, including the freight. Any discount terms do not apply to the prepaid freight.

To illustrate, assume that NetSolutions sells merchandise as follows:

June 20. Sold merchandise to Planter Company on account, $800, terms FOB shipping point. NetSolutions paid freight of $45, which was added to the invoice. The cost of the goods sold is $360.

NetSolutions records the sale, the cost of the sale, and the freight cost as follows:

2016				
June	20	Accounts Receivable—Planter Company	800	
		Sales		800
		Sold merchandise, terms FOB shipping point.		
	20	Cost of Goods Sold	360	
		Inventory		360
		Recorded cost of goods sold to Planter Company.		
	20	Accounts Receivable—Planter Company	45	
		Cash		45
		Prepaid shipping cost on goods sold.		

Shipping terms, the passage of title, and whether the buyer or seller is to pay the freight costs are summarized in Exhibit 8.

Exhibit 8

Freight Terms

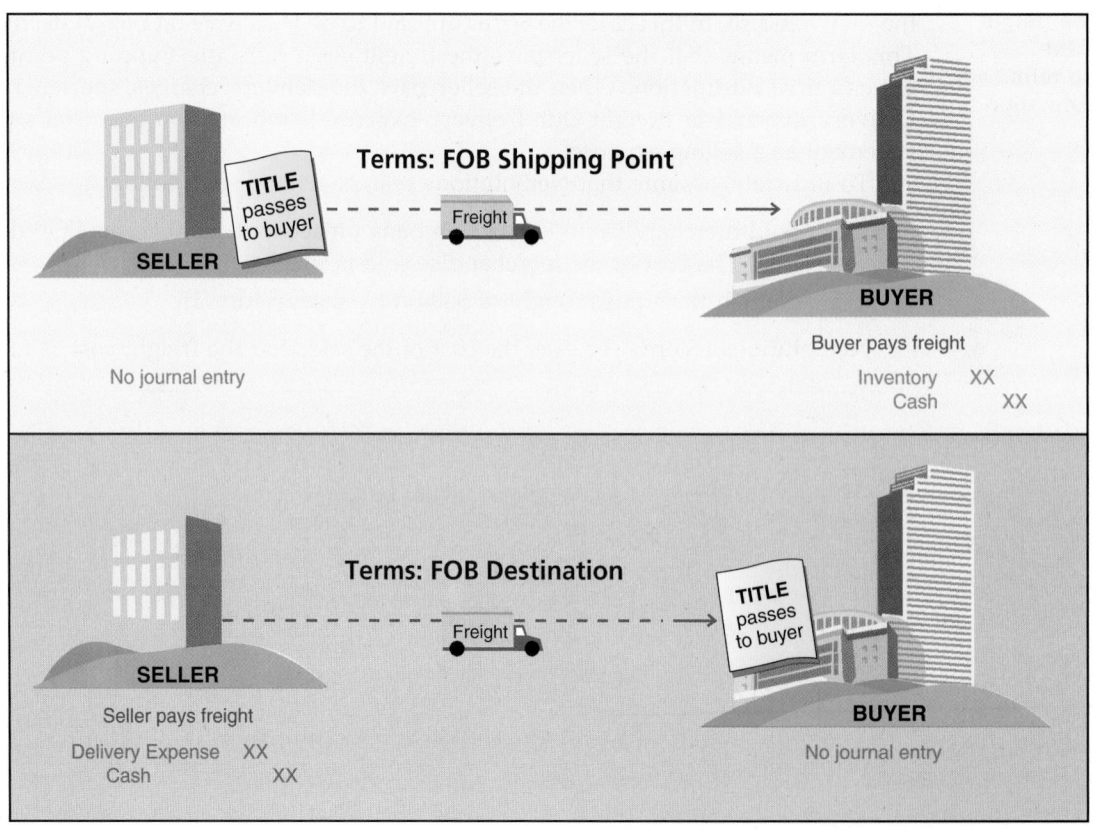

2

EXAMPLE EXERCISE 5-4   Freight Terms

Determine the amount to be paid in full settlement of each of invoices (a) and (b), assuming that credit for returns and allowances was received prior to payment and that all invoices were paid within the discount period.

	Merchandise	Freight Paid by Seller	Freight Terms	Returns and Allowances
a.	$4,500	$200	FOB shipping point, 1/10, n/30	$ 800
b.	5,000	60	FOB destination, 2/10, n/30	2,500

FOLLOW MY EXAMPLE 5-4

a. $3,863. Purchase of $4,500 less return of $800 less the discount of $37 [($4,500 – $800) × 1%] plus $200 of shipping.

b. $2,450. Purchase of $5,000 less return of $2,500 less the discount of $50 [($5,000 – $2,500) × 2%].

For Practice: PE 5-4

Trade Discounts *Wholesalers* are companies that sell merchandise to other businesses rather than to the public. Many wholesalers publish sales catalogues. Instead of updating their catalogues, wholesalers may publish price updates. These updates may include large discounts from the catalogue list prices. In addition, wholesalers often offer special discounts to government agencies or businesses that order large quantities. Such discounts are called **trade discounts**.

Sellers and buyers do not normally record the list prices of merchandise and trade discounts in their accounts. For example, assume that an item has a list price of $1,000 and a 40% trade discount. The seller records the sale of the item at $600 [$1,000 less the trade discount of $400 ($1,000 × 40%)]. Likewise, the buyer records the purchase at $600.

Summary: Recording Purchase of Inventory Recording inventory purchase transactions under the perpetual inventory system has been described and illustrated in the preceding sections. These transactions involved purchases, purchases discounts, purchases returns and allowances, and freight. Exhibit 9 summarizes how these transactions are recorded in T account form.

Exhibit 9

Recording Inventory

Inventory

Purchases of goods for sale	XXX	Purchases discounts	XXX
Freight for merchandise purchased FOB shipping point	XXX	Purchases returns and allowances	XXX
		Cost of goods sold	XXX
Goods returned from customer	XXX		

Cost of Goods Sold

Cost of goods sold	XXX	Goods returned from customer	XXX

Dual Nature of Merchandise Transactions

Each merchandising transaction affects a buyer and a seller. In the illustration below, we show how the same transactions are recorded by the seller and the buyer. In this example, the seller is Scully Company and the buyer is Burton Co. Keep in mind that the seller is using the perpetual system as described on page 238.

Transaction	Scully Company (Seller)		Burton Co. (Buyer)	

July 1. Scully Company sold merchandise on account to Burton Co., $7,500, terms FOB shipping point, n/45. The cost of the merchandise sold was $4,500.	Accounts Receivable—Burton Co. 7,500
	  Sales
	Sale to Burton Co. on account.
	
	Cost of Goods Sold 4,500
	  Inventory
	To record the cost of merchandise sold.
		7,500
		
		4,500
			Inventory 7,500
			  Accounts Payable—Scully Co.
			Purchase of goods from Scully.
				
				7,500

July 2. Burton Co. paid freight of $150 on July 1 purchase from Scully Company.	No entry.		Inventory 150 Cash Payment of freight on inventory.	 150

July 5. Scully Company sold merchandise on account to Burton Co., $5,000, terms FOB destination, n/30. The cost of the merchandise sold was $3,500. It was delivered today.	Accounts Receivable—Burton Co. 5,000
	  Sales
	Sale to Burton Co. on account.
	
	Cost of Goods Sold 3,500
	  Inventory
	To record the cost of merchandise sold.
		5,000
		
		3,500
			Inventory 5,000
			  Accounts Payable—Scully Co.
			Purchase of goods from Scully.
				
				5,000

July 7. Scully Company paid freight of $250 for delivery of merchandise sold to Burton Co. on July 5.	Delivery Expense 250 Cash Paid for delivery expense.	 250	No entry.	

July 13. Scully Company issued Burton Co. a credit memo for merchandise returned, $1,000. The merchandise had been purchased by Burton Co., on account on July 5. The cost of the merchandise returned was $700.	Sales Returns and Allowances 1,000
	  Accounts Receivable—
	  Burton Co.
	To record credit memo.
	
	Inventory 700
	  Cost of Goods Sold
	To record cost of merchandise returned.
		
		1,000
		
		700
			Accounts Payable—Scully Co. 1,000
			  Inventory
			Return of merchandise to Scully.
				
				1,000

(continued)

Transaction	Scully Company (Seller)	Burton Co. (Buyer)

July 15. Scully Company received payment from Burton Co. for purchase of July 5.	Cash 4,000
	  Accounts Receivable— 4,000
	   Burton Co.
	Received cash on account from Burton Co.
		Accounts Payable—Scully Co. 4,000
		  Cash 4,000
		Payment to Scully.

July 18. Scully Company sold merchandise on account to Burton Co., $12,000, terms FOB shipping point, 2/10, n/eom. Scully Company prepaid freight of $500, which was added to the invoice. The cost of the merchandise sold was $7,200.	Accounts Receivable—Burton Co. 12,000
	  Sales 12,000
	Sale to Burton Co. on account.
	
	Accounts Receivable—Burton Co. 500
	  Cash 500
	Prepaid freight for Burton Co.
	
	Cost of Goods Sold 7,200
	  Inventory 7,200
	To record the cost of merchandise sold.
		Inventory 12,500
		  Accounts Payable—Scully Co. 12,500
		Purchase of goods from Scully.

July 28. Scully Company received payment from Burton Co. for purchase on July 18, less discount (2% × $12,000).	Cash 12,260
	Sales Discounts 240
	  Accounts Receivable—Burton Co. 12,500
	Received cash from Burton less discount.
		Accounts Payable—Scully Co. 12,500
		  Inventory 240
		  Cash 12,260
		Payment to Scully less discount.

Describe the adjusting process for a merchandising business under the perpetual inventory system.

The Adjusting Process

We have described and illustrated the chart of accounts and the recording of transactions for a merchandising business. We now describe the adjusting process, the financial statements, and the closing process for a merchandising business. In this discussion, we focus on the elements of the accounting cycle that differ from those of a service business.

Adjusting Entry for Inventory Shrinkage

⊜netsolutions

Under the perpetual inventory system, the inventory account is continually updated for purchase and sales transactions. As a result, the balance of the inventory account is the amount of merchandise available for sale at that point in time. However, retailers normally experience some loss of inventory due to shoplifting, employee theft, or errors. Thus, the physical inventory on hand at the end of the accounting period is usually less than the balance of Inventory. This difference is called **inventory shrinkage** or **inventory shortage**.

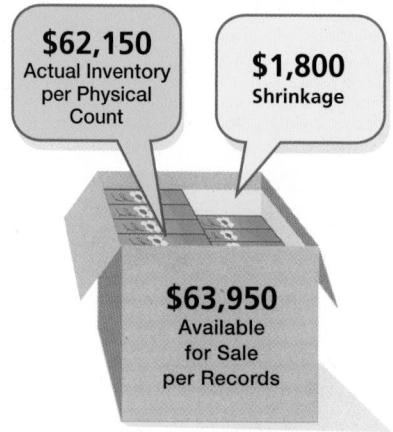

To illustrate, NetSolutions' inventory records indicate the following on December 31, 2016:

	Dec. 31, 2016
Account balance of Inventory	$63,950
Physical inventory on hand	62,150
Inventory shrinkage	$ 1,800

At the end of the accounting period, inventory shrinkage is recorded by the following adjusting entry:

2016					
Dec.	31	Adjusting Entry			
		Cost of Goods Sold		1,800	
		Inventory			1,800
		Inventory shrinkage ($63,950 − $62,150).			

After the preceding entry is recorded, the balance of Inventory agrees with the physical inventory on hand at the end of the period. Because inventory shrinkage cannot be totally eliminated, it is considered a normal cost of operations. If, however, the amount of the shrinkage is unusually large, it may be disclosed separately on the income statement. In such cases, the shrinkage may be recorded in a separate account, such as Loss from Inventory Shrinkage.[5]

---

5 The adjusting process for a merchandising business may be aided by preparing an end-of-period spreadsheet (work sheet). An end-of-period spreadsheet (work sheet) for a merchandising business is described and illustrated in Appendix F of the textbook.

EXAMPLE EXERCISE 5-6 Inventory Shrinkage   ③

Magnolia Company's perpetual inventory records indicate that $382,800 of merchandise should be on hand on December 31, 2015. The physical inventory indicates that $371,250 of merchandise is actually on hand. Journalize the adjusting entry for the inventory shrinkage for Magnolia Company for the year ended December 31, 2015. Assume that the inventory shrinkage is a normal amount.

FOLLOW MY EXAMPLE 5-6

Dec. 31	Cost of Goods Sold...	11,550	
	Inventory...		11,550
	Inventory shrinkage ($382,800 − $371,250).		

For Practice: PE 5-6

---

④ # Financial Statements for a Merchandising Business

Describe and illustrate the financial statements of a merchandising business under the perpetual inventory system.

In this section, we illustrate the financial statements for NetSolutions after it becomes a retailer of computer hardware and software.

The income statement of a merchandiser differs from a service provider's income statement. The users of the merchandiser's income statement want to be able to identify key financial numbers such as gross profit, sales expenses, or operating expenses. A multiple-step income statement provides this information.

Single-Step Income Statement

ⓐnetsolutions

The first form of income statement exhibited is the **single-step income statement.** As shown in Exhibit 10, the income statement for NetSolutions deducts the total of all expenses *in one step* from the total of all revenues.

The single-step form emphasizes total revenues and total expenses in determining net income. A criticism of the single-step form is that gross profit and income from operations are not reported.

Multiple-Step Income Statement

The second form of income statement for NetSolutions is shown in Exhibit 11. This form of income statement, called a **multiple-step income statement**, contains several sections, subsections, and subtotals.

Revenue from Sales This section of the multiple-step income statement consists of sales, sales returns and allowances, sales discounts, and net sales. This section, as shown in Exhibit 11, is as follows:

Revenue from sales:			
Sales..		$720,185	
Less: Sales returns and allowances................	$6,140		
Sales discounts	5,790	11,930	
Net sales..			$708,255

Sales is the total amount charged customers for goods sold, including cash sales and sales on account. During 2016, NetSolutions sold merchandise of $720,185 for cash or on account.

Sales returns and allowances are granted by the seller to customers for damaged or defective merchandise. In such cases, the customer may either return the merchandise or accept an allowance from the seller. The seller would return the inventory to the inventory account if the items can be resold. If the items cannot be resold they would not be returned to inventory. NetSolutions reported $6,140 of sales returns and allowances during 2016.

Exhibit 10

Single-Step Income Statement

NetSolutions Income Statement For the Year Ended December 31, 2016		
Revenues:		
Net sales		$708,255
Rent revenue		600
Total revenues		708,855
Expenses:		
Cost of goods sold	$525,305	
Selling expenses	70,820	
Administrative expenses	34,890	
Interest expense	2,440	
Total expense		633,455
Net income		$ 75,400

Exhibit 11

Multiple-Step Income Statement—Perpetual Method

NetSolutions Income Statement For the Year Ended December 31, 2016			
Revenue from sales:			
Sales		$720,185	
Less: Sales returns and allowances	$ 6,140		
Sales discounts	5,790	11,930	
Net sales			$708,255
Cost of goods sold			525,305
Gross profit			182,950
Operating expenses:			
Selling expenses:			
Sales salaries expense	53,430		
Advertising expense	10,860		
Depreciation expense—store equipment	3,100		
Delivery expense	2,800		
Miscellaneous selling expense	630		
Total selling expenses		70,820	
Administrative expenses:			
Office salaries expense	21,020		
Rent expense	8,100		
Depreciation expense—office equipment	2,490		
Insurance expense	1,910		
Misc. administrative expense	760		
Office supplies expense	610		
Total administrative expenses		34,890	
Total operating expenses			105,710
Income from operations			77,240
Other income and expense:			
Rent revenue		600	
Interest expense		(2,440)	(1,840)
Net income			$ 75,400

EXAMPLE EXERCISE 5-7   Multiple-Step Income Statement Compared with a Single-Step Income Statement (4)

Using the following data, determine the Revenues section of the Income Statement in a multiple-step form and in a single-step form.

Rent revenue	$ 3,000
Purchase discounts	2,544
Sales	453,991
Cost of goods sold	221,882
Sales discounts	2,972
Sales returns and allowances	2,577

FOLLOW MY EXAMPLE 5-7

Multiple-Step Form

Revenue from sales:		
Sales		$453,991
Less: Sales returns and allowances	$2,577	
Sales discounts	2,972	5,549
Net sales		448,442
Cost of goods sold		221,882
Gross profit		$226,560

(Note that rent revenue appears at the end of the statement in Other income and expenses.)

Single-Step Form

Revenues:	
Net sales	$448,442
Rent revenue	3,000
Total revenues	$451,442

For Practice PE 5-7

Sales discounts are granted by the seller to customers for early payment of amounts owed. For example, a seller may offer a customer a 2% discount on a sale of $10,000 if the customer pays within 10 days. If the customer pays within the 10-day period, the seller receives cash of $9,800, and the buyer receives a discount of $200 ($10,000 × 2%). NetSolutions reported $5,790 of sales discounts during 2016.

Net sales is determined by subtracting sales returns and allowances and sales discounts from sales. As shown above, NetSolutions reported $708,255 of net sales during 2016. Some companies report only net sales and report sales, sales returns and allowances, and sales discounts in notes to the financial statements.

Cost of Goods Sold   Businesses using a perpetual inventory system report the cost of goods sold as a single line on the income statement. An example of such reporting is illustrated in Exhibit 11 for NetSolutions.

Gross Profit   Gross profit is computed by subtracting the cost of goods sold from net sales, as shown below.

Net sales	$708,255
Cost of goods sold	525,305
Gross profit	$182,950

As shown above and in Exhibit 11, NetSolutions has gross profit of $182,950 in 2016.

Income from Operations   Income from operations, sometimes called **operating income**, is determined by subtracting operating expenses from gross profit.

Operating expenses are normally classified as either selling expenses or administrative expenses.

Selling expenses are incurred directly in the selling of merchandise. Examples of selling expenses include sales salaries, store supplies used, depreciation of store equipment, delivery expense, and advertising.

Administrative expenses, sometimes called **general expenses**, are incurred in the administration or general operations of the business. Examples of administrative expenses include office salaries, depreciation of office equipment, and office supplies used.

Each selling and administrative expense may be reported separately as shown in Exhibit 11. However, many companies report selling, administrative, and operating expenses as single line items as shown below for NetSolutions.

Gross profit		$182,950
Operating expenses:		
Selling expenses	$70,820	
Administrative expenses	34,890	
Total operating expenses		105,710
Income from operations		$ 77,240

Other Income and Expense Other income and expense items are not related to the primary operations of the business. **Other income** is revenue from sources other than the primary operating activity of a business. Examples of other income include income from interest, rent, and gains resulting from the sale of capital assets. **Other expense** is an expense that cannot be traced directly to the normal operations of the business. Examples of other expenses include interest expense and losses from the sale of or disposal of capital assets.

Other income and other expense are offset against each other on the income statement. If the total of other income exceeds the total of other expense, the difference is added to income from operations to determine net income. If the reverse is true, the difference is subtracted from income from operations. The other income and expense items of NetSolutions are reported as shown below and in Exhibit 11.

Income from operations		$77,240
Other income and expense:		
Rent revenue	$ 600	
Interest expense	(2,440)	
		(1,840)
Net income		$75,400

Accounting Standards for Private Enterprises (ASPE) require a category for "inventories recognized as an expense,"[6] which is often referred to as cost of goods sold or cost of sales. International Financial Reporting Standards (IFRS) gives the option of "inventories recognized as an expense" or a further breakdown into "raw materials" and other categories.[7] The standards do not require a category for "gross profit". It is presented here as it provides more relevant information to users. For example, Tim Hortons does not report its gross profit, but users can calculate gross profit from the cost of sales reported in the Costs and Expenses section of the income statement.

Statement of Owner's Equity

@netsolutions

The statement of owner's equity for NetSolutions is shown in Exhibit 12. This statement is prepared in the same manner as for a service business.

---

6 *CICA Handbook–Accounting*, 2012 edition, Part II, 1520, Income statement para. 4(o).

7 *CICA Handbook–Accounting*, 2013 edition, Part I, IAS 2, para. 36(d) and 39.

Exhibit 12

Statement of Owner's Equity for a Merchandising Business

NetSolutions Statement of Owner's Equity For the Year Ended December 31, 2016		
Chris Clark, capital, January 1, 2016		$153,800
Net income for the year	$75,400	
Less withdrawals	18,000	
Increase in owner's equity		57,400
Chris Clark, capital, December 31, 2016		$211,200

Balance Sheet

The balance sheet is usually presented in a downward sequence in three sections. This form of balance sheet is called the report form. The balance sheet for NetSolutions is shown in Exhibit 13. In Exhibit 13, inventory is reported as a current asset and the current portion of the note payable of $5,000 is reported as a current liability.

Exhibit 13

Balance Sheet

NetSolutions Balance Sheet December 31, 2016			
Assets			
Current assets:			
Cash		$52,950	
Accounts receivable.		91,080	
Inventory................................		62,150	
Office supplies.		480	
Prepaid insurance		2,650	
Total current assets			$209,310
Property, plant, and equipment:			
Store equipment	$27,100		
Less accumulated depreciation.	5,700	21,400	
Office equipment........................	15,570		
Less accumulated depreciation.	4,720	10,850	
Land		20,000	
Total property, plant, and equipment			52,250
Total assets.............................			$261,560
Liabilities			
Current liabilities:			
Accounts payable.		$22,420	
Note payable (current portion)		5,000	
Salaries payable.		1,140	
Unearned rent...........................		1,800	
Total current liabilities.			$ 30,360
Long-term liabilities:			
Note payable (final payment due 2026)			20,000
Total liabilities.........................			50,360
Owner's Equity			
Chris Clark, capital			211,200
Total liabilities and owner's equity.............			$261,560

Why would a company create a multiple-step income statement?

The sections, subsections, and subtotals of a multiple-step income statement provide additional information for the users. This additional information helps the users of the financial statements to make investing or lending decisions that are appropriate for a retail company that sells inventory.

The Closing Process

Describe the closing process for a merchandising business.

The closing entries for a merchandising business are similar to those for a service business. Refer to page 175 for a review of closing entries. Similar to the closing entries for a service industry, these entries are required to transfer revenue and expenses to the Capital account on the balance sheet. This transfer can be done directly or through the Income Summary account. The only difference for merchandise companies is their greater number of expense accounts. The four closing entries for a merchandising business are as follows:

1. Debit each temporary account with a credit balance, such as Sales, for its balance and credit Income Summary.

2. Credit each temporary account with a debit balance, such as the various expenses, for its balance and debit Income Summary. Because Sales Returns and Allowances, Sales Discounts, and Cost of Goods Sold are temporary accounts with debit balances, they are credited for their balances.

3. Debit Income Summary for the amount of its balance (net income) and credit the owner's capital account. The accounts debited and credited are reversed in the case of a net loss.

4. Debit the owner's capital account for the balance of the withdrawals account and credit the withdrawals account.

The four closing entries for NetSolutions are shown below.

Journal					Page 29
Date		**Item**	**Post. Ref.**	**Debit**	**Credit**
2016		Closing Entries			
Dec.	31	Sales	4010	720,185	
		Rent Revenue	6010	600	
		Income Summary	3030		720,785
	31	Income Summary	3030	645,385	
		Sales Returns and Allowances	4020		6,140
		Sales Discounts	4030		5,790
		Cost of Goods Sold	5010		525,305
		Sales Salaries Expense	5100		53,430
		Advertising Expense	5110		10,860
		Depr. Expense—Store Equipment	5120		3,100
		Delivery Expense	5130		2,800
		Miscellaneous Selling Expense	5140		630
		Office Salaries Expense	5200		21,020
		Rent Expense	5210		8,100
		Depr. Expense—Office Equipment	5220		2,490
		Insurance Expense	5230		1,910
		Office Supplies Expense	5240		610
		Misc. Administrative Expense	5250		760
		Interest Expense	7010		2,440
	31	Income Summary	3030	75,400	
		Chris Clark, Capital	3010		75,400
	31	Chris Clark, Capital	3010	18,000	
		Chris Clark, Withdrawals	3020		18,000

NetSolutions' income summary account after the closing entries have been posted is as follows:

Account	Income Summary				Account No. 3030	
					Balance	
Date	Item	Post. Ref.	Debit	Credit	Debit	Credit
2016 Dec. 31	Revenues	29		720,785		720,785
31	Expenses	29	645,385			75,400
31	Net income	29	75,400		—	—

After the closing entries are posted to the accounts, a post-closing trial balance is prepared. The only accounts that should appear on the post-closing trial balance are the asset, contra asset, liability, and owner's capital accounts with balances. These are the same accounts that appear on the end-of-period balance sheet.

The third closing entry, shown above, adds $75,400 to Chris Clark, Capital. This $75,400 is reported as net income for the year in the Statement of Owner's Equity in Exhibit 12. The fourth closing entry, shown above, decreases Chris Clark, Capital by $18,000. The $18,000 is reported as withdrawals in the Statement of Owner's Equity in Exhibit 12.

FINANCIAL ANALYSIS AND INTERPRETATION f·a·i

LE CHÂTEAU'S GROSS MARGIN

The gross margin, also referred to as the *gross profit margin* and as the *gross profit percentage*, is a comparison of sales and cost of goods sold. The ratio assesses a company's ability to earn a return on items sold before other expenses are considered. Gross profit is computed by subtracting the cost of goods sold from net sales. The gross margin is calculated as follows:

$$\text{Gross margin} = \frac{\text{Gross Profit}}{\text{Net Sales}}$$

As noted earlier, IFRS does not require a line item for Cost of Goods Sold or Cost of Sales. If the company has elected not to include that information, there may be no way to calculate gross profit or gross margin. ASPE does require a line for Cost of Goods Sold. Both IFRS and ASPE do not require a line item titled Gross Margin or Gross Profit, but companies may elect to disclose that information.

When users of the financial statements are interested in the gross profit or gross margin of the company, they may need to search for the information within the income statement or the notes to the financial statements. For instance, Le Château Inc. does not present the gross profit, but it can be calculated, as they do report "Cost of sales" in the "Cost of sales and expenses" section of the income statement. Using information from Le Château's 2011 and 2010 income statements, gross profit and gross margin can be calculated as follows:

	2011	2010
	(in thousands)	
Sales	$302,707	$319,039
Cost of sales	96,145	98,327
Gross profit	206,562	220,712

$$2011\ \text{Gross margin} = \frac{206,562}{302,707} = 68.24\%$$

$$2010\ \text{Gross margin} = \frac{220,712}{319,039} = 69.18\%$$

The margin decreased from 2010 to 2011. On page 11 of their Annual Report, Le Chateau reports that the decrease in the company's gross margin percentage to 68.23% from 69.2% was due to increased promotional activity.

Le Château Inc.
Consolidated Statements of Earnings (partial)
(in thousands of Canadian dollars)

	2011	2010
Sales	$302,707	$319,039
Costs of sales and expenses		
Cost of sales	96,145	98,327
Selling	168,035	155,891
General and administrative	39,752	36,283

Appendix D includes the gross margin in the profitability measures.

EXAMPLE EXERCISE 5-8 Gross Profit and Gross Margin

a. Using the information from Example Exercise 5-7 on page 257, calculate the gross margin percentage.

b. Suppose this company's competitor has a gross margin of 40%. Is this company's gross margin better or worse than that of its competitor?

FOLLOW MY EXAMPLE 5-8

a. $\dfrac{\$226,560}{\$448,442} = 51\%$

b. This company has a better gross margin than its competitor. Of each dollar earned, 50 cents is profit before operating expenses are considered. The competitor has higher inventory expense and so it shows profits of only 40 cents on each dollar (before considering operating expenses).

For Practice PE 5-8

INTEGRITY, OBJECTIVITY, AND ETHICS IN BUSINESS

THE COST OF EMPLOYEE THEFT

One survey reported that the 24 largest U.S. retail store chains have lost more than $6.7 billion to shoplifting and employee theft. Of this amount, only 2.2% of the losses resulted in any recovery. The stores apprehended more than 709,000 shoplifters and dishonest employees. Approximately 1 out of every 28 employees was apprehended for theft from his or her employer. Each dishonest employee stole approximately 6.6 times the amount stolen by shoplifters ($808 vs. $133).

The Canadian statistics are comparable to the American statistics. Retail crime, including shoplifting and employee theft, costs Canadians billions of dollars each year. Canadian retailers lose US$3.6 billion annually (1.49% of sales).

Source: Jack L. Hayes International, 20th Annual Retail Theft Survey, 2008; Retail Council of Canada, Retail Organized Crime: Report and Recommendations, 2008.

A P P E N D I X   1

The Periodic Inventory System

Throughout this chapter, the perpetual inventory system was used to record purchases and sales of merchandise. Not all merchandise businesses, however, use the perpetual inventory system. For example, small merchandise businesses, such as a local hardware store, may use a manual accounting system. A manual perpetual inventory system is time consuming and costly to maintain. In this case, the periodic inventory system may be used.

Cost of Goods Sold Using the Periodic Inventory System

@netsolutions

In the periodic inventory system, sales are recorded in the same manner as in the perpetual inventory system. However, cost of goods sold is not recorded on the date of sale. Instead, cost of goods sold is determined as shown in Exhibit 14 for NetSolutions.

Chart of Accounts under the Periodic Inventory System

The chart of accounts under a periodic inventory system is shown in Exhibit 15. The specific accounts used to record transactions under the periodic inventory system are highlighted in Exhibit 15.

Determining Cost of Goods Sold Using the Periodic System

Inventory, January 1, 2016			$ 59,700
Purchases...		$521,980	
Less: Purchases returns and allowances	$9,100		
Purchases discounts.........................	2,525	11,625	
Net purchases		510,355	
Add freight in		17,400	
Cost of goods purchased...................			527,755
Goods available for sale...........................			587,455
Less inventory,			
December 31, 2016			62,150
Cost of goods sold................................			$525,305

Chart of Accounts under the Periodic Inventory System

Balance Sheet Accounts		Income Statement Accounts	
Assets		**Revenues**	
1010	Cash	4010	Sales
1015	Notes Receivable	4020	Sales Returns and Allowances
1020	Accounts Receivable	4030	Sales Discounts
1050	Inventory	**Costs and Expenses**	
1060	Office Supplies	5010	Purchases
1070	Prepaid Insurance	5020	Purchases Returns and Allowances
1230	Store Equipment	5030	Purchases Discounts
1240	Accumulated Depreciation—	5040	Freight In
	Store Equipment	5100	Sales Salaries Expense
1250	Office Equipment	5110	Advertising Expense
1260	Accumulated Depreciation—	5120	Depreciation Expense—Store
	Office Equipment		Equipment
1270	Land	5130	Delivery Expense
Liabilities		5140	Miscellaneous Selling Expense
2010	Accounts Payable	5200	Office Salaries Expense
2020	Salaries Payable	5210	Rent Expense
2030	Unearned Rent	5220	Depreciation Expense—Office
2050	Notes Payable		Equipment
Owner's Equity		5230	Insurance Expense
3010	Chris Clark, Capital	5240	Office Supplies Expense
3020	Chris Clark, Withdrawals	5250	Misc. Administrative Expense
3030	Income Summary	**Other Income**	
		6010	Rent Revenue
		Other Expense	
		7010	Interest Expense

Recording Merchandise Transactions under the Periodic Inventory System

Using the periodic inventory system, purchases of inventory are not recorded in the inventory account. Instead they are recorded in purchases, purchases discounts, and purchases returns and allowances accounts. In addition, the sales of merchandise are not recorded in the inventory account. Thus, there is no detailed record of the amount of inventory on hand at any given time. At the end of the period, a physical count of

Exhibit 16

Periodic Inventory Equation

$$BI + P = GAFS$$

$$GAFS - EI = COGS$$

Alternatively

$$BI + P - EI = COGS$$

merchandise inventory on hand is taken. This physical count is used to determine the cost of goods sold as shown in Exhibit 16.

The equation that is used is found in Exhibit 16. The components of the equation are beginning inventory (BI), purchases (P), goods available for sale (GAFS), ending inventory (EI), and cost of goods sold (COGS).

To illustrate how cost of goods sold is determined, we use data from July 1, 2015, when NetSolutions began its merchandising operations.

Purchases July 1—December 31, 2015	$340,000
Inventory on December 31, 2015	59,700

Because NetSolutions had only $59,700 of merchandise on December 31, 2015, it must have sold goods that cost $280,300 during 2015 as shown below.

Purchases	$340,000
Less inventory, December 31, 2015	59,700
Cost of goods sold	$280,300

To continue, assume the following 2016 data for NetSolutions:

Purchases of merchandise	$521,980
Purchases returns and allowances	9,100
Purchases discounts	2,525
Freight In on merchandise	17,400

Sellers may grant a buyer sales returns and allowances for returned or damaged merchandise. From a buyer's perspective, such allowances are called **purchases returns and allowances**. Likewise, sellers may grant a buyer a sales discount for early payment of the amount owed. From a buyer's perspective, such discounts are called **purchases discounts**. Purchases returns and allowances and purchases discounts are subtracted from purchases to arrive at **net purchases** as shown below for NetSolutions.

Purchases		$521,980
Less: Purchases returns and allowances	$9,100	
Purchases discounts	2,525	11,625
Net purchases		$510,355

Freight costs incurred in obtaining the merchandise increase the cost of the goods purchased. These costs are called **Freight In**. Adding Freight In to net purchases yields the cost of goods purchased as shown below for NetSolutions.

Net purchases	$510,355
Add Freight In	17,400
Cost of goods purchased	$527,755

The beginning inventory is added to the **cost of goods purchased** to determine the **goods available for sale** for the period. The ending inventory of NetSolutions on December 31, 2015, $59,700, becomes the beginning (January 1, 2016) inventory for 2016. Thus, the cost of goods available for sale for NetSolutions during 2016 is $587,455 as shown below.

Inventory, January 1, 2016	$ 59,700
Cost of goods purchased	527,755
Cost of goods available for sale	$587,455

The ending inventory is then subtracted from the goods available for sale to yield the cost of goods sold. Assuming the ending inventory on December 31, 2016, is $62,150, the cost of goods sold for NetSolutions is $525,305 as shown in Exhibit 14 and below.

Cost of goods available for sale	$587,455
Less inventory, December 31, 2016	62,150
Cost of goods sold	$525,305

In the preceding computation, inventory at the end of the period is subtracted from the goods available for sale to determine the cost of goods sold. The inventory at the end of the period is determined by taking a physical count of inventory on hand. This system of determining the cost of goods sold and the amount of inventory on hand is called the periodic inventory system. Under the periodic inventory system, the inventory records do not show the amount available for sale or the amount sold during the period. Instead, the cost of goods sold is computed and reported as shown in Exhibit 14.

The use of purchases, purchases discounts, purchases returns and allowances, and freight in accounts is described below.

Purchases Purchases of inventory are recorded in a purchases account rather than in the inventory account. Purchases is debited for the invoice amount of a purchase.

Purchases Discounts Purchases discounts are normally recorded in a separate purchases discounts account. The balance of the purchases discounts account is reported as a deduction from Purchases for the period. Thus, Purchases Discounts is a contra (or offsetting) account to Purchases.

Purchases Returns and Allowances Purchases returns and allowances are recorded in a similar manner as purchases discounts. A separate purchases returns and allowances account is used to record returns and allowances. Purchases returns and allowances are reported as a deduction from Purchases for the period. Thus, Purchases Returns and Allowances is a contra (or offsetting) account to Purchases.

Freight In When merchandise is purchased FOB shipping point, the buyer pays for the freight. Under the periodic inventory system, freight paid when purchasing merchandise FOB shipping point is debited to Freight In, Transportation In, or a similar account.

The preceding periodic inventory accounts and their effect on the cost of merchandise purchased are summarized below.

Account	Entry to Increase	Normal Balance	Effect on Cost of Goods Purchased
Purchases	Debit	Debit	Increases
Purchases Discounts	Credit	Credit	Decreases
Purchases Returns and Allowances	Credit	Credit	Decreases
Freight In	Debit	Debit	Increases

Exhibit 17 illustrates the recording of merchandise transactions using the periodic system. As a review, Exhibit 17 also illustrates how each transaction would have been recorded using the perpetual system.

Financial Statements under the Periodic Inventory System

The financial statements for businesses that use the periodic system for inventory appear different from the financial statements for businesses that use the perpetual system of accounting for inventory. The focus is placed on an expansion of the cost

Exhibit 17

Transactions Using the Periodic and Perpetual Inventory Systems

Transaction	Periodic Inventory System	Perpetual Inventory System

June 5. Purchased $30,000 of merchandise on account, terms 2/10, n/30.	Purchases 30,000
	   Accounts Payable 30,000
	Purchase of goods on account.
		Inventory 30,000
		   Accounts Payable 30,000
		Purchase of goods on account.

June 8. Returned goods purchased on account on June 5, $500.	Accounts Payable 500
	   Purchases Returns and Allowances 500
	Return of goods.
		Accounts Payable 500
		   Inventory 500
		Return of goods.

June 15. Paid for purchase of June 5, less return of $500 and discount of $590 [($30,000 − $500) × 2%].	Accounts Payable 29,500
	   Cash 28,910
	   Purchases Discounts 590
	Payment of goods on account.
		Accounts Payable 29,500
		   Cash 28,910
		   Inventory 590
		Payment of goods on account.

June 18. Sold merchandise on account, $12,500, 1/10, n/30. The cost of the goods sold was $9,000.	Accounts Receivable 12,500
	   Sales 12,500
	Sale on account.
		Accounts Receivable 12,500
		   Sales 12,500
		Sale on account.
		Cost of Goods Sold 9,000
		   Inventory 9,000
		To record the cost of merchandise sold.

June 21. Received merchandise returned on account, $4,000. The cost of the goods returned was $2,800.	Sales Returns and Allowances 4,000
	   Accounts Receivable 4,000
	Merchandise return.
		Sales Returns and Allowances 4,000
		   Accounts Receivable 4,000
		Merchandise return.
		Inventory 2,800
		   Cost of Goods Sold 2,800
		To record return of merchandise.

June 22. Purchased merchandise, $15,000, terms FOB shipping point, 2/15, n/30, with prepaid freight of $750 added to the invoice.	Purchases 15,000
	Freight In 750
	   Accounts Payable 15,750
	Purchase of goods on account.
		Inventory 15,750
		   Accounts Payable 15,750
		Purchase of goods on account.

June 28. Received $8,415 as payment on account from June 18 sale less return of June 21 and less discount of $85 [($12,500 − $4,000) × 1%].	Cash 8,415
	Sales Discounts 85
	   Accounts Receivable 8,500
	Received payment on account.
		Cash 8,415
		Sales Discounts 85
		   Accounts Receivable 8,500
		Received payment on account.

June 29. Received $19,600 from cash sales. The cost of the goods sold was $13,800.	Cash 19,600
	   Sales 19,600
	To record cash sale.
		Cash 19,600
		   Sales 19,600
		To record cash sale.
		Cost of Goods Sold 13,800
		   Inventory 13,800
		To record the cost of merchandise sold.

of goods sold to include the "extra" accounts related to purchases, as highlighted in Exhibit 17. An example of an income statement for NetSolutions if they used a periodic inventory system is illustrated in Exhibit 18.

Adjusting Process under the Periodic Inventory System

The adjusting process is the same under the periodic and perpetual inventory systems except for the inventory shrinkage adjustment. The ending inventory is determined by a physical count under both systems.

Under the perpetual inventory system, the ending inventory physical count is compared to the balance of Inventory. The difference is the amount of inventory shrinkage. The inventory shrinkage is then recorded as a debit to Cost of Goods Sold and a credit to Inventory.

Under the periodic inventory system, the inventory account is not kept up to date for purchases and sales. As a result, the inventory shrinkage cannot be directly determined. Instead, any inventory shrinkage is included indirectly in the computation of cost of goods sold as shown in Exhibit 14. This is a major disadvantage of the periodic inventory system. That is, under the periodic inventory system, inventory shrinkage is not separately determined.

Exhibit 18

Multiple-Step Income Statement under the Periodic Inventory System

NetSolutions Income Statement For the Year Ended December 31, 2016			
Revenue from sales:			
Sales			$720,185
Less: Sales returns and allowances		$ 6,140	
Sales discounts		5,790	11,930
Net sales			708,255
Cost of goods sold:			
Inventory, January 1, 2016		59,700	
Purchase	$521,980		
Less: Purchases returns and allowances	9,100		
Purchases discounts	2,525		
Net purchases	510,355		
Add Freight In	17,400		
Cost of goods purchased		527,755	
Goods available for sale		587,455	
Less inventory, December 31, 2016		62,150	
Cost of goods sold			525,305
Gross profit			182,950
Operating expenses:			
Selling expenses:			
Sales salaries expense	53,430		
Advertising expense	10,860		
Depreciation expense—store equipment	3,100		
Delivery expense	2,800		
Miscellaneous selling expense	630		
Total selling expenses		70,820	
Administrative expenses:			
Office salaries expense	21,020		
Rent expense	8,100		
Depreciation expense—office equipment	2,490		
Insurance expense	1,910		
Misc. administrative expense	760		
Office supplies expense	610		
Total administrative expenses		34,890	
Total operating expenses			105,710
Income from operations			77,240
Other income and expense:			
Rent revenue		600	
Interest expense		(2,440)	(1,840)
Net income			$ 75,400

Closing Entries under the Periodic Inventory System

The closing entries differ in the periodic inventory system because there is no cost of goods sold account to close to Income Summary. Instead, the purchases, purchases discounts, purchases returns and allowances, and freight in accounts are closed to Income Summary. In addition, the inventory account is adjusted to the end-of-period physical inventory count during the closing process.

The four closing entries under the periodic inventory system are as follows:

1. Debit each temporary account with a credit balance, such as Sales, for its balance and credit Income Summary. Because Purchases Discounts and Purchases Returns and Allowances are temporary accounts with credit balances, they are debited for their balances. In addition, Inventory is debited for its end-of-period balance based on the end-of-period physical inventory.

2. Credit each temporary account with a debit balance, such as the various expenses, for its balance and debit Income Summary. Because Sales Returns and Allowances, Sales Discounts, Purchases, and Freight In are temporary accounts with debit balances, they are credited for their balances. In addition, Inventory is credited for its balance as at the beginning of the period.

3. Debit Income Summary for the amount of its balance (net income) and credit the owner's capital account. The accounts debited and credited are reversed in the case of a net loss.

4. Debit the owner's capital account for the balance of the withdrawals account and credit the withdrawals account.

The four closing entries for NetSolutions under the periodic inventory system are:

		Journal			
Date		**Item**	**Post. Ref.**	**Debit**	**Credit**
2016		Closing Entries			
Dec.	31	Inventory	1050	62,150	
		Sales	4010	720,185	
		Purchases Returns and Allowances	5020	9,100	
		Purchases Discounts	5030	2,525	
		Rent Revenue	6010	600	
		Income Summary	3030		794,560
	31	Income Summary	3030	719,160	
		Inventory	1050		59,700
		Sales Returns and Allowances	4020		6,140
		Sales Discounts	4030		5,790
		Purchases	5010		521,980
		Freight In	5040		17,400
		Sales Salaries Expense	5100		53,430
		Advertising Expense	5110		10,860
		Depreciation Expense—Store Equipment	5120		3,100
		Delivery Expense	5130		2,800
		Miscellaneous Selling Expense	5140		630
		Office Salaries Expense	5200		21,020
		Rent Expense	5210		8,100
		Depreciation Expense—Office Equipment	5220		2,490
		Insurance Expense	5230		1,910
		Office Supplies Expense	5240		610
		Miscellaneous Administrative Expense	5250		760
		Interest Expense	7010		2,440
	31	Income Summary	3030	75,400	
		Chris Clark, Capital	3010		75,400
	31	Chris Clark, Capital	3010	18,000	
		Chris Clark, Withdrawals	3020		18,000

In the first closing entry, Inventory is debited for $62,150. This amount is the ending physical inventory count on December 31, 2016. In the second closing entry, Inventory is credited for its January 1, 2016, balance of $59,700. In this way, the closing entries highlight the importance of the beginning and ending balances of Inventory in determining cost of goods sold, as shown in Exhibit 14. After the closing entries are posted, Inventory will have a balance of $62,150. This is the amount reported on the December 31, 2016, balance sheet.

In the preceding closing entries, the periodic accounts are highlighted in colour. Under the perpetual inventory system, the highlighted periodic inventory accounts are replaced by the Cost of Goods Sold account.

A P P E N D I X 2

Provincial Sales Tax (PST), Goods and Services Tax (GST), and Harmonized Sales Tax (HST)

Provincial Sales Tax (PST)

Many provinces and territories levy a tax on sales of merchandise to the final consumer, called **provincial sales tax,** or PST. Alberta, Nunavut, Northwest Territories, and Yukon do not charge provincial or territorial sales taxes. Businesses that purchase merchandise for resale to others are normally exempt from paying PST on their purchases. Only final buyers of merchandise pay PST. The liability for the sales tax is incurred when the sale is made.

The seller collects the PST at the time of sale. When a sale is made on account, the seller charges the tax to the buyer by debiting Accounts Receivable. The seller credits the sales account for the amount of the sale and credits the tax to Provincial Sales Tax (PST) Payable. For example, the seller would record a sale of $100 on account, subject to a tax of 6%, as follows:

Aug.	12	Accounts Receivable—Lemon Co.	106	
		Sales		100
		PST Payable		6
		Invoice No. 339, 2/10, n/30		

On a regular basis, the seller pays to the province the amount of the PST owing. In the following example, suppose the seller has collected $2,900 of PST. The seller records such a payment as follows:

Sep.	30	PST Payable	2,900	
		Cash		2,900
		Payment for provincial sales taxes collected during August.		

A company pays PST when it is the final buyer of the merchandise. When a company plans to resell the inventory purchased, it does not pay PST. However, when a company purchases supplies, it is usually not planning to resell those supplies. The company will record the tax to the asset, because the tax is part of the purchase price and will not be recovered from the provincial government. For example, suppose a retailer purchases $400 of supplies and $5,000 of inventory from a wholesaler. The retailer will pay PST on the supplies but not on the inventory. The retailer is the final user of the supplies, but will be reselling the inventory. Let us assume an 8% PST rate. The purchaser would record the following:

Inventory		5,000	
Supplies		432*	
Accounts Payable			5,432
* $400 + ($400 × 0.08) = $432			

The provinces choose their own tax rates. They also have the option of combining their tax with the federal goods and services tax (GST), in which case the Canada Revenue Agency (CRA) will collect the full amount and remit to the provinces their portion. This tax is called a **harmonized sales tax**, or HST. See Exhibit 19 (page 272) for a map of the taxes collected in the provinces and territories.

Goods and Services Tax (GST)

The federal government also levies taxes on most items. This tax is called the **goods and services tax**, or GST. GST is a value-added tax. The GST has complexities but basically most goods are subject to the tax. Manufacturers and retailers offset the GST owed by paying GST on their purchases. A significant difference between GST and PST is that GST is charged on services, such as accounting, whereas PST is charged only on merchandise. GST is also included in merchandise purchases. We also cover these journal entries for GST in Chapter 10.

Two accounts are required to track GST: GST Paid on Purchases and GST Charged on Sales.

To illustrate, suppose Coleman Company purchases $800 of inventory from a wholesaler and uses a perpetual inventory system; the GST rate is 5% and the PST rate is 7%. The journal entry to record the transaction is as follows:

Inventory		800	
GST Paid on Purchases		40*	
Accounts Payable			840
To record inventory purchase.			
* 800 × 0.05 = $40			

Because Coleman Company is a reseller and will be selling the inventory to another party, PST is not charged to Coleman Company on this purchase. Coleman Company will charge both GST and PST when it resells the inventory.

To illustrate, Coleman Company now sells the inventory to a customer for $1,500 cash, plus GST and PST. The journal entry is shown below:

Cash		1,680	
Sales			1,500
GST Charged on Sales			75*
PST Payable			105**
Sale of inventory.			
* 1,500 × 0.05 = $75			
** 1,500 × 0.07 = $105			

Also, under the perpetual inventory method, the purchase price of $800 is moved to the Cost of Goods Sold account.

Cost of Goods Sold		800	
Inventory			800
To record cost of goods sold.			

The sales account is not affected by the GST or PST because the GST and PST collected are to be remitted to the government. To illustrate, assume the above transactions for Coleman Company are the only transactions for the month. The entries to record remittance of taxes are as follows:

PST Payable	105	
Cash		105
Remittance of PST.		

GST Charged on Sales	75	
GST Paid on Purchases		40
Cash		35
Remittance of GST.		

The balance of the two GST accounts can result in a credit or a debit. When the balance is a credit, as in the case above, then that amount is remitted to the federal government. When the balance is a debit, it is recorded as a receivable, and the government will refund that amount to Coleman Company.

To illustrate the entry for a refund, assume that in the example above the total GST paid on purchases is $95. When the GST is due to be remitted, the following journal entry is recorded.

Accounts Receivable—CRA	20	
GST Charged on Sales	75	
GST Paid on Purchases		95
Recording refund of GST from CRA.		

Harmonized Sales Tax (HST)

Harmonized sales tax combines PST and GST into one tax that is collected by the federal government, which then remits the provincial portion to the provinces. A single percentage is applied to both sales and purchases. The names of the accounts change to HST Paid on Purchases and HST Charged on Sales. The amount to be remitted will require either a payment to the CRA or a refund from the CRA.

To illustrate, suppose Coleman Company purchases $800 of inventory from a wholesaler and uses a perpetual inventory system; the HST rate is 13%. The journal entry to record the transaction is as follows:

Inventory	800	
HST Paid on Purchases	104*	
Accounts Payable		904
To record inventory purchase.		
* 800 × 0.13 = $104		

Coleman Company will charge HST when it resells the inventory.

To illustrate, Coleman Company now sells the inventory to a customer for $1,500 cash, plus HST. The journal entry is shown below:

Cash	1,695	
Sale		1,500
HST Charged on Sales		195*
Sale of inventory.		
* 1,500 × 0.13 = $195		

Exhibit 19

Tax Map of Canada

*At the time of publication, British Columbia planned to switch back to PST and GST on April 1, 2013.
**At the time of publication, Prince Edward Island planned to switch to HST on April 1, 2013.
†In Quebec, PST is referred to as Quebec Sales Tax.

Also, under the perpetual inventory method, the cost of goods sold, which is the purchase price of $800, is moved to the Cost of Goods Sold account.

Cost of Goods Sold		800	
Inventory			800
To record cost of goods sold.			

The sales account is not affected by the HST because the HST collected is to be remitted to the government. To illustrate, assume the above transactions for Coleman Company are the only transactions for the month. The entry to record remittance of taxes is as follows:

HST Charged on Sales		195	
HST Paid on Purchases			104
Cash			91
Remittance of HST.			

The balance of the two HST accounts can result in a credit or a debit. When the balance is a credit, as in the case above, then that amount is remitted to the federal government. When the balance is a debit, it is recorded as a receivable, and the government will refund that amount to Coleman Company.

To illustrate the entry for a refund, assume that in the example above the total HST paid on purchases is $200. When the HST is due to be remitted, the following journal entry is recorded.

Accounts Receivable—CRA	5	
HST Charged on Sales	195	
HST Paid on Purchases		200
Recording refund of HST from CRA.		

APPENDIX PROBLEM

This problem is similar to the Illustrative Problem at the end of the chapter, completed here with PST, GST and PST, or HST. The following transactions were completed by Montrose Company during May of the current year. Montrose Company uses a perpetual inventory system.

May 3. Purchased merchandise on account from Floyd Co., $4,000, terms FOB shipping point, 2/10, n/30, with prepaid freight of $120 added to the invoice.

    6. Sold merchandise on account to C. F. Howell Co., list price $4,000, trade discount 30%, terms 2/10, n/30. The cost of the goods sold was $1,125.

    8. Purchased office supplies for cash, $150.

  13. Paid Floyd Co. on account for purchase of May 3, less discount.

  14. Purchased merchandise for cash, $10,500.

  16. Received cash on account from sale of May 6 to C. F. Howell Co., less discount.

Instructions

1. Journalize the preceding transactions.
    a. PST of 6% is applicable.
    b. PST of 6% and GST of 5% are applicable.
    c. HST of 13% is applicable.
2. Journalize the adjusting entry for inventory shrinkage, $3,750.

Solution

1. a.

May	3	Inventory	4,120	
		Accounts Payable—Floyd Co.		4,120
	6	Accounts Receivable—C.F. Howell Co.	2,968	
		Sales		2,800*
		PST Payable		168
		*2,800 = $4,000 − (30% × $4,000)		
	6	Cost of Goods Sold	1,125	
		Inventory		1,125
	8	Office Supplies	159	
		Cash		159*
		*159 = $150 + (6% × $150)		
	13	Accounts Payable—Floyd Co.	4,120	
		Inventory		80
		Cash		4,040*
		*4,040 = $4,000 − (2% × $4,000) + $120		
	14	Inventory	10,500	
		Cash		10,500
	16	Cash	2,912	
		Sales Discounts	56*	
		Accounts Receivable—C. F. Howell Co.		2,968
		*56 = $2,800 × 2%		

1. b.

May	3	Inventory	4,120	
		GST Paid on Purchases ($4,120 × 0.05)	206	
		Accounts Payable—Floyd Co.		4,326
	6	Accounts Receivable—C.F. Howell Co.	3,108	
		Sales		2,800*
		PST Payable ($2,800 × 0.06)		168
		GST Charged on Sales ($2,800 × 0.05)		140
		*$2,800 = $4,000 − ($4,000 × 30%)		
	6	Cost of Goods Sold	1,125	
		Inventory		1,125
	8	Office Supplies	159.00*	
		GST Paid on Purchases ($150 × 0.05)	7.50	
		Cash		166.50
		*$159 = $150 + ($150 × 0.06)		
	13	Accounts Payable—Floyd Co.	4,120	
		Inventory		80
		Cash		4,040
		*$4,040 = $4,000 − (2% × $4,000) + $120		
	14	Inventory	10,500	
		GST Paid on Purchases ($10,500 × 0.05)	525	
		Cash		11,025
	16	Cash	3,052	
		Sales Discounts	56*	
		Accounts Receivable—C.F. Howell Co.		3,108
		* $56 = $2,800 × 2%		

1. c.

May	3	Inventory	4,120.00	
		HST Paid on Purchases ($4,120 × 0.13)	535.60	
		Accounts Payable—Floyd Co.		4,655.60
	6	Accounts Receivable—C.F. Howell Co.	3,164.00	
		Sales		2,800.00*
		HST Charged on Sales ($2,800 × 0.13)		364.00
		*$2,800 = $4,000 − ($4,000 × 30%)		
	6	Cost of Goods Sold	1,125.00	
		Inventory		1,125.00
	8	Office Supplies	150.00	
		HST Paid on Purchases ($150 × 0.13)	19.50	
		Cash		169.50
	13	Accounts Payable—Floyd Co.	4,655.60	
		Inventory		80.00*
		Cash		4,575.60
		*$80 = $4,000 × 2%		
	14	Inventory	10,500.00	
		HST Paid on Purchases ($10,500 × 0.13)	1,365.00	
		Cash		11,865.00
	16	Cash	3,108.00	
		Sales Discounts	56.00*	
		Accounts Receivable—C.F. Howell Co.		3,164.00
		* $56 = $2,800 × 2%		

At a Glance 5

1 Distinguish between the activities and financial statements of service and merchandising businesses.

Key Points	Key Learning Outcomes	Page	Example Exercises
The primary differences between a service business and a merchandising business relate to revenue activities. Merchandising businesses purchase merchandise for selling to customers.	• Describe how the activities of a service and a merchandising business differ, and how those differences are reflected on the income statement.	236	
	• Compute gross profit.	237	5-1

2 Describe and illustrate the accounting for merchandise transactions under the perpetual inventory system.

Key Points	Key Learning Outcomes	Page	Example Exercises
Purchases of merchandise for cash or on account are recorded by debiting inventory.	• Prepare journal entries to record the purchase of merchandise.	239	5-2
	• Prepare journal entries to record purchases discounts, purchases returns and allowances, and freight.	241	
Sales of merchandise for cash or on account are recorded by crediting sales. A second entry is made to record cost of goods sold and to remove the amount from inventory.	• Prepare journal entries to record sales of merchandise.	244	5-3
	• Prepare journal entries to record sales discounts and sales returns and allowances.	245	
	• Determine the impact of FOB shipping and FOB destination on inventory.	249	5-4
	• Record the same merchandise transactions for the buyer and seller.	252	5-5

3 Describe the adjusting process for a merchandising business under the perpetual inventory system.

Key Points	Key Learning Outcomes	Page	Example Exercises
The accounting cycle for a merchandising business is similar to that of a service business. However, a merchandiser is likely to experience inventory shrinkage, which must be recorded.	• Prepare the adjusting journal entry for inventory shrinkage	254	5-6

Describe and illustrate the financial statements of a merchandising business under the perpetual inventory system.

Key Points	Key Learning Outcomes	Page	Example Exercises
The multiple-step income statement of a merchandiser reports sales, sales returns and allowances, sales discounts, and net sales. The cost of goods sold is subtracted from net sales to determine the gross profit. Operating income is determined by subtracting operating expenses from gross profit. Net income is determined by adding or subtracting the net of other income and expense. The income statement may also be reported in a single-step form.	• Prepare a single-step income statement.	255	5-7
	• Prepare a multiple-step income statement for a merchandising business.	255	
	• Consider the requirements of IFRS and ASPE.	258	

5 **Describe the closing process for a merchandising business.**

Key Points	Key Learning Outcomes	Page	Example Exercises
The closing entries for a merchandising business are similar to those for a service business.	• Prepare the closing entries for a merchandising business.	260	
	• Financial Analysis and Interpretation	261	5-8

GLOSSARY

administrative expenses (general expenses) – Expenses incurred in the administration or general operations of the business. (p. 258)

controlling account – The account in the general ledger that summarizes the balances of the accounts in a subsidiary ledger. (p. 239)

cost of goods purchased – The cost of net purchases plus transportation costs. (p. 264)

cost of goods sold – The cost that is reported as an expense when merchandise is sold. (p. 237)

credit memorandum (credit memo) – A form used by a seller to inform the buyer of the amount the seller proposes to credit to the account receivable due from the buyer. (p. 246)

credit period – The amount of time the buyer is allowed in which to pay the seller. (p. 240)

credit terms – Terms for payment on account by the buyer to the seller. (p. 240)

debit memorandum (debit memo) – A form used by a buyer to inform the seller of the amount the buyer proposes to debit to the account payable due the seller. (p. 243)

FOB (free on board) destination – Freight terms in which the seller pays the transportation costs from the shipping point to the final destination. (p. 249)

FOB (free on board) shipping point – Freight terms in which the buyer pays the transportation costs from the shipping point to the final destination. (p. 249)

freight in – Costs of transportation. (p. 264)

goods and services tax (GST) – A value-added tax applied by the federal government to most goods and services. (p. 270)

goods available for sale – The cost of merchandise available for sale to customers calculated by adding the beginning inventory to the cost of goods purchased. (p. 264)

gross profit – Sales minus the cost of goods sold. (p. 237)

harmonized sales tax (HST) – Provincial option to combine the goods and services tax with the provincial sales tax, in which case Canada Revenue Agency administers this combined tax for the province. (p. 270)

income from operations (operating income) – Gross profit less operating expenses and service department charges for a profit or an investment centre. (p. 257)

inventory – Merchandise on hand (not sold) at the end of an accounting period. (p. 237)

inventory shrinkage (inventory shortage) – The amount by which the merchandise for sale, as indicated by the balance of the inventory account, is larger than the total amount of merchandise counted during the physical inventory. (p. 254)

invoice – The bill that the seller sends to the buyer. (p. 240)

multiple-step income statement – A form of income statement that contains several sections, subsections, and subtotals. (p. 255)

net purchases – Total purchases less purchases discounts and purchases returns and allowances. (p. 264)

net sales – Revenue received for merchandise sold to customers less any sales returns and allowances and sales discounts. (p. 257)

other expense – An expense that cannot be traced directly to operations. (p. 258)

other income – Revenue from sources other than the primary operating activity of a business. (p. 258)

periodic inventory system – The inventory system in which the inventory records do not show the amount available for sale or sold during the period. (p. 238)

perpetual inventory system – The inventory system in which each purchase and sale of merchandise is recorded in an inventory account. (p. 238)

provincial sales tax (PST) – A tax on sales of merchandise applied by many provinces to the final consumer. (p. 269)

purchases discounts – Discounts taken by the buyer for early payment of an invoice. (p. 264)

purchases returns and allowances – From the buyer's perspective, returned merchandise or an adjustment for defective merchandise. (p. 264)

sales – The total amount charged customers for merchandise sold, including cash sales and sales on account. (p. 244)

sales discounts – From the seller's perspective, discounts that a seller may offer the buyer for early payment. (p. 257)

sales returns and allowances – From the seller's perspective, returned merchandise or an adjustment for defective merchandise. (p. 255)

selling expenses – Expenses that are incurred directly in the selling of merchandise. (p. 258)

single-step income statement – A form of income statement in which the total of all expenses is deducted from the total of all revenues. (p. 255)

subsidiary ledger – A ledger containing individual accounts with a common characteristic. (p. 239)

trade discounts – Discounts from the list prices in published catalogues or special discounts offered to certain classes of buyers. (p. 251)

ILLUSTRATIVE PROBLEM

The following transactions were completed by Montrose Company during May of the current year. Montrose Company uses a perpetual inventory system.

May 3. Purchased merchandise on account from Floyd Co., $4,000, terms FOB shipping point, 2/10, n/30, with prepaid freight of $120 added to the invoice.

5. Purchased merchandise on account from Kramer Co., $8,500, terms FOB destination, 1/10, n/30.

6. Sold merchandise on account to C. F. Howell Co., list price $4,000, trade discount 30%, terms 2/10, n/30. The cost of the goods sold was $1,125.

May 8. Purchased office supplies for cash, $150.
9. Received the Kramer Co. purchase made on May 5.
10. Returned merchandise purchased on May 5 from Kramer Co., $1,300.
13. Paid Floyd Co. on account for purchase of May 3, less discount.
14. Purchased merchandise for cash, $10,500.
15. Paid Kramer Co. on account for purchase of May 5, less return of May 10 and discount.
16. Received cash on account from sale of May 6 to C. F. Howell Co., less discount.
19. Sold merchandise on MasterCard credit cards, $2,450. The cost of the goods sold was $980.

Instructions

1. Journalize the preceding transactions.
2. Journalize the adjusting entry for inventory shrinkage, $3,750.

Solution

1.

May	3	Inventory	4,120	
		Accounts Payable—Floyd Co.		4,120
	5	As the inventory was purchased FOB destination it is not yet our inventory and should not be recorded until it is received.		
	6	Accounts Receivable—C.F. Howell Co.	2,800*	
		Sales		2,800
		*$4,000 − (30% × $4,000)		
	6	Cost of Goods Sold	1,125	
		Inventory		1,125
	8	Office Supplies	150	
		Cash		150
	9	Inventory	8,500	
		Accounts Payable—Kramer Co.		8,500
	10	Accounts Payable—Kramer Co.	1,300	
		Inventory		1,300
	13	Accounts Payable—Floyd Co.	4,120	
		Inventory		80
		Cash		4,040*
		*[$4,000 − (2% × $4,000) + $120]		
	14	Inventory	10,500	
		Cash		10,500
	15	Accounts Payable—Kramer Co.	7,200	
		Inventory		72*
		Cash		7,128**
		*72 = ($8,500 − $1,300) × 1%		
		**7,128 = $8,500 − $1,300 − $72		
	16	Cash	2,744	
		Sales Discounts	56*	
		Accounts Receivable—C.F. Howell Co.		2,800
		*56 = $2,800 × 2%		
	19	Cash	2,450	
		Sales		2,450
	19	Cost of Goods Sold	980	
		Inventory		980
2.	31	Cost of Goods Sold	3,750	
		Inventory		3,750

EYE OPENERS

1. What distinguishes a merchandising business from a service business?
2. Can a business earn a gross profit but incur a net loss? Explain.
3. Does each of the following items increase or decrease the cost of goods sold? (a) freight in, (b) beginning inventory, (c) purchases discounts, (d) ending inventory
4. How are sales recorded when customers pay by using their MasterCard and VISA?
5. What date usually begins the credit period during which the buyer of merchandise is allowed to pay?
6. What is the meaning of (a) 1/15, n/60; (b) n/30; (c) n/eom?
7. What is the nature of (a) a credit memo issued by the seller of merchandise, (b) a debit memo issued by the buyer of merchandise?
8. Who bears the freight when the terms of sale are (a) FOB shipping point, (b) FOB destination?
9. Desk Outfitters Inc., which uses a perpetual inventory system, experienced a normal inventory shrinkage of $8,050. What accounts are debited and credited to record the adjustment for the inventory shrinkage at the end of the accounting period?
10. Assume that Desk Outfitters Inc. in Eye Opener 9 experienced an abnormal inventory shrinkage of $70, 750. Desk Outfitters Inc. has decided to record the abnormal inventory shrinkage so that it is separately disclosed on the income statement. What account is debited for the abnormal inventory shrinkage?
11. Differentiate between the single-step and the multiple-step forms of the income statement.
12. What are the major advantages and disadvantages of the single-step form of income statement compared to the multiple-step statement?
13. What type of revenue is reported in the other income section of the multiple-step income statement?
14. Name at least three accounts that would normally appear in the chart of accounts of a merchandising business but would not appear in the chart of accounts of a service business.
15. What is the advantage of the perpetual inventory system over the periodic inventory system?

PRACTICE EXERCISES

(1)

PE 5-1
Gross profit

During the current year, merchandise is sold for $32,800 cash and $379,500 on account. The cost of the goods sold is $250,000. What is the amount of the gross profit?

EE 5-1 p. 238

---

(2)

PE 5-2
Purchase transactions

Elite Company purchased merchandise on account from a supplier for $23,500 terms 1/10, n/30. Elite Company returned $1,700 of the merchandise and received full credit.

a. If Elite Company pays the invoice within the discount period, what is the amount of cash required for the payment?

EE 5-2 p. 244

b. Under a perpetual inventory system, what account is debited by Elite Company to record the return?

---

(2)

PE 5-3
Sales transactions

Journalize the following merchandise transactions:

a. Sold merchandise on account, $41,000 with terms 1/10, n/30. The cost of the goods sold was $22,500.
b. Received payment less the discount.

EE 5-3 p. 247

PE 5-4
Freight terms

EE 5-4 p. 251

Determine the amount to be paid in full settlement of invoice (a) and invoice (b), assuming that credit for returns and allowances was received prior to payment and that all invoices were paid within the discount period.

	Merchandise	Freight Paid by Seller	Freight Terms	Returns and Allowances
a.	$13,150	$450	FOB destination, 1/10, n/30	$4,150
b.	32,100	900	FOB shipping point, 2/10, n/30	5,000

PE 5-5
Transactions for buyer and seller

EE 5-5 p. 253

West Co. sold merchandise to J.S. Custom Co. on account, $20,500, terms FOB shipping point, 2/10, n/30. The cost of the goods sold is $10,000. West Co. paid freight of $500 and later received the amount due within the discount period. Journalize West Co.'s and J.S. Custom Co.'s entries for the payment of the amount due.

PE 5-6
Inventory shrinkage

EE 5-6 p. 255

Merrill Company's perpetual inventory records indicate that $975,000 of merchandise should be on hand on October 31, 2015. The physical inventory indicates that $894,750 of merchandise is actually on hand. Journalize the adjusting entry for the inventory shrinkage for Merrill Company for the year ended October 31, 2015. Assume that the inventory shrinkage is a normal amount.

PE 5-7
Multiple-step and single-step income statement

EE 5-7 p. 257

Using the following data, determine the Revenues section of the income statement in a multiple-step form and in a single-step form.

Rental revenue	$ 3,600
Purchase discounts	2,987
Sales	672,121
Cost of goods sold	314,434
Sales discounts	2,732
Sales returns and allowances	3,212

PE 5-8
Gross profit and gross margin

f·a·i

EE 5-8 p. 262

a. Using the information from Practice Exercise 5-7, calculate the gross margin percentage.
b. If the previous year's gross margin was 60%, has this company's gross margin improved or declined?

EXERCISES

EX 5-1
Determining gross profit

During the current year, merchandise is sold for $750,000. The cost of the goods sold is $450,000.
a. What is the amount of the gross profit?
b. Compute the gross profit percentage (gross profit divided by sales).
c. Will the income statement necessarily report a net income? Explain.

EX 5-2
Determining cost of goods sold

In 2011, Best Buy reported sales of $50,272 million. Its gross profit was $12,637 million. What was Best Buy's cost of goods sold?

EX 5-3
Chart of accounts

Frazee Paints Co. is a newly organized business with a list of accounts arranged in alphabetical order below.

Accounts Payable	Miscellaneous Administrative Expense
Accounts Receivable	Miscellaneous Selling Expense
Accumulated Depreciation—Office Equipment	Notes Payable
Accumulated Depreciation—Store Equipment	Office Equipment
Advertising Expense	Office Salaries Expense
Cash	Office Supplies
Cost of Goods Sold	Office Supplies Expense
Delivery Expense	Prepaid Insurance
Depreciation Expense—Office Equipment	Rent Expense
Depreciation Expense—Store Equipment	Salaries Payable
Income Summary	Sales
Insurance Expense	Sales Discounts
Interest Expense	Sales Returns and Allowances
Inventory	Sales Salaries Expense
Jim Frazee, Capital	Store Equipment
Jim Frazee, Withdrawals	Store Supplies
Land	Store Supplies Expense

Construct a chart of accounts, assigning account numbers and arranging the accounts in balance sheet and income statement order, as illustrated in Exhibit 2. Each account number is four digits: the first digit is to indicate the major classification ("1"for assets, and so on); the second digit is to indicate the subclassification ("11" for current assets, and so on); and the third and fourth digits are to identify the specific account ("1110" for Cash, and so on).

EX 5-4
Purchase-related transactions

Newgen Company purchased merchandise on account from a supplier for $9,000, terms 2/10, n/30. Newgen Company returned $1,200 of the merchandise and received full credit.

a. If Newgen Company pays the invoice within the discount period, what is the amount of cash required for the payment?

b. Under a perpetual inventory system, what account is credited by Newgen Company to record the return?

EX 5-5
Purchase-related transactions

A retailer is considering the purchase of 100 units of a specific item from either of two suppliers. Their offers are as follows:

A: $200 a unit, total of $20,000, 2/10, n/30, no charge for freight.
B: $195 a unit, total of $19,500, 1/10, n/30, plus freight of $400.

Which of the two offers, A or B, yields the lower price?

EX 5-6
Purchase-related transactions

The debits and credits from four related transactions are presented in the following T accounts. Describe each transaction.

Cash		
(2)	250	
(4)	7,350	

Accounts Payable		
(3)	500	(1) 8,000
(4)	7,500	

Inventory		
(1)	8,000	(3) 500
(2)	250	(4) 150

EX 5-7

Purchase-related transactions

DEJ Co., a women's clothing store, purchased $25,000 of merchandise from a supplier on account, terms FOB destination, 2/10, n/30. DEJ Co. returned $3,500 of the merchandise, receiving a credit memo, and then paid the amount due within the discount period. Journalize DEJ Co.'s entries to record (a) the purchase, (b) the merchandise return, and (c) the payment.

EX 5-8

Purchase-related transactions

Journalize entries for the following related transactions of Westcoast Apparel Company:
a. Purchased $25,000 of merchandise from President Co. on account, terms 2/10, n/30.
b. Paid the amount owed on the invoice within the discount period.
c. Discovered that $5,000 of the merchandise was defective and returned items, receiving credit.
d. Purchased $4,000 of merchandise from President Co. on account, terms n/30.
e. Received a cheque for the balance owed from the return in (c), after deducting for the purchase in (d).

EX 5-9

Determining amounts to be paid on invoices

Determine the amount to be paid in full settlement of each of the following invoices, assuming that credit for returns and allowances was received prior to payment and that all invoices were paid within the discount period.

	Merchandise	Freight Paid by Seller		Returns and Allowances
a.	$15,000	—	FOB destination, n/30	$ 800
b.	10,000	$400	FOB shipping point, 2/10, n/30	1,200
c.	8,250	—	FOB shipping point, 1/10, n/30	750
d.	2,900	125	FOB shipping point, 2/10, n/30	400
e.	3,850	—	FOB destination, 2/10, n/30	—

EX 5-10

Sales-related transactions, including the use of credit cards

Journalize the entries for the following transactions, for the perpetual inventory system:
a. Sold merchandise for cash, $18,500. The cost of the goods sold was $11,000.
b. Sold merchandise on account, $12,000. The cost of the goods sold was $7,200.
c. Sold merchandise to customers who used MasterCard and VISA, $115,200. The cost of the goods sold was $70,000.
d. Received an invoice from National Credit Co. for $5,600, representing a service fee paid for processing MasterCard and VISA.

EX 5-11

Sales returns and allowances

During the year, sales returns and allowances totalled $65,900. The cost of the goods returned was $40,000. The accountant recorded all the returns and allowances by debiting the sales account and crediting Cost of Goods Sold for $40,000.

Was the accountant's method of recording returns acceptable? Explain. In your explanation, include the advantages of using a sales returns and allowances account.

EX 5-12

Sales-related transactions

After the amount due on a sale of $25,000, terms 1/10, n/eom, is received from a customer within the discount period, the seller consents to the return of the entire shipment. The cost of the goods returned was $15,000. (a) What is the amount of the refund owed to the customer? (b) Journalize the entries made by the seller to record the return and the refund.

EX 5-13

Sales-related transactions

The debits and credits for five journal entries, for three related transactions are presented in the following T accounts. Describe each transaction.

Cash				Sales	
(5)	17,640			(1)	20,000

Accounts Receivable				Sales Discounts	
(1)	20,000	(3)	2,000	(5)	360
		(5)	18,000		

Inventory				Sales Returns and Allowances	
(4)	1,000	(2)	12,000	(3)	2,000

				Cost of Goods Sold	
				(2) 12,000	(4) 1,000

---

② EX 5-14
Sales-related transactions

Merchandise is sold on account to a customer for $12,500, terms FOB shipping point, 1/10, n/30. The seller paid the freight of $400. Determine the following: (a) amount of the sale, (b) amount debited to Accounts Receivable, (c) amount of the discount for early payment, and (d) amount due within the discount period.

✔ d. $12,775

---

② EX 5-15
Sales-related transactions

Pitt Co., a furniture wholesaler using the perpetual method to record inventory, sells merchandise to Jeevan Co. on account, $25,600, terms 2/10, n/30. The cost of the goods sold is $14,000. Pitt Co. issues a credit memo for $4,000 for merchandise returned and subsequently receives the amount due within the discount period. The cost of the merchandise returned is $2,000. Journalize Pitt Co.'s entries for (a) the sale, including the cost of the goods sold, (b) the credit memo, including the cost of the returned merchandise, and (c) the receipt of the cheque for the amount due from Jeevan Co.

---

② EX 5-16
Purchase-related transactions

Using the data presented in Exercise 5-15, journalize Jeevan Co.'s entries for (a) the purchase, (b) the return of the merchandise for credit, and (c) the payment of the invoice within the discount period. Jeevan also uses the perpetual method.

---

② EX 5-17
Normal balances of merchandise accounts

For the following accounts, identify whether the normal balance is a credit or a debit: (a) Cost of Goods Sold, (b) Delivery Expense, (c) Inventory, (d) Sales, (e) Sales Discounts, (f) Sales Returns and Allowances, (g) Provincial Sales Tax Payable.

---

③ EX 5-18
Adjusting entry for inventory shrinkage

Iverson Tile Co.'s perpetual inventory records indicate that $675,150 of merchandise should be on hand on December 31, 2015. The physical inventory indicates that $649,780 of merchandise is actually on hand. Journalize the adjusting entry for the inventory shrinkage for Iverson Tile Co. for the year ended December 31, 2015.

---

④ EX 5-19
Income statement for merchandiser

For the fiscal year, sales were $5,280,000, sales discounts were $100,000, sales returns and allowances were $75,000, and the cost of goods sold was $3,000,000.

a. What was the amount of net sales?
b. What was the amount of gross profit?

---

④ EX 5-20
Income statement for merchandiser

The following expenses were incurred by a merchandising business during the year. In which expense section of the income statement should each be reported: (a) selling, (b) administrative, or (c) other?

1. Advertising expense
2. Depreciation expense on store equipment
3. Insurance expense on office equipment
4. Interest expense on notes payable

(continued)

5. Rent expense on office building
6. Salaries of office personnel
7. Salary of sales manager
8. Sales supplies used

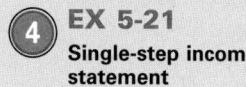

EX 5-21

Single-step income statement

✔ Net income:
$1,095,000

Summary operating data for Pens Plus Company during the year ended December 31, 2015, are as follows: cost of goods sold, $3,000,000; administrative expenses, $500,000; interest expense, $30,000; rent revenue, $100,000; net sales, $5,200,000; and selling expenses, $675,000. Prepare a single-step income statement.

EX 5-22

Multiple-step income statement

Identify the errors in the following multiple-step income statement:

Armortec Company
Income Statement
For the Year Ended December 31, 2015

Revenue from sales:			
Sales....................................			$5,345,800
Add: Sales returns and allowances	$120,000		
Sales discounts...........................	60,000	180,000	
Gross sales....................................			$5,525,800
Cost of goods sold...........................			3,100,800
Income from operations			2,425,000
Expenses:			
Selling expenses............................		800,000	
Administrative expenses......................		600,000	
Delivery expense		50,000	
Total expenses...........................			1,450,000
			975,000
Other expense:			
Interest revenue			40,000
Gross profit....................................			$ 935,000

EX 5-23

Determining amounts for items omitted from income statement

✔ a. $15,000
✔ h. $520,000

Two items are omitted in each of the following four lists of income statement data. Determine the amounts of the missing items, identifying them by letter.

Sales	$250,000	$600,000	$1,000,000	(g)
Sales returns and allowances	(a)	30,000	(e)	$ 7,500
Sales discounts	10,000	18,000	40,000	11,500
Net sales	225,000	(c)	910,000	(h)
Cost of goods sold	(b)	330,000	(f)	400,000
Gross profit	90,000	(d)	286,500	120,000

EX 5-24

Multiple-step income statement

✔ a. Net income:
$335,000

On December 31, 2015, the balances of the accounts appearing in the ledger of Arbutus Furnishings Company, a furniture wholesaler, are as follows:

Administrative Expenses	$ 250,000	Notes Payable	59,000
Breana Greva, Capital	$ 1,137,600	Office Supplies	21,200
Breana Greva, Withdrawals	50,000	Salaries Payable	6,000
Building	1,025,000	Sales	2,250,000
Cash	97,000	Sales Discounts	40,000
Cost of Goods Sold	1,200,000	Sales Returns and Allowances	160,000
Interest Expense	15,000	Selling Expenses	350,000
Inventory	260,000	Store Supplies	15,400

a. Prepare a multiple-step income statement for the year ended December 31, 2015.
b. Compare the major advantages and disadvantages of the multiple-step and single-step forms of income statements.

EX 5-25

Multiple-step income statement

a. How is cost of goods sold presented in the financial statements of Morning Java, Leon's, and Shoppers Drug Mart? These statements are found in the appendixes at the end of the textbook.
b. What is the most useful presentation of information for users of financial statements?

EX 5-26

Closing the accounts of a merchandiser

From the following list, identify the accounts that should be closed to Income Summary at the end of the fiscal year under a perpetual inventory system: (a) Accounts Payable, (b) Advertising Expense, (c) Cost of Goods Sold, (d) Inventory, (e) Sales, (f) Sales Discounts, (g) Sales Returns and Allowances, (h) Supplies, (i) Supplies Expense, (j) Talia Greenly, Withdrawals, (k) Wages Payable.

EX 5-27

Closing entries; net income

Based on the data presented in Exercise 5-24 for Arbutus Furnishings Company, journalize the closing entries.

EX 5-28

Closing entries

On December 31, 2015, the balances of the accounts appearing in the ledger of Champion Interiors Company, a furniture wholesaler, are as follows:

Accumulated Depr.—Building	$30,460	Notes Payable	$ 24,000
Administrative Expenses	65,300	Provincial Sales Tax Payable	4,900
Building	55,680	Salaries Payable	680
Cash	8,840	Sales	313,540
Cost of Goods Sold	188,000	Sales Discounts	18,000
Interest Expense	1,920	Sales Returns and Allowances	12,000
Inventory	26,000	Selling Expenses	124,000
Jessica Duerr, Capital	141,155	Store Supplies	4,580
Jessica Duerr, Withdrawals	7,950	Store Supplies Expenses	2,465

Prepare the December 31, 2015, closing entries for Champion Interiors Company.

Appendix 1
EX 5-29

Identify items missing in determining cost of goods sold

For (a) through (d), identify the items designated by X and Y.
a. Purchases − (X + Y) = Net purchases.
b. Net purchases + X = Cost of goods purchased.
c. Inventory (beginning) + Cost of goods purchased = X.
d. Goods available for sale − X = Cost of goods sold.

Appendix 1
EX 5-30

Cost of goods sold and related items

✔ a. Cost of goods sold, $1,298,600

The following data were extracted from the accounting records of Ruttan Company for the year ended December 31, 2015:

Inventory, January 1, 2015	$ 225,000
Inventory, December 31, 2015	175,000
Purchases	1,200,000
Purchases returns and allowances	18,000
Purchases discounts	16,500
Sales	2,180,000
Freight In	14,100

a. Using the periodic inventory system, prepare the cost of goods sold section of the income statement for the year ended December 31, 2015.
b. Determine the gross profit to be reported on the income statement for the year ended December 31, 2015.

Appendix 1
EX 5-31

Accounts for periodic and perpetual inventory systems

Indicate which of the following accounts would be included in the chart of accounts of a merchandising company using (a) the periodic inventory system or (b) the perpetual inventory system. If the account would be included in the chart of accounts of a company using either the periodic or perpetual systems, indicate (c) for both.

(1) Cost of Goods Sold	(6) Purchases Returns and Allowances
(2) Delivery Expense	(7) Sales
(3) Inventory	(8) Sales Discounts
(4) Purchases	(9) Sales Returns and Allowances
(5) Purchases Discounts	(10) Freight In

Appendix 1
EX 5-32

Rules of debit and credit for periodic inventory accounts

Complete the following table by indicating whether each item, (a) through (g), is a debit or credit.

Account	Increase	Decrease	Normal Balance
Purchases	debit	(a)	(b)
Purchases Discounts	(c)	debit	credit
Purchases Returns and Allowances	credit	(d)	(e)
Freight In	(f)	credit	(g)

Appendix 1
EX 5-33

Journal entries using the periodic inventory system

The following selected transactions were completed by Cold Company during February of the current year. Cold Company uses the periodic inventory system.

Feb. 2. Purchased $17,500 of merchandise on account, FOB shipping point, terms 2/15, n/30.
   5. Paid freight of $300 on the February 2 purchase.
   6. Returned $2,000 of the merchandise purchased on February 2.
   13. Sold goods on account, $9,000, FOB destination, 2/10, n/30. The cost of goods sold was $6,600.
   15. Paid freight of $100 for the merchandise sold on February 13.
   17. Paid for the purchase of February 2 less the return and discount.
   23. Received payment on account for the sale of February 13 less the discount.

Journalize the entries to record the transactions of Cold Company.

Appendix 1
EX 5-34

Journal entries using perpetual inventory system

Using the data shown in Exercise 5-33, journalize the entries for the transactions assuming that Cold Company uses the perpetual inventory system.

Appendix 1
EX 5-35

Cost of goods sold

Based on the following data, determine the cost of goods sold for April:

Inventory, April 1	$ 15,000
Inventory, April 30	28,000
Purchases	290,000
Purchases returns and allowances	10,000
Purchases discounts	5,800
Freight In	4,200

Appendix 1
EX 5-36

Cost of goods sold

Based on the following data, determine the cost of goods sold for March:

Inventory, March 1	$100,000
Inventory, March 31	90,000
Purchases	800,000
Purchases returns and allowances	15,000
Purchases discounts	12,000
Freight In	8,000

Appendix 1
EX 5-37

Cost of goods sold—periodic method

✔ Correct cost of goods sold, $953,500

Identify the errors in the following schedule of cost of goods sold for the current year ended December 31, 2015:

Cost of goods sold:			
Inventory, December 31, 2015			$ 140,000
Purchases		$975,000	
Plus: Purchases returns and allowances	$12,000		
Purchases discounts	8,000	20,000	
Gross purchases		995,000	
Less freight In		13,500	
Cost of goods purchased			981,500
Goods available for sale			1,121,500
Less goods inventory, January 1, 2015			125,000
Cost of goods sold			$ 996,500

Appendix 1
EX 5-38

Closing entries using periodic inventory system

Aladdin Company is a small rug retailer owned and operated by Lin Endsley. After the accounts have been adjusted on December 31, the following account balances were taken from the ledger:

Advertising Expense	$ 16,500
Depreciation Expense	4,000
Freight In	8,000
Inventory, December 1	43,800
Inventory, December 31	35,750
Lin Endsley, Withdrawals	30,000
Miscellaneous Expense	1,750
Purchases	560,000
Purchases Discounts	12,000
Purchases Returns and Allowances	6,000
Salaries Expense	80,000
Sales	890,000
Sales Discounts	5,000
Sales Returns and Allowances	10,000

Journalize the closing entries on December 31.

Appendix 1
Ex 5-39

Closing entries using periodic inventory system

Pyramid Company is a small rug retailer owned and operated by Rosemary Endecott. After the accounts have been adjusted on January 31, the following selected account balances were taken from the ledger:

Advertising Expense	$ 40,000
Depreciation Expense	15,000
Freight In	8,000
Inventory, January 1	250,000
Inventory, January 31	300,000
Miscellaneous Expense	29,000
Purchases	750,000
Purchases Discounts	12,000
Purchases Returns and Allowances	8,000
Rosemary Endecott, Withdrawals	60,000
Salaries Expense	175,000
Sales	1,200,000
Sales Discounts	20,000
Sales Returns and Allowances	30,000

Journalize the closing entries on January 31.

Appendix 2
EX 5-40

Sales transactions with PST

✔ c. $14,850

A sale of merchandise on account for $13,750 is subject to an 8% provincial sales tax. (a) Should the sales tax be recorded at the time of sale or when payment is received? (b) What is the amount of the sale? (c) What is the amount debited to Accounts Receivable? (d) What is the title of the account to which the $1,100 ($13,750 × 8%) is credited?

Appendix 2
EX 5-41

PST and GST

A sale of merchandise on account to a final user for $13,750 is subject to a 6% PST and a 5% GST. (a) Should the PST and the GST be recorded at the time of sale or when payment is received? (b) What is the amount of the sale? (c) What is the amount debited to Accounts Receivable? (d) What are the titles of the accounts to which the $825 ($13,750 × 6%) and $687.50 ($13,750 × 5%) are credited?

Appendix 2
EX 5-42

HST

A sale of merchandise on account to a final user for $13,750 is subject to an 13% HST. (a) Should the HST be recorded at the time of sale or when payment is received? (b) What is the amount of the sale? (c) What is the amount debited to Accounts Receivable? (d) What is the title of the account to which the $1,787.50 ($13,750 × 13%) is credited?

Appendix 2
EX 5-43

Purchase transactions including PST, PST and GST, and HST

Purchases of inventory and supplies on account were made for $2,000 and $3,000, respectively.

a. The province has an 8% PST. Journalize the entry.
b. The province has a 6% PST and a 5% GST. Journalize the entry.
c. The province has a 13% HST. Journalize the entry.

Appendix 2
EX 5-44

PST, PST and GST, and HST sales transactions, perpetual inventory system

Journalize the entries to record a sale in each of the scenarios below. The sale was for $3,400 of merchandise on account. The cost of goods sold was $2,000. Assume a perpetual inventory system. On the same day, remittance was made for taxes collected.

a. The goods were subject to a PST of 5%. The company remitted $41,950 to the provincial government for taxes collected.
b. The goods were subject to a PST of 7% and a GST of 5%. The company remitted $41,950 to the provincial government for taxes collected and the difference between $58,730 for federal taxes collected and $45,333 for federal taxes paid.
c. The goods were subject to an HST of 9%. The company remitted the difference between $58,730 for federal taxes collected and $45,333 for federal taxes paid.

Appendix 2
EX 5-45

PST, PST and GST, and HST sales transactions, perpetual inventory system

Journalize the following merchandise transactions in each of the scenarios below.

1. Sold merchandise on account, $41,000, terms 1/10, n/30. The cost of goods sold was $22,500. Assume a perpetual inventory system.
2. Received payment with a discount.
3. Remit taxes to the appropriate government bodies as follows.
   a. The goods were subject to a PST of 7%. The company remitted $4,500 to the provincial government for taxes collected.
   b. The goods were subject to a PST of 7% and a GST of 5%. The company remitted $4,500 to the province for the PST. The company remitted to the federal government for the GST collected. The balance in the GST Charged on Sales account is $9,326, and the balance in the GST Paid on Purchases account is $6,452. What would happen if the balances were reversed? Record the journal entry and explain the result.
   c. The goods were subject to an HST of 13%. The company remitted to the federal government for the HST collected. The balance in the HST Charged on Sales account is $8,326, and the balance in the HST Paid on Purchases account is $5,512. What would happen if the balances were reversed? Record the journal entry and explain the result.

Appendix 2
EX 5-46

Gross profit considering PST, PST and GST, and HST

During the current year, merchandise is sold for $795,000. The cost of goods sold is $477,000. For each of the scenarios (a), (b), and (c), answer the following questions:

1. What is the amount of gross profit?
2. What would the total cash amount be if all the cash is collected?
3. What amount of taxes collected will be remitted to the government?
   a. The PST is 6%.
   b. The PST is 7% and the GST is 5%. The GST paid on purchases is $48,850.
   c. The HST is 10%. The HST paid on purchases is $97,000.

PROBLEMS SERIES A

PR 5-1A
Purchase-related transactions

The following selected transactions were completed by Suzy Co. during October of the current year, using the perpetual inventory system.

Oct. 1.   Purchased merchandise from Wood Co., $15,500, terms FOB shipping point, 2/10, n/eom. Prepaid freight of $400 was added to the invoice.
      5.   Purchased merchandise from Davis Co., $14,150, terms FOB destination, n/30.
     10.   Paid Wood Co. for invoice of October 1, less discount.
     18.   Purchased merchandise from Smith Company, $12,250, terms FOB shipping point, n/eom.
     18.   Paid freight of $180 on October 18 purchase from Smith Company.
     31.   Paid Smith Company for invoice of October 18.
     31.   Paid Davis Co. for invoice of October 5.

Instructions

Journalize the entries to record the transactions of Suzy Co. for October.

PR 5-2A
Purchase-related transactions

The following selected transactions were completed by Marcel Co. during November of the current year, using the perpetual inventory system.

Nov. 13.   Purchased merchandise from Folts Co., $8,000, terms FOB destination, 1/10, n/30.
     14.   Issued debit memo to Folts Co. for $1,500 of merchandise returned from purchase on November 13.
     18.   Purchased merchandise from Lakey Company, $12,250, terms FOB shipping point, n/eom.
     18.   Paid freight of $180 on November 18 purchase from Lakey Company.
     19.   Purchased merchandise from Noman Co., $11,150, terms FOB destination, 2/10, n/30.
     23.   Paid Folts Co. for invoice of November 13, less debit memo of November 14 and discount.
     29.   Paid Noman Co. for invoice of November 19, less discount.
     30.   Paid Lakey Company for invoice of November 18.

Instructions

Journalize the entries to record the transactions of Marcel Co. for November.

PR 5-3A
Sales-related transactions

The following selected transactions were completed by Vancouver Island Irrigation Co., which sells irrigation supplies primarily to wholesalers and occasionally to retail customers:

Aug. 1.   Sold merchandise on account to Fir Co., $12,500, terms FOB shipping point, n/eom. The cost of goods sold was $7,500.
      2.   Sold merchandise for $20,000 to retail cash customers. The cost of goods sold was $13,100.
     13.   Sold merchandise to customers who used MasterCard, $8,000. The cost of goods sold was $5,000.
     18.   Sold merchandise on account to Horton Company, $6,850, terms FOB shipping point, 2/10, n/30. Paid $210 for freight and added it to the invoice. The cost of goods sold was $4,100.
     28.   Received cheque for amount due from Horton Company for sale of August 18.
     31.   Paid Piper Delivery Service $2,100 for merchandise delivered during August to customers under shipping terms of FOB destination.
     31.   Received cheque for amount due from Fir Co. for sale of August 1.
Sep. 3.   Paid bank $980 for service fees for handling MasterCard sales during August.

Instructions

Journalize the entries to record the transactions of Vancouver Island Irrigation Co., assuming the use of the perpetual inventory system.

PR 5-4A

Sales-related transactions

The following selected transactions were completed by Minty Supplies Co., which sells irrigation supplies primarily to wholesalers and occasionally to retail customers:

Jul. 5.   Sold merchandise on account to Epworth Company, $30,000, terms FOB destination, 1/10, n/30. The cost of goods sold was $19,500.

8.   Sold merchandise for $11,500 to retail customers who used VISA. The cost of goods sold was $7,000.

14.   Sold merchandise on account to Osgood Co., $11,800, terms FOB shipping point, 1/10, n/30. The cost of goods sold was $7,000.

15.   Received cheque for amount due from Epworth Company for sale on July 5.

16.   Issued credit memo for $1,800 to Osgood Co. for merchandise returned from sale on July 14. The cost of the goods returned was $1,000.

24.   Received cheque for amount due from Osgood Co. for sale on July 14 less credit memo of July 16 and discount.

31.   Paid Stewart Delivery Service $2,100 for merchandise delivered during July to customers under shipping terms of FOB destination.

Aug. 4.   Paid bank $400 for service fees for handling VISA sales during July.

Instructions

Journalize the entries to record the transactions of Minty Supplies Co., assuming the use of the perpetual inventory system.

PR 5-5A

Sales-related and purchase-related transactions

The following were selected from among the transactions completed by East Coast Trading Post during December of the current year:

Dec. 3.   Purchased merchandise on account from Hillsboro Co., list price $38,000, trade discount 25%, terms FOB shipping point, 2/10, n/30, with prepaid freight of $900 added to the invoice.

6.   Sold merchandise on account to Zion Co., list price $27,000, trade discount 35%, terms 2/10, n/30. The cost of the goods sold was $14,000.

13.   Paid Hillsboro Co. on account for purchase of December 3, less discount.

16.   Received cash on account from sale of December 6 to Zion Co., less discount.

19.   Sold merchandise on MasterCard, $58,000. The cost of the goods sold was $34,800.

23.   Sold merchandise for cash, $33,600. The cost of the goods sold was $20,000.

31.   Paid MasterCard service fee of $1,750.

Instructions

Journalize the transactions, assuming the use of the perpetual inventory system.

PR 5-6A

Sales-related and purchase-related transactions

The following were selected from among the transactions completed by Hamel Company during December of the current year:

Dec. 5.   Purchased merchandise on account from Deepwater Co., $18,750, terms FOB destination, 2/10, n/30.

6.   Sold merchandise on account to Breck Co., list price $21,000, trade discount 30%, terms 3/10, n/30. The cost of the goods sold was $9,000.

7.   Returned $3,000 of merchandise purchased on December 5 from Deepwater Co.

15.   Paid Deepwater Co. on account for purchase of December 5, less return of December 7 and discount.

16.   Received cash on account from sale of December 6 to Breck Co., less discount.

22.   Sold merchandise on account to Smith River Co., $15,400, terms 2/10, n/30. The cost of the goods sold was $9,000.

28.   Received merchandise returned by Smith River Co. from sale on December 22, $2,400. The cost of the returned merchandise was $1,400.

Instructions

Journalize the transactions, assuming the use of the perpetual inventory system.

PR 5-7A

Sales-related and purchase-related transactions for seller and buyer

The following selected transactions were completed during November between R & R Projectz Co. and Creative Company:

Nov. 8. R & R Projectz sold merchandise on account to Creative Company, $24,750, terms FOB destination, 1/15, n/eom. The cost of the goods sold was $14,850.

8. R & R Projectz paid freight of $640 for delivery of merchandise sold to Creative Company on November 8.

12. Creative Company returned $5,750 of merchandise purchased on account on November 8 from R & R Projectz. The cost of the goods returned was $3,000.

23. Creative Company paid R & R Projectz for purchase of November 8, less discount and less return of November 12.

Instructions

Journalize the November transactions for (1) R & R Projectz and (2) Creative Company, assuming both companies use the perpetual inventory system.

PR 5-8A

Sales-related and purchase-related transactions for seller and buyer

The following selected transactions were completed during May between Stewart Company and Frang Company:

May 2. Stewart Company sold merchandise on account to Frang Company, $16,000, terms FOB shipping point, 2/10, n/30. Stewart Company paid freight of $375, which was added to the invoice. The cost of the goods sold was $10,000.

12. Frang Company paid Stewart Company for purchase of May 2, less discount.

24. Stewart Company sold merchandise on account to Frang Company, $13,200, terms FOB shipping point, n/eom. The cost of the goods sold was $8,000.

26. Frang Company paid freight of $290 on May 24 purchase from Stewart Company.

30. Frang Company paid Stewart Company on account for purchase of May 24.

Instructions

Journalize the May transactions for (1) Stewart Company and (2) Frang Company, assuming both companies use the perpetual inventory system.

PR 5-9A

Single-step income statement and balance sheet

✔ 1. Net income: $120,000

The following selected accounts and their current balances appear in the ledger of Case-It Co. for December 31, 2015:

Cash	$ 37,700	Sales Returns and Allowances	$ 37,800
Accounts Receivable	111,600	Sales Discounts	19,800
Inventory	180,000	Cost of Goods Sold	1,926,000
Office Supplies	5,000	Sales Salaries Expense	378,000
Prepaid Insurance	12,000	Advertising Expense	50,900
Office Equipment	115,200	Depreciation Expense—	
Accumulated Depreciation—		Store Equipment	8,300
Office Equipment	49,500	Miscellaneous Selling Expense	2,000
Store Equipment	311,500	Office Salaries Expense	73,800
Accumulated Depreciation—		Rent Expense	39,900
Store Equipment	87,500	Insurance Expense	22,950
Accounts Payable	48,600	Depreciation Expense—	
Salaries Payable	3,600	Office Equipment	16,200
Note Payable	54,000	Office Supplies Expense	1,650
(final payment due 2030)		Miscellaneous Administrative	
Gina Hennessy, Capital	454,800	Expense	1,900
Gina Hennessy, Withdrawals	45,000	Interest Expense	4,400
Sales	2,703,600		

Instructions

1. Prepare a single-step income statement.
2. Prepare a statement of owner's equity.
3. Prepare a balance sheet, assuming that the current portion of the note payable is $8,000.
4. Briefly explain how single-step and multiple-step income statements differ. Which do you prefer? Why?

PR 5-10A

Multiple-step income statement and closing entries

Selected accounts and related amounts for Case-It Co. for the fiscal year ended December 31, 2015, are presented in Problem 5-9A.

Instructions

1. Prepare a multiple-step income statement in the format shown in Exhibit 11 on page 256.
2. Prepare closing entries as at December 31, 2015.

Appendix 1
PR 5-11A

Purchase-related transactions using periodic inventory system

Selected transactions for Suzy Co. during October of the current year are listed in Problem 5-1A.

Instructions

Journalize the entries to record the transactions of Suzy Co. for October using the periodic inventory system.

Appendix 1
PR 5-12A

Sales-related and purchase-related transactions using periodic inventory system

Selected transactions for East Coast Trading Post during December of the current year are listed in Problem 5-5A.

Instructions

Journalize the entries to record the transactions of East Coast Trading Post for December using the periodic inventory system.

Appendix 1
PR 5-13A

Sales-related and purchase-related transactions for buyer and seller using periodic inventory system

Selected transactions during November between R & R Projectz Co. and Creative Company are listed in Problem 5-7A.

Instructions

Journalize the entries to record the transactions for (1) R & R Projectz and (2) Creative Company assuming that both companies use the periodic inventory system.

Appendix 1
PR 5-14A

Periodic inventory accounts, multiple-step income statement, closing entries

✔ 2. Net income, $362,600

On December 31, 2015, the balances of the accounts appearing in the ledger of Andover Company are as follows:

Cash	$ 36,600	Sales Discounts	$ 18,750
Accounts Receivable	144,250	Purchases	1,073,000
Inventory, January 1, 2015	175,450	Purchases Returns and Allowances	12,000
Office Supplies	6,050	Purchases Discounts	9,000
Prepaid Insurance	9,000	Freight In	21,800
Store Equipment	341,550	Sales Salaries Expense	312,500
Accumulated Depreciation—		Advertising Expense	110,000
Store Equipment	11,800	Delivery Expense	18,000
Office Equipment	157,000	Depreciation Expense—	
Accumulated Depreciation—		Store Equipment	11,800
Office Equipment	32,500	Miscellaneous Selling Expense	21,400
Land	70,000	Office Salaries Expense	200,000
Accounts Payable	55,650	Rent Expense	62,500
Salaries Payable	5,900	Insurance Expense	6,000
Unearned Rent	16,600	Office Supplies Expense	4,600
Notes Payable	25,000	Depreciation Expense—	
Vanessa Andover, Capital	380,100	Office Equipment	3,000
Vanessa Andover, Withdrawals	37,500	Miscellaneous Administrative Expense	11,700
Sales	2,212,900	Rent Revenue	12,500
Sales Returns and Allowances	20,000	Interest Expense	1,500

Instructions

1. Does Andover Company use a periodic or perpetual inventory system? Explain.
2. Prepare a multiple-step income statement for Andover Company for the year ended December 31, 2015. The inventory as at December 31, 2015, was $188,200.
3. Prepare the closing entries for Andover Company as at December 31, 2015.

Appendix 2
PR 5-15A

Purchase- and sales-
related transactions
with PST, GST and
PST, and HST

The following selected transactions were completed by Drains Co. during November of the current year. The company sells irrigation supplies to both wholesalers and retail customers.

Nov. 2. Sold merchandise on account to Tree Co. (a wholesaler), $11,000, terms FOB shipping point, n/eom. The cost of the goods sold was $6,000.

6. Sold merchandise for $18,000 to retail cash customers. The cost of goods sold was $7,000.

7. Sold merchandise on account to Magnolia Inc. (a retail company), $25,000, terms FOB destination, 2/10, n/30. The cost of goods sold was $12,500.

12. Purchased supplies and inventory on account from Morin Company for $3,000 and $3,500 respectively.

16. Received cheque for amount due from Magnolia Inc. for the sale on November 7.

16. Issued credit memo for $1,800 to Tree Co. for merchandise returned from the sale on November 2. The cost of the goods returned was $900.

28. Received cheque for amount due from Tree Co. for the November 2 sale, less returned merchandise.

Instructions

Choose the scenario below that best matches the tax rate in your province. Journalize the entries to record the selected transactions for November and the tax remittances in December, assuming the perpetual inventory system.

a. The PST rate is 7%. On December 31, Drains Co. paid provincial sales taxes payable of $6,300.

b. The PST is 6% and the GST is 5%. On December 31, Drains Co. paid provincial sales tax payable of $3,500. Also on December 31, Drains Co. filed its GST return. The GST Paid on Purchases account balance was $6,300, and the GST Charged on Sales account balance was $8,300.

c. The HST is 13%. On December 31, Drains Co. filed its HST return. The HST Paid on Purchases account balance was $6,300, and the HST Charged on Sales account balance was $8,300.

Appendix 2
PR 5-16A

Purchase- and sales-
related transactions
with PST, GST and
PST, and HST

The following selected transactions were completed by Chao Co. during May and June of the current year. The company sells to wholesalers and retail customers. The wholesalers resell the inventory.

May 4. Sold merchandise on account to Robson Co. (a wholesaler), $7,000, terms FOB shipping point, n/eom. The cost of the goods sold was $4,000.

7. Sold merchandise for $15,000 to retail cash customers. The cost of goods sold was $6,000.

10. Sold merchandise on account to Lewis Inc. (a wholesaler), $20,000, terms FOB destination, 3/15, eom. The cost of goods sold was $10,000. The freight charge of $800 was paid.

13. Purchased supplies and inventory on account from Amin Company, for $2,000 and $2,500, respectively.

17. Received cheque for amount due from Lewis Inc. for the sale on May 10.

17. Issued credit memo for $1,000 to Robson Co. for merchandise returned from the sale on May 4. The cost of the goods returned was $600.

Jun. 30. Paid appropriate taxes.

Instructions

Choose the scenario below that best matches the tax rate in your province. Journalize the entries to record the selected transactions for May and June, assuming the perpetual inventory system.

a. The PST is 6%. Paid provincial sales tax payable of $5,500.

b. The PST is 7% and the GST is 5%. Paid provincial sales tax payable of $3,500. Filed GST return. The GST Paid on Purchases account balance was $7,200, and the GST Charged on Sales account balance was $9,300.

c. The HST is 12%. Chao Co. filed its HST return. The HST Paid on Purchases account balance was $5,200, and the HST Charged on Sales account balance was $7,300.

PROBLEM SERIES B

PR 5-1B
Purchase-related transactions

The following selected transactions were completed by Silvertree Company during January of the current year:

Jan. 1. Purchased merchandise from Guinn Co., $13,600, terms FOB destination, n/30.
   3. Purchased merchandise from Cybernet Co., $18,000, terms FOB shipping point, 2/10, n/eom. Prepaid freight of $300 was added to the invoice.
   13. Paid Cybernet Co. for invoice of January 3, less discount.
   31. Paid Guinn Co. for invoice of January 1.

Instructions

Journalize the entries to record the transactions of Silvertree Company for January, assuming the company uses the perpetual inventory system.

PR 5-2B
Purchase-related transactions

The following selected transactions were completed by Burrell Co. during December of the current year, using the perpetual inventory system.

Dec. 13. Purchased merchandise from Hammond Co., $8,000, terms FOB destination, 1/10, n/30.
   14. Issued debit memo to Hammond Co. for $1,500 of merchandise returned from purchase on December 13.
   18. Purchased merchandise from Nieuwkerk Company, $12,250, terms FOB shipping point, n/eom.
   18. Paid freight of $180 on December 18 purchase from Nieuwkerk Company.
   19. Purchased merchandise from Noman Co., $11,150, terms FOB destination, 2/10, n/30.
   23. Paid Hammond Co. for invoice of December 13, less debit memo of December 14 and discount.
   29. Paid Noman Co. for invoice of December 19, less discount.
   30. Paid Nieuwkerk Company for invoice of December 18.

Instructions

Journalize the entries to record the transactions of Burrell Co. for December.

PR 5-3B
Sales-related transactions

The following selected transactions were completed by Yukon Supply Co., which sells office supplies primarily to wholesalers and occasionally to retail customers:

Jan. 2. Sold merchandise on account to Oakley Co., $8,000, terms FOB destination, 1/10, n/30. The cost of the goods sold was $4,500.
   3. Sold merchandise for $21,800 to retail cash customers. The cost of goods sold was $13,000.
   12. Received cheque for amount due from Oakley Co. for sale on January 2.
   14. Sold merchandise to customers who used American Express cards, $6,000. The cost of goods sold was $3,200.
   19. Sold merchandise on account to Cooney Co., $15,750, terms FOB shipping point, 2/10, n/30. Added $400 to the invoice for prepaid freight. The cost of goods sold was $9,500.
   28. Received cheque for amount due from Cooney Co. for sale of January 19.
   31. Paid Black Hawk Delivery Service $3,875 for merchandise delivered during January to customers under shipping terms of FOB destination.
Feb. 3. Paid bank $1,150 for service fees for handling MasterCard and American Express sales during January.

Instructions

Journalize the entries to record the transactions of Yukon Supply Co., assuming use of the perpetual inventory system.

PR 5-4B

Sales-related transactions

The following selected transactions were completed by Wong Supply Co., which sells office supplies primarily to wholesalers and occasionally to retail customers:

Jan. 4. Sold merchandise on account to Liversedge Co., $7,500, terms FOB shipping point, n/eom. The cost of goods sold was $4,200.

 5. Sold merchandise for $10,000 to retail customers who used MasterCard. The cost of goods sold was $6,000.

14. Sold merchandise to customers who used American Express cards, $6,000. The cost of goods sold was $3,200.

16. Sold merchandise on account to Antonik Co., $16,500, terms FOB shipping point, 1/10, n/30. The cost of goods sold was $10,000.

18. Issued credit memo for $2,000 to Antonik Co. for merchandise returned from sale on January 16. The cost of the goods returned was $1,200.

26. Received cheque for amount due from Antonik Co. for sale on January 16 less credit memo of January 18 and discount.

31. Received cheque for amount due from Liversedge Co. for sale of January 4.

31. Paid Adams Delivery Service $2,134 for merchandise delivered during January to customers under shipping terms of FOB destination.

Feb. 3. Paid bank $950 for service fees for handling MasterCard and American Express sales during January.

Instructions

Journalize the entries to record the transactions of Wong Supply Co., assuming use of the perpetual inventory system.

PR 5-5B

Sales-related and purchase-related transactions

The following were selected from among the transactions completed by Calworks Company during April of the current year:

Apr. 3. Purchased merchandise on account from Prescott Co., list price $42,000, trade discount 40%, terms FOB destination, 2/10, n/30.

 4. Sold merchandise for cash, $18,200. The cost of the goods sold was $11,000.

 6. Returned $6,000 of merchandise purchased on April 3 from Prescott Co.

11. Sold merchandise on account to Logan Co., list price $8,500, trade discount 20%, terms 1/10, n/30. The cost of the goods sold was $4,500.

13. Paid Prescott Co. on account for purchase of April 3, less return of April 6 and discount.

21. Received cash on account from sale of April 11 to Logan Co., less discount.

Instructions

Journalize the transactions of Calworks Company, assuming use of the perpetual inventory system.

PR 5-6B

Sales-related and purchase-related transactions

The following were selected from among the transactions completed by Albinati Company during February of the current year:

Feb. 5. Purchased merchandise on account from Peng Co., $21,300, terms FOB shipping point, 2/10, n/30, with prepaid freight of $600 added to the invoice.

14. Sold merchandise on VISA, $60,000. The cost of the goods sold was $36,000.

15. Paid Peng Co. on account for purchase of February 5, less discount.

24. Sold merchandise on account to Matheson Co., $9,200, terms 1/10, n/30. The cost of the goods sold was $5,500.

28. Paid VISA service fee of $1,800.

28. Received merchandise returned by Matheson Co. from sale on February 24, $1,200. The cost of the returned merchandise was $720.

Instructions

Journalize the transactions, assuming use of the perpetual inventory system.

PR 5-7B

Sales-related and purchase-related transactions for seller and buyer

The following selected transactions were completed during August between Schlosser Company and Rock Co.:

Aug. 5. Schlosser Company sold merchandise on account to Rock Co., $18,000, terms FOB shipping point, n/eom. The cost of the goods sold was $10,800.

9. Rock Co. paid freight of $350 on August 5 purchase from Schlosser Company.

15. Schlosser Company sold merchandise on account to Rock Co., $36,200, terms FOB shipping point, 1/10, n/30. Schlosser Company paid freight of $900, which was added to the invoice. The cost of the goods sold was $19,600.

25. Rock Co. paid Schlosser Company on account for purchase of August 15, less discount.

31. Rock Co. paid Schlosser Company on account for purchase of August 5.

Instructions

Journalize the August transactions for (1) Schlosser Company and (2) Rock Co., assuming both companies use the perpetual inventory system.

PR 5-8B

Sales-related and purchase-related transactions for seller and buyer

The following selected transactions were completed during January between McGowan Company and Xi Co.:

Jan. 1. McGowan Company sold merchandise on account to Xi Co., $28,600, terms FOB destination, 2/15, n/eom. The cost of the goods sold was $17,000.

2. McGowan Company paid freight of $500 for delivery of goods sold to Xi Co. on January 1.

6. Xi Co. returned $1,600 of merchandise purchased on account on January 1 from McGowan Company. The cost of the goods returned was $960.

16. Xi Co. paid McGowan Company for purchase of January 1, less discount and less return of January 6.

Instructions

Journalize the January transactions for (1) McGowan Company and (2) Xi Co., assuming both companies use the perpetual inventory system.

PR 5-9B

Single-step income statement and balance sheet

✔ 1. Net income: $300,000

The following selected accounts and their current balances appear in the ledger of Drapery Land Co. for the fiscal year ended December 31, 2015:

Cash	$ 161,250	Sales Returns and Allowances	$ 69,300
Accounts Receivable	363,000	Sales Discounts	65,700
Inventory	525,000	Cost of Goods Sold	2,325,000
Office Supplies	16,800	Sales Salaries Expense	519,600
Prepaid Insurance	10,200	Advertising Expense	131,400
Office Equipment	255,000	Depreciation Expense—	
Accumulated Depreciation—		Store Equipment	19,200
Office Equipment	138,400	Miscellaneous Selling Expense	4,800
Store Equipment	759,000	Office Salaries Expense	252,450
Accumulated Depreciation—		Rent Expense	94,050
Store Equipment	102,600	Depreciation Expense—	
Accounts Payable	166,800	Office Equipment	38,100
Salaries Payable	7,200	Insurance Expense	11,700
Note Payable		Office Supplies Expense	3,200
(final payment due 2025)	168,000	Miscellaneous Administrative	
Tanya Xavier, Capital	1,312,250	Expense	5,500
Tanya Xavier, Withdrawals	105,000	Interest Expense	15,000
Sales	3,855,000		

Instructions

1. Prepare a single-step income statement.
2. Prepare a statement of owner's equity.
3. Prepare a balance sheet, assuming that the current portion of the note payable is $16,800.
4. Briefly explain how single-step and multiple-step income statements differ. Which is a better presentation for the user?

PR 5-10B

④ **Multiple-step income statement and closing**
⑤ **entries**

Selected accounts and related amounts for Drapery Land Co. for the fiscal year ended December 31, 2015, are presented in Problem 5-9B.

Instructions

1. Prepare a multiple-step income statement in the format shown in Exhibit 11.
2. Prepare closing entries as at December 31, 2015.

Appendix 1
PR 5-11B

Purchase-related transactions using periodic inventory system

Selected transactions for Silvertree Company during January of the current year are listed in Problem 5-1B.

Instructions

Journalize the entries to record the transactions of Silvertree Company for January using the periodic inventory system.

Appendix 1
PR 5-12B

Sales-related and purchase-related transactions using periodic inventory system

Selected transactions for Calworks Company during April of the current year are listed in Problem 5-5B.

Instructions

Journalize the entries to record the transactions of Calworks Company for April using the periodic inventory system.

Appendix 1
PR 5-13B

Sales-related and purchase-related transactions for buyer and seller using periodic inventory system

Selected transactions during August between Schlosser Company and Rock Co. are listed in Problem 5-7B.

Instructions

Journalize the entries to record the transactions for (1) Schlosser Company and (2) Rock Co., assuming both companies use the periodic inventory system.

Appendix 1
PR 5-14B

Periodic inventory accounts, multiple-step income statement, closing entries

✔ 2. Net income, $181,350

On December 31, 2015, the balances of the accounts appearing in the ledger of Triple Creek Company are as follows:

Cash	$ 18,300	Sales Discounts	$ 9,300
Accounts Receivable	72,000	Purchases	536,500
Inventory,		Purchases Returns and Allowances	6,000
January 1, 2015	87,700	Purchases Discounts	4,500
Office Supplies	3,000	Freight In	10,900
Prepaid Insurance	4,500	Sales Salaries Expense	156,250
Store Equipment	170,000	Advertising Expense	55,000
Accumulated Depreciation—		Delivery Expense	9,000
Store Equipment	55,900	Depreciation Expense—	
Office Equipment	78,500	Store Equipment	5,900
Accumulated Depreciation—		Miscellaneous Selling Expense	10,700
Office Equipment	16,250	Office Salaries Expense	100,000
Land	35,000	Rent Expense	31,250
Accounts Payable	27,800	Insurance Expense	3,000
Salaries Payable	3,000	Office Supplies Expense	2,300
Unearned Rent	8,300	Depreciation Expense—	
Notes Payable	12,500	Office Equipment	1,500
Shawn Hayes, Capital	189,050	Miscellaneous Administrative Expense	5,850
Shawn Hayes, Withdrawals	18,750	Rent Revenue	6,250
Sales	1,106,400	Interest Expense	750
Sales Returns and Allowances	10,000		

(continued)

Instructions

1. Does Triple Creek Company use a periodic or perpetual inventory system? Explain.
2. Prepare a multiple-step income statement for Triple Creek Company for the year ended December 31, 2015. The inventory as at December 31, 2015, was $94,100.
3. Prepare the closing entries for Triple Creek Company as at December 31, 2015.

Appendix 2
PR 5-15B

Purchase- and sales-related transactions with PST, GST Cost and PST, and HST

The following selected transactions were completed by Gutters Co. during May and June of the current year. The company sells irrigation supplies to both wholesalers and retail customers. The PST rate is 6%.

May 2. Sold merchandise on account to Tamarack Co. (a wholesaler), $13,000, terms FOB shipping point, n/eom. The cost of the goods sold was $7,000.

6. Sold merchandise for $15,000 to retail cash customers. The cost of goods sold was $6,500.

7. Sold merchandise on account to Fir Inc. (a retail company), $20,000, terms FOB destination, 2/10, n/30. The cost of goods sold was $11,000.

12. Purchased supplies and inventory on account from Boyd Company, for $2,000 and $2,500, respectively.

17. Received cheque for amount due from Fir Inc. for sale on May 7.

17. Issued credit memo for $1,600 to Tamarack Co. for merchandise returned from sale on May 2. The cost of the goods returned was $900.

29. Received cheque for amount due from Tamarack Co. for May 2 sale, less returned merchandise.

Jun. 30. Paid appropriate taxes.

Instructions

Journalize the entries in one of the scenarios below to record the selected transactions for the month of May and the July payment, assuming the use of the perpetual inventory system.

a. The PST rate is 4 %. On December 31, paid provincial sales taxes payable of $6,000.

b. The PST is 4% and the GST is 5%. On December 31, paid provincial sales tax payable of $3,000. Also on December 31, filed goods and services tax - GST Paid on Purchases was $6,000 and GST Charged on Sales was $8,000.

c. The HST is 11%. Filed harmonized sales tax - HST Paid on Purchases was $6,000 and HST Charged on Sales was $8,000.

Appendix 2
PR 5-16B

Purchase- and sales-related transactions with PST, GST and PST, and HST

The following selected transactions were completed by MacGillivray Co. during June and July of the current year. The company sells to both wholesalers and retail customers.

Jun. 6. Sold merchandise for cash to Bisset Co. (a wholesaler), $5,000, terms FOB shipping point, n/eom. The cost of the goods sold was $2,000.

8. Sold merchandise for $12,000 to retail cash customers. The cost of goods sold was $5,000.

10. Sold merchandise on account to Bruce Inc. (a wholesaler), $15,000, terms FOB destination, 3/15, eom. The cost of goods sold was $8,000. Freight paid was $700.

13. Purchased supplies and inventory on account from Calvin Company for $2,800 and $2,900, respectively.

18. Received cheque for amount due from Bruce Inc. for sale on June 10.

19. Issued cheque for $1,000 to Bissett Co. for merchandise returned from sale on June 6. The cost of the goods returned was $600.

Jul. 31. Paid appropriate taxes.

Instructions

Choose the scenario below that best matches the tax rate in your province. Journalize the entries to record the selected transactions for June and July, assuming the perpetual inventory system.

a. The PST is 6%. Paid provincial sales tax payable of $5,000.
b. The PST is 7% and the GST is 5%. Paid provincial sales tax payable of $3,500. MacGillivray Co. filed its GST return. The GST Paid on Purchases account balance was $7,200, and the GST Charged on Sales account balance was $9,400.
c. The HST is 13%. MacGillivray Co. filed its HST return. The HST Paid on Purchases account balance was $6,000, and the HST Charged on Sales account balance was $7,000.

COMPREHENSIVE PROBLEM

✔ 8. Net income: $667,150

Coastal Boards Co. is a merchandising business. The account balances for Coastal Boards Co. as at December 1, 2015 (unless otherwise indicated), are as follows:

1010	Cash	$ 63,600
1020	Accounts Receivable	153,900
1030	Inventory	602,400
1050	Store Supplies	11,400
1100	Store Equipment	469,500
1110	Accumulated Depreciation—Store Equipment	56,700
2010	Accounts Payable	96,600
2020	Salaries Payable	—
3010	Rocky Hansen, Capital, January 1, 2015	518,100
3020	Rocky Hansen, Withdrawals	135,000
3030	Income Summary	—
4010	Sales	3,221,100
4020	Sales Returns and Allowances	92,700
4030	Sales Discounts	59,400
5010	Cost of Goods Sold	1,623,000
5110	Sales Salaries Expense	334,800
5120	Advertising Expense	81,000
5130	Depreciation Expense	—
5140	Store Supplies Expense	—
5210	Office Salaries Expense	182,100
5220	Rent Expense	83,700

During December, the following transactions were completed.

Dec. 1. Paid rent for December, $5,000.
 6. Sold merchandise on account to Modesto Co., terms 2/10, n/30, FOB shipping point, $25,000. The cost of the goods sold was $15,000.
 7. Received $26,500 cash from Yuba Co. on account, no discount.
 14. Received merchandise returned on sale of December 6, $6,000. The cost of the goods returned was $4,500.
 15. Paid advertising expense for last half of December, $7,500.
 16. Received cash from sale of December 6, less return of December 14 and discount.
 19. Paid $18,000 to Bakke Co. on account, no discount.
 21. Purchased merchandise on account from Nye Co., terms 1/10, n/30, FOB destination, $20,000.
 24. Returned $2,000 of damaged merchandise purchased on December 21, receiving credit from the seller.
 28. Paid sales salaries of $22,800 and office salaries of $15,200.
 29. Purchased store supplies for cash, $2,400.
 31. Paid for purchase of December 21, less return of December 24 and discount.

Instructions

1. Enter the balances of each of the accounts in the appropriate balance column of a three-column account. Write *Balance* in the item section, and place a check mark (✓) in the Posting Reference column. Journalize the transactions for December.
2. Post the journal to the general ledger, extending the month-end balances to the appropriate balance columns after all posting is completed. You are not required to update or post to the accounts receivable and accounts payable subsidiary ledgers.

(continued)

3. Prepare an unadjusted trial balance.
4. At the end of December, the following adjustment data were assembled. Analyze and use these data to complete (5) and (6).

a. Inventory on December 31		$589,850
b. Store supplies on hand on December 31		4,700
c. Depreciation for the current year		18,800
d. Accrued salaries on December 31:		
Sales salaries	$4,400	
Office salaries	2,700	7,100

5. **Optional:** Enter the unadjusted trial balance on a 10-column end-of-period spread-sheet (work sheet), and complete the spreadsheet. See Appendix F for how to prepare an end-of-period spreadsheet (work sheet) for a merchandising business.
6. Journalize and post the adjusting entries.
7. Prepare an adjusted trial balance.
8. Prepare a multiple-step income statement, a statement of owner's equity, and a balance sheet.
9. Prepare and post the closing entries. Indicate closed accounts by inserting a line in the Balance column opposite the closing entry. Insert the new balance in the owner's capital account.
10. Prepare a post-closing trial balance.

SPECIAL ACTIVITIES

SA 5-1

Ethics and professional conduct in business

On February 15, 2015, Tropical Connection Company, a garden retailer, purchased $25,000 of seed, terms 2/10, n/30, from Midwest Seed Co. Although the discount period had expired, Lydia DeLay subtracted the discount of $500 when she processed the documents for payment on March 16, 2015.

Discuss whether Lydia DeLay behaved in a professional manner by subtracting the discount, after the discount period had expired.

SA 5-2

Purchases discounts and accounts payable

The Encore Video Store Co. is owned and operated by Debbie Popp. The following is an excerpt from a conversation between Debbie Popp and Suzie Engel, the chief accountant for The Encore Video Store.

Debbie: Suzie, I've got a question about this recent balance sheet.

Suzie: Sure, what's your question?

Debbie: Well, as you know, I'm applying for a bank loan to finance our new store in Regina, and I noticed that the accounts payable are listed as $120,000.

Suzie: That's right. Approximately $100,000 of that represents amounts due our suppliers, and the remainder is miscellaneous payables to creditors for utilities, office equipment, supplies, etc.

Debbie: That's what I thought. But as you know, we have an option of receiving a 2% discount from our suppliers for earlier payment, We've never taken it because we are always tight for cash.

Suzie: That's right. I can't remember the last time we received a discount.

Debbie: Well, it seems to me the accounts payable could be listed minus the 2% discount. Let's list the accounts payable due suppliers as $98,000, rather than $100,000. Every little bit helps. You never know. It might make the difference between getting the loan and not.

How would you respond to Debbie Popp's request?

SA 5-3
Determining cost of purchase

The following is an excerpt from a conversation between Ted Mackie and Laurie Van Dorn. Ted is debating whether to buy a stereo system from Classic Audio, a locally owned electronics store, or Sound Unlimited, an online electronics company.

Ted: Laurie, I don't know what to do about buying my new stereo.

Laurie: What's the problem?

Ted: Well, I can buy it locally at Classic Audio for $490.00. However, Sound Unlimited has the same system listed for $499.99.

Laurie: So what's the big deal? Buy it from Classic Audio.

Ted: It's not quite that simple. Sound Unlimited said something about not having to pay sales tax because I live out of province.

Laurie: Yes, that's a good point. If you buy it at Classic Audio, they'll charge you 6% sales tax.

Ted: But Sound Unlimited charges $13.99 for shipping and handling. If I have them send it next-day air, it'll cost $24.99 for shipping and handling.

Laurie: I guess it is a little confusing.

Ted: That's not all. Classic Audio will give an additional 1% discount if I pay cash. Otherwise, they will let me use my VISA, or I can pay it off in three monthly installments.

Laurie: Anything else?

Ted: Well ... Sound Unlimited says I have to charge it on my VISA. They don't accept cheques.

Laurie: I am not surprised. Many online stores don't accept cheques.

Ted: I give up. What would you do?

1. Assuming that Sound Unlimited doesn't charge sales tax on the sale to Ted, which company is offering a better buy?
2. What considerations other than price might influence Ted's decision on where to buy the stereo system?

SA 5-4
Sales discounts

Your sister operates Ennis Parts Company, an online boat parts distributorship that is in its third year of operation. The income statement is shown below and was recently prepared for the year ended December 31, 2015.

Ennis Parts Company
Income Statement
For the Year Ended December 31, 2015

Revenues:		
Net sales		$400,000
Interest revenue		5,000
Total revenues		405,000
Expenses:		
Cost of goods sold	$260,000	
Selling expenses	45,000	
Administrative expenses	24,275	
Interest expense	7,500	
Total expenses		336,775
Net income		$ 68,225

Your sister is considering a proposal to increase net income by offering sales discounts of 2/15, n/30, and by shipping all merchandise FOB shipping point. Currently, no sales discounts are allowed and merchandise is shipped FOB destination. The new credit terms are estimated to increase net sales by 15%. The ratio of the cost of goods sold to net sales is expected to be 65%. All selling and administrative expenses are expected to remain unchanged, except for store supplies, miscellaneous selling, office supplies, and miscellaneous administrative expenses, which are expected to increase proportionately with increased net sales. The amounts of these preceding items for the year ended December 31, 2015, were as follows:

(continued)

Store supplies expense	$6,000
Miscellaneous selling expense	1,500
Office supplies expense	1,000
Miscellaneous administrative expense	500

The other income and other expense items will remain unchanged. The shipment of all merchandise FOB shipping point will eliminate all delivery expenses, which for the year ended December 31, 2015, were $9,375.

1. Prepare a projected single-step income statement for the year ending December 31, 2016, based on the proposal. Assume all sales are collected within the discount period.

2. a. Based on the projected income statement in (1), would you recommend the implementation of the proposed changes?
   b. Describe any concerns related to the proposed changes described in (1).

SA 5-5

Shopping for a television

Group Project

Assume that you are planning to purchase a 50-inch plasma television. In groups of three or four, determine the lowest cost for the television, considering the available alternatives and the advantages and disadvantages of each alternative. For example, you could purchase locally, through mail order, or through an Internet shopping service. Consider such factors as delivery charges, interest-free financing, discounts, coupons, and availability of warranty services. Prepare a report for presentation to the class.

SA 5-6

Answer the following questions by referring to the financial statements of Leon's Furniture Limited and Shoppers Drug Mart Corporation, in Appendixes B and C:

1. Do you expect the gross margin of each company to be the same?
2. What is the gross margin for each company?
3. The gross margins for Leon's and Shoppers are much lower than the gross margin for Le Chateau, as noted on page 261. Explain the difference.

CANADIAN TIRE

Assume that in June you purchased camping equipment for your summer vacation from Canadian Tire, paying $110. You liked the sleeping bag so much that your roommate went back and bought the same one in July, when it was on sale for $90. In September, you both moved to a new apartment and, in the process of unpacking, discovered that a lot of camping equipment, including one of the sleeping bags, was missing. Luckily, your renters/homeowners insurance policy covers the theft, but the insurance company needs to know the cost of the sleeping bag that was stolen.

The sleeping bags were identical. However, to respond to the insurance company, you will need to identify which one was stolen. Was it the first one, at $110, or was it the second one, which cost $90? Whichever assumption you make may determine the amount that you receive from the insurance company.

Merchandising businesses, such as Canadian Tire, make similar assumptions when identical merchandise is purchased at different costs. For example, Canadian Tire may have purchased thousands of sleeping bags over the past year at different costs. At the end of the period, some of the sleeping bags will still be in inventory, and some will have been sold. But which costs relate to the sold bags, and which costs relate to the bags still in inventory? Canadian Tire's assumption about inventory costs can involve large dollar amounts and, thus, can have a significant impact on the financial statements. For example, Canadian Tire reported $1,448.6 million of inventory on December 31, 2011, and net income of $467.0 million for the year.

In this chapter, we will discuss such issues as how to determine the cost of merchandise in inventory and cost of goods sold. However, we begin this chapter by discussing the importance of control over inventory.

After studying this chapter, you should be able to:

1 Describe the importance of control over inventory.

Control of Inventory	Safeguarding Inventory	
	Reporting Inventory	

2 Describe three inventory cost flow methods and their impact on the income statement and balance sheet.

Inventory Cost Flow Methods		EXAMPLE EXERCISE 6-1 (page 307)
	Consigned Inventory	
	Inventory Ownership	
	Inventory Over/Short	EXAMPLE EXERCISE 6-2 (page 309)

3 Determine the cost of inventory under the perpetual inventory system using the FIFO and average cost methods.

Inventory Costing Methods under a Perpetual Inventory System	First-In, First-Out Method	EXAMPLE EXERCISE 6-3 (page 311)
	Average Cost Method (Moving Weighted Average Cost Method)	EXAMPLE EXERCISE 6-4 (page 312)
	Computerized Perpetual Inventory Systems	

4 Compare and contrast two of the inventory costing methods.

Comparing Inventory Costing Methods		

5 Describe and illustrate the reporting of inventory in the financial statements.

Reporting Inventory in the Financial Statements	Valuation at Lower of Cost and Net Realizable Value	EXAMPLE EXERCISE 6-5 (page 316)
	Inventory on the Balance Sheet	
	Cost of Goods Sold on the Income Statement	
	Effect of Inventory Errors on the Financial Statements	EXAMPLE EXERCISE 6-6 (page 320)
	Financial Analysis and Interpretation	EXAMPLE EXERCISE 6-7 (page 322)

APPENDIX 1 Estimating Inventory Cost

APPENDIX 2 Inventory Costing Methods under a Periodic Inventory System

For the chapter *At a Glance*, turn to page 326.

Control of Inventory

Describe the importance of control over inventory.

Two primary objectives of control over inventory are as follows:[1]

1. Safeguarding the inventory from damage or theft.
2. Reporting inventory in the financial statements.

Safeguarding Inventory

Controls for safeguarding inventory begin as soon as the inventory is ordered. The following documents are often used for inventory control:

> Purchase order
> Receiving report
> Vendor's invoice

---

1 Additional controls used by businesses are described and illustrated in Chapter 7, "Internal Control and Cash."

The **purchase order** authorizes the purchase of the inventory from an approved vendor. As soon as the inventory is received, a receiving report is completed. The **receiving report** establishes an initial record of the receipt of the inventory. The **vendor's invoice** is sent by the seller to the buyer. It states the quantity, price, description, and terms of the sale. An example of a vendor's invoice is given in Chapter 5, Exhibit 3, on page 241. To make sure the inventory received is what was ordered, the receiving report is compared to the company's purchase order. The price, quantity, and description of the item on the purchase order and receiving report are then compared to the vendor's invoice. If the receiving report, purchase order, and vendor's invoice agree, the inventory is recorded in the accounting records. If any differences exist, they should be investigated and reconciled.

Recording inventory using a perpetual inventory system versus a periodic inventory system is also an effective means of control. The amount of inventory is always available in the **subsidiary inventory ledger**. This helps keep inventory quantities at proper levels. For example, comparing inventory quantities with maximum and minimum levels allows for the timely reordering of inventory and prevents ordering excess inventory.

Finally, controls for safeguarding inventory should include security measures to prevent damage and customer or employee theft. Some examples of security measures include the following:

1. Storing inventory in areas that are restricted to authorized employees.
2. Locking high-priced inventory in cabinets.
3. Using two-way mirrors, cameras, security tags, and guards.
4. Periodic test counts during the year, in addition to the end-of-year count.
5. Segregation of duties to ensure that employees with access to bookkeeping do not have access to inventory, to prevent employees from stealing inventory and making entries to cover the theft.

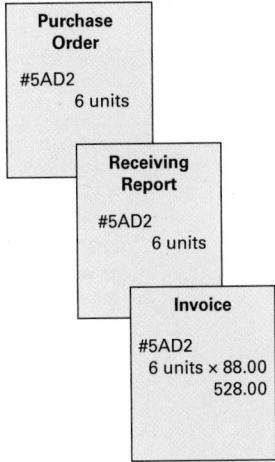

Reporting Inventory

A **physical inventory**, or count of inventory, should be taken near year-end to ensure that the quantity of inventory reported in the financial statements is accurate. After the quantity of inventory on hand is determined, the cost of the inventory is assigned for reporting in the financial statements. Most companies assign costs to inventory using one of three inventory cost flow methods.

2 Inventory Cost Flow Methods

The inventory cost method chosen by a company should be the method that best represents economic reality. For example, if each inventory item is unique and can be specifically identified, then a method is used to reflect that reality (specific identification). If each inventory item is identical and also perishable, such as milk, then the method chosen reflects that older items will be sold first, or first-in, first-out (FIFO).

If each inventory item is identical and is not perishable, such as office supplies, then the method chosen reflects that it does not matter which item is sold and so the average cost would be suitable (average cost).

Under the **specific identification inventory cost flow method,** the unit sold is identified with a specific purchase. For example, an automobile dealer may use the specific identification method because each automobile has a unique serial number. The cost of goods sold (COGS) is simply the cost of the unique items. For instance, a car with vehicle number 233255 has a sunroof, a design paint package, and expensive rims for a total cost of $32,778.12. When this vehicle is sold, the total cost of $32,778.12 becomes the cost of goods sold. This cost is specifically related to that car. Other businesses that use specific identification are jewellery stores and art galleries. However, most businesses cannot identify each inventory unit separately. In such cases, one of the two following inventory cost flow methods is used.

The first-in, first-out and average cost methods are designed to deal with an accounting issue that arises when identical units of merchandise are acquired at different unit costs during a period. In such cases, when an item is sold, it is necessary to determine its cost using a cost flow assumption and related inventory cost flow method.

To illustrate, assume that identical units of merchandise are purchased during May, as follows:

			Units	Unit Cost	Total Cost
May	10	Purchase	1	$ 9	$ 9
	18	Purchase	3	13	39
	24	Purchase	2	14	28
Total			6		$76

Inventory Cost Flow Methods

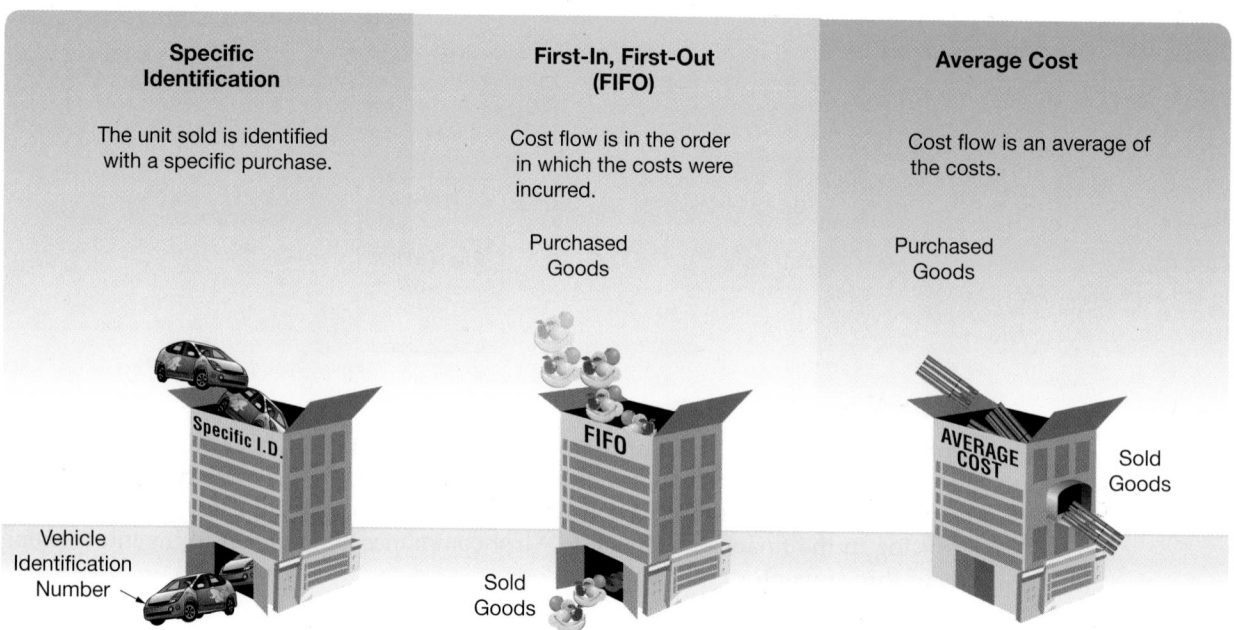

Specific Identification

The unit sold is identified with a specific purchase.

Vehicle Identification Number

First-In, First-Out (FIFO)

Cost flow is in the order in which the costs were incurred.

Purchased Goods

Sold Goods

Average Cost

Cost flow is an average of the costs.

Purchased Goods

Sold Goods

Assume that one unit is sold on May 30 for $20.

The specific identification inventory cost flow method is not practical unless each inventory unit can be separately identified.

Under the **first-in, first-out (FIFO) inventory cost flow method,** the first units purchased are assumed to be sold, and the ending inventory is made up of the most recent purchases.

In the preceding example, the May 10 unit would be assumed to have been sold. Thus, the gross profit would be $11, and the ending inventory would be $67 ($76 − $9).[2]

	May 10 Unit Sold
Sales	$20
Cost of goods sold	9
Gross profit	$11
Ending inventory	$67*

*($76 − $9)

Under the **average cost method**, the cost of both the units sold and the units in the ending inventory is an average of the purchase costs. In the preceding example, the cost of the unit sold would be $12.67 ($76 ÷ 6 units), the gross profit would be $7.33 ($20 − $12.67), and the ending inventory would be $63.33 ($76 − $12.67).

	May 10 Unit Sold
Sales	$20.00
Cost of goods sold	12.67
Gross profit	$ 7.33
Ending inventory	$63.33*

*($76 − $12.67)

EXAMPLE EXERCISE 6-1 Inventory Cost Flow Methods   **2**

Given the following three different scenarios, which costing method would best reflect economic reality?

a. High-end jewellery store

b. Dollar store

c. Grocery store

FOLLOW MY EXAMPLE 6-1

a. Specific identification

b. First-in, first-out or average cost

c. First-in, first-out

For Practice: PE 6-1

The inventory cost flow methods, specific identification, FIFO, and average cost using the example are shown in Exhibit 1.

Exhibit 2 shows the frequency with which the cost methods are used in Canada.

Consigned Inventory

As mentioned in Chapter 5, inventory needs to be owned by the business in order to be recorded in the accounting records. A retail business may have items for sale that it does not own. These are consigned items and are called **consigned inventory**. For instance, an outdoor equipment store may have a display case full of sunglasses. The store may have an arrangement with the manufacturer of those sunglasses that the store will sell them, take a commission on the sale, and forward the net amount to the manufacturer. Because the store has not bought the sunglasses, it does not have the risk of ownership. If the sunglasses do not sell, they will be returned to the manufacturer.

---

2 Another inventory method is last-in, first-out (LIFO). This method is not allowed under Accounting Standards for Private Enterprises or International Financial Reporting Standards (IFRS), but you may see this method in American financial statements.

Exhibit 1

Inventory Costing Methods

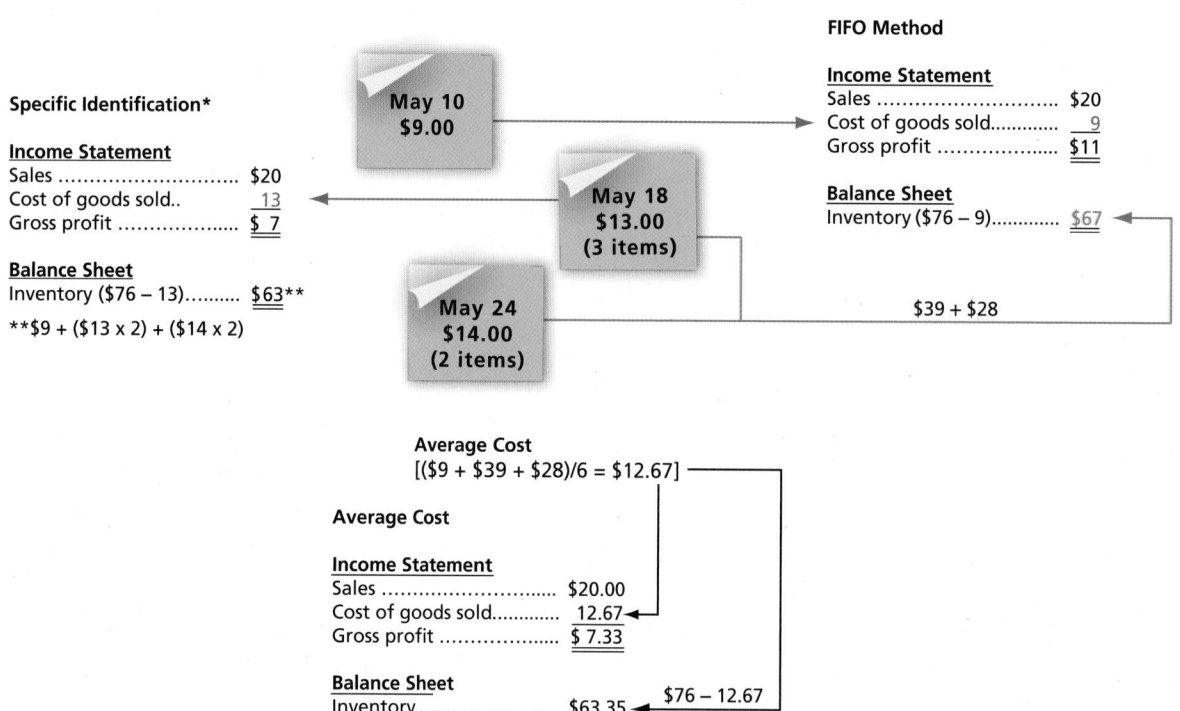

Purchases

Specific Identification*

Income Statement
Sales $20
Cost of goods sold.. 13
Gross profit .... $ 7

Balance Sheet
Inventory ($76 – 13)........... $63**

**$9 + ($13 x 2) + ($14 x 2)

May 10
$9.00

May 18
$13.00
(3 items)

May 24
$14.00
(2 items)

FIFO Method

Income Statement
Sales $20
Cost of goods sold............. 9
Gross profit $11

Balance Sheet
Inventory ($76 – 9)............. $67

$39 + $28

Average Cost
[($9 + $39 + $28)/6 = $12.67]

Average Cost

Income Statement
Sales $20.00
Cost of goods sold............. 12.67
Gross profit .... $ 7.33

Balance Sheet
Inventory $63.35

$76 – 12.67

*Only used if item is identifiable. Assumes the item sold on May 30 was one of the items purchased on May 18.

Exhibit 2

Use of Inventory Costing Methods*

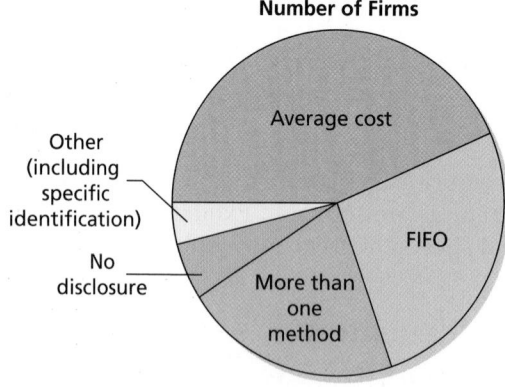

Number of Firms

Average cost

FIFO

More than one method

No disclosure

Other (including specific identification)

*Of 129 companies reporting inventory surveyed by *Financial Reporting in Canada: A Survey of Annual Reports of 200 Canadian Public Companies*, 32nd edition, 2007.

Inventory Ownership

The FOB shipping point and destination point, discussed in Chapter 5, also have an impact on the recording of inventory. Inventory is recorded when there is ownership of the items, which is determined by how the inventory is shipped. To review, if the inventory is transported FOB shipping point, then the inventory is owned by the purchaser from the day it leaves the seller, and the purchaser is responsible for freight and insurance. If the inventory is shipped FOB destination, then the inventory is owned by the purchaser when it is received, and the seller is responsible for the freight and insurance. As noted in Chapter 5, in practise we enter the invoice when created or received and at year end, we may need to review to ensure that they are recorded in the correct period.

Inventory Over/Short

As discussed in Chaper 5, at the end of the year when the physical count occurs, the actual count may differ from the recorded count for the perpetual method. This discrepancy may be the result of an error or theft. To keep track of the difference, it is debited either to Cost of Goods Sold or to an account known as Loss from Inventory Shrinkage. If the periodic inventory system is used, no entry is required because the inventory is not tracked on an ongoing basis.

EXAMPLE EXERCISE 6-2   Cost Flow Methods   **2**

Seven identical units of Item QBM are purchased during February, as shown below.

	Item QBM	Units	Cost	Total Cost
Feb. 8	Purchase	2	$46.00	$ 92.00
15	Purchase	1	48.00	48.00
26	Purchase	4	50.00	200.00
Total		7		$340.00
	Average cost per unit		$48.57 ($340 ÷ 7 units)	

Assume that two units are sold on February 27 for $70 each.

Determine the gross profit for February and ending inventory on February 28 using (a) the first-in, first-out (FIFO) method and (b) the average cost method.

FOLLOW MY EXAMPLE 6-2

		Gross Profit	Ending Inventory
a.	First-in, first-out (FIFO)..............................	$48 ($140 – ($46 × 2))	$248 ($48 + $200)
b.	Average cost..	$42.86 ($140 – ($48.57 × 2))	$242.85 ($48.57 × 5)

For Practice: PE 6-2

 Inventory Costing Methods under a Perpetual Inventory System

Determine the cost of inventory under the perpetual inventory system, using the FIFO and average cost methods.

As illustrated in the prior section, when identical units of an item are purchased at different unit costs, an inventory cost flow method must be used. This is true regardless of whether the perpetual or periodic inventory system is used.

In this section, the FIFO and average cost methods are illustrated under a perpetual inventory system. The FIFO and average cost methods are illustrated under a periodic inventory system in Appendix 2 of this chapter. For purposes of illustration, the data for Item 127B is used, as shown below.

	Item 127B	Units	Cost
Jan. 1	Inventory	100	$20
4	Sale	70	
10	Purchase	80	21
22	Sale	40	
28	Sale	20	
30	Purchase	100	22

First-In, First-Out Method

Note: Using FIFO, costs are included in cost of goods sold in the order in which the items were incurred.

When the FIFO method is used, costs are included in cost of goods sold in the order in which the items were purchased. This sequence is often the same as the physical flow of the merchandise. Thus, the FIFO method often provides results that are about the same as the results that would have been obtained using the specific identification method. For example, grocery stores shelve milk and other perishable products by expiration dates. Products with early expiration dates are stocked in front. In this way, the oldest products (earliest purchases) are sold first.

To illustrate, Exhibit 3 shows the use of FIFO under a perpetual inventory system for Item 127B. The journal entries and the subsidiary inventory ledger for Item 127B are shown in Exhibit 3 as follows:

1. The beginning balance on January 1 is $2,000 (100 units at a unit cost of $20).
2. On January 4, 70 units were sold at a price of $30 each for sales of $2,100 (70 units × $30). The cost of goods sold is $1,400 (70 units at a unit cost of $20). After the sale, $600 of inventory remains (30 units at a unit cost of $20).
3. On January 10, $1,680 of goods are purchased (80 units at a unit cost of $21). After the purchase, the inventory is reported on two lines, $600 (30 units at a unit cost of $20) from the beginning inventory and $1,680 (80 units at a unit cost of $21) from the January 10 purchase.
4. On January 22, 40 units are sold at a price of $30 each for sales of $1,200 (40 units × $30). Using FIFO, the cost of goods sold of $810 consists of $600 (30 units at a unit cost of $20) from the beginning inventory plus $210 (10 units at a unit cost of $21) from the January 10 purchase. After the sale, $1,470 of inventory remains (70 units at a unit cost of $21) from the January 10 purchase.
5. The January 28 sale and January 30 purchase are recorded in a similar manner.
6. The ending balance on January 31 is $3,250. This balance is made up of two layers of inventory as follows:

	Date of Purchase	Quantity	Unit Cost	Total Cost
Layer 1:	Jan. 10	50	$21	$1,050
Layer 2:	Jan. 30	100	22	2,200
Total		150		$3,250

Exhibit 3

Entries and Perpetual Inventory Account (FIFO)

Jan. 4 Accounts Receivable	2,100	
Sales		2,100
4 Cost of Goods Sold	1,400	
Inventory		1,400

10 Inventory	1,680	
Accounts Payable		1,680

22 Accounts Receivable	1,200	
Sales		1,200
22 Cost of Goods Sold	810	
Inventory		810

28 Accounts Receivable	600	
Sales		600
28 Cost of Goods Sold	420	
Inventory		420

30 Inventory	2,200	
Accounts Payable		2,200

Item 127B

		Purchases			Cost of Goods Sold			Inventory		
Date	Quantity	Unit Cost	Total Cost	Quantity	Unit Cost	Total Cost	Quantity	Unit Cost	Total Cost	
Jan. 1							100	20	2,000	
4				70	20	1,400	30	20	600	
10	80	21	1,680				30	20	600	
							80	21	1,680	
22				30	20	600				
				10	21	210	70	21	1,470	
28				20	21	420	50	21	1,050	
30	100	22	2,200				50	21	1,050	
							100	22	2,200	
31	Balances					2,630			3,250	

Cost of goods sold

January 31 inventory

EXAMPLE EXERCISE 6-3 Perpetual Inventory Using FIFO   **3**

Beginning inventory, purchases, and sales for Item ER27 are as follows:

Nov.	1	Inventory	40 units at $5
	5	Sale	32 units
	11	Purchase	60 units at $7
	21	Sale	45 units

Assuming a perpetual inventory system and using the first-in, first-out (FIFO) method, determine (a) the cost of goods sold on November 21 and (b) the inventory on November 30.

FOLLOW MY EXAMPLE 6-3

a. Cost of goods sold (November 21):   b. Inventory, November 30:

8 units at $5	$ 40
37 units at $7	259
45 units	$299

$161 = (23 units × $7)

For Practice: PE 6-3

Average Cost Method (Moving Weighted Average Cost Method)

When the average cost method, more correctly called the **moving weighted average cost method**, is used in a perpetual inventory system, an average unit cost for each item is computed each time a purchase is made. This unit cost is then used to determine the cost of each sale until another purchase is made and a new average is computed.

To illustrate, Exhibit 4 shows use of the moving weighted average cost method under a perpetual inventory system. The journal entries and the subsidiary ledger system for Item 127B are shown in Exhibit 4 as follows:

1. The beginning balance on January 1 is $2,000 (100 units at a cost of $20), and the average cost per unit is $20.

2. On January 4, 70 units were sold at a price of $30 each for sales of $2,100 (70 units × $30). The cost of goods sold is $1,400 (70 units at an average unit cost of $20). In this case, the COGS is the same as under the FIFO method. After the sale, $600 of inventory remains ($2,000 − $1,400). This is not calculated by multiplying 30 units by $20. Instead, it is the $2,000 − $1,400 as shown by the different titles of this table compared to the FIFO table. Again this cost is the same as under the FIFO method.

3. On January 10, $1,680 of goods are purchased (80 units at a unit cost of $21). After the purchase, the inventory is reported on one line instead of the two lines in the FIFO method. The total cost is calculated at $2,280 ($600 from the items remaining after the sale plus $1,680 from the purchase), and the total number of units is calculated at 110 (30 from the balance remaining after the sale and 80 new items). The $2,280 is then divided by the 110 to give an average unit cost of 20.727272. This amount is then rounded up to $20.73. The $20.73 is used to calculate cost of goods sold and then subtraction is used to calculate the remaining inventory.

4. On January 22, 40 units are sold at a price of $30 each for sales of $1,200 (40 units × $30). Using the average cost method, the cost of goods sold of $829.20 consists of the 40 units multiplied by the average price of $20.73. After the sale, $1,450.80 of inventory remains ($2,280.00 − $829.20).

5. The January 28 sale with a sale price of $30, and January 30 purchase are recorded in a similar manner.

6. The ending balance for inventory on January 31 is $3,236.20 ($1,036.20 + $2,200.00).

Exhibit 4

Entries and Perpetual Inventory Account (Moving Weighted Average Cost)

Jan. 4 Accounts Receivable	2,100.00
Sales	2,100.00
4 Cost of Goods Sold	1,400.00
Inventory	1,400.00

10 Inventory	1,680.00
Accounts Payable	1,680.00

22 Accounts Receivable	1,200.00
Sales	1,200.00
22 Cost of Goods Sold	829.20
Inventory	829.20

28 Accounts Receivable	600.00
Sales	600.00
28 Cost of Goods Sold	414.60
Inventory	414.60

30 Inventory	2,200.00
Accounts Payable	2,200.00

Item 127B

	Purchases			Cost of Goods Sold			Inventory		
Date	Quantity	Unit Cost	Total Cost	Quantity	Unit Cost	Total Cost	Quantity	Total Cost	New Average Unit Cost
Jan. 1							100	2,000.00	20.00
4				70	20.00	1,400.00	30	600.00	20.00
10	80	21.00	1,680.00				110	2,280.00	20.73*
22				40	20.73	829.20	70	1,450.80	20.73
28				20	20.73	414.60	50	1,036.20	20.72**
30	100	22.00	2,200.00				150	3,236.20	21.57†
31	Balances					2,643.80		3,236.20	

Cost of goods sold ⟶ 2,643.80

January 31 inventory ⟶ 3,236.20

$$*\frac{(\$600.00 + \$1,680.00)}{(30 + 80)} = \$20.727272 = \$20.73$$

$$**\frac{(\$1,450.80 - \$414.60)}{70 - 20} = \$20.72$$

$$†\frac{(\$1,036.20 + \$2,200.00)}{50 + 100} = \$21.5746$$

EXAMPLE EXERCISE 6-4 Perpetual Inventory Using Average Cost   ③

Beginning inventory, purchases, and sales for Item ER27 are as follows:

Nov.	1	Inventory	40 units at $5.00
	5	Purchase	10 units at $4.50
	8	Sale	32 units
	11	Purchase	60 units at $7.00
	21	Sale	45 units

Assuming a perpetual inventory system and using the moving weighted average cost method, determine (a) the cost of the goods sold on November 21 and (b) the inventory on November 30.

FOLLOW MY EXAMPLE 6-4

a. Cost of goods sold (November 21) is $293.40.

b. Inventory on November 30 is $214.80.

	Purchases			Cost of Goods Sold			Inventory		
Date	Quantity	Unit Cost	Total Cost	Quantity	Unit Cost	Total Cost	Quantity	Total Cost	New Average Unit Cost
Nov. 1							40	200.00	5.00
5	10	4.50	45.00				50	245.00	4.90*
8				32	4.90	156.80	18	88.20	4.90**
11	60	7.00	420.00				78	508.20	6.52†
21				45	6.52	293.40	33	214.80	6.51‡
30	Balances					450.20		214.80	

$$*4.90 = 245.00 \div 50$$
$$**4.90 = 88.20 \div 18$$
$$†6.52 = 508.20 \div 78$$
$$‡6.51 = 214.80 \div 33$$

For Practice: PE 6-4

Computerized Perpetual Inventory Systems

A perpetual inventory system may be used in a manual accounting system. However, if a business has many inventory transactions, such a system is costly and time consuming. In most cases, perpetual inventory systems are computerized. Walmart, Canadian Tire, and other retailers use bar code scanners as part of their perpetual inventory systems.

A computerized perpetual inventory system for a retail store could be used as follows:

1. Each inventory item, including description, quantity, and unit size, is stored electronically in an inventory file. The total of the file equals the balance of Inventory in the general ledger.

2. Each time an item is purchased or returned by a customer, the inventory file is updated by scanning the item's bar code.

3. Each time an item is sold, the item's bar code is scanned at the cash register, and the inventory files are updated.

4. After a physical inventory is taken, the inventory count data are used to update the inventory file. A listing of inventory overages and shortages is printed, and any unusual amounts are investigated.

Computerized perpetual inventory systems are useful to managers in controlling and managing inventory. For example, fast-selling items can be reordered before the stock runs out. Sales patterns can also be analyzed to determine when to mark down merchandise or when to restock seasonal merchandise. Finally, inventory data can be used in evaluating advertising campaigns and sales promotions.

INTEGRITY, OBJECTIVITY, AND ETHICS IN BUSINESS

LIQUID INVENTORY SHRINKAGE

A bartender offering a free drink to a friend seems like a fairly innocent event, but it is actually theft. Offering a free drink is one of the behaviours that costs companies as much as 30% of gross sales. Liquid inventory theft, or shrinkage, can result from the outright theft of bottles of alcohol or pouring a drink for a customer and pocketing the cash. More likely, the shrinkage results from overpouring customers so that they will tip a higher amount or pouring extra drinks for friends. With alcohol and beer sales in Canada of $14.5 billion annually, this shrinkage represents a large dollar amount and can make the difference between a restaurant or bar being profitable or not.

 ## Comparing Inventory Costing Methods

Compare and contrast two of the inventory costing methods.

A different cost flow is assumed for the FIFO and average inventory cost flow methods. As a result, the methods normally yield different amounts for the following:

1. Cost of goods sold
2. Gross profit
3. Net income
4. Ending inventory

Using the perpetual inventory system illustration above, with sales of $3,900 (130 units × $30), these differences are illustrated below.

Partial Income Statements

	First-In, First-Out	Average Cost
Sales	$3,900.00	$3,900.00
COGS	$2,630.00	2,643.80
Gross profit	$1,270.00	$1,256.20

The preceding difference shows the effect of increasing costs. If costs remain the same, the two methods yield the same results. However, costs normally do change.

FIFO reports higher gross profit and net income than the average method when costs are increasing. However, in periods of rapidly rising costs, the inventory that is sold must be replaced at increasingly higher costs. In such cases, the larger FIFO gross profit and net income are sometimes called *inventory profits* or *illusory profits*.

When using the average cost method, the effect of cost trends is averaged to determine the cost of goods sold and the ending inventory. For a series of purchases, the average cost will be the same, regardless of whether costs are increasing or decreasing.

Unlike FIFO, increases or decreases in prices do not result in the reporting of a higher cost of goods sold or inventory under the average cost method. In the average cost method, the effects of price increases or decreases are averaged between both accounts.

CRITICAL THINKING

How does an accountant choose between accounting options such as FIFO and average inventory cost flow methods?

An accountant needs to be mindful of the accounting principles and concepts such as representational faithfulness and comparability. As accountants, we want the financial statements to reflect the economic reality of the business. If FIFO represents the actual pattern of sales for the inventory that is being sold, then the use of FIFO is representationally faithful. For a grocery store, FIFO may better reflect the pattern of sales for most of the inventory. Because other grocery stores are also likely to use the FIFO method to record their inventory, the comparability principle is also met.

MID-CHAPTER ILLUSTRATIVE PROBLEM

Bob's Bicycles sells specialized bikes with many different options on each bike. Each one is unique in its features. It is a one-person shop, and Robert, the owner, does not have a computerized inventory system.
a. What method of inventory costing does he likely use?
b. In addition to selling these unique bikes, Robert sells a line of bikes that are identical. Which costing method does he likely use for these bikes?
c. If he did have a computerized inventory system and cash register, what kind of inventory costing method would he likely use?

MID-CHAPTER ILLUSTRATIVE SOLUTION

a. Robert likely uses specific identification. This costing method is used when each item is unique and the costs related to that item can be identified and allocated to it. He also likely keeps track using a perpetual method because he has few enough sales that he can keep track of them as they occur. This method is a manual perpetual method with specific identification.
b. Robert likely uses either the average cost or FIFO method for these bikes because they are identical. The average cost of the bikes can be interpreted as representing the flow of goods. An argument can also be made for first in, first out. Given that both these methods are possible, he might choose a method on the basis of other factors.
c. He is still likely to use the specific identification costing method for the unique bikes. The issue of whether Robert uses one method over another is not related to whether he is computerized. The choice of an inventory costing method is based on the product type and whether it is unique or whether each inventory item is identical.

Reporting Inventory in the Financial Statements

Cost is the primary basis for valuing and reporting inventories in the financial statements. However, inventory may be valued at other than cost in the following cases:

1. The cost of the inventories cannot be recovered. This can occur because they are damaged, have become obsolete, or the selling prices have declined.
2. The costs of selling the inventories has increased.[3]

Valuation at Lower of Cost and Net Realizable Value

In either case above, the **net realizable value** of the inventory is used. Net realizable value is determined as follows:

Net Realizable Value = Estimated Selling Price − Direct Costs of Disposal

Direct costs of disposal include selling expenses, such as special advertising or sales commissions on sales. To illustrate, assume the following data about an item of damaged merchandise:

Original cost	$1,000
Estimated selling price	800
Selling expense	150

The merchandise should be valued at its net realizable value of $650, as shown below.

Net Realizable Value = $800 − $150 = $650

This valuation is usually applied on an item-by-item basis. The valuation may be made by similar groups or related items. In both ASPE and IFRS, the net realizable value of the inventory is assessed at the end of the year. If the inventory has increased in value, the items can be written up to their original costs.[4]

The amount of any price decline is included in the cost of goods sold. This amount, in turn, reduces gross profit and net income either in the period in which the price declines occur or when the obsolescence is identified.

Exhibit 5 illustrates applying the lower of cost and net realizable value to each inventory item (A, B, C, and D). As applied on an item-by-item basis, the total lower of cost and net realizable value is $14,330, a decline of $1,190, which is the amount that would be debited to COGS. The journal entry follows:

Cost of Goods Sold	1,190	
Inventory		1,190
To reduce inventory to NRV.		

Computer equipment and cellphones are inventory items that may suffer from technological obsolescence, thereby requiring them to be written down.

3 *CICA Handbook—Accounting*, 2013 Edition, Part I, IAS 2.28, 2012 Edition, Part II, 3031.27.

4 *CICA Handbook—Accounting*, 2013 Edition, Part I, IAS 2.33, 2012 Edition, Part II, 3031.32.

Determining Inventory by the Lower of Cost and NRV

	A	B	C	D	E	F	G	H
1			Unit	Unit	Direct		Total	
2		Inventory	Cost	Selling	Selling			Lower
3	Item	Quantity	Price	Price	Costs	Cost*	NRV**	of Cost and NRV
4	A	400	$10.25	$ 9.50	$500	$ 4,100	$ 3,300	$ 3,300
5	B	120	22.50	24.10	0	2,700	2,892	2,700
6	C	600	8.00	7.75	0	4,800	4,650	4,650
7	D	280	14.00	14.75	450	3,920	3,680	3,680
8	Total					$15,520		$14,330
9								

* Column F = Column B x Column C.

** Column G = (Column B x Column D) – Column E.

EXAMPLE EXERCISE 6-5 **Lower of Cost and Net Realizable Value**   **5**

Using the following data, determine the value of the inventory at the lower of cost and net realizable value (NRV). Apply lower of cost and NRV to each inventory item as shown in Exhibit 5.

Item	Inventory Quantity	Unit Cost Price	Unit Selling Price	Direct Selling Costs
C17Y	10	$ 39	$ 40	$ 300
B563	7	110	98	250

Record the journal entry to adjust the inventory.

FOLLOW MY EXAMPLE 6-5

	A	B	C	D	E	F	G	H
1							Total	
2			Unit	Unit	Direct			Lower
3		Inventory	Cost	Selling	Selling			of Cost
4	Item	Quantity	Price	Price	Costs	Cost*	NRV**	and NRV
5	C17Y	10	$ 39	$ 40	$ 300	$ 390	$ 100	$ 100
6	B563	7	110	98	250	770	436	436
7	Total					$1,160		$ 536
8								
9								
10								

* Column F = Column B x Column C.

** Column G = (Column B x Column D) – Column E.

Cost of Goods Sold	624	
Inventory		624
$1,160 – $536		

For Practice: PE 6-5

CRITICAL THINKING

If you paid $50,000 for a shipment of iPads, would you ever record it in your books at $40,000?

Yes, it is possible. Assume, for example, another manufacturer creates a product with more capabilities than the iPad and offers it for a lower retail price. If this event lowers the retail price of the iPad, then all iPads in stock would need to be recorded at the lower of cost and net realizable value. Such a transaction occurred at Dell Inc., a manufacturer of computers. Dell Inc. lowered the value of its notebook computer inventory by $39.3 million.

Inventory on the Balance Sheet

Inventory is usually reported in the Current Assets section of the balance sheet.

Both ASPE and IFRS require that the method of determining the cost of the inventory (specific identification, FIFO, or weighted average cost) be disclosed in the notes to the financial statements.

In addition, IFRS requires the following:

1. The method of valuing inventories (cost or the lower of cost and NRV) and the value of inventories.
2. The amount of any write-down or reversal of write-down recognized in the period.
3. The amount of inventories pledged as security.[5]

The financial statement reporting for the topics covered in Chapters 6 to 15 are illustrated using excerpts from the financial statements of Morning Java. Morning Java is a fictitious company that offers drip and espresso coffee in a coffeehouse setting. The complete financial statements of Morning Java are illustrated in Appendix A.

The balance sheet presentation for inventory for Morning Java is as follows:

Morning Java
Balance Sheet
December 31, 2015

Current assets:		
Cash and cash equivalents		$235,000
Trading investments (at fair value)		465,000
Accounts receivable	$305,000	
Less allowance for doubtful accounts	12,300	292,700
Inventory		120,000

In Morning Java's financial statements, the notes would indicate that the inventory was reported using the first-in, first-out method.

It is not unusual for a large business to use different costing methods for segments of its inventories. Also, a business may change its inventory costing method. In such cases, the effect of the change and the reason for the change are disclosed in the financial statements.

Cost of Goods Sold on the Income Statement

Cost of goods sold, or Cost of sales, is reported as a line item in the income statement of private companies. Accounting Standards for Private Enterprises (ASPE) requires this line item for "inventories recognized as an expense." For companies that choose to use IFRS, this method of disclosing information is offered as an alternative. These companies can choose to exclude the line Cost of goods sold or Cost of sales.[6]

The income statement presentation for cost of goods sold for Morning Java is as follows:

---

5 *CICA Handbook—Accounting;* 2013 Edition, Part I, IAS 2.36, 2012 Edition, Part II, 3031.35

6 *CICA Handbook—Accounting;* 2013 Edition; Part I, IAS 1.99–103; 2012 Edition, Part II 1520.04 (o).

Morning Java Income Statement For the Year Ended December 31, 2015			
Revenue from sales:			
Sales		$5,450,000	
Less: Sales returns and allowances	$26,500		
Sales discounts	21,400	47,900	
Net sales			$5,402,100
Cost of goods sold			2,160,000
Gross profit			3,242,100
Operating expenses:			
Selling expenses:			

Effect of Inventory Errors on the Financial Statements

Any errors in inventory will affect the balance sheet and income statement. Inventory errors may occur for the following reasons:

1. Physical inventory on hand was miscounted.
2. Costs were incorrectly assigned to inventory. For example, the FIFO or average cost method was incorrectly applied.
3. Inventory in transit was incorrectly included or excluded from inventory.
4. Consigned inventory was incorrectly included or excluded from inventory.

Inventory errors often arise from merchandise that is in transit at year-end. As discussed earlier in this chapter and in Chapter 5, shipping terms determine when the title to merchandise passes. When goods are purchased or sold *FOB shipping point*, title passes to the buyer when the goods are shipped. When the terms are *FOB destination*, title passes to the buyer when the goods are received.

To illustrate, assume that SysExpress ordered the following merchandise from Canadian Products:

Date ordered:	December 27, 2014
Amount:	$10,000
Terms:	FOB shipping point, 2/10, n/30
Date shipped by seller:	December 30
Date delivered:	January 3, 2015

When SysExpress counts its physical inventory on December 31, 2014, the merchandise is still in transit. In such cases, it would be easy for SysExpress to not include the $10,000 of merchandise in its December 31 physical inventory. However, because the merchandise was purchased *FOB shipping point*, SysExpress owns the merchandise. Thus, it should be included in the ending December 31 inventory even though it is not on hand. Likewise, any merchandise *sold* by SysExpress *FOB destination* is still SysExpress's inventory even if it is in transit to the buyer on December 31.

Inventory errors often arise from consigned inventory. As mentioned earlier in this chapter, manufacturers sometimes ship merchandise to retailers who act as the manufacturer's selling agent. The manufacturer, called the **consignor**, retains title until the goods are sold. Such merchandise is said to be shipped *on consignment* to the retailer, called the **consignee**. Any unsold merchandise at year-end is a part of the manufacturer's (consignor's) inventory, even though the merchandise is in the hands of the retailer (consignee). At year-end, it is easy for the retailer (consignee) to incorrectly include the consigned merchandise in its physical inventory. Likewise, the manufacturer (consignor) should include consigned inventory in its physical inventory even though the inventory is not on hand.

Exhibit 6

Effect of Inventory Errors on Current Period's Income Statement

	Income Statement Effect		
Inventory Error	**Cost of Goods Sold**	**Gross Profit**	**Net Income**
Beginning inventory is:			
Understated	*Understated*	*Overstated*	*Overstated*
Overstated	*Overstated*	*Understated*	*Understated*
Ending inventory is:			
Understated	*Overstated*	*Understated*	*Understated*
Overstated	*Understated*	*Overstated*	*Overstated*

Income Statement Effects Inventory errors misstate the income statement amounts for cost of goods sold, gross profit, and net income. The effects of inventory errors on the current period's income statement are summarized in Exhibit 6.

To illustrate, we use the income statements of SysExpress shown in Exhibit 7.[7]

On December 31, 2014, assume that SysExpress incorrectly records its physical inventory as $50,000 instead of the correct amount of $60,000. Thus, the December 31, 2014, inventory is understated by $10,000 ($60,000 − $50,000). As a result, the cost of goods sold is overstated by $10,000. The gross profit and the net income for the year will both be understated by $10,000.

Exhibit 7

Effects of Inventory Errors on Two Years' Income Statements

SysExpress
Income Statement
For the Years Ended December 31, 2014 and 2015

	2014		2015	
	Correct	**Incorrect**	**Incorrect**	**Correct**
Net sales		$980,000	$980,000	$1,100,000	$1,100,000
Inventory, January 1	$ 55,000	$ 55,000	$ 50,000	$ 60,000
Purchases	650,000	650,000	700,000	700,000
Goods available for sale	705,000	705,000	750,000	760,000
Less inventory, December 31	60,000	50,000	70,000	70,000
Cost of goods sold		645,000	655,000	680,000	690,000
Gross profit		335,000	325,000	420,000	410,000
Operating expenses		100,000	100,000	120,000	120,000
Net income		$235,000	$225,000	$ 300,000	$ 290,000

$10,000
Understatement
of Net Income

$10,000
Overstatement
of Net Income

Net Effect Is Zero for Two Years
The inventory errors reverse (or cancel) so that the combined net income for the two years of $525,000 ($225,000 + $300,000) is correct.

7 We illustrate the effect of inventory errors using the periodic system. This system makes it easier to see the impact of inventory errors on the income statement. The effect of inventory errors would be the same under the perpetual inventory system.

Exhibit 8

Effect of Inventory Errors on Current Period's Balance Sheet

	Balance Sheet Effect			
Ending Inventory Error	Inventory	Current Assets	Total Assets	Owner's Equity (Capital)
Understated	Understated	Understated	Understated	Understated
Overstated	Overstated	Overstated	Overstated	Overstated

The December 31, 2014, ending inventory becomes the January 1, 2015, beginning inventory. Thus, the beginning inventory for 2015 is understated by $10,000. As a result, the cost of goods sold is understated by $10,000 for 2015. The gross profit and net income for 2015 will be overstated by $10,000.

As shown in Exhibit 7, because the ending inventory of one period is the beginning inventory of the next period, the effects of inventory errors carry forward to the next period. Specifically, if uncorrected, the effects of inventory errors reverse themselves in the next period. In Exhibit 7, the combined net income for the two years of $525,000 is correct even though the 2014 and 2015 income statements were incorrect.

Balance Sheet Effects Inventory errors misstate the inventory, current assets, total assets, and owner's equity on the balance sheet. The effects of inventory errors on the current period's balance sheet are summarized in Exhibit 8.

For the SysExpress illustration shown in Exhibit 7, the December 31, 2014, ending inventory was understated by $10,000. As a result, the inventory, current assets, and total assets are understated by $10,000 on the December 31, 2014, balance sheet. Because the ending physical inventory is understated, the cost of goods sold for 2014 is overstated by $10,000. Thus, the gross profit and the net income for 2014 are understated by $10,000. Because the net income is closed to owner's equity (capital) at the end of the period, the owner's equity on the December 31, 2014, balance sheet is also understated by $10,000.

As discussed above, inventory errors reverse themselves the following year. As a result, the balance sheet will be correct as at December 31, 2015. Using the SysExpress illustration from Exhibit 7, these effects are summarized below.

	Amount of Misstatement	
Balance Sheet:	December 31, 2014	December 31, 2015
Inventory overstated (understated)	$(10,000)	Correct
Current assets overstated (understated)	(10,000)	Correct
Total assets overstated (understated)	(10,000)	Correct
Owner's equity overstated (understated)	(10,000)	Correct
Income Statement:	2014	2015
Cost of goods sold overstated (understated)	$ 10,000	$(10,000)
Gross profit overstated (understated)	(10,000)	10,000
Net income overstated (understated)	(10,000)	10,000

EXAMPLE EXERCISE 6-6 Effect of Inventory Errors   (5)

Zula Repair Shop incorrectly counted its December 31, 2015, inventory as $250,000 instead of the correct amount of $220,000. Indicate the effect of the misstatement on Zula's December 31, 2015, balance sheet and income statement for the year ended December 31, 2015.

(continued)

FOLLOW MY EXAMPLE 6-6

	Amount of Misstatement Overstatement (Understatement)
Balance Sheet:	
Inventory overstated	$ 30,000
Current assets overstated	30,000
Total assets overstated	30,000
Owner's equity overstated	30,000
Income Statement:	
Cost of goods sold understated	$(30,000)
Gross profit overstated	30,000
Net income overstated	30,000

For Practice: PE 6-6

FINANCIAL ANALYSIS AND INTERPRETATION

A merchandising business should keep enough inventory on hand to meet the needs of its customers. A failure to do so may result in lost sales. At the same time, too much inventory ties up funds that could be used to improve operations. In addition, excess inventory increases expenses such as storage, insurance, and property taxes. Finally, excess inventory increases the risk of losses due to price declines, damage, or changes in customers' tastes.

Two measures to analyze the efficiency and effectiveness of inventory are the inventory turnover and the days' sales in inventory.

Inventory turnover measures the relationship between cost of goods sold and the amount of inventory carried during the period. It is computed as follows:

$$\text{Inventory Turnover} = \frac{\text{Cost of Goods Sold}}{\text{Average Inventory}}$$

To illustrate, the following data (in thousands) have been taken from annual reports for SUPERVALU Inc. and Zale Corporation:

	SUPERVALU	Zale
Cost of goods sold	$29,267,000	$1,194,399
Inventories:		
Beginning of year	$ 954,200	$ 903,294
End of year	$ 2,749,000	$1,021,164
Average	$ 1,851,600	$ 962,229
Inventory turnover	15.8	1.2

The inventory turnover is 15.8 for SUPERVALU and 1.2 for Zale. Generally, the larger the inventory turnover, the more efficient and effective the management of inventory. However, differences in companies and industries may be too great to allow specific statements as to what is a good inventory turnover. For example,

SUPERVALU is a leading food distributor in the United States. Because SUPERVALU's inventory is perishable, we would expect it to have a high inventory turnover. In contrast, Zale Corporation is a large retailer of fine jewellery in the United States and owns both Peoples Jewellers and Mappins Jewellers in Canada. Thus, we would expect Zale to have a lower inventory turnover than SUPERVALU.

The **days' sales in inventory** is a rough measure of the time it takes to acquire, sell, and replace the inventory. It is computed as follows:

Days' Sales in Inventory

$$= \frac{\text{Average Inventory}}{\text{Average Daily Cost of Goods Sold}}$$

The average daily cost of goods sold is determined by dividing the cost of goods sold by 365. Days' sales in inventory for SUPERVALU and Zale is computed as shown below.

	SUPERVALU	Zale
Average daily cost of goods sold:		
$29,267,000/365	$ 80,184	
$1,194,399/365		$ 3,272
Average inventory	$1,851,600	$962,229
Days' sales in inventory	23.1 days	294.1 days

Generally, the lower the days' sales in inventory, the better. As with inventory turnover, we should expect differences among industries, such as those for SUPERVALU and Zale.

Appendix D includes the inventory turnover and days' sales in inventory ratios.

EXAMPLE EXERCISE 6-7 Inventory Turnover ⑤

The following data were taken from the annual report of Kayi's Inc.

Cost of goods sold	$178,000
Inventory at end of year	30,000
Inventory at start of year	50,000

a. Determine the inventory turnover for Kayi's Inc.

b. Kayi's competitor, Gary and Goal Inc., has a turnover of 5. Which company is more efficient?

FOLLOW MY EXAMPLE 6-7

a. $\dfrac{178,000}{(30,000 + 50,000)/2} = 4.45$

b. Gary and Goal Inc. has a higher turnover rate, which indicates that it is the more efficient company.

For Practice: PE 6-7

A P P E N D I X 1

Estimating Inventory Cost

A business may need to estimate the amount of inventory for the following reasons:

1. Perpetual inventory records are not maintained.
2. A disaster such as a fire or flood has destroyed the inventory records and the inventory.
3. Monthly or quarterly financial statements are needed, but a physical inventory is taken only once a year.

This appendix describes and illustrates two widely used methods of estimating inventory cost. The retail method is accepted by ASPE and IFRS if the results approximate cost.[8]

Retail Method of Inventory Costing

The **retail inventory method** of estimating inventory cost requires costs and retail prices to be maintained for the goods available for sale. A ratio of cost to retail price is then used to convert ending inventory at retail to estimate the ending inventory cost.

The retail inventory method is applied as follows:

Step 1. Determine the total goods available for sale at cost and retail.
Step 2. Determine the ratio of the cost to retail price of the goods available for sale.
Step 3. Determine the ending inventory at retail by deducting the net sales from the goods available for sale at retail.
Step 4. Estimate the ending inventory cost by multiplying the ending inventory at retail by the cost-to-retail ratio.

Exhibit 9 illustrates the retail inventory method.

When estimating the cost-to-retail ratio, the mix of items in the ending inventory is assumed to be the same as the goods available for sale. If the ending inventory is

---

8 *CICA Handbook—Accounting*, 2013 Edition, Part I, IAS 2.21 and .22, 2012 Edition, Part II, 3031.20 and .21.

Exhibit 9

Determining Inventory by the Retail Method

	A	B	C
		Cost	**Retail**
1			
2	Inventory, January 1	$ 19,400	$ 36,000
3	Purchases in January (net)	42,600	64,000
Step 1 → 4	Goods available for sale	$ 62,000	100,000
Step 2 → 5	Ratio of cost to retail price: $\dfrac{\$62,000}{\$100,000} = 62\%$		
6	Sales for January (net)		70,000
Step 3 → 7	Inventory, January 31, at retail		$ 30,000
Step 4 → 8	Inventory, January 31, at estimated cost		
9	($30,000 × 62%)	$ 18,600	
10			

made up of different classes of merchandise, cost-to-retail ratios may be developed for each class of inventory.

An advantage of the retail method is that it provides inventory figures for preparing monthly statements. Department stores and similar retailers often determine gross profit and operating income each month but may take a physical inventory only once or twice a year. Thus, the retail method allows management to monitor operations more closely.

The retail method may also be used as an aid in taking a physical inventory. In this case, the items are counted and recorded at their retail (selling) prices instead of their costs. The physical inventory at retail is then converted to cost by using the cost-to-retail ratio.

Gross Profit Method of Inventory Costing

The **gross profit method** uses the estimated gross profit for the period to estimate the inventory at the end of the period. The gross profit is estimated from the preceding year, adjusted for any current-period changes in the cost and sales prices.

The gross profit method is applied as follows:

Step 1. Determine the goods available for sale at cost.
Step 2. Determine the estimated gross profit by multiplying the net sales by the gross profit percentage.
Step 3. Determine the estimated cost of goods sold by deducting the estimated gross profit from the net sales.
Step 4. Estimate the ending inventory cost by deducting the estimated cost of goods sold from the goods available for sale.

Exhibit 10 illustrates the gross profit method.

The gross profit method is useful for estimating inventories for monthly or quarterly financial statements. It is also useful in estimating the cost of goods destroyed by fire or other disasters.

Exhibit 10

Estimating Inventory by Gross Profit Method

	A	B	C
			Cost
1			
2	Inventory, January 1		$ 57,000
3	Purchases in January (net)		180,000
Step 1 → 4	Goods available for sale		237,000
5	Sales for January (net)	$250,000	
Step 2 → 6	Less estimated gross profit ($250,000 × 30%)	75,000	
Step 3 → 7	Estimated cost of goods sold		175,000
Step 4 → 8	Estimated inventory, January 31		$ 62,000
9			

A P P E N D I X 2

Inventory Costing Methods under a Periodic Inventory System

When the periodic inventory system is used, only revenue is recorded each time a sale is made. No entry is made at the time of the sale to record the cost of the goods sold. At the end of the accounting period, a physical inventory is taken to determine the cost of the inventory and the cost of the goods sold.[9]

Like the perpetual inventory system, a cost flow assumption must be made when identical units are acquired at different unit costs during a period. In such cases, either the FIFO or weighted average cost method is used.

First-In, First-Out Method

To illustrate the use of the FIFO method in a periodic inventory system, we use the same data for Item 127B as in the perpetual inventory example in the body of this chapter on page 309. The beginning inventory entry and purchases of Item 127B in January are as follows:

Jan. 1	Inventory	100 units at	$20	$2,000
10	Purchase	80 units at	21	1,680
30	Purchase	100 units at	22	2,200
Available for sale during month		280		$5,880

The physical count on January 31 shows that 150 units are on hand. Using the FIFO method, the cost of the goods on hand at the end of the period is made up of the most recent costs. The cost of the 150 units in ending inventory on January 31 is determined as follows:

Most recent costs, January 30 purchase	100 units at	$22	$2,200
Next most recent costs, January 10 purchase	50 units at	$21	1,050
Inventory, January 31	150 units		$3,250

Deducting the cost of the January 31 inventory of $3,250 from the cost of goods available for sale of $5,880 yields the cost of goods sold of $2,630, as shown below.

Beginning inventory, January 1	$2,000
Purchases ($1,680 + $2,200)	3,880
Cost of goods available for sale in January	5,880
Less ending inventory, January 31	3,250
Cost of goods sold	$2,630

The $3,250 cost of the ending inventory on January 31 is made up of the most recent costs. The $2,630 cost of goods sold is made up of the beginning inventory and the earliest costs. Exhibit 11 shows the relationship of the cost of goods sold for January and the ending inventory on January 31.

Average Cost Method (Weighted Average Cost Method)

The average cost method for a periodic inventory system is sometimes called the **weighted average cost method**. The average cost method uses the average unit cost for determining the cost of goods sold and the ending inventory. If purchases are relatively

---

9 Determining the cost of goods sold using the periodic system was illustrated in Appendix 2 of Chapter 5.

First-In, First-Out Flow of Costs

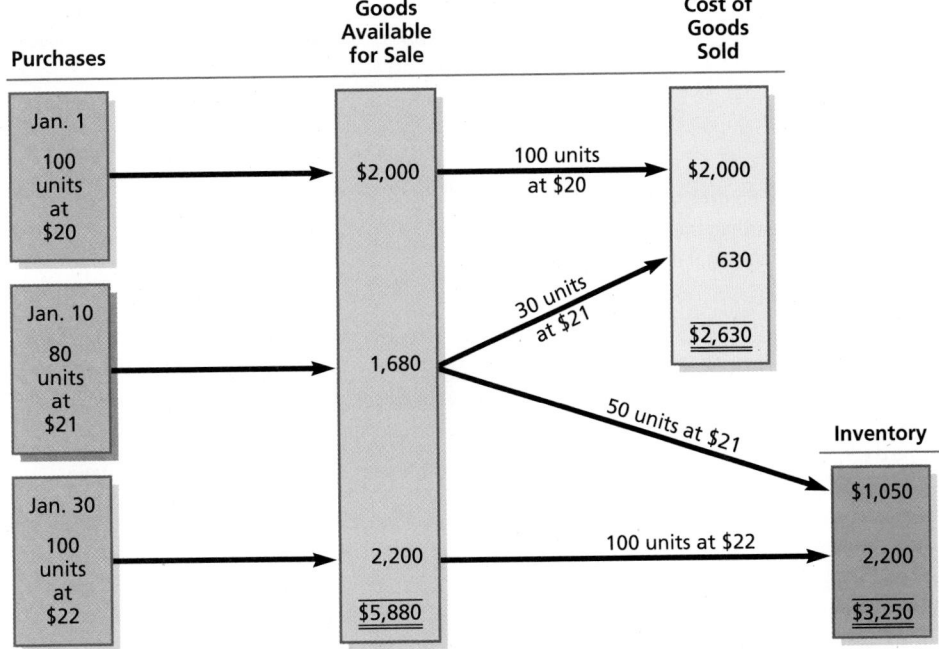

uniform during a period, the average cost method provides results that are similar to the physical flow of goods.

The weighted average unit cost is determined as follows:

$$\text{Average Unit Cost} = \frac{\text{Total Cost of Units Available for Sale}}{\text{Units Available for Sale}}$$

To illustrate, we use the data for Item 127B as follows:

$$\text{Average Unit Cost} = \frac{\text{Total Cost of Units Available for Sale}}{\text{Units Available for Sale}} = \frac{\$5,880}{280 \text{ units}}$$

$$\text{Average Unit Cost} = \$21 \text{ per unit}$$

The cost of the January 31 ending inventory is as follows:

Inventory, January 31: $3,150 (150 units × $21)

Deducting the cost of the January 31 inventory of $3,150 from the cost of goods available for sale of $5,880 yields the cost of goods sold of $2,730, as shown below.

Beginning inventory, January 1	$2,000
Purchases ($1,680 + $2,200)	3,880
Cost of goods available for sale in January	5,880
Less ending inventory, January 31	3,150
Cost of goods sold	$2,730

The cost of goods sold can also be computed by multiplying the number of units sold by the average cost as follows:

Cost of goods sold: $2,730 (130 units × $21)

At a Glance 6

1 Describe the importance of control over inventory.

Key Points	Key Learning Outcomes	Page	Example Exercises
Two primary objectives of control over inventory are safeguarding the inventory and properly reporting it in the financial statements.	• Describe controls for safeguarding inventory.	304	

2 Describe three inventory cost flow methods and their impact on the income statement and balance sheet.

Key Points	Key Learning Outcomes	Page	Example Exercises
The three common inventory cost flow methods used in business are (1) specific identification; (2) the first-in, first-out method (FIFO); and (3) the average cost method.	• Describe specific identification, FIFO, and average cost flow methods.	305	6-1 6-2

3 Determine the cost of inventory under the perpetual inventory system using the FIFO and average cost methods.

Key Points	Key Learning Outcomes	Page	Example Exercises
In a perpetual inventory system, the number of units and the cost of each type of merchandise are recorded in a subsidiary inventory ledger, with a separate account for each type of merchandise.	• Determine the cost of inventory and cost of goods sold using a perpetual inventory system under the FIFO and average cost methods.	309	6-3 6-4

4 Compare and contrast two of the inventory costing methods.

Key Points	Key Learning Outcomes	Page	Example Exercises
The FIFO and average inventory costing methods will normally yield different amounts for (1) the ending inventory, (2) the cost of goods sold for the period, and (3) the gross profit (and net income) for the period.	• Indicate which inventory cost flow method will yield the higher and lower ending inventory and net income during periods of increasing and decreasing prices.	313	

5 Describe and illustrate the reporting of inventory in the financial statements.

Key Points	Key Learning Outcomes	Page	Example Exercises
The lower of cost and net realizable value is used to value inventory. Inventory that is out of date, spoiled, or damaged is valued at its net realizable value.	• Determine inventory using lower of cost and net realizable value (NRV).	315	6-5
	• Describe ASPE and IFRS reporting requirements.	316	6-6
Errors in reporting inventory based on the physical inventory will affect the balance sheet and income statement.	• Determine the effect of inventory errors on the balance sheet and income statement.	318	
	• Calculate inventory turnover.	321	6-7

GLOSSARY

average cost method – The method of inventory costing based on the assumption that costs should be charged against revenue by using the weighted average unit cost of the items sold. (p. 307)

consigned inventory – Merchandise shipped by manufacturers to retailers who act as the manufacturer's selling agent. (p. 307)

consignee – The name for the retailer in a consigned inventory arrangement. (p. 318)

consignor – The name for the manufacturer in a consigned inventory arrangement. (p. 318)

days' sales in inventory – The relationship between the volume of sales and inventory, computed by dividing the inventory at the end of the year by the average daily cost of goods sold. (p. 321)

first-in, first-out (FIFO) inventory cost flow method – The method of inventory costing based on the assumption that the costs of merchandise sold should be charged against revenue in the order in which the costs were incurred. (p. 307)

gross profit method – A method of estimating inventory cost based on the relationship of gross profit to sales. (p. 323)

inventory turnover – The relationship between the cost of goods sold and inventory, computed by dividing the cost of goods sold by the average inventory. (p. 321)

moving weighted average cost method – Application of the average inventory cost flow method when using a perpetual inventory system. (p. 311)

net realizable value – The estimated selling price of an item of inventory less any direct costs of disposal, such as sales commissions. (p. 315)

physical inventory – A detailed listing of merchandise on hand. (p. 305)

purchase order – The purchase order authorizes the purchase of the inventory from an approved vendor. (p. 305)

receiving report – The form or electronic transmission used by the receiving personnel to indicate that materials have been received and inspected. (p. 305)

retail inventory method – A method of estimating inventory cost based on the ratio of cost to retail price. (p. 322)

specific identification inventory cost flow method – Inventory method in which the unit sold is identified with a specific purchase. (p. 306)

subsidiary inventory ledger – The subsidiary ledger containing individual accounts for items of inventory. (p. 305)

vendor's invoice – A document sent by the seller to the purchaser, stating quantity, price, description, and terms of sale. (p. 305)

weighted average cost method – Application of the average inventory cost flow method when using a periodic inventory system. (p. 325)

END-OF-CHAPTER ILLUSTRATIVE PROBLEM

Perpetual inventory using FIFO and weighted average

Periodic inventory using FIFO and average cost

Gross profit inventory method

Stewart Co.'s beginning inventory and purchases during the year ended December 31, 2015, were as follows:

		Units	Unit Cost	Total Cost
January 1	Inventory	1,000	$50.00	$ 50,000
March 10	Purchase	1,200	52.50	63,000
June 25	Sold 800 units			
September 30	Purchase	800	55.00	44,000
December 5	Sold 1,500 units			
Total		3,000		$157,000

Instructions

1. Determine the cost of inventory on December 31, 2015, using the perpetual inventory system and the following inventory costing methods:
   a. first-in, first-out
   b. average cost
2. Appendix 2: Determine the cost of inventory on December 31, 2015, using the periodic inventory system and the following inventory costing methods:
   a. first-in, first-out
   b. average cost
3. Appendix 1: Assume that during the fiscal year ended December 31, 2015, sales were $190,000 and the estimated gross profit rate was 40%. Estimate the ending inventory at December 31, 2015, using the gross profit method.

Solution

1. a. First-in, first-out method: $38,500

Date	Purchases Quantity	Unit Cost	Total Cost	Cost of Goods Sold Quantity	Unit Cost	Total Cost	Inventory Quantity	Unit Cost	Total Cost
2015 Jan. 1							1,000	50.00	50,000
Mar. 10	1,200	52.50	63,000				1,000	50.00	50,000
							1,200	52.50	63,000
Jun. 25				800	50.00	40,000	200	50.00	10,000
							1,200	52.50	63,000
Sep. 30	800	55.00	44,000				200	50.00	10,000
							1,200	52.50	63,000
							800	55.00	44,000
Dec. 5				200	50.00	10,000	700	55.00	38,500
				1,200	52.50	63,000			
				100	55.00	5,500			
31 Balances						118,500			38,500

b. Average cost: $36,877

Date	Purchases Quantity	Unit Cost	Total Cost	Cost of Goods Sold Quantity	Unit Cost	Total Cost	Inventory Quantity	Total Cost	New Average Unit Cost
2015 Jan. 1							1,000	50,000	50.00
Mar. 10	1,200	52.50	63,000				2,200	113,000	51.36
Jun. 25				800	51.36	41,088	1,400	71,912	51.37*
Sep. 30	800	55.00	44,000				2,200	115,912	52.69
Dec. 5				1,500	52.69	79,035	700	36,877	52.68*
31 Balances						120,123		36,877	

*Rounding difference

2. a. First-in, first-out method:
   700 units at $55 = $38,500
   b. Average cost method:
   Average cost per unit: $157,000/3,000 units = $52.33
   Inventory, December 31, 2015:   700 units at $52.33 = $36,631

3. Appendix 1:

Inventory, January 1, 2015	$ 50,000
Purchases (net)	107,000
Goods available for sale	157,000
Sales (net).. $190,000	
Less estimated gross profit ($190,000 3 40%) 76,000	
Estimated cost of goods sold	114,000
Estimated inventory, December 31, 2015.....................	$ 43,000

EYE OPENERS

1. Before inventory purchases are recorded, what documents should the receiving report be reconciled to?
2. What security measures may be used by retailers to protect inventory from customer theft?
3. Which inventory system provides the more effective means of controlling inventories (perpetual or periodic)? Why?
4. Why is it important to periodically take a physical inventory if the perpetual system is used?

5. Does the term *FIFO* refer to techniques used in determining quantities of the various classes of merchandise on hand? Explain.
6. Does the term *first-in* in the FIFO method mean that the items in the inventory are assumed to be the oldest (first) acquisitions? Explain.
7. If inventory is being valued at cost and the price level is decreasing, which method of costing—FIFO or average cost—will yield (a) the higher inventory cost, (b) the lower inventory cost, (c) the higher gross profit, and (d) the lower gross profit?
8. Which method of inventory costing—FIFO or average cost—will, in general, yield an inventory cost nearly approximating the current replacement cost?
9. If inventory is valued at cost and the price level is steadily rising, which method of costing—FIFO or average cost—yields the lower annual income tax expense? Explain.
10. Can a company change its method of costing inventory? Explain.
11. Because of imperfections, an item of merchandise cannot be sold at its normal selling price. How should this item be valued for financial statement purposes?
12. How do companies disclose their method of determining the cost of the inventory and their method of valuing it under ASPE and IFRS?
13. The inventory at the end of the year was understated by $13,500. (a) Did the error cause an overstatement or an understatement of the gross profit for the year? (b) Which items on the balance sheet at the end of the year were overstated or understated as a result of the error (ignore income taxes)?
14. Funtime Co. sold merchandise to Jaffe Company on December 31, FOB shipping point. If the merchandise is in transit on December 31, the end of the fiscal year, which company would report the merchandise in its financial statements? Explain.
15. A manufacturer shipped merchandise to a retailer on a consignment basis. If the merchandise is unsold at the end of the period, in whose inventory should the merchandise be included?

PRACTICE EXERCISES

(2) PE 6-1

Inventory cost flow methods

EE 6-1 p. 307

For each of the following three businesses, which costing method would better reflect the business's economic reality?
a. Art dealer
b. Automobile manufacturer
c. Specialty liquor store

---

(2) PE 6-2

Cost flow methods

EE 6-2 p. 309

Four identical units of Item KL3 are purchased during June, as shown below.

Item KL3		Units	Cost Per Unit	Total Cost
Jun. 3	Purchase	1	$20.00	$ 20.00
10	Purchase	2	35.00	70.00
19	Purchase	1	44.00	44.00
Total		4		$134.00
Average cost per unit			$33.50 ($134 ÷ 4 units)	

Assume that one unit is sold on June 23 for $55.

Determine the gross profit for June and the ending inventory on June 30 using (a) the first-in, first-out (FIFO) method and (b) the average cost method.

---

(3) PE 6-3

Perpetual inventory using FIFO

EE 6-3 p. 311

Beginning inventory, purchases, and sales for Item VX48 are as follows:

Jul. 1	Inventory	100 units at $8
8	Sale	90 units
15	Purchase	125 units at $12
25	Sale	60 units

Assuming a perpetual inventory system and using the first-in, first-out (FIFO) method, determine (a) the cost of goods sold on July 25 and (b) the inventory on July 31.

PE 6-4
③
Perpetual inventory using average cost

Beginning inventory, purchases, and sales for Item CJ10 are as follows:

Apr. 1	Inventory	30 units at $70
8	Sale	18 units
15	Purchase	25 units at $72
24	Sale	15 units

EE 6-4 p. 312

Assuming a perpetual inventory system and using the moving weighted average cost method, determine (a) the cost of goods sold on April 24 and (b) the inventory on April 30.

PE 6-5
⑤
Lower of cost and NRV method

Using the following data, determine the value of the inventory at the lower of cost and net realizable value (NRV). Apply lower of cost and NRV to each inventory item as shown in Exhibit 5.

Item	Inventory Quantity	Unit Cost Price	Unit Market Price	Selling Costs
Red	300	$ 7	$ 6	$ 0
Blue	310	12	14	500

EE 6-5 p. 316

Record the journal entry to adjust the inventory.

PE 6-6
⑤
Effect of inventory errors

During the taking of its physical inventory on December 31, 2015, Euro Bath Company incorrectly counted its inventory as $496,000 instead of the correct amount of $480,000. Indicate the effect of the misstatement on Euro Bath's December 31, 2015, balance sheet and income statement for the year ended December 31, 2015.

EE 6-6 p. 320

PE 6-7
⑤
Inventory turnover

The following data were taken from the annual report of Quinton Inc.

Cost of goods sold	$212,000
Inventory at end of year	25,000
Inventory at start of year	75,000

f·a·i

a. Determine the inventory turnover for Quinton Inc.

EE 6-7 p. 321

b. Quinton's competitor, Ng Inc., has a turnover of 3. Which company is more efficient?

EXERCISES

EX 6-1
①
Control of inventories

Hammer & Nails Hardware Store currently uses a periodic inventory system. Alice Asaki, the owner, is considering the purchase of a computer system that would make it feasible to switch to a perpetual inventory system.

Alice is unhappy with the periodic inventory system because it does not provide timely information on inventory levels. Alice has noticed on several occasions that the store runs out of fast-selling items, whereas too many slow-selling items are on hand.

Alice is also concerned about lost sales while a physical inventory is being taken. Hammer & Nails Hardware currently takes a physical inventory twice a year. To minimize distractions, the store is closed on the day inventory is taken. Alice believes that closing the store is the only way to get an accurate inventory count.

Will switching to a perpetual inventory system strengthen Hammer & Nails Hardware's control over inventory items? Will switching to a perpetual inventory system eliminate the need for a physical inventory count? Explain.

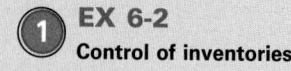

EX 6-2

Control of inventories

Fly Away Luggage Shop is a small retail establishment located in a large shopping mall. This shop has implemented the following procedures regarding inventory items:

a. Whenever Fly Away receives a shipment of new inventory, the items are taken directly to the stockroom. Fly Away's accountant uses the vendor's invoice to record the amount of inventory received.

b. Because the shop carries high-quality, designer luggage, all inventory items are tagged with a control device that activates an alarm if a tagged item is removed from the store.

c. Because the display area of the store is limited, only a sample of each piece of luggage is kept on the selling floor. Whenever a customer selects a piece of luggage, the salesclerk retrieves the appropriate piece from the store's stockroom. Because all salesclerks need access to the stockroom, it is not locked. The stockroom is adjacent to the break room used by all mall employees.

State whether each of these procedures is appropriate or inappropriate. If it is inappropriate, state why.

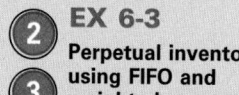

EX 6-3

Perpetual inventory using FIFO and weighted average

✔ a. Inventory balance, April 30, $3,750

Beginning inventory, purchases, and sales data for pillows are as follows:

Apr.	1	Inventory	50 units at $35
	5	Sale	40 units
	14	Purchase	60 units at $36
	21	Sale	35 units
	23	Sale	10 units
	30	Purchase	75 units at $38

a. Assume the business maintains a perpetual inventory system, costing by the first-in, first-out method. Determine the cost of the goods sold for each sale and the inventory balance after each sale, presenting the data in the form illustrated in Exhibit 3, on page 310.

b. The April 30 inventory count is $3,712. Record the journal entry required.

c. Assume the business maintains a perpetual inventory system, costing by the weighted average method. Determine the cost of goods sold for each sale and the inventory balance after each sale, presenting the data in the form illustrated in Exhibit 4, on page 311.

d. The April 30 inventory count is $3,712. Record the journal entry required.

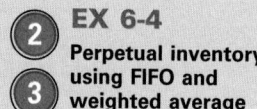

EX 6-4

Perpetual inventory using FIFO and weighted average

✔ a. Inventory balance, June 30, $2,964

Beginning inventory, purchases, and sales data for hammocks are as follows:

Jun.	1	Inventory	15 units at $112
	6	Sale	9 units
	8	Purchase	22 units at $120
	10	Sale	13 units
	20	Sale	12 units
	30	Purchase	21 units at $124

a. Assume the business maintains a perpetual inventory system, costing by the first-in, first-out method. Determine the cost of the goods sold for each sale and the inventory balance after each sale, presenting the data in the form illustrated in Exhibit 3, on page 310.

b. The June 30 inventory count is $2,840. Record the journal entry required.

c. Assume the business maintains a perpetual inventory system, costing by the weighted average method. Determine the cost of goods sold for each sale and the inventory balance after each sale, presenting the data in the form illustrated in Exhibit 4, on page 311.

d. The June 30 inventory count is $2,840. Record the journal entry required.

EX 6-5

2
3

Perpetual inventory using FIFO and weighted average

Beginning inventory, purchases, and sales data for cellphones are as follows:

Inventory		Purchases		Sales	
Mar. 1	1,000 units at $40	Mar. 5	500 units at $42	Mar. 8	700 units
		20	450 units at $44	14	600 units
				31	300 units

✔ a. Inventory balance, March 31, $15,400

a. Assuming that the perpetual inventory system is used, costing by the FIFO method, determine the cost of goods sold for each sale and the inventory balance after each sale, presenting the data in the form illustrated in Exhibit 3, on page 310.

b. Assuming that the perpetual inventory system is used, costing by the weighted average method, determine the cost of goods sold for each sale and the inventory balance after each sale, presenting the data in the form illustrated in Exhibit 4, on page 311.

EX 6-6

2
3

Perpetual inventory using FIFO and weighted average

Beginning inventory, purchases, and sales data for watches are as follows:

Inventory		Purchases		Sales	
May 1	850 units at $112	May 8	320 units at $120	May 10	600 units
		19	98 units at $132	15	405 units
				30	172 units

✔ a. Inventory balance, May 31, $12,012

a. Assuming that a perpetual inventory system is used, costing by the FIFO method, determine the cost of goods sold for each sale and the inventory balance after each sale, presenting the data in the form illustrated in Exhibit 3, on page 310.

b. Assuming that the perpetual inventory system is used, costing by the weighted average method, determine the cost of goods sold for each sale and the inventory balance after each sale, presenting the data in the form illustrated in Exhibit 4, on page 311.

EX 6-7

2
3

Perpetual inventory using FIFO

The following units of a particular item were available for sale during the year:

Beginning inventory	150 units at $75
Sale	120 units at $125
First purchase	400 units at $78
Sale	200 units at $125
Second purchase	300 units at $80
Sale	290 units at $125

✔ $19,200

Assume the firm uses the perpetual inventory system, and 240 units of the item are on hand at the end of the year. What is the total cost of the ending inventory, assuming use of the FIFO costing method?

EX 6-8

4

Comparing inventory methods

Assume that a firm separately determined inventory under FIFO and average cost methods and then compared the results.

1. In each space below, place the correct sign [less than (<), greater than (>), or equal (=)] for each comparison, assuming periods of rising prices.

a. FIFO inventory	_____	average cost inventory
b. FIFO cost of goods sold	_____	average cost COGS
c. FIFO net income	_____	average cost net income
d. FIFO income tax	_____	average cost income tax

2. Why might management prefer to use average cost over FIFO in periods of rising prices?

EX 6-9

Lower of cost and NRV inventory

✔ Lower of cost and NRV $16,440

On the basis of the following data, determine the value of the inventory at the lower of cost and NRV on an individual basis. Assemble the data in the form illustrated in Exhibit 5, on page 315.

Commodity	Inventory Quantity	Unit Cost Price	Unit Market Price	Direct Selling Costs
Aquarius	20	$80	$92	$ 0
Capricorn	50	70	65	250
Leo	8	300	280	0
Scorpio	30	40	30	300
Taurus	100	90	94	0

EX 6-10

Inventory on the balance sheet

Based on the data in Exercise 6-9 and assuming that cost was determined by the FIFO method, show how the inventory would appear on the balance sheet.

EX 6-11

Inventory on the balance sheet

How are inventories presented in the balance sheets of Morning Java (ASPE), Leon's Furniture Limited, and Shoppers Drug Mart Corporation? Check the significant accounting policy notes for any additional information regarding inventories. These statements are found in Appendixes A, B, and C at the end of the textbook.

EX 6-12

Inventory on the income statement

How are inventories presented in the income statements of Morning Java (ASPE), Leon's Furniture Limited, and Shoppers Drug Mart Corporation? Is there additional information provided in the notes to the financial statements for Leon's Furniture and Shoppers Drug Mart. These statements are found in Appendixes A, B, and C at the back of the textbook.

EX 6-13

Effect of errors in physical inventory

White Water Co. sells canoes, kayaks, whitewater rafts, and other boating supplies. During the taking of its physical inventory on December 31, 2015, White Water incorrectly counted its inventory as $315,600 instead of the correct amount of $325,000.

a. State the effect of the error on the December 31, 2015, balance sheet.
b. State the effect of the error on the income statement for the year ended December 31, 2015.
c. State the effect of the error on the 2016 balance sheet and the 2016 income statement.

EX 6-14

Effect of errors in physical inventory

Boss Motorcycle Shop sells motorcycles, ATVs, and other related supplies and accessories. During the taking of its physical inventory on December 31, 2015, Boss Motorcycle Shop incorrectly counted its inventory as $195,750 instead of the correct amount of $188,200.

a. State the effect of the error on the December 31, 2015, balance sheet.
b. State the effect of the error on the income statement for the year ended December 31, 2015.
c. State the effect of the error on the 2016 balance sheet and the 2016 income statement.

EX 6-15

Error in inventory

During 2015, the accountant discovered that the physical inventory at the end of 2014 had been understated by $11,900. Instead of correcting the error, however, the accountant assumed that an $11,900 overstatement of the physical inventory in 2015 would balance out the error.

Are there any flaws in the accountant's assumption? Explain.

Appendix 1

EX 6-16

Retail inventory method

A business uses the retail method of inventory costing for preparation of its quarterly statements. The business determines that its inventory at retail is $950,000. If the ratio of cost to retail price is 66%, what is the amount of inventory to be reported on the financial statements?

Appendix 1
EX 6-17
Retail inventory
method

A business uses the retail method of inventory costing. When preparing its quarterly statements, the business determines that its inventory at retail is $880,000. If the ratio of cost to retail price is 65%, what is the amount of inventory to be reported on the financial statements?

Appendix 1
EX 6-18
Retail inventory
method

A business uses the retail method of inventory costing. When preparing its quarterly statements, the business determines that its inventory at retail is $375,000. If the ratio of cost to retail price is 60%, what is the amount of inventory to be reported on the financial statements?

Appendix 1
EX 6-19
Retail inventory
method

On the basis of the following data, estimate the cost of the inventory at April 30 by the retail method:

		Cost	Retail
Apr. 1	Inventory	$ 180,000	$ 300,000
Apr. 1–30	Purchases (net)	1,200,000	2,000,000
Apr. 1–30	Sales (net)		2,025,000

✔ Inventory,
April 30, $165,000

Appendix 1
EX 6-20
Gross profit method

The inventory was destroyed by fire on October 11. The following data were obtained from the accounting records:

Jan. 1	Inventory	$ 260,000
Jan. 1–Oct. 11	Purchases (net)	1,900,000
	Sales (net)	3,200,000
	Estimated gross profit rate	40%

a. Estimate the cost of the merchandise destroyed.
b. Briefly describe the situations in which the gross profit method is useful.

Appendix 1
EX 6-21
Gross profit method

Based on the following data, estimate the cost of ending inventory:

Sales (net)	$4,800,000
Estimated gross profit rate	40%
Beginning inventory	$ 250,000
Purchases (net)	2,900,000
Goods available for sale	$3,150,000

Appendix 1
EX 6-22
Gross profit method

Based on the following data, estimate the cost of ending inventory:

Sales (net)	$1,500,000
Estimated gross profit rate	38%
Beginning inventory	$ 80,000
Purchases (net)	948,000
Goods available for sale	$1,028,000

Appendix 2
EX 6-23
Periodic inventory
using FIFO and
average cost methods

The units of an item available for sale during the year were as follows:

Jan. 1	Inventory	5 units at $120	$ 600
Feb. 13	Purchase	65 units at $114	7,410
Oct. 30	Purchase	10 units at $119	1,190
	Available for sale	80 units	$9,200

There are 24 units of the item in the physical inventory at December 31. The periodic inventory system is used. Determine the inventory cost using (a) the first-in, first-out method and (b) the average cost method.

Appendix 2
EX 6-24

Periodic inventory by two methods

✔ a. $8,124

The units of an item available for sale during the year were as follows:

Jan. 1	Inventory	27 units at $120
Feb. 17	Purchase	54 units at $138
Jul. 21	Purchase	63 units at $156
Nov. 23	Purchase	36 units at $165

There are 50 units of the item in the physical inventory at December 31. The periodic inventory system is used. Determine the inventory cost by (a) the first-in, first-out method and (b) the average cost method.

Appendix 2
EX 6-25

Periodic inventory by two methods; cost of goods sold

✔ a. Inventory, $2,508

The units of an item available for sale during the year were as follows:

Jan. 1	Inventory	42 units at $60
Mar. 10	Purchase	58 units at $65
Aug. 30	Purchase	20 units at $68
Dec. 12	Purchase	30 units at $70

There are 36 units of the item in the physical inventory at December 31. The periodic inventory system is used. Determine the inventory cost and the cost of goods sold by both FIFO and average cost methods, presenting your answers in the following form:

Inventory Method	Inventory Cost	Cost of Goods Sold
a. First-in, first-out	$	$
b. Average cost		

EX 6-26

Inventory turnover

f·a·i

The following data were taken from annual reports of Apple Computer, Inc., a manufacturer of personal computers and related products, and American Greetings Corporation, a manufacturer and distributor of greeting cards and related products:

	Apple	American Greetings
Cost of goods sold	$13,717,000,000	$826,791,000
Inventory, end of year	270,000,000	187,817,000
Inventory, beginning of year	165,000,000	230,308,000

a. Determine the inventory turnover for Apple and American Greetings. Round to one decimal place.
b. Would you expect American Greetings' inventory turnover to be higher or lower than Apple's? Why?

EX 6-27

Inventory turnover and number of days' sales in inventory

f·a·i

✔ a. Kroger, 33.1 days' sales in inventory

Kroger and Safeway Inc. are grocery chains in the United States. Inventory management is an important aspect of the grocery retail business. Balance sheets for these companies indicated the following inventory information:

	Inventory	
	End of Year (in millions)	Beginning of Year (in millions)
Kroger	$4,609	$4,486
Safeway	2,643	2,766

The cost of goods sold for each company were:

	Cost of Goods Sold (in millions)
Kroger	$50,115
Safeway	28,604

a. Determine the days' sales in inventory and inventory turnover for the companies. Round to the nearest day and one decimal place.
b. Which company has the faster inventory turnover?

PROBLEMS SERIES A

PR 6-1A
FIFO perpetual inventory

✔ 3. $624,000

The beginning inventory of merchandise at Chris Smith Co. and data on purchases and sales for a two-month period are as follows:

Date		Transaction	Number of Units	Per Unit	Total
Mar.	3	Inventory	60	$1,500	$ 90,000
	8	Purchase	120	1,800	216,000
	11	Sale	80	5,000	400,000
	30	Sale	50	5,000	250,000
Apr.	8	Purchase	100	2,000	200,000
	10	Sale	60	5,000	300,000

Instructions

1. Record the inventory, purchases, and cost of goods sold data in a perpetual inventory record similar to the one illustrated in Exhibit 3, on page 310, using the FIFO method.
2. Determine the total sales and the total cost of goods sold for the period. Journalize the entries in the sales and cost of goods sold accounts. Assume that all sales were on account.
3. Determine the gross profit from sales for the period.
4. Determine the ending inventory cost.
5. Record the entry necessary when the inventory count is $175,200 at the end of April.

PR 6-2A
FIFO perpetual inventory

✔ 3. $760,000

The beginning inventory of merchandise at Jackson Co. and data on purchases and sales for a two-month period are as follows:

Date		Transaction	Number of Units	Per Unit	Total
May	5	Inventory	70	$1,300	$ 91,000
	8	Sale	50	4,350	217,500
	16	Sale	10	4,350	43,500
	21	Purchase	150	1,500	225,000
Jun.	3	Sale	90	4,700	423,000
	10	Purchase	40	1,600	64,000
	23	Sale	100	4,400	440,000

Instructions

1. Record the inventory, purchases, and cost of goods sold data in a perpetual inventory record similar to the one illustrated in Exhibit 3, on page 310, using the FIFO method.
2. Determine the total sales and the total cost of goods sold for the period. Journalize the entries in the sales and cost of goods sold accounts. Assume that all sales were on account.
3. Determine the gross profit from sales for the period.
4. Determine the ending inventory cost.
5. Record the entry necessary when the inventory count is $12,600 at the end of June.

PR 6-3 A
FIFO perpetual inventory

✔ 3. $312,000

The beginning inventory of merchandise at Tschabold Co. and data on purchases and sales for a two-month period are as follows:

(continued)

Date	Transaction	Number of Units	Per Unit	Total
May 5	Inventory	60	$1,500	$ 90,000
19	Sale	30	5,000	150,000
28	Purchase	100	2,200	220,000
Jun. 5	Sale	60	5,250	315,000
16	Sale	30	5,250	157,500
21	Purchase	180	2,400	432,000
28	Sale	90	5,250	472,500

Instructions

1. Record the inventory, purchases, and cost of goods sold data in a perpetual inventory record similar to the one illustrated in Exhibit 3, on page 310, using the FIFO method.
2. Determine the total sales and the total cost of goods sold for the period. Journalize the entries in the sales and cost of goods sold accounts. Assume that all sales were on account.
3. Determine the gross profit from sales for the period.
4. Determine the ending inventory cost.
5. Record the entry necessary when the inventory count is $310,000 at the end of June.

PR 6-4A

Moving weighted average perpetual inventory

✔ 2. Gross profit, $615,000

The beginning inventory for Chris Smith Co. and data on purchases and sales for a two-month period are shown in Problem 6-1A. Round the average cost to two decimal places.

Instructions

1. Record the inventory, purchases, and cost of goods sold data in a perpetual inventory record similar to the one illustrated in Exhibit 4, on page 311, using the moving weighted average cost method.
2. Determine the total sales, the total cost of goods sold, and the gross profit from sales for the period.
3. Determine the ending inventory cost.

PR 6-5A

Moving weighted average perpetual inventory

✔ 2. Gross profit, $759,284

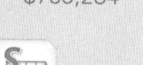

The beginning inventory for Jackson Co. and data on purchases and sales for a two-month period are shown in Problem 6-2A. Round the average cost to two decimal places.

Instructions

1. Record the inventory, purchases, and cost of goods sold data in a perpetual inventory record similar to the one illustrated in Exhibit 4, on page 311, using the moving weighted average cost method.
2. Determine the total sales, the total cost of goods sold, and the gross profit from sales for the period.
3. Determine the ending inventory cost.

PR 6-6A

Moving weighted average perpetual inventory

✔ 2. Gross profit, $656,454.30

The beginning inventory for Tschabold Co. and data on purchases and sales for a two-month period are shown in Problem 6-3A. Round the average cost to two decimal places.

Instructions

1. Record the inventory, purchases, and cost of goods sold data in a perpetual inventory record similar to the one illustrated in Exhibit 4, on page 311, using the moving weighted average cost method.
2. Determine the total sales, the total cost of goods sold, and the gross profit from sales for the period.
3. Determine the ending inventory cost.

5 **PR 6-7A**
Lower of cost and net
realizable value

If the working papers correlating with this textbook are not used, omit Problem 6-7A.
Data on the physical inventory of Winesap Co. as at December 31, 2015, are presented
in the working papers. The quantity of each commodity on hand has been determined
and recorded on the inventory sheet. Unit market prices have also been determined as
at December 31 and recorded on the sheet. The inventory is to be determined at the
lower of cost and net realizable value, using the first-in, first-out method; there are no
selling costs. Quantity and cost data from the last and the next-to-the-last purchases
invoices of the year are summarized as follows:

	Last Purchases Invoice		Next-to-the-Last Purchases Invoice	
Description	Quantity Purchased	Unit Cost	Quantity Purchased	Unit Cost
Alpha 10	30	$ 60	40	$ 59
Beta 30	25	170	15	180
Charlie 4	20	132	15	131
Echo 9	150	25	100	27
Frank 6	6	550	15	540
George 15	90	16	100	15
Killo 6	8	400	4	398
Quebec 12	500	6	500	7
Romeo 7	75	25	80	26
Sierra 3	5	250	4	260
Washbum 2	100	15	115	14
X-Ray 4	10	750	8	740

Instructions

Record the appropriate unit costs on the inventory sheet and complete the pricing of
the inventory. When two different unit costs are applicable to an item:

1. Draw a line through the quantity and insert the quantity and unit cost of the last purchase.
2. On the following line, insert the quantity and unit cost of the next-to-the-last
   purchase.
3. Total the cost and market columns and insert the lower of the two totals in the Lower
   of C and NRV column. The first item on the inventory sheet has been completed
   as an example.

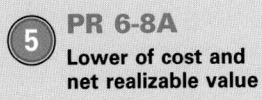 **PR 6-8A**
Lower of cost and
net realizable value

Using the following data regarding clothing inventory, determine the value of the
inventory at the lower of cost and NRV. Complete the calculation on an individual
basis for model numbers 236, 238, and 135 and for the whole of the 333 series.

Model Number	Inventory Quantity	Cost per Unit	Price per Unit	Direct Selling Costs
236	55	$53.21	$99.99	$550
238	82	12.33	9.99	
135	42	24.21	19.99	
333 – a	12	25.00	29.99	60
333 – b	9	30.00	29.99	
333 – c	15	35.00	49.99	

a. At what amount should the inventory be valued?
b. What possible reasons can explain the changes in the price? What are selling costs?
c. Will the company sell the inventory for its value as calculated in (a) above?

Appendix 1
PR 6-9A

Retail method; gross
profit method

Selected data on inventory, purchases, and sales for Hamiota Co. and Miniota Co. are
as follows:

✔ 1. $351,500

(continued)

	Cost	Retail
Hamiota Co.		
Inventory, July 1	$ 300,000	$ 400,000
Transactions during July:		
Purchases (net)	3,400,000	4,600,000
Sales		4,715,000
Sales returns and allowances		190,000
Miniota Co.		
Inventory, February 1	$ 225,000	
Transactions during February and March:		
Purchases (net)	3,200,000	
Sales	5,200,000	
Sales returns and allowances	95,000	
Estimated gross profit rate	38%	

Instructions

1. Determine the estimated cost of the inventory of Hamiota Co. on July 31 by the retail method, presenting details of the computations.
2. a. Estimate the cost of the inventory of Miniota Co. on March 31 by the gross profit method, presenting details of the computations.
   b. Assume that Miniota Co. took a physical inventory on March 31 and discovered that $243,250 of merchandise was on hand. What was the estimated loss of inventory due to theft or damage during February and March?

Appendix 1
PR 6-10A

Retail method; gross profit method

✔ 1. $300,656
✔ 3. $300,758

A clothing store, Space Inc., presents monthly statements with gross profit figures and counts its inventory twice a year.

1. Estimate inventory cost using the retail inventory method, based on the following data (round all dollar figures to one decimal place and percentage figures to one decimal place):

   Net sales for the month of February = $123,000
   Inventory at cost, February 1 = $298,900
   Purchases at cost during month = $70,000
   Inventory at retail, February 1 = $545,700
   Purchases at retail during the month = $120,000

2. Is additional information required to estimate inventory cost using the gross profit method?
3. Estimate inventory cost using the gross profit method.

---

(2) (4)
Appendix 2
PR 6-11A

Periodic inventory by two methods

✔ 1. $8,252

Arctic Appliances uses the periodic inventory system. Details regarding the inventory of appliances at January 1, 2015; purchases invoices during the year; and the inventory count at December 31, 2015, are summarized as follows:

Model	Inventory, January 1	Purchases Invoices			Inventory Count December 31
		1st	2nd	3rd	
BB900	27 at $213	21 at $215	18 at $222	18 at $225	30
C911	10 at 60	6 at 65	2 at 65	2 at 70	4
L100	6 at 305	3 at 310	3 at 316	4 at 317	4

Instructions

1. Determine the cost of the inventory on December 31, 2015, using the first-in, first-out method. Present data in columnar form, using the following headings:

Model	Quantity	Unit Cost	Total Cost

   If the inventory of a particular model comprises one entire purchase plus a portion of another purchase acquired at a different unit cost, use a separate line for each purchase.
2. Determine the cost of the inventory on December 31, 2015, using the average cost method and using the columnar headings indicated in (1).

Appendix 2
PR 6-12A

Periodic inventory by two methods

✔ 1. $7,331

McMonnies Company uses the periodic inventory system. The table below summarizes details regarding the inventory at January 1, 2015; purchases invoices during the year; and the inventory count at December 31, 2015.

| Model | Inventory, January 1 | Purchases Invoices | | | Inventory Count December 31 |
		1st	2nd	3rd	
N201	2 at $520	2 at $527	2 at $530	2 at $535	4
Q73	6 at 520	8 at 531	4 at 549	6 at 542	7
Z120	–	4 at 222	4 at 232	–	2
ZZRF	8 at 70	12 at 72	16 at 74	14 at 78	12

Instructions

1. Determine the cost of the inventory on December 31, 2015, using the first-in, first-out method. Present data in columnar form, using the following headings:

Model	Quantity	Unit Cost	Total Cost

If the inventory of a particular model comprises one entire purchase plus a portion of another purchase acquired at a different unit cost, use a separate line for each purchase.

2. Determine the cost of the inventory on December 31, 2015, using the average cost method and using the columnar headings indicated in (1).

PROBLEMS SERIES B

PR 6-1B

FIFO perpetual inventory

✔ 3. $4,525

The beginning inventory at Matt Meyer Office Supplies and data on purchases and sales for a two-month period are as follows:

Date		Transaction	Number of Units	Per Unit	Total
Jan.	1	Inventory	75	$20	$1,500
	10	Purchase	200	21	4,200
	28	Sale	100	40	4,000
	30	Sale	110	40	4,400
Feb.	5	Sale	20	44	880
	10	Purchase	120	22	2,640

Instructions

1. Record the inventory, purchases, and cost of goods sold data in a perpetual inventory record similar to the one illustrated in Exhibit 3, on page 310, using the FIFO method.
2. Determine the total sales and the total cost of goods sold for the period. Journalize the entries in the sales and cost of goods sold accounts. Assume that all sales were on account.
3. Determine the gross profit from sales for the period.
4. Determine the ending inventory cost.
5. Record the entry necessary when the inventory count is $3,500 on February 28.

PR 6-2B

FIFO perpetual inventory

✔ 3. $379,000

The beginning inventory of merchandise at Martin Co. and data on purchases and sales for a two-month period are as follows:

Date		Transaction	Number of Units	Per Unit	Total
Jul.	5	Inventory	80	$1,100	$ 88,000
	8	Sale	40	3,000	120,000
	16	Sale	20	3,000	60,000
	21	Purchase	70	1,300	91,000
Aug.	3	Sale	80	3,500	280,000
	10	Purchase	40	1,400	56,000
	23	Sale	40	3,500	140,000

(continued)

Instructions

1. Record the inventory, purchases, and cost of goods sold data in a perpetual inventory record similar to the one illustrated in Exhibit 3, on page 310, using the first-in, first-out method.
2. Determine the total sales and the total cost of goods sold for the period. Journalize the entries in the sales and cost of goods sold accounts. Assume that all sales were on account.
3. Determine the gross profit from sales for the period.
4. Determine the ending inventory cost.
5. Record the entry necessary when the inventory count is $13,000 at the end of August.

PR 6-3B

FIFO perpetual inventory

✔ 3. $7,805

The beginning inventory of merchandise at Cave Co. and data on purchases and sales for a two-month period are as follows:

Date		Transaction	Number of Units	Per Unit	Total
Jul.	5	Inventory	100	$20	$2,000
	16	Sale	90	42	3,780
	28	Sale	5	45	225
Aug.	5	Purchase	175	24	4,200
	14	Sale	120	50	6,000
	25	Purchase	150	25	3,750
	30	Sale	100	50	5,000

Instructions

1. Record the inventory, purchases, and cost of goods sold data in a perpetual inventory record similar to the one illustrated in Exhibit 3, on page 310, using the first-in, first-out method.
2. Determine the total sales and the total cost of goods sold for the period. Journalize the entries in the sales and cost of goods sold accounts. Assume that all sales were on account.
3. Determine the gross profit from sales for the period.
4. Determine the ending inventory cost.
5. Record the entry necessary when the inventory count is $2,700 at the end of August.

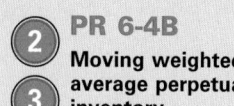

PR 6-4B

Moving weighted average perpetual inventory

✔ 2. Gross profit, $4,512.10

The beginning inventory for Matt Meyer Office Supplies and data on purchases and sales for a two-month period are shown in Problem 6-1B. Round the average cost to two decimal places.

Instructions

1. Record the inventory, purchases, and cost of goods sold data in a perpetual inventory record similar to the one illustrated in Exhibit 4, on page 311, using the moving weighted average cost method.
2. Determine the total sales, the total cost of goods sold, and the gross profit from sales for the period.
3. Determine the ending inventory cost.

PR 6-5B

Moving weighted average perpetual inventory

✔ 2. Gross profit, $378,711.20

The beginning inventory for Martin Co. and data on purchases and sales for a two-month period are shown in Problem 6-2B. Round the average cost to two decimal places.

Instructions

1. Record the inventory, purchases, and cost of goods sold data in a perpetual inventory record similar to the one illustrated in Exhibit 4, on page 311, using the moving weighted average cost method.
2. Determine the total sales, the total cost of goods sold, and the gross profit from sales for the period.
3. Determine the ending inventory cost.

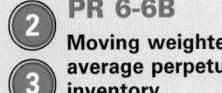

PR 6-6B

Moving weighted average perpetual inventory

✔ 2. Gross profit, $7,770.20

The beginning inventory for Cave Co. and data on purchases and sales for a two-month period are shown in Problem 6-3B. Round the average cost to two decimal places.

Instructions

1. Record the inventory, purchases, and cost of goods sold data in a perpetual inventory record similar to the one illustrated in Exhibit 4, on page 311, using the moving weighted average cost method.
2. Determine the total sales, the total cost of goods sold, and the gross profit from sales for the period.
3. Determine the ending inventory cost.

PR 6-7B

Lower of cost and NRV

✔ Lower of cost and NRV $44,146

If the working papers correlating with this textbook are not used, omit Problem 6-7B.

Data on the physical inventory of Zircon Company as at December 31, 2015, are presented in the working papers. The quantity of each commodity on hand has been determined and recorded on the inventory sheet. Unit market prices have also been determined as at December 31 and recorded on the sheet. The inventory is to be determined at the lower of cost and net realizable value, using the first-in, first-out method. Quantity and cost data from the last and the next-to-the-last purchases invoices of the year are summarized as follows:

Description	Last Purchases Invoice		Next-to-the-Last Purchases Invoice	
	Quantity Purchased	Unit Cost	Quantity Purchased	Unit Cost
Alpha 10	30	$ 60	30	$ 59
Beta 30	35	175	20	180
Charlie 4	20	130	25	129
Echo 9	150	26	100	27
Frank 6	10	565	10	560
George 15	100	15	100	14
Killo 6	10	385	5	384
Quebec 12	400	7	500	6
Romeo 7	80	22	50	21
Sierra 3	5	250	4	260
Washburn 2	90	24	80	22
X-Ray 4	10	750	9	745

Instructions

Record the appropriate unit costs on the inventory sheet and complete the pricing of the inventory. When two different unit costs are applicable to an item:

1. Draw a line through the quantity and insert the quantity and unit cost of the last purchase.
2. On the following line, insert the quantity and unit cost of the next-to-the-last purchase.
3. Total the cost and market columns and insert the lower of the two totals in the Lower of C and NRV column. The first item on the inventory sheet has been completed as an example.

PR 6-8B

Lower of cost and net realizable value

Using the following data related to automobile parts inventory, determine the value of the inventory at the lower of cost and NRV. Complete the calculation on an individual basis for model numbers 524, 526, and 455 and for the whole of the 555 series.

Model Number	Inventory Quantity	Cost per Unit	Price per Unit	Direct Selling Costs
524	42	$49.12	$99.99	$300
526	79	13.43	15.99	
455	53	18.55	10.99	
555 – a	16	20.00	29.99	40
555 – b	12	15.00	19.99	
555 – c	10	30.00	49.99	

(continued)

a. At what amount should the inventory be valued?

b. What possible reasons can explain the changes in the price? What are selling costs?

c. Will the company sell the inventory for its value as calculated in (a) above?

Appendix 1
PR 6-9B

Retail method; gross profit method

✔ 1. $340,000

Selected data on inventory, purchases, and sales for Oxbow Co. and Alameda Co. are as follows:

	Cost	Retail
Oxbow Co.		
Inventory, April 1	$ 200,000	$ 300,000
Transactions during April:		
Purchases (net)	2,520,000	3,700,000
Sales		3,550,000
Sales returns and allowances		50,000
Alameda Co.		
Inventory, October 1	$ 300,000	
Transactions during October through December:		
Purchases (net)	1,800,000	
Sales	2,796,000	
Sales returns and allowances	96,000	
Estimated gross profit rate	36%	

Instructions

1. Determine the estimated cost of the inventory of Oxbow Co. on April 30 by the retail method, presenting details of the computations.

2. a. Estimate the cost of the inventory of Alameda Co. on December 31 by the gross profit method, presenting details of the computations.

   b. Assume that Alameda Co. took a physical inventory on December 31 and discovered that $358,500 of merchandise was on hand. What was the estimated loss of inventory due to theft or damage during October through December?

Appendix 1
PR 6-10B

Retail method; gross profit method

✔ 1. $319,700
✔ 3. $319,700

A clothing store, Interlude Inc., had a fire at the end of February, and so used the gross profit method to estimate inventory cost.

1. Estimate the ending inventory cost based on the following data:

   Net sales for the month of February = $123,000
   Inventory at cost February 1 = $298,900
   Purchases at cost during month = $70,000
   Gross profit = 60%

2. Is additional information needed to estimate inventory cost using the retail method?

3. Estimate inventory cost using the retail method.

Appendix 2
PR 6-11B

Periodic inventory by two methods

✔ 1. $4,053

Bulldog Appliances uses the periodic inventory system. Details regarding the inventory of appliances at August 1, 2014; purchases invoices during the year; and the inventory count at July 31, 2015, are summarized as follows:

Model	Inventory, August 1	Purchases Invoices 1st	2nd	3rd	Inventory Count, July 31
ALN3	16 at $88	8 at $79	6 at $85	12 at $92	16
UGA1	1 at 75	1 at 65	5 at 68	3 at 70	4
SL89	7 at 242	6 at 250	5 at 260	10 at 259	9

Instructions

1. Determine the cost of the inventory on July 31, 2015, using the first-in, first-out method. Present data in columnar form, using the following headings:

Model	Quantity	Unit Cost	Total Cost

If the inventory of a particular model comprises one entire purchase plus a portion of another purchase acquired at a different unit cost, use a separate line for each purchase.

2. Determine the cost of the inventory on July 31, 2015, using the weighted average cost method and using the columnar headings indicated in (1).

Appendix 2
PR 6-12B

Periodic inventory by two methods

✔ 1. $3,528

Laker Company uses the periodic inventory system. The table below summarizes details regarding the inventory at January 1, 2015; purchases invoices during the year; and the inventory count at December 31, 2015.

| Model | Inventory, January 1 | Purchases Invoices | | | Inventory Count, December 31 |
		1st	2nd	3rd	
F69	6 at 80	5 at 82	8 at 89	8 at 90	6
H60W	2 at 108	2 at 110	3 at 128	3 at 130	5
J600T	5 at 160	4 at 170	4 at 175	7 at 180	8
ZZHO	–	7 at 75	7 at 100	7 at 101	9

Instructions

1. Determine the cost of the inventory on December 31, 2015, using the first-in, first-out method. Present data in columnar form, using the following headings:

| Model | Quantity | Unit Cost | Total Cost |

If the inventory of a particular model comprises one entire purchase plus a portion of another purchase acquired at a different unit cost, use a separate line for each purchase.

2. Determine the cost of the inventory on December 31, 2015, using the average cost method and using the columnar headings indicated in (1).

SPECIAL ACTIVITIES

SA 6-1

Ethics and professional conduct in business

Ebba Co. is experiencing a decrease in sales and operating income for the fiscal year ending December 31, 2015. Cody Bryant, controller of Ebba Co., has suggested that all orders received before the end of the fiscal year be shipped by midnight, December 31, 2015, even if the shipping department must work overtime. Because Ebba Co. ships all merchandise FOB shipping point, it would record all such shipments as sales for the year ending December 31, 2015, thereby offsetting some of the decreases in sales and operating income.

Discuss whether Cody Bryant is behaving in a professional manner.

SA 6-2

FIFO and inventory flow

The following is an excerpt from a conversation between Chad Lindy, the warehouse manager for House of Foods Wholesale Co., and its accountant, Summer Roseberry. House of Foods Wholesale operates a large regional warehouse that supplies produce and other grocery products to grocery stores in smaller communities.

Chad: Summer, can you explain what's going on here with these monthly statements?

Summer: Sure, Chad. How can I help you?

Chad: I don't understand this first-in, first-out inventory procedure. It just doesn't make sense.

Summer: Well, what it means is that we assume that the first items we received in inventory are the first ones sold. So the inventory is made up of the most recent costs. For most of our products we ensure that the oldest items are sold first. Produce, for instance, is perishable. We can't keep it very long or it will spoil.

Chad: But for some items such as candles, dishes, baskets, and cooking utensils, we don't worry about their age. These are not first-in, first-out. We aren't reporting what is really happening!

(continued)

Respond to Chad's concerns. First, discuss the need for an assumption of some sort regarding the flow of goods. Second, discuss what accounting principles allow for use as methods of keeping track of the flow of goods. And third, discuss the idea of materiality.

SA 6-3

Costing inventory periodic & perpetual

Mimotopes Company began operations in 2014 by selling a single product. Data on purchases and sales for the first four months were as follows:

Purchases:

Date	Units Purchased	Unit Cost	Total Cost
April 6	15,500	$12.20	$189,100
May 18	16,500	13.00	214,500
June 6	20,000	13.20	264,000
July 10	20,000	14.00	280,000
	72,000		$947,600

Sales:

April	8,000 units
May	8,000
June	10,000
July	12,000
Total units	38,000
Total sales	$608,000

On August 6, 2014, the president of the company, Mohammad Zanelli, asked for your advice on costing the 34,000-unit physical inventory that was taken on July 31, 2014. Moreover, because the firm plans to expand its product line, he asked for your advice on the use of a perpetual inventory system in the future.

1. Determine the cost of the July 31, 2014, inventory under the periodic system, using the (a) first-in, first-out method and (b) average cost method.
2. Determine the gross profit for the year under both of the methods in (1).
3. Which of the inventory costing methods better reflects the movement of the inventory?

SA 6-4

Inventory ratios

f·a·i

Dell Inc. and Hewlett-Packard Development Company, L.P. (HP) are both manufacturers of computer equipment and peripherals. However, the two companies follow two different strategies. Dell follows primarily a build-to-order strategy, where the consumer orders the computer from a Web page. The order is then manufactured and shipped to the customer within days of the order. In contrast, HP follows a build-to-stock strategy, where the computer is first built for inventory, then sold from inventory to retailers, such as Best Buy. The two strategies can be seen in the difference between the inventory turnover ratios and days' sales in inventory for the two companies. The following financial statement information is provided for Dell and HP for a fiscal year (in millions):

	Dell	HP
Inventory, beginning of period	$ 459	$ 6,877
Inventory, end of period	576	7,750
Cost of goods sold	45,958	69,178

a. Determine the inventory turnover ratio and days' sales in inventory for each company. Round to one decimal place.
b. Interpret the difference between the results for the two companies. Consider the timing of production and the risks related to designing the computer options.

SA 6-5

Comparing inventory ratios for two companies

f·a·i

Tiffany Co. is a high-end jewellery retailer, whereas Amazon.com is an online retailer that uses e-commerce services, features, and technologies to sell its products through the Internet. Balance sheet inventory disclosures for Tiffany and Amazon.com (in thousands) are as follows:

	End-of-Period Inventory	Beginning-of-Period Inventory
Tiffany Co.	$1,601,263	$1,372,397
Amazon.com	1,399,000	1,200,000

The cost of goods sold reported by each company was as follows:

	Tiffany Co.	Amazon.com
Cost of goods sold	$1,214,577	$14,896,000

a. Determine the inventory turnover ratios and days' sales in inventory for Tiffany and Amazon.com. Round to two decimal places.
b. Interpret your results. Consider how their different business models are reflected in these ratios.

SA 6-6

Comparing inventory ratios for three companies

f·a·i

The general merchandise retail industry has a number of segments represented by the following companies:

Company Name	Merchandise Concept
Costco Wholesale Corporation	Membership warehouse
Walmart	Discount general merchandise
JCPenney	Department store

The following cost of goods sold and beginning and ending inventories have been provided from corporate annual reports (in millions) for these three companies:

	Costco	Walmart	JCPenney
Cost of goods sold	$52,746	$264,152	$12,078
Inventory, beginning	4,015	32,191	3,210
Inventory, ending	4,569	33,685	3,400

a. Determine the inventory turnover ratio for all three companies. Round to one decimal place.
b. Determine the days' sales in inventory for all three companies. Round to one decimal place.
c. Interpret these results based on each company's merchandise concept.

SA 6-7

Reporting inventory in the financial statements

Using the financial statements of Leon's Furniture Limited and Shoppers Drug Mart Corporation in Appendixes B and C, answer the following question:

Shoppers Drug Mart identifies a note related to the Cost of Goods Sold. What information did Shoppers Drug Mart need to provide users that Leon's did not?

Internal Control and Cash

Debbie Yea/Nelson Education Ltd.

eBAY INC.

Controls are a part of your everyday life. At one extreme, laws are used to limit your behaviour. For example, the speed limit is a control on your driving, designed for traffic safety. In addition, you are also affected by many nonlegal controls. For example, you can keep credit card receipts in order to compare your transactions to the monthly credit card statement. Comparing receipts to the monthly statement is a control designed to catch mistakes made by the credit card company. In addition, banks give you a personal identification number (PIN) as a control against unauthorized access to your cash if you lose your automated teller machine (ATM) card. Dairies use freshness dating on their milk containers as a control to prevent the purchase or sale of soured milk. As you can see, you use and encounter controls every day.

Just as there are many examples of controls throughout society, businesses must also implement controls to help guide the behaviour of their managers, employees, and customers. For example, eBay Inc. maintains an Internet-based marketplace for the sale of goods and services. Using eBay's online platform, buyers and sellers can browse, buy, and sell a wide variety of items, including antiques and used cars. However, in order to maintain the integrity and trust of its buyers and sellers, eBay must have controls to ensure that buyers pay for their items and sellers don't misrepresent their items or fail to deliver sales. One such control eBay uses is a feedback forum that establishes buyer and seller reputations. A prospective buyer or seller can view the member's reputation and feedback comments before completing a transaction. Dishonest or unfair trading can lead to a negative reputation and even suspension or cancellation of the member's ability to trade on eBay.

The Canada Revenue Agency (CRA) also uses controls to ensure revenue from online sales is properly reported as taxable income. The CRA was successful in gaining access to eBay Canada's list of sellers and their sales records. The CRA uses this information to determine whether eBay sellers reported income from their eBay sales.

In this chapter, we will discuss controls that can be included in accounting systems to provide reasonable assurance that the financial statements are reliable. We also discuss controls over cash that you can use to determine whether your bank has made any errors in your account. We begin this chapter by discussing the Sarbanes-Oxley Act of 2002 and its impact on controls, financial reporting, and how it affects Canadian companies.

After studying this chapter, you should be able to:

1 Describe and illustrate the objectives and elements of internal control.

Internal Control	Objectives of Internal Control	
	Elements of Internal Control	
	Control Environment	
	Risk Assessment	
	Control Procedures	
	Monitoring	
	Information and Communication	EXAMPLE EXERCISE 7-1 (page 356)
	Limitations of Internal Control	

2 Describe the accounting for petty cash funds.

Petty Cash Funds		EXAMPLE EXERCISE 7-2 (page 358)

3 Describe and illustrate the application of internal controls to cash.

Cash Controls over Receipts and Payments	Control of Cash Receipts	
	Control of Cash Payments	

4 Describe the nature of a bank account and its use in controlling cash.

Bank Accounts	Bank Statement	EXAMPLE EXERCISE 7-3 (page 364)
	Using the Bank Statement as a Control over Cash	

5 Describe and illustrate the use of a bank reconciliation in controlling cash.

Bank Reconciliation		EXAMPLE EXERCISE 7-4 (page 369)

6 Describe and illustrate the reporting of cash and cash equivalents in the financial statements.

Financial Statement Reporting of Cash	Financial Analysis and Interpretation	EXAMPLE EXERCISE 7-5 (page 372)

For the chapter *At a Glance*, turn to page 372.

Internal Control

Describe and illustrate the objectives and elements of internal control.

A business that has weak internal controls leaves itself open to errors in its records and vulnerable to fraud, theft, and costly losses.

During the financial scandals of the early 2000s, shareholders, creditors, and other investors lost billions of dollars. Investors also lost their trust in the financial statements of companies. As a result, the United States Congress passed the Sarbanes-Oxley Act of 2002 (SOX), and Canadian regulations increased. SOX affects any Canadian companies that wish to trade on the American stock exchanges.

SOX and the Canadian regulations, such as the Canadian Securities Administrators National Instrument 52-109 Certification of Disclosure in Issuer's Annual and Interim

Management's Discussion and Analysis Regarding Controls from Shoppers Drug Mart Annual Report

---

Internal Controls over Financial Reporting

The CEO and CFO have designed, or caused to be designed under their supervision, internal controls over financial reporting to provide reasonable assurance regarding the reliability of financial reporting and the preparation of financial statements for external purposes in accordance with Canadian GAAP.

The Company's internal controls over financial reporting include policies and procedures that:

- pertain to the maintenance of records that, in reasonable detail, accurately and fairly reflect transactions and dispositions of assets of the Company;
- provide reasonable assurance that transactions are recorded as necessary to permit preparation of financial statements in accordance with Canadian GAAP and that receipts and expenditures of the Company are made only in accordance with authorizations of management and directors of the Company; and
- provide reasonable assurance regarding prevention or timely detection of unauthorized acquisition, use or disposition of the Company's assets that could have a material effect on the financial statements.

Internal control systems, no matter how well designed, have inherent limitations. Therefore, even those systems determined to be designed effectively can provide only reasonable assurance with respect to financial reporting and financial statement preparation.

Management, with the participation of the CEO and CFO, has evaluated the effectiveness of the Company's internal controls over financial reporting as at December 31, 2011 and has concluded that internal controls over financial reporting are designed and operating effectively to provide reasonable assurance regarding the reliability of financial reporting and the preparation of financial statements for external purposes in accordance with Canadian GAAP. Management's assessment was based on the framework established in *Internal Control – Integrated Framework* issued by the Committee of Sponsoring Organizations of the Treadway Commission.

There were no changes in internal controls over financial reporting that occurred during the Company's most recent interim period that have materially affected, or are reasonably likely to materially affect, the Company's internal controls over financial reporting.

Source: Reprinted with permission of Shoppers Drug Mart

Filings (NI 52-109), stress that effective internal controls are a major factor in deterring fraud and preventing misleading financial statements. They also stress the vital importance of communicating the findings regarding the effectiveness of the controls to shareholders, creditors, and other investors. This communication occurs in the *management discussion and analysis* (MD&A) section of the annual report. An example of a portion of the MD&A from the annual report of Shoppers Drug Mart is found in Exhibit 1.

Businesses may choose from a number of frameworks when considering their **internal control**. The Canadian Institute of Chartered Accountants' framework, *Risk Management and Governance: Guidance on Control (COCO Framework)*, considers all parts of the organization. *Internal Control—Integrated Framework* is an American standard that more narrowly focuses on financial reporting. It details how companies design, analyze, and evaluate internal control for financial reporting purposes.[1]

Objectives of Internal Control

The objectives of internal control are to ensure efficient operations and provide reasonable assurance of the following:

1. Assets are safeguarded and used for business purposes.
2. Business information is accurate.
3. Employees and managers comply with laws and regulations.

---

1 In this section, the objectives of internal control are described, followed by a discussion of how these objectives can be achieved using the *Integrated Framework's* five elements of internal control.

These objectives are illustrated below.

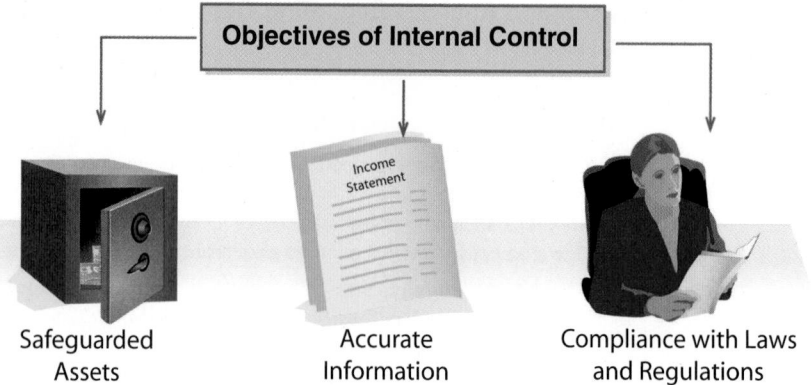

Internal control can safeguard assets by preventing theft, fraud, misuse, or misplacement. A serious concern of internal control is preventing employee fraud. **Employee fraud** is the intentional act of deceiving an employer for personal gain. Such fraud may range from minor overstating of a travel expense report to stealing millions of dollars. Employees stealing from a business often adjust the accounting records to hide their fraud. Thus, employee fraud usually affects the accuracy of business information.

Elements of Internal Control

The three internal control objectives can be achieved by applying the five **elements of internal control** set forth by the *Integrated Framework*.[2] These elements are as follows:

1. Control environment
2. Risk assessment
3. Control procedures
4. Monitoring
5. Information and communication

The elements of internal control are illustrated in Exhibit 2.

Exhibit 2

Elements of Internal Control

2 *Internal Control—Integrated Framework* by the Committee of Sponsoring Organizations of the Treadway Commission, 1992, pp. 16–18.

In Exhibit 2, the elements of internal control form an umbrella over the business to protect it from control threats. The control environment is the size of the umbrella. Risk assessment, control procedures, and monitoring are the fabric of the umbrella, which keep it from leaking. Information and communication connect the umbrella to management.

Control Environment

The **control environment** is the overall attitude of management and employees regarding the importance of controls. Three factors influencing a company's control environment are as follows:

1. *Management's philosophy and operating style* relate to whether management emphasizes the importance of internal controls or whether they place more emphasis on operating goals and tolerate deviations from control policies.

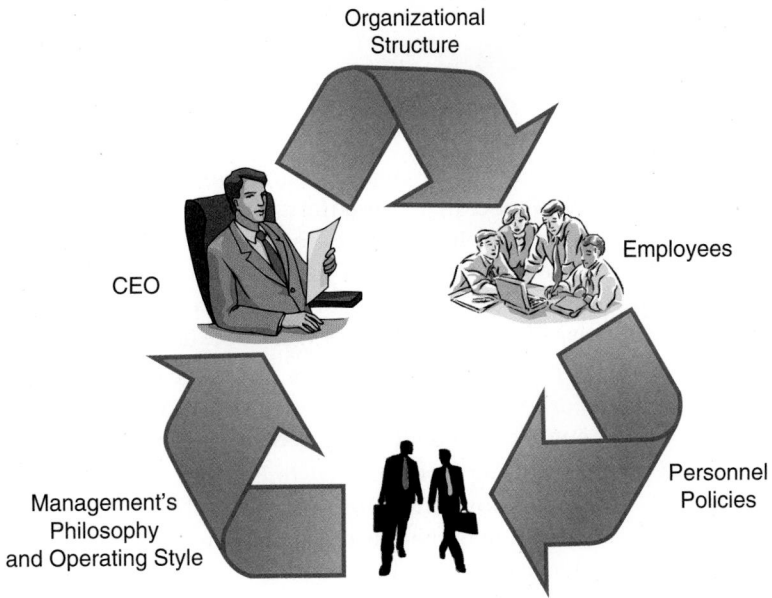

Control Environment

2. *The company's organizational structure* sets the responsibility and authority structure to ensure that employees know both their responsibilities and the responsibilities of other employees.
3. *The company's personnel policies* involve hiring, training, evaluation, compensation, and promotion of employees. These policies give reasonable assurance that competent, honest employees are hired and retained.

Risk Assessment

All businesses face risks such as changes in customer requirements, competitive threats, regulatory changes, and changes in economic factors. Management should identify such risks, analyze their significance, assess their likelihood of occurring, and take any necessary actions to minimize them.

Control Procedures

Control procedures provide reasonable assurance that business goals will be achieved, including the prevention of fraud. Control procedures, which constitute one of the most important elements of internal control, include the following, as shown in Exhibit 3.

Exhibit 3

Internal Control Procedures

1. *Competent personnel, rotating duties, and mandatory vacations* all increase the likelihood that procedures set in place are being followed. Employees who are trained in their duties are more likely to follow procedures when they know that other people will be replacing them regularly and during their vacation time. Cases of employee fraud are often discovered when a long-term employee, who has never taken vacations, misses work because of an illness or another unavoidable reason.

2. *Separating responsibilities for related operations* is called segregation of duties. For example, opportunities for fraud are limited by having one employee order supplies, another verify receipt of those supplies, and a third pay suppliers.

3. *Separating operations, custody of assets, and accounting* is another form of segregation of duties. Ensuring that custody of assets, such as inventory, is separate from recording of the sale of that asset reduces the chance that someone misappropriates the inventory and then makes an entry in the records to account for it. It also ensures that independent checks occur on the work of each employee.

4. *Proofs and security measures such as authorization, approval, and reconciliation* safeguard assets and ensure reliable accounting data. The use of bank reconciliations, an important control for cash, is described and illustrated later in this chapter.

5. *Encryption of data transmitted over the Internet and the use of computer firewalls* protect accounting information stored on the computer. **Data encryption** can be achieved through a well-designed software program that translates the information being sent over the Internet into a code that is able to be read only by the authorized receiving party. Firewalls block unwanted computer viruses from entering the system.

INTEGRITY, OBJECTIVITY, AND ETHICS IN BUSINESS

OCCUPATIONAL FRAUD PREVENTION MEASURES AND TECHNIQUES USED BY SMALL AND MEDIUM-SIZED ENTERPRISES

- Existence of clear and uniform accounting procedures
- Frequent financial reviews and/or reconciliations
- Existence of physical safeguards to secure company assets
- Segregation of duties and authorization policies for transactions
- Pre-employment screening of employees

- Existence and enforcement of the formal code of employee conduct
- Mandatory job or assignment rotation/mandatory vacations
- Fraud awareness and ethics training among management
- Fraud awareness and ethics training among employees

Source: Certified General Accountants Association of Canada, "Does Canada Have a Problem with Occupational Fraud?" (2011) www.cga-canada.org/enca/ResearchReports/ca_rep_2011-12_fraud.pdf

Monitoring

Monitoring of the internal control system is used to improve controls and to locate weaknesses, such as policies that are not being adhered to. Monitoring often includes observing both employee behaviour and the accounting system for indicators of control problems. Some such indicators are shown in Exhibit 4.

Evaluations of controls are often performed when major changes occur in strategy, senior management, business structure, or operations. Internal auditors, who are independent of operations, usually perform such evaluations. Internal auditors are also responsible for day-to-day monitoring of controls. External auditors also evaluate and report on internal control as part of their annual financial statement audit.

Internal Auditors Large corporations have an internal auditing department responsible for ensuring proper recording of the company's financial transactions. The auditing department is independent of the business operations and performs periodic, random spot checks to verify the accuracy of the records. **Internal auditors** are also responsible for day-to-day monitoring of the internal control system. The internal auditing department reports its findings to senior management.

External Auditors While internal auditors are independent of the operations, they are not independent of the company. To provide stronger assurance as to the validity of the financial statements, many companies hire an external auditor to review the records. Public corporations are required by law to have an annual independent audit of their financial records. **External auditors** are independent public accountants hired to test the reasonableness of the records and verify the accuracy of the financial statements. Having the external auditors verify each transaction would be too time-consuming and expensive; instead, they verify random transactions. The independent auditors' report for Leon's Furniture Limited can be found in Appendix B. In this report, the external auditor is responsible for obtaining *reasonable assurance* regarding the accuracy of the financial statements.

Information and Communication

Information and communication are essential elements of internal control. Information about the control environment, risk assessment, control procedures, and monitoring is used by management for guiding operations and ensuring compliance with reporting, legal, and regulatory requirements. Management also uses external information to

Warning Signs of Internal Control Problems

Warning signs with regard to people

Warning signs from the accounting system

1. Living beyond their means.
2. Finanicial difficulties.
3. Control issues and/or unwillingness to share duties.
4. Defensiveness, suspiciousness, and/or irritability.
5. Not taking annual leave/holidays.

1. Unexplained decreases in cash flows.
2. Unexplained increases in expenses.
3. Unusual adjustments at period end.
4. Round dollar payments being made to suppliers to "part pay" invoices.
5. Unreconciled bank accounts or suspense accounts.
6. Lack of complete and timely reconciliations and financial reports.

Source: The Association of Certified Fraud Examiners' 2010 *Report to the Nations on Occupational Fraud and Abuse*, pp 15, 70–71. Used with permission.

assess events and conditions that can affect decision making and external reporting. For example, management uses pronouncements of the Accounting Standards Board (AcSB) to assess the impact of changes in reporting standards on the financial statements.[3]

Limitations of Internal Control

Internal control systems can provide only reasonable assurance for safeguarding assets, processing accurate information, and compliance with laws and regulations. In other words, internal controls are not a guarantee. This is due to the following factors:

1. The human element of controls
2. Cost-benefit considerations

The *human element* recognizes that controls are applied and used by humans. As a result, human errors can occur because of fatigue, carelessness, confusion, or misjudgment. For example, an employee may unintentionally shortchange a customer or miscount the amount of inventory received from a supplier. In addition, two or more employees may collude to defeat or circumvent internal controls. **Collusion** often involves fraud and the theft of assets. For example, the cashier and the accounts receivable clerk might collude to steal customer payments on account.

Cost-benefit considerations recognize that costs of internal controls should not exceed their benefits. For example, retail stores could eliminate shoplifting by searching all customers before they leave the store. However, such a control procedure would upset customers and result in lost sales. Instead, retailers often prefer to install cameras, use electronic security tags, or post signs saying *We prosecute all shoplifters*.

 ## Petty Cash Funds

Describe the accounting for petty cash funds.

A company often has to pay small amounts for such items as postage, office supplies, or minor repairs. Although small, such payments may occur often enough to total a significant amount. Thus, it is desirable to control such payments. However, writing a cheque for each small payment is not practical. Instead, a special cash fund, called a **petty cash fund**, is used.

A petty cash fund is established by estimating the amount of payments needed from the fund during a period, such as a week or a month. A cheque is then written and cashed for this amount. The money obtained from cashing the cheque is then

---

3 With the transition to International Financial Reporting Standards, accounting pronouncements are issued by the International Accounting Standards Board (IASB), effective January 1, 2011.

given to an employee, called the *petty cash custodian*. The petty cash custodian disburses monies from the fund as needed. For control purposes, the company may place restrictions on the maximum amount and the types of payments that can be made from the fund. As an additional control, a company may require two employees to sign for all petty cash disbursements; alternatively, the petty cash custodian is the only employee who is assigned access to the fund. Each time money is paid from petty cash, the custodian records the details on a petty cash receipts form, and places the receipt in the petty cash box. The petty cash fund should be audited periodically to ensure the receipts plus cash on hand equal the established petty cash fund balance.

The petty cash fund is normally replenished at periodic intervals, when it is depleted or reaches a minimum amount. When a petty cash fund is replenished, the accounts debited are determined by summarizing the petty cash receipts. A cheque is then written for this amount, payable to Petty Cash.

To illustrate, assume that a petty cash fund of $500 is established on August 1. The entry to record this transaction is as follows:

Aug.	1	Petty Cash	500	
		Cash		500
		Establish petty cash fund.		

The only time Petty Cash is debited is when the fund is initially established, as shown in the preceding entry, or when the fund is being increased. The only time Petty Cash is credited is when the fund is being decreased.

At the end of August, the petty cash receipts indicate payments for the following items:

Office supplies	$380
Postage (debit Office Supplies)	22
Store supplies	35
Miscellaneous administrative expense	30
Total	$467

The entry to replenish the petty cash fund on August 31 is as follows:

Aug.	31	Office Supplies	402	
		Store Supplies	35	
		Miscellaneous Administrative Expense	30	
		Cash		467
		Replenish petty cash fund.		

Petty Cash is not debited when the fund is replenished. Instead, the accounts affected by the petty cash disbursements are debited, as shown in the preceding entry. Replenishing the petty cash fund restores the cash available to its original amount of $500. If money is missing or there is extra cash when the fund is balanced to replenish it, this amount is debited (when missing) or credited (when over) to a **cash over and short account** or a cash over/short account.

Companies often use other cash funds for special needs, such as payroll or travel expenses. Such funds are called **special-purpose funds**. For example, each salesperson might be given $1,000 for travel-related expenses. Periodically, each salesperson submits an expense report, and the fund is replenished. Special-purpose funds are established and controlled in a manner similar to that of the petty cash fund.

CRITICAL THINKING

If separating responsibilities for related operations is a control procedure, why is the petty cash custodian the only employee with access to the petty cash fund?

The petty cash custodian has sole custody over the fund, making this employee responsible to account for any cash that may go missing. If two or more employees have access to the fund and cash is missing, it is more difficult to determine which employee took the cash.

EXAMPLE EXERCISE 7-2 Petty Cash Fund   2

Prepare journal entries for each of the following:

a. Issued a cheque to establish a petty cash fund of $500.

b. The amount of cash in the petty cash fund is $120. Issued a cheque to replenish the fund, based on the following summary of petty cash receipts: office supplies, $300, and miscellaneous administrative expense, $75. Record any missing funds in the cash over/short account.

FOLLOW MY EXAMPLE 7-2

a.	Petty Cash	500	
	Cash..		500
	Establish petty cash fund.		
b.	Office Supplies...	300	
	Miscellaneous Administrative Expense.	75	
	Cash Over/Short	5	
	Cash..		380
	Replenish petty cash fund.		

For Practice: PE 7-2

MID-CHAPTER ILLUSTRATIVE PROBLEM

Doug's Boat Launch and Marina had a petty cash fund of $600. At July 31, the remaining cash was $175.62. The following receipts for July were found in the cash box. Sales taxes have been ignored.

July 8. Gas receipt for company truck. The gas portion of the receipt was $44.20. There was also an $8.96 cigarette charge. One of the employees filled up the truck and paid with petty cash.

July 15. Office supply store receipt with a total of $276.38. The large items were a $70 calculator and a $25 garbage can to be recorded in equipment. The remaining expenses were office supplies.

July 23. Receipt from the grocery store for $72 to stock up on chocolate bars for sale because the marina's inventory was getting low.

Instructions:

a. Record a journal entry to replenish the fund to $600 on July 31.

b. Identify how the controls over petty cash can be improved.

MID-CHAPTER ILLUSTRATIVE SOLUTION

a. Jul. 31	Automobile Expense	44.20	
	Employee Receivable	8.96*	
	Equipment	95.00	
	Office Supplies	181.38	
	Inventory	72.00	
	Cash Over/Short	22.84**	
	Cash		424.38†
	Replenish petty cash fund.		

*The employee owes the company for the cigarettes, which are not related to the operations of the business.

**Because no receipts are available for the remaining amount of $22.84, this amount is debited to the cash over/short account. This amount is calculated as follows: cash on hand + receipts − original fund balance ($175.62 + $401.54 − $600.00 = −$22.84). A negative result indicates the cash is short (debit) and a positive result indicates the cash is over (credit).

†The credit to cash is calculated as follows: required fund balance − cash on hand ($600.00 − $175.62 = $424.38).

b. If a petty cash shortfall is a regular occurrence, greater controls over petty cash may be required:

- The cash box should be in a locked drawer.
- Two signatures could be required for dispensing money.
- A policy regarding the personal purchases made by employees using petty cash funds should be developed and discussed with employees.

Cash Controls over Receipts and Payments

Describe and illustrate the application of internal controls to cash.

Cash includes coins, currency (paper money), cheques, and money orders. Also included in cash are deposited electronic funds transfers, debit card deposits, and credit card deposits. Any funds on deposit with a bank or other financial institution that are available for withdrawal are also considered cash. Normally, cash is anything that a bank would accept for deposit in your account. For example, a cheque made payable to you could normally be deposited in a bank and, thus, is considered cash.

Businesses usually have several bank accounts. For example, a business might have one bank account for general cash payments and another for payroll. A separate ledger account is normally used for each bank account. For example, a bank account at Scotiabank could be identified in the ledger as *Cash in Bank—Scotiabank*. To simplify, we will assume in this chapter that a company has only *one* bank account, which is identified in the ledger as *Cash*.

Appendix E discusses the use of special journals. Special journals are one tool companies use to monitor cash receipts and cash payments. The **cash receipts journal** is used to record all cash received by the business from any source. All cash payments made by the business are recorded in the **cash disbursements journal**. A scan of the cash disbursements journal will quickly identify any missing cheque numbers. Missing cheques should be investigated immediately to determine whether the cheque was voided or used inappropriately by an employee.

Cash is the asset most likely to be stolen or used improperly in a business. For this reason, businesses must carefully control cash and cash transactions.

Control of Cash Receipts

To protect cash from theft and misuse, a business must control cash from the time it is received until it is deposited in a bank. Businesses normally receive cash from two main sources:

1. Customers purchasing products or services
2. Customers making payments on account

Cash Received from Cash Sales An important control to protect cash received in over-the-counter sales is a cash register. The use of a cash register to control cash is shown below.

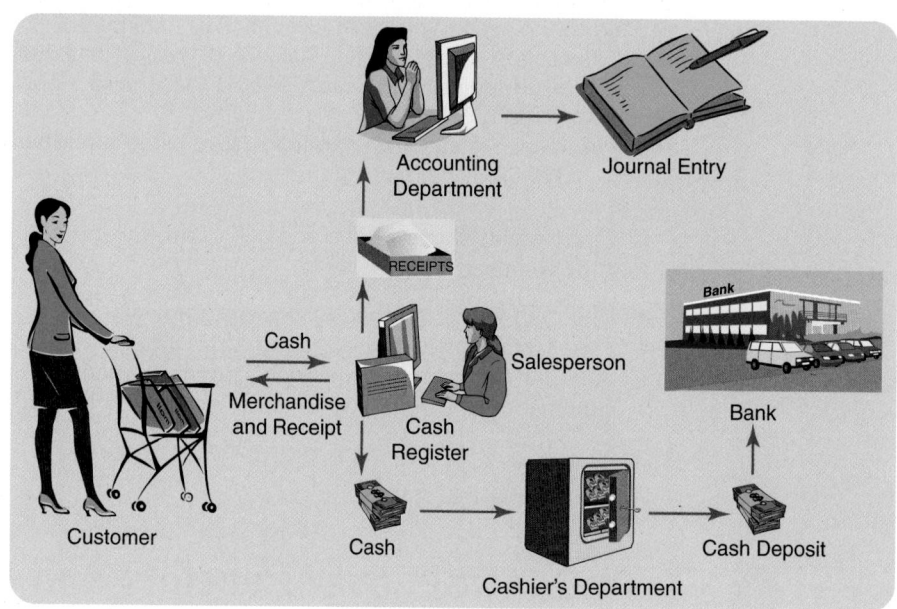

A cash register controls cash as follows:

1. At the beginning of every work shift, each clerk is given a cash drawer containing a predetermined amount of cash. This amount is used for making change for customers and is sometimes called a *float*.
2. When a salesperson enters the amount of a sale, the cash register accumulates the total sale and displays the amount to the customer. This display allows the customer to verify that the clerk has charged the correct amount. The customer also receives a cash receipt.
3. At the end of the shift, the clerk and the supervisor count the cash in the clerk's cash drawer. The amount of cash in each drawer should equal the beginning amount of cash plus the cash sales recorded by the cash register for the day.
4. The supervisor takes the cash to the Cashier's Department, where it is placed in a safe, and forwards the clerk's cash register receipts to the Accounting Department.
5. The Accounting Department summarizes the cash receipts and records the day's cash sales.

Salespersons may make errors when providing change for customers or when ringing up cash sales. As a result, the amount of cash on hand may differ from the amount of cash sales. Such differences are recorded in a cash over and short account, or a cash over/short account.

To illustrate, assume the following cash register data for May 3:

Cash register total for cash sales	$35,690
Cash receipts from cash sales	35,668

The cash sales, receipts, and shortage of $22 ($35,690 – $35,668) are recorded as follows:

May	3	Cash		35,668	
		Cash Over/Short		22	
		Sales			35,690
		To record cash sales.			

If the difference had been cash over, Cash Over/Short would have been credited for the overage. At the end of the accounting period, a debit balance in Cash Over/Short is included in Miscellaneous Expense on the income statement. A credit balance is included in the Other income section. If a salesperson consistently has large cash over/short amounts, the supervisor may require the clerk to take additional training.

Cash Received in the Mail Cash is received in the mail when customers pay their bills. This cash is usually in the form of cheques and money orders. Most companies design their invoices so that customers return a portion of the invoice, called a *remittance advice*, with their payment. Remittance advices may be used to control cash received in the mail as follows:

1. An employee opens the incoming mail and compares the amount of cash received with the amount shown on the remittance advice. If a customer does not return a remittance advice, the employee prepares one. The remittance advice serves as a record of the cash initially received. It also helps ensure that the posting to the customer's account is for the amount of cash received.
2. The employee opening the mail stamps cheques and money orders "For Deposit Only" to the bank account of the business.
3. The remittance advices and their summary totals are delivered to the Accounting Department.
4. All cash and money orders are delivered to the Cashier's Department.
5. An accounting clerk records the cash received and posts the amounts to the customer accounts.

Whether cash is received from cash sales or in the mail, it should be deposited into the bank on a regular basis. Many businesses deposit cash daily. The cashier prepares a bank deposit slip and deposits the cash in the bank, or the cash is picked up by an armoured car service, such as Brink's Canada. When cash is deposited in the bank, the teller normally stamps a duplicate copy of the deposit slip with the amount received. This bank receipt is returned to the Accounting Department, where it is compared to the total amount that should have been deposited. This control helps to ensure that all cash is deposited and that no cash is lost or stolen on the way to the bank. Any shortages are thus promptly detected.

Separating the duties of the Cashier's Department, which handles cash, and the Accounting Department, which records cash, is a control. If Accounting Department employees both handle and record cash, an employee could steal cash and change the accounting records to hide the theft.

Cash Received by EFT Cash may be received from customers through **electronic funds transfer (EFT)**. For example, customers may authorize automatic electronic transfers from their chequing accounts to pay monthly bills for such items as cellphone, Internet, and electric services. In such cases, the company sends the customer's bank a signed form from the customer authorizing the monthly electronic transfers. Each month, the company notifies the customer's bank of the amount of the transfer and the date the transfer should take place. On the due date, the company records the electronic transfer as a receipt of cash to its bank account and posts the amount paid to the customer's account.

Companies encourage customers to use EFT for the following reasons:

1. EFTs cost less than receiving cash payments through the mail.
2. EFTs enhance internal controls over cash because the cash is received directly by the bank without any employees handling cash.
3. EFTs reduce late payments from customers and speed up the processing of cash receipts.

Cash Received by Debit Card and Credit Card Cash may also be received from customers through **debit card** and **credit card** transactions. These transactions can also be made electronically. The debit card transfers the money from the customer's bank account to the business's bank account when the customer makes the purchase. The credit card transfers the money from a third party to the business's bank account. Businesses pay a fee to banks and credit card companies for allowing their customers to use debit cards and credit cards. Accounting for these fees was discussed in Chapter 5.

Control of Cash Payments

The control of cash payments should provide reasonable assurance of the following:

1. Payments are made for only authorized transactions.
2. Cash is used effectively and efficiently. For example, controls should ensure that all available purchase discounts are taken.

In a small business, an owner/manager may authorize payments based on personal knowledge. In a large business, however, purchasing goods, inspecting the goods received, and verifying the invoices are usually performed by different employees. These duties must be coordinated to ensure that proper payments are made to creditors. One system used for this purpose is the voucher system.

Voucher System A **voucher system** is a set of procedures for authorizing and recording liabilities and cash payments. A **voucher** is any document that serves as proof of authority to pay cash or issue an electronic funds transfer. An invoice that has been approved for payment could be considered a voucher. In many businesses, however, a voucher is a special form used to record data about a liability and the details of its payment.

In a manual system, a voucher is normally prepared after all necessary supporting documents have been received. For the purchase of goods, a voucher is supported by the supplier's invoice, a purchase order, and a receiving report. After a voucher is prepared, it is submitted for approval. Once approved, the voucher is recorded in the accounts and filed by due date. Upon payment, the voucher is recorded in the same manner as the payment of an account payable.

In a computerized system, data from the supporting documents (such as purchase orders, receiving reports, and suppliers' invoices) are entered directly into computer files. At the due date, the cheques are automatically generated and mailed to creditors. At that time, the voucher is electronically transferred to a paid voucher file.

Cash Paid by EFT Cash can also be paid by electronic funds transfer systems. For example, many companies pay their employees by EFT. Under such a system, employees authorize the deposit of their payroll cheques directly into their chequing accounts. Each pay period, the company transfers the employees' net pay to their chequing accounts through the use of EFT. Many companies also use EFT systems to pay their suppliers and other vendors.

Cash Paid by Debit Card and Credit Card Debit cards and credit cards can also be used to pay for travel expenses, supplies, inventory, or other expenses of the business. The debit card transactions will appear on the business bank statement. The credit card transactions will appear on the business credit card statement, and will be paid on a monthly basis.

Bank Accounts

A major reason that companies use bank accounts is for internal control. Some of the control advantages of using bank accounts are as follows:

1. Bank accounts reduce the amount of cash on hand.
2. Bank accounts provide an independent recording of cash transactions. Reconciling the balance of the cash account in the company's records with the cash balance according to the bank is an important control.
3. Use of bank accounts facilitates the transfer of funds using EFT systems.
4. The use of separate bank accounts helps to segregate cash used for a specific purpose. For example, many businesses use a separate payroll bank account in which only the net pay for a payroll period is deposited.

Bank Statement

Banks maintain a record of all chequing account transactions. A summary of all transactions, called a **bank statement**, is made available online, usually each month, or mailed to the company (depositor). The bank statement shows the beginning balance, additions, deductions, and the ending balance. A typical bank statement is shown in Exhibit 5.

Images of the cheques are made available online, or the cheques or copies of the cheques are listed in the order that they were paid by the bank and may accompany the bank statement. If paid cheques are returned with the statements, they are stamped "Paid," together with the date of payment. These cheques are considered "cancelled" by the bank to avoid a cheque being cashed more than once. Many banks no longer return cheques or cheque copies. Instead, the cheque payment information is available online.

The company's chequing account balance *in the bank records* is a liability. This concept is contrary to everything you have learned to this point in your course. The banks consider company (and personal) accounts a liability because the company is "lending" the money to the bank and may decide to take the money out of the account at any time. For this reason, the bank "owes" the money to the company, making it a liability to the bank. Thus, in the bank's records, the company's account has a credit balance. Because the bank statement is prepared from the bank's point of view, a credit memo entry on the bank statement indicates an increase (a credit) to the company's account. Likewise, a debit memo entry on the bank statement indicates a decrease (a debit) in the company's account. This relationship is shown below.

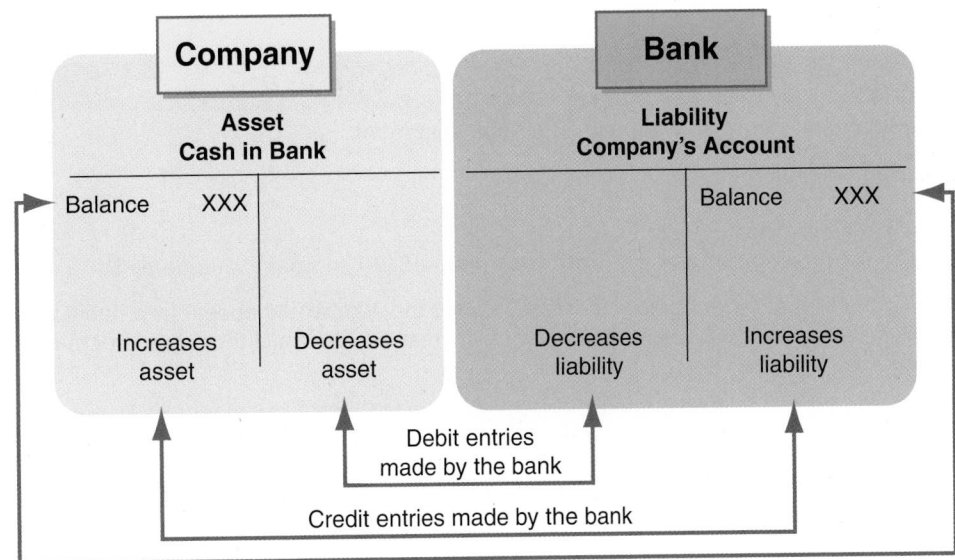

Exhibit 5

Bank Statement

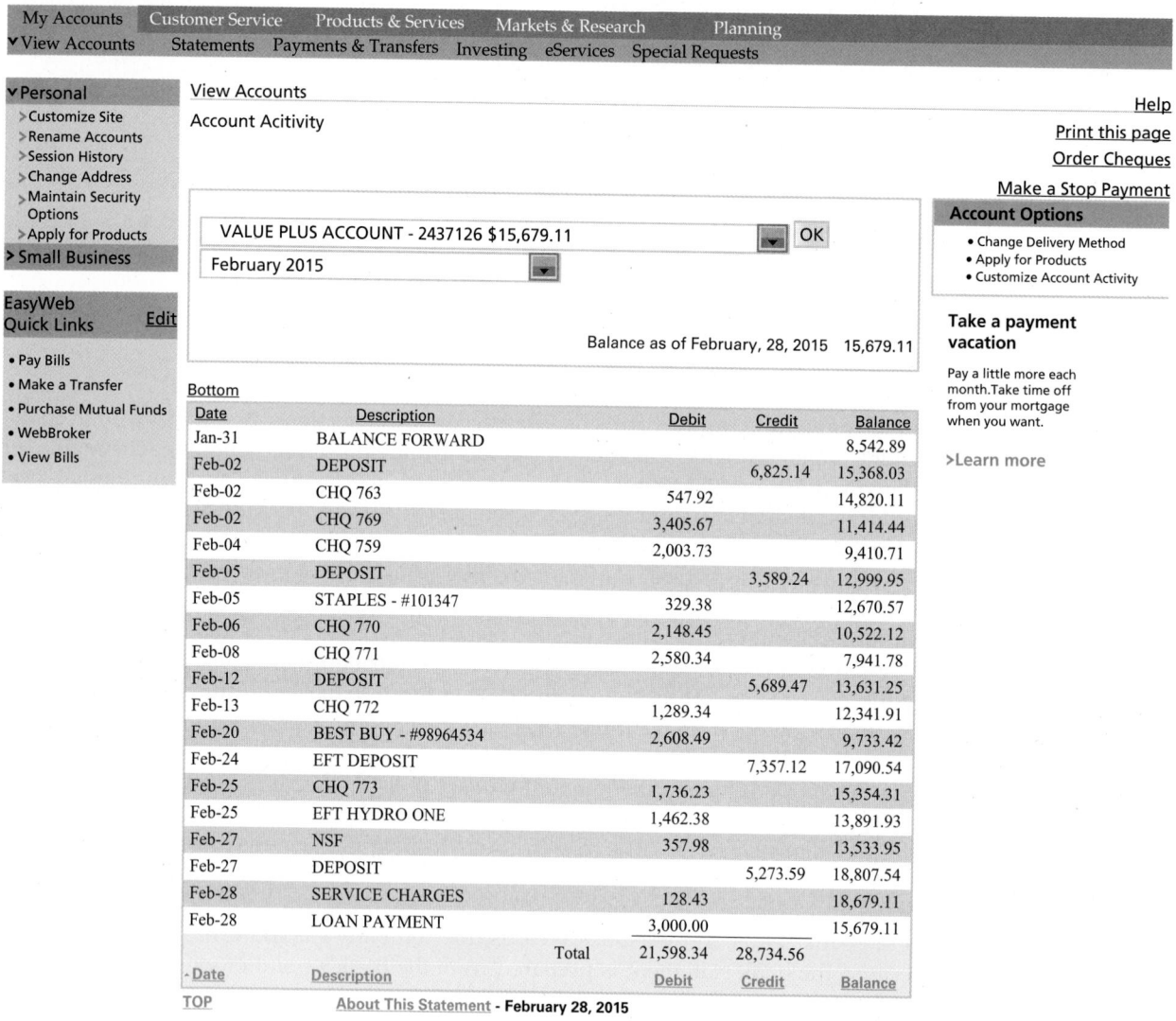

(continued)

EXAMPLE EXERCISE 7-3 Items on Company's Bank Statement   ④

The following items may appear on a bank statement:

1. NSF cheque
2. EFT deposit
3. Service charge
4. Bank correction of an error from recording a $400 company cheque as $40

Using the format shown below, indicate whether the item would appear as a debit or credit memo on the bank statement and whether the item would increase or decrease the balance of the company's bank account.

Item No.	Appears on the Bank Statement as a Debit or Credit Memo	Increases or Decreases the Balance of the Company's Bank Account

Item No.	Appears on the Bank Statement as a Debit or Credit Memo	Increases or Decreases the Balance of the Company's Bank Account
1	debit memo	decreases
2	credit memo	increases
3	debit memo	decreases
4	debit memo	decreases

For Practice: PE 7-3

Customers' cheques that are returned for not sufficient funds, called **NSF cheques**, are cheques that were initially deposited by the company upon receiving the cheques from the customer. The customer's bank returned the cheque because the issuer of the cheque did not have enough funds to cover the amount. When the cheque was initially deposited into the company's account, the bank credited (increased) the account. When the customer's bank returned the cheque marked NSF, the company's bank debited (decreased) the account. EFT indicates electronic funds transfer and may represent a withdrawal or a deposit.

Using the Bank Statement as a Control over Cash

The bank statement is used by a company as a primary control over cash. A company uses the bank's statement as a control by comparing the company's recording of cash transactions to those recorded by the bank.

The cash balance shown by a bank statement is usually different from the company's cash balance, as shown in Exhibit 6.

Differences between the company's records and the bank balance may arise because of a delay by either the company or the bank in recording transactions. For example, a time lag of one or more days is normal between the date a cheque is written and the date it is paid by the bank. Uncashed cheques are referred to as *outstanding cheques*. A time lag is also normal between when the company mails a deposit to the bank

Exhibit 6

Power Networking's Records and Bank Statement

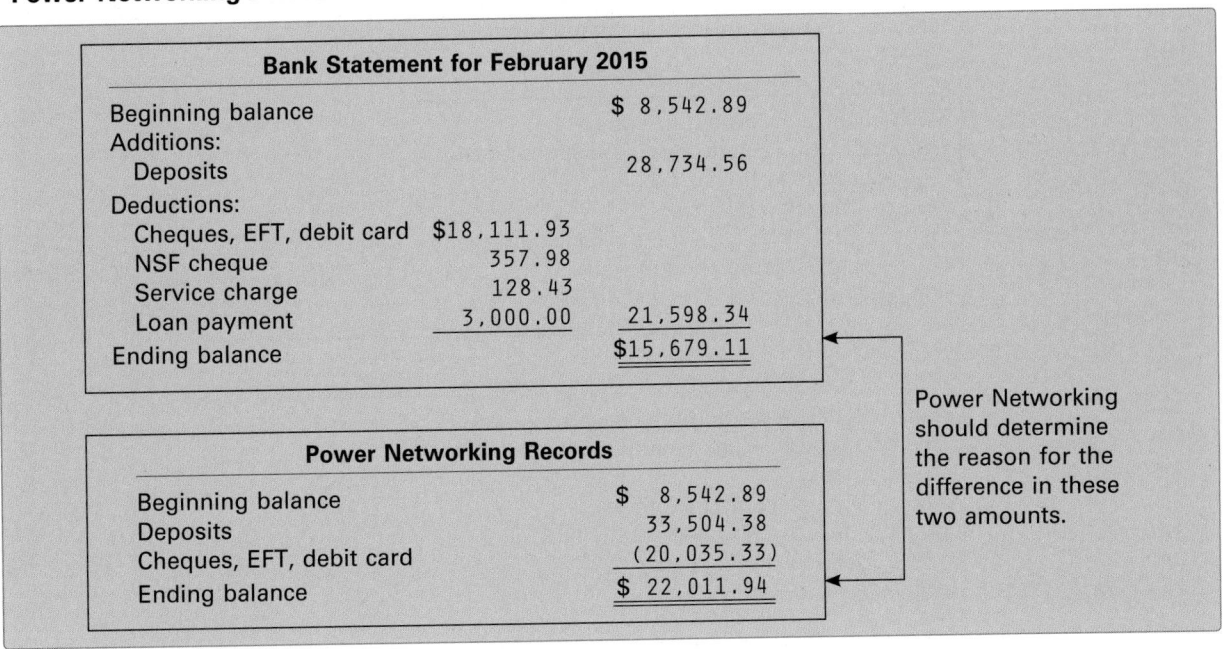

Bank Statement for February 2015		
Beginning balance		$ 8,542.89
Additions:		
Deposits		28,734.56
Deductions:		
Cheques, EFT, debit card	$18,111.93	
NSF cheque	357.98	
Service charge	128.43	
Loan payment	3,000.00	21,598.34
Ending balance		$15,679.11

Power Networking Records	
Beginning balance	$ 8,542.89
Deposits	33,504.38
Cheques, EFT, debit card	(20,035.33)
Ending balance	$ 22,011.94

Power Networking should determine the reason for the difference in these two amounts.

(or uses the night depository) and when the bank receives and records the deposit. Deposits that do not appear on the bank statement due to time lags are referred to as *deposits in transit*.

Differences may also arise because the bank has debited or credited the company's account for transactions that the company will not know about until the bank statement is received. Finally, differences may arise from errors made by either the company or the bank. For example, the company may incorrectly post to Cash a cheque written for $4,500 as $450. Likewise, a bank may incorrectly record the amount of a cheque.

INTEGRITY, OBJECTIVITY, AND ETHICS IN BUSINESS

CHEQUE FRAUD

Cheque fraud involves counterfeiting, altering, or otherwise manipulating the information on cheques in order to fraudulently cash a cheque. Fraud and counterfeiting are among the fastest-growing problems affecting the financial system, generating more than $10 billion in losses annually. Criminals perpetrate the fraud by taking blank cheques from your chequebook, finding a cancelled cheque in the garbage, or removing a cheque you have mailed to pay bills. Consumers can prevent cheque fraud by carefully storing blank cheques, placing outgoing mail in postal mailboxes, and shredding cancelled cheques.

 # Bank Reconciliation

Describe and illustrate the use of a bank reconciliation in controlling cash.

A **bank reconciliation** is an analysis of the items that result in the cash balance in the bank statement differing from the balance of the cash account in the ledger. The adjusted cash balance determined in the bank reconciliation is reported on the balance sheet.

A bank reconciliation is usually divided into two sections as follows:

1. The *bank section* begins with the cash balance according to the bank statement and ends with the *adjusted balance*.

2. The *company section* begins with the cash balance according to the company's records and ends with the *adjusted balance*.

The *adjusted balance* from the bank and company sections must be equal. The format of the bank reconciliation is shown below.

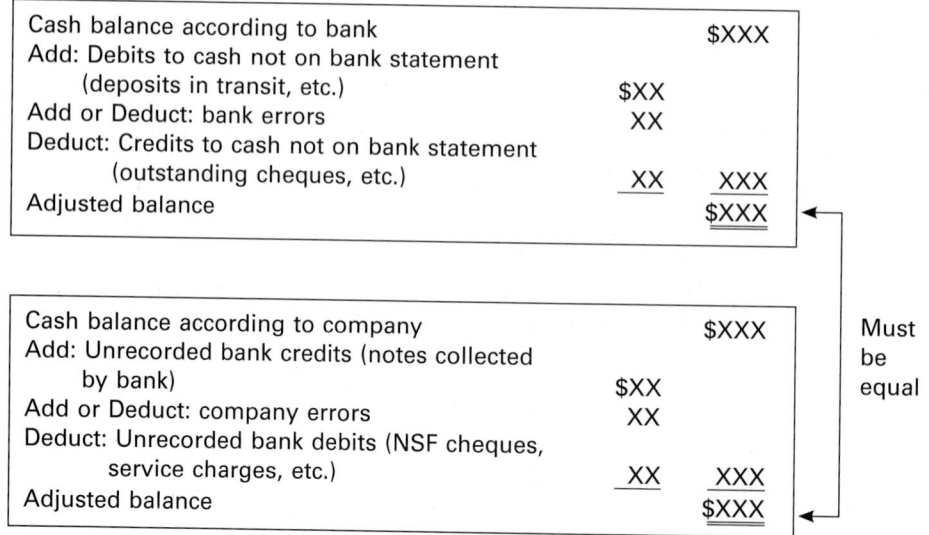

A bank reconciliation is prepared using the following steps:

To begin the reconciliation process, compare each item on the bank statement with each item in the company records. Add a check mark to each item on the bank statement that agrees with the company records. The unmarked items will need to be accounted for in the reconciliation. For items that show different amounts in the bank statement and the company records, determine which amount is correct.

Bank Section of Reconciliation

Step 1. Enter the ending *Cash balance according to the bank statement.*

Step 2. *Add deposits recorded by the company but not recorded by the bank.*
Identify deposits not recorded by the bank by comparing each deposit listed on the bank statement with unrecorded deposits appearing in the preceding period's reconciliation and with the current period's deposits.
Examples: Deposits in transit at the end of the period.

Step 3. *Add or deduct bank recording errors.*
Examples: Deposits or cheques recorded incorrectly on the bank statement.

Step 4. *Deduct outstanding cheques that have not been paid by the bank.*
Examples: Outstanding cheques at the end of the period.

Step 5. Determine the *Adjusted balance.*

Company Section of Reconciliation

Step 6. Enter the ending *Cash balance according to the company ledger.*

Step 7. *Add credit memos that have not been recorded.*
Examples: Notes receivable and interest that the bank has collected for the company.

Step 8. *Add or deduct company recording errors.*
Examples: Deposits or cheques recorded incorrectly in the company records.

Step 9. *Deduct debit memos that have not been recorded.*
Examples: Customers' not sufficient funds (NSF) cheques, bank service charges, EFT payments not recorded by the company.

Step 10. Determine the *Adjusted balance.*

Step 11. Verify that the Adjusted balances determined in steps 5 and 10 are equal.

The adjusted balances in the bank and company sections of the reconciliation must be equal. If the balances are not equal, an item has been overlooked and must be found.

Any bank or company errors discovered should be added or deducted from the bank or company section of the reconciliation. Adjust bank errors on the bank side and company errors on the company side. For example, assume the bank incorrectly recorded a company cheque for $50 as $500. This bank error of $450 ($500 − $50) is added to the bank balance in the bank section of the reconciliation. In addition, the bank is notified of the error so that it can be corrected. On the other hand, assume the company recorded a deposit of $1,200 as $2,100. This company error of $900 ($2,100 − $1,200) is deducted from the cash balance in the company section of the bank reconciliation. The company later corrects the error using a journal entry.

To illustrate, we will use the bank statement for Power Networking in Exhibit 5. This bank statement shows a balance of $15,679.11 as at February 28. The cash balance in Power Networking's records on the same date is $22,011.94 (see Exhibit 6). Using the preceding steps, the following reconciling items were identified:

Step 2. Deposit of February 28, not recorded on bank statement: $4,769.82
Step 4. Outstanding cheques:

Cheque No. 774	$ 416.98
Cheque No. 775	1,236.42
Total	$1,653.40

Step 8. An error of $270 was discovered. This error occurred when Cheque No. 771 for $2,580.34 to Taylor Co., on account, was recorded in the company's journal as $2,850.34.

Step 9. Cheque from customer (Thomas Ivey) for $357.98 returned by the bank because of not sufficient funds (NSF), as indicated by a debit memo.
Bank service charges of $128.43 not recorded in the journal, as indicated by a debit memo.
Loan payment of $3,000, paid by the bank on the company's behalf for the company's note payable to the bank, not recorded in the journal.

The bank reconciliation, based on the bank statement in Exhibit 5 and the preceding reconciling items, is shown in Exhibit 7.

The company's records do not need to be updated for any items in the *bank section* of the reconciliation. This section begins with the cash balance according to the bank statement. However, the bank should be notified of any errors that need to be corrected.

The company's records do need to be updated for any items in the *company section* of the bank reconciliation. The company's records are updated using journal entries. For example, journal entries should be made for any unrecorded bank memos and any company errors.

Exhibit 7

Bank Reconciliation for Power Networking

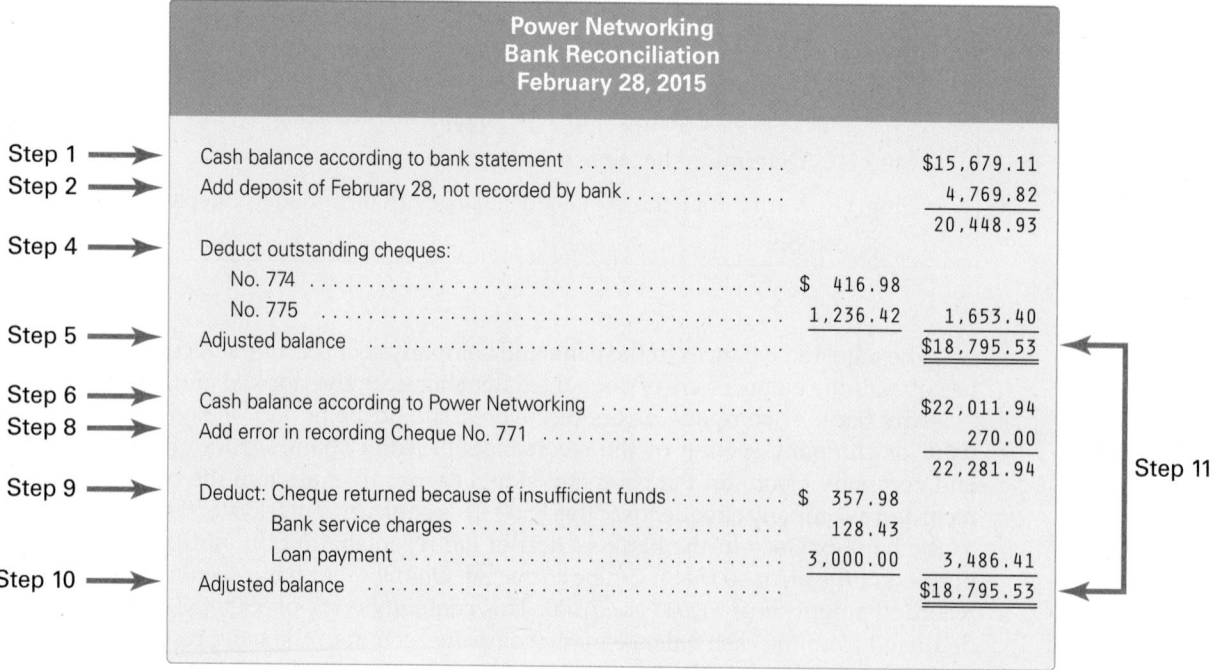

Power Networking
Bank Reconciliation
February 28, 2015

Step 1 → Cash balance according to bank statement $15,679.11
Step 2 → Add deposit of February 28, not recorded by bank 4,769.82
20,448.93

Step 4 → Deduct outstanding cheques:
No. 774 .... $ 416.98
No. 775 .... 1,236.42 | 1,653.40
Step 5 → Adjusted balance $18,795.53

Step 6 → Cash balance according to Power Networking $22,011.94
Step 8 → Add error in recording Cheque No. 771 .... 270.00
22,281.94

Step 9 → Deduct: Cheque returned because of insufficient funds .... $ 357.98
Bank service charges 128.43
Loan payment .... 3,000.00 | 3,486.41
Step 10 → Adjusted balance $18,795.53

Step 11

The journal entries for Power Networking, based on the bank reconciliation shown in Exhibit 7, are as follows:

Feb.	28	Cash	270.00	
		Accounts Payable-Taylor Co.		270.00
		Error in recording cheque No. 771.		
	28	Accounts Receivable—Thomas Ivey	357.98	
		Miscellaneous Expense	128.43	
		Note Payable	3,000.00	
		Cash		3,486.41
		Bank reconciliation adjustments.		

After the preceding journal entries are recorded and posted, the cash account will have a debit balance of $18,795.53. This cash balance agrees with the adjusted balance shown on the bank reconciliation. This is the amount of cash on February 28 and is the amount reported on Power Networking's February 28 balance sheet.

Businesses may reconcile their bank accounts in a slightly different format from that shown in Exhibit 7. Regardless, the objective is to control cash by reconciling the company's records with the bank statement. In doing so, any errors or misuse of cash may be detected.

To enhance internal control, the bank reconciliation should be prepared by an employee who does not take part in or record cash transactions. Otherwise, mistakes may occur, and cash is more likely to be stolen or misapplied. For example, an employee who handles cash and also reconciles the bank statement could steal a cash deposit, omit the deposit from the accounts, and omit it from the reconciliation.

Bank reconciliations are also important in computerized systems where deposits and cheques are stored in electronic files and records. Some systems use computer software to determine the difference between the bank statement and company cash balances. The software then adjusts for deposits in transit and outstanding cheques. Any remaining differences are reported for further analysis.

EXAMPLE EXERCISE 7-4 Bank Reconciliation ⑤

The following data were gathered to use in reconciling the bank account of Photo Op:

Balance per bank	$14,500
Balance per company records	13,875
Bank service charges	75
Deposit in transit	3,750
NSF cheque	800
Outstanding cheques	5,250

a. Prepare a bank reconciliation for Photo Op.

b. Journalize any necessary entries for Photo Op based on the bank reconciliation.

(continued)

FOLLOW MY EXAMPLE 7-4

a.

PHOTO OP
Bank Reconciliation
DATE

Cash balance according to bank statement...............................		$14,500
Add deposit in transit, not recorded by bank		3,750
		18,250
Deduct outstanding cheques..		5,250
Adjusted balance..		$13,000
Cash balance according to company's records......................		$13,875
Deduct bank service charges......................................	$ 75	
Deduct NSF cheque	800	875
Adjusted balance..		$13,000
b. Accounts Receivable...	800	
Miscellaneous Expense	75	
Cash		875
Bank reconciliation adjustments.		

For Practice: PE 7-4

 Financial Statement Reporting of Cash

Describe and illustrate the reporting of cash and cash equivalents in the financial statements.

Cash is normally listed as the first asset in the Current Assets section of the balance sheet. Most companies present only a single cash amount on the balance sheet by combining all their bank and cash fund accounts.

A company may temporarily have excess cash. In such cases, the company normally invests in highly liquid investments in order to earn interest. These investments are called **cash equivalents**. Cash equivalents are defined as "short-term, highly liquid investments that are readily convertible to known amounts of cash and that are subject to an insignificant risk of changes in value."[4] Examples of cash equivalents include

4 *CICA Handbook–Accounting*, 2012, Part II, S.1540.06(b); 2013, Part I, IAS 7.6.

certificates of deposit, notes issued by major corporations (referred to as commercial paper), and money market funds. In such cases, companies usually report *Cash and cash equivalents* as one amount on the balance sheet.

The balance sheet presentation for cash for Morning Java is shown below.

Morning Java Balance Sheet December 31, 2015	
Assets	
Current assets:	
Cash and cash equivalents	$235,000

Banks may require that companies maintain minimum cash balances in their bank accounts. Such a balance is called a **compensating balance**. This balance is often required by the bank as part of a loan agreement or line of credit. A *line of credit* is a preapproved amount the bank is willing to lend to a customer upon request. Compensating balance requirements are normally disclosed in notes to the financial statements.

FINANCIAL ANALYSIS AND INTERPRETATION

Cash is vitally important for businesses. For companies that are either starting up or in financial distress, cash is critical for their survival. In their first few years of operations, start-up companies often report losses and negative net cash flows. In these cases, the ratio of **cash to monthly cash expenses** (negative cash flow for operating activities) is useful for assessing how long a company can continue to operate without additional financing or without generating positive cash flows from operations. Likewise, this ratio can be used to assess how long a business may continue to operate when experiencing financial distress. In computing cash to monthly cash expenses, the amount of cash on hand can be taken from the balance sheet, and the monthly cash expenses can be estimated from the operating activities section of the statement of cash flows.

The ratio of cash to monthly cash expenses is computed by first determining the monthly cash expenses. The monthly cash expenses are determined as follows:

$$\text{Monthly Cash Expenses} = \frac{\text{Negative Cash Flows from Operations}}{12}$$

The ratio of cash to monthly cash expenses can then be computed as follows:

$$\text{Ratio of Cash to Monthly Cash Expenses} = \frac{\text{Cash and Cash Equivalents as at Year-End}}{\text{Monthly Cash Expenses}}$$

To illustrate these ratios, we use Le Château Inc., a Canadian retail store specializing in men's and women's clothing and accessories. For the year ended January 28, 2012, Le Château reported the following data:

Negative cash flows from operations	$ (11,304,000)
Cash and cash equivalents as at January 28, 2012	7,193,000

Based on the preceding data, the monthly cash expenses, sometimes referred to as **cash burn**, were $942,000 per month ($11,304,000/12). Thus, as at January 28, 2012, the cash to monthly cash expenses ratio was 7.6 ($7,193,000/$942,000). That is, as of January 28, 2012, Le Château will run out of cash in less than eight months unless it changes its operations, sells investments, or raises additional financing. In a press release on January 2, 2012, Le Château Inc. announced it had made arrangements for long-term financing of $10 million. Time will tell whether this financing will enable Le Château to turn its negative cash flows from operations into positive cash flows.

EXAMPLE EXERCISE 7-5 Ratio of Cash to Monthly Cash Expenses   6

Financial data for Hauser Company are shown below.

	For Year Ended December 31, 2015
Cash on December 31, 2015	$58,800
Cash flow from operations	(72,000)

1. Compute the ratio of cash to monthly cash expenses.
2. What will Hauser need to do to improve their cash position?

FOLLOW MY EXAMPLE 7-5

1. $\text{Monthly Cash Expenses} = \dfrac{\text{Negative Cash Flow from Operations}}{12}$

$$= \dfrac{\$72,000}{12} = \$6,000 \text{ per month}$$

$\dfrac{\text{Ratio of Cash to}}{\text{Monthly Cash Expenses}} = \dfrac{\text{Cash and Cash Equivalents as at Year-End}}{\text{Monthly Cash Expenses}}$

$$= \dfrac{\$58,800}{\$6,000} = 9.8 \text{ months}$$

2. The preceding computations indicate that Hauser Company has 9.8 months of cash remaining as at December 31, 2015. Hauser Company will need to generate positive cash flow from operations, raise additional financing from its owners, or issue debt.

For Practice: PE 7-5

At a Glance 7

1   Describe and illustrate the objectives and elements of internal control.

Key Points	Key Learning Outcomes	Page	Example Exercises
The objectives of internal control are to provide reasonable assurance that (1) assets are safeguarded and used for business purposes, (2) business information is accurate, and (3) laws and regulations are complied with. The elements of internal control are the control environment, risk assessment, control procedures, monitoring, and information and communication.	• List the objectives of internal control.	351	
	• List the elements of internal control.	352	7-1
	• Describe each element of internal control and factors influencing each element.	353	

2 Describe the accounting for petty cash funds.

Key Points	Key Learning Outcomes	Page	Example Exercises
Petty cash funds, or special-purpose funds, such as travel funds, are used by businesses to meet specific needs. Each fund is established by cashing a cheque for the amount of cash needed. At periodic intervals, the fund is replenished and the disbursements recorded.	• Describe the use of petty cash funds.	356	
	• Journalize the entry to establish a petty cash fund.	357	7-2

3 Describe and illustrate the application of internal controls to cash.

Key Points	Key Learning Outcomes	Page	Example Exercises
Controls over cash include use of a cash register, remittance slips, segregation of duties, voucher systems, and EFTs.	• Describe and give examples of controls for cash received from cash sales, cash received in the mail, and cash received by EFT, debit cards, and credit cards.	360	
	• Describe and give examples of controls for cash payments made using a voucher system and cash payments made by EFT, debit cards, and credit cards.	362	

4 Describe the nature of a bank account and its use in controlling cash.

Key Points	Key Learning Outcomes	Page	Example Exercises
Bank accounts help control cash by reducing the amount of cash on hand and facilitating the transfer of cash between businesses and clients. In addition, the bank statement allows a business to reconcile the cash transactions recorded in the accounting records to those recorded by the bank.	• Describe how the use of bank accounts helps control cash.	363	
	• Describe a bank statement and provide examples of items that appear on a bank statement as debit and credit memos.	363	7-3

5 Describe and illustrate the use of a bank reconciliation in controlling cash.

Key Points	Key Learning Outcomes	Page	Example Exercises
The cash balance on the bank statement is adjusted for the company's changes in cash that do not appear on the bank statement and for any bank errors. The cash balance according to the company's records is adjusted for the bank's changes in cash that do not appear on the company's records and for any company errors. The adjusted balances for the two sections must be equal. The items in the company section must be journalized on the company's records.	• Describe a bank reconciliation.	366	
	• Prepare a bank reconciliation.	367	7-4
	• Journalize any necessary entries on the company's records based on the bank reconciliation.	369	7-4

6 Describe and illustrate the reporting of cash and cash equivalents in the financial statements.

Key Points	Key Learning Outcomes	Page	Example Exercises
Cash is listed as the first asset in the Current Assets section of the balance sheet. Companies that have invested excess cash in highly liquid investments usually report *Cash and cash equivalents* on the balance sheet.	• Describe the reporting of cash and cash equivalents in the financial statements.	370	
	• Illustrate the reporting of cash and cash equivalents in the financial statements.	371	
	• Calculate the ratio of cash to monthly cash expenses.	371	7-5

GLOSSARY

bank reconciliation – The analysis that details the items responsible for the difference between the cash balance reported in the bank statement and the balance of the cash account in the ledger. (p. 366)

bank statement – A summary of all bank transactions, which is made available online or mailed to the account holder each month. (p. 363)

cash – Coins, currency (paper money), cheques, money orders, and money on deposit that is available for unrestricted withdrawal from banks and other financial institutions. (p. 359)

cash burn – A company's monthly cash expenses often used in the calculation of cash to monthly cash expenses ratio. (p. 371)

cash disbursements journal – A record of all cash payments made by the business. (p. 359)

cash equivalents – Highly liquid investments that are usually reported with cash on the balance sheet. (p. 370)

cash over and short account – An account that records errors in cash sales or errors in making change that cause the amount of actual cash on hand to differ from the beginning amount of cash plus the cash sales for the day. (p. 357)

cash receipts journal – A record of all cash received by the business from any source. (p. 359)

cash to monthly cash expenses – A company's monthly cash expenses in relation to its cash on hand, often

used to assess how long a company can continue to operate without additional financing, positive cash flow, or financial distress. (p. 371)

collusion – An illegal agreement or cooperation to defraud others of their legal rights. (p. 356)

compensating balance – A requirement by some banks requiring account holders to maintain minimum cash balances in their bank accounts. (p. 371)

control environment – The overall attitude of management and employees about the importance of controls. (p. 353)

credit card – A card allowing customers to electronically withdraw cash or pay for purchases. The funds increase the amount the customer owes to a third party. (p. 362)

data encryption – The process of translating computer information into code. (p. 354)

debit card – A card allowing customers to electronically withdraw cash or pay for purchases. The funds are immediately withdrawn from the customer's bank account. (p. 362)

electronic funds transfer (EFT) – A system in which computers rather than paper (money, cheques, etc.) are used to effect cash transactions. (p. 361)

elements of internal control – The control environment, risk assessment, control procedures, information and

communication, and monitoring. (p. 352)

employee fraud – The intentional act of deceiving an employer for personal gain. (p. 352)

external auditors – Independent public accountants who test the reasonableness of a company's financial records and verify the accuracy of the financial statements. (p. 355)

internal auditors – Internal employees responsible for ensuring proper recording of a company's financial transactions and day-to-day monitoring of the internal control system. (p. 355)

internal control – The policies and procedures used to safeguard assets, ensure accurate business information, and ensure compliance with laws and regulations. (p. 351)

NSF cheques – A term used when a cheque is written on an account with not sufficient funds. (p. 365)

petty cash fund – A special cash fund to pay relatively small amounts. (p. 356)

special-purpose fund – A cash fund used for a special business need. (p. 357)

voucher – A form for recording relevant data about a liability and the details of its payment. (p. 362)

voucher system – A set of procedures for authorizing and recording liabilities and cash payments. (p. 362)

ILLUSTRATIVE PROBLEM

The bank statement for Urethane Company for June 30, 2015, indicates a balance of $9,143.11. All cash receipts are deposited each evening in a night depository, after banking hours. The accounting records indicate a balance as at June 30, 2015 of $4,706.25. Comparing the bank statement and the accompanying cancelled cheques and memos with the records reveals the following reconciling items:

a. The bank had collected for Urethane Company $1,030 on a note left for collection. The face amount of the note was $1,000.

b. A deposit of $1,852.21, representing receipts of June 30, had been made through the night deposit, too late to appear on the bank statement.

c. Cheques outstanding totalled $5,265.27.

d. A cheque drawn for $139 had been incorrectly charged by the bank as $157.

e. A cheque for $30 returned with the statement had been recorded in the company's records as $60. The cheque was for the payment of an obligation to Avery Equipment Company for the purchase of office supplies on account.

f. Bank service charges for June amounted to $18.20.

Instructions

1. Prepare a bank reconciliation for June.
2. Journalize the entries that should be made by Urethane Company.

Solution

1.

Urethane Company Bank Reconciliation June 30, 2015		
Cash balance according to bank statement		$ 9,143.11
Add: Deposit of June 30 not recorded by bank	$1,852.21	
Bank error in charging cheque as $157 instead of $139	18.00	1,870.21
		11,013.32
Deduct: Outstanding cheques		5,265.27
Adjusted balance		$ 5,748.05
Cash balance according to company's records		$ 4,706.25
Add: Proceeds of note collected by bank, including $30 interest . . .	$1,030.00	
Error in recording cheque	30.00	1,060.00
		5,766.25
Deduct: Bank service charges		18.20
Adjusted balance		$ 5,748.05

2.

2015				
June	30	Cash	1,060.00	
		Notes Receivable		1,000.00
		Interest Revenue		30.00
		Accounts Payable—Avery Equipment Company		30.00
		Bank reconciliation adjustment.		
	30	Miscellaneous Administrative Expense	18.20	
		Cash		18.20
		Bank reconciliation adjustment.		

EYE OPENERS

1. What is the purpose of the Canadian regulations pertaining to internal controls?
2. What are the objectives of *internal control*?
3. (a) Name and describe the five elements of internal control. (b) Is any one element of internal control more important than another?
4. How does a policy of rotating clerical employees from job to job aid in strengthening the control procedures within the control environment? Explain.
5. Why should the responsibility for a sequence of related operations be divided among different persons? Explain.
6. Oak Grove Ltd. has a petty cash fund of $1,500. (a) Because the petty cash fund is only $1,500, should Oak Grove Ltd. implement controls over petty cash? (b) What controls, if any, could be used for the petty cash fund?
7. Why should the employee who handles cash receipts not have the responsibility for maintaining the accounts receivable records? Explain.
8. In an attempt to improve operating efficiency, one employee was made responsible for all purchasing, receiving, and storing of supplies. Is this organizational change wise from an internal control standpoint? Explain.

9. The ticket seller at a movie theatre doubles as a ticket taker for a few minutes each day while the ticket taker is on a break. Which control procedure of a business's system of internal control is violated in this situation?

10. Why should the responsibility for maintaining the accounting records be separated from the responsibility for operations? Explain.

11. Assume that Yvonne Dauphin, accounts payable clerk for Bedell Ltd., stole $73,250 by paying fictitious invoices for goods that were never received. The clerk set up accounts in the names of the fictitious companies and cashed the cheques at a local bank. Describe a control procedure that would have prevented or detected the fraud.

12. Before a voucher for the purchase of merchandise is approved for payment, supporting documents should be compared to verify the accuracy of the liability. Give an example of supporting documents for the purchase of merchandise.

13. The accounting clerk pays all obligations by prenumbered cheques and signs the cheques. What are the strengths and weaknesses in the internal control over cash payments in this situation?

14. The balance of Cash is likely to differ from the bank statement balance. What two factors are likely to be responsible for the difference?

15. What is the purpose of preparing a bank reconciliation?

16. Do items reported as credits on the bank statement represent (a) additions made by the bank to the company's balance or (b) deductions made by the bank from the company's balance? Explain.

17. (a) How are cash equivalents reported in the financial statements? (b) What are some examples of cash equivalents?

PRACTICE EXERCISES

① PE 7-1
Internal control elements

EE 7-1 p. 356

Identify each of the following as relating to (a) the control environment, (b) control procedures, or (c) monitoring.

1. Hiring of external auditors to review the adequacy of controls
2. Personnel policies
3. Safeguarding inventory in a locked warehouse

---

② PE 7-2
Petty cash fund

EE 7-2 p. 358

Prepare journal entries for each of the following:

a. Issued a cheque to establish a petty cash fund of $300.

b. The amount of cash in the petty cash fund is $95. Issued a cheque to replenish the fund, based on the following summary of petty cash receipts: store supplies, $120, and miscellaneous selling expense, $75. Record any missing funds in the cash over/short account.

---

④ PE 7-3
Items on company's bank statement

EE 7-3 p. 364

The following items may appear on a bank statement:

1. Bank correction of an error from posting another customer's cheque to the company's account
2. EFT deposit
3. Loan proceeds
4. NSF cheque

Using the format shown below, indicate whether each item would appear as a debit or credit memo on the bank statement and whether the item would increase or decrease the balance of the company's bank account.

Item No.	Appears on the Bank Statement as a Debit or Credit Memo	Increases or Decreases the Balance of the Company's Bank Account

⑤ PE 7-4

Bank reconciliation

EE 7-4 p. 369

The following data were gathered to use in reconciling the bank account of East Meets West Company:

Balance per bank	$18,340
Balance per company records	6,480
Bank service charges	50
Deposit in transit	2,500
Note collected by bank with $250 interest	8,250
Outstanding cheques	7,160
NSF cheque for Scott accounts receivable	1,000

1. Prepare a bank reconciliation for East Meets West Company.
2. Journalize any necessary entries for East Meets West Company based on the bank reconciliation.

⑥ PE 7-5

Ratio of cash to monthly cash expenses

EE 7-5 p. 372

Financial data for Preston Company are shown below.

	For Year Ended December 31, 2015
Cash on December 31, 2015	$184,800
Cash flow from operations	(158,400)

1. Compute the ratio of cash to monthly cash expenses.
2. What will Preston need to do to improve their cash position?

EXERCISES

① ③ EX 7-1

Internal control report

Publicly traded corporations are required to have their financial statements audited by an independent auditor. The Canadian Securities Administrators National Instrument 52-109 Certification of Disclosure in Issuers' Annual and Interim Filings requires the chief executive officer (CEO) and chief financial officer (CFO) of a corporation to certify that they have evaluated the effectiveness of the company's internal control over financial reporting. Why would the CEO and CFO be responsible for certifying the effectiveness of the controls and not the independent auditor?

① ③ EX 7-2

Internal controls

Courtney Linge has recently been hired as the manager of Jittery Jim's Coffee. Jittery Jim's Coffee is a national chain of franchised coffee shops. During her first month as store manager, Courtney encountered the following internal control situations:

a. Courtney caught an employee putting a case of 100 single-serving tea bags in his car. Not wanting to create a scene, Courtney smiled and said, "I don't think you're putting those tea bags on the right shelf. Don't they belong inside the coffee shop?" The employee returned the tea bags to the stockroom.

b. Jittery Jim's Coffee has one cash register. Prior to Courtney's joining the coffee shop, each employee working on a shift would take a customer order, accept payment, and then prepare the order. Courtney made one employee on each shift responsible for taking orders and accepting the customer's payment. Other employees prepare the orders.

c. Because only one employee uses the cash register, that employee is responsible for counting the cash at the end of the shift and verifying that the cash in the drawer matches the amount of cash sales recorded by the cash register. Courtney expects each cashier to balance the drawer to the penny *every* time—no exceptions.

State whether you agree or disagree with Courtney's method of handling each situation and explain your answer.

EX 7-3

Internal controls

Anasazi Earth Clothing is a retail store specializing in women's clothing. The store has established a liberal return policy for the holiday season in order to encourage gift purchases. Any item purchased during November and December may be returned through January 31, with a receipt, for cash or exchange. If the customer does not have a receipt, cash will still be refunded for any item less than $100. If the item is more than $100, a cheque is mailed to the customer.

Whenever an item is returned, a store clerk completes a return slip, which the customer signs. The return slip is placed in a special box. The store manager visits the return counter approximately once every two hours to authorize the return slips. Clerks are instructed to place the returned merchandise on the proper rack on the selling floor as soon as possible.

This year, returns at Anasazi Earth Clothing have reached an all-time high. The store has received a large number of returns of less than $100 without receipts.

1. How can sales clerks employed at Anasazi Earth Clothing use the store's return policy to steal money from the cash register?
2. What internal control weaknesses in the return policy make cash thefts easier?
3. Would the possibility of theft be reduced by issuing a store credit in place of a cash refund for all merchandise returned without a receipt? List the advantages and disadvantages of issuing a store credit in place of a cash refund.
4. Assume that Anasazi Earth Clothing is committed to the current policy of issuing cash refunds without a receipt. What changes in the store's procedures for customer refunds would improve internal control?

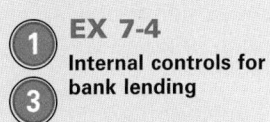

EX 7-4

Internal controls for bank lending

A bank provides loans to businesses in the community through its Commercial Lending Department. Small loans (less than $100,000) may be approved by an individual loan officer, whereas larger loans (greater than $100,000) must be approved by a board of loan officers. Once a loan is approved, the funds are made available to the loan applicant under agreed-upon terms. The president of the bank has instituted a policy whereby he has the individual authority to approve loans up to $5,000,000. The president believes this policy will allow flexibility to approve loans to valued clients much quicker than under the previous policy.

As an internal auditor of the bank, how would you respond to this change in policy?

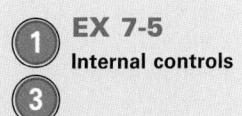

EX 7-5

Internal controls

One of the largest losses in history from unauthorized securities trading involved a securities trader for the French bank Société Générale. The trader was able to circumvent internal controls and create more than $7 billion in trading losses in six months. The trader apparently escaped detection by using knowledge of the bank's internal control systems learned from a previous back-office monitoring job. Much of this monitoring involved the use of software to monitor trades. In addition, traders are usually kept to tight spending limits. Apparently, these controls failed in this case.

What general weaknesses in Société Générale's internal controls contributed to the occurrence and size of the losses?

EX 7-6

Internal controls

An employee of JHT Holdings Inc., a trucking company, was responsible for resolving roadway accident claims of less than $25,000. The employee created fake accident claims and wrote settlement cheques of between $5,000 and $25,000 to friends or acquaintances acting as phony "victims." One friend recruited subordinates at his place of work to cash some of the cheques. The JHT employee also recruited lawyers, whom he paid to represent both the trucking company and the fake victims in the bogus accident settlements. When the lawyers cashed the cheques, they allegedly split the money with the corrupt JHT employee. This fraud went undetected for two years.

Why would it take so long to discover such a fraud?

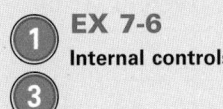

EX 7-7
Internal controls

Bizarro Sound Co. discovered a fraud whereby one of its front-office administrative employees used company funds to purchase goods, such as computers, digital cameras, compact disc players, and other electronic items, for her own use. The fraud was discovered when employees noticed an increase in delivery frequency from vendors and the use of unusual vendors. After some investigation, it was discovered that the employee had altered the description or changed the quantity on an invoice in order to explain the cost on the bill.

What general internal control weaknesses contributed to this fraud?

EX 7-8
Internal controls

South Shore TV and Audio was busier than usual during the month of May, but the income statement showed sales for the month were lower than usual. An investigation revealed that one of the checkout employees had been involved in theft. The employee would override the cash register sales price when her friends purchased televisions and stereo equipment. She would identify the items as sale items when they were not on sale.

1. Identify the store's weakness in internal control.
2. What steps could be taken to correct this weakness?

EX 7-9
Financial statement fraud

A former chairman, the CFO, and the controller of Donnkenny, Inc., an apparel company that makes sportswear for Pierre Cardin and Victoria Jones, pleaded guilty to financial statement fraud. These managers used false journal entries to record fictitious sales, hid inventory in public warehouses so that it could be recorded as "sold," and required sales orders to be backdated so that the sales could be moved back to an earlier period. The combined effect of these actions caused $25 million out of $40 million in quarterly sales to be phony.

1. Why might control procedures listed in this chapter be insufficient in stopping this type of fraud?
2. How could this type of fraud be stopped?

EX 7-10
Petty cash fund entries

1. Journalize the entries to record the following:
   a. Cheque No. 732 is issued to establish a petty cash fund of $800.
   b. The amount of cash in the petty cash fund is now $294. Cheque No. 857 is issued to replenish the fund, based on the following summary of petty cash receipts: office supplies, $295; miscellaneous selling expense, $120; miscellaneous administrative expense, $91.
2. Discuss the advantages and disadvantages of maintaining a large petty cash fund.

EX 7-11
Petty cash fund entries

Journalize the entries to record the following:
a. Cheque No. 356 is issued to establish a petty cash fund of $500.
b. Cheque No. 429 is issued to replenish the fund. A summary of the receipts in the fund shows the following: office supplies, $176; delivery charges, $120; cash advance to an employee, $75; cash advance to the owner for lunch with his spouse, $50. At the time the fund was replenished, it had $79 cash remaining.

EX 7-12
Petty cash fund entries

Shawnees Boat Club has never maintained a petty cash fund. The owner has decided that the club should have some funds available for small purchases. On May 1, a cheque for $200 was issued to establish the fund.

On May 13, the fund had $2 remaining, so a cheque was issued to replenish the fund, based on the following summary of petty cash receipts: office supplies, $75; delivery charges for clothes that will be resold to customers, $28; miscellaneous administrative expense, $95.

On May 31, the fund had $5 remaining, so another cheque was issued to replenish the fund. The owner decided to increase the fund to $400 to avoid having to replenish it twice a month. A summary of the petty cash receipts showed the following: office supplies, $38; meals for the owner, $49; postage expense, $27; newspaper advertising, $78. Prepare journal entries to record the transactions related to petty cash.

---

2 **EX 7-13**
Petty cash fund entries

The owner of Jake's Hardware Supply has decided to set up a petty cash fund for small purchases. On July 1, a cheque for $500 was issued to establish the fund.

On July 31, the fund had $305 remaining. A summary of the petty cash receipts showed the following: equipment repair expense, $72; a movie for the owner, $25; postage expense, $15; newspaper advertising, $52; miscellaneous administrative expense, $37. The owner decided the store did not need this much money left in the office and asked to have the fund reduced to $350 when the fund was reimbursed on July 31. Prepare journal entries to record the transactions related to petty cash.

---

2 **EX 7-14**
Petty cash fund entries

Journalize the entries to record the following:
a. Cheque No. 1054 is issued to establish a petty cash fund of $700.
b. Cheque No. 1259 is issued to replenish the fund. A summary of the receipts in the fund shows the following: vehicle expense, $173; advertising expense, $69; cash advance to an employee, $75; cash advance to the owner for office supplies, $65. There was $329 cash in the fund at the time it was replenished and the company decided to reduce the fund by $200.

---

1 **EX 7-15**
3 **Internal control of cash receipts**

The procedures used for over-the-counter receipts are as follows. At the close of each day's business, the sales clerks count the cash in their respective cash drawers. Next, they determine the amount recorded by the cash register and prepare the memo cash form, noting any discrepancies. An employee from the cashier's office counts the cash, compares the total with the memo, and takes the cash to the cashier's office.

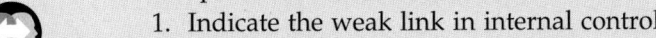

1. Indicate the weak link in internal control.
2. How can the weakness be corrected?

---

1 **EX 7-16**
3 **Internal control of cash receipts**

Victor Blackmon works at the drive-through window of Buffalo Bob's Burgers. Occasionally, when a drive-through customer orders, Victor fills the order and pockets the customer's money. He does not ring up the order on the cash register.

Identify the internal control weaknesses at Buffalo Bob's Burgers. Discuss what can be done to prevent this theft.

---

1 **EX 7-17**
3 **Internal control of cash receipts**

The mailroom employees send all remittances and remittance advices to the cashier. The cashier deposits the cash in the bank and forwards the remittance advices and duplicate deposit slips to the Accounting Department.

1. Indicate the weak link in internal control in the handling of cash receipts.
2. How can the weakness be corrected?

---

1 **EX 7-18**
3 **Entry for cash sales; cash short**

The actual cash received from cash sales was $36,183, and the amount indicated by the cash register total was $36,197. Journalize the entry to record the cash receipts and cash sales.

---

1 **EX 7-19**
3 **Entry for cash sales; cash over**

The actual cash received from cash sales was $11,279, and the amount indicated by the cash register total was $11,256. Journalize the entry to record the cash receipts and cash sales.

EX 7-20
Internal control of cash payments

Cordova Co. is a small merchandising company with a manual accounting system. An investigation revealed that in spite of a sufficient bank balance, a significant amount of available cash discounts had been lost because of failure to make timely payments. In addition, it was discovered that the invoices for several purchases had been paid twice.

Outline procedures for the payment of vendors' invoices so that the possibilities of losing available cash discounts and of paying an invoice a second time will be minimized.

EX 7-21
Internal control of cash payments

Digital Com Company, a communications equipment manufacturer, recently fell victim to a fraud scheme developed by one of its employees. To understand the scheme, it is necessary to review Digital Com's procedures for the purchase of services.

The purchasing agent is responsible for ordering services (such as repairs to a photocopy machine or office cleaning) after receiving a service requisition from an authorized manager. However, because no tangible goods are delivered, a receiving report is not prepared. When the Accounting Department receives an invoice billing Digital Com for a service call, the accounts payable clerk calls the manager who requested the service to verify the work was performed.

The fraud scheme involves Matt DuBois, the manager of plant and facilities. Matt arranged for his uncle's company, Urban Industrial Supply and Service, to be placed on Digital Com's approved vendor list. Matt did not disclose the family relationship.

On several occasions, Matt would submit a requisition for services to be provided by Urban Industrial Supply and Service. However, the service requested was not needed and was never performed. Urban would bill Digital Com for the service and then split the cash payment with Matt.

Explain what changes should be made to Digital Com's procedures for ordering and paying for services to prevent such occurrences in the future.

EX 7-22
Bank reconciliation

Identify each of the following reconciling items as (a) an addition to the cash balance according to the bank statement, (b) a deduction from the cash balance according to the bank statement, (c) an addition to the cash balance according to the company's records, or (d) a deduction from the cash balance according to the company's records. (None of the transactions reported by bank debit and credit memos has been recorded by the company.)

1. Bank service charges, $15.
2. Cheque drawn by company for $160 but incorrectly recorded as $610.
3. Cheque for $500 incorrectly charged by bank as $5,000.
4. Cheque of a customer returned by bank to company because of insufficient funds (NSF), $3,000.
5. Deposit in transit, $15,500.
6. Outstanding cheques, $9,600.
7. Note collected by bank, $10,000.

EX 7-23
Entries based on bank reconciliation

Which of the reconciling items listed in Exercise 7-22 require an entry in the company's accounts?

EX 7-24
Bank reconciliation

✔ Adjusted balance: $16,280

The following data were accumulated for use in reconciling the bank account of Watson's Mill for March:

a. Cash balance according to the company's records at March 31, $16,085.
b. Cash balance according to the bank statement at March 31, $17,350.
c. Cheques outstanding, $6,170.
d. Deposit in transit, not recorded by bank, $5,100.
e. A cheque for $180 in payment of an account was erroneously recorded in the cheque register as $810.
f. Bank debit memo for service charges, $35.
g. NSF cheque, $400.

Prepare a bank reconciliation, using the format shown in Exhibit 7.

EX 7-25

Entries for bank reconciliation

Using the data presented in Exercise 7-24, journalize the entry or entries that should be made by the company.

EX 7-26

Entries for bank reconciliation

Included with CarCo.'s bank statement for July was a debit memo for $372, representing the hydro payment that is automatically withdrawn from CarCo.'s bank account each month. Since the hydro charges are based on actual usage, CarCo. does not know the amount of its monthly bill until it receives the debit memo from the bank. Journalize the entry that CarCo. should make to properly record the hydro payment.

EX 7-27

Entries for note collected by bank

Accompanying a bank statement for Aubertson's Company is a credit memo for $15,300, representing the principal ($15,000) and interest ($300) on a note that had been collected by the bank. The company had not been notified by the bank at the time of the collection and so had made no entries. Journalize the entry that should be made by the company to bring the accounting records up to date.

EX 7-28

Bank reconciliation

An accounting clerk for Carson Office Supplies prepared the following bank reconciliation:

✔ Adjusted balance: $14,221

Carson Office Supplies
Bank Reconciliation
August 31, 2015

Cash balance according to company's records		$ 7,386
Add: Outstanding cheques.	$3,110	
Error by Carson Office Supplies in recording Cheque		
No. 875 as $740 instead of $470	270	
Note for $6,500 collected by bank, including interest	6,630	10,010
		17,396
Deduct: Deposit in transit on August 31	3,685	
Bank service charges	65	3,750
Cash balance according to bank statement.		$13,646

1. From the data in the above bank reconciliation, prepare a new bank reconciliation for Carson Office Supplies, using the format shown in the illustrative problem, on page 376.
2. If a balance sheet were prepared for Carson Office Supplies on August 31, 2015, what amount should be reported for cash?

EX 7-29

Bank reconciliation

The bookkeeper for Octagon Flowers discovered the following data for use in reconciling the bank account for July:

✔ Adjusted balance: $16,000

a. Cash balance according to the company's records at July 31, $15,600.
b. Cash balance according to the bank statement at July 31, $16,230.
c. Cheques outstanding, $3,180.
d. Deposit in transit, not recorded by bank, $1,950.
e. A $3,500 deposit received by the bank was recorded as $2,500 on the bank statement.
f. A cheque for $270 in payment of Telephone Expense was erroneously recorded in the cheque register as $720.
g. Bank debit memo for service charges, $50.

1. Prepare a bank reconciliation, using the format shown in Exhibit 7.
2. If a balance sheet were prepared for Octagon Flowers on July 31, what amount should be reported for cash?
3. Must a bank reconciliation always balance (reconcile)?

EX 7-30

Entries for bank reconciliation

Using the data presented in Exercise 7-29, journalize the entry or entries that the company should make.

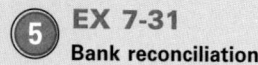

EX 7-31

Bank reconciliation

Identify the errors in the following bank reconciliation:

Alma Co.
Bank Reconciliation
For the Month Ended November 30, 2015

✔ Corrected adjusted
balance: $13,000

Cash balance according to bank statement			$12,090
Add: Outstanding cheques:			
No. 915		$ 850	
960		615	
964		850	
965		775	3,090
			15,180
Deduct deposit of November 30, not recorded by bank			4,000
Adjusted balance			$11,180
Cash balance according to company's records			$ 4,430
Add: Proceeds of note collected by bank:			
Principal	$5,000		
Interest	200	5,200	
Service charges		30	5,230
			9,660
Deduct: Cheque returned because of insufficient funds		1,100	
Error in recording November 23 deposit of $6,100 as $1,600		4,500	5,600
Adjusted balance			$ 4,060

EX 7-32

Using bank reconciliation to determine cash receipts stolen

Lasting Impressions Co. records all cash receipts on the basis of its cash register tapes. Lasting Impressions Co. discovered during June 2015 that one of its sales clerks had stolen an undetermined amount of cash receipts when she took the daily deposits to the bank. The following data have been gathered for June:

Cash in bank according to the general ledger	$ 8,900
Cash according to the June 30, 2015, bank statement	20,500
Outstanding cheques as at June 30, 2015	6,800
Bank service charge for June	100
Note receivable, including interest collected by bank in June	10,400

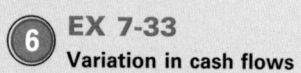

No deposits were in transit on June 30.
a. Determine the amount of cash receipts stolen by the sales clerk.
b. What accounting controls would have prevented or detected this theft?

EX 7-33

Variation in cash flows

Mattel, Inc. designs, manufactures, and markets toy products worldwide. Mattel's toys include Barbie™ fashion dolls and accessories, Hot Wheels™, and Fisher-Price brands. For 2011, Mattel reported the following net cash flows from operating activities (in thousands):

First quarter ended March 31	$ (41,844)
Second quarter ended June 30	(184,934)
Third quarter ended September 30	(95,307)
Fourth quarter ended December 31	986,724

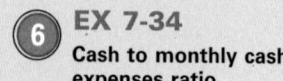

Explain why Mattel reports negative net cash flows from operating activities during the first three quarters, yet reports positive cash flows for the fourth quarter and net positive cash flows for the year.

EX 7-34

Cash to monthly cash expenses ratio

f·a·i

During 2015, Copper Coal Inc. has monthly cash expenses of $275,000. On December 31, 2015, the cash balance is $1,787,500.
a. Compute the ratio of cash to monthly cash expenses.
b. Based on a. what are the implications for Copper Coal Inc.?

6 **EX 7-35**
Cash to monthly cash expenses ratio

f·a·i

Indigo Books & Music Inc., Canada's largest book, gift, and specialty toy retailer, operates throughout Canada and online at www.chapters.indigo.ca. Indigo reported the following financial data (in thousands) for the year ended March 31, 2012:

| Net cash flows from operating activities | $(12,493) |
| Cash and cash equivalents, March 31, 2012 | 207,601 |

a. Determine the monthly cash expenses.
b. Determine the ratio of cash to monthly cash expenses. Round to one decimal place.
c. Based on your analysis, do you believe that Indigo will remain in business?

---

6 **EX 7-36**
Cash to monthly cash expenses ratio

f·a·i

Shorthills Co. reported the following data (in thousands) for the years ended December 31, 2013, 2012, 2011, and 2010:

	2013	**2012**	**2011**	**2010**
Cash as at December 31*	$59,750	$51,112	$45,180	$54,562
Net cash flows from operating activities	(48,089)	(30,683)	(19,319)	(15,507)

*Includes cash equivalents and short-term investments.

1. Determine the monthly cash expenses for 2013, 2012, 2011, and 2010. Round to one decimal place.
2. Determine the ratio of cash to monthly cash expenses as at December 31, 2013, 2012, 2011, and 2010. Round to one decimal place.
3. Based on instructions (1) and (2), comment on Shorthills Co.'s ratio of cash to monthly cash expenses for 2013, 2012, 2011, and 2010.

PROBLEMS SERIES A

1 **2** **3** **PR 7-1A**
Evaluate internal control of cash

The following procedures were recently installed by The Louver Shop:

a. Each cashier is assigned a separate cash register drawer to which no other cashier has access.
b. At the end of a shift, each cashier counts the cash in his or her cash register, unlocks the cash register record, and compares the amount of cash with the amount on the record to determine cash overages and shortages.
c. Vouchers and all supporting documents are perforated with a PAID designation after being paid by the treasurer.
d. Disbursements are made from the petty cash fund only after a petty cash receipt has been completed and signed by the payee.
e. All sales are rung up on the cash register, and a receipt is given to the customer. All sales are recorded on a record locked inside the cash register.
f. Cheques received through the mail are given daily to the accounts receivable clerk for recording collections on account and for depositing in the bank.
g. The bank reconciliation is prepared by the accountant.

Instructions

Indicate whether each of the procedures of internal control over cash represents (1) a strength or (2) a weakness. For each weakness, explain why it is a weakness.

---

1 **2** **3** **PR 7-2A**
Evaluate internal control of cash

Sharon Coulson was recently hired as the new director of accounting at SunShine Minerals. Sharon's first responsibility was to examine the internal control procedures and implement stronger controls where she found weaknesses. Sharon found two weaknesses and implemented new controls in the following areas:

1. Keith was responsible for ordering, receiving, and paying for all supplies.
2. Karen was responsible for counting the cash, recording the daily sales and cash receipts in the journal, and making all the bank deposits.

(continued)

Instructions

1. Indicate the two weaknesses Sharon found.
2. Explain the controls Sharon would likely put in place to protect against these weaknesses.
3. Discuss why these steps may not fully correct the weaknesses in the internal control procedures.

PR 7-3A

Transactions for petty cash, cash over/short

Crimson Company completed the following selected transactions during June 2015:

Jun. 1. Established a petty cash fund of $600.

12. The cash sales for the day, according to the cash register records, totalled $14,683. The actual cash received from cash sales was $14,732.

30. Petty cash on hand was $138. Replenished the petty cash fund for the following disbursements, each evidenced by a petty cash receipt:

Jun. 2. Store supplies, $55.

10. Express charges on merchandise purchased, $80 (Inventory).

14. Office supplies, $35.

15. Office supplies, $40.

18. Postage stamps, $42 (Office Supplies).

20. Repair to fax, $100 (Miscellaneous Administrative Expense).

21. Repair to office door lock, $35 (Miscellaneous Administrative Expense).

22. Postage due on special delivery letter, $27 (Miscellaneous Administrative Expense).

28. Express charges on merchandise purchased, $40 (Inventory).

30. The cash sales for the day, according to the cash register records, totalled $19,320. The actual cash received from cash sales was $19,143.

30. Increased the petty cash fund by $150.

Instructions

Journalize the transactions.

PR 7-4A

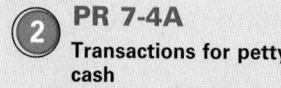

Transactions for petty cash

Lady Bug Express established a petty cash fund of $225 on August 1, 2015. On August 15, 2015, the petty cash fund was increased by $50. On August 31, 2015, the cash box contained $16 and receipts for the following purchases:

Aug. 7. Office supplies, $12.28.

12. Gas for company car, $20.00 (Automobile Expense).

18. Printer ink, $105.60 (Office Supplies).

21. Repair to office printer, $65.00 (Miscellaneous Expenses) and office supplies, $8.96.

28. Store supplies, $44.18 (Inventory).

Instructions

Journalize the necessary entries.

PR 7-5A

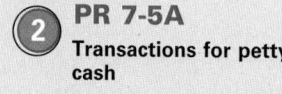

Transactions for petty cash

Kathy's Landscaping established a petty cash fund of $450 on February 1, 2015. On February 28, 2015, the petty cash on hand was $140.65, and the following receipts were found in the cash box:

Feb. 2. Inventory, $166.82.

9. Office supplies, $24.64.

16. IOU from Willie Smith, $40.00.

26. Paper, $72.53 (Office Supplies).
28. The company decided to close the petty cash fund.

Instructions

Journalize the necessary entries.

PR 7-6A

2

Transactions for petty cash

Cold Ice Ltd. established a petty cash fund of $450 on October 1, 2015. The petty cash is replenished when the cash on hand is less than $100. On October 17, 2015, the petty cash on hand was $62.73. The following receipts were found in the cash box:

1. Office supply store receipts, $117.14.
2. Receipts from a grocery store for coffee and creamer, $42.58.
3. Gas receipts for company delivery trucks, $208.24.

On October 31, 2015, the petty cash on hand was $96.47. The following receipts were found in the cash box:

1. Gas receipts for company trucks, $165.73.
2. Receipts from a grocery store for coffee, creamer, and sugar, $47.26.
3. Found receipt from October 2 for office supplies, $19.31.
4. Receipt for 70 bags of ice from competitor to fill emergency customer order, $140.54.

Instructions

Journalize the necessary entries.

PR 7-7A

2

Petty cash funds

Jocelyn is the owner of Jocelyn's Thai Food. She has a policy that all payments must be made by cheque, and she is the only person authorized to sign the cheques. Jocelyn is planning a two-week holiday and is very concerned about a few small deliveries that are expected during her vacation. A friend suggested Jocelyn use a petty cash system to pay for these small deliveries. Jocelyn has come to you for advice about a petty cash system. Specifically she would like answers to the following concerns:

1. If she records the petty cash payments each time the fund is replenished, she will end up with a very large balance in petty cash at the end of the year.
2. What is the best way to control the payments from the fund? Should all employees have access to the petty cash fund? What types of payments should be made out of petty cash?
3. How often should the fund be replenished?

Instructions

Advise Jocelyn on each of her concerns over the petty cash fund.

PR 7-8A

5

Bank reconciliation and entries

✔ 1. Adjusted balance: $15,045

The cash account for Computer Systems at February 28, 2015, indicated a balance of $10,635. The bank statement indicated a balance of $14,933 on February 28, 2015. Comparing the bank statement and the accompanying cancelled cheques and memos with the records reveals the following reconciling items:

a. Cheques outstanding totalled $2,118.
b. A deposit of $2,500, representing receipts of February 28, had been made too late to appear on the bank statement.
c. The bank had collected $4,200 on a note left for collection. The principal amount of the note was $4,000.
d. A cheque for $290 returned with the statement had been incorrectly recorded by Computer Systems as $920. The cheque was for the payment of an obligation to Busser Co. for the purchase of office supplies on account.
e. A cheque drawn for $415 had been incorrectly charged by the bank as $145.
f. Bank service charges for February amounted to $20.
g. An NSF cheque $400, from a client, Karen Guttormson, reported on the bank statement.

(continued)

Instructions

1. Prepare a bank reconciliation.
2. Journalize the necessary entries. The accounts have not been closed.

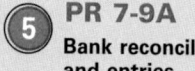

PR 7-9A

Bank reconciliation and entries

✔ 1. Adjusted balance: $15,430

The cash account for Jenny's Sports Co. on June 1, 2015, indicated a balance of $16,515. During June, the total cash deposited was $42,150, and cheques written totalled $45,600. The bank statement indicated a balance of $18,175 on June 30, 2015. Comparing the bank statement, the cancelled cheques, and the accompanying memos with the records revealed the following reconciling items:

a. Cheques outstanding totalled $4,840.

b. A deposit of $2,275, representing receipts of June 30, had been made too late to appear on the bank statement.

c. A cheque for $640 had been incorrectly charged by the bank as $460.

d. A cheque for $80 returned with the statement had been recorded by Jenny's Sports Co. as $800. The cheque was for the payment of an obligation to Miliski Co. on account.

e. The bank had collected for Jenny's Sports Co. $4,350 on a note left for collection. The principal amount of the note was $4,000.

f. Bank service charges for June amounted to $35.

g. A cheque for $2,670 from ChimTech Co. was returned by the bank because of insufficient funds.

Instructions

1. Prepare a bank reconciliation as at June 30.
2. Journalize the necessary entries. The accounts have not been closed.

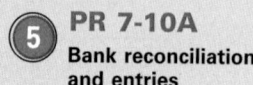

PR 7-10A

Bank reconciliation and entries

✔ 1. Adjusted balance: $16,716

Shelly has just been hired as the bookkeeper for Robinson's Grocery. Her first responsibility is to reconcile the bank account for September 30, 2015. Shelly gathered all the necessary documents and has discovered the following information.

The bank statement had an ending balance at September 30 of $15,693. The previous bookkeeper had recorded total deposits to cash during September of $34,760, and total payments from cash during September of $28,370. The reconciled cash balance on August 31, 2015, was $7,349. An NSF cheque for $548, written by P. Grossman in payment of its account, was returned with the September bank statement. September service charges were $75. Cheque No. 538 had been recorded by the previous bookkeeper as $5,100, but it was correctly cashed by the bank as $1,500. Cheque No. 538 was written to the building's owner for September rent. Four cheques written in September had not yet cleared the bank account, totalling $2,856. A deposit of $3,879, made after banking hours on September 30, did not appear on the bank statement.

Instructions

1. Prepare a bank reconciliation as at September 30, 2015.
2. Journalize the necessary entries. The accounts have not been closed.

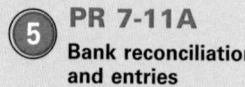

PR 7-11A

Bank reconciliation and entries

✔ 1. Adjusted balance: $15,101.03

The accountant for Jerico Co. has provided you with the following information for the month of March 2015.

March Bank Statement:

EXAMPLE BANK

Statement of Account	Account Type	Statement From - To
8304857	Business	Mar 01/15 - Mar 31/15

DATE	DESCRIPTION	WITHDRAWALS	DEPOSITS	BALANCE
Feb-28	BALANCE FORWARD			8,255.37
Mar-01	DEPOSIT		3,840.24	12,095.61
Mar-03	EFT		1,834.76	13,930.37
Mar-07	CHQ 3396	1,734.28		12,196.09
Mar-13	CHQ 3398	236.45		11,959.64
Mar-14	DEPOSIT		5,295.46	17,255.10
Mar-20	CHQ 3397	2,735.49		14,519.61
Mar-21	EFT	735.29		13,784.32
Mar-26	CHQ 3400	3,026.13		10,758.19
Mar-31	CHQ 3402	2,603.46		8,154.73
Mar-31	DEPOSIT		7,294.34	15,449.07
Mar-31	SERVICE CHARGE	73.25		15,375.82
		11,144.35	**18,264.80**	

Cash Account Transactions for March:

GL ACCOUNT: 1020 Cash Account
For the period of March 01-15 to March 31-15

DATE	REFERENCE	DEBIT	CREDIT	BALANCE Dr. (Cr.)
Opening Balance				8,255.37
Mar-01	Deposit	3,840.24		12,095.61
Mar-07	NO. 3396		1,734.28	10,361.33
Mar-07	NO. 3397		2,735.49	7,625.84
Mar-09	NO. 3398		236.45	7,389.39
Mar-14	Deposit	5,795.46		13,184.85
Mar-20	NO. 3399		1,495.34	11,689.51
Mar-22	NO. 3400		3,026.13	8,663.38
Mar-24	NO. 3401		836.18	7,827.20
Mar-27	NO. 3402		2,630.46	5,196.74
Mar-29	Deposit	7,294.34		12,491.08
Mar-31	Deposit	3,782.36		16,273.44
Mar-31	NO. 3403		1,725.63	14,547.81

Instructions

1. Prepare a bank reconciliation as at March 31, 2015. Assume that any errors in recording deposits or cheques were made by the company, all deposits are from sales, Cheque No. 3402 was paid to a supplier on account, EFT collections are from customer accounts, and EFT payments are to supplier accounts.
2. Journalize any necessary entries.

PR 7-12A

Bank reconciliation and entries

✔ 1. Adjusted balance: $11,178.59

Rocky Mountain Interiors deposits all cash receipts each Wednesday and Friday in a night depository, after banking hours. The data required to reconcile the bank statement as at July 31 have been taken from various documents and records and are reproduced as follows. The sources of the data are printed in capital letters. All cheques were written for payments on account.

BANK RECONCILIATION FOR PRECEDING MONTH (DATED JUNE 30):

Cash balance according to bank statement		$ 9,422.80
Add deposit of June 30, not recorded by bank		780.80
		10,203.60
Deduct outstanding cheques:		
No. 580	$310.10	
No. 602	85.50	
No. 612	92.50	
No. 613	137.50	625.60
Adjusted balance		$ 9,578.00
Cash balance according to company's records		$ 9,605.70
Deduct service charges		27.70
Adjusted balance		$ 9,578.00

CASH ACCOUNT:

Balance as at July 1	$ 9,578.00

CHEQUES WRITTEN:

Number and amount of each cheque issued in July:

Cheque No.	Amount	Cheque No.	Amount	Cheque No.	Amount
614	$243.50	621	$309.50	628	$ 837.70
615	350.10	622	Void	629	329.90
616	279.90	623	Void	630	882.80
617	395.50	624	707.01	631	1,081.56
618	435.40	625	158.63	632	62.40
619	320.10	626	550.03	633	310.08
620	328.87	627	318.73	634	503.30

Total amount of cheques issued in July	$8,405.01

```
                                                        PAGE    1

                                      ACCOUNT NUMBER

  Example Bank
  Calgary, AB                          FROM  7/01/2015  TO  7/31/2015

                                      BALANCE            9,422.80

                                    9 DEPOSITS           6,086.35

                                   20 WITHDRAWALS        8,237.41

  ROCKY MOUNTAIN INTERIORS
  Calgary, AB                        4 OTHER DEBITS
                                      AND CREDITS        3,685.00  CR

                                      NEW BALANCE       10,956.74
```

```
* -- DATE -- * -- CHEQUES AND OTHER DEBITS -- * -- DEPOSITS -- * -- BALANCE-- *

  July 1      No. 580      310.10                              9,112.70
              No. 612       92.50                              9,020.20
              Deposit                          780.80          9,801.00
  July 3      No. 602       85.50                              9,715.50
              No. 614      243.50                              9,472.00
              Deposit                          569.50         10,041.50
  July 6      No. 615      350.10                              9,691.40
              No. 616      279.90                              9,411.50
              Deposit                          701.80         10,113.30
  July 11     No. 617      395.50                              9,717.80
              No. 618      435.40                              9,282.40
              Deposit                          819.24         10,101.64
  July 13     No. 619      320.10                              9,781.54
              No. 620      238.87                              9,542.67
              Deposit                          580.70         10,123.37
  July 14     No. 621      309.50                              9,813.87
              No. 624      707.01                              9,106.86
              Miscellaneous              4,000.00             13,106.86
              No. 625      158.63                             12,948.23
              No. 626      550.03                             12,398.20
              Miscellaneous                160.00             12,558.20
  July 17     No. 627      318.73                             12,239.47
              No. 629      329.90                             11,909.57
              Deposit                          600.10         12,509.67
  July 20     No. 630      882.80                             11,626.87
              No. 631    1,081.56                             10,545.31
              NSF          450.00                             10,095.31
  July 21     No. 628      837.70                              9,257.61
              No. 633      310.08                              8,947.53
              Deposit                          701.26          9,648.79
  July 24     Deposit                          731.45         10,380.24
  July 28     Deposit                          601.50         10,981.74
  July 31     Service charge 25.00                            10,956.74
  * * *                        * * *                          * * *
```

RECONCILING THIS STATEMENT WITH YOUR RECORDS IS ESSENTIAL.
ANY ERROR OR EXCEPTION SHOULD BE REPORTED IMMEDIATELY.

CASH RECEIPTS FOR MONTH OF JULY $6,230.60

DUPLICATE DEPOSIT SLIPS:
  Date and amount of each deposit in July:

Date	Amount	Date	Amount	Date	Amount
July 2	$569.50	July 12	$580.70	July 23	$731.45
5	701.80	16	600.10	26	601.50
9	819.24	19	701.26	31	925.05

(continued)

Instructions

1. Prepare a bank reconciliation as at July 31. If errors in recording deposits or cheques are discovered, assume that the errors were made by the company except for the miscellaneous items, which represent a $4,000 note and the $160 of interest collected on the note. Assume that all deposits are from cash sales. All cheques are written to satisfy accounts payable.
2. Journalize the necessary entries. The accounts have not been closed.
3. What is the amount of Cash that should appear on the balance sheet as at July 31?
4. Assume that a cancelled cheque for $125 has been incorrectly recorded by the bank as $1,250. Briefly explain how the error would be included in a bank reconciliation and how it should be corrected.

PR 7-13A

Bank reconciliation and entries

✔ 1. Adjusted
balance $6,057.48

The Green Box Company has just received its September bank statement from Example Bank. You gather the following information to prepare the September 30, 2015, bank reconciliation.

SEPTEMBER BANK STATEMENT:

EXAMPLE BANK

Statement of Account	Account Type	Statement From - To
7531-3437568	Business	Sept 01/15 - Sept 30/15

DESCRIPTION	DATE	WITHDRAWALS	DEPOSITS	BALANCE
BALANCE FORWARD	AUG 31			5,391.43
No. 257	SEPT 03	406.40		4,985.03
No. 261	SEPT 03	31.73		4,953.30
No. 262	SEPT 03	191.30		4,762.00
Deposit	SEPT 03		351.25	5,113.25
No. 256	SEPT 05	88.73		5,024.52
Deposit	SEPT 10		739.43	5,763.95
No. 242	SEPT 11	130.23		5,633.72
No. 259	SEPT 11	90.20		5,543.52
No. 258	SEPT 17	234.53		5,308.99
No. 265	SEPT 17	111.25		5,197.74
NSF	SEPT 17	335.95		4,861.79
Deposit	SEPT 17		788.92	5,650.71
No. 263	SEPT 20	38.44		5,612.27
No. 267	SEPT 20	3,805.30		1,806.97
No. 268	SEPT 20	34.53		1,772.44
Deposit	SEPT 24		610.59	2,383.03
No. 239	SEPT 28	131.39		2,251.64
Service Charge	SEPT 28	30.00		2,221.64
		5,659.98	**2,490.19**	

CASH ACCOUNT TRANSACTIONS FOR SEPTEMBER:

GL ACCOUNT: 1080 Bank Account
For the period of Sept 01/15 to Sept 30/15

DATE	REFERENCE	DEBIT	CREDIT	BALANCE Dr. (Cr.)
Opening Balance				5,414.98
September 3	No. 256		88.73	5,326.25
	No. 257		406.40	4,919.85
	No. 258		234.53	4,685.32
	No. 259		90.20	4,595.12
	No. 260		84.01	4,511.11
	No. 261		31.73	4,479.38
	No. 262		191.30	4,288.08
September 7	Deposit Slip	739.43		5,027.51
September 14	Deposit Slip	788.92		5,816.43
September 17	No. 263		38.44	5,777.99
	No. 264		469.99	5,308.00
	No. 265		111.25	5,196.75
	No. 266		38.44	5,158.31
	No. 267		380.53	4,777.78
	No. 268		34.53	4,743.25
September 21	Deposit Slip	610.59		5,353.84
September 28	Deposit Slip	1,069.59		6,423.43
		3,208.53	**2,200.08**	

BANK RECONCILIATION FOR PRECEDING MONTH (DATED AUGUST 31):

Cash balance according to bank statement		$5,391.43
Add deposit of August 31, not recorded by bank.		351.25
		5,742.68
Deduct outstanding cheques:		
No. 239	$131.39	
240	66.08	
242	130.23	327.70
Adjusted balance		$5,414.98
Cash balance according to company's records.		$5,444.98
Deduct: Service charges		30.00
Adjusted balance		$5,414.98

Instructions

1. Prepare a bank reconciliation as at September 30, 2015. Assume that any errors in recording deposits or cheques were made by the bank. Deposits are made on Friday evenings.
2. Briefly explain how any errors were reflected in the bank reconciliation and how they should be corrected.
3. Journalize any necessary entries.
4. What should be the balance of the Cash Account as at September 30, 2015?

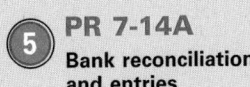

PR 7-14A
Bank reconciliation and entries

Helena's House of Toys banks online with Example Bank. It is March 2, 2015, and you have been asked to reconcile the bank statement as at February 28. You gather the following information:

(continued)

FEBRUARY BANK STATEMENT (note that the later dates are at the top because it is a copy of the online statement):

✔ 1. Adjusted
balance: $7,424.40

EXAMPLE BANK

BUSINESS ACCOUNT - 11980660
February 2015   Balance as at February 28, 2015: $(113.73)

DATE	DESCRIPTION	WITHDRAWALS	DEPOSITS	BALANCE
Feb 28, 2015	Bank Charges	43.75		(113.73)
Feb 28, 2015	EFT	10,954.32		(69.98)
Feb 28, 2015	CHQ#1543	713.00		10,884.34
Feb 28, 2015	CHQ#1542	541.24		11,597.34
Feb 24, 2015	CHQ#1539	54.24		12,138.58
Feb 24, 2015	CHQ#1525	1,221.50		12,192.82
Feb 23, 2015	DEPOSIT		6,528.53	13,414.32
Feb 21, 2015	CHQ#1541	446.98		6,885.79
Feb 20, 2015	CHQ#1538	742.96		7,332.77
Feb 16, 2015	CHQ#1540	9,089.53		8,075.73
Feb 16, 2015	DEPOSIT		9,035.81	17,165.26
Feb 15, 2015	EFT	11,545.50		8,129.45
Feb 09, 2015	DEPOSIT		4,593.28	19,674.95
Feb 07, 2015	CHQ#1536	544.92		15,081.67
Feb 06, 2015	CHQ#1535	693.96		15,626.59
Feb 03, 2015	CHQ#1537	2,481.09		16,320.55
Feb 01, 2015	DEPOSIT		9,014.35	18,801.64
		39,072.99	**29,171.97**	

CASH ACCOUNT TRANSACTIONS FOR FEBRUARY:

GL ACCOUNT: 1060 Cash Account
For the period of February 01-15 to February 28-15

DATE	REFERENCE	DEBIT	CREDIT	BALANCE Dr. (Cr.)
Opening Balance				7,119.80
February 1	NO. 1535		693.96	6,425.84
	NO. 1536		544.92	5,880.92
	NO. 1537		2,481.09	3,399.83
	Bank Deposit	9,014.35		12,414.18
February 2	NO. 1538		742.96	11,671.22
February 8	NO. 1539		45.24	11,625.98
	Bank Deposit	4,953.28		16,579.26
February 15	NO. 1540		9,089.53	7,489.73
	NO. 1541		446.98	7,042.75
	Bank Deposit	9,035.81		16,078.56
	Payroll		11,545.50	4,533.06
February 22	Bank Deposit	6,528.53		11,061.59
February 23	NO. 1542		541.24	10,520.35
February 27	NO. 1543		713.00	9,807.35
February 28	NO. 1545		63.60	9,743.75
	Bank Deposit	9,047.72		18,791.47
	Payroll		10,954.32	7,837.15
		38,579.69	**37,862.34**	

BANK RECONCILIATION FOR PRECEDING MONTH (DATED JANUARY 31):

Cash balance according to bank statement...........		$9,787.29
Deduct outstanding cheques:		
No. 1525................................	$1,221.50	
1526...............................	1,445.99	2,667.49
Adjusted balance.....................		$7,119.80
Cash balance according to company's records........		$7,163.55
Deduct: Service charges........................		43.75
Adjusted balance.....................		$7,119.80

Instructions

1. Prepare a bank reconciliation as at February 28, 2015. Assume that any errors in recording deposits or cheques were made by the company. Bank deposits are made Wednesday evenings.
2. Journalize any necessary entries.
3. What should be the balance of the Cash Account as at February 28, 2015?

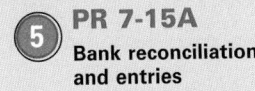

PR 7-15A

Bank reconciliation and entries

✔ 1. Adjusted balance $3,100.78

You recently started work in the accounting department at Fagan Industries. Your first task is to reconcile the bank statement as at December 31, 2015. You have been provided with the required information to reconcile the bank statement, and you notice that the date of the previous bank reconciliation is October 31.

DECEMBER BANK STATEMENT:

EXAMPLE BANK

Statement of Account	Account Type	Statement From - To
7257193-00	Business	DEC 01/15 - DEC 31/15

DESCRIPTION	DATE	WITHDRAWALS	DEPOSITS	BALANCE
BALANCE FORWARD	NOV 30			5,509.42
DEPOSIT	DEC 03		2,592.27	8,101.69
CHQ 447	DEC 04	102.18		7,999.51
CHQ 454	DEC 04	321.28		7,678.23
CHQ 462	DEC 04	221.73		7,456.50
CHQ 464	DEC 06	480.92		6,975.58
DEPOSIT	DEC 06		1,976.87	8,952.45
CHQ 463	DEC 07	1,370.91		7,581.54
DEPOSIT	DEC 10		861.54	8,443.08
DEPOSIT	DEC 13		922.24	9,365.32
EFT	DEC 13	3,107.08		6,258.24
CHQ 466	DEC 14	2,468.26		3,789.98
CHQ 467	DEC 14	683.21		3,106.77
DEPOSIT	DEC 17		2,577.29	5,684.06
DEPOSIT	DEC 20		1,216.01	6,900.07
DEPOSIT	DEC 27		785.99	7,686.06
EFT	DEC 31	3,978.61		3,707.45
DEPOSIT	DEC 31		734.93	4,442.38
Service Charge	DEC 31	72.75		4,369.63
		12,806.93	**11,667.14**	

(continued)

NOVEMBER BANK STATEMENT:

Statement of Account	Account Type	Statement From - To
7257193-00	Business	NOV 01/15 - NOV 30/15

DESCRIPTION	DATE	WITHDRAWALS	DEPOSITS	BALANCE
BALANCE FORWARD	OCT 31			5,291.78
CHQ 443	NOV 01	448.29		4,843.49
CHQ 451	NOV 01	1,935.60		2,907.89
CHQ 452	NOV 01	1,304.40		1,603.49
DEPOSIT	NOV 01		3,753.71	5,357.20
CHQ 453	NOV 02	962.35		4,394.85
DEPOSIT	NOV 05		2,674.38	7,069.23
NSF	NOV 07	881.83		6,187.40
DEPOSIT	NOV 08		976.55	7,163.95
DEPOSIT	NOV 12		716.91	7,880.86
CHQ 455	NOV 13	379.68		7,501.18
CHQ 456	NOV 15	2,470.18		5,031.00
CHQ 458	NOV 15	426.88		4,604.12
CHQ 459	NOV 15	499.80		4,104.32
EFT	NOV 15	3,201.09		903.23
DEPOSIT	NOV 15		2,765.83	3,669.06
DEPOSIT	NOV 19		3,791.96	7,461.02
DEPOSIT	NOV 22		893.38	8,354.40
DEPOSIT	NOV 26		902.12	9,256.52
CHQ 457	NOV 27	884.16		8,372.36
CHQ 460	NOV 28	70.18		8,302.18
DEPOSIT	NOV 29		901.58	9,203.76
EFT	NOV 30	3,621.59		5,582.17
Service Charge	NOV 30	72.75		5,509.42
		17,158.78	**17,376.42**	

CASH ACCOUNT TRANSACTIONS FOR NOVEMBER AND DECEMBER:

GL Account: CASH IN BANK 1040
For the period of NOV-01-15 to DEC-31-15

DATE	REFERENCE	DEBIT	CREDIT	BALANCE Dr. (Cr.)
Opening Balance				6,559.42
NOV 1	Chq. 452		1,304.40	5,255.02
	Chq. 453		962.35	4,292.67
	Chq. 454		321.28	3,971.39
NOV 2	Deposit	2,674.38		6,645.77
NOV 7	Deposit	976.55		7,622.32
NOV 8	Chq. 455		379.68	7,242.64
NOV 9	Deposit	716.91		7,959.55
NOV 14	Deposit	2,765.83		10,725.38
NOV 15	Chq. 456		2,470.18	8,255.20
	Chq. 457		884.16	7,371.04
	Chq. 458		426.88	6,944.16
	Chq. 459		499.80	6,444.36
	Payroll		3,201.09	3,243.27
NOV 16	Deposit	3,791.96		7,035.23
NOV 21	Deposit	893.38		7,928.61
NOV 22	Chq. 460		70.18	7,858.43
NOV 23	Deposit	902.12		8,760.55
NOV 28	Deposit	901.58		9,662.13
NOV 29	Chq. 461		573.75	9,088.38
	Chq. 462		221.73	8,866.65
NOV 30	Payroll		3,621.59	5,245.06
	Deposit	2,592.27		7,837.33
DEC 5	Deposit	976.87		8,814.20
DEC 6	Chq. 463		1,370.91	7,443.29
	Chq. 464		480.92	6,962.37
DEC 7	Deposit	861.54		7,823.91
DEC 12	Deposit	922.24		8,746.15
DEC 13	Chq. 465		50.00	8,696.15
	Chq. 466		2,468.26	6,227.89
	Chq. 467		683.21	5,544.68
	Payroll		3,107.08	2,437.60
DEC 14	Deposit	2,577.29		5,014.89
DEC 19	Deposit	1,216.01		6,230.90
DEC 20	Chq. 468		65.73	6,165.17
	Chq. 469		579.37	5,585.80
DEC 21	Deposit	785.99		6,371.79
DEC 28	Deposit	734.93		7,106.72
DEC 31	Payroll		3,978.61	3,128.11
		24,289.85	**27,721.16**	

(continued)

PRECEDING BANK RECONCILIATION (DATED OCTOBER 31):

Cash balance according to bank statement.............		$5,291.78
Add deposit of October 31 not recorded by bank.......		3,753.71
....		9,045.49
Deduct outstanding cheques:		
No. 443	$ 448.29	
447	102.18	
451	1,935.60	2,486.07
Adjusted balance..................................		$6,559.42
Cash balance according to company's records		$6,632.17
Deduct: Service charges...........................		72.75
Adjusted balance..................................		$6,559.42

Instructions

1. Prepare a bank reconciliation as at December 31, 2015. Assume that any errors in recording deposits were made by the company and any errors in recording cheques were made by the bank.
2. Journalize any necessary entries.
3. What should be the balance of the Cash Account as at December 31, 2015?

PROBLEMS SERIES B

PR 7-1B

①
②
③

Evaluating internal control of cash

The following procedures were recently installed by C&G Hydraulics Company:

a. The bank reconciliation is prepared by the cashier, who works under the supervision of the treasurer.
b. All mail is opened by the mail clerk, who forwards all cash remittances to the cashier. The cashier prepares a listing of the cash receipts and forwards a copy of the list to the accounts receivable clerk for recording in the accounts.
c. At the end of the day, cash register clerks are required to use their own funds to make up any cash shortages in their registers.
d. At the end of each day, all cash receipts are placed in the bank's night depository.
e. At the end of each day, an accounting clerk compares the duplicate copy of the daily cash deposit slip with the deposit receipt obtained from the bank.
f. The accounts payable clerk prepares a voucher for each disbursement. The voucher along with the supporting documentation is forwarded to the treasurer's office for approval.
g. After necessary approvals have been obtained for the payment of a voucher, the treasurer signs and mails the cheque. The treasurer then stamps the voucher and supporting documentation as paid and returns the voucher and supporting documentation to the accounts payable clerk for filing.
h. Along with petty cash expense receipts for postage, office supplies and so on, several postdated employee cheques are in the petty cash fund.

Instructions

Indicate whether each of the procedures of internal control over cash represents (1) a strength or (2) a weakness. For each weakness, explain why it is a weakness.

PR 7-2B

①
②
③

Evaluate internal control of cash

Jonathan Stallman was recently hired as the new director of accounting at SouthSide Charlies Grill. Jonathan's first responsibility was to examine the internal control procedures and implement stronger controls where he noted weaknesses. Jonathan found two weaknesses and implemented new controls in the following areas:

1. Cassandra was extremely dedicated to her bookkeeping job and the company, so much so, that she never took vacations.
2. Adam had been employed at SouthSide Charlies Grill for more than 30 years and was the sole employee responsible for reconciling the bank account on a monthly basis.

Instructions
1. Indicate the two weaknesses Jonathan identified.
2. Explain the controls Jonathan could put in place to protect against these weaknesses.
3. Discuss why these steps may not fully correct the weaknesses in the internal control procedures.

PR 7-3B

Transactions for petty cash, cash over/short

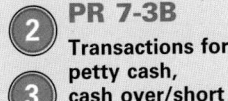

Baker's Restoration Company completed the following selected transactions during March 2015:

Mar. 1. Established a petty cash fund of $700.

10. The cash sales for the day, according to the cash register records, totalled $13,427. The actual cash received from cash sales was $13,592.

31. Petty cash on hand was $93. Replenished the petty cash fund for the following disbursements, each evidenced by a petty cash receipt:

Mar. 3. Store supplies, $175.

7. Express charges on merchandise sold, $220 (Delivery Expense).

9. Office supplies, $15.

13. Office supplies, $16.

19. Postage stamps, $15 (Office Supplies).

21. Repair to office file cabinet lock, $35 (Miscellaneous Administrative Expense).

22. Postage due on special delivery letter, $18 (Miscellaneous Administrative Expense).

24. Express charges on merchandise sold, $97 (Delivery Expense).

30. Office supplies, $9.

31. The cash sales for the day, according to the cash register records, totalled $15,720. The actual cash received from cash sales was $15,717.

31. Decreased the petty cash fund by $50.

Instructions
Journalize the transactions.

PR 7-4B

Transactions for petty cash

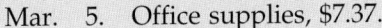

Mini Truck Transports established a petty cash fund of $80 on March 1, 2015. On March 12, 2015, the company increased the petty cash fund by $40. On March 31, 2015, the cash box contained $11.14 and receipts for the following purchases:

Mar. 5. Office supplies, $7.37.

11. Repair of a flat tire, $32.80, and gas for company truck, $40.

16. Office supplies, $11.06.

27. Gas for company truck, $15.

Instructions
Journalize the necessary entries.

PR 7-5B

Transactions for petty cash

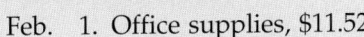

Sami's Composting established a petty cash fund of $160 on February 1, 2015. On February 28, 2015, the petty cash on hand was $31.80. The following receipts were found in the cash box:

Feb. 1. Office supplies, $11.52.

4. Inventory, $64.96.

19. IOU from Ken Doe, $10.

20. Inventory, $28.18.

28. The company decided to close the petty cash fund.

(continued)

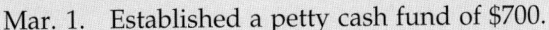

Instructions

Journalize the necessary entries.

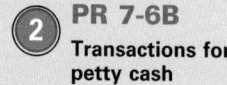

PR 7-6B
Transactions for petty cash

Tie-Dye T-Shirt Co. established a petty cash fund of $675 on May 1, 2015. The petty cash is replenished when the cash on hand is less than $200. On May 16, the petty cash on hand was $170.23. The following receipts were found in the cash box:

1. 25 kg of elastic bands, $293.73 (Inventory).
2. Office supply store receipts, $85.90.
3. Gas receipts for company delivery trucks, $106.58.

On May 31, the petty cash on hand was $190.88. The following receipts were found in the cash box:

1. Receipts from a grocery store for coffee, creamer, and sugar, $53.59.
2. Found receipt from May 3 for office supplies, $18.56.
3. Gas receipts for company trucks, $93.51.
4. Receipt for 100 T-shirts from competitor to fill emergency customer order, $337.02.

Instructions

Journalize the necessary entries.

PR 7-7B
Petty cash funds

Dirkson has been using a petty cash fund in his company for five years. The fund is locked in the supply cabinet, maintained at $2,000, and is used to pay for regular deliveries of supplies. Dirkson has 10 employees working at his company, and each employee has a key to the supply cabinet. Recently Dirkson has had to replenish the fund more frequently than normal. In the past, he replenished it at the end of each month but lately it has been running low every two weeks. Dirkson has asked you for some advice for controlling the petty cash. Specifically, he would like answers to the following concerns:

1. How many employees should have a key to the petty cash fund?
2. What types of payments should be made from petty cash?
3. How much cash should be maintained in the fund?
4. How often should the fund be replenished?

Instructions

Advise Dirkson on each of his concerns regarding the petty cash fund.

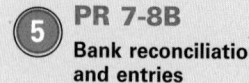

PR 7-8B
Bank reconciliation and entries

✔ 1. Adjusted balance: $8,613

The cash account for Discount Co. at April 30, 2015, indicated a balance of $5,605. The bank statement indicated a balance of $9,158 on April 30, 2015. Comparing the bank statement and the accompanying cancelled cheques and memos with the records revealed the following reconciling items:

a. Cheques outstanding totalled $5,225.
b. A deposit of $3,150, representing receipts of April 30, had been made too late to appear on the bank statement.
c. The bank had collected $4,120 on a note left for collection. The principal amount of the note was $4,000.
d. A cheque for $2,490 returned with the statement had been incorrectly recorded by Discount Co. as $2,409. The cheque was for the payment of an obligation to Goldstein Co. for the purchase of office equipment on account.
e. A cheque drawn for $170 had been erroneously charged by the bank as $1,700.
f. Bank service charges for April amounted to $30.
g. An NSF cheque, $1,001, from Tamara Gold for a sale, appeared on the bank statement.

Instructions

1. Prepare a bank reconciliation.
2. Journalize the necessary entries. The accounts have not been closed.

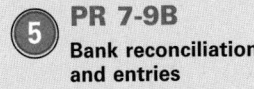

PR 7-9B

Bank reconciliation and entries

✔ 1. Adjusted balance: $10,480

The cash account for Junkey's Salvage at July 1, 2015, indicated a balance of $14,590. During July, the total cash deposited was $28,680, and cheques written totalled $33,500. The bank statement indicated a balance of $16,750 on July 31. Comparing the bank statement, the cancelled cheques, and the accompanying memos with the records revealed the following reconciling items:

a. Cheques outstanding totalled $11,730.
b. A deposit of $5,100, representing receipts of July 31, had been made too late to appear on the bank statement.
c. The bank had collected for Junkey's Salvage $1,675 on a note left for collection. The principal amount of the note was $1,500.
d. A cheque for $370 returned with the statement had been incorrectly charged by the bank as $730.
e. A cheque for $320 returned with the statement had been recorded by Junkey's Salvage as $230. The cheque was for the payment of an obligation to Ranchwood Co. on account.
f. Bank service charges for July amounted to $25.
g. A cheque for $850 from Hallock Co. was returned by the bank because of insufficient funds.

Instructions

1. Prepare a bank reconciliation as at July 31.
2. Journalize the necessary entries. The accounts have not been closed.

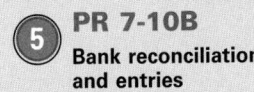

PR 7-10B

Bank reconciliation and entries

✔ 1. Adjusted balance $28,105

Arman has just been hired as the bookkeeper for Smart Drive Co. His first responsibility is to reconcile the bank account for July 31, 2015. Arman gathered all the necessary documents and has discovered the following information.

The bank statement had an ending balance at July 31 of $22,497. The bank had collected on a note on behalf of the company. The total collection was $2,250, including $250 of interest. The previous bookkeeper had recorded total deposits to cash during July of $56,930, and total payments from cash during July of $44,750. The reconciled cash balance on June 30, 2015, was $15,858. An NSF cheque for $1,700, written by P. Grenier in payment of its account, was returned with the July bank statement. July service charges were $52. Cheque No. 1225 had been recorded by the previous bookkeeper as $6,700, but it was correctly cashed by the bank as $7,600. Cheque No. 1225 was written to the utility company for July utilities. Three cheques written in July had not yet cleared the bank account, totalling $2,638. Cheque No. 1243 had been incorrectly cashed by the bank for $2,000, but it had actually been written for $5,000. A deposit of $5,246, made after banking hours on July 31, did not appear on the bank statement. Included with the bank statement were two EFT transactions: one for a $256 payment to a supplier, Office Supply Co., on account, and one for a $725 deposit from a customer, Bob's Grill Co., on account.

Instructions

1. Prepare a bank reconciliation as at September 30, 2015.
2. Journalize the necessary entries. The accounts have not been closed.

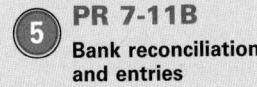

PR 7-11B

Bank reconciliation and entries

✔ 1. Adjusted balance: $7,170.57

The accountant for Spring Board Co. has provided you with the following information for the month of October 2015.

(continued)

October Bank Statement:

EXAMPLE BANK

Statement of Account	Account Type	Statement From - To
11763894	Business	Oct 01/15 - Oct 31/15

DATE	DESCRIPTION	WITHDRAWALS	DEPOSITS	BALANCE
Sep-30	BALANCE FORWARD			4,723.64
Oct-02	DEPOSIT		934.23	5,657.87
Oct-03	EFT		433.27	6,091.14
Oct-08	CHQ 329	245.67		5,845.47
Oct-14	CHQ 331	203.73		5,641.74
Oct-15	DEPOSIT		2,020.48	7,662.22
Oct-22	CHQ 330	28.45		7,633.77
Oct-22	EFT	174.38		7,459.39
Oct-27	CHQ 333	1,289.34		6,170.05
Oct-31	CHQ 335	208.49		5,961.56
Oct-31	DEPOSIT		1,273.59	7,235.15
Oct-31	SERVICE CHARGE	24.50		7,210.65
		2,174.56	**4,661.57**	

Cash Account Transactions for October:

GL ACCOUNT: 1020 Cash Account
For the period of October 01-15 to October 31-15

DATE	REFERENCE	DEBIT	CREDIT	BALANCE Dr. (Cr.)
Opening Balance				4,723.64
Oct-02	Deposit	934.23		5,657.87
Oct-07	NO. 329		245.67	5,412.20
Oct-12	NO. 330		28.45	5,383.75
Oct-13	NO. 331		203.73	5,180.02
Oct-15	Deposit	220.48		5,400.50
Oct-16	NO. 332		148.58	5,251.92
Oct-23	NO. 333		2,189.34	3,062.58
Oct-24	NO. 334		485.56	2,577.02
Oct-27	NO. 335		208.49	2,368.53
Oct-30	Deposit	1,273.59		3,642.12
Oct-31	Deposit	1,852.64		5,494.76
Oct-31	NO. 336		1,258.58	4,236.18

Instructions

1. Prepare a bank reconciliation as at October 31, 2015. Assume that any errors in recording deposits or cheques were made by the company, all deposits are from sales, Cheque No. 333 was paid to a supplier on account, EFT collections are from customer accounts, and EFT payments are to supplier accounts.
2. Journalize any necessary entries.

PR 7-12B
Bank reconciliation and entries

✔ 1. Adjusted balance: $13,893.32

Reydell Furniture Company deposits all cash receipts each Wednesday and Friday in a night depository, after banking hours. The data required to reconcile the bank statement as at June 30 have been taken from various documents and records and are reproduced as follows. The sources of the data are printed in capital letters. All cheques were written for payments on account.

JUNE BANK STATEMENT:

PAGE   1

EXAMPLE BANK
WINNIPEG, MB

ACCOUNT NUMBER

FROM 6/01/2015   TO   6/30/2015

BALANCE   9,447.20

9 DEPOSITS   8,691.77

20 WITHDRAWALS   8,014.37

REYDELL FURNITURE COMPANY
WINNIPEG, MB

4 OTHER DEBITS
AND CREDITS   3,370.00CR

NEW BALANCE   13,494.60

* – – – CHEQUES AND OTHER DEBITS – – – *		– – DEPOSITS – – *	– DATE – *	– – BALANCE– – *
No.731 162.15 No.736 345.95		690.25	6/01	9,629.35
No.739 60.55 No.740 237.50		1,080.50	6/02	10,411.80
No.741 495.15 No.742 501.90		854.17	6/04	10,268.92
No.743 671.30 No.744 506.88		840.50	6/09	9,931.24
No.745 117.25 No.746 298.66		MS 3,500.00	6/09	13,015.33
No.748 450.90 No.749 640.13		MS 210.00	6/09	12,134.30
No.750 276.77 No.751 299.37		896.61	6/11	12,454.77
No.752 537.01 No.753 380.95		882.95	6/16	12,419.76
No.754 449.75 No.755 272.75		1,606.74	6/18	13,304.00
No.757 407.95 No.759 901.50		897.34	6/23	12,891.89
		942.71	6/25	13,834.60
NSF 300.00			6/28	13,534.60
SC 40.00			6/30	13,494.60

EC — ERROR CORRECTION   OD — OVERDRAFT
MS — MISCELLANEOUS   PS — PAYMENT STOPPED
NSF — NOT SUFFICIENT FUNDS   SC — SERVICE CHARGE

* * *   * * *   * * *

RECONCILING THIS STATEMENT WITH YOUR RECORDS IS ESSENTIAL.
ANY ERROR OR EXCEPTION SHOULD BE REPORTED IMMEDIATELY.

CASH ACCOUNT:
Balance as at June 1 $9,317.40

CASH RECEIPTS FOR MONTH OF JUNE   9,601.58

DUPLICATE DEPOSIT SLIPS:
Date and amount of each deposit in June:

Date	Amount	Date	Amount	Date	Amount
June 1	$1,080.50	June 10	$ 896.61	June 22	$ 987.34
3	854.17	15	882.95	24	942.71
8	840.50	17	1,606.74	30	1,510.06

CHEQUES WRITTEN:
Number and amount of each cheque issued in June:

Cheque No.	Amount	Cheque No.	Amount	Cheque No.	Amount
740	$237.50	747	Void	754	$ 449.75
741	495.15	748	$450.90	755	272.75
742	501.90	749	640.13	756	113.95
743	671.30	750	276.77	757	407.95
744	506.88	751	299.37	758	259.60
745	117.25	752	537.01	759	901.50
746	298.66	753	830.95	760	486.39
Total amount of cheques issued in June					$8,755.66

(continued)

BANK RECONCILIATION FOR PRECEDING MONTH:

Reydell Furniture Company
Bank Reconciliation
May 31, 2015

Cash balance according to bank statement		$ 9,447.20
Add deposit for May 31, not recorded by bank		690.25
		10,137.45
Deduct outstanding cheques:		
No. 731	$162.15	
736	345.95	
738	251.40	
739	60.55	820.05
Adjusted balance		$ 9,317.40
Cash balance according to company's records		$ 9,352.50
Deduct service charges		35.10
Adjusted balance		$ 9,317.40

Instructions

1. Prepare a bank reconciliation as at June 30. If errors in recording deposits or cheques are discovered, assume that the errors were made by the company. Assume that all deposits are from cash sales, except for the MS (miscellaneous) items, which represent a $3,500 note and the $210 of interest collected on the note. All cheques are written to satisfy accounts payable.
2. Journalize the necessary entries. The accounts have not been closed.
3. What is the amount of Cash that should appear on the balance sheet as at June 30?
4. Assume that a cancelled cheque for $260 has been incorrectly recorded by the bank as $620. Briefly explain how the error would be included in a bank reconciliation and how it should be corrected.

---

5 **PR 7-13B**
Bank reconciliation and entries

Crabapple Catering has just received its April bank statement from Example Bank. You gather the following information to prepare the April 30, 2015, bank reconciliation.

APRIL BANK STATEMENT:

EXAMPLE BANK

✔ 1. Adjusted balance $8,556.41

Statement of Account	Account Type	Statement From - To
2197-0459036	Business	April 01/15 - April 30/15

DESCRIPTION	DATE	WITHDRAWALS	DEPOSITS	BALANCE
BALANCE FORWARD	MAR 31			10,126.95
No. 379	APR 02	430.02		9,696.93
No. 383	APR 02	89.40		9,607.53
No. 384	APR 02	960.00		8,647.53
Deposit	APR 02		1,267.83	9,915.36
No. 378	APR 04	44.39		9,870.97
Deposit	APR 09		387.28	10,258.25
No. 376	APR 10	64.74		10,193.51
No. 381	APR 10	33.71		10,159.80
No. 380	APR 16	871.27		9,288.53
No. 387	APR 16	561.70		8,726.83
NSF	APR 16	816.58		7,910.25
Deposit	APR 16		926.50	8,836.75
No. 385	APR 19	40.76		8,795.99
No. 389	APR 19	6,761.50		2,034.49
No. 390	APR 19	56.70		1,977.79
Deposit	APR 23		660.03	2,637.82
No. 364	APR 27	456.86		2,180.96
Service Charge	APR 30	18.75		2,162.21
		11,206.38	**3,241.64**	

CASH ACCOUNT TRANSACTIONS FOR APRIL:

GL ACCOUNT: 1080 Bank Account
For the period of April 01/15 to April 30/15

DATE	REFERENCE	DEBIT	CREDIT	BALANCE Dr. (Cr.)
Opening Balance				10,797.40
April 2	No. 378		44.39	10,753.01
	No. 379		430.02	10,322.99
	No. 380		871.27	9,451.72
	No. 381		33.71	9,418.01
	No. 382		24.49	9,393.52
	No. 383		89.40	9,304.12
	No. 384		960.00	8,344.12
April 6	Deposit Slip	387.28		8,731.40
April 13	Deposit Slip	926.50		9,657.90
April 16	No. 385		40.76	9,617.14
	No. 386		296.47	9,320.67
	No. 387		561.70	8,758.97
	No. 388		40.76	8,718.21
	No. 389		676.15	8,042.06
	No. 390		56.70	7,985.36
April 20	Deposit Slip	660.03		8,645.39
April 27	Deposit Slip	746.35		9,391.74
		2,720.16	**4,125.82**	

BANK RECONCILIATION FOR PRECEDING MONTH (DATED MARCH 31):

Cash balance according to bank statement $10,126.95
Add deposit of March 31, not recorded by bank.............. 1,267.83
11,394.78

Deduct outstanding cheques:
No. 364 .... $456.86
371... 75.78
376 .... 64.74   597.38
Adjusted balance... $10,797.40

Cash balance according to company's records................. $10,816.15
Deduct: Service charges... 18.75
Adjusted balance... $10,797.40

Instructions

1. Prepare a bank reconciliation as at April 30, 2015. Assume that any errors in recording deposits or cheques were made by the bank. Deposits are made on Friday evenings.
2. Briefly explain how any errors were reflected in the bank reconciliation and how they should be corrected.
3. Journalize any necessary entries.
4. What should be the balance of the Cash Account as at April 30, 2015?

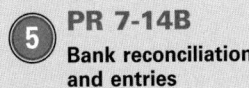

PR 7-14B
Bank reconciliation and entries

Makoika Children's Wear banks online with Example Bank. It is August 3, 2015, and you have been asked to reconcile the bank statement as at July 31. You gather the following information:

✔ 1. Adjusted balance $9,748.57

(continued)

JULY BANK STATEMENT (note that the later dates are at the top because it is a copy of the online statement):

EXAMPLE BANK

BUSINESS ACCOUNT - 30423442	
July 2015	Balance as at July 31, 2015: $(67.29)

DATE	DESCRIPTION	WITHDRAWALS	DEPOSITS	BALANCE
Jul 31, 2015	Bank Charge	49.95		(67.29)
Jul 31, 2015	EFT	7,214.41		(17.34)
Jul 31, 2015	CHQ#1388	870.35		7,197.07
Jul 30, 2015	CHQ#1387	373.15		8,067.42
Jul 27, 2015	CHQ#1384	31.89		8,440.57
Jul 27, 2015	CHQ#1371	945.21		8,472.46
Jul 26, 2015	DEPOSIT		6,310.17	9,417.67
Jul 24, 2015	CHQ#1386	418.45		3,107.50
Jul 23, 2015	CHQ#1383	789.08		3,525.95
Jul 19, 2015	CHQ#1385	2,997.34		4,315.03
Jul 19, 2015	DEPOSIT		7,871.04	7,312.37
Jul 18, 2015	EFT	9,286.49		(558.67)
Jul 12, 2015	DEPOSIT		1,168.37	8,727.82
Jul 10, 2015	CHQ#1381	202.16		7,559.45
Jul 09, 2015	CHQ#1380	438.39		7,761.61
Jul 06, 2015	CHQ#1382	6,727.91		8,200.00
Jul 04, 2015	DEPOSIT		8,458.50	14,927.91
		30,344.78	**23,808.08**	

CASH ACCOUNT TRANSACTIONS FOR JULY:

GL ACCOUNT: 1060 Cash Account
For the period of July 01-15 to July 31-15

DATE	REFERENCE	DEBIT	CREDIT	BALANCE Dr. (Cr.)
Opening Balance				4,482.27
July 4	NO. 1380		438.39	4,043.88
	NO. 1381		202.16	3,841.72
	Bank Deposit	8,458.50		12,300.22
	NO. 1382		6,727.91	5,572.31
July 5	NO. 1383		789.08	4,783.23
July 11	NO. 1384		13.89	4,769.34
	Bank Deposit	1,618.37		6,387.71
July 18	NO. 1385		2,997.34	3,390.37
	NO. 1386		418.45	2,971.92
	Bank Deposit	7,871.04		10,842.96
	Payroll		9,286.49	1,556.47
July 25	Bank Deposit	6,310.17		7,866.64
July 26	NO. 1387		373.15	7,493.49
July 30	NO. 1388		870.35	6,623.14
July 31	NO. 1390		84.82	6,538.32
	Bank Deposit	10,942.61		17,480.93
	Payroll		7,214.41	10,266.52
		35,200.69	**29,416.44**	

BANK RECONCILIATION FOR PRECEDING MONTH (DATED JUNE 30):

Cash balance according to bank statement......................		$6,469.41
Deduct outstanding cheques:		
No. 1371	$ 945.21	
1372	1,041.93	1,987.14
Adjusted balance..		$4,482.27
Cash balance according to company's records................		$4,532.22
Deduct: Service charges..		49.95
Adjusted balance..		$4,482.27

Instructions

1. Prepare a bank reconciliation as at July 31, 2015. Assume that any errors in recording deposits or cheques were made by the company.
2. Journalize any necessary entries.
3. What should be the balance of the Cash Account as at July 31, 2015?

PR 7-15B
Bank reconciliation and entries

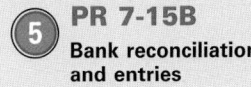

✔ 1. Adjusted balance $5,906.88

You recently started work in the accounting department at MM Industries. Your first task is to reconcile the bank statement as at June 30, 2015. You have been provided with the required information to reconcile the bank statement, and you notice that the date of the previous bank reconciliation is April 30.

JUNE BANK STATEMENT:

EXAMPLE BANK

Statement of Account	Account Type	Statement From - To
7043159-00	Business	JUN 01/15 -JUN 30/15

DESCRIPTION	DATE	WITHDRAWALS	DEPOSITS	BALANCE
BALANCE FORWARD	MAY 31			8,484.86
DEPOSIT	JUN 01		2,881.26	11,366.12
DEPOSIT	JUN 04		1,726.60	13,092.72
CHQ 567	JUN 04	285.33		12,807.39
CHQ 574	JUN 04	292.50		12,514.89
CHQ 582	JUN 04	466.23		12,048.66
CHQ 584	JUN 06	960.99		11,087.67
CHQ 583	JUN 07	2,042.06		9,045.61
DEPOSIT	JUN 07		3,481.41	12,527.02
DEPOSIT	JUN 11		825.19	13,352.21
EFT	JUN 15	5,247.25		8,104.96
CHQ 586	JUN 15	1,733.48		6,371.48
CHQ 587	JUN 18	204.65		6,166.83
DEPOSIT	JUN 18		2,472.51	8,639.34
DEPOSIT	JUN 21		738.96	9,378.30
DEPOSIT	JUN 25		772.69	10,150.99
DEPOSIT	JUN 28		2,309.79	12,460.78
EFT	JUN 29	5,647.05		6,813.73
Service Charge	JUN 29	63.00		6,750.73
		16,942.54	**15,208.41**	

(continued)

MAY BANK STATEMENT:

EXAMPLE BANK

Statement of Account	Account Type	Statement From - To
7043159-00	Business	MAY 01/15 - MAY 31/15

DESCRIPTION	DATE	WITHDRAWALS	DEPOSITS	BALANCE
BALANCE FORWARD	APR 30			7,257.00
CHQ 563	MAY 01	327.32		6,929.68
CHQ 571	MAY 01	413.58		6,516.10
CHQ 572	MAY 01	2,017.34		4,498.76
DEPOSIT	MAY 01		6,549.13	11,047.89
CHQ 573	MAY 02	672.65		10,375.24
DEPOSIT	MAY 03		3,744.05	14,119.29
NSF	MAY 07	335.41		13,783.88
DEPOSIT	MAY 07		613.09	14,396.97
DEPOSIT	MAY 10		2,600.18	16,997.15
CHQ 575	MAY 11	210.90		16,786.25
DEPOSIT	MAY 14		893.56	17,679.81
CHQ 576	MAY 15	1,557.89		16,121.92
CHQ 578	MAY 15	773.19		15,348.73
CHQ 579	MAY 15	662.08		14,686.65
EFT	MAY 15	5,707.07		8,979.58
DEPOSIT	MAY 17		4,549.56	13,529.14
DEPOSIT	MAY 21		735.06	14,264.20
DEPOSIT	MAY 24		1,100.55	15,364.75
CHQ 577	MAY 25	1,436.49		13,928.26
CHQ 580	MAY 25	93.36		13,834.90
DEPOSIT	MAY 28		378.24	14,213.14
EFT	MAY 31	5,665.28		8,547.86
Service Charge	MAY 31	63.00		8,484.86
		19,935.56	**21,163.42**	

CASH ACCOUNT TRANSACTIONS FOR MAY AND JUNE:

GL Account: CASH IN BANK 1040
For the period of MAY-01-15 to JUN-30-15

DATE	REFERENCE	DEBIT	CREDIT	BALANCE Dr. (Cr.)
Opening Balance				12,779.90
MAY 1	Chq.572		2,017.34	10,762.56
	Chq.573		672.65	10,089.91
	Chq.574		292.50	9,797.41
MAY 2	Deposit	3,744.05		13,541.46
MAY 4	Deposit	613.09		14,154.55
MAY 8	Chq.575		210.90	13,943.65
MAY 9	Deposit	2,600.18		16,543.83
MAY 11	Deposit	893.56		17,437.39
MAY 15	Chq.576		1,557.89	15,879.50
	Chq.577		1,436.49	14,443.01
	Chq.578		773.19	13,669.82
	Chq.579		662.08	13,007.74
	Payroll		5,707.07	7,300.67
MAY 16	Deposit	4,549.56		11,850.23
MAY 18	Deposit	735.06		12,585.29
MAY 22	Chq.580		93.36	12,491.93
MAY 23	Deposit	1,100.55		13,592.48
MAY 25	Deposit	378.24		13,970.72
MAY 29	Chq.581		371.36	13,599.36
	Chq.582		466.23	13,133.13
MAY 30	Deposit	2,881.26		16,014.39
MAY 31	Payroll		5,665.28	10,349.11
JUN 1	Deposit	726.60		11,075.71
JUN 6	Chq.583		2,042.06	9,033.65
	Chq.584		960.99	8,072.66
	Deposit	3,481.41		11,554.07
JUN 8	Deposit	825.19		12,379.26
JUN 15	Chq.585		70.00	12,309.26
	Chq.586		1,733.48	10,575.78
	Chq.587		204.65	10,371.13
	Payroll		5,247.25	5,123.88
	Deposit	2,472.51		7,596.39
JUN 20	Deposit	738.96		8,335.35
	Chq.588		95.28	8,240.07
	Chq.589		307.21	7,932.86
JUN 22	Deposit	772.69		8,705.55
JUN 27	Deposit	2,309.79		11,015.34
JUN 29	Payroll		5,647.05	5,368.29
		28,822.70	**36,234.31**	

(*continued*)

PRECEDING BANK RECONCILIATION (DATED APRIL 30):

Cash balance according to bank statement		$ 7,257.00
Add deposit of April 30 not recorded by bank		6,549.13
		13,806.13
Deduct outstanding cheques:		
No. 563	$327.32	
567	285.33	
571	413.58	1,026.23
Adjusted balance		$12,779.90
Cash balance according to company's records		$12,842.90
Deduct: Service charges		63.00
Adjusted balance		$12,779.90

Instructions

1. Prepare a bank reconciliation as at June 30, 2015. Assume that any errors in recording deposits were made by the company and any errors in recording cheques were made by the bank.
2. Journalize any necessary entries.
3. What should be the balance of the Cash Account as at June 30, 2015?

SPECIAL ACTIVITIES

SA 7-1

Ethics and professional conduct in business

During the preparation of the bank reconciliation for New Concepts Co., Peter Fikes, the assistant controller, discovered that the bank incorrectly recorded a $710 cheque written by New Concepts Co. as $170. Peter has decided not to notify the bank but to wait for the bank to detect the error. Peter plans to record the $540 error as Other Income if the bank fails to detect the error within the next three months.

Discuss whether Peter is behaving in a professional manner.

SA 7-2

Internal controls

Effective internal controls are a major factor in deterring fraud and preventing misleading financial statements. Communicating the findings regarding the effectiveness of the controls to shareholders, creditors, and other investors is vitally important. Refer to Exhibit 1 on page 351, Management's Discussion and Analysis Regarding Controls, from Shoppers Drug Mart's annual report, to answer the following questions:

1. Who is responsible for internal controls over financial reporting?
2. What framework was used as the basis for the assessment of the effectiveness of the internal controls?
3. Do the internal controls established at Shoppers Drug Mart guarantee accurate financial statements?
4. What policies and procedures are included in Shoppers Drug Mart's internal controls?

SA 7-3

Internal controls

The following is an excerpt from a conversation between two sales clerks, Ross Maas and Shu Lyons. Both Ross and Shu are employed by Hawkins Electronics, a locally owned and operated electronics retail store.

Ross: Did you hear the news?

Shu: What news?

Ross: Jane and Rachel were both arrested this morning.

Shu: What? Arrested? You're putting me on!

Ross: No, really! The police arrested them first thing this morning. Put them in handcuffs, told them they can contact a lawyer—the whole works. It was unreal!

Shu: What did they do?

Ross: Well, apparently they were filling out merchandise refund forms for fictitious customers and then taking the cash.

Shu: I guess I never thought of that. How did they catch them?

Ross: The store manager noticed that returns were twice that of last year and seemed to be increasing. When he confronted Jane, she became flustered and admitted to taking the cash, apparently over $7,000 in just three months. They're going over the last six months' transactions to try to determine how much Rachel stole. She apparently started stealing first.

Suggest appropriate control procedures that would have prevented or detected the theft of cash.

SA 7-4
Internal controls

The following is an excerpt from a conversation between the store manager of Yoder Brothers Grocery Stores, Lori Colburn, and Terry Whipple, president of Yoder Brothers Grocery Stores.

Terry: Lori, I'm concerned about this new scanning system.

Lori: What's the problem?

Terry: Well, how do we know the clerks are ringing up all the merchandise?

Lori: That's one of the strong points about the system. The scanner automatically rings up each item, based on its bar code. We update the prices daily, so we're sure that the sale is rung up for the right price.

Terry: That's not my concern. What keeps a clerk from pretending to scan items and then simply not charging his friends? If his friends were buying 10 to 15 items, it would be easy for the clerk to pass through several items with his finger over the bar code or just pass the merchandise through the scanner with the wrong side showing. It would look normal for anyone observing. In the old days, we at least could hear the cash register ringing up each sale.

Lori: I see your point.

Suggest ways that Yoder Brothers Grocery Stores could prevent or detect the theft of merchandise as described.

SA 7-5
Ethics and professional conduct in business

Ryan Egan and Jack Moody are both cash register clerks for Organic Markets and Lee Sorrell is the store manager. The following is an excerpt of a conversation between Ryan and Jack:

Ryan: Jack, how long have you been working for Organic Markets?

Jack: Almost five years this November. You just started two weeks ago . . . right?

Ryan: Yes. Do you mind if I ask you a question?

Jack: No, go ahead.

Ryan: What I want to know is, have they always had this rule that if your cash register is short at the end of the day, you have to make up the shortage out of your own pocket?

Jack: Yes, as long as I've been working here.

Ryan: Well, it's the pits. Last week I had to pay almost $40.

Jack: It's not that big a deal. I just make sure that I'm not short at the end of the day.

Ryan: How do you do that?

Jack: I just shortchange a few customers early in the day. There are a few jerks that deserve it anyway. Most of the time, their attention is elsewhere and they don't think to check their change.

Ryan: What happens if you're over at the end of the day?

Jack: Lee lets me keep it as long as it doesn't get to be too large. I've not been short in over a year. I usually clear about $20 to $30 extra per day.

Discuss this case from the viewpoint of proper controls and professional behaviour.

SA 7-6
Bank reconciliation and internal control

The records of Anacker Company indicate a July 31 cash balance of $9,400, which includes undeposited receipts for July 30 and 31. The cash balance on the bank statement as of July 31 is $6,575. This balance includes a note of $4,000 plus $160 interest collected by the bank but not recorded in the journal. Cheques outstanding on July 31 were as follows: No. 370, $580; No. 379, $615; No. 390, $900; No. 1148, $225; No. 1149, $300; and No. 1151, $750.

(continued)

On July 3, the cashier resigned, effective at the end of the month. Before leaving on July 31, the cashier prepared the following bank reconciliation:

Cash balance per books, July 31		$ 9,400
Add outstanding cheques:		
No. 1148	$225	
1149	300	
1151	750	1,175
		10,575
Less undeposited receipts		4,000
Cash balance per bank, July 31		6,575
Deduct unrecorded note with interest		4,160
True cash, July 31.		$ 2,415

```
Calculator Tape of Outstanding
           Cheques:
              0 *
            225 +
            300 +
            750 +
          1,175 *
```

Subsequently, the owner of Anacker Company discovered that the cashier had stolen an unknown amount of undeposited receipts, leaving only $1,000 to be deposited on July 31. The owner, a close family friend, has asked for your help in determining the amount that the former cashier has stolen.

1. Determine the amount the cashier stole from Anacker Company. Show your computations in good form.
2. How did the cashier attempt to conceal the theft?
3. a. Identify two major weaknesses in internal controls that allowed the cashier to steal the undeposited cash receipts.
   b. Recommend improvements in internal controls so that similar types of thefts of undeposited cash receipts can be prevented.

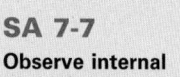

SA 7-7

Observe internal controls over cash

Group Project

Select a business in your community and observe its internal controls over cash receipts and cash payments. The business could be a bank, bookstore, restaurant, department store, or other retailer. In groups of three or four, identify and discuss the similarities and differences in each business's cash internal controls.

SA 7-8

Cash to monthly cash expenses ratio

Light Co. reported the following data (in thousands) for the years ended December 31, 2013, 2012, 2011, and 2010:

	2013	2012	2011	2010
Cash as at December 31*	$15,536	$41,268	$60,040	$1,239
Net cash flows from operating activities	(14,548)	(18,710)	(5,382)	(2,375)

*Includes cash equivalents and short-term investments.

1. Determine the monthly cash expenses for 2013, 2012, 2011, and 2010. Round to one decimal place.
2. Determine the ratio of cash to monthly cash expenses as at December 31, 2013, 2012, 2011, and 2010. Round to one decimal place.
3. Based on (1) and (2), comment on Light Co.'s ratio of cash to monthly cash expenses for 2013, 2012, 2011, and 2010.

Receivables

MOUNTAIN EQUIPMENT CO-OP

The sale and purchase of merchandise involves the exchange of goods for cash. However, the point at which cash actually changes hands varies with the transaction. Consider transactions by Mountain Equipment Co-op (MEC), a leading Canadian supplier of quality outdoor gear, clothing, and camping equipment. Not only does the company sell its products through 15 different retail stores, but it also sells online and by mail order.

If you were to buy camping equipment at an MEC store, you would need to pay cash or use a debit or credit card to pay for the gear before you left the store. However, MEC allows groups, such as sports teams, schools, search and rescue groups, and other companies and government agencies, to place orders "on account."

As a group, you would first need to build up a trusted financial history to allow you to purchase merchandise on account with MEC. MEC will check your group's credit rating to assess the likelihood that cash will be received for the sales over time. MEC is trying to prevent uncollectible accounts receivable by pre-screening their credit customers.

These sales on account are recorded as accounts receivable due from the group. Such credit transactions facilitate sales and are a significant current asset for many businesses. In this chapter, we will describe common classifications of receivables, illustrate how to account for uncollectible receivables, and demonstrate the reporting of receivables on the balance sheet.

After studying this chapter, you should be able to:

1 Describe the common classes of receivables.

Classification of Receivables	Accounts Receivable	
	Notes Receivable	
	Other Receivables	

2 Describe the accounting for uncollectible receivables.

Uncollectible Receivables		

3 Describe and illustrate the direct write-off method of accounting for uncollectible receivables.

Direct Write-Off Method for Uncollectible Receivables		EXAMPLE EXERCISE 8-1 (page 417)

4 Describe and illustrate the allowance method of accounting for uncollectible receivables.

Allowance Method for Uncollectible Receivables	Write-Offs to the Allowance Account	
	Recovery of a Bad Debt	EXAMPLE EXERCISE 8-2 (page 420)
	Estimating Uncollectibles	
	Percent of Sales Method	EXAMPLE EXERCISE 8-3 (page 421)
	Aging of Receivables Method	EXAMPLE EXERCISE 8-4 (page 423)
	Percent of Receivables Method	EXAMPLE EXERCISE 8-5 (page 425)
	Comparing Estimation Methods	

5 Describe the accounting for notes receivable.

Notes Receivable	Characteristics of Notes Receivable	
	Accounting for Notes Receivable	EXAMPLE EXERCISE 8-6 (page 430)

6 Describe and analyze the reporting of receivables on the balance sheet.

Reporting Receivables on the Balance Sheet		EXAMPLE EXERCISE 8-7 (page 431)
	Financial Analysis and Interpretation	EXAMPLE EXERCISE 8-8 (page 433)

For the chapter *At a Glance*, turn to page 433.

 Classification of Receivables

Describe the common classes of receivables.

The receivables that result from sales on account are normally accounts receivable or notes receivable. The term **receivables** includes all money claims against other entities, including people, companies, and other organizations. Receivables are usually a significant portion of the total current assets. For example, Canadian Tire Corporation, Limited recently reported that receivables made up more than 70% of its current assets.

Accounts Receivable

The most common transaction creating a receivable is selling merchandise or services on account (on credit). The receivable is recorded as a debit to Accounts Receivable. Such **accounts receivable**, or **trade receivables**, are normally collected within a short period, such as 30 or 60 days. They are classified on the balance sheet as a current asset.

Notes Receivable

Notes receivable are amounts that customers owe for which a formal, written instrument of credit has been issued. If notes receivable are expected to be collected within a year, they are classified on the balance sheet as a current asset.

Notes are often used for credit periods of more than 60 days. For example, an automobile dealer may require a down payment at the time of sale and accept a note or a series of notes for the remainder. Such notes usually provide for monthly payments. Notes may also be used to settle a customer's account receivable.

Other Receivables

Other receivables include interest receivable, taxes receivable, and receivables from owners or employees. Other receivables are normally reported separately on the balance sheet. If receivables are expected to be collected within one year, they are classified as current assets. If collection is expected beyond one year, they are classified as noncurrent assets.

 # Uncollectible Receivables

Describe the accounting for uncollectible receivables.

In prior chapters, the accounting for sales of merchandise or services on account (on credit) was described and illustrated. A major issue that has not yet been discussed is that some customers will not pay their accounts. That is, some accounts receivable will be uncollectible.

Companies may shift the risk of uncollectible receivables to other companies. For example, some retailers do not accept sales on account but require immediate payment by cash, debit cards, or credit card. Such policies shift the risk to the credit card companies.

Companies may also sell their receivables. Selling receivables is called **factoring** the receivables. The buyer of the receivables is called a *factor*. An advantage of factoring is that the company selling its receivables immediately receives cash for operating and other needs. Also, depending on the factoring agreement, some of the risk of uncollectible accounts is shifted to the factor.

The percentage of uncollectible accounts will vary across companies and industries. For example, in their recent annual reports, Deere & Company (manufacturer of John Deere tractors, etc.) reported only 1% of its dealer receivables as uncollectible, and Bell Canada Enterprises (a telecommunications company) reported about 4% of its receivables as uncollectible.

Regardless of how careful a company is in granting credit, some credit sales will be uncollectible. The operating expense recorded from uncollectible receivables is called **bad debt expense**, *uncollectible accounts expense*, or *doubtful accounts expense*.

There is no general rule for when an account becomes uncollectible. Some indications that an account may be uncollectible include the following:

1. The receivable is past due.
2. The customer does not respond to the company's attempts to collect.
3. The customer files for bankruptcy.
4. The customer closes its business.
5. The company cannot locate the customer.

If a customer doesn't pay, a company may turn the account over to a collection agency. After the collection agency attempts to collect payment, any remaining balance in the account is considered worthless.

The two methods of accounting for uncollectible receivables are as follows:

1. The **direct write-off method** records bad debt expense only when an account is determined to be worthless.
2. The **allowance method** records bad debt expense by estimating uncollectible accounts at the end of the accounting period.

The direct write-off method is sometimes used by small companies and companies with few receivables. Companies with a large amount of receivables, however, use the allowance method so they can more accurately record the actual value of this asset. As a result, most well-known companies, such as General Electric, Pepsi, IBM, and Purolator, use the allowance method.

Describe and illustrate the direct write-off method of accounting for uncollectible receivables.

Direct Write-Off Method for Uncollectible Receivables

Under the direct write-off method, Bad Debt Expense is not recorded until the customer's account is determined to be worthless. At that time, the customer's account receivable is written off.

To illustrate, assume that a $4,200 account receivable from D. L. Ross has been determined to be uncollectible. The entry to write off the account is as follows:

May	10	Bad Debt Expense	4,200	
		Accounts Receivable—D. L. Ross		4,200
		To write off accounts receivable.		

An account receivable that has been written off may be collected later. In such cases, the account is reinstated by an entry that reverses the write-off entry. The cash received in payment is then recorded as a receipt on account.

To illustrate, assume that the D. L. Ross account of $4,200 written off on May 10 is later collected on November 21. The reinstatement and receipt of cash is recorded as follows:

Nov.	21	Accounts Receivable—D. L. Ross	4,200	
		Bad Debt Expense		4,200
		To reinstate accounts receivable.		
	21	Cash	4,200	
		Accounts Receivable—D. L. Ross		4,200
		Received cash on account.		

The direct write-off method is used by businesses that sell most of their goods or services for cash or accept only MasterCard or VISA, which are recorded as cash sales. In such cases, receivables are a small part of the current assets, and any bad debt expense is small or immaterial.

An amount is considered **immaterial** when it does not affect the users of the financial statements or change their decisions regarding the company. Examples of businesses that might use the direct write-off method are convenience stores, small retail stores, and small restaurants.

EXAMPLE EXERCISE 8-1   Direct Write-Off Method

Journalize the following transactions using the direct write-off method of accounting for uncollectible receivables:

Jul. 9. Collected $1,200 from Jay Burke and wrote off the remainder owed of $3,900 as uncollectible.

Oct. 11. Reinstated the account of Jay Burke and received $3,900 cash in full payment.

FOLLOW MY EXAMPLE 8-1

Jul. 9	Cash	1,200	
	Bad Debt Expense..	3,900	
	Accounts Receivable—Jay Burke................................		5,100
	Partial collection and write-off of remainder.		
Oct. 11	Accounts Receivable—Jay Burke	3,900	
	Bad Debt Expense		3,900
	To reinstate accounts receivable.		
11	Cash	3,900	
	Accounts Receivable—Jay Burke...............................		3,900
	Received cash on account.		

For Practice: PE 8-1

---

4 Describe and illustrate the allowance method of accounting for uncollectible receivables.

Allowance Method for Uncollectible Receivables

The allowance method estimates the uncollectible accounts receivable at the end of the accounting period. Based on this estimate, Bad Debt Expense is recorded by an adjusting entry.

To illustrate, assume that ExTone Company began operations August 1. As at the end of its accounting period on December 31, 2014, ExTone has an accounts receivable balance of $200,000. This balance includes some past due accounts. Based on industry averages, ExTone estimates that $30,000 of the December 31 accounts receivable will be uncollectible. However, on December 31, ExTone doesn't know which customer accounts will be uncollectible. Thus, specific customer accounts cannot be decreased or credited. Instead, a contra asset account, **Allowance for Doubtful Accounts**, is credited for the estimated bad debts.

Using the $30,000 estimate, the following adjusting entry is made on December 31:

2014				
Dec.	31	Bad Debt Expense	30,000	
		Allowance for Doubtful Accounts		30,000
		Uncollectible accounts estimate.		

Note: The adjusting entry reduces receivables to their net realizable value.

The preceding adjusting entry affects the income statement and balance sheet. On the income statement, the $30,000 of Bad Debt Expense will be matched against the related revenues of the period. Exhibit 1 illustrates the presentation of these two accounts on the financial statements for ExTone Company.

On the balance sheet, the value of the receivables is reduced to the amount that is expected to be collected or realized. This amount is called the **net realizable value** of the receivables. To illustrate, using ExTone Company as an example:

Net realizable value = Accounts Receivable less Allowance for Doubtful Accounts

$$= \$200,000 - \$30,000$$
$$= \$170,000$$

After the preceding adjusting entry is recorded, Accounts Receivable still has a debit balance of $200,000. This balance is the total amount owed by customers on account on December 31 as supported by the accounts receivable subsidiary ledger.

Exhibit 1

Presentation on Financial Statements

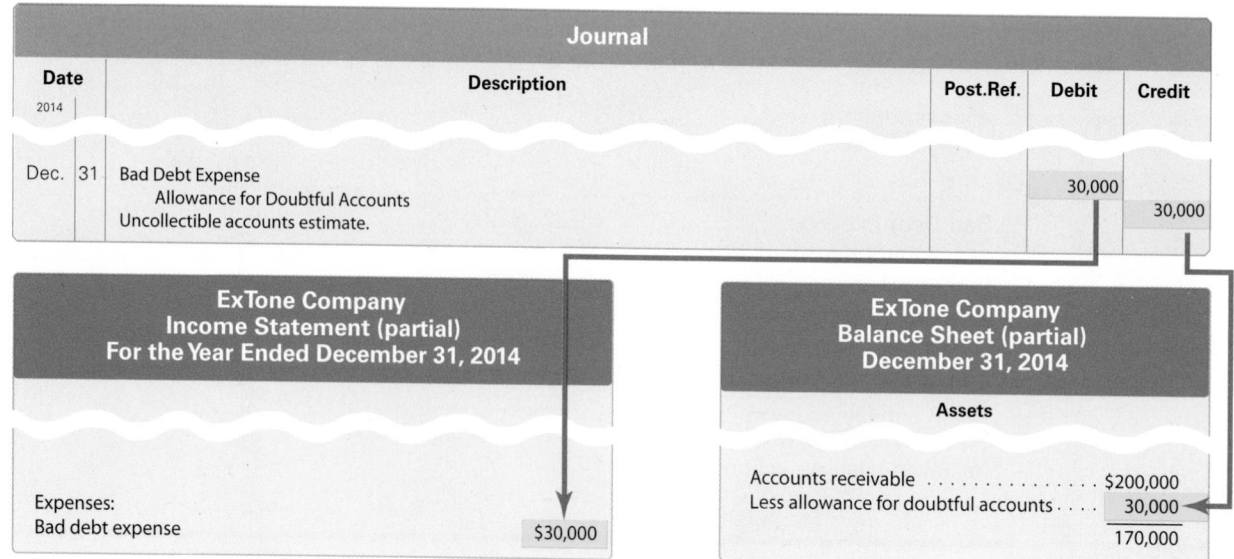

Journal					
Date 2014	**Description**		**Post.Ref.**	**Debit**	**Credit**
Dec. 31	Bad Debt Expense			30,000	
	Allowance for Doubtful Accounts				30,000
	Uncollectible accounts estimate.				

ExTone Company
Income Statement (partial)
For the Year Ended December 31, 2014

Expenses:
Bad debt expense $30,000

ExTone Company
Balance Sheet (partial)
December 31, 2014

Assets

Accounts receivable $200,000
Less allowance for doubtful accounts   30,000
                                           170,000

CRITICAL THINKING

Why do companies allow customers to pay "on account"?

If companies insisted that all customers pay cash for their service or product, they could avoid having bad debt expense—so why do they expose themselves to the risk of not collecting on receivables? Companies expect that the increased sales, as a result of offering credit to customers, will more than offset the bad debt expense.

The accounts receivable contra account, Allowance for Doubtful Accounts, has a credit balance of $30,000.

Write-Offs to the Allowance Account

When a customer's account is identified as uncollectible, it is written off against the allowance account. This write-off requires the company to remove the specific accounts receivable and an equal amount from the allowance account.

To illustrate, on January 21, 2015, John Parker's account of $6,000 with ExTone Company is written off as follows:

2015				
Jan. 21	Allowance for Doubtful Accounts		6,000	
	Accounts Receivable—John Parker			6,000
	To write off accounts receivable.			

At the end of a period, Allowance for Doubtful Accounts will normally have a balance. This is because Allowance for Doubtful Accounts is based on an estimate. As a result, the total write-offs to the allowance account during the period will rarely equal the balance of the account at the beginning of the period. The allowance account will have a credit balance at the end of the period if the write-offs during the period are less than the beginning balance. It will have a debit balance if the write-offs exceed the beginning balance.

To illustrate, assume that during 2015 ExTone Company writes off $26,750 of uncollectible accounts, including the $6,000 account of John Parker recorded on January 21. Allowance for Doubtful Accounts will have a credit balance of $3,250 ($30,000 − $26,750), as shown below.

ALLOWANCE FOR DOUBTFUL ACCOUNTS					
			Jan. 1	Balance	30,000
Total accounts written off $26,750	Jan. 21	6,000			
	Feb. 2	3,900			
	⋮	⋮			
			Dec. 31	Unadjusted balance	3,250

If ExTone Company had written off $32,100 in accounts receivable during 2015, Allowance for Doubtful Accounts would have a debit balance of $2,100, as shown below.

ALLOWANCE FOR DOUBTFUL ACCOUNTS					
			Jan. 1	Balance	30,000
Total accounts written off $32,100	Jan. 21	6,000			
	Feb. 2	3,900			
	⋮	⋮			
Dec. 31 2015	Unadjusted balance	2,100			

The allowance account balances (credit balance of $3,250 and debit balance of $2,100) in the preceding illustrations are *before* the end-of-period adjusting entry. After the end-of-period adjusting entry is recorded, Allowance for Doubtful Accounts should always have a credit balance.

Recovery of a Bad Debt

An account receivable that has been written off against the allowance account may be collected later. The account is reinstated by an entry that reverses the write-off entry. The cash received in payment is then recorded as a receipt on account.

To illustrate, assume that Nancy Smith's account of $5,000, which was written off on April 2, is collected later on June 10. ExTone Company records the reinstatement and the collection as follows:

Jun.	10	Accounts Receivable—Nancy Smith	5,000	
		Allowance for Doubtful Accounts		5,000
		To reinstate accounts receivable.		
	10	Cash	5,000	
		Accounts Receivable—Nancy Smith		5,000
		Received cash on account.		

EXAMPLE EXERCISE 8-2 **Allowance Method**   4

Journalize the following transactions using the allowance method of accounting for uncollectible receivables.

Jul. 9.   Collected $1,200 from Jay Burke and wrote off the remainder owed of $3,900 as uncollectible.
Oct. 11.   Reinstated the account of Jay Burke and received $3,900 cash in full payment.

FOLLOW MY EXAMPLE 8-2

Jul.	9	Cash	1,200	
		Allowance for Doubtful Accounts	3,900	
		Accounts Receivable—Jay Burke		5,100
		Partial collection and write-off of remainder.		
	Oct. 11	Accounts Receivable—Jay Burke	3,900	
		Allowance for Doubtful Accounts		3,900
		To reinstate accounts receivable.		
	11	Cash	3,900	
		Accounts Receivable—Jay Burke		3,900
		Received cash on account.		

For Practice: PE 8-2

Estimating Uncollectibles

The allowance method requires an estimate of uncollectible accounts at the end of the period. This estimate is normally based on past experience, industry averages, and forecasts of the future.

The three methods used to estimate uncollectible accounts are as follows:

1.   Percent of sales method.
2.   Aging of receivables method.
3.   Percent of receivables method.

Percent of Sales Method

Because accounts receivable are created by credit sales, uncollectible accounts can be estimated as a percent of credit sales, known as the **percent of sales** method. If the portion of credit sales to sales is relatively constant, the percent may be applied to total sales or net sales.

To illustrate, assume the following data for ExTone Company on December 31, 2015, before any adjustments:

Balance of Accounts Receivable	$ 240,500
Balance of Allowance for Doubtful Accounts	3,250 (Cr.)
Total credit sales	3,000,000
Bad debt as a percent of credit sales	¾%

Bad Debt Expense of $22,500 is estimated as follows:

Bad Debt Expense = Credit Sales × Bad Debt as a Percent of Credit Sales
Bad Debt Expense = $3,000,000 × ¾% = $22,500

The adjusting entry for uncollectible accounts on December 31, 2015, is as follows:

2015 Dec.	31	Bad Debt Expense	22,500	
		Allowance for Doubtful Accounts		22,500
		Uncollectible accounts estimate.		
		($3,000,000 × 0.0075 = $22,500)		

After the adjusting entry is posted to the ledger, Bad Debt Expense will have an adjusted balance of $22,500. Allowance for Doubtful Accounts will have an adjusted balance of $25,750 ($3,250 + $22,500). Both T accounts are shown below.

BAD DEBT EXPENSE

Dec. 31	Adjusting entry	22,500	
Dec. 31	Adjusted balance	22,500	

ALLOWANCE FOR DOUBTFUL ACCOUNTS

			Jan. 1	Balance	30,000
Total accounts written off $26,750	Jan. 21	6,000			
	Feb. 2	3,900			
	⋮	⋮			
			Dec. 31	Unadjusted balance	3,250
			Dec. 31	Adjusting entry	22,500
					25,750

Note: The estimate based on sales is added to any balance in Allowance for Doubtful Accounts.

Under the percent of sales method, the amount of the adjusting entry is the amount estimated for Bad Debt Expense. This estimate is credited to the unadjusted balance for Allowance for Doubtful Accounts.

To illustrate, assume that in the preceding example the unadjusted balance of Allowance for Doubtful Accounts on December 31, 2015, had been a $2,100 debit balance instead of a $3,250 credit balance. The adjustment would still have been $22,500. However, the December 31, 2015, ending adjusted balance of Allowance for Doubtful Accounts would have been $20,400 ($22,500 – $2,100).

EXAMPLE EXERCISE 8-3   Percent of Sales Method   ④

At the end of the current year, Accounts Receivable has a balance of $800,000, Allowance for Doubtful Accounts has a credit balance of $7,500, and net sales for the year total $3,500,000. Bad debt expense is estimated at ½ of 1% of net sales.

Determine (a) the amount of the adjusting entry for uncollectible accounts; (b) the adjusted balances of Accounts Receivable, Allowance for Doubtful Accounts, and Bad Debt Expense; and (c) the net realizable value of accounts receivable.

FOLLOW MY EXAMPLE 8-3

a. $17,500 ($3,500,000 × 0.005)

	Adjusted Balance
b. Accounts Receivable...	$800,000
Allowance for Doubtful Accounts ($7,500 + $17,500)	25,000
Bad Debt Expense..	17,500

c. $775,000 ($800,000 – $25,000)

For Practice: PE 8-3

Aging of Receivables Method

The **aging of receivables method** is based on the assumption that the longer an account receivable is outstanding, the less likely it will be collected. The aging of receivables method is applied as follows:

Step 1. The due date of each account receivable is determined.

Step 2. The number of days each account is past due is determined. This is the number of days between the due date of the account and the date of the analysis.

Step 3. Each account is placed in an aged class according to its days past due. Typical aged classes include the following:

> Not past due
> 1–30 days past due
> 31–60 days past due
> 61–90 days past due
> Over 90 days past due

Step 4. The totals for each aged class are determined.

Step 5. The total for each aged class is multiplied by an estimated percentage of uncollectible accounts for that class.

Step 6. The estimated total of uncollectible accounts is determined as the sum of the uncollectible accounts for each aged class.

The preceding steps are summarized in an aging schedule, in an overall process called aging the receivables.

To illustrate, assume that ExTone Company uses the aging of receivables method instead of the percent of sales method. ExTone prepared an aging schedule for its accounts receivable of $240,500 as at December 31, 2015, as shown in Exhibit 2 below.

Note: The estimate based on aged receivables is compared to the balance in the allowance account to determine the amount of the adjusting entry.

The sum of the estimated uncollectible accounts in each aged class (step 6) is the estimated uncollectible accounts on December 31, 2015. This amount is the desired adjusted balance for Allowance for Doubtful Accounts. For ExTone Company, this amount is $26,490, as shown in Exhibit 2 below.

Comparing the estimate of $26,490 with the unadjusted balance of the allowance account determines the amount of the adjustment for Bad Debt Expense. For ExTone, the unadjusted balance of the allowance account is a credit balance of $3,250. The amount to be added to this balance is therefore $23,240 ($26,490 – $3,250). The adjusting entry is as follows:

2015				
Dec.	31	Bad Debt Expense	23,240	
		Allowance for Doubtful Accounts		23,240
		Uncollectible accounts estimate.		
		($26,490 – $3,250)		

Exhibit 2

ExTone Company Aging of Receivables Schedule December 31, 2015

	A	B	C	D	E	F	G
1			**Not**		**Days Past Due**		
2			**Past**				
3	**Customer**	**Balance**	**Due**	**1–30**	**31–60**	**61–90**	**Over 90**
4	Ashby & Co.	1,500			1,500		
5	B. T. Barr	6,100					6,100
6	Brock Co.	4,700	4,700				
21							
22	Total	240,500	125,000	64,000	13,100	8,900	29,500
23	Percent uncollectible			2%	5%	10%	20%	60%
24	Estimate of uncollectible accounts	26,490	2,500	3,200	1,310	1,780	17,700

Steps 1–3

Step 4 → 22

Step 5 → 23

Step 6 → 24

After the preceding adjusting entry is posted to the ledger, Bad Debt Expense will have an adjusted balance of $23,240. Allowance for Doubtful Accounts will have an adjusted balance of $26,490, and the net realizable value of the receivables is $214,010 ($240,500 − $26,490). Both T accounts are shown below.

BAD DEBT EXPENSE

Dec. 31, 2015 Adjusting entry	23,240	
Dec. 31 Adjusted balance	23,240	

ALLOWANCE FOR DOUBTFUL ACCOUNTS

	Dec. 31, 2015	Unadjusted balance	3,250
	Dec. 31	Adjusting entry	23,240
	Dec. 31	Adjusted balance	26,490

Under the aging of receivables method, the amount of the adjusting entry is the amount that will yield an adjusted balance for Allowance for Doubtful Accounts equal to that estimated by the aging schedule.

To illustrate, if the unadjusted balance of the allowance account had been a debit balance of $2,100, the amount of the adjustment would have been $28,590 ($26,490 + $2,100). In this case, Bad Debt Expense would have an adjusted balance of $28,590. However, the adjusted balance of Allowance for Doubtful Accounts would still have been $26,490. After the adjusting entry is posted, both T accounts are shown below.

BAD DEBT EXPENSE

Dec. 31	Adjusting entry	28,590
Dec. 31	Adjusted balance	28,590

ALLOWANCE FOR DOUBTFUL ACCOUNTS

Dec. 31	Unadjusted balance 2,100	
	Dec. 31 Adjusting entry	28,590
	Dec. 31 Adjusted balance	26,490

EXAMPLE EXERCISE 8-4   Aging of Receivables Method   4

At the end of the current year, Accounts Receivable has a balance of $800,000, Allowance for Doubtful Accounts has a credit balance of $7,500, and net sales for the year total $3,500,000. Using the aging of receivables method, the balance of Allowance for Doubtful Accounts is estimated as $30,000.

Determine (a) the amount of the adjusting entry for uncollectible accounts; (b) the adjusted balances of Accounts Receivable, Allowance for Doubtful Accounts, and Bad Debt Expense; and (c) the net realizable value of accounts receivable.

FOLLOW MY EXAMPLE 8-4

a. $22,500 ($30,000 − $7,500)

	Adjusted Balance
b. Accounts Receivable	$800,000
Allowance for Doubtful Accounts	30,000
Bad Debt Expense	22,500

c. $770,000 ($800,000 − $30,000)

For Practice: PE 8-4

Percent of Receivables Method

The **percent of receivables method** is similar to the aging of receivables method. Both methods are based on the assumption that the longer an account receivable is outstanding, the less likely it will be collected. Rather than use an aging schedule, the uncollectible accounts are estimated as a percent of receivables.

To illustrate, assume the following data for ExTone Company on December 31, 2015, before any adjustments:

Balance of Accounts Receivable	$240,500
Balance of Allowance for Doubtful Accounts	3,250 (Cr.)
Bad debt as a percent of receivables	11%

The estimated uncollectible accounts on December 31, 2015, total $26,455 ($240,500 × 11%). Comparing the estimate of $26,455 with the unadjusted balance of the allowance account determines the amount of the adjustment for Bad Debt Expense. Since the unadjusted balance for ExTone is a credit balance of $3,250, the amount to be added to this balance is $23,205 ($26,455 − $3,250). The adjusting entry is as follows:

2015					
Dec.	31	Bad Debt Expense		23,205	
		Allowance for Doubtful Accounts			23,205
		Uncollectible accounts estimate.			
		($26,455 − $3,250)			

After the preceding adjusting entry is posted to the ledger, Bad Debt Expense will have an adjusted balance of $23,205. Allowance for Doubtful Accounts will have an adjusted balance of $26,455, and the net realizable value of the receivables is $214,045 ($240,500 − $26,455). Both T accounts are shown below.

	BAD DEBT EXPENSE					
Dec. 31	Adjusting entry	23,205				
Dec. 31	Adjusted balance	23,205				

	ALLOWANCE FOR DOUBTFUL ACCOUNTS					
			Dec. 31	Unadjusted balance	3,250
			Dec. 31	Adjusting entry	23,205
			Dec. 31	Adjusted balance	26,455

Under the percent of receivables method, the amount of the adjusting entry is the amount that will yield an adjusted balance for Allowance for Doubtful Accounts equal to that estimated by the percent of receivables calculation.

To illustrate, if the unadjusted balance of the allowance account had been a debit balance of $2,100, the amount of the adjustment would have been $28,555 ($26,455 + $2,100). In this case, Bad Debt Expense would have an adjusted balance of $28,555. However, the adjusted balance of Allowance for Doubtful Accounts would still have been $26,455. After the adjusting entry is posted, both T accounts are shown below.

	BAD DEBT EXPENSE					
Dec. 31	Adjusting entry	28,555				
Dec. 31	Adjusted balance	28,555				

	ALLOWANCE FOR DOUBTFUL ACCOUNTS					
Dec. 31	Unadjusted balance	2,100				
			Dec. 31	Adjusting entry	28,555
			Dec. 31	Adjusted balance	26,455

EXAMPLE EXERCISE 8-5 Percent of Receivables Method 4

At the end of the current year, Accounts Receivable has a balance of $800,000, Allowance for Doubtful Accounts has a credit balance of $7,500, and net sales for the year total $3,500,000.

Assuming that uncollectible accounts are estimated to be 2% of receivables, determine (a) the amount of the adjusting entry for uncollectible accounts; (b) the adjusted balances of Accounts Receivable, Allowance for Doubtful Accounts, and Bad Debt Expense; and (c) the net realizable value of accounts receivable.

FOLLOW MY EXAMPLE 8-5

a. $8,500 [($800,000 × 0.02) – $7,500]

	Adjusted Balance
b. Accounts Receivable...	$800,000
Allowance for Doubtful Accounts ($800,000 × 0.02).......................	16,000
Bad Debt Expense..	8,500

c. $784,000 ($800,000 – $16,000)

For Practice: PE 8-5

Comparing Estimation Methods

The percent of sales, the aging of receivables, and the percent of receivables methods all estimate uncollectible accounts. However, each method has a slightly different focus and financial statement emphasis.

Under the percent of sales method, Bad Debt Expense is the focus of the estimation process and so more emphasis is placed on the income statement. The amount of the adjusting entry is based on the estimate of Bad Debt Expense for the period.

Under the aging of receivables and the percent of receivables methods, Allowance for Doubtful Accounts is the focus of the estimation process, with both methods placing more emphasis on the net realizable value of the receivables and, thus, emphasizing the balance sheet. The amount of the adjusting entry is the amount that will yield an adjusted balance for Allowance for Doubtful Accounts based upon the aging schedule or the percentage estimation. There is usually a strong correlation between the age of receivables and their collectability, and so the aging method is often the best estimate of the realizable value of the receivables. However, since the percent of sales method and the percent of receivables method are easier to apply, companies often use these methods for interim financial reporting and use the aging of receivables method for annual reporting.

Exhibit 3 summarizes these differences between the percent of sales, the aging of receivables, and the percent of receivables methods. Exhibit 3 also shows the results of the ExTone Company illustration for the percent of sales, the aging of receivables, and the percent of receivables methods. The amounts shown in Exhibit 3 assume an unadjusted credit balance of $3,250 for Allowance for Doubtful Accounts. Although the methods normally yield different amounts for any one period, over several periods the amounts should be similar.

CRITICAL THINKING

Company XYZ had an allowance for doubtful accounts of $22,500 at December 31, 2014. During 2015, the company wrote off $26,000 of accounts receivable, resulting in a debit balance of $3,500 at December 31, 2015. **Did Company XYZ's accountant make a mistake when establishing the allowance in 2014?**

No. Bad debt expense is an estimate. Company XYZ's accountant used professional judgment to establish an allowance for doubtful accounts that reflects the approximate value of the accounts receivable. The company experienced more bad debts than expected, resulting in the debit balance. The increase in bad debts could result from a number of factors, such as a downturn in the economy or a change in the risk levels of Company XYZ's credit customers. Expecting a company to precisely estimate its bad debts is unrealistic.

Exhibit 3

Differences between Estimation Methods

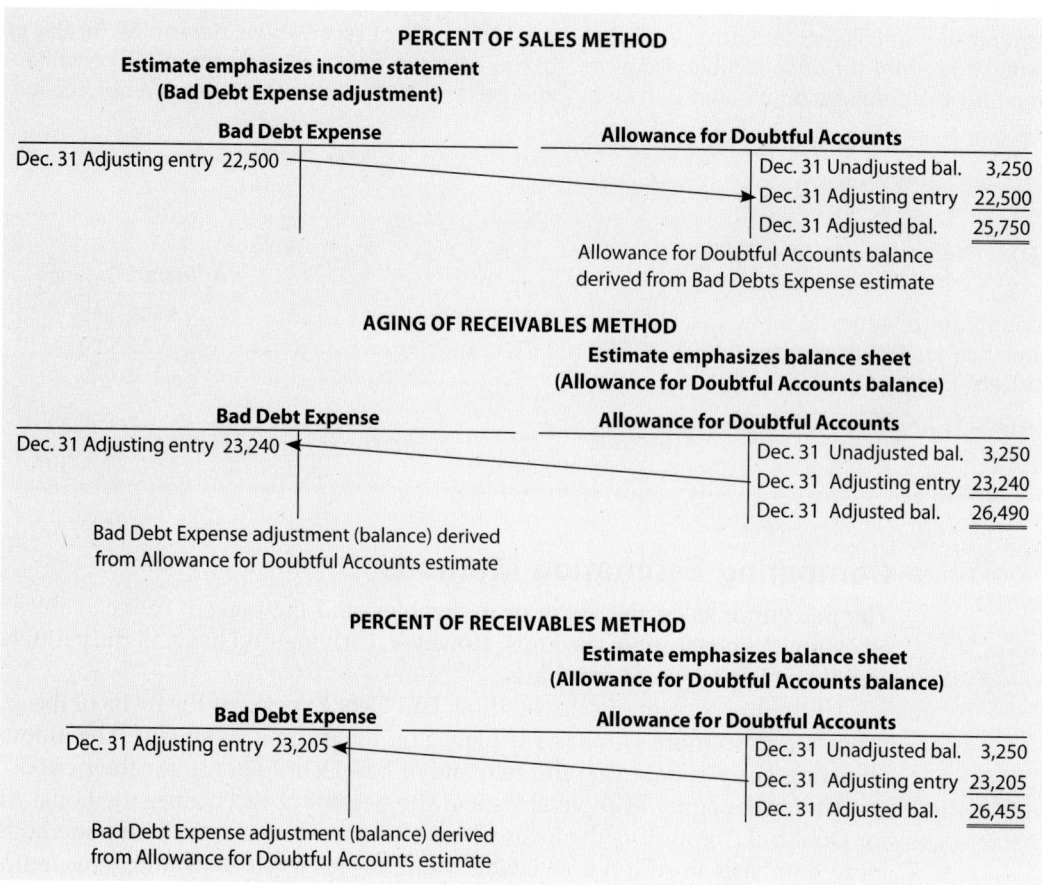

MID-CHAPTER ILLUSTRATIVE PROBLEM

At January 1, 2014, Hobbs Company's Accounts Receivable had a balance of $900,000, and the Allowance for Doubtful Accounts had a credit balance of $5,000. The company had the following transactions:

Mar. 1.	Wrote off account of C. York, $3,650.
Apr. 12.	Received $2,250 as a partial payment on the $5,500 account of Cary Bradshaw. Wrote off the remaining balance as uncollectible.
Jun. 22.	Received the $3,650 from C. York, which had been written off on March 1. Reinstated the account and recorded the cash receipt.
Sep. 7.	Wrote off the following accounts as uncollectible (record as one journal entry):

Jason Bigg	$1,100
Steve Bradey	2,220
Samantha Neeley	1,360

Dec. 31.	Hobbs Company uses the percent of sales method of estimated uncollectible expenses. Based on past history and industry averages, 1.25% of sales are expected to be uncollectible. Hobbs recorded $3,400,000 of sales during 2014.

Instructions

Journalize the transactions.

MID-CHAPTER ILLUSTRATIVE SOLUTION

2014 Mar.	1	Allowance for Doubtful Accounts	3,650	
		Accounts Receivable—C. York		3,650
		Wrote off account.		
Apr.	12	Cash	2,250	
		Allowance for Doubtful Accounts	3,250	
		Accounts Receivable—Cary Bradshaw		5,500
		Partial collection and write-off of remainder.		
Jun.	22	Accounts Receivable—C. York	3,650	
		Allowance for Doubtful Accounts		3,650
		To reinstate accounts receivable.		
		Cash	3,650	
		Accounts Receivable—C. York		3,650
		Received cash on account.		
Sep.	7	Allowance for Doubtful Accounts	4,680	
		Accounts Receivable—Jason Bigg		1,100
		Accounts Receivable—Steve Bradey		2,220
		Accounts Receivable—Samantha Neeley		1,360
		To write off accounts receivable.		
Dec.	31	Bad Debt Expense	42,500	
		Allowance for Doubtful Accounts		42,500
		($3,400,000 × 1.25%)		
		Uncollectible accounts estimate.		

INTEGRITY, OBJECTIVITY, AND ETHICS IN BUSINESS

THE PROFIT THAT WASN'T

Financial reporting frauds are often tied to accounts receivable because receivables allow companies to record revenue before cash is received. Take, for example, the case of Canada's technology giant, Nortel Networks Corp., which started making telephones in 1895, shortly after Alexander Graham Bell invented the telephone, and shifted its focus to Internet communications in the 1990s. Nortel, with phenomenal sales growth during the technology explosion of the 1990s, went on a spending spree, purchasing other companies, many of which would prove to be overvalued. When the technology "bubble" burst in 2000, Nortel was struggling to maintain sales. To cover up the losses and to receive bonuses tied to profit targets, Nortel executives accelerated recognition of revenues and booked false receivables of approximately $4 billion. An investigation by the Royal Canadian Mounted Police (RCMP) resulted in the CEO and senior executives being charged and fined $36 million.

 Notes Receivable

Describe the accounting for notes receivable.

A note has some advantages over an account receivable. By signing a note, the debtor recognizes the debt and agrees to pay according to the terms in the note. Thus, a note is a stronger legal claim.

Characteristics of Notes Receivable

A promissory note is a written promise to pay the principal, usually with interest, on demand or at a date in the future.[1] Characteristics of a promissory note are as follows:

1. The *maker* is the party making the promise to pay.
2. The *payee* is the party to whom the note is payable.

---

1 You may see references to non-interest-bearing notes. Such notes are not widely used and carry an assumed or implicit interest rate.

3. The *principal* is the amount the note is written for.
4. The *issuance date* is the date a note is issued.
5. The *due date* or *maturity date* is the date the note is to be paid.
6. The *term* of a note is the amount of time between the issuance and due dates and can be expressed as days or months.
7. The *interest rate* is that rate of interest that must be paid on the principal amount for the term of the note.

Exhibit 4 illustrates a promissory note. The maker of the note is Selig Company, and the payee is Pearland Company. The principal of the note is $2,000, and the issuance date is March 16, 2014. The term of the note is 90 days, which results in a due date of June 14, 2014, as shown below.

Days in March	31 days
Minus issuance date of note	16
Days remaining in March	15 days
Add days in April	30
Add days in May	31
Add days in June (due date of June 14)	14
Term of note	90 days

Due Date of 90-Day Note

MARCH 16-31	APRIL 1-30	MAY 1-31	JUNE 1-14
15 days	+ 30 days	+ 31 days	+ 14 days

Mar. 16   **Total of 90 days**   June 14

In Exhibit 4, the term of the note is 90 days, and it has an interest rate of 5%. If the term of the note had been three months, then the due date would have been June 16, 2014, three months from the issuance date.

Exhibit 4

Promissory Note

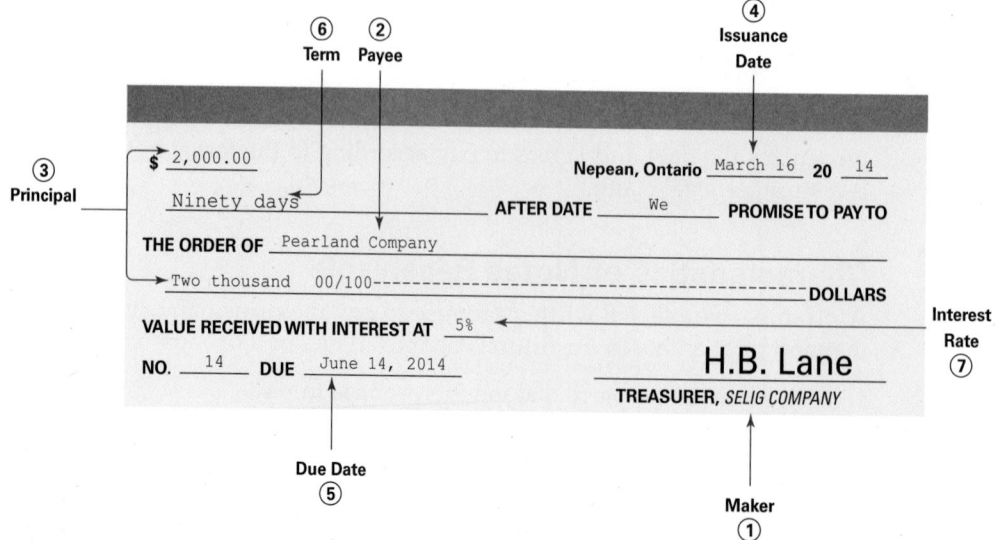

The interest on a note is computed as follows:

Interest = Principal × Interest Rate × (Term/365 days) or (Term/12 months)

The interest rate is stated on an annual (yearly) basis, whereas the term is expressed either as days or months. If the term is expressed in days, then the term is divided by 365 days in the interest calculation. If the term is expressed in months, then the term is divided by 12 months to determine the interest. In both cases, the interest is rounded to the nearest whole cent. Thus, the interest on the note in Exhibit 4 is computed as follows:

Interest = $2,000 × 5% × 90/365 = $24.658 or $24.66

If the note in Exhibit 4 had been for a term of three months rather than 90 days, then the interest would be computed as follows:

Interest = $2,000 × 5% × 3/12 = $25

The **maturity value** is the amount that must be paid at the due date of the note, which is the sum of the principal and the interest. The maturity value of the note in Exhibit 4 is $2,024.66 ($2,000 + $24.66).

Accounting for Notes Receivable

A promissory note may be received by a company from a customer to replace an account receivable. A promissory note may also be received in exchange for a sale on account or for a loan. In all three cases, the promissory note is recorded as a note receivable.

To illustrate, assume that a company accepts a 30-day, 6% note dated November 21, 2015, in settlement of the account of W. A. Bunn Co., which is past due and has a balance of $6,000. The company records the receipt of the note as follows:

2015				
Nov.	21	Notes Receivable—W. A. Bunn Co.	6,000	
		Accounts Receivable—W. A. Bunn Co.		6,000
		To record receipt of a note.		

At the due date, the company records the receipt of $6,029.59 ($6,000 principal amount plus $29.59 interest) as follows:

2015				
Dec.	21	Cash	6,029.59	
		Notes Receivable—W. A. Bunn Co.		6,000.00
		Interest Revenue		29.59
		To record payment of note.		
		$6,029.59 = [$6,000 + ($6,000 × 6% × 30/365)]		

If the maker of a note fails to pay the note on the due date, the note is a **dishonoured note receivable**. If a company that holds a dishonoured note believes the amount is still collectible, then the principal of the note plus any interest due are transferred to an accounts receivable account. For example, assume that the $6,000, 30-day, 6% note received from W. A. Bunn Co. and recorded on November 21 is dishonoured. The company holding the note, believing W. A. Bunn Co. will pay the amount owed, transfers the note and interest back to the customer's account as follows:

2015				
Dec.	21	Accounts Receivable—W. A. Bunn Co.	6,029.59	
		Notes Receivable—W. A. Bunn Co.		6,000.00
		Interest Revenue		29.59
		To record receipt of an accounts receivable.		

The company has earned the interest of $29.59, even though the note is dishonoured. If the account receivable is uncollectible, the company will write off $6,029.59 against Allowance for Doubtful Accounts.

A company receiving a note should record an adjusting entry for any accrued interest at the end of the period. For example, assume that Crawford Company issues a $4,000, three-month, 5% note dated December 1, 2015, in exchange for merchandise costing $2,400.

Assuming the company receiving the note has a December 31 year-end and uses a perpetual inventory system, the following entries would be recorded:

2015					
Dec.	1	Notes Receivable—Crawford Company		4,000.00	
		Sales			4,000.00
		Cost of Goods Sold		2,400.00	
		Inventory			2,400.00
		Sold merchandise in exchange for note.			
	31	Interest Receivable		16.67	
		Interest Revenue			16.67
		To record accrued interest.			
		($4,000 × 5% × 1/12).			
2016					
Mar.	1	Cash		4,050.00	
		Notes Receivable—Crawford Company			4,000.00
		Interest Receivable			16.67
		Interest Revenue			33.33*
		To record payment of note.			
		*[($4,000 × 5% × 3/12) − $16.67].			

The interest revenue account is closed at the end of each accounting period. The amount of interest revenue is normally reported in the Other Income section of the income statement.

EXAMPLE EXERCISE 8-6 **Notes Receivable** **5**

Optical Surgery Centre received a 60-day, 6% note for $4,000 dated March 14 from a patient on account.

a. Determine the due date of the note.

b. Determine the maturity value of the note.

c. Journalize the entry to record the receipt of the payment of the note at maturity.

FOLLOW MY EXAMPLE 8-6

a. The due date of the note is May 13, determined as follows:

March	17 days (31 − 14)
April	30 days
May	13 days
Total	60 days

b. $4,039.45 [$4,000 + ($4,000 × 6% × 60/365)]

c. May 13   Cash..   4,039.45

        Notes Receivable..   4,000.00

        Interest Revenue...   39.45

    To record payment of note.

For Practice: PE 8-6

 Reporting Receivables on the Balance Sheet

Describe and analyze the reporting of receivables on the balance sheet.

All receivables that are expected to be realized in cash within a year are reported in the Current Assets section of the balance sheet. Current assets are normally reported in the order of their liquidity, beginning with cash and cash equivalents.

The balance sheet presentation for receivables for Morning Java is shown on the following page.

Morning Java
Balance Sheet
December 31, 2015

Assets

Current assets:

Cash and cash equivalents		$235,000
Trading investments (at fair value)		465,000
Accounts receivable	$305,000	
Less allowance for doubtful accounts	12,300	292,700

In Morning Java's financial statements, the allowance for doubtful accounts is subtracted from accounts receivable. Some companies report receivables at their net realizable value. Under both IFRS and ASPE, disclosure of the allowance is not required and so either of these methods of presentation may be used.[2]

Other disclosures related to receivables are reported either on the face of the financial statements or in the financial statement notes. If unusual credit risks exist within the receivables, the nature of the risks is disclosed. For example, if the majority of the receivables are due from one customer or are due from customers located in one area of the country or one industry, these facts are disclosed.

EXAMPLE EXERCISE 8-7 Reporting Receivables   6

For the fiscal year ended December 31, 2015, Simple Solution had the following account balances:

	Dr (Cr)
Accounts receivable	120,000
Notes receivable, due Sept. 2016	65,000
Notes receivable, due Oct. 2017	119,500
Allowance for doubtful accounts	(5,400)
Bad debt expense	4,900
Cash	43,799
Inventory	238,600
Cost of goods sold	628,376
Office supplies	1,850

Prepare the current asset section of the balance sheet.

FOLLOW MY EXAMPLE 8-7

Simple Solution
Balance Sheet (partial)
December 31, 2015

Assets

Current assets:

Cash		$43,799
Accounts receivable	$120,000	
Less allowance for doubtful accounts	5,400	114,600
Notes receivable		65,000
Inventory		238,600
Office supplies		1,850
Total current assets		$463,849

For Practice: PE 8-7

2 *CICA Handbook–Accounting*, 2012 edition, Part I, IAS 1; and Part II, Section 3856.39.

Two financial measures that are especially useful in evaluating efficiency in collecting receivables are (1) the accounts receivable turnover and (2) the days' sales in receivables.

The **accounts receivable turnover** measures how frequently during the year the accounts receivable are being converted to cash. For example, with credit terms of 2/10, n/30, the accounts receivable should turn over more than 12 times per year. The accounts receivable turnover is computed as follows:[3]

$$\text{Accounts Receivable Turnover} = \frac{\text{Net Sales}}{\text{Average Accounts Receivable}}$$

The average accounts receivable can be determined by using monthly data or by simply adding the beginning and ending accounts receivable balances and dividing by two. For example, using the following financial data (in millions) for Air Canada, the 2011 and 2010 accounts receivable turnovers are computed as 17.2 and 16.1, respectively.

	2011	2010	2009
Net sales	$11,612	$10,786	
Accounts receivable	$713	$641	$701
Average accounts receivable	$677 ($713 + $641)/2	$671 ($641 + $701)/2	
Accounts receivable turnover	17.2 ($11,612/$677)	16.1 ($10,786/$671)	

Comparing 2011 and 2010 indicates that the accounts receivable turnover has increased from 16.1 to 17.2. Thus, Air Canada's management of accounts receivable has improved in 2011.

The **days' sales in receivables** is an estimate of the length of time the accounts receivable have been outstanding. It is computed as follows:

$$\text{Days' Sales in Receivables} = \frac{\text{Average Accounts Receivable}}{\text{Average Daily Sales}}$$

Average daily sales are determined by dividing net sales by 365 days. For example, using the preceding data for Air Canada, the days' sales in receivables is 21.3 and 22.7 for 2011 and 2010, respectively, as shown below.

	2011	2010
Net sales	$11,612	$10,786
Average accounts receivable	$677 ($713 + $641)/2	$671 ($641 + $701)/2
Average daily sales	$31.8 ($11,612/365)	$29.6 ($10,786/365)
Days' sales in receivables	21.3 ($677/$31.8)	22.7 ($671/$29.6)

The days' sales in receivables confirms an improvement in managing accounts receivable during 2011. That is, the efficiency in collecting accounts receivable improved when the days' sales in receivables decreased. Air Canada's days' sales in receivables decreased from 22.7 days in 2010 to 21.3 days in 2011. However, these measures should also be compared with similar companies within the industry, for a fuller understanding of the ratios' significance.

---

3 If known, credit sales can be used in the numerator. However, because credit sales are not normally disclosed to external users, most analysts use net sales in the numerator.

EXAMPLE EXERCISE 8-8   Accounts Receivable Turnover and Days' Sales in Receivables   ⑥

Financial statement data for the years ended December 31 for Osterman Company are as follows:

	2015	2014
Net sales	$4,284,000	$3,040,000
Accounts receivable:		
Beginning of year	550,000	400,000
End of year	640,000	550,000

a. Determine accounts receivable turnover for 2015 and 2014.

b. Determine the days' sales in receivables for 2015 and 2014.

c. Does the change in accounts receivable turnover and the days' sales in receivable from 2014 to 2015 indicate a favourable or an unfavourable trend?

FOLLOW MY EXAMPLE 8-8

a. Accounts receivable turnover:

	2015	2014
Average accounts receivable:		
($550,000 + $640,000)/2	$595,000	
($400,000 + $550,000)/2		$475,000
Accounts receivable turnover:		
$4,284,000/$595,000	7.2	
$3,040,000/$475,000		6.4

b. Days' sales in receivables:

	2015	2014
Average daily sales:		
$4,284,000/365 days	$11,737	
$3,040,000/365 days		$8,329
Days' sales in receivables:		
$595,000/$11,737	50.7 days	
$475,000/$8,329		57.0 days

c. The increase in the accounts receivable turnover from 6.4 to 7.2 and the decrease in the days' sales in receivables from 57.0 days to 50.7 days indicate favourable trends in the efficiency of collecting accounts receivable.

Practice Exercises: PE 8-8

At a Glance 8

①   Describe the common classes of receivables.

Key Points	Key Learning Outcomes	Page	Example Exercises
Receivables are normally classified as accounts receivable, notes receivable, or other receivables.	• Define the term receivables.	414	
	• List some common classifications of receivables.	414	

2 Describe the accounting for uncollectible receivables.

Key Points	Key Learning Outcomes	Page	Example Exercises
The operating expense recorded from uncollectible receivables is called *bad debt expense*. The two methods of accounting for uncollectible receivables are the direct write-off method and the allowance method.	• Describe the two methods of accounting for uncollectible accounts receivable.	416	

3 Describe and illustrate the direct write-off method of accounting for uncollectible receivables.

Key Points	Key Learning Outcomes	Page	Example Exercises
Under the direct write-off method, the entry to write off an account debits Bad Debt Expense and credits Accounts Receivable. The direct write-off method is acceptable only when the amount of bad debt expense is immaterial.	• Prepare journal entries to write off an account using the direct write-off method.	416	8-1
	• Prepare journal entries for the reinstatement and collection of an account previously written off using the direct write-off method.	416	8-1

4 Describe and illustrate the allowance method of accounting for uncollectible receivables.

Key Points	Key Learning Outcomes	Page	Example Exercises
Under the allowance method, an adjusting entry is made for uncollectible accounts. When an account is determined to be uncollectible, it is written off against the allowance account. The allowance account normally has a credit balance after the adjusting entry has been posted and is a contra asset account.	• Prepare journal entries to write off an account using the allowance method.	417	8-2
	• Prepare journal entries for the reinstatement and collection of an account previously written off using the allowance method.	419	8-2
The estimate of uncollectibles may be based on a percent of sales, an aging of receivables, or a percent of receivables.	• Determine the adjustment, bad debt expense, and net realizable value of accounts receivable using the percent of sales method.	420	8-3
While all three estimation methods are acceptable, the aging method is preferred because it provides the best estimate of the net realizable value of the receivables.	• Determine the adjustment, bad debt expense, and net realizable value of accounts receivable using the aging of receivables method.	422	8-4
	• Determine the adjustment, bad debt expense, and net realizable value of accounts receivable using the percent of receivables method.	424	8-5
	• Compare the three estimation methods.	425	

5 | Describe the accounting for notes receivable.

Key Points	Key Learning Outcomes	Page	Example Exercises
A note may be received in settlement of an account receivable or in exchange for a sale or a loan. If the maker of a note fails to pay the debt on the due date and if the payee believes the amount is collectible, the dishonoured note is recorded as an accounts receivable account for the amount of the claim against the maker of the note.	• Describe the characteristics of a note receivable.	427	
	• Determine the due date and maturity value of a note receivable.	428	8-6
	• Prepare journal entries for the receipt of the payment of a note receivable.	429	8-6
	• Prepare a journal entry for a dishonoured note receivable.	429	

6 | Describe and analyze the reporting of receivables on the balance sheet.

Key Points	Key Learning Outcomes	Page	Example Exercises
All receivables that are expected to be realized in cash within a year are reported in the Current Assets section of the balance sheet in the order in which they can be converted to cash in normal operations. Additional receivable disclosures include unusual credit risks. The accounts receivable turnover and the days' sales in receivable ratios measure how frequently accounts receivable are being converted to cash.	• Describe how receivables are reported in the Current Assets section of the balance sheet.	430	8-7
	• Describe disclosures related to receivables that should be reported in the financial statements.	431	
	• Describe two financial measures useful in evaluating efficiency in collecting receivables.	432	8-8

GLOSSARY

accounts receivable – Claims against customers created by selling merchandise or services on credit. (p. 415) Also known as *trade receivables*.

accounts receivable turnover – The measure of how frequently during the year the accounts receivable are being converted to cash. (p. 432)

aging of receivables method – The process of estimating uncollectible accounts based upon the age of the receivables. (p. 422)

allowance for doubtful accounts – The contra asset account for accounts receivable. (p. 417)

allowance method – The method of accounting for uncollectible accounts that provides an expense for uncollectible receivables in advance of their write-off. (p. 416)

bad debt expense – The operating expense incurred because of the failure to collect receivables. (p. 415)

days' sales in receivables – An estimate of the length of time the accounts receivable have been outstanding. (p. 432)

direct write-off method – The method of accounting for uncollectible accounts that recognizes the expense only when accounts are judged to be worthless. (p. 416)

dishonoured note receivable – A note that the maker fails to pay on the due date. (p. 429)

factoring – Selling of receivables. (p. 415)

immaterial – Description of an amount that does not affect the users of the financial statements or change their decision regarding the company. (p. 416)

maturity value – The amount that is due at the maturity or due date of a note. (p. 429)

net realizable value – The amount of receivables expected to be collected. (p. 417)

notes receivable – Customers' written promises to pay an amount and interest at an agreed-upon rate. (p. 415)

percent of receivables method – The process of estimating uncollectible accounts as a percent of all accounts receivable. (p. 424)

percent of sales method – The process of estimating uncollectible accounts as a percent of either credit sales or total sales. (p. 420)

receivables – All money claims against other entities, including people, business firms, and other organizations. (p. 414)

trade receivables – Claims against customers created by selling merchandise or services on credit. (p. 415) Also known as *accounts receivable*.

END-OF-CHAPTER ILLUSTRATIVE PROBLEM

Ditzler Company, a construction supply company, uses the allowance method of accounting for uncollectible accounts receivable and a perpetual inventory system. Selected transactions completed by Ditzler Company are as follows:

Feb. 1.	Sold merchandise on account to Ames Co., $8,000. The cost of the goods sold was $4,500.
Mar. 15.	Accepted a 60-day, 5% note for $8,000 from Ames Co. on account.
Apr. 9.	Wrote off a $2,500 account from Dorset Co. as uncollectible.
May 14.	Received from Ames Co. the amount due on its note of March 15.
Jun. 13.	Reinstated the account of Dorset Co., written off on April 9, and received $2,500 in full payment.
Dec. 31.	It is estimated that 3% of the credit sales of $1,375,000 for the year ended December 31 will be uncollectible.

Instructions

Journalize the transactions, rounding all transactions to the nearest cent.

Solution

Feb.	1	Accounts Receivable—Ames Co.	8,000.00	
		Sales		8,000.00
	1	Cost of Goods Sold	4,500.00	
		Inventory		4,500.00
Mar.	15	Notes Receivable—Ames Co.	8,000.00	
		Accounts Receivable—Ames Co.		8,000.00
Apr.	9	Allowance for Doubtful Accounts	2,500.00	
		Accounts Receivable—Dorset Co.		2,500.00
May	14	Cash	8,065.75	
		Notes Receivable—Ames Co.		8,000.00
		Interest Revenue		65.75
		($8,000 × 5% × 60/365)		
Jun.	13	Accounts Receivable—Dorset Co.	2,500.00	
		Allowance for Doubtful Accounts		2,500.00
	13	Cash	2,500.00	
		Accounts Receivable—Dorset Co.		2,500.00
Dec.	31	Bad Debt Expense	41,250.00	
		Allowance for Doubtful Accounts		41,250.00
		($1,375,000 × 3%)		

EYE OPENERS

1. What are the three classifications of receivables?
2. What types of transactions give rise to accounts receivable?
3. In what section of the balance sheet should a note receivable be listed if its term is (a) 90 days, (b) six years?
4. Give two examples of other receivables.
5. Gallatin Hardware is a small hardware store in the rural township of East Hawkesbury that rarely extends credit to its customers in the form of an account receivable. The few customers that are allowed to carry accounts receivable are longtime residents of East Hawkesbury and have a history of doing business at Gallatin Hardware. Which method of accounting for uncollectible receivables should Gallatin Hardware use? Why?
6. What kind of an account (asset, liability, etc.) is Allowance for Doubtful Accounts? Is its normal balance a debit or a credit?
7. After the accounts are adjusted and closed at the end of the fiscal year, Accounts Receivable has a balance of $298,150, and Allowance for Doubtful Accounts has a balance of $31,200. Describe how the accounts receivable and the allowance for doubtful accounts are reported on the balance sheet.
8. A firm has consistently adjusted its allowance account at the end of the fiscal year by adding a fixed percent of the period's net sales on account. After seven years, the balance in Allowance for Doubtful Accounts has become very large in relation to the balance in Accounts Receivable. Give two possible explanations.
9. Which of the three methods of estimating uncollectibles provides the most accurate estimate of the current net realizable value of the receivables?
10. For a business, what are the advantages of a note receivable compared with an account receivable?
11. Blanchard Company issued a note receivable to Tucker Company. (a) Who is the payee? (b) What is the title of the account used by Tucker Company in recording the note?

12. If a note provides for payment of principal of $90,000 and interest at the rate of 7%, will the interest amount to $6,300? Explain.

13. The maker of a $10,000, 4%, 90-day note receivable failed to pay the note on the due date of June 30. What accounts should be debited and credited by the payee to record the dishonoured note receivable, assuming the payee believes the amount is collectible?

14. The note receivable dishonoured in Eye Opener 13 is paid on July 30 by the maker, plus interest for 30 days at 5%. What entry should be made to record the receipt of the payment?

PRACTICE EXERCISES

③ PE 8-1
Direct write-off method

EE 8-1 p. 417

Journalize the following transactions using the direct write-off method of accounting for uncollectible receivables:

Sep. 19. Collected $100 from Ron Enns and wrote off the remainder owed of $500 as uncollectible.

Nov. 22 Reinstated the account of Ron Enns and received $500 cash in full payment.

---

④ PE 8-2
Allowance method

EE 8-2 p. 420

Journalize the following transactions using the allowance method of accounting for uncollectible receivables:

Sep. 19. Collected $100 from Ron Enns and wrote off the remainder owed of $500 as uncollectible.

Dec. 20. Reinstated the account of Ron Enns and received $500 cash in full payment.

---

④ PE 8-3
Percent of sales method

EE 8-3 p. 421

At the end of the current year, Accounts Receivable has a balance of $1,400,000, Allowance for Doubtful Accounts has a debit balance of $2,250, and net sales for the year total $9,500,000. Bad debt expense is estimated at ¼ of 1% of net sales.

Determine (1) the amount of the adjusting entry for uncollectible accounts; (2) the adjusted balances of Accounts Receivable, Allowance for Doubtful Accounts, and Bad Debt Expense; and (3) the net realizable value of accounts receivable.

---

④ PE 8-4
Aging of receivables method

EE 8-4 p. 423

At the end of the current year, Accounts Receivable has a balance of $1,400,000, Allowance for Doubtful Accounts has a debit balance of $2,250, and net sales for the year total $9,500,000. Using the aging of receivables method, the balance of Allowance for Doubtful Accounts is estimated as $24,000.

Determine (1) the amount of the adjusting entry for uncollectible accounts; (2) the adjusted balances of Accounts Receivable, Allowance for Doubtful Accounts, and Bad Debt Expense; and (3) the net realizable value of accounts receivable.

---

④ PE 8-5
Percent of receivables method

EE 8-5 p. 425

At the end of the current year, Accounts Receivable has a balance of $650,000, Allowance for Doubtful Accounts has a credit balance of $11,500, and net sales for the year total $3,850,000. Assuming that uncollectible accounts are estimated to be 5% of receivables, determine (a) the amount of the adjusting entry for uncollectible accounts; (b) the adjusted balances of Accounts Receivable, Allowance for Doubtful Accounts, and Bad Debt Expense; and (c) the net realizable value of accounts receivable.

---

⑤ PE 8-6
Note receivable

EE 8-6 p. 430

Cannondale Supply Company received a 60-day, 4% note for $200,000, dated March 13 from a customer on account.

a. Determine the due date of the note.

b. Determine the maturity value of the note.

c. Journalize the entry to record the receipt of the payment of the note at maturity.

PE 8-7
6
**Reporting
receivables**

EE 8-7 p. 431

For the fiscal year ended April 30, 2015, Interform Corp. had the following account balances:

	Dr (Cr)
Accounts receivable	$ 5,102,050
Notes receivable, due January 2016	6,209,564
Notes receivable, due October 2016	488,390
Allowance for doubtful accounts	(43,600)
Bad debt expense	59,200
Cash	329,504
Accounts payable	(32,416)
Inventory	2,584,933
Cost of goods sold	11,940,382
Equipment	2,689,900
Prepaid expenses	25,742

Prepare the current asset section of the balance sheet.

PE 8-8
6
**Accounts receivable
turnover and days'
sales in receivables**

EE 8-8 p. 433

f·a·i

Financial statement data for the years ended December 31 for Blum Company are shown below.

For the years ended	2015	2014
Net sales	$2,430,000	$1,920,000
Accounts receivable:		
Beginning of year	180,000	120,000
End of year	225,000	180,000

a. Determine the accounts receivable turnover for 2015 and 2014. Round to one decimal place.
b. Determine the days' sales in receivables for 2015 and 2014. Round to one decimal place.
c. Does the change in accounts receivable turnover and the days' sales in receivables from 2014 to 2015 indicate a favourable or an unfavourable trend?

EXERCISES

EX 8-1
1
Terminology
2
3
4
5

Match the following terms with the best description.

1. Direct write-off method
2. Aging of receivables method
3. Percent of sales method

4. Notes receivable

5. Factoring

6. Bad debt expense

a. An estimation method often used for interim reporting as it is easier to apply.
b. Sale of receivables.
c. The method used by businesses with few receivables or a history of good collection of receivables.
d. The method that is based on the assumption that the longer an account receivable is outstanding, the less likely it will be collected.
e. The amount incurred because of the failure to collect receivables.
f. A written promise to pay that often includes interest and a due date.

EX 8-2
2
**Nature of
uncollectible
accounts**

Bell Canada Enterprises (BCE) is Canada's largest communications company and a leading provider of wireline and wireless communications services, Internet access, and data and video services to residential, business, and wholesale customers. As at December 31, 2011, BCE reported trade accounts receivable of $3,069,000,000 and allowance for doubtful accounts of $105,000,000. Vecima Networks Inc., founded in Saskatoon, Saskatchewan in 1988, designs, manufactures, and sells products that enable broadband access to cable, wireless, and telephone networks. Vecima sells its products

(continued)

through offices across Canada, the United States, and internationally, to original equipment manufacturers, system integrators, cable operators, and other service providers. As at June 30, 2011, Vecima reported trade accounts receivable of $16,497,000 and allowance for doubtful accounts of $841,000.

a. Compute the percentage of the allowance for doubtful accounts to the accounts receivable as at December 31, 2011, for BCE.

b. Compute the percentage of the allowance for doubtful accounts to the accounts receivable as at June 30, 2011, for Vecima.

c. Discuss possible reasons for the difference in the two ratios computed in a. and b.

EX 8-3

Entries for uncollectible accounts, using direct write-off method

Journalize the following transactions in the accounts of Laser Tech Co., a medical equipment company that uses the direct write-off method of accounting for uncollectible receivables and a perpetual inventory system:

Feb. 23.   Sold merchandise on account to Dr. James Solomon, $31,500. The cost of the goods sold was $17,500.

May 10.   Received $10,000 from Dr. James Solomon and wrote off the remainder owed on the sale of February 23 as uncollectible.

Dec. 2.   Reinstated the account of Dr. James Solomon that had been written off on May 10 and received $21,500 cash in full payment.

EX 8-4

Entries for uncollectible receivables, using allowance method

Journalize the following transactions in the accounts of Food Unlimited Company, a restaurant supply company that uses the allowance method of accounting for uncollectible receivables and a perpetual inventory system.

Jan. 18.   Sold merchandise on account to Wings Co., $13,200. The cost of the goods sold was $9,500.

Mar. 31.   Received $5,000 from Wings Co. and wrote off the remainder owed on the sale of January 18 as uncollectible.

Sep. 3.   Reinstated the account of Wings Co. that had been written off on March 31 and received $8,200 cash in full payment.

EX 8-5

Entries to write off accounts receivable

On February 4, Tech Savvy, a computer consulting firm, decided to write off the $8,375 balance of an account owed by a customer, Nick Wadle. Journalize the entry to record the write-off, assuming that (a) the direct write-off method is used and (b) the allowance method is used.

EX 8-6

Providing for doubtful accounts

At the end of the current year, Accounts Receivable has a debit balance of $825,000, and net sales for the year total $9,000,000.

1. Determine the amount of the adjusting entry to provide for doubtful accounts under each of the following assumptions:

   a. The allowance account before adjustment has a credit balance of $12,000. Bad debt expense is estimated at ¼ of 1% of net sales.

   b. The allowance account before adjustment has a credit balance of $12,000. An aging of the accounts in the customer ledger indicates estimated doubtful accounts of $36,000.

   c. The allowance account before adjustment has a credit balance of $12,000. The uncollectible portion of receivables is estimated at 4% of the receivables balance.

   d. The allowance account before adjustment has a debit balance of $6,000. Bad debt expense is estimated at ½ of 1% of net sales.

   e. The allowance account before adjustment has a debit balance of $6,000. An aging of the accounts in the customer ledger indicates estimated doubtful accounts of $49,500.

   f. The allowance account before adjustment has a debit balance of $6,000. The uncollectible portion of receivables is estimated at 5% of the receivables balance.

2. In all of the above scenarios, bad debt expense does not match the allowance for doubtful accounts established at the start of the current year. Has the accountant made a mistake? Explain.

3. Identify a few events that might cause a debit balance in the allowance account.

EX 8-7

Entries for receivables and reporting receivables

Sloan Company's unadjusted trial balance for the fiscal year ended March 31, 2015, had the following account balances:

	Dr (Cr)
Accounts receivable	$ 6,122,460
Note receivable, due August 31, 2015	7,451,477
Allowance for doubtful accounts	(12,578)
Bad debt expense	71,040
Cash	395,404
Inventories	3,101,920
Accounts payable	(1,245,728)
Cost of goods sold	14,328,458
Prepaid expenses	30,890

An analysis of the accounts receivable identified $125,000 of the receivables as uncollectible. Once these accounts are written off, an allowance of $42,355 is required, based on an aging analysis of receivables.

Interest has not been recorded on the note. It is a 6-month, 6% note.

a. Prepare the adjusting journal entries to write off the uncollectible accounts, adjust the allowance to a final balance of $42,355, and record the accrued interest on the note.

b. Prepare the current asset section of the balance sheet.

EX 8-8

Estimating allowance for doubtful accounts

The accounts receivable clerk for Summit Industries prepared the following partially shown aging of receivables schedule as at the end of business on November 30:

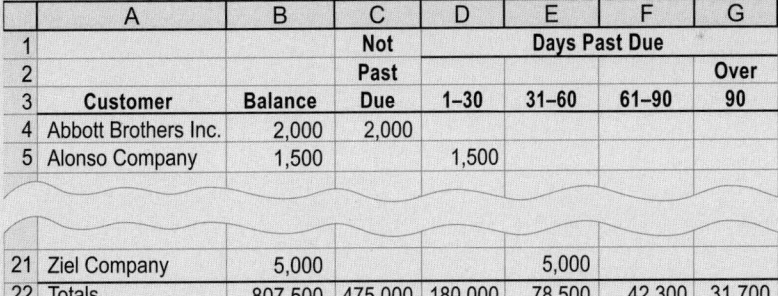

	A	B	C	D	E	F	G
1			Not		Days Past Due		
2			Past				Over
3	Customer	Balance	Due	1–30	31–60	61–90	90
4	Abbott Brothers Inc.	2,000	2,000				
5	Alonso Company	1,500		1,500			
21	Ziel Company	5,000			5,000		
22	Totals	807,500	475,000	180,000	78,500	42,300	31,700

Summit Industries has a past history of uncollectible accounts, as shown below. Estimate the allowance for doubtful accounts, based on the aging of receivables schedule.

Age Class	Percent Uncollectible
Not past due	1%
1–30 days past due	6
31–60 days past due	20
61–90 days past due	35
Over 90 days past due	50

EX 8-9

Adjustment for uncollectible accounts

Using the data in Exercise 8-8, assume that the allowance for doubtful accounts for Summit Industries has a credit balance of $16,175 before adjustment on November 30. Journalize the adjusting entry for uncollectible accounts as at November 30.

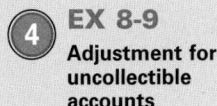

EX 8-10

Estimating doubtful accounts

Fontaine Bikes Co. is a wholesaler of motorcycle supplies. An aging of the company's accounts receivable on December 31, 2015, and a historical analysis of the percentage of uncollectible accounts in each age category are as follows:

Age Class	Balance	Percent Uncollectible
Not past due	$567,000	½%
1–30 days past due	58,000	3
31–60 days past due	29,000	7
61–90 days past due	20,500	15
Over 90 days past due	25,500	60
	$700,000	

Estimate the proper balance of the allowance for doubtful accounts as at December 31, 2015.

EX 8-11

Entry for uncollectible accounts

Using the data in Exercise 8-10, assume that the allowance for doubtful accounts for Fontaine Bikes Co. had a debit balance of $3,000 as at December 31, 2015.

a. Journalize the adjusting entry for uncollectible accounts as at December 31, 2015.
b. Determine the net realizable value of accounts receivable as at December 31, 2015.

EX 8-12

Entries for bad debt expense under the percent of sales method

The following selected transactions were taken from the records of Niagara Company for the year ended December 31, 2015:

Jan. 24. Wrote off account of J. Coleman, $3,000.
Feb. 17. Received $1,500 as partial payment on the $4,000 account of Karlene Solomon. Wrote off the remaining balance as uncollectible.
May 29. Received $3,000 from J. Coleman, which had been written off on January 24. Reinstated the account and recorded the cash receipt.
Nov. 30. Wrote off the following accounts as uncollectible (record as one journal entry):

Don O'Leary	$2,000
Kim Snider	1,500
Jennifer Kerlin	900

Dec. 31. Niagara Company uses the percent of sales method of estimating uncollectible accounts expense. Based on past history and industry averages, 1% of sales are expected to be uncollectible. Niagara Company recorded $975,000 of sales during 2015.

Journalize the transactions for 2015 under the percent of sales method assuming that the allowance account had a beginning balance of $10,000 on January 1, 2015.

EX 8-13

Entries for bad debt expense under the aging of receivables method

The following selected transactions were taken from the records of Bingham Company for the year ended December 31, 2015:

Mar. 13. Wrote off account of H. Ballard, $4,200.
Apr. 19. Received $3,000 as partial payment on the $7,500 account of M. Rainey. Wrote off the remaining balance as uncollectible.
Jul. 9. Received the $4,200 from H. Ballard, which had been written off on March 13. Reinstated the account and recorded the cash receipt.
Nov. 23. Wrote off the following accounts as uncollectible (record as one journal entry):

J. Shaw	$1,200
P. Newman	750
Nichole Chan	480

Dec. 31.   The company prepared the following aging schedule for its accounts receivable:

Aging Class	Receivables Balance on December 31	Estimated Percent of Uncollectible Accounts
0–30 days	$200,000	2%
31–60 days	75,000	8
61–90 days	24,000	25
More than 90 days	21,000	60
Total receivables	$320,000	

a. Journalize the transactions for 2015 under the allowance method, assuming that the allowance account had a beginning balance of $12,000 on January 1, 2015, and the company uses the aging of receivables method.

b. Determine the net realizable value of accounts receivable as at December 31, 2015.

---

④ EX 8-14

Entries for bad debt expense under the percent of receivables method

The following selected transactions were taken from the records of Gunn Corporation for the month of December 2015:

Dec. 16.   Billed Norwood and Company for $32,500 in services.

16.   Received $1,500 as partial payment on the $2,000 account of Dan Wade. Wrote off the remaining balance as uncollectible.

18.   Wrote off the following accounts as uncollectible (record as one journal entry):

G. Lenarduzzi	$1,250
J. Raymond	500
N. Clark	3,300
D. Johnson	1,675

22.   Received $500 from Dan Wade, which had been written off on December 16. Reinstated the account and recorded the cash receipt.

31.   Gunn Corporation uses the percent of receivables method of estimating uncollectible accounts expense. Based on past history, 4% of receivables are expected to be uncollectible.

Journalize the transactions for the month of December under the percent of receivables method, assuming that the allowance account had a balance of $5,400 and the accounts receivable account had a balance of $125,600 on December 1, 2015.

---

④ EX 8-15

Entries for bad debt expense under the percent of sales method

Isner Company wrote off the following accounts receivable as uncollectible for the first year of its operations ended December 31, 2015:

Customer	Amount
L. Hearn	$10,000
Carrie Murray	9,500
Kelly Salkin	13,100
Shana Wagnon	2,400
Total	$35,000

Journalize the write-offs for 2015 under the allowance method. Also, journalize the adjusting entry for uncollectible accounts. The company recorded $2,400,000 of credit sales during 2015. Based on past history and industry averages, 1¾% of credit sales are expected to be uncollectible.

---

④ EX 8-16

Entries for bad debt expense under the aging of receivables method

JD Industries wrote off the following accounts receivable as uncollectible for the year ended December 31, 2015:

Customer	Amount
Eva French	$ 1,500
Lance Landau	11,200
Marcie Moffet	3,800
Jose Rennie	3,500
Total	$20,000

(continued)

The company prepared the following aging schedule for its accounts receivable on December 31, 2015:

Aging Class	Receivables Balance on December 31	Estimated Percent of Uncollectible Accounts
0–30 days	$480,000	1%
31–60 days	100,000	3
61–90 days	40,000	20
More than 90 days	30,000	40
Total receivables	$650,000	

a. Journalize the write-offs and the year-end adjusting entry for 2015 under the allowance method, assuming that the allowance account had a beginning balance of $17,000 on January 1, 2015, and the company uses the aging of receivables method.

b. Determine the net realizable value of accounts receivable as at December 31, 2015.

---

(4)

EX 8-17

Entries for bad debt expense under the percent of receivables method

Braeburn Company wrote off the following accounts receivable as uncollectible for the year ended December 31, 2015:

Customer	Amount
Brandon Peele	$ 5,000
Clyde Stringer	9,000
Ned Berry	13,000
Mary Adams	2,000
Gina Bowers	4,500
	$33,500

a. Journalize the write-offs under the allowance method. Also, journalize the adjusting entry for uncollectible accounts under the percent of receivables method. The company recorded $2,750,000 of credit sales during 2015. The balances of Accounts Receivable and Allowance for Doubtful Accounts prior to the write-offs are $480,000 and $12,400, respectively, and the company expects 5% of the receivables to be uncollectible.

b. Determine the net realizable value of accounts receivable as at December 31, 2015.

---

(5)

EX 8-18

Entries for notes receivable

Oak Bay Interior Decorators issued a 90-day, 6% note for $40,000, dated April 15, to Victoria Furniture Company in exchange for an account receivable.

Journalize the entries to record the following: (1) receipt of the note by Victoria Furniture and (2) receipt of payment of the note at maturity.

---

(5)

EX 8-19

Entries for notes receivable

The series of seven transactions recorded in the following T accounts were related to a sale to a customer on account and the receipt of the amount owed. Briefly describe each transaction.

	CASH				NOTES RECEIVABLE		
(7)	30,955			(5)	30,000	(6)	30,000

	ACCOUNTS RECEIVABLE				SALES RETURNS AND ALLOWANCES		
(1)	35,000	(3)	5,000	(3)	5,000		
(6)	30,750	(5)	30,000				
		(7)	30,750				

	INVENTORY				COST OF GOODS SOLD		
(4)	3,000	(2)	21,000	(2)	21,000	(4)	3,000

	SALES				INTEREST REVENUE		
		(1)	65,000			(6)	750
						(7)	205

 **EX 8-20**

Entries for notes receivable, including year-end entries

The following selected transactions were completed by Alcor Co., a supplier of Velcro™ for clothing:

2014

Dec. 13.   Received from Pendray Clothing & Bags Co., in exchange for an account receivable, an $84,000, 90-day, 5% note dated December 13.

31.   Recorded an adjusting entry for accrued interest on the note of December 13.

31.   Recorded the closing entry for interest revenue.

2015

Mar. 12.   Received payment of note and interest from Pendray Clothing & Bags Co. at maturity.

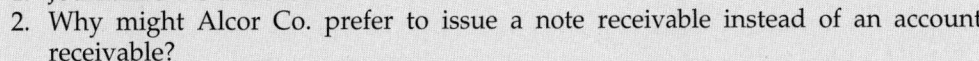

1. Journalize the transactions.
2. Why might Alcor Co. prefer to issue a note receivable instead of an account receivable?

EX 8-21

Entries for receipt and dishonour of note receivable

Journalize the following transactions of Funhouse Productions:

Jul. 8.   Received a $120,000, 90-day, 4% note dated July 8 from Mystic Mermaid Company for services.

Oct. 6.   The note is dishonoured by Mystic Mermaid Company. Funhouse Productions' accountant believes the amount owing is collectible.

Nov. 5.   Received the amount due on the dishonoured note plus interest for 30 days at 5% on the total amount charged to Mystic Mermaid Company on October 6.

 EX 8-22

Entries for receipt and dishonour of notes receivable

Journalize the following transactions in the accounts of Duncan Casino Co:

Mar. 1.   Received a $30,000, 60-day, 3% note dated March 1 from Bradshaw Co. in exchange for an account receivable.

18.   Received a $25,000, 60-day, 4% note dated March 18 from Soto Co. in exchange for an account receivable.

Apr. 30.   The note dated March 1 from Bradshaw Co. is dishonoured, and the customer's account is charged for the note, including interest.

May 17.   The note dated March 18 from Soto Co. is dishonoured, and the customer's account is charged for the note, including interest.

Jul. 29.   Cash is received for the amount due on the dishonoured note dated March 1 plus interest for 90 days at 4% on the total amount debited to Bradshaw Co. on April 30.

Aug. 23.   Wrote off against the allowance account the amount charged to Soto Co. on May 17 for the dishonoured note dated March 18.

EX 8-23

Receivables on the balance sheet (partial)

The partial balance sheet for Jennett Company is presented below.

a. List any errors you find in the partial balance sheet.
b. Prepare a corrected partial balance sheet.

Jennett Company
Balance Sheet (partial)
For the Year Ended December 31, 2015

Current assets:		
Notes receivable	$250,000	
Less interest receivable	15,000	$235,000
Accounts receivable	398,000	
Plus allowance for doubtful accounts	36,000	434,500
Cash		95,000

 EX 8-24

Accounts receivable turnover and days' sales in receivables

Polo Ralph Lauren Corporation designs, markets, and distributes a variety of apparel, home decor, accessory, and fragrance products. The company's products include such

(continued)

brands as Polo by Ralph Lauren, Ralph Lauren Purple Label, Ralph Lauren, Polo Jeans Co., and Chaps. Polo Ralph Lauren reported the following (in millions):

	For the Period Ended	
	April 2, 2011	April 3, 2010
Net sales	$5660.3	$4,978.9
Accounts receivable	673.7	588.0

The accounts receivable (in millions) were $665.8 at the beginning of the 2010 fiscal year.

a. Compute the accounts receivable turnover for 2011 and 2010. Round to one decimal place.

b. Compute the days' sales in receivables for 2011 and 2010. Round to one decimal place.

c. Do the ratios indicate an improvement or a decline in Polo Ralph Lauren's ability to manage accounts receivable?

d. Assuming an industry average accounts receivable turnover of 13.8 times, is Polo Ralph Lauren more or less efficient than other companies in the industry?

EX 8-25

Accounts receivable turnover and days' sales in receivables

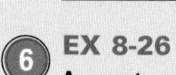

WestJet Airlines Ltd. pioneered low-cost flying in Canada, offering service throughout its 71-city North American and Caribbean network. WestJet reported the following (in millions of dollars):

	Year Ended	
	Dec. 31, 2010	Dec. 31, 2009
Net sales	$2,609	$2,281
Accounts receivable at end of year	18	28

The accounts receivable (in millions) were $17 at the beginning of the year ended December 31, 2009.

a. Compute the accounts receivable turnover for 2010 and 2009. Round to one decimal place.

b. Compute the days' sales in receivables for 2010 and 2009. Round to one decimal place.

c. Do the ratios indicate an improvement or a decline in WestJet Airlines Ltd.'s ability to manage accounts receivable?

d. Assuming an industry average accounts receivable turnover of 21.0 times, is WestJet Airlines Ltd. more or less efficient than other companies in the industry?

EX 8-26

Accounts receivable turnover and days' sales in receivables

Bombardier Inc., with headquarters in Montreal, is a world-leading manufacturer of innovative transportation equipment, including aircraft and rail transportation equipment, systems, and services. Bombardier has production and distribution centres in 23 countries and employs approximately 65,400 workers. Bombardier reported the following (in millions of U.S. dollars):

	Year Ended	
	Jan. 31, 2011	Jan. 31, 2010
Net sales	$17,712	$19,366
Accounts receivable at end of year	2,022	1,897

The accounts receivable (in millions) were $1,981 at the beginning of the year ended January 31, 2010.

a. Compute the accounts receivable turnover for 2011 and 2010. Round to one decimal place.

b. Compute the days' sales in receivables for 2011 and 2010. Round to one decimal place.

c. Do the ratios indicate an improvement or a decline in Bombardier Inc.'s ability to manage accounts receivable?

6 **EX 8-27**

Accounts receivable turnover

Use the data in Exercises 8-25 and 8-26 to analyze the accounts receivable turnover ratios of WestJet Airlines Ltd. and Bombardier Inc.

a. Compute the average accounts receivable turnover ratio for WestJet Airlines Ltd. and Bombardier Inc. for the years shown in Exercises 8-25 and 8-26.

b. What might explain why WestJet has an accounts receivable turnover ratio much higher than that of Bombardier? What differences in these businesses would affect their receivable turnover ratio?

PROBLEMS SERIES A

4 **PR 8-1A**

Entries for bad debt expense under the percent of sales method

✔ 3. $68,240

Acton Accountants Ltd. had the following account balances on December 1, 2015: Accounts Receivable, $72,344; Allowance for Doubtful Accounts, $(2,355). Acton Accountants completed the following selected transactions during the final two weeks of the current fiscal year:

Dec. 16.   Billed Davies and Company for $12,500 in accounting services.

16.   Received $3,500 as partial payment on the $4,000 account of Kathy Solomon. Wrote off the remaining balance as uncollectible.

18.   Received a $1,000 deposit for accounting work to be performed in January for Mars Inc.

22.   Received $500 from Kathy Solomon, which had been written off on December 16. Reinstated the account and recorded the cash receipt.

31.   Wrote off the following accounts as uncollectible (record as a compound journal entry):

Pat O'Higgins	$1,575
Matt Westby	4,600
Shan Treadwell	895
Wang Chu	1,255

31.   Acton Accountants Ltd. uses the percent of sales method of estimating uncollectible accounts expense. Based on past history, 1% of sales are expected to be uncollectible. Acton Accountants Ltd. recorded sales of $1,024,900 during 2015.

Instructions

1. Record the December 1 balances in T accounts for Accounts Receivable and for Allowance for Doubtful Accounts.
2. Journalize the transactions. Post each entry that affects the above-mentioned T accounts and determine the new balances.
3. Determine the net realizable value of the accounts receivable as at December 31, 2015.

4 **PR 8-2A**

Entries related to uncollectible accounts

✔ 3. $918,750

The following transactions were completed by Axiom Management Company during the current fiscal year ended December 31:

Jun.   6.   Reinstated the account of Ian Gillespie, which had been written off in the preceding year as uncollectible. Journalized the receipt of $1,945 cash in full payment of Ian's account.

Jul.   19.   Wrote off the $11,150 balance owed by Dunbar Rigging Co., which is bankrupt.

Aug. 13.   Received 35% of the $20,000 balance owed by Renaud Co., a bankrupt business, and wrote off the remainder as uncollectible.

Sep.   2.   Reinstated the account of Sheryl Capers, which had been written off two years earlier as uncollectible. Recorded the receipt of $3,170 cash in full payment.

(continued)

Dec. 31. Wrote off the following accounts as uncollectible (compound entry): Jacob Co., $8,390; Garcia Co., $2,500; Summit Furniture, $6,400; Jill DePuy, $1,800.

31. Based on an aging of the $960,750 of accounts receivable, it was estimated that $42,000 will be uncollectible. Journalized the adjusting entry.

Instructions

1. Record the January 1 credit balance of $40,000 in a T account for Allowance for Doubtful Accounts.
2. Journalize the transactions. Post each entry that affects the following T accounts and determine the new balances:

Allowance for Doubtful Accounts
Bad Debt Expense

3. Determine the net realizable value of the accounts receivable as at December 31.

PR 8-3A

Aging of receivables; estimating allowance for doubtful accounts

✔ 1. $63,730

Miller Equipment Ltd. supplies cooking equipment to restaurants throughout Canada. The accounts receivable clerk for Miller Equipment Ltd. prepared the following partially shown aging of receivables schedule as at the end of business on December 31, 2015:

	A	B	C	D	E	F	G
1			Not		Days Past Due		
2			Past				Over
3	Customer	Balance	Due	1–30	31–60	61–90	90
4	Alice's Restaurant	20,000	20,000				
5	Dell Restaurant	11,000			11,000		
21	Zeus' Grill	2,900		2,900			
22	Totals	900,010	498,600	217,260	98,750	33,300	52,100

Miller Equipment Ltd. has a past history of uncollectible accounts by age category, as follows:

Age Class	Percent Uncollectible
Not past due	2%
1–30 days past due	5
31–60 days past due	12
61–90 days past due	15
Over 90 days past due	50

Instructions

1. Estimate the allowance for doubtful accounts, based on the aging of receivables schedule.
2. Assume that the allowance for doubtful accounts for Miller Equipment Ltd. has a credit balance of $1,710 before adjustment on December 31, 2015. Journalize the adjustment for uncollectible accounts.
3. Determine the net realizable value of accounts receivable as at December 31, 2015.

PR 8-4A

Entries for bad debt expense under the aging of receivables method

✔ 2. $19,425

The following selected transactions were taken from the records of Keyes Advertising Company for the year ended September 30, 2015:

Oct. 23. Wrote off account of T. Stein, $1,025.

Nov. 15. Received $13,500 as partial payment on the $18,000 account of Drive Train Inc. Wrote off the remaining balance as uncollectible.

Dec. 31. Recorded a sale on account of $24,900 to Gibbons Hardware Ltd.

Feb. 15. Received $5,000 from Emerging Energy Sources for an advertising campaign to be launched in July.

Jul. 31. Invoiced Emerging Energy Sources for $10,750 for the July advertising campaign.

Sep. 30.   Wrote off the following accounts as uncollectible (record as a compound journal entry):

Trimark Planners	$ 975
Capital Innovations	1,860
Weatherby's	8,692
Sharp Ltd.	3,277

30.   Prepared the adjusting entry, using the following aging schedule for its accounts receivable:

Age Class	Receivables Balance on September 30	Estimated Percent of Uncollectible Accounts
0–30 days	$410,000	1%
31–60 days	37,500	5
61–90 days	28,000	20
Over 90 days	10,500	50

Instructions

1. Journalize the transactions. Record the September 30 adjusting entry, assuming the allowance account had a credit balance of $2,000 after recording the September 30 write-off of uncollectible accounts (prior entry).
2. Record the September 30 adjusting entry, assuming the allowance account had a debit balance of $2,600 after recording the September 30 write-off of uncollectible accounts.

---

④ PR 8-5A

Entries for bad debt expense using two allowance methods

✔ Dec. 31 Bad Debt Expense, $13,500

Grimm's Hardware Company uses the percent of sales method of estimating uncollectible accounts expense for its monthly financial reporting and the aging of receivables method for its year-end reporting. The company had a $9,500 credit balance in Allowance For Doubtful Accounts on November 1, 2015. The following selected transactions were completed during the final two months of the current fiscal year by Grimm's Hardware Company:

Nov. 15.   Recorded a sale on account of $9,664 to Hart House Inc.; cost of goods sold was $5,800.

23.   Wrote off account of Traders Ltd., $675.

27.   Received $9,500 as partial payment on the $20,000 account of Olds Distributors Ltd.

30.   Based on past history, 2% of sales are expected to be uncollectible. Grimm's Hardware Company recorded sales of $125,800 during November.

Dec. 1.   Recorded a sale on account of $22,900 to Chang Construction Ltd; cost of goods sold was $15,550.

5.   Received $675 from Traders Ltd., which had been written off on Nov. 23. Reinstated the account and recorded the cash receipt.

31.   Wrote off the following accounts as uncollectible (record as a compound journal entry):

Bill's Construction Co.	$ 425
Trenton Construction Ltd.	10,600
G. Schroeder	864

31.   Prepared the adjusting entry, using the following accounts receivable aging schedule:

Age Class	Receivables Balance on December 31	Estimated Percent of Uncollectible Accounts
0–30 days	$104,800	1%
31–60 days	62,900	5
61–90 days	20,960	20
Over 90 days	10,484	50

Instructions

Journalize the transactions, assuming Grimm's Hardware Company uses a perpetual inventory system.

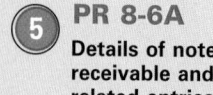

PR 8-6A

Details of notes receivable and related entries

✔ 1. Note 2:
Due date, Dec. 4;
Interest due at
maturity, $150

Old Town Co. wholesales bathroom fixtures. During the last six months of the current fiscal year, Old Town Co. received the following notes:

	Date	Principal	Term	Interest Rate
1.	Aug. 5	$45,000	3 months	3%
2.	Sep. 4	20,000	3 months	3
3.	Nov. 28	13,500	60 days	4
4.	Dec. 16	21,600	60 days	5

Instructions

1. Determine for each note (a) the due date and (b) the amount of interest due at maturity, identifying each note by number.
2. Journalize the entry to record the dishonouring of Note (1) on its due date, assuming it is unlikely to be collectible.
3. Journalize the adjusting entry to record the accrued interest on Notes (3) and (4) on December 31.
4. Journalize the entries to record the receipt of the amounts due on Notes (3) and (4) in January and February.

PR 8-7A

Notes receivable entries

✔ June 30; cash
$25,061.64

The following data relate to notes receivable and interest for Vidovich Co., a financial services company with an August 31 fiscal year-end. All notes are dated as of the day they are received.

May 16. Received a $40,000, 4%, 90-day note on account.
    31. Received a $25,000, 3%, 30-day note on account.
    ? Received principal and interest on note of May 31.
Jul. 1. Received a $7,500, 6%, 30-day note on account.
    15. Received a $72,000, 4%, 60-day note on account.
    ? Received principal and interest on note of July 1.
Aug. 14. The note of May 16 is dishonoured. Vidovich Co.'s accountant feels the amount owing is collectible.
    31. Recorded an adjusting entry for accrued interest on the notes outstanding.
    ? Received principal and interest on note of July 15.

Instructions

Journalize the entries to record the transactions.

PR 8-8A

Sales and notes receivable transactions

✔ June 20, Cash
$13,328

The following were selected from among the transactions completed during the current year by Booker Co., a wholesale appliance company with a June 30 fiscal year-end. Booker Co. had the following account balances on January 1, 2015:

Notes receivable, 3%, 60-day, issued Dec. 15, 2014	$ 10,000
Accounts receivable	465,932
Allowance for doubtful accounts	(5,128)

Jan. 20. Sold merchandise on account to Weeks Co., $32,750. The cost of goods sold was $19,000.
Feb. 13. Received the amount due on the note of December 15.
Mar. 3. Accepted a 60-day, 4% note for $32,750 from Weeks Co. on account.
    ? Received from Weeks Co. the amount due on the note of March 3.
Jun. 10. Sold merchandise on account to Foyers for $13,600 with terms 2/10, n/30. The cost of goods sold was $8,200.
    15. Loaned $18,000 cash to Mike Hobson, receiving a 30-day, 6% note.
    20. Received from Foyers the amount due on the invoice of June 10, less 2% discount.
    30. Wrote off the following accounts as uncollectible (compound entry): Clark, $2,540; Faulkner, $1,168; Perch, $1,754.
    30. Recorded an adjusting entry for the allowance for doubtful accounts. Based on an aging of the $493,220 of accounts receivable, it was estimated that $12,500 will be uncollectible.
    30. Recorded an adjusting entry for accrued interest on the note outstanding.

? Received the interest due from Mike Hobson and a new 60-day, 7% note as a renewal of the loan of June 15. (Record both the debit and the credit to the notes receivable account.)

? Received from Mike Hobson the amount due on his note of June 15.

Instructions

Journalize the transactions, assuming Booker Co. uses a perpetual inventory system.

PR 8-9A
4
Accounts and notes receivable entries
5

✔ June 30, Interest revenue $1,504.44

The following transactions were completed by Fullerton Farm Equipment Ltd., a distributor with a June 30 fiscal year-end. Fullerton Farm Equipment Ltd. had the following account balances on February 28, 2015:

Notes receivable	$ 50,000
Accounts receivable	136,740
Allowance for doubtful accounts	(12,080)

Mar. 1. Cash is received for a $35,000 note due, plus interest for 60 days at 4%.

10. Wrote off the remaining note receivable of $15,000 as uncollectible. No interest had been accrued for this note.

12. Sold merchandise on account to Amery Co., $12,500. The cost of goods sold was $7,500.

13. Received a $20,000, 60-day, 4% note dated March 13 from Stewart Co., in exchange for a rotary tiller. The cost of goods sold was $11,500.

18. Received a $132,000, 120-day, 4% note dated March 18 from Tanner Ltd., in exchange for a tractor. The cost of goods sold was $72,200.

Apr. 15. Cash is received for the transaction of March 12.

May 12. The note dated March 13 from Stewart Co. is dishonoured. Fullerton believes the amount is collectible and transfers the balance owing, including interest, to accounts receivable.

Jun. 16. Cash is received for the amount from Stewart Co.

30. Recorded an adjusting entry for accrued interest on the note outstanding.

30. Recorded an adjusting entry for the allowance for doubtful accounts. Based on an aging of the accounts receivable balance of $136,740, it was estimated that $15,760 will be uncollectible.

Instructions

Journalize the entries to record the transactions, assuming Fullerton Farm Equipment Ltd. uses a perpetual inventory system.

PR 8-10A
4
Sales and notes receivable entries
5
6

✔ Dec. 31, Interest revenue $43.15

The following were selected from among the transactions completed during the final two months of the year ended December 31, 2015, by M. Martin Ltd., a clothing retailer. M. Martin Ltd. had the following account balances on November 1, 2015:

Notes receivable	$58,000
Accounts receivable	67,433
Allowance for doubtful accounts	(8,105)

Nov. 2. Cash is received for a $40,000 note due, plus interest for 60 days at 4%.

10. Wrote off the remaining note receivable of $18,000 as uncollectible. No interest had been accrued for this note.

12. Sold merchandise on account to Lynn Wharram, $15,000. The cost of goods sold was $8,550.

13. Loaned $3,000 cash to Hugh Dobson, receiving a 30-day, 5% note.

Dec. 10. Accepted a 30-day, 5% note for $15,000 from Wharram on account.

? Cash is received for the amount owing on the Dobson note.

31. Wrote off the following accounts as uncollectible (compound entry): Trask, $254; Chung, $178; Stephens, $754.

31. Recorded an adjusting entry for accrued interest on the note outstanding.

31. Recorded an adjusting entry for the allowance for doubtful accounts. Based on an aging of the accounts receivable balance of $66,247, it was estimated that $5,500 will be uncollectible.

(continued)

Instructions

1. Journalize the entries to record the transactions, assuming M. Martin Ltd. uses a perpetual inventory system.
2. Prepare a partial balance sheet for M. Martin Ltd. as at December 31, 2015, for the related accounts. Round to the nearest whole dollar.
3. Journalize the receipt of cash in January 2016 for the $15,000 note receivable outstanding at year-end from Wharram.

PROBLEMS SERIES B

PR 8-1B

Entries for bad debt expense under the percent of sales method

✔ 3. $138,536

Arcade Systems Ltd. had the following account balances on October 1, 2015: Accounts Receivable, $132,304; Allowance for Doubtful Accounts, $(8,350). Arcade Systems completed the following selected transactions during the final month of the current fiscal year:

Oct. 4.   Invoiced Chamber Company for $28,760 of services.
   15.   Received $2,500 as partial payment on the $4,000 account of Steve Walker. Wrote off the remaining balance as uncollectible.
   18.   Received a $6,000 deposit for systems work to be performed in November for Templeton Ltd.
   25.   Received $500 from Steve Walker, which had been written off on October 15. Reinstated $500 of the account and recorded the cash receipt.
   31.   Wrote off the following accounts as uncollectible (record as a compound journal entry):

Oak Furnishings	$1,075
Weavers Guild Ltd.	2,346
T. Thomas	900

   31.   Arcade Systems Ltd. uses the percent of sales method of estimating uncollectible accounts expense. Based on past history, 1.5% of sales are expected to be uncollectible. Arcade Systems Ltd. recorded sales of $745,200 during 2015.

Instructions

1. Record the October 1 balances in T accounts for Accounts Receivable and for Allowance for Doubtful Accounts.
2. Journalize the transactions. Post each entry that affects the above-mentioned T accounts and determine the new balances.
3. Determine the net realizable value of the accounts receivable as at October 31, 2015.

PR 8-2B

Entries related to uncollectible accounts—aging method

✔ 3. $750,375

The following transactions were completed by The Spencer Gallery during the current fiscal year ended December 31:

Feb. 24.   Received 40% of the $18,000 balance owed by Coastal Co., a bankrupt business, and wrote off the remainder as uncollectible.
May 3.   Reinstated the account of Irma Austin, which had been written off in the preceding year as uncollectible. Journalized the receipt of $1,725 cash in full payment of Austin's account.
Aug. 9.   Wrote off the $3,600 balance owed by McHale Co., which has no assets.
Nov. 20.   Reinstated the account of Petty Co., which had been written off in the preceding year as uncollectible. Journalized the receipt of $6,140 cash in full payment of the account.
Dec. 31.   Wrote off the following accounts as uncollectible (compound entry): Chung Co., $2,400; Kommers Co., $1,800; Chase Distributors, $6,000; Ed Ballantyne, $1,750.
   31.   Based on an aging of the $768,375 of accounts receivable, it was estimated that $18,000 will be uncollectible. Journalized the adjusting entry.

Instructions

1. Record the January 1 credit balance of $15,500 in a T account for Allowance for Doubtful Accounts.
2. Journalize the transactions. Post each entry that affects the following selected T accounts and determine the new balances:

> Allowance for Doubtful Accounts
> Bad Debt Expense

3. Determine the net realizable value of the accounts receivable as at December 31.

PR 8-3B

Aging of receivables; estimating allowance for doubtful accounts

✔ 1. $56,549

Angler's Dream Company supplies flies and fishing gear to sporting goods stores and outfitters throughout the western provinces. The accounts receivable clerk for Angler's Dream prepared the following partially shown aging of receivables schedule as at the end of business on December 31, 2015:

	A	B	C	D	E	F	G
1			Not		Days Past Due		
2			Past				
3	Customer	Balance	Due	1–30	31–60	61–90	Over 90
4	AAA Fishery	15,000	15,000				
5	Blue Ribbon Flies	5,500			5,500		
30	Z Fish Co.	2,900		2,900			
31	Totals	850,050	422,450	247,300	103,850	33,300	43,150

Angler's Dream Company has a past history of uncollectible accounts by age category, as follows:

Age Class	Percent Uncollectible
Not past due	2%
1–30 days past due	4
31–60 days past due	8
61–90 days past due	25
Over 90 days past due	50

Instructions

1. Estimate the allowance for doubtful accounts, based on the aging of receivables schedule.
2. Assume that the allowance for doubtful accounts for Angler's Dream Company has a debit balance of $1,370 before adjustment on December 31, 2015. Journalize the adjusting entry for uncollectible accounts.
3. Determine the net realizable value of the accounts receivable as at December 31, 2015.

PR 8-4B

Entries for bad debt expense under the aging of receivables method

✔ 2. $11,984.50

The following selected transactions were taken from the records of Simcoe Services Ltd. for the year ended October 31, 2015:

Dec. 31. Recorded a sale on account of $37,350 to ABC Electric Ltd., terms 1/10, net 30. The cost of goods sold was $18,000.

Jan. 9. Cash is received for the amount owing from ABC Electric Ltd. The discount was taken.

Feb. 23. Wrote off account of B. Parker, $1,538.

Mar. 17. Received $10,125 as partial payment on the $13,500 account of Lance's Appliances. Wrote off the remaining balance as uncollectible.

Jun. 30. Recorded a sale on account of $120,350 to ABC Electric Ltd., terms 1/10, net 30. The cost of goods sold was $78,100.

Jul. 25. Cash is received for the amount owing from ABC Electric Ltd.

(continued)

Oct. 31. Wrote off the following accounts as uncollectible (record as a compound journal entry); Waterton Electric, $550; Capital Systems, $1,200; Trimark Supplies, $765.

     31. Prepared the adjusting entry, using the following aging schedule for its accounts receivable:

Age Class	Receivables Balance on October 31	Estimated Percent of Uncollectible Accounts
0–30 days	$110,600	1%
31–60 days	42,710	5
61–90 days	14,340	20
Over 90 days	8,750	50

Instructions

1. Journalize the transactions, assuming Simcoe Services Ltd. uses a periodic inventory system. Record the October 31 adjusting entry, assuming the allowance account had a credit balance of $6,540 after recording the October 31 write-off of uncollectible accounts (prior entry).
2. Record the October 31 adjusting entry, assuming the allowance account had a debit balance of $1,500 after recording the October 31 write-off of uncollectible accounts.

PR 8-5B

Entries for bad debt expense using two allowance methods

✔ Dec. 31, Bad debt expense, $9,522.52

Max's Plumbing Supplies Ltd. uses the percent of sales method to estimate the uncollectible accounts expense for its monthly financial reporting, the aging of receivables method for its year-end reporting, and a perpetual inventory system. The company had a $1,500.50 credit balance in the Allowance for Doubtful Accounts on November 1, 2015. The following selected transactions were completed during the final two months of the current fiscal year by Max's Plumbing Supplies Ltd.:

Nov. 10. Received $525 as partial payment on the $750 account of T. Robson Construction Co. Wrote off the balance as uncollectible.

Nov. 15. Recorded a sale on account of $10,564 to B. Merck. The cost of goods sold was $6,500.

     16. Wrote off account of Cutlers Ltd., $1,025.50.

     22. Received $9,500 as partial payment on the $20,000 account of Master Distributors Ltd. Max's accountant believes the account balance is collectible.

     30. Based on past history, 3% of sales are expected to be uncollectible. Max's Plumbing Supplies Ltd. recorded sales of $105,677 during November.

Dec. 1. Recorded a sale on account of $2,290 to Smith Construction Ltd; cost of goods sold was $1,550.

     5. Received $600 from Cutlers Ltd., which had been written off on November 16. Reinstated the portion of the account and recorded the cash receipt.

     31. Wrote off the following accounts as uncollectible (record as a compound journal entry):

B. Paxton	$ 576.10
Western Construction Co.	1,377.25
Able Construction Ltd.	10,600.00

     31. Prepared the adjusting entry using the following accounts receivable aging schedule:

Age Class	Receivables Balance on December 31	Estimated Percent of Uncollectible Accounts
0–30 days	$63,800.00	2%
31–60 days	43,988.50	8
61–90 days	22,126.00	20
Over 90 days	8,645.10	50

Instructions

Journalize the transactions.

PR 8-6B

Details of notes receivable and related entries

✔ 1. Note 2: Due date, Dec. 30; Interest due at maturity, $236.71

Media Ads Co. produces advertising videos. During the current fiscal year, Media Ads Co. received the following notes:

	Date	Principal	Term	Interest Rate
1.	Jul. 5	$18,000	4 months	3%
2.	Oct. 31	36,000	60 days	4
3.	Nov. 23	21,000	60 days	4
4.	Dec. 21	40,500	30 days	5

Instructions

1. Determine for each note (a) the due date and (b) the amount of interest due at maturity, identifying each note by number.
2. Journalize the entry to record the dishonouring of Note (1) on its due date.
3. Journalize the adjusting entry to record the accrued interest on Notes (3) and (4) on December 31.
4. Journalize the entries to record the receipt of the amounts due on Notes (3) and (4) in January.

PR 8-7B

Notes receivable entries

✔ Nov. 3; cash $24,157.81

The following data relate to notes receivable and interest for Optic Co., a financial services company with a December 31 fiscal year-end. All notes are dated as of the day they are received.

Sep. 4. Received a $24,000, 4%, 60-day note on account.
     ?   Received principal and interest on note of September 4.
Nov. 5. Received a $24,000, 3%, 30-day note on account.
     30. Received a $15,000, 5%, 30-day note on account.
     ?   Received principal and interest on note of November 5.
Dec. 9. Received a $15,000, 4%, 60-day note on account.
     ?   Note of November 30 is dishonoured, but the payee's accountant believes the amount owing is collectible.
     31. Recorded an adjusting entry for accrued interest on the notes outstanding.
     ?   Received principal and interest on note of December 9.

Instructions

Journalize the entries to record the transactions.

PR 8-8B

Sales and notes receivable transactions

✔ June 30, Interest revenue, $159.78

The following were selected from among the transactions completed during the current year by Wei Peng Co., a business security systems company with a June 30 fiscal year-end. Wei Peng Co. had the following account balances on January 1, 2015:

Notes receivable, 3%, 60-day, issued Dec. 10, 2014	$20,000
Accounts receivable	1,770
Allowance for doubtful accounts	(6,580)

Jan. 10. Loaned $12,000 cash to Jane Clarke, receiving a 90-day, 4% note.
Feb. 4. Sold a security system on account to Pietro & Co., $35,000. The cost of goods sold was $15,000.
     ?   Received the amount due on the note of December 10.
     13. Sold a security system on account to Centennial Co., $30,000, terms 1/15, n/30. The cost of goods sold was $12,500.
     28. Received from Centennial Co. the amount of the invoice of February 13, less 1% discount.
Mar. 6. Accepted a 30-day, 6% note for $35,000 from Pietro & Co. on account.
     ?   Received from Pietro & Co. the amount due on the note of March 6.
     ?   Received the interest due from Jane Clarke and a new 90-day, 6% note as a renewal of the loan of January 10. (Record both the debit and the credit to the notes receivable account.)
Jun. 30. Recorded an adjusting entry for accrued interest on the note outstanding.

(continued)

30. Recorded an adjusting entry for the allowance for doubtful accounts. Based on an aging of the accounts receivable balance of $36,770, it was estimated that $5,700 will be uncollectible.

Jul. 9. Received from Jane Clarke the amount due on her note.

Instructions

Journalize the transactions, assuming Wei Peng Co. uses a perpetual inventory system.

---

4 **5**

PR 8-9B

Accounts and notes receivable entries

✔ Sept. 30, Interest revenue, $878.73

The following transactions were completed by Comfort Distributors Ltd., a furniture distributor with a September 30 fiscal year-end. Comfort Distributors Ltd. had the following account balances on May 31, 2015:

Notes receivable	$500,000
Accounts receivable	336,400
Allowance for Doubtful Accounts	(22,560)

Jun. 1. Received cash for a $475,000 note due, plus interest for 60 days at 3%.

10. Wrote off the remaining note receivable of $25,000 as uncollectible. No interest had been accrued for this note.

12. Sold merchandise on account to Waller Co., $112,500, terms 1/15, net/30. The cost of goods sold was $87,500.

13. Received a $210,000, 60-day, 3% note dated June 13 from Maver Co., in exchange for merchandise. The cost of goods sold was $141,500.

18. Received a $102,800, 120-day, 3% note dated June 18 from Tatum Ltd., in exchange for merchandise. The cost of goods sold was $61,680.

26. Cash is received for the transaction of June 12. The discount was taken.

Aug. 12. The note dated June 13 from Maver Co. is dishonoured. Comfort Distributors believes the amount is collectible and the balance owing, including interest, is transferred to accounts receivable.

Sep. 16. Cash is received for the amount owing from Maver Co.

30. Recorded an adjusting entry for accrued interest on the note outstanding.

30. Recorded an adjusting entry for the allowance for doubtful accounts. Based on an aging of the accounts receivable balance of $336,400, it was estimated that $28,960 will be uncollectible.

Instructions

Journalize the entries to record the transactions, assuming Comfort Distributors Ltd. uses a perpetual inventory system.

---

4 **5**

PR 8-10B

Sales and notes receivable entries

✔ Dec. 31, Interest revenue, $8.56

The following were selected from among the transactions completed during the final two months of the year ended December 31, 2015, by C. Archibald Ltd., a clothing retailer. C. Archibald Ltd. had the following account balances on November 1, 2015:

Notes receivable	$45,000
Accounts receivable	50,403
Allowance for Doubtful Accounts	(8,080)

Nov. 2. Received cash for a $40,000 note due, plus interest for 60 days at 5%.

10. Wrote off the remaining note receivable of $5,000 as uncollectible. No interest had been accrued for this note.

12. Sold merchandise on account to Marshall Minton, $2,125. The cost of goods sold was $1,250.

13. Loaned $7,000 cash to Hilary Schmidt, receiving a 30-day, 6% note.

Dec. 10. Accepted a 30-day, 7% note for $2,125 from Minton on account.

? Cash is received for the amount owing on the Schmidt note.

31. Wrote off the following accounts as uncollectible (compound entry): Smith, $788; Magnan, $1,304; Olsen, $550.

31. Recorded an adjusting entry for accrued interest on the note outstanding.

31. Recorded an adjusting entry for the allowance for doubtful accounts. Based on an aging of the accounts receivable, it was estimated that $6,100 will be uncollectible.

Instructions

Journalize the transactions, assuming C. Archibald Ltd. uses a perpetual inventory system.

SPECIAL ACTIVITIES

SA 8-1

Classifications of receivables

Boeing is one of the world's major aerospace firms, with operations involving commercial aircraft, military aircraft, missiles, satellite systems, and information and battle management systems. As at December 31, 2011, Boeing had $2,950 million of receivables involving U.S government contracts and $1,390 million of receivables involving commercial aircraft customers, such as Delta Air Lines and United Airlines.

Should Boeing report these receivables separately in the financial statements, or combine them into one overall accounts receivable amount? Explain.

SA 8-2

Estimate uncollectible accounts

For several years, Halsey Co.'s sales have been on a "cash only" basis. On January 1, 2012, however, Halsey Co. began offering credit on terms of n/30. The amount of the adjusting entry to record the estimated uncollectible receivables at the end of each year has been ¼ of 1% of credit sales, which is the rate reported as the average for the industry. Credit sales and the year-end credit balances in Allowance for Doubtful Accounts for the past four years are as follows:

Year	Credit Sales	Allowance for Doubtful Accounts
2012	$6,120,000	$ 6,390
2013	6,300,000	11,880
2014	6,390,000	17,000
2015	6,540,000	24,600

John Carter, president of Halsey Co., is concerned that the method used to account for and write off uncollectible receivables is unsatisfactory. He has asked for your advice in the analysis of past operations in this area and for recommendations for change.
1. Determine the amount of (a) the addition to Allowance for Doubtful Accounts and (b) the accounts written off for each of the four years.
2. a. Advise John Carter whether the estimate of ¼ of 1% of credit sales appears reasonable.

   b. Assume that after discussing (a) with John Carter, he asked you what action might be taken to determine what the balance of Allowance for Doubtful Accounts should be at December 31, 2015, and what possible changes, if any, you might recommend in accounting for uncollectible receivables. How would you respond?

SA 8-3

Accounts receivable turnover and days' sales in receivables

f·a·i

RONA inc. is a leading Canadian retailer and distributor of hardware, home renovation, and garden products, operating out of more than 680 franchised, affiliated, and corporate stores. For two recent years, RONA reported the following (in millions):

	Year Ended	
	Dec. 25, 2011	Dec. 26, 2010
Net sales	$4,805	$4,820
Accounts receivable at end of year	370	300

The accounts receivable (in millions) were $251 at the beginning of the year ended December 26, 2010.
1. Compute the accounts receivable turnover for 2011 and 2010. Round to one decimal place.
2. Compute the days' sales in receivables at the end of 2011 and 2010. Round to one decimal place.

(continued)

3. What conclusions can be drawn from 1. and 2. regarding RONA's efficiency in collecting receivables?
4. For its years ended in 2011 and 2010, Canadian Tire Corporation, Limited has an accounts receivable turnover of 14.0 and 12.1, respectively. Compare RONA's efficiency in collecting receivables with that of Canadian Tire.

SA 8-4

Accounts receivable turnover and days' sales in receivables

f·a·i

Rogers Communications Inc. is one of Canada's largest communications companies, particularly in the field of wireless communications and cable television, with additional telecommunications and mass media assets. For two recent years, Rogers reported the following:

	Year Ended	
	Dec. 31, 2011	**Dec. 31, 2010**
Net sales	$12,428	$12,142
Accounts receivable at end of year	1,574	1,443

Assume that the accounts receivable (in millions) were $1,310 at the beginning of the year ended December 31, 2010.

1. Compute the accounts receivable turnover for 2011 and 2010. Round to one decimal place.
2. Compute the days' sales in receivables at the end of 2011 and 2010. Round to one decimal place.
3. What conclusions can be drawn from (1) and (2) regarding Rogers' efficiency in collecting receivables?

SA 8-5

Accounts receivable turnover

f·a·i

The accounts receivable turnover ratio will vary across companies, depending on the nature of the company's operations. For example, an accounts receivable turnover of 6 for an Internet service provider is unacceptable but might be excellent for a manufacturer. A list of well-known companies follows.

Apple Computer	Coca-Cola	RONA
Bombardier	The Home Depot	Sears Canada
The Brick Group	IBM	Walmart
Canadian Tire	Procter & Gamble	Whirlpool

1. For each of the preceding companies, identify whether its turnover ratio is likely to be greater than or less than 15.
2. Based on your answers to instruction 1, identify a characteristic of companies with accounts receivable turnover ratios greater than 15.

SA 8-6

Financial reporting for receivables

f·a·i

Using the financial statements for Leon's Furniture Limited and Shoppers Drug Mart Corporation in Appendixes B and C, answer the following questions:

1. When reporting receivables, companies must disclose any unusual credit risks. Both companies include a note regarding credit risk—is either company exposed to any unusual credit risk?
2. Are the receivables reported at their gross or net realizable values?
3. Which company would you expect to be more efficient in collecting receivables? Why?
4. Compute the accounts receivable turnover for the past two years for both companies.
5. Which company is more efficient in collecting receivables?

Property, Plant, and Equipment and Other Long-Term Assets

TIM HORTONS

If you were to go looking for a coffee shop in most towns or cities in Canada, you would likely find a Tim Hortons. With its new slogan, "It's Time For Tims," Tim Hortons is one of the largest fast-food restaurants in Canada, with more than 3,800 locations in Canada and the United States.

But in 1964, when the first Tim Hortons coffee shop was opened, it almost didn't stay open. Tim Horton knew how to play hockey and was a Canadian hockey legend, but he was skating on thin ice when it came to running a business. Fortunately, Tim became friends and then a business partner with a local police officer, Ron Joyce, who did have some business experience.

The first Tim Hortons stores offered only two products—coffee and doughnuts. Although the now legendary Tim Hortons coffee remains the biggest drawing card, the menu has grown to include Timbits, muffins, sandwiches, soups, smoothies, and many other products.

So, how much would it cost you to open a Tim Hortons restaurant? The total investment begins at approximately $500,000 per restaurant. Thus, in starting a Tim Hortons restaurant, you would be making a significant investment that would affect your life for years to come. In this chapter, we discuss the accounting for investments in long-term assets, such as those used to open a Tim Hortons restaurant. We also explain how to determine the portion of the asset that becomes an expense over time. Finally, we discuss the accounting for the disposal of these assets and accounting for intangible assets, such as patents and copyrights, and for goodwill.

After studying this chapter, you should be able to:

1 Define, classify, and account for the cost of property, plant, and equipment.

Nature of Property, Plant, and Equipment	Classifying Costs	
	The Cost of Property, Plant, and Equipment	EXAMPLE EXERCISE 9-1 (page 462)
	Cost Model versus Revaluation Model	
	Lump-Sum Purchases	EXAMPLE EXERCISE 9-2 (page 463)
	Capital and Revenue Expenditures	EXAMPLE EXERCISE 9-3 (page 465)

2 Compute depreciation using the following methods: straight-line method, units-of-production method, and double-declining-balance method.

Accounting for Depreciation	Factors in Computing Depreciation Expense	
	Straight-Line Method	EXAMPLE EXERCISE 9-4 (page 467)
	Units-of-Production Method	EXAMPLE EXERCISE 9-5 (page 468)
	Double-Declining-Balance Method	EXAMPLE EXERCISE 9-6 (page 469)
	Depreciation for Partial Years	EXAMPLE EXERCISE 9-7 (page 470)
	Comparing Depreciation Methods	
	Impairment of Long-Term Assets	EXAMPLE EXERCISE 9-8 (page 472)
	Revising Depreciation Estimates	EXAMPLE EXERCISE 9-9 (page 473)
	Depreciation for Income Tax Purposes	

3 Journalize entries for the disposal of property, plant, and equipment.

Disposal of Property, Plant, and Equipment	Discarding Property, Plant, and Equipment	
	Selling Property, Plant, and Equipment	EXAMPLE EXERCISE 9-10 (page 477)

4 Compute depletion and journalize the entry for amortization of natural resources.

Natural Resources		EXAMPLE EXERCISE 9-11 (page 478)

5 Describe the accounting for intangible assets and for goodwill.

Intangible Assets and Goodwill	Patents	
	Copyrights and Trademarks	
	Goodwill	
	Impairment of Intangible Assets and Goodwill	EXAMPLE EXERCISE 9-12 (page 480)

6 Describe how depreciation and amortization expense and impairment losses are reported in an income statement and prepare a balance sheet that includes property, plant, and equipment and other long-term assets.

Financial Reporting for Property, Plant, and Equipment and Other Long-Term Assets	Financial Analysis and Interpretation	EXERCISE EXERCISE 9-13 (page 482)

For the chapter *At a Glance*, turn to page 483.

Nature of Property, Plant, and Equipment

Define, classify, and account for the cost of property, plant, and equipment.

Property, plant, and equipment are long-term or relatively permanent assets such as equipment, machinery, buildings, and land. Other descriptive titles for property, plant, and equipment are **tangible capital assets** and **fixed assets**. These terms are used interchangeably by organizations and throughout this textbook. Property, plant, and equipment have the following characteristics:

1. They exist physically and, thus, are *tangible* assets.
2. They are owned and used by the company in its normal operations.
3. They are not offered for sale as part of normal operations.
4. They are expected to be used for more than one year.

Classifying Costs

Costs that are recorded as property, plant, and equipment include the purchase of land, buildings, or equipment. Such assets normally last more than a year and are used in the normal operations. However, standby equipment for use during peak periods or when other equipment breaks down is still classified as property, plant, and equipment even though it is not used very often. In contrast, property, plant, and equipment does not include assets that have been abandoned or are no longer used in operations.

Although property, plant, and equipment may be sold, they should not be offered for sale as part of normal operations. For example, cars and trucks offered for sale by an automotive dealership are not property, plant, and equipment of the dealership; instead, they are inventory of the dealership. On the other hand, a tow truck used in

---

Exhibit 1

Costs of Acquiring Property, Plant, and Equipment

Building	Machinery and Equipment	Land
• Purchase price	• Purchase price	• Purchase price
• Sales taxes	• Sales taxes	• Sales taxes
• Permits	• Permits	• Permits
• Sales commission	• Sales commission	• Broker's commission
• Modifying for use	• Modifying for use	• Modifying for use, such as removing unwanted buildings, grading, and levelling
• Interest on money borrowed to finance construction	• Interest on money borrowed to finance purchase	
• Insurance during construction	• Insurance while in transit	
• Repairs to existing building	• Repairs to used equipment	
• Architect's and engineer's fees		• Title and surveying fees
	• Freight	
	• Installation	
	• Assembly and testing for use	

Land Improvements

• Trees and shrubs
• Fences
• Outdoor lighting
• Paved parking areas

the normal operations of the dealership is part of property, plant, and equipment of the dealership.

A company might own land or buildings that are not used in the normal operations or are no longer used in the business and are held for sale or for capital appreciation. Such assets are reported on the balance sheet in a section entitled **Investment Property**. For example, undeveloped land acquired for future resale would be classified and reported at either cost or fair value as an investment property. The details of accounting for investment properties are discussed in more advanced accounting texts.

The Cost of Property, Plant, and Equipment

The costs of acquiring long-term assets include all amounts spent to get the asset in place and ready for use. For example, freight costs and the costs of installing equipment are part of the asset's total cost.

Exhibit 1 summarizes some of the common costs of acquiring property, plant, and equipment. These costs are recorded by debiting the related asset account, such as Building, Machinery and Equipment, Land,[1] or Land Improvements.

Land improvements are structural additions made to the property, such as paving, fencing, and landscaping. Unlike land, these structural additions deteriorate over time and require maintaining. Establishing a separate account for land improvements allows these items to be depreciated over their useful life. The Land account includes the costs to prepare the land for use, such as grading and *razing*, or removing old structures.

Only costs necessary for preparing the capital asset for use are included as a cost of the asset. Incidental costs that do not increase the asset's usefulness are recorded as an expense. For example, costs related to vandalism, damage or breakage during installation, and uninsured theft do not increase the asset's usefulness. Such costs are recorded as an expense as they are incurred.

A company may incur costs associated with constructing an asset such as a new building. The direct costs incurred in the construction, such as labour and materials, should be capitalized as a debit to an account entitled Construction in Progress. When the construction is complete, the costs are reclassified by crediting Construction in Progress and debiting the proper asset account, such as Building. For some companies, construction in progress can be significant.

EXAMPLE EXERCISE 9-1   Classifying Costs   ①

During March 2014, Comeau Lake Company decided to build a new retail outlet and purchased land for $125,000. An existing building was removed ($15,000), fencing was installed ($10,000), building permits were obtained ($1,200), and an architect developed plans for the new building ($25,000). An additional $500 was spent repainting the fence as the wrong paint had been applied initially. Determine the amounts to be allocated to the various accounts. Use Construction in Progress for the new building costs.

FOLLOW MY EXAMPLE 9-1

Construction in Progress = $26,200 ($1,200 + $25,000)
Land = $140,000 ($125,000 + $15,000)
Land Improvements = $10,000
Miscellaneous Expense = $500 (the repainting cost is expensed as it does not increase the asset's usefulness)

For Practice: PE 9-1

---

1 As discussed here, land is assumed to be used only as a location or site and not for its mineral deposits or other natural resources.

Cost Model versus Revaluation Model

Under International Financial Reporting Standards (IFRS), a company can use either the cost model or the revaluation model as its accounting policy and apply that policy to an entire class of property, plant, and equipment.[2] Under the **cost model**, a long-term asset is carried at its carrying amount, similar to the treatment a company would follow under Accounting Standards for Private Enterprises (ASPE).[3] The **revaluation model** allows long-term assets whose fair value can be measured reliably to be carried at their fair value.[4] The increase in fair value is recorded by reducing accumulated depreciation and recognizing the gain as *other comprehensive income*. An example of a revaluation gain is shown on the IFRS version of Morning Java's financial statements in Appendix A. The cost model will be discussed in this textbook as the revaluation model is used by few Canadian companies and is beyond the scope of an introductory course.

Lump-Sum Purchases

A **lump-sum purchase,** or **basket purchase,** occurs when a group of assets is purchased in one transaction for a lump-sum amount. For example, suppose a company paid $1,100,000 for the purchase of a building. The company is really purchasing three separate assets: the building; the land on which the building sits; and land improvements, such as landscaping, fencing, and pavement. These assets have different expected useful lives and different residual values. As a result, they will be depreciated over different time frames, or not at all, in the case of land. Thus, the $1,100,000 purchase price needs to be allocated to the individual asset accounts. If the fair value of an asset is known, it can be used to pro-rate the purchase price. Assuming fair values of $450,000, $600,000, and $150,000 for the building, land, and land improvements respectively, the purchase price would be pro-rated over the $1,200,000 total fair value as follows:

Asset	Calculation	Allocated Purchase Price
Building	$450,000/$1,200,000 × $1,100,000	$ 412,500
Land	$600,000/$1,200,000 × $1,100,000	550,000
Land Improvements	$150,000/$1,200,000 × $1,100,000	137,500
Total		$1,100,000

The journal entry to record the lump-sum purchase would be as follows:

Building	412,500	
Land	550,000	
Land Improvements	137,500	
Cash		1,100,000
To record lump-sum purchase of assets.		

EXAMPLE EXERCISE 9-2   Lump-Sum Purchase   (1)

Biddell Construction Company paid $750,000 on June 12, 2014, for the assets of a company going out of business. The equipment, vehicles, and inventory were valued at $60,000, $280,000, and $460,000, respectively. Prepare the journal entry for the lump-sum purchase.

(continued)

2 *CICA Handbook–Accounting, 2013,* Part I, IAS 16, para. 29.

3 *CICA Handbook–Accounting, 2013,* Part I, IAS 16, para. 30.

4 *CICA Handbook–Accounting, 2013,* Part I, IAS 16, para. 31.

FOLLOW MY EXAMPLE 9-2

2014 Jun. 12	Equipment	56,250*
	Vehicles	262,500**
	Inventory	431,250†
	Cash	
	To record lump-sum purchase of assets.	750,000
	*[($60,000/$800,000) × $750,000]	
	**[($280,000/$800,000) × $750,000]	
	†[($460,000/$800,000) × $750,000]	

For Practice: PE 9-2

Capital and Revenue Expenditures

Once an asset has been acquired and placed in service, costs may be incurred for ordinary maintenance and repairs. In addition, costs may be incurred for improving an asset or for extending the asset's useful life.

Ordinary Maintenance and Repairs Costs related to the ordinary maintenance and repairs of an asset are recorded as an expense of the current period. Such expenditures are **revenue expenditures** and are recorded as an expense. For example, $300 paid for a tune-up of a delivery truck is recorded as follows:

	Repairs and Maintenance Expense	300
	Cash	300
	Paid for truck tune-up.	

Asset Improvements After an asset has been placed in service, costs may be incurred to improve the asset. Such costs may increase the output of the asset, lower its operating costs, extend its useful life, or improve the quality of its output. For example, the service value of a delivery truck might be improved by adding a $5,500 hydraulic lift to allow for easier and quicker loading of cargo. Such costs are **betterments** or **capital expenditures** and are recorded as increases to the asset account. In the case of the hydraulic lift, the expenditure is recorded as follows:

	Delivery Truck	5,500
	Cash	5,500
	Paid for hydraulic lift for truck.	

CRITICAL THINKING

What is the difference between an ordinary repair and a betterment?

It can sometimes be difficult to determine whether a cost improves the asset or relates to an ongoing repair. For example, when a company replaces an old asphalt roof with a metal roof, part of that cost can be treated as a repair and part can be treated as a betterment. The metal roof will both extend the life of the asset and replace an existing asset. Professional judgment is required to make these decisions.

INTEGRITY, OBJECTIVITY, AND ETHICS IN BUSINESS

CAPITAL CRIME

An accounting fraud in Canada involved the improper accounting for capital expenditures. Atlas Cold Storage, the second largest refrigerated warehouse network in North America at the time, improperly treated more than $5 million of expenses as capital expenditures in order to understate expenses and overstate profit. As a result, the company had to restate its prior years' earnings downward by more than $5 million to correct this error, and Atlas Cold Storage's senior executives were charged.

EXAMPLE EXERCISE 9-3 Capital and Revenue Expenditures　①

On June 18, GTS Co. paid $1,200 to upgrade a hydraulic lift and $45 for an oil change for one of its delivery trucks. Journalize the entries for the hydraulic lift upgrade and oil change expenditures.

FOLLOW MY EXAMPLE 9-3

Jun. 18	Delivery Truck..	1,200	
	Repairs and Maintenance Expense..............................	45	
	Cash..		1,245
	To record hydraulic lift and oil change.		

For Practice: PE 9-3

② Accounting for Depreciation

Compute depreciation using the following methods: straight-line method, units-of-production method, and double-declining-balance method.

Property, plant, and equipment, with the exception of land, lose their ability, over time, to provide services. Thus, the costs of assets such as equipment and buildings should be recorded as an expense over their useful lives. This periodic recording of the cost of assets as an expense is called **depreciation** or **amortization.** Under ASPE, the terms *depreciation* and *amortization* are used interchangeably for depreciating tangible assets, intangible assets, and goodwill; the term *depletion* may be used for depreciating natural resources.[5] Under IFRS, the term *depreciation* is used for tangible capital assets, and the term *amortization* is used for natural resources and intangible capital assets.[6] This textbook uses the terminology followed under IFRS. Because land has an unlimited life, it is not depreciated.

To illustrate, the adjusting entry to record depreciation on a building is as follows:

	Depreciation Expense		XXX	
	Accumulated Depreciation—Building			XXX
	To record depreciation.			

Note: The adjusting entry to record depreciation debits Depreciation Expense and credits Accumulated Depreciation.

Accumulated depreciation is a contra asset account, allowing for the original cost of the asset to remain unchanged in the asset account. Instead of expensing an asset when purchased, depreciation allows the cost of the asset to be spread over the duration of its use, thereby making earnings more reflective of the true costs.

Two common misunderstandings exist about *depreciation* as used in accounting:

1. Depreciation does not measure a decline in the market value of these assets. Instead, depreciation is an allocation of an asset's cost to expense over the asset's useful life. Thus, the **carrying amount** or **book value** of an asset (cost less accumulated depreciation) usually does not equal the asset's market value. The difference between an asset's book value and its market value is justified in accounting because property, plant, and equipment are for use in a company's operations rather than for resale. Carrying amounts of assets may also be adjusted for impairment losses, which will be discussed later in this chaper.

2. Depreciation does not provide cash to replace assets as they wear out. This misunderstanding may occur because depreciation, unlike most expenses, does not require an outlay of cash when it is recorded.

5 *CICA Handbook–Accounting, 2012,* Part II, Section 3061.17.

6 *CICA Handbook–Accounting, 2013,* Part I, IAS 16, para. 6, and IAS 38, para. 8.

Factors in Computing Depreciation Expense

Three factors determine the depreciation expense for a depreciable capital asset. These three factors are as follows:

1. The asset's initial cost
2. The asset's expected useful life
3. The asset's estimated residual value

The initial *cost* of a capital asset is determined using the concepts discussed and illustrated earlier in this chapter.

The *expected useful life* of a capital asset is estimated at the time the asset is placed into service. Estimates of expected useful lives are available from industry trade associations. However, it is not uncommon for different companies to use a different useful life for similar assets. Canadian Tire, for example, depreciates buildings over five to 25 years, while Sears Canada depreciates buildings over 10 to 50 years.

The **residual value** of an asset at the end of its useful life is also estimated at the time the asset is placed into service. Residual value is sometimes referred to as *scrap value, salvage value,* or *trade-in value.* The difference between a capital asset's initial cost and its residual value is called the asset's depreciable amount. The **depreciable amount** is the amount of the asset's cost that is allocated over its useful life as depreciation expense. If a capital asset has no residual value, then its entire cost should be allocated to depreciation.

The three depreciation methods used most often are as follows:

1. Straight-line depreciation
2. Units-of-production depreciation
3. Double-declining-balance depreciation

It is not necessary that a company use one method of computing depreciation for all of its capital assets. For example, a company may use one method for depreciating equipment and another method for depreciating buildings. The method of depreciation should reflect the pattern in which the economic benefits of the asset are consumed or otherwise used up. The chosen method should be applied consistently over the life of the asset in order to produce rational, consistent results.

Straight-Line Method

The **straight-line method** provides for the same amount of depreciation expense for each year of the asset's useful life. The straight-line method, which reflects a constant charge for the service as a function of time, is the most widely used depreciation method in Canada.

To illustrate, assume that equipment was purchased on January 1 as follows:

Initial cost	$24,000
Expected useful life	5 years
Estimated residual value	$2,000

The annual straight-line depreciation of $4,400 is computed below.

$$\text{Annual Depreciation} = \frac{\text{Cost} - \text{Residual Value}}{\text{Useful Life}} = \frac{\$24,000 - \$2,000}{5 \text{ Years}} = \$4,400$$

The journal entry for the first year is recorded as follows:

2015				
Dec.	31	Depreciation Expense	4,400	
		Accumulated Depreciation—Equipment		4,400
		To record depreciation for equipment.		

At the end of the first year, $4,400 will be included on the income statement as depreciation expense. The carrying amount of the asset (cost less accumulated depreciation) has been reduced to $19,600 at the end of the first year. The carrying amount will be further reduced each year by the depreciation expense of $4,400. The equipment will appear on the balance sheet at the end of each of the first three years as follows:

	Year 1	Year 2	Year 3
Equipment	$24,000	$24,000	$24,000
Less accumulated depreciation	(4,400)	(8,800)	(13,200)
Equipment, net	$19,600	$15,200	$10,800

The computation of straight-line depreciation may be simplified by converting the annual depreciation to a percentage of depreciable cost.[7] The **straight-line rate** is determined by dividing 100% by the number of years of expected useful life, as shown below.

Expected Years of Useful Life	Straight-Line Rate
5 years	20% (100% ÷ 5)
8 years	12.5% (100% ÷ 8)
10 years	10% (100% ÷ 10)
20 years	5% (100% ÷ 20)
25 years	4% (100% ÷ 25)

For the preceding equipment, the annual depreciation of $4,400 can be computed by multiplying the depreciable amount of $22,000 by 20% (100%/5).

EXAMPLE EXERCISE 9-4   Straight-Line Depreciation   (2)

Equipment acquired on January 1, 2014, at a cost of $125,000, has an estimated residual value of $5,000 and an estimated useful life of 10 years. (a) Determine the annual straight-line depreciation and (b) journalize the end-of-year entry to record depreciation.

FOLLOW MY EXAMPLE 9-4

a. $12,000 [($125,000 – $5,000)/10]

b.
2014			
Dec. 31	Depreciation Expense	12,000	
	Accumulated Depreciation—Equipment......................		12,000
	To record depreciation of equipment.		

For Practice: PE 9-4

Units-of-Production Method

The **units-of-production method** provides the same amount of depreciation expense for each unit of production. Depending on the asset, the units of production can be expressed in terms of hours, kilometres driven, or quantity produced. Canadian Pacific Railway Limited, for instance, depreciates its train tracks based on volume of traffic.

The units-of-production method is applied in two steps.

---

7 The depreciation rate may also be expressed as a fraction. For example, the annual straight-line rate for an asset with a three-year useful life is 1/3.

Step 1. Determine the depreciation per unit as follows:

$$\text{Depreciation per Unit} = \frac{\text{Cost} - \text{Residual Value}}{\text{Total Units of Production}}$$

Step 2. Compute the depreciation expense as follows:

Depreciation Expense = Depreciation per Unit × Total Units of Production Used

To illustrate, assume that the equipment in the preceding example is expected to have a useful life of 10,000 operating hours. During the year, the equipment was operated 2,100 hours. The units-of-production depreciation for the year is $4,620, as shown below.

Step 1. Determine the depreciation per hour as follows:

$$\text{Depreciation per Unit} = \frac{\text{Cost} - \text{Residual Value}}{\text{Total Units of Production}} = \frac{\$24,000 - \$2,000}{10,000 \text{ Hours}}$$

$$= \$2.20 \text{ per Hour}$$

Step 2. Compute the depreciation expense as follows:

Depreciation Expense = Depreciation per Unit × Total Units of Production Used

Depreciation Expense = $2.20 per Hour × 2,100 Hours = $4,620

The units-of-production method is often used when an asset's in-service time (or use) varies from year to year.

EXAMPLE EXERCISE 9-5 Units-of-Production Depreciation ②

Equipment acquired at a cost of $180,000 has an estimated residual value of $10,000 and an estimated useful life of 40,000 hours and was operated 3,600 hours during the first year and 5,200 hours during the second year. Determine (a) the depreciable cost, (b) the depreciation per unit and the depreciation expense for (c) the first year and (d) the second year.

FOLLOW MY EXAMPLE 9-5

a. $170,000 ($180,000 – $10,000)

b. $4.25 per hour ($170,000/40,000 hours)

c. $15,300 (3,600 hours × $4.25)

d. $22,100 (5,200 hours × $4.25)

For Practice: PE 9-5

Double-Declining-Balance Method

The **double-declining-balance method** provides for a declining periodic expense over the expected useful life of the asset and may be appropriate when the operating efficiency of the asset declines over time. The double-declining-balance method is applied in three steps.

Step 1. Determine the straight-line rate using the expected useful life.

Step 2. Determine the double-declining-balance rate by multiplying the straight-line rate from step 1 by two.

Step 3. Compute the depreciation expense by multiplying the double-declining-balance rate from step 2 by the carrying amount of the asset.

Return to the details found on page 466 for the equipment purchase depreciated under the straight-line method. We will use this equipment purchase to illustrate the double-declining balance method. For the first year, the depreciation is $9,600, as shown on the following page.

Step 1. Straight-line rate = 20% (100%/5)
Step 2. Double-declining-balance rate = 40% (20% × 2)
Step 3. Depreciation expense = $9,600 ($24,000 × 40%)

For the first year, the carrying amount of the equipment is its initial cost of $24,000. After the first year, the carrying amount declines, and thus the depreciation also declines. The double-declining-balance depreciation for the full five-year life of the equipment is shown below.

Year	Cost	Acc. Deprec. at Beginning of Year	Carrying Amount at Beginning of Year	Double-Declining-Balance Rate	Depreciation for Year	Carrying Amount at End of Year
1	$24,000		$24,000.00 ×	40%	$9,600.00	$14,400.00
2	24,000	$ 9,600.00	14,400.00 ×	40%	5,760.00	8,640.00
3	24,000	15,360.00	8,640.00 ×	40%	3,456.00	5,184.00
4	24,000	18,816.00	5,184.00 ×	40%	2,073.60	3,110.40
5	24,000	20,889.60	3,110.40	—	1,110.40	2,000.00

When the double-declining-balance method is used, the estimated residual value is *not* considered. However, the asset should not be depreciated below its estimated residual value. In the above example, the estimated residual value was $2,000. Therefore, the depreciation for the fifth year is $1,110.40 ($3,110.40 – $2,000.00) instead of $1,244.16 (40% × $3,110.40).

The double-declining-balance method provides a higher depreciation in the first year of the asset's use, followed by declining depreciation amounts. For this reason, the double-declining-balance method is called an **accelerated depreciation method**.

An asset's service is often greater in the early years of its use than in later years. In such cases, the double-declining-balance method provides a good allocation of depreciation expense in relation to the asset's usefulness.

EXAMPLE EXERCISE 9-6 Double-Declining-Balance Depreciation ②

Equipment acquired at the beginning of the year at a cost of $125,000 has an estimated residual value of $5,000 and an estimated useful life of 10 years. Determine (a) the double-declining-balance rate and the double-declining-balance depreciation for (b) the first year and (c) the second year.

FOLLOW MY EXAMPLE 9-6

a. 20% [(100%/10) × 2]
b. $25,000 ($125,000 × 20%)
c. $20,000 [($125,000 – $25,000) × 20%]

For Practice: PE 9-6

Depreciation for Partial Years

The example used to illustrate depreciation so far in this chapter assumes the asset was purchased on January 1, the first day of the company's fiscal year. It is more likely that assets will be purchased and disposed of throughout the fiscal year and that depreciation will need to be calculated for partial years. There are a few methods used by companies to handle partial year purchases and sales. The practice used in this textbook is to treat asset purchases and disposals that occur during the month as having been purchased or sold on the first day of that month.

Straight-line Method for Partial Years If an asset is used for only part of a year, the annual depreciation is pro-rated. For example, assume that the preceding equipment was purchased and available for use on October 6. In this textbook, the practice is to treat asset purchases and sales occurring during the month as having occurred on the first day of that month. The depreciation for the year ended December 31 would be $1,100, computed as follows:

First-Year Partial Depreciation = $4,400 × 3/12 = $1,100

Units-of-Production Method for Partial Years Because the units-of-production method calculates depreciation based on production, no adjustment is required for purchases and sales of assets made throughout the year.

Double-Declining-Balance Method for Partial Years Similar to the treatment under straight-line depreciation, if an asset is used for only part of a year, the annual depreciation is pro-rated. Using the previous example of purchasing the equipment on October 6, the depreciation for the year ended December 31 would be $2,400, computed as follows:

First-Year Partial Depreciation = $9,600 × 3/12 = $2,400

The depreciation for the second year would then be $8,640, computed as follows:

Second-Year Depreciation = [40% × ($24,000 − $2,400)] = $8,640

EXAMPLE EXERCISE 9-7 Double-Declining-Balance Method for Partial Years ②

Refer to the information in Example Exercise 9-6. Assume the equipment was acquired on April 24. Determine (a) the double-declining-balance rate and (b) the double-declining-balance depreciation for the first year, and (c) for the second year.

FOLLOW MY EXAMPLE 9-7

a. 20% [(100%/10) × 2]

b. $18,750 ($125,000 × 20% × 9/12)

c. $21,250 [($125,000 − $18,750) × 20%]

For Practice: PE 9-7

Comparing Depreciation Methods

The three depreciation methods are summarized in Exhibit 2. All three methods allocate a portion of the total cost of an asset to an accounting period but never depreciate an asset below its residual value.

Exhibit 2

Summary of Depreciation Methods

	Straight-Line Method	Units-of-Production Method	Double-Declining-Balance Method
Useful life expressed in	Years	Total units of production	Years
Depreciation rate	Straight-line rate (100%/useful life)	(Cost − Residual value)/Total units of production	Straight-line rate × 2
Depreciation expense	Constant	Variable	Declining
Adjustment required for partial years	Yes	No	Yes

Exhibit 3

Comparing Depreciation Methods

	Depreciation Expense		
Year	Straight-Line Method	Units-of-Production Method	Double-Declining-Balance Method
1	$ 4,400*	$ 4,620 ($2.20 × 2,100 hrs.)	$ 9,600.00 ($24,000 × 40%)
2	4,400	3,300 ($2.20 × 1,500 hrs.)	5,760.00 ($14,400 × 40%)
3	4,400	5,720 ($2.20 × 2,600 hrs.)	3,456.00 ($8,640 × 40%)
4	4,400	3,960 ($2.20 × 1,800 hrs.)	2,073.60 ($5,184 × 40%)
5	4,400	4,400 ($2.20 × 2,000 hrs.)	1,110.40**
Total	$22,000	$22,000	$22,000.00

*$4,400 = ($24,000 − $2,000)/5 years

**$3,110.40 − $2,000.00 because the equipment cannot be depreciated below its residual value of $2,000.

The straight-line method provides for the same periodic amounts of depreciation expense over the life of the asset. The units-of-production method provides for periodic amounts of depreciation expense that vary, depending on the amount the asset is used. The double-declining-balance method provides for a higher depreciation amount in the first year of the asset's use, followed by declining amounts.

The depreciation for the straight-line, units-of-production, and double-declining-balance methods is shown in Exhibit 3. The depreciation in Exhibit 3 is based on the equipment purchased in our previous illustrations. For the units-of-production method, we assume that the equipment was used as follows:

Year 1	2,100 hours
Year 2	1,500
Year 3	2,600
Year 4	1,800
Year 5	2,000
Total	10,000 hours

Impairment of Long-Term Assets

Although the carrying amount of an asset usually does not agree with the asset's market value, it is important to ensure that the carrying amount doesn't exceed the asset's market value. If the carrying amount exceeds the market value, the asset has suffered an *impairment*. An **impairment loss** can result from an adverse change, such as a decline in the market for the asset, obsolescence, and abnormal wear and tear. The asset's carrying amount is adjusted to market value by increasing accumulated depreciation and recording a loss.

To illustrate, assume the following data for a building that was purchased on January 1, 2014.

Initial building cost	$1,200,000
Expected useful life	25 years
Estimated residual value	$ 200,000
Annual depreciation using the straight-line method	$ 40,000
[($1,200,000 − $200,000) /25 years]	

At the end of 2016, the building's carrying amount (the undepreciated cost) is $1,080,000, as shown below.

Initial building cost	$1,200,000
Less accumulated depreciation ($40,000 per year × 3 years)	120,000
Carrying amount (undepreciated cost), end of third year	$1,080,000

On January 1, 2017, an appraisal indicates that the building's value has decreased to $942,000 and that its residual value is likely to be $150,000. The journal entry for the impairment loss of $138,000 ($1,080,000 – $942,000) is recorded as follows:

2017					
Jan.	1	Impairment Loss		138,000	
		Accumulated Depreciation—Building			138,000
		To record an impairment loss on the building.			

For companies that report under IFRS, impairment losses for all assets other than goodwill can be reversed up to the original carrying value if market values suggest a reversal is appropriate.[8] Impairment losses are not reversible for companies reporting under ASPE.[9]

EXAMPLE EXERCISE 9-8 Impairment Loss of Long-Term Assets   2

In January 2005, Athabasca Mining Company acquired equipment for $545,000 that had an estimated useful life of 25 years and an expected residual value of $55,000. An appraisal of the equipment at the end of 2014 indicated the market value of the equipment was $300,000. Using this information, (a) calculate the annual depreciation expense up to and including 2014, (b) calculate the equipment's carrying amount at December 31, 2014, and (c) journalize the impairment loss.

FOLLOW MY EXAMPLE 9-8

a. $19,600 [($545,000 – $55,000)/25]

b. $349,000 [$545,000 – ($19,600 × 10)]

c.
2014			
Dec. 31	Impairment Loss..	49,000	
	Accumulated Depreciation—Equipment........................		49,000
	To record an impairment loss on the equipment.		

For Practice: PE 9-8

Revising Depreciation Estimates

Depreciation estimates may need to be revised because of impairment losses, such as those previously illustrated, or because circumstances suggest the original estimates need to be adjusted to reflect abnormal wear, obsolescence, or a change in the estimate of the useful life.

To illustrate, using the example on page 471, the depreciation on the building will need to be revised for periods starting in 2017. The depreciation expense for each of the remaining 22 years (25 years – 3 years) is $36,000, computed as follows:

Carrying amount (undepreciated cost), end of third year	$1,080,000
Less impairment loss	138,000
Carrying amount, adjusted	$ 942,000
Revised annual depreciation expense [($942,000 – $150,000)/22 years]	$ 36,000

---

8 *CICA Handbook–Accounting, 2013,* Part I, IAS 36, paras. 110–124.

9 *CICA Handbook–Accounting, 2012,* Part II, Section 3063.06.

Does a revision of depreciation indicate an accounting error?

No. Accountants need to make many estimates and, thus, they need to apply professional judgment. When depreciating an asset, an accountant estimates the length of the asset's useful life and its residual value. Over time, as more accurate information is acquired, accountants may need to adjust or revise both current and future depreciation expenses.

EXAMPLE EXERCISE 9-9   Revision of Depreciation   ②

A warehouse with a cost of $500,000 has an estimated residual value of $120,000 and an estimated useful life of 40 years and is depreciated by the straight-line method. (a) Determine the amount of the annual depreciation. (b) Determine the carrying amount at the end of the 20th year of use. (c) Assuming that at the start of the 21st year the remaining life is estimated to be 25 years and the residual value is estimated to be $150,000, determine the depreciation expense for each of the remaining 25 years.

FOLLOW MY EXAMPLE 9-9

a. $9,500 [($500,000 − $120,000)/40]

b. $310,000 [$500,000 − ($9,500 × 20)]

c. $6,400 [($310,000 − $150,000)/25]

For Practice: PE 9-9

Depreciation for Income Tax Purposes

The Income Tax Act requires companies to use a declining-balance method, with the maximum rate predetermined, depending upon the type of asset being depreciated. **Capital cost allowance (CCA)** is the term used for depreciation for income tax purposes.

When using CCA rates, residual value is ignored. Also, because all assets are assumed to be put in service in the middle of the year, for most asset categories, only 50% of the normal CCA rate is allowed in the first year. Examples of maximum rates available for various types of assets are shown below.

Class	Assets in Class	Rate
1	Buildings	4%
8	Office furniture and fixtures	20%
10	Automobiles, computers	30%
12	Computer software	100%

To simplify, a company will sometimes use CCA rates for both financial statements and tax purposes. This method is acceptable if the CCA rates do not result in significantly different amounts than would have been reported using one of the three depreciation methods discussed in this chapter.

Can a company keep two sets of books for its long-term assets?

Yes. A company can use one depreciation method and rate for accounting purposes and another for income tax purposes. For example, a company can depreciate buildings using a 4% rate for its tax returns and can choose to use a 5% rate to prepare its financial statements. The tax rates are set by law, whereas the accounting rate is determined by professional judgment.

MID-CHAPTER ILLUSTRATIVE PROBLEM

On May 10, 2013, Marmite Company purchased manufacturing equipment for $66,000. The equipment was expected to have a useful life of three years, or 10,000 operating hours, and a residual value of $3,000. The equipment was used for 2,200 hours during 2013, 3,100 hours during 2014, 3,400 hours in 2015, and 1,800 hours in 2016.

Instructions

1. Determine the amount of depreciation expense for the years ended December 31, 2013 through 2016 by (a) the straight-line method, (b) the units-of-production method, and (c) the double-declining-balance method.
2. Determine the total depreciation expense for the four years by each method.
3. Journalize the entry to record depreciation for 2015, using the double-declining-balance method.
4. Show the balance sheet presentation for the equipment at the 2014 and 2015 year-ends, using the straight-line method.

MID-CHAPTER ILLUSTRATIVE SOLUTION

1. and 2.

	Straight-Line Method	Units-of-Production Method	Double-Declining-Balance Method
2013	$14,000*	$13,860 ($6.30† × 2,200 hrs.)	$29,333 ($66,000 × 66 2/3% × 8/12)
2014	$21,000	$19,530 ($6.30 × 3,100 hrs.)	$24,445 ($66,000 − $29,333) × 66 2/3%
2015	$21,000	$21,420 ($6.30 × 3,400 hrs.)	$ 8,148 ($66,000 − $29,333 − $24,445) × 66 2/3%
2016	$ 7,000**	$ 8,190††	$ 1,074††
Total	$63,000	$63,000	$63,000

* ($66,000 − $3,000) ÷ 3 years × 8/12 = $14,000
** ($66,000 − $3,000) ÷ 3 years × 4/12 = $7,000
† ($66,000 − $3,000) ÷ 10,000 hours = $6.30 per hour
†† The equipment cannot be depreciated below its residual value of $3,000.

3.

2015				
Dec.	31	Depreciation Expense	8,148	
		Accumulated Depreciation–Equipment		8,148
		To record depreciation of the equipment.		

4.

	2015	2014
Equipment	$66,000	$66,000
Less accumulated depreciation	(56,000)	(35,000)
Equipment, net	$10,000	$31,000

Disposal of Property, Plant, and Equipment

Journalize entries for the disposal of property, plant, and equipment.

Property, plant, and equipment that are no longer useful may be discarded or sold. In such cases, the asset is removed from the accounts. Just because an asset is fully depreciated, however, does not mean that it should be removed from the accounts.

If an asset is still being used, its cost and accumulated depreciation should remain in the ledger even if the asset is fully depreciated. This approach maintains account-ability for the asset in the ledger. If the asset was removed from the ledger, the accounts would contain no evidence of the continued existence of the asset.

Discarding Property, Plant, and Equipment

If property, plant, and equipment are no longer used and have no residual value, they are discarded. For example, assume that an asset that is fully depreciated and has no residual value is discarded. The entry to record the discarding removes the asset and its related accumulated depreciation from the ledger.

To illustrate, assume that equipment acquired at a cost of $25,000 is fully depreci-ated at December 31, 2014. Using T accounts, the equipment and accumulated depre-ciation account balances at December 31, 2014, would appear as shown in the margin. On February 14, 2015, the equipment is discarded. The entry to record the discard and the changes to the T accounts are as follows:

Equipment		Accum. Dep.— Equipment	
25,000			25,000

Equipment		Accum. Dep.— Equipment	
25,000			25,000
	25,000	25,000	
Ø			Ø

2015				
Feb.	14	Accumulated Depreciation—Equipment	25,000	
		Equipment		25,000
		To record the discarding of equipment.		

If an asset has not been fully depreciated, depreciation should be recorded before removing the asset from the accounting records.

To illustrate, assume that equipment costing $6,000 with no estimated residual value is depreciated at a straight-line rate of 10%. On December 31, 2014, the accumulated deprecia-tion balance, after adjusting entries, is $4,750. Using T accounts, the equipment and accu-mulated depreciation account balances at December 31, 2014, would appear as shown in the margin. On April 4, 2015, the asset is removed from service and discarded. The entry to record the depreciation for the three months of 2015 before the asset is discarded and the changes to the Accumulated Depreciation—Equipment account are as follows:

Equipment		Accum. Dep.— Equipment	
6,000			4,750

Equipment		Accum. Dep.— Equipment	
6,000			4,750
			150
			4,900

2015				
Apr.	4	Depreciation Expense	150	
		Accumulated Depreciation—Equipment		150
		To record depreciation on equipment discarded		
		($ 6,000 × 10% × $^{3}/_{12}$).		

The entry to record the discarding of the equipment and the changes to the T accounts are as follows:

Equipment		Accum. Dep.— Equipment	
6,000			4,900
	6,000	4,900	
Ø			Ø

Apr.	4	Accumulated Depreciation—Equipment	4,900	
		Loss on Disposal of Equipment	1,100	
		Equipment		6,000
		To record the discarding of equipment.		

The loss of $1,100 is recorded because the balance of the accumulated depreciation account ($4,900) is less than the balance in the equipment account ($6,000). Losses on the discarding of assets are nonoperating items and are normally reported in the Other Expense section of the income statement.

Selling Property, Plant, and Equipment

The entry to record the sale of an asset is similar to the entries for discarding an asset. The only difference is that the receipt of cash is also recorded. If the selling price is more than the carrying amount of the asset, a gain is recorded. If the selling price is less than the carrying amount, a loss is recorded.

To illustrate, assume that equipment is purchased at a cost of $10,000 with no estimated residual value and is depreciated at a straight-line rate of 10%. The equipment is sold for cash on October 12, 2015, during the eighth year of its use. The balance of the accumulated depreciation account as at December 31, 2014, is $7,000. Using T accounts, the equipment and accumulated depreciation account balances at December 31, 2014, would appear as shown in the margin. The entry to update the depreciation for the nine months of 2015 and the changes to the T accounts are as follows:

Equipment		Accum. Dep.—Equipment	
10,000			7,000

Equipment		Accum. Dep.—Equipment	
10,000			7,000
			750
			7,750

2015 Oct.	12	Depreciation Expense		750	
		Accumulated Depreciation—Equipment			750
		To record depreciation on equipment sold			
		($10,000 × 10% × 9/12).			

After the current depreciation is recorded, the carrying amount of the asset is $2,250 ($10,000 − $7,750). The entries to record the sale, and the changes to the T accounts, assuming three different selling prices, are as follows:

Sold at carrying amount, for $2,250. No gain or loss.

Equipment		Accum. Dep.—Equipment	
10,000			7,750
	10,000	7,750	
Ø			Ø

Oct.	12	Cash		2,250	
		Accumulated Depreciation—Equipment		7,750	
		Equipment			10,000
		Sale of equipment.			

Sold at less than the carrying amount, for $1,000. Loss of $1,250.

Equipment		Accum. Dep.—Equipment	
10,000			7,750
	10,000	7,750	
Ø			Ø

Oct.	12	Cash		1,000	
		Accumulated Depreciation—Equipment		7,750	
		Loss on Sale of Equipment		1,250	
		Equipment			10,000
		Sale of equipment.			

Sold at more than the carrying amount, for $2,800. Gain of $550.

Equipment		Accum. Dep.—Equipment	
10,000			7,750
	10,000	7,750	
Ø			Ø

Oct.	12	Cash		2,800	
		Accumulated Depreciation—Equipment		7,750	
		Equipment			10,000
		Gain on Sale of Equipment			550
		Sale of equipment.			

EXAMPLE EXERCISE 9-10 Sale of Equipment

Equipment was acquired at the beginning of the year at a cost of $91,000. The equipment was depreciated using the straight-line method based on an estimated useful life of nine years and an estimated residual value of $10,000.

a. What was the depreciation for the first year?

b. Assuming the equipment was sold at the end of the second year for $78,000, determine the gain or loss on sale of the equipment.

c. Journalize the entry to record the sale.

FOLLOW MY EXAMPLE 9-10

a. $9,000 [($91,000 – $10,000)/9]

b. $5,000 gain {$78,000 – [$91,000 – ($9,000 × 2)]}

c. Cash... 78,000
   Accumulated Depreciation—Equipment................................. 18,000
       Equipment   91,000
       Gain on Sale of Equipment..   5,000
   Sale of equipment.

For Practice: PE 9-10

4 Natural Resources

Compute depletion and journalize the entry for amortization of natural resources.

The assets of some companies include timber, metal ores, minerals, or other natural resources. Because these resources are harvested or mined and then sold, a portion of their cost is debited to an expense account. This process of transferring the cost of these assets to an expense account is called amortization, or **depletion**.[10]

Amortization is determined as follows:[11]

Step 1. Determine the amortization rate as follows:

$$\text{Amortization Rate} = \frac{\text{Cost of Resource}}{\text{Estimated Total Units of Resource}}$$

Step 2. Multiply the amortization rate by the quantity extracted from the resource during the period.

Amortization Expense = Amortization Rate × Quantity Extracted

To illustrate, assume that Karst Company purchased mining rights as follows:

Cost of mineral deposit	$ 400,000
Estimated total units of resource	1,000,000 tonnes
Tonnes mined during year	90,000 tonnes

The amortization expense of $36,000 for the year is computed, as shown below.

Step 1.

$$\text{Amortization Rate} = \frac{\text{Cost of Resource}}{\text{Estimated Total Units of Resource}} = \frac{\$400,000}{1,000,000 \text{ Tonnes}} = \$0.40 \text{ per Tonne}$$

---

10 As mentioned earlier, the terms *amortization*, *depreciation*, and *depletion* may be used under ASPE.

11 We assume that no significant residual value remains after all the natural resource is extracted.

Step 2.

Amortization Expense = $0.40 per Tonne × 90,000 Tonnes = $36,000

The adjusting entry to record the amortization is shown below.

Dec.	31	Amortization Expense	36,000	
		Accumulated Amortization—Mineral Deposit		36,000
		Amortization of mineral deposit.		

EXAMPLE EXERCISE 9-11   Amortization of Natural Resource   4

Earth's Treasures Mining Co. acquired mineral rights for $45,000,000. The mineral deposit is estimated at 50,000,000 tonnes. During the current year, 12,600,000 tonnes were mined and sold.

a. Determine the amortization rate.

b. Determine the amount of amortization expense for the current year.

c. Journalize the adjusting entry on December 31 to recognize the amortization expense.

FOLLOW MY EXAMPLE 9-11

a. $0.90 per tonne ($45,000,000/50,000,000 tonnes)

b. $11,340,000 (12,600,000 tonnes × $0.90 per tonne)

c. Dec. 31   Amortization Expense...................................... 11,340,000
         Accumulated Amortization—Mineral Deposit   11,340,000
         Amortization of mineral deposit.

For Practice: PE 9-11

 Intangible Assets and Goodwill

Describe the accounting for intangible assets and for goodwill.

Patents, copyrights, trademarks, computer software, and customer lists are examples of long-term assets that are called **intangible assets**. Like tangible assets, they are used in the operations of a business and are not held for sale; because they do not exist physically, they are intangible. Intangible assets may have a finite life, such as patents, or may exist indefinitely, such as trademarks.

The accounting for intangible assets is similar to that for property, plant, and equipment. The major issues are the following:

1. determining the initial cost
2. for finite life intangibles, determining the amortization
3. testing for impairment losses, if any

Patents

Manufacturers may acquire exclusive rights to produce and sell goods with one or more unique features. Such rights are granted by **patents,** which the federal government issues to inventors. These rights continue in effect for 20 years. A business may purchase patent rights from others, or it may obtain patents developed by its own research and development.

The initial cost of a purchased patent, including any legal fees, is debited to an asset account. This cost is written off, or amortized, over the years of the patent's expected useful life. The expected useful life of a patent may be less than its legal life. For example, a patent may become worthless because of changing technology or consumer tastes.

Patent amortization is normally computed using the straight-line method. The amortization is recorded by debiting an amortization expense account and crediting a separate contra asset account.

To illustrate, assume that at the beginning of its fiscal year, a company acquires patent rights for $100,000. Although the patent will not expire for 14 years, it is expected to be useful for only five years. The adjusting entry to amortize the patent at the end of the year is as follows:

Dec.	31	Amortization Expense	20,000	
		Accumulated Amortization—Patents		20,000
		Patent amortization ($100,000/5).		

Copyrights and Trademarks

The exclusive right to publish and sell a literary, artistic, or musical composition is granted by a **copyright**. Copyrights are issued by the federal government and extend for 50 years beyond the author's death. The costs of a copyright include all costs of creating the work plus any other costs of obtaining the copyright. A copyright that is purchased is recorded at the price paid for it. Copyrights are amortized over their estimated useful lives. Sony Corporation of America, for instance, amortizes its artist contracts and music catalogues over 16 years and 21 years, respectively.

A **trademark** is a name, term, or symbol used to identify a business and its products. Most businesses identify their trademarks with ® in their advertisements and on their products.

Businesses can protect their trademarks by registering them with the government's patent office. Like a copyright, the legal costs of registering a trademark are recorded as an asset. A trademark that is purchased is recorded at the price paid for it. Trademarks are amortized over their estimated useful lives. Trademarks can potentially exist forever and so these **indefinite life assets** are not amortized. They must, however, be evaluated annually for impairment.

INTEGRITY, OBJECTIVITY, AND ETHICS IN BUSINESS

21ST-CENTURY PIRATES

Pirated software is a major concern of software companies. It is estimated that as much as 28% of all software sold in Canada is pirated. For example, during an electronic sweep, a major organization in Canada appeared to be using hundreds of copies of pirated Microsoft software. The search utilized a program that probed thousands of networked computers to detect whether they contained certain software products. The results were then compared with the number of software licences purchased by the department.

Businesses should honour the copyrights held by software companies by eliminating pirated software

from corporate computers. The Business Software Alliance (BSA) represents the largest software companies in campaigns to investigate illegal use of unlicensed software by businesses. The BSA estimates software industry losses of nearly $59 billion annually from software piracy. BSA alleges that one in three software programs on Canadian computers is pirated. Employees using pirated software on business assets risk bringing legal penalties to themselves and their employers.

Source: "Emerging Markets Drive Software Piracy to a Record $59 Billion in 2010, BSA Reports," May 12, 2011, http://www.bsa.org/country/News%20 and%20Events/News%20Archives/global/05062011-idc-globalpiracystudy .aspx.

Goodwill

Goodwill refers to an asset of a business that is created from such favourable factors as location, product quality, reputation, and managerial skill. Goodwill allows a business to earn a greater rate of return than normal. Because goodwill does not exist separately from the business entity, it is not considered an intangible asset, despite sharing many other characteristics of intangible assets.

Goodwill may be recorded only if it is objectively determined by a transaction. An example of such a transaction is the purchase of a business at a price in excess of the fair value of its net assets (assets – liabilities). The excess is recorded as goodwill.

Goodwill is an indefinite-life asset and is not amortized. However, goodwill and intangible assets should be evaluated each year, and a loss recorded if they are determined to be impaired. This loss is normally disclosed in the Other Expense section of the income statement.

Impairment of Intangible Assets and Goodwill

Similar to the treatment for tangible long-term assets, the carrying amounts of intangible assets and goodwill need to be adjusted for any impairment losses. An impairment loss can result from an adverse change, such as a decline in the market for the asset or a change in the asset's useful life. The asset's carrying amount needs to be adjusted to market value, and the difference is recorded as a loss.

An impairment loss for goodwill occurs when the carrying amount of the business exceeds the fair value of the business; goodwill is then reduced by the difference between these two values. Events that might impair goodwill include unanticipated competition, a loss of key personnel, and a significant adverse change in either legal factors or the business climate.[12] As previously mentioned, impairment losses for all assets other than goodwill can be reversed up to the original carrying value if market values improve and the company reports under IFRS. Impairment losses for goodwill are not reversible under either IFRS or ASPE.

For example, eBay determined that $1.39 billion of the goodwill created from the purchase of Skype is impaired. The entry to record the impairment is as follows:

Impairment Loss		1,390,000,000	
Goodwill			1,390,000,000
Impaired goodwill.			

EXAMPLE EXERCISE 9-12 Impaired Goodwill and Amortization of Patent   (5)

On December 31, it was estimated that goodwill of $40,000 was impaired. In addition, a patent with an estimated useful economic life of 12 years was acquired for $84,000 on July 1.

a. Journalize the adjusting entry on December 31 for the impaired goodwill.

b. Journalize the adjusting entry on December 31 for the amortization of the patent rights.

FOLLOW MY EXAMPLE 9-12

a.	Dec. 31	Impairment Loss...	40,000	
		Goodwill..		40,000
		Impaired goodwill.		
b.	Dec. 31	Amortization Expense	3,500	
		Accumulated Amortization—Patents		3,500
		Amortized patent rights [($84,000/12) × (6/12)].		

For Practice: PE 9-12

12 *CICA Handbook–Accounting, 2013*, Part I, IAS 36, para. 12, and Part II, Section 3064.73.

NEL

WHEN DOES GOODWILL BECOME WORTHLESS?

The timing and amount of goodwill write-offs can be very subjective. Managers and their accountants should fairly estimate the value of goodwill and record goodwill impairment when it occurs. It is unethical to delay a write-down of goodwill when it is determined that the asset is impaired.

 6

Describe how depreciation and amortization expense and impairment losses are reported in an income statement and prepare a balance sheet that includes property, plant, and equipment and other long-term assets.

Financial Reporting for Property, Plant, and Equipment and Other Long-Term Assets

In the income statement, depreciation expense, amortization expense, and impairment losses should be reported or disclosed in a note. A description of the methods used in computing these expenses should also be reported.

In the balance sheet, each class of long-term assets should be disclosed on the face of the statement or in the notes. The related accumulated depreciation or amortization or impairment losses should also be disclosed, either by class or in total. The assets may be shown at their carrying amount (cost less accumulated depreciation or amortization less accumulated impairment losses), which can also be described as their *net* amount. If the assets are shown at their carrying amount, then details of the accumulated depreciation, amortization, and impairment losses should be disclosed in the notes.

If there are many classes of assets, a single amount may be presented in the balance sheet, supported by a note with a separate listing.

Intangible assets are usually reported in the balance sheet in a separate section following property, plant, and equipment. Natural resources are normally shown as part of the property, plant, and equipment sections. Goodwill should be presented as a separate line item on the balance sheet.

Under IFRS, a company may choose to report some or all of its property, plant, and equipment at fair value. An example of an increase in the fair value of a long-term asset is shown on the IFRS version of Morning Java's financial statements in Appendix A.

The balance sheet presentation for Morning Java's property, plant, and equipment and intangible assets is shown below.

Morning Java
Balance Sheet
December 31, 2015

Property, plant, and equipment:			
Buildings	$2,650,000		
Less accumulated depreciation	420,000	$2,230,000	
Office equipment	350,000		
Less accumulated depreciation	102,000	248,000	
Land		1,850,000	
Total property, plant, and equipment			$4,328,000
Intangible assets:			
Patents	160,000		
Less accumulated amortization	20,000		140,000

FINANCIAL ANALYSIS AND INTERPRETATION f·a·i

Long-term assets can be evaluated by their ability to generate income. The **return on assets** ratio measures the profitability of total assets used within the company and is computed as follows:

$$\text{Return on Assets} = \frac{\text{Net Income}}{\text{Average Total Assets}}$$

To illustrate, the following information is used for WestJet:

	December 31, 2011 (in millions)	December 31, 2010 (in millions)
Total assets	$3,474	$3,384
Net income	149	

Thus, the return on assets ratio is calculated as follows:

$$\text{Return to Assets} = \frac{\$149}{(\$3,384 + \$3,474)/2} = 4.3\%$$

The larger this ratio, the more efficiently a business is using its assets. This ratio can be compared across time within a single company or to other companies in the industry to evaluate overall asset performance.

The return on assets for a number of different companies is shown below. The smaller ratios are associated with companies that require large investments in long-term assets. The larger ratios are associated with firms that are more labour intensive and require smaller investments in long-term assets.

Company (Industry)	Return on Assets
Canadian Pacific Railway Ltd. (railroad)	4.7%
Google Inc. (Internet)	17.3%
Tim Hortons Inc. (restaurant)	28.3%

EXAMPLE EXERCISE 9-13 Return on Assets Ratio   6

Shown below is information for Broadwater Company for the years ended December 31 (in thousands).

	2014	2013	2012
Total assets	$28,620	$20,250	$19,780
Net income	2,534	2,311	

a. Determine the return on assets ratio for 2014 and 2013.

b. Does the change in the return on assets ratio from 2013 to 2014 indicate a favourable or an unfavourable trend?

FOLLOW MY EXAMPLE 9-13

a. Return on assets ratio:

Net income	$2,534	$2,311
Average total assets	$24,435 [($28,620 + $20,250)/2]	$20,015 [($19,780 + $20,250)/2]
Return on assets ratio	10.4% ($2,534 ÷ $24,435)	11.5% ($2,311 ÷ $20,015)

b. The decrease in the return on assets ratio from 11.5% to 10.4% indicates an unfavourable trend in the efficiency of using long-term assets to generate a profit.

For Practice: PE 9-13

At a Glance 9

1 Define, classify, and account for the cost of property, plant, and equipment.

Key Points	Key Learning Outcomes	Page	Example Exercises
Property, plant, and equipment are long-term tangible assets that are owned by the business and are used in the normal operations of the business, such as equipment, buildings, and land. The initial cost of an asset includes all amounts spent to get the asset in place and ready for use. Under IFRS, a company may choose to use either the cost model or the revaluation model. Revenue expenditures include ordinary repairs and maintenance. Capital expenditures include asset improvements.	• Define property, plant, and equipment.	461	
	• List types of costs that should and should not be included in the asset cost.	462	9-1
	• Describe the cost model and the revaluation model.	463	9-2
	• Compute and journalize a lump-sum asset purchase.	463	
	• Provide examples and journal entries of ordinary repairs and asset improvements.	464	9-3

2 Compute depreciation using the following methods: straight-line method, units-of-production method, and double-declining-balance method.

Key Points	Key Learning Outcomes	Page	Example Exercises
All property, plant, and equipment except land lose their ability to provide services and should be depreciated over time. The three depreciation methods used most often for property, plant, and equipment are straight-line, units-of-production, and double-declining-balance. Depreciation may be revised for changes in an asset's useful life, residual value, or for impairment losses. Such changes affect current and future depreciation.	• Define and describe depreciation.	465	
	• Compute and prepare the journal entry for straight-line depreciation.	466	9-4
	• Compute units-of-production depreciation.	467	9-5
	• Compute double-declining-balance depreciation.	468	9-6
	• Compute depreciation for a partial year.	469	9-7
	• Compare the three depreciation methods.	470	
	• Compute and prepare the journal entry for an impairment loss.	471	9-8
	• Compute revised depreciation for a change in an asset's useful life and residual value.	472	9-9
	• Describe depreciation for income tax purposes.	473	

3 Journalize entries for the disposal of property, plant, and equipment.

Key Points	Key Learning Outcomes	Page	Example Exercises
Assets that are no longer used in operations, because they have been discarded or sold, are removed from the accounts. A gain or loss may result from the transaction.	• Prepare the journal entry for discarding an asset.	474	
	• Prepare journal entries for the sale of an asset.	476	9-10

4 Compute depletion and journalize the entry for amortization of natural resources.

Key Points	Key Learning Outcomes	Page	Example Exercises
The process of transferring the cost of a natural resource to an expense account is called amortization, or depletion.	• Define and describe amortization of natural resources.	477	
	• Compute an amortization rate.	477	9-11
	• Prepare the journal entry to record amortization.	478	9-11

5 Describe the accounting for intangible assets and for goodwill.

Key Points	Key Learning Outcomes	Page	Example Exercises
Long-term assets, such as patents, copyrights, and trademarks, that are without physical attributes but are used in the business, are intangible assets. Because goodwill does not exist separately from the business unit, it is not an intangible asset. The cost of intangible assets should be amortized over the years of the asset's expected usefulness. Goodwill and indefinite-life intangibles are not amortized, but are written down only upon impairment.	• Define, describe, and provide examples of intangible assets.	478	
	• Define goodwill.	479	
	• Prepare a journal entry to amortize the costs of patents, copyrights, and trademarks.	480	9-12
	• Prepare the journal entry to record an impairment loss.	480	9-12

6 Describe how depreciation and amortization expense and impairment losses are reported in an income statement and prepare a balance sheet that includes property, plant, and equipment and other long-term assets.

Key Points	Key Learning Outcomes	Page	Example Exercises
The amount of depreciation expense, amortization expense, and any impairment losses, and the method or methods used in computing these amounts should be disclosed in the financial statements. In addition, each major class of long-term assets should be disclosed, along with the related accumulated depreciation and amortization and any impairment losses.	• Describe and illustrate how property, plant, and equipment, intangible assets, and goodwill are reported in the income statement and balance sheet.	481	
	• Calculate and interpret the return on assets ratio	482	9-13

GLOSSARY

accelerated depreciation method – A depreciation method that provides for a higher depreciation amount in the first year of the asset's use, followed by a gradually declining amount of depreciation. (p. 469)

amortization – The systematic periodic transfer of the cost of natural resources and intangible assets to expense accounts during their expected useful life. (p. 465)

basket purchase – A purchase of a group of assets in one transaction. (p. 463) Also known as a *lump-sum purchase.*

betterments – Costs that increase the output of an asset, lower its operating costs, extend its useful life, or improve the quality of its output. (p. 464) Also known as *capital expenditures.*

book value – The cost of an asset minus any accumulated depreciation or amortization and accumulated impairment losses. (p. 465) Also known as *carrying amount.*

capital cost allowance (CCA) – The term used for depreciation for income tax purposes. (p. 473)

capital expenditures – Costs that increase the output of an asset, lower its operating costs, extend its useful life, or improve the quality of its output. (p. 464) Also known as *betterments.*

carrying amount – The cost of an asset minus any accumulated depreciation or amortization and accumulated impairment losses. (p. 465) Also known as *book value.*

copyright – An exclusive right to publish and sell a literary, artistic, or musical composition. (p. 479)

cost model – The measurement method whereby a long-term asset is carried at its carrying amount. (p. 463)

depletion – The process of transferring the cost of a natural resource

to an expense account. (p. 477) May also be called *amortization.*

depreciable amount – The amount of an asset that will be depreciated, being the cost of an asset, or other amount substituted for cost, less its residual value. (p. 466)

depreciation – The systematic periodic transfer of the cost of a capital asset to an expense account during its expected useful life. (p. 465)

double-declining-balance method – A method of depreciation that provides periodic depreciation expense based on the declining book value of an asset over its estimated life. (p. 468)

fixed assets – Long-term or relatively permanent tangible assets such as equipment, machinery, buildings, and land that are used in the normal business operations. (p. 461) Also known as *property, plant, and equipment* and *tangible capital assets.*

goodwill – An asset that is created from such favourable factors as location, product quality, reputation, and managerial skill. (p. 479)

impairment loss – Condition that exists when the carrying amount of a long-term tangible asset, intangible asset, or goodwill exceeds its fair value. (p. 471)

indefinite life assets – Long-term assets that can potentially exist forever. (p. 479)

intangible assets – Long-term assets that are useful in the operations of a business, are not held for sale, and are without physical qualities. (p. 478)

investment property – Assets that are not used in the normal operations or are no longer used in the business and are held for sale or for capital appreciation. (p. 462)

land improvements – Structural additions to land, such as paving, landscaping, and fencing. (p. 462)

lump-sum purchase – A purchase of a group of assets in one transaction.

(p. 463) Also known as a *basket purchase.*

patents – Exclusive rights to produce and sell goods with one or more unique features. (p. 478)

property, plant, and equipment – Long-term or relatively permanent tangible assets such as equipment, machinery, buildings, and land that are used in the normal business operations. (p. 461) Also known as *tangible capital assets* and *fixed assets.*

residual value – The estimated value of a capital asset at the end of its useful life. (p. 466) Also known as *salvage value, scrap value,* or *trade-in value.*

return on assets – A measure of the profitability of total assets used within a business. (p. 482)

revaluation model – The measurement method that allows a long-term asset to be carried at its fair value (p. 463)

revenue expenditures – Costs that benefit only the current period or costs incurred for normal maintenance and repairs of assets. (p. 464)

straight-line method – A method of depreciation that provides for equal periodic depreciation expense over the estimated life of an asset. (p. 466)

straight-line rate – The rate determined by dividing 100% by the number of years of expected useful life. (p. 467)

tangible capital assets – Long-term or relatively permanent tangible assets such as equipment, machinery, buildings, and land that are used in the normal business operations. (p. 461) Also known as *property, plant, and equipment* and *fixed assets.*

trademark – A name, term, or symbol used to identify a business and its products. (p. 479)

units-of-production method – A method of depreciation that provides for depreciation expense based on the expected productive capacity of an asset. (p. 467)

END-OF-CHAPTER ILLUSTRATIVE PROBLEM

McDonald Company, a furniture wholesaler, acquired new equipment, paying $150,000 cash on January 10, 2013. The equipment has an estimated life of five years and an estimated residual value of $10,000. At the end of 2015, McDonald's accountant determined that the equipment's value had declined by $20,000 and that the asset would likely be used for another three years. On January 7, 2018, the equipment was sold for $15,000.

Instructions

1. Journalize the following entries:
   a. purchase of the equipment
   b. depreciation at the end of 2013
   c. impairment loss in 2015
   d. depreciation at the end of 2016
   e. sale of the equipment in 2018
2. Show the balance sheet presentation for the equipment as at December 31, 2015, and December 31, 2016.

Solution

1.

a.	2013 Jan. 10	Equipment	150,000	
		Cash		150,000
b.	Dec. 31	Depreciation Expense	28,000	
		Accumulated Depreciation—Equipment		28,000
		[($150,000 − $10,000)/5]		
c.	2015 Dec. 31	Impairment Loss	20,000	
		Accumulated Depreciation—Equipment		20,000
d.	2016 Dec. 31	Depreciation Expense	12,000	
		Accumulated Depreciation—Equipment		12,000
		[($150,000 − ($28,000 × 3 years) − $20,000 − $10,000)/3 years]		
e.	2018 Jan. 7	Cash	15,000	
		Accumulated Depreciation—Equipment	128,000*	
		Loss on Sale of Equipment	7,000	
		Equipment		150,000
		*[($28,000 × 3 years) + $20,000 + ($12,000 × 2 years)]		

2.

	2016	2015
Equipment	$150,000	$150,000
Less accumulated depreciation	(116,000)	(104,000)
Equipment, net	$ 34,000	$ 46,000

EYE OPENERS

1. Which of the following describe characteristics of property, plant, and equipment? (a) tangible, (b) capable of repeated use in the operations of the business, (c) held for sale in the normal course of business, (d) used rarely in the operations of the business, (e) long term.

2. Mancini Office Supplies has a fleet of automobiles and trucks for use by salespersons and for delivery of office supplies and equipment. East Village Auto Sales Co. has automobiles and trucks for sale. Under what caption would the automobiles and trucks be reported in the balance sheet of (a) Mancini Office Supplies and (b) East Village Auto Sales Co.?

3. Just Animals Co. acquired an adjacent vacant lot with the hope of selling it in the future at a gain. The lot is not intended to be used in Just Animals' business operations. Where should such real estate be listed in the balance sheet?

4. My Mother's Closet Company solicited bids from several contractors to construct an addition to its office building. The lowest bid received was for $375,000.

My Mother's Closet Company decided to construct the addition itself at a cost of $298,500. What amount should be recorded in the building account?

5. Distinguish between the accounting for capital expenditures and for revenue expenditures.

6. Immediately after a used truck is acquired, a new motor is installed at a total cost of $3,175. Is this cost a capital expenditure or a revenue expenditure?

7. Are long-term assets reported in the balance sheet at their approximate market values as at the date of the balance sheet? Discuss.

8. a. Does the recognition of depreciation in the accounts provide a special cash fund for the replacement of the assets? Explain.

   b. Describe the nature of depreciation as the term is used in accounting.

9. Pac Vac Company purchased a machine that has a manufacturer's suggested life of 15 years. The company plans to use the machine on a special project that will last 12 years. At the completion of the project, the machine will be sold. Over how many years should the machine be depreciated?

10. Is it necessary for a business to use the same method of computing depreciation (a) for all classes of its depreciable assets and (b) for financial statement purposes and in determining income taxes?

11. Under what conditions is the use of an accelerated depreciation method most appropriate?

12. Distinguish between the accounting for impairment losses under IFRS and under ASPE. How do IFRS and ASPE account for impairment losses for goodwill?

13. For some of the long-term assets of a business, the balance in Accumulated Depreciation is exactly equal to the cost of the asset. (a) Is it permissible to record additional depreciation on the assets if they are still useful to the business? Explain. (b) When should an entry be made to remove the cost and the accumulated depreciation from the accounts?

14. a. Over what period of time should the cost of a patent acquired by purchase be amortized?

    b. How should goodwill be amortized?

    c. Why is goodwill not an intangible asset?

PRACTICE EXERCISES

① PE 9-1
Classifying costs

EE 9-1 p. 462

During June 2014, Green Grocer Inc. decided to build a new warehouse and purchased land for $850,000. By the end of the month, $72,000 has been spent on excavation costs, $12,000 on paving, and $30,000 on architect-developed plans. Green Grocer Inc. also spent $400 to replace a tree on a neighbouring property that was damaged by the excavator. Determine the amounts to be allocated to the various accounts, using Construction in Progress for the new building costs.

---

① PE 9-2
Lump-sum purchase

EE 9-2 p. 463

On October 11, 2014, Usher Company purchased a building for $2,250,000. The building, land, and land improvements were valued at $1,440,000, $840,000, and $120,000 respectively. Prepare the journal entry for the lump-sum purchase.

---

① PE 9-3
Capital and revenue expenditures

EE 9-3 p. 465

On May 27, Linoleum Associates Co. paid $250 to repair the brakes on one of its delivery vans. In addition, Linoleum Associates paid $450 to install a GPS system in its van. Journalize the entries for the brakes and GPS system expenditures.

PE 9-4
Straight-line depreciation

A building acquired on January 1, 2014, at a cost of $485,000, has an estimated residual value of $75,000 and an estimated useful life of 25 years. (a) Determine the annual straight-line depreciation and (b) journalize the end-of-year entry to record depreciation.

EE 9-4 p. 467

PE 9-5
Units-of-production depreciation

A truck acquired at a cost of $134,000 has an estimated residual value of $35,000 and an estimated useful life of 300,000 kilometres and was driven 52,000 kilometres during the first year and 48,000 kilometres during the second year. Determine (a) the depreciable cost, (b) the depreciation per unit, and (c) the depreciation expense for the first year and (d) for the second year.

EE 9-5 p. 468

PE 9-6
Double-declining-balance depreciation

A building acquired at the beginning of the year at a cost of $650,000 has an estimated residual value of $125,000 and an estimated useful life of 40 years. Determine (a) the double-declining-balance rate and (b) the double-declining-balance depreciation for the first year and (c) for the second year.

EE 9-6 p. 469

PE 9-7
Double-declining-balance method for partial years

Refer to the information in PE 9-6. Assume the building was acquired on April 8, 2014. Determine (a) the double-declining-balance rate and (b) the double-declining-balance depreciation for the first year and (c) for the second year.

EE 9-7 p. 470

PE 9-8
Impairment loss of long-term assets

In January 2010, Trenton Tents Ltd. paid $345,000 for equipment that had an estimated useful life of 16 years and an expected residual value of $25,000. At the end of 2014, an appraisal of the equipment indicated a market value of $200,000 and a residual value of $13,000. Determine (a) the annual depreciation expense to 2014 and (b) the equipment's carrying amount at December 31, 2014. (c) Journalize the impairment loss.

EE 9-8 p. 472

PE 9-9
Revision of depreciation

Equipment with a cost of $250,000 has an estimated residual value of $34,000 and an estimated useful life of 18 years and is depreciated by the straight-line method. (a) Determine the amount of the annual depreciation. (b) Determine the carrying amount at the end of the 10th year of use. (c) Assuming that at the start of the 11th year, the remaining life is estimated to be nine years, and the residual value is estimated to be $26,500, determine the depreciation expense for each of the remaining nine years.

EE 9-9 p. 473

PE 9-10
Sale of equipment

Equipment was acquired at the beginning of the year at a cost of $324,000. The equipment was depreciated using the double-declining-balance method based on an estimated useful life of eight years and an estimated residual value of $43,000.

a. What was the depreciation for the first year?
b. Assuming the equipment was sold at the end of the second year for $200,000, determine the gain or loss on the sale of the equipment.
c. Journalize the entry to record the sale.

EE 9-10 p. 477

PE 9-11
④
Amortization of natural resource

Montana Mining Co. acquired mineral rights for $120,000,000. The mineral deposit is estimated at 200,000,000 tonnes. During the current year, 31,155,000 tonnes were mined and sold.

a. Determine the amortization rate.
b. Determine the amount of amortization expense for the current year.
EE 9-11 p. 478   c. Journalize the adjusting entry on December 31 to recognize the amortization expense.

PE 9-12
⑤
Impaired goodwill and amortization of patent

On December 31, it was estimated that goodwill of $500,000 was impaired. In addition, a patent with an estimated useful economic life of eight years was acquired for $388,000 on July 1.

a. Journalize the adjusting entry on December 31 for the impaired goodwill.
b. Journalize the adjusting entry on December 31 for the amortization of the patent rights.

EE 9-12 p. 480

PE 9-13
⑥
Return on assets ratio

f·a·i

Fallon Company had the following information for the years ended December 31.

	2014	2013	2012
Total assets	$5,620,000	$4,250,000	$3,780,000
Net income	$ 234,000	$ 211,000	

a. Determine the return on assets ratio for 2014 and 2013.
b. Does the change in the return on assets ratio from 2013 to 2014 indicate a favourable or unfavourable trend?

EE 9-13 p. 482

EXERCISES

EX 9-1
①
Costs of acquiring property, plant, and equipment

Les Bancroft owns and operates Crown Print Co. During February, Crown Print Co. incurred the following costs in acquiring a printing press.

Costs related to the new printing press:

1. Provincial sales tax on purchase price
2. Freight
3. Special foundation
4. Insurance while in transit
5. New parts to replace those damaged in unloading
6. Fee paid to factory representative for installation.

Indicate which costs incurred in acquiring the new printing press should be debited to the asset account.

EX 9-2
①
Costs of acquiring property, plant, and equipment

Able Warehousing Co. decided to tear down and rebuild one of its storage units. The company spent $50,000 constructing the new storage units, $3,000 on paving, and $1,200 on new landscaping. Able Warehousing sold scrap materials from the old storage units to the building contractor for $900. Able Warehousing also spent $500 to repair damage done to an employee's truck during teardown of the old storage units. Determine the amounts to be allocated to various accounts.

EX 9-3
①
Determine cost of land

Alpine Ski Co. has developed a tract of land into a ski resort. The company has cut the trees, cleared and graded the land and hills, and constructed ski lifts. (a) Should the tree cutting, land clearing, and grading costs of constructing the ski slopes be debited to the land account? (b) If such costs are debited to Land, should they be depreciated?

EX 9-4
Determine cost of land

Discount Delivery Company acquired an adjacent lot to construct a new warehouse, paying $25,000 and giving a short-term note for $300,000. Legal fees paid were $2,100, grading and levelling costs were $14,000, and fees paid to remove an old building from the land were $9,000. Materials salvaged from the demolition of the building were sold for $3,500. A contractor was paid $800,000 to construct a new warehouse. Determine the cost of the land to be reported on the balance sheet.

EX 9-5
Lump-sum purchase

On April 17, 2014, Sanford Printing Co. Ltd. purchased a printing operation in Newmarket, Ontario, paying $1,450,000 in total. The purchase included a building valued at $800,000, land valued at $600,000, and printing presses valued at $200,000. Prepare the journal entry for the lump-sum purchase.

EX 9-6
Lump-sum purchase

Crane Company purchased a company on November 11, 2014, paying $1,150,000 for assets with the following fair values:

Asset	Fair Value
Land	$ 200,000
Buildings	350,000
Factory equipment	550,000
Office equipment	150,000
Total	$1,250,000

Prepare the journal entry for the lump-sum purchase.

EX 9-7
Capital and revenue expenditures

Link Lines Co. incurred the following costs related to trucks and vans used in operating its delivery service:

1. Replaced a truck's suspension system with a new suspension system that allows for the delivery of heavier loads.
2. Installed a hydraulic lift to a van.
3. Repaired a flat tire on one of the vans.
4. Removed a two-way radio from one of the trucks and installed a new radio with a greater range of communication.
5. Tinted the back and side windows of one of the vans to discourage theft of contents.
6. Changed the oil and greased the joints of all the trucks and vans.
7. Installed security systems on four of the newer trucks.

Classify each of the costs as a capital expenditure or a revenue expenditure.

EX 9-8
Capital and revenue expenditures

John Shaw owns and operates Shaw Transport Co. During the past year, John incurred the following costs related to an 18-wheel truck:

1. Changed engine oil.
2. Installed a wind deflector on top of the cab to increase fuel efficiency.
3. Replaced fog and cab light bulbs.
4. Modified the factory-installed turbo charger with a special-order kit designed to improve engine performance.
5. Replaced a headlight that had burned out.
6. Replaced the hydraulic brake system that had begun to fail during his latest trip through the Rocky Mountains.
7. Installed a television in the sleeping compartment of the truck.

Classify each of the costs as a capital expenditure or a revenue expenditure.

EX 9-9
Capital and revenue expenditures

Reliable Move Company made the following expenditures on one of its delivery trucks:

Feb. 16.   Replaced transmission at a cost of $4,300.
Jul. 15.   Paid $1,000 for installation of a hydraulic lift.
Oct. 3.   Paid $60 to change the oil and air filter.

Prepare journal entries for each expenditure.

② EX 9-10
Nature of depreciation

Butterfield Ironworks Co. reported $7,500,000 for equipment and $6,175,000 for accumulated depreciation—equipment on its balance sheet.

Does this mean (a) that the replacement cost of the equipment is $7,500,000 and (b) that $6,175,000 is set aside in a special fund for the replacement of the equipment? Explain to welders who have no accounting background what depreciation is.

---

② EX 9-11
Straight-line depreciation rates

Convert each of the following estimates of useful life to a straight-line depreciation rate, stated as a percentage: (a) 4 years, (b) 8 years, (c) 10 years, (d) 25 years, (e) 40 years, (f) 50 years.

---

② EX 9-12
Straight-line depreciation

A refrigerator used by a meat processor has a cost of $93,750, an estimated residual value of $10,000, and an estimated useful life of 25 years. What is the amount of the annual depreciation computed by the straight-line method?

---

② EX 9-13
Depreciation by units-of-production method

A diesel-powered tractor with a cost of $145,000 and estimated residual value of $7,000 is expected to have a useful operating life of 75,000 hours. During July, the generator was operated 150 hours. Determine the depreciation for the month.

---

② EX 9-14
Depreciation by units-of-production method

Prior to adjustment at the end of the year, the balance in Trucks is $275,900 and the balance in Accumulated Depreciation—Trucks is $91,350. Details of the subsidiary ledger are as follows:

Truck No.	Cost	Estimated Residual Value	Estimated Useful Life (in kilometres)	Accumulated Depreciation at Beginning of Year	Kilometres Operated During Year
1	$75,000	$15,000	200,000	—	19,500
2	38,000	3,000	200,000	$ 8,050	36,000
3	72,900	9,900	300,000	60,900	25,000
4	90,000	20,000	250,000	22,400	26,000

a. Determine the depreciation rates per kilometre and the amount to be credited to the accumulated depreciation section of each of the subsidiary accounts for the kilometres operated during the current year.

b. Journalize the entry to record depreciation for the year.

---

② EX 9-15
Depreciation by two methods

A Kubota tractor acquired on January 9 at a cost of $80,000 has an estimated useful life of 20 years. Assuming that it will have no residual value, determine the depreciation for each of the first two years (a) by the straight-line method and (b) by the double-declining-balance method. Journalize the entries to record depreciation for each of the first two years by the double-declining-balance method.

---

② ⑥ EX 9-16
Depreciation by two methods

A storage tank acquired at the beginning of the fiscal year at a cost of $344,000 has an estimated residual value of $50,000 and an estimated useful life of 16 years. Determine the following: (a) the amount of annual depreciation by the straight-line method and (b) the amount of depreciation for the first and second years computed by the double-declining-balance method. Show the balance sheet presentation for the storage tank for the first two years by the straight-line method.

---

② EX 9-17
Partial-year depreciation

Sandblasting equipment acquired at a cost of $85,000 has an estimated residual value of $5,000 and an estimated useful life of 10 years. It was placed in service on October 11 of the current fiscal year, which ends on December 31. Determine the depreciation for the current fiscal year and for the following fiscal year by (a) the straight-line method

(*continued*)

and (b) the double-declining-balance method. Journalize the entries to record depreciation for each of the first two years by the straight-line method.

EX 9-18

(2) (6)

Partial-year depreciation by three methods

A printing press acquired at a cost of $880,000 has an estimated useful life of 10 years, or 75,000 hours, and an expected residual value of $40,000. The press was put into operation on May 21, 2013. Determine the depreciation for 2013 and 2014 by (a) the straight-line method, (b) the double-declining-balance method, and (c) the unit-of-production method, assuming the press operated for 3,000 hours in 2013 and 7,000 hours in 2014. The company has a December 31 year-end. Show the balance sheet presentation for the printing press for 2013 and 2014, using the units-of-production method.

EX 9-19

(2)

Revision of depreciation

A building with a cost of $900,000 has an estimated residual value of $250,000, an estimated useful life of 40 years, and is depreciated by the straight-line method. (a) What is the amount of the annual depreciation? (b) What is the carrying amount at the end of the 24th year of use? (c) If at the start of the 25th year it is estimated that the remaining life is nine years and that the residual value is $240,000, what is the depreciation expense for each of the remaining nine years?

EX 9-20

(2)

Revision of depreciation and impairment loss

Farm equipment with a cost of $225,000 has an estimated residual value of $15,000, an estimated useful life of six years, and is depreciated by the straight-line method.

a. What is the amount of annual depreciation?
b. What is the carrying amount at the end of the fourth year of use?
c. At the start of the fifth year, $25,000 is spent on an engine upgrade so that the remaining useful life is four years and the estimated residual value is $5,000. What is the depreciation expense for the fifth year?
d. At the start of the sixth year, the appraised value of the farm equipment is $60,000. What is the impairment loss?

EX 9-21

(3)

Entries for sale of property, plant, and equipment

Equipment acquired on January 3, 2012, at a cost of $380,000, has an estimated useful life of 16 years, an estimated residual value of $40,000, and is depreciated by the straight-line method.

a. What was the carrying amount of the equipment at December 31, 2015, the end of the fiscal year?

b. Assuming that the equipment was sold on July 1, 2016, for $270,000, journalize the entries to record (1) depreciation for the six months until the sale date and (2) the sale of the equipment.

EX 9-22

(3)

Entries of sale of property, plant, and equipment

Equipment acquired on January 11, 2012, at a cost of $265,500, has an estimated useful life of eight years and an estimated residual value of $31,500.

a. What was the total amount of depreciation for the years 2012, 2013, and 2014, using the straight-line method of depreciation?
b. What was the carrying amount of the equipment on January 1, 2015?
c. Assuming that the equipment was sold on January 4, 2015, for $168,500, journalize the entry to record the sale.
d. Assuming that the equipment had been sold on January 4, 2015, for $180,000 instead of $168,500, journalize the entry to record the sale.

4 **EX 9-23**
Natural resources

Ashwood Mining Co. acquired mineral rights for $15,000,000. The mineral deposit is estimated at 120,000,000 tonnes. During the current year, 24,000,000 tonnes were mined and sold.

a. Determine the amount of amortization expense for the current year.

b. Journalize the adjusting entry to recognize the amortization expense.

5 **EX 9-24**
Intangible assets

Greanleaf Company acquired patent rights on January 4, 2012, for $300,000. The patent has a useful life equal to its legal life of 12 years. On January 7, 2015, Greanleaf successfully defended the patent in a lawsuit at a cost of $72,000.

a. Determine the patent amortization expense for the current year ended December 31, 2015.

b. Journalize the adjusting entry to recognize the amortization.

6 **EX 9-25**
Carrying amount of long-term assets

The following information was taken from an annual report of Falconer Corporation, a manufacturer and wholesaler of farm equipment:

Property, Plant, and Equipment (in millions):

	2015	2014
Land and buildings	2,060	1,470
Machinery	6,926	3,590
Office furniture and equipment	184	144
Leasehold improvements	2,600	2,030
Accumulated depreciation and amortization	(3,990)	(2,465)

a. Compute the carrying amount of the assets for the current year and the preceding year and explain the differences, if any.

b. What transactions cause the carrying amount of long-term assets to increase or decrease during the year?

c. Would you normally expect the carrying amount of long-term assets to increase or decrease during the year?

6 **EX 9-26**
Balance sheet presentation

List the errors you find in the following property, plant, and equipment note to the financial statements:

Note xx:

	Replacement Cost	Accumulated Amortization	Carrying Amount
Property, plant, and equipment:			
Land	$ 60,000	$ 12,000	$ 48,000
Buildings...........................	156,000	45,600	110,400
Factory equipment	330,000	175,200	154,800
Office equipment	72,000	48,000	24,000
Patents	48,000	—	48,000
Goodwill	27,000	3,000	24,000
Total property, plant, and equipment....................	$693,000	$283,800	$409,200

6 **EX 9-27**
Return on assets ratio

Rogers Communications is a major telecommunications company in Canada. Rogers' balance sheet disclosed the following information:

(continued)

	Dec. 31, 2010 (in millions)	Dec. 31, 2009 (in millions)
Net income	$ 1,528	$ 1,478
Total assets	17,330	17,018

Rogers' total assets for 2008 were $17,082 million. The return on assets ratio for the telecommunications industry averages –1.867%.

a. Determine Rogers' return on assets ratio for 2010 and 2009. Round to two decimal places.

b. Has Rogers' return on assets ratio improved since 2009? Is it using its assets more or less efficiently than other telecommunications companies?

---

6 **EX 9-28**

Return on assets ratio

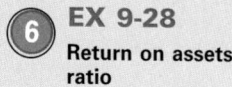

The following table shows the net income and average total assets (in millions) for a recent fiscal year for RONA inc. and Canadian Tire Corporation, Limited:

	Net Income	Average Total Assets
RONA	$143	$2,862
Canadian Tire	454	8,818

a. Compute the return on assets ratio for each company. Round to two decimal places.

b. Which company uses its assets more efficiently? Explain.

PROBLEMS SERIES A

1 **PR 9-1A**

Allocate payments and receipts to asset accounts

✔ Land, $390,500

The following payments and receipts are related to land, land improvements, and buildings acquired for use in a wholesale ceramic business. The receipts are identified by an asterisk.

a.	Fee paid to lawyer for title search	$ 3,000
b.	Cost of real estate acquired as a plant site: Land	320,000
	Building	30,000
c.	Special assessment paid to city for extension of water main to the property	18,000
d.	Cost of razing and removing building	5,000
e.	Proceeds from sale of salvage materials from old building	3,000*
f.	Advertising costs for announcing new location	12,000
g.	Premium on one-year insurance policy during construction	4,200
h.	Cost of filling and grading land	17,500
i.	Architect's and engineer's fees for plans and supervision	44,000
j.	Money borrowed to pay building contractor	750,000*
k.	Cost of repairing windstorm damage during construction	5,500
l.	Cost of paving parking lot to be used by customers	15,000
m.	Cost of trees and shrubbery planted	9,000
n.	Cost of floodlights installed on parking lot	1,000
o.	Cost of repairing vandalism damage during construction	2,500
p.	Proceeds from insurance company for windstorm and vandalism damage	6,000*
q.	Payment to building contractor for new building	800,000
r.	Interest incurred on building loan during construction	37,500

Instructions

1. Assign each payment and receipt to Land, Land Improvements, Building, or Other Accounts. Indicate receipts by an asterisk. Identify each item by letter and list the amounts in columnar form, as follows:

Item	Land	Land Improvements	Building	Other Accounts

2. Determine the amount debited to Land, Land Improvements, and Building.
3. The costs assigned to the land, which is used as a plant site, will not be depreciated, while the costs assigned to land improvements will be depreciated. Explain this seemingly contradictory application of the concept of depreciation.
4. What would be the effect on the income statement and balance sheet if the cost of filling and grading land of $17,500 [payment (h)] was incorrectly classified as Land Improvements rather than Land? Assume Land Improvements are depreciated over a 20-year life using the double-declining-balance method.

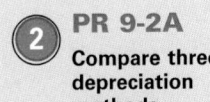

PR 9-2A

Compare three depreciation methods

✔ 1.b. 2014: $31,500

Breyer Company purchased packaging equipment on January 3, 2013, for $101,250. The equipment was expected to have a useful life of three years, or 25,000 operating hours, and a residual value of $7,500. The equipment was used for 9,500 hours during 2013, 8,400 hours in 2014, and 7,100 hours in 2015.

Instructions

1. Determine the amount of depreciation expense for the years ended December 31, 2013, 2014, and 2015, by (a) the straight-line method, (b) the units-of-production method, and (c) the double-declining-balance method. The following columnar headings are suggested for recording the depreciation expense amounts:

	Depreciation Expense		
Year	Straight-Line Method	Units-of-Production Method	Double-Declining-Balance Method

2. What method yields the highest depreciation expense for 2013?
3. What method yields the most depreciation over the three-year life of the equipment?

PR 9-3A

Depreciation by three methods; partial years

✔ a. 2013, $7,600

Razar Sharp Company purchased tool-sharpening equipment on July 1, 2013, for $48,600. The equipment was expected to have a useful life of three years, or 7,500 operating hours, and a residual value of $3,000. The equipment was used for 1,800 hours during 2013, 2,600 hours in 2014, 2,000 hours in 2015, and 1,100 hours in 2016.

Instructions

Determine the amount of depreciation expense for the years ended December 31, 2013, 2014, 2015, and 2016, by (a) the straight-line method, (b) the units-of-production method, and (c) the double-declining-balance method.

PR 9-4A

Depreciation by two methods; sale of asset

✔ b. Year 1: $315,000 depreciation expense

New lithographic equipment, acquired at a cost of $787,500 at the beginning of a fiscal year, has an estimated useful life of five years and an estimated residual value of $67,500. The manager requested information regarding the effect of alternative methods on the amount of depreciation expense each year. On the basis of the data presented to the manager, the double-declining-balance method was selected.

In the first week of the fifth year, the equipment was sold for $115,000.

Instructions

1. Determine the annual depreciation expense for each of the estimated five years of use, the accumulated depreciation at the end of each year, and the carrying amount of the equipment at the end of each year by (a) the straight-line method and (b) the double-declining-balance method. The following columnar headings are suggested for each schedule:

Year	Depreciation Expense	Accumulated Depreciation, End of Year	Carrying Amount, End of Year

2. Journalize the entry to record the sale.
3. Journalize the entry to record the sale, assuming that the equipment was sold for $98,900 instead of $115,000.

PR 9-5A

Transactions for property, plant, and equipment, including sale

✔ July 30, 2014, gain on sale of equipment, $2,766

The following transactions and adjusting entries were completed by Kitchener Furniture Co. during a two-year period. All are related to the use of delivery equipment. The double-declining-balance method of depreciation is used.

2013
Feb. 7. Purchased a used delivery truck for $30,000, paying cash.
     27. Paid garage $130 for changing the oil, replacing the oil filter, and tuning the engine on the delivery truck.
Dec. 31. Recorded depreciation on the truck for the fiscal year. The estimated useful life of the truck is eight years, with a residual value of $10,000.

2014
Mar. 8. Purchased a new truck for $75,000, paying cash.
     13. Paid garage $200 to tune the engine and make other minor repairs on the used truck.
Jul. 30. Sold the used truck for $23,000. (Record depreciation to date in 2014 for the truck.)
Dec. 31. Recorded depreciation for the new truck. It has an estimated trade-in value of $13,500 and an estimated life of 10 years.

Instructions

Journalize the transactions and the adjusting entries. (Hint: Treat all purchases and sales as if they occurred on the first day of the month.)

PR 9-6A

Transactions for long-term assets, including revision of depreciation and sale

✔ Dec. 31, 2013, Depreciation expense–equipment, $21,170

The following transactions and adjusting entries were completed by Brand Construction Co. over a two-year period. The company has a December 31 year-end and records depreciation on an annual basis.

2013
Feb. 25. Purchased equipment for $125,000 and office furniture for $23,040.
Mar. 5. Paid garage $525 for maintenance of the equipment.
Apr. 25. Installed air-conditioning unit for the equipment, paying $2,020.
Dec. 31. Recorded depreciation on the equipment for the fiscal year, using the double-declining-balance method. The estimated useful life of the equipment is 10 years, with a residual value of $20,000. Recorded depreciation on the office furniture using the straight-line method, assuming an estimated life of 12 years and no residual value.

2014
May 10. Paid $150 to repair minor water damage to furniture due to a burst pipe in the office.
Dec. 31. Recorded depreciation on the office furniture, which is now expected to have a useful life of 10 years. Recorded depreciation on the equipment.

Instructions

1. Journalize the transactions and the adjusting entries.
2. Journalize the entry to record the sale of the office furniture, assuming it is sold on July 10, 2020, for $5,000.

PR 9-7A

Amortization and impairment entries

✔ 1. b. $33,750

Data related to the acquisition of timber rights and intangible assets during the current year ended December 31 are as follows:

a. On December 31, the company determined that $20,000,000 of goodwill was impaired.

b. Governmental and legal costs of $675,000 were incurred on July 30 in obtaining a patent with an estimated economic life of 10 years.

c. Timber rights on a tract of land were purchased for $1,665,000 on February 16. The stand of timber is estimated at 9,000,000 board feet. During the current year, 2,400,000 board feet of timber were cut and sold.

Instructions

1. Determine the amount of the amortization or impairment for the current year for each of the foregoing items. (Hint: Treat all purchases and sales as if they occurred on the first day of the month.)
2. Journalize the adjusting entries to record the amortization or impairment for each item.

---

②③④⑤⑥ PR 9-8A

Transactions for tangible assets, intangible assets, and goodwill, including impairment entries and sale

✔ Furniture and equipment, net, Dec. 31, 2015, $163,900

Stark Communications Ltd. had the following account balances on January 1, 2015:

	Cost	Accumulated Depreciation/Amortization
Land	$ 500,000	
Building	1,350,000	528,000
Furniture and equipment	240,000	100,000
Artist contracts	4,000,000	2,400,000
Goodwill	6,600,000	

During the year, the corporation completed the following transactions and adjusting entries affecting long-term assets.

Mar. 10. Purchased an artist contract from another company for $900,000.

Jul. 5. Sold furniture for $15,000 that was purchased on January 5, 2010, at a cost of $42,000. The furniture was depreciated on a straight-line basis over 10 years with an expected residual value of $4,000. (Record depreciation to date of sale.)

Sep. 12. Purchased recording equipment for $69,000.

Dec. 31. The recording industry is experiencing a minor recession. Stark's accountant feels the carrying amount of the business exceeds its fair value by $500,000.

31. Recorded depreciation on the building using the straight-line method, assuming an estimated useful life of 10 years and a residual value of $250,000.

31. Recorded depreciation on the furniture and equipment using the straight-line method, assuming an estimated useful life of 10 years and no residual value.

31. Recorded amortization on the artists' contracts using the double-declining-balance method, assuming an estimated life of 10 years and a $1,000,000 residual value.

Instructions

1. Journalize the transactions and the adjusting entries.
2. Prepare the balance sheet presentation for Stark Communications' long-term assets as at December 31, 2015, with comparative amounts for December 31, 2014.

---

⑥ PR 9-9A

Financial reporting for long-term assets

✔ Property, plant, and equipment, $2,645,400

At August 31, 2015, the end of the current fiscal year, Beady Engineering Inc. had the following account balances:

	Cost	Accumulated Depreciation/Amortization
Building	$2,350,000	624,000
Furniture and equipment	267,000	97,600
Land	750,000	
Patents	2,800,000	2,080,000
Goodwill	2,650,000	

Instructions

Prepare the balance sheet presentation for Beady Engineering Inc.'s long-term assets.

PROBLEMS SERIES B

PR 9-1B

Allocate payments and receipts to asset accounts

✔ Land, $582,500

The following payments and receipts are related to land, land improvements, and buildings acquired for use in a wholesale apparel business. The receipts are identified by an asterisk.

a.	Finder's fee paid to real estate agency.	$ 5,000
b.	Cost of real estate acquired as a plant site: Land.	500,000
	Building	40,000
c.	Fee paid to lawyer for title search	2,500
d.	Advertising costs for announcing new location.	15,000
e.	Architect's and engineer's fees for plans and supervision	36,000
f.	Cost of removing building purchased with land in (b)	10,000
g.	Proceeds from sale of salvage materials from old building.	4,000*
h.	Cost of filling and grading land.	20,000
i.	Premium on one-year insurance policy during construction	6,000
j.	Money borrowed to pay building contractor	750,000*
k.	Special assessment paid to city for extension of water main to the property. . . .	9,000
l.	Cost of repairing windstorm damage during construction.	3,000
m.	Cost of repairing vandalism damage during construction	2,000
n.	Cost of trees and shrubbery planted	12,000
o.	Cost of paving parking lot to be used by customers.	14,500
p.	Interest incurred on building loan during construction	45,000
q.	Proceeds from insurance company for windstorm and vandalism damage.	3,000*
r.	Payment to building contractor for new building.	800,000

Instructions

1. Assign each payment and receipt to Land, Land Improvements, Building, or Other Accounts. Indicate receipts by an asterisk. Identify each item by letter and list the amounts in columnar form, as follows:

Item	Land	Land Improvements	Building	Other Accounts

2. Determine the amount debited to Land, Land Improvements, and Building.
3. The costs assigned to the land, which is used as a plant site, will not be depreciated, while the costs assigned to land improvements will be depreciated. Explain this seemingly contradictory application of the concept of depreciation.
4. What would be the effect on the income statement and balance sheet if the cost of paving the parking lot of $14,500 [payment (o)] was incorrectly classified as Land rather than Land Improvements? Assume Land Improvements are depreciated over a 10-year life using the double-declining-balance method.

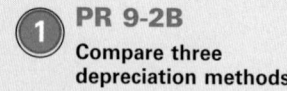

PR 9-2B

Compare three depreciation methods

✔ 1.c. 2015, $112,500

Plum Coatings Company purchased waterproofing equipment on January 2, 2014, for $450,000. The equipment was expected to have a useful life of four years, or 10,000 operating hours, and a residual value of $50,000. The equipment was used for 3,000 hours during 2014, 4,000 hours in 2015, 2,500 hours in 2016, and 500 hours in 2017.

Instructions

1. Determine the amount of depreciation expense for the years ended December 31, 2014, 2015, 2016, and 2017, by (a) the straight-line method, (b) the units-of-production method, and (c) the double-declining-balance method. Also determine the total depreciation expense for the four years by each method. The following columnar headings are suggested for recording the depreciation expense amounts:

	Depreciation Expense		
Year	Straight-Line Method	Units-of-Production Method	Double-Declining-Balance Method

2. What method yields the highest depreciation expense for 2014?
3. What method yields the most depreciation over the four-year life of the equipment?

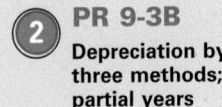

PR 9-3B

Depreciation by three methods; partial years

✔ a. 2013, $2,510

Quality IDs Company purchased plastic laminating equipment on July 1, 2013, for $15,660. The equipment was expected to have a useful life of three years, or 18,825 operating hours, and a residual value of $600. The equipment was used for 3,750 hours during 2013, 7,500 hours in 2014, 5,000 hours in 2015, and 2,575 hours in 2016.

Instructions

Determine the amount of amortization expense for the years ended December 31, 2013, 2014, 2015, and 2016, by (a) the straight-line method, (b) the units-of-production method, and (c) the double-declining-balance method.

PR 9-4B

Depreciation by two methods; sale of asset

✔ 1. b. Year 1, $36,000 depreciation expense

New tire-retreading equipment, acquired at a cost of $72,000 at the beginning of a fiscal year, has an estimated useful life of four years and an estimated residual value of $5,400. The manager requested information regarding the effect of alternative methods on the amount of depreciation expense each year. On the basis of the data presented to the manager, the double-declining-balance method was selected.

In the first week of the fourth year, the equipment was sold for $13,750.

Instructions

1. Determine the annual depreciation expense for each of the estimated four years of use, the accumulated depreciation at the end of each year, and the carrying amount of the equipment at the end of each year by (a) the straight-line method and (b) the double-declining-balance method. The following columnar headings are suggested for each schedule:

Year	Depreciation Expense	Accumulated Depreciation, End of Year	Carrying Amount, End of Year

2. Journalize the entry to record the sale.
3. Journalize the entry to record the sale, assuming that the equipment sold for $3,700 instead of $13,750.

PR 9-5B

Transactions for property, plant, and equipment, including sale

✔ July 1, 2014, loss on sale of equipment, $7,915

The following transactions and adjusting entries were completed by Fraser Furniture Co. during a two-year period. All transactions are related to the use of delivery equipment. The double-declining-balance method of depreciation is used.

2013
Mar. 6. Purchased a used delivery truck for $41,520, paying cash.
Jul. 19. Paid garage $500 for miscellaneous repairs to the truck.
Dec. 31. Recorded depreciation on the truck for the year. The estimated useful life of the truck is four years, with a residual value of $4,000.

2014
Jan. 2. Purchased a new truck for $69,000, paying cash.
Jul. 1. Sold the used truck for $10,250. (Record depreciation to date in 2014 for the truck.)
Oct. 24. Paid garage $415 for miscellaneous repairs to the truck.
Dec. 31. Recorded depreciation for the new truck. It has an estimated residual value of $15,000 and an estimated life of four years.

Instructions

Journalize the transactions and the adjusting entries. (Hint: Treat all purchases and sales as if they occurred on the first day of the month.)

PR 9-6B

Transactions for long-term assets, including revision of depreciation and sale

✔ Dec. 31,2014, depreciation expense—lawn mower, $7,336

The following transactions and adjusting entries were completed by Brandon Lawn Service over a two-year period. The company has a December 31 year-end and records depreciation on an annual basis.

2013
Mar. 26. Purchased ride-on lawn mower for $25,000 and office furniture for $10,000.
     28. Paid garage $525 for maintenance of the equipment.
     30. Installed air-conditioning unit for the lawn mower, paying $1,200.
Dec. 31. Recorded depreciation on the equipment for the fiscal year, using the double-declining-balance method. The estimated useful life of the equipment is five years, with a residual value of $2,000. Recorded depreciation on the office furniture using the straight-line method, assuming a useful life of 10 years and a $1,000 residual value.

2014
May 10. Paid $150 to repair minor damage to furniture.
Dec. 31. Recorded depreciation on the office furniture, which is now expected to last for five years in total. Recorded depreciation on the lawn mower.

Instructions

1. Journalize the transactions and the adjusting entries.
2. Journalize the entry to record sale of the office furniture, assuming it is sold on January 5, 2018, for $2,000.

PR 9-7B

Amortization and impairment entries

✔ 1. a. $356,200

Data related to the acquisition of timber rights and intangible assets during the current year ended December 31 are as follows:

a. Timber rights on a tract of land were purchased for $1,170,000 on July 5. The stand of timber is estimated at 4,500,000 board feet. During the current year, 1,370,000 board feet of timber were cut and sold.
b. On December 31, the company determined that $5,000,000 of goodwill was impaired.
c. Governmental and legal costs of $234,000 were incurred on April 4 in obtaining a patent with an estimated economic life of 12 years.

Instructions

1. Determine the amount of the amortization or impairment for the current year for each of the foregoing items. (Hint: Treat all purchases and sales as if they occurred on the first day of the month.)
2. Journalize the adjusting entries required to record the amortization or impairment for each item.

PR 9-8B

Transactions for tangible assets, intangible assets, and goodwill, including impairment entries and sale

✔ Patents, net, Dec. 31, 2015, $1,233,680

Innovative Inventions Ltd. had the following account balances on January 1, 2015:

	Cost	Accumulated Depreciation/Amortization
Land	$ 750,000	
Building	2,900,000	1,160,000
Furniture and equipment	640,000	512,000
Patents	4,921,000	4,028,900
Goodwill	1,800,000	

During the year, the corporation completed the following transactions and adjusting entries affecting long-term assets.

May 1. Purchased a patent from another company for $600,000.
Jul. 5. Sold furniture for $24,000 that was purchased on January 9, 2010, at a cost of $67,200. The furniture was depreciated on a straight-line basis over 10 years with an expected residual value of $2,000. (Record depreciation to date of sale.)

Oct. 1. Purchased equipment for $52,000.

Dec. 31. Innovative Inventions Ltd.'s accountant feels the carrying amount of the business exceeds its fair value by $220,000.

31. Recorded depreciation on the building using the straight-line method, assuming an estimated life of 25 years and a residual value of $300,000.

31. Recorded depreciation on the furniture and equipment using the straight-line method, assuming an estimated useful life of 10 years and no residual value.

31. Recorded amortization on the patents using the double-declining balance method, assuming an estimated useful life of 10 years and a $100,000 residual value.

Instructions

1. Journalize the transactions and the adjusting entries.
2. Prepare the balance sheet presentation for Innovative Inventions' long-term assets as at December 31, 2015, with comparative amounts for December 31, 2014.

PR 9-9B

Financial reporting for long-term assets

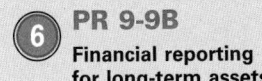 Property, plant, and equipment, $10,901,600

At October 31, 2015, the end of the current fiscal year, Lafontaine Engineering Inc. had the following account balances:

	Cost	Accumulated Depreciation/Amortization
Building	$ 9,400,000	2,496,000
Furniture and equipment	1,068,000	390,400
Land	3,320,000	
Trademarks	11,200,000	8,320,000
Goodwill	1,650,000	

Instructions

Prepare the balance sheet presentation for Lafontaine Engineering Inc.'s long-term assets.

SPECIAL ACTIVITIES

SA 9-1

Ethics and professional conduct in business

Steven Appleby, CA, is an assistant to the controller of Summerfield Consulting Co. In his spare time, Steven also prepares tax returns and performs general accounting services for clients. Frequently, Steven performs these services after his normal working hours, using Summerfield Consulting Co.'s computers and laser printers. Occasionally, Steven's clients will call him at the office during regular working hours.

Discuss whether Steven is behaving in a professional manner.

SA 9-2

Depreciation vs. capital cost allowance

The following is an excerpt from a conversation between two employees of Quantum Technologies, Pat Gapp and Faye Dalby. Pat is the accounts payable clerk, and Faye is the cashier.

Pat: Faye, could I get your opinion on something?

Faye: Sure, Pat.

Pat: Do you know Julie, the fixed assets clerk?

Faye: I know who she is, but I don't know her really well. Why?

Pat: Well, I was talking to her at lunch last Monday about how she liked her job. You know, the usual ... and she mentioned something about having to keep two sets of books ... one for taxes and one for the financial statements. That can't be good accounting, can it? What do you think?

Faye: Two sets of books? It doesn't sound right.

Pat: It doesn't seem right to me either. I was always taught that you had to use generally accepted accounting principles. How can there be two sets of books? What can be the difference between the two?

How would you respond to Faye and Pat if you were Julie?

SA 9-3

Applying for patents, copyrights, and trademarks

Internet Project

Log on to the Internet and review the procedures for applying for a patent, a copyright, and a trademark. One Internet site that is useful for this purpose is www.ipic .ca, of the Intellectual Property Institute of Canada. Prepare a written summary of these procedures.

SA 9-4

Return on assets: three industries

f·a·i

The following table shows the net income and average total assets for a recent fiscal year for three different companies from three different industries: retailing, manufacturing, and communications.

	Net Income (in millions)	Average Total Assets (in millions)
Canadian Tire Corporation	$467	$11,694
Nova Chemicals Corporation	615	5,892
Bell Aliant Regional Communications Inc.	336	8,156

a. For each company, determine the return on assets ratio. Round to two decimal places.
b. Explain Canadian Tire's ratio relative to the other two companies.

SA 9-5

Financial reporting for long-term assets

Using the financial statements of Leon's Furniture Limited and Shoppers Drug Mart Corporation in Appendixes B and C, answer the following questions:

1. What depreciation methods are used for property, plant, and equipment assets?
2. What depreciation methods are used for intangible assets?
3. Did either company value any of its long-term assets at fair value?
4. Has either company recorded an impairment loss for any of its long-term assets in the past? In this year?

Current Liabilities and Payroll

PREMIÈRE MOISSON

Banks and other financial institutions provide loans or credit to buyers for purchases of various items. Using credit to purchase items is probably as old as commerce itself. In fact, the Babylonians were lending money to support trade as early as 1300 BCE. The use of credit provides *individuals* convenience and buying power. Credit cards provide individuals convenience over writing cheques and make purchasing over the Internet easier. Credit cards also provide individuals control over cash by providing documentation of the purchases through monthly credit card statements, by avoiding the need to carry large amounts of cash, and by enabling the purchase of items before they are paid.

Short-term credit is also used by *businesses* to provide convenience in purchasing items for manufacture or resale. More importantly, short-term credit gives a business control over the payment for goods and services. For example, Première Moisson, a chain of bakeries located in Quebec, uses short-term trade credit, or accounts payable, to purchase ingredients for making bread products in its bakeries. Short-term trade credit gives Première Moisson control over cash payments by separating the purchase function from the payment function. Thus, the employee responsible for purchasing the bakery ingredients is separated from the employee responsible for paying for the purchase. This separation of duties can help prevent unauthorized purchases or payments.

In addition to having accounts payable, a business such as Première Moisson can also have current liabilities related to payroll, payroll deductions, short-term notes, unearned revenue, and contingencies. We will discuss each of these types of current liabilities in this chapter.

After studying this chapter, you should be able to:

1 Describe and illustrate known liabilities, estimated liabilities, contingent liabilities, and provisions.

Current Liabilities	Known Liabilities	EXAMPLE EXERCISE 10-1 (page 509) EXAMPLE EXERCISE 10-2 (page 511)
	Estimated Liabilities	EXAMPLE EXERCISE 10-3 (page 513)
	Contingent Liabilities	EXAMPLE EXERCISE 10-4 (page 515)
	Provisions	

2 Determine employer liabilities for payroll, including liabilities arising from employee earnings and deductions from earnings.

Payroll and Payroll Deductions	Liability for Employee Earnings	
	Deductions from Employee Earnings	
	Steps for Completing Payroll	
	Step 1: Calculating Gross Pay, Deductions, and Net Pay	EXAMPLE EXERCISE 10-5 (page 520)
	Step 2: Recording Distribution of Gross Pay	EXAMPLE EXERCISE 10-6 (page 523)
	Step 3: Recording Employer's Portion of Payroll Expenses	
	Step 4: Recording Payment of Net Pay to Employees	
	Step 5: Recording Remittance of Payroll Deductions	

3 Describe payroll accounting systems and apply steps to completing payroll within a payroll accounting system.

Steps to Completing Payroll with a Payroll System	Step 1: Calculating Gross Pay, Deductions, and Net Pay	
	Step 2: Recording Distribution of Gross Pay	EXAMPLE EXERCISE 10-7 (page 529)
	Step 3: Recording Employer's Portion of Payroll Expenses	EXAMPLE EXERCISE 10-8 (page 530)
	Step 4: Recording Payment of Net Pay to Employees	
	Step 5: Recording Remittance of Payroll Deductions	EXAMPLE EXERCISE 10-9 (page 531)
	Payroll System Elements	
	Internal Controls for Payroll Systems	

4 Present current liabilities on the balance sheet.

| Balance Sheet Presentation | Current Liabilities on the Balance Sheet | |
| | Financial Analysis and Interpretation | EXAMPLE EXERCISE 10-10 (page 533) |

For the chapter *At a Glance*, turn to page 534.

Current Liabilities

Describe and illustrate known liabilities, estimated liabilities, contingent liabilities, and provisions.

This chapter is a good place to review the definition of a liability, as discussed in Chapter 1, on page 10. A liability is a present obligation to pay for a transaction that has occurred in the past and cannot be avoided in the future. When a company buys merchandise from a supplier with a promise to pay for the inventory in the future, this transaction is referred to as a purchase *on account*.

Accrued liabilities are liabilities arising from accrued expenses. Accrued expenses, as discussed in Chapter 3, are unrecorded expenses that have been incurred and for which cash has yet to be paid. Since the expense has been incurred, it must be recorded, creating an accrued liability. Utility costs and payroll costs are examples of accrued expenses that create accrued liabilities.

Interest owing on notes payable is another example of an accrued liability that must be recorded at year-end. An obligation exists to pay out cash in the near future.

Unearned revenues represent the advance receipt of *future* revenues and are recorded as liabilities when cash is received from the customer. The company has an obligation to perform the work, or return the cash to the customer, creating a current liability that must be fulfilled within the following 12 months.

When a company or a bank advances *credit*, it is making a loan. The company or bank is called a *creditor* (or *lender*). The individuals or companies receiving the loan are called *debtors* (or *borrowers*).

Debt is recorded as a liability by the debtor. *Long-term liabilities* are debts due beyond one year. Thus, a 25-year mortgage used to purchase property is a long-term liability. *Current liabilities* are debts that will normally be paid out of current assets and are due within one year. Current liabilities discussed in earlier chapters include accrued expenses, unearned revenue, and interest payable. The size of current liabilities and current assets is of great concern to users of the financial statements, who are interested in knowing the business's ability to pay its current debts. Numerous ratios can assist users in assessing the company's current liabilities in relation to its current assets. The quick ratio is covered in the Financial Analysis and Interpretation on page 533, and analysis of other ratios will be covered in Chapter 17.

Four types of current liabilities will be discussed in this chapter. These are **known liabilities**, **estimated liabilities**, **contingent liabilities**, and **provisions**. Known liabilities usually arise when a transaction occurs, such as a purchase on account (accounts payable), and normally have a source document generating the transaction (purchase invoice). Payroll liabilities are a type of known liability, and they will be discussed more extensively in the next section in this chapter. Estimated liabilities are not generated by source documents. Instead, estimated liabilities relate to items for which a liability is known to exist but the amount is unknown. Examples of estimated liabilities are warranty expenses and income taxes. Professional judgment is required to estimate the amounts that should be recorded. Contingent liabilities and provisions are liabilities that may occur if another event occurs. They also require professional judgment to assess whether they should be recorded and, if so, the amount to be recorded. Estimated liabilities, contingent liabilities, and provisions will be discussed in more detail later in this chapter.

Known Liabilities

Accounts Payable Accounts payable transactions have been described and illustrated in earlier chapters. These transactions involved a variety of purchases on account, including the purchase of merchandise and supplies. For most companies, accounts payable is the largest current liability. Exhibit 1 shows the accounts payable balance as a percent of total current liabilities for a number of companies.

Maintaining control of accounts payable is crucial. As noted in Chapter 5, a controlling account is the account in the general ledger that summarizes the details found in the respective subsidiary ledger. Accounts payable is a control account in the general ledger but this account shows only the total amount owing to suppliers. To avoid overpaying a supplier or paying late, an accounts payable subsidiary ledger is also maintained. The subsidiary ledger shows specific details regarding both the purchases from and the payments to all the individual suppliers. The **accounts payable subsidiary ledger** is a secondary ledger that supports the accounts payable controlling account in the general ledger. The balances in the individual subsidiary ledgers must total the balance in the control account. Thus, if the balance in the accounts payable control account is $7,250, the accounts payable subsidiary balances must total $7,250 as follows:

Accounts Payable Subsidiary Ledger	
Office Supply Co.	$2,900
Barkers Supplies Co.	1,850
Jemini Office Systems	2,500
Total Accounts Payable	$7,250

Exhibit 1

Accounts Payable as a Percent of Total Current Liabilities

Company	Accounts Payable as a Percent of Total Current Liabilities
General Motors Company	50%
Leon's Furniture Limited	45
Sears Canada Inc.	45
Canadian Tire Corporation, Limited	38
Reitmans (Canada) Limited	29
Cineplex Inc.	18
lululemon athletica inc.	14

Provincial Sales Tax (PST) Payable As introduced in Chapter 5, provincial sales tax (PST) is an end-user tax. Thus, a retailer who purchases inventory for resale is not charged PST on the purchase of inventory. The retailer does, however, charge PST on the inventory when it is sold to the end user.

To illustrate, Smith Corporation purchases $600 worth of inventory using a perpetual inventory system. Because Smith intends to resell the inventory, no PST is paid on the purchase, and the following entry is made:

Inventory		600	
Accounts Payable			600
Purchase of inventory on account.			

Assuming a PST rate of 8% and a perpetual inventory system, Smith makes the following entries when the item is sold for $1,000 plus PST.

Cash		1,080	
PST Payable			80
Sales			1,000
Sale of inventory.			

Cost of Goods Sold		600	
Inventory			600
To remove sold items from inventory.			

PST Payable is a current liability account, which is normally remitted to the provincial government on a monthly basis. Assuming this sale is Smith's only taxable transaction for the month, the accountant would make the following entry when remitting the tax:

PST Payable		80	
Cash			80
Paid PST to government.			

If a retailer purchases items, such as office supplies or equipment, to be used in the business and not for resale, the retailer pays PST because the retailer is the end user. The PST is then included in the price of the office supplies or equipment.

To illustrate, Smith Corporation purchases office furniture for $500 plus PST of 8%. Notice there is no separate entry for PST since Smith intends to use the office furniture in the business. The entry is as follows:

Office Furniture	540	
Cash		540
Purchase of furniture. $540 = $500 + ($500 × 0.08)		

Goods and Services Tax (GST) Payable

The federal government collects a goods and services tax (GST) on most products and services. There are three classifications and many complicating factors in the classification of products under GST. These details will be covered more thoroughly in a tax class.

The main difference between PST and GST is that a business both collects GST on sales and pays GST on purchases, whereas PST is only collected on sales. Similar to the treatment for PST, the company acts as a tax collector and remits the GST to the federal government. The two GST accounts offset each other, and the company either pays the balance or is paid the balance by the Receiver General for Canada. In Quebec, these taxes are administered by Revenu Québec.

In practice, these two accounts are known by many different names. For recording GST collected on sales, commonly used names are *GST Charged on Sales, GST Collected,* or *GST Payable*. The textbook uses GST Charged on Sales. For recording GST paid on purchases, commonly used names are *GST Paid on Purchases, GST Input Tax Credits,* and *GST Receivable*. The textbook uses GST Paid on Purchases. GST has been referred to as a "flow-through" tax because it flows through the company to the final customer. In 2012, the GST rate was 5%.

To illustrate, Smith Corporation purchases $1,000 worth of inventory from a wholesaler and uses the perpetual inventory system.

GST Paid on Purchases	50*	
Inventory	1,000	
Cash or Accounts Payable		1,050
To record inventory purchase.		
*($1,000 × 0.05 = $50)		

The purchase is exempt from PST because Smith Corporation is not the end user of the inventory. Smith Corporation sells the inventory to a customer for $1,700 plus 5% GST and 8% PST, recorded as follows:

Cash	1,921	
Sales		1,700
GST Charged on Sales		85*
PST Payable		136**
Sale of inventory.		
*($1,700 × 0.05 = $85)		
**($1,700 × 0.08 = $136)		

Cost of Goods Sold	1,000	
Inventory		1,000
To remove sold item from inventory.		

Neither tax amount is included in the sales revenue because the taxes will eventually be paid to the government by Smith Corporation, which is simply acting as a tax collector. When reporting the GST on the balance sheet, the two GST account balances are netted; if an amount is owed to the Receiver General (a credit balance), it is reported as a current liability; if it is owed from the Receiver General (a debit balance), it is reported as a current asset. At the end of the month, assuming this transaction is Smith Corporation's only GST-taxable sale, the difference between the two GST account balances is remitted to the Receiver General, and the following entry is made:

GST Charged on Sales	85	
GST Paid on Purchases		50
Cash		35
GST remittance to CRA.		

This entry sets the GST account balances to zero, so the account is ready to track the GST charged on sales and paid on purchases in the following month or quarter. Only the end consumer is out of pocket for the GST; the amount of GST paid by Smith Corporation, $50, has been reimbursed because Smith Corporation pays the government only $35 of the $85 collected from the customer. In addition, Smith Corporation will make an entry similar to the entry shown on page 508 when it remits the PST to the provincial government.

The provincial sales tax is applied slightly differently in Quebec and Prince Edward Island (PEI). Although PEI's provincial sales tax is still called PST, Quebec's provincial sales tax is called Quebec Sales Tax (QST). In both provinces the taxes are applied to the selling price including the GST of 5%. Using the GST rate of 5%, and a QST rate of 9.5%, assume Marco's Toys, operating in Quebec, sold $3,000 of merchandise to a customer for cash. Marco would record the sale as follows:

Cash	3,449.25	
Sales		3,000.00
GST Charged on Sales		150.00*
QST Payable		299.25**
Sale of Inventory.		
*($3,000 × 5%)		
**($3,000 + $150) × 9.5%		

The calculation for PEI is the same as Quebec, using a PST rate of 10%.

Harmonized Sales Tax (HST) Payable Some provinces have harmonized their PST with the GST, resulting in one tax being collected, the harmonized sales tax (HST). Exhibit 19 on page 272 shows which taxes are collected for all provinces and territories.

Suppose Smith Corporation operates in a province that charges the 13% HST. The company would make the following entry to record the purchase of inventory for $1,000 plus HST:

HST Paid on Purchases	130*	
Inventory	1,000	
Cash or Accounts Payable		1,130
To record inventory purchase.		
*($1,000 × 0.13 = $130)		

The following journal entries record the sale of inventory to a customer for $1,700 plus 13% HST:

Cash	1,921	
Sales		1,700
HST Charged on Sales		221*
Sale of inventory.		
*($1,700 × 0.13 = $221)		
Cost of Goods Sold	1,000	
Inventory		1,000
To remove sold items from inventory.		

The difference between the HST charged on sales and the HST paid on purchases is remitted to the Receiver General and recorded by the following entry:

HST Charged on Sales	221	
HST Paid on Purchases		130
Cash		91
HST remittance to CRA.		

EXAMPLE EXERCISE 10-1   PST Payable and GST Charged on Sales   ①

Peter Plumbing Store purchased 10 sinks on May 4 for its inventory, paying $750 per sink. The sinks retail for $1,100 each. GST is 5%, PST is 8%, and Peter Plumbing Store keeps track of its inventory using the perpetual inventory method. The store sold one of these sinks the next day for cash.

a) Record the purchase of the sinks including PST and GST, if appropriate.

b) Record the sale of the sink including PST and GST, if appropriate.

FOLLOW MY EXAMPLE 10-1

a) May 4	Inventory	7,500	
	GST Paid on Purchases	375*	
	Accounts Payable..		7,875
	To record purchase of inventory on account.		
	*($7,500 × 0.05 = $375)		
b) May 5	Cash	1,243	
	Sales..		1,100
	GST Charged on Sales.....................................		55*
	PST Payable..		88**
	To record cash sale.		
	* ($1,100 × 0.05 = $55)		
	** ($1,100 × 0.08 = $88)		
	Cost of Goods Sold..	750	
	Inventory..		750
	To record the cost of goods sold.		

For Practice: PE 10-1

Current Portion of Long-Term Debt

Long-term liabilities are often paid back in periodic payments, called *installments*. Such installments that are due *within* the coming year are classified as a current liability. The installments due *after* the coming year are classified as a long-term liability.

To illustrate, Shoppers Drug Mart reported the following debt payments schedule in its December 31, 2011, annual report to shareholders:

Medium-term notes

Series 2 Notes	June 2013	$449,298,000
Series 3 Notes	January 2012	249,971,000
Series 4 Notes	January 2014	249,081,000
		948,350,000
Less: current portion of long-term notes		(249,971,000)
		$698,379,000

SOURCE: Courtesy of Shoppers Drug Mart

The debt of $249,971,000, due January 2012, is reported as a current liability on the December 31, 2011, balance sheet. This $249,971,000 represents the principal on long-term debt that is due within the next 12 months. The remaining debt of $698,379,000 ($948,350,000 – $249,971,000) is reported as a long-term liability on the balance sheet.

Short-Term Notes Payable Notes may be issued to purchase merchandise or other assets. Notes may also be issued to creditors to satisfy an account payable created earlier.[1]

To illustrate, assume that Nature's Sunshine Company issued a 90-day, 6% note for $1,000, dated August 1, 2014, to Murray Co. for a $1,000 overdue account. The entry, on Sunshine Company's books, to record the issuance of the note is as follows:

2014				
Aug.	1	Accounts Payable—Murray Co.	1,000	
		Notes Payable		1,000
		Issued a 90-day, 6% note on account.		

When the note matures, the entry to record the payment of $1,000 plus $14.79 interest ($1,000 × 6% × 90/365) is as follows:

2014				
Oct.	30	Notes Payable	1,000.00	
		Interest Expense	14.79	
		Cash		1,014.79
		Paid principal and interest due on note.		

The interest expense is reported in the Other Expense section of the income statement for the year ended December 31, 2014.

Each note transaction affects a debtor (borrower) and a creditor (lender). The following illustration shows how the same transactions are recorded by the debtor and creditor. In this illustration, the debtor (borrower) is Bowden Co., and the creditor (lender) is Coker Co.

	Bowden Co. (Debtor)		Coker Co. (Creditor)	

May 1. Bowden Co. purchased merchandise on account from Coker Co., $10,000, 2/10, n/30. The merchandise cost Coker Co. $7,500.	Inventory
	  Accounts Payable
		10,000.00
		10,000.00
			Accounts Receivable
			  Sales
			
			Cost of Goods Sold
			  Inventory
				10,000.00
				10,000.00
				
				7,500.00
				7,500.00

May 31. Bowden Co. issued a 60-day, 6% note for $10,000 to Coker Co. on account.	Accounts Payable
	  Notes Payable
		10,000.00
		10,000.00
			Notes Receivable
			  Accounts Receivable
				10,000.00
				10,000.00

July 30. Bowden Co. paid Coker Co. the amount due on the note of May 31. Interest: $10,000 × 6% × 60/365.	Notes Payable
	Interest Expense
	  Cash
		10,000.00
		98.63
		10,098.63
			Cash
			  Interest Revenue
			  Notes Receivable
				10,098.63
				98.63
				10,000.00

1 The accounting for notes received in exchange for an account receivable, a sale on account, or a loan was described and illustrated in Chapter 8, Receivables, and included a discussion of partial periods of interest.

A company may borrow from a bank by issuing a note. To illustrate, assume that on September 19, Iceburg Company issues a $4,000, 90-day, 7% note to Royal Bank of Canada. The entry to record the issuance of the note is as follows:

Sept.	19	Cash	4,000.00	
		Notes Payable		4,000.00
		Issued a 90-day, 7% note to Royal Bank.		

On the due date of the note (December 18), Iceburg Company owes $4,000 plus interest of $69.04 ($4,000 × 7% × 90/365). The entry to record the payment of the note is as follows:

Dec.	18	Notes Payable	4,000.00	
		Interest Expense	69.04	
		Cash		4,069.04
		Paid principal and interest due on note.		

EXAMPLE EXERCISE 10-2 Proceeds from Notes Payable ①

On July 1, Bella Salon Company issued a 60-day note with a principal amount of $60,000 to Delilah Hair Products Company for inventory.

a. Determine the due date of the note.

b. Determine the proceeds of the note, assuming the note carries an interest rate of 4%.

c. Record the journal entries to issue the note and pay the note.

FOLLOW MY EXAMPLE 10-2

a. The note is due to be repaid on August 30 (30 days in July + 30 days in August)

b. $60,000

c. July 1	Cash..	60,000.00	
	Notes Payable		60,000.00
	Issued a 60-day note to Delilah Hair Products Company.		
Aug. 30	Notes Payable......................................	60,000.00	
	Interest Expense..................................	394.52*	
	Cash..		60,394.52
	Paid principal and interest due on note.		
	*($60,000 × 0.04 × 60/365 = $394.52)		

For Practice: PE 10-2

MID-CHAPTER ILLUSTRATIVE PROBLEM

Ruby Rose Company, which has a December 31 year-end, issued a 60-day note on December 1, 2014, at 3%, to cover an account payable owed to Benjamin Buck Ltd., for $1,300. Journalize the transactions for all the important dates for Ruby Rose Company. The amount was paid when it was due. On February 10, 2015, Ruby Rose bought inventory of $1,500 on account from Benjamin Buck Ltd. and sold it on February 14 to Marina Quilty-Peters for $2,600. Ruby Rose uses the perpetual inventory system. HST is 13%.

MID-CHAPTER ILLUSTRATIVE SOLUTION

2014					
Dec.	1	Accounts Payable—Benjamin Buck Ltd.		1,300.00	
		Notes Payable			1,300.00
Dec.	31	Interest Expense		3.21*	
		Interest Payable			3.21
		*($1,300 × 0.03 × 30/365)			
2015					
Jan.	30	Notes Payable		1,300.00	
		Interest Expense		3.21*	
		Interest Payable		3.21	
		Cash			1,306.42
		*($1,300 × 0.03 × 30/365)			
Feb.	10	Inventory		1,500.00	
		HST Paid on Purchases		195.00	
		Accounts Payable—Benjamin Buck Ltd.			1,695.00
Feb.	14	Accounts Receivable—Marina Quilty-Peters		2,938.00	
		HST Charged on Sales			338.00
		Sales			2,600.00
		Cost of Goods Sold		1,500.00	
		Inventory			1,500.00

Estimated Liabilities

Examples of estimated liabilities are warranty liabilities and income tax liabilities. If a product offers a warranty, the warranty expense is recorded in the same period in which the sale is recorded. In this way, warranty expense is matched with the related revenue (sales). This approach fulfills the matching principle discussed in earlier chapters. The liability is known to exist, but the amount is based on an estimate. It is recorded in the same manner as other liabilities, by debiting an expense account and crediting a liability account.

To illustrate, assume that during 2014 (with a year-end of December 31), a company sold product for $60,000 that includes a 12-month warranty for repairs. The average cost of repairs expected over the next year is estimated at 5% of the sales price. The entry to record the estimated product liability for the year is shown below:

2014				
Dec.	31	Product Warranty Expense	3,000	
		Product Warranty Liability		3,000
		Estimated warranty liability for 2015, 5% of $60,000.		

If the product is repaired under warranty, the repair costs are recorded by debiting Product Warranty Liability and crediting Cash, Supplies, Wages Payable, or other accounts. Thus, if a $200 part is replaced under warranty on January 16, 2015, the entry is as follows:

2015				
Jan.	16	Product Warranty Liability	200	
		Supplies		200
		Replaced defective part under warranty.		

Research In Motion Limited explains its handling of warranties in the significant policies section of the notes to the financial statements as follows:

Warranty

> *The Company provides for the estimated costs of product warranties at the time revenue is recognized. BlackBerry devices are generally covered by a time-limited warranty for varying periods of time. The Company's warranty obligation is affected by product failure rates, differences in warranty periods, regulatory developments with respect to warranty obligations in the countries in which the Company carries on business, freight expense, and material usage and other related repair costs.*

> *The Company's estimates of costs are based upon historical experience and expectations of future return rates and unit warranty repair costs. If the Company experiences increased or decreased warranty activity, or increased or decreased costs associated with servicing those obligations, revisions to the estimated warranty liability would be recognized in the reporting period when such revisions are made.*

EXAMPLE EXERCISE 10-3 Estimated Warranty Liability ①

Cook-Rite Co. sold $140,000 of kitchen appliances during August under a six-month warranty. The cost to repair defects under the warranty is estimated at 6% of the sales price. On September 11, a customer required a $200 part replacement, plus $90 of labour under the warranty.

Provide the journal entry for (a) the estimated warranty expense on August 31 and (b) the September 11 warranty work.

FOLLOW MY EXAMPLE 10-3

a. Product Warranty Expense	8,400	
Product Warranty Liability..		8,400
To record estimated warranty expense for August, 6% × $140,000.		
b. Product Warranty Liability	290	
Supplies..		200
Wages Payable..		90
Replaced defective part under warranty.		

For Practice: PE 10-3

Contingent Liabilities

Some liabilities may arise from past transactions if certain events occur in the future. These *potential* liabilities are called contingent liabilities.

The accounting for contingent liabilities depends on the following two factors:

1. Likelihood of occurring: Likely, unlikely, and not determinable
2. Measurement: Estimable or not estimable

The likelihood of the event creating the liability occurring is classified as *likely*, *unlikely*, or *not determinable*. The ability to estimate the potential liability is classified as *estimable* or *not estimable*.

Likely and Estimable If a contingent liability is *likely* and the amount of the liability can be *reasonably estimated*, it is recorded and disclosed. The liability is recorded by debiting an expense and crediting a liability.

To illustrate, assume that a lawsuit has been evaluated as likely to be lost with a cost of $10,000. The entry to record the contingent liability is as shown below.

	Contingent Loss	10,000	
	Contingent Liability		10,000
	To record a likely and estimable contingent loss.		

The preceding entry fulfills the conservatism principle. When there is uncertainty, we choose estimates of a conservative nature to ensure that assets, revenues, and gains are not overstated and that liabilities, expenses, and losses are not understated.[2] The liability is recognized because this amount will likely need to be paid in the future. This contingent loss decreases net income, but because it is not a part of the main operations of the business, it is included on the income statement after the income from operations subtotal.

If the contingency is a gain, conservatism is also applied. Even if the gain is likely and estimable, it is not recorded in the general ledger. Instead, the contingent gain is disclosed in the notes to the financial statements. This is an application of conservatism, in that the asset is not being overestimated.[3]

Likely and Not Estimable A contingent liability may be likely but cannot be estimated. In this case, the contingent liability is disclosed in the notes to the financial statements. For example, a company may have accidentally polluted a local river by dumping waste products. At the end of the period, the company may not be able to estimate the cost of the cleanup and any fines.

Not Determinable If the liability cannot be determined to be either likely or unlikely, it is *not determinable*. For example, a company may be sued for infringing on another company's patent rights. However, the verdict is pending, and the company's lawyers are uncertain about the lawsuit's outcome. In this case, the potential liability is not recorded in the general ledger but is disclosed in the notes to the financial statements.

Unlikely If a contingent liability is unlikely, it is not recorded in the financial statements or disclosed in the notes. However, an exception to this approach is made when the contingent liability would have an extreme effect on the business. In this case, the contingent liability is disclosed in the notes because it could affect the business's future viability.

The accounting treatment of contingent liabilities is summarized in Exhibit 2.

Exhibit 2

Accounting Treatment of Contingent Liabilities

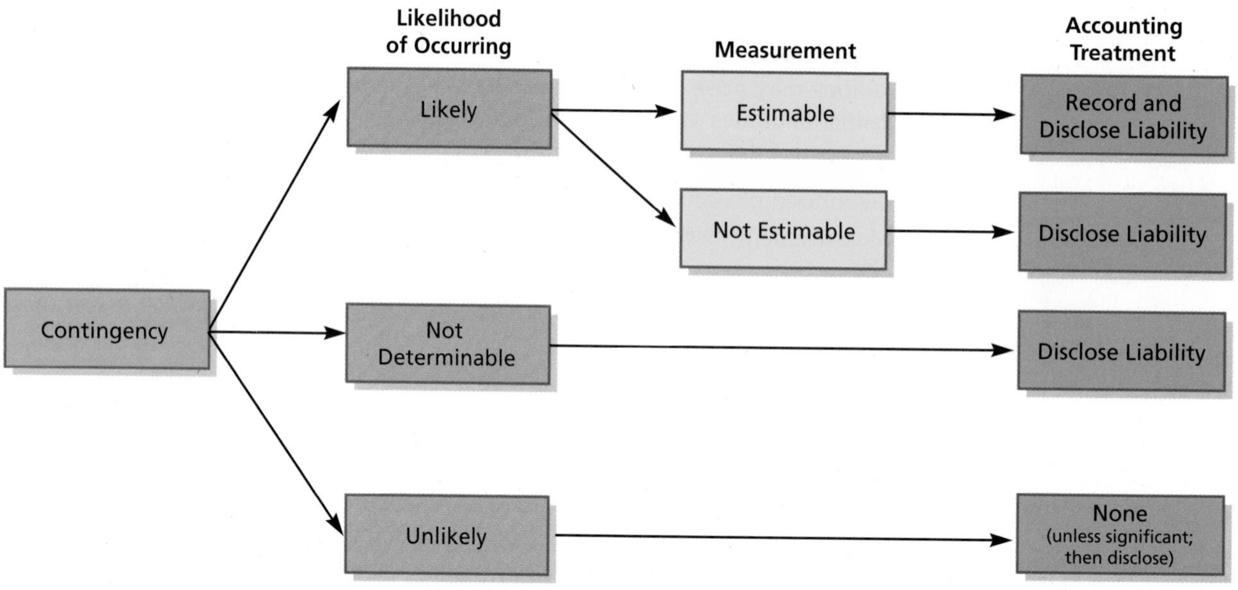

2 *CICA Handbook—Accounting*, 2012, Part II, 1000.18

3 *CICA Handbook—Accounting*, 2012, Part II, 3290.22

Common examples of contingent liabilities disclosed in notes to the financial statements are litigation, environmental matters, guarantees, and contingencies from the sale of receivables.

CRITICAL THINKING

Why do we bother to record a future event that may or may not occur?

To represent the economic reality of the decisions that the business has made, accountants need to consider the effect of those decisions on the future. This consideration reflects the principle of representational faithfulness. The purpose of financial statements is to present information to help users of the statements in their decision making. Current and future investors and lenders need to be aware of all possible future liabilities.

INTEGRITY, OBJECTIVITY, AND ETHICS IN BUSINESS

TODAY'S MISTAKES CAN BE TOMORROW'S LIABILITY

Environmental and public health claims are quickly becoming some of the largest contingent liabilities facing companies. For example, tobacco, asbestos, and environmental cleanup claims have reached billions of dollars and have led to numerous corporate bankruptcies. Managers must be careful that today's decisions do not become tomorrow's nightmare.

EXAMPLE EXERCISE 10-4   Contingent Liabilities

Thomson Aluminum Plant experienced the following events in the past year. Identify the correct accounting treatment for each item.

a. Thomson is being sued by a nearby town for $50 million because it polluted the town's water supply. Thomson's lawyers estimate the lawsuit will result in a settlement of $12 million.

b. Thomson is also being sued by an environmental group that believes aluminum products should not be produced because of their negative impact on the environment. Although Thomson's lawyers suspect the group will probably receive some payment, they are not sure of the amount.

c. Because some individuals have adverse health reactions to the use of aluminum, a remote chance exists that Thomson could be sued by an end user of its products.

FOLLOW MY EXAMPLE 10-4

a. Because this item is likely and estimable, Thomson should record the expected loss of $12 million.

b. Because this item is likely and not estimable, the item will be disclosed in the notes to the financial statements.

c. Because this item is determinable but unlikely, no disclosure needs to be made in the notes to the financial statements, if the business would be viable even if it did occur.

For Practice: PE 10-4

Provisions

IFRS defines provisions as liabilities of uncertain timing or amount.[4] Accounts payable, sales taxes payable, and the accruals previously discussed in this chapter are liabilities but they are not provisions. We know the amount and timing of the future payments for liabilities, but the amount and timing are uncertain for the payments for provisions.

4 *CICA Handbook—Accounting,* 2013, Part I, IAS 37, 10.

For example, in its 2011 financial statements, Shoppers Drug Mart recorded its best estimate for provisions resulting from legal claims that it may eventually need to pay.

All of the following three criteria must be met to recognize a liability as a provision in the financial statements: the company has a present obligation as a result of a past event, it is "probable" that the company will be required to pay cash, and a reliable estimate can be made of the amount.[5]

Under International Financial Reporting Standards (IFRS), if all three conditions are not met, the company is required to disclose the event as a *contingent liability* in the notes to the financial statements. Contingent liabilities are not recorded (recognized) in the books because their existence will be confirmed only by the occurrence or non-occurrence of one or more uncertain future events not wholly within the control of the entity.[6] In circumstances where the possibility of future payments is *remote*, the contingent liability is not disclosed in the notes. A great deal of professional judgment is necessary.

Professional judgment is also necessary when distinguishing between classes of contingent liabilities or provisions. This is especially the case when distinguishing between likely and unlikely contingent liabilities, or more likely than not provisions.

Payroll and Payroll Deductions

Determine employer liabilities for payroll, including liabilities arising from employee earnings and deductions from earnings.

In accounting, **payroll** refers to the amount paid to employees for services they provided during the period. A company's payroll is important for the following reasons:

1. Employees are sensitive to payroll errors and irregularities.
2. Good employee morale requires payroll to be paid on time and with accuracy.
3. Payroll is subject to federal, provincial, and territorial regulations.
4. Payroll and related payroll deductions significantly affect the net income of most companies.

Five steps will be introduced to complete payroll. Payroll will be reviewed for an individual and for a group of employees.

Liability for Employee Earnings

Note: Employee salaries and wages are expenses to an employer.

Salary usually refers to payment for managerial and administrative services. Salary is normally expressed in terms of a month or a year. *Wages* usually refers to payment for employee manual labour. The rate of wages is normally stated on an hourly or a weekly basis. The salary or wage of an employee may be increased by bonuses, commissions, profit sharing, or cost-of-living adjustments.

Companies must comply with the Employment Standards Act, and with the Canada Labour Code if the business operates within multiple provinces and territories. These acts establish regulations for employers, such as minimum rates of pay for regular hours and for overtime, minimum number of paid vacation days, and their responsibility for withholding and remitting income tax.

Businesses will also be registered with the Workers' Compensation Board (WCB), or the Workplace Safety and Insurance Board (WSIB), and pay insurance premiums based on the gross pay of the business and the type of work done by the employees. The Workers' Compensation Act falls under provincial and territorial jurisdictions. This act requires payments to be made to sick or injured employees when they cannot attend work. To fund these payments, employers insure their employees by paying premiums to their provincial or territorial WCB or WSIB. These payments are set by the WCB or WSIB on the basis of the industry classification and total payroll of the company. The rates vary from $1 to $3 for every $100 of payroll.

---

5 *CICA Handbook—Accounting*, 2013, Part I, IAS 37, 14.
6 *CICA Handbook—Accounting*, 2013, Part I, IAS 37, 12.

These additional amounts—premium payments to WCB or WSIB and to other insurance providers and for vacation pay—are called employee benefits. Another possible benefit is an employer's contribution to a pension plan for employees. These plans set aside funds for employees, to be paid on their retirement.

By law, employees are entitled to an annual vacation allowance. Labour laws are regulated by each province, and the minimum vacation allowance varies. Generally, the minimum vacation allowance is the equivalent of two weeks' work, or 4% of an employee's gross earnings. Many companies allow their employees more than two weeks' vacation per year. Companies should accrue the amount of vacation that is owing to employees each period to properly match the vacation expense to the period it was earned by the employee.

Deductions from Employee Earnings

The total earnings of an employee for a payroll period, including any overtime pay, are called **gross pay**. From this amount is subtracted one or more *deductions* to arrive at the **net pay**. Net pay is the amount paid to the employee.

The deductions normally include Canada Pension Plan (CPP), employment insurance (EI), and federal and provincial, or territorial, income taxes.

Income Taxes
Employers withhold a portion of employee earnings for payment of the employees' federal and provincial, or territorial, income tax, and remit it to the Receiver General for Canada. Employees declare information that will be used to calculate their personal tax credits by completing a Personal Tax Credit Return, or TD1 form, for both the provincial, or territorial, and the federal governments. To illustrate, assume that John T. McGrath is a salesperson employed by McDermott Supply Co. Exhibit 3 is the federal TD1 form submitted by John T. McGrath.

It may be of interest to note that income tax was introduced in 1917 by Sir Thomas White, then federal minister of finance, as a "temporary" tax on income to fund the war efforts. It was White's hope that this temporary tax, now known as "income tax," which has been in place for almost 100 years, would be rescinded a year or two following the war.

Canada Pension Plan (CPP) or Quebec Pension Plan (QPP)
Employees between the ages of 18 and 70 are required to make contributions to the Canada Pension Plan (CPP) or the Quebec Pension Plan (QPP). In 2012, employees contributed 4.95% of their gross wages to the CPP for annual wages greater than $3,500 and less than $50,100. The first $3,500 of wages that an individual earns does not require CPP contributions. Because the maximum pensionable earnings is an indexed amount, it is adjusted each year. The employer matches the employee's contribution. Self-employed individuals are responsible for both the employee and the employer portions, when they file their personal income tax return.

The employer deducts the employee's CPP contribution from the employee's payroll cheque. The employer is responsible for calculating the amount, deducting it from the gross pay, and remitting it to Canada Revenue Agency. Of course, the employer is also responsible for remitting its portion of the CPP contribution.

Tables provided by CRA are used to calculate the CPP contribution payable. Alternatively, CPP contribution payable can be calculated by subtracting the $3,500 personal exemption from gross wages and multiplying by 4.95%. To calculate the CPP contribution payable on weekly wages, the $3,500 personal exemption is first divided by 52. For example, if an employee's weekly wage was $600, the calculation would be $26.37 = [$600 − ($3,500/52)] × 4.95%.

Employment Insurance (EI)
The federal government also has an employment insurance plan. This plan provides for temporary payments to individuals who become unemployed. All employees make contributions to the employment insurance plan based on income earned, up to a maximum contribution. The employer contributes 1.4

Exhibit 3

Personal Tax Credits Return (TD1 Form)

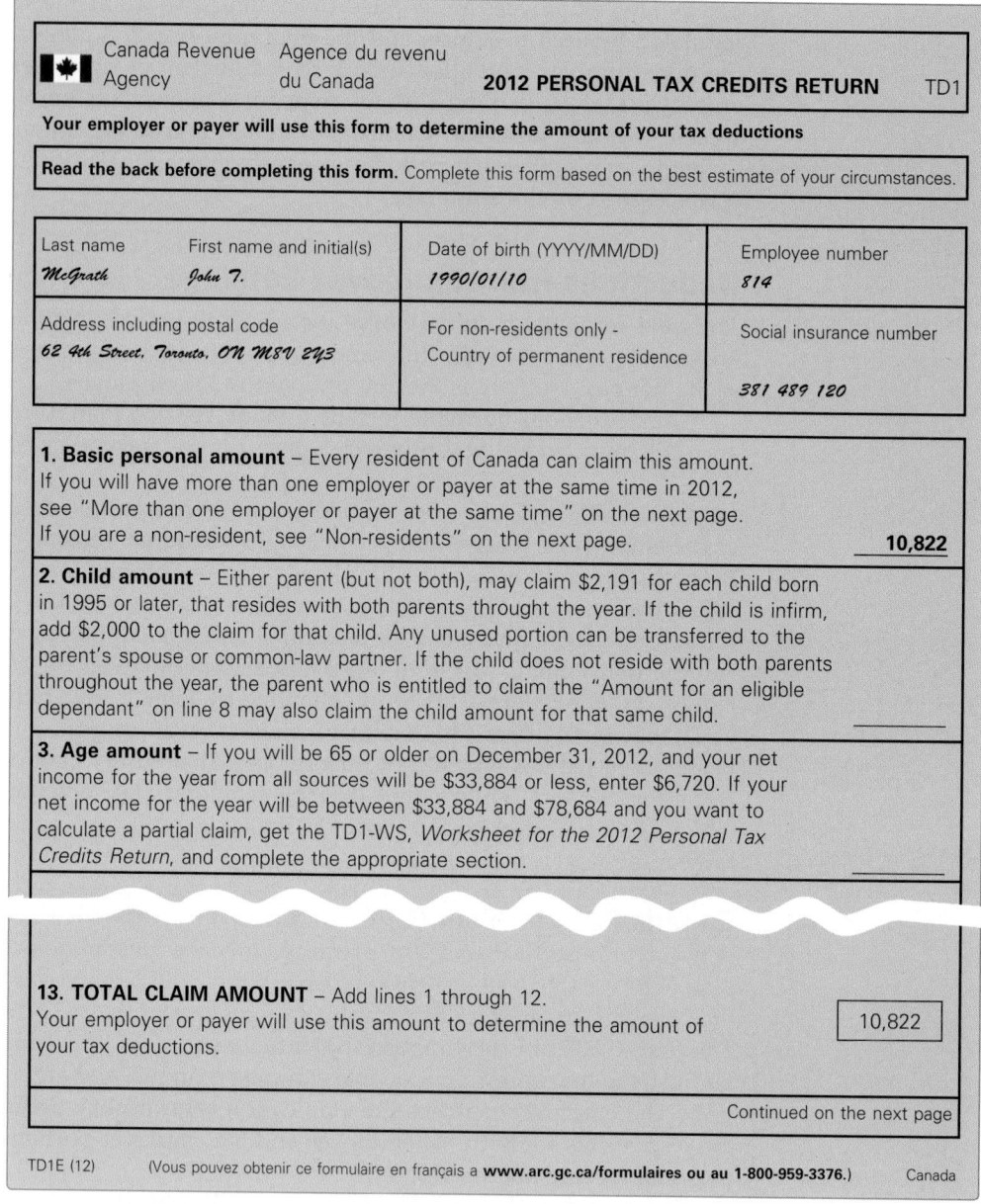

Source: Canada Revenue Agency. Reproduced with permission of the Minister of Public Works and Government Services Canada, 2012.

times the amount that the employee contributes. In 2012, the employee's contribution was 1.83% (1.47% in Quebec) of gross earnings paid up to the maximum earnings of $45,900. CRA also provides tables for employment insurance calculations. Alternatively, EI can be calculated by multiplying the gross wage by 1.83%. For example, if an employee's weekly wage was $600, the calculation would be as follows: $10.98 = $600 × 1.83%. Again, the employer is responsible for calculating the amounts for both the employee and the business, deducting the employee's portion from the employee's gross payroll, and remitting it to CRA.

Other Deductions Payroll may have numerous other deductions. For example, an employee may authorize deductions for retirement savings, charitable contributions, parking fees, or life insurance. A union contract may also require the deduction of union dues.

Steps for Completing Payroll

Although many complexities are involved in completing a payroll, five basic steps and four basic entries are required to complete a payroll run. These five steps and the related entries are summarized in Exhibit 4. This exhibit will be referred to throughout this section.

As well, if the payroll period extends over the year-end, an accrual is required for the days owing to the employees.

To illustrate computing an employee's earnings, John T. McGrath, the salesperson mentioned earlier, will be used. John's regular rate is $20 per hour, and any hours worked in excess of 40 hours per week are paid at 1½ times the regular rate. John worked 42 hours for the week ended January 30, 2015.

Step 1: Calculating Gross Pay, Deductions, and Net Pay

Gross earnings less payroll deductions equals *net pay*, sometimes called *take-home pay*. John's information would be compiled to first calculate the gross pay for the week.

His earnings of $860 for the week are computed as follows:

Earnings at regular rate (40 hrs. × $20)	$800.00
Earnings at overtime rate [2 hrs. × ($20 × 1.5)]	60.00
Total earnings	$860.00

Exhibit 4

Steps to Completing Payroll

1. **Calculating gross pay, deductions, and resulting net pay.**

2. **Recording distribution of gross pay.**

Salaries or Wages Expense	XX	
CPP Payable		XX
EI Payable		XX
Provincial Income Taxes Payable		XX
Federal Income Taxes Payable		XX
Other Benefits Payable		XX
Salaries or Wages Payable		XX

3. **Recording employer's portion of payroll expenses.**

CPP Expense	XX	
EI Expense	XX	
Other Benefits Expense	XX	
CPP Payable		XX
EI Payable		XX
Other Benefits Payable		XX

4. **Recording payment of net pay to employees.**

Salaries or Wages Payable	XX	
Cash		XX

5. **Recording remittance of payroll deductions.**
   This amount includes remittances to Canada Revenue Agency and any other optional deductions paid to third parties.

CPP Payable (employee and employer shares)	XX	
EI Payable (employee and employer shares)	XX	
Provincial Income Taxes Payable (employee share)	XX	
Federal Income Taxes Payable (employee share)	XX	
Cash		XX
Other Benefits Payable	XX	
Cash		XX

Some companies track the overtime premiums they pay. In this example, the gross earnings are calculated as follows:

Earnings at regular rate (42 hrs. × $20)	$840.00
Overtime premium [2 hrs. × ($20 × 0.5)]	20.00
Total earnings	$860.00

The two calculations result in the same gross earnings for the employee, but the second method allows the employer to track the payment of overtime premiums.

John's gross earnings are $860. Because he is older than 18, he is required to pay premiums both to Employment Insurance and to Canada Pension Plan. As well, he will have income taxes deducted from his paycheque.

Canada Pension Plan [$860 − ($3,500/52)] × 4.95%	$39.24
Employment Insurance ($860 × 1.83%)	15.74
Provincial income taxes	44.65
Federal income taxes	89.75

Assuming that John T. McGrath authorized weekly deductions for retirement savings of $20 and for a United Way contribution of $5, John's net pay for the week ended January 30, 2015, is $645.62, as shown below.

Gross earnings for the week		$860.00
Deductions:		
CPP	$39.24	
EI	15.74	
Provincial income taxes	44.65	
Federal income taxes	89.75	
Retirement savings	20.00	
United Way	5.00	
Total deductions		214.38
Net pay		$645.62

EXAMPLE EXERCISE 10-5 Calculating Gross Pay and Deductions
2

Sharon's pay rate is $22 per hour, and she worked 43 hours last week. CPP contributions are deducted at a rate of 4.95%, and EI contributions are deducted at a rate of 1.83%. Overtime premiums are paid at 50% of the regular rate for hours worked in excess of 40.

a. Calculate Sharon's gross pay.

b. Calculate Sharon's CPP and EI contributions.

FOLLOW MY EXAMPLE 10-5

a.
Earnings at regular rate (40 hrs. × $22)	$880.00
Earnings at overtime rate [3 hrs. × ($22 × 1.5)]	99.00
Total earnings	$979.00

b. CPP = [$979.00 − ($3,500/52)] × 4.95% = $45.13
   EI = $979.00 × 1.83% = $17.92

For Practice: PE 10-5

Canada Revenue Agency publishes payroll deduction tables annually. The tables can be used as an alternative method of calculating payroll deductions for CPP, EI, and income taxes. Excerpts from the 2012 Ontario payroll deduction tables are shown in Exhibit 5. Full tables are available on the CRA website and are updated annually.[7]

---

7 To access the CRA payroll deduction tables, visit www.cra-arc.gc.ca/tx/bsnss/tpcs/pyrll/t4032/menu-eng.html

To determine the deductions, begin by selecting the appropriate tables. CPP tables are created with the $3,500 basic exemption already taken into account. Thus, the tables are provided for weekly, biweekly, semi-monthly, and monthly payroll periods. The income tax tables are created based on the provincial and territorial tax rates. These tables are provided for each province and territory, and include one table for the provincial or territorial tax and one for the federal tax. Two tables are available for EI deductions: one for Quebec and one for the other provinces and the territories.

Using John T. McGrath's gross pay of $860.00, search for the gross amount in the *pay (or insurable earnings)* column and use the entry in the withholding column to determine the deduction. You will notice that the CPP and EI deductions from the tables are the same as our calculations in the previous section.

Step 2: Recording Distribution of Gross Pay

The journal entry to record John T. McGrath's weekly pay is:

2015					
Jan.	30	Wages Expense		860.00	
		Provincial Income Taxes Payable			44.65
		Federal Income Taxes Payable			89.75
		CPP Payable			39.24
		EI Payable			15.74
		United Way Payable			5.00
		RRSP Contribution Payable			20.00
		Wages Payable			645.62
		To record distribution of gross pay.			

Exhibit 5

2012 Payroll Deduction Tables Excerpts

Canada Pension Plan Contributions
Weekly (52 pay periods a year)

Cotisations au Régime de pensions du Canada
Hebdomadaire (52 périodes de paie par année)

Pay Rémunération		CPP RPC	Pay Rémunération		CPP RPC	Pay Rémunération		CPP RPC	Pay Rémunération		CPP RPC
From - De	To - À		From - De	To - À		From - De	To - À		From - De	To - À	
829.02 -	829.21	37.71	843.57 -	843.76	38.43	858.11 -	858.31	39.15	872.66 -	872.85	39.87
829.22 -	829.42	37.72	843.77 -	843.96	38.44	858.32 -	858.51	39.16	872.86 -	873.05	39.88
829.43 -	829.62	37.73	843.97 -	844.16	38.45	858.52 -	858.71	39.17	873.06 -	873.25	39.89
829.63 -	829.82	37.74	844.17 -	844.37	38.46	858.72 -	858.91	39.18	873.26 -	873.46	39.90
829.83 -	830.02	37.75	844.38 -	844.57	38.47	858.92 -	859.11	39.19	873.47 -	873.66	39.91
830.03 -	830.22	37.76	844.58 -	844.77	38.48	859.12 -	859.32	39.20	873.67 -	873.86	39.92
830.23 -	830.43	37.77	844.78 -	844.97	38.49	859.33 -	859.52	39.21	873.87 -	874.06	39.93
830.44 -	830.63	37.78	844.98 -	845.17	38.50	859.53 -	859.72	39.22	874.07 -	874.26	39.94
830.64 -	830.83	37.79	845.18 -	845.38	38.51	859.73 -	859.92	39.23	874.27 -	874.47	39.95
830.84 -	831.03	37.80	845.39 -	845.58	38.52	859.93 -	860.12	39.24	874.48 -	874.67	39.96
831.04 -	831.23	37.81	845.59 -	845.78	38.53	860.13 -	860.33	39.25	874.68 -	874.87	39.97
831.24 -	831.44	37.82	845.79 -	845.98	38.54	860.34 -	860.53	39.26	874.88 -	875.07	39.98
831.45 -	831.64	37.83	845.99 -	846.18	38.55	860.54 -	860.73	39.27	875.08 -	875.27	39.99
831.65 -	831.84	37.84	846.19 -	846.39	38.56	860.74 -	860.93	39.28	875.28 -	875.48	40.00
831.85 -	832.04	37.85	846.40 -	846.59	38.57	860.94 -	861.13	39.29	875.49 -	875.68	40.01
832.05 -	832.24	37.86	846.60 -	846.79	38.58	861.14 -	861.34	39.30	875.69 -	875.88	40.02
832.25 -	832.45	37.87	846.80 -	846.99	38.59	861.35 -	861.54	39.31	875.89 -	876.08	40.03
832.46 -	832.65	37.88	847.00 -	847.19	38.60	861.55 -	861.74	39.32	876.09 -	876.28	40.04

Employee's maximum CPP contribution for the year 2012 is $2,306.70
La cotisation maximale de l'employé au RPC pour l'année 2012 est de 2 306.70 $

(continued)

Source: Canada Revenue Agency. Reproduced with permission of the Minister of Public Works and Government Services Canada, 2012.

Exhibit 5

2012 Payroll Deduction Tables Excerpts (*continued*)

Employment Insurance Premiums   Cotisations à l'assurance-emploi

Insurable Earnings Rémunération assurable		EI premium Cotisation d'AE	Insurable Earnings Rémunération assurable		EI premium Cotisation d'AE	Insurable Earnings Rémunération assurable		EI premium Cotisation d'AE	Insurable Earnings Rémunération assurable		EI premium Cotisation d'AE
From - De	To - À		From - De	To - À		From - De	To - À		From - De	To - À	
816.67 -	817.21	14.95	856.02 -	856.55	15.67	895.36 -	895.90	16.39	934.70 -	935.24	17.11
817.22 -	817.75	14.96	856.56 -	857.10	15.68	895.91 -	896.44	16.40	935.25 -	935.79	17.12
817.76 -	818.30	14.97	857.11 -	857.65	15.69	896.45 -	896.99	16.41	935.80 -	936.33	17.13
818.31 -	818.85	14.98	857.66 -	858.19	15.70	897.00 -	897.54	16.42	936.34 -	936.88	17.14
818.86 -	819.39	14.99	858.20 -	858.74	15.71	897.55 -	898.08	16.43	936.89 -	937.43	17.15
819.40 -	819.94	15.00	858.75 -	859.28	15.72	898.09 -	898.63	16.44	937.44 -	937.97	17.16
819.95 -	820.49	15.01	859.29 -	859.83	15.73	898.64 -	899.18	16.45	937.98 -	938.52	17.17
820.50 -	821.03	15.02	859.84 -	860.38	15.74	899.19 -	899.72	16.46	938.53 -	939.07	17.18
821.04 -	821.58	15.03	860.39 -	860.92	15.75	899.73 -	900.27	16.47	939.08 -	939.61	17.19
821.59 -	822.13	15.04	860.93 -	861.47	15.76	900.28 -	900.81	16.48	939.62 -	940.16	17.20
822.14 -	822.67	15.05	861.48 -	862.02	15.77	900.82 -	901.36	16.49	940.17 -	940.71	17.21
822.68 -	823.22	15.06	862.03 -	862.56	15.78	901.37 -	901.91	16.50	940.72 -	941.25	17.22
823.23 -	823.77	15.07	862.57 -	863.11	15.79	901.92 -	902.45	16.51	941.26 -	941.80	17.23
823.78 -	824.31	15.08	863.12 -	863.66	15.80	902.46 -	903.00	16.52	941.81 -	942.34	17.24
824.32 -	824.86	15.09	863.67 -	864.20	15.81	903.01 -	903.55	16.53	942.35 -	942.89	17.25
824.87 -	825.40	15.10	864.21 -	864.75	15.82	903.56 -	904.09	16.54	942.90 -	943.44	17.26
825.41 -	825.95	15.11	864.76 -	865.30	15.83	904.10 -	904.64	16.55	943.45 -	943.98	17.27
825.96 -	826.50	15.12	865.31 -	865.84	15.84	904.65 -	905.19	16.56	943.99 -	944.53	17.28

Yearly maximum insurable earnings are $45,900
Yearly maximum employee premiums are $839.97
The premium rate for 2012 is 1.83 %
Source: Canada Revenue Agency. Reproduced with permission of the Minister of Public Works and Government Services Canada, 2012.

Le maximum annuel de la rémunération assurable est de 45 900 $
La cotisation maximale annuella de l'employé est de 839,97$
Le taux de cotisation pour 2012 est de 1.83 %

Ontario provincial tax deductions
Effective January 1, 2012
Weekly (52 pay periods a year)
Also look up the tax deductions in the federal table

Retenues d'impôt provincial de l'Ontario
En vigueur le 1er janvier 2012
Hebdomadaire (52 périodes de paie par année)
Cherchez aussi les retenues d'impôt dans la table fédérale

Pay Rémunération		Provincial claim codes/Codes de demande provinciaux										
		0	1	2	3	4	5	6	7	8	9	10
From - De	Less than Moins de	Deduct from each pay / Retenez sur chaque paie										
808 -	816	49.55	40.45	39.45	37.50	35.50	33.55	31.60	29.60	27.65	25.70	23.70
816 -	824	50.30	41.15	40.15	38.20	36.20	34.25	32.30	30.30	28.35	26.40	24.40
824 -	832	51.00	41.85	40.85	38.90	36.95	34.95	33.00	31.00	29.05	27.10	25.10
832 -	840	51.70	42.55	41.55	39.60	37.65	35.65	33.70	31.75	29.75	27.80	25.85
840 -	848	52.40	43.25	42.25	40.30	38.35	36.35	34.40	32.45	30.45	28.50	26.55
848 -	856	53.10	43.95	43.00	41.00	39.05	37.05	35.10	33.15	31.15	29.20	27.25
856 -	864	53.80	44.65	43.70	41.70	39.75	37.80	35.80	33.85	31.90	29.90	27.95
864 -	872	54.50	45.35	44.40	42.40	40.45	38.50	36.50	34.55	32.60	30.60	28.65
872 -	880	55.20	46.05	45.10	43.10	41.15	39.20	37.20	35.25	33.30	31.30	29.35
880 -	888	55.90	46.80	45.80	43.85	41.85	39.90	37.95	35.95	34.00	32.00	30.05
888 -	896	56.65	47.50	46.50	44.55	42.55	40.60	38.65	36.65	34.70	32.75	30.75
896 -	904	57.35	48.20	47.20	45.25	43.30	41.30	39.35	37.40	35.40	33.45	31.50
904 -	912	58.05	48.90	47.95	45.95	44.00	42.05	40.05	38.10	36.15	34.15	32.20
912 -	920	58.75	49.65	48.65	46.70	44.70	42.75	40.75	38.80	36.85	34.85	32.90
920 -	928	59.70	50.55	49.60	47.60	45.65	43.70	41.70	39.75	37.80	35.80	33.85

Source: Canada Revenue Agency. Reproduced with permission of the Minister of Public Works and Government Services Canada, 2012.

(*continued*)

Exhibit 5

2012 Payroll Deduction Tables Excerpts (*concluded*)

Federal tax deductions	Retenues d'impôt fédéral
Effective January 1, 2012	En vigueur le 1er janvier 2012
Weekly (52 pay periods a year)	Hebdomadaire (52 périodes de paie par année)
Also look up the tax deductions in the provincial table	Cherchez aussi les retenues d'impôt dans la table provinciale

Pay Rémunération		Federal claim codes/Codes de demande fédéraux										
		0	1	2	3	4	5	6	7	8	9	10
From - De	Less than Moins de	Deduct from each pay / Retenez sur chaque paie										
811 - 819		111.30	80.10	77.10	71.15	65.15	59.20	53.25	47.30	41.30	35.35	29.40
819 - 827		112.55	81.35	78.35	72.40	66.40	60.45	54.50	48.50	42.55	36.60	30.65
827 - 835		114.25	83.00	80.05	74.05	68.10	62.15	56.15	50.20	44.25	38.25	32.30
835 - 843		115.90	84.70	81.70	75.75	69.80	63.80	57.85	51.90	45.90	39.95	34.00
843 - 851		117.60	86.35	83.40	77.40	71.45	65.50	59.50	53.55	47.60	41.65	35.65
851 - 859		119.25	88.05	85.05	79.10	73.15	67.15	61.20	55.25	49.25	43.30	37.35
859 - 867		120.95	89.75	86.75	80.80	74.80	68.85	62.90	56.90	50.95	45.00	39.00
867 - 875		122.60	91.40	88.40	82.45	76.50	70.55	64.55	58.60	52.65	46.65	40.70
875 - 883		124.30	93.10	90.10	84.15	78.15	72.20	66.25	60.25	54.30	48.35	42.40
883 - 891		126.00	94.75	91.80	85.85	79.85	73.90	67.95	61.95	56.00	50.05	44.05
891 - 899		127.70	96.45	93.50	87.55	81.55	75.60	69.65	63.65	57.70	51.75	45.75
899 - 907		129.40	98.20	95.20	89.25	83.25	77.30	71.35	65.35	59.40	53.45	47.45
907 - 915		131.10	99.90	96.90	90.95	84.95	79.00	73.05	67.05	61.10	55.15	49.15
915 - 923		132.80	101.60	98.60	92.65	86.65	80.70	74.75	68.75	62.80	56.85	50.85
923 - 931		134.50	103.30	100.30	94.35	88.35	82.40	76.45	70.45	64.50	58.55	52.55

Source: Canada Revenue Agency. Reproduced with permission of the Minister of Public Works and Government Services Canada, 2012.

EXAMPLE EXERCISE 10-6   Employee Net Pay   ②

Karen Dunn's weekly gross earnings for the week ended April 3 were $850. CPP contributions of $38.74, EI contributions of $15.55, provincial income taxes of $41.30, and federal income taxes of $80.45 are to be deducted from her gross earnings.
   Calculate Dunn's net pay.

FOLLOW MY EXAMPLE 10-6

Gross wage		$850.00
Less: Provincial income taxes	$41.30	
Federal income taxes	80.45	
CPP	38.74	
EI	15.55	176.04
Net pay		$673.96

For Practice: PE 10-6

Each employee's earnings to date must be determined at the end of each payroll period. This total is necessary for computing the employee's CPP and EI contributions and the employer's payroll taxes. As well, the earnings-to-date total is used as the basis for the amounts declared on the T4 statement. An example of John T. McGrath's T4 statement for the prior year is shown in Exhibit 6. Thus, detailed payroll records must be kept for each employee. This record is called an **employee's earnings record**.

Exhibit 7, on pages 524 and 525, shows a portion of the employee's earnings record for John T. McGrath. An employee's earnings record and the payroll register are interrelated. For example, John's earnings record for January 30 can be traced to the fourth line of the payroll register in Exhibit 10 on page 528.

Exhibit 6

T4-Statement of Remuneration Paid

Employer's name – Nom de l'employeur	
McDermott Supply Co. 411 5th Ave. Toronto, Ontario M8V 3X4	

I✦I Canada Revenue Agency   Agence du revenu du Canada

T4

Year / Année **2014**

STATEMENT OF REMUNERATION PAID
ÉTAT DE LA RÉMUNÉRATION PAYÉE

Employment income – line 101 Revenus d'emploi – ligne 101	Income tax deducted – line 437 Impôt sur le revenu retenu – ligne 437
14 44,230	00	**22** 14,153	60

Business Number
Numéro d'entreprise

54

Province of employment Province d'emploi	Employee's CPP contributions – line 308 Cotisations de l'employé au RPC – ligne 308	EI insurable earnings Gains assurables d'AE
10	**16** 2,016	35	**24** 44,230	00

Social insurance number
Numéro d'assurance sociale

Exempt – Exemption
CPP/QPP   EI   PPIP

12 381 489 120

28

RPC/RRQ   AE   RPAP

Employment code Code d'emploi	Employee's QPP contributions – line 308 Cotisations de l'employé au RRQ – ligne 308	CPP/QPP pensionable earnings Gains ouvrant droit à pension – RPC/RRQ
29	**17**	**26** 44,230	00

	Employee's name and address – Nom et adresse de l'employé	

Last name (in capital letters) – Nom de famille (en lettres moulées)	First name – Prénom	Initials – Initiales
McGrath	John	T.

62 4th St.
Toronto, Ontario
M8V 2Y3

Employee's EI premiums – line 312 Cotisations de l'employé à l'AE – ligne 312	Union dues – line 212 Cotisations syndicales – ligne 212
18 809	41	**44**

RPP contributions – line 207 Cotisations à un RPA – ligne 207	Charitable donations – see the back Dons de bienfaisance – voir au verso
20	**46**

Pension adjustment – line 206 Facteur d'équivalence – ligne 206	RPP or DPSP registration number N° d'agrément d'un RPA ou d'un RPDB
52	**50**

Employee's PPIP premiums – see the back Cotisations de l'employé au RPAP – voir au verso	PPIP insurable earnings Gains assurables du RPAP
55	**56**

Other information (see the back)	Box – Case	Amount – Montant	Box – Case	Amount – Montant	Box – Case	Amount – Montant
Autres renseignements (voir au verso)	Box – Case	Amount – Montant	Box – Case	Amount – Montant	Box – Case	Amount – Montant

T4 (06)

Source: Canada Revenue Agency. Reproduced with permission of the Minister of Public Works and Government Services Canada, 2012.

Exhibit 7

Employee's Earnings Record

John T. McGrath
62 4th St.
Toronto, Ontario M8V 2Y3

PHONE: 416-555-3148

CLAIM CODE: 1		**PAY RATE:**	**$800.00 per Week**
OCCUPATION:	**Salesperson**	**EQUIVALENT HOURLY RATE: $20**	

				Earnings		
	Period Ending	Total Hours	Regular Earnings	Overtime Earnings	Total Earnings	Cumulative Total
42	JAN. 9	46	800.00	180.00	980.00	980.00	42
43	JAN. 16	45	800.00	150.00	950.00	1,930.00	43
44	JAN. 23	44	800.00	120.00	920.00	2,850.00	44
45	JAN. 30	42	800.00	60.00	860.00	3,710.00	45

(continued)

Exhibit 7

Employee's Earnings Record (*concluded*)

										Paid		
SIN: 381 489 120											EMPLOYEE NO.: 814	
DATE OF BIRTH: January 10, 1990												
DATE EMPLOYMENT TERMINATED:												
			Deductions							Paid		
	CPP	EI	Prov. Income Taxes	Fed. Income Taxes	Retirement Savings	Other		Total		Net Amount	Cheque No.	
42	45.18	17.93	58.25	115.35	20.00			256.71		723.29	6175	42
43	43.69	17.39	55.35	108.40	20.00			244.83		705.17	6225	43
44	42.21	16.84	49.65	101.60	20.00			230.30		689.70	6344	44
45	39.24	15.74	44.65	89.75	20.00	UW	5.00	214.38		645.62	6860	45

Step 3: Recording Employer's Portion of Payroll Expenses

The employer deducts and remits employee premiums for CPP and EI. The employer also is required to remit the employer portion of the CPP and EI premiums. As noted earlier, the employer matches the CPP deduction and pays 1.4 times the employee's EI deduction. The employee portion of the remittance is not a separate expense of the business, as it is included in the wage expense. The employer portion of the payroll expenses, however, is a separate expense of the company.

To illustrate, McDermott Supply Co. would need to pay the following amounts for John T. McGrath's payroll for the week ended January 30.

McDermott Supply Co.'s contribution:

CPP (matched)	$39.24
EI ($15.74 × 1.4)	22.04
Total	$61.28

The entry for the payroll deductions that the employer pays is as follows:

2015					
Jan.	30	CPP Expense		39.24	
		EI Expense		22.04	
		CPP Payable			39.24
		EI Payable			22.04
		To record employer's portion of payroll deductions.			

The preceding employer deductions are an operating expense of the company. The employer is responsible for remitting to the government both the employee and the employer contributions for income taxes, CPP, and EI. Exhibit 8 summarizes the responsibility for employee and employer payroll taxes.

Exhibit 8

Responsibility for Source Deductions

	Employee Costs	Employer Costs	
Provincial Income Tax	✓		
Federal Income Tax	✓		
Canada Pension Plan	✓	✓	× 1.0
Employment Insurance	✓	✓	× 1.4
WCB or WSIB		✓	
Other Deductions*	✓	✓	

*There are other deductions, such as charitable donations, that are employee costs only.

INTEGRITY, OBJECTIVITY, AND ETHICS IN BUSINESS

TAXING ISSUES

Both owners of sole proprietorships and directors of corporations can be held liable for amounts owing to the government. Owners of sole proprietorships are responsible for payments to the provincial Minister of Finance for PST collected, and to the Receiver General for employee taxes, employer and employee portions of EI and CPP, and remittance of GST, or HST, collected. If businesses do not submit payments by their due dates, they are charged fines and interest that increase with each late payment or missed payment. If the business should fail and these amounts are outstanding, the owner is personally liable for the payment in full. Directors of corporations are in the same position: they may be held liable for payroll deductions and for GST, PST, and HST remittances that have not been paid to the government when the company fails.

Step 4: Recording Payment of Net Pay to Employees

Usually within days of recording the salary payable, the salary is paid to the employee. An electronic funds transaction is made, moving the funds from the company bank account to John's bank account. If electronic funds transactions are not used, a physical cheque is printed and signed.

The journal entry is as follows:

2015				
Jan.	30	Wages Payable	645.62	
		Cash		645.62
		To record payment of salary.		

John will also receive a pay advice, as shown in Exhibit 9. If electronic funds transactions are not used, the paycheque will include a detachable statement showing how the net pay was computed.

Step 5: Recording Remittance of Payroll Deductions

Within the next month, the source deductions withheld from employees and the employer's portion are remitted to CRA. Fines and penalties are levied if this remittance is not completed on time.

Exhibit 9

Pay Advice

McDermott Supply Co. MS			Cheque Number: 6860 Pay Period Ending: 30/01/15

McDermott Supply Co.
411 5th Ave.
Toronto, ON
M8V 3X4

John T. McGrath
62 4th St.
Toronto, ON M8V 2Y3

Cheque Number: 6860
Pay Period Ending: 30/01/15

HOURS AND EARNINGS		TAXES AND DEDUCTIONS		
DESCRIPTION	AMOUNT	DESCRIPTION	CURRENT AMOUNT	Y-T-D AMOUNT
Rate of Pay Reg.	20	Canada Pension Plan	39.24	170.32
Rate of Pay O.T.	30	Employment Insurance	15.74	67.90
Hours Worked Reg.	40	Provincial Income Taxes	44.65	207.90
Hours Worked O.T.	2	Federal Income Taxes	89.75	415.10
		Savings	20.00	80.00
Net Pay	645.62	United Way	5.00	5.00
Total Gross Pay	860.00			
Total Gross Y-T-D	3,710.00	Total	214.38	946.22

The entry is as follows:

Feb.	15	CPP Payable	78.48*	
		EI Payable	37.78**	
		Provincial Income Taxes Payable	44.65	
		Federal Income Taxes Payable	89.75	
		Cash		250.66
		Remittance of source deductions to CRA.		
		*($39.24 + 39.24)		
		**($15.74 + $22.04)		

The other deductions are remitted to the correct organizations. The remittances required for John are as follows:

2015 Jan.	30	United Way Payable	5.00	
		Cash		5.00
		Remittance of employee donation to United Way.		
Jan.	30	RRSP Contribution Payable	20.00	
		Cash		20.00
		Remittance of RRSP funds to pension fund manager.		

Steps to Completing Payroll with a Payroll System

Describe payroll accounting systems and apply steps to completing payroll within a payroll accounting system.

A payroll system that handles numerous employees is illustrated using the five steps to complete payroll. These same five steps were illustrated earlier with one employee, John T. McGrath.

Payroll systems should be designed to do the following:

1. Pay employees accurately and in a timely fashion.
2. Meet regulatory requirements of federal and provincial, or territorial, governments.
3. Provide useful data for management decision-making needs.

Although payroll systems differ among companies, most payroll systems comprise the following major elements:

1. A payroll register
2. An employee's earnings record
3. Pay advice or payroll cheques

Step 1: Calculating Gross Pay, Deductions, and Net Pay

The **payroll register** is a multicolumn report used for summarizing the data for each payroll period. The register tracks the gross pay, deductions, and resulting net pay of employees. Although payroll registers vary by company, a payroll register normally contains the columns shown in Exhibit 10.

Note: Payroll deductions become a liability to the employer when the payroll is earned by the employees.

Step 2: Recording Distribution of Gross Pay

The column totals of the payroll register provide the basis for recording the journal entry for payroll. This is the equivalent entry to step 2 for John T. McGrath's entry, combined for everyone in the company. Payroll deductions are recorded as liabilities

Exhibit 10

Payroll Register

January 30		Earnings			
Employee Name	**Total Hours**	**Regular**	**Overtime**	**Total**	
1 Abrams, Julie S.	40	500.00		500.00	1
2 Elrod, Fred G.	44	392.00	58.80	450.80	2
3 Gauvreau, Micheline	40	840.00		840.00	3
4 McGrath, John T.	42	800.00	60.00	860.00	4
5 Wilkes, Glenn K.	40	480.00		480.00	5
6 Zumpano, Michael W.	40	600.00		600.00	6
Total		3,612.00	118.80	3,730.80	

	Deductions								Paid	Accounts Debited		
	CPP	**EI**	**Prov. Income Taxes**	**Fed. Income Taxes**	**RRSP**	**Misc.**		**Total**	**Net Pay**	**Sales Salaries Expense**	**Office Salaries Expense**	
1	21.42	9.15	20.25	36.20	20.00	UW	10.00	117.02	382.98	500.00		1
2	18.98	8.25	16.15	28.90		AR	50.00	122.28	328.52		450.80	2
3	38.25	15.37	42.55	84.70	25.00	UW	10.00	215.87	624.13	840.00		3
4	39.24	15.74	44.65	89.75	20.00	UW	5.00	214.38	645.62	860.00		4
5	20.43	8.78	19.15	33.40	10.00	UW		91.76	388.24	480.00		5
6	26.37	10.98	24.95	49.90	5.00	UW	2.00	119.20	480.80		600.00	6
	164.69	68.27	167.70	322.85	80.00	UW	27.00	880.51	2,850.29	2,680.00	1,050.80	
						AR	50.00					

Miscellaneous Deductions: UW—United Way; AR—Accounts Receivable

when the payroll is earned by the employees. The entry based on the payroll register in Exhibit 10 is shown below.

2015					
Jan.	30	Sales Salaries Expense		2,680.00	
		Office Salaries Expense		1,050.80	
		CPP Payable			164.69
		EI Payable			68.27
		Provincial Income Taxes Payable			167.70
		Federal Income Taxes Payable			322.85
		RRSP Contribution Payable			80.00
		United Way Payable			27.00
		Accounts Receivable—Fred G. Elrod (emp.)			50.00
		Salaries Payable			2,850.29
		Payroll for week ended January 30.			

EXAMPLE EXERCISE 10-7   Journalize Period Payroll   ③

The payroll register of Chen Engineering Services indicates $900 of CPP contributions withheld and $225 of EI contributions withheld on total salaries of $15,000 for the period. Income taxes for the period included provincial tax of $1,015 and federal tax of $1,910.

   Provide the journal entry for the period's payroll.

FOLLOW MY EXAMPLE 10-7

Salaries Expense...	15,000	
CPP Payable...		900
EI Payable		225
Provincial Income Taxes Payable.......................................		1,015
Federal Income Taxes Payable...		1,910
Salaries Payable...		10,950

For Practice: PE 10-7

Step 3: Recording Employer's Portion of Payroll Expenses

To illustrate, the journal entry for the employer portion of the January 30 payroll for McDermott Supply Co. is as follows:

2015					
Jan.	30	EI Expense ($68.27 × 1.4)		95.58	
		CPP Expense		164.69	
		EI Payable			95.58
		CPP Payable			164.69

The same EI and CPP payable accounts are used to record both the employer's and the employees' portions of these deductions. These amounts are due from the business to the government, and the total amount is remitted to the Receiver General for Canada. See the T accounts below.

EI Payable

		68.27	For the employees' portion
		95.58	For the employer's portion
		163.85	
To pay the Receiver General	163.85		
		0	

CPP Payable

		164.69	For the employees' portion
		164.69	For the employer's portion
		329.38	
To pay the Receiver General	329.38		
		0	

EXAMPLE EXERCISE 10-8 **Journalize Payroll Deductions**   ③

The payroll register of Chen Engineering Services indicates $900 of CPP contributions and $225 of EI contributions withheld on total salaries of $15,000 for the period. Provincial taxes of $1,015 and federal taxes of $1,910 were deducted. Provide the journal entry to record the employer's payroll deductions liability for the period.

FOLLOW MY EXAMPLE 10-8

CPP Expense	900	
EI Expense	315*	
CPP Payable		900
EI Payable		315
*$225 × 1.4		

For Practice: PE 10-8

Step 4: Recording Payment of Net Pay to Employees

To illustrate, the journal entry for the January 30 McDermott Supply Co. net pay is as follows:

2015				
Jan.	30	Salaries Payable	2,850.29	
		Cash		2,850.29
		Payment of weekly payroll.		

Step 5: Recording Remittance of Payroll Deductions

The following entry is made when the cheque is written for payment to the Receiver General for Canada.

2015				
Feb.	15	EI Payable (68.27 + 95.58)	163.85	
		CPP Payable (164.69 + 164.69)	329.38	
		Provincial Income Taxes Payable	167.70	
		Federal Income Taxes Payable	322.85	
		Cash		983.78
		Remittance of payroll deductions.		

EXAMPLE EXERCISE 10-9 **Recording Remittance of Payroll Deductions**   ③

Archer Transportations withheld CPP of $391.24, EI of $152.64, provincial income taxes of $732.58, and federal income taxes of $1,408.39 from its employees' pay during a recent pay period.

Provide the journal entry to record the remittance of payroll deductions to the Receiver General.

FOLLOW MY EXAMPLE 10-9

CPP Payable ($391.24 + $391.24)	782.48	
EI Payable [$152.64 + ($152.64 × 1.4)]	366.34	
Provincial Income Taxes Payable	732.58	
Federal Income Taxes Payable	1,408.39	
Cash		3,289.79
Remittance of source deductions for payroll.		

For Practice: PE 10-9

Payroll System Elements

The inputs into a payroll system may be classified as follows:

1. Constants, which are data that remain unchanged from payroll to payroll.

   Examples: Employee names, social insurance numbers, rates of pay, tax rates, and withholding tables.

2. Variables, which are data that may change from payroll to payroll.

   Examples: Number of hours or days worked for each employee, accrued days of sick leave, vacation credits, total earnings to date, and total withholdings.

In a computerized accounting system, constants are stored within a payroll file. The variables are input each pay period by a payroll clerk. In some systems, employees swipe their identification (ID) cards when they report for and leave work. In such cases, the hours worked by each employee are automatically updated.

A computerized payroll system also maintains electronic versions of the payroll register and employee earnings records. Payroll system outputs, such as payroll cheques, EFTs, and tax records, are automatically produced each pay period.

Internal Controls for Payroll Systems

The cash payment controls described in Chapter 7, Internal Control and Cash, also apply to payrolls. Some examples of payroll controls include the following:

1. If a cheque-signing machine is used, blank payroll cheques and access to the machine should be restricted to prevent their theft or misuse.
2. The hiring and firing of employees should be properly authorized and approved in writing.
3. All changes in pay rates should be properly authorized and approved in writing.
4. Employees should be observed when arriving for work to verify that employees are "checking in" for work only once and only for themselves. Employees may "check in" for work by using a time card or by swiping their employee ID card.
5. Payroll cheques should be distributed by someone other than employee supervisors.
6. A special payroll bank account should be used. An advantage of using a separate payroll bank account is that reconciling the bank statements is simplified. In addition, a payroll bank account establishes control over payroll cheques and, thus, prevents their theft or misuse.

INTEGRITY, OBJECTIVITY, AND ETHICS IN BUSINESS

WATCH OUT FOR GHOSTS ON YOUR PAYROLL

Ghost employees are fictitious employees that exist on the payroll register. In one case, a former bookkeeper in Manitoba managed to steal more than $1.1 million by manipulating the payroll records. It is alleged that she maintained employee records for employees who had died or no longer worked for the organization, cashed the cheques to the ghost employees, and eventually transferred the funds into her personal account. Who was responsible to check the payroll? The bookkeeper!

The theft was discovered by the bank when money in the organization's account started to get low and the bank began scrutinizing each transaction. This organization lacked strong internal controls for its payroll system.

Sources: CBC News, "Former Band Council Employee Charged in $1M Theft," December 10, 2009, http://www.cbc.ca/news/canada/manitoba/story/2009/12/10/mb-theft-norway-house-money-manitoba.html; Aldo Santin, "First Nation Victim of $1-M Fraud: Police," *Winnipeg Free Press*, December 11, 2009, http://www.winnipegfreepress.com/local/first-nation-victim-of-1-m-fraud-police-79038552.html.

 # Balance Sheet Presentation

Present current liabilities on the balance sheet.

Current Liabilities on the Balance Sheet

Accounts payable, the current portion of long-term debt, notes payable, and any other debts that are due within one year are reported as current liabilities on the balance sheet. The balance sheet presentation of current liabilities for Morning Java is as follows:

Morning Java
Balance Sheet
December 31, 2015

Liabilities	
Current liabilities:	
Accounts payable	$133,000
Notes payable (current portion)	200,000
Salaries and wages payable	42,000
Source deductions payable	16,400
Interest payable	40,000
Total current liabilities	$431,400

FINANCIAL ANALYSIS AND INTERPRETATION   f·a·i

The Current Assets and Current Liabilities sections of the balance sheet for Noble Co. and Hart Co. are illustrated as follows:

	Noble Co.	Hart Co.
Current assets:		
Cash	$147,000	$120,000
Accounts receivable (net)	84,000	472,000
Inventory	150,000	200,000
Total current assets	$381,000	$792,000
Current liabilities:		
Accounts payable	$ 75,000	$227,000
Wages payable	30,000	193,000
Notes payable	115,000	320,000
Total current liabilities	$220,000	$740,000

We can use this information to evaluate Noble's and Hart's ability to pay their current liabilities within a short period of time, using the **quick ratio** or **acid-test ratio**. The quick ratio is computed as follows:

$$\text{Quick Ratio} = \frac{\text{Quick Assets}}{\text{Current Liabilities}}$$

The quick ratio measures the "instant" debt-paying ability of a company, using quick assets. **Quick assets** are cash, receivables, and other current assets that can quickly be converted into cash. It is often considered desirable to have a quick ratio exceeding 1.0. A ratio less than 1.0 would indicate that current liabilities cannot be covered by cash and "near cash" assets.

To illustrate, the quick ratios for both companies would be as follows:

$$\text{Noble Co.} = \frac{\$147,000 + \$84,000}{\$220,000} = 1.05$$

$$\text{Hart Co.} = \frac{\$120,000 + \$472,000}{\$740,000} = 0.80$$

As you can see, Noble Co. has quick assets in excess of current liabilities, or a quick ratio of 1.05. The ratio exceeds 1.0, indicating that the quick assets should be sufficient to meet current liabilities. Hart Co., however, has a quick ratio of 0.8. Its quick assets will not be sufficient to cover the current liabilities. Hart could solve this problem by working with a bank to convert its short-term debt of $320,000 into a long-term obligation. This would remove the notes payable from current liabilities. If Hart did this, then its quick ratio would improve to 1.4 ($592,000/ $420,000), which would be sufficient for quick assets to cover current liabilities.

EXAMPLE EXERCISE 10-10 Quick Ratio   ④

Moncton Company reported the following current assets and liabilities for December 31, 2015 and 2014:

	Dec. 31, 2015	Dec. 31, 2014
Cash	$ 620	$ 560
Temporary investments	1,330	1,250
Accounts receivable	850	830
Inventory	1,000	1,000
Accounts payable	2,800	2,200

1. Compute the quick ratio for December 31, 2015 and 2014.
2. Interpret the company's quick ratio. Is the quick ratio improving or declining?

FOLLOW MY EXAMPLE 10-10

1. December 31, 2015
   Quick Ratio = Quick Assets ÷ Current Liabilities
   Quick Ratio = ($620 + $1,330 + $850) ÷ $2,800
   Quick Ratio = 1.0

   December 31, 2014
   Quick Ratio = Quick Assets ÷ Current Liabilities
   Quick Ratio = ($560 + $1,250 + $830) ÷ $2,200
   Quick Ratio = 1.2

2. The quick ratio of Moncton Company has declined from 1.2 in 2014 to 1.0 in 2015. This decrease is the result of a large increase in accounts payable compared to relatively smaller increases in the three types of quick assets (cash, short-term investments, and accounts receivable).

For Practice: PE 10-10

At a Glance 10

1   Describe and illustrate known liabilities, estimated liabilities, contingent liabilities, and provisions.

Key Points	Key Learning Outcomes	Page	Example Exercises
Current liabilities are obligations that are to be paid out of current assets and are due within a short time, usually within one year. Types of current liabilities are known liabilities, estimated liabilities, contingent liabilities, and provisions.	• Identify and define the most frequently reported current liabilities on the balance sheet.	504	
	• Journalize known liabilities.	506	10-1, 2
	• Journalize estimated liabilities.	512	10-3
	• Describe the accounting for contingent liabilities.	513	10-4
	• Describe the accounting for provisions.	515	

2   Determine employer liabilities for payroll, including liabilities arising from employee earnings and deductions from earnings.

Key Points	Key Learning Outcomes	Page	Example Exercises
An employer's liability for payroll is determined from employee total earnings, including overtime pay. From this amount, employee deductions are subtracted to arrive at the net pay to be paid to each employee. Employers also incur liabilities for their premiums for employment insurance (EI), Canada Pension Plan (CPP), Workers' Compensation Board (WCB), and Workplace Safety and Insurance Board (WSIB).	• Five steps to completing payroll:		
	1. Calculating gross pay, deductions, and net pay.	519	10-5
	2. Recording distribution of gross pay.	521	10-6
	3. Recording employer's portion of payroll expenses.	525	
	4. Recording payment of net pay to employees.	526	
	5. Recording remittance of payroll deductions.	526	
	• Describe the employees' earnings record and payroll advice.		

3   Describe payroll accounting systems and apply steps to completing payroll within a payroll accounting system.

Key Points	Key Learning Outcomes	Page	Example Exercises
The payroll register is used in assembling and summarizing the data needed for each payroll period. The payroll register is supported by a detailed payroll record for each employee, called an employee's earnings record.	• Five steps to completing payroll:		
	1. Calculating gross pay, deductions, and net pay.	528	
	2. Recording distribution of gross pay.	528	10-7
	3. Recording employer's portion of payroll expenses.	529	10-8
	4. Recording payment of net pay to employees.	530	
	5. Recording remittance of payroll deductions.	530	10-9
	• Describe elements of a payroll system and internal controls.		

Present current liabilities on the balance sheet.

Key Points	Key Learning Outcomes	Page	Example Exercises
Accounts payable, the current portion of long-term debt, notes payable, and any other debts that are due within one year are reported as current liabilities on the balance sheet.	• Describe the presentation of current liabilities on the balance sheet.	532	
	• Calculate the quick ratio.	533	10-10

GLOSSARY

accounts payable subsidiary ledger – A secondary ledger that supports the accounts payable controlling account. (p. 505)

acid-test ratio – A financial ratio that measures the ability to pay current liabilities with quick assets (cash, marketable securities, accounts receivable). (p. 533) Also known as *quick ratio*.

contingent liabilities – Liabilities that may arise from past transactions if certain events occur in the future. (p. 505)

employee's earnings record – A detailed record of each employee's earnings. (p. 523)

estimated liabilities – Liabilities whose existence is known but the amount is an estimate. (p. 505)

gross pay – The total earnings of an employee for a payroll period. (p. 517)

known liabilities – Liabilities that arise when a transaction occurs (e.g., a purchase on account). (p. 505)

net pay – Gross pay less payroll deductions; the amount the employer is obligated to pay the employee. (p. 517)

payroll – The total amount paid to employees for a certain period. (p. 516)

payroll register – A multicolumn report used to assemble and summarize payroll data at the end of each payroll period. (p. 528)

provisions – Liabilities of uncertain timing or amount. (p. 505)

quick assets – Cash and other current assets that can be quickly converted to cash, such as marketable securities and receivables. (p. 533)

quick ratio – A financial ratio that measures the ability to pay current liabilities with quick assets (cash, marketable securities, accounts receivable). (p. 533) Also known as *acid-test ratio*.

ILLUSTRATIVE PROBLEM

Selected transactions of Taylor Company, completed during the fiscal year ended December 31, are as follows:

Apr. 10. Purchased merchandise on account from Kelvin Co. and issued a 60-day, 5% note for $20,000 in exchange for the inventory.

Jun. 9. Paid Kelvin Co. the amount owed on the note of April 10.

Aug. 1. Issued a $50,000, 90-day, 7% note to Harold Co. in exchange for a building.

Oct. 30. Paid Harold Co. the amount due on the note of August 1.

Dec. 27. Journalized the entry to record the biweekly payroll. A summary of the payroll record follows:

Salary distribution:

Sales	$63,400	
Officers	36,600	
Office	10,000	
		$110,000

Deductions:

CPP	$ 5,050	
EI	1,650	
Provincial income taxes	6,900	
Federal income taxes	13,700	
Savings bond deductions	850	
		28,150
Net amount		$ 81,850

27. Journalized the entry to record the employer's expenses from the biweekly payroll.

30. Issued a cheque in payment of liabilities for federal and provincial income taxes, CPP, and EI.

31. Journalized an entry to record the estimated accrued product warranty liability, $37,240.

Instructions

Journalize the preceding transactions. Omit explanations.

Solution

Apr.	10	Inventory	20,000.00	
		Notes Payable		20,000.00
Jun.	9	Notes Payable	20,000.00	
		Interest Expense ($20,000 × 5% × 60/365)	164.38	
		Cash		20,164.38
Aug.	1	Building	50,000.00	
		Notes Payable		50,000.00
Oct.	30	Notes Payable	50,000.00	
		Interest Expense	863.01*	
		Cash		50,863.01
		*($50,000 × 7% × 90/365)		
Dec.	27	Sales Salaries Expense	63,400.00	
		Officers Salaries Expense	36,600.00	
		Office Salaries Expense	10,000.00	
		CPP Payable		5,050.00
		EI Payable		1,650.00
		Provincial Income Taxes Payable		6,900.00
		Federal Income Taxes Payable		13,700.00
		Bond Deductions Payable		850.00
		Salaries Payable		81,850.00
	27	CPP Expense	5,050.00	
		EI Expense	2,310.00	
		CPP Payable		5,050.00
		EI Payable ($1,650 × 1.4)		2,310.00
	30	Provincial Income Taxes Payable	6,900.00	
		Federal Income Taxes Payable	13,700.00	
		CPP Payable ($5,050 + $5,050)	10,100.00	
		EI Payable ($1,650 + $2,310)	3,960.00	
		Cash		34,660.00
	31	Product Warranty Expense	37,240.00	
		Product Warranty Payable		37,240.00

EYE OPENERS

1. On April 30, Hartwell Co. had a balance in the GST Paid on Purchases account of $32,458.29. The balance in the GST Charged on Sales account was $26,405.31. What amount should Hartwell remit to the Receiver General on May 15?
2. When should the liability associated with a product warranty be recorded? Discuss.
3. General Motors Company reported $6.6 billion of product warranties in the Liabilities section of a recent balance sheet. How would costs of repairing a defective product be recorded?
4. The "Questions and Answers Technical Hotline" in the *Journal of Accountancy* included the following question:

   Several years ago, Company B instituted legal action against Company A. Under a memorandum of settlement and agreement, Company A agreed to pay Company B a total of $17,500 in three installments—$5,000 on March 1, $7,500 on July 1, and the remaining $5,000 on December 31. Company A paid the first two installments during its fiscal year ended September 30. Should the unpaid amount of $5,000 be presented as a current liability at September 30?

How would you answer this question?

5. Employees are subject to deductions withheld from their paycheques.

    a. List the deductions withheld from most employee paycheques.

    b. Give the title of the accounts credited by amounts withheld.

6. For each of the following payroll-related deductions, indicate whether there is a ceiling on the annual earnings subject to the deduction: (a) income tax; (b) EI; (c) CPP.

7. Why are deductions from employees' earnings classified as liabilities for the employer?

8. Taylor Company, with 20 employees, is expanding operations. It needs to decide whether to hire one full-time employee for $60,000 or two part-time employees for a total of $60,000. Would any of the employer's payroll deductions discussed in this chapter have a bearing on this decision? Explain.

9. For each of the following payroll-related deductions, indicate whether they generally apply to (a) employees only, (b) employers only, or (c) both employees and employers:

    1. Federal income tax

    2. EI

    3. CPP

    4. WCB/WSIB

10. What are the principal reasons for using a special payroll chequing account?

11. In a payroll system, what types of input data are referred to as (a) constants and (b) variables?

12. Explain how a payroll system that is properly designed and operated works to ensure that (a) wages paid are based on hours actually worked and (b) payroll cheques are not issued to fictitious employees.

13. To match revenues and expenses properly, should the expense for employee vacation pay be recorded in the period during which the vacation privilege is earned or during the period in which the vacation is taken? Discuss.

PRACTICE EXERCISES

① PE 10-1
GST and PST payable

EE 10-1 p. 509

Whitehall Doll Company purchased 15 dolls for its inventory, paying $86 per doll. The dolls retail for $145 each. GST is 5%, PST is 8%, and Whitehall Doll Company keeps track of its inventory using the perpetual method.

a. Record the purchase of the dolls including PST and GST, if appropriate.

b. Record the sale of one doll including PST and GST, if appropriate.

① PE 10-2
Proceeds from notes payable

EE 10-2 p. 511

On November 1, Cats Co. issued a 60-day note with a face amount of $70,000 to Nip Co. for inventory.

a. Determine the due date of the note.

b. Determine the proceeds of the note, assuming the note carries an interest rate of 4%.

c. Record the journal entries to issue the note and pay the note.

① PE 10-3
Estimated warranty liability

EE 10-3 p. 513

Akine Co. sold $600,000 of equipment during April under a one-year warranty. The cost to repair defects under the warranty is estimated at 6% of the sales price. On August 4, a customer required a $140 part replacement, plus $80 of labour under the warranty.

Provide the journal entry for (a) the estimated warranty expense on April 30 and (b) the August 4 warranty work.

PE 10-4
Contingent liabilities

EE 10-4 p. 515

Baffinland Smelting Co. experienced the following events in the past year. Identify the correct accounting treatment for each item.

a. Baffinland is being sued for $5 million by citizens living within a five-kilometre radius of the plant who claim the plant has violated air pollution laws. Baffinland's lawyers believe the lawsuit, which is not yet settled, will result in a settlement of $1.4 million.

b. A remote chance exists that Baffinland could be sued by an end user of its products for ill health caused by the metal products produced in the smelter.

c. Baffinland is also being sued by an environmental group that believes metal products should not be produced because of their negative impact on the environment. Baffinland's lawyers believe that the group will probably receive some payment, but they are not sure of the amount.

PE 10-5
Calculating gross pay and deductions

EE 10-5 p. 520

Jonathan's pay rate is $24 per hour, and he worked 45 hours last week. CPP contributions are deducted at a rate of 4.95%, and EI contributions are deducted at a rate of 1.83%. Overtime premiums are paid at 50% of the regular rate for hours worked in excess of 40.

a. Calculate Jonathan's gross pay.
b. Calculate Jonathan's CPP and EI contributions.

PE 10-6
Employee net pay

EE 10-6 p. 523

Matthew Burdick's weekly gross earnings for the week ended April 18 were $2,000, his provincial income taxes were $125.14, and his federal income taxes were $271.05. Assuming his CPP contribution is $95.60, EI contribution is $36.60, and he donates $30 per week through automatic deductions to Big Brothers Big Sisters, what is Matthew's net pay?

PE 10-7
Journalize period payroll

EE 10-7 p. 529

The payroll register of Westward Construction Co. indicates $3,464 of CPP contributions and $862 of EI contributions withheld on total salaries of $73,000 for the period. Income taxes for the period included provincial tax of $2,418 and federal tax of $5,020.

   Provide the journal entry for the period's payroll.

PE 10-8
Journalize payroll deductions

EE 10-8 p. 530

The payroll register of Westward Construction Co. indicates $3,464 of CPP contributions and $862 of EI contributions withheld on total salaries of $73,000 for the period. Income taxes for the period included provincial tax of $2,418 and federal tax of $5,020.

   Provide the journal entry to record the employer's payroll deductions liability for the period.

PE 10-9
Recording remittance of payroll deductions

EE 10-9 p. 531

Bingham's Custom Woodworking withheld CPP contributions of $587.25, EI contributions of $251.65, provincial income taxes of $827.61, and federal income taxes of $1,845.62 from its employees' pay during a recent pay period.

   Provide the journal entry to record the remittance of payroll deductions to the Receiver General.

PE 10-10
Quick ratio

EE 10-10 p. 533

NEL

Crosser Company reported the following current assets and liabilities for December 31, 2015, and December 31, 2014:

(continued)

	Dec. 31, 2015	Dec. 31, 2014
Cash	$ 990	$ 860
Temporary investments	1,910	1,500
Accounts receivable	1,600	1,280
Inventory	2,000	1,400
Accounts payable	3,000	2,800

1. Compute the quick ratio for December 31, 2015 and December 31, 2014.
2. Interpret the company's quick ratio. Is the quick ratio improving or declining?

EXERCISES

① EX 10-1
Current liabilities

✔ Total current liabilities, $790,000

I-Generation Co. sold 14,000 annual subscriptions of *Climber's World* for $60 during December 2015. These new subscribers will receive monthly issues, beginning in January 2016. In addition, the business had taxable income of $400,000 during the first calendar quarter of 2016. The income tax rate is 40%. A quarterly tax payment will be made on April 7, 2016.

Prepare the Current Liabilities section of the balance sheet for I-Generation Co. on March 31, 2016. Ignore GST and PST.

① EX 10-2
PST and GST charged on sales

Extreme Games Ltd. bought 10 consoles for its inventory for $1,800 and a display case, which will not be resold, for $2,700. Extreme Games sold one console for $240 on that same day. The company keeps track of its inventory using the perpetual method. Assuming GST of 5% and PST of 6%, record the entries.

① EX 10-3
PST, GST, and HST charged on sales

Inigma Boutiques bought $4,600 of inventory, a new cash register for $5,200, and office supplies of $1,450. Inigma Boutiques uses the perpetual inventory method to track its purchases and sales. Two days later, Inigma Boutiques sold inventory costing $750 for $1,250.

a. Assuming GST of 5% and PST of 8%, record the entries.
b. Assuming HST of 13%, record the entries.
c. Assuming GST of 5% and QST of 9.5%, record the entries.

① EX 10-4
PST and GST charged on sales

An architect, We Build It, provides planning services in the province of Manitoba. GST of 5% and PST of 7% apply. Transactions are shown below:

May 1. Purchased a large-format scanner on account for $2,000 for use in the office.
     8. Purchased from a computer store the necessary cords to install the scanner, paying $120 plus taxes.
    15. Billed a client for services provided of $1,500, plus applicable taxes.
Jun. 15. Remitted GST to the Receiver General and PST to the Minister of Finance. The balance for GST Charged on Sales was $1,480.12 and for GST Paid on Purchases was $986.15. The PST collected was $1,057.22.

Record the entries.

① EX 10-5
HST charged on sales

My Nook sells unique household items and books in the province of Ontario. HST of 13% applies. Select transactions are shown below:

Jul. 1. Purchased a new computer to track inventory on account from Office Supply Co. for $1,750, plus applicable taxes.
    10. Purchased inventory from a local supplier for $6,500, plus applicable taxes.
    23. Sold three items from inventory for $874 cash, plus applicable taxes. The inventory had cost My Nook $528.
Aug. 15. Remitted HST to the Receiver General. My Nook had collected $738 in HST from customers during July and had paid $1,396 in HST during July.

Record the entries.

EX 10-6

Entries for discounting notes payable

U-Construct It Warehouse issues a 30-day, 5% note for $700,000 to Thornton Home Furnishings Co. for inventory.

a. Journalize U-Construct It Warehouse's entries to record:
   1. the issuance of the note.
   2. the payment of the note at maturity.
b. Journalize Thornton Home Furnishings Co.'s entries to record:
   1. the receipt of the note.
   2. the receipt of the payment of the note at maturity.

EX 10-7

Evaluate alternative notes

A borrower has two alternatives for a loan: (1) issue a $240,000, 60-day, 8% note or (2) issue a $240,000, 120-day, 4% note.

a. Calculate the amount of the interest expense for each option.
b. Determine the proceeds received by the borrower in each situation.
c. Which alternative is more favourable to the borrower? Explain.

EX 10-8

Entries for notes payable

A business issued a 45-day, 7% note for $75,000 to a creditor on account. Journalize the entries to record (a) the issuance of the note and (b) the payment of the note at maturity, including interest.

EX 10-9

Entries for notes payable

A business issued a 60-day, 6% note for $45,000 to a creditor on account. Journalize the entries to record (a) the issuance of the note and (b) the payment of the note at maturity, including interest.

EX 10-10

Fixed asset purchases with note

On June 30, New Wave Company purchased land for $250,000, equipment for $325,000, and a building for $500,000, paying $500,000 cash and issuing a 5% note for the balance, secured by a mortgage on the property. The terms of the note provide for 23 semiannual payments of $25,000 on the principal plus the interest accrued from the date of the preceding payment. Journalize the entry to record (a) the transaction on June 30, (b) the payment of the first installment on December 31, and (c) the payment of the second installment the following June 30.

EX 10-11

Current portion of long-term debt

On August 1, 2015, Frank's Deli purchased a new building to expand the business. The purchase price was $680,000. Frank paid $100,000 cash and issued a 4% note for the balance. Frank agreed to pay 25 semiannual payments of $23,200 on the principal plus the interest accrued from the date of the preceding payment. The semiannual payments are to be paid on the last day of December and June each year. Suppose Frank's Deli has a December 31 year-end. How will the note be shown in the financial statements on December 31, 2015?

EX 10-12

Current portion of long-term debt

French Bistro reported the following information about its long-term debt in the notes to a recent financial statement:

Long-term debt comprises the following:

	December 31	
	2015	**2014**
Notes payable	$19,210,000	$10,470,000
Less current portion	(5,487,000)	(5,110,000)
Long-term debt	$13,723,000	$ 5,360,000

a. How much of the notes payable was disclosed as a current liability on the December 31, 2015, balance sheet?

(continued)

b. How much did the total current liabilities change between 2014 and 2015 as a result of the current portion of long-term debt?

c. If French Bistro did not issue additional notes payable during 2016, what would be the total notes payable on December 31, 2016?

d. During 2016, what is the average principal that French Bistro will pay each month? Explain why interest is not included in this amount.

EX 10-13

Accrued product warranty

Lachgar Industries warrants its products for one year. The estimated product warranty is 4% of sales. Assume that sales were $210,000 for June. In July, a customer received warranty repairs requiring $140 of parts and $95 of labour.

a. Journalize the adjusting entry required at June 30, the end of the first month of the current fiscal year, to record the accrued product warranty.

b. Journalize the entry to record the warranty work provided in July.

EX 10-14

Accrued product warranty

General Motors Company disclosed estimated product warranty payable for comparative years as follows:

	(in millions)	
	12/31/11	**12/31/10**
Current policy, product warranty, and recall campaigns	$3,061	$2,587
Noncurrent policy, product warranty, and recall campaigns	3,539	4,202
Total	$6,600	$6,789

GM's sales were $135,311 million in 2010 and increased to $148,866 million in 2011. Assume that the total paid on warranty claims during 2011 was $4,000 million.

a. Why are short- and long-term estimated warranty liabilities separately disclosed?

b. Provide the journal entry for the 2011 product warranty expense.

EX 10-15

Accrued product warranty

Loco Camping Supplies offers a 60-day exchange policy on all of the products it sells. Loco estimates that 2.5% of its total sales will be returned for exchange each month. During May, Loco sold 1,000 tents for $250 each. Loco had purchased the tents from a regional supplier for $100 each. In June, 20 tents were returned for exchange by customers.

a. Provide the journal entry to record the warranty expense related to tent sales for May.

b. Provide the journal entry to record the 20 tents exchanged in June.

EX 10-16

Accrued product warranty

✔ Balance in Product Warranty Payable at the end of August = $3,975

Munchko Office Supplies offers a 90-day exchange policy on all of the products it sells. Munchko estimates that 3% of its total sales will be returned for exchange each month. At the beginning of July, Munchko had a balance in its Product Warranty Payable account of $4,500. During July, Munchko sold 800 office chairs for $350 each, and 25 office chairs were returned for exchange by customers. Munchko had purchased the office chairs from a regional supplier for $175 each. In August, Munchko sold another 700 office chairs, and 23 office chairs were returned for exchange by customers.

a. Provide the journal entry to record the 25 office chairs exchanged in July.

b. Provide the journal entry to record the warranty expense related to office chairs sold in July.

c. Provide the journal entry to record the 23 office chairs exchanged in August.

d. Provide the journal entry to record the warranty expense related to office chairs sold in August.

e. Determine the balance in the Product Warranty Payable account at the end of August.

EX 10-17
Unearned revenue

① Crankshaw Co. is in the home renovation business. Crankshaw Co. received $325,000 from customers during January. Of the $325,000 received, $100,000 was for work performed during November and December of the previous year, $175,000 was for work performed during January, and the balance was for work to be performed during February and March.

a. Prepare the journal entry to record the money received in January.
b. How will the cash received for work to be performed in February and March be shown in the financial statements?

EX 10-18
Accrued liabilities

① Janzen Yard Works received the following during October: September utility bill of $325.67; October equipment purchases, $2,745; September telephone bill, $168.25; new loan statement documenting a $500 principal payment per month for the next 48 months starting in November; quote for office renovations, $3,800; cash deposits from customers, $5,800.

How should these amounts be reported on the financial statements?

EX 10-19
Contingent liabilities

① Several months ago, Welker Chemical Company experienced a hazardous materials spill at one of its plants. As a result, the Environmental Protection Branch (EPB), Atlantic Region, fined the company $410,000. The company is contesting the fine. In addition, an employee is seeking $400,000 for damages related to the spill. Lastly, a homeowner has sued the company for $260,000. The homeowner lives 30 km from the plant but claims that the incident has reduced the home's resale value by $260,000.

Welker's legal counsel believes that the EPB fine will probably stand. In addition, counsel indicates that an out-of-court settlement of $170,000 has recently been reached with the employee. The final papers will be signed next week. Counsel believes that the homeowner's case is much weaker and will be decided in favour of Welker. Other litigation related to the spill is possible, but the damage amounts are uncertain.

a. Journalize the contingent liabilities associated with the hazardous materials spill. Use the account "Damage Awards and Fines" to recognize the expense for the period.
b. Prepare a note disclosure relating to this incident.

EX 10-20
Contingent liabilities

① As the new chief financial officer (CFO) for a tobacco company, you are required to review the company's contingencies. Many lawsuits are in different stages and categories, and they include both class-action and individual plaintiff cases. Some contingencies for which decisions are required are as follows:

1. An appeal is pending regarding the verdict of a lawsuit that awarded $3 million in damages to an individual. In like cases, the appeal has not been successful.
2. A class-action suit, the only one of its kind, is in its second phase of multiple expected phases, and damages of $70 billion have been requested.
3. The tobacco company has a suit against a competitor for infringing on a patent. The company's lawyers believe it will be won, with a resulting $2 million payment and recovery of all legal expenses.

How would you record and disclose these items?

EX 10-21
Provisions

① Expedite Chemical Shipping Ltd. ships toxic chemicals around the world for use in research. In May 2015, one of its transport vehicles was involved in an accident causing a chemical spill near a residential development. Expedite Chemical Shipping is being sued for $7,000,000 by the local residents who claim their health is at risk as a result of the chemical spill. The lawyer acting on behalf of Expedite Chemical Shipping is arguing that the company requires its customers to sign a waiver stating that the customer assumes responsibility for properly sealing all transportation containers and releases Expedite Chemical Shipping from all liability in the event of chemical leakage.

In a private conversation between the lawyer and the CEO of Expedite Chemical Shipping, the lawyer suggests that the company has a good case but four similar cases

(continued)

recently settled in favour of the injured party (the local residents), and the courts are leaning toward protecting the environment. If Expedite Chemical Shipping loses, the lawyer believes the company will have to pay 50% of the claim based on the four recent court cases. Expedite Chemical Shipping prepares their financial statements using IFRS.

Does this lawsuit meet the criteria of a provision or a contingent liability? Explain your answer.

---

① EX 10-22
Provisions

Casablanca On-Line Inc. provides free counselling advice for those in need. This past year, the company was sued for $2,000,000 by a client who claims he was given bad advice by one of Casablanca On-Line's counsellors who suggested he quit his job and move out West to start over. The lawyer for Casablanca On-Line feels very strongly that the company will not have to pay. In the past five years, only three similar claims were made. Two of those cases were thrown out of court and the third is ongoing. Casablanca On-Line was not involved in any of the three other cases. Casablanca On-Line prepares its financial statements using IFRS.

Does this lawsuit meet the criteria of a provision or a contingent liability? Explain your answer.

---

② EX 10-23
Calculate payroll

✔ b. Net pay,
$711.30

An employee earns $22 per hour and 1.5 times that rate for all hours in excess of 40 hours per week. Assume that the employee worked 50 hours during the week. Assume further that the CPP contribution was $56.56, the EI contribution was $22.14, and income taxes were $150.00 provincial and $270.00 federal.

a. Determine the gross pay for the week.
b. Determine the net pay for the week.
c. Record the journal entries for the payroll and the employer's payroll deductions.

---

② EX 10-24
Calculate payroll

✔ Administrator
net pay, $782.82

Reaves Professional Services has three employees—a consultant, a computer programmer, and an administrator. The following payroll information is available for each employee:

	Consultant	Computer Programmer	Administrator
Regular earnings rate	$2,000 per week	$18 per hour	$20 per hour
Overtime earnings rate	Not applicable	2 times hourly rate	2 times hourly rate
Provincial income taxes withheld	$110	$ 75	$ 60
Federal income taxes withheld	$230	$125	$130

For the current pay period, the computer programmer worked 50 hours and the administrator worked 46 hours. The CPP contribution is 4.95%, the EI contribution is 1.83%, and the employees have not exceeded the maximums. The overtime rate applies to all hours in excess of 40 hours per week.

Determine the gross pay and the net pay for each of the three employees for the current pay period.

---

② EX 10-25
③
Summary payroll data

✔ a. (3) Total
earnings, $400,000

In the following summary of data for a payroll period, some amounts have been intentionally omitted:

Earnings:		
1. At regular rate	?	
2. At overtime rate	$ 60,000	
3. Total earnings	?	
Deductions:		
4. CPP	9,900	
5. EI	3,400	
6. Provincial income taxes withheld	32,400	
7. Federal income taxes withheld	67,200	
8. Union dues	?	
9. Total deductions	128,600	
10. Net amount paid	271,400	
Accounts debited:		
11. Factory Wages	210,000	
12. Sales Salaries	?	
13. Office Salaries	80,000	

a. Calculate the amounts omitted in lines (1), (3), (8), and (12).
b. Journalize the entry to record the payroll accrual.
c. Journalize the entry to record the payment of the payroll.
d. From the data given in this exercise and your answer to (a), would you conclude that this payroll was paid sometime during the first few weeks of the calendar year? Explain.

EX 10-26
Payroll entries

According to a summary of the payroll of Peterson's Construction Ltd., $780,000 was subject to 4.95% CPP contributions and 1.83% EI contributions for the employees' portions of these deductions. The provincial income taxes are $62,000 and the federal income taxes are $133,000.

✔ a. $247,884 Total

a. Calculate the employees' payroll deductions.
b. Journalize the entries to record the payroll including accrual of employer payroll expenses.

EX 10-27
Payroll entries

The payroll register for Gentry Company for the week ended December 17 indicated the following:

Salaries	$540,000
CPP withheld	26,730
EI withheld	9,882
Provincial income taxes withheld	32,000
Federal income taxes withheld	76,000

In addition, union dues and the company pension plan contributions were calculated at the rate of 1.8% and 8% of salaries, respectively.

a. Journalize the entry to record the payroll for the week of December 17.
b. Journalize the entry to record the employer payroll expenses incurred for the week of December 17.

EX 10-28
Payroll entries

Thorup Company had gross wages of $200,000 during the week ended December 10. The amount of wages subject to CPP was $195,000. Tax rates are as follows:

CPP	4.95%
EI	1.83%

✔ Employee CPP payable = $9,652.50

The total amount withheld from employee wages for provincial taxes was $12,000, and for federal taxes was $28,000.

a. Journalize the entry to record the payroll for the week of December 10.
b. Journalize the entry to record the employer payroll expenses incurred for the week of December 10.

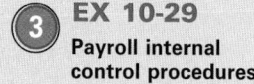

EX 10-29

Payroll internal control procedures

Hillman Pizza is a restaurant specializing in the sale of pizza by the slice. The store employs 7 full-time and 13 part-time workers. The store's weekly payroll averages $3,800 for all 20 workers.

Hillman Pizza uses a personal computer to assist in preparing paycheques. Each week, the store's accountant collects the employee time cards and enters the hours worked into the payroll program. The payroll program calculates each employee's pay and prints a paycheque. The accountant uses a cheque-signing machine to sign the paycheques. Next, the restaurant's owner authorizes the transfer of funds from the restaurant's regular bank account to the payroll account.

For the week of July 11, the accountant accidentally recorded 250 hours worked instead of 40 hours for one of the full-time employees.

Does Hillman Pizza have internal controls in place to catch this error? If so, how will this error be detected?

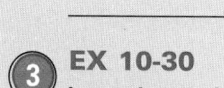

EX 10-30

Internal control procedures

Kailua Motors is a small manufacturer of specialty electric motors. The company employs 26 production workers and 7 administrative personnel. The following procedures are used to process the company's weekly payroll:

a. All employees are required to record their hours worked by clocking in and out on a time clock. Employees must clock out for their lunch breaks. Because of congestion around the time clock area at lunchtime, management has not objected to having one employee clock in and out for an entire department.

b. Whenever a salaried employee is terminated, Personnel authorizes Payroll to remove the employee from the payroll system. However, this procedure is not required when an hourly worker is terminated. Hourly employees receive a paycheque only if their time cards show hours worked. The computer automatically drops an employee from the payroll system when that employee has six consecutive weeks with no hours worked.

c. Whenever an employee receives a pay raise, the supervisor must fill out a wage adjustment form, which is signed by the company president. This form is used to change the employee's wage rate in the payroll system.

d. Kailua Motors maintains a separate chequing account for payroll cheques. Each week, the total net pay for all employees is transferred from the company's regular bank account to the payroll account.

e. Paycheques are signed by using a cheque-signing machine. This machine is located in the main office so that it can be easily accessed by anyone needing a cheque signed.

State whether each of the procedures is appropriate or inappropriate after considering the principles of internal control. If a procedure is inappropriate, describe the appropriate procedure.

EX 10-31

Payroll procedures

The fiscal year for Grain-Crop Stores Inc. ends on June 30. The company's accountant computes and reports payroll taxes on a fiscal-year basis. Thus, Grain-Crop applies CPP and EI maximum earnings limitations to the fiscal-year payroll.

What is wrong with these procedures for accounting for payroll expenses?

EX 10-32

Accrued vacation pay

A business provides its employees with varying amounts of vacation per year, depending on the length of employment. The estimated amount of the current year's vacation pay is $80,400. Journalize the adjusting entry required on January 31, the end of the first month of the current year, to record the accrued vacation pay.

EX 10-33

Accrued vacation pay

Employees at Custom Woodworking Co. are entitled to two weeks' vacation every year, which is equivalent to 4% of their gross earnings. The annual gross earnings for the employees average $570,000. Provide the journal entry required each month to accrue employee vacation pay.

EX 10-34
Quick ratio

✔ a. 2015: 1.10

f·a·i

Antigonish Technology Co. had the following current assets and liabilities for two comparative years:

	Dec. 31, 2015	Dec. 31, 2014
Current assets:		
Cash	$370,000	$ 448,000
Accounts receivable	400,000	410,000
Inventory	220,000	180,000
Total current assets	$990,000	$1,038,000

	Dec. 31, 2015	Dec. 31, 2014
Current liabilities:		
Current portion of long-term debt	$110,000	$100,000
Accounts payable	220,000	200,000
Accrued and other current liabilities	370,000	360,000
Total current liabilities	$700,000	$660,000

a. Determine the quick ratio for December 31, 2015 and 2014.
b. Interpret the change in the quick ratio between the two balance sheet dates.

EX 10-35
Quick ratio

f·a·i

The current assets and current liabilities for Dell Inc. are shown as follows at the end of two recent periods (in millions)[†]:

	Feb. 3, 2012	Jan. 28, 2011
Current assets:		
Cash and cash equivalents	$13,852	$13,913
Short-term investments	966	452
Accounts receivable, net	6,476	6,493
Short-term financing receivables, net	3,327	3,643
Inventories, net	1,404	1,301
Other current assets*	3,423	3,219
Total current assets	$29,448	$29,021
Current liabilities:		
Short-term debt	$ 2,867	$ 851
Accounts payable	11,656	11,293
Accrued and other	3,934	4,181
Short-term deferred services revenue	3,544	3,158
Total current liabilities	$22,001	$19,483

*These represent prepaid expenses and other nonquick current assets.

a. Determine the quick ratio for both years.
b. Interpret the quick ratio difference between the two years.

†© 2012 Dell Inc. All Rights Reserved.

PROBLEMS SERIES A

PR 10-1A
Liability transactions

The following selected transactions occurred at Quayle Gardens during the year; sales taxes apply. Quayle Gardens uses the perpetual method to record inventory.

Jan. 10.   Purchased Evergrow lights for use in the greenhouses on account from White Light Co., $190,000, terms n/30.
Feb. 5.   Purchased plants with a value of $40,000 from Green Thumb, terms n/30.
       9.   Paid White Light Co. the amount owed.
Jun. 7.   Sued White Light because two of the lights burst and burned the arm of an employee. The lawyer says Quayle Gardens will likely win the cost of the employee's time off and compensation for mental distress, for a total of $30,000.

(continued)

Jul. 15. Initiated a promotion for customers, whereby, if their plants die within three months of purchase, Quayle Gardens will reimburse the customer.

31. Total reimbursed to customers between July 15 and July 31 for the death of plants is $2,500 (use Miscellaneous Expense).

31. Quayle accrued another $4,000 for anticipated reimbursements for sales to July 31 (use Plant Replacement Liability).

Aug. 31. Total reimbursed to customers during the month is $3,200.

Instructions

Journalize the transactions with the following taxes.
a. GST of 5%
b. GST of 5% and PST of 7%
c. HST of 13%
d. GST of 5% and QST of 9.5%

---

① PR 10-2A
Liability transactions

The following items were selected from among the transactions completed by Echo Mountain Co. during the current year:

Jan. 15. Purchased merchandise on account from Hood Co., $250,000 plus taxes, terms n/30.

Feb. 14. Issued a 90-day, 6% note for balance due to Hood Co., on account.

May 15. Paid Hood Co. the amount owed on the note of February 14.

Jun. 2. Borrowed $260,000 from Capital Credit Union, issuing a 120-day, 7% note.

Jul. 25. Purchased tools from Columbia Supply Co., $220,000 plus taxes, issuing a 120-day, 6% note.

Sep. 30. Paid Capital Credit Union the interest due on the note of June 2 and renewed the loan by issuing a new 45-day, 10% note for the amount due. (Journalize both the debit and credit to the notes payable account.)

Nov. 14. Paid Capital Credit Union the amount due on the note of September 30.

Nov. 22. Paid Columbia Supply Co. the amount due on the note of July 25.

Dec. 1. Purchased office equipment from Mariko's Office Solutions for $150,000 plus taxes, paying $69,500 and issuing a 5% note for the balance, coming due in 60 days.

Instructions

1. Journalize the transactions with the following taxes.
   a. GST of 5%
   b. GST of 5% and PST of 7%
   c. HST of 13%
   d. GST of 5% and QST of 9.5%
2. Journalize the adjusting entry for each of the following accrued expenses at the end of the current year: (a) product warranty cost, $16,400; (b) interest on the note owed to Mariko's Office Solutions.

---

① PR 10-3A
Liability transactions

The following items were selected from among the transactions completed by Isis Co. during the current year:

Feb. 15. Purchased merchandise on account from Viper Co., $260,000 plus $13,000 GST, terms n/30.

Mar. 17. Issued a 45-day, 5% note for the balance owed to Viper Co., on account.

May 1. Paid Viper Co. the amount owed on the note of March 17.

Jun. 15. Borrowed $300,000 from Local Credit Union, issuing a 60-day, 9% note.

Jul. 21. Purchased tools from Charger Co. for $240,000 plus 5% GST, issuing a 60-day, 7% note.

Aug. 14. Paid Local Credit Union the interest due on the note of June 15 and renewed the loan by issuing a new 30-day, 10% note for the balance due. (Journalize both the debit and credit to the notes payable account.)

Sep. 13. Paid Local Credit Union the amount due on the note of August 14.

19. Paid Charger Co. the amount due on the note of July 21.

Dec. 1. Purchased office equipment from Challenger Office Supplies for $235,000 plus 5% GST and 8% PST, paying $65,550 and issuing a series of ten 7.5% notes for $20,000 each, coming due at 30-day intervals.

   12. Settled a product liability lawsuit with a customer for $121,600, payable in January. Isis Co. accrued the loss in a litigation claims payable account.

   31. Paid the amount due Challenger Office Supplies on the first note in the series issued on December 1.

Instructions

1. Journalize the transactions.
2. Journalize the adjusting entry for each of the following accrued expenses at the end of the current year: (a) product warranty cost, $26,240; (b) interest on the nine remaining notes owed to Challenger Office Supplies.

PR 10-4A

Entries for payroll and payroll deductions

The following information about the payroll for the week ended December 26 was obtained from the records of Amherst Equipment Co.:

Salaries:		Deductions:	
Sales salaries	$244,000	Provincial taxes withheld	$ 27,100
Warehouse salaries	135,000	Federal taxes withheld	61,604
Office salaries	125,000	CPP withheld	22,216
	$504,000	EI withheld	7,560
		Canada Savings Bonds	11,088
		Group insurance	9,072
			$138,640

Instructions

Amherst Equipment Co.'s employees are paid on the Friday of every week and work a five-day workweek. Journalize the following entries:

1. December 26, to record the payroll.
2. December 26, to record the employer's payroll expenses.
3. December 31, to accrue for pay to the company's year-end of December 31. (Assume the December 26 payroll amounts represent a typical payroll amount.)
4. December 31, to accrue for the employer's payroll expenses up to the year-end.
5. January 2, to record the payroll for the week, using the same numbers for the week ended December 26.
6. January 2, to record the employer's payroll deduction liability.
7. January 15, to remit source deductions for the payroll for December (assume four pays equal to the December 26 pay).

PR 10-5A

Entries for payroll and payroll deductions

Carson Brothers pays its employees weekly. Information for the week ended May 29, 2015, is given below.

Employee	Gross Pay	Claim Code
J. Carson	$859.32	1
R. Docker	$861.30	2

Instructions

1. Determine the deductions for CPP, EI, and provincial and federal income taxes using the payroll deduction tables found in Exhibit 5.
2. Journalize the entry to record the payroll for the week.
3. Journalize the entry to record the employer payroll expenses for the week.

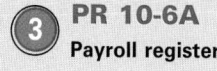

PR 10-6A

Payroll register

✔ 3. Dr. CPP
Expense, $538.60

If the working papers correlating with this textbook are not used, omit Problem 10-6A.
The payroll register for Cupcake Co. for the week ended April 10, 2015, is presented in the working papers.

Instructions

1. Journalize the entry to record the payroll for the week.
2. Journalize the entry to record the issuance of the cheques to employees.
3. Journalize the entry to record the employer's payroll expenses for the week.
4. Journalize the entry to record a cheque issued on April 15 to the Receiver General for March payroll, deductions. Provincial income taxes are $2,132.41, federal income taxes are $5,442.25, employees' portion of CPP is $1,276.49, and employees' portion of EI is $548.75.

PR 10-7A

Payroll entries

The payroll information for Computer Consultants Co. for the week ended April 24, 2015, is given below.

Employee	Pay Rate	Hours Worked	United Way Deductions	Department
J. Chasson	25	40	15	Office
R. Franks	32	44	10	Sales
S. Ingrams	26	40	10	Office
L. Toner	30	46	25	Sales
F. Ventresca	45	40	0	Sales
K. Wong	25	40	15	Office

The following rates apply to deductions for all employees: CPP, 4.95%; EI, 1.83%; provincial income tax, 10%; federal income tax, 15%; Registered Retirement Savings Plan (RRSP), 5%. The overtime premium is calculated at a rate of 1.5 times the regular rate for all hours worked in excess of 40 hours per week. None of the employees has reached the ceiling for CPP or EI.

Instructions

1. Complete a payroll register similar to the one in Exhibit 10.
2. Journalize the entry to record the payroll for the week.
3. Journalize the entry to record the issuance of the cheques to the employees.
4. Journalize the entry to record the employer payroll expenses for the week.

PR 10-8A

Payroll accounts and year-end entries

The following accounts, with the balances indicated, appear in the ledger of Wadsley Gifts Co. on December 1 of the current year:

2110	Salaries Payable	—	6110	Operations Salaries Expense	$766,000
2120	CPP Payable	$ 7,234	7110	Sales Salaries Expense	504,000
2130	EI Payable	1,904	7120	Office Salaries Expense	126,000
2140	Provincial Income Taxes Payable	7,051	7180	CPP Expense	68,879
2150	Federal Income Taxes Payable	16,110	7190	EI Expense	34,439
2180	Canada Savings Bond Deductions Payable	2,800			

The following selected transactions relating to payroll, payroll deductions, and employer payroll expenses occurred during December:

Dec. 2. Issued cheque for $2,800 to the Bank of Canada to purchase Canada Savings Bonds for employees.

3. Issued cheques to various agencies in payment of balances owing for CPP payable, EI payable, and income taxes payable.

14. Journalized the entry to record the biweekly payroll. A summary of the payroll record follows:

Salary distribution:

Operations	$34,800	
Sales	22,900	
Office	5,700	$63,400

Deductions:

CPP withheld	2,550	
EI withheld	951	
Provincial income taxes withheld	4,162	
Federal income taxes withheld	7,123	
Savings bond deductions	1,400	16,186
Net amount		$47,214

14. Journalized the entry to record the employer payroll expenses for the December 14 payroll.

Dec. 28. Journalized the entry to record the biweekly payroll. A summary of the payroll record follows:

Salary distribution:

Operations	$34,200	
Sales	22,400	
Office	5,400	$62,000

Deductions:

CPP withheld	3,348	
EI withheld	930	
Provincial income taxes withheld	3,921	
Federal income taxes withheld	7,115	
Savings bond deductions	1,400	16,714
Net amount		$45,286

28. Journalized the entry to record the employer payroll expenses for the December 28 payroll.

31. Journalized the adjusting entry for one day's pay for December 31. (Record one-fifth of the most recent payroll.)

31. Journalized the adjusting entry for the employer's payroll expenses for one day's pay for December 31.

Instructions

Journalize the transactions.

PROBLEMS SERIES B

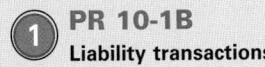

PR 10-1B

Liability transactions

The following selected transactions occurred at Home Staging by Clarissa during the year; sales taxes apply:

Jan. 20. Purchased three living room sofas on account from Sofas R Us, $7,500, terms n/30, for use by Home Staging in show homes.

Feb. 1. Purchased silk plants with a value of $1,500 from Your Green Thumb, for resale to clients.

5. Paid Sofas R Us the amount owed.

Jun. 1. Sued Sofas R Us because a sofa leg collapsed, injuring a real estate agent. The lawyer says Home Staging by Clarissa will likely win the cost of the real estate agent's time off and compensation for her mental distress, a total of $40,000.

Jul. 1. Issued a deal to customers: if their house does not receive an offer to purchase within 21 days of being staged, Home Staging by Clarissa will reimburse the customer for the staging cost.

31. Total reimbursed to customers for lack of offers to purchase is $1,000 (use Miscellaneous Expense).

31. Home Staging by Clarissa accrued another $5,000 for anticipated reimbursements for sales to July 31 (use Reimbursement Liability).

Aug. 31. Total reimbursed to customers during the month is $2,800.

(continued)

Instructions

Journalize the transactions with the following taxes.
a. GST of 5%
b. GST of 5% and PST of 6%
c. HST of 13%
d. GST of 5% and QST of 9.5%

PR 10-2B
Liability transactions

The following items were selected from among the transactions completed by Jameson's Inc. during the current year:

Apr. 1. Borrowed $75,000 from McGrath Company, issuing a 60-day, 5% note for that amount.

Apr. 26. Purchased $200,000 of equipment by issuing a 180-day, 5% note to Hudson Bay Manufacturing Co. Taxes apply.

May 31. Paid McGrath Company the interest due on the note of April 1 and renewed the loan by issuing a new 45-day, 7% note for $75,000. (Record both the debit and credit to the notes payable account.)

Jul. 15. Paid McGrath Company the amount due on the note of May 31.

Sep. 3. Purchased inventory on account from Oakland Co., $95,000 plus taxes, terms n/30.

Oct. 3. Issued a 30-day, 10% note to Oakland Co. for the amount owing on account.

23. Paid Hudson Bay Manufacturing Co. the amount due on the note of April 26.

Nov. 2. Paid Oakland Co. the amount owed on the note of October 3.

10. Purchased store equipment from Baden Technology Co. for $110,000 plus taxes, paying $20,000 and issuing a 120-day, 8% note for the balance.

Instructions

1. Journalize the transactions with the following taxes.
   a. GST of 5%
   b. GST of 5% and PST of 6%
   c. HST of 13%
   d. GST of 5% and QST of 9.5%
2. Journalize the adjusting entry for each of the following accrued expenses at the end of the current year:
   a. Product warranty cost, $10,400.
   b. Accrued interest on the Baden note issued November 10.

PR 10-3B
Liability transactions

The following items were selected from among the transactions completed by Javelin Inc. during the current year:

Mar. 1. Borrowed $80,000 from Nova Company, issuing a 30-day, 9% note for that amount.

15. Purchased equipment by issuing a $165,000, 180-day, 7.5% note to Shelby Manufacturing Co. The purchase price includes GST and PST of $7,500 each.

31. Paid Nova Company the interest due on the note of March 1 and renewed the loan by issuing a new 60-day, 9% note for $80,000. (Record both the debit and credit to the notes payable account.)

May 30. Paid Nova Company the amount due on the note of March 31.

Jul. 6. Purchased merchandise on account from Pacer Co., $56,000 plus GST of 5%, terms n/30.

Aug. 5. Issued a 45-day, 8% note to Pacer Co., for the amount owing on account.

Sep. 11. Paid Shelby Manufacturing Co. the amount due on the note of March 15.

19. Paid Pacer Co. the amount owed on the note of August 5.

Nov. 16. Purchased store equipment from Gremlin Co. for a total of $187,000, paying $37,000 cash and issuing a series of 15, 6% notes for $10,000 each coming due at 30-day intervals. The purchase price includes PST and GST of $8,500 each.

Dec. 16. Paid the amount due Gremlin Co. on the first note in the series issued on November 16.

21. Settled a personal injury lawsuit with a customer for $55,250, to be paid in January. No previous entry had been made for this lawsuit. Javelin Inc. accrued the loss in a litigation claims payable account.

Instructions

1. Journalize the transactions.
2. Journalize the adjusting entry for each of the following accrued expenses at the end of the current year: (a) product warranty cost, $13,520; (b) interest on the 14 remaining notes owed to Gremlin Co.

PR 10-4B

Entries for payroll and payroll deductions

The following information about the payroll for the week ended December 26 was obtained from the records of Vienna Co.:

Salaries:		Deductions:	
Sales salaries	$ 670,000	Provincial taxes withheld	$ 63,122
Warehouse salaries	110,000	Federal taxes withheld	135,622
Office salaries	234,000	CPP withheld	48,714
	$1,014,000	EI withheld	15,210
		Canada Savings Bonds	30,420
		Group insurance	45,630
			$338,718

Instructions

Vienna Co.'s employees are paid at the end of every week, and they work a five-day workweek. Journalize the following entries:

1. December 26, to record the payroll.
2. December 26, to record the employer's payroll expenses.
3. December 31, to accrue for pay to the company's year-end of December 31. (Assume the December 26 payroll amounts represent a typical payroll amount.)
4. December 31, to accrue for the employer's payroll expenses up to the year-end.
5. January 2, to record the payroll for the week.
6. January 2, to record the employer's payroll deduction liability.
7. January 15, to remit source deductions for the payroll for December (assume four pays equal to the December 26 pay).

PR 10-5B

Entries for payroll and payroll deductions

Johnson's Supplies pays its employees weekly. Information for the week ended July 24, 2015, is given below.

Employee	Gross Pay	Claim Code
S. Munroe	$858.12	3
L. Whyte	$861.42	1

Instructions

1. Determine the deductions for CPP, EI, and provincial and federal income taxes using the payroll deduction tables found in Exhibit 5.
2. Journalize the entry to record the payroll for the week.
3. Journalize the entry to record the employer payroll expenses for the week.

PR 10-6B

Payroll register

✔ 3. Dr. CPP
Expenses $597.82

If the working papers correlating with this textbook are not used, omit Problem 10-6B.

The payroll register for Gogol Manufacturing Co. for the week ended July 3, 2015, is presented in the working papers.

Instructions

1. Journalize the entry to record the payroll for the week.
2. Journalize the entry to record the issuance of the cheques to employees.

(continued)

3. Journalize the entry to record the employer's portion of the payroll expenses for the week.

4. Journalize the entry to record the cheque issued on July 15 to the Receiver General for June payroll deductions. Provincial income taxes are $3,721.20, federal income taxes are $4,271.21, employees' portion of CPP is $1,426.32, and employees' portion of EI is $569.72.

---

③ PR 10-7B

The payroll information for Jaspers Rock Climbing for the week ended July 3, 2015, is given below.

Employee	Pay Rate	Hours Worked	United Way Deductions	Department
A. Abrahams	27	43	15	Office
D. Clarke	31	41	10	Sales
F. Johnson	28	40	10	Office
M. Musson	28	40	25	Sales
L. Roberts	42	46	0	Sales
T. Tomison	29	42	15	Office

The following rates apply to deductions for all employees: CPP, 4.95%; EI, 1.83%; provincial income tax, 10%; federal income tax, 15%, Registered Retirement Savings Plan (RRSP), 5%. The overtime premium is calculated at a rate of 1.5 times the regular rate for all hours worked in excess of 40 hours per week. None of the employees has reached the ceiling for CPP or EI.

Instructions

1. Complete a payroll register similar to the one in Exhibit 10.
2. Journalize the entry to record the payroll for the week.
3. Journalize the entry to record the issuance of the cheques to the employees.
4. Journalize the entry to record the employer payroll expenses for the week.

---

③ PR 10-8B

Payroll accounts and year-end entries

The following accounts, with the balances indicated, appear in the ledger of Thompson Kayak Co. on December 1 of the current year:

2110	Salaries Payable	—	6110	Operations Salaries Expense	$556,000
2120	CPP Payable	$ 4,880	7110	Sales Salaries Expense	266,400
2130	EI Payable	1,236	7120	Office Salaries Expense	99,200
2140	Provincial Income Taxes Payable	3,216	7180	CPP Expense	44,544
2150	Federal Income Taxes Payable	11,362	7190	EI Expense	22,772
2180	Canada Savings Bond Deductions Payable	1,800			

The following selected transactions relating to payroll, payroll deductions, and employer payroll expenses occurred during December:

Dec. 2. Issued cheque for $1,800 to the Bank of Canada to purchase Canada Savings Bonds for employees.

3. Issued cheques to various agencies in payment of balances owing for CPP payable, EI payable, and income taxes payable.

14. Journalized the entry to record the biweekly payroll. A summary of the payroll record follows:

Salary distribution:		
Operations	$25,000	
Sales	12,100	
Office	4,500	$41,600
Deductions:		
CPP withheld	$ 1,988	
EI withheld	624	
Provincial income taxes withheld	3,015	
Federal income taxes withheld	6,262	
Savings bond deductions	900	12,789
Net amount		$28,811

14. Journalized the entry to record the employer's payroll expenses for the December 14 payroll.
28. Journalized the entry to record the biweekly payroll. A summary of the payroll record follows:

Salary distribution:		
Operations	$25,400	
Sales	12,400	
Office	4,800	$42,600
Deductions:		
CPP withheld	$ 2,000	
EI withheld	639	
Provincial income taxes withheld	2,200	
Federal income taxes withheld	7,300	
Savings bond deductions	900	13,039
Net amount		$29,561

28. Journalized the entry to record the employer payroll expenses for the December 28 payroll.
31. Journalized the adjusting entry for one day's pay for December 31. (Record one-fifth of the most recent payroll.)
31. Journalized the adjusting entry for the employer's payroll expenses for one day's pay for December 31.

Instructions

Journalize the transactions.

COMPREHENSIVE PROBLEM 3

Selected transactions completed by Blackwell Company during its first fiscal year ended December 31, 2015, were as follows:

Jan.   2. Issued a cheque to establish a petty cash fund of $2,000.

Mar. 4. Replenished the petty cash fund, based on the following summary of petty cash receipts: office supplies, $724; miscellaneous selling expense, $256; miscellaneous administrative expense, $378; HST paid, $176.54.

Apr. 5. Purchased $14,000 of merchandise on account, terms 1/10, n/30. The perpetual inventory system is used to account for inventory. HST is $1,820.

May 7. Paid the invoice of April 5 after the discount period had passed.

     10. Received cash from daily cash sales for $10,695.85. The amount indicated by the cash register was $9,545. HST of $1,240.85 is collected.

Jun. 2. Received a 60-day, 9% note for $80,000 on the Stevens account.

Aug. 1. Received amount owed on June 2 note, plus interest at the maturity date.

     8. Received $3,400 on the Jacobs account and wrote off the remainder owed on a $4,000 accounts receivable balance. (The allowance method is used in accounting for uncollectible receivables.)

     25. Reinstated the Jacobs account written off on August 8 and received $600 cash in full payment.

Sep. 2. Purchased land by issuing a $300,000, 90-day, 10% note to Ace Development Co. Purchase price includes HST of $14,286.

Oct. 2. Sold office equipment in exchange for $60,000 cash plus receipt of a $40,000, 120-day, 6% note. The equipment had cost $140,000 and had accumulated depreciation of $25,000 as at October 1. HST is $13,000.

     15. Paid the Receiver General for Canada for the third quarter HST remittance. All entries have been recorded. HST Paid on Purchases balance is $18,286; HST Charged on Sales balance is $84,000.

Nov. 30. Journalized the monthly payroll for November, based on the following data:

(continued)

Salaries		Deductions	
Sales salaries	$60,400	Provincial income taxes withheld	$ 5,161
Office salaries	34,500	Federal income taxes withheld	11,921
	$94,900	CPP withheld	4,450
		EI withheld	1,424

30. Journalized the employer payroll expenses on the payroll.

Dec. 1. Journalized the payment of the September 2 note at maturity.

Instructions

1. Journalize the selected transactions.
2. Based on the following data, prepare a bank reconciliation for December of the current year:
   a. Balance according to the bank statement at December 31, $126,400.
   b. Balance according to the ledger at December 31, $109,650.
   c. Cheques outstanding at December 31, $30,600.
   d. Deposit in transit, not recorded by bank, $13,200.
   e. Bank debit memo for service charges, $350.
   f. A cheque for $530 in payment of an invoice was incorrectly recorded in the accounts as $230.
3. Based on the bank reconciliation prepared in (2), journalize the entry or entries to be made by Blackwell Company.
4. Based on the following selected data, journalize the adjusting entries as at December 31 of the current year:
   a. Estimated uncollectible accounts at December 31, $7,200, based on an aging of accounts receivable. The balance of Allowance for Doubtful Accounts at December 31 was $750 (debit).
   b. The physical inventory on December 31 indicated an inventory shrinkage of $1,480.
   c. Prepaid insurance expired during the year, $10,200.
   d. Office supplies used during the year, $1,760.
   e. Depreciation is computed using the nearest whole month as follows:

Asset	Cost	Residual Value	Acquisition Date	Useful Life in Years	Depreciation Method Used
Buildings	$400,000	$ 0	January 2	40	Straight-line
Office Equip.	110,000	10,000	July 1	4	Straight-line
Store Equip.	50,000	5,000	January 3	8	Double-declining-balance (at twice the straight-line rate)

   f. A patent costing $22,500 when acquired on January 2 has a remaining legal life of 10 years and is expected to have value for five years.
   g. The cost of mineral rights was $220,000. Of the estimated deposit of 400,000 tonnes of ore, 24,000 tonnes were mined and sold during the year.
   h. Vacation pay expense for December, $4,800.
   i. A product warranty was granted beginning December 1 and covering a one-year period. The estimated cost is 2.5% of sales, which totalled $840,000 in December.
   j. Interest was accrued on the note receivable received on October 2.
5. Based on the following information and the post-closing trial balance shown below, prepare a balance sheet in report form at December 31 of the current year.

The inventory is stated at cost by the FIFO method.

The product warranty payable is a current liability.

Vacation pay payable:
  Current liability $ 3,200
  Long-term liability   1,600

Notes payable:
  Current liability $25,000
  Long-term liability   75,000

Blackwell Company
Post-Closing Trial Balance
December 31, 2015

	Debit Balances	Credit Balances
Petty Cash	2,000	
Cash	109,000	
Notes Receivable	40,000	
Accounts Receivable	210,000	
Allowance for Doubtful Accounts...................		7,200
Inventory...	144,200	
Interest Receivable................................	592	
Prepaid Insurance..................................	20,400	
Office Supplies	6,000	
Buildings	400,000	
Accumulated Depreciation—Buildings		10,000
Office Equipment	110,000	
Accumulated Depreciation—Office Equipment		12,500
Store Equipment....................................	50,000	
Accumulated Depreciation—Store Equipment.........		12,500
Land	292,500	
Mineral Rights.....................................	220,000	
Accumulated Amortization—Mineral Rights..........		13,200
Patents	22,500	
Accumulated Amortization—Patents		4,500
CPP Payable		10,420
EI Payable..		2,550
Provincial Income Taxes Payable		5,120
Federal Income Taxes Payable......................		12,140
HST Paid on Purchases	37,382	
HST Charged on Sales		168,300
Salaries Payable		85,000
Accounts Payable		140,000
Interest Payable		3,200
Product Warranty Payable		21,000
Vacation Pay Payable		4,800
Notes Payable......................................		100,000
J. Crane, Capital		1,052,144
	1,664,574	1,664,574

6. On February 7 of the following year, the inventory was destroyed by fire. Based on the following data obtained from the accounting records, estimate the cost of goods destroyed:

Jan. 1 Inventory	$144,200
Jan. 1–Feb. 7 Purchases (net)	40,000
Jan. 1–Feb. 7 Sales (net)	70,000
Estimated gross profit rate	40%

SPECIAL ACTIVITIES

SA 10-1

Quick ratio

Refer to the financial statements in Appendix B for Leon's Furniture Limited and in Appendix C for Shoppers Drug Mart.

a. Calculate the quick ratio for both companies as at December 31, 2011.

b. Comment on the ratios. Which company is in a better position when considering the quick ratio?

SA 10-2

Ethics and
professional conduct
in business

Suzanne Thompson is a chartered accountant (CA) and senior accountant for Deuel and Soldner, a local CA firm. It had been the policy of the firm to provide a holiday bonus equal to two weeks' salary to all employees. The firm's new management team announced on November 15 that a bonus equal to only one week's salary would be made available to employees this year. Suzanne thought that this policy was unfair because she and her coworkers planned on the full two-week bonus. The two-week bonus had been given for 10 straight years, so it seemed as though the firm had breached an implied commitment. Thus, Suzanne decided that she would make up the lost bonus week by working an extra six hours of overtime per week over the next five weeks until the end of the year. Deuel and Soldner's policy is to pay overtime at 150% of straight time.

Suzanne's supervisor was surprised to see overtime being reported because the company's clients generally made very few additional or unusual service demands at the end of the calendar year. However, the overtime was not questioned because firm employees are on the "honour system" in reporting their overtime.

Discuss whether the firm is acting in an ethical manner by changing the bonus. Is Suzanne behaving in an ethical manner?

SA 10-3

Contingent liabilities

Internet Project

Altria Group, Inc. has more than 20 pages dedicated to describing contingent liabilities in the notes to recent financial statements. These pages include extensive descriptions of multiple contingent liabilities. Use the Internet to research Altria Group, Inc., at **www.altria.com**.

a. What are the major business units of Altria Group?
b. Based on your understanding of this company, why would Altria Group require more than 20 pages of contingency disclosure?

SA 10-4

Ethics and
professional conduct
in business

Paul Sheile, the owner of Sheile Trucking Company, initiated an executive bonus plan for his chief executive officer (CEO). The new plan provides a bonus to the CEO equal to 3% of the income before taxes. Upon learning of the new bonus arrangement, the CEO issued instructions to change the company's accounting for trucks. The CEO has asked the controller to make the following two changes:

a. Change from the double-declining-balance method to the straight-line method of depreciation.
b. Add 50% to the useful lives of all trucks.

Why did the CEO ask for these changes? How would you respond to the CEO's request?

SA 10-5

Ethics and
professional conduct
in business

Theo Barellis was discussing summer employment with Sara Rida, president of Xanadu Construction Service:

Sara: I'm glad that you're thinking about joining us for the summer. We could certainly use the help.

Theo: Sounds good. I enjoy outdoor work, and I could use the money to help with next year's school expenses.

Sara: I've got a plan that can help you out on that. As you know, I'll pay you $12 per hour, but in addition, I'd like to pay you with cash. You're only working for the summer, so it really doesn't make sense for me to go to the trouble of formally putting you on our payroll system. In fact, I do some jobs for my clients on a strictly cash basis, so it would be easy to just pay you that way.

Theo: Well, that's a bit unusual, but I guess money is money.

Sara: Yeah, not only that, it's tax-free!

Theo: What do you mean?

Sara: Didn't you know? Any money that you receive in cash is not reported to the CRA on a T4 form; therefore, the CRA doesn't know about the income—hence, it's the same as tax-free earnings.

a. Why does Sara Rida want to conduct business transactions using cash (not cheque or credit card)?
b. How should Theo respond to Sara's suggestion?

SA 10-6

Payroll forms

Group Project

Internet Project

Payroll accounting involves the use of government-supplied forms and tables to account for payroll deductions and expenses. Two common forms are the TD1 and T4, and two common tables are the federal and provincial tax deduction tables. Form a team with three of your classmates and retrieve copies of each of these forms and tables. They may be obtained from a local CRA office or a library or downloaded from the Internet at **www.cra-arc.gc.ca** (go to Forms and publications) and search for CPP deduction tables.

Briefly describe the purpose of the two forms and the tables.

APPENDICES

Financial Statements for Morning Java (ASPE)

The financial statements of Morning Java are provided in the following pages. Morning Java is a fictitious coffeehouse chain featuring drip and espresso coffee in a café setting. The financial statements of Morning Java are provided to illustrate the completed financial statements of a corporation using the terms, formats and presentation style illustrated throughout this text. In addition, excerpts of the Morning Java financial statements are used to illustrate the financial reporting presentation for the topics discussed in Chapters 6–10. Thus, you can refer to the complete financial statements or the excerpts near the end of each of Chapters 6–10. We provide this fictitious financial statement illustration to avoid the additional complexity introduced by different terms, formats, concepts, and style used in real world financial statements. Leon's Furniture Limited and Shoppers Drug Mart Corporation are provided in Appendix B and Appendix C, respectively. The financial statements for Morning Java are illustrated in Volume 2 using International Financial Reporting Standards.

A "Cost of goods sold" line indicates this is a merchandising business.

ASPE requires an inventory expense line, which may be called "Cost of goods sold"; IFRS does not.

"Gross profit" subtotal is not required by ASPE or IFRS.

The term "Profit for the year" may be used in IFRS.

IFRS includes the word "Comprehensive" in the statement title.

This is a multiple-step presentation.

Earnings per share is not required under ASPE.

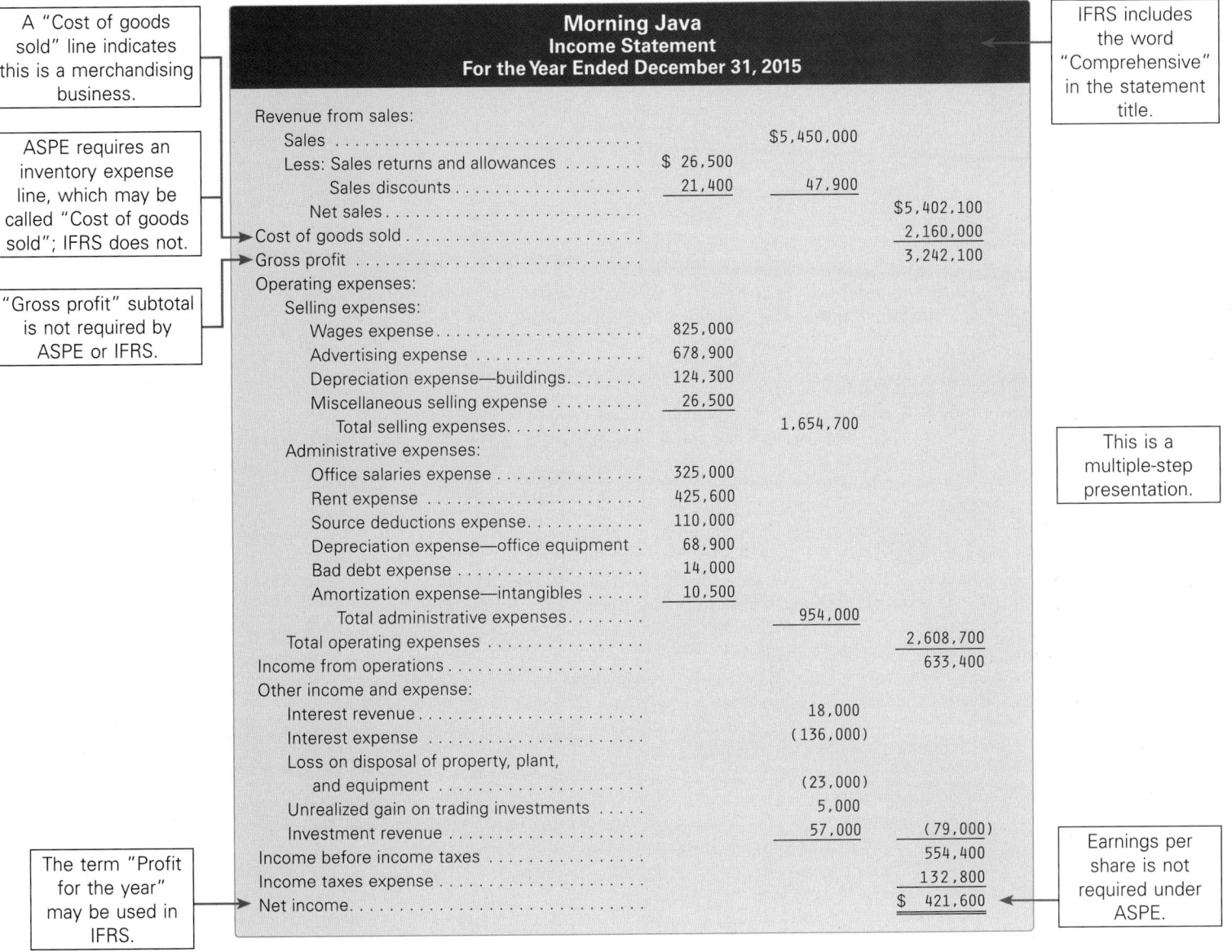

Morning Java
Income Statement
For the Year Ended December 31, 2015

Revenue from sales:			
Sales		$5,450,000	
Less: Sales returns and allowances	$ 26,500		
Sales discounts	21,400	47,900	
Net sales			$5,402,100
Cost of goods sold			2,160,000
Gross profit			3,242,100
Operating expenses:			
Selling expenses:			
Wages expense	825,000		
Advertising expense	678,900		
Depreciation expense—buildings	124,300		
Miscellaneous selling expense	26,500		
Total selling expenses		1,654,700	
Administrative expenses:			
Office salaries expense	325,000		
Rent expense	425,600		
Source deductions expense	110,000		
Depreciation expense—office equipment	68,900		
Bad debt expense	14,000		
Amortization expense—intangibles	10,500		
Total administrative expenses		954,000	
Total operating expenses			2,608,700
Income from operations			633,400
Other income and expense:			
Interest revenue		18,000	
Interest expense		(136,000)	
Loss on disposal of property, plant, and equipment		(23,000)	
Unrealized gain on trading investments		5,000	
Investment revenue		57,000	(79,000)
Income before income taxes			554,400
Income taxes expense			132,800
Net income			$ 421,600

Title of statement may be "Statement of Financial Position" under IFRS.

"Allowance for doubtful accounts" line is not required by ASPE or IFRS. It is often included because it provides additional information to users.

Inventory requires a note to describe the method of determining cost. IFRS also requires the method of valuation, whether write-down has occurred, and whether inventory is pledged as security.

Under ASPE, cost is used to value property, plant, and equipment. Under IFRS, a company may choose to report some or all of its PPE at fair value.

This is a report form of the balance sheet using a classified method of presentation.

Morning Java
Balance Sheet
December 31, 2015

Assets

Current assets:		
Cash and cash equivalents		$ 235,000
Trading investments (at fair value)		465,000
Accounts receivable	$ 305,000	
Less allowance for doubtful accounts	12,300	292,700
Inventory		120,000
Prepaid insurance		24,000
Total current assets		$1,136,700
Investments:		
Investment in *AM Coffee* (equity method)		565,000
Property, plant, and equipment:		
Buildings	2,650,000	
Less accumulated depreciation	420,000	2,230,000
Office equipment	350,000	
Less accumulated depreciation	102,000	248,000
Land	1,850,000	
Total property, plant, and equipment		4,328,000
Intangible assets:		
Patents	160,000	
Less accumulated amortization	20,000	140,000
Total assets		$6,169,700

Liabilities

Current liabilities:		
Accounts payable		$ 133,000
Notes payable (current portion)		200,000
Salaries and wages payable		42,000
Source deductions payable		16,400
Interest payable		40,000
Total current liabilities		$ 431,400
Long-term liabilities:		
Bonds payable, 8%, due December 31, 2035	500,000	
Less unamortized discount	16,000	484,000
Notes payable		1,400,000
Total long-term liabilities		1,884,000
Total liabilities		2,315,400

Shareholders' Equity

Contributed capital:	
$5 preferred shares (6,000 shares authorized, issued, and outstanding)	350,000
Common shares (50,000 shares authorized, 45,000 shares issued and outstanding)	2,350,000
Total contributed capital	2,700,000
Retained earnings	1,154,300
Total shareholders' equity	3,854,300
Total liabilities and shareholders' equity	$6,169,700

Title of statement may be "Statement of Changes in Equity" under IFRS.

Morning Java Statement of Retained Earnings For the Year Ended December 31, 2015		
Retained earnings, January 1, 2015		$ 806,700
Net income.	$421,600	
Less dividends:		
Preferred.	$30,000	
Common.	44,000	74,000
Increase in retained earnings		347,600
Retained earnings, December 31, 2015		$1,154,300

A complete set of financial statements would also include a Statement of Cash Flows and notes to the financial statements.

Leon's Furniture Limited, 2011 Financial Statements

MANAGEMENT'S DISCUSSION & ANALYSIS

Financial Review

The following Management's Discussion and Analysis ("MD&A") is prepared as at February 23, 2012 and is based on the consolidated financial position and operating results of Leon's Furniture Limited/Meubles Leon Ltée (the "Company") as of December 31, 2011, and for the year ended December 31, 2011. It should be read in conjunction with the fiscal year 2011 consolidated financial statements and the notes thereto. For additional details and information relating to the Company, readers are referred to the fiscal 2011 quarterly financial statements and corresponding MD&As, which are published separately and available at www.sedar.com.

Cautionary Statement Regarding Forward-Looking Statements

This MD&A is intended to provide readers with the information that management believes is required to gain an understanding of Leon's Furniture Limited's current results and to assess the Company's future prospects. This MD&A, and in particular the section under the heading "Outlook", includes forward-looking statements, which are based on certain assumptions and reflect Leon's Furniture Limited's current plans and expectations. These forward-looking statements are subject to a number of risks and uncertainties that could cause actual results and future prospects to differ materially from current expectations. Some of the factors that can cause actual results to differ materially from current expectations are: a continuing slowdown in the Canadian economy; a further drop in consumer confidence; and dependency on product from third-party suppliers. Given these risks and uncertainties, investors should not place undue reliance on forward-looking statements as a prediction of actual results. Readers of this report are cautioned that actual events and results may vary.

Financial Statements Governance Practice

The consolidated financial statements of the Company have been prepared in accordance with International Financial Reporting Standards ("IFRS") as issued by the International Accounting Standards Board ("IASB"). These consolidated financial statements represent the first annual financial statements of the Company prepared in accordance with IFRS. The Company adopted IFRS in accordance with International Financial Reporting Standards 1, *First time Adoption of International Financial Reporting Standards* ("IFRS 1"). Further details, including the effects of the transition from the previous Canadian generally accepted accounting principles ("Canadian GAAP") to IFRS, are explained in Note 22 to these accompanying consolidated financial statements. Certain comparative figures have been reclassified to conform to the basis of presentation adopted in fiscal 2010.

Leon's Furniture Limited 2010 financial results included in this MD&A have been restated to be in accordance with IFRS.

The Audit Committee of the Board of Directors of the Company reviewed the MD&A and the consolidated financial statements, and recommended that the Board of Directors approve them. Following review by the full Board, the consolidated financial statements and MD&A were approved on February 23, 2012.

Introduction

Leon's Furniture Limited has been in the furniture retail business for over 100 years. The Company's 43 corporate and 32 franchise stores can be found in every province across Canada except British Columbia. Main product lines sold at retail include furniture, appliances and electronics.

14

LEON'S FURNITURE LIMITED
Management's Discussion & Analysis

Revenues and Expenses

For the year ended December 31, 2011, total Leon's sales were $879,561,000 including $196,725,000 of franchise sales ($907,497,000 including $197,062,000 of franchise sales in 2010), a decrease of 3.1%.

The decrease in sales for the year compared to the prior year reflected a continuation of waning consumer confidence and a decrease in housing starts. These factors also resulted in downward pressure on retail pricing. In particular electronics have experienced declines in same product pricing for the past four years. Overall same store sales decreased by 6.4% (see section on "Non-IFRS Financial Measures").

Leon's franchise sales for 2011 were flat compared to 2010. Overall store for store franchise sales decreased by 1.8%. The sales difference in 2011 was the result of the successful opening of two new franchise stores in Bathurst, New Brunswick and Drummondville, Quebec.

Our gross margin for the year 2011 of 42.3% was up approximately 0.3% from the prior year 2010. The increase in gross margin was mainly attributable to the conscientious effort to reduce damaged and discounted product sales and a reduction in our sales finance expenses, which are deducted from sales.

For the year, net operating expenses of $213,395,000 were up $1,159,000, or 0.55% as compared to 2010. General and administrative expenses decreased $2,646,000 from the prior year. The decrease was mainly the result of lower depreciation cost on buildings. Under IFRS, buildings are now being depreciated over a useful life of 30 years, which resulted in a depreciation expense reduction of approximately $2,600,000 compared to the prior year. Sales and marketing expenses were basically flat with the prior year. We did see lower sales commission costs as a result of decreased sales for the year. This cost reduction was offset by the increase of advertising expenses of $1,400,000 or 4.5% from the prior year. Additional marketing dollars were spent during the year to increase consumer traffic into our stores and to promote the opening of four new corporate stores in 2011 being Guelph, Ontario; Mississauga, Ontario; Rosemère, Quebec; and Regina, Saskatchewan. These new stores plus some significant increases in existing store property assessments led to higher property and business taxes in 2011. As a result, we saw occupancy expenses increase by $3,180,000 or 10.8% as compared to 2010.

As a result of the above, net income for the year ended 2011 was $56,666,000, $0.81 per common share ($63,284,000, $0.90 per common share in 2010), a decrease of 10% per common share.

For the three months ended December 31, 2011, total Leon's sales were $254,989,000 including $61,166,000 of franchise sales ($257,708,000 including $59,820,000 of franchise sales in 2010), a decrease of 1.1%.

Leon's corporate sales of $193,823,000 in the fourth quarter of 2011, decreased by $4,065,000, or 2.1%, compared to the fourth quarter of 2010. Same store corporate sales decreased by 7.4% compared to the prior year's quarter.

Leon's franchise sales of $61,166,000 in the fourth quarter of 2011 increased by $1,346,000, or 2.25% compared to 2010. The sales increase is mainly attributable to the two new franchise stores opened during 2011.

Net income for the fourth quarter of 2011 was $19,872,000, $0.28 per common share ($21,360,000, $0.30 per common share in 2010), a decrease of 6.7% per common share.

Annual Financial Information

($ in thousands, except earnings per share and dividends)	2011	2010	2009
Net corporate sales	$ 682,836	$ 710,435	$ 703,180
Leon franchise sales	196,725	197,062	194,290
Total Leon's sales	$ 879,561	$ 907,497	$ 897,470
Net income	56,666	63,284	56,864
Earnings per share			
Basic	$ 0.81	$ 0.90	$ 0.80
Diluted	$ 0.78	$ 0.87	$ 0.78
Total assets	$ 595,339	$ 566,674	$ 529,156
Common share dividends declared	$ 0.37	$ 0.32	$ 0.28
Special common share dividends declared	$ 0.15	$ –	$ 0.20
Convertible, non-voting shares dividends declared	$ 0.20	$ 0.18	$ 0.14

The year ended 2010 has been restated to IFRS while the year ended 2009 is as originally reported under Canadian GAAP. Furthermore, the year ended 2010 figures have been revised, from previously reported IFRS amounts, to reflect an immaterial adjustment to the amount of foreign exchange that is required to be recorded within comprehensive income as it relates to the Company's foreign denominated non-monetary available-for-sale financial assets. Any foreign denominated monetary available-for-sale financial assets were appropriately recorded in the consolidated income statement.

Liquidity and Financial Resources

($ in thousands, except dividends per share)	Dec 31, 2011	Dec 31, 2010	Dec 31, 2009
Cash, cash equivalents, available-for-sale financial assets	$ 221,823	$ 211,813	$ 170,726
Trade and other accounts receivable	28,937	28,569	31,501
Inventory	87,830	85,423	83,957
Total assets	595,339	566,674	529,156
Working capital	204,649	200,826	164,759

For the 3 Months Ended	Current Quarter Dec 31, 2011	Prior Quarter Sept 30, 2011	Prior Quarter June 30, 2011
Cash flow provided by operations	$ 26,230	$ 26,857	$ 12,770
Purchase of property, plant and equipment	6,336	9,386	6,401
Repurchase of capital stock	219	1,615	3,785
Dividends paid	6,292	6,305	6,317
Dividends paid per share	$ 0.09	$ 0.09	$ 0.09

In the third quarter of 2011, the Company celebrated a grand opening of a new corporate store in Guelph, Ontario. That was followed by grand openings in the fourth quarter of 2011 of three additional corporate stores in Mississauga, Ontario; Rosemère, Quebec; and Regina, Saskatchewan. As well, during the fourth quarter of 2011, new Leon's franchise locations had grand openings in Bathurst, New Brunswick; and Drummondville, Quebec, our first franchise located in Quebec.

In addition to these new locations, the Company and our existing franchisees continue to replace, renovate and expand existing stores in order to serve our customers better. Renovations are well underway in our Sudbury and Sault Ste. Marie, Ontario corporate stores. Our Trenton, Ontario franchise recently completed a renovation of their store and a renovation and expansion will commence shortly at our Simcoe, Ontario franchise. Our Kentville franchise has recently completed construction of a new and larger replacement store in Coldbrook, Nova Scotia. Finally, construction has started for a brand new franchise store to replace our existing St. John, New Brunswick store.

16

LEON'S FURNITURE LIMITED
Management's Discussion & Analysis

The Company continues to explore new opportunities across Canada. The Company has recently secured sites for four new corporate stores in: Orangeville and Brantford, Ontario; Sherbrooke, Quebec; and Rocky View County, which is just north of Calgary, Alberta. Our current plan is to open these locations during 2012 and 2013. All funding for new store projects and renovations is planned to come from our existing cash resources.

Common Shares

At December 31, 2011, there were 69,815,734 common shares issued and outstanding. During 2011, 484,727 shares were repurchased at an average cost of $13.07 and then cancelled by the Company through its Normal Course Issuer Bid. In addition, during the year ended December 31, 2011, 145,583 convertible, non-voting series 2002 shares and 79,545 convertible, non-voting series 2005 shares were converted into common shares. There were 53,017 convertible, non-voting series 2009 shares cancelled. For details on the Company's commitments related to its redeemable shares, please refer to Note 13 to the accompanying consolidated financial statements.

Commitments

($ in thousands)

CONTRACTUAL OBLIGATIONS		Total		Less than 1 Year		2-3 Years		4-5 Years		Payments Due by Period After 5 Years
Operating Leases[1]	$	44,131	$	5,860	$	10,329	$	9,660	$	18,282
Purchase Obligations		4,407		4,407		–		–		–
Total Contractual Obligations	$	48,538	$	10,267	$	10,329	$	9,660	$	18,282

(1) The Company is obligated under operating leases to future minimum rental payments for various land and building sites across Canada.

Recent Accounting Pronouncements

Please refer to Note 3 to the accompanying consolidated financial statements for the accounting standards and amendments issued but not yet adopted.

Impact of New Accounting Policies – Adoption of IFRS

Leon's Furniture Limited was required to prepare financial statements in accordance with IFRS starting with the unaudited interim condensed consolidated financial statements for the quarter ended March 31, 2011. These statements required the 2010 results to be presented in accordance with IFRS.

Further details, including the effects of the transition from the previous Canadian GAAP to IFRS, are explained in Note 22 to the accompanying consolidated financial statements.

Critical Accounting Estimates

Please refer to Note 4 to the accompanying consolidated financial statements for the Company's critical accounting estimates and assumptions.

Related Party Transactions

Please refer to Note 21 to the accompanying consolidated financial statements for the Company's related party transactions.

Risks and Uncertainties

For a complete discussion of the risks and uncertainties that apply to the Company's business and operating results, please refer to the Company's Annual Information Form dated March 31, 2011 available on www.sedar.com.

Quarterly Results (2011, 2010)

Quarterly Income Statement

($ in thousands, except per share data)	Quarter Ended December 31		Quarter Ended September 30		Quarter Ended June 30		Quarter Ended March 31	
	2011	2010	**2011**	2010	**2011**	2010	**2011**	2010
Leon's corporate sales	**$ 193,823**	$ 197,888	**$ 174,373**	$ 182,125	**$ 163,857**	$ 168,952	**$ 150,783**	$ 161,470
Leon's franchise sales	**61,166**	59,820	**49,273**	49,421	**45,477**	45,493	**40,809**	42,328
Total Leon's sales	**254,989**	257,708	**223,646**	231,546	**209,334**	214,445	**191,592**	203,798
Net income per share	**$ 0.28**	$ 0.30	**$ 0.22**	$ 0.26	**$ 0.16**	$ 0.17	**$ 0.15**	$ 0.17
Fully diluted per share	**$ 0.27**	$ 0.29	**$ 0.21**	$ 0.25	**$ 0.15**	$ 0.16	**$ 0.14**	$ 0.16

Net income per share and fully diluted per share amounts presented in the above table, with the exception of the fourth quarter ended December 31, 2011, have been revised from previously reported IRFS reports to reflect an immaterial adjustment to the amount of foreign exchange that is required to be recorded within comprehensive income as it relates to the Company's foreign denominated non-monetary available-for-sale financial assets. Any foreign denominated monetary available-for-sale financial assets were appropriately recorded in the consolidated income statement.

The following table provides selected 2010 results by quarter.

IFRS 2010 Results by Quarter

($ in thousands, except per share data)	First Quarter	Second Quarter	Third Quarter	Fourth Quarter	Full Year 2010
Revenue	$ 161,470	$ 168,952	$ 182,125	$ 197,888	$ 710,435
Cost of sales	93,498	100,187	106,564	112,130	412,379
Gross profit	67,972	68,765	75,561	85,758	298,056
Operating expenses					
General and administrative expenses	23,293	25,432	24,484	25,475	98,684
Sales and marketing expenses	18,572	18,008	19,297	22,344	78,221
Occupancy expenses	7,630	7,490	7,214	7,217	29,551
Other operating expenses	1,558	1,281	1,464	1,477	5,780
	51,053	52,211	52,459	56,513	212,236
Operating profit	16,919	16,554	23,102	29,245	85,820
Gain on sale of capital property	–	–	1,231	–	1,231
Finance income	691	663	789	991	3,134
Profit before income tax	17,610	17,217	25,122	30,236	90,185
Income tax expense	5,640	5,344	7,041	8,876	26,901
Profit for the period attributable to the shareholders of the Company	$ 11,970	$ 11,873	$ 18,081	$ 23,360	$ 63,284
Earnings per share					
Basic	$ 0.17	$ 0.17	$ 0.26	$ 0.30	$ 0.90
Diluted	$ 0.16	$ 0.16	$ 0.25	$ 0.29	$ 0.87

The Full Year 2010 and Quarters ended March 31, 2010, June 30, 2010, September 30, 2010 and December 31, 2010 figures above have been revised, from previously reported IFRS amounts, to reflect an immaterial adjustment to the amount of foreign exchange that is required to be recorded within comprehensive income as it relates to the Company's foreign denominated non-monetary available-for-sale financial assets. Any foreign denominated monetary available-for-sale financial assets were appropriately recorded in the consolidated income statement.

18
LEON'S FURNITURE LIMITED
Management's Discussion & Analysis

Disclosure Controls and Procedures

Management is responsible for establishing and maintaining a system of disclosure controls and procedures to provide reasonable assurance that all material information relating to the Company is gathered and reported on a timely basis to senior management, including the Chief Executive Officer and Chief Financial Officer so that appropriate decisions can be made by them regarding public disclosure. Based on the evaluation of disclosure controls and procedures, the CEO and CFO have concluded that the Company's disclosure controls and procedures were effective as at December 31, 2011.

Internal Controls Over Financial Reporting

Management is also responsible for establishing and maintaining adequate internal control over financial reporting to provide reasonable assurance regarding the reliability of financial reporting and the preparation of consolidated financial statements for external purposes in accordance with IFRS. The Company's internal control over financial reporting may not prevent or detect all misstatements because of inherent limitations. The Company assessed the effectiveness of its internal control over financial reporting as of December 31, 2011, based on the framework established in the publications, Internal Control – Integrated Framework and specifically in Internal Control over Financial Reporting – Guidance for Smaller Public Companies published by the Committee of Sponsoring Organizations of the Treadway Commission. Based on this assessment, the CEO and the CFO concluded that the Company maintained effective internal control over financial reporting as of December 31, 2011.

Changes in Internal Control Over Financial Reporting

Management has also evaluated whether there were changes in the Company's internal control over financial reporting that occurred during the period beginning on October 1, 2011 and ended on December 31, 2011 that have materially affected, or are reasonably likely to materially affect, the Company's internal control over financial reporting. The Company has determined that no material changes in internal controls have occurred during this period.

Outlook

We have been experiencing a slowdown in our economy, which began in 2009, and we don't see any signs of any major improvement moving into 2012. As such, we anticipate that consumer discretionary spending will remain soft in 2012. To help counter this, we plan an even more robust marketing and merchandising campaign for 2012. The recent opening of four new stores in the latter part of 2011 should also aid our sales in 2012. Even with these measures in place, growing profits in 2012 will be challenging. Despite this, our strong financial position coupled with our experience in adjusting to changing market conditions, provide us with the confidence to adapt to the prevailing economic conditions.

Non-IFRS Financial Measures

In order to provide additional insight into the business, the Company has provided the measure of same store sales, in the revenue and expenses section above. This measure does not have a standardized meaning prescribed by IFRS but it is a key indicator used by the Company to measure performance against prior period results. Comparable store sales are defined as sales generated by stores that have been open or closed for more than 12 months on a yearly basis. The reconciliation between total corporate sales (an IFRS measure) and comparable store sales is provided below:

($ in thousands)	2011	2010
Net corporate sales	$ 682,836	$ 710,435
Adjustments for stores not in both fiscal periods	(20,555)	(2,516)
Comparable store sales	$ 662,281	$ 707,919

MANAGEMENT'S RESPONSIBILITY FOR FINANCIAL REPORTING

The accompanying consolidated financial statements are the responsibility of management and have been approved by the Board of Directors.

The accompanying consolidated financial statements have been prepared by management in accordance with International Financial Reporting Standards ("IFRS") and incorporate the requirements of IFRS 1, *First time adoption of IFRS*. Financial statements are not precise since they include certain amounts based upon estimates and judgments. When alternative methods exist, management has chosen those it deems to be the most appropriate in the circumstances.

Leon's Furniture Limited/Meubles Leon Ltee ("Leon's" or the "Company") maintains systems of internal accounting and administrative controls, consistent with reasonable costs. Such systems are designed to provide reasonable assurance that the financial information is relevant and reliable and that Leon's assets are appropriately accounted for and adequately safeguarded.

The Board of Directors is responsible for ensuring that management fulfils its responsibilities for financial reporting and is ultimately responsible for reviewing and approving the financial statements. The Board carries out this responsibility through its Audit Committee.

The Audit Committee is appointed by the Board and reviews these consolidated financial statements; considers the report of the external auditors; assesses the adequacy of the internal controls of the Company; examines the fees and expenses for audit services; and recommends to the Board the independent auditors for appointment by the shareholders. The Committee reports its findings to the Board of Directors for consideration when approving these consolidated financial statements for issuance to the shareholders.

These consolidated financial statements have been audited by Ernst & Young, the external auditors, in accordance with Canadian generally accepted auditing standards on behalf of the shareholders. Ernst & Young has full and free access to the Audit Committee.

Terrence T. Leon
President and CEO

Dominic Scarangella
Vice President and CFO

20

LEON'S FURNITURE LIMITED

INDEPENDENT AUDITORS' REPORT

To the Shareholders of

Leon's Furniture Limited/Meubles Leon Ltée

We have audited the accompanying consolidated financial statements of Leon's Furniture Limited/Meubles Leon Ltée, which comprise the consolidated statements of financial position as at December 31, 2011 and 2010, and January 1, 2010, and the consolidated income statements, comprehensive income, changes in equity and cash flows for the years ended December 31, 2011 and 2010, and a summary of significant accounting policies and other explanatory information.

Management's Responsibility for the Consolidated Financial Statements

Management is responsible for the preparation and fair presentation of these consolidated financial statements in accordance with International Financial Reporting Standards, and for such internal control as management determines is necessary to enable the preparation of consolidated financial statements that are free from material misstatement, whether due to fraud or error.

Auditors' Responsibility

Our responsibility is to express an opinion on these consolidated financial statements based on our audits. We conducted our audits in accordance with Canadian generally accepted auditing standards. Those standards require that we comply with ethical requirements and plan and perform the audit to obtain reasonable assurance about whether the consolidated financial statements are free from material misstatement.

An audit involves performing procedures to obtain audit evidence about the amounts and disclosures in the consolidated financial statements. The procedures selected depend on the auditors' judgment, including the assessment of the risks of material misstatement of the consolidated financial statements, whether due to fraud or error. In making those risk assessments, the auditors consider internal control relevant to the entity's preparation and fair presentation of the consolidated financial statements in order to design audit procedures that are appropriate in the circumstances, but not for the purpose of expressing an opinion on the effectiveness of the entity's internal control. An audit also includes evaluating the appropriateness of accounting policies used and the reasonableness of accounting estimates made by management, as well as evaluating the overall presentation of the consolidated financial statements.

We believe that the audit evidence we have obtained in our audits is sufficient and appropriate to provide a basis for our audit opinion.

Opinion

In our opinion, the consolidated financial statements present fairly, in all material respects, the financial position of Leon's Furniture Limited/Meubles Leon Ltée as at December 31, 2011 and 2010, and January 1, 2010, and its financial performance and its cash flows for the years ended December 31, 2011 and 2010 in accordance with International Financial Reporting Standards.

Ernst & Young LLP

Chartered Accountants
Licensed Public Accountants

Toronto, Canada
February 23, 2012

CONSOLIDATED STATEMENTS OF FINANCIAL POSITION

Leon's Furniture Limited / Meubles Leon Ltée Incorporated under the laws of Ontario	As at December 31	As at December 31	As at January 1
($ in thousands)	2011	2010	2010
		(Note 22)	(Note 22)
Assets			
Current			
Cash and cash equivalents (Notes 5 and 7)	$ 72,505	$ 71,589	$ 58,301
Available-for-sale financial assets (Notes 5 and 19(e))	149,318	140,224	112,425
Trade receivables (Note 5)	28,937	28,569	31,501
Income taxes receivable	5,182	–	–
Inventories	87,830	85,423	83,957
Total current assets	$ 343,772	$ 325,805	$ 286,184
Other assets	1,431	1,574	1,560
Property, plant and equipment, net (Note 8)	214,158	201,492	203,653
Investment properties (Note 9)	8,366	8,417	8,545
Intangible assets, net (Note 10)	3,958	4,902	5,334
Goodwill (Note 10)	11,282	11,282	11,282
Deferred income tax assets (Note 17)	12,372	13,202	12,598
Total assets	$ 595,339	$ 566,674	$ 529,156
Liabilities and Shareholders' Equity			
Current			
Trade and other payables (Notes 5 and 11)	$ 75,126	$ 71,724	$ 72,603
Provisions (Note 12)	11,231	12,341	11,277
Income taxes payable	–	524	1,958
Customers' deposits	19,157	17,198	15,632
Dividends payable (Note 14)	17,457	6,310	4,938
Deferred warranty plan revenue	16,152	16,882	16,150
Total current liabilities	$ 139,123	$ 124,979	$ 122,558
Deferred warranty plan revenue	19,445	21,392	22,248
Redeemable share liability (Notes 5 and 13)	382	172	383
Deferred income tax liabilities (Note 17)	10,928	9,845	8,829
Total liabilities	$ 169,878	$ 156,388	$ 154,018
Shareholders' equity attributable to the shareholders of the Company			
Common shares (Note 14)	$ 20,918	$ 19,177	$ 17,704
Retained earnings	404,647	390,629	357,576
Accumulated other comprehensive income (loss)	(104)	480	(142)
Total shareholders' equity	$ 425,461	$ 410,286	$ 375,138
	$ 595,339	$ 566,674	$ 529,156

Commitments and contingencies (Note 19)

The accompanying notes are an integral part of these consolidated financial statements.

On behalf of the Board:

Mark Leon
Director

Peter Eby
Director

22

LEON'S FURNITURE LIMITED
Consolidated Financial Statements

CONSOLIDATED INCOME STATEMENTS

Years ended December 31 ($ in thousands, except shares outstanding and earnings per share)	2011	2010
Revenue (Notes 15 and 22)	$ 682,836	$ 710,435
Cost of sales	394,099	412,379
Gross profit	$ 288,737	$ 298,056
Operating expenses (Notes 16 and 22)		
General and administrative expenses	96,038	98,684
Sales and marketing expenses	78,387	78,221
Occupancy expenses	32,731	29,551
Other operating expenses	6,260	5,785
	$ 213,416	$ 212,241
Operating profit	75,321	85,815
Gain on sale of capital property	21	1,236
Finance income	3,506	3,134
Profit before income tax	78,848	90,185
Income tax expense (Note 17)	22,182	26,901
Profit for the year attributable to the shareholders of the Company	$ 56,666	$ 63,284
Weighted average number of common shares outstanding		
Basic	69,969,417	70,371,744
Diluted	72,305,424	73,133,906
Earnings per share		
Basic	$ 0.81	$ 0.90
Diluted	$ 0.78	$ 0.87
Dividends declared per share		
Common	$ 0.52	$ 0.32
Convertible, non-voting	$ 0.20	$ 0.18

The accompanying notes are an integral part of these consolidated financial statements.

CONSOLIDATED STATEMENTS OF COMPREHENSIVE INCOME

Year ended December 31 ($ in thousands)	2011	2011 Tax Effect	2011
Profit for the year	$ 56,666	$ –	$ 56,666
Other comprehensive loss, net of tax			
Unrealized (losses) on available-for-sale financial assets arising during the year	(621)	(87)	(534)
Reclassification adjustment for net gains and losses included in net income	(58)	(8)	(50)
Change in unrealized gains on available-for-sale financial assets arising during the year	(679)	(95)	(584)
Comprehensive income for the year	$ 55,987	$ (95)	$ 56,082

Year ended December 31 ($ in thousands)	2010	2010 Tax Effect	2010
Profit for the year	$ 63,284	$ –	$ 63,284
Other comprehensive income, net of tax			
Unrealized gains on available-for-sale financial assets arising during the year	917	144	773
Reclassification adjustment for net gains and losses included in net income	(178)	(27)	(151)
Change in unrealized gains on available-for-sale financial assets arising during the year	739	117	622
Comprehensive income for the year	$ 64,023	$ 117	$ 63,906

The accompanying notes are an integral part of these consolidated financial statements.

24
LEON'S FURNITURE LIMITED
Consolidated Financial Statements

CONSOLIDATED STATEMENTS OF CHANGES IN EQUITY

($ in thousands)	Common Shares	Accumulated Other Comprehensive Income (Loss)	Retained Earnings	Total
At January 1, 2010	$ 17,704	$ (142)	$ 357,576	$ 375,138
Comprehensive income				
Profit for the period	–	–	63,284	63,284
Change in unrealized gains on available-for-sale financial assets arising during the period	–	622	–	622
Total comprehensive income	–	622	63,284	63,906
Transactions with shareholders				
Dividends declared	–	–	(22,492)	(22,492)
Management share purchase plan (Note 13)	1,768	–	–	1,768
Repurchase of common shares (Note 14)	(295)	–	(7,739)	(8,034)
Total transactions with shareholders	1,473	–	(30,231)	(28,758)
At December 31, 2010	$ 19,177	$ 480	$ 390,629	$ 410,286
At January 1, 2011	$ 19,177	$ 480	$ 390,629	$ 410,286
Comprehensive income				
Profit for the period	–	–	56,666	56,666
Change in unrealized (losses) on available-for-sale financial assets arising during the period	–	(584)	–	(584)
Total comprehensive income	–	(584)	56,666	56,082
Transactions with shareholders				
Dividends declared	–	–	(36,371)	(36,371)
Management share purchase plan (Note 13)	1,798	–	–	1,798
Repurchase of common shares (Note 14)	(57)	–	(6,277)	(6,334)
Total transactions with shareholders	1,741	–	(42,648)	(40,907)
At December 31, 2011	$ 20,918	$ (104)	$ 404,647	$ 425,461

The accompanying notes are an integral part of these consolidated financial statements.

CONSOLIDATED STATEMENTS OF CASH FLOWS

Years ended December 31 ($ in thousands)	2011	2010
Operating Activities		
Profit for the year	$ 56,666	$ 63,284
Add (deduct) items not involving an outlay of cash		
Depreciation of property, plant and equipment and investment properties (Note 16)	12,705	15,354
Amortization of intangible assets (Note 16)	880	802
Amortization of deferred warranty plan revenue	(17,271)	(16,838)
Gain on sale of property, plant and equipment (Note 16)	(21)	(1,236)
Deferred income taxes	2,008	295
Gain (loss) on sale of available-for-sale financial assets	35	(337)
Cash received on warranty plan sales	14,594	16,714
	69,596	78,038
Net change in non-cash working capital balances related to operations (Note 20)	(4,426)	1,391
Cash provided by operating activities	65,170	79,429
Investing Activities		
Purchase of property, plant and equipment (Note 8)	(24,999)	(13,567)
Purchase of intangible assets (Note 10)	64	(370)
Proceeds on sale of property, plant and equipment (Note 8)	39	2,117
Purchase of available-for-sale financial assets	(569,050)	(524,414)
Proceeds on sale of available-for-sale financial assets	559,242	497,691
Decrease in employee share purchase loans (Note 13)	2,008	1,556
Cash used in investing activities	(32,696)	(36,987)
Financing Activities		
Dividends paid	(25,224)	(21,120)
Repurchase of common shares (Note 14)	(6,334)	(8,034)
Cash used in financing activities	(31,558)	(29,154)
Net increase in cash and cash equivalents during the year	916	13,288
Cash and cash equivalents, beginning of year	71,589	58,301
Cash and cash equivalents, end of year	$ 72,505	$ 71,589

The accompanying notes are an integral part of these consolidated financial statements.

26

LEON'S FURNITURE LIMITED

NOTES TO THE CONSOLIDATED FINANCIAL STATEMENTS

For the years ended December 31, 2011 and 2010
(Tabular amounts in thousands of Canadian dollars except shares outstanding and earnings per share)

1. General Information

Leon's Furniture Limited/Meubles Leon Ltée was incorporated by Articles of Incorporation under the Business Corporations Act on February 28, 1969. Leon's Furniture Limited/Meubles Leon Ltée and its subsidiaries ("Leon's" or the "Company") is a public company with its common shares listed on the Toronto Stock Exchange and is incorporated and domiciled in Canada. The address of the Company's head and registered office is 45 Gordon Mackay Road, Toronto, Ontario, M9N 3X3.

Leon's is a retailer of home furnishings, electronics and appliances across Canada from Alberta to Newfoundland and Labrador. The Company owns a chain of forty-one retail stores operating as Leon's Home Furnishings Super Stores, two retail stores operating under the brand of Appliance Canada and operates an ecommerce internet site www.leons.ca. In addition, the Company has twenty-seven franchisees operating thirty-two Leon's Furniture franchise stores.

2. Basis of Preparation and Adoption of IFRS

The consolidated financial statements of the Company have been prepared in accordance with International Financial Reporting Standards ("IFRS") as issued by the International Accounting Standards Board ("IASB"). These consolidated financial statements represent the first annual financial statements of the Company prepared in accordance with IFRS. The Company adopted IFRS in accordance with International Financial Reporting Standards 1 First-time Adoption of International Financial Reporting Standards ("IFRS 1"). The first date at which IFRS was applied was January 1, 2010. Further details, including the effects of the transition from the previous Canadian generally accepted accounting principles ("Canadian GAAP") to IFRS, are explained in Note 22 to these consolidated financial statements. The accounting policies were consistently applied to all periods presented unless otherwise noted.

Use of Judgment and Estimates

Management has exercised judgment in the process of applying the Company's accounting policies. The preparation of consolidated financial statements in accordance with IFRS requires management to make estimates and assumptions that affect the reported amounts of assets and liabilities and disclosure of contingent assets and liabilities at the consolidated balance sheet date and the reported amounts of revenue and expenses during the reporting period. Key areas where management has made estimates include allowance for doubtful accounts, valuation of inventory, fair values and impairment of financial assets, investment properties, goodwill and intangible assets, income taxes, and useful lives of capital assets and intangible assets. Actual results could differ from those estimates.

These consolidated financial statements were approved by the Board of Directors for issuance on February 23, 2012.

3. Summary of Significant Accounting Policies

The significant accounting policies used in the preparation of these consolidated financial statements are as follows:

Basis of Measurement

The consolidated financial statements have been prepared under the historical cost convention, except for available-for-sale financial assets, which are measured at fair value.

Consolidation

The financial statements consolidate the accounts of the Company and its wholly owned subsidiaries, Murlee Holdings Limited, Leon Holdings (1967) Limited and Ablan Insurance Corporation. Subsidiaries are all those entities over which the Company has the power to govern the financial and operating policies generally accompanying a shareholding of more than one half of the voting rights. The existence and effect of potential voting rights that are currently exercisable or convertible are considered when assessing whether the Company controls another entity. Subsidiaries are fully consolidated from the date on which control is transferred to the Company and de-consolidated from the date that control ceases. Intercompany transactions, balances, income and expenses, and profits and losses are eliminated.

Segment Reporting

Operating segments are reported in a manner consistent with the internal reporting provided to the chief operating decision-maker. The chief operating decision-maker, who is responsible for allocating resources and assessing performance of the operating segments, has been identified as the President and Chief Executive Officer. The Company operates in one geographical segment (Canada) and one industry (sale of home furnishings, appliances and electronics). Accordingly, no segment information has been provided in these consolidated financial statements.

Foreign Currency Translation

Functional and Presentation Currency

Items included in the consolidated financial statements are measured using the currency of the primary economic environment in which the Company operates (the functional currency). These consolidated financial statements are presented in Canadian dollars, which is the Company's functional and presentation currency and is also the functional currency of each of the Company's subsidiaries.

Foreign Currency Transactions

Foreign currency transactions are translated into the respective functional currencies of the Company's subsidiaries using the exchange rate at the dates of transactions. Merchandise imported from the United States and South East Asia, paid for in U.S. dollars, is recorded at its equivalent Canadian dollar value upon receipt. U.S. dollar trade payables are translated at the year-end exchange rate. The Company is subject to gains and losses due to fluctuations in the U.S. dollar. Foreign exchange gains and losses resulting from translation of U.S. dollar accounts payable are included in the consolidated income statement within cost of sales.

Any foreign exchange gains and losses on monetary available-for-sale financial assets are recognized in the consolidated income statement, and other changes in the carrying amounts are recognized in other comprehensive income. For available-for-sale assets that are not monetary items, the gain or loss that is recognized in other comprehensive income includes any related foreign exchange component.

Financial Assets and Liabilities

A financial asset or liability is recognized if the Company becomes a party to the contractual provisions of the asset or liability. A financial asset or liability is recognized initially (at trade date) at its fair value plus, in the case of a financial asset or liability not at fair value through profit or loss, transaction costs that are directly attributable to the acquisition or issue of the instrument. Financial assets and liabilities carried at fair value through profit or loss are initially recognized at fair value and transaction costs are expensed in the consolidated income statement.

After initial recognition, financial assets are measured at their fair values except for loans and receivables, which are measured at amortized cost using the effective interest method. After initial recognition, financial liabilities are measured at amortized cost except for financial liabilities at fair value through profit or loss, which are measured at fair value.

The Company classifies its financial assets and liabilities according to their characteristics and management's choices and intentions related thereto for the purposes of ongoing measurement.

Classifications that the Company has used for financial assets include:

(a) **Available-for-sale** – financial assets that are non-derivatives that are either designated in this category or not classified in any other category and include marketable securities, which consist primarily of quoted bonds, equities and debentures. These assets are measured at fair value with changes in fair value recognized in other comprehensive income for the current period until realized through disposal or impairment; and

(b) **Loans and receivables** – are non-derivative financial assets with fixed or determinable payments that are not quoted in an active market. Loans and receivables include trade receivables and recorded at amortized cost with gains and losses recognized in the consolidated income statement in the period that the asset is no longer recognized or impaired.

28
LEON'S FURNITURE LIMITED
Notes to the Consolidated Financial Statements

Classification choice that the Company has used for financial liabilities includes:

> **Other financial liabilities** – measured at amortized cost with gains and losses recognized in the consolidated income statement in the period that the liability is no longer recognized.

Financial assets are derecognized if the Company's contractual rights to the cash flows from the financial assets expire or if the Company transfers the financial asset to another party without retaining control or substantially all risks and rewards of the asset. Financial liabilities are derecognized if the Company's obligations specified in the contract expire or are discharged or cancelled.

Impairment of Financial Assets

The Company assesses at the end of each reporting period whether there is objective evidence that a financial asset or group of financial assets is impaired. A financial asset or group of financial assets is impaired and impairment losses are incurred only if there is objective evidence of impairment as a result of one or more events that occurred after the initial recognition of the asset (a loss event) and that loss event has an impact on the estimated future cash flows of the financial asset or group of financial assets that can be reliably estimated.

The amount of the loss is measured as the difference between the asset's carrying amount and the present value of estimated future cash flows discounted at the financial asset's original effective interest rate. The asset's carrying amount is reduced and the amount of the loss is recognized in the consolidated income statement.

If, in a subsequent period, the amount of the impairment loss decreases and the decrease can be related objectively to an event occurring after the impairment was recognized, the reversal of the previously recognized impairment is recognized in the consolidated income statement.

Cash and Cash Equivalents

Cash and cash equivalents include cash on hand, balances with banks and short-term market investments with a remaining term to maturity of less than 90 days from the date of purchase.

Trade Receivables

Trade receivables are amounts due for goods sold in the ordinary course of business. If collection is expected in one year or less, they are classified as current assets. If not, they are presented as non-current assets.

Trade receivables are initially recognized at fair value and subsequently measured at amortized cost using the effective interest method, less provision for impairment.

Inventories

Inventories are valued at the lower of cost, determined on a first-in, first-out basis, and net realizable value.

The Company receives vendor rebates on certain products based on the volume of purchases made during specified periods. The rebates are deducted from the inventory value of goods received and are recognized as a reduction of cost of sales upon sale of the goods. Incentives received for a direct reimbursement of costs incurred to sell the vendor's products such as marketing and advertising funds are recorded as a reduction of those related costs in the consolidated income statement, provided certain conditions are met.

Property, Plant and Equipment

Property, plant and equipment are initially recorded at cost. Historical cost includes expenditure that is directly attributable to the acquisition of items. Subsequent costs are included in the asset's carrying amount or recognized as a separate asset, as appropriate, only when it is probable that future economic benefits associated with the asset will flow to the Company and the cost can be measured reliably. When significant parts of property, plant and equipment are required to be replaced at intervals, the Company derecognizes the replaced part, and recognizes the new part with its own associated useful life and depreciation. Normal repair and maintenance expenditures are expensed as incurred.

Land and construction in progress are not depreciated. Depreciation on other assets is provided over the estimated useful lives of the assets using the following annual rates and methods:

Buildings	30 years straight-line
Equipment	20% to 30% declining balance
Vehicles	30% declining balance
Computer hardware	5 years straight-line
Building improvements	Over the estimated useful life to a maximum of 15 years

The Company allocates the amount initially recognized in respect of an item of property, plant and equipment to its significant parts and depreciates separately each such part. The Company reviews the condition and consistently maintains items of property, plant and equipment to maximize the useful life of these items. However, residual values, method of depreciation and useful lives of items of property, plant and equipment are reviewed annually by the Company and adjusted if appropriate.

Gains and losses on disposals of property, plant and equipment are determined by comparing the proceeds with the carrying amount of the asset and are included as part of other expenses in the consolidated income statement.

Leases

The determination of whether an arrangement is, or contains, a lease is based on the substance of the arrangement at the inception date, whether fulfillment of the arrangement is dependent on the use of a specific asset or assets or the arrangement conveys a right to use the asset, even if that right is not explicitly specified in an arrangement.

Leased Assets – Leon's is the Lessee
Leases that are not finance leases are classified as operating leases and the assets are not recognized on the Company's consolidated statements of financial position. Operating lease payments are recognized as an expense in the consolidated income statement on a straight-line basis over the period of the lease.

Leased Assets – Leon's is the Lessor
Assets leased to third parties under operating leases are classified as investment property in the consolidated statements of financial position. They are depreciated over their expected useful lives on a basis consistent with similar owned investment property. Rental income (net of any incentives given to lessees) is recognized on a straight-line basis over the period of the lease.

Investment Properties

Assets that are held for long-term rental yields or for capital appreciation or both, and that are not occupied by either the Company or any of its subsidiaries, are classified as investment properties. Investment properties are measured initially at cost, including related transaction costs. Subsequent to initial recognition, investment properties are carried at cost and depreciated over the estimated useful lives of the properties using the following annual rates and methods:

Buildings	30 years straight-line
Building improvements	Over the estimated useful life to a maximum of 15 years

Land held by the Company and classified as investment property is not depreciated.

Subsequent expenditures on investment properties are capitalized to the properties' carrying amount only when it is probable that future economic benefits associated with the expenditures will flow to the Company and the cost of the item can be measured reliably. All other repairs and maintenance costs are expensed when incurred. When part of an investment property is replaced, the carrying amount of the replaced part is derecognized.

If an investment property becomes owner-occupied, it is reclassified as property, plant and equipment.

Goodwill and Intangible Assets

Goodwill
Goodwill is the residual amount that results when the purchase price of an acquired business exceeds the sum of the amounts allocated to the tangible and intangible assets acquired, less liabilities assumed, based on their fair value. Goodwill is assigned as of the date of the business acquisition. The Company assesses at least annually, or at any time if an indicator of impairment exists, whether there has been an impairment loss in the carrying value of goodwill and it is carried at cost less accumulated impairment losses. Impairment losses on goodwill are not reversed.

30

LEON'S FURNITURE LIMITED
Notes to the Consolidated Financial Statements

Goodwill is allocated to cash-generating units ("CGUs"), or groups of CGUs, that are expected to benefit from the business combination for the purpose of impairment testing. A group of CGUs represents the lowest level within the Company at which goodwill is monitored for internal management purposes.

Finite-Lived Intangible Assets

Intangible assets with finite useful lives are amortized on a straight-line basis over their estimated useful lives using the following annual rates:

Customer relationships	8 years
Brand name	10 years
Non-compete agreement	8 years
Computer software	7 years

The Company identifies and measures intangible assets acquired in business acquisitions and accounts for these assets separately from goodwill.

Impairment of Non-Financial Assets

Property, plant and equipment and finite lived intangible assets are reviewed quarterly for impairment and whenever events or changes in circumstances indicate that the carrying amount may not be recoverable. If the estimated recoverable amount of an asset is less than its carrying amount, the asset is written down to its estimated recoverable amount and an impairment loss is recognized. The recoverable amount of an asset is the higher of its fair value less costs to sell and value in use. For the purposes of assessing impairment, assets are grouped at the lowest level for which there are separately identifiable cash inflows (CGU). The Company has identified the CGU to be at the store level. Non-financial assets, other than goodwill, that suffered impairment are reviewed for possible reversal of the impairment at each reporting date.

Income Taxes

Income tax expense for the period comprises current and deferred income tax. Income tax is recognized in the consolidated income statement except to the extent it relates to items recognized in other comprehensive income or directly in equity, in which case the related tax is recognized in equity. Levies other than income taxes, such as taxes on real estate, are included in occupancy expenses.

Current Income Tax

Current income tax expense is based on the results of the period as adjusted for items that are not taxable or not deductible. Current tax is calculated using tax rates and laws that were substantively enacted at the end of the reporting period. Management periodically evaluates positions taken in tax returns with respect to situations in which applicable tax regulation is subject to interpretation. It establishes provisions where appropriate on the basis of amounts expected to be paid to the tax authorities.

Deferred Income Tax

Deferred income tax is recognized, using the liability method, on temporary differences arising between the tax bases of assets and liabilities and their carrying amounts in the consolidated statement of financial position. Deferred income tax is determined using tax rates (and laws) that have been enacted or substantively enacted by the consolidated statement of financial position date and are expected to apply when the related deferred income tax asset is realized or the deferred income tax liability is settled.

Deferred income tax assets are recognized only to the extent that it is probable that future taxable profit will be available against which the temporary differences can be utilized.

Deferred income tax assets and liabilities are offset when there is a legally enforceable right to offset current income tax assets against current income tax liabilities and when the deferred income tax assets and liabilities relate to income taxes levied by the same taxation authority where there is an intention to settle the balances on a net basis.

Trade and Other Payables

Trade and other payables are obligations to pay for goods or services that have been acquired in the ordinary course of business from suppliers. Trade and other payables are classified as current liabilities if payment is due within one year or less.

Provisions

Provisions are recognized only in those circumstances where the Company has a present legal or constructive obligation as a result of a past event, when it is probable that an outflow of resources will be required to settle the obligation, and a reliable estimate of the amount can be made.

Provisions are measured at the present value of the expenditures expected to be required to settle the obligation using a pre-tax discount rate that reflects current market assessments of the time value of money and the risks specific to the obligation.

Share Capital

Common shares are classified as equity. Incremental costs directly attributable to the issuance of new shares are shown in equity as a deduction, net of income tax, from the proceeds.

Revenue Recognition

Revenue comprises the fair value of consideration received or receivable for the sale of goods and services in the ordinary course of the Company's activities. Revenue is shown net of sales tax and financing charges. The Company recognizes revenue when the amount of revenue can be reliably measured and it is probable that future economic benefits will flow to the Company.

In addition to the above general principles, the Company applies the following specific revenue recognition policies:

Sale of Goods
Revenue from the sale of goods is recognized either when the customer picks up the merchandise ordered or when merchandise is delivered to the customer's home. Any payments received in advance of delivery are deferred and recorded as customers' deposits.

Extended Warranty
The Company recognizes extended warranty plan revenue on a straight-line basis over the contract period. The service costs associated with the warranty obligations are expensed as incurred.

Franchise Fees
Leon's franchisees operate principally as independent owners. The Company charges each franchisee a royalty fee based on a percentage of the franchisee's gross revenue. This royalty income is recorded by the Company on an accrual basis and presented within revenue.

Rent on Investment Properties
Rental income arising on investment properties is accounted for on a straight-line basis over the lease term and is presented within revenue.

Sale of Gift Cards
Revenue from the sale of gift cards is recognized when the gift cards are redeemed (the customer purchases merchandise), or when the gift cards are no longer expected to be redeemed, based on an analysis of historical redemption rates, if any. Revenue from unredeemed gift cards is deferred and included in trade and other payables.

Store Pre-Opening Costs

Store pre-opening costs are expensed as incurred.

Earnings per Share

Basic earnings per share have been calculated using the weighted average number of common shares outstanding during the year. Diluted earnings per share are calculated using the "if converted" method. The dividends declared on the redeemable share liability under the Company's Management Share Purchase Plan (the Plan) are included in net income for the year. The redeemable shares convertible under the Plan are included in the calculation of diluted number of common shares to the extent the redemption price was less than the average annual market price of the Company's common shares.

Accounting Standards and Amendments Issued But Not Yet Adopted

Unless otherwise noted, the following revised standards and amendments are effective for annual periods beginning on or after January 1, 2013, with earlier application permitted. The Company has not yet assessed the impact of these standards and amendments or determined whether it will early adopt them.

i.   IFRS 7, *Financial Instruments: Disclosures*, has been amended to include additional disclosure requirements in the reporting of transfer transactions and risk exposures relating to transfers of financial assets and the effect of those risks on an entity's financial position, particularly those involving securitization of financial assets. The amendment is applicable for annual periods beginning on or after July 1, 2011, with earlier application permitted.

32

LEON'S FURNITURE LIMITED
Notes to the Consolidated Financial Statements

ii. IFRS 9, *Financial Instruments,* was issued in November 2009 and addresses classification and measurement of financial assets. It replaces the multiple category and measurement models in IAS 39 for debt instruments with a new mixed measurement model having only two categories: amortized cost and fair value through profit or loss. IFRS 9 also replaces the models for measuring equity instruments. Such instruments are either recognized at fair value through profit or loss or at fair value through other comprehensive income. Where equity instruments are measured at fair value through other comprehensive income, dividends are recognized in profit or loss to the extent that they do not clearly represent a return of investment; however, other gains and losses (including impairments) associated with such instruments remain in accumulated other comprehensive income (loss) indefinitely.

Requirements for financial liabilities were added to IFRS 9 in October 2010 and they largely carried forward existing requirements in IAS 39, *Financial Instruments – Recognition and Measurement,* except that fair value changes due to credit risk for liabilities designated at fair value through profit and loss are generally recorded in other comprehensive income.

iii. IFRS 10, *Consolidated Financial Statements,* requires an entity to consolidate an investee when it has power over the investee, is exposed, or has rights, to variable returns from its involvement with the investee and has the ability to affect those returns through its power over the investee. Under existing IFRS, consolidation is required when an entity has the power to govern the financial and operating policies of an entity so as to obtain benefits from its activities. IFRS 10 replaces SIC-12, *Consolidation – Special Purpose Entities* and parts of IAS 27, *Consolidated and Separate Financial Statements.*

iv. IFRS 11, *Joint Arrangements,* requires an entity to classify its interest in a joint arrangement as a joint operation or a joint venture. The standard eliminates the use of the proportionate consolidation method to account for joint ventures. Joint ventures will be accounted for using the equity method of accounting, while for a joint operation the entity will recognize its share of the assets, liabilities, revenues and expenses of the joint operation. IFRS 11 supersedes SIC-13, *Jointly Controlled Entities – Non-Monetary Contributions by Venturers* and IAS 31 *Joint Ventures.*

v. IFRS 12, *Disclosure of Interests in Other Entities,* establishes disclosure requirements for interests in other entities, such as subsidiaries, joint arrangements, associates, and unconsolidated structured entities. The standard carries forward existing disclosures and also introduces significant additional disclosure that address the nature of, and risks associated with, an entity's interests in other entities.

vi. IFRS 13, *Fair Value Measurement,* is a comprehensive standard for fair value measurement and disclosure for use across all IFRS standards. The new standard clarifies that fair value is the price that would be received to sell an asset, or paid to transfer a liability in an orderly transaction between market participants, at the measurement date. Under existing IFRS, guidance on measuring and disclosing fair value is dispersed among the specific standards requiring fair value measurements and does not always reflect a clear measurement basis or consistent disclosures.

vii. There have been amendments to existing standards, including IAS 27, *Separate Financial Statements* (IAS 27), and IAS 28, *Investments in Associates and Joint Ventures* (IAS 28). IAS 27 addresses accounting for subsidiaries, jointly controlled entities and associates in non-consolidated financial statements. IAS 28 has been amended to include joint ventures in its scope and to address the changes in IFRS 10-13.

viii. IAS 1, *Presentation of Financial Statements,* has been amended to require entities to separate items presented in OCI into two groups, based on whether or not items may be recycled in the future. Entities that choose to present OCI items before tax will be required to show the amount of tax related to the two groups separately. The amendment is effective for annual periods beginning on or after July 1, 2012, with earlier application permitted.

ix. IFRS 1, *First-time Adoption of International Financial Reporting Standards,* has been amended for two changes. The first replaces references to a fixed date of January 1, 2004 with 'the date of transition to IFRSs'. This eliminates the need for entities adopting IFRSs for the first time to restate derecognition transactions that occurred before the date of transition to IFRS. The second amendment provides guidance on how an entity should resume presenting financial statements in accordance with IFRSs after a period when the entity was unable to comply with IFRSs because its functional currency was subject to severe hyperinflation. The amendment is effective for annual periods beginning on or after July 1, 2011, with earlier application permitted.

x. IAS 12, *Income Taxes,* was amended to introduce an exception to the existing principle for the measurement of deferred tax assets or liabilities arising on investment property measured at fair value. As a result of the amendment, there is a rebuttable presumption that the carrying amount of the investment property will be recovered through sale when considering the expected manner or recovery or settlement. SIC-21, *Income Taxes – Recovery of Revalued Non-Depreciable Assets,* will no longer apply to investment properties carried at fair value. The amendment also incorporates into IAS 12 the remaining guidance previously contained in SIC-21, which is withdrawn. The amendment is effective for annual periods beginning on or after January 1, 2012, with earlier application permitted.

4. Critical Accounting Estimates and Assumptions

The preparation of consolidated financial statements requires management to use judgment in applying its accounting policies and estimates and assumptions about the future. Estimates and other judgments are continuously evaluated and are based on management's experience and other factors, including expectations about future events that are believed to be reasonable under the circumstances. The following discusses the most significant accounting judgments and estimates that the Company has made in the preparation of the consolidated financial statements:

Revenue Recognition

Revenue is recognized for accounting purposes upon the customer either picking up the merchandise or when merchandise is delivered to the customer's home. The Company offers the option to finance purchases through various third-party financing companies. In situations where a customer elects to take advantage of delayed payment terms, the costs of financing this revenue are deducted from revenue.

Inventories

The Company estimates the net realizable value as the amount at which inventories are expected to be sold by taking into account fluctuations of retail prices due to prevailing market conditions. If required, inventories are written down to net realizable value when the cost of inventories is estimated to not be recoverable due to obsolescence, damage or declining sales prices.

Reserves for slow moving and damaged inventory are deducted in the Company's evaluation of inventories. The reserve for slow moving inventory is based on many years of historic retail experience. The reserve is calculated by analyzing all inventory on hand older than one year. The amount of reserve for damaged inventory is determined by specific product categories.

The amount of inventory recognized as an expense for the year ended December 31, 2011 was $385,495,000 (year ended December 31, 2010 – $402,685,000), which is presented within cost of sales in the consolidated income statements. There were $535,000 inventory write-downs (2010 – $67,000) recognized as an expense during 2011.

As at December 31, 2011, the inventory markdown provision totalled $4,846,000 (as at December 31, 2010 – $4,311,000 and as at January 1, 2010 – $4,244,000). None of the Company's inventory has been pledged as security for any liabilities of the Company.

Extended Warranty Revenue

Extended warranty revenue is deferred and taken into revenue on a straight-line basis over the life of the extended warranty period.

Franchise Royalties

Leon's franchisees operate as independent owners. The Company charges the franchisee a royalty fee based primarily on a percentage of the franchisee's gross revenues. This royalty revenue is recorded by the Company on an accruals basis and is classified as revenue within the consolidated income statements.

Volume Rebates

The Company receives vendor rebates on certain products based on the volume of purchases made during specified periods. The rebates are deducted from the inventory value of goods received and are recognized as a reduction in cost of goods sold as revenue is recognized.

Income Taxes

The Company computes an income tax provision. However, actual amounts of income tax expense only become final upon filing and acceptance of the tax return by the relevant taxation authorities, which occur subsequent to the issuance of the annual consolidated financial statements. Additionally, estimation of income taxes includes evaluating the recoverability of deferred income tax assets based on an assessment of the ability to use the underlying future tax deductions before they expire against future taxable income. The assessment is based upon existing tax laws and estimates of future taxable income. To the extent estimates differ from the final tax return, earnings would be affected in a subsequent period.

Impairment

The Company reviews goodwill at least annually and other non-financial assets when there is any indication that the asset might be impaired. The Company has estimated the recoverable amount of Appliance Canada, a division of the Company, to which goodwill is allocated using a discounted cash flow model that required assumptions about future cash flows, margins, and discount rates.

34

LEON'S FURNITURE LIMITED
Notes to the Consolidated Financial Statements

5. Financial Risk Management

Classification of Financial Instruments and Fair Value

The classification of the Company's financial instruments, as well as their carrying amounts and fair values are disclosed in the table below.

Financial Instrument	Designation	Measurement	December 31 2011	December 31 2010	January 1 2010
Cash and cash equivalents	Available-for-sale	Fair value	$ 72,505	$ 71,589	$ 58,301
Available-for-sale financial assets	Available-for-sale	Fair value	$ 149,318	$ 140,224	$ 112,425
Trade receivables	Loans and receivables	Amortized cost	$ 28,937	$ 28,569	$ 31,501
Trade and other payables	Other financial liabilities	Amortized cost	$ 75,126	$ 71,724	$ 72,603
Redeemable share liability	Other financial liabilities	Amortized cost	$ 382	$ 172	$ 383

Fair Value Hierarchy

The following table classifies financial assets and liabilities that are recognized on the consolidated statements of financial position at fair value in a hierarchy that is based on significance of the inputs used in making the measurements. The levels in the hierarchy are:

Level 1:   Quoted prices (unadjusted) in active markets for identical assets or liabilities.
Level 2:   Inputs other than quoted prices included within level 1 that are observable for the asset or liability, either directly (that is, as prices) or indirectly (that is, derived from prices).
Level 3:   Inputs for the asset or liability that are not based on observable market data (that is, unobservable inputs).

Financial Instruments at Fair Value

	Fair Value Measurement at December 31, 2011		
	Level 1	Level 2	Level 3
Cash and cash equivalents	$ 72,505	$ –	$ –
Available-for-sale financial assets – Bonds	–	118,171	–
Available-for-sale financial assets – Equities	31,147	–	–
	$ 103,652	$ 118,171	$ –

	Fair Value Measurement at December 31, 2010		
	Level 1	Level 2	Level 3
Cash and cash equivalents	$ 71,589	$ –	$ –
Available-for-sale financial assets – Bonds	–	117,817	–
Available-for-sale financial assets – Equities	22,407	–	–
	$ 93,996	$ 117,817	$ –

	Fair Value Measurement at January 1, 2010		
	Level 1	Level 2	Level 3
Cash and cash equivalents	$ 58,301	$ –	$ –
Available-for-sale financial assets – Bonds	–	92,884	–
Available-for-sale financial assets – Equities	19,541	–	–
	$ 77,842	$ 92,884	$ –

Financial Risks Factors

The Company's activities expose it to a variety of financial risks: market risk (including foreign currency risk, interest rate risk and other price risk), credit risk and liquidity risk. Risk management is carried out by the Company by identifying and evaluating the financial risks inherent within its operations. The Company's overall risk management activities seek to minimize potential adverse effects on the Company's financial performance.

(a) Market Risk

i.   **Foreign exchange risk** – The Company is exposed to foreign currency risk. Certain merchandise is paid for in U.S. dollars. This foreign exchange cost is included in the inventory cost. The Company does not believe it has significant foreign currency risk with respect to its trade payables in U.S. dollars.

   The Company is also exposed to foreign currency risk on its foreign currency denominated portfolio of available-for-sale financial assets, primarily related to actively traded international equities. As at December 31, 2011, the Company's investment portfolio included 10% of foreign currency denominated assets (as at December 31, 2010 – 8% and as at January 1, 2010 – 8%). This risk is monitored by the Company's investment managers in an effort to reduce the Company's exposure to foreign currency exchange rate risk.

ii. **Interest rate risk** – The Company is exposed to interest rate risk through its portfolio of available-for-sale financial assets by holding cash, cash equivalents and actively traded Canadian and international Bonds. At December 31, 2011, 86% of the Company's investment portfolio was made up of cash, cash equivalents and Canadian and international Bonds (as at December 31, 2010 – 89% and as at January 1, 2010 – 89%). This risk is monitored by the Company's investment managers in an effort to reduce the Company's exposure to interest rate risk. The exposure to this risk is minimal due to the short-term maturities of the bonds held. The Company is not subject to any other interest rate risk.

iii. **Price risk** – The Company is exposed to fluctuations in the market prices of its portfolio of available-for-sale financial assets. Changes in the fair value of the available-for-sale financial assets are recorded, net of income taxes, in accumulated other comprehensive income as it relates to unrecognized gains and losses. The risk is managed by the Company and its investment managers by ensuring a conservative asset allocation of bonds and equities.

(b) Credit Risk

Credit risk arises from cash and cash equivalents, available-for-sale financial assets and trade receivables. The Company places its cash and cash equivalents and available-for-sale financial assets with institutions of high credit worthiness. Maximum credit risk exposure represents the loss that would be incurred if all of the Company's counterparties were to default at the same time.

The Company has some credit risk associated with its trade receivables as it relates to the Appliance Canada division that is partially mitigated by the Company's credit management practices.

The Company's trade receivables total $28,937,000 as at December 31, 2011 (as at December 31, 2010 – $28,569,000 and as at January 1, 2010 – $31,501,000). The amount of trade receivables that the Company has determined to be past due (which is defined as a balance that is more than 90 days past due) is $191,000 as at December 31, 2011 (as at December 31, 2010 – $158,000 and as at January 1, 2010 – $431,000), which relates entirely to the Appliance Canada division. The Company's provision for impairment of trade receivables, established through ongoing monitoring of individual customer accounts, was $500,000 as at December 31, 2011 (as at December 31, 2010 – $470,000 and as at January 1, 2010 – $300,000).

The majority of the Company's sales are paid through cash, credit card or non-recourse third-party finance. The Company relies on one third-party credit supplier to supply financing to its customers.

(c) Liquidity Risk

The Company has no outstanding borrowings and does not rely upon available credit facilities to finance operations or to finance committed capital expenditures. The portfolio of available-for-sale financial assets consists primarily of actively traded Canadian and international bonds. There is no immediate need for cash by the Company from its investment portfolio.

The Company expects to settle its trade and other payables within 30 days of the period end date. The redeemable share liability does not have any fixed terms of repayment.

36

LEON'S FURNITURE LIMITED
Notes to the Consolidated Financial Statements

6. Capital Risk Management

The Company defines capital as shareholders' equity. The Company's objectives when managing capital are to:

- ensure sufficient liquidity to support its financial obligations and execute its operating and strategic plans; and
- utilize working capital to negotiate favourable supplier agreements both in respect of early payment discounts and overall payment terms.

The Company is not subject to any externally imposed capital requirements.

7. Cash and Cash Equivalents

	As at December 31 2011	As at December 31 2010	As at January 1 2010
Cash at bank and on hand	$ 2,181	$ 19,642	$ 7,620
Short-term investments	70,324	51,947	50,681
	$ 72,505	$ 71,589	$ 58,301

8. Property, Plant and Equipment

	Land	Buildings	Equipment	Vehicles	Computer Hardware	Building Improvements	Total
At January 1, 2010							
Cost	$ 56,156	$ 163,680	$ 34,730	$ 20,853	$ 8,604	$ 78,175	$ 362,198
Accumulated depreciation	–	86,277	23,112	16,726	7,297	25,133	158,545
Net book value	$ 56,156	$ 77,403	$ 11,618	$ 4,127	$ 1,307	$ 53,042	$ 203,653
Year ended December 31, 2010							
At January 1, 2010	$ 56,156	$ 77,403	$ 11,618	$ 4,127	$ 1,307	$ 53,042	$ 203,653
Additions	45	11,685	1,323	484	347	98	13,982
Disposals	870	–	–	10	–	–	880
Depreciation	–	6,484	1,880	1,253	537	5,109	15,263
Closing net book value	55,331	82,604	11,061	3,348	1,117	48,031	201,492
At December 31, 2010							
Cost	55,331	175,365	36,053	20,900	8,951	78,273	374,873
Accumulated depreciation	–	92,761	24,992	17,552	7,834	30,242	173,381
Net book value	$ 55,331	$ 82,604	$ 11,061	$ 3,348	$ 1,117	$ 48,031	$ 201,492
Year ended December 31, 2011							
At January 1, 2011	$ 55,331	$ 82,604	$ 11,061	$ 3,348	$ 1,117	$ 48,031	$ 201,492
Additions	100	9,165	4,403	2,253	164	9,253	25,338
Disposals	–	–	–	18	–	–	18
Depreciation	–	3,563	2,029	1,271	538	5,253	12,654
Closing net book value	55,431	88,206	13,435	4,312	743	52,031	214,158
At December 31, 2011							
Cost	55,431	184,530	40,456	23,051	9,115	87,526	400,109
Accumulated depreciation	–	96,324	27,021	18,739	8,372	35,495	185,951
Net book value	$ 55,431	$ 88,206	$ 13,435	$ 4,312	$ 743	$ 52,031	$ 214,158

Included in the above balances at December 31, 2011 are assets not being amortized with a net book value of approximately $2,638,000 (as at December 31, 2010 – $2,400,000 and as at January 1, 2010 – $Nil) being construction-in-progress.

The Company assessed for an indicator of impairment of each CGU by comparing the CV (carrying value)/EBITDA (earnings before interest, depreciation and amortization) multiple to that of comparable public companies. Where the impairment indicator existed, the carrying value of the assets within a CGU was compared with its estimated recoverable value, which was generally considered to be the CGU's value-in-use.

When determining the CGU's value-in-use, the Company estimated the future cash flows and discounted them at an appropriate pre-tax rate for the individual CGU. Where the carrying value of the CGU's assets exceeded the recoverable amounts, as represented by the CGU's value-in-use, the store's property and equipment assets were written down.

For the year ended December 31, 2011 and 2010, there has been no impairment loss recognized.

9. Investment Properties

		Land		Buildings		Building Improvements		Total
At January 1, 2010								
Cost	$	8,286	$	8,039	$	1,494	$	17,819
Accumulated depreciation		–		8,039		1,235		9,274
Net book value	$	8,286	$	–	$	259	$	8,545
Year ended December 31, 2010								
At January 1, 2010	$	8,286	$	–	$	259	$	8,545
Additions		–		–		–		–
Disposals		–		–		37		37
Depreciation		–		–		91		91
At December 31, 2010		8,286		–		131		8,417
As at December 31, 2010								
Cost		8,286		8,039		1,457		17,782
Accumulated depreciation		–		8,039		1,326		9,365
Net book value	$	8,286	$	–	$	131	$	8,417
Year ended December 31, 2011								
At January 1, 2011	$	8,286	$	–	$	131	$	8,417
Additions		–		–		–		–
Disposals		–		–		–		–
Depreciation		–		–		51		51
Closing net book value		8,286		–		80		8,366
As at December 31, 2011								
Cost		8,286		8,039		1,457		17,782
Accumulated depreciation		–		8,039		1,377		9,416
Net book value	$	8,286	$	–	$	80	$	8,366

The fair value of the investment property portfolio as at December 31, 2011 was $29,750,000 (as at December 31, 2010 – $29,750,000 and as at January 1, 2010 – $29,750,000). The fair value was compiled internally by management based on available market evidence.

38

LEON'S FURNITURE LIMITED
Notes to the Consolidated Financial Statements

10. Intangible Assets and Goodwill

	Customer Relationships		Brand Name		Non-Compete Agreement		Computer Software		Total
At January 1, 2010									
Cost	$	2,000	$	2,500	$	1,000	$	3,896	$ 9,396
Accumulated amortization		500		500		250		2,812	4,062
Net book value	$	1,500	$	2,000	$	750	$	1,084	$ 5,334
Year ended December 31, 2010									
At January 1, 2010	$	1,500	$	2,000	$	750	$	1,084	$ 5,334
Additions		–		–		–		370	370
Disposals		–		–		–		–	–
Amortization for the year		250		250		125		177	802
Closing net book value		1,250		1,750		625		1,277	4,902
As at December 31, 2010									
Cost		2,000		2,500		1,000		4,266	9,766
Accumulated amortization		750		750		375		2,989	4,864
Net book value	$	1,250	$	1,750	$	625	$	1,277	$ 4,902
Year ended December 31, 2011									
At January 1, 2011	$	1,250	$	1,750	$	625	$	1,277	$ 4,902
Additions		–		–		–		(64)	(64)
Disposals		–		–		–		–	–
Amortization for the year		250		250		125		255	880
Closing net book value		1,000		1,500		500		958	3,958
At December 31, 2011									
Cost		2,000		2,500		1,000		4,202	9,702
Accumulated amortization		1,000		1,000		500		3,244	5,744
Net book value	$	1,000	$	1,500	$	500	$	958	$ 3,958

Impairment Test of Goodwill

The Company performed impairment tests of goodwill at December 31, 2011, December 31, 2010 and January 1, 2010 in accordance with the accounting policy as described in note 3 and IFRS transitional provisions. The recoverable amount of the Appliance Canada CGU, where all goodwill is allocated, was determined based on value-in-use calculations. These calculations used cash flow projections based on financial budgets approved by management covering a one-year period. Cash flows beyond the one-year period are extrapolated using the estimated growth rates stated below. The key assumptions used for the value-in-use calculation at December 31, 2010 and January 1, 2010 were as follows:

	Growth Rate %	After-Tax Discount Rate %
December 31, 2011	3.0	10.0
December 31, 2010	2.0	9.7
January 1, 2010	3.0	9.9

The impairment tests performed resulted in no impairment of the goodwill as at December 31, 2011, December 31, 2010 or January 1, 2010.

11. Trade and Other Payables

	As at December 31 2011	As at December 31 2010	As at January 1 2010
Trade payables	$ 62,485	$ 60,127	$ 69,495
Other payables	12,641	11,597	3,108
	$ 75,126	$ 71,724	$ 72,603

12. Provisions

	Profit Sharing and Bonuses	Vacation Pay	Totals
As at January 1, 2010	$ 10,775	$ 502	$ 11,277
Additional provisions	11,880	3,302	15,182
Unused amounts reversed	(598)	–	(598)
Utilized during the year	(10,057)	(3,463)	(13,520)
As at December 31, 2010	$ 12,000	$ 341	$ 12,341
Additional provisions	10,860	3,365	14,225
Unused amounts reversed	(1,019)	–	(1,019)
Utilized during the year	(10,981)	(3,335)	(14,316)
As at December 31, 2011	$ 10,860	$ 371	$ 11,231

(a)   The provision for profit sharing and bonuses is payable within the first half of the following fiscal year.

(b)   The provision for vacation pay represents employee entitlements to vacation time not taken at each reporting date.

13. Redeemable Share Liability

	As at December 31 2011	As at December 31 2010	As at January 1 2010
Authorized			
2,284,000 convertible, non-voting, series 2002 shares			
806,000 convertible, non-voting, series 2005			
1,224,000 convertible, non-voting, series 2009 shares			
Issued and fully paid			
667,748 series 2002 shares			
(December 31, 2010 – 813,331 and January 1, 2010 – 969,033)	$ 4,799	$ 5,846	$ 6,965
541,248 series 2005 shares			
(December 31, 2010 – 620,793 and January 1, 2010 – 689,513)	5,111	5,862	6,511
1,115,107 series 2009 shares			
(December 31, 2010 – 1,168,124 and January 1, 2010 – 1,207,000)	9,869	10,339	10,683
Less employee share purchase loans	(19,397)	(21,875)	(23,776)
	$ 382	$ 172	$ 383

Under the terms of the Plan, the Company advanced non-interest bearing loans to certain of its employees in 2002, 2005 and 2009 to allow them to acquire convertible, non-voting, series 2002 shares, series 2005 shares and series 2009 shares, respectively, of the Company. These loans are repayable through the application against the loans of any dividends on the shares, with any remaining balance repayable on the date the shares are converted to common shares. Each issued and fully paid for series 2002, 2005 and

40

LEON'S FURNITURE LIMITED
Notes to the Consolidated Financial Statements

2009 share may be converted into one common share at any time after the fifth anniversary date of the issue of these shares and prior to the tenth anniversary of such issue. Series 2002 shares may also be redeemed at the option of the holder or by the Company at any time after the fifth anniversary date of the issue of these shares and must be redeemed prior to the tenth anniversary of such issue. The series 2005 and series 2009 shares are redeemable at the option of the holder for a period of one business day following the date of issue of such shares. The Company has the option to redeem the series 2005 and series 2009 shares at any time after the fifth anniversary date of the issue of these shares and must redeem them prior to the tenth anniversary of such issue. The redemption price is equal to the original issue price of the shares adjusted for subsequent subdivisions of shares plus accrued and unpaid dividends. The purchase prices of the shares are $7.19 per series 2002 share, $9.44 per series 2005 share and $8.85 per series 2009 share.

Dividends paid to holders of series 2002, 2005 and 2009 shares of approximately $470,000 (2010 – $401,000) have been used to reduce the respective shareholder loans.

During the year ended December 31, 2011, 145,583 series 2002 shares (year ended December 31, 2010 – 155,702) and 79,545 series 2005 shares (year ended December 31, 2010 – 68,720) were converted into common shares with a stated value of approximately $1,047,000 (year ended December 31, 2010 – $1,119,000) and $751,000 (year ended December 31, 2010 – $475,000), respectively.

During the year ended December 31, 2011, the Company cancelled 53,017 series 2009 shares (year ended December 31, 2010 – 38,876) in the amount of $470,000 (year ended December 31, 2010 – $344,000).

Employee share purchase loans have been netted against the redeemable share liability as the Company has the legally enforceable right of offset and the positive intent to settle on a net basis.

The Plan represents a compensatory plan under IFRS 2 as the terms of the series 2002, 2005 and 2009 shares and related employee share purchase loans collectively give the employees that ability, but not the obligation, to acquire common shares of the Company.

14. Common Shares

	As at December 31 2011	As at December 31 2010	As at January 1 2010
Authorized			
Unlimited common shares			
Issued			
69,815,734 common shares			
(December 31, 2010 – 70,075,333 and January 1, 2010 – 70,477,611)	**20,918**	19,177	17,704

During the year ended December 31, 2011, 145,583 series 2002 shares (year ended December 31, 2010 – 155,702) and 79,545 series 2005 shares (year ended December 31, 2010 – 68,720) were converted into common shares with a stated value of approximately $1,047,000 (year ended December 31, 2010 – $1,119,000) and $751,000 (year ended December 31, 2010 – $475,000), respectively.

During the year ended December 31, 2011, the Company repurchased 484,727 (year ended December 31, 2010 – 626,700) of its common shares on the open market pursuant to the terms and conditions of Normal Course Issuer Bid at a net cost of approximately $6,334,000 (year ended December 31, 2010 – $8,034,000). All shares repurchased by the Company pursuant to its Normal Course Issuer Bid have been cancelled. The repurchase of common shares resulted in a reduction of share capital in the amount of approximately $57,000 (year ended December 31, 2010 – $295,000). The excess net cost over the average carrying value of the shares of approximately $6,277,000 (year ended December 31, 2010 – $7,739,000) has been recorded as a reduction in retained earnings.

As at December 31, 2011, the dividends payable were $17,457,000 ($0.25 per share) and December 31, 2010, $6,310,000 ($0.09 per share) and as at January 1, 2010 $4,938,000 ($0.07 per share).

15. Revenue

	Year Ended December 31 2011	Year Ended December 31 2010
Sale of goods by corporate stores	$ 663,607	$ 691,079
Royalty income from franchisees	10,434	10,663
Extended warranty revenue	8,055	8,007
Rental income from investment property	740	686
	$ 682,836	$ 710,435

16. Operating Expenses by Nature

	Year Ended December 31 2011	Year Ended December 31 2010
Depreciation of property, plant and equipment and investment properties	$ 12,705	$ 15,354
Amortization of intangible assets	$ 880	$ 802
Operating lease payments	$ 3,631	$ 3,300
Gain on disposal of property, plant and equipment	$ 21	$ 1,236

17. Income Tax Expense

(a) The Major Components of Income Tax Expense for the Year Ended are:

INCOME STATEMENT	December 31 2011	December 31 2010
Current income tax expense:		
Based on taxable income of the current year	$ 20,636	$ 26,606
Adjustments in respect of prior years	(368)	–
	20,268	26,606
Deferred income tax expense (benefit):		
Origination and reversal of temporary differences	1,758	(2)
Impact of change in tax rates/new tax laws	156	297
	1,914	295
Income tax expense reported in the income statement	$ 22,182	$ 26,901

(b) Reconciliation of Effective Tax Rate:

	2011		2010	
Income before income taxes	$ 78,848		$ 90,185	
Income tax expense based on statutory rate	22,219	28.18%	27,507	30.50%
Increase (decrease) in income taxes resulting from non-taxable items or adjustments of prior year taxes:				
Non-deductible items	86	0.11%	(158)	(0.17%)
Rate differences related to origination and reversal of temporary differences	156	0.20%	298	0.33%
Remeasurement of deferred tax asset for rate changes	66	0.08%	(286)	(0.32%)
Other	(345)	(0.44%)	(460)	(0.51%)
Total income tax expense	$ 22,182	28.13%	$ 26,901	29.83%

42

LEON'S FURNITURE LIMITED
Notes to the Consolidated Financial Statements

(c) Deferred Taxes:

i. DEFERRED TAX RELATES TO THE FOLLOWING:	December 31 2011		December 31 2010		January 1 2010
Deferred income tax assets					
Deferred warranty plan revenue	$	**4,245**	$	4,739	$	4,644
Unrealized gains/losses on available-for-sale investments		**(25)**		(38)		42
Fixed assets		**8,152**		8,501		7,912
		12,372		13,202		12,598
Deferred income tax liabilities					
Deferred warranty plan direct costs		**(617)**		–		–
Fixed assets		**(10,311)**		(9,845)		(8,829)
		(10,928)		(9,845)		(8,829)
Net deferred tax asset position		**1,444**		3,357		3,769
Reported in:					
Deferred income tax assets		**12,372**		13,202		12,598
Deferred income tax liabilities	$	**(10,928)**	$	(9,845)	$	(8,829)

ii. DEFERRED TAX MOVEMENT IN THE INCOME STATEMENT IS AS FOLLOWS:	2011		2010
Expense (benefit)			
Deferred warranty plan revenue	$	**494**	$	(95)
Unrealized gains/losses on available-for-sale investments		**(13)**		81
Fixed assets		**815**		426
Deferred warranty plan direct costs		**617**		–
Net deferred income tax expense	$	**1,913**	$	412

iii. RECONCILIATION OF NET DEFERRED TAX ASSET:	2011		2010
Opening balance as of January 1	$	**3,357**	$	3,769
Tax expense during the period recognized in profit or loss		**(1,913)**		(412)
Closing balance as of December 31	$	**1,444**	$	3,357

18. Earnings per Share

Earnings per share are calculated using the weighted average number of shares outstanding. The weighted average number of shares used in the basic earnings per share calculations amounted to 69,969,417 for the year ended December 31, 2011 (year ended December 31, 2010 – 70,371,744).

The following table reconciles the profit for the period and the number of shares for the basic and diluted earnings per share calculations:

Year Ended December 31, 2011	**Profit for the Period Attributed to Common Shareholders**	**Weighted Average Number of Shares**	**Per Share Amount**
Basic	$ 56,666	69,969,417	$ 0.81
Dilutive effect (Note 13)	–	2,336,007	–
Diluted	$ 56,666	72,305,424	$ 0.78

Year Ended December 31, 2010	Profit for the Period Attributed to Common Shareholders	Weighted Average Number of Shares	Per Share Amount
Basic	$ 63,284	70,371,744	$ 0.90
Dilutive effect (Note 13)	–	2,762,162	–
Diluted	$ 63,284	73,133,906	$ 0.87

19. Commitments and Contingencies

(a) The cost to complete all construction-in-progress as at December 31, 2011 totals $4,407,000 at two locations (December 31, 2010 – to complete at two locations at an approximate cost of $9,609,000).

(b) The Company is obligated under operating leases for future minimum annual rental payments for certain land and buildings as follows:

No later than 1 year	$ 5,860
Later than 1 year and no later than 5 years	19,989
Later than 5 years	18,282
	$ 44,131

(c) The future minimum lease payments receivable under non-cancellable operating leases for certain land and buildings classified as investment property are as follows:

No later than 1 year	$ 712
Later than 1 year and no later than 5 years	2,027
Later than 5 years	427
	$ 3,166

(d) The Company has issued approximately $255,000 in letters of credit primarily with respect to buildings under construction (as at December 31, 2010 – $2,400,000).

(e) Pursuant to a reinsurance agreement relating to the extended warranty sales, the Company has pledged available-for-sale financial assets amounting to $20,257,000 (as at December 31, 2010 – $19,498,000) and provided a letter of credit of $1,500,000 (as at December 31, 2010 – $1,500,000) for the benefit of the insurance company.

44

LEON'S FURNITURE LIMITED
Notes to the Consolidated Financial Statements

20. Consolidated Statements of Cash Flows

(a) The net change in non-cash working capital balances related to operations consists of the following:

	Year Ended December 31 2011		Year Ended December 31 2010
Trade receivables	$ (368)	$	2,932
Inventory	(2,407)		(1,466)
Other assets	143		(14)
Trade, other payables and provisions	1,953		(193)
Income taxes payable	(5,706)		(1,434)
Customers' deposits	1,959		1,566
	$ (4,426)	$	1,391

(b) Supplemental cash flow information:

	Year Ended December 31 2011		Year Ended December 31 2010
Income taxes paid	$ 26,076	$	28,541
Interest paid	$ –	$	24

(c) During the year, property, plant and equipment were acquired at an aggregate cost of $25,338,000 (2010 – $13,946,000), of which $874,000 (2010 – $536,000) is included in trade and other payables as at December 31, 2011.

21. Related Party Transactions

Key Management Compensation

Key management includes the Directors and the five senior executives of the Company. The compensation expense paid to key management for employee services during each period is shown below:

	Year Ended December 31 2011	Year Ended December 31 2010
Salaries and other short-term employee benefits	$ 3,416,188	$ 3,706,894

22. Transition to IFRS

The effect of the Company's transition to IFRS, described in note 2, is summarized in this note as follows:

(a) Transition elections

The Company has applied the following transition exceptions and exemptions to full retrospective application of IFRS:

Business combinations – In accordance with IFRS transitional provisions, the Company elected to apply IFRS relating to business combinations prospectively from January 1, 2010. As such, Canadian GAAP balances relating to the acquisition of Appliance Canada Ltd. on January 2, 2008, including goodwill, have been carried forward without adjustment.

Share-based payments – In accordance with IFRS transitional provisions, the Company elected not to apply IFRS 2, *Share-based Payments*, to convertible shares issued under the Management Share Purchase Plan that were still outstanding at January 1, 2010 but had fully vested.

Estimates – Hindsight is not used to create or revise estimates. The estimates previously made by the Company under Canadian GAAP were not revised for application of IFRS except where necessary to reflect any difference in accounting policies.

(b) Effect of material transition adjustments on the consolidated statements of financial positions, consolidated income statements, consolidated statements of comprehensive income and consolidated statements of cash flows:

i. Consolidated Statements of Financial Position

	As at December 31, 2010			As at January 1, 2010		
	Cdn. GAAP	Adj. (revised*)	IFRS	Cdn. GAAP	Adj. (revised*)	IFRS
Assets						
Cash and cash equivalents	$ 71,589	$ –	$ 71,589	$ 58,301	$ –	$ 58,301
Available-for-sale financial assets	140,224	–	140,224	112,425	–	112,425
Trade receivables	28,569	–	28,569	31,501	–	31,501
Inventory	85,423	–	85,423	83,957	–	83,957
Deferred income tax assets (Note (a))	1,251	(1,251)	–	1,133	(1,133)	–
Total current assets	$ 327,056	$ (1,251)	$ 325,805	$ 287,317	$ (1,133)	$ 286,184
Other assets	1,574	–	1,574	1,560	–	1,560
Property, plant and equipment (Note (b))	209,909	(8,417)	201,492	212,198	(8,545)	203,653
Investment properties (Note (b))	–	8,417	8,417	–	8,545	8,545
Intangible assets	4,902	–	4,902	5,334	–	5,334
Goodwill	11,282	–	11,282	11,282	–	11,282
Deferred income tax assets (Note (a))	11,951	1,251	13,202	11,465	1,133	12,598
Total assets	$ 566,674	$ –	$ 566,674	$ 529,156	$ –	$ 529,156
Liabilities and Shareholders' Equity						
Trade and other payables (Note (c))	$ 84,065	$ (12,341)	$ 71,724	$ 83,880	$ (11,277)	$ 72,603
Provisions (Note (c))	–	12,341	12,341	–	11,277	11,277
Income taxes payable	524	–	524	1,958	–	1,958
Customers' deposits	17,198	–	17,198	15,632	–	15,632
Dividends payable	6,310	–	6,310	4,938	–	4,938
Deferred warranty plan revenue	16,882	–	16,882	16,150	–	16,150
Total current liabilities	$ 124,979	$ –	$ 124,979	$ 122,558	$ –	$ 122,558
Deferred warranty plan revenue	21,392	–	21,392	22,248	–	22,248
Redeemable share liability	172	–	172	383	–	383
Deferred income tax liabilities (Note (a))	9,845	–	9,845	8,829	–	8,829
Total liabilities	$ 156,388	$ –	$ 156,388	$ 154,018	$ –	$ 154,018
Common shares	19,177	–	19,177	17,704	–	17,704
Retained earnings	390,629	–	390,629	357,576	–	357,576
Accumulated other comprehensive income (loss)	480	–	480	(142)	–	(142)
Total shareholders' equity	$ 410,286	$ –	$ 410,286	$ 375,138	$ –	$ 375,138
Total liabilities and shareholders' equity	$ 566,674	$ –	$ 566,674	$ 529,156	$ –	$ 529,156

* *The above figures have been revised, from previously reported IFRS amounts, to reflect an immaterial adjustment to the amount of foreign exchange that is required to be recorded within comprehensive income as it relates to the Company's foreign denominated non-monetary available-for-sale financial assets. Any foreign denominated monetary available-for-sale financial assets were appropriately recorded in the consolidated income statement.*

46

LEON'S FURNITURE LIMITED
Notes to the Consolidated Financial Statements

ii. Consolidated Statement of Comprehensive Income

		Cdn. GAAP	Reclasses (revised*)		IFRS
			As at December 31, 2010		
Revenue (Note (e))	$	699,772	$ 10,663	$	710,435
Cost of sales		412,379	–		412,379
Gross profit	$	287,393	$ 10,663	$	298,056
Operating expenses (Note (f))					
General and administrative expenses		–	98,684		98,684
Sales and marketing expenses		–	78,221		78,221
Occupancy expenses		–	29,551		29,551
Other operating expenses		–	5,780		5,780
Salaries and commissions		105,368	(105,368)		–
Advertising		31,565	(31,565)		–
Rent and property taxes		14,000	(14,000)		–
Amortization		16,156	(16,156)		–
Employee profit-sharing plan		4,746	(4,746)		–
Other operating expenses		41,495	(41,495)		–
Interest income		(3,134)	3,134		–
Other income		(12,988)	12,988		–
	$	197,208	$ 15,028	$	212,236
Operating profit		90,185	(4,365)		85,820
Gain on disposal		–	1,231		1,231
Finance income		–	3,134		3,134
Profit before income tax		90,185	–		90,185
Income tax expense		26,901	–		26,901
Profit for the period attributable to the shareholders of the Company	$	63,284	$ –	$	63,284
Other comprehensive income, net of tax					
Unrealized gains on available-for-sale financial assets arising during the period (Note (d))		773	–		773
Reclassification adjustment for net gains and losses included in profit for the period		(151)	–		(151)
Change in unrealized gains on available-for-sale financial assets arising during the period		622	–		622
Comprehensive income for the period attributable to the Shareholders of the Company	$	63,906	$ –	$	63,906

* *The above figures have been revised, from previously reported IFRS amounts, to reflect an immaterial adjustment to the amount of foreign exchange that is required to be recorded within comprehensive income as it relates to the Company's foreign denominated non-monetary available-for-sale financial assets. Any foreign denominated monetary available-for-sale financial assets were appropriately recorded in the consolidated income statement.*

Shoppers Drug Mart Corporation, 2011 Financial Statements Information

Consolidated Statements of Earnings

For the 52 weeks ended December 31, 2011 and January 1, 2011
(in thousands of Canadian dollars, except per share amounts)

	Note	2011	2010[1]
Sales		$ 10,458,652	$ 10,192,714
Cost of goods sold	9	(6,416,208)	(6,283,634)
Gross profit		4,042,444	3,909,080
Operating and administrative expenses	10, 11, 13	(3,131,539)	(3,011,758)
Operating income		910,905	897,322
Finance expenses	12	(64,038)	(60,633)
Earnings before income taxes		846,867	836,689
Income taxes	14		
Current		(208,696)	(238,779)
Deferred		(24,237)	(6,059)
		(232,933)	(244,838)
Net earnings		$ 613,934	$ 591,851
Net earnings per common share			
Basic	25	$ 2.84	$ 2.72
Diluted	25	$ 2.84	$ 2.72
Weighted average common shares outstanding (millions):			
Basic	25	216.4	217.4
Diluted	25	216.5	217.5
Actual common shares outstanding (millions)	24	212.5	217.5

[1] In preparing its 2010 comparative information, the Company has adjusted amounts reported previously in financial statements prepared in accordance with Canadian Generally Accepted Accounting Principles ("previous Canadian GAAP"). See Note 30 to these consolidated financial statements for an explanation of the transition to International Financial Reporting Standards ("IFRS").

The accompanying notes are an integral part of these consolidated financial statements.

Consolidated Statements of Comprehensive Income

For the 52 weeks ended December 31, 2011 and January 1, 2011
(in thousands of Canadian dollars)

	Note	2011	2010[1]
Net earnings		$ 613,934	$ 591,851
Other comprehensive income (loss), net of tax			
Effective portion of changes in fair value of hedges on interest rate derivatives (net of tax of $nil (2010: $525))	18	–	1,120
Effective portion of changes in fair value of hedges on equity forward derivatives (net of tax of $12 (2010: $205))	18	(39)	(521)
Net change in fair value of hedges on interest rate and equity forward derivatives transferred to earnings (net of tax of $163 (2010: $13))	18	411	33
Retirement benefit obligations actuarial losses (net of tax of $7,433 (2010: $2,905))	21	(21,943)	(8,150)
Other comprehensive loss, net of tax	7	(21,571)	(7,518)
Total comprehensive income		$ 592,363	$ 584,333

[1] In preparing its 2010 comparative information, the Company has adjusted amounts reported previously in financial statements prepared in accordance with previous Canadian GAAP. See Note 30 to these consolidated financial statements for an explanation of the transition to IFRS.

The accompanying notes are an integral part of these consolidated financial statements.

Source: Used with permission of Shoppers Drug Mart.

Consolidated Balance Sheets

As at December 31, 2011, January 1, 2011 and January 3, 2010
(in thousands of Canadian dollars)

	Note	December 31, 2011	January 1, 2011[1]	January 3, 2010[1]
Current assets				
Cash		$ 118,566	$ 64,354	$ 44,391
Accounts receivable		493,338	432,089	470,935
Inventory		2,042,302	1,957,525	1,852,441
Income taxes recoverable		–	20,384	–
Prepaid expenses and deposits		41,441	68,468	74,206
Total current assets		2,695,647	2,542,820	2,441,973
Non-current assets				
Property and equipment	15	1,767,543	1,677,340	1,541,841
Investment property	15	16,372	12,770	5,884
Goodwill	16	2,499,722	2,493,108	2,483,430
Intangible assets	17	281,737	272,217	258,766
Other assets		18,214	19,678	16,716
Deferred tax assets	14	21,075	26,264	28,456
Total non-current assets		4,604,663	4,501,377	4,335,093
Total assets		$ 7,300,310	$ 7,044,197	$ 6,777,066
Liabilities				
Bank indebtedness	19	$ 172,262	$ 209,013	$ 270,332
Commercial paper	19	–	127,828	260,386
Accounts payable and accrued liabilities	18	1,109,444	990,244	970,831
Income taxes payable		26,538	–	17,046
Dividends payable	24	53,119	48,927	46,748
Current portion of long-term debt	20	249,971	–	–
Provisions	22	12,024	12,562	11,009
Associate interest		152,880	138,993	130,189
Total current liabilities		1,776,238	1,527,567	1,706,541
Long-term debt	20	695,675	943,412	946,098
Other long-term liabilities	23	520,188	442,124	386,262
Provisions	22	1,701	1,852	1,062
Deferred tax liabilities	14	38,678	26,607	25,219
Total long-term liabilities		1,256,242	1,413,995	1,358,641
Total liabilities		3,032,480	2,941,562	3,065,182
Shareholders' equity				
Share capital	24	1,486,455	1,520,558	1,519,870
Treasury shares	24	(4,735)	–	–
Contributed surplus	26	10,246	11,702	10,274
Accumulated other comprehensive loss	7	(30,214)	(8,643)	(1,125)
Retained earnings		2,806,078	2,579,018	2,182,865
Total shareholders' equity		4,267,830	4,102,635	3,711,884
Total liabilities and shareholders' equity		$ 7,300,310	$ 7,044,197	$ 6,777,066

[1] In preparing its 2010 comparative information, the Company has adjusted amounts reported previously in financial statements prepared in accordance with previous Canadian GAAP. See Note 30 to these consolidated financial statements for an explanation of the transition to IFRS.

The accompanying notes are an integral part of these consolidated financial statements

On behalf of the Board of Directors:

Domenic Pilla
Director

Holger Kluge
Director

Consolidated Statements of Changes in Shareholders' Equity

For the 52 weeks ended December 31, 2011 and January 1, 2011
(in thousands of Canadian dollars)

	Note	Share Capital	Treasury Shares	Contributed Surplus	Accumulated Other Comprehensive Loss (Notes 18 and 21)	Retained Earnings	Total
Balance as at January 1, 2011[1]		$ 1,520,558	$ –	$ 11,702	$ (8,643)	$ 2,579,018	$ 4,102,635
Total comprehensive income		–	–	–	(21,571)	613,934	592,363
Dividends	24	–	–	–	–	(215,671)	(215,671)
Share repurchases	24	(35,576)	(4,735)	–	–	(171,203)	(211,514)
Share-based payments	26	–	–	(1,210)	–	–	(1,210)
Share options exercised	26	1,466	–	(246)	–	–	1,220
Repayment of share-purchase loans		7	–	–	–	–	7
Balance as at December 31, 2011		**$ 1,486,455**	**$ (4,735)**	**$ 10,246**	**$ (30,214)**	**$ 2,806,078**	**$ 4,267,830**
Balance as at January 3, 2010[1]		$ 1,519,870	$ –	$ 10,274	$ (1,125)	$ 2,182,865	$ 3,711,884
Total comprehensive income		–	–	–	(7,518)	591,851	584,333
Dividends	24	–	–	–	–	(195,698)	(195,698)
Share-based payments	26	–	–	1,592	–	–	1,592
Share options exercised	26	655	–	(164)	–	–	491
Repayment of share-purchase loans		33	–	–	–	–	33
Balance as at January 1, 2011[1]		$ 1,520,558	$ –	$ 11,702	$ (8,643)	$ 2,579,018	$ 4,102,635

[1] In preparing its 2010 comparative information, the Company has adjusted amounts reported previously in financial statements prepared in accordance with previous Canadian GAAP. See Note 30 to these consolidated financial statements for an explanation of the transition to IFRS.

The accompanying notes are an integral part of these consolidated financial statements.

Consolidated Statements of Cash Flows

For the 52 weeks ended December 31, 2011 and January 1, 2011
(in thousands of Canadian dollars)

	Note	2011	2010[1]
Cash flows from operating activities			
Net earnings		$ 613,934	$ 591,851
Adjustments for:			
Depreciation and amortization	13, 15, 17	296,464	278,421
Finance expenses	12	64,038	60,633
Loss on sale or disposal of property and equipment, including impairments	15, 17	2,015	3,880
Share-based payment transactions	26	(1,210)	1,592
Recognition and reversal of provisions, net	22	9,218	12,160
Other long-term liabilities	23	296	18,491
Income tax expense	14	232,933	244,838
		1,217,688	1,211,866
Net change in non-cash working capital balances	27	32,166	(34,824)
Provisions used	22	(9,907)	(9,817)
Interest paid		(63,853)	(62,916)
Income taxes paid		(202,256)	(276,108)
Net cash from operating activities		973,838	828,201
Cash flows from investing activities			
Proceeds from disposition of property and equipment and investment property		55,459	60,538
Business acquisitions	8	(10,496)	(11,779)
Deposits		105	1,534
Acquisition or development of property and equipment	15	(341,868)	(415,094)
Acquisition or development of intangible assets	17	(53,836)	(56,625)
Other assets		1,464	(3,249)
Net cash used in investing activities		(349,172)	(424,675)
Cash flows from financing activities			
Repurchase of own shares	24	(206,779)	–
Proceeds from exercise of share options	26	1,220	491
Repayment of share-purchase loans	24	7	33
Repayment of bank indebtedness, net	19	(36,714)	(61,319)
Repayment of commercial paper, net	19	(128,000)	(133,000)
Revolving term debt, net	20	152	(1,298)
Payment of transaction costs for debt refinancing	20	(575)	(2,792)
Repayment of financing lease obligations	23	(2,173)	(1,436)
Associate interest		13,887	9,277
Dividends paid	24	(211,479)	(193,519)
Net cash used in financing activities		(570,454)	(383,563)
Net increase in cash		54,212	19,963
Cash, beginning of the year		64,354	44,391
Cash, end of the year		$ 118,566	$ 64,354

[1] In preparing its 2010 comparative information, the Company has adjusted amounts reported previously in financial statements prepared in accordance with previous Canadian GAAP. See Note 30 to these consolidated financial statements for an explanation of the transition to IFRS.

The accompanying notes are an integral part of these consolidated financial statements.

Notes to the Consolidated Financial Statements ◄─────────

December 31, 2011 and January 1, 2011 (in thousands of Canadian dollars, except per share data)

> In order to save space, only notes that are referenced in the textbook are included.

1. GENERAL INFORMATION

Shoppers Drug Mart Corporation (the "Company") is a public company incorporated and domiciled in Canada, whose shares are publicly traded on the Toronto Stock Exchange. The Company's registered address is 243 Consumers Road, Toronto, Ontario M2J 4W8, Canada.

The Company is a licensor of 1,199 Shoppers Drug Mart®/Pharmaprix® full-service retail drug stores across Canada. The Shoppers Drug Mart®/Pharmaprix® stores are licensed to corporations owned by pharmacists ("Associates"). The Company also licenses or owns 58 Shoppers Simply Pharmacy®/Pharmaprix Simplement Santé® medical clinic pharmacies and eight Murale™ beauty stores. In addition, the Company owns and operates 63 Shoppers Home Health Care® stores. In addition to its store network, the Company owns Shoppers Drug Mart Specialty Health Network Inc., a provider of specialty drug distribution, pharmacy and comprehensive patient support services, and MediSystem Technologies Inc., a provider of pharmaceutical products and services to long-term care facilities in Ontario and Alberta.

The majority of the Company's sales are generated from the Shoppers Drug Mart®/Pharmaprix® full-service retail drug stores and the majority of the Company's assets are used in the operations of these stores. As such, the Company presents one operating segment in its consolidated financial statement disclosures. The revenue generated by Shoppers Drug Mart®/Pharmaprix Simplement Santé®, MediSystem Technologies Inc. and Shoppers Drug Mart Specialty Health Network Inc. is included with prescription sales of the Company's retail drug stores. The revenue generated by Shoppers Home Health Care® and Murale™ is included with the front store sales of the Company's retail drug stores.

These consolidated financial statements of the Company as at and for the financial year ended December 31, 2011 include the accounts of Shoppers Drug Mart Corporation, its subsidiaries, and the Associate-owned stores that comprise the majority of the Company's store network. The financial year of the Company consists of a 52 or 53 week period ending on the Saturday closest to December 31. The current financial year is the 52 weeks ended December 31, 2011. The comparative financial year is the 52 weeks ended January 1, 2011. The Company has also presented the consolidated balance sheet as at January 3, 2010, the Company's date of transition to International Financial Reporting Standards ("IFRS").

2. BASIS OF PREPARATION

(a) Statement of Compliance

These consolidated financial statements have been prepared in accordance with Canadian Generally Accepted Accounting Principles ("Canadian GAAP"). These consolidated financial statements also comply with International Financial Reporting Standards ("IFRS") as issued by the International Accounting Standards Board ("IASB").

These are the Company's first consolidated financial statements prepared in accordance with IFRS. IFRS 1, "First-time Adoption of International Financial Reporting Standards", has been applied in the preparation of these financial statements. Consolidated financial statements of the Company had been prepared under previous Canadian GAAP, which differs in certain respects from IFRS. When preparing the Company's 2011 consolidated financial statements, management has amended certain accounting methods in order to comply with IFRS. The comparative consolidated financial statements reflect the adoption of IFRS.

An explanation of how the transition from previous Canadian GAAP to IFRS has affected the reported financial position, financial performance and cash flows of the Company is provided in Note 30 to these consolidated financial statements.

These consolidated financial statements were authorized for issuance by the Board of Directors of the Company on February 9, 2012.

(b) Use of Estimates and Judgements

The preparation of these consolidated financial statements in conformity with IFRS requires management to make certain judgements, estimates and assumptions that affect the application of accounting policies and the reported amounts of assets and liabilities and disclosure of contingent assets and liabilities at the date of these consolidated financial statements and the reported amounts of revenues and expenses during the reporting period.

2. BASIS OF PREPARATION (continued)

Judgement is commonly used in determining whether a balance or transaction should be recognized in the consolidated financial statements and estimates and assumptions are more commonly used in determining the measurement of recognized transactions and balances. However, judgement and estimates are often interrelated.

The Company has applied judgement in its assessment of the appropriateness of the consolidation of the Associate-owned stores, classification of items such as leases and financial instruments, the recognition of tax losses and provisions, determining the tax rates used for measuring deferred taxes, determining cash-generating units, identifying the indicators of impairment for property and equipment and intangible assets with finite useful lives, and the level of componentization of property and equipment.

Estimates are used when estimating the useful lives of property and equipment and intangible assets for the purpose of depreciation and amortization, when accounting for or measuring items such as inventory provisions, Shoppers Optimum® loyalty card program deferred revenue, assumptions underlying the actuarial determination of retirement benefit obligations, income and other taxes, provisions, certain fair value measures including those related to the valuation of business combinations, share-based payments and financial instruments and when testing goodwill, indefinite useful life intangible assets and other assets for impairment. Actual results may differ from these estimates.

Estimates and underlying assumptions are reviewed on an ongoing basis. Revisions to accounting estimates are recognized in the period in which the estimates are revised and in any future periods affected.

3. SIGNIFICANT ACCOUNTING POLICIES

The accounting policies set out in these consolidated financial statements have been applied consistently to all periods presented in these consolidated financial statements.

(a) Basis of Consolidation

(i) Subsidiaries

Subsidiaries are entities controlled by the Company. Control exists where the Company has the power to govern the financial and operating policies of an entity so as to obtain benefits from its activities. All of the Company's subsidiaries are wholly-owned. The financial statements of subsidiaries are included in the Company's consolidated financial statements from the date that control commences until the date that control ceases.

(ii) Associate-owned Stores

Associate-owned stores comprise the majority of the Company's store network. The Company does not have any direct or indirect shareholdings in these Associates' corporations. The Associates' corporations remain separate legal entities. The Company consolidates the Associate-owned stores under IAS 27, "Consolidated and Separate Financial Statements" ("IAS 27"). The consolidation of the stores under IAS 27 was determined based on the concept of control under IAS 27 and determined primarily through the agreements with Associates ("Associate Agreements") that govern the relationship between the Company and the Associates.

(iii) Transactions Eliminated on Consolidation

Intra-company balances and transactions and any unrealized earnings and expenses arising from intra-company transactions, including those of the Associate-owned stores, are eliminated in preparing the consolidated financial statements.

(b) Basis of Measurement

These consolidated financial statements have been prepared on the historical cost basis except for certain financial instruments, deferred revenue related to the Shoppers Optimum® loyalty card program and the liabilities for the Company's long-term incentive plan and restricted share unit plan, which are measured at fair value (see Note 26 to these consolidated financial statements for further information on the long-term incentive plan and the restricted share unit plan). Any recognized impairment losses will also impact the historical cost of certain balances.

The methods used to measure fair values are discussed further in Note 4 to these consolidated financial statements.

(c) Revenue

(i) Sale of Goods and Services

Revenue is comprised primarily of retail sales, including prescription sales. Retail sales are recognized as revenue when the goods are sold to the customer. Revenue is net of returns and amounts deferred related to the issuance of points under the Shoppers Optimum® Loyalty Card Program (the "Program"). Where a sales transaction includes points awarded under the Program, revenue allocated to the Program points is deferred based on the fair value of the awards and recognized as revenue when the Program points are redeemed and the Company fulfills its obligations to supply the awards.

Revenue is measured at the fair value of the consideration received or receivable from the customer for products sold or services supplied.

(ii) Shoppers Optimum® Loyalty Card Program

The Shoppers Optimum® Loyalty Card Program allows members to earn points on their purchases in Shoppers Drug Mart®, Pharmaprix®, Shoppers Simply Pharmacy®, Pharmaprix Simplement Santé®, Shoppers Home Health Care® and Murale™ stores at a rate of 10 points for each dollar spent on eligible products and services, plus any applicable bonus points. Members can then redeem points, in accordance with the Program rewards schedule or other offers, for qualifying merchandise at the time of a future purchase transaction.

When points are earned by Program members, the Company defers revenue equal to the fair value of the awards. The Program's deferred revenue is recognized within accounts payable and accrued liabilities in the Company's consolidated balance sheets. When awards are redeemed by Program members, the redemption value of the awards is charged against the deferred revenue balance and recognized as revenue.

The estimated fair value per point is determined based on the expected weighted average redemption levels for future redemptions based on the program reward schedule, including special redemption events. The trends in redemption rates (points redeemed as a percentage of points issued) are reviewed on an ongoing basis and the estimated fair value per point is adjusted based upon expected future activity.

(d) Vendor Rebates

The Company classifies rebates and other consideration received from vendors as a reduction to the cost of inventory. These amounts are recognized in cost of goods sold when the associated inventory is sold. Certain exceptions apply where the consideration received from the vendor is a reimbursement of a selling cost or a payment for services delivered to the vendor, in which case the consideration is reflected in cost of goods sold or operating and administrative expenses dependent on where the related expenses are recorded.

(e) Finance Expenses

Finance expenses are comprised of interest expense on borrowings and the amortization of transaction costs incurred in conjunction with debt transactions. All borrowing costs are recognized in earnings on an accrual basis using the effective interest method, net of amounts capitalized as part of the cost of qualifying property and equipment.

The Company's finance income is not significant.

(f) Borrowing Costs

Borrowing costs that are directly attributable to the acquisition, construction or development of a qualifying asset are recognized as part of the cost of that asset. Qualifying assets are those that require a substantial period of time to prepare for their intended use. All other borrowing costs are recognized as finance expenses in the period in which they are incurred.

The Company capitalizes borrowing costs at the weighted average interest rate on borrowings outstanding for the period. The Company commences capitalization of borrowing costs as part of the cost of a qualifying asset when activities are undertaken to prepare the asset for its intended use and when expenditures, including borrowing costs, are incurred for the asset. Capitalization of borrowing costs ceases when substantially all of the activities necessary to prepare the asset for its intended use are complete.

December 31, 2011 and January 1, 2011 (in thousands of Canadian dollars, except per share data)

3. SIGNIFICANT ACCOUNTING POLICIES (continued)

(g) Income Taxes

Income tax expense is comprised of taxes currently payable on earnings and changes in deferred tax balances, excluding those changes related to business acquisitions. Income tax expense is recognized in net earnings except to the extent that it relates to items recognized either in other comprehensive income (loss) or directly in equity, in which case it is recognized in other comprehensive income (loss) or in equity respectively.

Current tax expense is comprised of the tax payable on the taxable income for the current financial year using tax rates enacted or substantively enacted at the reporting date, and any adjustment to income taxes payable in respect of previous years.

Deferred tax is recognized using the balance sheet method in respect of taxable temporary differences arising from differences between the carrying amount of assets and liabilities for tax purposes and their carrying amounts in the financial statements. Deferred tax is calculated at the tax rates that are expected to apply to temporary differences in the year they are expected to reverse and are based on the tax legislation that has been enacted or substantively enacted by the reporting date. Deferred tax is not recognized for the following temporary differences: the initial recognition of goodwill and the initial recognition of assets or liabilities in a transaction that is not a business acquisition and that affects neither accounting nor taxable earnings; and, differences relating to investments in subsidiaries to the extent that it is probable that they will not reverse in the foreseeable future. Deferred tax assets and liabilities are offset if there is a legally enforceable right to offset the recognized amounts and the Company intends to settle on a net basis or to realize the asset and settle the liability simultaneously.

A deferred tax asset is recognized to the extent that it is probable that future taxable earnings will be available against which the temporary difference can be utilized. Deferred tax assets are reviewed at each reporting date and are reduced to the extent that it is no longer probable that all or part of the related tax benefit will be realized.

(h) Earnings per Common Share

The Company presents basic and diluted earnings per share ("EPS") amounts for its common shares. Basic EPS is calculated by dividing the net earnings attributable to common shareholders of the Company by the weighted average number of common shares outstanding during the period. Diluted EPS is determined by dividing the net earnings attributable to common shareholders of the Company by the weighted average number of common shares outstanding after adjusting both amounts for the effects of all potential dilutive common shares, which are comprised of share options granted to employees. Anti-dilutive options are not included in the calculation of diluted EPS.

(i) Financial Instruments

(i) Classification of Financial Instruments

Financial instruments are recognized when the Company becomes a party to the contractual provisions of a financial instrument. Financial instruments are classified into one of the following categories: held for trading, held-to-maturity investments, loans and receivables, available-for-sale financial assets or financial liabilities. The classification determines the accounting treatment of the instrument. The classification is determined by the Company when the financial instrument is initially recorded, based on the underlying purpose of the instrument.

The Company's financial instruments are classified and measured as follows:

Financial Asset/Liability	Category	Measurement
Cash	Loans and receivables	Amortized cost
Accounts receivable	Loans and receivables	Amortized cost
Deposits[1]	Loans and receivables	Amortized cost
Long-term receivables[2]	Loans and receivables	Amortized cost
Bank indebtedness	Financial liabilities	Amortized cost
Commercial paper	Financial liabilities	Amortized cost
Accounts payable and accrued liabilities	Financial liabilities	Amortized cost
Dividends payable	Financial liabilities	Amortized cost
Long-term debt	Financial liabilities	Amortized cost
Other long-term liabilities	Financial liabilities	Amortized cost

Derivatives	Classification	Measurement
Interest rate derivatives[3]	Effective cash flow hedge	Fair value through other comprehensive income (loss)
Equity forward derivatives[3][4]	Derivative financial instrument	Fair value through earnings
Equity forward derivatives[3][4]	Effective cash flow hedge	Fair value through other comprehensive income (loss)

[1] The carrying value of deposits is recognized within prepaid expenses and deposits in the consolidated balance sheets.

[2] The carrying value of long-term receivables is recognized within other assets in the consolidated balance sheets.

[3] The carrying values of the Company's derivatives are recognized within other assets, accounts payable and accrued liabilities and other long-term liabilities in the consolidated balance sheets.

[4] The portion of the equity forward derivative agreements relating to the earned long-term incentive plan units and earned restricted share unit plan units is considered a derivative financial instrument. The portion of the equity forward derivative agreements relating to the unearned long-term incentive plan units and unearned restricted share unit plan units is considered an effective cash flow hedge. See Note 26 to these consolidated financial statements for further discussion of the long-term incentive plan and the restricted share unit plan.

Financial instruments measured at amortized cost are initially recognized at fair value and then subsequently at amortized cost using the effective interest method, less any impairment losses, with gains and losses recognized in earnings in the period in which the gain or loss occurs. Changes in the fair value of the Company's derivative instruments designated as effective cash flow hedges are recognized in other comprehensive income (loss) and changes in derivative instruments not designated as effective hedges are recognized within operating and administrative expenses in the Company's consolidated statements of earnings in the period of the change.

The Company categorizes its financial assets and financial liabilities that are recognized in the consolidated balance sheets at fair value using the fair value hierarchy. The fair value hierarchy has the following levels:

- Level 1 – quoted market prices in active markets for identical assets or liabilities;

- Level 2 – inputs other than quoted market prices included in Level 1 that are observable for the asset or liability, either directly (as prices) or indirectly (derived from prices); and

- Level 3 – unobservable inputs such as inputs for the asset or liability that are not based on observable market data.

The level in the fair value hierarchy within which the fair value measurement is categorized in its entirety is determined on the basis of the lowest level input that is significant to the fair value measurement in its entirety.

3. SIGNIFICANT ACCOUNTING POLICIES (continued)

(ii) Transaction Costs

Transaction costs are added to the initial fair value of financial assets and liabilities when those financial assets and liabilities are not measured at fair value subsequent to initial measurement. Transaction costs are amortized to net earnings, within finance expenses, using the effective interest method.

(iii) Derivative Financial Instruments and Hedge Accounting

The Company is exposed to fluctuations in interest rates by virtue of its borrowings under its bank credit facilities, commercial paper program and financing programs available to its Associates. Increases and decreases in interest rates will negatively or positively impact the financial performance of the Company. The Company may use, from time to time, interest rate derivatives to manage this exposure. The earnings or expense arising from the use of these instruments is recognized within finance expenses for the financial year.

The Company uses cash-settled equity forward agreements to limit its exposure to future price changes in the Company's share price for share unit awards under the Company's long-term incentive plan ("LTIP") and restricted share unit plan ("RSU Plan"). The earnings or expense arising from the use of these instruments is included in other comprehensive income (loss) and in operating and administrative expenses, based on the amounts considered to be a hedge or a derivative, respectively, for the financial year. See Note 26 to these consolidated financial statements for further discussion of the LTIP and RSU Plan.

The Company formally identifies, designates and documents all relationships between hedging instruments and hedged items, as well as its risk assessment objective and strategy for undertaking various hedge transactions. The Company assesses, both at the inception of the hedge and on an ongoing basis, including on re-designation, whether the derivatives that are used in hedging transactions are highly effective in offsetting changes in fair values or cash flows of hedged items. When such derivative instruments cease to exist or to be effective as hedges, or when designation of a hedging relationship is terminated, any associated deferred gains or losses are recognized in earnings in the same period as the corresponding gains or losses associated with the hedged item. When a hedged item ceases to exist, any associated deferred gains or losses are recognized in earnings in the period the hedged item ceases to exist.

(iv) Embedded Derivatives

Embedded derivatives (elements of contracts whose cash flows move independently from the host contract) are required to be separated and measured at their respective fair values unless certain criteria are met. The Company does not have any significant embedded features in contractual arrangements that require separate accounting or presentation from the related host contracts.

(v) Share Capital

Common Shares   Common shares issued by the Company are recorded in the amount of the proceeds received, net of direct issue costs.

Repurchase of Share Capital   The Company, from time to time, will repurchase its common shares under a Normal Course Issuer Bid. When common shares are repurchased, the amount of the consideration paid which includes directly attributable costs and is net of any tax effects, is recognized as a deduction from share capital. Any repurchased common shares are cancelled. The premium paid over the average book value of the common shares repurchased is charged to retained earnings. At the end of a reporting period, if there are shares that have not yet been cancelled, they are recognized as treasury shares at the purchase price of the transaction.

(j) Business Combinations

The Company applies the acquisition method in accounting for business combinations.

On acquisition, the assets, including intangible assets, and any liabilities assumed are measured at their fair value. Purchase price allocations may be preliminary when initially recognized and may change pending finalization of the valuation of the assets acquired. Purchase price allocations are finalized within one year of the acquisition and prior periods are restated to reflect any adjustments to the purchase price allocation made subsequent to the initial recognition.

The determination of fair values, particularly for intangible assets, is based on management's estimates and includes assumptions on the timing and amount of future cash flows. The Company recognizes as goodwill the excess of the purchase price of an acquired business over the fair value of the underlying net assets, including intangible assets, at the date of acquisition. Transaction costs are expensed as incurred. The date of acquisition is the date on which the Company obtains control over the acquired business.

(k) Inventory

Inventory is comprised of merchandise inventory, which includes prescription inventory, and is valued at the lower of cost and estimated net realizable value. Cost is determined on the first-in, first-out basis. Cost includes all direct expenditures and other appropriate costs incurred in bringing inventory to its present location and condition. The Company classifies rebates and other consideration received from a vendor as a reduction to the cost of inventory unless the rebate relates to the reimbursement of a selling cost or a payment for services.

Net realizable value is the estimated selling price in the ordinary course of business, less the estimated selling expenses.

(l) Property and Equipment and Investment Property

(i) Recognition and Measurement

Items of property and equipment are carried at cost less accumulated depreciation and any recognized impairment losses (see (p) Impairment).

Cost includes expenditures that are directly attributable to the acquisition of the asset. The cost of self-constructed assets includes the cost of materials and direct labour, any other costs directly attributable to bringing the assets to a working condition for their intended use, and, where applicable, the costs of dismantling and removing the items and restoring the site on which they are located. Borrowing costs are recognized as part of the cost of an asset, where appropriate.

Purchased software that is integral to the functionality of the related equipment is capitalized as part of that equipment.

When components of property and equipment have different useful lives, they are accounted for as separate items of property and equipment.

Gains and losses on disposal of an item of property and equipment are determined by comparing the proceeds from disposal with the carrying amount of property and equipment and are recognized net, within operating and administrative expenses, in net earnings.

Fully-depreciated items of property and equipment that are still in use continue to be recognized in cost and accumulated depreciation.

(ii) Subsequent Costs

The cost of replacing part of an item of property and equipment is recognized in the carrying amount of the item if it is probable that the future economic benefits embodied within the part will flow to the Company and its cost can be measured reliably. The carrying amount of the replaced part is de-recognized. The costs of repairs and maintenance of property and equipment are recognized in earnings as incurred.

3. SIGNIFICANT ACCOUNTING POLICIES (continued)

(iii) Depreciation

Depreciation is recognized in earnings on a straight-line basis over the estimated useful lives of each component of an item of property and equipment. Land is not depreciated. The Company commences recognition of depreciation in earnings when the item of property and equipment is ready for its intended use.

The estimated useful lives for the current and comparative periods are as follows:

Buildings and their components	10 to 40 years
Equipment and fixtures	3 to 10 years
Computer equipment	2 to 10 years
Leasehold improvements	Lesser of term of the lease and useful life
Assets under financing leases	Lesser of term of the lease and useful life

Depreciation methods and useful lives are reviewed at each reporting date.

(iv) Investment Property

Investment property is carried at cost less accumulated depreciation and any recognized impairment losses.

(m) Goodwill

(i) Recognition and Measurement

The Company recognizes goodwill as the excess amount of the purchase price of an acquired business over the fair value of the underlying net assets, including intangible assets, at the date of acquisition. Goodwill is not amortized but is tested for impairment on an annual basis or more frequently if there are indicators that goodwill may be impaired (see (p) Impairment).

(ii) Acquisitions Prior to January 3, 2010

As described in Note 30 to these consolidated financial statements, as part of its transition to IFRS, the Company elected to apply IFRS 3, "Business Combinations" ("IFRS 3"), only to those business combinations that occurred on or after January 3, 2010. In respect of acquisitions prior to January 3, 2010, goodwill represents the amount recognized under previous Canadian GAAP.

(iii) Subsequent Measurement

Goodwill is measured at cost less any accumulated impairment losses.

(n) Intangible Assets

(i) Computer Software

The Company acquires computer software through purchases from vendors and internal development. Computer software that is an integral part of computer equipment is presented in property and equipment. All other computer software is treated as an intangible asset. The Company includes computer software under development in intangible assets. The assessment of whether computer software is an integral part of computer hardware is made when the software development project is complete and placed into use. Costs for internally developed computer software include directly attributable costs including direct labour and overheads associated with the software development project. Expenditures on research activities as part of internally developed computer software are recognized in earnings when incurred.

(ii) Other Intangible Assets

Other intangible assets that are acquired by the Company, other than as a result of a business acquisition, which have finite useful lives, are measured at cost less accumulated amortization and any accumulated impairment losses (see (p) Impairment). Other intangible assets that are acquired by the Company as a result of a business acquisition are measured at their fair values as at the date of acquisition.

(iii) Amortization

Amortization is recognized in earnings on a straight-line basis over the estimated useful lives of intangible assets from the date that they are available for their intended use. The estimated useful lives are as follows:

Prescription files	7 to 12 years
Customer relationships	5 to 25 years
Computer software	3 to 10 years
Other	Term of the lease or 3 years

Computer software under development is not amortized. Amortization methods and useful lives are reviewed at each reporting date.

(o) Leases

The Company leases most of its store locations and office space. Terms vary in length and typically permit renewal for additional periods. Leases for which substantially all the benefits and risks of ownership are transferred to the Company based on certain criteria are recorded as financing leases and classified as property and equipment, accounts payable and accrued liabilities and other long-term liabilities. All other leases are classified as operating leases under which minimum rent, including scheduled escalations, is expensed on a straight-line basis over the term of the lease, including any rent-free periods. Landlord inducements are deferred and amortized as reductions to rent expense on a straight-line basis over the same period.

In the normal course of business, the Company sells certain real estate properties and enters into leaseback arrangements for the area occupied by the Associate-owned stores. The leases are assessed as financing or operating in nature as applicable, and are accounted for accordingly. The gains realized on the disposal of the real estate properties related to sale-leaseback transactions, which are financing in nature, are deferred and amortized on a straight-line basis over the shorter of the lease term and the estimated useful life of the leased asset. The gains realized on the disposal of real estate properties related to sale-leaseback transactions, which are transacted at fair value and are operating in nature, are recognized within operating and administrative expenses in the consolidated statements of earnings. In the event the fair value of the asset at the time of the sale-leaseback transaction is less than its carrying value, the difference would be recognized within operating and administrative expenses in the consolidated statements of earnings.

Leases may include additional payments for real estate taxes, maintenance and insurance. These amounts are expensed in the period to which they relate.

(p) Impairment

(i) Financial Assets

A financial asset is assessed at each reporting date to determine whether there is any objective evidence that it is impaired. A financial asset is considered to be impaired if objective evidence indicates that one or more events, which have a negative effect on the estimated future cash flows of that asset, have occurred.

An impairment loss in respect of a financial asset measured at amortized cost is calculated as the difference between its carrying amount and the present value of the estimated future cash flows, discounted at the original effective interest rate.

Individually significant financial assets are tested for impairment on an individual basis. The remaining financial assets are assessed collectively in groups that share similar credit risk characteristics.

All impairment losses are recognized in the consolidated statements of earnings.

An impairment loss is reversed if the reversal can be objectively related to an event occurring after the impairment loss was recognized. For financial assets measured at amortized cost, the reversal is recognized in earnings.

3. SIGNIFICANT ACCOUNTING POLICIES (continued)

(ii) Property and Equipment and Intangible Assets with Finite Useful Lives

The carrying amount of property and equipment and intangible assets with finite useful lives is reviewed at each reporting date to determine whether there are any indicators of impairment. If any such indicators exist, then the recoverable amount of the asset is estimated as the higher of the fair value of the asset less costs to sell, or value-in-use. An impairment loss is recognized in net earnings for the amount by which the carrying amount of the asset exceeds its recoverable amount. For the purposes of assessing impairment, when an individual asset does not generate cash flows in and of itself, assets are then grouped and tested at the lowest level for which there are separately identifiable cash flows, called a cash-generating unit. The Company has determined that its cash generating units are primarily its retail stores.

(iii) Goodwill and Intangible Assets with Indefinite Useful Lives

For goodwill and intangible assets that have indefinite useful lives or that are not yet available for use, the carrying value is reviewed for impairment on an annual basis, or more frequently if there are indicators that impairment may exist.

Goodwill is allocated to cash-generating units expected to benefit from the synergies created from a business combination and to the lowest level at which management monitors goodwill. To review for impairment, the recoverable amount of each cash-generating unit to which goodwill is allocated is compared to its carrying value, including goodwill.

(iv) Recoverable Amount

The recoverable amount of an asset or cash-generating unit is the greater of its value-in-use and its fair value less costs to sell. In assessing value-in-use, the estimated future cash flows are discounted to their present value using a pre-tax discount rate that reflects current market assessments of the time value of money and the risks specific to the asset.

(v) Impairment Losses

An impairment loss is recognized if the carrying amount of an asset or its cash-generating unit exceeds its estimated recoverable amount. Impairment losses are recognized in operating and administrative expenses in the consolidated statements of earnings. Impairment losses recognized in respect of cash-generating units are allocated first to reduce the carrying amount of any goodwill allocated to the cash-generating units and, then, to reduce the carrying amounts of the other assets in the cash-generating unit (group of cash-generating units) on a pro rata basis.

An impairment loss in respect of goodwill is not reversed. In respect of other assets, impairment losses recognized in prior periods are assessed at each reporting date for any indicators that the loss has decreased or no longer exists. An impairment loss is reversed if there has been a change in the estimates used to determine the recoverable amount. An impairment loss is reversed only to the extent that the carrying amount of the asset does not exceed the carrying amount that would have been determined, net of depreciation or amortization, if no impairment loss had been recognized.

(q) Bank Indebtedness

Bank indebtedness is comprised of corporate bank overdraft balances, corporate and Associate-owned store bank lines of credit and outstanding cheques.

5. FINANCIAL RISK MANAGEMENT OBJECTIVES AND POLICIES RELATED TO FINANCIAL INSTRUMENTS

Financial Risk Management Objectives and Policies

In the normal course of business, the Company is exposed to financial risks that have the potential to negatively impact its financial performance. The Company may use derivative financial instruments to manage certain of these risks. The Company does not use derivative financial instruments for trading or speculative purposes. These risks are discussed in more detail below.

Interest Rate Risk

Interest rate risk is the risk that fair value or future cash flows associated with the Company's financial assets or liabilities will fluctuate due to changes in market interest rates.

The Company, including its Associate-owned store network, is exposed to fluctuations in interest rates by virtue of its borrowings under its bank credit facilities, commercial paper program and financing programs available to its Associates. Increases or decreases in interest rates will positively or negatively impact the financial performance of the Company.

The Company monitors market conditions and the impact of interest rate fluctuations on its fixed and floating rate debt instruments on an ongoing basis and may use interest rate derivatives to manage this exposure. Until December 2010, the Company used interest rate derivatives to manage a portion of the interest rate risk on its commercial paper. The Company was party to an agreement converting an aggregate notional principal amount of $50,000 of floating rate commercial paper debt into fixed rate debt at a rate of 4.18%, which expired in December 2010. Throughout 2011, the Company no longer had interest rate derivative agreements to convert its floating rate debt into fixed rate debt. See Note 18 to these consolidated financial statements for further discussion of the derivative agreement.

As at December 31, 2011, the Company had $166,592 (2010: $304,410) of unhedged floating rate debt. During the current financial year, the Company's average outstanding unhedged floating rate debt was $386,193 (2010: $538,243). Had interest rates been higher or lower by 50 basis points during the current financial year, net earnings for the financial year would have decreased or increased, respectively, by approximately $1,396 (2010: $1,885) as a result of the Company's exposure to interest rate fluctuations on its unhedged floating rate debt.

Credit Risk

Credit risk is the risk that the Company's counterparties will fail to meet their financial obligations to the Company, causing a financial loss.

Accounts receivable arise primarily in respect of prescription sales billed to governments and third-party drug plans and, as a result, collection risk is low. There is no concentration of balances with debtors in the remaining accounts receivable. The Company does not consider its exposure to credit risk to be material.

Liquidity Risk

Liquidity risk is the risk that the Company will be unable to meet its obligations relating to its financial liabilities.

The Company prepares cash flow budgets and forecasts to ensure that it has sufficient funds through operations, access to bank facilities and access to debt and capital markets to meet its financial obligations, capital investment program requirements and fund new investment opportunities or other unanticipated requirements as they arise. The Company manages its liquidity risk as it relates to financial liabilities by monitoring its cash flow from operating activities to meet its short-term financial liability obligations and planning for the repayment of its long-term financial liability obligations through cash flow from operating activities and/or the issuance of new debt or equity.

Notes to the Consolidated Financial Statements (continued)

December 31, 2011 and January 1, 2011 (in thousands of Canadian dollars, except per share data)

5. FINANCIAL RISK MANAGEMENT OBJECTIVES AND POLICIES RELATED TO FINANCIAL INSTRUMENTS (continued)

The contractual maturities of the Company's financial liabilities in the consolidated balance sheet as at December 31, 2011 are as follows:

	Carrying Amount	Payments Due in the Next 90 Days	Payments Due Between 90 Days and Less Than a Year	Payments Due Between 1 Year and Less Than 2 Years	Payments Due After 2 Years	Total Contractual Cash Flows
Bank indebtedness	$ 172,262	$ 172,262	$ –	$ –	$ –	$ 172,262
Accounts payable and accrued liabilities	1,055,891	1,032,431	23,460	–	–	1,055,891
Derivatives	915	–	793	122	–	915
Dividends payable	53,119	53,119	–	–	–	53,119
Medium-term notes	945,494	262,488	28,943	474,202	256,487	1,022,120
Revolving-term debt	152	–	–	–	152	152
Other long-term liabilities	231,970	–	–	18,478	213,492	231,970
Total	**$ 2,459,803**	**$ 1,520,300**	**$ 53,196**	**$ 492,802**	**$ 470,131**	**$ 2,536,429**

The contractual maturities of the Company's financial liabilities in the consolidated balance sheet as at January 1, 2011, were as follows:

	Carrying Amount	Payments Due in the Next 90 Days	Payments Due Between 90 Days and Less Than a Year	Payments Due Between 1 Year and Less Than 2 Years	Payments Due After 2 Years	Total Contractual Cash Flows
Bank indebtedness	$ 209,013	$ 209,013	$ –	$ –	$ –	$ 209,013
Commercial paper	127,828	128,000	–	–	–	128,000
Accounts payable and accrued liabilities	930,910	920,384	10,526	–	–	930,910
Derivatives	2,257	–	674	1,583	–	2,257
Dividends payable	48,927	48,927	–	–	–	48,927
Medium-term notes	946,641	12,488	34,943	291,430	730,690	1,069,551
Other long-term liabilities	167,709	–	–	19,207	148,502	167,709
Total	$ 2,433,285	$ 1,318,812	$ 46,143	$ 312,220	$ 879,192	$ 2,556,367

The accounts payable and accrued liabilities and other long-term liabilities amounts exclude certain liabilities that are not considered financial liabilities. The medium-term note amounts, which are recognized within long-term debt in the consolidated balance sheets, include principal and interest liabilities.

9. COST OF GOODS SOLD

During the current financial year, the Company recorded $39,943 (2010: $37,884) as an expense for the write-down of inventory as a result of net realizable value being lower than cost in cost of goods sold in the consolidated statements of earnings.

During the financial years ended December 31, 2011 and January 1, 2011, the Company did not reverse any significant inventory write-downs recognized in previous years.

15. PROPERTY AND EQUIPMENT AND INVESTMENT PROPERTY

	Properties Under Development	Land	Buildings	Equipment, Fixtures and Computer Equipment	Leasehold Improvements	Assets Under Financing Leases (Note 23)	Total
Cost							
Balance at January 1, 2011	$ 72,035	$ 70,411	$ 206,472	$ 1,135,805	$ 1,179,795	$ 83,082	$ 2,747,600
Additions:							
– Asset acquisitions	9,979	–	–	–	–	43,952	53,931
– Development	9,990	3,688	25,738	168,204	131,667	–	339,287
Transfers	(20,662)	6,147	8,791	752	320	–	(4,652)
Computer software transfers from intangible assets	–	–	–	1,330	–	–	1,330
Disposals	–	(14,768)	(26,958)	(23,563)	(20,337)	–	(85,626)
Retirements	–	–	–	534	–		534
Balance at December 31, 2011	**$ 71,342**	**$ 65,478**	**$ 214,043**	**$ 1,283,062**	**$ 1,291,445**	**$ 127,034**	**$ 3,052,404**
Depreciation							
Balance at January 1, 2011	$ –	$ –	$ 16,102	$ 655,467	$ 355,523	$ 11,446	$ 1,038,538
Depreciation for the financial year	–	–	11,542	140,537	92,423	4,965	249,467
Transfers	–	–	(216)	375	(123)	–	36
Computer software transfers from intangible assets	–	–	–	(18)	–	–	(18)
Disposals	–	–	(3,103)	(19,792)	(11,807)	–	(34,702)
Retirements	–	–	–	(182)	–	–	(182)
Balance at December 31, 2011	**$ –**	**$ –**	**$ 24,325**	**$ 776,387**	**$ 436,016**	**$ 16,411**	**$ 1,253,139**
Impairment losses							
Balance at January 1, 2011	$ –	$ –	$ –	$ 16,257	$ 15,465	$ –	$ 31,722
Impairment loss	–	–	–	–	–	–	–
Balance at December 31, 2011	**$ –**	**$ –**	**$ –**	**$ 16,257**	**$ 15,465**	**$ –**	**$ 31,722**
Net book value							
At December 31, 2011	**$ 71,342**	**$ 65,478**	**$ 189,718**	**$ 490,418**	**$ 839,964**	**$ 110,623**	**$ 1,767,543**
Cost							
Balance at January 3, 2010	$ 113,478	$ 57,683	$ 144,515	$ 1,048,056	$ 1,022,868	$ 59,382	$ 2,445,982
Additions:							
– Asset acquisitions	11,139	531	695	–	–	23,700	36,065
– Development	94,745	327	5,206	135,454	166,986	–	402,718
Transfers	(143,302)	27,880	97,365	(1,223)	11,943	–	(7,337)
Computer software transfers from intangible assets	–	–	–	1,395	–	–	1,395
Disposals	(4,025)	(16,010)	(41,309)	(45,515)	(22,002)	–	(128,861)
Retirements	–	–	–	(2,362)	–	–	(2,362)
Balance at January 1, 2011	**$ 72,035**	**$ 70,411**	**$ 206,472**	**$ 1,135,805**	**$ 1,179,795**	**$ 83,082**	**$ 2,747,600**
Depreciation							
Balance at January 3, 2010	$ –	$ –	$ 24,412	$ 561,691	$ 288,519	$ 8,135	$ 882,757
Depreciation for the financial year	–	–	8,759	136,933	85,487	3,311	234,490
Transfers	–	–	732	(439)	(293)	–	–
Disposals	–	–	(17,801)	(41,255)	(18,190)	–	(77,246)
Retirements	–	–	–	(1,463)	–	–	(1,463)

Notes to the Consolidated Financial Statements (continued)

December 31, 2011 and January 1, 2011 (in thousands of Canadian dollars, except per share data)

15. PROPERTY AND EQUIPMENT AND INVESTMENT PROPERTY (continued)

	Properties Under Development	Land	Buildings	Equipment, Fixtures and Computer Equipment	Leasehold Improvements	Assets Under Financing Leases (Note 23)	Total
Balance at January 1, 2011	$ –	$ –	$ 16,102	$ 655,467	$ 355,523	$ 11,446	$ 1,038,538
Impairment losses							
Balance at January 3, 2010	$ –	$ –	$ –	$ 10,502	$ 10,882	$ –	$ 21,384
Impairment loss	–	–	–	5,755	4,583	–	10,338
Balance at January 1, 2011	$ –	$ –	$ –	$ 16,257	$ 15,465	$ –	$ 31,722
Net book value							
At January 1, 2011	$ 72,035	$ 70,411	$ 190,370	$ 464,081	$ 808,807	$ 71,636	$ 1,677,340
At January 3, 2010	$ 113,478	$ 57,683	$ 120,103	$ 475,863	$ 723,467	$ 51,247	$ 1,541,841

During the financial year ended December 31, 2011, the Company recognized depreciation expense of $249,467 (2010: $234,490), an impairment loss on store assets of $nil (2010: $10,338) and a loss on disposal of property and equipment of $1,498 (2010: a net gain of $6,818) within operating and administrative expenses in the consolidated statements of earnings.

Impairment Loss

During the financial year ended December 31, 2011, the Company reviewed its long-lived assets for indicators of impairment at the cash-generating unit level and determined that an impairment test was not necessary.

During the financial year ended January 1, 2011, the Company reviewed its long-lived assets for indicators of impairment at the cash-generating unit level and determined that a test for impairment was necessary on certain of its store assets. This resulted in the identification of an impairment charge of $7,554, which is net of taxes of $2,784. The impaired assets consist primarily of equipment, fixtures, computer equipment and leasehold improvements at certain of the Company's newer stores. The recoverable amount of the impaired assets was determined through a value-in-use methodology using a pre-tax discount rate of 8 percent.

During the financial years ended December 31, 2011 and January 1, 2011, the Company did not record any reversals of previously recorded impairment charges.

Property under Development

During the financial year ended December 31, 2011, the Company acquired properties with the intention of developing retail stores on the sites. The cost of acquisition was $9,979 (2010: $11,139).

Investment Property

	Land	Building	Total	Land	Building	Total
			2011			2010
Cost						
Balance, beginning of financial year $	**8,084** $	**5,995** $	**14,079** $	3,729 $	3,044 $	6,773
Transfers	**4,325**	**327**	**4,652**	4,386	2,951	7,337
Disposals	**(723)**	**(2)**	**(725)**	(31)	–	(31)
Balance, end of financial year $	**11,686** $	**6,320** $	**18,006** $	8,084 $	5,995 $	14,079
Amortization						
Balance, beginning of financial year $	**–** $	**1,309** $	**1,309** $	– $	889 $	889
Amortization for the financial year	**–**	**325**	**325**	–	420	420
Transfers	**–**	**–**	**–**	–	–	–
Balance, end of financial year $	**–** $	**1,634** $	**1,634** $	– $	1,309 $	1,309
Net book value		$	**16,372**		$	12,770
Net book value at January 3, 2010					$	5,884

The fair value of investment property approximates its carrying value.

24. SHARE CAPITAL

Share Capital and Contributed Surplus

Authorized

Unlimited number of common shares

Unlimited number of preferred shares, issuable in series without nominal or par value

Outstanding

	Number of Common Shares	Stated Value	Number of Common Shares	Stated Value
		2011		2010
Beginning balance	**217,452,068** $	**1,520,558**	217,431,898 $	1,519,870
Shares issued for cash	**109,729**	**1,220**	20,170	491
Shares repurchased in cash	**(5,086,200)**	**(35,576)**	–	–
Repayment of share purchase loans	**–**	**7**	–	33
Exercise of share options	**–**	**246**	–	164
Ending balance	**212,475,597** $	**1,486,455**	217,452,068 $	1,520,558

The Company also has issued share options. See Note 26 to these consolidated financial statements for further details on the Company's issued share options.

24. SHARE CAPITAL (continued)

Individual shareholder agreements address matters related to the transfer of certain shares issued to the Company's management and Associates, including shares issued under certain options granted to management. In particular, each provides, subject to certain exceptions, for a general prohibition on any transfer of a member of management's or Associate's shares for a period of five years from the date that the individual entered into the shareholder agreement.

The holders of common shares are entitled to receive dividends as declared from time to time and are entitled to one vote per share at meetings of the Company.

Normal Course Issuer Bid

On February 10, 2011, the Company implemented a normal course issuer bid to repurchase, for cancellation, up to 8,700,000 of its common shares, representing approximately 4.0% of the Company's then outstanding common shares. Repurchases will be effected through the facilities of the Toronto Stock Exchange (the "TSX") and may take place over a 12-month period ending no later than February 14, 2012. Repurchases will be made at market prices in accordance with the requirements of the TSX.

From February 10, 2011 to December 31, 2011, the Company purchased and cancelled 5,086,200 common shares under the normal course issuer bid at a cost of $206,779. The premium paid over the average book value of the common shares repurchased of $171,203 has been charged to retained earnings. The Company purchased an additional 115,900 shares at the end of the financial year at a cost of $4,735. These shares were cancelled subsequent to the end of the financial year. The cost of this latter purchase is recorded as treasury shares in Shareholders' Equity as at December 31, 2011.

Dividends

The following table provides a summary of the dividends declared by the Company:

Declaration Date	Record Date	Payment Date	Dividend per Common Share
February 10, 2011	March 31, 2011	April 15, 2011	$ 0.250
April 27, 2011	June 30, 2011	July 15, 2011	$ 0.250
July 21, 2011	September 30, 2011	October 14, 2011	$ 0.250
November 9, 2011	December 30, 2011	January 13, 2012	$ 0.250
February 11, 2010	March 31, 2010	April 15, 2010	$ 0.225
April 28, 2010	June 30, 2010	July 15, 2010	$ 0.225
July 22, 2010	September 30, 2010	October 15, 2010	$ 0.225
November 9, 2010	December 31, 2010	January 14, 2011	$ 0.225

On February 9, 2012, the Board of Directors declared a dividend of 26.5 cents per common share payable April 13, 2012 to shareholders of record as of the close of business on March 30, 2012.

25. EARNINGS PER COMMON SHARE

Basic Net Earnings per Common Share

The calculation of basic net earnings per common share at December 31, 2011 was based on net earnings for the financial year of $613,934 (2010: $591,851) and a weighted average number of shares outstanding (basic) of 216,420,096 (2010: 217,435,868). The weighted average number of shares outstanding (basic) is calculated as follows:

Weighted Average Shares Outstanding (Basic)

	Note	2011	2010
Issued shares, beginning of the financial year	24	217,452,068	217,431,898
Effect of share options exercised		52,350	8,094
Effect of shares repurchased		(1,082,326)	–
Effect of share purchase loans		(1,996)	(4,124)
Weighted average number of shares outstanding (basic), end of the financial year		216,420,096	217,435,868

Diluted Net Earnings per Common Share

The calculation of diluted net earnings per common share at December 31, 2011 was based on net earnings for the financial year of $613,934 (2010: $591,851) and a weighted average number of shares outstanding, after adjustment for the effects of all potentially dilutive shares, of 216,504,784 (2010: 217,537,709). The weighted average number of shares outstanding (diluted) is calculated as follows:

Weighted Average Shares Outstanding (Diluted)

	2011	2010
Weighted average number of shares outstanding (basic), end of the financial year	216,420,096	217,435,868
Potentially dilutive share options	84,688	101,841
Weighted average number of shares outstanding (diluted), end of the financial year	216,504,784	217,537,709

The average market value of the Company's shares for purposes of calculating the effect of dilutive share options was based on quoted market prices for the period that the stock options were outstanding. Anti-dilutive stock options have been excluded.

Financial Statements Analysis Ratios

Exhibit

Financial Statement Analysis Ratios

	Method of Computation	Use
Liquidity measures:		
Working Capital	Current Assets − Current Liabilities	To indicate the ability to meet currently maturing obligations
Current Ratio	$\dfrac{\text{Current Assets}}{\text{Current Liabilities}}$	
Quick Ratio	$\dfrac{\text{Quick Assets}}{\text{Current Liabilities}}$	To indicate instant debt-paying ability
Efficiency measures:		
Accounts Receivable Turnover	$\dfrac{\text{Net Sales}}{\text{Average Net Accounts Receivable}}$	To assess the efficiency in collecting receivables and in the management of credit
Days' Sales in Receivables	$\dfrac{\text{Average Net Accounts Receivable}}{\text{Average Daily Sales}}$	
Inventory Turnover	$\dfrac{\text{Cost of Goods Sold}}{\text{Average Inventory}}$	To assess the efficiency in the management of inventory
Days' Sales in Inventory	$\dfrac{\text{Average Inventory}}{\text{Average Daily Cost of Goods Sold}}$	
Total Asset Turnover	$\dfrac{\text{Net Sales}}{\text{Average Total Assets}}$	To assess the efficiency in the management of assets
Solvency measures:		
Debt Ratio	$\dfrac{\text{Total Liabilities}}{\text{Total Assets}}$	To indicate the percentage of assets financed with debt
Times Interest Earned Ratio	$\dfrac{\text{Income Before Income Taxes} + \text{Interest Expense}}{\text{Interest Expense}}$	To assess the risk to debtholders in terms of number of times interest charges were earned
Profitability measures:		
Profit Margin	$\dfrac{\text{Net Income}}{\text{Net Sales}}$	To assess the overall profitability of a company
Gross Margin	$\dfrac{\text{Gross Profit}}{\text{Net Sales}}$	To assess the ability to earn a return on items sold
Return on Assets	$\dfrac{\text{Net Income}}{\text{Average Total Assets}}$	To assess the profitability of the assets
Return on Common Shareholders' Equity	$\dfrac{\text{Net Income} - \text{Preferred Dividends}}{\text{Average Common Shareholders' Equity}}$	To assess the profitability of the investment by common shareholders
Earnings per Share (EPS)	$\dfrac{\text{Net Income} - \text{Preferred Dividends}}{\text{Weighted Average Number of Common Shares}}$	
Price-Earnings Ratio	$\dfrac{\text{Market Price per Common Share}}{\text{Earnings per Share}}$	To indicate future earnings prospects, based on the relationship between market value of common shares and earnings
Dividend Yield	$\dfrac{\text{Annual Dividends per Share}}{\text{Market Price per Share}}$	To indicate the rate of return to common shareholders in terms of dividends

Accounting Systems

Basic Accounting Systems

In Chapters 1 through 4, an accounting system for NetSolutions was described and illustrated. An accounting system is the methods and procedures for collecting, classifying, summarizing, and reporting a business's financial and operating information. Most accounting systems, however, are more complex than NetSolutions'.

As a business grows and changes, its accounting system also changes in a three-step process. This three-step process is as follows:

Step 1. *Analyze* user information needs.
Step 2. *Design* the system to meet the user needs.
Step 3. *Implement* the system.

For NetSolutions, our analysis determined that Chris Clark needed financial statements for the new business. We designed the system, using a basic manual system that included a chart of accounts, a two-column journal, and a general ledger. Finally, we implemented the system to record transactions and prepare financial statements.

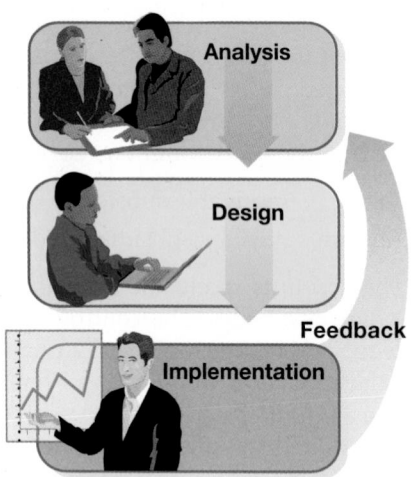

Once a system has been implemented, *feedback,* or input, from users is used to analyze and improve the system. For example, in later chapters, NetSolutions expands its chart of accounts to record more complex transactions.

Internal controls and information processing methods are essential in an accounting system. Internal controls are the policies and procedures that protect assets from misuse, ensure that business information is accurate, and ensure that laws and regulations are being followed. Internal controls are discussed in Chapter 7.

Processing methods are the means by which the system collects, summarizes, and reports accounting information. These methods may be either *manual* or *computerized.* In the following sections, manual accounting systems that use special journals and subsidiary ledgers are described and illustrated. This is followed by a discussion of computerized accounting systems.

Manual Accounting Systems

Accounting systems are manual or computerized. Understanding a manual accounting system is useful in identifying relationships between accounting data and reports. Also, most computerized systems use principles from manual systems.

In Chapters 1 through 4, the transactions for NetSolutions were manually recorded in an all-purpose (two-column) journal. The journal entries were then posted individually to the accounts in the ledger, called the general ledger. This ledger contains all of the balance sheet and income statement accounts. Such a system is simple to use and easy to understand when there are a small number of transactions. However, when a business has a large number of *similar*, repetitive transactions, using an all-purpose journal is inefficient and impractical. For example, in a given day, a company might earn fees on account from 20 customers. Recording each fee earned by debiting Accounts Receivable and crediting Fees Earned would be inefficient. Also, a record of the amount each customer owes must be kept. In such cases, subsidiary ledgers and special journals are useful. The special journals also improve internal controls by including a summary account that the special journal is matched to. This process ensures that mistakes are identified.

Subsidiary Ledgers

An accounting system should be designed to provide information on the amounts due from various customers (accounts receivable) and amounts owed to various suppliers (accounts payable). A separate account for each customer and supplier can be added to the ledger. However, as the number of customers and suppliers increases, the ledger can become awkward.

Note: Subsidiary ledgers are a method of summarizing individual accounts.

A large number of individual accounts with a common characteristic can be grouped together in a separate ledger called a subsidiary ledger. Each subsidiary ledger is represented in the general ledger by a summarizing account, called a controlling account. The sum of the balances of the accounts in a subsidiary ledger must equal the balance of the related controlling account. Thus, a subsidiary ledger is a secondary ledger that supports a controlling account in the general ledger.

Two of the most common subsidiary ledgers are as follows:

1. Accounts receivable subsidiary ledger
2. Accounts payable subsidiary ledger

The accounts receivable subsidiary ledger lists the individual customer accounts in alphabetical order. The controlling account in the general ledger that summarizes the debits and credits to the individual customer accounts is Accounts Receivable. This subsidiary ledger is discussed in Chapter 8.

The accounts payable subsidiary ledger lists individual supplier accounts in alphabetical order. The related controlling account in the general ledger is Accounts Payable. This subsidiary ledger is discussed in Chapter 10.

Special Journals

One method of processing data more efficiently in a manual accounting system is to expand the all-purpose two-column journal to a multicolumn journal. Each column in a multicolumn journal is used only for recording transactions that affect a certain account.

Note: Special journals are a method of summarizing transactions.

For example, a special column can be used only for recording debits to the cash account. The addition of the special column eliminates the writing of *Cash* in the journal for every receipt of cash. Also, there is no need to post each individual debit to the cash account. Instead, the *Cash Dr.* column can be totalled periodically and only the total posted. In a similar way, special columns can be added for recording credits to cash and Fees Earned, for reporting debits and credits to Accounts Receivable and Accounts Payable, and for other entries that are repeated.

An all-purpose multicolumn journal may be adequate for a small business that has many transactions of a similar nature. However, a journal that has many columns for recording many different types of transactions is impractical for larger businesses.

The next logical extension of the accounting system is to replace the single multicolumn journal with several special journals. Each special journal is designed to be used for recording a single kind of transaction that occurs frequently. For example, because most businesses have many transactions in which cash is paid out, they will likely use a special journal for recording cash payments. Likewise, they will use another special journal for recording cash receipts. Special journals are a method of summarizing frequent transactions, which is a basic feature of any accounting system.

The format and number of special journals that a business uses depends on the nature of the business. A business that gives credit might use a special journal designed for recording only revenue from services provided on credit. In contrast, a business that does not give credit will have no need for such a journal.

The transactions that occur most often in a small service business and the special journals in which they are recorded are as follows:

Providing services on account	recorded in →	Sales journal (S)*
Receipt of cash from *any* source	recorded in →	Cash receipts journal (CR)*
Purchase of items on account	recorded in →	Purchases journal (P)*
Payment of cash for *any* purpose	recorded in →	Cash disbursements journal (CD)*

*These are common abbreviations, used for these journals.

See Exhibit 1 for a graphic representation of how to decide which journal to use in most cases.

The all-purpose two-column journal, called the general journal or simply the *journal,* can be used for entries that do not fit into any of the special journals. For example, adjusting and closing entries are recorded in the general journal. The abbreviation GJ will be used.

Exhibit 1

Decision Tree for Choosing the Appropriate Journal

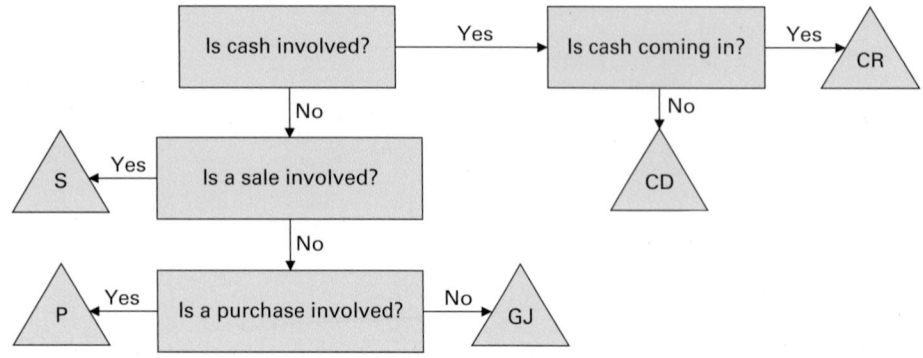

Next, the following types of transactions, special journals, and subsidiary ledgers are described and illustrated for NetSolutions:

Transaction	Special Journal	Subsidiary Ledger
Fees earned on account	Sales journal	Accounts receivable subsidiary ledger
Cash receipts	Cash receipts journal	Accounts receivable subsidiary ledger
Purchases on account	Purchases journal	Accounts payable subsidiary ledger
Cash payments	Cash disbursements journal	Accounts payable subsidiary ledger

As shown above, most transactions that are recorded in the sales and cash receipts journals will affect the accounts receivable subsidiary ledger. Likewise, most transactions that are recorded in the purchases and cash disbursements journals will affect the accounts payable subsidiary ledger. The cash receipts journal includes all transactions involving the receipt of cash and includes a column for recording transactions that do not affect accounts receivable, such as rent revenue received, loan proceeds received, deposits made by the owner, and cash sales. The cash payments journal includes all transactions involving the payment of cash and includes a column for recording transactions that do not affect accounts payable, such as rent paid, loan payments, withdrawals made by the owner, cash equipment purchases, and other miscellaneous payments.

We will assume that NetSolutions had the following selected general ledger balances on March 1, 2015:

Account Number	Account	Balance
1010	Cash	$6,200
1020	Accounts Receivable	3,400
1040	Supplies	2,500
1070	Office Equipment	2,500
2010	Accounts Payable	1,230

Sales Journal

Fees earned on account are recorded in the sales journal. *Cash fees earned* are recorded in the cash receipts journal.

To illustrate the efficiency of using a sales journal, an example for NetSolutions is used. Specifically, assume that NetSolutions recorded the following four revenue transactions for March in its general journal:

2015					
Mar.	2	Accounts Receivable—Accessories by Claire	1020/✓	2,200	
		Fees Earned	4010		2,200
	6	Accounts Receivable—RapZone	1020/✓	1,750	
		Fees Earned	4010		1,750
	18	Accounts Receivable—Web Cantina	1020/✓	2,650	
		Fees Earned	4010		2,650
	27	Accounts Receivable—Accessories by Claire	1020/✓	3,000	
		Fees Earned	4010		3,000

For the above entries, NetSolutions recorded eight account titles and eight amounts. In addition, NetSolutions made 12 postings to the ledgers—four to Accounts Receivable in the general ledger, four to the accounts receivable subsidiary ledger (indicated by each check mark), and four to Fees Earned in the general ledger.

Exhibit 2

Sales Journal

			Sales Journal		Page 35
Date	**Invoice No.**		**Account Debited**	**Post. Ref.**	**Accts. Rec. Dr. Fees Earned Cr.**
2015					
Mar. 2		615	Accessories by Claire		2,200
6		616	RapZone		1,750
18		617	Web Cantina		2,650
27		618	Accessories by Claire		3,000
31					9,600

The preceding sales transactions could be recorded more efficiently in a sales journal, as shown in Exhibit 2. In each revenue transaction, the amount of the debit to Accounts Receivable is the same as the amount of the credit to Fees Earned. Thus, only a single amount column is necessary. The date, invoice number, customer name, and amount are entered separately for each transaction.

Revenues are normally recorded in the sales journal when the company sends an invoice to the customer. An invoice is the bill that is sent to the customer by the company. Each invoice is normally numbered in sequence for future reference.

To illustrate, assume that on March 2, NetSolutions issued Invoice No. 615 to Accessories by Claire for fees earned of $2,200. This transaction is entered in the sales journal, shown on the first line in Exhibit 2.

The process of posting from a sales journal, shown in Exhibit 3, is as follows:

1. Each transaction is posted individually to a customer account in the accounts receivable subsidiary ledger. Postings to customer accounts should be made on a regular basis. In this way, the customer's account will show a current balance, as shown in Exhibit 3.

2. To provide a trail of the entries posted to the subsidiary and general ledger, the source of these entries is indicated in the Posting Reference column of each account by inserting the letter S (for sales journal) and the page number of the sales journal.

3. To indicate that the transaction has been posted to the accounts receivable subsidiary ledger, a check mark (✓) is inserted in the Post. Ref. column of the sales journal, as shown in Exhibit 3.

4. A single monthly total is posted to Accounts Receivable and Fees Earned in the general ledger. This total is equal to the sum of the month's debits to the individual accounts in the subsidiary ledger. It is posted in the general ledger as a debit to Accounts Receivable and a credit to Fees Earned, as shown in Exhibit 3. The accounts receivable account number (1020) and the fees earned account number (4010) are then inserted below the total in the sales journal to indicate that the posting is completed.

Exhibit 3 illustrates the efficiency gained by using the sales journal instead of the general journal. Specifically, all of the transactions for fees earned during the month are posted to the general ledger only once—at the end of the month. As noted above, if NetSolutions had used the general journal, it would have made 12 postings. Using the sales journal required only six postings.

Internal Control Impact The sales journal improves internal controls. Because the sales invoice numbers are recorded in numerical order, missing or duplicate invoices can be immediately identified and corrected.

Exhibit 3

Sales Journal and Postings

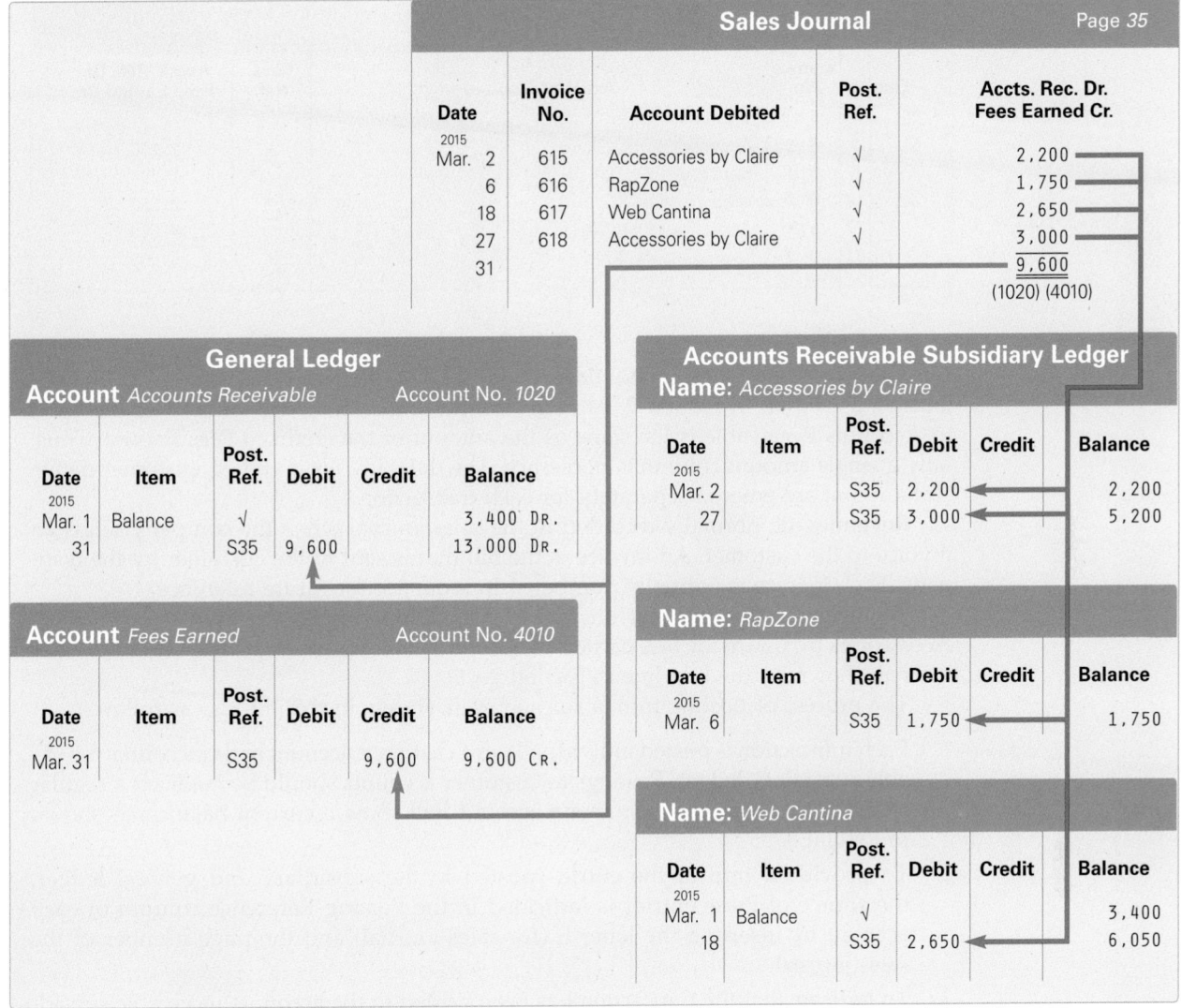

Cash Receipts Journal

All transactions that involve the receipt of cash are recorded in a cash receipts journal. The cash receipts journal for NetSolutions is shown in Exhibit 4.

The cash receipts journal shown in Exhibit 4 has a Cash Dr. column. The titles of the other columns are determined by the kinds of transactions in which cash is received and how often they occur. For example, NetSolutions often receives cash from customers on account. Thus, the cash receipts journal in Exhibit 4 has an Accounts Receivable Cr. column.

To illustrate, on March 28, Accessories by Claire made a payment of $2,200 on its account. This transaction is recorded on the third line in the cash receipts journal, shown in Exhibit 4.

The Other Accounts Cr. column in Exhibit 4 is used for recording credits to any account that does not have a special credit column. For example, NetSolutions received cash on March 1 for rent. Because no special column exists for Rent Revenue, Rent Revenue is entered in the Account Credited column. This transaction is recorded on the first line in the cash receipts journal, shown in Exhibit 4.

At the end of the month, all of the amount columns are totalled. The debits must equal the credits. If the debits do not equal the credits, an error has occurred. Before proceeding further, the error must be found and corrected.

Exhibit 4

Cash Receipts Journal

				Cash Receipts Journal			Page *14*
Date		Account Credited	Post. Ref.	Other Accounts Cr.	Accounts Receivable Cr.	Cash Dr.	
2015							
Mar.	1	Rent Revenue	4020	400		400	
	19	Web Cantina	✓		3,400	3,400	
	28	Accessories by Claire	✓		2,200	2,200	
	30	RapZone	✓		1,750	1,750	
	31			400	7,350	7,750	
				(✓)	(1020)	(1010)	

The process of posting from the cash receipts journal is similar to the process of posting from the sales journal. A summary of the steps for posting from all the special journals is as follows:

1. Each transaction involving a customer or supplier is posted individually, on a regular basis, to the customer's or supplier's account in the appropriate subsidiary ledger.

2. To provide a trail of the entries posted to the subsidiary ledger and the general ledger, the source of these entries is indicated in the Posting Reference column of each account by inserting the special journal's letter (S for Sales, CR for Cash Receipts, P for Purchases, and CD for Cash Disbursements) and its page number.

3. To indicate that the transaction has been posted to the subsidiary ledger, a check mark (✓) is inserted in the Posting Reference column of the special journal.

4. A single monthly total of any individual column is posted to the respective general ledger account, along with the letters of the special journal (S, CR, P, or CD). The account number of the general ledger account is then inserted below the column total in the special journal to indicate that the posting is complete.

5. The accounts listed in the Other Accounts columns are posted on a regular basis as a separate debit or credit to each account. The general ledger account number is then inserted in the Posting Reference column to indicate that the posting is complete. Because accounts in the Other Accounts columns are posted individually, a check mark is placed below the column total at the end of the month to show that no further action is needed.

Internal Control Impact Because cash is easily stolen, controls for cash transactions are essential. The cash receipts journal improves the business's internal control of cash because a reviewer can easily follow the transactions related to cash. Using the general journal to track particular types of transactions is not a straightforward task. A reviewer can more easily check the cash receipts journal to see whether there were any days that no cash was received and then assess whether that pattern makes sense for the business. Alternatively, a reviewer can check to ensure that any cash received was deposited promptly. The owner (reviewer) can also keep track of the cash flow by analyzing the receipts for cash sales and sales on account.

Accounts Receivable Control Account and Subsidiary Ledger

After all posting has been completed for the month, the balances in the accounts receivable subsidiary ledger should be totalled. This total should then be compared with the balance of the accounts receivable control account in the general ledger. If the control account and the subsidiary ledger do not agree, an error has occurred. Before proceeding further, the error must be located and corrected.

After posting the cash receipts journal, the total of NetSolutions' accounts receivable subsidiary ledger is $5,650. This total agrees with the balance of its accounts receivable control account on March 31, 2015, as shown below.

Accounts Receivable (Control)		NetSolutions Accounts Receivable Subsidiary Ledger March 31, 2015	
Balance, March 1, 2015	$ 3,400	Accessories by Claire	$3,000
Total debits (from sales journal)	9,600	RapZone	0
Total credits (from cash receipts journal)	(7,350)	Web Cantina	2,650
Balance, March 31, 2015	$ 5,650	Total accounts receivable	$5,650

Purchases Journal

All *purchases on account* are recorded in the purchases journal. *Cash purchases are recorded in the cash disbursements journal.* The purchases journal for NetSolutions is shown in Exhibit 5.

The amounts purchased on account are recorded in the purchases journal in an Accounts Payable Cr. column. The items most often purchased on account determine the titles of the other columns. For example, NetSolutions often purchases supplies on account. Thus, the purchases journal in Exhibit 5 has a Supplies Dr. column.

To illustrate, on March 3, NetSolutions purchased $600 of supplies on account from Howard Supplies. This transaction is recorded on the first line in the purchases journal, shown in Exhibit 5.

The Other Accounts Dr. column in Exhibit 5 is used to record purchases, on account, of any item that does not have a debit column. The title of the account to be debited is entered in the Other Accounts Dr. column, and the amount is entered in the Amount column.

To illustrate, on March 12, NetSolutions purchased office equipment on account from Jewett Business Systems for $2,800. This transaction is recorded on the third line in the purchases journal shown in Exhibit 5.

At the end of the month, all of the amount columns are totalled. The debits must equal the credits. If the debits do not equal the credits, an error has occurred. Before proceeding further, the error must be found and corrected.

The process of posting from the purchases journal is similar to the process of posting from the sales or cash receipts journals. Refer to the steps described for the cash receipts journal.

Exhibit 5

Purchases Journal

							Page *11*
			Purchases Journal				
Date	Account Credited	Post. Ref.	Accounts Payable Cr.	Supplies Dr.	Other Accounts Dr.	Post. Ref.	Amount
2015 Mar. 3	Howard Supplies	✓	600	600			
7	Donnelly Supplies	✓	420	420			
12	Jewett Business Systems	✓	2,800		Office Equipment	1070	2,800
19	Donnelly Supplies	✓	1,450	1,450			
27	Howard Supplies	✓	960	960			
31			6,230 (2010)	3,430 (1040)			2,800 (✓)

Cash Disbursements Journal

All transactions that involve the payment of cash are recorded in a cash disbursements journal. The cash disbursements journal for NetSolutions is shown in Exhibit 6.

The cash disbursements journal shown in Exhibit 6 has a Cash Cr. column. The titles of the other columns are determined by the kinds of transactions in which cash is paid and how often they occur. For example, NetSolutions often pays cash to suppliers on account. Thus, the cash disbursements journal in Exhibit 6 has an Accounts Payable Dr. column. In addition, NetSolutions makes all payments by cheque. Thus, a cheque number is entered for each payment in the Ch. No. (Cheque Number) column to the right of the Date column. Some companies may use a debit card instead of a cheque when making small purchases. To record these purchases, the company would enter a short form such as "DB" in the Ch. No. column, in place of the cheque number.

To illustrate, on March 15, NetSolutions issued Cheque No. 151 for $1,230 to Grayco Supplies for payment on its account. This transaction is recorded on the second line in the cash disbursements journal shown in Exhibit 6.

The Other Accounts Dr. column in Exhibit 6 is used for recording debits to any account that does not have a special debit column. For example, NetSolutions issued Cheque No. 150 on March 2 for $1,600 in payment of the March rent. This transaction is recorded on the first line in the cash disbursements journal, shown in Exhibit 6.

At the end of the month, all of the amount columns are totalled. The debits must equal the credits. If the debits do not equal the credits, an error has occurred. Before proceeding further, the error must be found and corrected.

The process of posting from the cash disbursements journal is similar to the process of posting from the sales, cash receipts, or purchases journals. Refer to the steps described for the cash receipts journal on page E-7.

Internal Control Impact The cash disbursements journal improves internal controls. Because the cheque numbers are recorded in numerical order, missing or duplicate cheques can be immediately identified and corrected.

Accounts Payable Control Account and Subsidiary Ledger

After all posting has been completed for the month, the balances in the accounts payable subsidiary ledger should be totalled. This total should then be compared with the balance of the accounts payable control account in the general ledger. If the control account and the subsidiary ledger do not agree, an error has occurred. Before proceeding, the error must be located and corrected.

At the beginning of March, the balance in the accounts payable control account for NetSolutions was $1,230. This balance was owed to Grayco Supplies. After posting

Exhibit 6

Cash Disbursements Journal

Cash Disbursements Journal						Page 7
Date	Ch. No.	Account Debited	Post. Ref.	Other Accounts Dr.	Accounts Payable Dr.	Cash Cr.
2015						
Mar. 2	150	Rent Expense	5020	1,600		1,600
15	151	Grayco Supplies	✓		1,230	1,230
21	152	Jewett Business Systems	✓		2,800	2,800
22	153	Donnelly Supplies	✓		420	420
30	154	Utilities Expense	5040	1,050		1,050
31	155	Howard Supplies	✓		600	600
31				2,650	5,050	7,700
				(✓)	(2010)	(1010)

the March transactions, the total of NetSolutions' accounts payable subsidiary ledger is $2,410. This total agrees with the balance of its accounts payable control account on March 31, 2015, as shown below:

Accounts Payable (Control)		NetSolutions Accounts Payable Subsidiary Ledger March 31, 2015	
Balance, March 1, 2015	$ 1,230	Donnelly Supplies	$1,450
Total credits (from purchases journal)	6,230	Grayco Supplies	0
Total debits		Howard Supplies	960
(from cash disbursements journal)	(5,050)	Jewett Business Systems	0
Balance, March 31, 2015	$ 2,410	Total	$2,410

Accounting Systems for Merchandisers

Merchandising companies may use either manual or computerized accounting systems, similar to those used by service businesses. In this section, we describe and illustrate special journals for the manual system.

Manual Accounting System

In a manual accounting system, a merchandise business normally uses the standard four special journals:

Special Journal	Type of Transaction
Sales journal	Sales on account
Purchases journal	Purchases on account
Cash receipts journal	Cash receipts
Cash disbursements journal	Cash payments

These journals can be adapted from the special journals that we just illustrated for a service business.

@netsolutions

Exhibit 7 illustrates NetSolutions' sales journal. In this sales journal, each transaction is recorded by entering the sales amount in the *Accounts Receivable Dr./Sales Cr.* column. The cost of the merchandise sold amount is entered in the *Cost of Goods Sold Dr./Inventory Cr.* column. The totals of the two columns are posted to the general ledger accounts at the end of the month. The inventory and accounts receivable subsidiary ledgers are updated when each transaction is recorded.

Exhibit 7

Sales Journal for a Merchandising Business

		Sales Journal				Page 35
Date	Invoice No.	Account Debited	Post. Ref.	Accts. Rec. Dr. Sales Cr.	Cost of Goods Sold Dr. Inventory Cr.	
2016						
Mar. 2	810	Berry Co.	✓	2,750	2,000	
14	811	Handler Co.	✓	4,260	3,470	
19	812	Jordan Co.	✓	5,800	4,650	
26	813	Kenner Co.	✓	4,500	3,840	
				17,310	13,960	
				(1020) (4010)	(5010) (1050)	

Exhibit 8

Purchases Journal for a Merchandising Business

									Purchases Journal								Page *11*

Date	Account Credited	Post. Ref.	Accounts Payable Cr.	Inventory Dr.	Other Accounts Dr.	Post. Ref.	Amount
2016							
Mar. 4	Compu-Tek	✓	13,880	13,880			
7	Omega Technologies	✓	4,650	4,650			
15	Dale Furniture Co.	✓	5,700		Store Equipment	1230	5,700
22	Delta Data Link	✓	3,840	3,840			
29	Power Electronics	✓	3,200	3,200			
			31,270	25,570			5,700
			(2010)	(1050)			(✓)

Exhibit 8 illustrates a purchases journal for NetSolutions' merchandising business. This journal is similar to the purchases journal for NetSolutions' service business illustrated in the previous section. It includes an *Accounts Payable Cr.* column and an *Inventory Dr.* column, rather than a *Supplies Dr.* column. At the end of the month, these two column totals are posted to the general ledger controlling accounts, Accounts Payable and Inventory. The amounts in *Other Accounts Dr.* are posted individually. The inventory and accounts payable subsidiary ledgers are updated when each transaction is recorded.

Exhibit 9 illustrates NetSolutions' cash receipts journal. Cash sales are recorded in a *Sales Cr.* column, rather than a *Fees Earned Cr.* column. In addition, the cost of goods sold for cash sales is recorded in a *Cost of Goods Sold Dr./Inventory Cr.* column. Sales discounts are recorded in a *Sales Discounts Dr.* column. At the end of the month, all the column totals except for *Other Accounts Cr.* are posted to the general ledger. The inventory and accounts receivable subsidiary ledgers are updated when each transaction is recorded.

Exhibit 10 illustrates NetSolutions' cash disbursements journal. This journal is modified for a merchandising business by adding an *Inventory Cr.* column for recording

Exhibit 9

Cash Receipts Journal for Merchandising Business

									Cash Receipts Journal								Page *14*

Date	Account Credited	Post. Ref.	Other Accounts Cr.	Cost of Goods Sold Dr. Inventory Cr.	Sales Cr.	Accounts Receivable Cr.	Sales Discounts Dr.	Cash Dr.
2016								
Mar. 3	Sales	✓		400	600			600
12	Berry Co.	✓				2,750	55	2,695

Exhibit 10

Cash Disbursements Journal for Merchandising Business

							Cash Disbursements Journal						Page *7*

Date	Ch. No.	Account Debited	Post. Ref.	Other Accounts Dr.	Accounts Payable Dr.	Inventory Cr.	Cash Cr.
2016							
Mar. 16	210	Compu-Tek	✓		13,880		13,880
17	211	Omega Technologies	✓		4,650	93	4,557

discounts on purchases paid within the discount period. The inventory and accounts payable subsidiary ledger are updated when each transaction is recorded. At the end of the month, all the column totals except for *Other Accounts Dr.* are posted to the general ledger.

Computerized Accounting Systems

Computerized accounting systems are widely used by even the smallest of companies. Computerized accounting systems have the following three main advantages over manual systems:

1. Computerized systems simplify the record-keeping process because transactions are recorded in electronic forms and, at the same time, posted electronically to general and subsidiary ledger accounts.
2. Computerized systems are generally more accurate than manual systems.
3. Computerized systems provide management with current account balance information to support decision making because account balances are posted when the transactions occur.

@netsolutions

A computerized system such as Simply Accounting® or QuickBooks® uses electronic forms that look much like their paper counterparts, such as invoices. An electronic version of the invoice is filled out in the computerized system and mailed to the customer. The electronic invoice is linked to the general ledger and the subsidiary ledgers, and all relevant information is posted automatically to the ledgers. When a payment is received, an electronic form is filled out, such as a "Customer payment" form. This transaction is connected to the ledgers by a debit to cash, a credit to accounts receivable for that client, and a credit to the accounts receivable control account. See Exhibit 11 for an illustration of QuickBooks® electronic forms and reports.

Computerized accounting systems generate financial and managerial reports that aid management in their decision making. These systems have the ability to generate the four financial statements, cash receipts and cash payments reports, and expense reports showing total payments by expense category. Typical reports generated through these systems include accounts receivable and accounts payable subsidiary ledgers. These subsidiary ledgers can generate aged reports detailing the length of time each receivable or payable has been outstanding, or a detailed report on fees earned by customer, or payments made to suppliers. The computer does not make journalizing, posting, or mathematical errors. For example, a computerized accounting system will not process a transaction unless the total debits for the transaction equal the total credits for a transaction. Instead, an error screen will notify the user that the transaction data must be corrected.

The discovery and correction of human errors, however, is important in a computerized system. Errors that can occur in a computerized system include the following:

1. Failing to record a transaction.
2. Recording a transaction more than once.
3. Recording a transaction in incorrect accounts.
4. Entering an incorrect number in both the debit and credit sides of the transaction.

The preceding errors are often discovered by reviewing the computerized trial balance for any account balances that are unusual or unreasonable. For example, a credit balance for Supplies indicates that an error has occurred. In addition, errors are often discovered when parties affected by the incorrect transaction complain. For example, an employee would likely complain about a missed or incorrect payroll cheque.

Incorrectly recorded transactions can be corrected in computerized accounting systems by correcting the electronic form, in this case, the invoice. The computer then makes a reversing entry and a correcting entry, as described in Chapter 2.

It is possible to set up standardized adjusting entries in the system that can be prepared and posted at the end of each accounting period with the click of a button. Computerized accounting systems also have the ability to prepare a bank reconciliation at the end of each month.

Exhibit 11

Revenue and Cash Receipts in QuickBooks®

1. Record fees by completing an electronic invoice form.

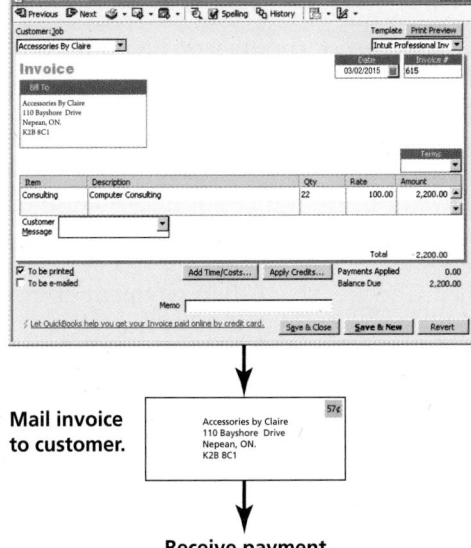

Automatic Postings	Dr.	Cr.
Accounts Receivable—		
Accessories by Claire....	2,200	
Fees Earned.........		2,200

Mail invoice to customer.

Receive payment

2. Record collection of payment by completing a "receive payment" form.

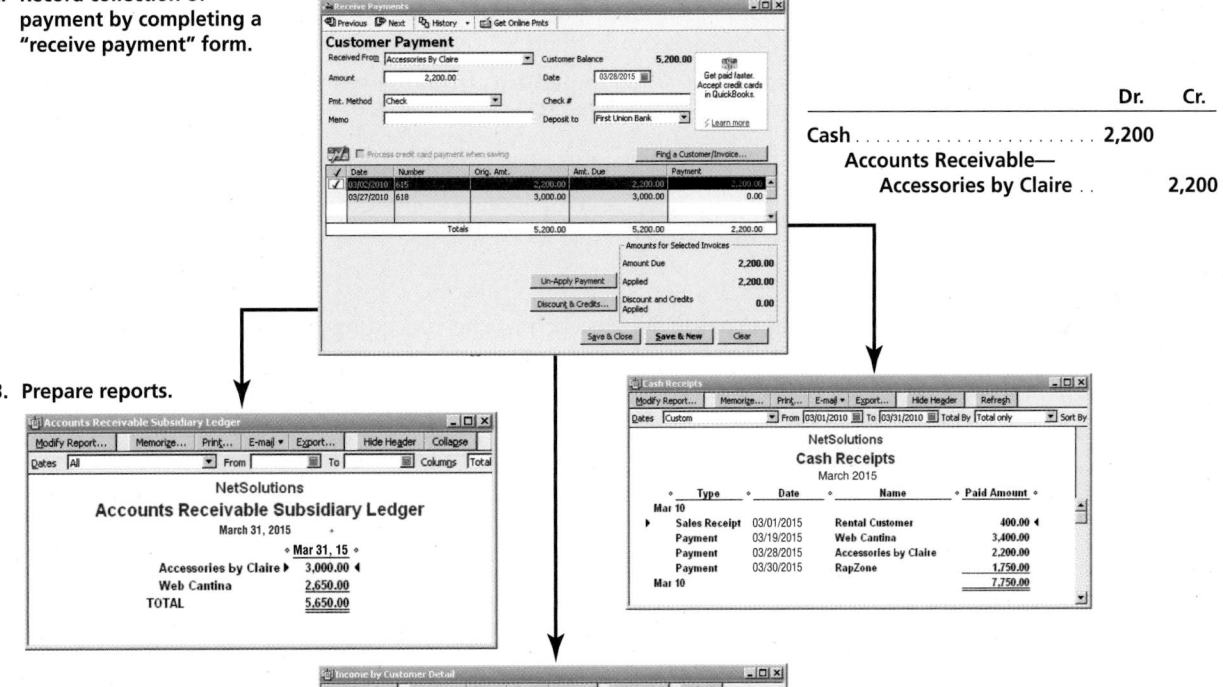

	Dr.	Cr.
Cash......................	2,200	
Accounts Receivable—		
Accessories by Claire ..		2,200

3. Prepare reports.

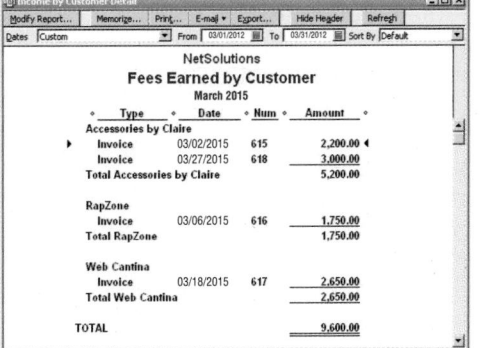

ILLUSTRATIVE PROBLEM

Selected transactions of O'Malley Co. for the month of May are as follows:

a.	May	1.	Issued Cheque No. 1001 in payment of rent for May, $1,200.
b.		2.	Purchased office supplies on account from McMillan Co., $3,600.
c.		4.	Issued Cheque No. 1003 in payment of freight charges on the supplies purchased on May 2, $320.
d.		8.	Provided services on account to Waller Co., Invoice No. 51, $4,500.
e.		9.	Issued Cheque No. 1005 for office supplies purchased, $450.
f.		10.	Received cash for office supplies sold to employees at cost, $120.
g.		11.	Purchased office equipment on account from Fender Office Products, $15,000.
h.		12.	Issued Cheque No. 1010 in payment of the supplies purchased from McMillan Co. on May 2, $3,600.
i.		16.	Provided services on account to Riese Co., Invoice No. 58, $8,000.
j.		18.	Received $4,500 from Waller Co. in payment of May 8 invoice.
k.		20.	Invested additional cash in the business, $10,000.
l.		25.	Provided services for cash, $15,900.
m.		30.	Issued Cheque No. 1040 for withdrawal of cash for personal use, $1,000.
n.		30.	Issued Cheque No. 1041 in payment of electricity and water invoices, $690.
o.		30.	Issued Cheque No. 1042 in payment of office and sales salaries for May, $15,800.
p.		31.	Journalized adjusting entries from the work sheet prepared for the fiscal year ended May 31.

O'Malley Co. maintains a sales journal, a cash receipts journal, a purchases journal, a cash disbursements journal, and a general journal. In addition, accounts receivable and accounts payable subsidiary ledgers are used.

Instructions

1. Indicate the journal in which each of the preceding transactions, (a) through (p), should be recorded.
2. Indicate whether an account in the accounts receivable or accounts payable subsidiary ledgers would be affected for each of the preceding transactions.
3. Journalize transactions (b), (c), (d), (h), and (j) in the appropriate journals.

Solution

	1. Journal	2. Subsidiary Ledger
a.	Cash disbursements journal	
b.	Purchases journal	Accounts payable ledger
c.	Cash disbursements journal	
d.	Sales journal	Accounts receivable ledger
e.	Cash disbursements journal	
f.	Cash receipts journal	
g.	Purchases journal	Accounts payable ledger
h.	Cash disbursements journal	Accounts payable ledger
i.	Sales journal	Accounts receivable ledger
j.	Cash receipts journal	Accounts receivable ledger
k.	Cash receipts journal	
l.	Cash receipts journal	
m.	Cash disbursements journal	
n.	Cash disbursements journal	
o.	Cash disbursements journal	
p.	General journal	

3.
Transaction (b):

			Purchases Journal				
Date	Account Credited	Post. Ref.	Accounts Payable Cr.	Office Supplies Dr.	Other Accounts Dr.	Post. Ref.	Amount
May 2	McMillan Co.		3,600	3,600			

Transactions (c) and (h):

				Cash Disbursements Journal		
Date	Ch. No.	Account Debited	Post. Ref.	Other Accounts Dr.	Accounts Payable Dr.	Cash Cr.
May 4	1003	Freight Expense		320		320
12	1010	McMillan Co.			3,600	3,600

Transaction (d):

			Sales Journal	
Date	Invoice No.	Account Debited	Post. Ref.	Accts. Rec. Dr. Fees Earned Cr.
May 8	51	Waller Co.		4,500

Transaction (j):

			Cash Receipts Journal		
Date	Account Credited	Post. Ref.	Other Accounts Cr.	Accounts Receivable Cr.	Cash Dr.
May 18	Waller Co.			4,500	4,500

PROBLEM

PR E-1

All journals and general ledger; trial balance

✔ 2. Total cash receipts, $73,230

The transactions completed by Over-Nite Express Company during January 2015 were as follows:

Jan. 1. Issued Cheque No. 205 for January rent, $1,000.
2. Purchased a vehicle on account from McIntyre Sales Co., $22,300.
3. Purchased office equipment on account from Office Mate Inc., $520.
5. Issued Invoice 91 to Martin Co., $5,200.
6. Received cheque for $5,610 from Baker Co. in payment of invoice.
7. Issued Invoice 92 to Trent Co., $8,150.
9. Issued Cheque No. 206 for fuel expense, $670.
10. Received cheque for $8,920 from Guttormson Co. in payment of invoice.
10. Issued Cheque No. 207 to Office City in payment of $490 invoice.
10. Issued Cheque No. 208 to Bastille Co. in payment of $1,350 invoice.
11. Issued Invoice 93 to Jarvis Co., $6,540.
11. Issued Cheque No. 209 to Porter Co. in payment of $325 invoice.

(continued)

Jan. 12. Received cheque for $5,200 from Martin Co. in payment of invoice.
13. Issued Cheque No. 210 to McIntyre Sales Co. in payment of $22,300 invoice.
16. Cash fees earned for January 1–16, $18,900.
16. Issued Cheque No. 211 for purchase of a vehicle, $22,400.
17. Issued Cheque No. 212 for miscellaneous administrative expense, $4,100.
18. Purchased maintenance supplies on account from Bastille Co., $1,680.
18. Received cheque for rent revenue on office space, $2,000.
19. Purchased the following on account from Master Supply Co.: maintenance supplies, $1,950, and office supplies, $2,050.
20. Issued Cheque No. 213 in payment of advertising expense, $7,250.
20. Used maintenance supplies with a cost of $2,400 to repair vehicles; use the expense account.
21. Purchased office supplies on account from Office City, $710.
24. Issued Invoice 94 to Guttormson Co., $7,890.
25. Received cheque for $11,900 from Baker Co. in payment of invoice.
25. Issued Invoice 95 to Trent Co., $5,030.
26. Issued Cheque No. 214 to Office Mate Inc. in payment of $520 invoice.
27. Issued Cheque No. 215 to J. Li as a personal withdrawal, $3,240.
30. Issued Cheque No. 216 in payment of driver salaries, $27,690.
31. Issued Cheque No. 217 in payment of office salaries, $18,600.
31. Issued Cheque No. 218 for office supplies, $450.
31. Cash fees earned for January 17–31, $20,700.
31. Recorded depreciation expense for January as follows: Office Equipment—$1,432; Vehicles—$4,860.

Instructions

1. Enter the following account balances in the general ledger and accounts receivable and accounts payable subsidiary ledgers as at January 1:

1010	Cash	$ 61,300	3020	J. Li, Withdrawals	—
1020	Accounts Receivable	26,430	4010	Fees Earned	—
1040	Maintenance Supplies	6,580	4020	Rent Revenue	—
1050	Office Supplies	3,150	5010	Driver Salaries Expense	—
1060	Office Equipment	15,390	5020	Maintenance Supplies Expense	—
1070	Accum. Depr.—Office Equip.	3,450	5030	Fuel Expense	—
1080	Vehicles	57,000	5040	Office Salaries Expense	—
1090	Accum. Depr.—Vehicles	15,460	5050	Rent Expense	—
2010	Accounts Payable	2,165	5060	Advertising Expense	—
3010	J. Li, Capital	148,775	5070	Miscellaneous Administrative Expense	—
			5080	Depreciation Expense	—

Opening Accounts Receivable balances

Baker Co.	17,510
Guttormson Co.	8,920

Opening Accounts Payable balances

Office City	490
Bastille Co.	1,350
Porter Co.	325

2. Journalize the transactions for January 2015, using the following journals similar to those illustrated in this appendix: single-column sales journal, cash receipts journal, purchases journal (with columns for Accounts Payable, Maintenance Supplies, Office Supplies, and Other Accounts), cash disbursements journal, and two-column general journal.
3. Post the appropriate individual entries to the general ledger and subsidiary ledgers.
4. Total each of the columns of the special journals and post the appropriate totals to the general ledger; insert the account balances.
5. Prepare a trial balance.
6. Verify the agreement of each subsidiary ledger with its controlling account. The sum of the balances of the accounts in the subsidiary ledgers as at January 31 are as follows:

Accounts Receivable	$27,610
Accounts Payable	6,390

End-of-Period Spreadsheet (Work Sheet) for a Merchandising Business

@netsolutions

A merchandising business may use an end-of-period spreadsheet (work sheet) for preparing financial statements and adjusting and closing entries. This appendix illustrates such a spreadsheet for the perpetual inventory system.

The end-of-period spreadsheet in Exhibit 1 is for NetSolutions on December 31, 2016. Exhibit 1 was prepared using the following steps that are described and illustrated in Appendix 2, at the end of Chapter 4.

Step 1. Enter the Title.
Step 2. Enter the Unadjusted Trial Balance.
Step 3. Enter the Adjustments.
Step 4. Enter the Adjusted Trial Balance.
Step 5. Extend the Accounts to the Income Statement and Balance Sheet columns.
Step 6. Total the Income Statement and Balance Sheet columns, compute the Net Income or Net Loss, and complete the spreadsheet.

The data needed for adjusting the accounts of NetSolutions are as follows:

Physical inventory on December 31, 2016.		$62,150
Office supplies on hand on December 31, 2016.		480
Insurance expired during 2016.		1,910
Depreciation during 2016 on: Store equipment.		3,100
Office equipment.		2,490
Salaries accrued on December 31, 2016: Sales salaries.	$780	
Office salaries	360	1,140
Rent earned during 2016.		600

There is no required order for analyzing the adjustment data and the accounts in the spreadsheet. However, the accounts are normally analyzed in the order in which they appear in the spreadsheet. Using this approach, the adjustment for inventory shrinkage is listed first as entry (a), followed by the adjustment for office supplies used as entry (b), and so on.

After all the adjustments have been entered, the Adjustments columns are totalled to prove the equality of debits and credits. The adjusted trial balance is entered by combining the adjustments with the unadjusted balances for each account.[1] The Adjusted Trial Balance columns are then totalled to prove the equality of debits and credits. The adjusted balances are then extended to the statement columns. The four statement columns are totalled, and the net income or net loss is determined.

For NetSolutions, the difference between the Credit and Debit columns of the Income Statement section is $75,400, the amount of the net income. The difference between the Debit and Credit columns of the Balance Sheet section is also $75,400, which is the increase in owner's equity as a result of the net income.

1 The Adjusted Trial Balance columns can be eliminated and the adjusted balances directly extended to the statement columns.

Exhibit 1

End-of-Period Spreadsheet (Work Sheet) for a Merchandising Business Using Perpetual Inventory System

	A	B	C	D	E	F	G	H	I	J	K
1				NetSolutions							
2				End-of-Period Spreadsheet (Work Sheet)							
3				For the Year Ended December 31, 2016							
4		Unadjusted Trial Balance		Adjustments		Adjusted Trial Balance		Income Statement		Balance Sheet	
5	Account Title										
6		Dr.	Cr.	Dr.	Cr.	Dr.	Cr.	Dr.	Cr.	Dr.	Cr.
7	Cash	52,950				52,950				52,950	
8	Accounts Receivable	91,080				91,080				91,080	
9	Inventory	63,950			(a)1,800	62,150				62,150	
10	Office Supplies	1,090			(b) 610	480				480	
11	Prepaid Insurance	4,560			(c)1,910	2,650				2,650	
12	Land	20,000				20,000				20,000	
13	Store Equipment	27,100				27,100				27,100	
14	Accum. Depr.—Store Equipment		2,600		(d)3,100		5,700				5,700
15	Office Equipment	15,570				15,570				15,570	
16	Accum. Depr.—Office Equipment		2,230		(e)2,490		4,720				4,720
17	Accounts Payable		22,420				22,420				22,420
18	Salaries Payable				(f)1,140		1,140				1,140
19	Unearned Rent		2,400	(g) 600			1,800				1,800
20	Notes Payable										
21	(final payment due 2026)		25,000				25,000				25,000
22	Chris Clark, Capital		153,800				153,800				153,800
23	Chris Clark, Withdrawals	18,000				18,000				18,000	
24	Sales		720,185				720,185		720,185		
25	Sales Returns and Allowances	6,140				6,140		6,140			
26	Sales Discounts	5,790				5,790		5,790			
27	Cost of Goods Sold	523,505		(a)1,800		525,305		525,305			
28	Sales Salaries Expense	52,650		(f) 780		53,430		53,430			
29	Advertising Expense	10,860				10,860		10,860			
30	Depr. Exp.—Store Equipment			(d)3,100		3,100		3,100			
31	Delivery Expense	2,800				2,800		2,800			
32	Miscellaneous Selling Expense	630				630		630			
33	Office Salaries Expense	20,660		(f) 360		21,020		21,020			
34	Rent Expense	8,100				8,100		8,100			
35	Depr. Exp.—Office Equipment			(e)2,490		2,490		2,490			
36	Insurance Expense			(c)1,910		1,910		1,910			
37	Office Supplies Expense			(b) 610		610		610			
38	Misc. Administrative Expense	760				760		760			
39	Rent Revenue				(g) 600		600		600		
40	Interest Expense	2,440				2,440		2,440			
41		928,635	928,635	11,650	11,650	935,365	935,365	645,385	720,785	289,980	214,580
42	Net income							75,400			75,400
43								720,785	720,785	289,980	289,980
44											

(a) Inventory shrinkage for period, $1,800 ($63,950 − $62,150).

(b) Office supplies used, $610 ($1,090 − $480).

(c) Insurance expired, $1,910.

(d) Depreciation of store equipment, $3,100.

(e) Depreciation of office equipment, $2,490.

(f) Salaries accrued but not paid (sales salaries, $780; office salaries, $360), $1,140.

(g) Rent earned from amount received in advance, $600.

The income statement, statement of owner's equity, and balance sheet can be prepared from the spreadsheet (work sheet). These financial statements are shown in Exhibits 11, 12, and 13 in Chapter 5. The Adjustments columns in the spreadsheet (work sheet) may be used as the basis for journalizing the adjusting entries. NetSolutions' adjusting entries at the end of 2016 are shown at the top of the following page.

		Journal			Page 28
Date		**Description**	**Post. Ref.**	**Debit**	**Credit**
2016		**Adjusting Entries**			
Dec.	31	Cost of Goods Sold	5010	1,800	
		Inventory	1050		1,800
		Inventory shrinkage.			
	31	Office Supplies Expense	5240	610	
		Office Supplies	1060		610
		Supplies used.			
	31	Insurance Expense	5230	1,910	
		Prepaid Insurance	1070		1,910
		Insurance expired.			
	31	Depr. Expense—Store Equipment	5120	3,100	
		Accumulated Depr.—Store Equipment	1240		3,100
		Store equipment amortization.			
	31	Depr. Expense—Office Equipment	5220	2,490	
		Accumulated Depr.—Office Equipment	1260		2,490
		Office equipment depreciation			
	31	Sales Salaries Expense	5100	780	
		Office Salaries Expense	5200	360	
		Salaries Payable	2020		1,140
		Accrued salaries.			
	31	Unearned Rent	2030	600	
		Rent Revenue	6010		600
		Rent earned.			

The Income Statement columns of the work sheet may be used as the basis for preparing the closing entries. The closing entries for NetSolutions at the end of 2016 are shown on page 258 of Chapter 5.

After the closing entries have been prepared and posted to the accounts, a post-closing trial balance may be prepared to verify the debit-credit equality. The only accounts that should appear on the post-closing trial balance are the asset, contra asset, liability, and owner's capital accounts with balances. These are the same accounts that appear on the end-of-period balance sheet.

PROBLEMS SERIES

PR F-1

End-of-period spreadsheet (work sheet), financial statements, and adjusting and closing entries for perpetual inventory system

✔ 2. Net income: $38,800

The accounts and their balances in the ledger of Rack Saver Co. as at December 31, 2015, are as follows:

Cash	$ 12,000		Sales	$800,000
Accounts Receivable	72,500		Sales Returns and Allowances	11,900
Inventory	170,000		Sales Discounts	7,100
Prepaid Insurance	9,700		Cost of Goods Sold	500,000
Store Supplies	4,200		Sales Salaries Expense	96,400
Office Supplies	2,100		Advertising Expense	25,000
Store Equipment	360,000		Depreciation Expense—	
Accumulated Depreciation—			Store Equipment	—
Store Equipment	60,300		Store Supplies Expense	—
Office Equipment	70,000		Miscellaneous Selling Expense	1,600
Accumulated Depreciation—			Office Salaries Expense	64,000
Office Equipment	17,200		Rent Expense	16,000
Accounts Payable	46,700		Insurance Expense	—
Salaries Payable	—		Depreciation Expense—	
Unearned Rent	3,000		Office Equipment	—
Note Payable			Office Supplies Expense	—
(final payment due 2023)	180,000		Miscellaneous Administrative	
Evan Hoffman, Capital	352,750		Expense	1,650
Evan Hoffman, Withdrawals	25,000		Rent Revenue	—
Income Summary	—		Interest Expense	10,800

The data needed for year-end adjustments on December 31 are as follows:

Physical inventory on December 31......................................	$162,500
Insurance expired during the year	3,600
Supplies on hand on December 31:	
Store supplies	1,050
Office supplies..	600
Depreciation for the year:	
Store equipment	6,000
Office equipment...	3,000
Salaries payable on December 31:	
Sales salaries.. $1,800	
Office salaries....................................... 1,200	3,000
Unearned rent on December 31.......................................	2,000

Instructions

1. Prepare an end-of-period spreadsheet (work sheet) for the fiscal year ended December 31, 2015. List all accounts in the order given.
2. Prepare a multiple-step income statement.
3. Prepare a statement of owner's equity.
4. Prepare a report form of balance sheet, assuming that the current portion of the note payable is $36,000.
5. Journalize the adjusting entries.
6. Journalize the closing entries.

PR F-2

End-of-period spreadsheet (work sheet), financial statements, and adjusting and closing entries for perpetual inventory system

✔ 1. Net income: $38,450

The accounts and their balances in the ledger of Quality Sports Co. on December 31, 2015, are as follows:

Cash	$ 18,000	Sales Discounts	$ 7,100
Accounts Receivable	42,500	Cost of Goods Sold	557,000
Inventory	218,000	Sales Salaries Expense	101,400
Prepaid Insurance	8,000	Advertising Expense	45,000
Store Supplies	4,200	Depreciation Expense—	
Office Supplies	2,100	Store Equipment	—
Store Equipment	282,000	Delivery Expense	6,000
Accumulated Depreciation—		Store Supplies Expense	—
Store Equipment	70,300	Miscellaneous Selling Expense	1,600
Office Equipment	60,000	Office Salaries Expense	64,000
Accumulated Depreciation—		Rent Expense	25,200
Office Equipment	17,200	Insurance Expense	—
Accounts Payable	26,700	Depreciation Expense—	
Salaries Payable	—	Office Equipment	—
Unearned Rent	2,500	Office Supplies Expense	—
Note Payable (final payment, 2023)	175,000	Miscellaneous Administrative	
Rosario Noe, Capital	286,450	Expense	1,650
Rosario Noe, Withdrawals	10,000	Rent Revenue	—
Sales	900,000	Interest Expense	10,500
Sales Returns and Allowances	13,900		

The data needed for year-end adjustments on December 31 are as follows:

Inventory on December 31		$211,000
Insurance expired during the year		5,000
Supplies on hand on December 31:		
Store supplies		1,150
Office supplies		750
Depreciation for the year:		
Store equipment		7,500
Office equipment		3,800
Salaries payable on December 31:		
Sales salaries	$1,500	
Office salaries	1,000	2,500
Unearned rent on December 31		500

Instructions

1. Prepare an end-of-period spreadsheet (work sheet) for the fiscal year ended December 31, listing all accounts in the order given.
2. Prepare a multiple-step income statement.
3. Prepare a statement of owner's equity.
4. Prepare a report form of balance sheet, assuming that the current portion of the note payable is $25,000.
5. Journalize the adjusting entries.
6. Journalize the closing entries.

Interest Tables

Present Value of $1 at Compound Interest Due in n Periods

Periods	2.5%	3%	3.5%	4%	5%	5.5%
1	0.97561	0.97087	0.96618	0.96154	0.95238	0.94787
2	0.95181	0.94260	0.93351	0.92456	0.90703	0.89845
3	0.92860	0.91514	0.90194	0.88900	0.86384	0.85161
4	0.90595	0.88849	0.87144	0.85480	0.82270	0.80722
5	0.88385	0.86261	0.84197	0.82193	0.78353	0.76513
6	0.86230	0.83748	0.81350	0.79031	0.74622	0.72525
7	0.84127	0.81309	0.78599	0.75992	0.71068	0.68744
8	0.82075	0.78941	0.75941	0.73069	0.67684	0.65160
9	0.80073	0.76642	0.73373	0.70259	0.64461	0.61763
10	0.78120	0.74409	0.70892	0.67556	0.61391	0.58543
11	0.76214	0.72242	0.68495	0.64958	0.58468	0.55491
12	0.74356	0.70138	0.66178	0.62460	0.55684	0.52598
13	0.72542	0.68095	0.63940	0.60057	0.53032	0.49856
14	0.70773	0.66112	0.61778	0.57748	0.50507	0.47257
15	0.69047	0.64186	0.59689	0.55527	0.48102	0.44793
16	0.67362	0.62317	0.57671	0.53391	0.45811	0.42458
17	0.65720	0.60502	0.55720	0.51337	0.43630	0.40245
18	0.64117	0.58740	0.53836	0.49363	0.41552	0.38147
19	0.62553	0.57029	0.52016	0.47464	0.39573	0.36158
20	0.61027	0.55368	0.50257	0.45639	0.37689	0.34273
21	0.59539	0.53755	0.48557	0.43883	0.35894	0.32486
22	0.58086	0.52189	0.46915	0.42196	0.34185	0.30793
23	0.56670	0.50669	0.45329	0.40573	0.32557	0.29187
24	0.55288	0.49193	0.43796	0.39012	0.31007	0.27666
25	0.53939	0.47761	0.42315	0.37512	0.29530	0.26223
26	0.52623	0.46369	0.40884	0.36069	0.28124	0.24856
27	0.51340	0.45019	0.39501	0.34682	0.26785	0.23560
28	0.50088	0.43708	0.38165	0.33348	0.25509	0.22332
29	0.48866	0.42435	0.36875	0.32065	0.24295	0.21168
30	0.47674	0.41199	0.35628	0.30832	0.23138	0.20064
31	0.46511	0.39999	0.34423	0.29646	0.22036	0.19018
32	0.45377	0.38834	0.33259	0.28506	0.20987	0.18027
33	0.44270	0.37703	0.32134	0.27409	0.19987	0.17087
34	0.43191	0.36604	0.31048	0.26355	0.19036	0.16196
35	0.42137	0.35538	0.29998	0.25342	0.18129	0.15352
40	0.37243	0.30656	0.25257	0.20829	0.14205	0.11746
45	0.32917	0.26444	0.21266	0.17120	0.11130	0.08988
50	0.29094	0.22811	0.17905	0.14071	0.08720	0.06877

Present Value of $1 at Compound Interest Due in n Periods

Periods	6%	6.5%	7%	8%	9%	10%
1	0.94334	0.93897	0.93458	0.92593	0.91743	0.90909
2	0.89000	0.88166	0.87344	0.85734	0.84168	0.82645
3	0.83962	0.82785	0.81630	0.79383	0.77218	0.75132
4	0.79209	0.77732	0.76290	0.73503	0.70842	0.68301
5	0.74726	0.72988	0.71290	0.68058	0.64993	0.62092
6	0.70496	0.68533	0.66634	0.63017	0.59627	0.56447
7	0.66506	0.64351	0.62275	0.58349	0.54703	0.51316
8	0.62741	0.60423	0.58201	0.54027	0.50187	0.46651
9	0.59190	0.56735	0.54393	0.50025	0.46043	0.42410
10	0.55840	0.53273	0.50835	0.46319	0.42241	0.38554
11	0.52679	0.50021	0.47509	0.42888	0.38753	0.35049
12	0.49697	0.46968	0.44401	0.39711	0.35554	0.31863
13	0.46884	0.44102	0.41496	0.36770	0.32618	0.28966
14	0.44230	0.41410	0.38782	0.34046	0.29925	0.26333
15	0.41726	0.38883	0.36245	0.31524	0.27454	0.23939
16	0.39365	0.36510	0.33874	0.29189	0.25187	0.21763
17	0.37136	0.34281	0.31657	0.27027	0.23107	0.19784
18	0.35034	0.32189	0.29586	0.25025	0.21199	0.17986
19	0.33051	0.30224	0.27651	0.23171	0.19449	0.16351
20	0.31180	0.28380	0.25842	0.21455	0.17843	0.14864
21	0.29416	0.26648	0.24151	0.19866	0.16370	0.13513
22	0.27750	0.25021	0.22571	0.18394	0.15018	0.12285
23	0.26180	0.23494	0.21095	0.17032	0.13778	0.11168
24	0.24698	0.22060	0.19715	0.15770	0.12640	0.10153
25	0.23300	0.20714	0.18425	0.14602	0.11597	0.09230
26	0.21981	0.19450	0.17211	0.13520	0.10639	0.08390
27	0.20737	0.18263	0.16093	0.12519	0.09761	0.07628
28	0.19563	0.17148	0.15040	0.11591	0.08955	0.06934
29	0.18456	0.16101	0.14056	0.10733	0.08216	0.06304
30	0.17411	0.15119	0.13137	0.09938	0.07537	0.05731
31	0.16426	0.14196	0.12277	0.09202	0.06915	0.05210
32	0.15496	0.13329	0.11474	0.08520	0.06344	0.04736
33	0.14619	0.12516	0.10724	0.07889	0.05820	0.04306
34	0.13791	0.11752	0.10022	0.07304	0.05331	0.03914
35	0.13010	0.11035	0.09366	0.06764	0.04899	0.03558
40	0.09722	0.08054	0.06678	0.04603	0.03184	0.02210
45	0.07265	0.05879	0.04761	0.03133	0.02069	0.01372
50	0.05429	0.04291	0.03395	0.02132	0.01345	0.00852

Present Value of Ordinary Annuity of $1 per Period

Periods	2.5%	3.0%	3.5%	4.0%	5%	5.5%
1	0.97561	0.97087	0.96618	0.96154	0.95238	0.94787
2	1.92742	1.91347	1.89969	1.88609	1.85941	1.84632
3	2.85602	2.82861	2.80164	2.77509	2.72325	2.69793
4	3.76197	3.71710	3.67308	3.62990	3.54595	3.50515
5	4.64583	4.57971	4.51505	4.45182	4.32948	4.27028
6	5.50813	5.41719	5.32855	5.24214	5.07569	4.99553
7	6.34939	6.23028	6.11454	6.00205	5.78637	5.68297
8	7.17014	7.01969	6.87396	6.73274	6.46321	6.33457
9	7.97087	7.78611	7.60769	7.43533	7.10782	6.95220
10	8.75206	8.53020	8.31661	8.11090	7.72174	7.53763
11	9.51421	9.25262	9.00155	8.76048	8.30641	8.09254
12	10.25776	9.95400	9.66333	9.38507	8.86325	8.61852
13	10.98318	10.63496	10.30274	9.98565	9.39357	9.11708
14	11.69091	11.29607	10.92052	10.56312	9.89864	9.58965
15	12.38138	11.93794	11.51741	11.11839	10.37966	10.03758
16	13.05500	12.56110	12.09412	11.65230	10.83777	10.46216
17	13.71220	13.16612	12.65132	12.16567	11.27407	10.86461
18	14.35336	13.75351	13.18968	12.65930	11.68959	11.24607
19	14.97889	14.32380	13.70984	13.13394	12.08532	11.60765
20	15.58916	14.87747	14.21240	13.59033	12.46221	11.95038
21	16.18455	15.41502	14.69797	14.02916	12.82115	12.27524
22	16.76541	15.93692	15.16712	14.45112	13.16300	12.58317
23	17.33211	16.44361	15.62041	14.85684	13.48857	12.87504
24	17.88499	16.93554	16.05837	15.24696	13.79864	13.15170
25	18.42438	17.41315	16.48151	15.62208	14.09394	13.41393
26	18.95061	17.87684	16.89035	15.98277	14.37518	13.66250
27	19.46401	18.32703	17.28536	16.32959	14.64303	13.89810
28	19.96489	18.76411	17.66702	16.66306	14.89813	14.12142
29	20.45355	19.18845	18.03577	16.98371	15.14107	14.33310
30	20.93029	19.60044	18.39205	17.29203	15.37245	14.53375
31	21.39541	20.00043	18.73628	17.58849	15.59281	14.72393
32	21.84918	20.38877	19.06887	17.87355	15.80268	14.90420
33	22.29188	20.76579	19.39021	18.14765	16.00255	15.07507
34	22.72379	21.13184	19.70068	18.41120	16.19290	15.23703
35	23.14516	21.48722	20.00066	18.66461	16.37420	15.39055
40	25.10278	23.11477	21.35507	19.79277	17.15909	16.04612
45	26.83302	24.51871	22.49545	20.72004	17.77407	16.54773
50	28.36231	25.72976	23.45562	21.48218	18.25592	16.93152

Present Value of Ordinary Annuity of $1 per Period

Periods	6%	6.5%	7%	8%	9%	10%
1	0.94340	0.93897	0.93458	0.92593	0.91743	0.90909
2	1.83339	1.82063	1.80802	1.78326	1.75911	1.73554
3	2.67301	2.64848	2.62432	2.57710	2.53130	2.48685
4	3.46511	3.42580	3.38721	3.31213	3.23972	3.16986
5	4.21236	4.15568	4.10020	3.99271	3.88965	3.79079
6	4.91732	4.84101	4.76654	4.62288	4.48592	4.35526
7	5.58238	5.48452	5.38923	5.20637	5.03295	4.86842
8	6.20979	6.08875	5.97130	5.74664	5.53482	5.33493
9	6.80169	6.65610	6.51523	6.24689	5.99525	5.75902
10	7.36009	7.18883	7.02358	6.71008	6.41766	6.14457
11	7.88688	7.68904	7.49867	7.13896	6.80519	6.49506
12	8.38384	8.15873	7.94269	7.53608	7.16072	6.81369
13	8.85268	8.59974	8.35765	7.90378	7.48690	7.10336
14	9.29498	9.01384	8.74547	8.22424	7.78615	7.36669
15	9.71225	9.40267	9.10791	8.55948	8.06069	7.60608
16	10.10590	9.76776	9.44665	8.85137	8.31256	7.82371
17	10.47726	10.11058	9.76322	9.12164	8.54363	8.02155
18	10.82760	10.43247	10.05909	9.37189	8.75562	8.20141
19	11.15812	10.73471	10.33560	9.60360	8.95012	8.36492
20	11.46992	11.01851	10.59401	9.81815	9.12855	8.51356
21	11.76408	11.28498	10.83553	10.01680	9.29224	8.64869
22	12.04158	11.53520	11.06124	10.20074	9.44242	8.77154
23	12.30338	11.77014	11.27219	10.37106	9.58021	8.88322
24	12.55036	11.99074	11.46933	10.52876	9.70661	8.98474
25	12.78336	12.19788	11.65358	10.67478	9.82258	9.07704
26	13.00317	12.39237	11.82578	10.80998	9.92897	9.16094
27	13.21053	12.57500	11.98671	10.93516	10.02658	9.23722
28	13.40616	12.74648	12.13711	11.05108	10.11613	9.30657
29	13.59072	12.90749	12.27767	11.15841	10.19828	9.36961
30	13.76483	13.05868	12.40904	11.25778	10.27365	9.42691
31	13.92909	13.20063	12.53181	11.34980	10.34280	9.47901
32	14.08404	13.33393	12.64656	11.43500	10.40624	9.52638
33	14.23023	13.45909	12.75379	11.51389	10.46444	9.56943
34	14.36814	13.57661	12.85401	11.58693	10.51784	9.60858
35	14.49825	13.68696	12.94767	11.65457	10.56682	9.64416
40	15.04630	14.14553	13.33171	11.92461	10.75736	9.77905
45	15.45583	14.48023	13.60552	12.10840	10.88118	9.86281
50	15.76186	14.72452	13.80075	12.23348	10.96168	9.91481

SUBJECT INDEX

COMPANY INDEX

Classification of Accounts

Account Title	Account Classification	Normal Balance	Financial Statement
Accounts Payable	Current liability	Credit	Balance sheet
Accounts Receivable	Current asset	Debit	Balance sheet
Accumulated Amortization	Contra asset	Credit	Balance sheet
Accumulated Depreciation	Contra asset	Credit	Balance Sheet
Accumulated Other Comprehensive Income	Shareholders' equity	Credit	Balance sheet
Advertising Expense	Operating expense	Debit	Income statement
Allowance for Doubtful Accounts	Contra current asset	Credit	Balance sheet
Amortization Expense	Operating expense	Debit	Income statement
Bad Debt Expense	Operating expense	Debit	Income statement
Bonds Payable	Long-term liability	Credit	Balance sheet
Building	Property, plant, and equipment	Debit	Balance sheet
CPP Expense	Operating expense	Debit	Income statement
CPP Payable	Current liability	Credit	Balance sheet
(Owner's name), Capital	Owner's equity	Credit	Statement of owner's equity/ Balance sheet
Cash	Current asset	Debit	Balance sheet
Cash Dividends	Shareholders' equity	Debit	Retained earnings statement
Cash Dividends Payable	Current liability	Credit	Balance sheet
Common Shares	Shareholders' equity	Credit	Balance sheet
Common Share Dividend Distributable	Shareholders' equity	Credit	Balance sheet
Contributed Capital from Retirement of Common Shares	Shareholders' equity	Credit	Balance sheet
Cost of Goods Sold	Cost of goods sold	Debit	Income statement
Current Portion of Long-Term Debt	Current liability	Credit	Balance sheet
Delivery Expense	Operating expense	Debit	Income Statement
Depreciation Expense	Operating expense	Debit	Income Statement
Discount on Bonds Payable	Contra long-term liability	Debit	Balance sheet
Discount on Notes Payable	Contra long-term liability	Debit	Balance sheet
Dividend Revenue	Other income	Credit	Income statement
Dividends Payable—Common	Current liability	Credit	Balance sheet
Dividends Payable—Preferred	Current liability	Credit	Balance sheet
EI Expense	Operating expense	Debit	Income statement
EI Payable	Current liability	Credit	Balance sheet
Equipment	Property, plant, and equipment	Debit	Balance sheet
Federal Income Taxes Payable	Current liability	Credit	Balance Sheet
Freight In	Cost of goods sold	Debit	Income statement
Freight Out	Operating expense	Debit	Income statement
Gain on Disposal of Property, Plant, and Equipment	Other income	Credit	Income statement
Gain on Sale of Investments	Other income	Credit	Income statement

Classification of Accounts

Account Title	Account Classification	Normal Balance	Financial Statement
Goodwill	Non-current asset	Debit	Balance sheet
GST Charged on Sales	Current liability	Credit	Balance sheet
GST Paid on Purchases	Contra current liability	Debit	Balance sheet
HST Charged on Sales	Current liability	Credit	Balance sheet
HST Paid on Purchases	Contra Current liability	Debit	Balance sheet
Impairment Loss	Other expense	Debit	Income Statement
Income Taxes Expense	Income tax	Debit	Income statement
Income Taxes Payable	Current liability	Credit	Balance sheet
Insurance Expense	Operating expense	Debit	Income statement
Interest Expense	Other expense	Debit	Income statement
Interest Payable	Current liability	Credit	Balance sheet
Interest Receivable	Current asset	Debit	Balance sheet
Interest Revenue	Other income	Credit	Income statement
Inventory	Current asset/Cost of goods sold	Debit	Balance sheet/Income statement
Investment in Bonds	Investment	Debit	Balance sheet
Investment in Shares	Investment	Debit	Balance sheet
Investment Revenue	Other income	Credit	Income statement
Land	Property, plant, and equipment	Debit	Balance sheet
Loss on Disposal of Property, Plant, and Equipment	Other expense	Debit	Income statement
Loss on Sale of Investments	Other expense	Debit	Income statement
Notes Payable	Current liability/Long-term liability	Credit	Balance sheet
Notes Receivable	Current asset/Investment	Debit	Balance sheet
Other Benefits Expense	Operating expense	Debit	Income statement
Other Benefits Payable	Current liability	Credit	Balance sheet
Patents	Intangible asset	Debit	Balance sheet
Pension Expense	Operating expense	Debit	Income statement
Petty Cash	Current asset	Debit	Balance sheet
Preferred Shares	Shareholders' equity	Credit	Balance sheet
Premium on Bonds Payable	Contra long-term liability	Credit	Balance sheet
Prepaid Insurance	Current asset	Debit	Balance sheet
Prepaid Rent	Current asset	Debit	Balance sheet
Product Warranty Expense	Operating expense	Debit	Income statement
Product Warranty Liability	Current liability	Credit	Balance sheet
Provincial Income Taxes Payable	Current liability	Credit	Balance Sheet
Provisions	Current liability/Long-term liability	Credit	Balance sheet
PST Payable	Current liability	Credit	Balance sheet
Purchases	Cost of goods sold	Debit	Income statement
Purchases Discounts	Cost of goods sold	Credit	Income statement
Purchases Returns and Allowances	Cost of goods sold	Credit	Income statement
Rent Expense	Operating expense	Debit	Income statement
Rent Revenue	Other income	Credit	Income statement
Retained Earnings	Shareholders' equity	Credit	Balance sheet/Retained earnings statement
Salaries Expense	Operating expense	Debit	Income statement
Salaries Payable	Current liability	Credit	Balance sheet
Sales	Revenue from sales	Credit	Income statement
Sales Discounts	Revenue from sales	Debit	Income statement
Sales Returns and Allowances	Revenue from sales	Debit	Income statement

Account Title	Account Classification	Normal Balance	Financial Statement
Share Dividends	Shareholders' equity	Debit	Retained earnings statement
Supplies	Current asset	Debit	Balance sheet
Supplies Expense	Operating expense	Debit	Income statement
Unearned Rent	Current liability	Credit	Balance sheet
Utilities Expense	Operating expense	Debit	Income statement
Vacation Pay Expense	Operating expense	Debit	Income statement
Vacation Pay Payable	Current liability/Long-term liability	Credit	Balance sheet
Wages Expense	Operating expense	Debit	Income statement
Wages Payable	Current liability	Credit	Balance sheet
(Owner's name), Withdrawals	Owner's equity	Debit	Statement of owner's equity

The Basics

1. Accounting Equation (page 10):

Assets = Liabilities + Owner's Equity

2. T Account (page 47):

Account Title	
Left side	Right side
debit	*credit*

3. Rules of Debit and Credit (page 51):

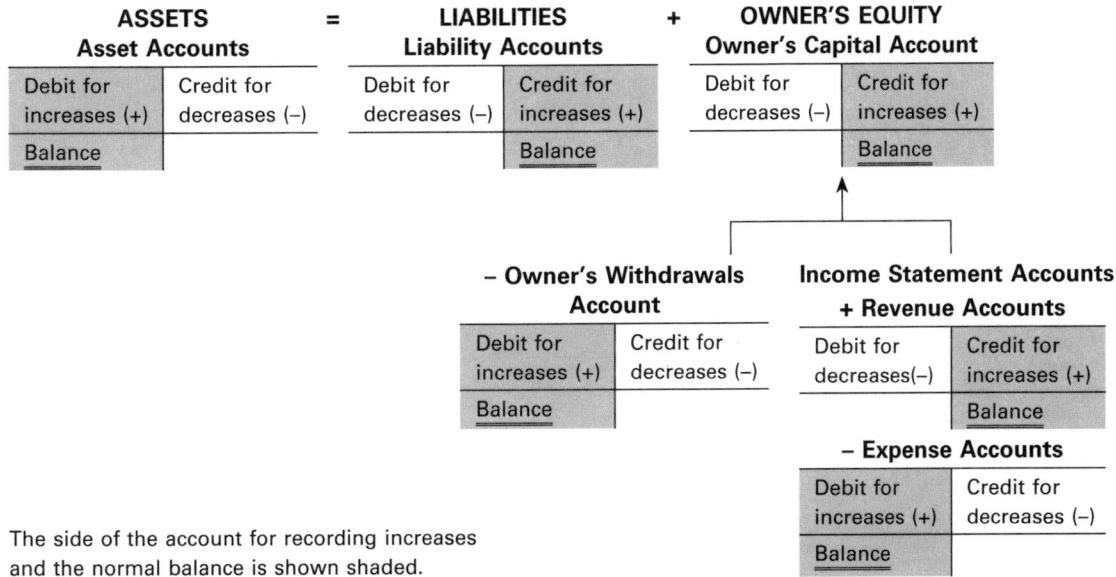

The side of the account for recording increases and the normal balance is shown shaded.

Net income or net loss

4. Analyzing and Journalizing Transactions (page 53)

A. Carefully read the description of the transaction to determine whether an asset, a liability, an owner's equity, a revenue, an expense, or a withdrawals account is affected.

B. For each account affected by the transaction, determine whether the account increases or decreases.

C. Determine whether each increase or decrease should be recorded as a debit or a credit, following the rules of debit and credit.

D. Record the transaction using a journal entry.

E. Periodically post journal entries to the accounts in the ledger.

F. Prepare an unadjusted trial balance at the end of the period.

5. Financial Statements—ASPE (page 16):

INCOME STATEMENT
A summary of the revenues and expenses of a business entity for a specific period of time, such as a month or a year.

STATEMENT OF OWNER'S EQUITY
A summary of the changes in the owner's equity of a business entity that have occurred during a specific period of time, such as a month or a year.

BALANCE SHEET
A list of the assets, liabilities, and owner's equity of a business entity as of a specific date, usually at the close of the last day of a month or a year.

CASH FLOW STATEMENT
A summary of the cash receipts and cash payments of a business entity for a specific period of time, such as a month or a year.

6. Accounting Cycle (page 52):

1. Source documents arrive.
2. Journal entries are recorded.
3. Transactions are posted to accounts.
4. Unadjusted trial balance is prepared.
5. Optional worksheet is prepared.
6. Adjusting entries are journalized and posted.
7. Adjusted trial balance is prepared.
8. Financial statements are prepared.
9. Closing entries are journalized and prepared.
10. Post-closing trial balance is prepared.

7. Types of Adjusting Entries (page 102):

1. Prepaid expenses
2. Unearned revenues
3. Accrued revenues
4. Accrued expenses
5. Depreciation of property, plant, and equipment

Each entry will always affect both a balance sheet and an income statement account.

8. Closing Entries (page 175):

1. Revenue account balances are transferred to an account called Income Summary.
2. Expense account balances are transferred to an account called Income Summary.
3. The balance of Income Summary (net income or net loss) is transferred to the owner's capital account.
4. The balance of the owner's withdrawals account is transferred to the owner's capital account.

9. Format for Bank Reconciliation (page 366):

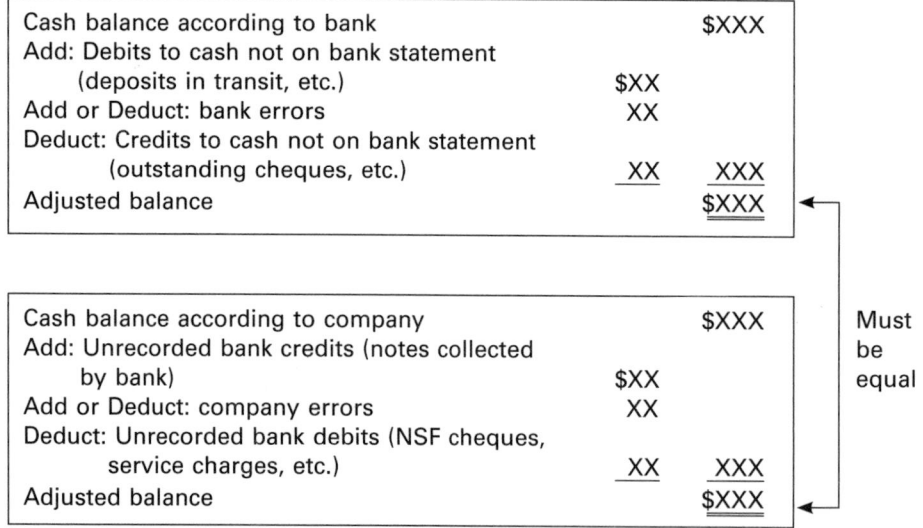

```
Cash balance according to bank                              $XXX
Add: Debits to cash not on bank statement
     (deposits in transit, etc.)                     $XX
Add or Deduct: bank errors                            XX
Deduct: Credits to cash not on bank statement
     (outstanding cheques, etc.)                      XX      XXX
Adjusted balance                                            $XXX
```

```
Cash balance according to company                          $XXX
Add: Unrecorded bank credits (notes collected
     by bank)                                        $XX
Add or Deduct: company errors                         XX
Deduct: Unrecorded bank debits (NSF cheques,
     service charges, etc.)                           XX      XXX
Adjusted balance                                            $XXX
```

Must be equal

10. Interest Computations (page 429):

$$\text{Interest} = \text{Principal} \times \text{Interest Rate} \times (\text{Term}/365 \text{ days})$$

11. Methods of Determining Annual Depreciation (page 465):

STRAIGHT-LINE: $\dfrac{\text{Cost} - \text{Residual Value}}{\text{Useful Life}}$

DOUBLE-DECLINING-BALANCE: Rate* × Carrying Amount at Beginning of Period

*Rate is commonly twice the straight-line rate (100%/Estimated Life).

12. Payroll Steps (page 519):

1. Calculating gross pay, deductions, and resulting net pay.
2. Recording distribution of gross pay.
3. Recording employer's portion of payroll expenses.
4. Recording payment of net pay to employees.
5. Recording remittance of payroll deductions.